Addison Wesley
Mathematics
Makes Sense

Program Overview

Making sense of your needs...

Addison Wesley Mathematics Makes Sense

Student understanding in a manageable and easy-to-use program

Addison Wesley Mathematics Makes Sense

Program Overview

Kindergarten to Grade 3 Authors

Pat Dickinson
Michelle Jackson
Maggie Martin Connell
Heather Spencer
Susan Gordon
Linden Gray
Nirmala Nutakki
Ken Harper
Lynn Bryan
Peggy Morrow
Ralph Connelly
Don Jones
Michael Davis
Trevor Brown
Brenda Lightburn
Cathy Anderson
Angie Harding
Jennifer Travis
Sharon Jeroski
Carole Saundry
Maureen Dockendorf
Steve Thomas
Jeananne Thomas
Michelle Skene
Sandra Ball
Donna Beaumont

Grade 4 to 8 Authors

Peggy Morrow
Bryn Keyes
Jason Johnston
Ken Harper
Margaret Sinclair
Angela D'Alessandro
Manuel Salvati
Ralph Connelly
Trevor Brown
Michael Davis
Don Jones
Cathy Heideman
Antonietta Lenjosek
Linden Gray
Sharon Jeroski
Maggie Martin Connell
Jeananne Thomas
Steve Thomas
Mary Doucette
Linda Edwards
Sue Gordon

PEARSON
Addison Wesley

Elementary Mathematics Publishing Team

Enid Haley
Lesley Haynes
Mei Lin Cheung
Lynne Gulliver
Tricia Carmichael
Susan Lishman
Ingrid D'Silva
Lynn Pereira
Keltie Thomas
Ellen Davidson
Rosalyn Steiner
Kirsten Vanstone
Susan Ginsberg
Alison Rieger
Kathleen ffolliott
Marg Bukta
Judy Wilson
Nicole Argyropoulos

Elementary Mathematics Production Coordinators

Stephanie Cox
Denise Wake

Product Manager

Anne-Marie Scullion

Mathematics Publishers

Claire Burnett
Susan Green

Program Overview Design

Ezio Lisi

Pages 10, 14-15: From John A. Van de Walle *Elementary and Middle School Mathematics: Teaching Developmentally,* 5e. Published by Allyn and Bacon, Boston, MA. Copyright (c) 2004 by Pearson Education. Reprinted by permission of the publisher.

Page 10: *Principles and Standards for School Mathematics.* Published by The National Council of Teachers of Mathematics, Inc. Reston, VA. Copyright (c) 2000.

Program Overview Publication 0-321-11825-1

This book contains recycled product and is acid free. Printed and bound in Canada

5 6 – TCP – 09 08 07 06 05

PEARSON
Addison Wesley

Table of Contents

Welcome to

Addison Wesley Mathematics Makes Sense

Addison Wesley Mathematics Makes Sense Kindergarten

Core

- Teacher Guide – binder with 8 modules
- Big Math Book

- *Addison Wesley Little Books*
- Audio
- Website www.pearsoned.ca/mathmakessense
- e-tools

Addison Wesley Mathematics Makes Sense Grades 1 and 2

Core

- Teacher Guide with CD – binder with 15 modules
- Student Book i.e. consumable or BLM
- Big Math Book

- *Addison Wesley Little Books*
- *Together Resource:* Support for Combined Grades
- Audio
- Website www.pearsoned.ca/mathmakessense
- e-tools

Addison Wesley Mathematics Makes Sense Grades 3 to 8

Core

- Teacher Guide with CD – binder with 14 modules
- Student Book – hard cover text

- Practice and Homework Book
- *Together Resource:* Support for Combined Grades
- *Addison Wesley Little Books*
- Website www.pearsoned.ca/mathmakessense
- e-tools

French Editions

Addison Wesley Mathematics recognizes the importance of developing a parallel French Edition of *Addison Wesley Mathematics Makes Sense* for French-speaking students.

- Les Editions de la Chenelière is translating all grade levels of *Addison Wesley Mathematics Makes Sense* K-8, therefore ensuring consistency in their translation, Chenelière Mathématiques Un choix logique. Les Editions de la Chenelière is Canada's leading publisher of resources for the French-speaking community outside of Quebec. We look forward to servicing the needs of your French and English students.

Chenelière Mathématiques

Program Principles

- All students need opportunities to learn mathematics in ways that are meaningful to them. A responsible mathematics program recognizes many learning styles and offers guidance to teachers as they plan for individual student differences.

- Teacher understanding of mathematics is a critical factor in their students' success. Teacher understanding can and must be supported in program methodology and pedagogy.

- Students best develop conceptual mathematical understanding when they have opportunities to "do" math, to engage in hands-on experiences in which they explore concepts in a rich mathematical context.

- Students demonstrate conceptual understanding by communicating and modelling their reasoning, and connecting a new concept or strategy to other contexts they have seen before.

- Problem solving is an integral part of learning mathematics. Students best learn new mathematical concepts when they pose and solve problems.

- Mathematics understanding is deepened and enhanced when students have opportunities to make connections between mathematical concepts and other mathematics strands, other disciplines, and the real world.

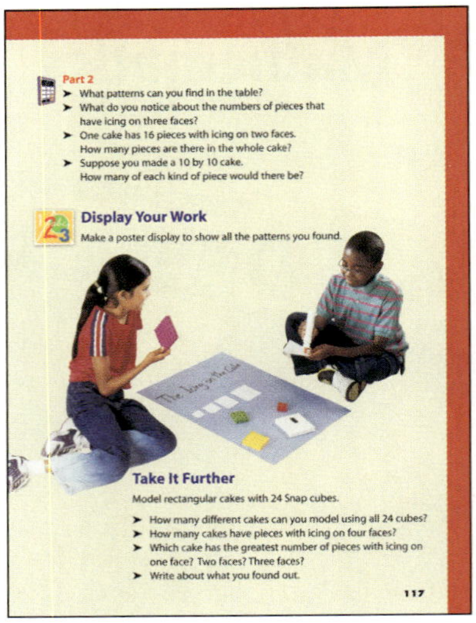
Part 2

- What patterns can you find in the table?
- What do you notice about the numbers of pieces that have icing on three faces?
- One cake has 16 pieces with icing on two faces. How many pieces are there in the whole cake?
- Suppose you made a 10 by 10 cake. How many of each kind of piece would there be?

Display Your Work

Make a poster display to show all the patterns you found.

Take It Further

Model rectangular cakes with 24 Snap cubes.

- How many different cakes can you model using all 24 cubes?
- How many cakes have pieces with icing on four faces?
- Which cake has the greatest number of pieces with icing on one face? Two faces? Three faces?
- Write about what you found out.

117

- Procedural fluency with number is an essential skill for life. Both mental and written computational strategies must be accurate, efficient, flexible, and adaptable.

- Parents have a significant role to play in student learning, in supporting and reinforcing what is learned in the classroom each day, and promoting a positive attitude toward mathematics in the home.

- The purposeful use of technology in the mathematics classroom can enrich learning experiences for students, allowing them to explore and develop concepts, and extend critical thinking and problem-solving skills.

- A mathematics program should support curriculum implementation and assessment with 100% curriculum fit and practical teacher support – pacing guidelines; combined grades strategies; models for independent and group learning; performance-based assessment suggestions.

- Teachers need a balance of diagnostic, formative, and summative assessment opportunities, with practical assessment tools to track student achievement and meet reporting requirements.

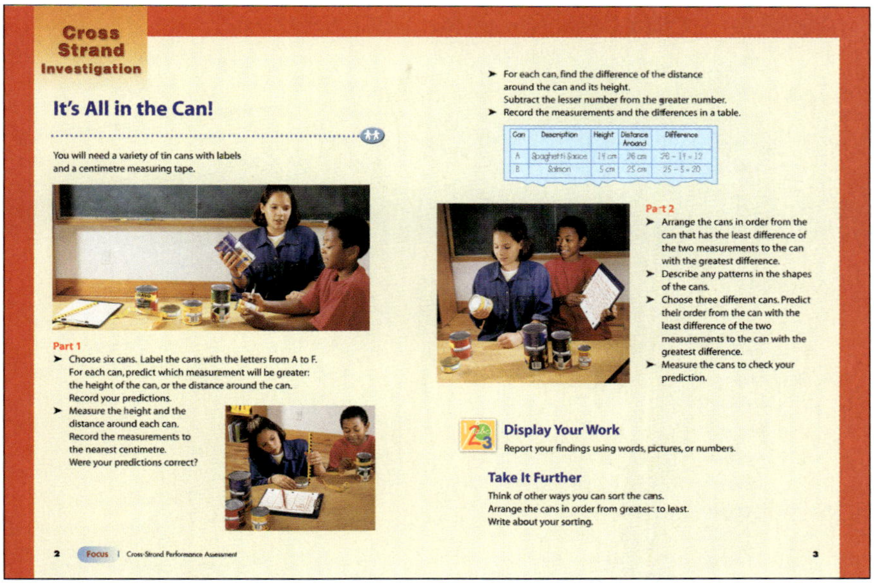

Cross Strand Investigation

It's All in the Can!

You will need a variety of tin cans with labels and a centimetre measuring tape.

Part 1

- Choose six cans. Label the cans with the letters from A to F. For each can, predict which measurement will be greater: the height of the can, or the distance around the can. Record your predictions.
- Measure the height and the distance around each can. Record the measurements to the nearest centimetre. Were your predictions correct?
- For each can, find the difference of the distance around the can and its height. Subtract the lesser number from the greater number.
- Record the measurements and the differences in a table.

Can	Description	Height	Distance Around	Difference
A	Spaghetti Sauce	14 cm	26 cm	26 – 14 = 12
B	Salmon	5 cm	25 cm	25 – 5 = 20

Part 2

- Arrange the cans in order from the can that has the least difference of the two measurements to the can with the greatest difference.
- Describe any patterns in the shapes of the cans.
- Choose three different cans. Predict their order from the can with the least difference of the two measurements to the can with the greatest difference.
- Measure the cans to check your prediction.

Display Your Work

Report your findings using words, pictures, or numbers.

Take It Further

Think of other ways you can sort the cans. Arrange the cans in order from greatest to least. Write about your sorting.

2 Focus | Cross-Strand Performance Assessment 3

From Research to Classroom Practice

Addison Wesley Mathematics Makes Sense is based on the most current research about how students learn. The Addison Wesley development team examined published academic research and professional development resources, while we learned about ongoing research into the impact of current issues on classroom practice.

This research was shared with educators across Canada, as the development team assessed its implications for the creation of new mathematics resources for the classroom.

The Addison Wesley development team also met with experienced and new teachers, with principals, parents, and consultants, in a series of symposia, focus groups, and one-on-one interviews. Our purpose was to define the resources that would best suit the needs of student learning and teacher instruction.

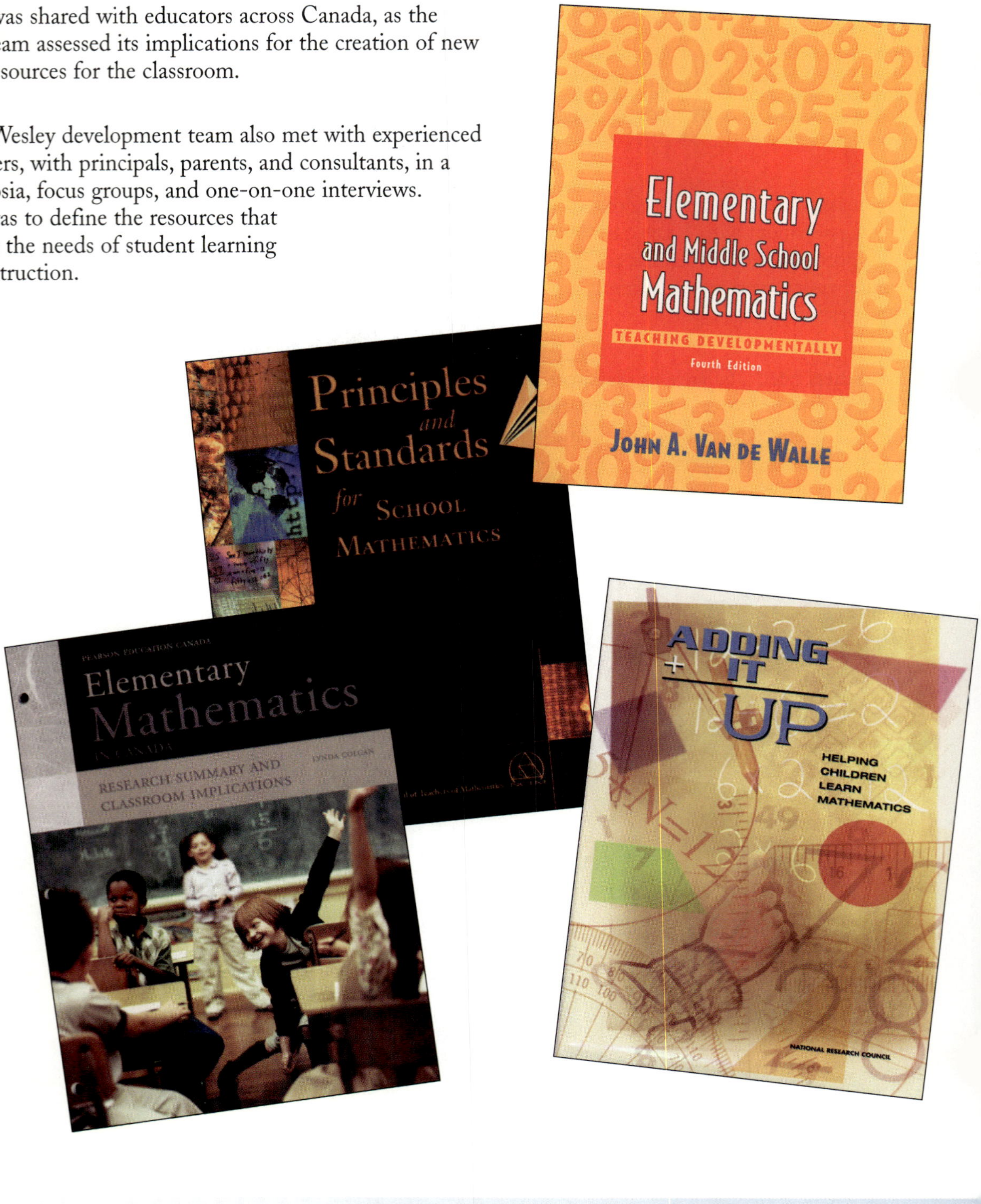

> Current research has profound implications for new classroom resources.
>
> – Lynda Colgan, Program Adviser

Program development included field tests at each grade level. In the first year of field testing, 200 classrooms across Canada participated, involving 10,000 students and their teachers to validate program content and organization.

The Addison Wesley development team incorporated field-test teacher input as we refined program design at all levels.

LESSON 1

Measuring Linear Dimensions

You can measure how long, how wide, how tall, how deep, or how thick an object is.

Shannon measures the width of the blackboard in metres.

Danny measures Seveen's height in centimetres.

Explore

You will need a 30-cm ruler and a metre stick or a measuring tape.

- Choose a classroom object.
- Estimate, then measure to the nearest unit.
- Record your work.

Repeat with other objects.
Include 2 objects you measure in centimetres and 2 in metres.

Show and Share

You can record your work in a table.

How did you use one measurement to help you estimate the next?
How did you use your ruler to measure?

Object	What We measured	Estimate	Approximate measurement
Table	Length	100 cm	83 cm

320 Lesson Focus | Estimate and measure in centimetres and metres.

Unit Problem Design a Backyard

Design a backyard for the Rizvi family.

360

Addison Wesley Mathematics Makes Sense is:

- Built from an understanding of current educational research
- Shaped against the backdrop of extensive market research into resource needs
- Field tested in hundreds of schools across Canada

Making Sense of...

Balanced Instruction

For real understanding, students need a combination of open-ended problem-solving opportunities, meaningful dialogue, and purposeful practice that reinforces, and extends, new learning.

Balanced instruction recognizes four key components that build mathematical literacy, as illustrated here.

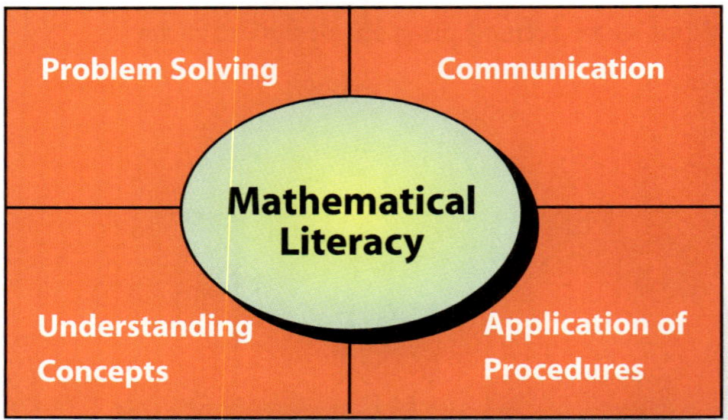

Addison Wesley Mathematics Makes Sense supports each key component in the following ways.

Problem Solving

- Introduces new concepts by presenting a problem to solve.
- Includes whole group, partner, and independent problem-solving activities.

Understanding Concepts

- A variety of activities allows students to bring their own experiences to new concepts.
- Question prompts guide the student dialogue that follows each new learning experience.
- Consolidates key concepts before moving to independent work.

Application of Procedures

- Gives purposeful practice for students to apply, clarify, and extend the learning.
- Provides regular opportunities for calculator or computer applications, or the introduction of new problem-solving strategies.

Communication

- Guides students to represent their thinking in pictures, numbers, or words.
- Provides a balance of oral and written communication opportunities.

> It's time for a program that simplifies teacher planning so teachers have more time with their students.
>
> – Peggy Morrow, Program Author

Balanced instruction is delivered in a consistent three-part lesson structure that supports the way students learn, and the way teachers teach.

How Students Learn:	How Teachers Teach:
Our Student Book Lesson	Our Teacher Guide Lesson

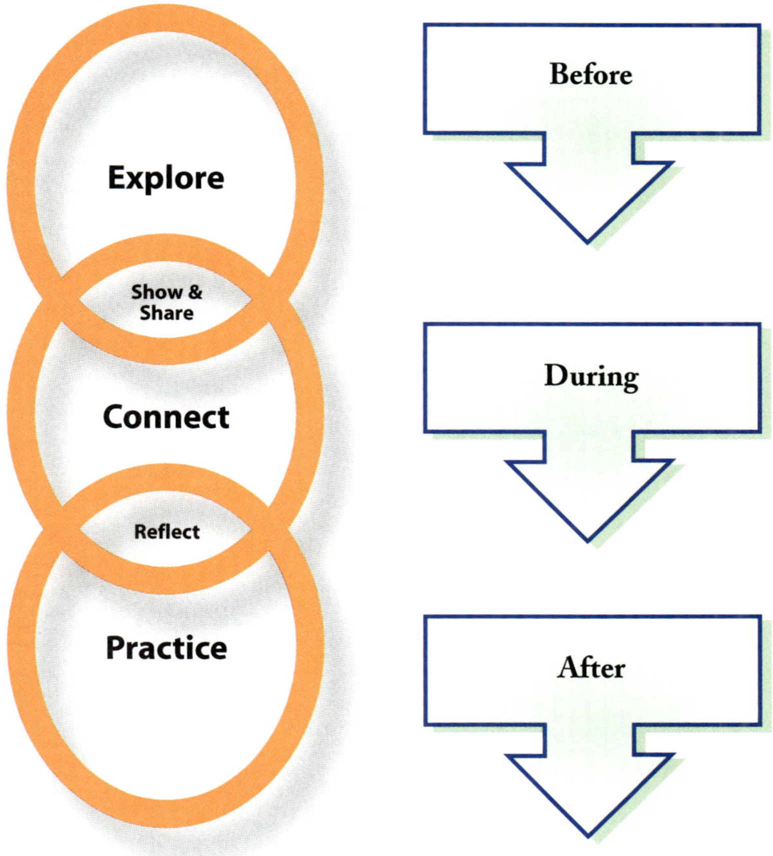

Manageable and Easy-to-Use

The problem-solving approach in *Addison Wesley Mathematics Makes Sense* is balanced with purposeful practice of skills and reinforcement of concepts. *Addison Wesley Mathematics Makes Sense* gives you quick access to ideas for instruction, while your students get clean, clear content appropriately paced.

- An "all-in-one-place" Teacher Guide
- Predictable, consistent format
- Open, readable design

Making Sense of...

Teaching and Learning for Understanding

Addison Wesley Mathematics Makes Sense has been built on the belief that mathematics is more than a list of isolated facts, that mathematics as a whole can make sense for students, teachers, and parents. Fundamental to this belief is our understanding of the importance of mathematical connections: Math makes sense for students when they see how mathematical ideas are connected to the real world, to other mathematical ideas, and to what they are learning in other subject areas.

Children come to us with experiences and understandings they have already developed into personal networks of understanding. As they work with new ideas, their active engagement leads them to fit new learning within their established understanding. The more ideas students connect, the more solid their understanding.

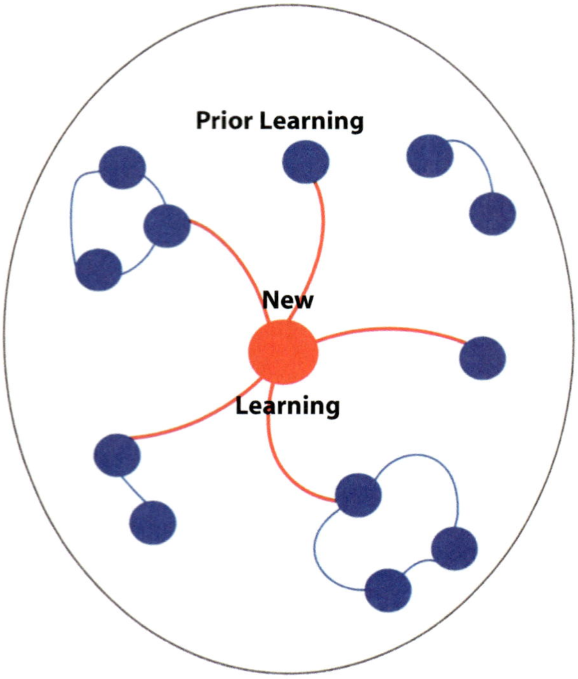

Teaching for understanding reaps many benefits for students:

- When students understand mathematical procedures, they can recall them easily and apply them in a variety of settings.
- When students understand the main concepts and connections of mathematical topics, they rely on reasoning more, and on memory less.
- Conceptual understanding provides the basis for acquiring new knowledge and solving unfamiliar problems.
- Conceptual understanding helps students spot and correct errors in their problem solutions.

> The tools that we use to build understanding are our existing ideas, the knowledge that we already possess.
> – John A. Van de Walle, Elementary Mathematics Consultant

In *Addison Wesley Mathematics Makes Sense*, the lesson framework delivers instruction in the way in which students learn most effectively.

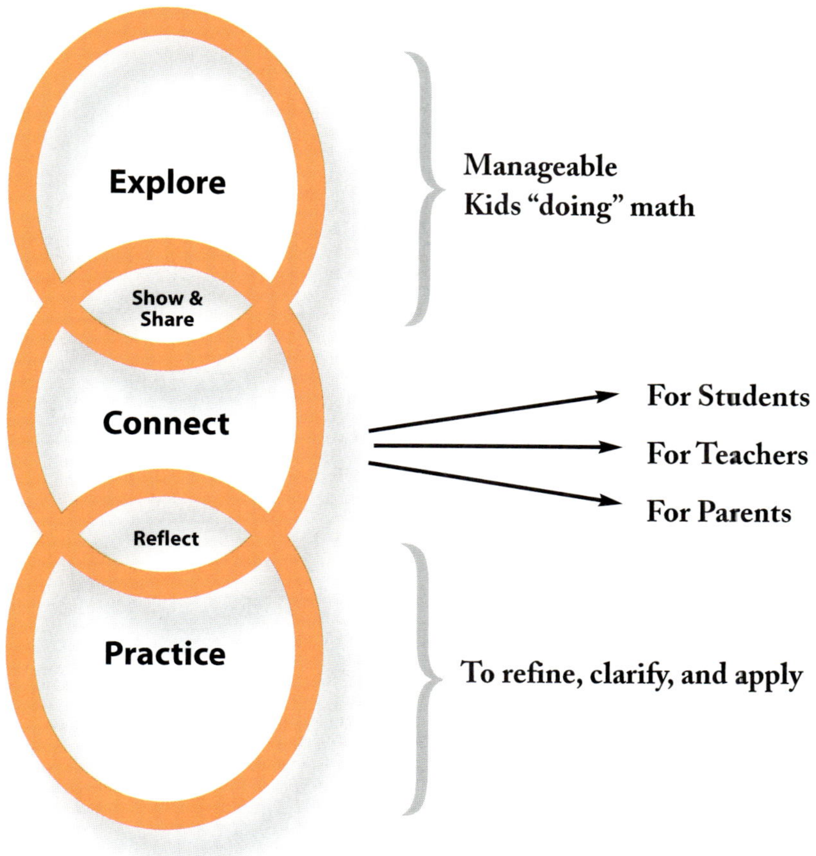

Supporting the lesson framework of *Addison Wesley Mathematics Makes Sense* is an over-arching understanding of how students' mathematical understanding, skills, and strategies develop from the early years (pre-school) through elementary school.

Developmental Continuum — A Useful Tool

- Based on current research on key developmental stages
- Enables teachers to view each student's achievements and challenges within a broader perspective
- Provides a tool for teachers to use with parents and supports teachers when discussing student progress

Making Sense of...

Purposeful Practice

Educators recognize the important role practice plays within a balanced program. Purposeful practice allows students to clarify, refine, consolidate, and apply new learning through a variety of experiences. In *Addison Wesley Mathematics Makes Sense*, purposeful practice is offered in every lesson to suit a range of learner needs.

At K to 2

Teacher Guide **Practice** suggestions for each core lesson include

- **Reinforcement** for all students
- **Extra Support** for students who may face ESL challenges, or need more experiences with early concepts, problem solving, or applying procedures
- *Extension* for students who are ready to take concepts further

Lessons also regularly include **Numbers Every Day,** and **Activity Banks.** These additional ideas for activities provide hands-on practice.

At grades 1 and 2, the Student Book provides a mechanism for students to record a selection of their mathematics practice.

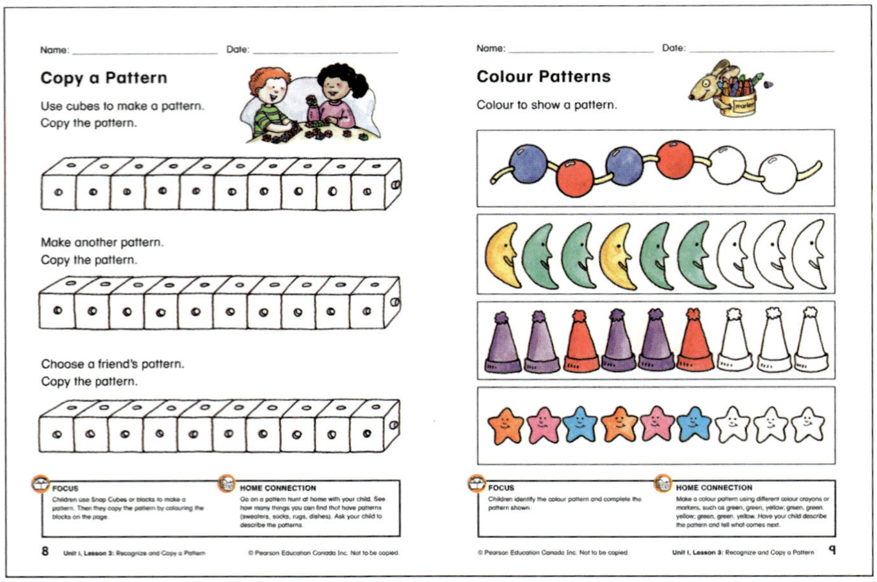

Name: ________ Date: ________

Copy a Pattern

Use cubes to make a pattern.
Copy the pattern.

Make another pattern.
Copy the pattern.

Choose a friend's pattern.
Copy the pattern.

FOCUS
Children use Snap Cubes or blocks to make a pattern. Then they copy the pattern by colouring the blocks on the page.

HOME CONNECTION
Go on a pattern hunt at home with your child. See how many things you can find that have patterns (sweaters, socks, rugs, dishes). Ask your child to describe the patterns.

8 Unit 1, Lesson 3: Recognize and Copy a Pattern © Pearson Education Canada Inc. Not to be copied.

Name: ________ Date: ________

Colour Patterns

Colour to show a pattern.

FOCUS
Children identify the colour pattern and complete the pattern shown.

HOME CONNECTION
Make a colour pattern using different colour crayons or markers, such as green, green, yellow; green, green, yellow; green, green, yellow. Have your child describe the pattern and tell what comes next.

© Pearson Education Canada Inc. Not to be copied. Unit 1, Lesson 3: Recognize and Copy a Pattern 9

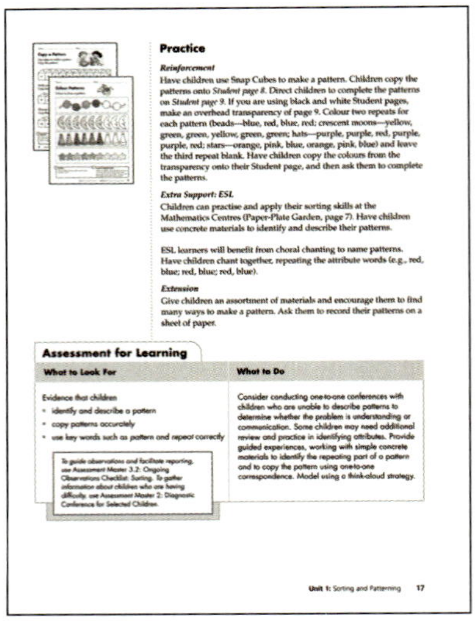

Practice

Reinforcement
Have children use Snap Cubes to make a pattern. Children copy the patterns onto *Student page 8*. Direct children to complete the patterns on *Student page 9*. If you are using black and white Student pages, make an overhead transparency of page 9. Colour two repeats for each pattern (beads—blue, red, blue, red; crescent moons—yellow, green, green, yellow, green, green; hats—purple, purple, red, purple, purple, red; stars—orange, pink, blue, orange, pink, blue) and leave the third repeat blank. Have children copy the colours from the transparency onto their Student page, and then ask them to complete the patterns.

Extra Support: ESL
Children can practise and apply their sorting skills at the Mathematics Centres (Paper-Plate Garden, page 7). Have children use concrete materials to identify and describe their patterns.

ESL learners will benefit from choral chanting to name patterns. Have children chant together, repeating the attribute words (e.g., red, blue; red, blue; red, blue).

Extension
Give children an assortment of materials and encourage them to find many ways to make a pattern. Ask them to record their patterns on a sheet of paper.

Assessment for Learning

What to Look For	What to Do
Evidence that children • identify and describe a pattern • copy patterns accurately • use key words such as *pattern* and *repeat* correctly	Consider conducting one-to-one conferences with children who are unable to describe patterns to determine whether the problem is understanding or communication. Some children may need additional review and practice in identifying attributes. Provide guided experiences, working with simple concrete materials to identify the repeating part of a pattern and to copy the pattern using one-to-one correspondence. Model using a think-aloud strategy.

To guide observations and facilitate reporting, use Assessment Master 3.2: Ongoing Observations Checklist: Sorting. To gather information about children who are having difficulty, use Assessment Master 2: Diagnostic Conference for Selected Children.

Unit 1: Sorting and Patterning 17

Students naturally solve mathematical problems daily.
Purposeful practice authenticates our classroom instruction.
– Jeanianne Thomas, Program Author

At Grades 3 and up

Each lesson in the Student Book provides one to two pages of **Practice**.

This exercise set includes patterning and visual estimation, as well as reinforcement and problem-solving opportunities.

One question in each Practice is identified as an **Assessment Focus:** it provides a good barometer of students' level of conceptual understanding.

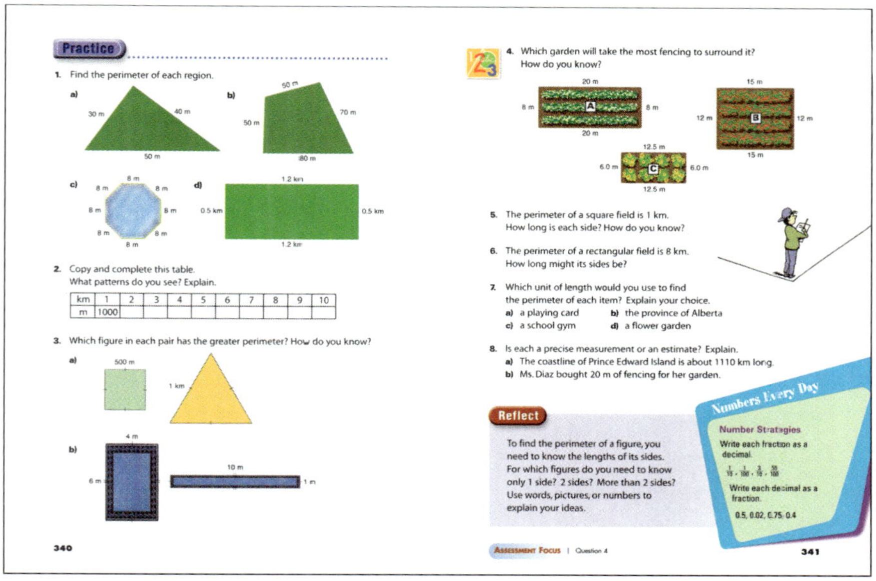

In each lesson, **Numbers Every Day** reinforces students'

- Number Sense
- Calculator Skills
- Mental Math

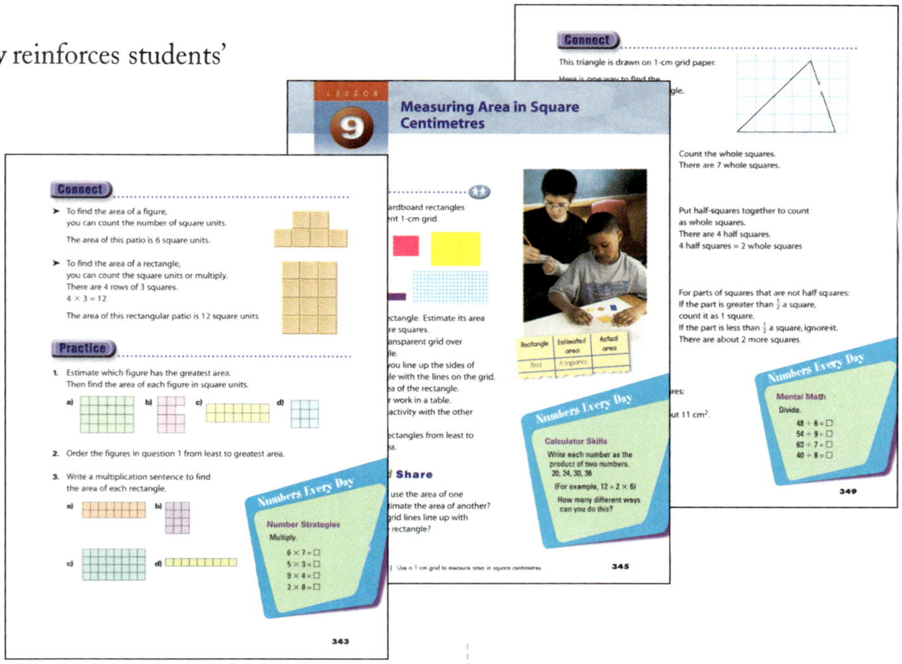

The **Teacher Guide** provides

- Answers and sample responses to **Practice** questions
- Answers and strategy suggestions for **Numbers Every Day**
- **Extra Practice** masters to support specific student needs

Also available at grade 3 and beyond: A **Practice and Homework Book** with two pages of additional support for each lesson in the Student Book

Making Sense of... Assessment for Learning

Assessment that informs instruction, with direct links to the curriculum and teacher reporting, is *purposeful, practical,* and *powerful* — a major contributor to how well students learn. In *Addison Wesley Mathematics Makes Sense,* assessment opportunities are woven right into the main flow of instruction, across every unit.

Unit Structure

Structure	Assessment
Unit Launch	Diagnostic
Core Lessons	Diagnostic, Formative
Strategies Toolkit	Formative
Show What You Know	Formative, Summative
Unit Problem (Grade 3 and up)	Summative

Term Structure

Structure	Assessment
Cross-Strand Investigation	Summative

Comprehensive Assessment Support

Your Teacher Guide provides detailed assessment support in each unit, with **Planning for Assessment** charts at the start of each unit, **Assessment for Learning** notes in each lesson, and a selection of **Assessment** masters specific to the unit content.

The **Assessment Module** in your Teacher Guide provides additional background support as well as generic assessment tools for use throughout the school year.

Assessment is not an event, but a continuous process embedded in instruction.

– Sharon Jeroski, Program Author

Diagnostic Assessment

- ☑ To identify students who are at risk in terms of acquiring concepts, procedures, and strategies required in the unit
- ☑ To develop insights into particular needs so that instruction can be adjusted to ensure students have the best possibility to succeed

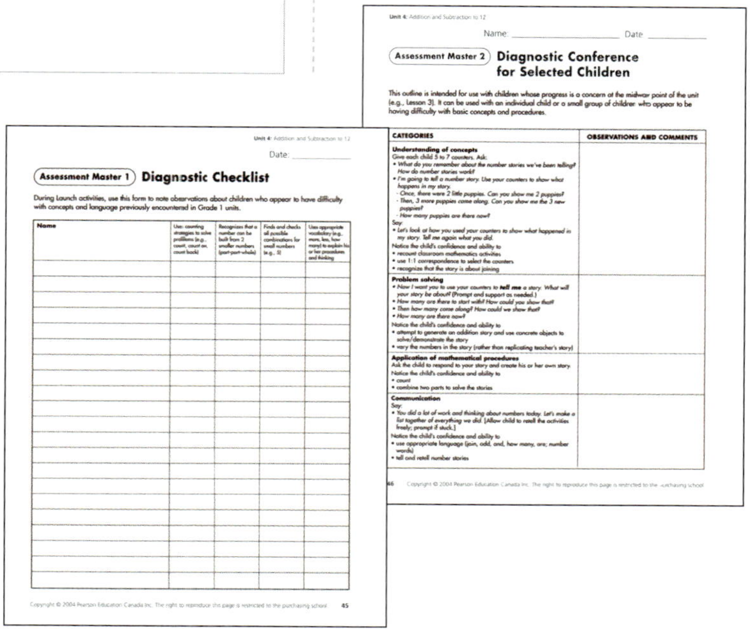

At Grades 1 and 2

- The **Diagnostic Checklist** lets you record your observations during the **Unit Launch.**
- Mid-unit, use the **Diagnostic Conference** outline with students who appear to be at risk. This form includes scaffolding and observation cues.

At Grades 3 to 8

- Each **Unit Launch** in the Student Book is designed to probe children's prior knowledge and skills. The Teacher Guide provides additional diagnostic questions and support.
- The first **Cross-Strand Investigation** in the text lets you start the year with a meaningful context in which students re-visit key concepts from the previous year.
- Use the **Diagnostic Assessment** form; it cues you regarding what to watch for and how to help.

Formative Assessment

- ☑ To gather ongoing information in a variety of ways
- ☑ To provide feedback to students about how they are doing, and how they might improve
- ☑ To adjust instruction
- ☑ To provide additional scaffolding to students who need it
- ☑ To engage students in their own learning and in self-assessment

- At all grades, during all parts of the lesson, the Teacher Guide offers specific questions to probe student understanding.
- Because each lesson engages students directly in **actively exploring** the key concept, teachers have opportunities to observe what students are able to do.

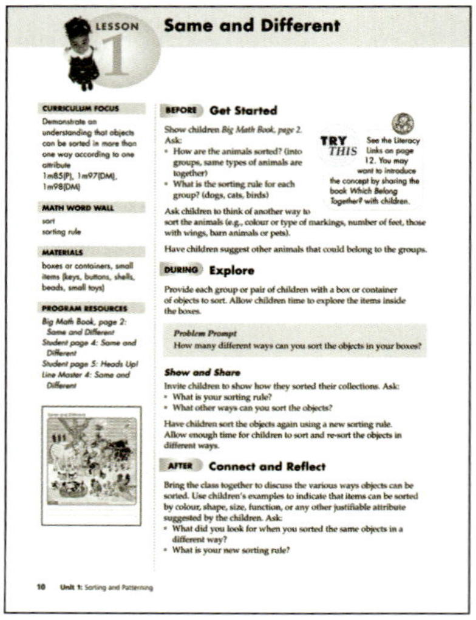

LESSON 1

Same and Different

CURRICULUM FOCUS

Demonstrate an understanding that objects can be sorted in more than one way according to one attribute
1m85(P), 1m97(DM), 1m98(DM)

MATH WORD WALL

sort
sorting rule

MATERIALS

boxes or containers, small items (keys, buttons, shells, beads, small toys)

PROGRAM RESOURCES

Big Math Book, page 2: Same and Different
Student page 4: Same and Different
Student page 5: Heads Up!
Line Master 4: Same and Different

BEFORE Get Started

Show children *Big Math Book, page 2.*
Ask:
- How are the animals sorted? (into groups, same types of animals are together)
- What is the sorting rule for each group? (dogs, cats, birds)

TRY THIS See the Literacy Links on page 12. You may want to introduce the concept by sharing the book *Which Belong Together?* with children.

Ask children to think of another way to sort the animals (e.g., colour or type of markings, number of feet, those with wings, barn animals or pets).

Have children suggest other animals that could belong to the groups.

DURING Explore

Provide each group or pair of children with a box or container of objects to sort. Allow children time to explore the items inside the boxes.

Problem Prompt
How many different ways can you sort the objects in your boxes?

Show and Share

Invite children to show how they sorted their collections. Ask:
- What is your sorting rule?
- What other ways can you sort the objects?

Have children sort the objects again using a new sorting rule. Allow enough time for children to sort and re-sort the objects in different ways.

AFTER Connect and Reflect

Bring the class together to discuss the various ways objects can be sorted. Use children's examples to indicate that items can be sorted by colour, shape, size, function, or any other justifiable attribute suggested by the children. Ask:
- What did you look for when you sorted the same objects in a different way?
- What is your new sorting rule?

10 **Unit 1:** Sorting and Patterning

- At all grades, **Show and Share** provides a key opportunity for eliciting students' understanding through communication.

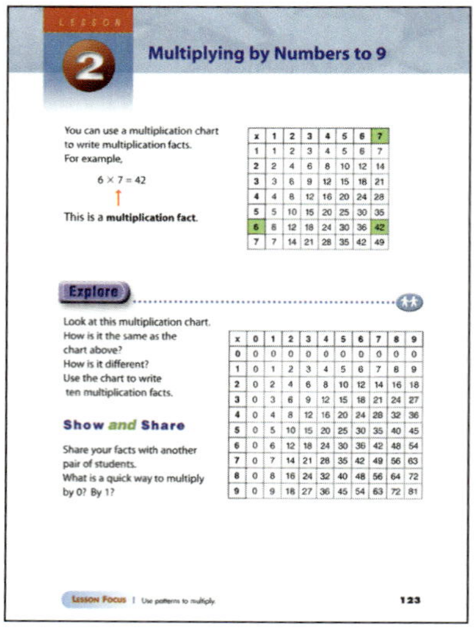

LESSON 2

Multiplying by Numbers to 9

You can use a multiplication chart to write multiplication facts.
For example,

$6 \times 7 = 42$

This is a **multiplication fact**.

x	1	2	3	4	5	6	7
1	1	2	3	4	5	6	7
2	2	4	6	8	10	12	14
3	3	6	9	12	15	18	21
4	4	8	12	16	20	24	28
5	5	10	15	20	25	30	35
6	6	12	18	24	30	36	42
7	7	14	21	28	35	42	49

Explore

Look at this multiplication chart.
How is it the same as the chart above?
How is it different?
Use the chart to write ten multiplication facts.

x	0	1	2	3	4	5	6	7	8	9
0	0	0	0	0	0	0	0	0	0	0
1	0	1	2	3	4	5	6	7	8	9
2	0	2	4	6	8	10	12	14	16	18
3	0	3	6	9	12	15	18	21	24	27
4	0	4	8	12	16	20	24	28	32	36
5	0	5	10	15	20	25	30	35	40	45
6	0	6	12	18	24	30	36	42	48	54
7	0	7	14	21	28	35	42	49	56	63
8	0	8	16	24	32	40	48	56	64	72
9	0	9	18	27	36	45	54	63	72	81

Show and Share

Share your facts with another pair of students.
What is a quick way to multiply by 0? By 1?

LESSON FOCUS | Use patterns to multiply. 123

Assessment has taken on new importance in its impact on instructional decisions.

– Ralph Connelly, Program Author

- In the Teacher Guide, **Assessment for Learning** directs your attention to specific behaviours you may see in students' work, and provides practical instructions about what to do to help students who may be struggling.
- **Practice** questions provide more opportunities for you to observe, probe, and provide feedback about student development.

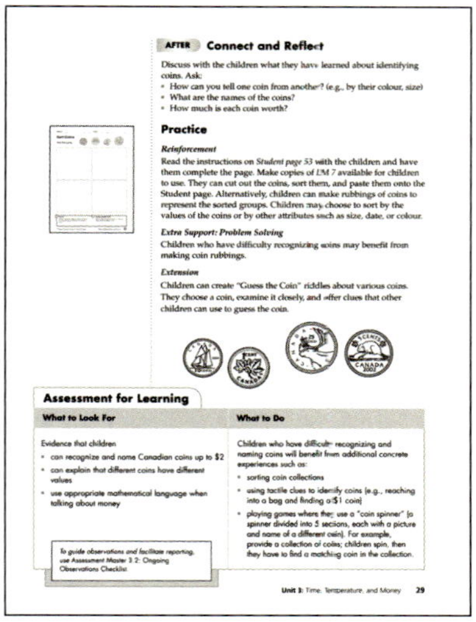

- At grades 3 to 8, Practice sets always include one exercise highlighted as an **Assessment Focus** question: this open-ended problem allows for a range of performance levels, and provides a quick touchstone for you as you circulate to observe students at work.

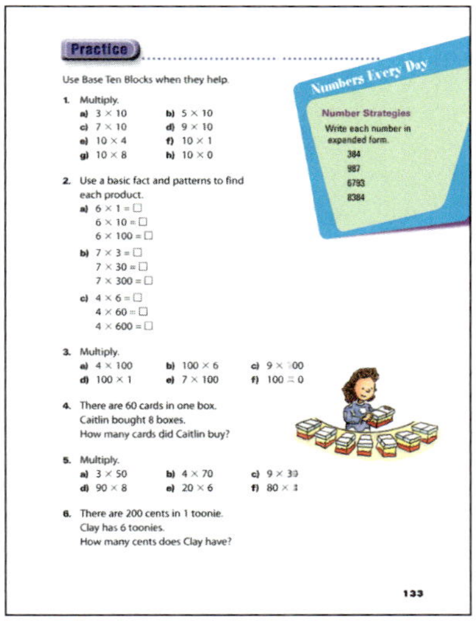

Practice

Use Base Ten Blocks when they help.

1. Multiply.
a) 3 × 10 b) 5 × 10
c) 7 × 10 d) 9 × 10
e) 10 × 4 f) 10 × 1
g) 10 × 8 h) 10 × 0

2. Use a basic fact and patterns to find each product.
a) 6 × 1 = □
6 × 10 = □
6 × 100 = □
b) 7 × 3 = □
7 × 30 = □
7 × 300 = □
c) 4 × 6 = □
4 × 60 = □
4 × 600 = □

3. Multiply.
a) 4 × 100 b) 100 × 6 c) 9 × 100
d) 100 × 1 e) 7 × 100 f) 100 × 0

4. There are 60 cards in one box. Caitlin bought 8 boxes. How many cards did Caitlin buy?

5. Multiply.
a) 3 × 50 b) 4 × 70 c) 9 × 30
d) 90 × 8 e) 20 × 6 f) 80 × 3

6. There are 200 cents in 1 toonie. Clay has 6 toonies. How many cents does Clay have?

Numbers Every Day

Number Strategies

Write each number in expanded form.

384
987
6793
8384

133

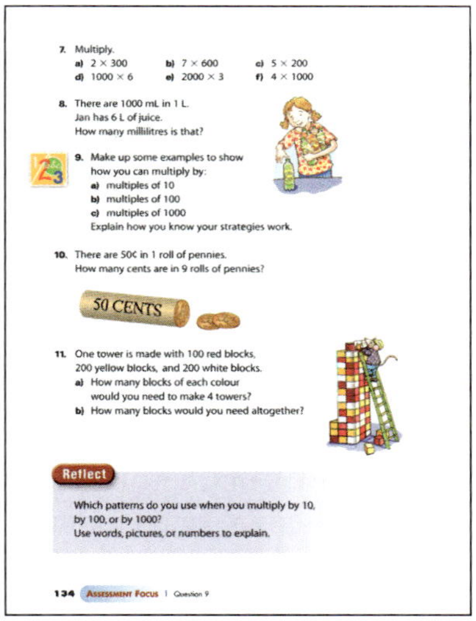

7. Multiply.
a) 2 × 300 b) 7 × 600 c) 5 × 200
d) 1000 × 6 e) 2000 × 3 f) 4 × 1000

8. There are 1000 mL in 1 L. Jan has 6 L of juice. How many millilitres is that?

9. Make up some examples to show how you can multiply by:
a) multiples of 10
b) multiples of 100
c) multiples of 1000
Explain how you know your strategies work.

10. There are 50¢ in 1 roll of pennies. How many cents are in 9 rolls of pennies?

11. One tower is made with 100 red blocks, 200 yellow blocks, and 200 white blocks.
a) How many blocks of each colour would you need to make 4 towers?
b) How many blocks would you need altogether?

Reflect

Which patterns do you use when you multiply by 10, by 100, or by 1000? Use words, pictures, or numbers to explain.

134 Assessment Focus | Question 9

- At grades 3 to 8, the Teacher Guide support for the Practice includes notes on **common misconceptions** and **opportunities for reteaching.**

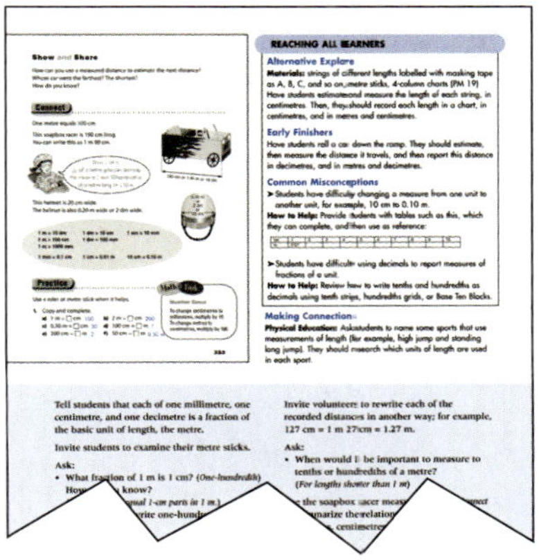

Summative Assessment

- ☑ To make a judgment about a student's achievement of the learning goals for the unit
- ☑ To facilitate reporting

Addison Wesley Mathematics Makes Sense provides a variety of options to meet your summative assessment needs.

At Grades 1 and 2

Show What You Know features performance tasks that enable students to work with concepts from the unit with new materials, or with a new context.

My Journal, in the Student Book, invites students to use pictures, words, or numbers to show their learning.

Cross-Strand Investigations appear once each term. These rich problems have a strong story element. They present an engaging context to students, and allow you to assess the extent to which students are able to synthesize and apply their learning in an integrated way.

The Teacher Guide provides a rubric and supporting notes for each Cross-Strand Investigation, in the **Additional Assessment Support** module that accompanies the Teacher Guide.

At Grades 3 and up

Show What You Know includes a combination of short answer and open-ended questions, all cross-referenced to relevant lessons of the unit.

A **Unit Problem** involves students in the context used to introduce the unit. A **Check List** in the Student Book tells students how their work will be assessed.

Reflect on the Unit presents a journal opportunity that asks students to consolidate their understanding of the big idea for the unit.

Cross-Strand Investigations appear once each term in the Student Book. These rich problems present an engaging context to students, and allow you to assess the extent to which students are able to synthesize and apply their learning in an integrated way.

The Teacher Guide provides a rubric and supporting notes for each Cross-Strand Investigation, in the **Additional Assessment Support** module that accompanies the Teacher Guide.

A three-part **Unit Test** in the Teacher Guide includes a short-answer section, conceptual items, and a problem to be solved.

> Teachers are facing increased pressures around accountability. They need some practical support to meet new reporting requirements.
> – Jason Johnston, Program Author

Reporting Opportunities

Managing your assessment strategies is a first step in your effective communication regarding student performance, whether informally through parent interviews, or through your preparation of student reports. *Addison Wesley Mathematics Makes Sense* supports your reporting requirements in a number of ways.

- By offering a **Scope and Sequence** that allows you to cover several strands in each term, with each strand appearing at least once in each grade
- With a **Learning Skills Checklist** that lets you summarize observations for possible use in report card comments
- With an **Ongoing Observations Checklist** for each unit that lets you track student performance lesson by lesson, with each lesson tied to your specific curriculum expectations/outcomes
- With specific **rubrics** that match your provincial reporting protocols
- With a **Unit Summary** tracking sheet that lets you record a student's most consistent achievement level in each block of lessons from the unit, with space for anecdotal comments

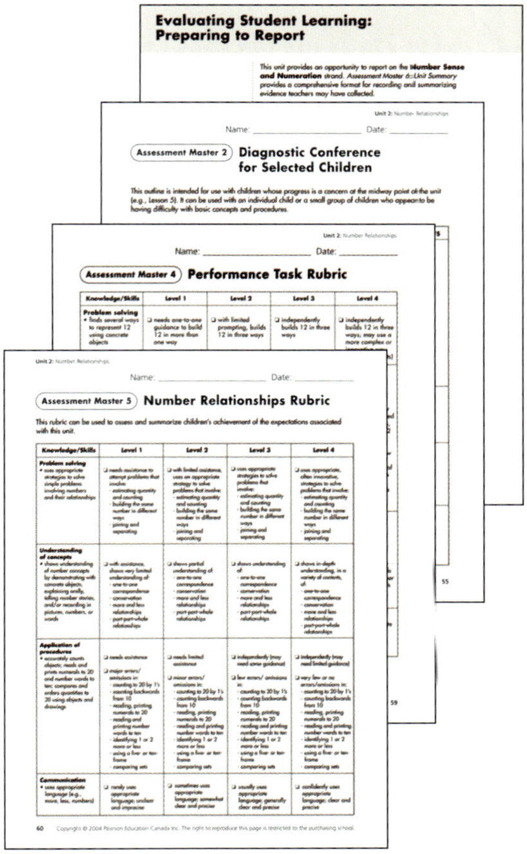

At the close of the unit, look for reporting guidelines and sample report card comments in **Evaluating Student Learning: Preparing to Report.**

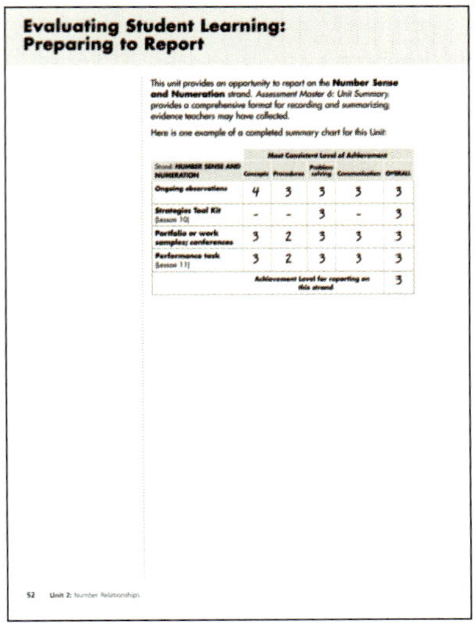

Making Sense of...

Your Curriculum Requirements

Addison Wesley Mathematics Makes Sense organizes your curriculum into clusters of expectations/outcomes across and within grades to create a logical, conceptual, and developmental progression of curriculum presentation.

The authors and development team have analyzed your curriculum document carefully, against the backdrop of sound conceptual development. The result is a carefully structured program that makes sense across the grades and, within each grade, designed to enhance student understanding and to recognize students' developmental stages.

Our scope and sequence is designed to meet the demands of your school year calendar. At each grade level, *Addison Wesley Mathematics Makes Sense* has 11 units to keep formal reporting needs to a minimum, while ensuring complete curriculum coverage.

At each grade level, unit by unit, the program filters your curriculum requirements into a selection of "curriculum clusters." Each curriculum cluster represents a "big idea," a building block to creating a deep understanding of mathematics concepts.

- The **Curriculum Overview** in each Teacher Guide unit reveals the "big ideas" of the unit at a glance.

At Grades 1 and 2

For each curriculum cluster at grades 1 and 2, we've organized a logical sequence of core **Lessons**, together with relevant **Activity Banks** to provide additional teaching options.

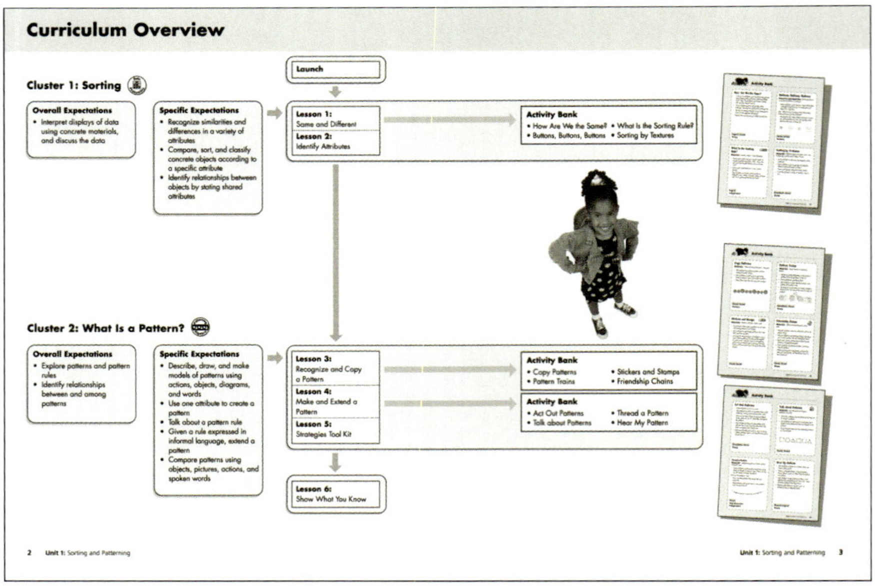

Curriculum Overview

Cluster 1: Sorting

Overall Expectations
- Interpret displays of data using concrete materials, and discuss the data

Specific Expectations
- Recognize similarities and differences in a variety of attributes
- Compare, sort, and classify concrete objects according to a specific attribute
- Identify relationships between objects by stating shared attributes

Launch

Lesson 1: Same and Different
Lesson 2: Identify Attributes

Activity Bank
- How Are We the Same?
- What Is the Sorting Rule?
- Buttons, Buttons, Buttons
- Sorting by Textures

Cluster 2: What Is a Pattern?

Overall Expectations
- Explore patterns and pattern rules
- Identify relationships between and among patterns

Specific Expectations
- Describe, draw, and make models of patterns using actions, objects, diagrams, and words
- Use one attribute to create a pattern
- Talk about a pattern rule
- Given a rule expressed in informal language, extend a pattern
- Compare patterns using objects, pictures, actions, and spoken words

Lesson 3: Recognize and Copy a Pattern
Lesson 4: Make and Extend a Pattern
Lesson 5: Strategies Tool Kit

Activity Bank
- Copy Patterns
- Stickers and Stamps
- Pattern Trains
- Friendship Chains

Activity Bank
- Act Out Patterns
- Thread a Pattern
- Talk about Patterns
- Hear My Pattern

Lesson 6: Show What You Know

2 **Unit 1:** Sorting and Patterning

Unit 1: Sorting and Patterning 3

> A curriculum document sets out overall content goals. It is our responsibility to make that content unfold in the classroom on a daily basis.
> – Bryn Keyes, Program Author

At Grades 3 and up

The Curriculum Overview in grades 3 and up shows how the lessons develop across the unit.

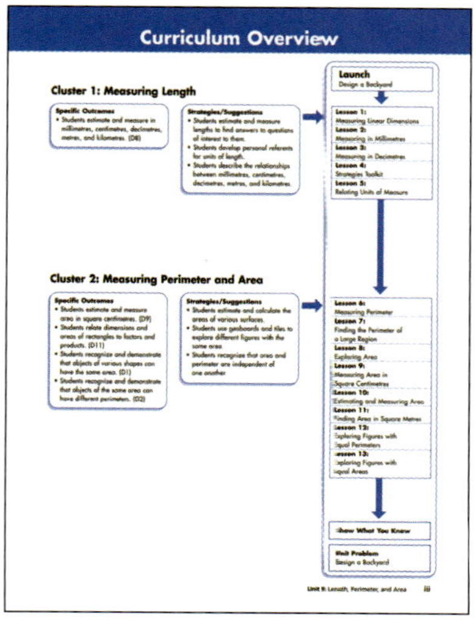

- The **Curriculum Focus** is summarized for each lesson and lists specific outcomes/expectations that relate to the lesson.

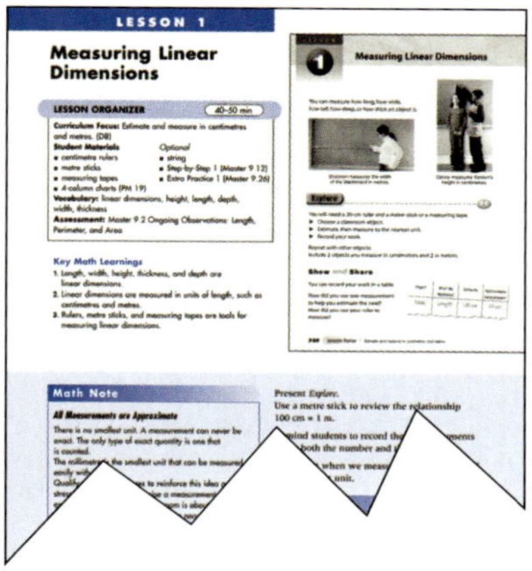

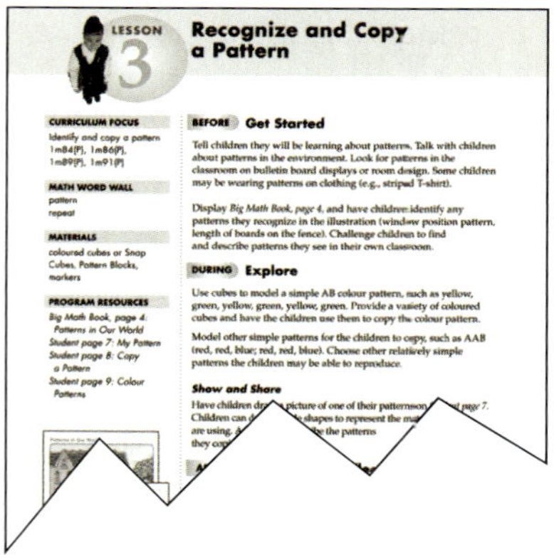

Your regional **Teacher Guide** highlights specific curriculum requirements and

- Year-long planning suggestions
- A **Curriculum Overview** in each unit that clusters and correlates your curriculum to specific lessons
- Specific lesson notes and suggestions
- The CD-ROM that accompanies your Teacher Guide

Making Sense of...

Solutions for Combined Grades

Teachers of combined grades have a special challenge in their task of providing full curriculum coverage for different grade levels, in the same classroom and during the same class period, while addressing the learning needs of all their students. *Addison Wesley Mathematics Makes Sense* offers planning tools for day-to-day support of combined grades classrooms.

Available as a supplement to your Teacher Guide, our **Together Resources** provide practical suggestions for planning and teaching combined grades.

- Background notes outline 3 general lesson approaches, depending on the nature of the content at hand and students' prior knowledge
- Specific unit suggestions identify a day-to-day unit plan with recommended lesson approaches, notes for specific activities, and homework assignments from the unit

In our earliest planning, combined grades have been considered in the creation of the **K to 8 Scope and Sequence.** Wherever the mathematical content allowed, and the curriculum requirements indicated, our development team strove to ensure that unit content aligned across the grades.

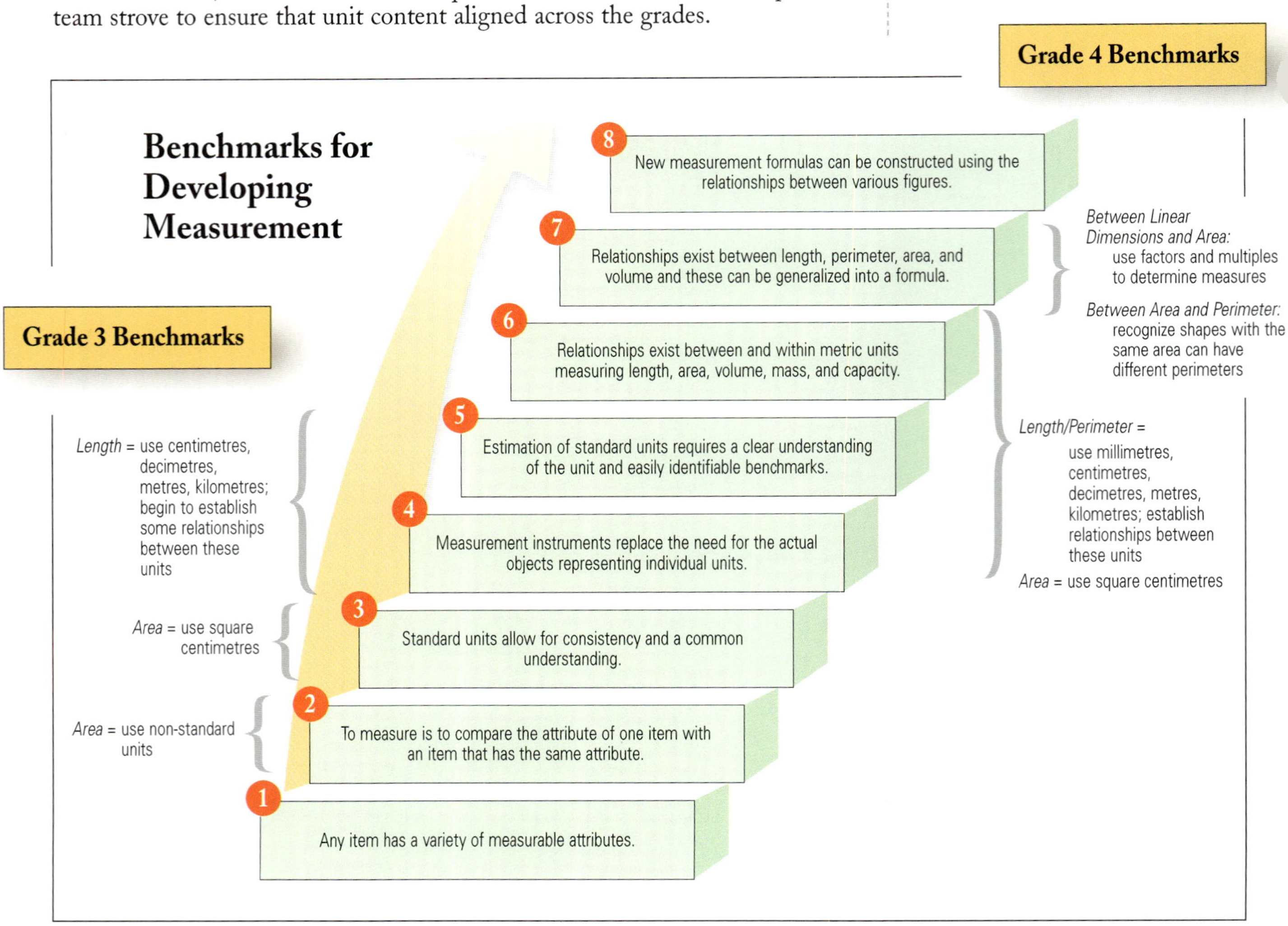

Understanding developmental stages provides a framework for planning effective mathematics lessons to meet the needs of all students.
– Craig Featherstone, Program Consultant

K to 2 Scope and Sequence: Supporting Combined Grades

Although headings may change, they accurately reflect content plans.

Kindergarten	Unit	Grade 1	Grade 2
Number Sense and Numeration	1	**Sorting and Patterning**	**Sorting and Patterning**
Measurement	2	**Number Development:** Number Relationships	**Number Development:** Counting and Patterns
Geometry	3	**Measurement:** Time, Temperature, and Money	**Measurement:** Time, Temperature, and Money
		Cross-Strand Investigation	Cross-Strand Investigation
Patterning and Algebra	4	**Number Operations:** Addition and Subtraction to 12	**Number Operations:** Exploring Addition and Subtraction
Data Management	5	**Data Management and Probability**	**Data Management and Probability**
	6	**3-Dimensional Geometry**	**3-Dimensional Geometry**
	7	**Number Operations:** Addition and Subtraction	**Number Operations:** Addition and Subtraction
		Cross-Strand Investigation	Cross-Strand Investigation
	8	**Measurement:** Linear Measurement and Area	**Measurement:** Linear Measurement and Area
	9	**2-Dimensional Geometry**	**2-Dimensional Geometry**
	10	**Number Operations:** Number and Applications	**Number Operations:** Number and Number Patterns
	11	**Measurement:** Mass and Capacity	**Measurement:** Mass and Capacity
		Cross-Strand Investigation	Cross-Strand Investigation

Grades 3 to 6 Scope and Sequence: Supporting Combined Grades

Although headings may change, they accurately reflect content plans.

Unit	Grade 3	Grade 4	Grade 5	Grade 6
1	**Patterns in Number:** Patterns and Place Value	**Patterns in Number**	**Patterns in Number**	**Patterns in Number:** Patterns and Algebra
2	**Number Operations:** Patterns in Addition and Subtraction	**Number Operations:** Whole Numbers and Operations	**Number Operations:** Whole Numbers and Operations	**Number Operations:** Whole Numbers and Operations
3	**Geometry**	**Geometry**	**Geometry**	**Geometry**
	Cross-Strand Investigation	Cross-Strand Investigation	Cross-Strand Investigation	Cross-Strand Investigation
4	**Number Operations:** Multiplication and Division	**Number Operations:** Multiplication and Division	**Number Development:** Decimals	**Number Development:** Fractions and Decimals
5	**Data Management**	**Data Management**	**Data Management**	**Data Management**
6	**Measurement:** Time, Money, and Mass	**Measurement:** Time, Money, and Mass	**Measurement:** Time, Money, and Mass	**Measurement:** Time, Money, and Mass
7	**Geometry:** Transformational Geometry	**Geometry:** Transformational Geometry	**Geometry:** 3-D Geometry and Measurement	**Geometry:** 3-D Geometry and Measurement
	Cross-Strand Investigation	Cross-Strand Investigation	Cross-Strand Investigation	Cross-Strand Investigation
8	**Fractions**	**Fractions and Decimals**	**Fractions and Decimals**	**Fractions:** Ratio, Rate, and Percent
9	**Measurement:** Length, Perimeter, and Area	**Measurement:** Length, Perimeter, and Area	**Measurement:** Length, Perimeter, and Area	**Measurement:** Length, Perimeter, and Area
10	**Patterns and Relationships:** Patterns in Geometry	**Patterns and Relationships:** Patterns in Number and Geometry	**Patterns and Relationships:** Patterns in Number and Geometry	**Patterns and Relationships:** Patterning and Algebra
11	**Probability**	**Probability**	**Probability**	**Probability**
	Cross-Strand Investigation	Cross-Strand Investigation	Cross-Strand Investigation	Cross-Strand Investigation

Grades 7 to 8 Scope and Sequence: Supporting Combined Grades

Although headings may change, they accurately reflect content plans.

Unit	Grade 7	Grade 8
1	**Whole Numbers and Patterns**	**Number and Patterns**
2	**Number Development:** Fractions and Decimals	**Number Development:** Fractions and Decimals
3	**Geometry**	**Geometry**
	Cross-Strand Investigation	Cross-Strand Investigation
4	**Number Development:** Working with Percent	**Number Development:** Working with Percent
5	**Data Management:** Collect, Analyse, and Display	**Data Management:** Collect, Analyse, Display, Infer from Data
6	**Measurement:** Perimeter and Area	**Measurement:** Circle and Triangle Measurement
7	**Geometry and Measurement**	**Geometry and Measurement**
	Cross-Strand Investigation	Cross-Strand Investigation
8	**Ratio and Proportion**	**Ratio and Proportion**
9	**Integers**	**Integers**
10	**Patterning and Algebra:** Linear Equations	**Patterning and Algebra:** Linear Equations
11	**Data Analysis and Probability**	**Data Analysis and Probability**
	Cross-Strand Investigation	Cross-Strand Investigation

Making Sense of...

Reaching All Learners

Addison Wesley Mathematics Makes Sense meets diverse needs in both the Student Book and Teacher Guide. Through the Teacher Guide, the program also provides strategies for creating an inclusive learning environment while supporting individual student needs.

From the ground up . . . the Lesson Model

A consistent lesson model simplifies the instructional design while offering a balanced approach to learning new concepts.

- **Explore** activities use a variety of groupings and types of materials; their exploratory nature allows for varying background knowledge
  - **Show and Share** highlights opportunities for students to support each other in developing new concepts
- **Connect** consolidates key concepts for all learners
- **Practice** questions cover a range of difficulty levels and learning styles

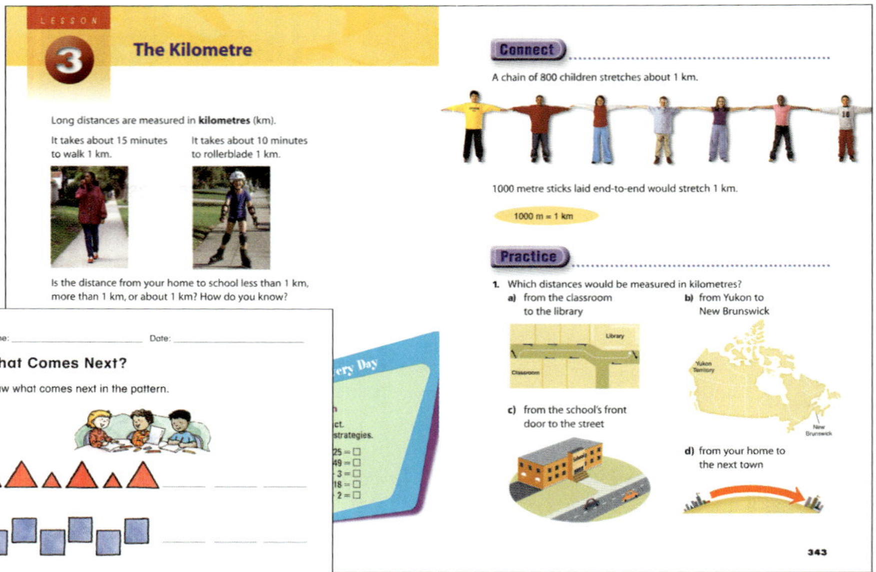

LESSON 3 The Kilometre

Long distances are measured in **kilometres** (km).

It takes about 15 minutes to walk 1 km.

It takes about 10 minutes to rollerblade 1 km.

Is the distance from your home to school less than 1 km, more than 1 km, or about 1 km? How do you know?

Connect

A chain of 800 children stretches about 1 km.

1000 metre sticks laid end-to-end would stretch 1 km.

1000 m = 1 km

Practice

1. Which distances would be measured in kilometres?
   a) from the classroom to the library
   b) from Yukon to New Brunswick
   c) from the school's front door to the street
   d) from your home to the next town

343

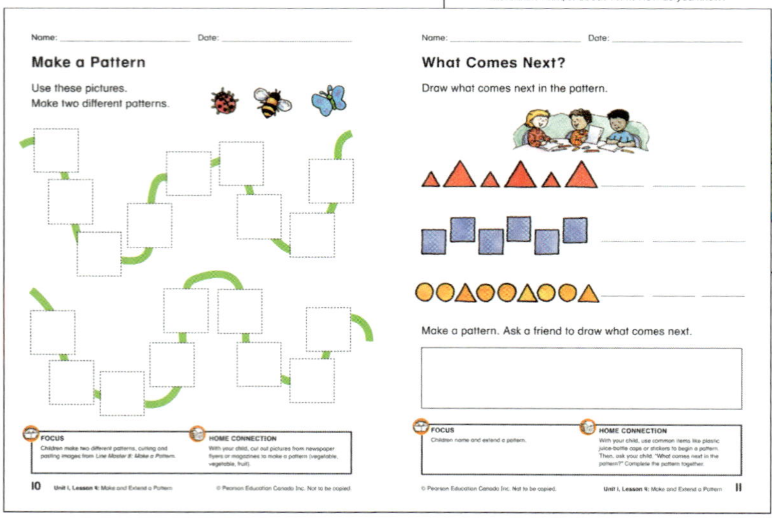

Name: Date:

Make a Pattern

Use these pictures. Make two different patterns.

FOCUS

HOME CONNECTION

10 Unit 1, Lesson 4: Make and Extend a Pattern © Pearson Education Canada Inc. Not to be copied.

Name: Date:

What Comes Next?

Draw what comes next in the pattern.

Make a pattern. Ask a friend to draw what comes next.

FOCUS

Children name and extend a pattern.

HOME CONNECTION

© Pearson Education Canada Inc. Not to be copied. Unit 1, Lesson 4: Make and Extend a Pattern 11

Understanding the elementary-level student:

- An open, inviting design with language at an appropriate reading level
- Content pacing that fits the developmental stage of the learner
- Contexts that are meaningful across cultures — from First Nations people to our multicultural mosaic
- Opportunities to communicate responses in a variety of ways — through words, numbers, pictures, or models

> All students need opportunities to apply mathematics skills and concepts in ways that are meaningful to them.
>
> – Sue Gordon, Author

Reaching all learners . . . through support in the Teacher Guide

In the Teacher Guide, additional activities address multiple intelligences, while teaching notes offer suggestions for supporting specific student needs.

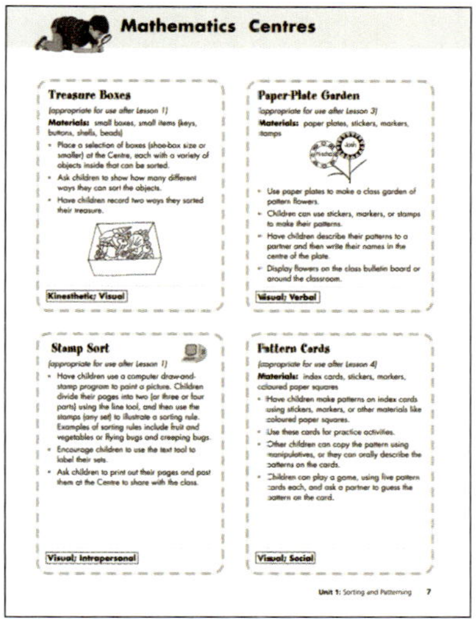

At Grades 1 and 2

- **Mathematics Centres** provide ideas for extra support and reinforcement throughout the unit
- **Practice** suggestions for core lessons include ideas for **Extra Support** for ESL learners or students who require additional reinforcement
- **Activity Banks** for core lessons identify multiple intelligences and grouping options
- **Assessment for Learning** provides suggestions for identifying and addressing specific student needs

At Grades 3 and up

- **Additional Activities** at the start of each unit provide ideas for extra support
- Notes in each lesson provide suggestions for **ESL Strategies; Alternative Explore; Common Misconceptions,** and **How to Help**
- **Assessment for Learning** provides suggestions for identifying and addressing specific student needs
- **Step by Step** offers a scaffolded problem in worksheet form, featuring the Assessment Focus question from the Practice set, provided for every lesson

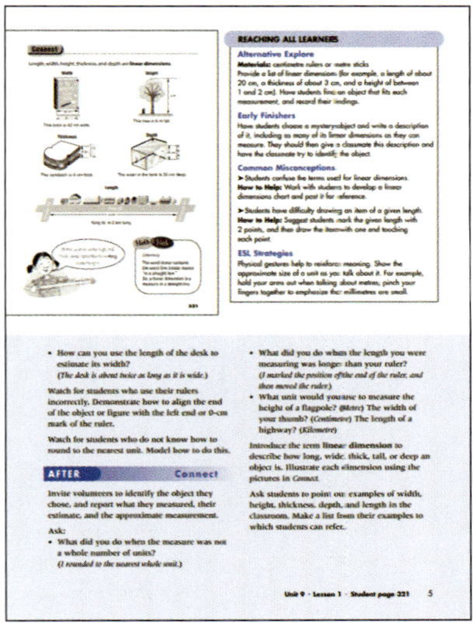

Building a Math Community

This section in the Grade 4 Planning and Program Masters module in your Teacher Guide gives you:

- Guidelines for creating a supportive environment for learning mathematics
- Suggestions for age-appropriate activities, games, and routines that help to create positive attitudes toward learning mathematics

Making Sense of...

Math Connections

Addison Wesley Mathematics Makes Sense recognizes that mathematical understanding is deepened and enhanced when students make connections between what they are learning and their own experience.

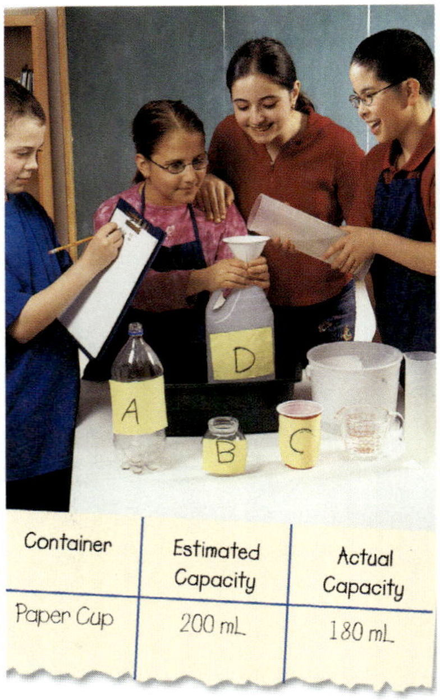

Real-World Contexts

- **Unit Launches** provide contexts to prompt mathematical conversation
- **Problem prompts** and activities in core lessons are relevant to the student's experience
- **Unit Problems** feature applied settings

Numbers Every Day

- Connects "number" to everyday class routines in Kindergarten to Grade 2, threading number concepts through all core learning in Grades 3-8

Cross-Curricular Connections

- At Kindergarten to grade 2, Teacher Guide notes in each lesson provide suggestions for relating mathematics to other subject areas – art, science, social studies, physical education, music
- At grades 3 and up, **Math Link** features in the student book highlight cross-curricular, mathematical, or real-world connections; the Teacher Guide details additional ideas

Across Strands

- Integration of strands occurs within units at the lesson level, and through the **Activity Banks** and **Mathematics Centres.**
- **Cross-Strand Investigations** appear each term, to provide opportunities for rich problem solving that draws on multiple strand concepts.

> Students better understand mathematical concepts when they make real-life connections and talk about personal experiences.
> – Angela D'Alessandro, Program Author

The Literacy and Numeracy Connection

At K to 2

- **Addison Wesley Mathematics Little Books** and **Lap Books** provide an alternative for launching or extending lessons.
- The **Big Math Book** appeals to primary-level children, many of whom may not yet be comfortable reading print. It includes chants, poems and songs that connect the kinesthetic to the linguistic.
- A take-home book with each **Investigation** in the Student Book provides a shared reading opportunity with mathematical elements.
- The **Literacy Links** feature in the Teacher Guide suggests titles that can be integrated with each lesson or used as a cross-over point with the teaching of language arts.
- Teacher Guide suggestions include use of **cooperative journals**, **pocket charts,** and a **Math Word Wall.**

At Grades 3 to 8

- **Key Words** are listed in the Student Book at the start of each unit
- Students' vocabulary is supported with an illustrated **Glossary** in the Student Book
- **Literature Opportunities** are listed in the Teacher Guide with each Unit Launch; share these literature suggestions before starting the unit to help motivate learning

Making Sense of...

Home Connections

Parents have a significant role to play in student learning, in supporting and reinforcing what is learned in the classroom each day, and promoting a positive attitude toward mathematics in the home.

Addison Wesley Mathematics Makes Sense provides several tools for communicating with parents, with a changing emphasis as the learner matures from grade 2 to grade 3, and beyond.

At Grades 1 and 2 ...in the Student Book

- Each unit includes a **Dear Family** letter regarding the upcoming unit.
- Each page presents a **Focus** statement to communicate the key learning, and a **Home Connection** suggestion for further reinforcement.
- Between selected units, **Math at Home** – a tear-out, take-home booklet – provides a magazine-style family connection with mathematical information, Canadian trivia, and game suggestions.

Name: Date:

Dear Family,

In this unit, your child will be learning about time, temperature, and money.

The Learning Goals for this unit are to

- Understand temperature as it relates to seasons and activities.
- Describe and order events, that happen in a day.
- Identify key events, such as birthdays.
- Compare the duration of events, such as recess and lunchtime.
- Name the seasons and days of the week.
- Tell time to the hour.
- Make groups of coins up to 10 cents.

You can help your child reach these goals by doing the activities suggested at the bottom of each page.

44

At K to 2 ...in the Teacher Guide

- Look for **At Home** line masters that provide a summary of the Big Ideas in the unit, with accompanying activities to reinforce key concepts at home.
- In each unit, content-specific **Assessment Tools** support the teacher when speaking with parents about children's progress.

Students, teachers, and parents are all partners in the learning process.

– Maggie Martin Connell, Program Author

At Grades 3 and up ...in the Student Book

- **Learning Goals** and **Key Words**, presented at the start of each unit, identify the content to be covered for parents as well as students.
- The **Lesson Focus** statement, on the first page of each lesson, identifies the key learning goal for the lesson.
- Parents can use the **Connect** section of each lesson to check the key concepts students have covered in class.
- Regular **At Home** features suggest activities for students to do with family members at home.

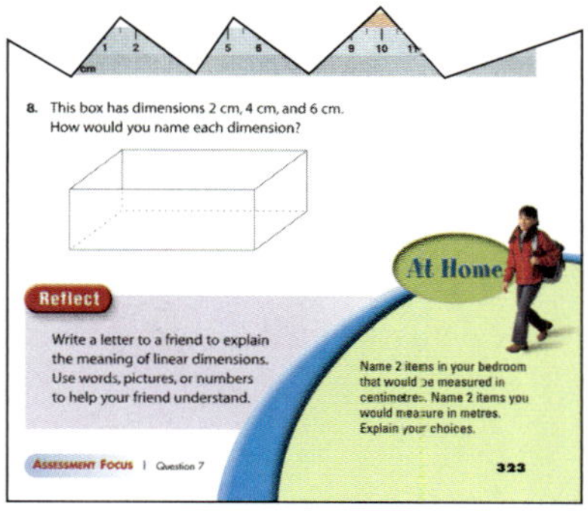

Practice and Homework Book for Grades 3 to 8

- For each lesson, a Quick Review of the key concepts
- For each lesson, graded practice questions that students can complete at home
- Games and activities used for practice when appropriate

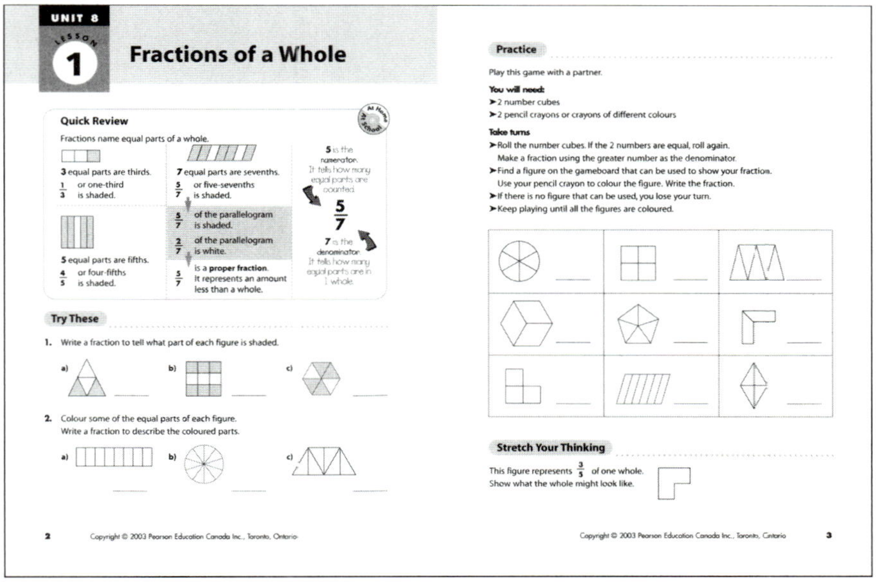

Across the Grades

The Pearson Education mathematics Website provides parent information and support.

Making Sense of...

Technology

Addison Wesley Mathematics Makes Sense integrates technology in the following ways.

- **Technology Lessons** in the student book highlight opportunities for learning new mathematical concepts through the use of the calculator or the computer.

Grade 1

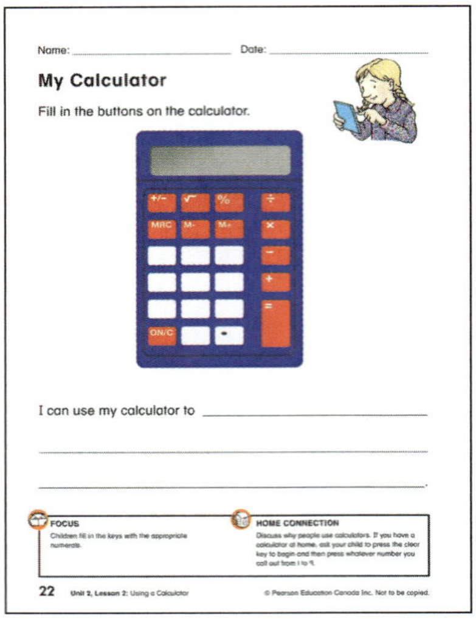

Name: ______________ Date: ______________

My Calculator

Fill in the buttons on the calculator.

I can use my calculator to ______________________________

____

______________________________.

FOCUS
Children fill in the keys with the appropriate numerals.

HOME CONNECTION
Discuss why people use calculators. If you have a calculator at home, ask your child to press the clear key to begin and then press whatever number you call out from 1 to 9.

22 **Unit 2, Lesson 2:** Using a Calculator © Pearson Education Canada Inc. Not to be copied.

Grade 4

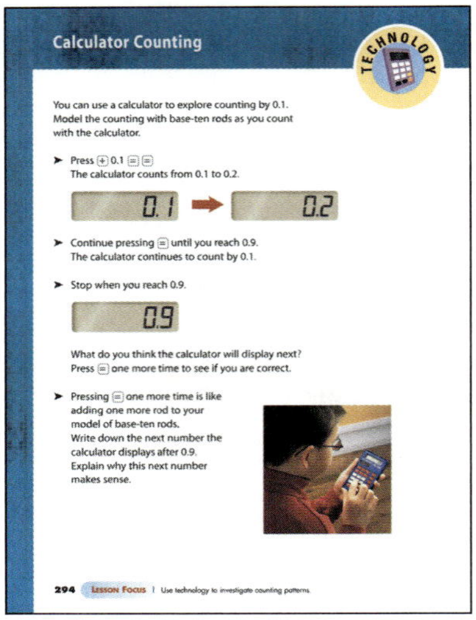

Calculator Counting

TECHNOLOGY

You can use a calculator to explore counting by 0.1.
Model the counting with base-ten rods as you count with the calculator.

➤ Press + 0.1 = =
The calculator counts from 0.1 to 0.2.

0.1 → 0.2

➤ Continue pressing = until you reach 0.9.
The calculator continues to count by 0.1.

➤ Stop when you reach 0.9.

0.9

What do you think the calculator will display next?
Press = one more time to see if you are correct.

➤ Pressing = one more time is like adding one more rod to your model of base-ten rods.
Write down the next number the calculator displays after 0.9.
Explain why this next number makes sense.

294 LESSON FOCUS | Use technology to investigate counting patterns.

- When appropriate, individual activities within the student book suggest the use of a calculator or computer application to enrich and extend the mathematics.
- Suggestions for Numbers Every Day regularly include suggestions related to Calculator Skills.

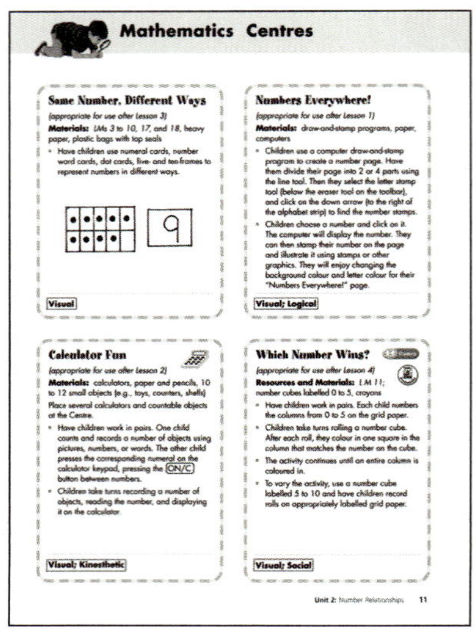

Mathematics Centres

Same Number, Different Ways
(appropriate for use after Lesson 3)
Materials: *LMs 3 to 10, 17, and 18,* heavy paper, plastic bags with top seals
- Have children use numeral cards, number word cards, dot cards, five- and ten-frames to represent numbers in different ways.

9

Visual

Numbers Everywhere!
(appropriate for use after Lesson 1)
Materials: draw-and-stamp programs, paper, computers
- Children use a computer draw-and-stamp program to create a number page. Have them divide their page into 2 or 4 parts using the line tool. Then they select the letter stamp tool (below the eraser tool on the toolbar), and click on the down arrow (to the right of the alphabet strip) to find the number stamps.
- Children choose a number and click on it. The computer will display the number. They can then stamp their number on the page and illustrate it using stamps or other graphics. They will enjoy changing the background colour and letter colour for their "Numbers Everywhere!" page.

Visual; Logical

Calculator Fun
(appropriate for use after Lesson 2)
Materials: calculators, paper and pencils, 10 to 12 small objects (e.g., toys, counters, shells)
Place several calculators and countable objects at the Centre.
- Have children work in pairs. One child counts and records a number of objects using pictures, numbers, or words. The other child presses the corresponding numeral on the calculator keypad, pressing the ON/C button between numbers.
- Children take turns recording a number of objects, reading the number, and displaying it on the calculator.

Visual; Kinesthetic

Which Number Wins?
(appropriate for use after Lesson 4)
Resources and Materials: *LM 11;* number cubes labelled 0 to 5, crayons
- Have children work in pairs. Each child numbers the columns from 0 to 5 on the grid paper.
- Children take turns rolling a number cube. After each roll, they colour in one square in the column that matches the number on the cube.
- The activity continues until an entire column is coloured in.
- To vary the activity, use a number cube labelled 5 to 10 and have children record rolls on appropriately labelled grid paper.

Visual; Social

Unit 2: Number Relationships 11

> The purposeful use of technology in the mathematics classroom can enrich student learning. It allows students to explore and develop concepts, to extend critical thinking and problem-solving skills.
>
> – Addison Wesley Mathematics Research Report

Addison Wesley Mathematics e-Tools (K-8) software helps students develop important math concepts using an electronic form of mathematics manipulatives.

- Use to guide class discussion
- Have students use e-Tools as an alternative to concrete materials
- Especially relevant for students who face motor challenges

- Place-Value Blocks
- Counters
- Money
- Time
- Fractions
- Probability
- Spreadsheet-data-grapher
- Geometry Shapes
- Geometry Drawing

Addison Wesley Mathematics Makes Sense **Website** provides a wealth of interactive online resources for teachers, students, and parents. Teachers can access their *Math Makes Sense* Teacher Guide making it easy to customize planning and assessment tools. On-line professional development opportunities, additional activities, samples of student work, sample report card comments, and parent letters in different languages are just a few of the resources teachers will find on this site. Support for students includes additional practice, activities, and web links correlated to their student book. Parents can download our *Math@Home* magazine filled with background information, Canadian math trivia, and fun games and activities the whole family can do together.

http://www.pearsoned.ca/mathmakessense/

Professional Development

Addison Wesley Mathematics Makes Sense integrates professional development for teachers throughout the program resources, and provides in-service and other tools to ensure success of program implementation.

Professional Development built right into the program. . .

Each unit in the Teacher Guide provides planning detail that includes

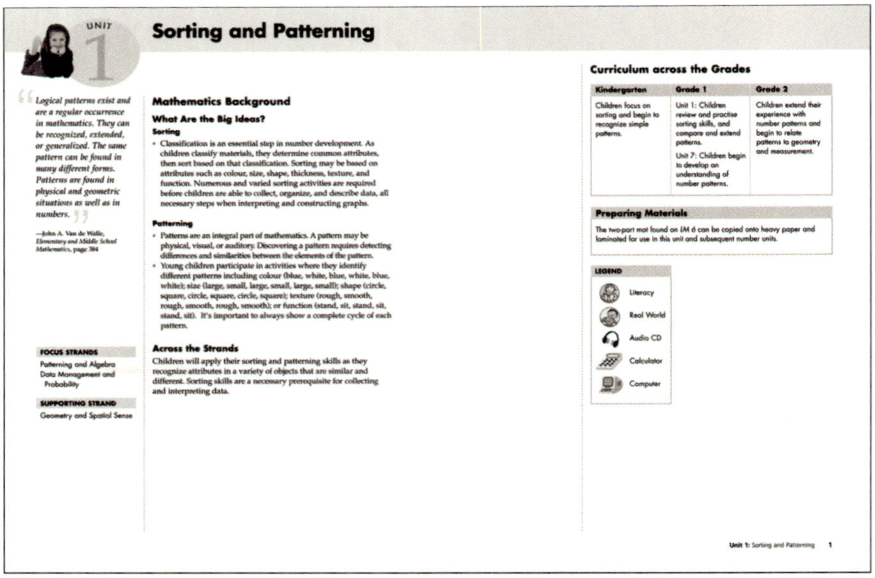

UNIT 1

Sorting and Patterning

"Logical patterns exist and are a regular occurrence in mathematics. They can be recognized, extended, or generalized. The same pattern can be found in many different forms. Patterns are found in physical and geometric situations as well as in numbers."

—John A. Van de Walle, *Elementary and Middle School Mathematics*, page 384

FOCUS STRANDS

Patterning and Algebra
Data Management and Probability

SUPPORTING STRAND

Geometry and Spatial Sense

Mathematics Background

What Are the Big Ideas?

Sorting

- Classification is an essential step in number development. As children classify materials, they determine common attributes, then sort based on that classification. Sorting may be based on attributes such as colour, size, shape, thickness, texture, and function. Numerous and varied sorting activities are required before children are able to collect, organize, and describe data, all necessary steps when interpreting and constructing graphs.

Patterning

- Patterns are an integral part of mathematics. A pattern may be physical, visual, or auditory. Discovering a pattern requires detecting differences and similarities between the elements of the pattern.
- Young children participate in activities where they identify different patterns including colour (blue, white, blue, white, blue, white); size (large, small, large, small, large, small); shape (circle, square, circle, square, circle, square); texture (rough, smooth, rough, smooth, rough, smooth); or function (stand, sit, stand, sit, stand, sit). It's important to always show a complete cycle of each pattern.

Across the Strands

Children will apply their sorting and patterning skills as they recognize attributes in a variety of objects that are similar and different. Sorting skills are a necessary prerequisite for collecting and interpreting data.

Curriculum across the Grades

Kindergarten	Grade 1	Grade 2
Children focus on sorting and begin to recognize simple patterns.	Unit 1: Children review and practise sorting skills, and compare and extend patterns. Unit 7: Children begin to develop an understanding of number patterns.	Children extend their experience with number patterns and begin to relate patterns to geometry and measurement.

Preparing Materials

The two-part mat found on *LM 6* can be copied onto heavy paper and laminated for use in this unit and subsequent number units.

LEGEND

Literacy
Real World
Audio CD
Calculator
Computer

Unit 1: Sorting and Patterning 1

- A **Mathematics Background** section, with information for the teacher about the key mathematics concepts to be developed
- **Across the Grades** summary, to show how the topic develops over a three-year window, from the previous grade, to this grade, to the next grade
- Information about how the unit makes connections between various mathematics strands, in **Across the Strands**
- Expert quotes that point to further reading for interested teachers

Each lesson further supports professional development in a lesson model that offers

- Connect section to establish the key mathematical understanding of the lesson
- Focus statement to identify the key concepts of the lesson to teachers as well as parents and children
- A variety of instructional strategies detailed in the supporting Teacher Guide notes

> Teachers' confidence and understanding of mathematics is an essential criterion for their students' success.
> – Trevor Brown, Program Author

Professional Development in direct support of the program

Pearson Education offers flexibility and choice with a range of professional development options.

Customized In-Service and Partnerships

- Workshops, institutes, and on-line in-service led by leading local, national and international math educators such as:

John A. Van de Walle
Elementary Mathematics Advisor

Craig Featherstone
Pearson Education Consultant

Trevor Brown
Toronto, Ontario

Mignonne Wood
Vancouver, British Columbia

Maggie Martin Connell
Atlantic Canada

Jodi Mackie
Edmonton, Alberta

Administrator's Handbook

- Authored by Mignonne Wood, Steve Cairns
- Designed to assist principals in implementing a new mathematics program
- Shows how to foster a positive attitude toward teaching mathematics by building understanding within the school community, with teachers and parents

Van de Walle Facilitator's Guide

- Based on *Elementary and Middle School Mathematics: Teaching Developmentally* by John A. Van de Walle, a teaching methodology resource for the elementary teacher of mathematics
- Provides an organization for a Van de Walle Book Study group model

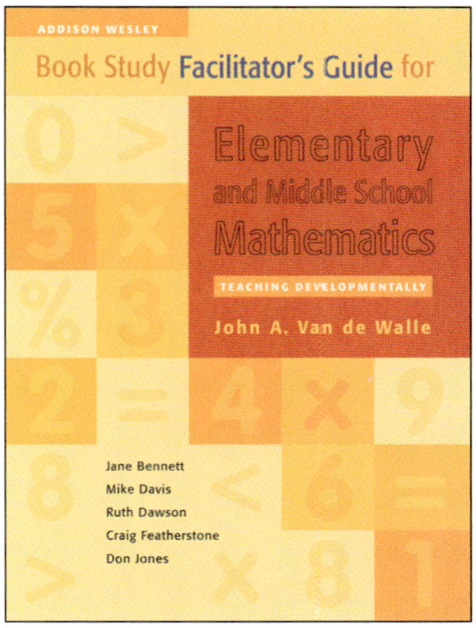

Pearson Professional Learning

- Quality, sustained, comprehensive teacher professional development at affordable prices

Using Your Teacher Guide...

Addison Wesley Mathematics Makes Sense recognizes that teachers need a program with quick access to ideas for instruction and teacher support features.

Your Teacher Guide has separate modules for each unit of instruction, with additional modules to support your year-long planning:

- **Program Overview** provides detailed information about the overall structure and features of the program.
- **Building a Math Community** (grades 1 and 2) provides a description of a positive environment, and practical suggestions for organizing your classroom and materials, as well as grade-specific ideas for routines and activities.
- The **Additional Assessment Support** module includes a selection of assessment tools that can be used throughout the program for your assessment and reporting needs.
- **Planning and Program Masters** (grades 3 to 8) provide year at a glance planning, materials list, literature connections, and generic program blackline masters. This module includes the feature "Building a Math Community."

The enclosed CD provides additional support and ensures ease of use, with

- A grade-level correlation showing our complete curriculum fit
- Editable versions of unit planning charts, rubrics, and other assessment tools
- Files for selected line masters

Planning a Unit

Each unit module in your Teacher Guide starts with several pages to support your planning for the unit. You'll see **Mathematics Background, Curriculum across the Grades,** and a **Curriculum Overview.**

Planning Charts provide overviews of lessons, materials requirements, assessment opportunities, and suggested times.

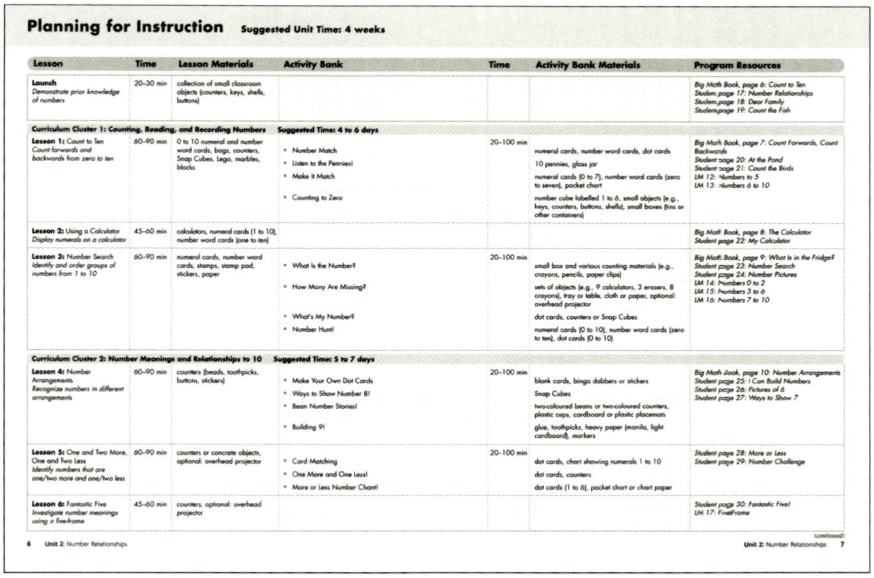

In grades 1 and 2, one of your planning pages describes **Mathematics Centres** that you can set up in advance for use at various points through the unit. Lesson notes reference centres for support in individualizing instruction.

Grade 1

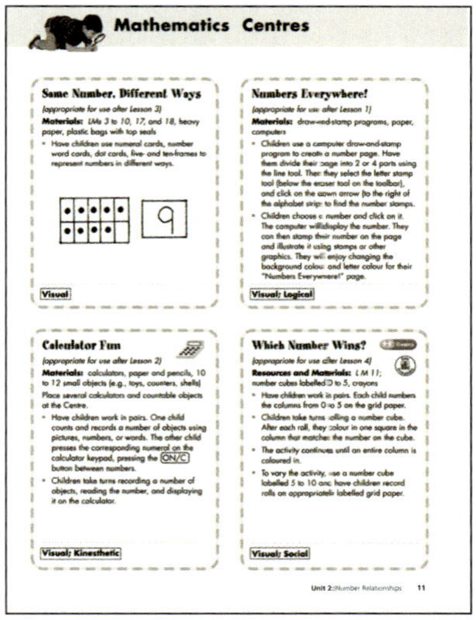

In grades 3 and up, one of your planning pages describes **Additional Activities** that you can organize for use at various points through the unit. Each **Additional Activity** comes with an accompanying activity **Master**, provided at the end of the module.

Grade 4

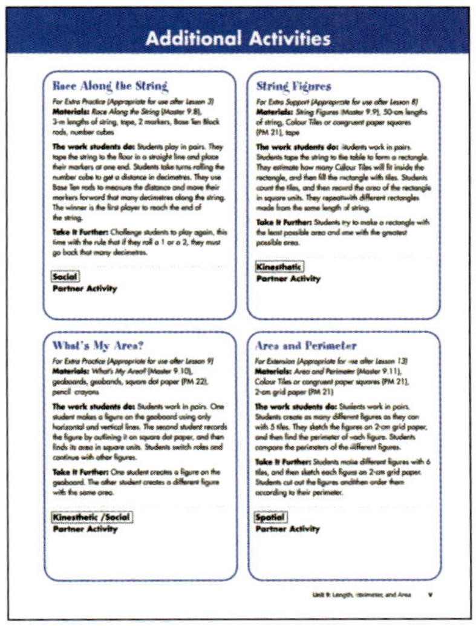

At Grades 1 and 2

When you're ready to start the unit, the Teacher Guide lessons provide professional choices within a consistent structure.

The suggested **Unit Launch** describes a 20-minute introduction to activate prior knowledge and engage the learner.

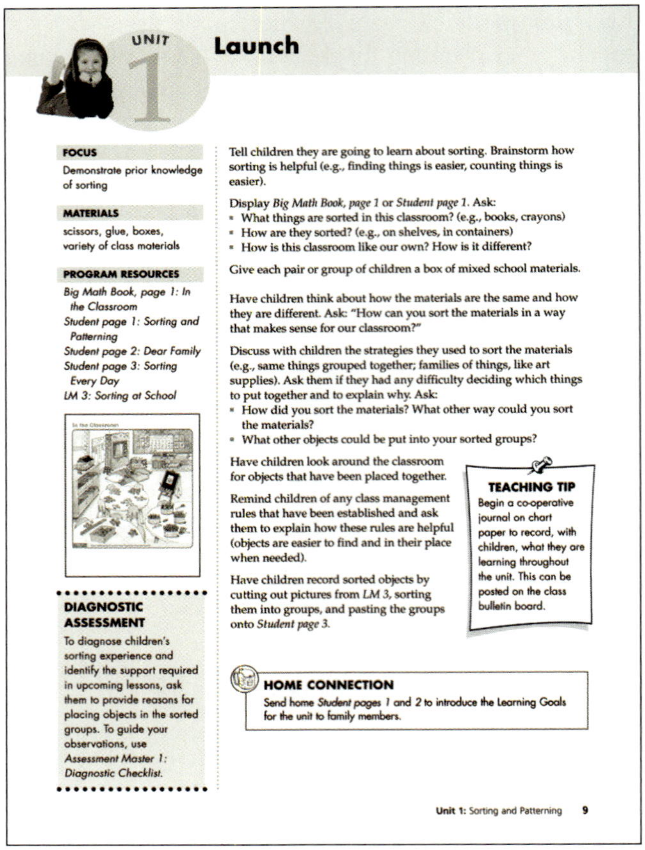

UNIT 1

Launch

FOCUS

Demonstrate prior knowledge of sorting

MATERIALS

scissors, glue, boxes, variety of class materials

PROGRAM RESOURCES

Big Math Book, page 1: In the Classroom
Student page 1: Sorting and Patterning
Student page 2: Dear Family
Student page 3: Sorting Every Day
LM 3: Sorting at School

DIAGNOSTIC ASSESSMENT

To diagnose children's sorting experience and identify the support required in upcoming lessons, ask them to provide reasons for placing objects in the sorted groups. To guide your observations, use *Assessment Master 1: Diagnostic Checklist.*

Tell children they are going to learn about sorting. Brainstorm how sorting is helpful (e.g., finding things is easier, counting things is easier).

Display *Big Math Book, page 1* or *Student page 1*. Ask:
- What things are sorted in this classroom? (e.g., books, crayons)
- How are they sorted? (e.g., on shelves, in containers)
- How is this classroom like our own? How is it different?

Give each pair or group of children a box of mixed school materials.

Have children think about how the materials are the same and how they are different. Ask: "How can you sort the materials in a way that makes sense for our classroom?"

Discuss with children the strategies they used to sort the materials (e.g., same things grouped together; families of things, like art supplies). Ask them if they had any difficulty deciding which things to put together and to explain why. Ask:
- How did you sort the materials? What other way could you sort the materials?
- What other objects could be put into your sorted groups?

Have children look around the classroom for objects that have been placed together.

Remind children of any class management rules that have been established and ask them to explain how these rules are helpful (objects are easier to find and in their place when needed).

Have children record sorted objects by cutting out pictures from *LM 3*, sorting them into groups, and pasting the groups onto *Student page 3*.

TEACHING TIP

Begin a co-operative journal on chart paper to record, with children, what they are learning throughout the unit. This can be posted on the class bulletin board.

HOME CONNECTION

Send home *Student pages 1* and *2* to introduce the Learning Goals for the unit to family members.

Unit 1: Sorting and Patterning 9

Notes on **Diagnostic Assessment** help you interpret students' responses, and provide support where needed. Use the supporting master available in the module.

Home Connection highlights opportunities for communication with the home that also appear in the Student Book.

Throughout the teaching notes for the unit, **Teaching Tip** highlights instructional strategies.

As a teacher, I'm looking for lessons I know I can deliver. As an author, I look for ways to embed professional development in the Teacher Guide, in student activities that are developmentally appropriate. – Michelle Jackson, Program Author

Lessons

Each lesson provides a consistent framework for teaching new concepts and procedural skills: **Explore, Connect and Reflect,** and **Practice.**

LESSON 1

Same and Different

CURRICULUM FOCUS

Demonstrate an understanding that objects can be sorted in more than one way according to one attribute
1m85(P), 1m97(DM), 1m98(DM)

MATH WORD WALL

sort
sorting rule

MATERIALS

boxes or containers, small items (keys, buttons, shells, beads, small toys)

PROGRAM RESOURCES

Big Math Book, page 2: Same and Different
Student page 4: Same and Different
Student page 5: Heads Up!
Line Master 4: Same and Different

BEFORE Get Started

Show children *Big Math Book, page 2.* Ask:

- How are the animals sorted? (into groups, same types of animals are together)
- What is the sorting rule for each group? (dogs, cats, birds)

Ask children to think of another way to sort the animals (e.g., colour or type of markings, number of feet, those with wings, barn animals or pets).

Have children suggest other animals that could belong to the groups.

TRY THIS See the Literacy Links on page 12. You may want to introduce the concept by sharing the book *Which Belong Together?* with children.

DURING Explore

Provide each group or pair of children with a box or container of objects to sort. Allow children time to explore the items inside the boxes.

Problem Prompt
How many different ways can you sort the objects in your boxes?

Show and Share

Invite children to show how they sorted their collections. Ask:

- What is your sorting rule?
- What other ways can you sort the objects?

Have children sort the objects again using a new sorting rule. Allow enough time for children to sort and re-sort the objects in different ways.

AFTER Connect and Reflect

Bring the class together to discuss the various ways objects can be sorted. Use children's examples to indicate that items can be sorted by colour, shape, size, function, or any other justifiable attribute suggested by the children. Ask:

- What did you look for when you sorted the same objects in a different way?
- What is your new sorting rule?

10 **Unit 1:** Sorting and Patterning

TEACHING TIP
Begin a math word wall of mathematical words. The children can refer to these words when they are writing. As *sort* and *sorting rule* are modelled, place them on the math word wall.

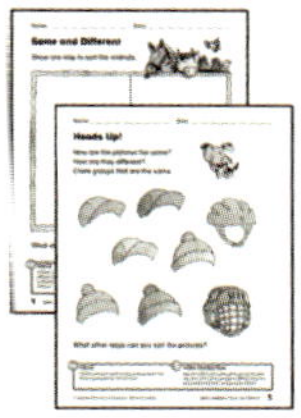

Practice

Reinforcement
Have children cut out pictures from *LM 4*, sort them into groups, and paste the groups onto *Student page 4*.

Read the directions on *Student page 5* with the children. After they have completed the page, discuss the different ways the pictures could have been sorted (summer/winter; brims/no brims; chin strap/no chin strap).

Extra Support: ESL
Children can practise and apply their sorting skills at the Mathematics Centres (Treasure Boxes and Stamp Sort, page 7). Have children describe the objects in detail to enable them to sort by more apparent attributes such as colour and size.

ESL learners will benefit from working with and describing one attribute at a time. Consider providing word cards to help reinforce some of the vocabulary they are learning.

Extension
Have early finishers work in pairs or on their own to create a secret sorting rule game using one attribute. Invite children to explain and share their games with the class or another pair of children.

Assessment for Learning

What to Look For	What to Do
Evidence that children ▪ sort accurately using one attribute ▪ find more than one way to sort ▪ use mathematical language appropriately	Conduct brief conferences to determine why some children are having difficulty. Support them by ▪ posing questions that help children to see that an object can be described by a variety of attributes and sorted accordingly; ▪ asking children to describe objects in detail to help them think of additional attributes for sorting; ▪ modelling mathematical language: "You have sorted these buttons by putting the same colours together. I think your sorting rule is dark colours/light colours.

To guide observations and facilitate reporting, use Assessment Master 3.1: Ongoing Observations Checklist: Sorting.

Unit 1: Sorting and Patterning 11

Here, and in all lessons, check the margin if you need information on curriculum match, or specific materials needed.

- Curriculum Focus
- Materials
- Program Resources

Assessment for Learning appears in every lesson with the main teaching notes, to help shape your formative assessment.

Then, turn the page for additional features that let you deepen the content, or spend additional focused time when needed.

Literacy Links
Providing an alternative way to begin some lessons, using literature and literacy as an entry point for learning

Numbers Every Day
Creating an awareness of number in classroom routine and day-to-day activities

Cross-Curricular Connections
Connecting math to other subject areas

Activity Banks provide up to four additional activity ideas related to the core content of the lesson. Select Activity Banks based on your class needs, and those of individual students. Each activity is keyed to learning style, and grouping requirements.

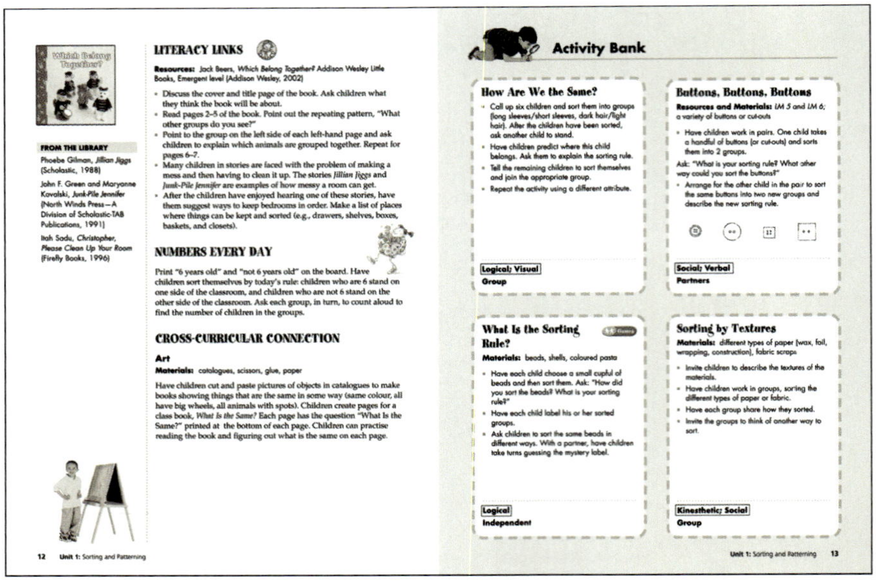

Each unit also provides ideas for teaching problem solving, and assessing student performance on the whole unit.

Strategies Tool Kit

Focusing on the strategies and processes children need to master to become effective problem solvers

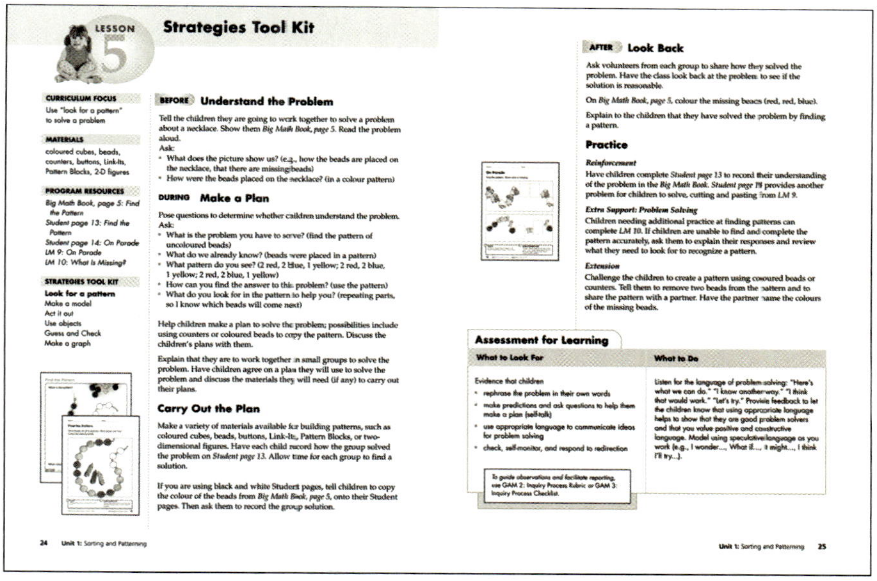

LESSON 5

Strategies Tool Kit

CURRICULUM FOCUS
Use "look for a pattern" to solve a problem

MATERIALS
coloured cubes, beads, counters, buttons, Link-Its, Pattern Blocks, 2-D figures

PROGRAM RESOURCES
Big Math Book, page 5: Find the Pattern
Student page 13: Find the Pattern
Student page 14: On Parade
LM 9: On Parade
LM 10: What Is Missing?

STRATEGIES TOOL KIT
Look for a pattern
Make a model
Act it out
Use objects
Guess and Check
Make a graph

BEFORE Understand the Problem

Tell the children they are going to work together to solve a problem about a necklace. Show them *Big Math Book, page 5.* Read the problem aloud.
Ask:
- What does the picture show us? (e.g., how the beads are placed on the necklace, that there are missing beads)
- How were the beads placed on the necklace? (in a colour pattern)

DURING Make a Plan

Pose questions to determine whether children understand the problem.
Ask:
- What is the problem you have to solve? (find the pattern of uncoloured beads)
- What do we already know? (beads were placed in a pattern)
- What pattern do you see? (2 red, 2 blue, 1 yellow; 2 red, 2 blue, 1 yellow; 2 red, 2 blue, 1 yellow)
- How can you find the answer to this problem? (use the pattern)
- What do you look for in the pattern to help you? (repeating parts, so I know which beads will come next)

Help children make a plan to solve the problem; possibilities include using counters or coloured beads to copy the pattern. Discuss the children's plans with them.

Explain that they are to work together in small groups to solve the problem. Have children agree on a plan they will use to solve the problem and discuss the materials they will need (if any) to carry out their plans.

Carry Out the Plan

Make a variety of materials available for building patterns, such as coloured cubes, beads, buttons, Link-Its, Pattern Blocks, or two-dimensional figures. Have each child record how the group solved the problem on *Student page 13.* Allow time for each group to find a solution.

If you are using black and white Student pages, tell children to copy the colour of the beads from *Big Math Book, page 5,* onto their Student pages. Then ask them to record the group solution.

24 Unit 1: Sorting and Patterning

AFTER Look Back

Ask volunteers from each group to share how they solved the problem. Have the class look back at the problem to see if the solution is reasonable.

On *Big Math Book, page 5,* colour the missing beads (red, red, blue).

Explain to the children that they have solved the problem by finding a pattern.

Practice

Reinforcement
Have children complete *Student page 13* to record their understanding of the problem in the *Big Math Book. Student page 14* provides another problem for children to solve, cutting and pasting from *LM 9.*

Extra Support: Problem Solving
Children needing additional practice at finding patterns can complete *LM 10.* If children are unable to find and complete the pattern accurately, ask them to explain their responses and review what they need to look for to recognize a pattern.

Extension
Challenge the children to create a pattern using coloured beads or counters. Tell them to remove two beads from the pattern and to share the pattern with a partner. Have the partner name the colours of the missing beads.

Assessment for Learning

What to Look For	What to Do
Evidence that children • rephrase the problem in their own words • make predictions and ask questions to help them make a plan (self-talk) • use appropriate language to communicate ideas for problem solving • check, self-monitor, and respond to redirection	Listen for the language of problem solving: "Here's what we can do." "I know another way." "I think that would work." "Let's try." Provide feedback to let the children know that using appropriate language helps to show that they are good problem solvers and that you value positive and constructive language. Model using speculative language as you work (e.g., I wonder..., What if..., it might..., I think I'll try...).

To guide observations and facilitate reporting, use GAM 2: Inquiry Process Rubric or GAM 3: Inquiry Process Checklist.

Unit 1: Sorting and Patterning 25

Show What You Know

Your Teacher Guide pages detail a performance task that will allow for demonstration of the learning through the unit.

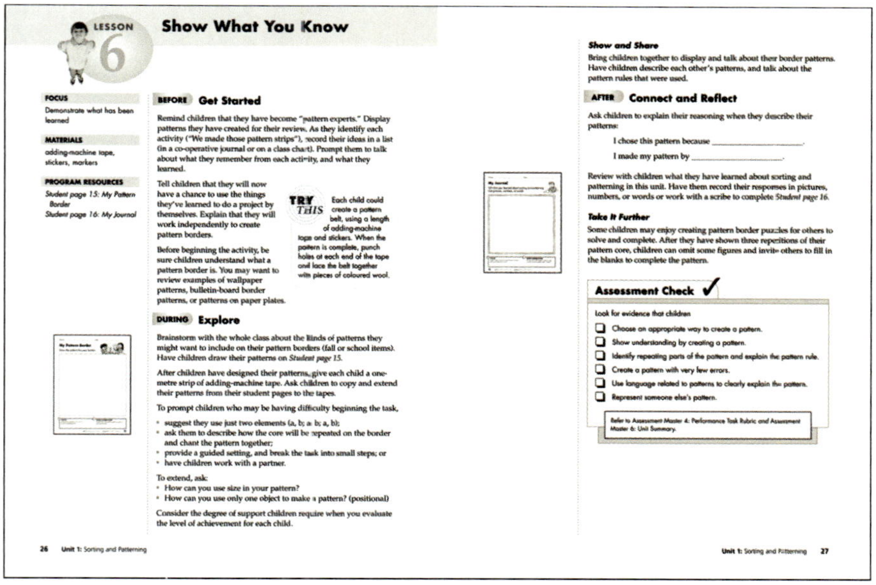

LESSON 6

Show What You Know

FOCUS
Demonstrate what has been learned

MATERIALS
adding-machine tape, stickers, markers

PROGRAM RESOURCES
Student page 15: My Pattern Border
Student page 16: My Journal

BEFORE Get Started

Remind children that they have become "pattern experts." Display patterns they have created for their review. As they identify each activity ("We made those pattern strips"), record their ideas in a list (in a co-operative journal or on a class chart). Prompt them to talk about what they remember from each activity, and what they learned.

Tell children that they will now have a chance to use the things they've learned to do a project by themselves. Explain that they will work independently to create pattern borders.

Before beginning the activity, be sure children understand what a pattern border is. You may want to review examples of wallpaper patterns, bulletin-board border patterns, or patterns on paper plates.

TRY THIS Each child could create a pattern belt, using a length of adding-machine tape and stickers. When the pattern is complete, punch holes at each end of the tape and lace the belt together with pieces of coloured wool.

DURING Explore

Brainstorm with the whole class about the kinds of patterns they might want to include on their pattern borders (fall or school items). Have children draw their patterns on *Student page 15.*

After children have designed their patterns, give each child a one-metre strip of adding-machine tape. Ask children to copy and extend their patterns from their student pages to the tapes.

To prompt children who may be having difficulty beginning the task,
- suggest they use just two elements (a, b; a, b; a, b);
- ask them to describe how the core will be repeated on the border and chant the pattern together;
- provide a guided setting, and break the task into small steps; or
- have children work with a partner.

To extend, ask:
- How can you use size in your pattern?
- How can you use only one object to make a pattern? (positional)

Consider the degree of support children require when you evaluate the level of achievement for each child.

26 Unit 1: Sorting and Patterning

Show and Share
Bring children together to display and talk about their border patterns. Have children describe each other's patterns, and talk about the pattern rules that were used.

AFTER Connect and Reflect

Ask children to explain their reasoning when they describe their patterns:

I chose this pattern because ________________.

I made my pattern by ________________.

Review with children what they have learned about sorting and patterning in this unit. Have them record their responses in pictures, numbers, or words or work with a scribe to complete *Student page 16.*

Take It Further
Some children may enjoy creating pattern border puzzles for others to solve and complete. After they have shown three repetitions of their pattern core, children can omit some figures and invite others to fill in the blanks to complete the pattern.

Assessment Check ✓

Look for evidence that children
- ☐ Choose an appropriate way to create a pattern.
- ☐ Show understanding by creating a pattern.
- ☐ Identify repeating parts of the pattern and explain the pattern rule.
- ☐ Create a pattern with very few errors.
- ☐ Use language related to patterns to clearly explain the pattern.
- ☐ Represent someone else's pattern.

Refer to Assessment Master 4: Performance Task Rubric and Assessment Master 6: Unit Summary.

Unit 1: Sorting and Patterning 27

Use the **Assessment Check** checklist to guide your assessment of students' performance. For a more detailed assessment, use the corresponding Assessment Master, which provides a specific rubric.

At Grades 3 and up

Addison Wesley Mathematics Makes Sense moves to a more mature student book format at grade 3. The hard-cover **Student Book** provides a resource for use in the classroom, and at home. For day-to-day planning, the **Teacher Guide** gives reduced pages of the Student Book with accompanying teaching notes.

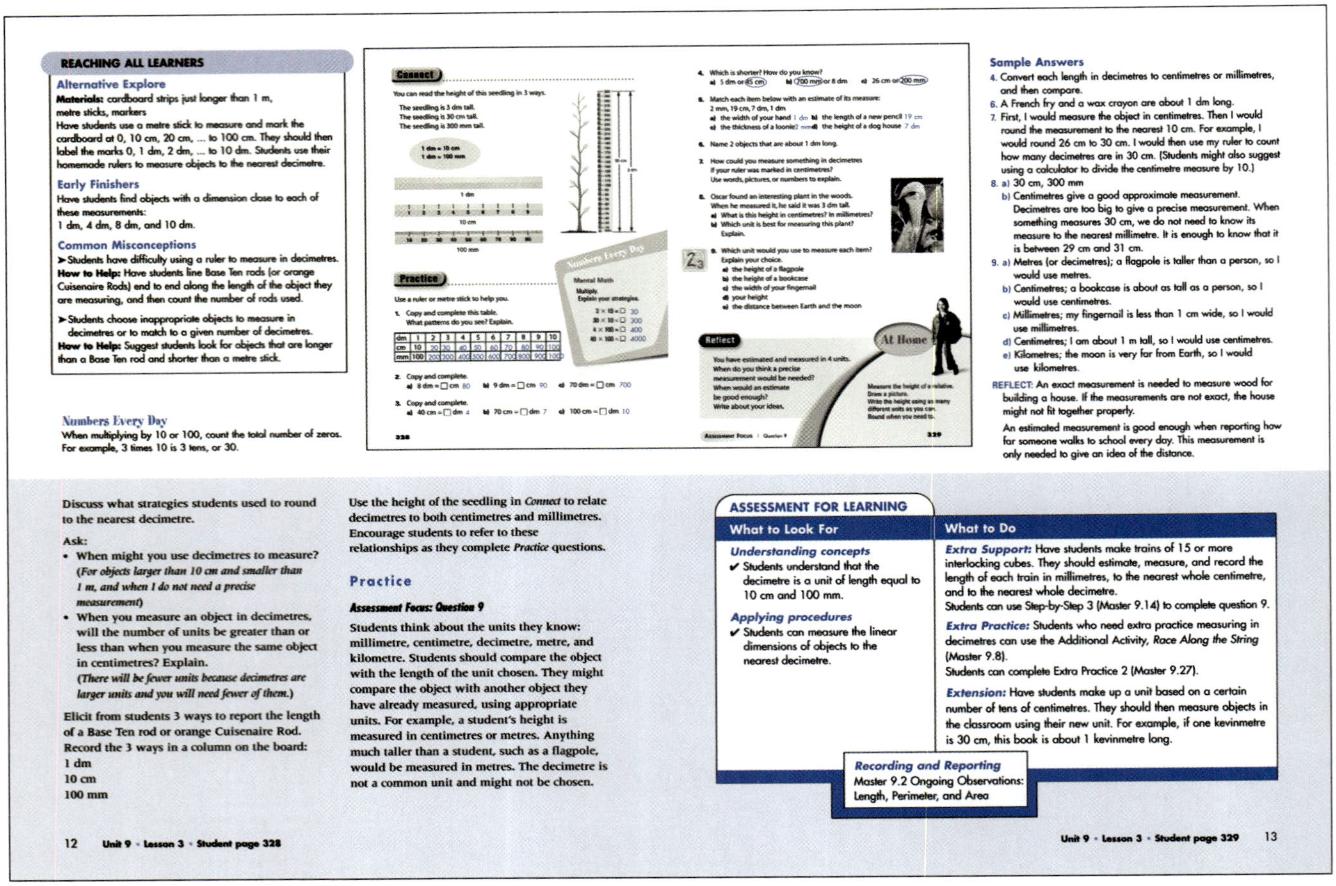

REACHING ALL LEARNERS

Alternative Explore
Materials: cardboard strips just longer than 1 m, metre sticks, markers
Have students use a metre stick to measure and mark the cardboard at 0, 10 cm, 20 cm, ... to 100 cm. They should then label the marks 0, 1 dm, 2 dm, ... to 10 dm. Students use their homemade rulers to measure objects to the nearest decimetre.

Early Finishers
Have students find objects with a dimension close to each of these measurements:
1 dm, 4 dm, 8 dm, and 10 dm.

Common Misconceptions
➤ Students have difficulty using a ruler to measure in decimetres.
How to Help: Have students line Base Ten rods (or orange Cuisenaire Rods) end to end along the length of the object they are measuring, and then count the number of rods used.
➤ Students choose inappropriate objects to measure in decimetres or to match to a given number of decimetres.
How to Help: Suggest students look for objects that are longer than a Base Ten rod and shorter than a metre stick.

Numbers Every Day
When multiplying by 10 or 100, count the total number of zeros. For example, 3 times 10 is 3 tens, or 30.

Sample Answers
4. Convert each length in decimetres to centimetres or millimetres, and then compare.
6. A French fry and a wax crayon are about 1 dm long.
7. First, I would measure the object in centimetres. Then I would round the measurement to the nearest 10 cm. For example, I would round 26 cm to 30 cm. I would then use my ruler to count how many decimetres are in 30 cm. (Students might also suggest using a calculator to divide the centimetre measure by 10.)
8. a) 30 cm, 300 mm
b) Centimetres give a good approximate measurement. Decimetres are too big to give a precise measurement. When something measures 30 cm, we do not need to know its measure to the nearest millimetre. It is enough to know that it is between 29 cm and 31 cm.
9. a) Metres (or decimetres); a flagpole is taller than a person, so I would use metres.
b) Centimetres; a bookcase is about as tall as a person, so I would use centimetres.
c) Millimetres; my fingernail is less than 1 cm wide, so I would use millimetres.
d) Centimetres; I am about 1 m tall, so I would use centimetres.
e) Kilometres; the moon is very far from Earth, so I would use kilometres.
REFLECT: An exact measurement is needed to measure wood for building a house. If the measurements are not exact, the house might not fit together properly.
An estimated measurement is good enough when reporting how far someone walks to school every day. This measurement is only needed to give an idea of the distance.

Discuss what strategies students used to round to the nearest decimetre.
Ask:
- When might you use decimetres to measure? *(For objects larger than 10 cm and smaller than 1 m, and when I do not need a precise measurement)*
- When you measure an object in decimetres, will the number of units be greater than or less than when you measure the same object in centimetres? Explain. *(There will be fewer units because decimetres are larger units and you will need fewer of them.)*

Elicit from students 3 ways to report the length of a Base Ten rod or orange Cuisenaire Rod. Record the 3 ways in a column on the board:
1 dm
10 cm
100 mm

Use the height of the seedling in *Connect* to relate decimetres to both centimetres and millimetres. Encourage students to refer to these relationships as they complete *Practice* questions.

Practice

Assessment Focus: Question 9
Students think about the units they know: millimetre, centimetre, decimetre, metre, and kilometre. Students should compare the object with the length of the unit chosen. They might compare the object with another object they have already measured, using appropriate units. For example, a student's height is measured in centimetres or metres. Anything much taller than a student, such as a flagpole, would be measured in metres. The decimetre is not a common unit and might not be chosen.

ASSESSMENT FOR LEARNING

What to Look For	What to Do
Understanding concepts ✔ Students understand that the decimetre is a unit of length equal to 10 cm and 100 mm.	*Extra Support:* Have students make trains of 15 or more interlocking cubes. They should estimate, measure, and record the length of each train in millimetres, to the nearest whole centimetre, and to the nearest whole decimetre. Students can use Step-by-Step 3 (Master 9.14) to complete question 9.
Applying procedures ✔ Students can measure the linear dimensions of objects to the nearest decimetre.	*Extra Practice:* Students who need extra practice measuring in decimetres can use the Additional Activity, *Race Along the String* (Master 9.8). Students can complete Extra Practice 2 (Master 9.27). *Extension:* Have students make up a unit based on a certain number of tens of centimetres. They should then measure objects in the classroom using their new unit. For example, if one kevinmetre is 30 cm, this book is about 1 kevinmetre long.

Recording and Reporting
Master 9.2 Ongoing Observations: Length, Perimeter, and Area

12 Unit 9 · Lesson 3 · Student page 328

Unit 9 · Lesson 3 · Student page 329 13

In the Teacher Guide, each **Unit Launch** provides suggestions to support your **Diagnostic Assessment** of students.

Look for **Literature Connections** that relate to the topics at hand.

In a Teacher Guide I look for daily support for content presentation, classroom management, assessment, and ideas for supporting all learners.

– Mary Doucette, Program Author

In core lessons, beside the reduced student pages you will find

- **Lesson Organizer** with curriculum information, materials, and vocabulary
- **Key Learnings** for the lesson
- **Reaching All Learners** with suggestions for an **Alternative Explore,** suggested **ESL Strategies,** and **Common Misconceptions/How to Help**
- **Sample Answers** to questions that require a written or diagrammatic response

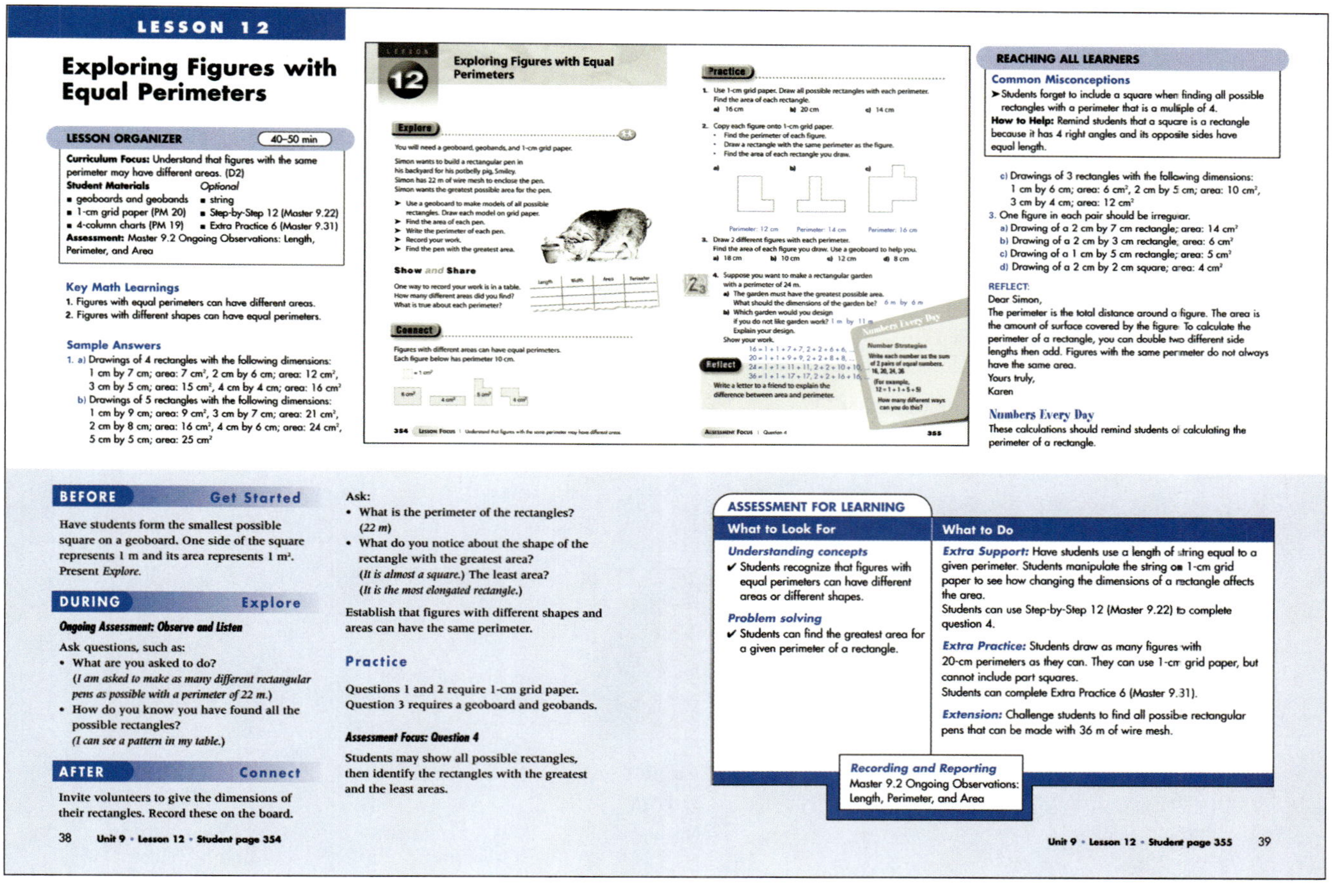

LESSON 12

Exploring Figures with Equal Perimeters

LESSON ORGANIZER — 40–50 min

Curriculum Focus: Understand that figures with the same perimeter may have different areas. (D2)

Student Materials	*Optional*
geoboards and geobands	string
1-cm grid paper (PM 20)	Step-by-Step 12 (Master 9.22)
4-column charts (PM 19)	Extra Practice 6 (Master 9.31)

Assessment: Master 9.2 Ongoing Observations: Length, Perimeter, and Area

Key Math Learnings

1. Figures with equal perimeters can have different areas.
2. Figures with different shapes can have equal perimeters.

Sample Answers

1. a) Drawings of 4 rectangles with the following dimensions: 1 cm by 7 cm; area: 7 cm², 2 cm by 6 cm; area: 12 cm², 3 cm by 5 cm; area: 15 cm², 4 cm by 4 cm; area: 16 cm²
   b) Drawings of 5 rectangles with the following dimensions: 1 cm by 9 cm; area: 9 cm², 3 cm by 7 cm; area: 21 cm², 2 cm by 8 cm; area: 16 cm², 4 cm by 6 cm; area: 24 cm², 5 cm by 5 cm; area: 25 cm²

REACHING ALL LEARNERS

Common Misconceptions

➤ Students forget to include a square when finding all possible rectangles with a perimeter that is a multiple of 4.

How to Help: Remind students that a square is a rectangle because it has 4 right angles and its opposite sides have equal length.

   c) Drawings of 3 rectangles with the following dimensions: 1 cm by 6 cm; area: 6 cm², 2 cm by 5 cm; area: 10 cm², 3 cm by 4 cm; area: 12 cm²

3. One figure in each pair should be irregular.
   a) Drawing of a 2 cm by 7 cm rectangle; area: 14 cm²
   b) Drawing of a 2 cm by 3 cm rectangle; area: 6 cm²
   c) Drawing of a 1 cm by 5 cm rectangle; area: 5 cm²
   d) Drawing of a 2 cm by 2 cm square; area: 4 cm²

REFLECT:
Dear Simon,
The perimeter is the total distance around a figure. The area is the amount of surface covered by the figure. To calculate the perimeter of a rectangle, you can double two different side lengths then add. Figures with the same perimeter do not always have the same area.
Yours truly,
Karen

Numbers Every Day

These calculations should remind students of calculating the perimeter of a rectangle.

BEFORE — Get Started

Have students form the smallest possible square on a geoboard. One side of the square represents 1 m and its area represents 1 m². Present *Explore.*

DURING — Explore

Ongoing Assessment: Observe and Listen

Ask questions, such as:

- What are you asked to do? (*I am asked to make as many different rectangular pens as possible with a perimeter of 22 m.*)
- How do you know you have found all the possible rectangles? (*I can see a pattern in my table.*)

AFTER — Connect

Invite volunteers to give the dimensions of their rectangles. Record these on the board.

Ask:

- What is the perimeter of the rectangles? (*22 m*)
- What do you notice about the shape of the rectangle with the greatest area? (*It is almost a square.*) The least area? (*It is the most elongated rectangle.*)

Establish that figures with different shapes and areas can have the same perimeter.

Practice

Questions 1 and 2 require 1-cm grid paper. Question 3 requires a geoboard and geobands.

Assessment Focus: Question 4

Students may show all possible rectangles, then identify the rectangles with the greatest and the least areas.

ASSESSMENT FOR LEARNING

What to Look For	What to Do
Understanding concepts ✔ Students recognize that figures with equal perimeters can have different areas or different shapes.	***Extra Support:*** Have students use a length of string equal to a given perimeter. Students manipulate the string on 1-cm grid paper to see how changing the dimensions of a rectangle affects the area. Students can use Step-by-Step 12 (Master 9.22) to complete question 4.
Problem solving ✔ Students can find the greatest area for a given perimeter of a rectangle.	***Extra Practice:*** Students draw as many figures with 20-cm perimeters as they can. They can use 1-cm grid paper, but cannot include part squares. Students can complete Extra Practice 6 (Master 9.31). ***Extension:*** Challenge students to find all possible rectangular pens that can be made with 36 m of wire mesh.

Recording and Reporting
Master 9.2 Ongoing Observations: Length, Perimeter, and Area

38 Unit 9 • Lesson 12 • Student page 354

Unit 9 • Lesson 12 • Student page 355 39

Your lesson plan appears across the bottom half of your lesson pages, with teaching suggestions to support the lesson structure established in the Student Book: **Explore, Connect,** and **Practice.**

Assessment for Learning appears in every lesson with the main teaching notes, to help shape your formative assessment.

Meet our *Addison Wesley Mathematics Makes Sense* In-Service and Professional Development Faculty

Trevor Brown
Toronto, Ontario

Steve Cairns
Burnaby, British Columbia

Lynda Colgan
Kingston, Ontario

Maggie Martin Connell
Atlantic Canada

Marg Craig
Southwestern Ontario

Craig Featherstone
Pearson Education Consultant

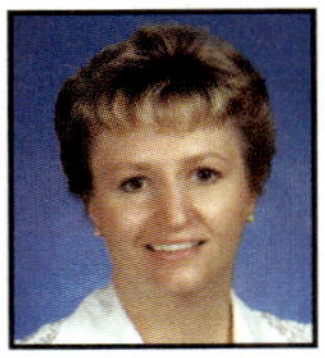

Angie Harding
Regina, Saskatchewan

Sharon Jeroski
Assessment Consultant

Jodi Mackie
Edmonton, Alberta

Bill Nimigon
Toronto, Ontario

Carole Saundry
Richmond, British Columbia

Michelle Skene
Ottawa, Ontario

Lynn Strangway
Toronto, Ontario

John A. Van de Walle
Elementary Mathematics Advisor

Mignonne Wood
Vancouver, British Columbia

ADDISON WESLEY

Ontario

Math Makes Sense 8

Ontario

Teacher Guide

Grade 8 Planning and Program Masters

ISBN 0-321-13868-6

9 780321 138682

Teacher Guide Modules

ISBN 0-321-13869-4

9 780321 138699

Complete Teacher Guide package

PEARSON Education Canada

Building a Math Community

Contents

Creating a Math Community in the Classroom

> *"Success in mathematics learning requires being positively disposed toward the subject."*
> (Kilpatrick and Swafford 2002, 16)

Each new school year provides fresh opportunities to create a community of learners in the classroom. The goal is to facilitate the development of an inclusive classroom where all students feel safe, valued, and supported in their learning.

As members of a classroom community, teacher and students:

- Demonstrate mutual respect.
- Take risks.
- Seek, evaluate, and apply information to solve problems.
- Make decisions.
- Learn successfully together.

> *"Community building is an ongoing process. Students who feel they are part of a cohesive group take more responsibility for what happens in the classroom and may perform better because of encouragement from their peers."*
> (Barnes 2002, 84)

Helping children acquire "mathematical power" means helping them develop the capacity to apply mathematical knowledge to new or familiar tasks. (Baroody and Coslick 1998, 1 and 2) Mathematics in the classroom must promote a positive disposition to learn and use mathematics.

> *"For students to be comfortable with the processes of mathematical inquiry, they need to explore, reason, solve problems, and communicate about mathematics—and they need regular feedback. When students have these learning opportunities, they begin to develop a deeper understanding of mathematics, enabling them to see connections between mathematical ideas, between mathematics and other subject areas, and between mathematics and everyday life situations."*
> (Baroody and Coslick 1998)

As facilitators of learning, teachers are responsible for creating a classroom environment that allows each student to experience success. The reward is in knowing that students will view math as fun, exciting, engaging, and something they are capable of doing.

Setting the Stage for Community Building

Central to the life of any community is a group meeting time—when the whole class meets to learn what it means to belong to a community. The group meeting should facilitate effective communication—each person has the opportunity to speak, to share successes and challenges, and to listen to and value the ideas of others. Group meetings also reinforce communication skills, such as listening with respect, and speaking clearly and in turn.

Regular meeting times demonstrate to students they have a voice in the classroom. You might consider creating a T-chart with students that describes what an effective meeting should "look like and sound like." Refer to this chart during meeting times through the day as you observe behaviour you identified together as important.

Using the Meeting Time

- Discuss difficulties that occur in the classroom or on the playground. As a community, discuss tools and strategies that may help resolve difficulties or conflicts.
- Share ideas, strategies, or completed work.
- Celebrate successes or provide encouragement.
- Share information about upcoming events in the class or school.
- Trade information about what happened outside the classroom after school hours.

OUR MEETING TIME

LOOKS LIKE	SOUNDS LIKE
• Everyone sits in an arrangement that is conducive to discussion (e.g., desks arranged in a horseshoe formation). • Students are attentive. • The atmosphere is one of respect. • Students come prepared with notebooks. • Student raises a hand to be heard.	• Everyone takes turns to talk. • The student/teacher talks clearly. • Offer positive feedback: "That is an interesting idea. Can you tell us more about it?" • Suggest questions: "Can you share how you solved the problem?"

A math meeting can be held any time. Your needs will direct the activity and discussion. Some possibilities are to:

- Introduce a new math concept.
- Brainstorm students' prior knowledge about a math topic.
- Share a new manipulative or technology and explore possible uses.
- Revisit a math concept to reinforce a specific skill.
- Introduce new math activities.
- Discuss any difficulties arising from the previous math period.
- Share and celebrate student work.

Classroom Seating

Arrange students' desks in groups. Students will then have a sense of belonging. In each group, include students with varied strengths and abilities. This encourages peer modelling and role definition within the group. These groups should not be static; however, they should stay together for at least four weeks so that students can become familiar with one another and feel comfortable in their group.

Regularly reinforce the classroom principles students have agreed to. These principles will be integral to the development of group cohesiveness and classroom norms.

To encourage students to sit beside different classmates have them:

- Sit in alphabetical order by first or last name.
- Sit in order of their birth dates.
- Randomly select name cards from a box, or number sticks from a box.
- Write a proposal of whom they would like to have sit in their groups, providing justification as to why that grouping would work well together.

"An effective mathematics learning environment is an environment that encourages the establishment of a community of mathematics learners."

(Ontario Ministry of Education 2003, 12)

Developing Common Principles

To create a successful classroom community, develop common principles. These principles should reflect the beliefs students and you have about an exemplary learning environment. All students should be encouraged to contribute; and all contributions should be respected.

Characteristics of a Community

- security
- open communication
- mutual liking
- shared goals or objectives
- connectedness
- trust

(Sapon-Shevin 1999, 16 and 17)

Establishing Community Principles

You and your students sit in a circle or horseshoe formation in the classroom.

- Make sure that everyone is together and can see one another. Explain that you are sitting in a circle so that everyone will have a chance to speak and to hear what the others are saying.
- Explain that the meeting you are having now is to decide what will help you learn together and get along in the classroom.
- Tell students that you are excited about beginning a new school year together. You want to make sure that it is a successful year for everyone. To make the class an enjoyable and positive environment to be in, there will be some expectations for all students. These will be your common principles.

Give an example of a class principle, such as, "It is important to help one another."

- Ask for a student volunteer to begin by suggesting a principle. Record the principles on chart paper.
- Go around the room giving each person a turn to contribute. Some students may feel reluctant to share; ensure that students have the opportunity to "pass" when it is their turn to speak. Return to these students later to invite them to participate.

Discuss the principles that were suggested.

- Note principles that were mentioned multiple times, and encourage additional suggestions.
- As the discussion progresses, note all principles mentioned on chart paper or on the blackboard. With the help of the students, summarize the ideas in three to six statements.

Divide students into groups, so that each group can discuss one principle.

- Print each principle on a strip of paper.
- Instruct each group to choose one principle and find a quiet spot in the room to discuss the importance of that principle. (You may need to reread each group's principle as it is selected.)
- Ask each group to decide if it feels that principle should or should not become part of the class rules. The group must provide justification for its decision.

Note

Circulate among the groups to ensure students understand the task and the principle. They may need some discussion prompts:

- Why do you think it is important to include that principle?
- What may happen if we don't include that principle?

This process allows students to take ownership of the class principles. Students are more likely to remember and apply these ideas when they are part of the decision-making process. Throughout the year, revisit these principles with students and discuss their effectiveness. Students may suggest which principles are working well, and which principles could be changed. Encourage students to give reasons.

Bring the groups back.

- Ask each group to put its principle on the chart or write it on the blackboard. Time should be provided for others to comment.
- As a class, decide if any of the groups' decisions should be changed (only after all ideas about the principles have been heard).
- Create the final list of principles based on student decisions. Record the list on chart paper and post it in the classroom.

An Inclusive Math Community

Support Different Learning Styles

Try to get to know your students so you can plan effectively. Students should leave a math class feeling their needs have been addressed and they are successful.

Students have a range of learning styles. To effectively teach all students, it is essential to provide a multitude of classroom experiences. *Addison Wesley Mathematics Makes Sense* uses a variety of approaches to reach all learners.

Different Learning Styles

LEARNING STYLE	STRENGTHS AND PREFERENCES	*MATH MAKES SENSE*
Linguistic	Reading, writing, telling stories, remembering, talking, interacting, hearing, seeing words	Provides learning opportunities to talk, discuss, explain, write, read, and see words
Logical/Mathematical	Experimenting, working with numbers, asking questions, exploring patterns and relationships, math reasoning, applying logic, problem solving, classifying	Provides learning opportunities to experiment, ask questions, explore patterns and relationships, reason mathematically, solve problems, classify items
Visual/Spatial	Drawing, building, designing, creating, visualizing, imagining, working with pictures/colours, doing mazes and puzzles, reading maps and charts	Provides learning opportunities to draw, build, design, create, visualize, imagine, work with pictures/colours, do puzzles, read maps and charts
Musical	Singing, humming, noticing pitches, responding to music, playing instruments, picking up sounds/rhythms/melodies	Provides learning opportunities to work with patterns and make music connections
Kinesthetic	Moving and doing, touching and talking, feeling objects, using body language, physical activities, sports/dance, acting, making crafts, interacting with space	Provides learning opportunities to move and do, touch and talk, feel objects, use body language, work with manipulatives, make models, interact with space
Social (Interpersonal)	Talking to people, joining groups, understanding/leading others, organizing, communicating, mediating, sharing, relating, cooperating, interviewing	Provides learning opportunities to talk to people, work in groups, understand/lead others, organize, communicate, mediate, share, relate, cooperate, interview
Individual (Intrapersonal)	Working alone, pursuing own interests, understanding self, focusing inward, following instincts, pursuing goals, being original, having own space, individual projects	Provides learning opportunities to work individually, build thinking skills, think critically, follow instincts, solve problems, find original solutions, pursue individual projects
Naturalistic	Interest in nature and the environment	Provides learning opportunities by working with objects from nature

Adapted from *Instructor*, Scholastic Inc., 1990.

Preparing Students for Success

"Valuing mathematics implies being productively disposed towards the subject. It involves seeing mathematics as sensible, useful and worthwhile, and seeing oneself as able to learn and use it. Teachers must create a climate whereby all students can make sense of the mathematics they are learning and gain confidence in their mathematics ability."

(*Leading Math Success*, 2004)

When students experience success at math and perceive themselves as doers of math, they can encourage their peers to participate actively in math as well.

Creating Positive Attitudes

Children are more likely to develop a positive attitude toward mathematics when the teacher models the same attitudes.

Activating Prior Knowledge

Students come to the classroom with different experiences and knowledge of math. By determining where students are starting out, you are in a better position to provide appropriate math experiences and to assess ongoing learning.

How to Activate Prior Knowledge

- Pose a question to initiate discussion. For example, "How do you think you would go about adding fractions that do not have like denominators?" "What do you already know about adding fractions that might help you?"
- Brainstorm a class chart when introducing a new concept. For example, provide students with centicubes and pose the question, "How could these manipulatives help you find the volume of a rectangular prism?" Brainstorm and record students' responses on chart paper.
- Use a manipulative to investigate a new type of problem. For example, use two-colour tiles to investigate integers.

Reaching All Learners

Since there is no single way to reach all students, we are challenged to provide a wide variety of instructional strategies and learning experiences. Through observation, you can determine the strengths of each student. This information, combined with what is known about a student's prior knowledge, can help you address learning needs.

The following classroom practices are recommended as appropriate for students' cognitive development:

- New learning must be connected to existing knowledge.
- Examples should be concrete.
- Experiences must be hands-on.
- Lessons need to be active.
- Students must be engaged.
- It is essential to use manipulatives and technology.
- There must be time for active exploration.

> ***Tools for Learning***
>
> Working with manipulatives and technology can facilitate math exploration and understanding among a range of learners, especially ESL students. You may also wish to provide each student with a math tool kit (or request that students provide their own) of basic equipment such as a ruler, calculator, two-colour counters, protractor, and so on.

Supporting ESL Students

To comprehend meaning and instruction, ESL students often require other resources in addition to words, such as manipulatives, drawings, and models. You can use these strategies to help ESL learners understand math concepts and language.

- Use facial expressions, gestures, and pantomime to help convey meaning. Repeat key language and concepts, rephrasing concepts in simple words.
- Use manipulatives, drawings, and real-world objects to demonstrate concepts, clarify instructions, and develop language.
- Use charts, graphs, and graphic organizers to introduce and explore concepts. Present additional examples and demonstrations.
- Provide a variety of ways for students to respond and/or show their findings.
- Provide brief previews and reviews of materials to reinforce language and concepts.
- Set a classroom tone that encourages and rewards students who interact, take risks, and use language to express their ideas.

Making Learning Meaningful

When learning is meaningful, students see the connections between themselves and the learning experience. Students do best with activities they find interesting and can actively engage in, including problem scenarios.

> To engage learners in meaningful math:
> - Use interesting materials.
> - Provide students with a choice of tools, manipulatives, and technology.
> - Connect new activities to what students already know.
> - Pose problems that relate to students, and involve their types of interests.

> *"Children's confidence, competence, and interest in mathematics flourish when new experiences are meaningful and connected with their prior knowledge and experience."*
>
> (NAEYC and NCTM 2002, 6)

Promoting Classroom Communication

It is important to encourage all students to participate in class discussions. As the year progresses, students tend to take more risks at these meetings, especially if they perceive that all ideas are accepted.

To create effective and inclusive collaborative groupings:

- Involve students in discussing and determining appropriate interpersonal and small group skills (class principles).
- Group heterogeneously to promote modelling and diverse thinking. (Include boys and girls.)
- Begin with pairs or with groups of three.
- Keep work groups to 4 students or fewer to encourage positive social behaviours.
- Group students in a way that will encourage positive social behaviours.
- Use strategies such as think-pair-share.
- Use cooperative learning strategies often, but for short periods of time.
- Change group members regularly to promote a variety of interactions. (Leading Math Success, 2004)

Fostering Collaborative Learning

Cooperative/collaborative learning involves students working together towards a common goal. There are five elements involved in successful cooperative/collaborative learning: positive interdependence, face-to-face interaction, individual and group accountability, interpersonal and small group skills. (Johnson and Johnson, 1994, as cited in Bennett and Rolheiser 2001)

It is always important to impress upon students that they are in the classroom together to help each other learn.

It is beneficial for students to experience a variety of groupings. When students work in pairs or small groups, they are provided with more opportunities for interaction and discussion than when they work in larger groups. Providing opportunities to experience math concepts in pairs or small groups enables students to:

- Observe one another.
- Build on one another's ideas by hearing and trying out different strategies.
- Discuss their findings and pose questions.
- Give explanations and demonstrations, using math vocabulary.
- Search for connections and commonalities.

As students work collaboratively, you can glean valuable information by observing their interactions, discussions, explanations, and active involvement. Question students to encourage deeper understanding and reflection. In this way, students identify their own misconceptions and adjust their activity/thinking to reflect their new knowledge.

> *"The kinds of experiences teachers provide clearly play a major role in determining the extent and quality of students' learning... Classroom discourse and social interaction can be used to promote the recognition of connections among ideas and the reorganization of knowledge."*
>
> (Lampert 1986, as cited in NCTM 2000, 21)

Questions to Prompt Discussion and Reflection

- What thought process (steps) did you follow?
- What are you doing right now?
- Why do you think that will work?
- What strategy did you use to solve that problem? How did you solve the problem?
- Is there another way you could solve that problem? Why did you try it that way?
- What are you stuck on?
- How did you figure that out?
- How did you make that happen?
- What are you going to do next?
- What would happen if...?
- What gave you that idea?

The NCTM standards state that mathematics programs should enable all students to:

- Organize and consolidate their math thinking through communication.
- Communicate their math thinking coherently and clearly to peers/teachers.
- Analyse and evaluate the math thinking and strategies of others.
- Use the language of math to express math ideas precisely.

"Although organizing instructions for heterogeneous groups definitely involves a different kind of planning and preparation, many teachers report increased enthusiasm in their students, as well as greater learning and deeper involvement when curricula and instruction are organized around diverse learners working together."

(Sapon-Shevin 1999, 68)

Sharing and Reflecting

Encourage classroom communication to give all students an opportunity to share their thinking and understanding. This also gives you an opportunity to gain an insight into what students are thinking and learning. By providing students with a sharing and reflecting time at the end of a math activity, you offer the opportunity for metacognition. *Reflect and Share* in each section in the Student Book encourages such sharing.

Students are encouraged to:

- Check their own thinking.
- Highlight their own ideas, and see that their solutions are valued.
- Validate their problem-solving strategies and share those ideas.
- Consolidate their learning by explaining it to their peers.
- Ask further questions and learn from their peers as they share their insights.

The Math Journal Entry

Students provide a written or visual reflection of their math experience for the day. You may provide a journal sentence starter to guide their thoughts. Encourage students to write about their thinking using the math vocabulary, pictures, diagrams, symbols, or charts. You may wish to have students respond to *Reflect* at the end of each section in the Student Book. Students may share their entries with a peer or their work group.

Math Routines

Students benefit from a classroom structure that is predictable, follows certain routines, and allows concepts to be revisited regularly. Incorporating math throughout the day gives students the chance to experience more success with math, since they gain more practice with concepts and develop an awareness that math is connected to everyday experiences.

Graph the Class's Favourite Sports Team

Record and graph the scores and win/loss record of a favourite sports team. Have students analyse the data regularly and discuss the probable outcomes of upcoming games based on the opposing teams' win/loss record.

Numbers Every Day

Have students do *Mental Math, Number Strategies,* or *Calculator Skills*, a five- to ten-minute activity in each lesson of the Student Book. Use these activities any time during the day to help students build number sense and skills.

Track a Stock

As a class, choose to buy a fictional stock option in a company. Track the progress of the stock in the newspaper and on the internet. Discuss the stock's profitability (percent increase, decrease, and so on) and make decisions on when it would be best to sell the stock or buy more options in the company.

Games

Incorporate games into your routine once a week to reinforce concepts and give students the opportunity to realize that math can be fun, and to develop strategies. The Student Book contains math games, such as *Fitting In*. You may also wish to have students play with jigsaw puzzles to develop spatial sense.

Math in the Picture

Have the students work together to select an appropriate photograph or picture that identifies each of the math concepts shown. In groups, students can glue the selected pictures on to chart paper and record their ideas about the math found in the picture and the significance of this mathematics.

Some ideas for Math in the Picture are:

- Sports
- Fashion
- Music
- Seasons
- Time of day
- Shapes
- Measuring tools/ devices
- Temperature
- Patterns
- Money

Creating the Learning Environment

> *"Students do not want to be embarrassed in front of their peers, and will not take risks unless they feel valued and supported. The classroom therefore must be a safe place. Routines should be established in the classroom that value such behaviours as attentive listening, appreciation, respect, and participation that leaves no occasion for put-downs."*
>
> (Gibbs 2001; Pugalee 2001b in *Leading Math Success* 2004)

A Problem-Solving Approach

Problem solving is a key instructional strategy that enables students to take risks, secure in the knowledge that their thoughts, queries, and ideas are valued. In time, students become well versed in the language of cooperation and collaboration.

After students share their solutions and justifications, you can elaborate on their methods and encourage students to comment or ask questions of their peers. Using student findings and solution methods as a means to guide instruction also allows students to see the value in their work, and encourages peers to share their strategies. While some strategies may be more efficient than others, you can note that several strategies may work and often a combination of strategies is required to solve a problem. Students must use strategies that are meaningful to them and make sense to them.

Classroom Management Tips for Intermediate Mathematics Learners

- Increase emotional safety by including strategies such as framing questions appropriately, using well-planned student groupings and inviting rather than demanding responses.
- Provide positive feedback whenever possible.
- Frequently use positive humour.
- Recognize that intermediate learners will behave inappropriately at times and develop a range of strategies for responding such as, speaking privately to students about inappropriate behaviour using a neutral (not angry) tone of voice. (*Leading Math Success* 2004)

Problem-Solving Strategies

Math Makes Sense 8 provides many opportunities for students to use problem-solving strategies such as:

- Make a table.
- Use a model.
- Draw a diagram.
- Solve a simpler problem.
- Work backward.
- Guess and check.
- Make an organized list.
- Use a pattern.
- Draw a graph.
- Use logical reasoning.

Here are some suggestions to empower students to become problem solvers.

Before

Before students begin:

- Prepare meaningful problem scenarios for students. These should be sufficiently challenging, but easy to solve.
- Ensure the problem is understood by all.
- Begin with a simpler version of the task. Brainstorm possible strategies to use.
- Estimate what the answer might be.
- Explain the expectations for the process and the product.

During

As students work through the problem:

- Let students approach the problem in a way that makes sense to them.
- Listen to conversations to observe student thinking.
- Provide hints or suggestions if students are on the wrong path.
- Encourage students to test their ideas.
- Ask questions to stimulate ideas.
- Assess student understanding of her/his solution.

After

After students have solved their problem:

- Gather for a group meeting to reflect and share.
- Provide ample time for all to discuss the solution.
- Highlight the variety of answers and methods.
- Encourage students to justify their solutions.
- Encourage students to comment positively or ask questions regarding their peers' solutions.

Note

For more details on using a problem-solving approach to teach mathematics, see John A. Van de Walle, *Elementary and Middle School Mathematics: Teaching Developmentally.* Boston: Allyn and Bacon, 2004, from which these ideas are drawn.

"Problem solving should be a primary goal of all mathematics instruction and an integral part of all mathematical activity."

(NCTM 1989, 23)

Creating the Physical Environment

Building a community of learners can begin with the physical arrangement of the classroom. Students should know where all necessary materials are so they can access them easily. They should also know they are responsible for collecting and returning any materials they have used, and that they are expected to cooperate with other members of the classroom. The classroom set-up should:

- Promote independence for students.
- Provide choices within a structured setting.
- Be organized to encourage sharing.

To set up the physical space:

- Create floor space where you and students can gather for lessons, discussions, and sharing.
- Arrange student desks or tables in groups (about four students per group) to facilitate working together.
- Create a variety of work areas so students have a selection (group areas, individual areas, floor spaces, table spaces, and so on).
- Set up a special area for you to conference with students individually.

Maximizing Classroom Space

Here are some suggestions for maximizing space.

- Establish a bulletin board as a Math Corner where students can display their work. Place a shelf underneath the bulletin board for work that cannot be posted. Include an area where students can write "I wonder about" questions.
- Post Bristol board or a white board to use as a message centre.
- Store math portfolios and games in stackable plastic crates or tubs. Or, turn desks upside down and tape Bristol board around the legs to create a filing cabinet for portfolios and games.
- Create an instant math centre by placing game(s) at a table or meeting space for students to play and work at math challenges or games.

Storage of Materials

Provide a variety of manipulative materials in labelled bins in an accessible area of the classroom. This ensures students know where to find and return what they need. Label the bins clearly.

Organize the mathematics tools. For example, you might want to have math toolkits for each group. These toolkits could contain rulers, measuring tapes, calculators, various counters stored in small plastic bags, string, elastic bands, math vocabulary and definitions, mathematics journal writing starters, and so on. Be sure there are enough items in the kits for the group to work together.

You could also create a materials centre containing pencils, scissors, tape, glue, erasers, crayons, markers, different sizes and types of paper (lined, unlined, graph paper, dot paper, centimetre grid paper), and so on.

You will need a variety of mathematics tools and manipulatives to address different math concepts throughout the year. Students should have access to these materials. Open access allows students to explore manipulatives in greater depth; for example, to further their understanding of a concept, to revisit an activity that was previously provided, or to experiment with their own math problem.

To recognize the importance of personal space while promoting the sharing of materials:

- Provide a personal place in the classroom for each student—for example, the inside of a desk, a cubby, or a mailbox.
- Use labelled bins or shelves to hold math books, workbooks, and journals.

Math Tubs

Math Tubs are a great way to extend and reinforce student learning daily. A Math Tub can be put together following any manipulative activity, game, or problem-solving scenario. Math Tubs should change as the year progresses, to reflect current math topics. You may also want to use these to revisit a particular concept over the course of the year.

Why Use Math Tubs?

- To provide an opportunity to revisit a math concept
- To increase student success by drawing on previously built knowledge
- To provide opportunities to attempt new strategies
- To provide extensions for students who have completed their daily activities
- To reuse materials you have already put together
- To provide further problem-solving activities

Recommended Math Materials

- Algebra Tiles (2-colour) — class set, clear plastic organizer trays, overhead or magnetic set
- Base-ten materials (clearview with interlocking pieces)
- Calculators with fraction key and problem-solving capabilities
- Circular fraction set and frames (decimal, degree, percent, time, fraction and compass points), translucent pieces and overhead set
- Coloured tiles and overhead set
- Coloured relational rods and overhead set (Cuisenaire Rods)
- Connecting cubes (1-cm, 2-cm)
- Connecting plastic figures to build 2-D figures and nets for 3-D solids (Polyhedrons)
- Full circle protractors
- Geoboards (minimum 15 cm by 15 cm) clear, 11 by 11, 5 by 5, circular
- Geobands
- Measuring cups
- Measuring tapes (minimum 150-cm, wind-up tape in protective case, calibrated in centimetres and millimetres)
- Metre sticks (unbreakable plastic, calibrated in centimetres and millimetres)
- Number cubes: 6-faces in two colours; 10-, 12- and 30-faces
- Operation cubes (cubes labelled with operation signs)
- Pattern Blocks and an overhead set
- Pentominoes
- Plastic transparent tools
- Playing cards
- Relational geometric 3-D solids and large demonstration set
- 30-cm rulers
- Safety compasses
- Spinners (number, colour)
- Tangrams
- Trundle wheels
- Two-colour counters and overhead set

(*Leading Math Success* 2004)

Each Math Tub should be in its own bin for easy organization and storage. Each tub should be labelled on the outside with the name of the activity and the number of students that can use that tub at one time. The tub should include:

- instructions for the activity
- any required manipulatives or technology
- a list of common materials required that are not in the tub; for example, glue, scissors
- expectations for the completed activity (whether it is a game or a created piece of work)

Illustrated Glossary

acute angle: an angle measuring less than 90°

acute triangle: a triangle with three acute angles

algebraic expression: a mathematical expression containing a variable: for example, $6x - 4$ is an algebraic expression

alternate angles: angles that are between two lines and are on opposite sides of the transversal that cuts the two lines

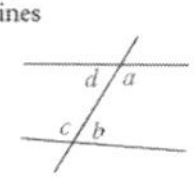

a and *c* are alternate angles.
d and *b* are alternate angles.

angle: the figure formed by two rays from the same endpoint

angle bisector: the line that divides an angle into two equal angles

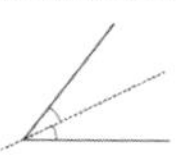

approximate: a number close to the exact value of an expression; the symbol ≐ means "is approximately equal to"

area: the number of square units needed to cover a region

array: an arrangement in rows and columns

assumption: something that is accepted as true, but has not been proved

average: a single number that represents a set of numbers; see *mean*, *median*, and *mode*

bar graph: a graph that uses horizontal or vertical bars to display data that can be counted (see page 195)

bar notation: the use of a horizontal bar over decimal digits to indicate that they repeat; for example, $1.\overline{34}$ means 1.343 434 …

base: the side of a polygon or the face of a solid from which the height is measured; the factor repeated in a power

bias: an emphasis on characteristics that are not typical of the entire population

bisector: a line that divides a line segment or an angle into two equal parts

capacity: the amount a container can hold

census: a method of data collection where all the people in a population are surveyed

circle graph: a graph in which a circle used to represent one whole is divided into sectors that represent parts of the whole

circumcentre: the point where the perpendicular bisectors of the sides of a triangle intersect; see *circumcircle*

circumcircle: a circle drawn through all vertices of a triangle and with its centre at the circumcentre of the triangle

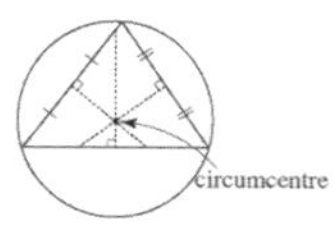

circumference: the distance around a circle, also known as the perimeter of the circle

commission: the percent paid to a salesperson based on the amount sold

common denominator: a number that is a multiple of each of the given denominators; for example, 12 is a common denominator for the fractions $\frac{1}{3}, \frac{5}{4}, \frac{7}{12}$

common factor: a number that is a factor of each of the given numbers; for example, 3 is a common factor of 15, 9, and 21

complementary angles: two angles whose sum is 90°

composite number: a number with three or more factors; for example, 8 is a composite number because its factors are 1, 2, 4, and 8

Illustrated Glossary 501

Math Terminology

Students should be exposed to mathematics terminology and definitions regularly. This will build their confidence in using mathematics terms and increase their knowledge of the meaning of such terms. You could create a mathematics terminology bulletin board that may include the mathematics term and its corresponding definition. Continue to add to this board throughout the school year. As new terminology is introduced during a lesson, identify the word, its meaning, and add it to the bulletin board. A picture or symbol may accompany the word, if appropriate. This board provides a visual connection for students and helps them identify the word and its meaning.

Another resource for students is the *Glossary* at the end of their text. Students could also create their own personal mathematics dictionaries where they record the terminology and definitions from the bulletin board. This will serve as their own personal reference and could be particularly helpful when students are working independently in class, or when working on homework, or studying for tests.

Key words are listed on the opening page of each unit of the Student Book. These words can be added to language lessons and spelling lists when a particular math concept is being developed.

At times through the year, you can choose a math word and ask students to "Explain what you know about _____" as a math journal entry. This checks prior knowledge or assesses knowledge (as students are using an open-ended forum to share what they know about a math term in pictures, numbers, or words).

Community-Building Activities

The following ideas provide opportunities for students to work together to develop relationships built on co-operation and mutual respect. These activities also provide opportunities to model classroom principles while using math concepts.

Co-operative Math Posters

Have students work co-operatively to create a math poster when you introduce new concepts/topics. Students can work in groups to develop a poster that shows what they know about the new concepts/topic. The group may wish to select pictures from magazines, draw pictures, print words, label diagrams, or use a combination of the above to create the poster.

Create a Math Bulletin Board

Devote a bulletin board to math. As students work through a concept, all students can contribute work to be displayed. Or, students can work together to create a bulletin board demonstrating a concept they have learned. For example, after a study of symmetry and congruency, students could make a mural depicting various similar, congruent, and symmetrical figures in a futuristic city.

Math Meetings

Use math meetings to gather first-hand information about student attitudes and feelings about math. This is the time to pose a question about a particular math activity, problem, or collaborative group work time. All student responses should be valued and considered for future planning. Students may also have suggestions that could be explored for future learning experiences.

Problem of the Week

At the beginning of the week, pose a math problem to the class and have small groups work on it. Toward the end of the week, invite groups to share their solutions and encourage the class to discuss and compare the different problem-solving strategies presented. You may also wish to have students create similar problems and trade with classmates to solve.

Math through the Day

Students have individual learning styles and strengths in different areas. When math is meaningfully integrated into other subject areas, it can provide significant learning connections for students. Students who demonstrate strengths in other areas of the curriculum can use these strengths to show what they know about mathematics. *Math Link* features in the Student Book highlight connections between the math students are learning and other subject areas as well as the real world.

The math curriculum is extensive; thus, some concepts may be taught early in the year and not revisited in a formal way for some time. By providing students with many opportunities to revisit concepts, you can enhance learning and encourage students to strengthen their understanding. Incorporating math into daily routines provides students with ongoing support and ways to connect math learning to real-life experiences.

LANGUAGE

- Use a math journal to record problem-solving strategies and students' thinking/reflecting on their processes and solutions.
- Read literature related to math concepts.
- Create word or letter patterns.
- Use poems or rhymes during shared reading that include math concepts.
- Create riddles involving math concepts.
- Use math vocabulary in spelling lists and lessons.

NUMBER SENSE AND NUMERATION

- Practise estimation whenever possible: "How much will you save if a $48 pair of jeans is on sale for 30% off?"
- Practise mental math strategies that include ratio, fractions, decimal, percents, integers and exponents: "What is the ratio of students in the class wearing running shoes to those who are not?"

MEASUREMENT

- Regularly have students calculate elapsed time from one activity or one class to the next. Express that time as a fraction, ratio, or percent of the school day, the regular day, the week, and so on.
- Estimate the perimeter and area of irregularly shaped rooms or spaces in and around the school.

PATTERNING AND ALGEBRA

- Begin having students translate simple patterns in the environment into symbolic (variable) representations.

DATA MANAGEMENT AND PROBABILITY

- Discuss relevant data in the media, such as sports statistics, the stock market, or record sales for a student's favourite artist.

GEOMETRY AND SPATIAL SENSE

- Discuss designs in the environment using motion geometry terminology (for example, images that are congruent, will tile a plane, can be translated, rotated or reflected).

Extending the Math Community

Parents and other adults at home need to understand the purpose of a math community in the classroom. Some family members feel uncomfortable with the "new way of doing math" and are unfamiliar with the principles that underlie it.

Here are some ways to open the lines of communication, while providing important information about your math program and each student's progress.

- Keep families informed of current math topics through a biweekly newsletter. Include what, why, and how you are teaching to ensure others understand your instructional strategies.
- Use newsletters to share classroom happenings, procedures, expectations, and celebrations. In each newsletter, publish one problem students have worked through and a few student solutions demonstrating different strategies. Ensure students' names are not published.
- Include in each newsletter an idea or two that families could try at home, to extend the classroom math experiences. Include calculator activities that parents and students can work on together.
- Use a student *Practice and Homework* book as a follow-up to a class experience so that students can re-create a similar experience at home with their families. This should involve interaction and activity, and not be a worksheet students would complete on their own.
- Send home celebratory notes comprising one or two sentences, sharing a student's mathematical success.
- Take photographs of students involved in a variety of math activities and create a photo album with captions. Send this home with students on a rotating basis, providing space for parents to comment, or with a comment sheet that would provide a focus for writing.
- Encourage families to play number games when travelling.
- If students have agendas or day planners, use them to share celebratory notes, as well as other "items."
- Send home mathematics web sites that include problems suitable for grade 8 students.

It is important for families to develop a comfort level with the "what, how, and why" of their children's math learning. Encourage families to become involved in a way that makes sense for them. Family attitudes will have a significant impact on student attitudes regarding math, and you are instrumental in helping others see this "new math" positively.

When you provide support and offer simple ideas about making math real for students at home, you will have succeeded in extending the classroom math community to the homes of students.

REFERENCES

Barnes, Peter. (2002). A Community of Support. *Teaching PreK-8*, August/September, 33, 1, page 84.

Baroody, Arthur J., and Ronald Coslick. (1998). *Fostering Children's Mathematical Power: An Investigative Approach to K-8 Mathematics Instruction.* Mahwah, NJ: Lawrence Erlbaum Associates, pages 1, 2.

Gibbs, J. (2001). *Tribes: A New Way of Learning and Being Together.* Windsor, CA: Center Source Systems.

Kilpatrick, J., and Swafford, J. (Eds.). (2002). *Helping Children Learn Mathematics.* Washington, DC: National Academy Press.

Leading Math Success. (2004). *Mathematical Literacy Grades 7 – 12: The Report of the Expert Panel on Student Success in Ontario.* Toronto: Ontario Ministry of Education

National Council of Teachers of Mathematics. (2000). *Principles and Standards for School Mathematics.* Reston, VA: Author.

National Association for the Education of Young Children (NAEYC) and National Council of Teachers of Mathematics (NCTM). (2002). *Early Childhood Mathematics: Promoting Good Beginnings.* A joint position statement. Adopted April 2002, pages 5, 6.

National Council of Teachers of Mathematics (NCTM). *Curriculum and Evaluation Standards for School Mathematics.* Reston, VA: NCTM, 1989, page 23.

Ontario Ministry of Education. (2003). *Early Math Strategy, The Report of the Expert Panel on Early Math in Ontario; 2003*, Toronto: Queen's Printer for Ontario, page 12.

Pugalee, D.K. (2001b). *Using Communication to Develop Students' Mathematical Literacy.* Mathematics Teaching in the Middle School, 6(5), 296-299.

Sapon-Shevin, Mara. (1999). *Because We Can Change The World; A Practical Guide to Building Cooperative, Inclusive Classroom Communities.* Boston: Allyn and Bacon, pages 16, 17, 68.

Van de Walle, John A. (2004). *Elementary and Middle School Mathematics: Teaching Developmentally.* Boston: Allyn and Bacon.

Addison Wesley Math Makes Sense 8 accommodates these planning needs:

- Each strand is addressed with a major emphasis at least twice through the school year, to provide a rich variety of math experiences for students and to accommodate provincial reporting requirements.
- All units can be completed in about 31 weeks – depending on the needs of the class – to accommodate the normal interruptions that occur during a regular 36-week school year.
- To support the teaching of combined grades, the grade 8 program aligns as much as possible with the grade 7 program. Unit by unit, students can work on the same strand across grades. Some teachers prefer to plan their own sequence of topics through the school year. *Addison Wesley Math Makes Sense 8* accommodates this, as well, within the larger framework of the mathematics to be developed across the grade 8 program. Some units need to remain in the sequence in which they are placed: for example, it is not wise to change the order of the number units. Other units are independent, and can be shifted if desired: for example, the units on geometry and probability can be shifted, although the teacher needs to bear in mind that the Probability unit does assume prior knowledge of fractions.

If you're teaching *Addison Wesley Math Makes Sense 8* for the first time, you may prefer to follow the order in the text. This will ensure that the grade-level prerequisites for each unit have been covered previously within the school year. Once you have taught the units in sequence, and become familiar with the content detail in each unit, you will be able to determine whether you prefer a different order.

Here is a suggested timing chart for *Addison Wesley Math Makes Sense 8*:

MONTH	SEPTEMBER	OCTOBER		NOVEMBER	DECEMBER		JANUARY
Text Unit	1 Numbers, Variables, and Equations	2 Applications of Ratio, Rate, and Percent	3 Geometry and Measurement	4 Fractions and Decimals	5 Data Management	Vacation	6 Circles
Suggested Timing (weeks)	About 3	4	About 1	About 4	About 3		About 2

This timing chart shows one possible alternative unit sequence:

MONTH	SEPTEMBER		OCTOBER	NOVEMBER	DECEMBER		JANUARY
Text Unit	3 Geometry and Measurement	1 Numbers, Variables, and Equations	2 Applications of Ratio, Rate, and Percent	5 Data Management	4 Fractions and Decimals	Vacation	6 Circles
Suggested Timing (weeks)	About 1	About 3	4	About 3	About 4		About 2

Cross Strand Investigations

The Cross Strand Investigations are designed for flexible use:

- at the end of each term, as they occur in the text
- to assign during periods of the school year that are prone to interruption of regular class schedules, such as the weeks leading up to holidays
- in a cluster as a closing project – with choice for students – at the end of the school year.

Each Investigation provides an opportunity for students to use the math they have learned in the preceding units, or in earlier years, to solve a problem in context or to investigate an intriguing question or pattern. They can be used to gather assessment information to enable you to fulfill reporting requirements.

Teaching notes, sample responses, and accompanying check lists for the Cross Strand Investigations are in the Additional Assessment Support module.

FEBRUARY	MARCH		APRIL	MAY		JUNE	MONTH
7 Geometry	8 Square Roots and Pythagoras	Vacation	9 Integers	10 Algebra	11 Probability		**Text Unit**
About 4	About 3		About 3–4	About 2–3	About 2		**Suggested Timing (weeks)**

FEBRUARY	MARCH		APRIL	MAY		JUNE	MONTH
8 Square Roots and Pythagoras	7 Geometry	Vacation	9 Integers	11 Probability	10 Algebra		**Text Unit**
About 3	About 4		About 3–4	About 2	About 2–3		**Suggested Timing (weeks)**

Materials List for *Math Makes Sense 8*

Recommended quantities of materials other than program resources provided on Black Line Masters.

For classroom use	For each group of 3 or 4 students	For each pair of students	For each student
• overhead algebra tiles • overhead Base Ten Blocks • overhead Pattern Blocks • overhead Cuisenaire Rods • models of geometric solids • newspapers, magazines • overhead counters • two-pan balances and masses • trundle wheel **Software** • *The Geometer's Sketchpad* • *Fathom* • *AppleWorks*	• atlas or almanac • 4 identical empty cereal boxes • objects with circular cross section • dental floss • regular polyhedrons with numbered faces	• deck of cards • Base Ten Blocks • measuring tape or metre stick • Interlocking cubes • Colour Tiles or congruent squares • number cubes • glue • Pattern Blocks • sticky tape • Tangram • spinner • opened metal paper clip • paper bags • cardboard • Cuisenaire Rods • cardboard tubes • cylindrical objects • Mira • coins	• calculator • scissors • 30-cm ruler • tracing paper • protractor • index cards • compass • counters of different colours • algebra tiles

Literature Connections – Grade 8 Math

Algebra For Everyone: Videotape and Discussion Guide. (NCTM, 1992, Third printing 2002) ISBN: 087353350X

Bokhari, Naila. *Piece of Pi: Wit-Sharpening, Brain-Bruising, Number Crunching Activities with Pi.* Prufrock Press, 2001. ISBN: 1883055431

Burns, Marilyn. *Lessons for Multiplying and Dividing Fractions: Grades 5-6.* Math Solutions Publications, 2003. ISBN: 0941355640

Haven, Kendall. *Marvels of Math: Fascinating Reads and Awesome Activities.* Teacher Ideas Press, 1998. ISBN: 1563085852

Hopfensperger, P., H. Kranendonk, and R. Scheaffer. *Data-Driven Mathematics: Probability through Data.* Dale Seymour Publications, 1999. ISBN: 157232225X
ISBN: 0534066968

Janes, Nancy Segal. *Problem Solving with Polyhedra Dice.* Cuisenaire Company of America Inc., 1994. ISBN: 0938587749

Kahn, Charles H. *Pythagoras and the Pythagoreans: A Brief History.* Hackett Publishing Company, 2001. ISBN: 0872205754

Lappan, Glenda, James T. Fey (Editor), William M. Fitzgerald (Editor), Catherine Anderson (Editor). *Looking for Pythagoras: The Pythagorean Theorem* (*Connected Mathematics Series*). Dale Seymour Publications, 1997. ISBN: 1572321806

Lee, Martin and Marcia Miller. *5-Minute Math Problem of the Day*. Scholastic Publishing, 2000. ISBN: 0439175399

Marcy, Steve and Janis. *Pre-Algebra with Pizzazz!* Creative Publications, 1978. ISBN: 0884881512

Muschla, Gary Robert, Judith A. Muschla. *Hands-On Math Projects with Real-Life Applications: Ready-to-Use Lessons and Materials for Grades 6-12.* Jossey-Bass, 1996. ISBN: 0876283849

Newman, Claire M., Thomas E. Obremski, and Richard L. Scheaffer. *Exploring Probability.* Dale Seymour Publications, 1987. ISBN: 0866513337

Phillips, Elizabeth, Glenda Lappan, Mary Jean Winter, and William Fitzgerald. *Middle Grades Mathematics Project: Probability.* Addison-Wesley Publishing Company, 1986. ISBN: 0201214784

Serra, Michael. *Patty Paper Geometry*. Key Curriculum Press, 1994. ISBN: 1559530723

Smith, Karl J. *The Nature of Mathematics* 5th edition. Brooks/Cole Publishing Company, 2003. ISBN: 053440023X

Van de Walle, John A. and LouAnn H. Lovin. *Teaching Student-Centered Mathematics Grades 5–8.* Pearson Education, Inc. (Allyn and Bacon), 2006. ISBN: 0205417973

Walch. *Daily Warm-Ups: Geometry*. J. Weston Walch Publishing, 2004. ISBN: 0825144981

Program Masters

Program Masters

Contents

Name ________________ Date ______________

Program Master 1

Inquiry Process Check List

	Understands Problem		Makes a Plan		Carries out Plan		Looks Back		
Name	Restates problem in own words.	Identifies information given.	Asks questions; makes predictions.	Chooses a strategy.	Applies procedures accurately.	Knows when plan is/is not working.	Explains solution.	Evaluates reasona-bleness of solution.	Describes processes.

Name ____________________ Date ________________

Program Master 2

Self-Assessment

Students can use this format to guide reflection and self-assessment at the end of an activity, lesson, or unit. They can record their ideas on the form or in a journal.

1. What was the main mathematical concept, procedure or strategy you learned?

2. Give an example to show how it works. You can use words, diagrams, symbols, or sketches.

3. Why is it important? When might it be useful to you or others?

4. Check the options below that describe how well you understand it.

- ☐ I could teach it to someone else.
- ☐ I know when and how to use it on my own.
- ☐ I can use it with a bit of help or reminding.
- ☐ I still need a lot of help and practice.

Name ____________________ Date ________________

Program Master 3

Self-Assessment: Problem Solving

Step 1. **Understand.**
State the problem in your own words. Make sure you tell exactly what you are supposed to find or solve.

What information are you given?

How well do you understand this problem?
not at all ☐ partly ☐ a lot ☐

Step 2. **Plan.**
How will you solve the problem? What strategy will you use?

How confident are you that your plan will work?
not at all ☐ partly ☐ a lot ☐

Step 3. **Solve.**
Solve the problem (in your notebook or on paper).
Explain your solution.

Step 4. **Look Back.**
Is your solution reasonable?
not at all ☐ maybe ☐
How certain are you that your solution is correct?
not at all ☐ somewhat ☐ a lot ☐

Describe another way to solve this problem. Compare it to the method you used.

Name ____________________ Date ________________

Program Master 4

Learning Skills Check List

Record ongoing observations of students' learning skills. Use check marks or dates to indicate when behaviours are observed, or use the following key:

Level 1 – very limited; Level 2 – somewhat or limited; Level 3 – satisfactory; Level 4 – thorough

Name	Works independently	Shows initiative	Completes tasks (work habits)	Asks questions (uses information)	Co-operates with others	Resolves conflicts appropriately	Participates in class and group activities	Assesses own work (sets goals)

Name ____________________ Date ______________

Program Master 5

Mathematical Dispositions and Learning Skills

Teachers can record observations about students' dispositions and learning skills once or twice during each unit by noting a rating (for example, 1 to 4) along with brief comments.

Learning Skill	Observation 1		Observation 2	
	Rating*	Date/Evidence	Rating*	Date/Evidence
Independent work • shows self-responsibility • completes work on time and with care				
Initiative • takes risks in performing mathematical tasks • exhibits curiosity • shows enjoyment of mathematical experiences • approaches new tasks confidently				
Work habits • puts forward consistent effort • perseveres in mathematical tasks and projects • shows flexibility				
Class participation • contributes to mathematical discussions • contributes to co-operative problem solving • shares responsibility				
Problem solving • mathematically represents and organizes information • devises plans • carries out plans • self-checks to verify solutions • makes connections among different problems and solutions				
Goal setting • assesses own work; evaluates success • identifies goals • identifies specific steps or actions needed to improve • uses criteria				

Level 1 – very limited; Level 2 – somewhat or limited; Level 3 – satisfactory; Level 4 – thorough

Name ____________________ Date ________________

Program Master 6

Observation Record 1

This form can be used to observe three students who are working together or who are in close proximity.

Unit_____ Lesson _____ Activity _______________

	Observation Notes
Name ____________ ***Focus: KU, T, CM, AP** **Observed strengths:** **Observed needs:**	
Name ____________ ***Focus: KU, T, CM, AP** **Observed strengths:** **Observed needs:**	
Name ____________ ***Focus: KU, T, CM, AP** **Observed strengths:** **Observed needs:**	

*Circle one or more to indicate the focus of your observations and notes:

KU – Knowledge and Understanding **T** – Thinking
CM – Communication **AP** – Application

Name ____________________ Date ________________

Program Master 7

Observation Record 2

Use this form to record ongoing observations over a period of time. You can record more than one date/observation in each category.

Observation period from __________ to __________

Observation Notes
Knowledge and Understanding
Thinking
Communication
Application
Summary ***Strengths:*** ***Needs:*** ***Next steps:***

Name ____________________ Date ______________

Program Master 8

Conference Prompts

Teachers can select and develop questions and prompts to use during both formal and informal conferences and interviews with students.
Answers will often provide evidence of more than one category.
Note: The questions are not intended to provide an overall sequence/conference outline. They are examples.

Knowledge and Understanding	Thinking
• Tell me what you know/learned about … • Tell me about your thinking … • How do you know …? • Why does …? • Tell me how you could … • Show me … • What do you predict/think will happen if …? Why? • Does that make sense to you? Tell me why/why not. • How could you explain this to someone who has not learned it yet? • Explain what you need to do … • About how much/how many …? Tell me about your thinking—how did you decide on your estimate? • What is the same/different …? What questions do you have about …?	• Explain the problem to me. • What have you tried? • How did you decide where to start/what to do? • Were there any places where you got stuck? How did you get going again? • Why did you choose …? • How did you solve …? • Show/tell me about your thinking. • Show me another way … • What other ways could someone solve this problem? • Have you found all possible solutions/answers? How do you know? • What advice would you give someone else who had to solve a problem like this? • Can you make up another problem like this for me to solve? Here's what I saw you do …
Communication	**Application**
Can be observed as students respond, through speech, writing, and drawing, to questions such as those listed above. Also: • Is there another way to say/show that? • What do you call that? Does it have another name? • How could you tell/show someone else what you learned/found out? • Tell me what you did.	• How many …? • Show me how to … • What answer/solution do you have? • Does that make sense to you? • How could you check? • How did you get that answer/solution? • Have you answered all the parts? • Why is this important? How could you use … outside of school? • How is … connected to …? • Have you done work like this before? Tell me about it.

Name ____________________ Date ______________

Program Master 9

Work Sample Records

Teachers can use this form to record key information about a portfolio or collection of work samples they select to keep as evidence of learning.

Unit ______

	Strand circle one or more	**Category** circle one or more*	**What this sample shows about student learning**
Date:________ **Work Sample:**	• Number Sense and Numeration • Measurement • Geometry and Spatial Sense • Patterning and Algebra • Data Management and Probability	KU T CM AP	
Date:_____ **Work Sample:**	• Number Sense and Numeration • Measurement • Geometry and Spatial Sense • Patterning and Algebra • Data Management and Probability	KU T CM AP	
Date:_____ **Work Sample:**	• Number Sense and Numeration • Measurement • Geometry and Spatial Sense • Patterning and Algebra • Data Management and Probability	KU T CM AP	

* **KU** – Knowledge and Understanding **T** – Thinking
CM – Communication **AP** – Application

Name ____________________ Date ________________

Program Master 10

Summary Class Records: Strands

Achievement Levels
1 – very limited; simple strategies; major errors; unclear
2 – somewhat or limited; somewhat appropriate strategies; several minor errors; some clarity
3 – satisfactory; appropriate strategies; few minor errors; clear
4 – thorough; rarely makes errors; innovative strategies; clear and precise

Unit ______

	Strand ________________				**Strand** ________________			
	Most consistent achievement level				**Most consistent achievement level**			
Name	Observations	Work samples	Performance Assessment	**Overall**	Observations	Work samples	Performance Assessment	**Overall**

Name ____________________ Date ________________

Program Master 11

Summary Class Records: Achievement Categories

Teachers can use this form to keep a class record of the levels achieved on various tasks and activities. Levels can be assigned based on observations, conferences, work samples, and/or performance assessment.

Achievement Levels
1 – very limited; simple strategies; major errors; unclear
2 – somewhat or limited; somewhat appropriate strategies; several minor errors; some clarity
3 – satisfactory; appropriate strategies; few minor errors; clear
4 – thorough; rarely makes errors; innovative strategies; clear and precise

Unit ____ Focus Strand ______________________________

	Level Achieved												
	Knowledge and Understanding			Thinking			Communication			Application			Overall
Name													

Name ____________________ Date ________________

Program Master 12

Summary Record: Individual

Teachers can use this form to maintain an ongoing record of student achievement. For each strand, use records of ongoing observations and conferences, work samples, and performance assessments to determine the level achieved for each category. Record category levels in the boxes, and comments in the space provided.

Achievement Levels

1 – very limited; simple strategies; major errors; unclear
2 – somewhat or limited; somewhat appropriate strategies; several minor errors; some clarity
3 – satisfactory; appropriate strategies; few minor errors; clear
4 – thorough; rarely makes errors; innovative strategies; clear and precise

	Most Consistent Level Achieved				
Category	**Knowledge and Understanding**	**Thinking**	**Communication**	**Application**	**Overall**
NUMBER SENSE AND NUMERATION	level ☐	level ☐	level ☐	level ☐	level ☐
MEASUREMENT	level ☐	level ☐	level ☐	level ☐	level ☐
GEOMETRY AND SPATIAL SENSE	level ☐	level ☐	level ☐	level ☐	level ☐
PATTERNING AND ALGEBRA	level ☐	level ☐	level ☐	level ☐	level ☐
DATA MANAGEMENT AND PROBABILITY	level ☐	level ☐	level ☐	level ☐	level ☐
OVERALL	level ☐	level ☐	level ☐	level ☐	level ☐

Name ______________________ Date ________________

Program Master 13

Hundred Chart

1	2	3	4	5	6	7	8	9	10
11	12	13	14	15	16	17	18	19	20
21	22	23	24	25	26	27	28	29	30
31	32	33	34	35	36	37	38	39	40
41	42	43	44	45	46	47	48	49	50
51	52	53	54	55	56	57	58	59	60
61	62	63	64	65	66	67	68	69	70
71	72	73	74	75	76	77	78	79	80
81	82	83	84	85	86	87	88	89	90
91	92	93	94	95	96	97	98	99	100

Name ____________________ Date ________________

Program Master 14

0.5-cm Grid Paper

Name ____________________ Date ________________

Program Master 15

12 × 12 Multiplication Chart

×	1	2	3	4	5	6	7	8	9	10	11	12
1	1	2	3	4	5	6	7	8	9	10	11	12
2	2	4	6	8	10	12	14	16	18	20	22	24
3	3	6	9	12	15	18	21	24	27	30	33	36
4	4	8	12	16	20	24	28	32	36	40	44	48
5	5	10	15	20	25	30	35	40	45	50	55	60
6	6	12	18	24	30	36	42	48	54	60	66	72
7	7	14	21	28	35	42	49	56	63	70	77	84
8	8	16	24	32	40	48	56	64	72	80	88	96
9	9	18	27	36	45	54	63	72	81	90	99	108
10	10	20	30	40	50	60	70	80	90	100	110	120
11	11	22	33	44	55	66	77	88	99	110	121	132
12	12	24	36	48	60	72	84	96	108	120	132	144

Name ____________________ Date ________________

Program Master 16

Blank 12 by 12 Chart

Name ____________________ Date ______________

Program Master 17

2-Column Chart

Name ____________________ Date ________________

Program Master 18

3-Column Chart

Name ____________________ Date ________________

Program Master 19

4-Column Chart

Name ____________________ Date _______________

Program Master 20

1-cm Grid Paper

Name ____________________ Date ________________

Program Master 21

2-cm Grid Paper

Name ____________________ Date ________________

Program Master 22

Square Dot Paper

Name ____________________ Date ______________

Program Master 23

Isometric Dot Paper

Name ____________________ Date ______________

Program Master 24

Isometric Grid Paper

Name ____________________ Date ________________

Program Master 25

Pattern Blocks

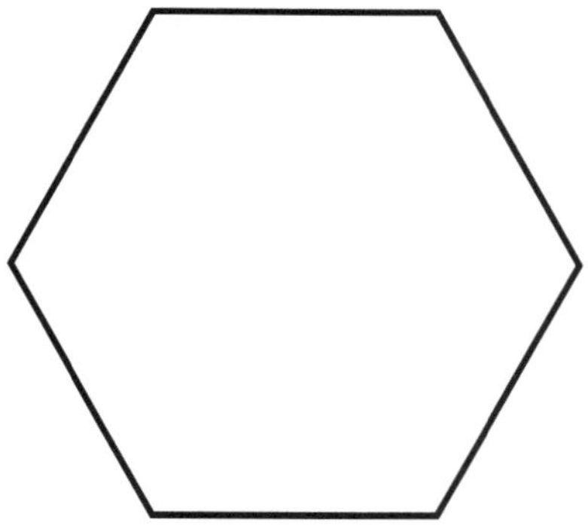

Yellow Hexagon

Orange Square

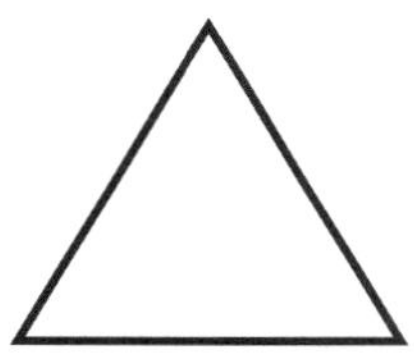

Green Triangle

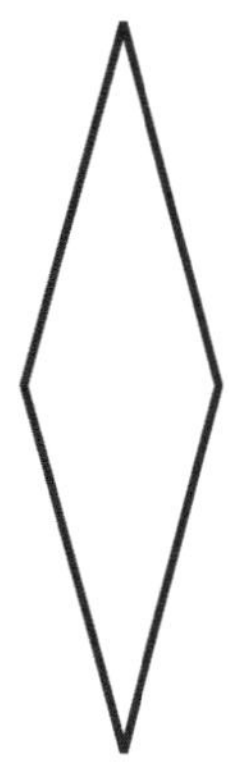

Tan Rhombus

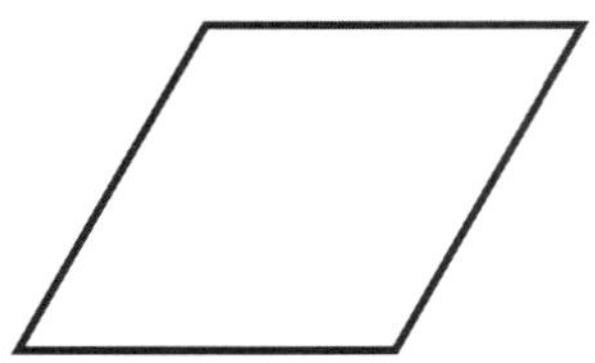

Blue Rhombus

Red Trapezoid

Name ____________________ Date ________________

Program Master 26

Tangram

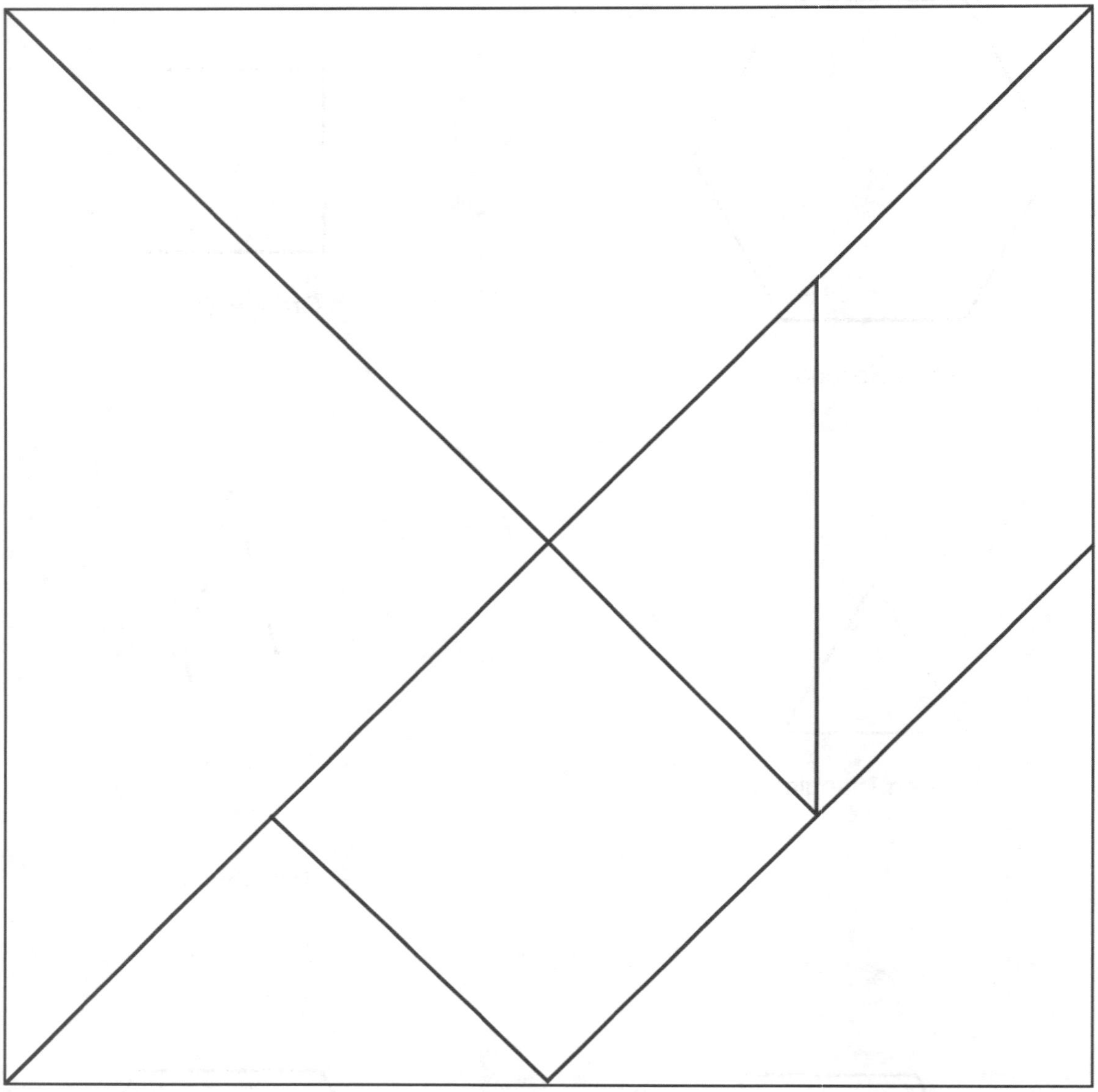

Name ____________________ Date ______________

Program Master 27

Algebra Tiles

Name ____________________ Date ________________

Program Master 28

Venn Diagram

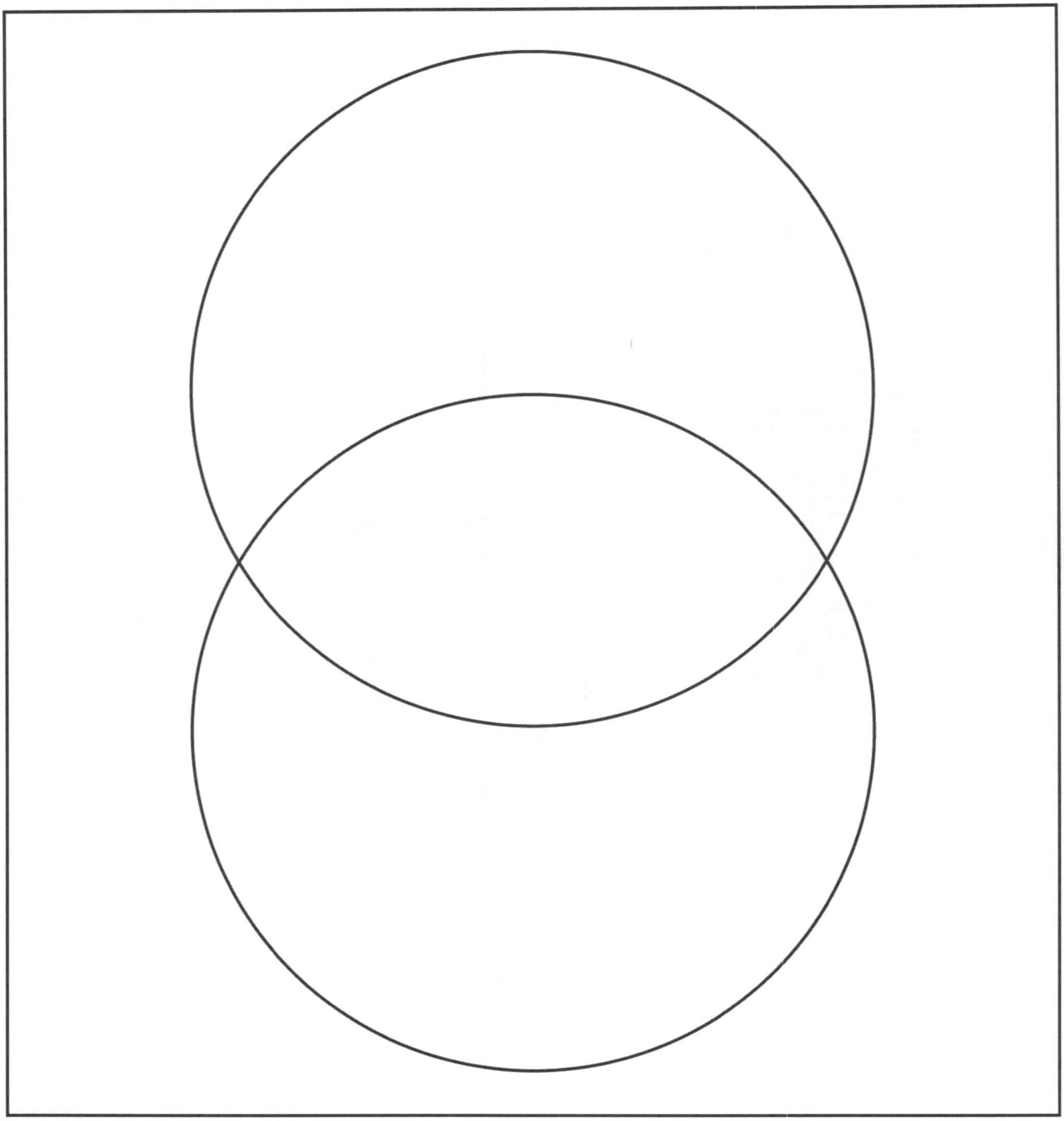

Name ____________________ Date ________________

Program Master 29

5-Column Chart

Name ____________________ Date ________________

Program Master 30

Number Lines

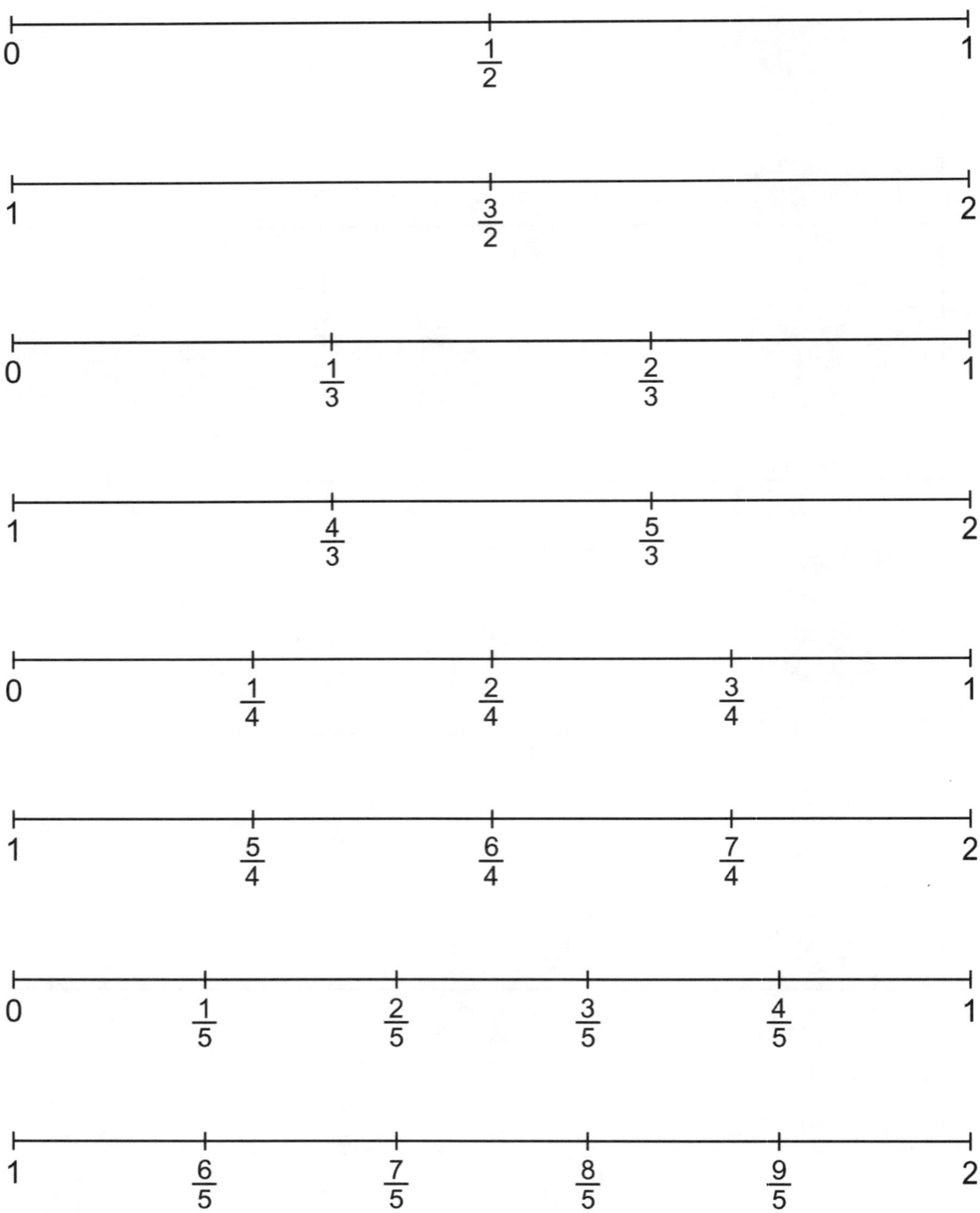

Addison Wesley **Mathematics** *Makes Sense*

Program Authors

Trevor Brown

Antonietta Lenjosek

Cathy Heideman

Jim Mennie

Georgia Konis-Chatzis

A.J. Keene

Margaret Sinclair

Craig Featherstone

Jason Johnston

Bryn Keyes

Elizabeth Wood

Elizabeth Milne

David Sufrin

Don Jones

Sharon Jeroski

Lynn Strangway

Printed and bound in Canada

2 3 4 5 – TC – 09 08 07 06

PEARSON
Education Canada

ADDISON WESLEY

Ontario

Math Makes Sense 8

Ontario
Teacher Guide

Additional Assessment Support

PEARSON Education Canada

ASSESSMENT BACKGROUND

1 An Introduction to Assessment

> *"A problem ... must begin where the students are ... Good* [assessment] *tasks should permit every student in the class ... to demonstrate some knowledge, skill, or understanding."*
>
> (Van de Walle 2004, 62)

Assessment and evaluation in *Addison Wesley Mathematics Makes Sense* are **purposeful** and **possible**—to ensure students are supported in reaching the highest possible levels of achievement, and teachers are supported with tools and strategies that enhance assessment and reporting. Assessment and evaluation reflect the exploratory, hands-on, problem-solving approach that is the foundation of *Addison Wesley Mathematics Makes Sense.*

Improving Student Learning

> *Assessment should support the learning of important mathematics and furnish useful information to both teachers and children.*
>
> (NCTM: *Assessment Principles*)

The primary purpose of assessment and evaluation is to improve student learning. *Diagnostic assessment* helps teachers and students identify learning needs and plan for excellence. *Formative assessment* provides descriptive feedback for teachers and students to monitor their efforts, make adjustments that lead to enhanced learning, and work toward successful achievement. *Summative assessment* allows students to demonstrate and document their achievements, and share them with families, to ensure future effective learning. Student reflection and self-assessment help students become self-directed learners—able to set, work toward, and monitor their own goals.

Assessment strategies and materials in *Addison Wesley Mathematics Makes Sense* reflect the NCTM assessment standards.

Problem Solving

The active, exploratory, problem-solving approach to learning mathematics central to *Addison Wesley Mathematics Makes Sense* is reflected in assessment strategies and techniques. Students demonstrate their knowledge and skills by *doing* mathematics. Many assessment activities focus on performance assessment, where students are asked to demonstrate their knowledge and skills through problems and investigations that connect mathematics to open-ended problems and real-world contexts and issues.

NCTM ASSESSMENT STANDARDS	ADDISON WESLEY MATHEMATICS MAKES SENSE
Standard 1: Assessment should reflect the mathematics that all students need to know and be able to do.	Assessment is aligned with the provincial curriculum expectations and content standards that specify what students are to learn at each grade.
Standard 2: Assessment should enhance mathematics learning.	Assessment *for* Learning, a feature in every lesson in the Teacher Guide, focuses on teacher implementation of effective practices to support student learning and performance.
Standard 3: Assessment should promote equity.	At the beginning of every unit, open-ended *diagnostic assessment* helps teachers build on students' prior learning to support student success. *Formative assessment* is particularly helpful in supporting low-achieving students.
Standard 4: Assessment should be an open process.	From grade 1, expectations and criteria are made clear to students and their families. As students gain experience, they are increasingly involved in discussing and setting criteria for their work.
Standard 5: Assessment should promote valid inferences about mathematics learning.	Assessment is based on students *doing* mathematics. To ensure the full spectrum of mathematics achievement is addressed, attention is focused on all aspects of mathematics: understanding concepts and making connections; applying procedures, using problem-solving strategies; and communicating.
Standard 6: Assessment should be a coherent process.	All assessment techniques, tools, and activities are related to the content strands and curriculum expectations, and to student performance.

2 Effective Assessment Practices

> *"Researchers and policy-makers are finally recognizing what teachers have long known: assessment has a powerful effect on student learning."*
>
> (Jeroski 2002)

Goal-Setting, Shared Criteria, Effective Tasks

Learning is enhanced when goals are understood and shared by teachers and students. Recognizing goals and criteria for success is crucial to formative assessment.

Effective performance tasks include complex thinking, where students make choices and decisions. Effective tasks also focus on what students are supposed to **learn** or demonstrate, (not just what they are supposed to **do**).

Self-Assessment

Providing structured, focused opportunities for self-assessment helps students learn, and increases their sense of responsibility. Students engaged in self-assessment become more interested in learning goals, criteria, feedback, and self-improvement.

Provide Meaningful Feedback

Descriptive feedback improves student achievement—feedback that focuses on:

- what students have or have not achieved (rather than comparisons to others)
- timely explanations and corrections (what is incorrect and what is correct and why)
- specific ways in which work can be improved

Adjust Instruction

Teachers who use ongoing assessment results to adjust their teaching help students achieve better results. Thus, teachers are open to adapting their instructional plans to reflect student needs. Teachers should select and develop assessments with a clear sense of purpose—knowing what specific information they and the students need to work toward specific results or expectations.

Motivate Students

Student motivation is one of the keys to learning and improvement. Where assessment results are conveyed in a way that supports learning (rather than questioning ability and effort), teachers have found significant learning gains.

Assessment for learning (formative assessment) and *assessment of learning (summative assessment)* ought first and foremost to support learning. Research by Wynne Harlen and Ruth Deakin Crick found that the effects of summative assessment could support students' learning *when:*

- Assessments were consistent with teacher expectations and student capabilities.
- Students had opportunities to develop self-assessment skills and learning goals.
- The school took a constructive and supportive stance about testing.
- Learning goals were made explicit to low-achieving students, who were shown how to direct effort in learning.
- Assessment results were used to convey a sense of learning progress to students.

3 Diagnostic, Formative, and Summative Assessment

Diagnostic Assessment

Teachers use diagnostic information to make choices about the nature and extent of the learning experiences they provide. Teachers have to consider the varying mathematical knowledge and skills of the whole class as well as individual students.

Purpose

- Help teachers identify students who have difficulty acquiring the necessary concepts, procedures, and strategies.
- Develop insights into particular needs to adjust instruction to ensure at-risk students have the best possibility to succeed.

Diagnostic Opportunities in Addison Wesley Math Makes Sense 8

- The Student Book begins with a group *Cross Strand Investigation* designed to give teachers and students an opportunity to revisit some key concepts and procedures from prior knowledge, and document any gaps or misconceptions. Each unit in the Student Book begins with a *Unit Launch*, designed to activate and build upon students' prior knowledge.
- The notes for the *Unit Launch* in the Teacher Guide include diagnostic questions, and a Diagnostic Assessment feature that cues teachers about what to watch for and what to do. The lesson teaching notes include prompts and questions to help teachers activate prior knowledge to determine whether a student has the skills and understanding required to work on the lesson content.

Generic Tools

The generic tools are available in the *Grade 8 Planning and Program Masters* module.

Helping Teachers Plan

The Planning for Assessment chart at the beginning of each unit in the Teacher Guide includes a section on diagnostic assessment.

Planning for Assessment

Purpose	Tools and Process	Recording and Reporting
Diagnostic	*Unit Launch* Question; conference; scaffold problems throughout the unit	PM 8: Conference Prompts
Formative	*Explore* – Ongoing Assessment: Observe and Listen	Master 1.2 Ongoing Observations: Numbers, Variables, and Equations PM 1: Inquiry Process Check List PM 6: Observation Record 1 PM 7: Observation Record 2 PM 8: Conference Prompts PM 2: Self-Assessment PM 3: Self-Assessment: Problem Solving PM 9: Work Sample Records
Summative	*Unit Review* *Unit Problem* – Performance Assessment *Unit Test* Review assessment records; add unit results to ongoing records	Master 1.1 Unit Rubric: Numbers, Variables, and Equations Master 1.3 Performance Assessment Rubric: Planning a Ski Trip Master 1.4 Unit Summary: Numbers, Variables, and Equations PM 10: Summary Class Records: Strands PM 11: Summary Class Records: Achievement Categories PM 12: Summary Record: Individual
Learning Skills/Mathematical Disposition	Observe and record throughout the unit.	PM 4: Learning Skills Check List PM 5: Mathematical Dispositions and Learning Skills

Program Masters (PM) are in the *Grade 8 Planning and Program Masters* module.
Extra Practice Masters are on the CD-ROM and printed in reduced format on page 66 of this module.

Formative Assessment (Assessment for Learning)

> *"Assessment for learning is the process of seeking and interpreting evidence for use by learners and their teachers to decide where the learners are in their learning, where they need to go and how best to get there."*
>
> (Assessment Reform Group 2002)

Assessment *for* learning, at the heart of *Addison Wesley Mathematics Makes Sense,* is designed to help students learn. A comprehensive research summary concluded that *formative assessment* (assessment for learning) improves student achievement substantially, particularly for low achievers (Black and Wiliam 1998). The research indicated that implementing effective formative assessment could be one of the most powerful intervention techniques ever identified, and estimated it could improve average student achievement between 1 to 2 levels.

Purpose

- Provide feedback to students so they know how they are doing, and how they might improve their learning.
- Gather information to adjust instruction for the group, and to provide additional scaffolding to students who need it.
- Engage students in their own learning, goal-setting, and self-assessment.
- Help teachers ensure students are provided with purposeful practice.

Formative Opportunities in Addison Wesley Math Makes Sense 8

Teachers can use the Planning for Assessment chart at the beginning of each unit to create a manageable and purposeful formative assessment plan.

- The Teacher Guide provides specific questions to probe student understanding at various stages of a lesson. Each lesson *(Explore/Show and Share)* engages students in *actively exploring* the key concept. This gives teachers opportunities to observe what students are able to do. *The Explore/Ongoing Assessment: Observe and Listen* sections of the Teacher Guide provide specific cues and questions.
- *Practice* in the Student Book provides opportunities for teachers to observe, probe, and provide feedback about student development. The *Assessment Focus* question in each lesson allows teachers to check various levels of achievement. Numerical and written answers in the Teacher Guide help teachers provide feedback. *Reflect* in the Student Book directs students to focus on what they have learned, and how well they understand the math. Teachers may choose to use these to prompt discussion, demonstration, or journal entries.
- In the Teacher Guide, *Assessment for Learning: What to Look For; What to Do* cues teachers' attention on specific behaviours in students' oral, concrete, or written work. It provides direct, practical instructions about what to do to provide extra support, extra practice, or extensions. *Reaching All Learners* helps teachers identify common misunderstandings and how to alleviate them.

Specific Tools in Each Unit

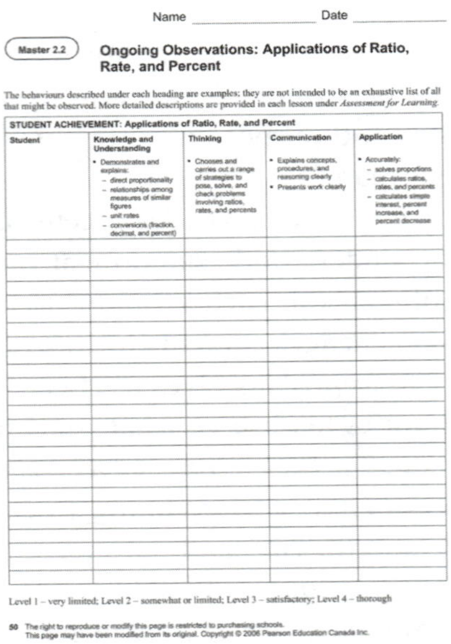

Name ______________ Date ____________

Master 2.2 **Ongoing Observations: Applications of Ratio, Rate, and Percent**

The behaviours described under each heading are examples; they are not intended to be an exhaustive list of all that might be observed. More detailed descriptions are provided in each lesson under *Assessment for Learning*.

STUDENT ACHIEVEMENT: Applications of Ratio, Rate, and Percent				
Student	**Knowledge and Understanding** • Demonstrates and explains: – direct proportionality – relationships among measures of similar figures – unit rates – conversions (fraction, decimal, and percent)	**Thinking** • Chooses and carries out a range of strategies to pose, solve, and check problems involving ratios, rates, and percents	**Communication** • Explains concepts, procedures, and reasoning clearly • Presents work clearly	**Application** • Accurately: – solves proportions – calculates ratios, rates, and percents – calculates simple interest, percent increase, and percent decrease

Level 1 – very limited; Level 2 – somewhat or limited; Level 3 – satisfactory; Level 4 – thorough

50

- The *Ongoing Observations* master provides a recording form for teachers to record evidence of student key behaviours in relation to the unit content and the four categories of achievement. Teachers should accumulate observations under each category over the course of the unit.
- The *Unit Rubric* master can be used for both formative and summative assessment. It is based on specific expectations for the entire unit. As a formative assessment master, it can be used to monitor student development during the unit (for example, use a highlighter to indicate which behaviours are observed at different times). It can also be used to assess open-ended tasks or problems, such as the *Assessment Focus* questions in the Student Book, although only parts of the rubric will apply to a specific task.

Generic Tools

The generic tools, *Program Masters*, in the *Grade 8 Planning and Program Masters* module support formative assessment, but are optional. They are not part of the core assessment, but allow teachers to tailor the assessment programs that best suit them.

- *Program Master 1: Inquiry Process Check List* provides criteria and recording forms for teachers to document student development.
- *Program Master 2: Self-Assessment,* and *Program Master 3: Self-Assessment: Problem Solving* can be used to prompt reflection and self-assessment.
- *Program Masters 6 and 7: Observation Records 1* and *2* are recording formats for making observational notes. They are not specific to a particular unit or activity.

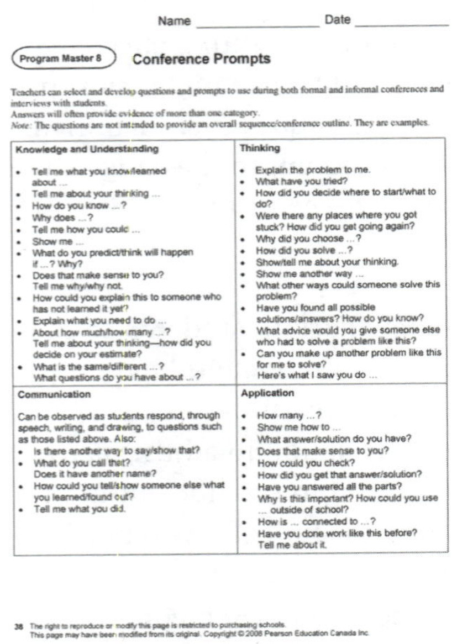

Name ______________ Date ____________

Program Master 8 **Conference Prompts**

Teachers can select and develop questions and prompts to use during both formal and informal conferences and interviews with students.
Answers will often provide evidence of more than one category.
Note: The questions are not intended to provide an overall sequence/conference outline. They are examples.

Knowledge and Understanding	Thinking
• Tell me what you know/learned about ... • Tell me about your thinking ... • How do you know ...? • Why does ...? • Tell me how you could ... • Show me ... • What do you predict/think will happen if ...? Why? • Does that make sense to you? Tell me why/why not. • How could you explain this to someone who has not learned it yet? • Explain what you need to do ... • About how much/how many ...? Tell me about your thinking—how did you decide on your estimate? • What is the same/different ...? What questions do you have about ...?	• Explain the problem to me. • What have you tried? • How did you decide where to start/what to do? • Were there any places where you got stuck? How did you get going again? • Why did you choose ...? • How did you solve ...? • Show/tell me about your thinking. • Show me another way ... • What other ways could someone solve this problem? • Have you found all possible solutions/answers? How do you know? • What advice would you give someone else who had to solve a problem like this? • Can you make up another problem like this for me to solve? Here's what I saw you do ...
Communication	**Application**
Can be observed as students respond, through speech, writing, and drawing, to questions such as those listed above. Also: • Is there another way to say/show that? • What do you call that? Does it have another name? • How could you tell/show someone else what you learned/found out? • Tell me what you did.	• How many ...? • Show me how to ... • What answer/solution do you have? • Does that make sense to you? • How could you check? • How did you get that answer/solution? • Have you answered all the parts? • Why is this important? How could you use ... outside of school? • How is ... connected to ...? • Have you done work like this before? Tell me about it.

38

- *Program Master 8: Conference Prompts* provides questions teachers can use to probe student understanding, and to help determine the strategies students are using.
- *Program Master 9: Work Sample Records* provides a format for documenting work samples as part of portfolios.

Summative Assessment (Assessment of Learning)

> *"The goal of assessment is to provide a valid set of inferences related to particular expectations for children and schools."*
>
> (Linn and Baker 2002, 3)

Summative assessment involves both assessment (gathering and documenting evidence) and evaluation (judging student development and achievement). Effective summative assessment balances teacher observations and conferences, and student work samples or portfolios, with more structured performance tasks. Effective summative assessment includes assessments that are cumulative and integrated—it allows students to apply what they have learned over a period of time, and to integrate their mathematical understanding across strands.

In *Addison Wesley Mathematics Makes Sense:*

- Students are encouraged to demonstrate and recognize what they have achieved.
- Teachers document evidence and make decisions about student achievement.
- Family members/adults at home understand and have confidence in the reports they receive.

The achievement chart in each *Unit Summary* master in the Teacher Guide provides the framework for most assessments, so teachers can readily combine evidence from various tasks and observations. At the same time, all assessments are linked to the strands and "big ideas" of the math curriculum, supported by references to specific expectations.

Purpose

- Evaluate and judge student achievement of the expectations in the unit.
- Document student achievement to facilitate reporting to families.

Summative Assessment Opportunities in Addison Wesley Math Makes Sense 8

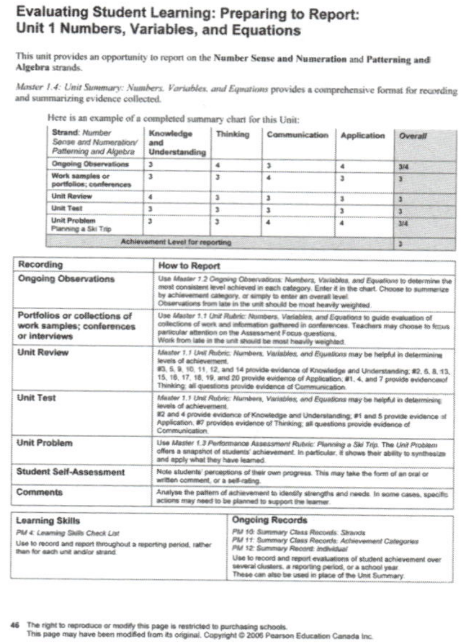

Evaluating Student Learning: Preparing to Report: Unit 1 Numbers, Variables, and Equations

This unit provides an opportunity to report on the **Number Sense and Numeration** and **Patterning and Algebra** strands.

Master 1.4: Unit Summary: Numbers, Variables, and Equations provides a comprehensive format for recording and summarizing evidence collected.

Here is an example of a completed summary chart for this Unit:

Strand: *Number Sense and Numeration/ Patterning and Algebra*	Knowledge and Understanding	Thinking	Communication	Application	*Overall*
Ongoing Observations	3	4	3	4	3/4
Work samples or portfolios; conferences	3	3	4	3	3
Unit Review	4	3	3	3	3
Unit Test	3	3	3	3	3
Unit Problem Planning a Ski Trip	3	3	4	4	3/4
Achievement Level for reporting					3

Recording	How to Report
Ongoing Observations	Use *Master 1.2 Ongoing Observations: Numbers, Variables, and Equations* to determine the most consistent level achieved in each category. Enter it in the chart. Choose to summarize by achievement category, or simply to enter an overall level. Observations from late in the unit should be most heavily weighted.
Portfolios or collections of work samples; conferences or interviews	Use *Master 1.1 Unit Rubric: Numbers, Variables, and Equations* to guide evaluation of collections of work and information gathered in conferences. Teachers may choose to focus particular attention on the Assessment Focus questions. Work from late in the unit should be most heavily weighted.
Unit Review	*Master 1.1 Unit Rubric: Numbers, Variables, and Equations* may be helpful in determining levels of achievement. #3, 5, 9, 10, 11, 12, and 14 provide evidence of Knowledge and Understanding; #2, 6, 8, 13, 15, 16, 17, 18, 19, and 20 provide evidence of Application; #1, 4, and 7 provide evidence of Thinking; all questions provide evidence of Communication.
Unit Test	*Master 1.1 Unit Rubric: Numbers, Variables, and Equations* may be helpful in determining levels of achievement. #2 and 4 provide evidence of Knowledge and Understanding; #1 and 5 provide evidence of Application; #7 provides evidence of Thinking; all questions provide evidence of Communication.
Unit Problem	Use *Master 1.3 Performance Assessment Rubric: Planning a Ski Trip*. The *Unit Problem* offers a snapshot of students' achievement. In particular, it shows their ability to synthesize and apply what they have learned.
Student Self-Assessment	Note students' perceptions of their own progress. This may take the form of an oral or written comment, or a self-rating.
Comments	Analyse the pattern of achievement to identify strengths and needs. In some cases, specific actions may need to be planned to support the learner.

Learning Skills	Ongoing Records
PM 4: Learning Skills Check List Use to record and report throughout a reporting period, rather than for each unit and/or strand.	*PM 10: Summary Class Records: Strands* *PM 11: Summary Class Records: Achievement Categories* *PM 12: Summary Record: Individual* Use to record and report evaluations of student achievement over several clusters, a reporting period, or a school year. These can also be used in place of the Unit Summary.

46 The right to reproduce or modify this page is restricted to purchasing schools.
This page may have been modified from its original. Copyright © 2006 Pearson Education Canada Inc.

The Planning for Assessment chart at the beginning of each unit helps teachers plan for summative assessment.

- In the Student Book, the *Unit Review* offers a set of short answer and open-ended questions, keyed to lessons in the unit. The *Practice Test* offers a page of questions that students can use to assess their conceptual understanding and procedural skills in preparation for a unit test. The *Unit Problem* in the Student Book presents a performance task that requires students to apply their learning to an engaging problem or problems. This task allows students to demonstrate various levels of achievement.
- In the Teacher Guide, the *Unit Test* is provided in line master form. The *Unit Test* assesses procedural skills, conceptual understanding, and problem solving skills.
- In each unit of the Teacher Guide, *Evaluating Student Learning: Preparing to Report* offers samples and suggestions on how teachers can summarize the evidence they collect, and make a summative judgment on student achievement. These are organized by strand.

- Each unit in the Student Book concludes with *Reflect,* which focuses student reflection on a key idea in the unit. Use *Reflect* to prompt demonstration, discussion, or journal entries.
- In the Student Book, there are four *Cross Strand Investigations,* one for the start of the school year, and one to close each term. These *Investigations* allow teachers to assess the extent to which students are able to synthesize and apply their learning in an integrated way.

Specific Tools in Each Unit

Name ______________ Date __________

Master 1.1 **Unit Rubric: Numbers, Variables, and Equations**

	Level 1	Level 2	Level 3	Level 4
Knowledge and Understanding • Shows understanding by demonstrating and explaining: – order of operations with brackets and exponents – ways of representing numbers (scientific notation; expanded form; products of prime factors) – how to solve equations using balance scales and algebra tiles	shows limited understanding; may be unable to demonstrate or explain: – order of operations with brackets and exponents – ways of representing numbers (scientific notation; expanded form; products of prime factors) – how to solve equations using balance scales and algebra tiles	shows some understanding; partially able to demonstrate or explain: – order of operations with brackets and exponents – ways of representing numbers (scientific notation; expanded form; products of prime factors) – how to solve equations using balance scales and algebra tiles	shows considerable understanding; able to clearly and appropriately demonstrate or explain: – order of operations with brackets and exponents – ways of representing numbers (scientific notation; expanded form; products of prime factors) – how to solve equations using balance scales and algebra tiles	shows a high degree of understanding; able to accurately and effectively demonstrate or explain: – order of operations with brackets and exponents – ways of representing numbers (scientific notation; expanded form; products of prime factors) – how to solve equations using balance scales and algebra tiles
Thinking • Chooses and carries out a range of strategies to solve and check multi-step problems involving numbers, variables, and equations; justifies the strategies used to produce an accurate solution	with assistance, chooses, carries out, and justifies a limited range of appropriate strategies to solve and check multi-step problems; rarely produces an accurate solution	with limited assistance, chooses, carries out, and justifies some appropriate strategies to solve and check problems; frequently produces an accurate solution	chooses, carries out, and justifies appropriate strategies to solve and check problems; usually produces an accurate solution	develops, carries out, and justifies effective, and often innovative, strategies to solve and check problems; always produces an accurate solution
Communication • Explains concepts, procedures, and reasoning clearly, using appropriate terms (e.g., variable)	unable to explain concepts, procedures, and reasoning clearly	partially explains concepts, procedures, and reasoning	explains concepts, procedures, and reasoning clearly	explains concepts, procedures, and reasoning clearly, precisely, and confidently
• Presents work clearly	presents work with little clarity	presents work with some clarity and precision	presents work with considerable clarity and precision	presents work with a high degree of clarity and precision
Application • Accurately: – represents whole numbers using prime factors, expanded form, and scientific notation – applies order of operations with brackets and exponents – evaluates algebraic expressions – solves equations using balance scales and tiles, and verifies solutions	limited accuracy; major errors or omissions in: – representing whole numbers using prime factors, expanded form, and scientific notation – applying order of operations with brackets and exponents – evaluating algebraic expressions – solving equations using balance scales and tiles, and verifying solutions	somewhat accurate; several minor errors or omissions in: – representing whole numbers using prime factors, expanded form, and scientific notation – applying order of operations with brackets and exponents – evaluating algebraic expressions – solving equations using balance scales and tiles, and verifying solutions	generally accurate; few minor errors or omissions in: – representing whole numbers using prime factors, expanded form, and scientific notation – applying order of operations with brackets and exponents – evaluating algebraic expressions – solving equations using balance scales and tiles, and verifying solutions	accurate and precise; no errors in: – representing whole numbers using prime factors, expanded form, and scientific notation – applying order of operations with brackets and exponents – evaluating algebraic expressions – solving equations using balance scales and tiles, and verifying solutions

- The *Unit Rubric* master highlights strategies, concepts, procedures, and communication students are expected to develop over the course of the unit. It can be used to judge the level of achievement demonstrated in portfolios, conference notes, or other tasks. It describes four levels of performance, taking into account the specific expectations for the entire unit. It can also be used to assess performance tasks.
- The *Performance Assessment Rubric* master supports the assessment of the unit problem.

- In the *Unit Summary* master, teachers summarize results of various assessments, and write an overall evaluation of student achievement. In addition to recording and summarizing levels of achievement, teachers are encouraged to comment on the patterns they observe—strengths, needs, and next steps—and to seek student self-assessment.

Generic Tools

The *Grade 8 Planning and Program Masters* module includes several Program Masters teachers may use as part of their summative assessment. These include self-assessment forms and optional summary forms.

Name ______________ Date __________

Program Master 2 **Self-Assessment**

Students can use this format to guide reflection and self-assessment at the end of an activity, lesson, or unit. They can record their ideas on the form or in a journal.

1. What was the main mathematical concept, procedure or strategy you learned?

2. Give an example to show how it works. You can use words, diagrams, symbols, or sketches.

3. Why is it important? When might it be useful to you or others?

4. Check the options below that describe how well you understand it.
   - ☐ I could teach it to someone else.
   - ☐ I know when and how to use it on my own.
   - ☐ I can use it with a bit of help or reminding.
   - ☐ I still need a lot of help and practice.

- *Program Master 2: Self-Assessment* prompts students to think about what they have learned and the progress they have made.
- *Program Master 10: Summary Class Records: Strands, Program Master 11: Summary Class Records: Achievement Categories,* and *Program Master 12: Summary Record: Individual,* offer options for record keeping. Teachers might choose one of these forms as an alternative to the *Unit Summary* master, or to create summary records over an extended time.

4 Assessing Student Progress

A. Observe and Listen

> *"Effective assessment involves ongoing, consistent, and focused observations. For a complete picture, we observe students at different times of the day, in different settings, doing different kinds of work."*
>
> (Stenmark and Bush 2001, 38)

Effective Observation

Skilful observation is one key to effective teaching. Teachers routinely adjust their lessons, offer support and feedback to students, modify tasks, ask probing questions, and make plans for future activities based on what they notice.

For many teachers, the most challenging part of observing is documenting what they see and hear. Experienced teachers have developed a variety of ways to observe and record.

Here are some suggestions for effective observation.

- Review provincial and professional documents that offer insights into the typical behaviour and development of students, including those younger and older than the ones you teach.
- Ensure students are actively engaged in exploring and problem solving. When students participate actively, they reveal their thinking and the strategies they use.
- Focus observations on a small number of behaviours or expectations that are central to the content of the lesson. Teachers who observe effectively plan their lessons at the same time as they observe. These lessons will focus on the strengths and weaknesses of students and help students develop the concepts and strategies they need.
- The top priority in observing is student understanding of concepts and use of strategies. Observation can be supplemented with assessment of student work samples and portfolios.
- For each section, choose 2 to 3 students to focus your observation. In this way, teachers ensure they have observed all students over each two- to three-week period.
  Use thoughtful prompts, such as:
  Tell me about your thinking.
  Show me what you have tried.
  How did you decide/know ...?
- Use a recording system compatible with the teaching style and other forms of record keeping.
  - Some teachers prefer to make anecdotal notes.
  - Often, teachers use a check list to identify specific behaviours associated with the lesson by entering a checkmark, date, or code to indicate what they observed.
  - Rubrics can also be used to guide observation and document behaviours.
- Be flexible. Not all observations can be planned and focused. Often, students reveal their mathematical thinking and development during other subjects or outside of class. Some teachers write one sentence at the end of morning, and one sentence immediately after school, to capture these important events and insights. Over time, this can become a rich source of information.
- Frequently skim or reread past observations, especially just before focusing observations on a particular student or group of students. This helps to provide context and continuity.

Observation Features and Tools in Addison Wesley Math Makes Sense 8

Assessment for Learning and Ongoing Observations Check List

- Each lesson includes the feature, *Assessment for Learning,* which cues teachers about key student behaviours. Over the course of a unit, these behaviours should focus on most of the key expectations, and reflect all aspects of achievement—Knowledge and Understanding, Thinking, Communication, and Application.
- In each unit, the *Ongoing Observations* master provides a manageable form for recording the observations, such as those identified in *Assessment for Learning*. Each aspect of achievement is briefly described, in terms of what to look for within the particular unit. Teachers can make brief notes, enter dates, or use a coding system of their choice.

The tools are tailored to your provincial requirements. Summarize these observations in the *Unit Summary* master to ensure that reporting incorporates a range of evidence.

Other Observation Tools

- *Program Master 6: Observation Record 1* provides a format for teachers to make anecdotal notes about three students who are working together. Teachers can note which strand students are working on, which category of achievement they are observing (for example, Knowledge and Understanding, Thinking, Communication, Application), and indicate specific strengths and needs they notice.
- *Program Master 7: Observation Record 2* is designed to help teachers accumulate anecdotal notes about an individual student over time—over an entire school term or reporting period. Four categories of achievements are identified: Knowledge and Understanding, Thinking, Communication, and Application. Teachers can use the final section of the form to summarize strengths, needs, and next steps.
- In each unit, the *Unit Rubric* master can be used to guide and record observations. It provides a comprehensive description of four levels of student achievement, and reflects the particular expectations associated with the unit. Some teachers copy a class set of rubrics, such as the *Unit Rubric* master, pre-code one copy with each student's name, then use a highlighter pen to record not only observations, but also evidence from conferences and work samples over the course of a unit. In some cases, teachers use a different colour highlighter pen for different occasions or sources of evidence.

B. Oral Questioning and Conferencing

Oral questioning plays a critical role in assessment:

- It prompts class and group discussion, where teachers are able to both stimulate student thinking and gain insights into their level of understanding.
- It is important in individual interviews or conferences, both formal and informal, where teachers prompt and support students as they explain and justify their thinking, the procedures they are using, and their results and conclusions.

Effective Questioning and Conferencing

- Keep a short list of key questions available for a conversation or short conference. Identify key questions for more formal interviews or conferences ahead of time.
- Respect the student. Focus carefully on what the student is saying.
- Accept the language students use without criticism or correction. Rephrase key ideas, and model appropriate terminology, so students become accustomed to hearing the language of mathematics.
- Ensure students understand that it is their *thinking* that is most interesting to you. Encourage through close attention, positive body language, and non-judgmental comments. However, clarify student language and misconceptions. Use student friendly language to establish comfort level so the student does not feel threatened. Consider prompts such as:
  Tell me about ... or *I wonder how we could* ... or *What if?* ...
- Give students time to think. They need to reflect, self-correct, or confirm what they have said.
- Invite students to pose questions. These questions often reveal more of student understanding than do the responses. Consider the linguistic abilities of the ESL student who may be able to demonstrate mathematical thinking in other ways than talking about it.
- All students, regardless of their language competence, should have access to manipulatives during both informal questioning, and conferences or interviews.

Using the Questioning and Conferencing Features and Tools

Conference and Interview Prompts

Program Master 8: Conference Prompts offers a variety of prompts and questions teachers may choose to use in conferences, interviews, or informal conversations with students. The questions and prompts are organized under four categories: Knowledge and Understanding; Thinking; Communication; and Application. They are intended to be samples only, and do not constitute a conference outline. Teachers can add to these from their own repertoire.

Ongoing Assessment: Observe and Listen

Each lesson includes prompts and questions designed to stimulate student thinking, provide scaffolding as needed, and offer insights into students' level of understanding. Under the heading, *Explore/Ongoing Assessment: Observe and Listen,* a short list of questions helps teachers determine how well students are developing lesson concepts. *Connect* often includes one or two key questions that help students formalize lesson concepts and allow teachers to gain insight into their understanding.

C. Performance Assessment

Addison Wesley Mathematics Makes Sense reflects the belief that students must *do* math to *learn* math, and focuses on exploration and problem solving. Performance assessment is a key component at all stages—students have opportunities to apply their learning and demonstrate their achievement through open-ended tasks and investigations.

Effective Performance Assessment

Effective performance assessment depends on effective tasks that help students, teachers, and parents focus on what is important in student learning, and gain insights into student development and achievement. Throughout the resource, a wide variety of open-ended problems, tasks, and investigations, along with rubrics and other scoring guides, have been designed to ensure that they meet the following criteria.

Using the Performance Assessment Features and Tools in Addison Wesley Math Makes Sense 8

Unit Rubric and Performance Assessment Rubric

- Each unit concludes with a performance assessment task linked to the *Unit Launch*.
- Teachers can choose to have students work independently, with a partner, or in a small group. Observing students working together often provides insights into their thinking—as students discuss and debate procedures, their thinking becomes "visible." On the other hand, it is also important to note individual student contributions. Teachers should clearly note on recording forms whether students worked independently, with the support of a peer, or with adult help. Where students work collaboratively, it is often best to have them record their solutions and justification independently.

EFFECTIVE PERFORMANCE ASSESSMENT CHECK LIST

Helps students, teachers, and families focus on learning goals and expectations

- ☑ Learning goals are specified.
- ☑ Expectations and criteria are clear, usually in the form of a rubric.
- ☑ Key mathematical concepts and skills for the grade level are emphasized.
- ☑ Tasks are meaningful to and valued by students and families.
- ☑ Rubrics and scoring guides are designed to provide meaningful feedback to help students see clearly what they are doing well and where they need to improve.

Engages students in applying what they have learned

- ☑ Students are engaged in realistic applications of their understanding and skill.
- ☑ Students are expected to think in complex ways, and to explain or justify their processes and results.

Allows for various levels of performance

- ☑ Tasks allow for a broad range of performance, and lead naturally to extensions—other problems, possibilities, and questions. They are complex and go beyond what could be assessed in a typical paper and pencil test.
- ☑ Students are required to make decisions about the strategies and procedures they use.
- ☑ Make the process open (multiple paths to a solution may be explored); thus the end product is open (multiple correct answers).

- In each unit, the *Performance Assessment Rubric* master can be used to assess students' level of achievement on the *Unit Problem*. The rubric incorporates all parts of the task, and considers concepts, procedures, strategies, and communication.
- The *Unit Summary* master includes space to record these results.

Investigations

- The Student Book has four *Cross Strand Investigations*, designed to take 2 to 4 days for students to complete. The teaching notes are in this *Assessment Module* (pp. 24–39). Each *Investigation* is accompanied by a sample response and check list.
- *Digital Roots* appears at the beginning of the Student Book and is designed for diagnostic assessment at the beginning of the year. An *Investigation* follows each of Units 3, 7, and 11. These three *Investigations* are placed approximately at the end of each term. Each *Investigation* draws on concepts, skills, and strategies students have already developed.
- The Teacher Guide support for each *Investigation* includes a check list that describes the strand and the expectations addressed by the task. The check lists are cross strand.
- **Option:** Teachers who wish to focus on a specific strand can use the *Unit Rubric* master from previous units. This rubric focuses on generic observations that apply across tasks. For example, the *Unit Rubric* from Unit 1: Numbers, Variables, and Equations could be used to assess the number aspects of *Cross Strand Investigation: Digital Roots*.

Reading and Writing in Math

- Each unit includes a *Reading and Writing in Math* feature, where students explore different aspects of problem solving and practise their skills.
- The optional assessment tools *Program Master 1: Inquiry Process Check List* helps teachers assess students' strategies for:
  - ➤ Understanding the problem
  - ➤ Making a plan
  - ➤ Carrying out the plan
  - ➤ Looking back

Other Opportunities for Performance Assessment

- One question in each *Practice* set is designated *Assessment Focus*. This question may be open-ended, and allows for various levels of achievement.
- Each *Unit Test* includes an open-ended problem. While this does not provide the scope of the *Unit Problem* or an *Investigation*, it does allow teachers to assess students' abilities to solve a problem. This item is particularly useful in assessing the problem-solving strategies students have developed.
- In each unit, the *Unit Rubric* master can be used to assess performance tasks based on unit content. This rubric provides an overall "standard" for the unit, outlining the concepts, procedures, strategies, and communication students are expected to develop. In some cases, teachers may wish to focus on only part of this rubric for a particular task.

D. Work Samples and Portfolios

Collections of student work over time provide both teachers and students with concrete evidence of progress. Portfolios and other collections are often best assessed in conjunction with an interview or conference. It is often difficult to make sense of a written sample without hearing the student's rationale. For ESL students and those who have not developed facility with written English, work samples may not offer an accurate representation of their learning.

Effective Portfolios and Work Samples

- Each item in a collection of work should illustrate something important about a student's development or progress; attitude; understanding of concepts; use of strategies; and application of procedures.
- Engage students in selecting work to collect. Schedule time for students to review, add, delete, and replace material from their portfolios regularly.
- Incorporate students' self-assessment because it is necessary to know the student's thought process. Self-assessment can address questions such as:
  - What does this work show about the math you learned?
  - What does it show about your learning skills or work habits—the way you approach and complete your work?
  - Which of these pieces was most challenging for you? How did you meet the challenge?
  - What are you most proud of in this collection?
  - What is one goal for improvement?
- Use the portfolios or collections as the basis for conferences with students and their parents.
- In assessing portfolios, look for patterns and trends, and try to make an overall or holistic assessment of the student's progress. The *Unit Rubric* master can help teachers make decisions. Some teachers work with students to develop criteria and a rubric for assessing portfolios.

Portfolio and Work Sample Features and Tools in Addison Wesley Math Makes Sense 8

Assessment Focus Questions

In each lesson, one *Practice* question is designated as *Assessment Focus*. These questions may be open ended, and allow students to show various levels of achievement. Responses to these questions can be an integral part of a collection of work samples over a unit.

Portfolio and Work Sample Records

- *Program Master 9: Work Sample Records* is a contents page for a collection of work. It provides space for recording information for up to three samples; teachers can add additional pages as needed. This form can help teachers keep track of the samples they collect, and summarize student achievement. For each unit, teachers record their insights and conclusions about student achievement in the *Unit Summary* master. Collectively, these insights will help teachers decide on a student's overall achievement.

Unit Rubric

- The *Unit Rubric* master guides teachers' decision making when they consider a portfolio or collection of work that reflects student learning over a unit. The *Unit Rubric* describes four levels of achievement, based on the unit expectations, and provides the basis for judging achievement on a collection of work, prior to completing the *Unit Summary*. Some teachers use one copy of the rubric for both observations and work samples.

E. Reflection and Self-Assessment

Opportunities to reflect, self-assess, and set goals improve student learning. Effective self-assessment is constructive and empowering. Students increase their sense of control and responsibility, and are able to focus on how they can improve. Through carefully structured reflection and self-assessment activities, students develop metacognition—they become increasingly aware of what is important in their learning and understand their own progress.

Writing is an important learning tool in mathematics. Students record their thinking, using a combination of pictures, words, or numbers.

Effective Reflection and Self-Assessment

- To become effective at reflection and self-assessment, students need frequent oral modelling and guided practice. Modelling helps students develop the language of self-assessment; they benefit from hearing and seeing examples from their peers, as well as from adults. A collaborative class journal is an excellent way of initiating self-assessment and reflection. In the Student Book, *Show and Share, Connect,* and *Reflect* highlight the importance of bringing students together to collaborate on their learning.
- Provide a variety of formats and media for self-assessment—oral, written, visual, kinesthetic—to ensure a comfort level for all students. It should not depend on a student's linguistic skills. *All* students should have opportunities to consider and assess their learning.
- When students are expected to provide written reflections, offer simple frames to help them get started, for example:
  - ➤ I want to get better at ...
  - ➤ I found out that ...
  - ➤ Look at these two pieces of work. What do you notice? What can you do now that you couldn't do before?
- Provide a concrete "anchor" for students as they self-assess and reflect. This may be a specific representation or piece of work, a portfolio, classroom charts, or a collaborative list of activities they have done. Students will find reflection and self-assessment easier and more natural if it is tied to the specific activities they have done. Provide opportunities for students to share their self-assessments with their families.
- If students are keeping math journals, ensure these are used only as places to share mathematical thinking and ideas. Students should be clear about their purpose and audience—what they are expected to share, to whom they are writing, and what result they can expect.

Reflection and Self-Assessment Features and Tools in Addison Wesley Math Makes Sense 8

Journals

There are questions and prompts for reflection at the end of each lesson, as well as at the end of every unit. Students can respond to these in their notebooks, or in special journals. Encourage students to record their ideas in any way they can. Emphasize that you are only interested in their *mathematical thinking*.

Self-assessment forms

- *Program Master 3: Self-Assessment: Problem Solving* provides a four-step outline for problem solving that includes: Understand, Plan, Solve, and Look Back. At each step, students are asked to assess their work. This form can be used with any problem-solving activity.
- *Program Master 2: Self-Assessment* guides reflection and self-assessment at the end of a lesson or activity. It prompts students to identify and

explain what they have learned, to tell why it is important, and to assess their understanding. It can be used after any activity.

Other reflection and self-assessment tools

Many conference prompts included in *Program Master 8: Conference Prompts* described in *Section 4B: Oral Questioning and Conferencing* (page 11) can be used to prompt reflection and self-assessment.

F. Learning Skills and Dispositions

Comprehensive assessment includes a focus on the learning skills and dispositions that enable student achievement and success. Students need to develop skills that support learning (for example, working independently, showing initiative, completing work, and participating in classroom activities). While these are important to mathematical achievement, they should be assessed and reported separately. It is also important for students to develop a positive attitude toward mathematics.

Effective Assessment of Learning Skills and Dispositions

- Document students' learning skills and dispositions separately from their mathematical development, and report on them separately, as outlined in provincial or local guidelines. Emphasize to students and their families the importance of assessing their skills and dispositions.
- Encourage students to assess their learning skills and set personal goals. Focus on one skill at a time, and focus on a short list of behaviours that a student can reflect on.
- Connect the learning skills students are focusing on in mathematics with those they are developing in other parts of their curriculum. Where possible, use the same recording or self-assessment formats and strategies, while ensuring that you include specific examples from mathematics. Students need to see the connections among various parts of their curriculum and their learning.

Using the Learning Skills and Dispositions Features and Tools in Addison Wesley Math Makes Sense 8

- Teachers can use *Program Master 5: Mathematical Dispositions and Learning Skills* to accumulate observations and notes about an individual student over time. As teachers notice specific behaviours, they can record the data and enter notes and/or a symbol (for example, Level 1 = very limited; Level 2 = somewhat or limited; Level 3 = satisfactory; Level 4 = thorough). Where teachers select specific students to observe each day (see *Section 4A: Observe and Listen,* page 9), they can record observations about learning skills as well as about mathematical development.
- *Program Master 4: Learning Skills Check List* focuses on information similar to that in *Program Master 5: Mathematical Dispositions and Learning Skills,* but in a more condensed form—a class check list. Teachers can use the check list to record assessments of an entire class, using a coding system such as the one described above.

G. Classroom Testing

Teachers recognize that tests have limited utility, and try to balance their assessments—collecting a range of evidence to ensure decisions about achievement are valid.

Effective Classroom Testing

- The development or selection of a test begins with a careful plan or set of specifications to ensure the test is a valid reflection of both the content (the topics and expectations) and the achievement categories (Knowledge and Understanding, Thinking, Application) of interest.
- Make sure each question poses a clear task. For this reason, when designing multiple-choice items, a question is usually better than an incomplete statement. After reading the stem, the students should know *exactly* what is required.
- Word questions clearly; use simple straightforward language and short sentences. This is important for ESL students, or others who have difficulty reading.
- Create your own bank of items, organized by topic or expectation.
- Allow students sufficient time to complete the test. A test of mathematics should be a test of *power* (the extent to which the student has acquired the skills, concepts, and strategies required), not a test of the *speed* with which the student answers.
- Before you begin assessing, create a set of sample answers and decide how you will score each item. Apply your criteria and guidelines consistently.

Using the Unit Tests

The Teacher Guide includes a *Unit Test* for each unit. The tests reflect both the content of the unit and the aspects of achievement reflected in the achievement chart. They also present students with a variety of item types.

Sample answers are provided in the Teacher Guide. Teachers can use these to assess each item, then record a raw score, or use the *Unit Rubric* to determine the level of achievement for each section. Teachers can also consider the overall level of mathematical communication students demonstrated in responding to questions throughout the test. Results can be recorded on the *Unit Summary* master. Teachers then determine a student's level of achievement.

Assessing All Learners

Assessment needs to be fair and valid for *all* learners. Teachers also need to be sensitive to the impact assessment can have on students who are struggling.

- Ensure that assessment opportunities include a range of ways that students can represent their learning. Emphasize that you are most interested in students' thinking, rather than in their particular answer or solution.
- Provide opportunities for ESL students and others with limited language skills to demonstrate their learning pictorially and with concrete materials.
- Conduct frequent one-on-one conferences to clarify and extend student learning.
- Look for patterns in students' work that may help to identify those who are having trouble with an aspect that is unrelated to mathematics, such as fine motor control, attention, or language.
- Ensure students are not asked to perform assessment tasks they are incapable of attempting. Select tasks that all students can attempt; then provide adaptations and scaffolding to support them.

5 Summarizing and Reporting Progress

Addison Wesley Mathematics Makes Sense supports a balanced approach to summarizing and reporting. Teachers are encouraged to include observations and portfolios or work samples, as well as formal assessments, in making decisions about a student's progress. In considering evidence from various sources, it is important that teachers:

- establish a tentative plan for reporting at the beginning of each unit or term that includes identifying key evidence that will be collected
- make decisions based on a variety of evidence, collected at various times and in various ways
- ensure the evidence comprehensively addresses the learning expectations
- establish the most consistent level of achievement, rather than the mathematical average
- weight assessments from the end of a cluster, unit, or group of units most heavily
- look for patterns in the results—areas of consistent strength or concern; increasing/ decreasing performance levels over time; characteristic differences from one type of assessment to another
- use a consistent rubric or definition of standards to guide decision making (for example, the *Unit Rubric*)
- invite students to offer their own assessments; conference with them to reconcile any discrepancies between their perceptions and the teacher's record
- base comments on the patterns of achievement noted through observation, conferences, work samples, and performance tasks; be as specific as possible about next steps

Record Keeping, Reporting Features, and Tools

Reporting by Strand

Assessment records and rubrics, as well as the *Unit Summary* master, are organized, first, by strand; then, within strand, by the categories of achievement (Knowledge and Understanding, Thinking, Communication, and Application). Teachers are given the flexibility to record and report on each category for a particular strand, or to report on overall level of achievement for the strand.

Features

- As part of *Planning for Assessment,* each unit begins with an outline of diagnostic and formative assessment opportunities and the available tools. This chart identifies both the core assessment tools that are included with the unit, and the optional *Program Masters* in the *Grade 8 Planning and Program Masters* module. The core set of assessment tools and features is consistent throughout.
- At the end of each unit, *Evaluating Student Learning: Preparing to Report* describes how teachers can summarize the evidence they have gathered to determine the most appropriate achievement level for each student. This description includes samples and is tied directly to the *Unit Summary* master. It offers suggestions about how teachers can summarize, record, and combine evidence from observations; problem-solving activities; conferences, portfolios or collections of student work; and performance tasks to complete the *Unit Summary* master.

Unit Rubric

Each unit includes a *Unit Rubric* that focuses on the content of the unit and can be used to assess a variety of student tasks. It can guide a teacher's decisions about the level each student has achieved and demonstrated. The *Unit Rubric* provides descriptions of four levels of achievement for each of the following categories: Knowledge and Understanding, Thinking, Communication, and Application.

Unit Summary: The Chart

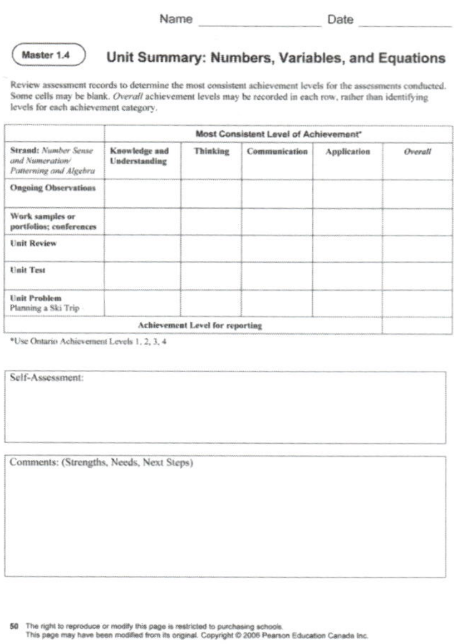
Name ______________ Date ____________

Master 1.4 **Unit Summary: Numbers, Variables, and Equations**

Review assessment records to determine the most consistent achievement levels for the assessments conducted. Some cells may be blank. *Overall* achievement levels may be recorded in each row, rather than identifying levels for each achievement category.

	Most Consistent Level of Achievement*				
Strand: *Number Sense and Numeration/ Patterning and Algebra*	**Knowledge and Understanding**	**Thinking**	**Communication**	**Application**	***Overall***
Ongoing Observations					
Work samples or portfolios; conferences					
Unit Review					
Unit Test					
Unit Problem Planning a Ski Trip					
Achievement Level for reporting					

*Use Ontario Achievement Levels 1, 2, 3, 4

Self-Assessment:

Comments: (Strengths, Needs, Next Steps)

50 The right to reproduce or modify this page is restricted to purchasing schools.
This page may have been modified from its original. Copyright © 2006 Pearson Education Canada Inc.

A *Unit Summary* master provides a chart to be completed for each student, summarizing the various types of summative evidence gathered. There is space to make notes about students' self-assessment, their strengths and needs, and the next steps needed to ensure their success. Teachers can choose to record information for each category of the achievement chart, or use the overall column.

Teachers use their assessment records to enter the following information:

Ongoing Observations—Teachers should use the *Ongoing Observations* master to determine the most consistent level of achievement observed.

Conferences and interviews; portfolios or collections of work samples—Teachers can use the *Unit Rubric* master to assess a student's level of achievement.

The Unit Review—Teachers can use the *Unit Rubric* master to determine a student's achievement level. *Evaluating Student Learning: Preparing to Report* includes suggestions about which item reflects which category of achievement.

Unit Test—Teachers can enter results of the *Unit Test* (see *Section 4G: Using the Unit Tests,* page 17). Teachers can enter the results as achievement levels, based on the *Unit Rubric,* or as raw scores.

Unit Problem—The *Unit Problem* can be assessed using the *Performance Assessment Rubric* master. This master provides a snapshot of a student's achievement related to the expectations addressed in the unit.

Unit Summary

- Teachers can use the *Unit Summary* master to record brief comments about a student's strengths and needs, and next steps for supporting student progress. The *Unit Rubric* master can help to guide these comments, to ensure they deal with key learnings or big ideas in the strand or unit, as well as specific expectations. For example:

  Strengths: Mohsan can perform the four basic operations on integers with reasonable accuracy and efficiency. His sound grasp of concepts and skills will provide a good foundation when he begins algebra in later years.

  Needs: Mohsan occasionally makes minor errors, and needs reminding to complete all parts of the work required.

Next steps: Mohsan may benefit from having a task broken into smaller parts, so that he can focus better on each procedure.

- A student's self-assessment can also be included in the *Unit Summary* master. It is preferable to quote a student's exact oral or written words. These may come from conferences, in-class discussions, journals, or other written reflections.

Report Card Comments

Teachers can synthesize their comments over 3 to 4 units when they are preparing to report. Comments should focus on the student's achievement of the curriculum, and describe areas of strength and growth made throughout the term. The comments should also communicate areas needing further growth and suggest ways to promote this growth.

Learning Skills and Dispositions

- Evidence of learning skills should be ongoing throughout a reporting period, rather than broken down by units or strands. At reporting time, teachers can transfer decisions about the level of students' learning skills directly from *Program Master 5: Mathematical Dispositions and Learning Skills* or *Program Master 4: Learning Skills Check List,* to the report. (See *Section 4F: Learning Skills and Disposition* for further information.)

6 District and Provincial Assessment Programs

In most regions, students at some grades participate in district and/or provincial assessments that are reported at the individual, school, and district level. Often, these are primarily designed to ensure accountability—that students are learning the required expectations or outcomes and achieving high standards.

In some cases—particularly at school and district levels—this may involve aggregating results from a standard performance assessment or test administered in all or a sample of classrooms at a particular grade. In other cases, the assessment is imposed by an external authority (for example, provincial assessments or examinations); the results are released to individual classrooms and students.

Impact of External Testing

While these tests generally have little impact on classroom assessment and reporting for elementary students, research suggests that they can have a powerful effect and (sometimes) negative effect on students' motivation and self-esteem. However, where the following instructional practices are in place, students can respond positively:

- Tests and other assessments are consistent with teacher expectations and student capability.
- Students have opportunities to develop self-assessment skills and learning goals.
- The school takes a constructive and supportive stance about testing.
- Low-achieving students are supported when teachers make learning goals explicit and show students how to direct effort in learning.
- Assessment results are used to convey a sense of learning progress to students.

Enhancing Student Performance on Provincial Assessments

- In the Student Book, assessment and evaluation materials are organized around these four categories of achievement.
  - sound conceptual understanding
  - procedural fluency
  - effective and flexible problem-solving strategies
  - clear and precise mathematical communication
- Each section and unit include assessment items and tasks similar to the types of questions presented on provincial tests. For example:
  - short answer procedural questions
  - items that require students to explain their thinking in words, pictures, or numbers
  - problems to solve
  - timed tests (optional)
  - open-ended performance tasks that integrate the four Achievement Categories
- In each lesson, at least one question in *Practice* provides opportunities for students to display all four levels of performance, which also offers scope for students to demonstrate a Level 4 performance.
- Four *Cross Strand Investigations,* presented at intervals during the year, ensure students approach mathematics as an integrated study. These mirror some question types in the provincial tests.

References

Assessment Reform Group. 1999. *Assessment for Learning: Beyond the Black Box.* Cambridge, UK: University of Cambridge School of Education.

———. 2002. *News/Events: Current activities.* http://www.assessment-reform-group.org.uk

Black, Paul, and Dylan Wiliam. 1998. *Inside the Black Box: Raising Standards through Classroom Assessment.* London, UK: King's College London, School of Education.

———. 1998. Assessment and Classroom Learning. *Assessment in Education* 5 (1): 7–74.

BC Ministry of Education. 2000; 2002. BC Performance Standards: Numeracy. Victoria, BC: Ministry of Education. Available at www.gov.bc.ca/bced

Harlen, Wynne, and Ruth Deakin Crick. 2002. *Review: What is the evidence of the impact of summative assessment and tests on students' motivation for learning?* Presentation, Invitational Conference, Assessment Reform Group, March 5, 2002.

Marzano, Robert J., Debra J. Pickering, and Jane E. Pollock. 2001. *Classroom instruction that works: Research-based strategies for increasing student achievement.* Alexandria, VA: ASCD.

National Education Association in collaboration with Rick Stiggins and the Assessment Training Institute. 2003. *Balanced Assessment.* Washington, DC: National Education Association.

Stenmark, Jean Kerr, and William S. Bush. eds. 2001. *Mathematics Assessment: A Practical Handbook.* Reston, VA: NCTM.

Stiggins, Rick. 2001. *Making Classroom Assessment Instructionally Relevant.* Paper presented at the annual meeting of the American Educational Research Association, Seattle, 2001.

Van de Walle, John A. 2004. *Elementary and Middle School Mathematics: Teaching Developmentally.* 5th ed. Boston: Allyn and Bacon.

Cross Strand Investigation Notes

Digital Roots

LESSON ORGANIZER (80–100 min)

Curriculum Focus: Cross Strand Performance Assessment: Number Sense and Numeration, Patterning and Algebra, Geometry and Spatial Sense, Measurement

Teacher Materials
- overhead transparency of blank 12 × 12 chart (PM 16)
- overhead transparency and markers

Student Materials
- blank 12 × 12 multiplication chart (PM 16)
- compass
- circular protractor

Vocabulary: digital root, line segment, degree

Assessment: Cross Strand Observations Check List: Digital Roots, PM 9 Work Sample Records

Key Math Learnings

1. Use patterns to make predictions.
2. Apply patterning strategies to solve problems.
3. Communicate patterns and pattern relationships using appropriate terminology.
4. Correctly use tools to construct and divide circles.

Cross Strand Investigation

Digital Roots

Materials:
- multiplication chart

Work with a partner.

The **digital root** of a number is the result of adding the digits of the number until a single-digit number is reached.

For example, the digital root of 27 is: $2 + 7 = 9$
To find the digital root of 168:
Add the digits: $1 + 6 + 8 = 15$
Since 15 is not a single-digit number, add the digits: $1 + 5 = 6$
Since 6 is a single-digit number, the digital root of 168 is 6.

A digital root can also be found for the product of a multiplication fact.
For the multiplication fact, 8×4:
$8 \times 4 = 32$
Add the digits in the product: $3 + 2 = 5$
Since 5 is a single-digit number, the digital root of 8×4 is 5.

You will explore the digital roots of the products in a multiplication table, then display the patterns you find.
As you complete the *Investigation*, include all your work in a report that you will hand in.

Part 1

×	1	2	3	4	…
1					
2					
3					
4				7	
⋮					

➢ Use a blank 12 × 12 multiplication chart.
Find each product.
Find the digital root of each product.
Record each digital root in the chart.
For example, for the product $4 \times 4 = 16$, the digital root is $1 + 6 = 7$.

➢ Describe the patterns in the completed chart.
Did you need to calculate the digital root of each product? Explain.
Did you use patterns to help you complete the table? Explain.

➢ Look down each column. What does each column represent?

2 Cross Strand Investigation

TEACHING TIP

At the beginning of the school year, it is worth taking the time to outline expectations and procedures for working with partners and writing reports.

BEFORE — Get Started

Remind students that there are many ways to describe a number. On the board or overhead projector, write the number 254, and ask students to tell what they know about the number (*it is even, it has three digits, it is divisible by 2, it is made up of two square numbers – 25 and 4*). If a student suggests that the sum of the digits is 11, use this comment to introduce digital roots.

Illustrate the meaning of a digital root using the examples in the text. Use other examples to ensure students understand the meaning of a digital root.

In Part 2, students will draw circles and mark points on the circles using a protractor. Draw a line segment on the board, and tell students that the line is 120 cm long. Ask:

- How do I divide this line into 10 equal parts? (*Divide the length, 120 cm, by the number of parts, 10. Each part will be 12 cm long.*)
- How do I divide a circle into 9 equal parts? (*Divide the number of degrees in a whole turn by 9.*)

DURING — Investigation

Encourage students to look at the patterns in the multiplication chart as they find the digital roots.

In Part 2, provide help to those students who have difficulty using the compass and protractor.

Part 2

➢ Use a compass to draw 12 circles.
Use a protractor to mark 9 equally spaced points on each circle.
Label these points in order, clockwise, from 1 to 9.
Use the first circle.
Look at the first two digital roots in the 1st column of your chart.
Find these numbers on the circle.
Use a ruler to join these numbers with a line segment.
Continue to draw line segments to join points that match the digital roots in the 1st column.
What figure have you drawn?

➢ Repeat this activity for each remaining column.
Label each circle with the number at the top of the column.

➢ Which circles have the same figure?
Which circle has a unique figure?
What is unique about the figure?
Why do some columns have the same pattern of digital roots? Explain.

Take It Further

➢ Investigate if similar patterns occur in each case:
- Digital roots of larger 2-digit numbers, such as 85 to 99
- Digital roots of 3-digit numbers, such as 255 to 269

Write a report on what you find out.

Digital Roots 3

REACHING ALL LEARNERS

Early Finishers

Encourage students to explore patterns in multiplication tables beyond 12s. When do patterns repeat? What figure would they expect the 23 times table to form on the circle?

Common Misconceptions

➤ Students have difficulty drawing and dividing the circles.
How to Help: Draw a circle and mark the points. Photocopy the circle for students' use.

ESL Strategies

Read the instructions while copying examples into a multiplication chart on the overhead projector. Illustrate marking points on a circle so students can see what the outcome should be.

Ongoing Assessment: Observe and Listen

Ask questions, such as:

- How did you fill in the multiplication chart? *(I started with the 1s and made my way across; each time I completed a column, I completed that row; I started with 1, 2, 3, 6, 9 then worked my way through the rest.)*
- What patterns do you see in the rows and columns? *(The numbers in the 1s row and column increase by 1 until they get to 9, then start at 1 again. The numbers in the 2s row and column are the even numbers to 8, then the odd numbers to 9, and this pattern seems to repeat.)*
- How did you mark the points on the circle? *(I divided 360° by 9 and got 40°. I put the protractor on the circle so the centre of the protractor coincided with the centre of the circle. I marked a point on the circle every 40°, starting at 0° and ending at 360°.)*
- What were some of the figures your number patterns created? *(Triangles, 9-sided polygon, star-shape)*

AFTER

Have students share their findings by completing the multiplication chart on the overhead projector. Encourage students to share their strategies for dividing the circle. (*For example, dividing the circle into thirds at 0, 120°, and 240°, and then divide each sector into thirds again.*)

Have students explain why the 9s column and row have only 9 in them. (*The sum of the digits of any multiple of 9 is 9 – this is the divisibility rule for 9.*)

Sample Response

Part 1

The completed chart will look like this:

×	1	2	3	4	5	6	7	8	9	10	11	12
1	1	2	3	4	5	6	7	8	9	1	2	3
2	2	4	6	8	1	3	5	7	9	2	4	6
3	3	6	9	3	6	9	3	6	9	3	6	9
4	4	8	3	7	2	6	1	5	9	4	8	3
5	5	1	6	2	7	3	8	4	9	5	1	6
6	6	3	9	6	3	9	6	3	9	6	3	9
7	7	5	3	1	8	6	4	2	9	7	5	3
8	8	7	6	5	4	3	2	1	9	8	7	6
9	9	9	9	9	9	9	9	9	9	9	9	9
10	1	2	3	4	5	6	7	8	9	1	2	3
11	2	4	6	8	1	3	5	7	9	2	4	6
12	3	6	9	3	6	9	3	6	9	3	6	9

- In the 1s row and column, the numbers increase by 1. In the 3s and 6s rows and columns, the numbers 3, 6, 9 and 6, 3, 9, respectively, are repeated. The pattern in the 4s row and column is "add 4, subtract 5" and in the 5s row and column, it is "subtract 4, add 5", that is, the numbers added and subtracted in the patterns are the numbers of the rows. In the 8s row and column, the numbers decrease by 1. I didn't always need to calculate each digital root, because I could use the pattern I recognized to complete the row. Also, once a row was finished, I could use it to complete a column.
- The number in each column is the digital root of the product of the number at the top of the column and the number at the left of the corresponding row.

Part 2

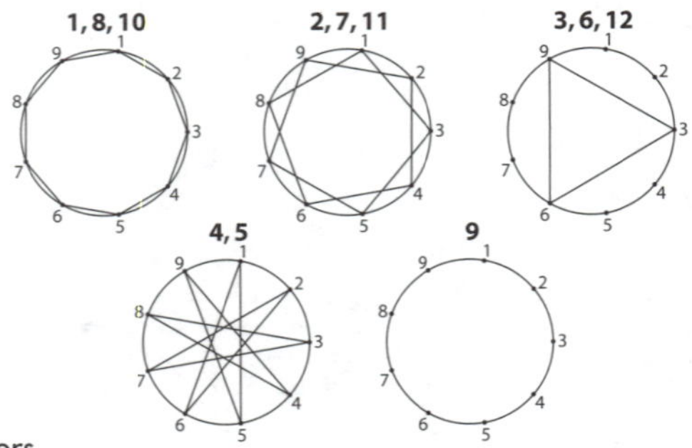

- Here are the completed circles.
- Circles: 1 and 8 have the same figure (a nonagon, or 9-sided polygon); 2 and 7 have the same figure; 3, 6, and 12 have the same figure; and 4 and 5 have the same figure. Circle 9 is unique because the digital root of all multiples of 9 is 9, so there is no figure, only a point. Columns 1 and 10 have the same pattern, as do 2 and 11, and 3 and 12. It appears that numbers have the same pattern when the sums of the digits in the number are equal.

Take It Further

The same patterns occur for multiplication tables with 2-digit and 3-digit numbers.

ASSESSMENT FOR LEARNING

What to Look For

Knowledge and Understanding

✔ Students can determine digital roots and can describe the patterns in the multiplication chart.

Thinking

✔ Students choose appropriate strategies to explore and use patterns.

Communication

✔ Students can explain the patterns they see using appropriate terminology.

Application

✔ Students can apply geometry and measurement skills to construct circles and divide them into equal sectors.

Recording and Reporting

PM 9 Work Sample Records

Cross Strand Observations Check List: Digital Roots

Name	Patterning		Number	Geometry and Measurement
	Recognizes patterns and uses them to make predictions; describes relationships between patterns KU/T/AP	Applies patterning strategies to solve problems T/AP/CM	Correctly multiplies numbers and adds digits KU	Correctly uses tools and strategies to construct and divide circles T/CM

KU – Knowledge and Understanding **T** – Thinking
CM – Communication **AP** – Application

Golden Rectangles

LESSON ORGANIZER 80–100 min

Curriculum Focus: Cross Strand Performance Assessment: Number Sense and Numeration, Patterning and Algebra, Geometry and Spatial Sense

Teacher Materials

- overhead transparency of 1-cm grid paper (PM 20)
- overhead transparency and markers

Student Materials

- 1-cm grid paper (PM 20)

Optional

- calculator

Vocabulary: ratio

Assessment: Cross Strand Observations Check List: Golden Rectangles, PM 9 Work Sample Records

Key Math Learnings

1. Use patterns to make predictions.
2. Describe patterns.
3. Identify and calculate ratios.

Cross Strand Investigation

Golden Rectangles

Materials:
- 1-cm grid paper

Work with a partner.

Similar polygons have the same shape, but different sizes.
These two rectangles are similar.

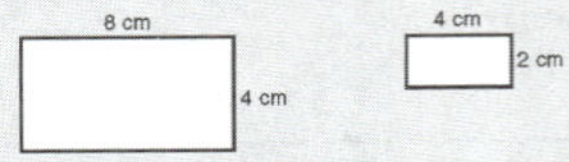

Similar rectangles have the same base:height ratio.
That is, 8 cm:4 cm = 4 cm:2 cm

In this *Investigation*, you will draw rectangles and compare the ratios of their side lengths.
As you complete the *Investigation*, include all your work in a report that you will hand in.

Part 1

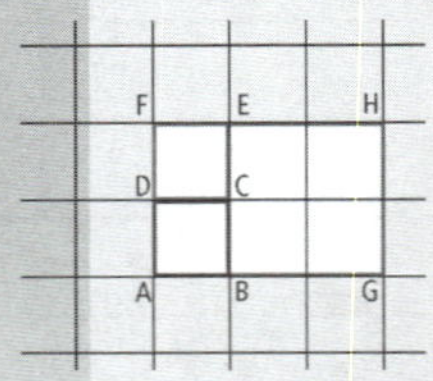

➢ Use 1-cm grid paper.
Turn your paper so the longer side is horizontal.
Draw a 1-cm square in the bottom left hand corner.
Label this square ABCD.
Draw another 1-cm square directly above the first.
You should now have a rectangle that measures 2 cm by 1 cm.
Label this rectangle ABEF.
Make a larger rectangle by drawing a square along a longer side of rectangle ABEF. Label this 3-cm by 2-cm rectangle AGH

➢ Continue to make larger rectangles by drawing squares along a longer side of the previous rectangle.
Continue to label the rectangles with letters.
Is there a pattern in the way you draw the rectangles? Explain.

➢ Stop drawing rectangles when you have no more room on the paper.
Record the base and height of each rectangle in a table.
For this *Investigation*, the base is always the longer side.

130 Cross Strand Investigation

BEFORE Get Started

On an overhead transparency, draw several rectangles and label them with their dimensions. Ensure that some rectangles are similar. Ask:

- What can you tell me about these rectangles?
- Are any of them similar rectangles? How do you know?

Use the illustration in the Student Book to remind students about similar rectangles.

Explain that students will be drawing rectangles and comparing their base:height ratios. Provide students with 1-cm grid paper.

DURING Investigation

Students may have difficulty getting started drawing their rectangles on the grid paper. Demonstrate by drawing the first few rectangles on an overhead transparency.

Ongoing Assessment: Observe and Listen

As students work, ask:

- How are you keeping track of the rectangles you have drawn? (*By labelling the vertices*)
- How do you know where to draw the next square?
(*The side length of the square is the longest side of the rectangle I just drew.*)
- What patterns do you see in the *Height* column? (*The sequence is the Fibonacci sequence – 1, 1, 2, 3, 5, 8, 13, ...*) The *Base* column?
(*The sequence is Fibonacci, with the first term missing.*)

➢ Write the ratio of the base to the height in fraction form.
Calculate the value of the ratio by dividing the base by the height. Use a calculator if you need to.
Round each number to 3 decimal places when necessary.
Include these numbers in the table.

Rectangle	Base	Height	Ratio $\frac{b}{h}$	Ratio Value
ABCD	1	1	$\frac{1}{1}$	1.0
ABEF	2	1	$\frac{2}{1}$	2.0

➢ What patterns do you see in the table?

➢ Extend the patterns. What are the dimensions of the next 3 rectangles? How do you know?

➢ Calculate the ratio of $\frac{b}{h}$ for each of the next 3 rectangles.
What do you notice about the value of the ratio as the rectangles get larger?

➢ Predict the value of the ratio for the 50th rectangle.
What do you think the ratio will be for the 100th rectangle? Explain.

➢ Are the rectangles in the table similar? Explain.

Part 2

➢ Look for rectangles around the room.
Some examples might be found in notebook paper, textbooks, and windows. Include these rectangles in your table.

➢ Measure the base and height of each rectangle you include.
What is the ratio of $\frac{b}{h}$ for each?
What is the value of this ratio?

Take It Further

Find some pictures of structures or buildings.
Look for rectangles in these structures.
Find the values of $\frac{b}{h}$ for each rectangle. Does any rectangle have the same ratio as the last rectangle in your table?

Golden Rectangles 131

REACHING ALL LEARNERS

Early Finishers

Assign *Take It Further* to students.

Common Misconceptions

➤ Students have difficulty naming and recording the rectangles they have created on the grid paper.

How to Help: Have students record each rectangle in the table after they create it. Once the rectangle is labelled, they should write the rectangle name into the table, then record its base and height.

➤ Students miscalculate ratio values of the rectangles around the room.

How to Help: Illustrate calculating two ratio values – long side:short side and short side:long side – for several rectangles, and ask students what they notice about the quotient in each case (*One value is always greater than 1; one value is always less than 1*). Explain that, since the golden ratio is 1.618, students must always write the ratio with the longer side as the first term.

- What do you notice about the ratio values? (*The ratios increase, then decrease. The ratio is never less than 1 or greater than 2. The ratio seems to end up at about 1.6.*)

In Part 2, students find rectangles around the room and determine the *b*:*h* ratio for each. This activity illustrates how common golden rectangles are in architecture and everyday objects. Ensure there are enough samples of rectangles in the room for students to include in their tables.

AFTER

Bring students together for a discussion about their investigation. Ask students if they recognized the Fibonacci sequence, and what they can remember about it. Review the terms *ratio* and *ratio value*. Ask students to describe in their own words the difference between the two terms. (*A ratio compares two numbers or quantities; a ratio value is the quotient of dividing the first term by the second.*) Make a connection to similar rectangles having equal ratio values. Refer to the original example. The ratio value of an 8 by 4 rectangle is 2; the ratio value of a 4 by 2 rectangle is also 2.

Ask students about their predictions of the ratio values of the 50th and 100th rectangles. Explain that the number the ratio values approach is known as *Phi* (ϕ) and has an approximate value of 1.618 033 99, but is commonly rounded to 1.618 (similar to the rounding of π to 3.14). This "golden ratio" was pervasive in ancient architecture, and can still be found in structures and buildings today. A rectangle whose ratio of sides is equal to the golden ratio is called a golden rectangle.

Sample Response

Part 1

Here is the completed table:

Rectangle	Base	Height	Ratio $\frac{b}{h}$	Ratio Value
ABCD	1	1	$\frac{1}{1}$	1.0
ABEF	2	1	$\frac{2}{1}$	2.0
AFHG	3	2	$\frac{3}{2}$	1.5
AGIJ	5	3	$\frac{5}{3}$	$1.\overline{66}$
AJKL	8	5	$\frac{8}{5}$	1.6
ALNM	13	8	$\frac{13}{8}$	1.625
AMOP	21	13	$\frac{21}{13}$	1.615
APQR	34	21	$\frac{34}{21}$	1.619
ARST	55	34	$\frac{55}{34}$	1.618
ATUV	89	55	$\frac{89}{55}$	1.618
AVWX	144	89	$\frac{144}{89}$	1.618

- There are many patterns in the table. The base in one row is the height in the next row. The base is always the sum of the base and height in the row above. The ratio values seem to settle at 1.618 after the first few rectangles, and I noticed the numbers in the table are the Fibonacci sequence.
- The dimensions of the next 3 rectangles are in the table. I know these are correct because I extended the pattern of adding the base and height to get the next base, and making the height the base from the row before.
- I noticed the ratio (1.618) was the same for each of the new rectangles when I rounded it to 3 decimal places.
- I predict the ratio value of the 50th and 100th rectangles to be 1.618 as well, though there might be some differences of a few thousandths. I think because the rectangles are larger, the ratios will become closer and closer. The ratio values differ most when the rectangles are smaller.
- The rectangles are not similar, because the ratio values are different. However, the larger the rectangles get, the closer they become to being similar.

Part 2

Some common examples might include:

- notepaper – 28:21.5, ratio value of 1.30
- window – 94:60, ratio value of 1.57
- desk – 65:40, ratio value of 1.625

The ratio value of the desk is closer to the last ratio value in the table.

Take It Further

Students should be able to find some examples of rectangles in architecture that have the golden ratio. Encourage students to look for rectangles that might not be as obvious as others (for example, the rectangle formed by several windows instead of one window).

ASSESSMENT FOR LEARNING

What to Look For

Knowledge and Understanding

✔ Students can draw rectangles and calculate ratio values. Students understand that rectangles with equal ratio values are similar.

Thinking

✔ Students use critical thinking skills effectively to make predictions from the table of ratio values.

Communication

✔ Students can explain the connection between ratio values and similar rectangles.

Application

✔ Students can apply their understanding of ratio values and the golden ratio to rectangles in the classroom and environment.

Recording and Reporting

PM 9 Work Sample Records

Cross Strand Observations Check List: Golden Rectangles

Name	Patterning		Number	Geometry
	Recognizes patterns and uses them to make predictions T/AP	Describes relationships between patterns KU/CM	Calculates and applies ratio values to identify similar rectangles KU/AP	Draws consecutive rectangles according to a given pattern KU/AP

KU – Knowledge and Understanding
CM – Communication
T – Thinking
AP – Application

Pack It Up!

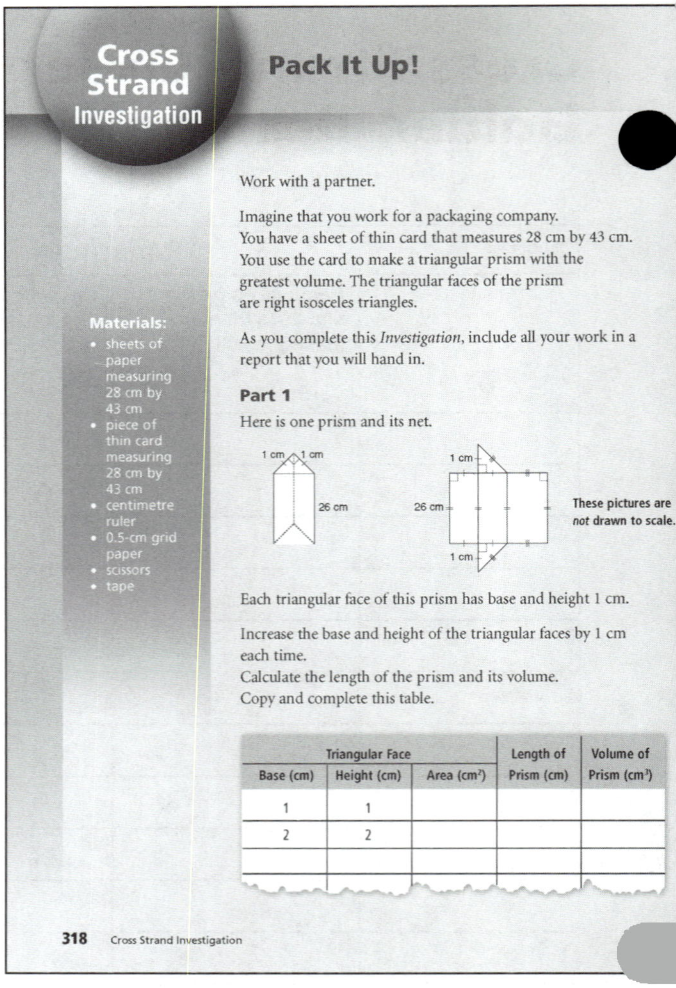
Cross Strand Investigation

Pack It Up!

Materials:
- sheets of paper measuring 28 cm by 43 cm
- piece of thin card measuring 28 cm by 43 cm
- centimetre ruler
- 0.5-cm grid paper
- scissors
- tape

Work with a partner.

Imagine that you work for a packaging company. You have a sheet of thin card that measures 28 cm by 43 cm. You use the card to make a triangular prism with the greatest volume. The triangular faces of the prism are right isosceles triangles.

As you complete this *Investigation*, include all your work in a report that you will hand in.

Part 1

Here is one prism and its net.

These pictures are *not* drawn to scale.

Each triangular face of this prism has base and height 1 cm.

Increase the base and height of the triangular faces by 1 cm each time.
Calculate the length of the prism and its volume.
Copy and complete this table.

Triangular Face			Length of Prism (cm)	Volume of Prism (cm^3)
Base (cm)	Height (cm)	Area (cm^2)		
1	1			
2	2			

318 Cross Strand Investigation

LESSON ORGANIZER

80–100 min

Curriculum Focus: Cross Strand Performance Assessment: Measurement, Data Management and Probability, Patterning and Algebra

Teacher Materials
- sample packages

Student Materials
- 28-cm by 43-cm sheets of paper
- 28-cm by 43-cm piece of thin card
- centimetre ruler
- 0.5-cm grid paper (PM 14)
- scissors
- tape

Vocabulary: volume, area, right isosceles triangle

Assessment: Cross Strand Observations Check List: Pack It Up!, PM 9 Work Sample Records

Key Math Learnings

1. Calculate surface area and volume of a prism.
2. Use patterns to describe relationships between area and volume.
3. Graph and analyse data.

BEFORE Get Started

Make connections to experiences students have had with packages and packaging. Discuss different packages and their shapes. Have some samples of packages to share with the class. Ask:

- What are some of the shapes of packages you see in the store?
  (*Cereal boxes are rectangular prisms. Toblerone chocolate bars are triangular prisms with equilateral triangular bases. Cleaning cloths come in hexagonal prisms. Water comes in a bottle, the bottom part of which is a cylinder.*)
- What determines the size of the package?
  (*Content size and shape, cost of materials*)
- What are other important things to think about when designing a package?
  (*Efficient use of materials to reduce the costs*)

Explain that this investigation looks at one type of package – a triangular prism – and that students will be using tables and graphs to make a choice for a package design. Provide students with the necessary materials and read through the instructions in Part 1 with the class. Ensure students are clear on the directions before proceeding.

DURING Investigation

Some students may have difficulty determining the dimensions of the second package. Each net fits on one sheet of paper, with the overall "height" of the net being 28 cm. The second net looks like this:

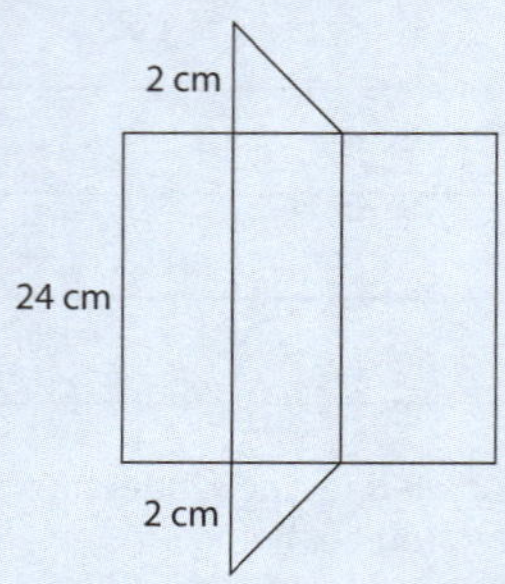

Continue to increase the base and height of the triangular face.
Use a sheet of paper to draw each net if you need to.
The length of the prism decreases each time, so the net always fits on the piece of paper.

- ➢ When do you know that the table is complete?
- ➢ What patterns do you see in the table? Explain.
- ➢ From the table, what is the greatest volume of the prism? What are its dimensions?

Part 2

Use 0.5-cm grid paper.
Draw a graph of *Volume* against *Base of triangular face*.
Join the points.

- ➢ What inferences can you make from the graph?
- ➢ How can you find the greatest volume from the graph?

Part 3

Use a piece of thin card that measures 28 cm by 43 cm.
Construct the net for your prism.
Cut out, then fold and tape the net to make the prism.

Take It Further

Does the prism with the greatest volume also have the greatest surface area?
Write about what you find out.

Pack It Up! 319

REACHING ALL LEARNERS

Early Finishers

Challenge students to find a prism with a greater volume by using dimensions that are decimals; for example, suggest they use values from 9.1 cm to 9.5 cm as the base and height of the triangular face. (The greatest volume is approximately 406.5 cm^3, when the base of the triangular face is $9.\overline{3}$ cm.)

Common Misconceptions

➤ Students may incorrectly calculate the area of the triangular face.

How to Help: Provide students with several right triangles drawn on 1-cm grid paper, with dimensions labelled. Ask students to count the squares and part squares to find the approximate area, and then use the formula to calculate the area.

➤ Students change the length of the prism without using a pattern.

How to Help: Demonstrate on the board that each time students draw a net, the overall height of the net must fit the vertical height of the page in landscape. As each triangular face increases, the length of the prism decreases.

Students should figure out that the orientation of the paper should always be landscape for the pattern to emerge.

Ongoing Assessment: Observe and Listen

As students work, ask:

- How are you calculating the area of the base of the prism?
  (*I multiply the base by the height, then divide by 2.*)
- What patterns did you use to complete the table? (*The numbers in the Base and Height columns increase by 1 each time. The numbers in the Length of Prism column decrease by 2 each time.*)
- How did using a net help you complete the table? (*Visualizing the net helped me see how the prism length decreases by 2 each time.*)

As students draw the graph in Part 2, ask:

- How did you find the greatest volume from your graph?
  (*When the vertical axis represents volume, the highest point in the graph is the greatest volume.*)

AFTER

Share students' findings in a class discussion. Some students can draw their graphs on an overhead transparency.

Ask:

- What can you tell me about the base and height of the triangular face and the length of the prism for the greatest volume?
  (*The dimensions are very close in value. When two of these prisms are placed to form a rectangular prism, the rectangular prism approximates a cube.*)
- What additional information would you like to have before deciding on which package to use?
  (*The surface area would be important to know, to determine the cost of materials in the package.*)

Have students display their graphs and prisms made from their nets somewhere in the room.

Sample Response

Part 1

Here is the completed table:

➤ I know the table is complete when the base and height of the triangular face are 13 cm, because the prism length is then 2 cm. If I were to make the base and height 14 cm, there would be no prism length (the net could not fit on the paper).

➤ There are many patterns in the table. The base and height of the triangular face always increase by 1 and are always equal. In the area column, the second prism has an area 1.5 cm^2 greater than the first, and the third is 2.5 cm^2 greater than the second, and the fourth is 3.5 cm^2 greater than the third, and so on. The prism length decreases by 2. The volume of the prism increases, then decreases.

➤ The prism with the greatest volume is the 9-cm by 9-cm by 10-cm prism, with a volume of 405 cm^3.

Triangular Face			Length of Prism (cm)	Volume of Prism (cm^3)
Base (cm)	Height (cm)	Area (cm^2)		
1	1	0.5	26	13
2	2	2.0	24	48
3	3	4.5	22	99
4	4	8.0	20	160
5	5	12.5	18	225
6	6	18.0	16	288
7	7	24.5	14	343
8	8	32.0	12	384
9	9	40.5	10	405
10	10	50.0	8	400
11	11	60.5	6	363
12	12	72.0	4	288
13	13	84.5	2	169

Part 2

Here is the graph.

➤ From my graph, I infer that as the triangular base increases, so does the volume of the prism. However, at a certain point, the volume begins to decrease. If I think about the prisms, they start off as long skinny prisms with small triangular bases. These prisms have small volumes. As the triangular bases get larger the volume increases, but eventually the prisms become "all base" with little or no length. These prisms have small volumes.

➤ The prism with the greatest volume is the one that corresponds to the highest point on my graph.

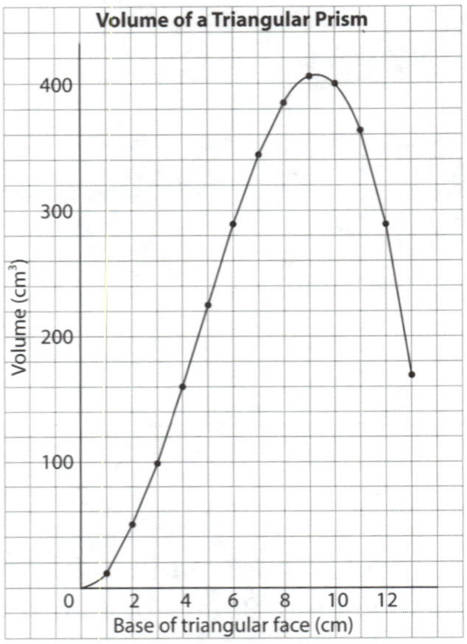

Take It Further

The prism with the greatest volume does not have the greatest surface area. I found the surface area of the largest prism to be about 388 cm^2 and then checked the prisms on either side of it. The prism before the largest prism (8 cm by 8 cm by 12 cm) has a larger surface area, about 392 cm^2.

ASSESSMENT FOR LEARNING

What to Look For

Knowledge and Understanding

✔ Students can complete the table by using appropriate formulas to determine area and volume.

Thinking

✔ Students use patterns to complete some columns in the table and make connections between area and volume.

Communication

✔ Students can describe the prism with the greatest volume.

Application

✔ Students can draw on experiences with packaging to relate to the math in the investigation.

Recording and Reporting

PM 9 Work Sample Records

Cross Strand Observations Check List: Pack It Up!

Name	Measurement	Patterning		Data Management
	Calculates area of base and volume of prism accurately KU/AP	Describes patterns in a table CM	Uses patterns to describe relationships between area and volume T/KU	Graphs and analyses data KU/AP

KU – Knowledge and Understanding
CM – Communication
T – Thinking
AP – Application

Integer Probability

LESSON ORGANIZER 80–100 min

Curriculum Focus: Cross Strand Performance Assessment: Data Management and Probability, Number Sense and Numeration
Student Materials
- four integer cards labelled −3, −2, +1, +2
- brown paper bag

Vocabulary: theoretical probability
Assessment: Cross Strand Observations Check List: Integer Probablility; PM 9 Work Sample Records

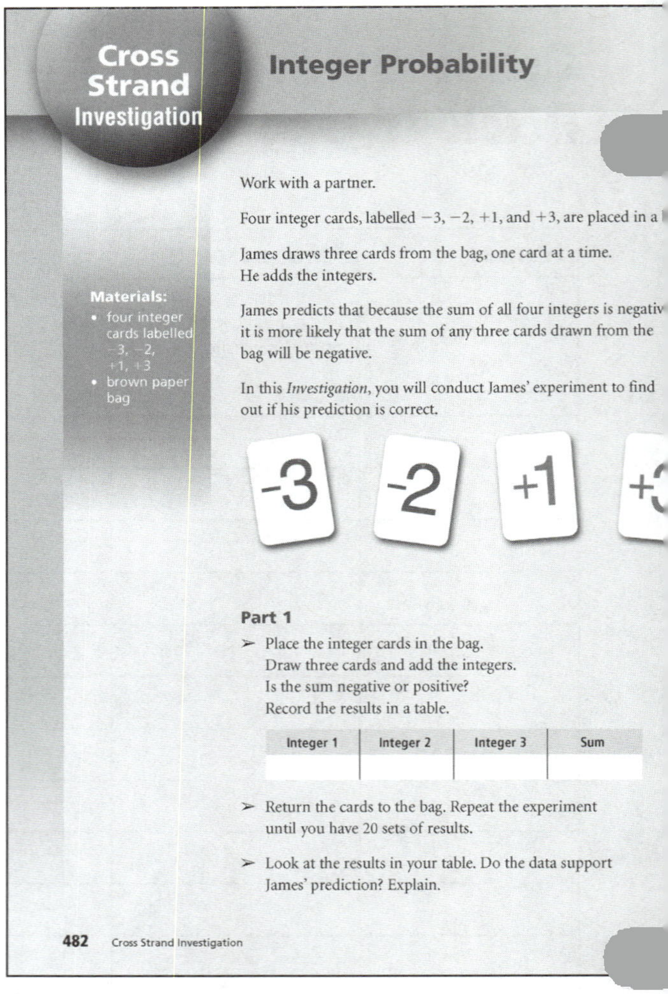

Cross Strand Investigation

Integer Probability

Materials:
- four integer cards labelled −3, −2, +1, +3
- brown paper bag

Work with a partner.

Four integer cards, labelled −3, −2, +1, and +3, are placed in a

James draws three cards from the bag, one card at a time.
He adds the integers.

James predicts that because the sum of all four integers is negativ
it is more likely that the sum of any three cards drawn from the
bag will be negative.

In this *Investigation*, you will conduct James' experiment to find
out if his prediction is correct.

-3 -2 +1 +

Part 1

➢ Place the integer cards in the bag.
Draw three cards and add the integers.
Is the sum negative or positive?
Record the results in a table.

Integer 1	Integer 2	Integer 3	Sum

➢ Return the cards to the bag. Repeat the experiment
until you have 20 sets of results.

➢ Look at the results in your table. Do the data support
James' prediction? Explain.

482 Cross Strand Investigation

Key Math Learnings

1. Add integers with and without the use of models.
2. Perform experiments to compare theoretical probability of events with experimental probability.
3. Explain differences in theoretical and experimental probability.

BEFORE Get Started

Review how to add integers.

The *Investigation* requires students use a model or diagram to determine theoretical probability – you may wish to review probability models with students before they begin the *Investigation*.

DURING Investigation

Ongoing Assessment: Observe and Listen

Observe students as they conduct their investigations. Students who struggle with integer addition may require integer tiles or number lines to help them. Ask:

- Do you have to add the integers to find the sign of their sum?
(I noticed that the sum of any two integers with the same sign is always numerically greater than the integer on the 3rd card. So, the sign of the sum is always the sign of the two cards with the same sign.)

Once groups of students have combined their data, ask:

- Do the results of the larger group differ from the results of the investigation you and your partner completed?
(With 20 sets of results, each pair of students might be leaning more toward confirming or refuting James' prediction. With 100 sets of results, they may be closer to 50% positive, 50% negative.)

As students determine the theoretical probability of drawing a negative sum, encourage them to record their model on chart paper for sharing.

➢ Combine your results with those of 4 other pairs of classmates.
You now have 100 sets of results.
Do the data support James' prediction?
Explain.

➢ Use a diagram or other model to find the theoretical probability of getting a negative sum.
Do the results match your experiment?

➢ Do you think the values of the integers make a difference?
Find 4 integers (2 positive, 2 negative) for which James' prediction is correct.

Part 2

Look at the results of your investigation in *Part 1*.

➢ If the first card James draws is negative, does it affect the probability of getting a negative sum?
Use the results of *Part 1* to support your thinking.

➢ If the first card James draws is positive, does it affect the probability of getting a negative sum?
Use the results of *Part 1* to support your thinking.

Take It Further

➢ Emma wonders if she will get a different result if she multiplies the three integers instead of adding them.
She predicts that she is more likely to get a negative product than a positive product.

➢ Design an experiment to find out if Emma's prediction is correct.
Perform the experiment. Was Emma's prediction correct?
Explain.

Integer Probability **483**

REACHING ALL LEARNERS

Early Finishers

Have students find three other combinations of 4 integer cards that produce a 50% probability of drawing a negative sum.

Common Misconceptions

➤ Students' theoretical models do not include all possible outcomes.

How to Help: Scaffold the problem by asking students:

- What if the first card you drew were −3. What could your next card be?
- How can you record this to keep track of your thinking?

Remind students how to use a tree diagram to record all possible results.

Sample Response

Part 1

Here is a sample completed table.

The data support James' prediction, but because the data are so close, James could be wrong.

➤ When I combined our data with those of my classmates, we got the following results: 58 negative sums, 42 positive sums. It appears that the data do support James' predictions of a negative sum more often than a positive sum.

(Sample Solutions continue below, right.)

AFTER

Bring the class together for a discussion of the *Investigation*. Ask:

- Was James correct in his hypothesis?
(No, the probability of drawing 3 cards with a negative sum is $\frac{12}{24}$, or 50%.)
- Why do you think the experimental probability was different from the theoretical probability?
(It is unlikely that our class results would produce exactly a 50% result. Each time you draw, you have a 50-50 chance of drawing a negative sum. You could draw 100 positive sums in a row, and still have a 50-50 chance that the next draw is negative.)

Ask students to share their models for determining the theoretical probability of drawing 3 cards with a negative sum. Ask students which model makes most sense to them and why.

(Sample Solutions, continued)

Draw	Integer 1	Integer 2	Integer 3	Sum	
1	−3	−2	+1	negative	
2	+3	−2	−3	negative	
3	−2	+3	+1	positive	
4	+1	−2	+3	positive	
5	+1	−3	−2	negative	
6	−2	−3	+1	negative	
7	+3	+1	−2	positive	
8	+3	+1	−3	positive	
9	−3	+1	+3	positive	
10	−2	+1	−3	negative	
11	+1	−3	−2	negative	
12	−2	+3	+1	positive	
13	−3	−2	+3	negative	
14	+3	+1	−3	positive	
15	−3	−2	+1	negative	
16	−2	+1	−3	negative	
17	+3	+1	−2	positive	
18	−2	+3	+1	positive	
19	−3	−2	+3	negative	
20	−3	+1	−2	negative	
TOTAL				11−	9+

➤ I used a table again to represent the theoretical probability of drawing a negative sum.

1st Card	−3						−2						+1						+3					
2nd Card	−2		+1		+3		−3		+1		+3		−3		−2		+3		−3		−2		+1	
3rd Card	+1	+3	−2	+3	−2	+1	+1	+3	−3	+3	−3	+1	−2	+3	−3	+3	−3	−2	−2	+1	−3	+1	−3	−2
Sum	−	−	−	+	−	+	−	−	−	+	−	+	−	+	−	+	+	+	−	+	−	+	+	+

The table shows that there are 24 possible outcomes: 12 positive and 12 negative. These results don't match the experiment, and show that James' hypothesis is not true, even though it appeared to be from the experiment. The table also explains why some other groups may have experiments with more positive sums than negative.

➤ I think the values of the integers do make a difference. If I used negative integers such as −10 and −12, and positive integers such as +1 and +2, then the sum of the 3 integers would always be negative.

Part 2

➤ In our experiment, we drew a negative card first 12 times, and 8 times the sum was negative. We drew a positive card first 8 times, and the sum was positive for 5 of those draws. Experimentally, it seems that if you draw a negative card first, you are more likely to get a negative sum, and if you draw a positive card first, you are more likely to get a positive sum. When we look at our theoretical model, it supports the experimental results.

There is an 8 in 12, or $66.\overline{6}\%$, chance that when you draw a negative card first, the sum will be negative, and the same probability of getting a positive sum when a positive card is drawn first.

Take It Further

We performed the same type of experiment, only this time we used coloured counters. The value of the integers doesn't matter in this experiment, because it is the sign of the integer that determines if the product is positive or negative. We put four counters in the bag, 2 yellow and 2 red. The red represents negative integers and the yellow represents positive integers. We used a tree diagram to show the theoretical results.

The theoretical probability indicates that there is a 3 in 6 or 50% probability that the product of three cards drawn will be negative. Emma was not correct.

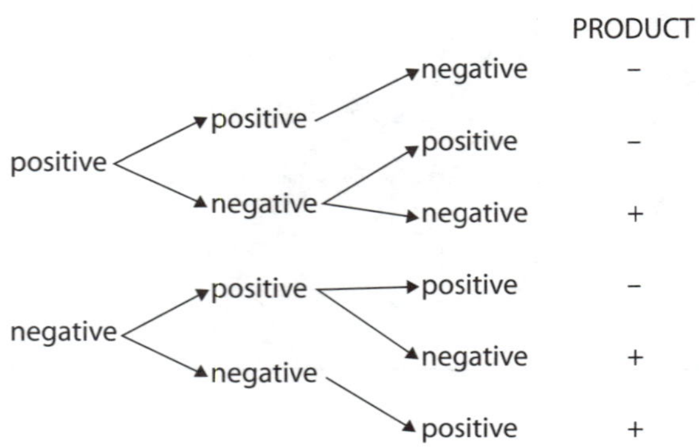

ASSESSMENT FOR LEARNING

What to Look For

Knowledge and Understanding

✔ Students can conduct and record the results of a probability experiment and use a model to explore theoretical probability.

Thinking

✔ Students make predictions based on critical thinking of quantity and operations with integers.

Communication

✔ Students can justify differences between experimental and theoretical probability.

Application

✔ Students apply an understanding of integer operations to determine experimental outcomes.

Recording and Reporting

PM 9 Work Sample Records

Cross Strand Observations Check List: Integer Probabilities

Name	Data Management and Probability			Number
	Predicts probability based on experimental results and mathematical reasoning T	Determines theoretical probability using an appropriate model KU/AP	Explains differences in theoretical and experimental probability KU/CM	Correctly finds the sum of 3 integers KU

KU – Knowledge and Understanding **T** – Thinking
CM – Communication **AP** – Application

Addison Wesley
Mathematics
Makes Sense

Program Authors

Trevor Brown
Antonietta Lenjosek
Cathy Heideman
Jim Mennie
Georgia Konis-Chatzis
A.J. Keene
Margaret Sinclair
Craig Featherstone
Jason Johnston
Bryn Keyes
Elizabeth Wood
Elizabeth Milne
David Sufrin
Don Jones
Sharon Jeroski
Lynn Strangway

Printed and bound in Canada

2 3 4 5 – TC – 09 08 07 06

PEARSON
Education Canada

ADDISON WESLEY

Ontario

Math Makes Sense 8

Ontario

Teacher Guide

Unit 1: Numbers, Variables, and Equations

PEARSON
Education Canada

UNIT 1

Numbers, Variables, and Equations

"Algebraic reasoning involves representing, generalizing, and formalizing patterns and regularity in all aspects of mathematics. As algebraic reasoning develops so must the language and symbolism that have been developed to support and communicate that thinking — specifically equations and variables."

— John A. Van de Walle

FOCUS STRANDS
Number Sense and Numeration
Patterning and Algebra

TIPS
Having flexible thinking skills empowers students and frees them to invent strategies that make sense to them.

Mathematics Background

What Are the Big Ideas?

- Numbers are used to describe our world. When we solve problems involving numbers, the method used depends on the context of the problem.
- Numbers can be expressed in standard form, as a product of prime numbers, in expanded form using powers of 10, and in scientific notation.
- An equation is used to express a relationship between two quantities. To solve an equation means to find the value of the variable that makes the equation true.

How Will the Concepts Develop?

Students learn to choose the most effective method for calculations. They use mental math, estimation, pencil and paper, and calculators to solve problems. Students justify their choice of method.

Students represent numbers as products of prime factors. Students use their knowledge of powers to write the factors in exponent form.

Students continue to use powers when they write large numbers in expanded form using powers of 10, and in scientific notation.

Students apply the order of operations to evaluate expressions involving brackets and exponents.

Students use a two-pan balance model and algebra tiles to solve equations, then record the solution process algebraically.

Why Are These Concepts Important?

Problem solving is an important skill. Students need to be able to select the most appropriate and efficient strategy when solving a problem.

Expressing a number in terms of prime factors improves numeracy, and helps make connections between and among sets of numbers. This skill is useful when operating with fractions. Students can simplify fractions by dividing the numerator and denominator by their common factors before they multiply.

Scientific notation provides an efficient way to write and use large numbers. Scientific calculators use scientific notation to display a number when it has more digits than the display can contain.

The use of variables in expressions and equations helps to generalize number patterns and relationships.

Curriculum Overview

The codes refer to the 2005 revised curriculum.

Cluster 1: Working with Numbers and Variables

Overall Expectations

- Represent, compare, and order equivalent representations of numbers, ... (8m8)
- Solve problems involving whole numbers, decimal numbers, ..., using a variety of computational strategies. (8m9)

Specific Expectations

- Express repeated multiplication using exponential notation. (8m11)
- Represent whole numbers in expanded form using powers of ten. (8m12)
- Represent, compare, and order rational numbers. (8m13)
- Determine common factors and common multiples using the prime factorization of numbers. (8m15)
- Solve multi-step problems arising from real-life contexts and involving whole numbers and decimals, using a variety of tools and strategies. (8m16)
- Use estimation when solving problems involving operations with whole numbers, decimals, ... to help judge the reasonableness of a solution. (8m18)
- Multiply and divide decimal numbers by various powers of ten. (8m24)
- Evaluate expressions ... that contain brackets and exponents, using order of operations. (8m23)
- Evaluate algebraic expressions with up to three terms, by substituting ... decimals, ... for the variables. (8m62)

Cluster 2: Solving Equations

Overall Expectation

- ...solve and verify algebraic equations, using a variety of strategies, including ... using a "balance" model. (8m55)

Specific Expectations

- Translate statements describing mathematical relationships into algebraic ... equations. (8m61)
- Solve and verify linear equations involving a one-variable term and having solutions that are integers, by using ... a "balance" model. (8m64)

Launch

Lesson 1.1: Numbers in the Media

Lesson 1.2: Prime Factors

Lesson 1.3: Expanded Form and Scientific Notation

Mid-Unit Review

Lesson 1.4: Order of Operations

Lesson 1.5: Using a Model to Solve Equations

Lesson 1.6: Using Algebra Tiles to Solve Equations

Unit Review
Practice Test

Unit Problem Planning a Ski Trip

Curriculum across the Grades

Grade 7	Grade 8
Students generate multiples and factors.	Students express repeated multiplication using exponential notation. They represent whole numbers in expanded form using powers of ten.
Students solve multi-step problems arising from real-life contexts and involving whole numbers and decimals.	Students represent, compare, and order rational numbers. They determine common factors and common multiples using the prime factorization of numbers.
Students use estimation when solving problems involving operations with whole numbers and decimals, to help judge the reasonableness of a solution.	Students solve multi-step problems arising from real-life contexts and involving whole numbers and decimals. They use estimation to help judge the reasonableness of a solution.
Students evaluate expressions that involve whole numbers and decimals, including expressions that contain brackets, using order of operations.	Students evaluate expressions that contain brackets and exponents, using order of operations.
Students translate phrases describing simple mathematical relationships into algebraic expressions, using concrete materials.	Students translate statements describing mathematical relationships into algebraic expressions and equations.
Students evaluate algebraic expressions by substituting natural numbers for the variables.	Students evaluate algebraic expressions with up to three terms, by substituting decimals for the variables.
Students solve simple linear equations by modelling with concrete materials, by inspection, or by guess and check.	Students solve and verify linear equations involving a one-variable term.

Materials for This Unit

If you do not have algebra tiles, use thin card or paper to prepare them from PM 27. Colour one side red, the other side yellow, then laminate the tiles if possible.

Additional Activities

Factor Fun

For Extra Support (Appropriate for use after Lesson 1.2)
Materials: *Factor Fun* (Master 1.5), a hundred chart (PM 13), a set of cards labelled 1 to 9, a set of cards labelled 0 to 9, 2 sets of counters (one colour per player)

Playing this game reinforces the skills of factoring whole numbers.

The work students do: Students play in pairs. Students take turns to make a 2-digit number with the number cards, then cover all the factors of that number on a hundred chart. A student receives 1 point for each correct factor. The student with the higher score after 5 rounds wins.

Take It Further: Students play the game again, this time covering only the prime factors of each number.

Mathematical/Social/Logical
Partner Activity

Size It Up

For Extra Practice (Appropriate for use after Lesson 1.3)
Materials: *Size It Up* (Master 1.6), a deck of playing cards with the tens and face cards removed

Playing this game provides practice in writing numbers in expanded form and in scientific notation.

The work students do: Students play in pairs. They arrange the black cards and red cards in separate piles. Students pick 3 black cards to make a 3-digit number, then 1 red card that is the exponent of a power of 10, which they multiply the 3-digit number by. The student with the greater number gets 1 point. Students then write their numbers in expanded form and scientific notation, and get 1 point for each correct answer. The first student to get 15 points wins.

Take It Further: Students play the game again. They arrange the 4 cards any way they wish to get the least number.

Mathematical/Social
Partner Activity

It All Adds Up

For Extra Practice (Appropriate for use after Lesson 1.4)
Materials: *It All Adds Up* (Master 1.7), 4 regular octahedrons labelled 1 to 8

Playing this game provides practice with the order of operations.

The work students do: Students play in pairs. Students take turns to roll the octahedrons. Students use the 4 numbers rolled and any operations or brackets to make as many of the whole numbers from 1 to 10 as they can. Students get 1 point for each correct expression. The student with the higher score after 5 rounds wins.

Take It Further: Students play the game again. This time, they make as many of the whole numbers from 10 to 20 as they can.

Logical/Mathematical/Social
Partner Activity

Solve It

For Extra Practice (Appropriate for use after Lesson 1.6)
Materials: *Solve It* (Master 1.8), coloured pencils or pens

Completing this activity provides practice with solving equations.

The work students do: Students work on their own. Each student solves the given equations to find sets of equations with the same solution.

Take It Further: Students create 5 equations, all of which have the same solution.

Mathematical/Logical
Individual Activity

Planning for Unit 1

Planning for Instruction

Suggested Unit time: About 3 weeks

Lesson	Time	Materials	Program Support
Launch, page 2	15–20 min		
Skills You'll Need, page 4	40–50 min	calculators (optional)	
1.1: Numbers in the Media, page 7 Justify the choice of strategy when solving problems.	80–100 min	calculators newspapers, magazines (optional)	Master 1.9: Step-by-Step 1 Master 1.18: Extra Practice 1
1.2: Prime Factors, page 12 Represent composite numbers as products of prime factors.	80–100 min	calculators factor squares	Master 1.15: Factor Square Master 1.10: Step-by-Step 2 Master 1.19: Extra Practice 2
1.3: Expanded Form and Scientific Notation, page 17 Represent whole numbers in expanded form and scientific notation.	80–100 min	calculators	Master 1.11: Step-by-Step 3 Master 1.20: Extra Practice 3
Mid-Unit Review, page 22		calculators	
1.4: Order of Operations, page 23 Understand the order of operations with brackets and exponents.	80–100 min	calculators	Master 1.12: Step-by-Step 4 Master 1.21: Extra Practice 4
1.5: Using a Model to Solve Equations, page 27 Solve equations by using a model and by inverse operations.	80–100 min	two-pan balances and masses (optional) diagrams of two-pan balance and masses (optional)	Master 1.13: Step-by-Step 5 Master 1.22: Extra Practice 5
1.6: Using Algebra Tiles to Solve Equations, page 32 Use algebra tiles and inverse operations to solve equations.	80–100 min	algebra tiles	PM 27: Algebra Tiles Master 1.14: Step-by-Step 6 Master 1.23: Extra Practice 6
Reading and Writing in Math: Visual Text Features, page 38			
Unit Review, page 40		calculators algebra tiles (optional)	PM 27: Algebra Tiles Extra Practice: Student Book page 488
Practice Test, page 43		calculators algebra tiles (optional)	PM 27: Algebra Tiles
Unit Problem: Planning a Ski Trip, page 44	80–100 min	calculators atlases, brochures for Mont Tremblant	

Planning for Assessment

Purpose	Tools and Process	Recording and Reporting
Diagnostic	*Unit Launch* Question; conference; scaffold problems throughout the unit	PM 8: Conference Prompts
Formative	*Explore* – Ongoing Assessment: Observe and Listen	Master 1.2 Ongoing Observations: Numbers, Variables, and Equations PM 1: Inquiry Process Check List PM 6: Observation Record 1 PM 7: Observation Record 2 PM 8: Conference Prompts PM 2: Self-Assessment PM 3: Self-Assessment: Problem Solving PM 9: Work Sample Records
Summative	*Unit Review* *Unit Problem* – Performance Assessment *Unit Test* Review assessment records; add unit results to ongoing records	Master 1.1 Unit Rubric: Numbers, Variables, and Equations Master 1.3 Performance Assessment Rubric: Planning a Ski Trip Master 1.4 Unit Summary: Numbers, Variables, and Equations PM 10: Summary Class Records: Strands PM 11: Summary Class Records: Achievement Categories PM 12: Summary Record: Individual
Learning Skills/Mathematical Disposition	Observe and record throughout the unit.	PM 4: Learning Skills Check List PM 5: Mathematical Dispositions and Learning Skills

Program Masters (PM) are in the *Grade 8 Planning and Program Masters* module.
Extra Practice Masters are on the CD-ROM and printed in reduced format on page 66 of this module.

LAUNCH

LESSON ORGANIZER

15–20 min

Curriculum Focus: Activate prior learning about numbers, variables, and equations.

ASSUMED PRIOR KNOWLEDGE

- ☑ Students can solve problems involving decimals, using estimation and calculation.
- ☑ Students can apply the rules for order of operations.

Teaching notes for Cross Strand Investigation *Digital Roots* are in the *Additional Assessment Support* module.

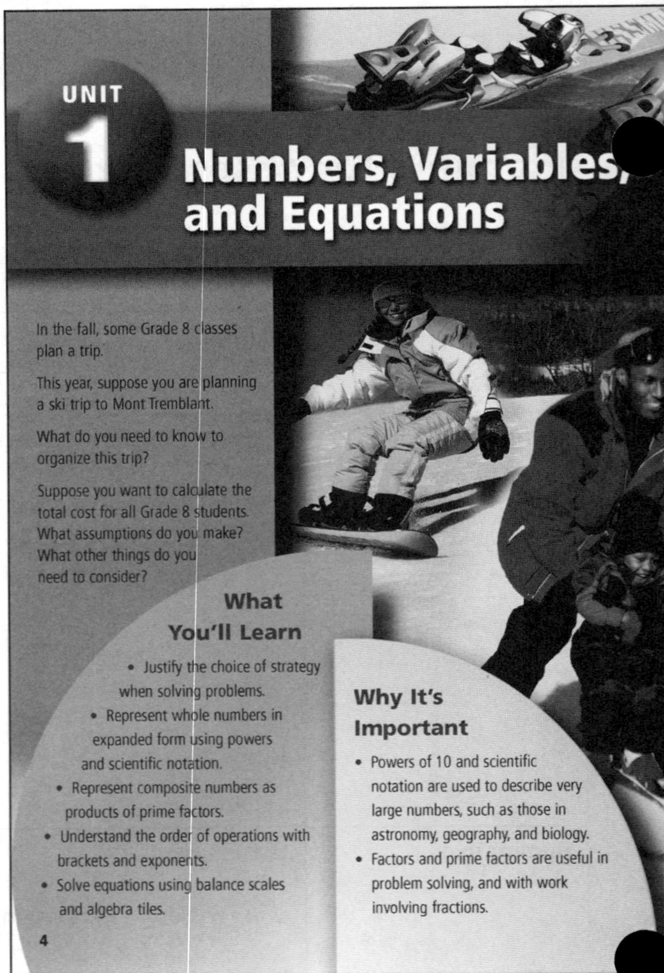

UNIT 1

Numbers, Variables, and Equations

In the fall, some Grade 8 classes plan a trip.

This year, suppose you are planning a ski trip to Mont Tremblant.

What do you need to know to organize this trip?

Suppose you want to calculate the total cost for all Grade 8 students. What assumptions do you make? What other things do you need to consider?

What You'll Learn

- Justify the choice of strategy when solving problems.
- Represent whole numbers in expanded form using powers and scientific notation.
- Represent composite numbers as products of prime factors.
- Understand the order of operations with brackets and exponents.
- Solve equations using balance scales and algebra tiles.

Why It's Important

- Powers of 10 and scientific notation are used to describe very large numbers, such as those in astronomy, geography, and biology.
- Factors and prime factors are useful in problem solving, and with work involving fractions.

4

ACTIVATE PRIOR LEARNING

After students have had time to read the *Launch*, ask questions about the data in the tables.

- How much would it cost for one person in our class to use the chair lift for one day? (*$40.95*)
- About how much would it cost for 5 days? (*About $200*) How did you estimate? (*I rounded $40.95 to $40, then multiplied by 5.*)
- How would you calculate how much it costs to use the lift and rent skis for 3 days? (*I would multiply $40.95 by 3, then multiply $12.99 by 3, and add the amounts.*)
- About how much does it cost? (*$40 × 3 = $120; $12 × 3 = $36; so it costs about $120 + $40 = $160*)
- Could you calculate the cost for the lift and skis a different way? (*Yes, I could add the costs for 1 day for each, then multiply by 3: ($40.95 + $12.99) × 3 = $161.82*)

Review students' responses to the question about what they need to know to organize the trip.
(*Other costs, such as transportation and accommodation*)

The costs for all Grade 8 students would depend upon whether the students own their own equipment, possibly insurance costs, costs for the teachers or parents who accompany the students, and spending money.

Have students make up their own problems about the given data. For example:

How much does it cost for 2 adults and 10 youths to ski for half a day, assuming they have their own equipment?
(*2 × $46.95 + 10 × $34.95 = $443.40*)

Suppose you have $200 to spend on lift tickets, and renting the complete package of equipment. Estimate how many days you could ski.

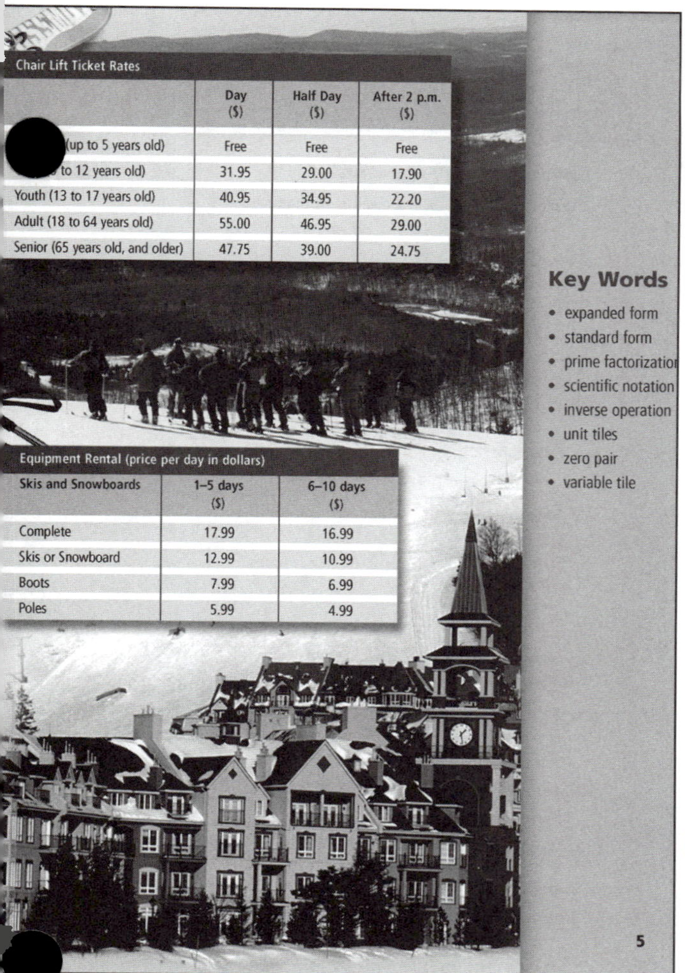

Chair Lift Ticket Rates	Day ($)	Half Day ($)	After 2 p.m. ($)
[illegible] (up to 5 years old)	Free	Free	Free
[illegible] to 12 years old)	31.95	29.00	17.90
Youth (13 to 17 years old)	40.95	34.95	22.20
Adult (18 to 64 years old)	55.00	46.95	29.00
Senior (65 years old, and older)	47.75	39.00	24.75

Equipment Rental (price per day in dollars)

Skis and Snowboards	1–5 days ($)	6–10 days ($)
Complete	17.99	16.99
Skis or Snowboard	12.99	10.99
Boots	7.99	6.99
Poles	5.99	4.99

Key Words

- expanded form
- standard form
- prime factorizatio
- scientific notation
- inverse operation
- unit tiles
- zero pair
- variable tile

5

FROM THE LIBRARY

Pre-Algebra with Pizzazz! by Steve and Janis Marcy. Creative Publications, 1996
ISBN: 0884881512
This book has interesting and enjoyable reproducibles involving riddles, jokes, and limericks to motivate students. The four sections cover:

- Integers, fractions, decimals, properties of operations
- Exponents, decimals, scientific notation, irrational numbers, ratio, proportion, percent, and probability
- Geometric figures, measurement, square roots, Pythagorean Theorem, trigonometric ratios, and statistics
- Variables, exponents, equations, problem solving, inequalities, and graphing

REACHING ALL LEARNERS

Some students may benefit from using the virtual manipulatives on the e-Tools CD-ROM. The e-Tool appropriate for this unit is *Place-Value Blocks.*

(*The complete package is $17.99 per day. The lift ticket is $40.95 per day. So, that is about $20 + $40 = $60. $200 ÷ $60 is about 3. So, I could ski for 3 days.*)

Tell students that, in this unit, they will learn more about working with large numbers, extending the order of operations to include brackets and exponents, and solving equations. At the end of this unit, students will plan a ski trip to Mont Tremblant.

DIAGNOSTIC ASSESSMENT

What to Look For	What to Do
	Extra Support:
✔ Students can solve problems involving decimals, using estimation and calculation.	Students who have difficulty working with decimals could round them to whole numbers, before operating with them, or use a calculator. *Work on this skill during Lesson 1.1.*
✔ Students can apply the rules for the order of operations.	Students who have difficulty with the order of operations should start by working on questions with only 2 operations. *Work on this skill during Lesson 1.4.*

LESSON ORGANIZER 40–50 min

Skills in Review
- Understanding exponents
- Understanding powers of 10
- Solving equations

Student Materials

Optional
- calculators

Alternative Example 1

Write 256 as a power in more than one way.

Solution

Since $256 = 4 \times 64 = 4 \times 4 \times 16 = 16 \times 16$,
then $256 = 16 \times 16 = 16^2$

Since $16 = 4 \times 4$,
then $256 = 4 \times 4 \times 4 \times 4 = 4^4$

Since $4 = 2 \times 2$,
then $256 = 2 \times 2 \times 2 \times 2 \times 2 \times 2 \times 2 \times 2 = 2^8$

Sample Solutions

2. a) $5 \times 5 \times 5 \times 5 = 625$
   b) $11 \times 11 = 121$
   c) $2 \times 2 \times 2 \times 2 \times 2 \times 2 \times 2 \times 2 = 256$
   d) $12 \times 12 \times 12 = 1728$

UNIT 1

Skills You'll Need

Understanding Exponents

The exponent 3 indicates how many 5s are multiplied.

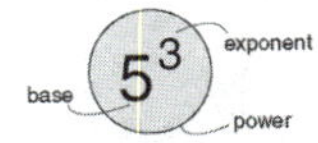

$5^3 = 5 \times 5 \times 5$ **expanded form**
$= 125$ **standard form**

5^3 is a power of 5.
We say: 5 to the power of 3, or 5 cubed

Example 1

Write 81 as a power in more than one way.

Solution

Since $81 = 9 \times 9$,
then $81 = 9^2$
Since $9 = 3 \times 3$,
then $81 = 3 \times 3 \times 3 \times 3$, or 3^4

✓ Check

1. Write in exponent form.
   a) $4 \times 4 \times 4$ 4^3
   b) $2 \times 2 \times 2 \times 2 \times 2 \times 2 \times 2$ 2^7
   c) 7×7 7^2
   d) $12 \times 12 \times 12 \times 12 \times 12$ 12^5
2. Write in expanded form, then in standard form.
   a) 5^4 b) 11^2 c) 2^8 d) 12^3
3. Write as a power. Do this more than one way, if possible.
   a) 27 3^3 b) 36 6^2 c) 64 $8^2, 4^3, 2^6$ d) 4 2^2
   e) 125 5^3 f) 8 2^3 g) 343 7^3 h) 625 $25^2, 5^4$

6 UNIT 1: Numbers, Variables, and Equations

Understanding Exponents

We use exponents to write a number as a power, when that number can be written as the product of equal factors. Ask students how they could identify whether a number could be written as a power.

- How do you know if you can write 243 as a power?
  (I would find the least number that divides into it. I know that 2 doesn't divide into 243 because it is an odd number. I know that 3 does divide into 243 because the sum of the digits: 2 + 4 + 3 = 9, is divisible by 3. I'd keep dividing by 3 until I can't divide by 3 any more. If the last quotient is 1, then I can write 243 as a power.)

Show students successive divisions:

$$\begin{array}{r|l} 3 & 243 \\ 3 & 81 \\ 3 & 27 \\ 3 & 9 \\ 3 & 3 \\ & 1 \end{array}$$

Then, $243 = 3 \times 3 \times 3 \times 3 \times 3 = 3^5$

Then ask:

- How do you know if you could write this power in a different way?
  (If there is an even number of factors, I can multiply pairs of factors to get a larger factor. I cannot do this with 243, because it has 5 factors.)
- How can you write any number as a power?
  (I can use the exponent 1. For example, 7 can be written as 7^1.)

Review the rules for divisibility for 4, 5, 6, 8, 9, and 10. These are listed on page 14.

It might help students to record certain powers, such as these:

$2^2 = 4$	$3^2 = 9$	$4^2 = 16$	$5^2 = 25$
$2^3 = 8$	$3^3 = 27$	$4^3 = 64$	$5^3 = 125$
$2^4 = 16$	$3^4 = 81$		$5^4 = 625$
⋮	$3^5 = 243$		
$2^{10} = 1024$			

Understanding Powers of 10

This place-value chart shows some of the powers of 10 written in words
…ent form.

One hundred million	Ten million	One million	One hundred thousand	Ten thousand	One thousand	One hundred	Ten
10^8	10^7	10^6	10^5	10^4	10^3	10^2	10^1

Example 2

Express each number in standard form and as a power of 10.

a) one hundred thousand
b) one hundred
c) one thousand
d) one hundred million

Solution

Use the place-value chart.

a) One hundred thousand is 100 000, which is 10^5.
b) One hundred is 100, which is 10^2.
c) One thousand is 1000, which is 10^3.
d) One hundred million is 100 000 000, which is 10^8.

✓ Check

a) Express each number as a power of 10.
  i) 10 000 10^4 **ii)** 10 000 000 10^7
  iii) $10 \times 10 \times 10$ 10^3 **iv)** $10 \times 10 \times 10 \times 10 \times 10 \times 10 \times 10 \times 10$ 10^8
b) What patterns do you see in part a?
How can you use these patterns to write a number as a power of 10?

Write in standard form.
a) 10^4 **b)** 10^6 **c)** 10^{10} **d)** 10^{12}

A student says that $10^6 - 10^4 = 10^2$.
Is the student correct? Explain. No

Add.
a) $10^2 + 10^3$ 1100 **b)** $10^3 + 10^4$ 11 000 **c)** $10^4 + 10^5$ 110 000

Skills You'll Need 7

Alternative Example 2

Express each number in standard form and as a power of 10.

a) ten thousand
b) ten
c) one million

Solution

Use the place-value chart.

a) Ten thousand is 10 000, which is 10^4.
b) Ten is 10, which can be written as 10^1.
c) One million is 1 000 000, which is 10^6.

4. b) For example: The exponent is the number of zeros in the standard form of the number.
5. a) 10 000 **b)** 1 000 000
  c) 10 000 000 000
  d) 1 000 000 000 000
6. $10^6 - 10^4 = 1\ 000\ 000 - 10\ 000 = 990\ 000$; $10^2 = 100$
7. Write the numbers in standard form, then add.
  a) 100 + 1000 = 1100
  b) 1000 + 10 000 = 11 000
  c) 10 000 + 100 000 = 110 000

Remind students how to use scientific calculators to write powers of large numbers in standard form.
For 15^2, key in:
15 [x^2] [ENTER =] to display 225.
For 15^6, key in:
15 [^] 6 [ENTER =] to display 11 390 625.

Common Misconceptions

➤ Students multiply the base by the exponent when writing a power in standard form.

How to Help: Encourage students to first write the power as a product of equal factors.

Understanding Powers of 10

Students need to understand powers of 10 to be able to write a number in scientific notation. Encourage students to copy the place-value chart, with names and powers, in their notebooks. They could write each number in standard form, in the relevant column.

Ask:

- How is a multiple of 10 related to how it is written as a power of 10? *(The number of zeros in the multiple of 10 is equal to the exponent when the number is written as a power of 10. For example, 10 000 has 4 zeros and 10 000 = 10^4.)*
- What is an easy way to write a power of 10 in standard form? *(Write 1, followed by zeros, where the number of zeros is equal to the exponent of the power. For example, 10^5 = 100 000)*

Have students make up, then solve, their own problems, where they add and/or subtract powers of 10, then check their answers with a calculator.

Common Misconceptions

➤ When students add or subtract powers of 10, they simply add or subtract the exponents.

How to Help: Have students write the numbers in standard form before they add or subtract. Or, have students use their calculators to find the sum or difference.

Alternative Example 3

Solve by systematic trial. $4x - 8 = 36$

Solution

$4x - 8 = 36$

Choose a value for x and substitute.

Try $x = 4$:	$4(4) - 8 = 16 - 8 = 8$	too low
Try $x = 8$:	$4(8) - 8 = 32 - 8 = 24$	too low
Try $x = 12$:	$4(12) - 8 = 48 - 8 = 40$	too high, but close
Try $x = 11$:	$4(11) - 8 = 44 - 8 = 36$	correct

The solution is $x = 11$.

Alternative Example 4

Solve by inspection. $70 + 3x = 91$

Solution

$70 + 3x = 91$

Think: 70 plus 3 times a number is 91.

We know: $70 + 21 = 91$; so, 3 times a number is 21.

We know: $3 \times 7 = 21$; so, the number is 7.

The solution is $x = 7$.

8. Solve either by systematic trial or by inspection. For example:
   a) Ten times a number subtract 9 is 81. So, ten times the number must be 90; $10 \times 9 = 90$.
   b) Try $x = 5$: $37 + 20(5) = 37 + 100 = 137$, slightly too high; try $x = 4$: $37 + 20(4) = 37 + 80 = 117$, correct.

Solving Equations

To solve an equation means to find the value of the variable that makes the equation true.
Two ways to solve an equation are:
- by systematic trial
- by inspection

Example 3

Solve by systematic trial. $3x + 4 = 28$

Solution

$3x + 4 = 28$

Choose a value for x and substitute.

Try: $x = 5$	$3(5) + 4 = 15 + 4 = 19$	too small
Try: $x = 10$	$3(10) + 4 = 30 + 4 = 34$	too large, but not by much
Try: $x = 8$	$3(8) + 4 = 24 + 4 = 28$	correct

The solution is $x = 8$.

Example 4

Solve by inspection. $100 - 7x = 58$

Solution

$100 - 7x = 58$

Think: 100 subtract 7 times a number is 58.

We know: $100 - 42 = 58$; so, 7 times a number is 42.

We know: $7 \times 6 = 42$; so, the number is 6.

The solution is $x = 6$.

✓ Check

8. Solve each equation.

a) $10x - 9 = 81$ $x = 9$	b) $37 + 20x = 117$ $x = 4$	c) $88 = 4 + 7x$ $x = 12$
d) $9 = 19x - 124$ $x = 7$	e) $x + 29 = 46$ $x = 17$	f) $x - 85 = 17$ $x = 102$
g) $\frac{x}{5} = 9$ $x = 45$	h) $\frac{3x}{10} = 6$ $x = 20$	i) $\frac{3x}{10} + 3 = 6$ $x = 10$

Solving Equations

Review the concept of a variable. In the equations that students solve in this text, a variable represents one number, in each case.

Remind students that the variable used does not affect the solution of an equation. For example, these three equations have the same solution: $3x + 4 = 28$; $3a + 4 = 28$; $3n + 4 = 28$.

Remind students that $3x$ means $3 \times x$, and encourage students to write the x as shown in their texts, and not as a multiplication sign.

Students must understand that the equal sign in an equation means that the quantity on the left side is the same as the quantity on the right side; that is, for the equation $3x + 4 = 28$, $3x + 4$ is another way to write 28, and the correct value of x makes this true.

Although the two ways to solve an equation are shown as separate examples, frequently we use both systematic trial and inspection to solve an equation. If the numbers are large, encourage students to use calculators to help.

For example, $372 + 4x = 596$

Use a calculator to find what adds to 372 to get 596; that is, $596 - 372 = 224$. Then use a calculator to find what we multiply 4 by to get 224:

$x = \frac{224}{4} = 56$

Common Misconceptions

➤ When students use systematic trial, they always begin by substituting $x = 1$; and increasing x by 1 each time.

How to Help: Encourage students to look at the numbers in the equation to find a reasonable estimate for x. For example, for $3x + 4 = 28$, 4 is much less than 28. We need a value of x that makes $3x$ a little less than 28.

1.1 Numbers in the Media

Focus Justify the choice of strategy when solving problems.

We use numbers to describe situations, to compare quantities, to make decisions, and to support points of view.

In the media, the numbers indicate that Canada is a good place to live.

How can we use the data in the table below to justify Canada's high ranking as a place to live?

Canada still ranked in the top 5 places to live — United Nations

Statistics indicate that most Canadians will finish high school

Life expectancy reaches a new high — 79.3 years

Literacy rate approaches 100%

Country	Estimated Annual Income ($)	Adult Literacy Rate (% of population)	Infant Mortality (per 1000 live births)	Number of Physicians (per 100 000 people)	Estimated Population (mid-2004)
Bangladesh	2 035	41.1	51	23	141 340 476
Brazil	10 879	86.4	30	206	184 101 109
Canada	36 299	99.9	5	187	31 964 434
China	5 435	90.9	31	164	1 298 847 624
Ethiopia	1 008	41.5	114	3	67 851 281
Mexico	12 967	90.5	24	156	104 959 594
New Zealand	26 481	99.9	6	219	3 993 817
Norway	42 340	99.9	4	367	4 574 560

Explore

Work with a partner.
Use the data in the table above.
Make up 4 problems for your partner to solve.
Try to write a problem that can be solved using each one of these methods:

- mental math
- pencil and paper
- estimation
- calculator

Reflect & Share

Compare problems and solutions with your partner.
Justify your choice of method for solving each problem.

1.1 Numbers in the Media 9

LESSON 1.1

Numbers in the Media

LESSON ORGANIZER 80–100 min

Curriculum Focus: Justify the choice of strategy when solving problems. (8m16, 8m18)

Student Materials
- calculators

Optional
- newspapers, magazines
- Step-by-Step 1 (Master 1.9)
- Extra Practice 1 (Master 1.18)

Assessment: Master 1.2 Ongoing Observations: Numbers, Variables, and Equations

Key Math Learnings

1. Numbers are used to provide information about our world.
2. There are many methods that can be used to solve problems: mental math, estimation, pencil and paper, and a calculator.

Assignment Guidelines

If your students do not have time to complete all the *Practice* questions on pages 11, 12, and 13, these questions provide minimum curriculum coverage: 1, 2, 4, 5, 6, 7, *Reflect*

To assess the 4 Achievement Chart categories listed in the curriculum document, have students complete these *Practice* questions:
Knowledge and Understanding: 2
Application: 6
Thinking: 7
Communication: 8

BEFORE Get Started

Review techniques for mental math and estimation.

Here are some examples.

For mental math, to find this sum:
251 + 375 + 185

Begin by adding the hundreds:
2 hundred + 3 hundred is 5 hundred;
then 5 hundred + 1 hundred is 6 hundred;
then add the tens: 600 → 650 → 720 → 800;
then add the ones: 800 → 801 → 806 → 811

For mental math, to find this product: 58 × 6
Think: 58 × 6 = 60 × 6 – 2 × 6;
then, 60 × 6 is 360 and 2 × 6 is 12, so 360 – 12 is 360 – 10 – 2 = 348

For estimation, round the numbers, then use mental math.

To estimate this sum: 251 + 375 + 185
Round to the nearest 25: 250 + 375 + 175;
then count hundreds, then twenty-fives:
200 → 500 → 600; then 650 → 725 → 800
The sum is approximately 800.

To estimate this product: 58 × 6
Round 58 to 60, then 60 × 6 = 360.
Since we rounded 58 up to 60, we round the product down to the nearest 50.
The product is approximately 350.

Invite students to list situations in which numbers are used in our world, such as large numbers of people and long distances. (Canada's national debt in billions of dollars; the population of Canada in millions of people; the distance from the east coast to the west coast in thousands of kilometres) Then ask students if these numbers are accurate or approximate.

Review the data on page 9 of the Student Book. Have students suggest why Canada ranks

REACHING ALL LEARNERS

Alternative Explore

Materials: newspapers and magazines

Have students work in pairs. They look through newspapers and magazines for situations that involve large numbers. Each pair makes up 2 problems that can be solved using mental math, pencil and paper, estimation, or a calculator. Students share the problems and their solutions with the class.

Common Misconceptions

➤ Students often believe that rounding and estimation are not valid ways to calculate.

How to Help: Have students randomly choose 10 numbers between 20 and 100. Students could roll a decahedron labelled 0 to 9 to generate 2-digit numbers.

- Round the numbers to the nearest 10 and add mentally.
- Round the numbers to the nearest 5 and add.
- Calculate the sum.

Have students compare the three answers. They should be close. (*Example: Ten numbers are: 73, 52, 81, 59, 67, 79, 47, 26, 34, 98; round, then add: 620; round, then add: 615; calculate: 616*)

ESL Strategies

Make a list of important words students need to know. Have students write the meaning of each word in English and in their native language.

Consider pairing each ESL student with a competent reader.

Connect

When calculating with rounded numbers, an estimated answer is appropriate.
Use mental math to solve a problem with numbers that are eas[y to]
handle, and when the solving requires few steps.
Use pencil and paper, or a calculator, when the problem requires more complex calculations.

Example

In North America, a new computer is purchased every two seconds.

Find how many new computers are purchased:
a) in two minutes **b)** in one month

Solution

a) Use mental math.
There are 120 s in 2 min.
One computer is purchased every 2 s;
so, the number purchased in 120 s is:
120 ÷ 2 = 60
60 computers are purchased in 2 min.

b) Use pencil and paper, or a calculator.
Use 30 for the number of days in one month.
There are 24 h in 1 day.
Number of hours in one month: 30 × 24 h = 720 h
Number of minutes in one month: 720 × 60 min = 43 200 min
Number of seconds in one month: 43 200 × 60 s = 2 592 000 s
Number of computers purchased in one month:
2 592 000 ÷ 2 = 1 296 000
In North America, about 1 300 000 computers are purchased in one month.
We can write this as 1.3 million.

There are 60 min in 1 h.
There are 60 s in 1 min.

10 UNIT 1: Numbers, Variables, and Equations

highly as a place to live. (Out of 8: 2nd highest in annual income, so people have a decent standard of living; ties for 1st in literacy rate, which enables people to participate fully in society; 2nd lowest in infant mortality, which means that the health care system is one of the best; 3rd highest in number of physicians per capita, which means that all people have access to health care.)

Present *Explore*. Encourage students to create problems that can be solved in different ways.

DURING Explore

Ongoing Assessment: Observe and Listen

In Grade 7, students worked with whole-number percents. Have students round the percents in the literacy rate column if they do not know how to deal with percents to 1 decimal place. This concept is taught in Unit 2.

As students work, ask questions, such as:

- Why are the populations given as estimates? (*The populations are constantly changing as children are born, people die, and people leave or arrive in the country.*)
- Which countries have very low mortality rates? Can you suggest a reason? (*Norway, Canada, and New Zealand have very low mortality rates. These countries have a high standard of living with good, low-cost health coverage. They also have a greater number of physicians per capita.*)
  Very high mortality rates?
  (*Ethiopia has a high mortality rate. This is a very poor country that has suffered a number of major disasters in recent years. There is a high rate of disease, poverty, and hunger, which means many mothers are sick and babies are born into an unhealthy environment.*)
- Approximately how many physicians are there in Canada?
  (*32 000 000 ÷ 100 000 × 200 = 64 000*)

Practice

"... means ... wer."

1. Use mental math to evaluate.
   Describe the strategies you used.
   a) 88 + 56 **144** b) 118 + 296 **414** c) 2958 − 1998 **960** d) 25 × 25 × 4 **2500**
2. State whether you will use mental math, paper and pencil, or a calculator; then evaluate.
   a) 29 + 41 **70** b) 19 × 21 **399** c) 7872 ÷ 1000 **7.872** d) 7850 − 6975 **875**
   e) 777 + 333 **1110** f) 9876 ÷ 3 **3292** g) 25% of 500 **125** h) 80% of 150 **120**
3. Explain whether you would need an exact answer or an estimate.
   a) You want to know the number of books read this year by Grade 8 students in Canada. **Estimate**
   b) You want to know the amount of money needed to pay for your Grade 8 graduation clothes. **Exact**
   c) You want to know how much money you collected for a charity walk-a-thon. **Exact**
4. **Assessment Focus** The table shows the U.S. and worldwide box office earnings for the top five movies of all time, as of 2004.

Movie	Year	U.S. Box Office Revenue ($ millions)	World Box Office Revenue ($ millions)
Titanic	1997	600.8	1835.4
Lord of the Rings—Return of the King	2003	377.0	1129.2
Harry Potter and the Sorcerer's Stone	2001	317.6	975.8
Star Wars Episode 1—The Phantom Menace	1999	431.1	925.5
Lord of the Rings—The Two Towers	2002	341.7	924.7

   a) What were the total earnings worldwide of the top five movies? **$5790.6 million**
   b) How much more money did *Titanic* earn in the world than each of the other movies?
   c) Name two movies that together earned about as much as *Titanic.*
   d) Which movies more than tripled their U.S. box office revenues?
   e) Is revenue a fair way to rank the top five movies? Explain.
   f) Pose a problem that could be solved using these data. Solve the problem you posed.

1.1 Numbers in the Media 11

Sample Solutions

1. For example:
   a) 88 + 56 = 90 + 54 = 144
   b) 118 + 296 = 114 + 300 = 414
   c) 2958 − 1998 = 2960 − 2000 = 960
   d) 25 × 25 × 4 = 25 × 100 = 2500
3. a) It would be impossible to poll every Grade 8 student in Canada.
   b) You would want to be sure you had enough money to pay for the clothes.
   c) You must find exactly how much money should be given to the charity.
4. b) Subtract each world revenue from $1835.4 million: $706.2 million; $859.6 million; $909.9 million; $910.7 million
   c) Three of the movies are in the $900 million range. Add in pairs to get closest to $1835.4 million: *Star Wars Episode 1–The Phantom Menace* and *Lord of the Rings–The Two Towers;* $1850.2 million
   d) Multiply each U.S. box office revenue by 3 and compare with the world box office revenue: *Titanic* and *Harry Potter and the Sorcerer's Stone*
   e) For example: Yes, if earnings are the criteria for ranking. However, there are other ways to rank movies.
   f) "Which 3 movies together earned about $1000 million in the U.S.?" Answer: *Harry Potter and the Sorcerer's Stone, Star Wars Episode 1–The Phantom Menace,* and *Lord of the Rings–The Two Towers*

- What problem did you write that involves the use of a calculator?
  (I wanted to find how many times as many people are in China as in New Zealand. I used a calculator to divide 1 298 847 624 by 3 993 817 to get 325.2. So, there are about 300 times as many people in China as in New Zealand.)
- Could you use estimation to get an answer?
  (Yes, I could round each population. I round China's population to the nearest trillion: 1 300 000 000. I round New Zealand's population to the nearest million: 4 000 000. Then I divide: 1 300 000 000 ÷ 4 000 000. This is the same as: 1300 ÷ 4 = 325. My estimated answer is very close to the actual answer.)
- Which of the 4 methods do you like best? Why?
  (I like estimating as it gives me a good idea of the answer without a lot of work. It also allows me to use mental math and pencil and paper.)

AFTER Connect

Invite students to share their problems, solutions, and their strategies. Ask:

- Does the strategy used by this pair of students seem reasonable?
- Does anyone have a different strategy for a similar problem?

Ask if any students managed to create a problem that involved the use of three of the methods.

Here are some sample problems and solutions.

Using mental math: "What percent of the population of Bangladesh is not literate?"
(100 – 41.1 = 58.9; 58.9%)

Using estimation: "Approximately how many physicians are there in Ethiopia?"
(The population is approximately 70 million. Divide by 100 000 to get 700. Multiply by 3 to get the total number of physicians, 2100.)

5. **b)** For example: If an aerial ladder on a fire truck is used (32 m), the answer would be approximately 620; if a 12-m ladder is used, the answer would be approximately 1640.

6. **a)** Mental math: 25 × 100 = 2500 L

   b) Pencil and paper and mental math:
   3.75 × 600 L = 3.75 × 6 × 100 = 22.5 × 100 = 2250 L

   c) Pencil and paper and mental math:
   2.45 × 40 000 L = 2.45 × 4 × 10 000 = 9.8 × 10 000 = 98 000 L

   d) Calculator: About 14.5 kg of rice, 0.7 kg of beef, 48 kg of wheat

7. For example: "What is the mean weekly income?"
   Answer: $916.25

8. **a)** For example: This may seem high for an individual, but more reasonable for a family of 2 or more.

   b) A bathtub filled to the brim would be about 90 L, so 300 L would more than fill 3 bathtubs; or a bucket holds about 8 L, so 300 L would fill almost 40 buckets.

9. **c)** For example: Round the population to 26 million. Assume one-half are male and one-half are female. Assume 1.9% of the females and 4.6% of the males chose basketball. 1.9% of 13 million + 4.6% of 13 million = 6.5% of 13 million = 845 000.

   d) "How many more females than males chose swimming?"
   Answer: 256 000

10. For example: Pair the numbers, 1 + 50, 2 + 49, and so on, to get 25 sets of 51. 25 sets of 50 = 1250, then add 25 to get 1275. Another way is to pair the numbers 1 + 49, 2 + 48, and so on, to get 24 sets of 50 = 1200, and then add 50 and 25 to get 1275.

5. The tallest mountain in the world is Mount Everest.
Its summit is about 8800 m above sea level.
The lowest point in the ocean is the Marianas Trench.
Its deepest point is about 10 900 m below sea level.

a) What is the distance between the highest point on land and the lowest point in the ocean? 19 700 m

b) About how many ladders would you need to bridge the distance in part a?
State your assumptions and show your work.

6. Here are some statistics about water use.
- 100 L for 1 bath
- 600 L to produce 1 kg of wheat
- 2000 L to produce 1 kg of rice
- 40 000 L to produce 1 kg of beef

Answer each question.
Explain which calculation method you used.

a) How much water would be needed for 25 baths?

b) How much water would be needed to produce 3.75 kg of wheat?

c) Suppose you bought 2.45 kg of beef. How much water was used to produce it?

d) Twenty-nine thousand litres of water would produce how much rice? How much beef? How much wheat?

7. In the year 2003, Statistics Canada reported that workers in the mining industry were paid a higher wage than those in other similar jobs.

Sector	Weekly Income ($)
Mining	1176
Forestry	840
Manufacturing	832
Construction	817

Make up a problem using the data above.
Trade your problem with a classmate.
Solve your classmate's problem.

12 UNIT 1: Numbers, Variables, and Equations

Using a calculator: "Which three countries together have a population that is 51 329 010 greater than that of Bangladesh?" (*Brazil, New Zealand, and Norway*)

Using pencil and paper: "How many more people are in Brazil than in Bangladesh?" (*184 101 109 – 141 340 476 = 42 760 633*)

Using estimation and mental math: "Estimate the weekly, then monthly income in Canada." (*Estimate $36 000 ÷ 50 = $720 weekly; $36 000 ÷ 12 = $3000 monthly*)

Using estimation, mental math, and pencil and paper: "What is the approximate ratio of income in Canada to income in Norway?" (*36 000:42 000 = 36:42 = 6:7*)

Use *Connect* to show how different methods can be used to obtain useful results.

Practice

Some useful data for question 8: a bath uses 100 L, a shower uses 55 L, a washing machine uses 135 L, a dishwasher uses 60 L, and a toilet uses 15 L of water per use.

Assessment Focus: Question 4

Students' work should include how they calculated (mental math, pencil and paper, or a calculator) and whether the answer is approximate or exact, and why. Students may realize that all answers are approximate because the revenues have been rounded to the nearest tenth of a million dollars; that is, to the nearest $100 000.

Students who need extra support to complete Assessment Focus questions may benefit from the Step-by-Step masters (Masters 1.9–1.14).

8. According to one source, the average Canadian uses between 300 L and 350 L of water per day.
   a) Does this sound reasonable? Explain.
   b) What would 300 L of water look like? What would 300 L fill?

9. Canadians were asked to choose their most popular participation sport. Here are the top five results in 1998 for people aged 15 and older.

The percents in the table have been rounded to the nearest tenth.

Sport	Females		Males	
	Number	%	Number	%
Golf	476 000	3.9	1 325 000	11.1
Ice Hockey	65 000	0.5	1 435 000	12.0
Baseball	386 000	3.1	953 000	8.0
Swimming	688 000	5.6	432 000	3.6
Basketball	237 000	1.9	550 000	4.6

In 1998, there were about 12 323 000 females aged 15 and older, and about 11 937 000 males aged 15 and older.
   a) For which sport is the number of females about 3 times the number for basketball? Swimming
   b) For which sport is the number of males about $\frac{2}{3}$ the number for ice hockey? Baseball
   c) In 2004, Canada's population aged 15 and older was about 25 849 000. How many people do you think chose basketball? What assumptions did you make?
   d) Write a problem that could be solved using these data. Solve your problem.

ntal Math

all these numbers with
tion and subtraction.
14, 21, 28, 30, 35, 40
e two different
essions equal to 100.

Take It Further

10. Describe how you could add the numbers from 1 to 50 quickly, without using a calculator.

Reflect

Give an example of a problem that requires an exact answer.
Give an example of a problem that requires estimation.
Solve each problem.
Show your solutions.

1.1 Numbers in the Media 13

REFLECT: A problem that requires an exact answer would be similar to question 10. "Add the numbers from 1 to 99 quickly, without using a calculator."

Solution

Add the numbers in pairs, where the sum of each pair is 100.

$(1 + 99) + (2 + 98) + (3 + 97) + \dots + (49 + 51) + 50 =$
$(49 \times 100) + 50 = 4950$

Another solution is to write the sum down twice; add, then divide by 2.

$$\begin{array}{ccccccccccccc} 1 & + & 2 & + & 3 & + & \dots & + & 97 & + & 98 & + & 99 \\ 99 & + & 98 & + & 97 & + & \dots & + & 3 & + & 2 & + & 1 \\ \hline 100 & + & 100 & + & 100 & + & \dots & + & 100 & + & 100 & + & 100 \end{array}$$

$= 99 \times 100$
$= 9900$

Divide by 2: $9900 \div 2 = 4950$

A problem that requires an estimated answer is:
"The attendance at four hockey games was: 19 284, 18 856, 19 176, 18 253
Approximately how many people attended the four games?"
Round each attendance to the nearest thousand, then add.
$19\,000 + 19\,000 + 19\,000 + 18\,000 = 75\,000$
About 75 000 people attended the games.

Mental Math

Encourage students to keep track of partial sums and differences rather than start from the beginning each time.

$5 + 7 + 14 + 21 + 28 + 30 + 35 - 40 = 100$
$7 + 28 + 30 + 35 + 40 - 5 - 14 - 21 = 100$

ASSESSMENT FOR LEARNING

What to Look For	What to Do
Knowledge and Understanding ✔ Students understand there are many different methods and strategies for solving problems. ✔ Students understand some methods are more effective than others. ***Communication*** ✔ Students can explain and justify the method they used when solving problems. ***Application*** ✔ Students can choose the best method to solve a problem, then solve the problem.	***Extra Support:*** Students who have difficulty choosing the most effective method may benefit from asking themselves questions such as: "Are the numbers exact or approximate?", "How accurate an answer do I need?", "Can I use estimation or should I use a calculator?" Students can use Step-by-Step 1 (Master 1.9) to complete question 4. ***Extra Practice:*** Have students check each part of *Practice* question 2 using a different method. The answers should be the same each time. Students can complete Extra Practice 1 (Master 1.18). ***Extension:*** Have students use the information in *Practice* question 6 to create similar problems, solve the problems, then exchange problems with a classmate and solve the classmate's problems.

Recording and Reporting
Master 1.2 Ongoing Observations: Numbers, Variables, and Equations

LESSON 1.2

Prime Factors

LESSON ORGANIZER — 80–100 min

Curriculum Focus: Represent composite numbers as products of prime factors. (8m11, 8m15)

Teacher Materials
- overhead transparency of factor square (Master 1.15)

Student Materials
- factor square (Master 1.15)
- calculators

Optional
- coloured pens or pencils
- Step-by-Step 2 (Master 1.10)
- Extra Practice 2 (Master 1.19)

Vocabulary: prime factorization

Assessment: Master 1.2 Ongoing Observations: Numbers, Variables, and Equations

Key Math Learnings

1. All composite numbers can be expressed as a product of prime factors.
2. Two or more numbers have a greatest common factor and a lowest common multiple.

1.2 Prime Factors

Focus Represent composite numbers as products of prime factors.

In earlier grades, you broke numbers apart by finding their factors. We will now further investigate these factors.

Explore

Work on your own.
Use a copy of this factor square.

4	×	15	×	2	×	9	×	40	×
×	18	×	2	×	2	×	5	×	3
2	×	3	×	24	×	36	×	20	×
×	16	×	10	×	30	×	10	×	12
2	×	60	×	6	×	4	×	2	×
×	11	×	50	×	28	×	5	×	4
2	×	15	×	20	×	3	×	24	×
×	8	×	2	×	5	×	2	×	6
2	×	10	×	3	×	7	×	18	×
×	3	×	5	×	60	×	24	×	5

Draw a loop around factors of 120.
Look for 2 factors, 3 factors, and so on, up to as many factors as possible.
One set of factors is looped for you: $2 \times 4 \times 15$
List all the factors you find.
Have you found all possible factors of 120?
Organize your results to justify your answer to this question.

Reflect & Share

Compare your results with those of a classmate.
Identify the factorization of 120 that has the most numbers.
What is special about these factors?
Use powers to write the product of these factors a simpler way.

BEFORE — Get Started

Have students write 48 as the product of three factors in as many ways as possible.

Ask:

- How many answers can you find? *(8: $1 \times 2 \times 24$, $1 \times 3 \times 16$, $1 \times 4 \times 12$, $1 \times 6 \times 8$, $2 \times 2 \times 12$, $2 \times 3 \times 8$, $2 \times 4 \times 6$, $3 \times 4 \times 4$)*
- Do not use 1 as a factor this time. Can you write 48 as the product of more than three factors? *(Yes: 4 factors: $2 \times 2 \times 2 \times 6$; $2 \times 2 \times 3 \times 4$; 5 factors: $2 \times 2 \times 2 \times 2 \times 3$)*

Present *Explore.* Encourage students to use one colour to draw loops containing two factors, a different colour to draw loops containing three factors, and so on. Alternatively, give students extra copies of the chart so they can use one chart for loops of two factors, another chart for loops of three factors, and so on.

DURING — Explore

Ongoing Assessment: Observe and Listen

As students work, ask questions, such as:

- What is the least factor you found? *(2)* The greatest factor? *(60)*
- What pairs of factors did you loop? *(2×60, 3×40, 4×30, 5×24, 6×20, 8×15, 10×12)*
- What is the greatest number of factors you looped? *(5: $2 \times 2 \times 2 \times 3 \times 5$)*
- How could you write this product using powers? *($2^3 \times 3 \times 5$)*
- How many different groups of three factors did you find? *(8: $2 \times 2 \times 30$, $2 \times 3 \times 20$, $2 \times 4 \times 15$, $2 \times 5 \times 12$, $2 \times 6 \times 10$, $3 \times 4 \times 10$, $3 \times 5 \times 8$, $4 \times 5 \times 6$)*

Connect

...osite number has more than two factors. A prime number has exactly two factors: itself and 1.

All numbers, except 1, can be written as the product of two different factors.
The number 36 can be written as: 1×36, 2×18, 3×12, 4×9, 6×6
36 can also be written as the product of three factors:
for example, $2 \times 2 \times 9$, $2 \times 3 \times 6$
And, as the product of four factors: $2 \times 2 \times 3 \times 3$
Each of these four factors is a prime number.
So, we say that $2 \times 2 \times 3 \times 3$ is a product of prime factors, or a **prime factorization** of 36.

The prime factors of 36 are 2 and 3.

Any composite number can be written as a product of prime factors.
For example, to write 144 as a product of prime factors, begin with 12×12.
Continue to factor 12×12 until all the factors are prime numbers.

$$12 \times 12 = (4 \times 3) \times (4 \times 3)$$
$$= (2 \times 2 \times 3) \times (2 \times 2 \times 3)$$
$$= 2 \times 2 \times 2 \times 2 \times 3 \times 3$$

The prime factors of 144 are 2 and 3.

Use powers to write the prime factorization a simpler way:
$144 = 2^4 \times 3^2$

Another method to find the prime factors is to divide by prime numbers.

Example 1

Find the prime factorization of 200.

Solution

Divide 200 by its least prime factor, which is 2.

2 ⌊ 200	Keep dividing by 2 until the quotient is an odd number.
2 ⌊ 100	
2 ⌊ 50	
5 ⌊ 25	Neither 2 nor 3 is a factor of 25.
5 ⌊ 5	So, divide by the next prime factor, 5.
1	Continue to divide by prime factors until the quotient is 1.

All the divisors are the prime factors of 200.

$$200 = 2 \times 2 \times 2 \times 5 \times 5$$
$$= 2^3 \times 5^2$$

The prime factors of 200 are 2 and 5.

1.2 Prime Factors 15

REACHING ALL LEARNERS

Alternative Explore

Have students write each even number from 30 to 50 as the product of different numbers of factors. Share the results with the class. Identify the prime factorization of each number.

Early Finishers

Have students find a number greater than 100 that is the product of exactly 2 different prime numbers. What is the least number they can find?
(*Answer*: $2 \times 53 = 106$)
Repeat for 3, 4, 5, and 6 prime numbers.
(*Answers*: *102, 210, 2310, 30 030*)

Common Misconceptions

➤ Students often confuse prime factorization and finding the prime factors of a number.

How to Help: Emphasize that finding prime factors involves listing the prime numbers that are factors; prime factorization is writing a product of prime numbers.
Have students write 54 as the product of its prime factors (2×3^3), then list the prime factors (2, 3).
Repeat for 72: $72 = 2^3 \times 3^2$; 2, 3
54 and 72 have the same prime factors (2, 3) but different prime factorizations.

- How many different groups of four factors did you find?
(*4:* $2 \times 2 \times 2 \times 15$, $2 \times 2 \times 3 \times 10$, $2 \times 2 \times 5 \times 6$, $2 \times 3 \times 4 \times 5$)
- Which groups of factors could be written using powers?
($2 \times 2 \times 2 \times 15 = 2^3 \times 15$, $2 \times 2 \times 3 \times 10 = 2^2 \times 3 \times 10$, $2 \times 2 \times 5 \times 6 = 2^2 \times 5 \times 6$)

AFTER Connect

Invite students to share their solutions on an overhead transparency of the factor square. List all the solutions on the board. Look for combinations that involve 3 or more prime numbers.

Review the meanings of prime and composite numbers, LCM, and GCF.

Ask:

- What do you know about prime numbers?
(*All prime numbers are odd except for 2, which is the only even prime number. The number 1 is neither composite nor prime.*)
- What is the least 2-digit prime number? (*11*)
The greatest 2-digit prime number? (*97*)
- What are the first 5 prime numbers?
(*2, 3, 5, 7, 11*)
- What is the least number that is the product of 3 of these factors?
($2 \times 2 \times 2 = 8$)
The greatest number?
($11 \times 11 \times 11 = 1331$)
- What is the least number that is the product of 3 different factors from this set?
($2 \times 3 \times 5 = 30$)
The greatest number?
($5 \times 7 \times 11 = 385$)

Sample Solutions

4. Find the factors of each number, then list the factors common to both numbers.
   a) 55 has factors 5 and 11. 88 has factors 2, 4, 8, 11. The common factor is 11.
   b) 48 has factors 2, 3, 4, 6, 8, 12, 16, 24, and 48. 120 has factors 2, 3, 4, 5, 6, 8, 10, 12, 15, 20, 24, 30, 40, 60, and 120. The common factors are 2, 3, 4, 6, 8, 12, and 24.
   c) 96 has factors 2, 3, 4, 6, 8, 12, 16, 24, 32, 48, and 96. 63 has factors 3, 7, 9, 21, and 63. The common factor is 3.
   d) 125 has factors 5, 25, and 125. 400 has factors 2, 4, 5, 8, 10, 16, 20, 25, 40, 50, 80, 100, 200, and 400. The common factors are 5 and 25.
5. Write each pair of numbers as a product of prime factors. List the factors that are common to both numbers, then list the factors that are unique to each number. Find the product of these numbers. This is the lowest common multiple of the numbers. This number multiplied by 2 and by 3 gives the three lowest common multiples.
   a) LCM = $2^4 \times 3 \times 7 = 336$; the next two multiples are $336 \times 2 = 672$ and $336 \times 3 = 1008$.
   b) LCM = $2^5 \times 3^2 = 288$; the next two multiples are $288 \times 2 = 576$ and $288 \times 3 = 864$.
   c) LCM = $2^3 \times 7 \times 11 = 616$; the next two multiples are $616 \times 2 = 1232$ and $616 \times 3 = 1848$.
   d) LCM = $2^2 \times 3^2 \times 7 = 252$; the next two multiples are $252 \times 2 = 504$ and $252 \times 3 = 756$.

We can use prime factors to find common factors and common multiples.

Example 2

a) Find all the common factors of 18 and 24.
b) Find the first 3 common multiples of 18 and 24.

Solution

The greatest common factor of 18 and 24 is 6.

a) Write each number as a product of its prime factors. Identify common factors.

$18 = 2 \times 3 \times 3$ $\qquad$ $24 = 2 \times 2 \times 2 \times 3$

common factors

The common factors are 2, 3; and $2 \times 3 = 6$.

Note that 2 and 3 are prime common factors, and 6 is a composite common factor.

The first common multiple is called the lowest common multiple.

b) Use the prime factors from part a.
The first common multiple is the product of all the prime factors, but the common factors are only included once.

common factors

$18 = 2 \times 3 \times 3$ $\qquad$ $24 = 2 \times 2 \times 2 \times 3$

remaining factors

The first common multiple is the product of the common factors and the remaining factors.
That is: $2 \times 3 \times 3 \times 2 \times 2 = 6 \times 12 = 72$

common factors $\qquad$ remaining factors

The second common multiple is: $72 \times 2 = 144$
The third common multiple is: $72 \times 3 = 216$

Since 1 is a factor of all numbers, when we list factors or common factors we do not need to include 1.

16 UNIT 1: Numbers, Variables, and Equations

Review *Connect* and a logical process for finding the prime factors of a number, then writing the prime factorization of that number.

Students might benefit from a review of these divisibility rules. A number is divisible by:
- 2 if the number is even
- 3 if the sum of its digits is divisible by 3
- 4 if the number represented by the last 2 digits is divisible by 4
- 5 if the last digit is 0 or 5
- 6 if the number is divisible by 2 and 3
- 8 if the number represented by the last 3 digits is divisible by 8
- 9 if the sum of the digits is divisible by 9
- 10 if the last digit is 0

After *Example 2*, check students' understanding of common factors and common multiples. Ask:
- What do we mean by the common factors of 2 numbers?
  (*Those factors that occur in both numbers*)
- What do we mean by the greatest common factor of 2 numbers?
  (*The greatest number that is a factor of both numbers*)
- What is true about the greatest common factor of two numbers?
  (*It is always equal to, or less than, the lesser of the two numbers.*)
- What do we mean by a common multiple of 2 numbers?
  (*Any number that has both numbers as factors*)
- What do we mean by the lowest common multiple of 2 numbers?
  (*The least number that can be divided exactly by both the given numbers*)
- What is true about the lowest common multiple of 2 numbers?
  (*It is always equal to, or greater than, the greater of the two given numbers.*)

Since several *Practice* questions require students to find the lowest common multiple of 3

Practice

1. Write each product as a number in standard form.
   a) $2^2 \times 3^2$ 36 b) $7^2 \times 2^3$ 392 c) $5^2 \times 3^3$ 675 d) $2^2 \times 3^2 \times 5$ 180
   e) $2^7 \times 3$ 384 f) 7×3^4 567 g) $3^2 \times 7^2$ 441 h) $10^2 \times 7$ 700
2. List the prime factors of each number.
   a) 21 3, 7 b) 14 2, 7 c) 100 2, 5 d) 125 5
   e) 19 19 f) 50 2, 5 g) 77 7, 11 h) 96 2, 3
3. Write each number as a product of prime factors. Use exponents where possible.
   a) 48 $2^4 \times 3$ b) 63 $3^2 \times 7$ c) 400 $2^4 \times 5^2$ d) 16 2^4
   e) 120 $2^3 \times 3 \times 5$ f) 55 5×11 g) 36 $2^2 \times 3^2$ h) 88 $2^3 \times 11$
4. Use the prime factors from questions 2 and 3. Find all the common factors of each pair of numbers.
   a) 55, 88 b) 48, 120 c) 96, 63 d) 125, 400
5. Use the prime factors from questions 2 and 3. Find the first 3 common multiples of each pair of numbers.
   a) 16, 21 b) 36, 96 c) 77, 88 d) 36, 63
6. A number has 2, 3, and 5 as factors.
   a) Which is the least possible number? 30
   b) Find two more numbers with these factors.
7. According to a student, the least number that has 2, 3, 4, and 5 as factors can be found by multiplying: $2 \times 3 \times 4 \times 5$
   Is the student correct? Explain.
8. Can you find the greatest number with factors 11, 23, and 37? Explain.
9. a) Find the least number with the factors 14, 27, and 38.
   b) Write the prime factorization of this number.
   $7182 = 2 \times 3^3 \times 7 \times 19$
10. a) Write a four-digit number that is divisible by 5 and 7. Explain how you did it.
    b) Write the prime factorization of this number.

Number Strategies

The six-digit number 678 □44 is divisible by 3. Which digits could go in the hundreds place? Explain your strategy.
1, 4, and 7

1.2 Prime Factors 17

6. b) Any multiples of 30 will have 2, 3, and 5 as factors; such as 90 and 180.
7. No. If 4 is a factor, then 2 is also a factor.
8. Since 11, 23, and 37 are prime numbers, the least number with these factors is $11 \times 23 \times 37 = 9361$. You can always find a greater number by multiplying 9361 by 2, by 3, by 4, or by any greater number.
9. a) Write the numbers as products of prime factors, then find the lowest common multiple of the three numbers.
10. a) There are many answers to this question. If the number is divisible by 5 and 7, then it has to be divisible by 35. Any four-digit number that is a multiple of 35 is acceptable. The least number is 1015 (35×29); the greatest number is 9975 (35×285).
    b) For example: $1015 = 5 \times 7 \times 29$
11. a) $21 = 3 \times 7$ and $77 = 7 \times 11$, so the least number is $3 \times 7 \times 11 = 231$.
    b) Other factors are the prime factors of the given factors, and factors formed by multiplying pairs of prime factors: 3, 7, 11, 33
12. a) The number is $4 \times 25 \times 7 = 100 \times 7 = 700$
    b) The factors are 2, 5, and 7, and all possible products of 2, 2, 5, 5, and 7.
    Multiply pairs of factors:
    $2 \times 2 = 4$; $2 \times 5 = 10$; $2 \times 7 = 14$; $5 \times 5 = 25$; $5 \times 7 = 35$
    Multiply sets of 3 factors:
    $2 \times 2 \times 5 = 20$; $2 \times 2 \times 7 = 28$; $2 \times 5 \times 5 = 50$;

(Sample Solutions continue below.)

numbers, show students how to do this with 3 numbers such as 15, 28, and 32.

$15 = 3 \times 5$ $28 = 2 \times 2 \times 7$

$32 = 2 \times 2 \times 2 \times 2 \times 2$

The lowest common multiple is:

$2 \times 2 \times 2 \times 2 \times 2 \times 3 \times 5 \times 7 = 3360$

Practice

Encourage students to show their work for finding the prime factors of a number.

Assessment Focus: Question 12

Students should know to multiply $2 \times 2 \times 5 \times 5 \times 7$ to get the number 700.

To find all the factors of 700, the prime factors are multiplied in different sets of 2, 3, and 4 factors. Students may notice that factors can be obtained in pairs. As each factor is found, another factor can be obtained by dividing 700 by that factor.

(Sample Solutions, continued)

$2 \times 5 \times 7 = 70$; $5 \times 5 \times 7 = 175$
Multiply sets of 4 factors:
$2 \times 2 \times 5 \times 5 = 100$; $2 \times 2 \times 5 \times 7 = 140$; $2 \times 5 \times 5 \times 7 = 350$
Multiply all 5 factors:
$2 \times 2 \times 5 \times 5 \times 7 = 700$

13. a) Since a perfect square is the product of two equal numbers, the prime factors of a perfect square will always occur in pairs. That is, if there is a certain prime factor in one of the numbers, it will also be in the other number. For example: 16 has 4 prime factors: $2 \times 2 \times 2 \times 2$; 9 has 2 prime factors: 3×3; 64 has 6 prime factors; $2 \times 2 \times 2 \times 2 \times 2 \times 2$; 2, 4, and 6 are all even numbers.
    b) $3025 = 5 \times 5 \times 11 \times 11 = 5^2 \times 11^2$; since 3025 has an even number of each prime factor, 3025 is a perfect square.
14. 4 is not a prime number.
    The correct answer is $4^2 \times 4^2 = 4 \times 4 \times 4 \times 4 = 2 \times 2 \times 2 \times 2 \times 2 \times 2 \times 2 \times 2 = 2^8$.
15. The least number with 4 different prime factors is $2 \times 3 \times 5 \times 7 = 210$.

16. Doors with square numbers will be open:
1, 4, 9, 16, 25, 36, 49, 64, 81, and 100.
Most doors will change position an even number of times, and so the lockers will end up closed. The exceptions are the lockers with square numbers. Their doors will change position an odd number of times, so the lockers will end up open.

REFLECT: For the prime factorization of a number, all its factors must be prime numbers. For example, $24 = 2 \times 2 \times 2 \times 3$ is the prime factorization while $24 = 2 \times 2 \times 6$ is not a prime factorization, since 6 is not prime.

Number Strategies

Guess and check is possible but time consuming. Use the divisibility rule for 3 (if the sum of the digits is divisible by 3, the number is divisible by 3). The sum of 6 + 7 + 8 + 4 + 4 is 29. To make a multiple of 3, add 1 (to get 30), add 4 (to get 33), or add 7 (to get 36). So, 1, 4, and 7 are possible digits.

Assignment Guidelines

If your students do not have time to complete all the *Practice* questions on pages 17 and 18, these questions provide minimum curriculum coverage: 2, 3, 4, 6, 9, 11, 12, *Reflect*

To assess the 4 Achievement Chart categories listed in the curriculum document, have students complete these *Practice* questions:
Knowledge and Understanding: 3
Application: 6
Thinking: 9
Communication: 11

11. A number has 21 and 77 as factors.
a) Which is the least possible number? 231
b) Which other numbers are factors of the number in pa
Explain your reasoning. 3, 7, 11, 33

12. **Assessment Focus** The prime factorization of a number is $2^2 \times 5^2 \times 7$.
a) What is the number? 700
b) Use the prime factors to list all the factors of that number. Show your work.

13. "The total number of prime factors for a perfect square is always an even number."
a) Do you agree or disagree with this statement? Justify your answer with at least three different perfect squares. Agree
b) Use prime factors to show that 3025 is a perfect square.

14. Is $4^2 \times 4^2$ a prime factorization of 256? Explain. No

Take It Further

15. Can you find a number less than 150 that is divisible by 4 different prime numbers? Justify your answer. No

16. On graduation day, 100 Grade 8 students lined up outside the school.
As they entered the school, they passed their lockers.
The first student opened all the locker doors.
The second student closed every second locker door.
The third student changed the position of every third locker door. If the door was open, the student closed it.
If the door was closed, the student opened it.
The fourth student changed the position of every fourth locker door. This pattern continues.
Which doors are open after 100 students have entered the school?
Explain how you know.

Reflect

What makes the factorization of a number a *prime* factorization?
Use examples in your explanation.

18 UNIT 1: Numbers, Variables, and Equations

ASSESSMENT FOR LEARNING

What to Look For	What to Do
Knowledge and Understanding ✔ Students understand how to generate the prime factors and the prime factorization of a given number. ✔ Students understand how to generate common factors and common multiples of pairs of numbers. ***Communication*** ✔ Students can explain how to find the prime factors of a number. ***Application*** ✔ Students can represent composite numbers as products of their prime factors, including the use of exponents.	***Extra Support:*** Students can do the Additional Activity, *Factor Fun* (Master 1.5). Students can use Step-by-Step 2 (Master 1.10) to complete question 12. ***Extra Practice:*** Students could find the lowest common multiple for each pair of numbers in *Practice,* question 4, and the greatest common factor for each pair of numbers in *Practice,* question 5. Students can complete Extra Practice 2 (Master 1.19). ***Extension:*** Have students make a factor square for a 3-digit number of their choice. Students trade squares with a classmate, then list all possible factors of their classmate's number.

Recording and Reporting
Master 1.2 Ongoing Observations: Numbers, Variables, and Equations

Expanded Form and Scientific Notation

LESSON ORGANIZER

80–100 min

Curriculum Focus: Represent whole numbers in expanded form and scientific notation. (8m12, 8m13, 8m24)

Student Materials
- calculators

Optional
- Step-by-Step 3 (Master 1.11)
- Extra Practice 3 (Master 1.20)

Vocabulary: scientific notation

Assessment: Master 1.2 Ongoing Observations: Numbers, Variables, and Equations

Key Math Learnings

1. Numbers can be expressed in expanded form using powers of 10.
2. Numbers can be expressed in scientific notation.

1.3 Expanded Form and Scientific Notation

Focus Represent whole numbers in expanded form and scientific notation.

…id-July, 2004, the population of Canada was estimated to be 31 964 434.
…can write this number in different ways.

In expanded form:
31 964 434 = 30 000 000 + 1 000 000 + 900 000 + 60 000 + 4000 + 400 + 30 + 4
Using powers of 10 in this expanded form:
First, write each number as a product of a whole number and a power of 10:
31 964 434 = (3 × 10 000 000) + (1 × 1 000 000) + (9 × 100 000) + (6 × 10 000) + (4 × 1000) + (4 × 100) + (3 × 10) + 4
Then, write each power of 10 in exponent form:
$31\ 964\ 434 = 3 \times 10^7 + 1 \times 10^6 + 9 \times 10^5 + 6 \times 10^4 + 4 \times 10^3 + 4 \times 10^2 + 3 \times 10^1 + 4$

Explore

Work with a partner.
Use a calculator if you need to.
Here are some headlines relating to the Internet in 2004.

Experts predict e-commerce will top $300 000 000 000

1 000 000 000 people will be connected to the Internet by 2005

In 2000, Canadian adolescents surfed an average of 197 hours

Connected schools in Canada reach 15 035

For each headline:
- Write each number in expanded form using powers of 10.
- Write each number as a product of two factors, where one factor is a power of 10.

Reflect & Share

Compare your results with those of another pair of classmates.
Talk about the different ways you wrote factors for each product.
How many ways could you do this for each number?
Was each expression correct? How could you check?

1.3 Expanded Form and Scientific Notation 19

BEFORE Get Started

If you have not done so already, review the *Skills You'll Need: Understanding Powers of 10*, on page 7.

Write the population of Canada, 31 964 434, on a place-value chart.

Ten millions	Millions	Hundred thousands	Ten thousands	Thousands	Hundreds	Tens	Ones
3	1	9	6	4	4	3	4

Review the different ways of writing expanded form, as on page 19 of the Student Book.

Repeat the process for a number such as 572 384.

Have a student write the number in a place-value chart on the board, then in standard form, using powers of 10 and exponents.

Present *Explore.*

DURING Explore

Ongoing Assessment: Observe and Listen

As students work, ask questions, such as:
- What is e-commerce?
  (*Buying and selling on the Internet*)
- How do you read this number? (Point to $300 000 000 000.)
  (*The number is three hundred thousand million, or three hundred billion.*)
- What is that number in expanded form?
  (3×10^{11})
- How do you read this number? (Point to 2005.)
  (*The number is two thousand five.*)
- What is that number in expanded form?
  (*2000 + 5, or* $2 \times 1000 + 5$, *or* $2 \times 10^3 + 5$)
- How could you write 2005 as a product with one factor of 10?
  ($2005 \div 10 = 200.5$, *so I could write 2005 as* 200.5×10.)

REACHING ALL LEARNERS

Alternative Explore

Materials: newspapers and magazines

Have students look through newspapers and magazines for large numbers. They use these numbers to complete the *Explore* on page 19.

Early Finishers

Have students round the estimated populations in *Lesson 1.1, Explore*, page 9, to the nearest million, then write each number in scientific notation.

Common Misconceptions

➤ Students have difficulty writing a number in scientific notation.

How to Help: Have students use a place-value chart with headings that include powers of 10, as in *Skills You'll Need*, page 7. They can extend the chart to the right, as necessary, to include the ones and tenths columns, and so on. Students write a number in the chart. The column heading of the first digit shows the power of 10 for scientific notation. The decimal point is placed between the first and second digits. For example, for 672 000:

HTh	TTh	Th	H	T	O	t
10^5	10^4	10^3	10^2	10^1		
6	7	2	0	0	0 •	

6.72×10^5

ESL Strategies

Students from other countries may have learned that 1 billion is 1 million million. Ensure they understand that 1 billion in Canada is 1 000 000 000, and 1 million million is 1 trillion: 1 000 000 000 000.

Connect

In *Lesson 1.1*, you learned that the U.S. box office revenue for movie *Titanic* was $600 800 000.
We can write large numbers like this in scientific notation.

A number expressed in **scientific notation** is written as a product of two factors:

- One factor is a number greater than or equal to 1, and less than 10.
- The other factor is a power of 10.

For example,

41	=	4.1×10^1	These numbers are written in scientific notation.
410	=	4.10×10^2	
4105	=	4.105×10^3	
41 057	=	4.1057×10^4	
410 578	=	$4.105\ 78 \times 10^5$	

The number of digits in the standard form of the number is 1 more than the exponent in scientific notation.

The exponent in the power of 10 indicates the number of places to the position of the decimal point when the number is written in standard form.

$4.105\ 78 \times 10^5 = 410\ 578.$

5 places

Example

1 barrel of oil is 159 L.

Norman Wells, Northwest Territories, is the fourth largest producing oil field in Canada. Its estimated reserves are 140 million barrels of oil. Write this number in scientific notation.

Solution

Write 140 million as 140 000 000.
For the factor greater than 1 and less than 10, mark a decimal point after the first digit:
1.40 000 000, or 1.4 ← Delete the zeros that indicate place value at the right of the number.

There are 9 digits in 140 000 000.
The exponent in the power of 10 is 1 less than 9, which is 8.
$140\ 000\ 000 = 1.4 \times 10^8$

- How could you write 2005 as a product with one factor of 100? (*$2005 \div 100 = 20.05$, so $2005 = 20.05 \times 100$, or 20.05×10^2*) As a product with one factor of 1000? (*$2005 = 2.005 \times 1000$, or 2.005×10^3*)
- How many different ways could you write 15 035 as a product of a number and a power of 10? (*15 035 is 1503.5×10, or 150.35×10^2, or 15.035×10^3, or 1.5035×10^4.*)
- How could you check that each expression does equal 15 035? (*Use a calculator.*)

AFTER Connect

Have student volunteers write their numbers on the board. Here are the numbers in standard and expanded forms:

$1\ 000\ 000\ 000 = 1 \times 10^9$
$2000 = 2 \times 10^3$
$197 = 1 \times 10^2 + 9 \times 10 + 7$
$15\ 035 = 1 \times 10^4 + 5 \times 10^3 + 3 \times 10 + 5$

Point out that the numbers 1×10^4, 1×10^9, and 2×10^3 are in scientific notation.

Use these examples to explain how a number is written in scientific notation.

If these numbers were not provided by the students, write them on the board:

2.005×10^3; 1.97×10^2; 1.5035×10^4, then have students explain how they know the numbers are in scientific notation.

Use *Connect* for further examples of writing a number in scientific notation. Point out that $41 = 4.1 \times 10$, which is written as 4.1×10^1. Make sure students understand that 10 can be written as 10^1.

Show students how to write a number, such as 4.81×10^6, in standard form. To multiply by 10^6, each digit is moved 6 places to the left on a place-value chart.

The *Example* illustrates that, when a large number is written in scientific notation, it is easier to read.
Calculators display scientific notation in different ways.
Key in: 1230000 [×] 1230000 [ENTER =] to see how your calculator displays 1.5129×10^{12}.

Practice

Calculator Skills

What is the greatest power with a base of 4 and a value less than 1000? 4^4

What is the greatest power with an exponent of 4 and a value less than 1000? 5^4

1. Write each number in expanded form using powers of 10. How could you check your answer?

a) 834 000 b) 98 977 183
c) 7 000 010 d) 23 232

2. Which is greater? Explain.

a) $4 \times 10^3 + 6 \times 10^2 + 6 \times 10^1 + 7$ or 4327
b) $2 \times 10^4 + 4 \times 10^3 + 2 \times 10^2 + 4 \times 10^1$ or 2432
c) $7 \times 10^7 + 7 \times 10^3$ or 777 777

3. For each power of 10, write the exponent that makes each statement true. How do you know?

a) $7000 = 7 \times 10^?$ 3 b) $400\,000 = 4 \times 10^?$ 5
c) $2\,890\,000 = 2.89 \times 10^?$ 6 d) $20\,000 = 2 \times 10^?$ 4
e) $704 = 7.04 \times 10^?$ 2 f) $71 = 7.1 \times 10^?$ 1

4. Write each number in scientific notation. Check with a calculator.

a) 1 532 000 b) 31 000
c) 4 600 000 000 d) 150
e) 6 000 100 f) 147 032

5. Order the numbers in each set from least to greatest.

a) 1.6×10^3, 1616, 6.1×10^2, 616
b) 2.453×10^6, 248 555, 2.4531×10^6, 2 453 101

6. Look at a number in scientific notation.
Why is the exponent in the power of 10 one less than the number of digits in the number?
Use a place-value chart or another way to show why this is true.

1.3 Expanded Form and Scientific Notation 21

Sample Solutions

1. a) $8 \times 10^5 + 3 \times 10^4 + 4 \times 10^3$
   b) $9 \times 10^7 + 8 \times 10^6 + 9 \times 10^5 + 7 \times 10^4 + 7 \times 10^3 + 1 \times 10^2 + 8 \times 10^1 + 3$
   c) $7 \times 10^6 + 1 \times 10^1$
   d) $2 \times 10^4 + 3 \times 10^3 + 2 \times 10^2 + 3 \times 10^1 + 2$
2. Write the first number in standard form, then compare.
   a) 4667 and 4327: hundreds digit in first number is greater. So, $4 \times 10^3 + 6 \times 10^2 + 6 \times 10^1 + 7$ is greater.
   b) 24 240 and 2432: first number is greater. $2 \times 10^4 + 4 \times 10^3 + 2 \times 10^2 + 4 \times 10^1$ is greater.
   c) 70 007 000 and 777 777: first number is greater. So, $7 \times 10^7 + 7 \times 10^3$ is greater.
4. a) 1.532×10^6 b) 3.1×10^4 c) 4.6×10^9
   d) 1.5×10^2 e) 6.0001×10^6 f) $1.470\,32 \times 10^5$
5. Write the numbers in each set in standard form, then compare.
   a) 610, 616, 1600, 1616: 6.1×10^2, 616, 1.6×10^3, 1616
   b) 248 555, 2 453 000, 2 453 100, 2 453 101: 248 555, 2.453×10^6, 2.4531×10^6, 2 453 101
6. For example: The number has to be divided by the power of 10 that reduces the number to a number less than 10 but greater than 1. This means the exponent of the power of 10 has to be 1 less than the number of digits in the number.
7. Multiply 12 756 by 4, then round the answer: 5.1024×10^4 km, or about 5.1×10^4 km
9. a) No. The number 12.756 is greater than 10, so the number is not in scientific notation. To write the number in scientific notation, 12.756 has to be divided by 10 and 10^3 multiplied by 10 to give 1.2756×10^4.

M	HTh	TTh	Th	H	T	O	t	h	
						4 •	8	1	4.81
4	8	1	0	0	0	0 •			4.81×10^6

Since it is tedious to draw a place-value chart each time, we move the decimal point 6 places to the right instead.

$4.81 \times 10^6 = 4\ 8\ 1\ 0\ 0\ 0\ 0$

We write zeros as place holders in the thousands to ones places.

Practice

Students should use calculators only to check their answers.

Question 1: Have students say the numbers in words, then use powers of 10. This reinforces the relationship between the numbers and powers of 10; for example, eight hundred thousand means 8×10^5.

Question 4: If the students say the number in words, they can more easily relate to the power of 10 required; for example, 1 million ... means the second factor in scientific notation will be 10^6.

Question 10: Students need to realize that since the mean of 5 numbers is 7.5×10^4, the sum of the 5 numbers must be $5 \times 7.5 \times 10^4 = 375\,000$, and the unknown fifth number can be obtained by subtracting the sum of the known numbers from the total.

Question 12b: Students should realize they have to add the populations, then convert the sum to scientific notation. It is only possible to add numbers in scientific notation if the powers of 10 are the same. For example, it is correct to add: $5.3 \times 10^3 + 1.8 \times 10^3$ to get 7.1×10^3, but to add: $5.3 \times 10^3 + 1.8 \times 10^4$ would require changing 1.8×10^4 to 18×10^3 before adding.

b) Scientific notation is a way to write and understand large numbers more easily.

10. The sum of the five numbers is $5 \times 7.5 \times 10^4 = 375\ 000$. The sum of the four numbers is 305 000. So, the missing number is $375\ 000 - 305\ 000 = 70\ 000 = 7 \times 10^4$.

11. a) The frequency of violet light is greater by 3.2×10^4 Hz.

 b) Yes, especially if the exponents are the same

12. a) New Brunswick: 7.514×10^5; Nova Scotia: 9.37×10^5; Ontario: $1.23\ 927 \times 10^7$; Quebec: 7.5428×10^6; Manitoba: 1.1703×10^6; Northwest Territories: 4.28×10^4; British Columbia: 4.1964×10^6; Prince Edward Island: 1.379×10^5; Yukon: 3.12×10^4; Alberta: 3.2019×10^6; Saskatchewan: 9.954×10^5; Newfoundland and Labrador: 5.17×10^5; Nunavut: 2.96×10^4

 c) New Brunswick, Prince Edward Island, and the Northwest Territories

 d) For example: In parts b and c, it was easier to add the numbers in standard form because the exponents were different.

13. Assuming a heart rate of 72 beats per minute and a life so far of 13 years, the number of beats would be
$72 \times 60 \times 24 \times 365 \times 13 = 491\ 961\ 600$
There will be a wide range of answers that depend on the number used for the heartbeats per minute.
491 961 600;
$4.919\ 616 \times 10^8$;
400 000 000 + 90 000 000 + 1 000 000 + 900 000 + 60 000 + 1000 + 600;

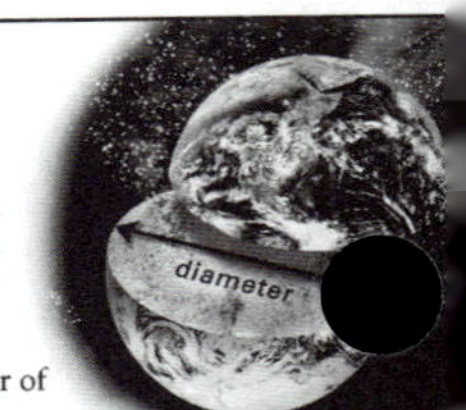

7. The diameter of Earth is 12 756 km.
The diameter of Uranus is approximately four times as great as Earth's diameter.
Write the approximate diameter of Uranus in scientific notation.
Justify your answer.

8. Here are some facts about the central nervous system.
Write the numbers that would complete the table.

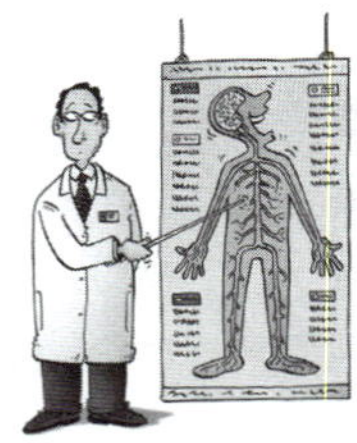

		Standard Form	Scientific Notation
a)	Number of neurons in the central nervous system	100 000 000 000	1×10^{11}
b)	Bits of information the brain is able to record in one day	8 600 000	8.6×10^6
c)	Approximate number of nerve cells in the body	30 000 000 000	3×10^{10}
d)	Average number of nerve endings per square centimetre in a human hand	208	2.08×10^2

9. **Assessment Focus**

 a) Is 12.756×10^3 in scientific notation?
 If your answer is yes, explain how you know.
 If your answer is no, how would you write the number in scientific notation?

 b) Why do we use scientific notation?

The mean of five numbers is the sum of the numbers divided by 5.

10. The mean of five numbers is 7.5×10^4.
Four of the numbers are: 50 000, 100 000, 75 000, 80 000
What is the 5th number? How do you know? 70 000 or 7 × 1

11. Different colours of light have different frequencies.
The frequency of red light is 4.3×10^{14} Hz.
The frequency of violet light is 7.5×10^{14} Hz.

The frequency of 1 Hz (one Hertz) means 1 wave per second.

 a) Which frequency is greater and by how much?

 b) Are numbers written in scientific notation easier to compare than numbers in standard form? Explain.

22 UNIT 1: Numbers, Variables, and Equations

Question 13: Students could work in pairs to measure each other's pulse, then calculate the number of heartbeats in one year, and from birth until now.

Assessment Focus: Question 9

Not every number written as a product, where one factor is a power of 10, is in scientific notation. Students should realize that since the first factor is greater than 10, the number is not in scientific notation. The first term has to be divided by 10, so the second term has to be multiplied by 10 to give an answer of 1.2756×10^4.

12. The table lists Canadian provinces and territories. It shows the year each joined Confederation, and the approximate 2004 population.

Premier Paul Okalik in Nunavut in 1999

	Date of Entry	Population
New Brunswick	1867	751 400
Nova Scotia	1867	937 000
Ontario	1867	12 392 700
Quebec	1867	7 542 800
Manitoba	1870	1 170 300
Northwest Territories	1870	42 800
British Columbia	1871	4 196 400
Prince Edward Island	1873	137 900
Yukon	1898	31 200
Alberta	1905	3 201 900
Saskatchewan	1905	995 400
Newfoundland and Labrador	1949	517 000
Nunavut	1999	29 600

a) Write each population in scientific notation.

b) Write the sum of the populations of the 4 original provinces in scientific notation. $2.162\ 39 \times 10^7$

c) Which 3 provinces or territories together have a population approximately equal to that of Nova Scotia?

d) For parts b and c, is it easier to add the numbers in standard form or in scientific notation? Explain.

Take It Further

13. Approximately how many times has your heart beaten in your lifetime? Give your answer in as many different forms as possible. Explain how you solved this problem.

14. Use only the operations of multiplication or division. Write 0.004 32 in terms of a number between 1 and 10, and a power of 10. $4.32 \div 10^3$

Reflect

How can you tell if a number is written in scientific notation? Give examples.

$4 \times 10^8 + 9 \times 10^7 + 1 \times 10^6 + 9 \times 10^5 + 6 \times 10^4 + 1 \times 10^3 + 6 \times 10^2$

REFLECT: For a number to be in scientific notation, it must be a product of 2 factors. The first factor must be greater than or equal to 1, but less than 10; and the second factor must be a power of 10. For example, 3.8×10^5 is in scientific notation. 38.1×10^5 is not in scientific notation, because the first factor is greater than 10.

Calculator Skills

□ has to be such that $4^{□}$ is less than 1000. Find □ by guess and check. $4^4 = 256$, $4^5 = 1024$, so 4^4 is the greatest power.
n has to be such that n^4 is less than 1000. Use guess and check. $5^4 = 625$, $6^4 = 1296$, so 5^4 is the greatest power.

Assignment Guidelines

If your students do not have time to complete all the *Practice* questions on pages 21, 22, and 23, these questions provide minimum curriculum coverage: 1, 3, 4, 6, 8, 10, 11, *Reflect*

To assess the 4 Achievement Chart categories listed in the curriculum document, have students complete these *Practice* questions:
Knowledge and Understanding: 4
Communication: 6
Application: 10
Thinking: 11

ASSESSMENT FOR LEARNING

What to Look For

Knowledge and Understanding

- ✔ Students recognize a number written in expanded form.
- ✔ Students recognize a number written in scientific notation.

Communication

- ✔ Students can explain how to convert a number from standard form to scientific notation, and vice versa.

Application

- ✔ Students can write numbers in expanded form using powers of 10.
- ✔ Students can write numbers in scientific notation.

What to Do

Extra Support: Students who have difficulty writing numbers in expanded form could write each number in a place-value chart, to help recognize the powers of 10.
Students can use Step-by-Step 3 (Master 1.11) to complete question 9.

Extra Practice: Students can do the Additional Activity, *Size It Up* (Master 1.6).
Students can complete Extra Practice 3 (Master 1.20).

Extension: Have students investigate ways to add or multiply numbers in scientific notation; for example, $(3 \times 10^4) + (2 \times 10^5)$ or $(3 \times 10^4) \times (2 \times 10^5)$.

Recording and Reporting

Master 1.2 Ongoing Observations: Numbers, Variables, and Equations

MID-UNIT REVIEW

LESSON ORGANIZER

Student Materials

- calculators

Assessment: Master 1.1 Unit Rubric: Numbers, Variables, and Equations
Master 1.4 Unit Summary: Numbers, Variables, and Equations

Mid-Unit Review

LESSON

1.1 **1.** Here is a list of the top 10 all-time point scorers in NHL history.

Player	Goals	Assists	Total Points
Gretzky	894	1963	2857
Messier	694	1193	1887
Howe	801	1049	1850
Francis	549	1249	1798
Dionne	731	1040	1771
Yzerman	678	1043	1721
Lemieux	683	1018	1701
Esposito	717	873	1590
Bourque	410	1169	1579
Coffey	396	1135	1531

a) Estimate the total number of goals scored by the top ten players. Explain how you estimated.
b) Which players have about twice as many assists as goals? Explain.
c) Write your own problem about the data. Solve your problem and describe how you solved it.

1.2 **2.** Write each number as a product of prime factors. Use exponents where possible.
a) 444 b) 162
c) 102 d) 1225

3. Find the first 2 common multiples of each pair of numbers.
135, 270 a) 15, 27 b) 16, 28 112, 224
288, 576 c) 18, 32 d) 20, 36 180, 360

4. Find the common factors of each pair of numbers.
a) 100, 120 b) 56, 80
c) 72, 27 d) 48, 92

5. a) Why is 2^3 a prime factorization of a number?
b) Why is 4^3 not a prime factorization of a number?

6. Write each number in standard form. Then, order the numbers from least to greatest.
$2^4 \times 5^2$, $5^2 \times 11$,
$3^2 \times 7 \times 11$,
$2^5 \times 7 \times 13^2$

7. a) Is it possible that 3 consecutive whole numbers can be prime factors? Explain. No
b) Is it possible that 2 consecutive whole numbers can be prime factors? Explain. Yes

1.3 **8.** Write each number in expanded form using powers of 10.
a) 806 087 137 b) 20 020 220

9. Write each number in scientific notation.
a) 5 600 000 b) 773 291
c) 9 200 000 000 d) 62

10. Which numbers are in scientific notation? Explain how you know.
a) 66.8×10^5 (b) 4.163×10^4)
c) 73×10^7 (d) 2×10^8)

24 UNIT 1: Numbers, Variables, and Equations

Sample Solutions

1. a) For example: 6550. I rounded each number to the nearest ten before adding.
   b) Gretzky: $900 \times 2 = 1800$, which is close to 1963; Francis: $550 \times 2 = 1100$, which is close to 1249
   c) For example: "The sum of the goals of two players is 8 less than the assists of a third player. Who are the 3 players?" Answer: Esposito: 717; Bourque: 410; and Coffey: 1135
2. a) $2^2 \times 3 \times 37$ b) 2×3^4
   c) $2 \times 3 \times 17$ d) $5^2 \times 7^2$
3. a) $15 = 3 \times 5$, $27 = 3 \times 3 \times 3$
   The first common multiple is the product of the common factors and the remaining factors:
   $3 \times 3 \times 3 \times 5 = 135$. The second common multiple is: $135 \times 2 = 270$
   b) $16 = 2 \times 2 \times 2 \times 2$; $28 = 2 \times 2 \times 7$
   The first common multiple is:
   $2 \times 2 \times 2 \times 2 \times 7 = 112$
   The second common multiple is: $112 \times 2 = 224$
   c) $18 = 2 \times 3 \times 3$; $32 = 2 \times 2 \times 2 \times 2 \times 2$
   The first common multiple is:
   $2 \times 2 \times 2 \times 2 \times 2 \times 3 \times 3 = 288$
   The second common multiple is: $288 \times 2 = 576$
   d) $20 = 2 \times 2 \times 5$; $36 = 2 \times 2 \times 3 \times 3$
   The first common multiple is:
   $2 \times 2 \times 3 \times 3 \times 5 = 180$
   The second common multiple is: $180 \times 2 = 360$
4. a) 2, 4, 5, 10, 20 b) 2, 4, 8
   c) 3, 9 d) 2, 4
5. a) 2^3 is a prime factorization of a number because 2^3 is a product of 2s, and 2 is a prime number.
   b) 4^3 is not a prime factorization of a number because 4 is not a prime number.
6. 400, 275, 693, 37 856; from least to greatest: 275, 400, 693, 37 856
7. a) For example: No. Two is the only even prime number. Three consecutive whole numbers will have at least one even number other than 2.
   b) Yes. Any set of two consecutive whole numbers will contain an odd number and an even number. The only even prime number is 2. So, the only 2 consecutive whole numbers that can be prime factors are 2 and 3.
8. a) $8 \times 10^8 + 6 \times 10^6 + 8 \times 10^4 + 7 \times 10^3 + 1 \times 10^2 + 3 \times 10^1 + 7$
   b) $2 \times 10^7 + 2 \times 10^4 + 2 \times 10^2 + 2 \times 10^1$
9. a) 5.6×10^6 b) $7.732\ 91 \times 10^5$
   c) 9.2×10^9 d) 6.2×10^1
10. b and d
    66.8×10^5 is not in scientific notation because the first factor is greater than 10.
    4.163×10^4 is in scientific notation because the first factor is greater than or equal to 1, and less than 10, and the second factor is a power of 10.
    73×10^7 is not in scientific notation because the first factor is greater than 10.
    2×10^8 is in scientific notation because the first factor is greater than or equal to 1, and less than 10, and the second factor is a power of 10.

1.4 Order of Operations

Focus Understand the order of operations with brackets and exponents.

Explore

Work on your own.
Two students evaluated this expression: $(3 + 5.4) + 5.2 \times 10^2$

Jinni did this:	Todd did this:
$(3 + 5.4) + 5.2 \times 10^2$	$(3 + 5.4) + 5.2 \times 10^2$
$= 8.4 + 5.2 \times 10^2$	$= 8.4 + 5.2 \times 10^2$
$= 13.6 \times 10^2$	$= 8.4 + 52^2$
$= 13.6 \times 100$	$= 8.4 + 2704$
$= 1360$	$= 2712.4$

Which student is correct?
Or, are the evaluations of both students incorrect?
If so, how was each evaluation incorrect?
How would you evaluate the expression?
Show your work.

Reflect & Share

Compare your answer to this problem with that of another student.
Who is correct: Jinni, Todd, your classmate, or you?
Explain how you know.

Connect

To avoid getting different answers when we evaluate an expression, mathematicians have agreed on the order in which operations should be performed:

- Do the operations in brackets.
- Do the exponents.
- Multiply and divide, in order, from left to right.
- Add and subtract, in order, from left to right.

So, when this order is followed, everyone should get the same answer.

1.4 Order of Operations 25

Order of Operations

LESSON ORGANIZER (80–100 min)

Curriculum Focus: Understand the order of operations with brackets and exponents. (8m23, 8m62)

Student Materials
- calculators

Optional
- Step-by-Step 4 (Master 1.12)
- Extra Practice 4 (Master 1.21)

Vocabulary: order of operations

Assessment: Master 1.2 Ongoing Observations: Numbers, Variables, and Equations

Key Math Learning

The order of operations is an arbitrary rule to ensure that operations in expressions are calculated the same way.

BEFORE — Get Started

On the board, randomly write these words: Brackets, Add, Divide, Multiply, and Subtract.

Ask students what the words mean and how they can put them in a logical order. Have students explain their order and give examples of expressions for other students to evaluate. Challenge the students to evaluate $24 + 3 \times (18 - 12 \div 3)$.
(*Answer:* $24 + 3 \times (18 - 4) = 24 + 3 \times 14 = 24 + 42 = 66$)

Present *Explore.*

DURING — Explore

Ongoing Assessment: Observe and Listen

As students work, ask questions, such as:

- Do you think Jinni is correct? Explain.
  (*She is correct in the first line where she adds the numbers in the brackets. However, she is wrong when she adds 8.4 and 5.2 before multiplying by* 10^2*. She should have multiplied 5.2 by* 10^2 *before adding 8.4.*)
- Do you think Todd is correct? Explain.
  (*He is correct in the first line when he adds the numbers in the brackets. However, he is wrong in writing* 5.2×10^2 *as* 52^2*. He should have squared 10 to get 100 before multiplying by 5.2.*)
- What is the correct solution?
  (*The correct solution is:* $(3 + 5.4) + 5.2 \times 10^2 = 8.4 + 5.2 \times 10^2 = 8.4 + 5.2 \times 100 = 8.4 + 520 = 528.4$)

REACHING ALL LEARNERS

Early Finishers

Have students make up a question similar to those in question 8. Students write 4 different expressions, then evaluate each expression, and order them from greatest to least.

Common Misconceptions

➤ Students confuse expressions such as $4 + 5^2$ and $(4 + 5)^2$.

How to Help: Have students write the power as a product and insert brackets around the product: $4 + 5^2 = 4 + (5 \times 5)$
Alternatively, insert brackets around the power: $4 + 5^2 = 4 + (5^2)$

Sample Solutions

2. c) $18.3 - (7.2 - 3.5)^2 = 18.3 - (3.7)^2 = 18.3 - 13.69 = 4.61$

d) $(22.3 + 1.1)^2 - (22.3 - 1.1)^2 = (23.4)^2 - (21.2)^2 = 547.56 - 449.44 = 98.12$

e) $10.8 + 6.3^2 - 1.2 \times 2.1 = 10.8 + 39.69 - 2.52 = 47.97$

f) $20.8 \div 1.3 \times (14.8 + 17.2) = 20.8 \div 1.3 \times 32 = 16 \times 32 = 512$

3. $3 \times \$24.99 + 2 \times \$14.99 = \$104.95$

5. a) $3 + 8.8 \times 0.5 - 4.9 \times (0.5)^2 = 3 + 4.4 - 4.9 \times 0.25 = 3 + 4.4 - 1.225 = 6.175$

Example 1

Evaluate.
$15.5^2 - 2.4 \times (3.1 + 4.7)^2$

Solution

Use a calculator.
Do the operation in brackets first.

$15.5^2 - 2.4 \times (3.1 + 4.7)^2$
$= 15.5^2 - 2.4 \times (7.8)^2$ Deal with the exponents.
$= 240.25 - 2.4 \times 60.84$ Then multiply.
$= 240.25 - 146.016$ Then subtract.
$= 94.234$

If you have a scientific calculator, you can input the expression in *Example 1* directly.
To evaluate $15.5^2 - 2.4 \times (3.1 + 4.7)^2$, key in:
15.5 [x^2] [−] 2.4 [×] [(] 3.1 [+] 4.7 [)] [x^2] [ENTER] to display 94.234

We also use the order of operations when we evaluate an algebraic expression by substituting for the variable.

Example 2

The power, in watts (W), supplied to a circuit by a 9-V battery is expressed as $9c - 0.5c^2$, where c is the current in amperes (A).
Find the power supplied when the current is 8 A.

Solution

Substitute $c = 8$.
$9c - 0.5c^2 = 9(8) - 0.5(8)^2$
Deal with the exponent first.
$9(8) - 0.5(8)^2 = 9 \times 8 - 0.5 \times 64$ Then multiply.
$= 72 - 32$
$= 40$
When the current is 8 A, the power is 40 W.

26 UNIT 1: Numbers, Variables, and Equations

AFTER Connect

Invite students to explain the errors in Jinni's and Todd's work, then show the correct method.

In earlier grades, students learned the order of operations with brackets and the four operations: add, subtract, multiply, and divide. The exponents are the new element in Grade 8.

As you work through *Example 1*, have students explain why each operation is being performed, as it is performed.

Students may not be able to identify their types of calculators. Typically, a 4-function calculator does *not* follow the order of operations.

Before reviewing *Example 2*, remind students that a term such as $9c$ means $9 \times c$, and when we substitute a number for c, the number is multiplied by 9. Also, $0.5c^2$ means $0.5 \times c \times c$.

The acronym BEDMAS may help students remember the order of operations.

Introduce students to the word *mnemonic* (the *m* is silent), which is a device, such as a verse or sentence, to help memory. Have students make up a mnemonic for BEDMAS, such as *Betty Enjoys Doing Math After Supper*.

Practice

1. Evaluate.
   a) $7 \times 12 - 48$ 36 b) $15 + 3 + 12 - 6$ 24 c) $(5 + 6) \times 11$ 121
   d) $(34 + 46) - 5 \times 11$ 25 e) $89 - (76 + 13)$ 0 f) $144 \div (36 \times 2)$ 2

2. Evaluate.
   a) 3.2×10^4 32 000 b) $66.15 \div 10.5^2$ 0.6
   c) $18.3 - (7.2 - 3.5)^2$ 4.61 d) $(22.3 + 1.1)^2 - (22.3 - 1.1)^2$ 98.12
   e) $10.8 + 6.3^2 - 1.2 \times 2.1$ 47.97 f) $20.8 \div 1.3 \times (14.8 + 17.2)$ 512

…culator Skills

…y the decimals below. …lace each comma with …r ÷ to make an …ression equal to 1.
0.5, 0.2, 0.25, 0.4, 0.1

3. Cody bought 3 DVDs at $24.99 each and 2 compact discs at $14.99 each.
   Write an expression to show how much he spent before taxes.

4. Forty metres of fencing are available to enclose a rectangular pen.
   When the length of the pen is l metres, the area of the pen, in square metres, is expressed as $20l - l^2$.
   What is the area of the pen for each value of l?
   a) 4 m $64\ m^2$ b) 10 m $100\ m^2$ c) 13 m $91\ m^2$

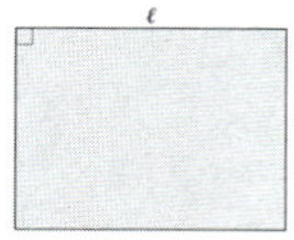

5. When a 3-m springboard diver leaves the diving board, her height above the water depends on the time since she left the board. When the time is t seconds, the diver's height above the water, in metres, is expressed as $3 + 8.8t - 4.9t^2$.
   Find the height of the diver after each time.
   a) 0.5 s 6.175 m b) 1 s 6.9 m c) 1.5 s 5.175 m

6. Copy each statement.
   Insert brackets to make each statement true.
   a) $(10 + 2) \times 3^2 - 2 = 106$ b) $10 + 2 \times (3^2 - 2) = 24$
   c) $(10 + 2) \times (3^2 - 2) = 84$ d) $(10 + 2 \times 3)^2 - 2 = 254$

7. Copy each statement.
   Insert brackets to make each statement true.
   a) $20 \div (2 + 2) \times 2^2 + 6 = 26$ b) $20 \div 2 + 2 \times (2^2 + 6) = 30$
   c) $20 \div (2 + 2 \times 2^2) + 6 = 8$ d) $(20 \div 2 + 2) \times (2^2 + 6) = 120$

1.4 Order of Operations 27

8. a) 49, 128, 1024, 625; from greatest to least: 4^5, 5^4, 2^7, 7^2
   b) 9, 8, 1, 25; from greatest to least: $(3 + 2)^2$, 3^2, 2^3, $(3 - 2)^2$
   c) 72.25, 90.25, 65.5, 102.5; from greatest to least: $103.5 - 1^2$, $(10.5 - 1)^2$, $(7.5 + 1)^2$, $61.5 + 2^2$
   d) 104.04, 33.64, 12, 3.16; from greatest to least: $(2.2 + 8)^2$, $(8 - 2.2)^2$, $8 + 2^2$, $8 - 2.2^2$
9. $100 + 39.99 \times 24 = 100 + 959.76 = 1059.76$
10. For example: a) $2 \times 6 + 4 + 8$ or $4 \times 8 - 2 - 6$
    b) $4 \times 8 + 2 + 6$ or $4 \times (6 + 2) + 8$
    c) $(8 - 2) \times (6 + 4)$ or $6 \times (8 + 4 - 2)$
    d) $(2 \times 6 + 8) \times 4$
11. For example: $(4 \times 4) \div (4 \times 4) = 1$; $(4 \times 4) \div (4 + 4) = 2$; $(4 + 4 + 4) \div 4 = 3$; $4 + 4 \times (4 - 4) = 4$; $(4 \times 4 + 4) \div 4 = 5$; $4 + (4 + 4) \div 4 = 6$; $4 + 4 - 4 \div 4 = 7$; $4 \times 4 - 4 - 4 = 8$; $4 + 4 + 4 \div 4 = 9$; $(44 - 4) \div 4 = 10$
12. No; for example, $(6 + 4)^2 = 10^2 = 100$, but $6^2 + 4^2 = 36 + 16 = 52$
13. For example: 92/11/26; $9 - 2 + 1 = (1 \times 2) + 6$
14. For example: $1 + 2 + 3 \times (4 + 5) + 6 \times 7 + 8 \times 9 = 144$ or $1 \times 6 \times (7 + 3) + 5 \times 8 + 4 \times (9 + 2) = 144$

Practice

Students will require calculators for some questions. Students with scientific calculators should be encouraged to read their manuals to learn how to use the calculators efficiently.

Students could talk their way through questions 1 and 2 to reinforce the logic of the order of operations.

Question 3: Students could find the total cost using mental math. ($104.95)

Question 5: Have students find the height after 0.3 s and compare the result with the height after 1.5 s. (*The height is 5.2 m, the same as at 1.5 s. At 0.3 s, the diver is rising and at 1.5 s the diver is falling.*)

Question 6: This question provides opportunities for students to insert brackets and apply the order of operations. Students who have difficulty could use guess and check, by inserting brackets at different places in the expression, then calculating the answer each time.

Assessment Focus: Question 10

Students should keep track of all their trials to avoid repetition. They could also be challenged to find more than one expression for each number.

REFLECT: We use the order of operations so we all get the same answer when we evaluate an expression that has different operations. For example, if we did not have the order of operations, this expression could be evaluated different ways:
$30 - 9 \times 3 + 5$
Here are different ways.
$30 - 9 \times 3 + 5 = 21 \times 3 + 5 = 63 + 5 = 68$
$30 - 9 \times 3 + 5 = 30 - 27 + 5 = 3 + 5 = 8$
$30 - 9 \times 3 + 5 = 30 - 9 \times 8 = 30 - 72 = -42$
The middle solution follows the order of operations.

Calculator Skills

Answers may vary. Sample:
$0.4 \times 0.5 \div 0.2 \div 0.25 \div 0.4 \times 0.1 = 1$

Assignment Guidelines

If your students do not have time to complete all the *Practice* questions on pages 27 and 28, these questions provide minimum curriculum coverage: 1, 2, 5, 6, 8, 10, 11, 12, *Reflect*

To assess the 4 Achievement Chart categories listed in the curriculum document, have students complete these *Practice* questions:
Knowledge and Understanding: 2
Application: 5
Thinking: 11
Communication: 12

8. Evaluate each expression.
Then write the expressions in order from greatest to least.
a) $7^2, 2^7, 4^5, 5^4$
b) $3^2, 2^3, (3 - 2)^2, (3 + 2)^2$
c) $(7.5 + 1)^2, (10.5 - 1)^2, 61.5 + 2^2, 103.5 - 1^2$
d) $(2.2 + 8)^2, (8 - 2.2)^2, 8 + 2^2, 8 - 2.2^2$

9. Skylar wants to join the local gym.
The cost in dollars for a membership can be expressed as:
$100 + 39.99m$
where 100 is the initiation fee in dollars,
39.99 is the monthly fee in dollars, and
m is the number of months for which a person signs up.
How much will it cost Skylar to join the gym for 24 months? $1059.76

10. Assessment Focus Use the numbers 2, 4, 6, 8, and any operations or brackets to make an expression that equals each number. Show your work.
a) 24 b) 40 c) 60 d) 80

11. Use four 4s and any operations or brackets to make each whole number from 1 to 10.

12. A student said: "The sum of the squares of two numbers is equal to the square of the sum of the numbers."
Do you agree with this statement? Justify your answer.

Take It Further

13. Write your birth date in this form: year/month/date
Use the digits in this number in the order they are written to make an equation.
For example, if your birth date is April 15, 1992, write it as 92/04/15, then use the numbers 9 2 0 4 1 5:
$9 \times (2 \times 0) = (4 + 1) - 5$

14. Use each digit from 1 to 9 once, and any operations, to write an expression with answer 144.

Reflect

Why is it necessary to follow the order of operations?
Include examples in your explanation.

28 UNIT 1: Numbers, Variables, and Equations

ASSESSMENT FOR LEARNING

What to Look For	What to Do
Knowledge and Understanding ✔ Students understand the rules for the order of operations when using brackets and exponents. ***Communication*** ✔ Students can describe the steps in calculations involving the order of operations. ***Application*** ✔ Students can apply the order of operations to evaluate an expression after substituting for a variable.	***Extra Support:*** Students who have difficulty should begin with evaluating expressions that have only two operations, then work up to brackets and exponents. Students can use Step-by-Step 4 (Master 1.12) to complete question 10. ***Extra Practice:*** Have students write the 4 digits of the year they were born. Use these digits together with any operations to try to write expressions with answers 0 to 10. Students can do the Additional Activity, *It All Adds Up* (Master 1.7). Students can complete Extra Practice 4 (Master 1.21). ***Extension:*** Have students write statements that are similar to those in questions 6 and 7, then trade with classmates to insert brackets to make the statements true.

Recording and Reporting
Master 1.2 Ongoing Observations: Numbers, Variables, and Equations

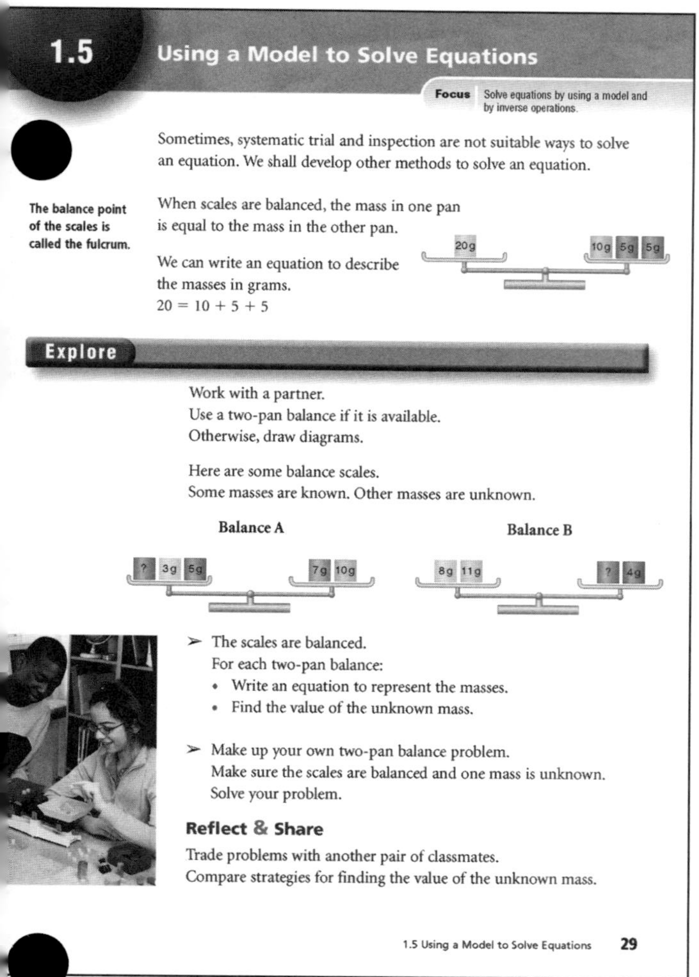

1.5 Using a Model to Solve Equations

Focus Solve equations by using a model and by inverse operations.

Sometimes, systematic trial and inspection are not suitable ways to solve an equation. We shall develop other methods to solve an equation.

The balance point of the scales is called the fulcrum.

When scales are balanced, the mass in one pan is equal to the mass in the other pan.

We can write an equation to describe the masses in grams.

$20 = 10 + 5 + 5$

Explore

Work with a partner.
Use a two-pan balance if it is available.
Otherwise, draw diagrams.

Here are some balance scales.
Some masses are known. Other masses are unknown.

➢ The scales are balanced.
For each two-pan balance:
- Write an equation to represent the masses.
- Find the value of the unknown mass.

➢ Make up your own two-pan balance problem.
Make sure the scales are balanced and one mass is unknown.
Solve your problem.

Reflect & Share

Trade problems with another pair of classmates.
Compare strategies for finding the value of the unknown mass.

1.5 Using a Model to Solve Equations 29

Using a Model to Solve Equations

LESSON ORGANIZER (80–100 min)

Curriculum Focus: Solve equations by using a model and by inverse operations. (8m64)

Teacher Materials *Optional*
- two-pan balance and masses
- overhead transparency of two-pan balance with masses

Student Materials *Optional*
- two-pan balances and masses
- diagrams of two-pan balance and masses
- Step-by-Step 5 (Master 1.13)
- Extra Practice 5 (Master 1.22)

Vocabulary: inverse operation

Assessment: Master 1.2 Ongoing Observations: Numbers, Variables, and Equations

Key Math Learnings

1. Some equations can be solved with a two-pan balance model.
2. Some equations can be solved with an algebraic model that uses inverse operations.

BEFORE Get Started

Review the scales at the top of page 29 in the Student Book.

Show a balance with these masses:

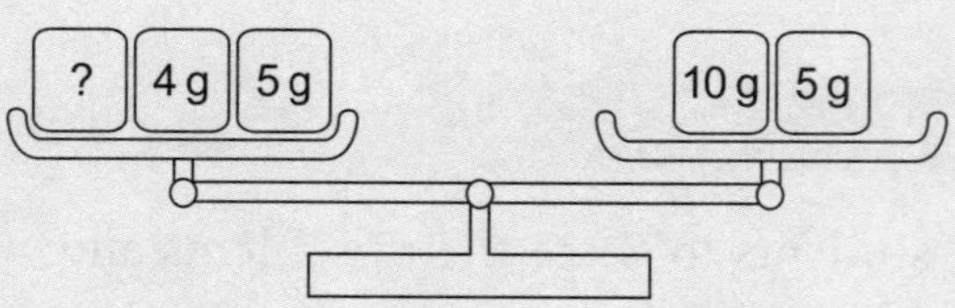

Ask:
- What happens if I remove the 5-g mass from the left pan?
  (*The balance tips to the right.*)
- What happens if, instead, I remove a 5-g mass from each pan?
  (*The balance doesn't move.*)
- What does this mean?
  (*The masses in the two pans are equal. The unknown mass plus the 4-g mass are balanced by the 10-g mass.*)

Present *Explore.*

DURING Explore

Ongoing Assessment: Observe and Listen

As students work, ask questions, such as:
- How could you find the unknown mass in Balance A?
  (*I could trade the 10-g mass for a 3-g, a 5-g, and a 2-g mass. Then I could remove a 3-g and a 5-g mass from each pan. This would leave the unknown mass balancing the 2-g and 7-g masses. So, the unknown mass is 9 g.*)

REACHING ALL LEARNERS

Alternative Explore

Have students choose a number, then write a number sentence, similar to that shown in the introduction. Encourage students to subtract as well as add. Students then erase one number and replace it with □ or x. Students trade sentences, and find the value of □ or x.

Early Finishers

Have students write equations for other students to solve. Students must ensure that the equations they write do have solutions.

Common Misconceptions

➤ Students attempt to verify a solution by substituting for x directly in the equation, instead of considering each side of the equation separately.

How to Help: Show how this can be misleading when the solution is incorrect. For example, a student erroneously solves the equation $x - 5 = 12$ as $x = 7$. If students substitute $x = 7$ in the equation, they get the statement $7 - 5 = 12$, which is incorrect and confuses some students.

Connect

➢ Here is another two-pan balance problem.
Mass A is an unknown mass.

We can remove the same mass from each pan, or add the same mass to each pan; and the scales will still be balanced.
We need to find out which mass balances Mass A.
If we remove 7 g from the left pan,
then Mass A is alone in that pan.
To remove 7 g from the right pan,
we replace 10 g with 3 g and 7 g; then remove 7 g.

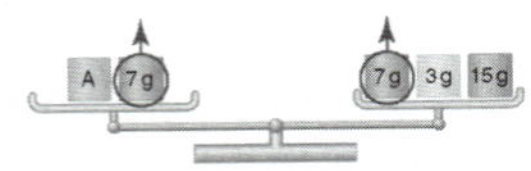

We are left with Mass A in the left pan balancing 18 g in the right pan. So, Mass A is 18 g.

We can write this problem as an equation.
Then, we solve the equation algebraically.
Let x grams represent the unknown mass.

Then: $x + 7 \quad = \quad 10 + 15$

Left pan ↑ balances ↑ right pan ↑

$x + 7 \quad = \quad 25$

Subtract 7 from each side of the equation.

$x + 7 - 7 = 25 - 7$

$x = 18$

In the solution of the equation $x + 7 = 10 + 15$, we used the **inverse operation**.
That is, to isolate x, we *subtracted* 7 from +7 to get $+7 - 7 = 0$ on the left side.

- Could you use different masses to find the unknown mass?
  (I could trade the 5-g and the 3-g masses for an 8-g mass and replace the 7-g and the 10-g masses with an 8-g and a 9-g mass. I can remove an 8-g mass from each pan, leaving the unknown mass balancing the 9-g mass. So, the unknown mass is 9 g.)
- What equations could you write for Balance A?
  ($\square + 3 + 5 = 7 + 10$ or $\square + 8 = 17$)
- What is one way you could solve the equation?
  (An unknown number plus 8 is equal to 17. I know 9 + 8 = 17, so the unknown number is 9.)
- How can you solve the equation a different way?
  (I could try different values for the unknown number until the equation balances; that is, use guess and check.)
- What equation could you write for Balance B?
  ($8 + 11 = x + 4$ or $19 = x + 4$)
- How could you solve the equation?
  (I could remove 4 from each side: $19 - 4 = x + 4 - 4$, to get $15 = x$. The unknown mass is 15 g.)
- What problem did you create?
  (*Sample answer:* $5 + \square + 7 = 6 + 9$)
- What is the unknown mass? (*3 g*)

AFTER Connect

Invite students to share their problems and solutions.

Use appropriate language to connect the two-pan balance model to the algebraic method. Have students verbalize the steps as they complete them.

Review *Connect* and ensure students understand the steps in solving equations.

Reinforce the importance of verifying solutions and checking the left side and the right side of an equation separately. Verifying solutions

We can verify the solution to this problem in two ways.

- Replace Mass A with 18 g.
  Then, in the left pan: 18 g + 7 g = 25 g
  And, in the right pan: 10 g + 15 g = 25 g
  Since the masses are equal, the solution is correct.
- Substitute $x = 18$ in the equation $x + 7 = 10 + 15$.
  Left side: $x + 7 = 18 + 7$ $= 25$ Right side $= 10 + 15$ $= 25$

Since the left side of the equation equals the right side, the solution is correct.

Example

Solve each equation. Verify the solution.

a) $10 + x = 5 + 8$ b) $x - 6 = 10 - 3$

Solution

a) $10 + x = 5 + 8$
Add the numbers on the right side.
$10 + x = 13$
Subtract 10 from each side to isolate x.
$10 + x - 10 = 13 - 10$
$x = 3$
To verify $x = 3$ is correct, substitute $x = 3$ in $10 + x = 5 + 8$.
Left side $= 10 + x$ $= 10 + 3$ $= 13$ Right side $= 5 + 8$ $= 13$
Since the left side equals the right side, $x = 3$ is correct.

b) $x - 6 = 10 - 3$
Subtract the numbers on the right side.
$x - 6 = 7$
Add 6 to each side to isolate x.
$x - 6 + 6 = 7 + 6$
$x = 13$
To verify $x = 13$ is correct, substitute $x = 13$ in $x - 6 = 10 - 3$.
Left side $= x - 6$ $= 13 - 6$ $= 7$ Right side $= 10 - 3$ $= 7$
Since the left side equals the right side, $x = 13$ is correct.

1.5 Using a Model to Solve Equations 31

Sample Solutions

1. The solution for an equation is shown on a line, with each successive step indicated with an arrow (⇨). Students' solutions should show one step per line, with equals signs aligned as per the *Example* in the text.
   a) 20 + A = 50 ⇨ 20 + A = 20 + 30 ⇨ A = 30
   b) 75 = B + 20 ⇨ 55 + 20 = B + 20 ⇨ B = 55
   c) 15 + C = 30 + 50 ⇨ 15 + C = 15 + 15 + 50 ⇨ C = 15 + 50 ⇨ C = 65
   d) 20 + 20 + 25 = D + 15 ⇨ 5 + 15 + 20 + 25 = D + 15 ⇨ 5 + 20 + 25 = D ⇨ D = 50
2. a) $x + 3 = 5$ ⇨ $x + 3 - 3 = 5 - 3$ ⇨ $x = 2$
   b) $x + 5 = 10$ ⇨ $x + 5 - 5 = 10 - 5$ ⇨ $x = 5$
   c) $x + 10 = 17$ ⇨ $x + 10 - 10 = 17 - 10$ ⇨ $x = 7$
   d) $x - 3 = 5$ ⇨ $x - 3 + 3 = 5 + 3$ ⇨ $x = 8$
   e) $x - 5 = 10$ ⇨ $x - 5 + 5 = 10 + 5$ ⇨ $x = 15$
   f) $x - 10 = 17$ ⇨ $x - 10 + 10 = 17 + 10$ ⇨ $x = 27$
3. a) $3 + x = 5 + 9$ ⇨ $3 + x = 14$ ⇨ $3 - 3 + x = 14 - 3$ ⇨ $x = 11$
   Verify: Left side = 3 + 11 = 14; Right side = 5 + 9 = 14; the solution is correct.
4. $5 + x = 24$ ⇨ $5 - 5 + x = 24 - 5$ ⇨ $x = 19$
5. a) For example: $x + 25 + 10 = 25 + 10 + 25$
   b) Remove 25 g and 10 g from each pan; $x = 25$
6. a) For example: In the left pan, x, x, x, x, x, 10 g; in the right pan, 105 g
   b) For example: $5x + 10 = 105$ ⇨ $5x + 10 - 10 = 105 - 10$ ⇨ $5x = 95$
   By inspection: $x = 19$, or $x + x + x + x + x = 19 + 19 + 19 + 19 + 19$; so, $x = 19$

becomes more important as equations become more complex and the likelihood of making mistakes in the solution increases.

All the equations in this lesson show x as positive, and the coefficient of x is always 1 (except *Take It Further*, question 6a).

In *Lesson 1.6*, students will solve equations where the coefficient of x is greater than 1.

In Unit 7, students will solve equations to find the measure of an angle in a triangle.
In Unit 10, students will solve equations where the coefficient of x is negative, and also where the solution is a fraction or a decimal.

With frequent experiences in solving equations in different contexts, students maintain and practise their skills.

Practice

Encourage students to show all the steps in their solutions.

Remind students they must show the verification of their solutions.

Question 1: Encourage students to draw diagrams to show their processes and solutions.

Questions 2 and 3: Have students verbalize the steps as they do them.

Assessment Focus: Question 5

Students may represent 35 as a sum of multiples of 5; and/or represent 60 as a sum of multiples of 5. There are many possible combinations; in fact, there are 14 ways to express 35 as a sum of multiples of 5.

REFLECT: The equation $x + 5 = 12$ can be solved using a two-pan balance.

$x + 5 = 7 + 5$

$x = 7$

(Students' work should include a sketch of the two-pan balance at each stage of the solution.)

The equation $x - 5 = 12$ cannot be solved using a two-pan balance because I cannot have a negative mass. So, I solve it using algebra and inverse operations.

$x - 5 + 5 = 12 + 5$

$x = 17$

Number Strategies

List all the 2-digit square numbers. (*16, 25, 36, 49, 64, 81*)
Add the squares in pairs to find the sum that is also a square number.

Assignment Guidelines

If your students do not have time to complete all the *Practice* questions on page 32, these questions provide minimum curriculum coverage: 2, 3, 4, 5, *Reflect*

To assess these 3 Achievement Chart categories, have students complete the *Practice* questions indicated.
Knowledge and Understanding: 2
Application: 4
Thinking: 5

Practice

1. Find the value of the unknown mass on each two-pan bala[nce.]
   a) A = 30

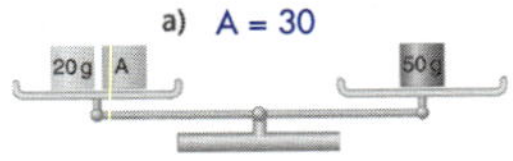

   b) B = 55

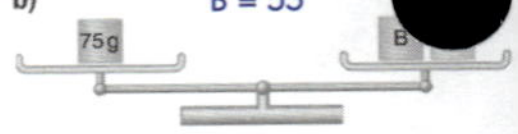

   c) C = 65

   d) D = 50

2. Solve each equation.
   a) $x + 3 = 5$ $x = 2$ b) $x + 5 = 10$ $x = 5$ c) $x + 10 = 17$ $x = 7$
   d) $x - 3 = 5$ $x = 8$ e) $x - 5 = 10$ $x = 15$ f) $x - 10 = 17$ $x = 2$[7]
3. Solve each equation. Verify the solution.
   a) $3 + x = 5 + 9$ $x = 11$ b) $x - 3 = 11 - 8$ $x = 6$
   c) $4 + 7 = x - 8$ $x = 19$ d) $21 - 13 = 7 + x$ $x = 1$

Number Strategies

Find a square number that is the sum of 2 two-digit square numbers.
How many numbers can you find?
$36 + 64 = 100$ or
$6^2 + 8^2 = 10^2$

4. Five more than a number is 24.
   Let x represent the number.
   Then an equation is $5 + x = 24$.
   Solve the equation. What is the number? 19
5. **Assessment Focus** The masses for a two-pan balance are multiples of 5 g.
   a) Sketch a two-pan balance to represent this equation:
      $x + 35 = 60$
      How many different balances can you sketch?
   b) Solve the equation. Verify the solution.
      Show your work. $x = 25$

Take It Further

6. a) Sketch a two-pan balance to represent the equation:
      $5x + 10 = 105$
   b) Solve the equation. Verify the solution. $x = 19$

Reflect

Write an equation, then solve it using a two-pan balance.
Write an equation you cannot solve using a two-pan balance.
Solve the equation algebraically.

ASSESSMENT FOR LEARNING

What to Look For	What to Do
Knowledge and Understanding ✔ Students understand how to solve an equation using a two-pan balance. ✔ Students understand how to solve an equation using algebra and inverse operations. ***Communication*** ✔ Students can describe the steps in solving an equation. ***Application*** ✔ Students can solve an equation using a two-pan balance model, and an algebraic method involving inverse operations.	***Extra Support:*** In questions 2 and 3, have students replace the x with □, and relate the process to the work students did in earlier grades. Students can use Step-by-Step 5 (Master 1.13) to complete question 5. ***Extra Practice:*** Have students use question 4 as a model. They rewrite each equation in questions 2 and 3 as a word sentence. Students can complete Extra Practice 5 (Master 1.22). ***Extension:*** Have students create and solve two-pan balance problems with 2 or more identical unknown masses on one pan.

Recording and Reporting
Master 1.2 Ongoing Observations: Numbers, Variables, and Equations

Code Makers and Breakers

One method for keeping information private is to encode it—that is, jumble or transform it so the original information is unreadable. But you can't just jumble it randomly. The encoding must be done in such a way that someone who holds the "key" can reverse the process and decode the information.

Bletchley Park, England, was the code-breaking centre of WW2. Thousands of men and women, including top mathematicians from many universities, worked night and day to break the top secret codes of the Germans. The success of the code breakers played a large part in the allied victory. Many machines, such as the Enigma machine, and the first electronic computer, the Colossus, were invented here, as aids for breaking the codes.

The Colossus, Bletchley Park, 1940s.

In 1977, three scientists (Rivest, Shamir, and Adleman) challenged the world to decode a message encoded by their new RSA-129 scheme. RSA-129 is a system that uses a computer-generated, 129-digit number when encoding a message. This number is the product of two very large prime numbers (with between 50 and 100 digits). To decode the message, you must know the two prime numbers.

In 1994, Arjen Lenstra, a computer scientist and factoring specialist, led a group of 600 Internet volunteers and their computers to decode the message. The project took eight months and over 15×10^{16} calculations!

The World of Work: Code Makers and Breakers 33

Code Makers and Breakers

Secret codes have been around since ancient times. Students may have worked with simple codes. Three of the more common codes or ciphers are:

- Write the letters of the alphabet. Underneath, write the alphabet in the reverse order. Write the message, then interchange the letters to encode the message.
- Write the letters of the alphabet. Underneath, write the alphabet with the letters moved a fixed number of places to the right. Write the message, then interchange the letters to encode the message.
- Replace the letters of the alphabet with the numbers 1 to 26.

Students could use these methods to try to translate these coded messages:
DVORPVNZGS
RZGDFAHVOC
23,5,12,9,11,6,13,1,20,8
(*Answer: we like math*)

Students could be given a project to create a code and challenge other students to break the code.

With the advances in technology, the creation of secret codes has become a sophisticated science. Code makers are known as **cryptologists** and code breakers are called **cryptanalysts,** although the common name is cryptologist as most people working on codes do both.

The use of secret codes has become common in our society and the development of "unbreakable" codes is a constant challenge. Codes are used in credit cards, bankcards, car security systems, bar codes, and many other situations. Many government agencies and large companies employ full-time cryptologists to design codes so that information can be transmitted securely through telephone lines, computer networks, or satellite links.

Most of the work in applying cryptography is done by cryptographic engineers who have knowledge of cryptography but spend most of their time applying known codes to create and check new secure systems. Every time a secure system is designed, code breakers are challenged to break the code. This way, any glitches can be found and fixed.

Often people who work with codes enjoy mathematics, music, classical languages, and chess.

There are many careers in the field of code making. Career paths vary from one-year college courses in working with coding systems (for example, in encoding medical data) to university courses and programs linked to business and engineering.

Have students create lists of all the places in which codes are used. The list could be separated into systems that recognize codes and those that recognize codes plus require the input of a personal code.

For more information on cryptology, visit *www.bletchleypark.net* (accessed July, 2005).

Using Algebra Tiles to Solve Equations

LESSON ORGANIZER

80–100 min

Curriculum Focus: Use algebra tiles and inverse operations to solve equations. (8m61, 8m64)

Teacher Materials
- overhead algebra tiles

Student Materials
- algebra tiles

Optional
- algebra tiles (PM 27)
- Step-by-Step 6 (Master 1.14)
- Extra Practice 6 (Master 1.23)

Vocabulary: unit tile, variable tile, zero pair

Assessment: Master 1.2 Ongoing Observations: Numbers, Variables, and Equations

Key Math Learnings

1. Some equations can be solved using algebra tiles.
2. Equations can be solved using algebraic methods, including inverse operations.

1.6 Using Algebra Tiles to Solve Equations

Focus Use algebra tiles and inverse operations solve equations.

Recall the integer tiles you have used.

This tile represents +1, or 1. This tile represents −1.

These two tiles are called **unit tiles.**

One red unit tile and one yellow unit tile combine to model 0.

−1, +1 These two unit tiles form a **zero pair.**

We also use tiles to represent variables.
This tile represents *x*.

We call it an *x*-tile, or a **variable tile.**
Unit tiles and variable tiles are collectively called algebra tiles.

Explore

Work with a partner.
You will need algebra tiles.
- ➢ Use algebra tiles to represent this equation: $x + 5 = 9$
  Use the tiles to solve the equation.
  Sketch the tiles you used.
- ➢ Repeat the process for the equation $x - 5 = 9$.
- ➢ Write your own equation to solve using algebra tiles.
  Solve your equation.

Reflect & Share

Share your strategies for solving an equation using algebra tiles with another pair of classmates.
Write the algebraic solutions for your equations.
How did you use zero pairs in your solutions?

34 UNIT 1: Numbers, Variables, and Equations

BEFORE Get Started

Review integer tiles.

Have students use integer tiles to create, then sketch, a "picture" worth zero.

Introduce the *x*-tile or variable tile.

Have students make a picture worth $x + 1$, $x - 1$, $2x + 1$, $2x - 1$, and so on.

Present *Explore*.

DURING Explore

Ongoing Assessment: Observe and Listen

Ensure students know how to lay out tiles to represent $x + 5 = 9$.

As students work, ask questions, such as:
- How do you know you have +5?
  (*I used 5 yellow tiles.*)
- How did you solve the equation?
  (*I removed 5 yellow tiles from each side and was left with x on one side and 4 yellow tiles on the other side, so x = 4.*)
- How will you show the equation $x - 5 = 9$?
  (*I need one x-tile, 5 red tiles, and 9 yellow tiles.*)

Connect

We extend the idea of balanced scales to model an equation with algebra tiles.

We draw a vertical line in the centre of the page: it represents the balance point of the scales and the equal sign in the equation.

We arrange tiles on each side of the line to represent an equation. Whatever we do to one side of the equation, we also do to the other side.
To solve the equation $x - 3 = 10$:

On the left side, put algebra tiles to represent $x - 3$.

On the right side, put algebra tiles to represent 10.

To isolate the x-tile, add 3 yellow unit tiles to make zero pairs. Remove zero pairs.

Add 3 yellow unit tiles to this side, too.

The tiles above show the solution $x = 13$.

Here is the algebraic solution.

$x - 3 = 10$ — Use the inverse operation.

$x - 3 + 3 = 10 + 3$ — Add 3 to each side to isolate x.

$x = 13$

Remember that: $-3 + 3 = 0$

We can use algebra tiles to solve an equation when the x-term is greater than $1x$.

REACHING ALL LEARNERS

Early Finishers

Have students write, then solve, equations similar to those in *Practice*, question 5. Challenge students to write equations with x-coefficients greater than 1, and the value of x positive.

Common Misconceptions

➤ Students get incorrect answers by failing to use inverse operations or zero pairs.

How to Help: Have students practise making zero pairs by beginning with different numbers of red or yellow tiles. For example, give a student 5 red tiles, he writes -5, then he picks the yellow tiles needed to make 0. After he picks 5 yellow tiles, he completes the sentence $-5 + 5 = 0$.
As students solve the equations, ask questions, such as, "To get 0, do you add 5 to + 5 or do you subtract 5 from +5?"; "When you subtract 5 from +5 to get 0, what must you do to the other side of the equation?"

- How do you know you have –5?
  (*I used 5 red tiles.*)
- How do you solve the equation?
  (*I do not have any red tiles on the right side so I cannot take 5 red tiles from each side. But, if I add 5 yellow tiles to each side, the red and yellow tiles on the left side make 5 zero pairs, so I just have x left on that side.*)
- What happens on the right side?
  (*I now have 9 + 5, or 14 yellow tiles.*)
- What is the solution of the equation?
  ($x = 14$)
- What equation did you write?
  ($x - 3 = 4$)
- How did you solve the equation?
  (*I added 3 yellow tiles to each side, then used zero pairs to get* $x = 7$.)

Encourage students to show what they did using sketches, numbers, and variables.

AFTER Connect

Invite students to share their equations and have the class solve them.

Introduce *Connect* and explain the process of solving equations using algebra tiles.

One way to link the use of algebra tiles to the algebraic method is to have students divide their page in half vertically. On the left side they can sketch the tiles and on the right side they can show the equivalent algebraic method. When students are comfortable with the algebraic method, they are ready to stop using the tiles. Emphasize the use of zero pairs when using the tiles.

Sample Solutions

2. a) $x + 4 = 8 \Rightarrow x + 4 - 4 = 8 - 4 \Rightarrow x = 4$
   b) $3 + x = 10 \Rightarrow 3 + x - 3 = 10 - 3 \Rightarrow x = 7$
   c) $12 = x + 2 \Rightarrow 12 - 2 = x + 2 - 2 \Rightarrow x = 10$
   d) $x - 4 = 8 \Rightarrow x - 4 + 4 = 8 + 4 \Rightarrow x = 12$
   e) $10 = x - 3 \Rightarrow 10 + 3 = x - 3 + 3 \Rightarrow x = 13$
   f) $12 = x - 2 \Rightarrow 12 + 2 = x - 2 + 2 \Rightarrow x = 14$
3. $5 + x = 11 \Rightarrow 5 + x - 5 = 11 - 5 \Rightarrow x = 6$
4. $x - 4 = 13 \Rightarrow x - 4 + 4 = 13 + 4 \Rightarrow x = 17$
5. i) $2x + 7 = 13 \Rightarrow 2x + 7 - 7 = 13 - 7 \Rightarrow 2x = 6 \Rightarrow \frac{2x}{2} = \frac{6}{2}$
   $\Rightarrow x = 3$
   Verify: Left side = $2 \times 3 + 7 = 13$ = right side
   ii) $11 = 3x - 1 \Rightarrow 11 + 1 = 3x - 1 + 1 \Rightarrow 12 = 3x \Rightarrow \frac{12}{3} = \frac{3x}{3}$
   $\Rightarrow x = 4$
   Verify: Right side = $3 \times 4 - 1 = 11$ = left side
   iii) $4x + 13 = 17 \Rightarrow 4x + 13 - 13 = 17 - 13 \Rightarrow 4x = 4$,
   $\frac{4x}{4} = \frac{4}{4} \Rightarrow x = 1$
   Verify: Left side = $4 \times 1 + 13 = 17$ = right side
   iv) $9 = 5x - 6 \Rightarrow 9 + 6 = 5x - 6 + 6 \Rightarrow 15 = 5x \Rightarrow \frac{15}{5} = \frac{5x}{5}$
   $\Rightarrow x = 3$
   Verify: Right side = $5 \times 3 - 6 = 9$ = left side
6. $5x = 30 \Rightarrow \frac{5x}{5} = \frac{30}{5} \Rightarrow x = 6$
7. $8x = 104 \Rightarrow \frac{8x}{8} = \frac{104}{8} \Rightarrow x = 13$
8. $7 + 3x = 28 \Rightarrow 7 + 3x - 7 = 28 - 7 \Rightarrow 3x = 21 \Rightarrow \frac{3x}{3} = \frac{21}{3}$
   $\Rightarrow x = 7$

Example 1

a) Use algebra tiles to solve this equation: $2x + 1 = 9$
b) Solve the equation in part a algebraically.
c) Verify the solution.

Solution

a) $2x + 1 = 9$

Add 1 red unit tile to each side.
Remove zero pairs.

Arrange the tiles on each side into 2 equal groups.

Compare groups.
One x-tile equals 4 unit tiles.
So, $x = 4$

b)

$$2x + 1 = 9 \quad \text{Subtract 1 from each side.}$$
$$2x + 1 - 1 = 9 - 1$$
$$2x = 8$$
$$\frac{2x}{2} = \frac{8}{2} \quad \text{Divide each side by 2.}$$
$$x = 4$$

36 UNIT 1: Numbers, Variables, and Equations

Some students may need more practice solving equations with 1 as the coefficient of x, before you introduce *Examples 1* and *2*. The algebraic solutions in *Examples 1* and *2* illustrate that an equation can be solved so that x is on the left side or the right side in the final line of the solution.

Ensure students understand the step in the algebraic solution that relates to arranging the tiles into equal groups. Remind students that whatever is done to one side of the equation must also be done to the other side.
In *Example 1*, we know what $2x$ is equal to, so, to find x, we divide $2x$ by 2. Then, we must also divide the other side of the equation by 2.

You may wish to introduce the words *constant* or *constant term* for any number in an equation. And, introduce the word *coefficient* for the number in front of a variable.

For example, in the equation $2 = 3x - 4$, 2 and 4 are constant terms, and 3 is the coefficient of the variable term. When no coefficient is shown, the coefficient is 1. That is, x can be written as $1x$.

An alternative way to introduce algebraic equations and their solutions is by using a question and answer format that introduces inverse operations. Students start by using mental math to answer the questions, then, as the questions become more complex, they start writing equations.

One possible sequence is:

- I am thinking of a number. I add 5 and get an answer of 8. What number was I thinking of? How did you find the number?
  (*The number is 3. I subtracted 5 from 8.*)
- What equation could I write?
  ($x + 5 = 8$)

c) To verify the solution, substitute $x = 4$ into $2x + 1 = 9$.

Left side $= 2x + 1$ Right side $= 9$

$= 2(4) + 1$

$= 8 + 1$

$= 9$

Since the left side equals the right side, $x = 4$ is correct.

Example 2

a) Use algebra tiles to solve this equation: $2 = 3x - 4$

b) Solve the equation in part a algebraically.

c) Verify the solution.

Solution

a) $2 = 3x - 4$

Add 4 yellow unit tiles to each side.
Remove zero pairs.

Arrange the tiles on each side into equal groups.

2 yellow unit tiles equal one x-tile.
So, $x = 2$

1.6 Using Algebra Tiles to Solve Equations 37

9. For example: Four more than twice a number is 18.
Let x represent the number. Twice the number is $2x$.
Four more than twice the number is $2x + 4$.
The equation is: $2x + 4 = 18$
$2x + 4 - 4 = 18 - 4 \Rightarrow 2x = 14 \Rightarrow \frac{2x}{2} = \frac{14}{2} \Rightarrow x = 7$
Verify: Left side $= 2 \times 7 + 4 = 18 =$ right side
(Student's solution should also include a sketch of the algebra tiles used.)

10. a) $3x + 12 = 6 \Rightarrow 3x + 12 - 12 = 6 - 12 \Rightarrow 3x = -6 \Rightarrow \frac{3x}{3} = \frac{-6}{3} \Rightarrow x = -2$

b) $5 - 2x = 11 \Rightarrow 5 - 2x - 5 = 11 - 5 \Rightarrow -2x = 6 \Rightarrow \frac{-2x}{-2} = \frac{6}{-2} \Rightarrow x = -3$

c) $-2 = 3x + 10 \Rightarrow -2 - 10 = 3x + 10 - 10 \Rightarrow -12 = 3x \Rightarrow \frac{-12}{3} = \frac{3x}{3} \Rightarrow x = -4$

11. a) Let x represent the number. Two times the number is $2x$.
Five more than 2 times the number is $5 + 2x$.
The equation is: $5 + 2x = 1$
$5 + 2x - 5 = 1 - 5 \Rightarrow 2x = -4 \Rightarrow \frac{2x}{2} = \frac{-4}{2} \Rightarrow x = -2$
Verify: Left side: $5 + 2 \times (-2) = 1 =$ right side

- I am thinking of a number. I subtract 5 and get an answer of 7. What number was I thinking of? How did you find the number? (*The number is 12. I added 5 to 7.*)
- What equation could I write? ($x - 5 = 7$)
- I am thinking of a number. I multiply by 3 and get an answer of 18. What number was I thinking of? How did you find the number? (*The number is 6. I divided 18 by 3.*)
- What equation could I write? ($3x = 18$)
- I am thinking of a number. I divide by 4 and get an answer of 7. What number was I thinking of? How did you find the number? (*The number is 28. I multiplied 7 by 4.*)
- What equation could I write? ($\frac{x}{4} = 7$)
- I am thinking of a number. I multiply by 3, then add 4. I get an answer of 19. What number was I thinking of? How did you find the number? (*The number is 5. I subtracted 4 from 19, then divided the answer by 3.*)
- What equation could I write? ($3x + 4 = 19$)
- I am thinking of a number. I multiply by 4, then subtract 5. I get an answer of 7. What number was I thinking of? How did you find the number? (*The number is 3. I added 5 to 7, then divided the answer by 4.*)
- What equation could I write? ($4x - 5 = 7$)

This method of introducing and solving equations links to a work backward strategy for solving problems.

b) Let x represent the number. Two times the number is $2x$.
Five less than 2 times the number is $2x - 5$.
The equation is: $2x - 5 = -1$
$2x - 5 + 5 = -1 + 5 \Rightarrow 2x = 4 \Rightarrow \frac{2x}{2} = \frac{4}{2} \Rightarrow x = 2$
Verify: Left side: $2 \times 2 - 5 = -1$ = right side

The algebraic solutions of the equations in questions 10 and 11 involve dividing integers. Students do not learn this until Unit 9. They could solve the equation using algebra tiles instead. The verification of the solutions in question 11 involves substituting integers for variables. Students do not learn this until Unit 10. They could use algebra tiles to verify, instead. Students replace the x-tile in the algebra-tile representation of the equation by the integer tiles it represents, then simplify by using zero pairs.

REFLECT: The equation $2x - 3 = 7$ cannot be solved with a two-pan balance because we cannot show a negative mass. (Students' responses should include sketches of the tiles and the steps in an algebra-tile solution: $x = 5$)
To verify, substitute $x = 5$ into $2x - 3 = 7$.

Left side $= 2x - 3$ $\quad$ Right side = 7
$= 2(5) - 3$
$= 10 - 3$
$= 7$

Since the left side equals the right side, $x = 5$ is correct.

b)
$2 = 3x - 4$ $\quad$ Add 4 to each side.
$2 + 4 = 3x - 4 + 4$
$6 = 3x$
$\frac{6}{3} = \frac{3x}{3}$ $\quad$ Divide each side by 3.
$2 = x$

c) To verify the solution, substitute $x = 2$ into $2 = 3x - 4$.
Left side = 2 $\quad$ Right side $= 3(2) - 4$
$= 6 - 4$
$= 2$
Since the left side equals the right side, $x = 2$ is correct.

Practice

1. Use algebra tiles to solve each equation.
   a) $x + 4 = 8$ x=4 b) $3 + x = 10$ x=7 c) $12 = x + 2$ x=10
   d) $x - 4 = 8$ x=12 e) $10 = x - 3$ x=13 f) $12 = x - 2$ x=14
2. Solve each equation in question 1 algebraically.
3. Five more than a number is 11.
   Let x represent the number.
   Then, an equation is $5 + x = 11$.
   Solve the equation.
   What is the number? 6
4. Four less than a number is 13.
   Let x represent the number.
   Then, an equation is $x - 4 = 13$.
   Solve the equation.
   What is the number? 17
5. a) Use algebra tiles to solve each equation.
   b) Solve each equation algebraically.
   c) Verify each solution.
      i) $2x + 7 = 13$ $x = 3$
      ii) $11 = 3x - 1$ $x = 4$
      iii) $4x + 13 = 17$ $x = 1$
      iv) $9 = 5x - 6$ $x = 3$

38 UNIT 1: Numbers, Variables, and Equations

Practice

Students should use algebra tiles and sketch the tiles to show their solutions.

Encourage students to show the intermediate steps in the algebraic solutions of equations. Emphasize the importance of verifying the solutions.

Assessment Focus: Question 9

Students may write an equation that cannot be solved using algebra tiles (the answer may be a fraction). However, students should solve it algebraically and explain why it cannot be solved using tiles.

6. Five times a number is 30.
Let x represent the number.
Then, an equation is $5x = 30$.
Solve the equation. What is the number? 6

umber Strategies

nd the least number that
beys these clues:
ne number is divisible
y 5 and by 11.
When the number is
vided by 9,
e remainder is 2.
110

7. The perimeter of a regular octagon is 104 cm.
Let x centimetres represent the length of one side.
Then, an equation to represent the perimeter is $8x = 104$.
Solve the equation.
What is the side length of the octagon? 13 cm

8. Seven more than three times a number is 28.
Let x represent the number.
Then, an equation is $7 + 3x = 28$.
Solve the equation. What is the number? 7

9. **Assessment Focus** Look at the problems in questions 3, 4, 6, 7, and 8.
Make up a problem similar to these.
Write an equation for your problem.
Solve the equation using algebra tiles, and algebraically.
Verify the solution. Show your work.

Take It Further

10. Solve each equation algebraically.
a) $3x + 12 = 6$ $x = -2$
b) $5 - 2x = 11$ $x = -3$
c) $-2 = 3x + 10$ $x = -4$

11. Write an equation for each number.
Solve the equation to find each number.
Verify the solution.
a) Five more than two times a number is 1.
What is the number? -2
b) Five less than two times a number is -1.
What is the number? 2

Reflect

Write an equation you can solve with algebra tiles but not with a two-pan balance.
Explain why the equation cannot be solved with a two-pan balance.
Solve the equation. Verify the solution.

Number Strategies

To be divisible by 5 and 11, the number must be 55 or a multiple of 55. To be divisible by 9 with a remainder of 2, the sum of the digits must be 2 more than a number divisible by 9.

Assignment Guidelines

If your students do not have time to complete all the *Practice* questions on pages 38 and 39, these questions provide minimum curriculum coverage: 1, 2, 4, 5, 7, 9, *Reflect*

To assess the 4 Achievement Chart categories listed in the curriculum document, have students complete these *Practice* questions:
Communication: 1
Knowledge and Understanding: 5
Thinking: 7
Application: 9

ASSESSMENT FOR LEARNING

What to Look For

Knowledge and Understanding
- ✔ Students understand that some equations can be solved using algebra tiles.
- ✔ Students should understand that all equations can be solved algebraically.

Communication
- ✔ Students can explain the process of solving equations using algebra tiles.
- ✔ Students can explain the process of solving equations using algebraic methods.

Application
- ✔ Students can solve equations using algebra tiles and drawings.
- ✔ Students can solve equations algebraically using inverse operations.

What to Do

Extra Support: Have students use algebra tiles as long as they need to, to solve equations.
Students can use Step-by-Step 6 (Master 1.14) to complete question 9.

Extra Practice: Students can do the Additional Activity, *Solve It* (Master 1.8).
Students can complete Extra Practice 6 (Master 1.23).

Extension: Challenge students to write an equation that they think has a negative solution and/or a fraction/decimal solution. Students then solve the equation to check.

Recording and Reporting
Master 1.2 Ongoing Observations: Numbers, Variables, and Equations

Visual Text Features

LESSON ORGANIZER

Teacher Materials	*Optional*
	▪ math textbooks from different decades

Sample Solutions

1. A circle shows the start of a new unit, *The World of Work*, *Reading and Writing in Math*, and *Technology*. A partial circle shows the start of a new lesson, or *Cross Strand Investigation*. A bar shows the start of *Explore*, *Connect*, and *Practice*.
2. For example: In the mid-unit reviews and unit reviews, there are small rectangles beside some of the questions, which indicate the lesson that the question and following questions pertain to. Each *Unit Problem* has a *Check List* in a rectangle on the second page to remind us what our work should show.
3. *Explore*, *Connect*, and *Practice* occur in every lesson.
4. Large fonts occur in the unit titles, *Skills You'll Need*, and other titles. Small fonts occur in the margins and as labels on art.
5. Sample: Name the topics covered in the green boxes at the sides of some of the *Practice* pages. (Answer: *Mental Math*, *Number Strategies*, *Calculator Skills*)

Visual Text Features

This textbook has visual features that help you find things easily and to know what type of information is found there. Matching colours, fonts (type, colour, and style), symbols, backgrounds, colour bars or banners, or pictures show similar information.

For example, in the upper left corner of a page indicates a new lesson. You should find it helpful to become familiar with the features of this book. Pages xi – xvii of this book explain some of these features.

Explore Visual Text Features

1. Here are some sample visual features. What does each one tell you?
2. Flip through your textbook. Find several other features that repeat throughout the book. Describe each feature. Explain what it means.
3. Which features appear most often? Why?
4. Where do you find the largest fonts? The smallest fonts? Describe a general pattern for how font size is used.
5. Create your own question about visual text features. Trade questions with a classmate. Answer your classmate's question.

40 UNIT 1: Numbers, Variables, and Equations

At the start of a new unit, have students read the lesson titles. Have them explain how these titles relate to work they have done previously. Ask them what they think they will learn.

At the start of a new lesson, ask students what they understand from the title. (They may have to check the *Glossary*.) Ask:
- What do you think the lesson is about?
- What do you already know about the topic?

Text book publishers spend much time and effort designing the layout of textbooks. Math books have to be attractive, colourful, and easy to read while presenting complex ideas.

It would be interesting to show students copies of textbooks from the 1980s, 1960s and, if possible, pre-1950s for comparison. Pre-1950s textbooks were usually sources of examples and questions; the development of concepts and skills was done by the teacher. A look at old textbooks shows that there was little change in the content and presentation of mathematics from the 1900s to the 1960s. Nowadays, textbooks are designed to include the development of the new ideas in a way that is understandable to students.

Textbooks have become more colourful due to various influences, including: advances in technology making it possible to include colour, diagrams, and different layouts of pages; changes in curriculum content making it necessary to redesign the layout; research on how students learn leading to more variations in textbooks to address different learning styles; external factors, such as colour TV, making traditional textbooks less interesting.

Every attempt is made to write textbooks in a logical sequential way so students can read and understand each topic. Many students do not

Reading and Writing in Math

Use Visual Text Features

With a partner, look through the book to find an example of each item below. Describe the visual feature that identifies it. The table of contents and index might help.

- Important key words used in a unit
- Reflect on the important ideas of a lesson or unit
- Tests to help practise skills
- Reviews in the middle of a unit
- Reviews of a unit
- Challenging problems to take a math idea further
- Practice questions to develop understanding
- Using technology
- Games
- Meanings of math words
- How people use math in their work
- Skills that you will need to help you work through a unit
- Math to practise in your head

Reading and Writing in Math: Visual Text Features 41

Use Visual Text Features

- Important key words are listed on the second page of each unit; they are printed in boldface text in the unit; and their meanings are explained in the *Glossary*.
- Reflect on the important ideas of a lesson is found at the end of each *Practice*. Reflect on the important ideas of a unit is found at the end of each *Unit Problem*. The heading is in a brown oval, and the text is on a purple background.
- A test to find out how much a student knows follows each *Unit Review*. It has the heading **Practice Test** on a purple banner.
- A **Mid-Unit Review** is part way through each unit, and has a purple banner.
- A review of a unit is titled **Unit Review**. It is found at the end of each unit and has a purple banner.
- Challenging problems to take a math idea further are found in most *Practice* sections, under the heading **Take It Further**. This heading is in purple.
- *Practice* questions to develop understanding follow each *Connect*. These questions are under the heading **Practice**, which is in a purple banner.
- A *Technology* lesson is indicated by a large blue and purple banner that contains a computer icon. There is a circle in the top left corner with the heading **Technology**.
- A *Game* is indicated by a large orange and purple banner. There is a circle in the top left corner that contains the heading **Game**.
- The meanings of math words are found in the *Glossary* near the end of the book. The **Glossary** has a purple banner.

(Sample Solutions continue below.)

know how to read a math text. Students should understand that reading a math text is different from reading a novel.

To read successfully, students have to learn and understand the symbols and be able to "translate" from English to mathematics and from mathematics to English.

Here are some additional activities:

1. On the board, write the headings Prime Factorization, Expanded Form, Scientific Notation, Order of Operations, and Solving Equations. Assign each title to a group of students. Have the students review the topic, then write a brief summary and an example on chart paper. Post and discuss the results to check for understanding.
2. Pick any lesson and have students summarize the *Connect* section.

(Sample Solutions, continued)

- How people use math in their work is found in **The World of Work**. The banner is purple and red, and the circle in the top left corner represents the Earth.
- Things that you need to know to be able to work through a unit are found in **Skills You'll Need** at the beginning of each unit. They have purple banners.
- Math to practise in your head is found in some of the green boxes that are in every *Practice* section. They have the heading **Mental Math**.

UNIT REVIEW

LESSON ORGANIZER

Student Materials
- calculators

Optional
- algebra tiles (PM 27)

Assessment:
Master 1.1 Unit Rubric: Numbers, Variables, and Equations
Master 1.4 Unit Summary: Numbers, Variables, and Equations

Unit Review

Review any lesson with etext online tutorial

What Do I Need to Know?

✓ **Prime Factorization**
Use repeated division to find prime factors.
Write the prime factors as powers when possible.
For example, $630 = 2 \times 3^2 \times 5 \times 7$

✓ **Expanded Form with Powers of 10**
Use place value to write a number as the sum of its parts.
For example, $4356 = 4 \times 10^3 + 3 \times 10^2 + 5 \times 10 + 6$

✓ **Scientific Notation**
It is used to write a large number as the product of a number greater than or equal to 1 and less than 10, and a power of 10.
For example, $7\ 500\ 000 = 7.5 \times 10^6$

✓ **Order of Operations**
To evaluate an expression with different operations, follow this order:
- Do the operations in brackets.
- Do the exponents.
- Multiply and divide, in order, from left to right.
- Add and subtract, in order, from left to right.

What Should I Be Able to Do?

For extra practice, go to page 488.

LESSON 1.1

1. Here are some data about voluntary organizations in 2003:
   - Canadians took out 139 000 000 memberships in these organizations.
   - Nineteen million Canadians contributed more than 2 000 000 000 h of voluntary time.
   - These organizations had $112 000 000 000 in revenues.

   Write a problem about these data. Solve your problem. Justify the strategy you used.

Correlation of Extra Practice questions on page 488:

Lesson	Questions
1.1	1
1.2	2, 3, 4
1.3	5, 6, 7
1.4	8
1.5	9, 10
1.6	9, 10

Sample Solutions

1. For example: "How many more people took out memberships than volunteered?"
   Answer: 139 million − 19 million = 120 million
   One hundred twenty million more people took out memberships than volunteered.
   I used mental math because I subtracted two numbers that were whole numbers of millions.

4. **a)** Since the factors are prime, the least number is their product: $11 \times 23 = 253$
   b) The greatest number a calculator displays is 9 999 999 999. Divide this number by 253 to get 39 525 691.7. Ignore the decimal part of this number. Multiply: $253 \times 39\ 525\ 691$ to get 9 999 999 823, which is the greatest number that can be displayed.

5. In part a, 1 is not a prime factor. In part b, $2^2 \times 3 \times 5^2 = 300$. In part d, 75 is not a prime factor.

6. **a) i)** $15 = 3 \times 5$, $35 = 5 \times 7$; the common factor is 5.
   ii) The first common multiple is: $5 \times 3 \times 7 = 105$
   The second common multiple is: $105 \times 2 = 210$
   The third common multiple is: $105 \times 3 = 315$
   b) i) $20 = 2 \times 2 \times 5$, $100 = 2 \times 2 \times 5 \times 5$; the common factors are: 2 and 5; and $2 \times 2 = 4$; $2 \times 5 = 10$; and $2 \times 2 \times 5 = 20$
   ii) The first common multiple is: $2 \times 2 \times 5 \times 5 = 100$
   The second common multiple is: $100 \times 2 = 200$
   The third common multiple is: $100 \times 3 = 300$
   c) i) $25 = 5 \times 5$, $75 = 3 \times 5 \times 5$; the common factors are: 5; and $5 \times 5 = 25$
   ii) The first common multiple is: $5 \times 5 \times 3 = 75$
   The second common multiple is: $75 \times 2 = 150$
   The third common multiple is: $75 \times 3 = 225$
   d) i) $30 = 2 \times 3 \times 5$, $36 = 2 \times 2 \times 3 \times 3$; the common factors are: 2 and 3; and $2 \times 3 = 6$
   ii) The first common multiple is: $2 \times 2 \times 3 \times 3 \times 5 = 180$
   The second common multiple is: $180 \times 2 = 360$
   The third common multiple is: $180 \times 3 = 540$

7. **a)** Any two numbers that do not have a common factor; for example, 6 and 11; or 28 and 15
   b) Any two numbers that have at least one common factor; for example, 8 and 10; or 24 and 80
   c) The lowest common multiple is less than the product of two numbers if the numbers have at least one common factor. If the numbers do not have any common factors, the lowest common multiple is the product of the two numbers.

LESSON

1.2 **2.** Write each number as a product of prime factors. $2^2 \times 3 \times 5$

a) 64 2^6 b) 42 $2 \times 3 \times 7$ c) 60 d) 30 $2 \times 3 \times 5$

Write each product in standard form.

a) $2^4 \times 3$ 48 b) $5^2 \times 2^2$ 100

4. A number has 11 and 23 as factors.

a) Which is the least number this could be? 253

b) Which is the greatest number with these factors that can be displayed on your calculator?

5. Which expression shows the prime factorization of 600? Explain.

a) $1 \times 2^3 \times 3 \times 5^2$

b) $2^2 \times 3 \times 5^2$

c) $2^3 \times 5^2 \times 3$ (circled)

d) $2 \times 2 \times 2 \times 75$

6. For each pair of numbers below:

i) Find all the common factors.

ii) Find the first 3 common multiples.

a) 15, 35 b) 20, 100

c) 25, 75 d) 30, 36

7. a) Find two pairs of numbers for which the lowest common multiple is the product of the numbers.

b) Find two pairs of numbers for which the lowest common multiple is less than the product of the numbers.

c) How can you tell if the lowest common multiple of two numbers is less than or equal to the product of the numbers?

1.3 **8.** Here are the areas of the ten largest lakes in the world, to the nearest 100 km².

Lake	Area (km²)
Huron, North America	5.96×10^4
Aral Sea, Asia	3.07×10^4
Caspian Sea, Asia-Europe	371 000
Great Bear, North America	31 300
Superior, North America	82 100
Baikal, Asia	3.15×10^4
Victoria, Africa	69 500
Malawi, Africa	28 900
Michigan, North America	57 800
Tanganyika, Africa	32 900

a) Order the lakes from greatest area to least area. Explain how you did this.

b) Which two lakes together have an area approximately equal to that of Lake Superior? How do you know?

9. Write each number in expanded form using powers of 10.

a) 9 337 000 b) 977 183

c) 106 040 055 d) 73 532

10. Write each number in scientific notation.

a) 1 500 000 1.5×10^6 b) 42 000 4.2×10^4

c) 600 000 000 6×10^8 d) 27 2.7×10^1

Unit Review 43

8. a) Caspian Sea, Superior, Victoria, Huron, Michigan, Tanganyika, Baikal, Great Bear, Aral, Malawi; I wrote each area in standard form, then ordered the numbers.

b) Malawi and Michigan; 28 900 is about 29 000. 57 800 is about 58 000.
58 000 + 29 000 = 60 000 + 27 000 = 87 000, which is close to 82 100.

9. a) $9 \times 10^6 + 3 \times 10^5 + 3 \times 10^4 + 7 \times 10^3$

b) $9 \times 10^5 + 7 \times 10^4 + 7 \times 10^3 + 1 \times 10^2 + 8 \times 10^1 + 3$

c) $1 \times 10^8 + 6 \times 10^6 + 4 \times 10^4 + 5 \times 10^1 + 5$

d) $7 \times 10^4 + 3 \times 10^3 + 5 \times 10^2 + 3 \times 10^1 + 2$

12. a) $83 - 6 \times 11 = 83 - 66 = 17$

b) $15 + (3 + 12) \times 6 = 15 + 15 \times 6 = 15 + 90 = 105$

c) $(20 - 9)^2 - 3 \times 2 = 11^2 - 6 = 121 - 6 = 115$

d) $1.3 + 4.1^2 - 15 = 1.3 + 16.81 - 15 = 18.11 - 15 = 3.11$

13. a) $30w - 2w^2$
Substitute: $w = 5$

$$30(5) - 2(5)^2 = 30(5) - 2(25) = 150 - 50 = 100$$

The area is 100 m².

14. a)
$$x + 2 = 7$$
$$x + 2 - 2 = 7 - 2$$
$$x = 5$$

b)
$$x - 3 = 5$$
$$x - 3 + 3 = 5 + 3$$
$$x = 8$$

c)
$$13 = 4 + x$$
$$13 - 4 = 4 - 4 + x$$
$$9 = x$$

d)
$$7 = x - 2$$
$$7 + 2 = x - 2 + 2$$
$$9 = x$$

16. a)
$$3 + 11 = 5 + x$$
$$14 = 5 + x$$
$$14 - 5 = 5 - 5 + x$$
$$9 = x$$

L.S. = 3 + 11 = 14 R.S. = 5 + x = 5 + 9 = 14

17. a)

$$6 + 3x = 17 - 2$$
$$6 + 3x = 15$$
$$6 - 6 + 3x = 15 - 6$$
$$3x = 9$$
$$\frac{3x}{3} = \frac{9}{3}$$
$$x = 3$$

L.S. $= 6 + 3x$ R.S. $= 17 - 2$
$= 6 + 3(3)$ $= 15$
$= 6 + 9$
$= 15$

LESSON

11. Write each number in standard form.
a) 6×10^3 6000 b) 8.43×10^6 8 430 000
c) 7.2×10^5 720 000 d) 3.28×10^8 328 000 000

1.4 **12.** Evaluate.
a) $83 - 6 \times 11$ 17
b) $15 + (3 + 12) \times 6$ 105
c) $(20 - 9)^2 - 3 \times 2$ 115
d) $1.3 + 4.1^2 - 15$ 3.11

13. A rectangular lot has a river along one side.

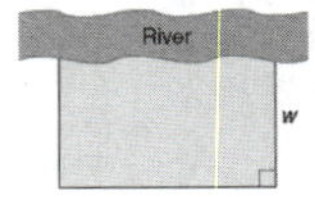

The fencing for the other 3 sides has a total length of 30 m. When the width of the lot is w metres, the area of the lot, in square metres, is expressed as $30w - 2w^2$.
What is the area of the lot for each value of w?
a) 5 m 100 m² b) 9 m 108 m² c) 12 m 72 m²

1.5 **14.** Solve each equation.
a) $x + 2 = 7$ $x = 5$ b) $x - 3 = 5$ $x = 8$
c) $13 = 4 + x$ $x = 9$ d) $7 = x - 2$ $x = 9$

15. Jan collects foreign stamps. Her friend gives her 8 stamps. Jan then has 21 stamps. How many stamps did Jan have to start with? 13
Let x represent the number of stamps.
Then, an equation is $8 + x = 21$.
Solve the equation.
Answer the question. 13 stam

16. Solve each equation. Verify the solution.
a) $3 + 11 = 5 + x$ $x = 9$
b) $x - 3 = 11 - 8$ $x = 6$
c) $16 - 9 = x + 4$ $x = 3$
d) $x - 7 = 8 - 5$ $x = 10$

1.6 **17.** Solve each equation. Verify the solution.
a) $6 + 3x = 17 - 2$ $x = 3$
b) $9 + 12 = 2x - 1$ $x = 11$
c) $5x - 3 = 9 - 2$ $x = 2$
d) $14 - 3 = 4x + 7$ $x = 1$

18. One paperback book costs $7. How many books can be bought for $133?
Let x represent the number of books.
Then, an equation is $7x = 133$.
Solve the equation. $x = 19$
Answer the question. 19 books

19. Jaya has 26 hockey cards. Jaya has 1 fewer than 3 times the number her brother, Kumar, has. How many cards does Kumar have?
Let x represent the number of cards Kumar has.
Then, an equation is $3x - 1 = 26$.
Solve the equation. $x = 9$
Answer the question. 9 cards

44 UNIT 1: Numbers, Variables, and Equations

ASSESSMENT FOR LEARNING

What to Look For

Knowledge and Understanding

✔ **Question 9:** Student can represent whole numbers in expanded form using powers of 10.
✔ **Question 10:** Student can represent whole numbers in scientific notation.
✔ **Question 12:** Student understands the order of operations with brackets and exponents.

Thinking

✔ **Question 7:** Student can solve a problem related to common multiples.

Communication

✔ **Question 1:** Student can justify the choice of strategy when solving a problem.

Application

✔ **Questions 2 and 6:** Student can represent composite numbers as products of prime factors.
✔ **Question 13:** Student can apply the concept of order of operations to simplify an algebraic expression after substituting for the variable.
✔ **Questions 14, 16, and 17:** Student can solve equations using a model, algebra tiles, or inverse operations.

Recording and Reporting

Master 1.1 Unit Rubric: Numbers, Variables, and Equations
Master 1.4 Unit Summary: Numbers, Variables, and Equations

Practice Test

1. Canada is rich in natural resources.
We have abundant water, yet we must conserve this resource.
The average Canadian toilet uses 20 L of water per flush.
   a) About how many litres of water are flushed in one household per day? Justify your answer.
   b) Suppose you installed a low-consumption toilet that used only 6 L of water per flush.
   How much water could you save in one day?
2. How is expanded form with powers of 10 like scientific notation? How are they different? Give examples to support your answer.
3. a) Write a 4-digit number that is divisible by 11 and 17.
   b) Write the prime factorization of this number.
4. A cell phone company has a monthly service charge of $25 plus 10¢ for each minute or part of a minute of air time.
   a) What is the cost if a person uses 100 min of air time in one month? $35
   b) In each expression below, m represents the number of minutes of air time.
   Which expression represents the monthly cost in dollars? Explain how you know.
   i) $10m + 0.25$ ii) $(25 + 0.10)m$
   iii) $25 + 0.10m$ (circled) iv) $0.10 + 25m$
   c) Find the cost if a person uses 175 min of air time in 3 months.
5. Solve each equation. Verify the solution.
   a) $5 + x = 20 - 3$ $x = 12$
   b) $11 = 2x - 9$ $x = 10$
   c) $6 + 3x = 40 - 1$ $x = 11$
6. Three less than 5 times a number is 62.
What is the number? 13
Show your work.

Practice Test 45

LESSON ORGANIZER

Student Materials
- calculators

Optional
- algebra tiles (PM 27)

Assessment:
Master 1.1 Unit Rubric: Numbers, Variables, and Equations
Master 1.4 Unit Summary: Numbers, Variables, and Equations

Assignment Guidelines

To assess the 4 Achievement Chart categories listed in the curriculum document, use these test questions:
Knowledge and Understanding: 1
Communication: 2
Application: 4
Thinking: 6

Sample Solutions

1. For example: I assumed there are 6 people in the household, and that each person flushes the toilet 5 times per day. Each flush uses 20 L.
   a) The volume of water in litres used in one day is:
   number of people × number of flushes per person × volume of water per flush = $6 \times 5 \times 20 = 600$
   The household uses 600 L per day.
   b) If each flush used only 6 L of water, the volume of water saved per flush is 20 L – 6 L = 14 L. So, the total volume of water saved is: $6 \times 5 \times 14$ L = 420 L
   I would save 420 L per day.
2. Both methods use powers of 10 multiplied by a number greater than or equal to 1 and less than 10. Expanded form shows the given number as the sum of numbers, each written as a product of a whole number and a power of 10; for example, 12 345 is written
$1 \times 10^5 + 2 \times 10^4 + 3 \times 10^2 + 4 \times 10^1 + 5$.
Scientific notation shows the number as a product of two factors: one factor is a number greater than or equal to 1, and less than 10; the other factor is a power of 10; for example, 12 345 is written as 1.2345×10^4.
3. a) The number must be a multiple of $11 \times 17 = 187$.
   I used a calculator. I multiplied 187 by a different whole number each time until I got a product that was a 4-digit number. For example: $8 \times 187 = 1496$
   b) $1496 = 2 \times 2 \times 2 \times 11 \times 17$, or $2^3 \times 11 \times 17$
4. a) Cost for 1 min = 10¢
   Cost for 100 min = 100 × 10¢
   = 1000¢
   = $10
   Add the service charge: $10 + $25 = $35
   b) $25 + 0.10m$; 25 represents the monthly service charge in dollars, 0.10 represents the cost of each additional minute or part of a minute, in dollars, and m represents the number of minutes of air time.
   To check, I substituted $m = 100$ in each expression to check which one equals 35, the answer in part a.
   i) $10m + 0.25 = 10 \times 100 + 0.25 = 1000.25$
   ii) $(25 + 0.10)m = (25 + 0.10)(100) = (25.1)(100) = 2510$
   iii) $25 + 0.10m = 25 + 0.10 \times 100 = 25 + 10 = 35$
   iv) $0.10 + 25m = 0.10 + 25(100) = 0.10 + 2500 = 2500.10$
   c) $3(25) + 0.10(175) = 92.50$, or $92.50; the monthly service charge must be multiplied by 3 because the 175 min of air time was used over a period of three months.
6. Let n represent the number.
Then 5 times the number is $5n$.
Three less than 5 times the number is $5n - 3$.
Then, an equation is: $5n - 3 = 62$
$$5n - 3 + 3 = 62 + 3$$
$$5n = 65$$
$$\frac{5n}{5} = \frac{65}{5}$$
$$n = 13$$

Planning a Ski Trip

LESSON ORGANIZER 80–100 min

Student Grouping: 2-4

Student Materials
- atlases
- brochures for Mont Tremblant
- calculators

Assessment:
Master 1.3 Performance Assessment Rubric: Planning a Ski Trip
Master 1.4 Unit Summary: Numbers, Variables, and Equations

Sample Response

Part 1

1. From greatest elevation to least elevation: Telluride, Aspen Highlands, Vail, Big Sky, Steamboat, Jackson Hole, Heavenly, Sun Valley, Kicking Horse, Whistler/Blackcomb
2. **a)** 4 students **b)** 8 students
   The number in each group is a factor of 96 between 4 and 10. Possible factors are 4, 6, and 8. So, the minimum number in each group is 4 and the maximum number is 8.
3. **a)** $10 - 1050 \div 150 = 10 - 7 = 3$; the temperature is 3°C.
   b) $0 - 900 \div 150 = 0 - 6 = -6$; the temperature is −6°C.
4. Company A: Cost = \$300 + \$55 × 104 = \$300 + \$5720 = \$6020
   Company B: Cost = \$100 + \$75 × 104 = \$100 + \$7800 = \$7900
   Company A is cheaper by almost \$2000.

Unit Problem Planning a Ski Trip

Part 1

1. The top ten North American ski resorts are listed, with their elevations.
   Whistler/Blackcomb, B.C.: 2.284×10^3 m
   Big Sky, Montana: 3.399×10^3 m
   Jackson Hole, Wyoming: 3185 m
   Kicking Horse, British Columbia: 2450 m
   Steamboat, Colorado: 3221 m
   Aspen Highlands, Colorado: 3559 m
   Telluride, Colorado: 3.737×10^3 m
   Heavenly, California: 3068 m
   Vail, Colorado: 3527 m
   Sun Valley, Idaho: 2789 m

   Order the resorts from greatest elevation to least elevation.

Suppose you are in charge of planning a four-day Grade 8 ski trip.

2. You decide to ski in Mont Tremblant, Quebec.
   Ninety-six students will go on the trip.
   They are organized in groups based on the following rules:
   - Groups must have an even number of students.
   - All groups must have the same number of students.
   - Groups cannot have fewer than 4 or more than 10 students.

   a) What is the minimum number of students that could be in each group? 4 students
   b) What is the maximum number of students that could be in each group? 8 students
3. When you are skiing, you must be aware of extreme temperatures. As you ascend the mountain, the temperature drops. An expression for calculating the temperature at a given elevation is: $c - e \div 150$; where
   c is the temperature in degrees Celsius at sea level, and
   e is the elevation in metres.
   a) Suppose the temperature at sea level is 10°C.
   What is the temperature at an elevation of 1050 m? 3°C

46 UNIT 1: Numbers, Variables, and Equations

Have students turn to pages 4 and 5 of the Student Book.

Review *What You'll Learn*, the learning goals of the unit, and discuss the meanings of the Key Words. Tell students they will use the skills and concepts they learned in this unit to complete the *Unit Problem*.

Present the *Unit Problem*. Have one student read the *Check List* aloud. Remind students that they should use the *Check List* to assess their work before handing it in.

You may also wish to provide students with copies of Master 1.3 Performance Assessment Rubric: Planning a Ski Trip so they will know how their work will be assessed.

After students have completed Part 1, they should discuss the proposed trip outlined in Part 2. Students should list their assumptions (number of students, adults, nights of stay, days skiing, lift passes, ski sets, and so on).

Students should be encouraged to include additional information, such as possible temperatures on the slopes, cost of food, and so on.

For more information on Mont Tremblant, visit www.tremblant.ca (accessed August, 2005).

REFLECT ON THE UNIT

Numbers can be written in standard form, expanded form, scientific notation, and as the product of prime factors.
For example:

$$2\,116\,800 = 2 \times 10^6 + 1 \times 10^5 + 1 \times 10^4 + 6 \times 10^3 + 8 \times 10^2$$
$$= 2.1168 \times 10^6 = 2^6 \times 3^3 \times 5^2 \times 7^2$$

Variables are used in expressions and equations. An equation can be solved by using a two-pan balance model, algebra tiles, or algebra and inverse operations.
For example: to solve $3x + 7 = 25$ using algebra:

$$3x + 7 - 7 = 25 - 7$$
$$3x = 18$$
$$\frac{3x}{3} = \frac{18}{3}$$
$$x = 6$$

I verify the solution by substituting $x = 6$ in each side of the equation.

b) Mont Tremblant has an elevation of 900 m. Suppose the temperature at sea level is 0°C. What is the temperature at the peak? −6°C

4. Two local bus companies, Company A and Company B, offer packages for school trips.
The rate for each company is given by these expressions:
Company A: $300 + 55n$
Company B: $100 + 75n$
where n is the number of people on a bus.
Suppose 96 students and 8 adults go on the trip.
Which company should you choose? Justify your answer.
Company A: $6020 Company B: $7900
Company A is cheaper by almost $2000.

Check List

Your work should show:
- ✓ all calculations in detail
- ✓ your understanding of algebraic expressions
- ✓ the strategies you used to solve the problems
- ✓ a clear explanation of the thinking behind your solutions

Part 2

Plan the ski trip for your class.
Decide how many adults will go with you.
There needs to be 1 adult for every 12 students.
The hotel accommodation in Mont Tremblant is $66 per person per night.
Use the information on these pages and on page 5.
Show all your work. Include costs for transportation, accommodation, and recreation.
State any assumptions you made.

Reflect on the Unit

Write about the different ways to represent a number, and how variables are used in expressions and equations.

Unit Problem: Planning a Ski Trip **47**

Part 2

We assumed 36 students will go. They are 13 and 14 years old. We will take 3 adults and stay in a hotel for 2 nights. We will rent ski equipment for 2 days. Each person will need 2 ski passes.
The cost of transportation:
Company A: Cost = $300 + $55 × 39 = $300 + $2145 = $2445
Company B: Cost = $100 + $75 × 39 = $100 + $2925 = $3025
We will use Company A as it is cheaper.
The cost of accommodation:
The hotel accommodation is $66 per person per night.
So, the total cost is: $66 × 39 × 2 = $5148
We assume that no one has her or his own ski equipment.
The cost of equipment rental:
The cost to rent a complete set of ski equipment is $17.99 per day. So, the total cost is: $17.99 × 39 × 2 = $1403.22
The cost of chair lift tickets:
A youth ticket costs $40.95 per day.
An adult ticket costs $55.00 per day.
So, the total cost is:
($40.95 × 36 × 2) + ($55.00 × 3 × 2) = $3278.40
The cost of food:
We allowed $30 per day per person.
So, the total cost is: $30 × 39 × 2 = $2340
The total cost of the ski trip will be:
$2445 + $5148 + $1403.22 + $3278.40 + $2340 = $14 614.62
The total cost is shared among 36 students.
The cost per student is $\frac{\$14\,614.62}{36}$ = $405.96.
Each student pays just over $400.
We will encourage each person to bring spending money.

ASSESSMENT FOR LEARNING

What to Look For	What to Do
Knowledge and Understanding ✔ Students understand how number concepts and algebra can be used to solve problems. ***Thinking*** ✔ Students can plan a ski trip for their class. ***Communication*** ✔ Students can use mathematical language to explain their solutions to problems. ***Application*** ✔ Students can use concepts, such as scientific notation and algebraic substitution, to solve problems.	***Extra Support:*** Make the problem accessible. For question 1, have students write each height in standard form, then use a place-value chart to order the heights. For question 2, have students write the factors of 96, then identify the least and greatest factors. For question 3, have students identify the value of each variable before substituting. For question 4, remind students to use the order of operations when evaluating the expressions.

Recording and Reporting
Master 1.3 Performance Assessment Rubric: Planning a Ski Trip
Master 1.4 Unit Summary: Numbers, Variables, and Equations

Evaluating Student Learning: Preparing to Report: Unit 1 Numbers, Variables, and Equations

This unit provides an opportunity to report on the **Number Sense and Numeration** and **Patterning and Algebra** strands.

Master 1.4: Unit Summary: Numbers, Variables, and Equations provides a comprehensive format for recording and summarizing evidence collected.

Here is an example of a completed summary chart for this Unit:

Strand: *Number Sense and Numeration/ Patterning and Algebra*	**Knowledge and Understanding**	**Thinking**	**Communication**	**Application**	***Overall***
Ongoing Observations	3	4	3	4	3/4
Work samples or portfolios; conferences	3	3	4	3	3
Unit Review	4	3	3	3	3
Unit Test	3	3	3	3	3
Unit Problem Planning a Ski Trip	3	3	4	4	3/4
Achievement Level for reporting					3

Recording	How to Report
Ongoing Observations	Use *Master 1.2 Ongoing Observations: Numbers, Variables, and Equations* to determine the most consistent level achieved in each category. Enter it in the chart. Choose to summarize by achievement category, or simply to enter an overall level. Observations from late in the unit should be most heavily weighted.
Portfolios or collections of work samples; conferences or interviews	Use *Master 1.1 Unit Rubric: Numbers, Variables, and Equations* to guide evaluation of collections of work and information gathered in conferences. Teachers may choose to focus particular attention on the Assessment Focus questions. Work from late in the unit should be most heavily weighted.
Unit Review	*Master 1.1 Unit Rubric: Numbers, Variables, and Equations* may be helpful in determining levels of achievement. #3, 5, 9, 10, 11, 12, and 14 provide evidence of Knowledge and Understanding; #2, 6, 8, 13, 15, 16, 17, 18, 19, and 20 provide evidence of Application; #1, 4, and 7 provide evidence of Thinking; all questions provide evidence of Communication.
Unit Test	*Master 1.1 Unit Rubric: Numbers, Variables, and Equations* may be helpful in determining levels of achievement. #2 and 4 provide evidence of Knowledge and Understanding; #1 and 5 provide evidence of Application; #7 provides evidence of Thinking; all questions provide evidence of Communication.
Unit Problem	Use *Master 1.3 Performance Assessment Rubric: Planning a Ski Trip.* The *Unit Problem* offers a snapshot of students' achievement. In particular, it shows their ability to synthesize and apply what they have learned.
Student Self-Assessment	Note students' perceptions of their own progress. This may take the form of an oral or written comment, or a self-rating.
Comments	Analyse the pattern of achievement to identify strengths and needs. In some cases, specific actions may need to be planned to support the learner.

Learning Skills	**Ongoing Records**
PM 4: Learning Skills Check List Use to record and report throughout a reporting period, rather than for each unit and/or strand.	*PM 10: Summary Class Records: Strands* *PM 11: Summary Class Records: Achievement Categories* *PM 12: Summary Record: Individual* Use to record and report evaluations of student achievement over several clusters, a reporting period, or a school year. These can also be used in place of the Unit Summary.

Name ____________________ Date ______________

Master 1.1

Unit Rubric: Numbers, Variables, and Equations

	Level 1	Level 2	Level 3	Level 4
Knowledge and Understanding • Shows understanding by demonstrating and explaining: – order of operations with brackets and exponents – ways of representing numbers (scientific notation; expanded form; products of prime factors) – how to solve equations using balance scales and algebra tiles	shows limited understanding; may be unable to demonstrate or explain: – order of operations with brackets and exponents – ways of representing numbers (scientific notation; expanded form; products of prime factors) – how to solve equations using balance scales and algebra tiles	shows some understanding; partially able to demonstrate or explain: – order of operations with brackets and exponents – ways of representing numbers (scientific notation; expanded form; products of prime factors) – how to solve equations using balance scales and algebra tiles	shows considerable understanding; able to clearly and appropriately demonstrate or explain: – order of operations with brackets and exponents – ways of representing numbers (scientific notation; expanded form; products of prime factors) – how to solve equations using balance scales and algebra tiles	shows a high degree of understanding; able to accurately and effectively demonstrate or explain: – order of operations with brackets and exponents – ways of representing numbers (scientific notation; expanded form; products of prime factors) – how to solve equations using balance scales and algebra tiles
Thinking • Chooses and carries out a range of strategies to solve and check multi-step problems involving numbers, variables, and equations; justifies the strategies used to produce an accurate solution	with assistance, chooses, carries out, and justifies a limited range of appropriate strategies to solve and check multi-step problems; rarely produces an accurate solution	with limited assistance, chooses, carries out, and justifies some appropriate strategies to solve and check problems; frequently produces an accurate solution	chooses, carries out, and justifies appropriate strategies to solve and check problems; usually produces an accurate solution	develops, carries out, and justifies effective, and often innovative, strategies to solve and check problems; always produces an accurate solution
Communication • Explains concepts, procedures, and reasoning clearly, using appropriate terms (e.g., variable)	unable to explain concepts, procedures, and reasoning clearly	partially explains concepts, procedures, and reasoning	explains concepts, procedures, and reasoning clearly	explains concepts, procedures, and reasoning clearly, precisely, and confidently
• Presents work clearly	presents work with little clarity	presents work with some clarity and precision	presents work with considerable clarity and precision	presents work with a high degree of clarity and precision
Application • Accurately: – represents whole numbers using prime factors, expanded form, and scientific notation – applies order of operations with brackets and exponents – evaluates algebraic expressions – solves equations using balance scales and tiles, and verifies solutions	limited accuracy; major errors or omissions in: – representing whole numbers using prime factors, expanded form, and scientific notation – applying order of operations with brackets and exponents – evaluating algebraic expressions – solving equations using balance scales and tiles, and verifying solutions	somewhat accurate; several minor errors or omissions in: – representing whole numbers using prime factors, expanded form, and scientific notation – applying order of operations with brackets and exponents – evaluating algebraic expressions – solving equations using balance scales and tiles, and verifying solutions	generally accurate; few minor errors or omissions in: – representing whole numbers using prime factors, expanded form, and scientific notation – applying order of operations with brackets and exponents – evaluating algebraic expressions – solving equations using balance scales and tiles, and verifying solutions	accurate and precise; no errors in: – representing whole numbers using prime factors, expanded form, and scientific notation – applying order of operations with brackets and exponents – evaluating algebraic expressions – solving equations using balance scales and tiles, and verifying solutions

Name ____________________ Date ________________

Master 1.2

Ongoing Observations: Numbers, Variables, and Equations

The behaviours described under each heading are examples; they are not intended to be an exhaustive list of all that might be observed. More detailed descriptions are provided in each lesson under *Assessment for Learning*.

STUDENT ACHIEVEMENT: Numbers, Variables, and Equations				
Student	**Knowledge and Understanding** • Demonstrates and explains: – order of operations, expanded form, scientific notation, and prime factors – solving equations using balance scales and algebra tiles	**Thinking** • Chooses, carries out, and justifies a range of appropriate strategies to solve and check multi-step problems; usually results in accurate solution	**Communication** • Explains concepts, procedures, and reasoning clearly • Presents work clearly	**Application** • Accurately: – represents numbers using prime factors, expanded form, and scientific notation – applies order of operations – solves equations; verifies solutions

Level 1 – very limited; Level 2 – somewhat or limited; Level 3 – satisfactory; Level 4 – thorough

Name ____________________ Date ______________

Master 1.3

Performance Assessment Rubric: Planning a Ski Trip

	Level 1	Level 2	Level 3	Level 4
Knowledge and Understanding • Shows understanding of algebraic expressions by appropriately justifying choice of bus company	shows limited understanding; may be unable to justify choice	shows some understanding; gives appropriate but incomplete explanations for choice	shows considerable understanding by giving appropriate and complete explanations for choice	shows a high degree of understanding by giving appropriate and thorough explanations for choice
Thinking • Uses appropriate strategies to: – group students (Part 1) – plan the ski trip, determine costs, and verify solutions using the information given (Part 2)	uses a limited range of appropriate strategies, with limited success to: – group students – plan the ski trip, determine costs, and verify solutions	uses some appropriate strategies to: – group students – plan the ski trip, determine costs, and verify solutions; some success	uses appropriate strategies to: – group students – plan the ski trip, determine costs, and verify solutions; considerable success	uses innovative and effective strategies to: – group students – plan the ski trip, determine costs, and verify solutions; high degree of success
Communication • Explains reasoning clearly using appropriate mathematical terminology (e.g., variable) • Presents work clearly	explains reasoning unclearly and imprecisely using few mathematical terms presents work with little clarity	explains reasoning with some clarity using some appropriate mathematical terms presents work with some clarity	explains reasoning clearly and precisely using appropriate mathematical terms presents work clearly	explains reasoning clearly, precisely, and confidently using a range of appropriate mathematical terminology presents work clearly and precisely
Application • Accurately: – orders elevations (interprets scientific notation) – uses factors to group students – evaluates algebraic expressions to determine temperature and choose a bus company – calculates costs of the trip they plan	limited accuracy; major errors or omissions in: – interpreting scientific notation – using factors – evaluating algebraic expressions – calculating costs of planned trip	somewhat accurate; several minor errors or omissions in: – interpreting scientific notation – using factors – evaluating algebraic expressions – calculating costs of planned trip	generally accurate; few minor errors or omissions in: – interpreting scientific notation – using factors – evaluating algebraic expressions – calculating costs of planned trip	accurate and precise; with no errors or omissions in: – interpreting scientific notation – using factors – evaluating algebraic expressions – calculating costs of planned trip

Name ____________________ Date ______________

Master 1.4

Unit Summary: Numbers, Variables, and Equations

Review assessment records to determine the most consistent achievement levels for the assessments conducted. Some cells may be blank. *Overall* achievement levels may be recorded in each row, rather than identifying levels for each achievement category.

	Most Consistent Level of Achievement*				
Strand: *Number Sense and Numeration/ Patterning and Algebra*	**Knowledge and Understanding**	**Thinking**	**Communication**	**Application**	***Overall***
Ongoing Observations					
Work samples or portfolios; conferences					
Unit Review					
Unit Test					
Unit Problem Planning a Ski Trip					
Achievement Level for reporting					

*Use Ontario Achievement Levels 1, 2, 3, 4

Self-Assessment:

Comments: (Strengths, Needs, Next Steps)

Name ____________________ Date ________________

Master 1.5

Additional Activity 1: Factor Fun

Play with a partner.

You will need a hundred chart, a set of cards labelled 1 to 9, a set of cards labelled 0 to 9, and 2 sets of counters (one colour per player).

How to Play:

1. Shuffle each set of cards. Place the cards face down in 2 piles.
2. Player A turns over the top card in each pile to make a 2-digit number.
   The first card is the tens digit and the second card is the ones digit.
3. Player A places her counters on the hundred chart to cover all the factors of that number.
   She gets 1 point for each correct factor.
   Player B uses his counters to cover any factors missed by Player A.
   He gets 1 point for each correct factor.
4. Change roles. Repeat *Steps 1* to *3*.
5. Continue to take turns.
   The player with the higher score after 5 rounds wins.

Take It Further:
Play the game again.
This time, cover only the prime factors of each number.

Name ____________________ Date ________________

Master 1.6

Additional Activity 2: Size It Up

Play with a partner.

You will need a deck of playing cards with the tens and face cards removed.

How to Play:

1. Separate the black cards from the red cards.
   Shuffle each set of cards and place them face down in 2 piles.

2. Each player draws 3 black cards and 1 red card.
   Use the 3 black cards to make a 3-digit number.
   Multiply the 3-digit number by 10 to the power of the number on the red card.
   Record the product.

3. The player with the greater number gets 1 point.

4. Write your number in expanded form and in scientific notation.
   Check each other's work.
   One point is awarded for each correct answer.

5. Return the cards to the piles and shuffle them.
   Repeat *Steps 2* to *4*.
   The first player to get 15 points wins.

Take It Further:
Play the game again.
This time, arrange the 4 cards any way you wish to get the least number.
Write the number in expanded form and in scientific notation.
Points are awarded as before.

Name ____________________ Date ________________

Master 1.7

Additional Activity 3: It All Adds Up

Play with a partner.

You will need 4 regular octahedrons, labelled 1 to 8.

How to Play:

1. Player A rolls the 4 octahedrons.
2. Player A uses the 4 numbers rolled and any operations or brackets to make as many of the whole numbers from 1 to 10 as he can.
   One point is awarded for each correct expression.
3. Player B has a turn.
4. The player with the higher score after 5 rounds wins.

Take It Further:
Play the game again.
This time, make as many of the whole numbers from 10 to 20 as you can.

Name ____________________ Date ________________

Master 1.8

Additional Activity 4: Solve It

Work on your own.

You will need coloured pencils.

Find sets of equations with the same solution.

Circle each set in a different colour.

A: $x + 3 = 5$	**B:** $3x - 2 = 7$	**C:** $11 = x + 5$
D: $2 = x - 3$	**E:** $21 = 5x + 1$	**F:** $x - 2 = 2$
G: $x - 3 = 3$	**H:** $3x - 7 = 8$	**I:** $2x - 7 = 9$
J: $8 = x + 5$	**K:** $14 = x + 9$	**L:** $1 = x - 1$
M: $3x - 8 = 10$	**N:** $x - 2 = 6$	**O:** $x + 8 = 12$
P: $11 = x + 3$	**Q:** $2x + 5 = 9$	**R:** $x - 3 = 0$

Take It Further:
Write 5 different equations that have the same solution.

Name ____________________ Date ______________

Master 1.9

Step-by-Step 1

Lesson 1.1, Question 4

Step 1 What were the total earnings worldwide of the top five movies?

____

Step 2 Subtract to find how much more money *Titanic* earned than each other movie.
Titanic – Lord of the Rings: Return of the King

____

Titanic – Harry Potter and the Sorcerer's Stone

____

Titanic – Star Wars Episode 1: The Phantom Menace

____

Titanic – Lord of the Rings: The Two Towers

____

Step 3 Add the world box office revenues in pairs.
Which sum is closest to $1835.4 million?

____

Which two movies together earned about as much as *Titanic*?

____

Step 4 Multiply each U.S. box office revenue by 3.
Which products are greater than their matching world box office revenues?

____

Which movies more than tripled their U.S. box office revenues?

____

Step 5 Is revenue a fair way to rank the top five movies? Explain.

____

____

Step 6 Use any of the ideas in parts a and b.
Write your own problem about these data.

____

____

Solve your problem.

Name ____________________ Date ________________

Master 1.10

Step-by-Step 2

Lesson 1.2, Question 12

Step 1 Write $2^2 \times 5^2 \times 7$ as a product of prime numbers without exponents.

____

Write the product as a number in standard form.

____

Step 2 Multiply the prime factors 2, 2, 5, 5, and 7 in pairs to get other factors of the number.

____

____

Step 3 Multiply the prime factors 2, 2, 5, 5, and 7 in groups of three to get other factors of the number.

____

____

Step 4 Multiply the prime factors 2, 2, 5, 5, and 7 in groups of four to get other factors of the number.

____

____

Step 5 List all the different factors of the number in *Step 1*.
Include the prime factors and the number itself.

____

____

Name ______________________ Date _________________

Master 1.11

Step-by-Step 3

Lesson 1.3, Question 9

Step 1 What is true about the first factor of a number written in scientific notation?

____

Step 2 What is true about the second factor of a number written in scientific notation?

____

Step 3 Use the number 12.756×10^3.

Is 12.756 greater than 1? ___________________________

Is 12.756 less than 10? ___________________________

Is 12.756×10^3 in scientific notation? ___________________________

Step 4 Write 12.756×10^3 in standard form, then in scientific notation.

____

Step 5 Give one reason why we use scientific notation.

____

____

Name ____________________ Date ________________

Master 1.12

Step-by-Step 4

Lesson 1.4, Question 10

Use the numbers 2, 4, 6, 8, and any operations or brackets.

Step 1 To make 24:

Use two of the numbers to make 12. ______________________

Use the other two numbers to make 12. ______________________

Use your answers to write an expression that equals 24.

____

Step 2 To make 40:

Use two of the numbers to make 32. ______________________

Use the other two numbers to make 8. ______________________

Use your answers to write an expression that equals 40.

____

Step 3 To make 60:

Use two of the numbers to make 10. ______________________

Use the other two numbers to make 6. ______________________

Use your answers to write an expression that equals 60.

____

Step 4 To make 80:

Use the numbers 2, 6, and 8 to make 20. ______________________

Use your answer and the number 4 to write an expression that equals 80.

____

Name ____________________ Date ______________

Master 1.13

Step-by-Step 5

Lesson 1.5, Question 5

Use masses that are multiples of 5 g.

Step 1 Sketch a two-pan balance to represent the equation $x + 35 = 60$.

Step 2 Write 3 different ways to get a sum of 35.

__________________ __________________ __________________

Step 3 Write 3 different ways to get a sum of 60.

__________________ __________________ __________________

Step 4 Use one way from *Step 2* and one way from *Step 3*.
Sketch a two-pan balance to represent the equation $x + 35 = 60$.
Do this 3 times.

Step 5 Use one of the balances in *Step 4*.
Remove the same masses from each pan to leave x alone in one pan.

What mass does x balance? ____________________

What is the solution of the equation $x + 35 = 60$? ________________

Step 6 Verify the solution by replacing x with the value of x from *Step 5*.

Name ____________________ Date ________________

Master 1.14

Step-by-Step 6

Lesson 1.6, Question 9

Step 1 Write an addition, subtraction, or multiplication fact. ________________________

Replace one of the numbers with x. ______________________________________

You now have an equation.

Step 2 Write the equation in words.

____

Step 3 Solve the equation using algebra tiles.

Step 4 Solve the equation algebraically.

Step 5 Verify the solution. Show your work.

Name ____________________ Date ________________

Master 1.15

Factor Square

4	×	15	×	2	×	9	×	40	×
×	18	×	2	×	2	×	5	×	3
2	×	3	×	24	×	36	×	20	×
×	16	×	10	×	30	×	10	×	12
2	×	60	×	6	×	4	×	2	×
×	11	×	50	×	28	×	5	×	4
2	×	15	×	20	×	3	×	24	×
×	8	×	2	×	5	×	2	×	6
2	×	10	×	3	×	7	×	18	×
×	3	×	5	×	60	×	24	×	5

Name ______________________ Date ________________

Master 1.16a

Unit Test: Unit 1
Numbers, Variables, and Equations

1. This table, from *Statistics Canada*, shows the Canadian cattle inventory as of January 1, 2005.

Type of cattle	Number (Thousands of cattle)
Bulls	272
Milk cows	1065
Beef cows	5320
Dairy heifers	523
Beef heifers for breeding	660
Beef heifers for market	950
Steers	1185
Calves	5115

State which strategy you use to solve each problem.

a) What is Canada's total cattle inventory?

b) How many more beef cows are there than milk cows?

c) Which two types of cattle together total about the same number as beef heifers for market?

d) About what fraction of the total number of cattle are calves?

e) Pose a problem that could be solved using these data.
Solve the problem you posed.

2. Write any 4-digit number.

a) Write the prime factorization of the number.

b) Write the number in expanded form.

c) Write the number in scientific notation.

Name ______________________ Date ________________

Master 1.16b

Unit Test continued

3. How many different answers can you find by inserting one pair of brackets in this expression? Show your work.
$24 \div 3 + 5 \times 2^2$

4. Describe the steps you would follow to solve $3x + 3 = 15$:
a) using algebra tiles **b)** algebraically

Name ____________________ Date ________________

Master 1.16c **Unit Test continued**

5. I think of a number and double it.
I then add 9 to get a sum of 27.
Write an equation.
Solve the equation to find the number.

6. How many seconds are there in one year?
Write your answer in scientific notation.
Show your work.

7. There are 100 m of fencing to enclose a rectangular vegetable plot.
When the width of the plot is w metres,
its area in square metres is expressed as $50w - w^2$.
What is the area of the plot when the width is 30 m?

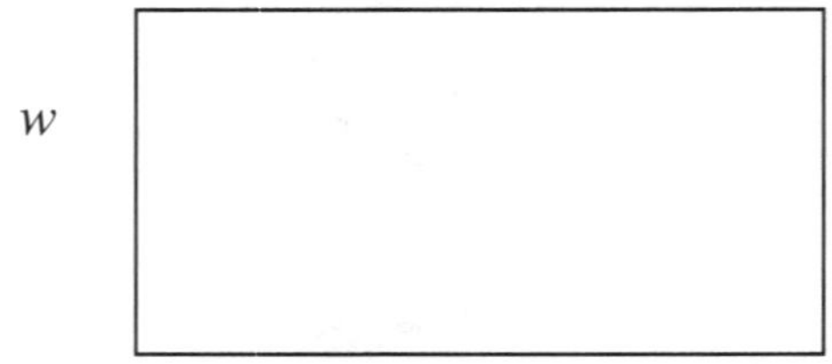

Name ______________________ Date ________________

Master 1.17

Sample Answers

Unit Test – Master 1.16

1. **a)** Use a calculator: 272 + 1065 + 5320 + 523 + 660 + 950 + 1185 + 5115 = 15 090; Canada has 15 090 000 cattle.

b) Use pencil and paper: 5320 – 1065 = 4255; there are 4 255 000 more beef cows.

c) Use pencil and paper: bulls and beef heifers for breeding; 272 + 660 = 932

d) Use estimation: $\frac{5000}{15000} = \frac{1}{3}$

e) For example: "Which type of cattle has about $\frac{1}{10}$ the number of beef cows?"
Answer: Dairy heifers

2. For example: 2464

a) $2464 = 2^5 \times 7 \times 11$

b) $2 \times 10^3 + 4 \times 10^2 + 6 \times 10^1 + 4$

c) 2.464×10^3

3. $(24 \div 3) + 5 \times 2^2 = 28$
$(24 \div 3 + 5) \times 2^2 = 52$
$(24 \div 3 + 5 \times 2)^2 = 324$
$24 \div (3 + 5) \times 2^2 = 12$
$24 \div (3 + 5 \times 2)^2 \doteq 0.142$
$24 \div 3 + (5 \times 2)^2 = 108$
$24 \div (3 + 5 \times 2^2) \doteq 1.043$

4. **a)** On the left side, put 3 x-tiles and 3 yellow unit tiles. On the right side, put 15 yellow unit tiles. To isolate the x-tiles, add 3 red unit tiles to each side. Remove zero pairs. There are 3 x-tiles on the left side, and 12 yellow unit tiles on the right side. Arrange the tiles on each side into 3 equal groups. One x-tile equals 4 unit tiles. So, $x = 4$

b) Add –3 to each side:

$3x + 3 - 3 = 15 - 3$

$3x = 12$

Divide both sides by 3:

$\frac{3x}{3} = \frac{12}{3}$

$x = 4$

5. Let x represent the number.
Twice the number is $2x$.
Twice the number, add 9, is $2x + 9$.
So, the equation is: $2x + 9 = 27$
$x = 9$; the number is 9.

6. Assume 365 days in one year.
365 days × 24 h/day = 8760 h
8760 h × 60 min/h = 525 600 min
525 600 min × 60 s/min = 31 536 000 s
There are about 3.1536×10^7 seconds in one year.

7. $50(30) - 30^2 = 600$; the area of the plot is 600 m^2.

Extra Practice Masters 1.18–1.24

Go to the CD-ROM to access editable versions of these Extra Practice Masters

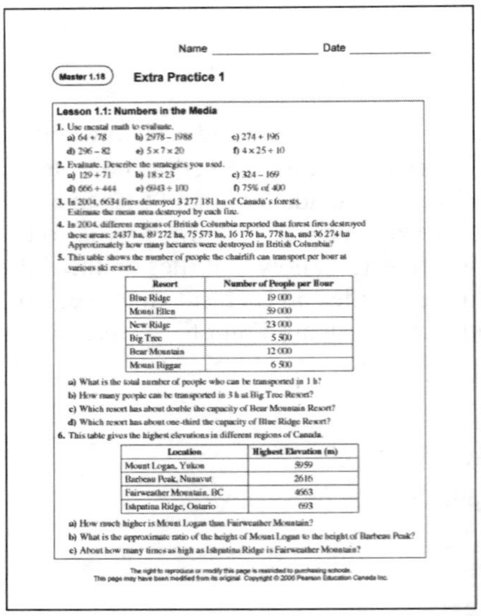

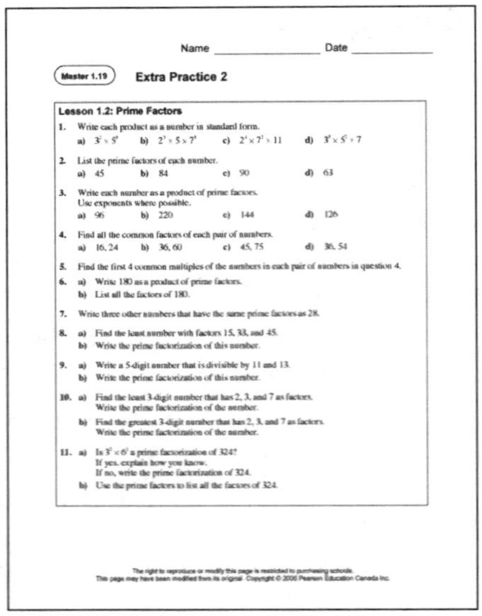

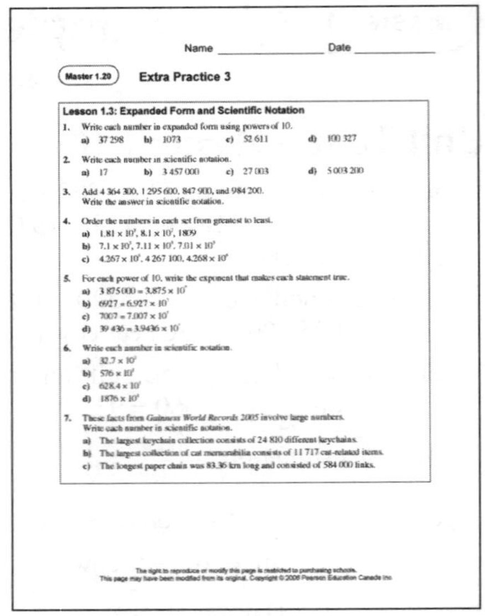

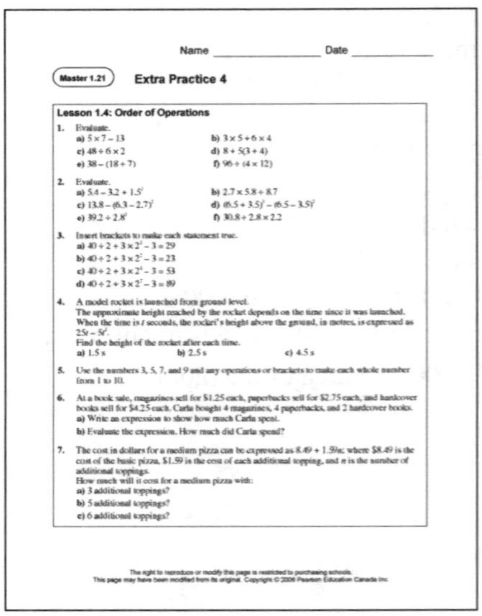

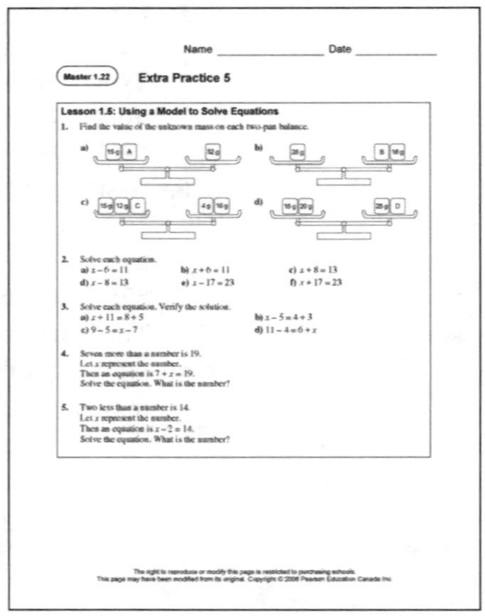

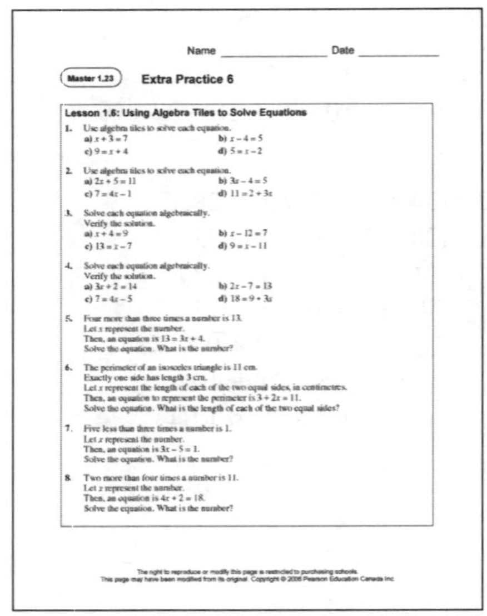

Addison Wesley

Mathematics Makes Sense

Program Authors

Trevor Brown

Antonietta Lenjosek

Cathy Heideman

Jim Mennie

Georgia Konis-Chatzis

A.J. Keene

Margaret Sinclair

Craig Featherstone

Jason Johnston

Bryn Keyes

Elizabeth Wood

Elizabeth Milne

David Sufrin

Don Jones

Sharon Jeroski

Lynn Strangway

Printed and bound in Canada

2 3 4 5 – TC – 09 08 07 06

PEARSON
Education Canada

ADDISON WESLEY

Ontario

Math Makes Sense 8

Ontario

Teacher Guide

Unit 2: Applications of Ratio, Rate, and Percent

PEARSON
Education Canada

UNIT 2 Applications of Ratio, Rate, and Percent

"The ability to understand ratios is one aspect of proportional reasoning, which is considered to be an indicator of a shift from concrete to formal operational levels of thought. Proportional reasoning involves both qualitative and quantitative thinking and concerns prediction and multiple comparisons."

– Lesh, Post, and Behr (1988) in Cathcart, Pothier, and Vance (2004), *Learning Mathematics in Elementary and Middle Schools*, Pearson Prentice Hall, p. 326

FOCUS STRAND
Number Sense and Numeration

SUPPORTING STRAND
Patterning and Algebra

TIPS
Mathematical activity should be balanced with time to investigate and explore as well as time to practise skills.

Mathematics Background

What Are the Big Ideas?

- A ratio is a comparison of two quantities. A student needs to be able to think of a ratio as a distinct entity, different from the two quantities that it comprises.
- A proportion is a statement that two ratios are equal. Equal ratios are related by multiplication or division, not addition or subtraction.
- Proportional thinking or proportional reasoning is the basis of many concepts, including similarity in geometry, and graphing in algebra.
- Simple interest can be calculated using a formula.

How Will the Concepts Develop?

Students set up and solve proportions involving equal ratios.

Students choose and apply appropriate scales to make scale drawings, and investigate scales on maps.

Students apply the concepts of ratio and proportion to investigate relationships among measures of similar figures.

Students calculate and apply unit rates to compare rates and solve problems.

Students estimate and calculate percents including those that are less than 1% and greater than 100% to solve problems. Students find: the percent of a number; a number when a percent of it is given; and percent increases and decreases.

Students estimate and calculate sales tax, discount, and commission and solve related problems.

Students investigate simple interest and use a formula to calculate it.

Why Are These Concepts Important?

Ratios, rates, and percents occur in our world, and have important applications in mathematics. Students need to understand the concepts of ratio, rate, and percent, and apply their understanding to a variety of problems involving tax, discount, commission, simple interest, scale drawings, and maps. The ability to create and solve problems is a useful skill, both in mathematics and the world outside school.

Curriculum Overview

The codes refer to the 2005 revised curriculum.

Cluster 1: Ratio and Rates

Overall Expectations
- Solve problems involving whole numbers, decimal numbers, fractions, ... using a variety of computational strategies. (8m9)
- Solve problems by using proportional reasoning in a variety of meaningful contexts. (8m10)
- Solve and verify algebraic equations ...(8m55)
- Develop geometric relationships involving ... triangles, and polyhedra ...(8m41)

Specific Expectations
- Identify and describe real-life situations involving two quantities that are directly proportional. (8m26)
- Solve problems involving proportions, using concrete materials, drawings, and variables. (8m27)
- Solve problems involving rates. (8m29)
- Solve multi-step problems arising from real-life contexts and involving whole numbers and decimals, using a variety of tools and strategies. (8m16)
- Translate between equivalent forms of a number. (8m14)
- Translate statements describing mathematical relationships into algebraic expressions and equations. (8m61)
- Solve and verify linear equations involving a one-variable term ...(8m64)
- Determine relationships among area, perimeter, corresponding side lengths ...(8m46)

Cluster 2: Percent and Simple Interest

Overall Expectations
- Solve problems involving whole numbers, decimal numbers, fractions, ... using a variety of computational strategies. (8m9)
- Solve problems by using proportional reasoning in a variety of meaningful contexts. (8m10)
- ...Solve and verify algebraic equations ...(8m55)

Specific Expectations
- Translate between equivalent forms of a number. (8m14)
- Solve multi-step problems arising from real-life contexts and involving whole numbers and decimals, using a variety of tools and strategies. (8m16)
- Solve problems involving percents expressed to one decimal place and whole percents greater than 100. (8m17)
- Use estimation when solving problems involving operations with whole numbers, decimals, percents, ... and fractions, to help judge the reasonableness of a solution. (8m18)
- Solve problems involving percents that arise from real-life contexts. (8m28)
- Describe different ways in which algebra can be used in real-life situations. (8m59)
- Translate statements describing mathematical relationships into algebraic expressions and equations. (8m61)
- Evaluate algebraic expressions with up to three terms, by substituting fractions, decimals, ... for the variables. (8m62)

Launch

Lesson 2.1: Using Proportions to Solve Ratio Problems

Lesson 2.2: Scale Drawings

Technology: Exploring Similar Figures

Lesson 2.3: Comparing Rates

Mid-Unit Review

Lesson 2.4: Calculating Percents

Lesson 2.5: Solving Percent Problems

Lesson 2.6: Sales Tax, Discount, and Commission

Lesson 2.7: Simple Interest

Unit Review
Practice Test

Unit Problem
Where to Live?

Curriculum across the Grades

Grade 7	Grade 8
Students determine the relationships among fractions, decimals, percents, and ratios. They solve problems that involve determining whole number percents. Students understand that a rate is a comparison, or ratio, of two measurements with different units. They solve problems involving the calculation of unit rates. Students use estimation when solving problems involving operations with whole numbers, decimals, and percents, to help judge the reasonableness of a solution.	Students identify and describe real-life situations involving two quantities that are directly proportional. They solve problems involving proportions and rates. Students apply the concepts of ratio and proportion to investigate relationships among measures of similar figures. Students solve problems involving percents expressed to one decimal place and whole percents greater than 100. Students solve problems involving whole numbers, decimals, and percents that arise from real-life contexts. They use estimation when solving problems to help judge the reasonableness of a solution. Students translate between equivalent forms of a number.

Additional Activities

Reductions

For Extra Support (Appropriate for use after Skills You'll Need)

Materials: *Reductions* (Master 2.5a), a set of *Reduction Cards* (Master 2.5b)

Playing this game provides practice in stating ratios in simplest form.

The work students do: Students play in pairs. Students take turns to pick two cards. The numbers are used to state the ratio of the first number to the second number in simplest form. One point is given for correctly stating the ratio in simplest form. The student with more points after 6 rounds wins.

Take It Further: Students play the game again, this time using the numbers to form a fraction, then an equivalent percent.

Mathematical/Social/Logical

Partner Activity

Triple Play

For Extra Practice (Appropriate for use after Skills You'll Need)

Materials: *Triple Play* (Master 2.6a), *Ratio Cards* (Master 2.6b)

Playing this game reinforces students' knowledge of equivalent ratios.

The work students do: Students play in pairs. Students take turns to pick a card and give the ratio in simplest form, as well as two other equivalent ratios. Students get 1 point for the ratio in simplest form and 1 point for each equivalent ratio. The student with more points after 6 rounds wins.

Take It Further: Students create a set of cards with the ratios in simplest form. The cards are combined with those on Master 2.6b. A student shuffles and deals 8 cards to each student. The aim of the game is to collect pairs of equivalent ratios. Students pick and discard a card each round.

Mathematical/Social/Logical

Partner Activity

Pair It Up

For Extra Practice (Appropriate for use after Skills You'll Need)

Materials: *Pair It Up* (Master 2.7a), *Pair It Up Cards* (Master 2.7b)

Playing this game reinforces the skills of recognizing equivalent fractions, decimals, and percents.

The work students do: Students play in pairs. All the cards are placed face down. Students turn 2 cards face up. If the cards show equivalent numbers, the student keeps the cards. If the numbers are not equivalent, the cards are turned face down. The students with more pairs after all the cards have been picked up wins.

Take It Further: Shuffle and deal 8 cards to each student. The aim of the game is to collect equivalent pairs. Students pick and discard a card each round.

Logical/Mathematical/Social

Partner Activity

Rate It

For Extra Support (Appropriate for use after Lesson 2.3)

Materials: *Rate It* (Master 2.8a), *Rate It Cards* (Master 2.8b)

Playing this game provides practice in stating unit rates.

The work students do: Students play in pairs. Students take turns turning over a card and stating the quantities as a unit rate. One point is awarded for each correct response.

Take It Further: Students use index cards to write another set of game cards.

Mathematical/Logical/Social

Partner Activity

Planning for Unit 2

Planning for Instruction

Suggested Unit time: About 4 weeks

Lesson	Time	Materials	Program Support
Launch, page 2	15–20 min	calculators	
Skills You'll Need, page 4	65–80 min	calculators	
2.1: Using Proportions to Solve Ratio Problems, page 7 Set up a proportion to solve a ratio problem.	80–100 min	calculators	Master 2.9: Step-by-Step 1 Master 2.19: Extra Practice 1
2.2: Scale Drawings, page 11 Solve problems involving scale drawings.	80–100 min	calculators 1-cm grid paper metre sticks, measuring tapes, or trundle wheels atlases or maps (optional)	PM 20: 1-cm Grid Paper Master 2.10: Step-by-Step 2 Master 2.20: Extra Practice 2
Technology: Exploring Similar Figures, page 15 Investigate relationships among side lengths, angles, perimeter, and area.	80–100 min	0.5-cm grid paper 1-cm grid paper square dot paper isometric dot paper 5-column charts	Master 2.18: Alternative Explore for Similar Figures PM 14: 0.5-cm Grid Paper PM 20: 1-cm Grid Paper PM 22: Square Dot Paper PM 23: Isometric Dot Paper PM 29: 5-Column Chart
2.3: Comparing Rates, page 19 Use unit rates to compare rates.	80–100 min	calculators	Master 2.11: Step-by-Step 3 Master 2.21: Extra Practice 3
Mid-Unit Review, page 23		calculators	
2.4: Calculating Percents, page 24 Calculate percents from less than 1% to greater than 100%.	80–100 min	calculators	Master 2.12: Step-by-Step 4 Master 2.22: Extra Practice 4
2.5: Solving Percent Problems, page 28 Find the whole, when given a percent, and find percent increase and decrease.	80–100 min	calculators	Master 2.13: Step-by-Step 5 Master 2.23: Extra Practice 5
2.6: Sales Tax, Discount, and Commission, page 32 Investigate the uses of percent in consumer math.	80–100 min	calculators	Master 2.14: Step-by-Step 6 Master 2.24: Extra Practice 6
2.7: Simple Interest, page 36 Investigate simple interest.	80–100 min	calculators	Master 2.15: Step-by-Step 7 Master 2.25: Extra Practice 7
Reading and Writing in Math: Posing Math Problems, page 40		calculators	
Unit Review, page 42		calculators	Extra Practice: Student Book page 489
Practice Test, page 45		calculators	
Unit Problem: Where to Live?, page 46	80–100 min	calculators	

Planning for Assessment

Purpose	Tools and Process	Recording and Reporting
Diagnostic	*Unit Launch* Question; conference; scaffold problems throughout the unit	PM 8: Conference Prompts
Formative	*Explore* – Ongoing Assessment: Observe and Listen	Master 2.2 Ongoing Observations: Applications of Ratio, Rate, and Percent PM 1: Inquiry Process Check List PM 6: Observation Record 1 PM 7: Observation Record 2 PM 8: Conference Prompts PM 2: Self-Assessment PM 3: Self-Assessment: Problem Solving PM 9: Work Sample Records
Summative	*Unit Review* *Unit Problem* – Performance Assessment Unit Test Review assessment records; add unit results to ongoing records	Master 2.1 Unit Rubric: Applications of Ratio, Rate, and Percent Master 2.3 Performance Assessment Rubric: Where to Live Master 2.4 Unit Summary: Applications of Ratio, Rate, and Percent PM 10: Summary Class Records: Strands PM 11: Summary Class Records: Achievement Categories PM 12: Summary Record: Individual
Learning Skills/Mathematical Disposition	Observe and record throughout unit	PM 4: Learning Skills Check List PM 5: Mathematical Dispositions and Learning Skills

Program Masters (PM) are in the *Grade 8 Planning and Program Masters* module.
Extra Practice Masters are on the CD-ROM and printed in reduced format on page 73 of this module.

LESSON ORGANIZER

15–20 min

Curriculum Focus: Activate prior learning about ratio, rate, and percent.

Student Materials

- calculators

ASSUMED PRIOR KNOWLEDGE

- ☑ Students can recognize and write ratios.
- ☑ Students can recognize and write rates.
- ☑ Students can understand what is meant by percent.

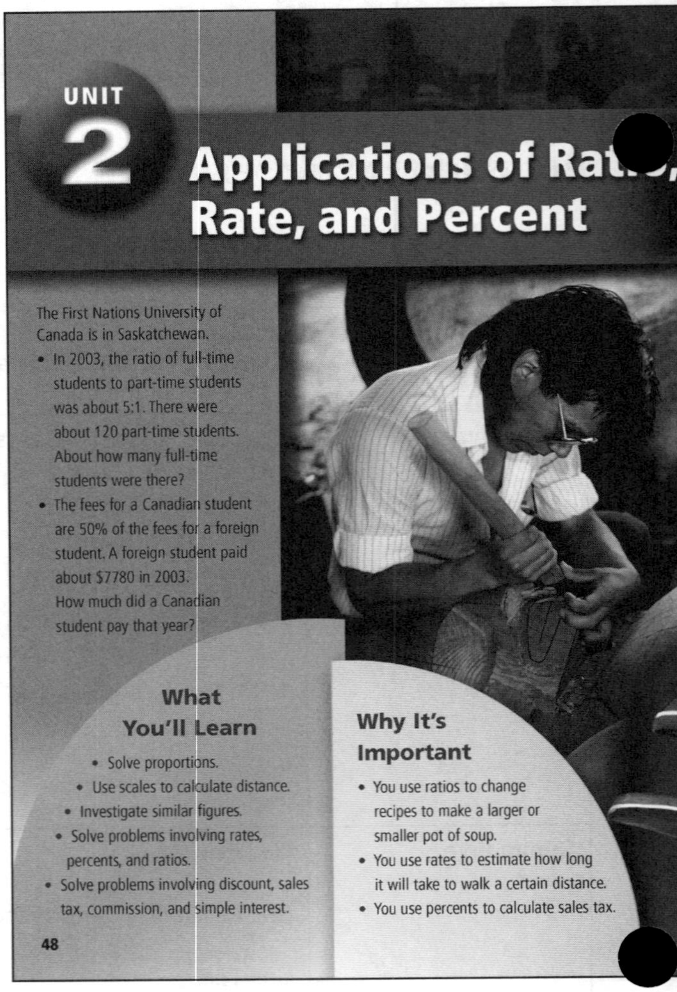

UNIT 2

Applications of Ratio, Rate, and Percent

The First Nations University of Canada is in Saskatchewan.

- In 2003, the ratio of full-time students to part-time students was about 5:1. There were about 120 part-time students. About how many full-time students were there?
- The fees for a Canadian student are 50% of the fees for a foreign student. A foreign student paid about $7780 in 2003. How much did a Canadian student pay that year?

What You'll Learn

- Solve proportions.
- Use scales to calculate distance.
- Investigate similar figures.
- Solve problems involving rates, percents, and ratios.
- Solve problems involving discount, sales tax, commission, and simple interest.

Why It's Important

- You use ratios to change recipes to make a larger or smaller pot of soup.
- You use rates to estimate how long it will take to walk a certain distance.
- You use percents to calculate sales tax.

48

ACTIVATE PRIOR LEARNING

Review the questions on page 48 of the Student Book.

The number of full-time students is 5 times the number of part-time students. So, the number of full-time students is $120 \times 5 = 600$.

Fifty percent is one-half.

So, to find 50% of $7780, divide it by 2:

$7780 ÷ 2 = $3890

A Canadian student pays $3890.

For more information about this university, visit www.firstnationsuniversity.ca (accessed June 2005).

Students should have prior knowledge of ratios, rates, and percents from their work in Grade 7 and from their everyday life experiences.

Ask questions, such as:

- Where have you come across ratios recently? (*Ratio of boys to girls in class; advertising, 9 out of 10 people prefer Brand X; ratio of water to concentrate in juice*)
- Where have you come across rates recently? (*Car speeds; running speed; growth rates of plants, of children, and of financial investments; unemployment rates*)
- Where have you seen percents used recently? (*Test and exam marks; weather forecasting; new condos sold; targets reached in fund-raising; sale prices in stores*)

Tell students that in this unit they will apply ratios to solve proportions, and use unit rates, rates, and percents to solve problems. They will learn about discount, sales tax, commission, and simple interest and how to calculate them.

At the end of the unit, students will apply their knowledge and skills to decide whether it is cheaper to stay at home and drive to college every day, or live in residence. This involves calculating the cost of purchasing a car together with the cost of driving and maintaining the vehicle, and comparing the costs with those of living in residence.

Key Words

- equivalent ratios
- unit rate
- proportion
- similar figures
- discount
- sales tax
- commission
- simple interest
- principal
- amount

49

FROM THE LIBRARY

The Nature of Mathematics (5th edition) by Karl J. Smith.
Brooks/Cole Publishing Company
ISBN: 0534066968
The book is designed to create interest and includes much additional interesting information. Chapter 1.4 deals with ratios applied to the human body and the Fibonacci sequence. Chapter 6.7 deals with ratio, proportion, and problem solving, while Chapter 6.8 deals with percents.

REACHING ALL LEARNERS

Some students may benefit from using the virtual manipulatives on the e-Tools CD-ROM. The e-Tools appropriate for this unit is *Counters*.

DIAGNOSTIC ASSESSMENT

What to Look For	What to Do
✔ Students can recognize and write ratios. ✔ Students can recognize and write rates. ✔ Students can understand what is meant by percent.	***Extra Support:*** Students who have difficulty working with ratios may benefit from sorting a box of counters by colour, then writing ratios to compare two groups, and to compare one group to the whole collection. *Work on this skill during Lesson 2.1.* Students who have difficulty with rates may benefit from explaining the meaning of simple rates in words, such as 60 km/h; 3 m/s; \$2.00/kg; \$8.00/h. *Work on this skill during Lesson 2.3.* Students who have difficulty understanding percents may benefit from colouring a hundredths chart with 5 different colours, then writing each coloured region as a percent of the whole. *Work on this skill during Lesson 2.4.*

LESSON ORGANIZER

65–80 min

Skills in Review
- What is a ratio?
- What is a rate?
- Relating fractions, decimals, and percents

Student Materials
- calculators

Alternative Example 1

Write each ratio in simplest form.

a) 20:45 **b)** 33:24 **c)** 28:42

Solution

a) 20:45
The greatest common factor of 20 and 45 is 5. Divide each term by 5.
20:45 = (20 ÷ 5):(45 ÷ 5) = 4:9

b) 33:24
The greatest common factor of 33 and 24 is 3. Divide each term by 3.
33:24 = (33 ÷ 3):(24 ÷ 3) = 11:8

c) 28:42
The factors of 28 are 2 × 2 × 7.
The factors of 42 are 2 × 3 × 7.
The greatest common factor of 28 and 42 is 2 × 7 = 14.
Divide each term by 14.
28:42 = (28 ÷ 14):(42 ÷ 14) = 2:3

UNIT 2

Skills You'll Need

What Is a Ratio?

Recall that a ratio is a comparison of two quantities measured in the same unit.

Here are some data for the 2002–2003 hockey season.

Northeast Division	Games Played	Wins	Losses	Ties	Overtime Losses
Ottawa	82	52	21	8	1
Toronto	82	44	28	7	3
Boston	82	36	31	11	4
Montreal	82	30	35	8	9
Buffalo	82	27	37	10	8

For the Toronto Maple Leafs:
The ratio of wins to games played was 44:82. This is a part-to-whole ratio.
The ratio of wins to losses was 44:28. This is a part-to-part ratio.

Example 1

Write each ratio in simplest form.
a) 44:82 **b)** 44:28

Solution

To write a ratio in simplest form, divide the terms by their greatest common factor.

a) 44:82 Divide each term by 2.
= (44 ÷ 2):(82 ÷ 2)
= 22:41

b) 44:28 Divide each term by 4.
= (44 ÷ 4):(28 ÷ 4)
= 11:7

In *Example 1*, the ratios 44:82 and 22:41 are **equivalent**, and the ratios 44:28 and 11:7 are equivalent.

50 UNIT 2: Applications of Ratio, Rate, and Percent

What Is a Ratio?

Remind students that a ratio can be used to compare one part of a collection to the whole collection (part-to-whole) or to compare one part of a collection with another part of the same collection (part-to-part). For example: On a school trip there are 15 boys, 18 girls, and 3 teachers.

Ask:
- What is the ratio of boys to girls? (*15:18, or 5:6*)
- What type of ratio is it? (*Part-to-part*)
- What is the ratio of students to students and teachers? (*33:36, or 11:12*)
- What type of ratio is it? (*Part-to-whole*)

Show students how a ratio can be written in fraction form. Note that we say "in fraction form" and not "as a fraction."

A part-to-whole ratio can be written as a fraction; for example, the ratio of students to students and teachers is $\frac{33}{36}$ or $\frac{11}{12}$. That is, $\frac{11}{21}$ of the people on the trip are students. We can say this as eleven-twelfths.

A part-to-part ratio can be written in fraction form; that is, the ratio of boys to girls can be written as $\frac{11}{85}$, or $\frac{5}{6}$. But, we cannot say this as "five-sixths," because that implies 5 parts out of a total of 6 parts, which is not correct.

For extra support, students can play *Reductions* (Master 2.5). For extra practice, students can play *Triple Play* (Master 2.6).

Common Misconceptions

➤ Students sometimes confuse part-to-part ratios with part-to-whole ratios.

How to Help: Give students coloured cubes (or counters). Have them write part-to-part ratios for pairs of colours and part-to-whole ratios for each group of coloured cubes to the whole group. Have students describe how part-to-part and part-to-whole ratios are related. (*If part-to-part is 3:5, then part-to-whole will be 3:8 or 5:8.*)

✓ Check

1. Use the table on page 50. For each team below, find:
 i) the ratio of wins to losses
 ii) the ratio of games played to ties
 Write each ratio in simplest form.
 a) Ottawa b) Boston c) Montreal d) Buffalo

a) i) 52:21 ii) 41:4
b) i) 36:31 ii) 82:11
c) i) 6:7 ii) 41:4
d) i) 27:37 ii) 41:5

2. Identify any pairs of equivalent ratios in question 1.
 82:8 and 41:4; 82:10 and 41:5; 30:35 and 6:7

What Is a Rate?

A rate is a comparison of two quantities measured in different units.

In 5 min, Ryan typed 425 words.
So, in $\frac{5}{5}$, or 1 min, Ryan typed: $\frac{425 \text{ words}}{5} = 85$ words
Ryan's typing rate is 85 words/min.
This is a **unit rate** because it represents the words typed in *one* minute.

Example 2

Meghan drove 300 km in 4 h.
a) What was her average speed?
b) Draw a graph to illustrate Meghan's journey.
 Explain how the average speed is represented in the graph.

Solution

a) In 4 h, Meghan drove 300 km.
 So, in 1 h, Meghan drove: $\frac{300 \text{ km}}{4} = 75$ km
 Meghan's average speed was 75 km/h.

b) On a grid, label the horizontal axis *Time* and the vertical axis *Distance*.
 Mark a point to represent 300 km in 4 h.
 Draw a line through this point and the origin.
 From the graph, the distance travelled after 1 h is 75 km.
 So, the average speed is 75 km/h.

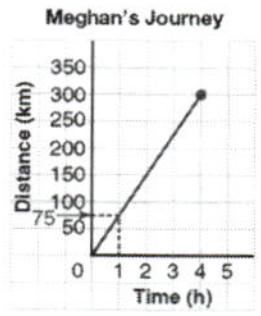

Skills You'll Need 51

Alternative Example 2

A large tank is filled with 900 L of water in 1 h.

a) What is the rate at which the tank was filled, in litres per minute?

b) Draw a graph to show how the volume of water in the tank changed. Explain how the rate is represented on the graph.

Solution

a) In 60 min, 900 L of water went in the tank.
 So, in 1 min, $\frac{900 \text{L}}{60} = 15$ L of water went in the tank.
 The rate at which the tank was filled was 15 L/min.

b) On a grid, mark a point to represent 900 L in 1 h. Draw a line through this point and the origin. From the graph, the volume of water in the tank after 10 min is 150 L.
 So, the volume after 1 min is 15 L.

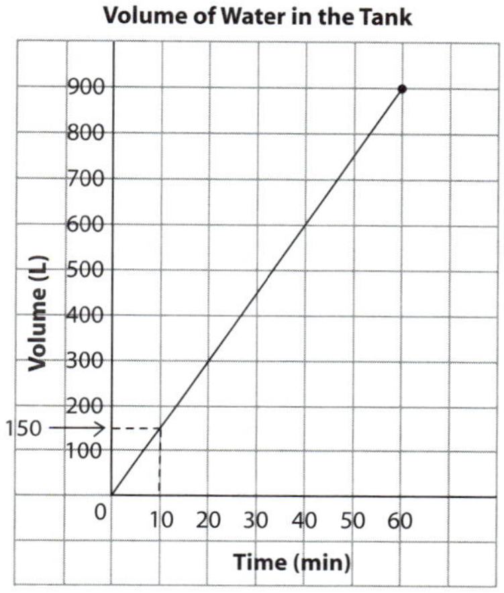

What Is a Rate?

Ask:

- How do you calculate the average speed of a car? (*Divide the distance travelled by the time taken.*)
- What two things do you need to know to calculate average speed? (*Distance and time*)
- What two things do you need to know to calculate typing speed? (*Number of words typed and the time taken to type them*)
- What two things do you need to know to calculate heart rate? (*Number of heartbeats and time taken to count them*)
- What are some other examples of rate? (*Unit cost, growth rate, production rate*)

Introduce the term "directly proportional." A graph that illustrates a rate always goes through the origin. For the graph in *Example 2*, we say that the distance is directly proportional to the time. That is, when the time doubles, the distance doubles. When the time is halved, the distance is halved. Have students use "directly proportional" to relate the items in question 3 (*The number of heartbeats is directly proportional to the time; the cost of tickets is directly proportional to the number of tickets; the cost of golf balls is directly proportional to the number of golf balls; the money earned for working is directly proportional to the time worked.*)

Common Misconceptions

➤ When writing a unit rate, students do not know which quantity goes first.

How to Help: Have students think about dividing the quantities, and which division makes more sense. For question 2a, we can say 225 heartbeats in 3 min is $\frac{225}{3}$, or 75 heartbeats per minute; or in 3 min, a heart beats 225 times, so $\frac{3}{225}$ min/heartbeat is the time in minutes for 1 heartbeat. Both expressions are unit rates, but the former expression makes more sense.

Alternative Example 3

Draw three 10 by 10 grids on grid paper.

a) Shade 40% of the first grid.

b) Shade $\frac{2}{5}$ of the second square.

c) Shade 0.4 of the third grid.

What do you notice? Explain.

Solution

All grids look like the one above.

The shaded areas on the grids are equal, so: $40\% = \frac{2}{5} = 0.4$.

✓ Check

3. Write each pair of quantities as a unit rate. a) 75 heartbeats/min b) \$9.35/ticket c) \$2.25/ball d) \$9.75/h

a) 225 heartbeats in 3 min　b) \$18.70 for 2 tickets

c) \$6.75 for 3 golf balls　d) \$78.00 for 8 h work

4. Jose travelled 480 km in 6 h.

a) Draw a graph to illustrate Jose's journey. Find his average speed. 80 km/h

b) At this average speed, how long will Jose take to travel 700 km? 8 h 45 min

Relating Fractions, Decimals, and Percents

This hundredths chart represents one whole, or 1.
The shaded part of this chart can be described three ways.

As a fraction: $\frac{24}{100}$
As a percent: 24%
As a decimal: 0.24

Each way above can be written in any of the other two ways.

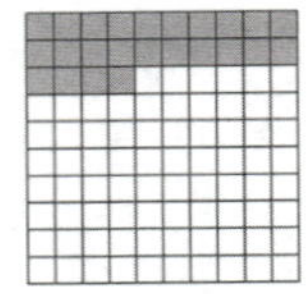

Recall that 1 whole is 100%.

Example 3

a) Write 5% as a decimal.　b) Write 1.65 as a percent.　c) Write $\frac{3}{8}$ as a decimal.

Solution

a) $5\% = \frac{5}{100} = 0.05$

b) $1.65 = 1\frac{65}{100} = \frac{165}{100} = 165\%$

c) $\frac{3}{8} = 3 \div 8 = 0.375$

✓ Check

5. a) Write each fraction as a decimal and as a percent.

i) $\frac{3}{10}$ 0.3, 30% ii) $\frac{4}{5}$ 0.8, 80% iii) $\frac{21}{20}$ 1.05, 105% iv) $\frac{3}{100}$ 0.03, 3%

b) Write each percent as a decimal and as a fraction.

i) 25% 0.25, $\frac{1}{4}$ ii) 34% 0.34, $\frac{17}{50}$ iii) 250% 2.5, $\frac{5}{2}$ iv) 2% 0.02, $\frac{1}{50}$

c) Write each decimal as a percent and as a fraction.

i) 0.15 15%, $\frac{3}{20}$ ii) 0.07 7%, $\frac{7}{100}$ iii) 0.4 40%, $\frac{2}{5}$ iv) 1.15 115%, $\frac{23}{20}$

52　UNIT 2: Applications of Ratio, Rate, and Percent

Relating Fractions, Decimals, and Percents

Ask:

- What does it mean when I say 25% of the Grade 8 students are absent? (*One-quarter of the students are absent.*)
- What if I say 50% are absent? (*$\frac{50}{100}$ or $\frac{1}{2}$ are absent.*)

  40% are absent? (*$\frac{40}{100}$ or $\frac{2}{5}$ are absent.*)

  35% are absent? (*$\frac{40}{100}$ or $\frac{7}{20}$ are absent.*)

Review percents greater than 100%. Ask:

- One whole is 100%. What is 150%?
  (*One whole plus $\frac{1}{2}$ of one whole, which is $1\frac{1}{2}$ or 1.5.*)
- What is 125%? (*One whole plus $\frac{1}{4}$ of one whole, which is $1\frac{1}{4}$, or 1.25.*)

For extra practice, students can play *Pair It Up* (Master 2.7).

Common Misconceptions

➤ Students do not know the relationship among the benchmark fractions, decimals, and percents.

How to Help: Have students draw a line segment 10 cm long, and label the end points 0, 0.0, 0% and 1, 1.0, 100%. Divide the segment into quarters. Label each point appropriately as: $\frac{1}{4}$, 0.25, 25%; $\frac{1}{2}$, 0.5, 50%; $\frac{3}{4}$, 0.75, 75%. Extend the segment a further 5 cm to the right. Label the new end point $1\frac{1}{2}$, 1.5, 150%.

2.1 Using Proportions to Solve Ratio Problems

Focus Set up a proportion to solve a ratio problem.

We use ratios when we change a recipe.

Explore

Work on your own.
Here is a recipe for apple pie.

500 mL flour
200 mL margarine
500 g sliced apples
125 g sugar

Each pie serves 6 people.
Frank has only 350 g of sliced apples.
How much of each other ingredient does Frank need to make the pie?
How many people will Frank's pie serve? Explain.

Reflect & Share

Compare your answers with those of a classmate.
What strategies did you use to solve the problems?

Connect

In a recycle drive last week at Cue Elementary School, Mr. Bozyk's Grade 8 class collected bottles and recycled some of them.
The ratio of bottles recycled to bottles collected was 3:4.
This week, his class collected 24 bottles.
Mr. Bozyk told the students that the ratio of bottles recycled to bottles collected is the same as the ratio the preceding week.
How can the students find how many bottles are recycled this week?

Last week's ratio of bottles recycled to bottles collected is 3:4.
This week's ratio of bottles recycled to bottles collected is ?:24.
These two ratios are equal.
Let r represent the number of bottles recycled.
Then, $r:24 = 3:4$
A statement that two ratios are equal is a **proportion**.

2.1 Using Proportions to Solve Ratio Problems 53

Using Proportions to Solve Ratio Problems

LESSON ORGANIZER (80–100 min)

Curriculum Focus: Set up a proportion to solve a ratio problem. (8m14, 8m27, 8m59)

Student Materials
- calculators

Optional
- Step-by-Step 1 (Master 2.9)
- Extra Practice 1 (Master 2.19)

Vocabulary: proportion

Assessment: Master 2.2 Ongoing Observations: Applications of Ratio, Rate, and Percent

Key Math Learnings

1. Equal ratios can be written as a proportion.
2. A proportion can be solved to find the value of an unknown term.

Calculator Skills

One method: Find sets of 3 prime numbers whose sum is 91, then calculate their products until you get 14 573.

Another method: Use division to find the prime factors of 14 573.

BEFORE Get Started

Invite students to give examples of ratio.

Ask:

- Have any of you changed recipes in cooking, baking, or mixing punch to make a greater or lesser amount? How did you do it?
  (*By doubling or halving the amount of each ingredient*)
- Suppose you need one bottle of juice for 3 people. How many bottles would you need for 9 people? Explain.
  (*The number of people has tripled, so the number of bottles must triple. So, I need 3 × 1, or 3 bottles for 9 people.*)

Present *Explore.*

DURING Explore

Ongoing Assessment: Observe and Listen

As students work, ask questions, such as:

- How much flour do you need?
  (*The volume of flour in the recipe is 500 mL. The mass of apples is 500 g. So, when the mass of apples is only 350 g, then the volume of flour is only 350 mL.*)
- What is the ratio of apples you have to apples in the recipe?
  (*350:500, or 35:50, or 7:10*)
- How can you find how much margarine you need? (*I find a ratio that is equivalent to 7:10; that is, the margarine I need to 200 is equal to 7 to 10. I multiply 10 by 20 to get 200, so I multiply 7 by 20 to find the margarine I need: 7 × 20 = 140, so I need 140 mL of margarine.*)
- How much sugar do you need?
  (*In the original recipe, 125 g is one-quarter of 500 g. So, in the new recipe, the sugar I need is $\frac{1}{4}$ of 350 g, which is 350 g ÷ 4 = 87.5 g.*)

REACHING ALL LEARNERS

Early Finishers

Have students use the information from the recipe in *Explore* to calculate the ingredients for:

a) Eight pies. How many people will this serve?

b) The number of pies for 35 people

(Answers: *a) 4 L flour, 1.6 L margarine, 4 kg sliced apples, 1 kg sugar; 48 people b) We cannot make part of a pie, so 6 pies are needed: 3 L flour, 1.2 L margarine, 3 kg sliced apples, 750 g sugar*)

Common Misconceptions

➤Students have difficulty solving proportions when the variable is in the denominator.

How to Help: Demonstrate that the terms of a proportion can be inverted without affecting the result:

The ratio 4:5 = 8:10 can be written $\frac{4}{5} = \frac{8}{10}$.

The ratio 5:4 = 10:8 can be written $\frac{5}{4} = \frac{10}{8}$.

Encourage students to invert the fractions before solving the proportion.

ESL Strategies

Have students write the words *ratio* and *proportion* and their meanings both in English and their own language. Have them describe, in English and their own language, the steps to write and solve a proportion.

We can write each ratio in the proportion in fraction form:

$\frac{r}{24} = \frac{3}{4}$

To find the value of *r*, solve the proportion.

To isolate *r*, multiply each side of the proportion by 24.

$24 \times \frac{r}{24} = \frac{3}{4} \times 24$

$\frac{24r}{24} = \frac{72}{4}$ — $\frac{72}{4}$ means 72 ÷ 4.

$r = 18$

18 bottles were recycled.

Example

These suitcases have the same length to width ratio.

Calculate the width of Suitcase B.

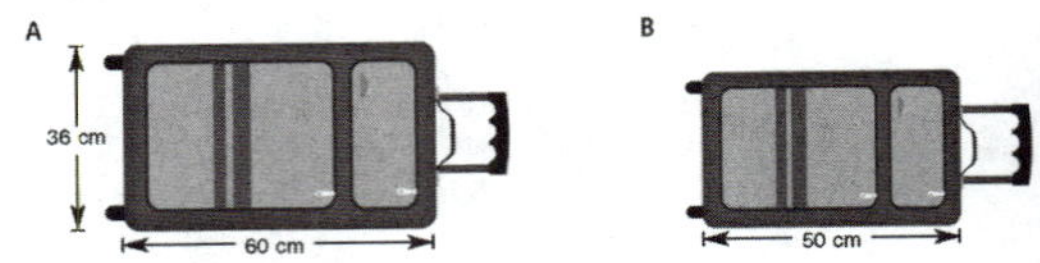

Solution

Let the width of Suitcase B be *w* centimetres.

For Suitcase B, width to length is *w*:50.

For Suitcase A, width to length is 36:60.

Write this ratio in simplest form.

Divide each term by 12.

36:60 = (36 ÷ 12):(60 ÷ 12)

= 3:5

The ratios for Suitcase A and Suitcase B are equal.

Write each ratio in fraction form.

Then write a proportion.

$\frac{w}{50} = \frac{3}{5}$

Multiply each side by 50.

$50 \times \frac{w}{50} = \frac{3}{5} \times 50$

$\frac{50w}{50} = \frac{150}{5}$

$w = 30$

Suitcase B is 30 cm wide.

Write the ratio with the variable as the first term of the ratio. This makes it easier to solve the proportion.

54 UNIT 2: Applications of Ratio, Rate, and Percent

- How can you find how many people the pie will serve?
  (*The pie could still serve 6 people, but each person would have less than before.*)
- How much less would each person have?
  (*Since the mass of apples is* $\frac{7}{10}$ *of what it was before, each person would get* $\frac{7}{10}$ *of what she had before.*)
- Suppose each person had about the same as before. How many people could the pie serve?
  (*Since the ingredients are only* $\frac{7}{10}$ *of what they were before, then the number of people the smaller pie will serve is* $\frac{7}{10}$ *of 6 = 0.7 × 6 = 4.2. Since we can't have 4.2 people, I round it to 4 people. Each person's share will be a little more than it was before.*)

AFTER Connect

Review students' methods for solving the problem. If they did not use ratios or fractions, show them how the problem is solved that way. You can use this problem to introduce proportions. Then, the volume of margarine needed to the volume of margarine in the recipe = the mass of apples available to the mass of apples in the recipe.

Let *m* represent the volume of margarine needed in millilitres.

Then, *m*:200 = 350:500

Write each ratio in fraction form.

$\frac{m}{200} = \frac{350}{500}$

$\frac{m}{200} = \frac{7}{10}$

$200 \times \frac{m}{200} = \frac{7 \times 200}{10}$

$m = 140$

So, the volume of margarine needed is 140 mL.

The volume of margarine is directly proportional to the mass of apples. That is, when the mass of apples is reduced, the volume of margarine is reduced proportionally.

Practice

1. Find each missing term.
   a) $\frac{t}{18} = \frac{6}{3}$ 36
   b) $\frac{y}{60} = \frac{3}{10}$ 18
   c) $\frac{x}{15} = \frac{2}{3}$ 10
   d) $a:7 = 30:70$ 3
   e) $b:45 = 5:15$ 15
   f) $l:8 = 15:6$ 20

2. In the NHL, the ratio of shots taken to goals scored by an all-star player is 9:2. The player has a 50-goal season. How many shots did he take? 225

3. Fatima plants 5 tree seedlings for every 3 that Shamar plants. Shamar plants 6 trees in 1 min.
   a) How many trees does Fatima plant in 1 min? 10
   b) Did you write a proportion to solve this problem? If so, how else could you have solved it?

4. An ad said that 4 out of 5 dentists recommend a certain chewing gum for their patients. Suppose 185 dentists were interviewed. Find the number of dentists who recommend this gum. 148

5. A bike is in fourth gear. When the pedals turn 3 times, the rear wheel turns 7 times. When the pedals turn twice, how many times does the rear wheel turn? $4\frac{2}{3}$ times

6. At the annual Grade 8 ski trip, for every 2 students who skied, 3 snowboarded. Ninety-six students snowboarded. How many students skied? 64

7. **Assessment Focus** In rectangle MNPQ, the ratio of the length of MN to the length of MP is 4:5.
   a) Does this ratio tell you how long MN is? Explain.
   b) What if MN is 12 cm long. How long is MP? Use a diagram to illustrate your answer.
   Show your work.

2.1 Using Proportions to Solve Ratio Problems 55

Assignment Guidelines

If your students do not have time to complete all the *Practice* questions on pages 55 and 56, these questions provide minimum curriculum coverage: 1, 3, 4, 6, 7, 8, 9, and *Reflect*

To assess the 4 Achievement Chart categories listed in the curriculum document, have students complete these *Practice* questions:
Knowledge and Understanding: 1
Communication: 3
Application: 5
Thinking: 9

Sample Solutions

2. Let the number of shots taken be s. Then, $s:50 = 9:2$
   In fraction form: $\frac{s}{50} = \frac{9}{2}$
   $\frac{s}{50} \times 50 = \frac{9}{2} \times 50 \rightarrow s = 9 \times 25 \rightarrow s = 225$;
   he took 225 shots.
3. a) Let the number of trees that Fatima plants in 1 min be n.
   Then, $n:6 = 5:3$
   In fraction form: $\frac{n}{6} = \frac{5}{3}$
   $\frac{n}{6} \times 6 = \frac{5}{3} \times 6 \rightarrow n = 5 \times 2 \rightarrow n = 10$;
   Fatina plants 10 trees in 1 min.
   b) I could also have used logical reasoning and equivalent ratios.
   I multiply 3 by 2 to get 6. So, I multiply 5 by 2 to get 10.
   Fatima plants 10 trees in 1 min.

Practice

When students write a proportion, encourage them to use a "helpful" variable for the unknown quantity; for example, *t* for time, *l* for length, *d* for distance, and so on.

Question 1: Remind students to write proportions in fraction form and, wherever possible, reduce fractions to simplest form before solving the proportion.

Question 3: Although the problem can be solved by writing a proportion, students should be encouraged to think about different strategies for every question. In this case, students could use proportional reasoning to see that Shamar plants 3 trees in 30 s, so Fatima plants 5 trees in 30 s and 2 × 5, or 10 trees in 2 × 30 s, or 1 min.

Question 4: Some students may obtain the correct answer by using logical/proportional reasoning.

Question 6: Remind students that the number of students who skied is directly proportional to the number of students who snowboarded, and vice versa.

Question 8: Remind students to write the given ratio (20:30) in simplest form (2:3).

Question 9: Students need to realize that there are 3 types of tickets: child, student, and adult.

Question 11: Students can use the proportion:

$$\frac{\text{height of flagpole}}{\text{length of its shadow}} = \frac{\text{height of student}}{\text{length of her shadow}}$$

Assessment Focus: Question 7

For part a, students should realize that the ratio 4:5 does not mean the sides MN and MP have lengths 4 cm and 5 cm respectively. The sides *may* have these lengths, but the ratio illustrates the lengths could be any multiples of 4 and 5 respectively. In part b, when the length of one side is given, the length of the other side can be found.

4. Let the number of dentists who recommend the gum be d.
Then, $d{:}185 = 4{:}5$
In fraction form: $\frac{d}{185} = \frac{4}{5}$
$\frac{d}{185} \times 185 = \frac{4}{5} \times 185 \rightarrow d = 4 \times 37 \rightarrow d = 148$;
148 dentists recommend this gum.

5. Let the number of times the rear wheel turns be n.
Then, $2{:}n = 3{:}7$
In fraction form: $\frac{2}{n} = \frac{3}{7}$
This can be written $\frac{n}{2} = \frac{7}{3}$
$\frac{n}{2} \times 2 = \frac{7}{3} \times 2 \rightarrow n = \frac{14}{3} \rightarrow n = 4\frac{2}{3}$;
the rear wheel turns $4\frac{2}{3}$ times.

6. Let the number of students who skied be n. Then, $n{:}96 = 2{:}3$
In fraction form: $\frac{n}{96} = \frac{2}{3}$
$\frac{n}{96} \times 96 = \frac{2}{3} \times 96 \rightarrow n = 2 \times 32 \rightarrow n = 64$;
64 students skied.

7. a) The ratio does not tell me how long MN is. It tells me how the length of MN compares with the length of MP. That is, MN is $\frac{4}{5}$ the length of MP.
b) If MN is 12 cm long, then MP is $\frac{5}{4}$ the length of MP.
I can set up a proportion. Let l represent the length of MP.
Then, $\frac{l}{12} = \frac{5}{4}$
$l = 15$
MP is 15 cm long.
I could have said MP is $\frac{5}{4} \times 12$ cm, or 15 cm.

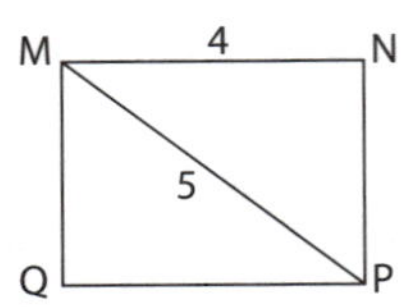

(Sample Solutions continue on page 17.)

Calculator Skills

Find 3 prime numbers that have a sum of 91 and a product of 14 573.
13, 19, 59

8. Last week, Marcia played goalkeeper for her hockey team. She stopped 20 out of 30 shots on goal. This week, Marcia faced 36 shots. She stopped shots on goal in the same ratio as the previous week. How many shots did Marcia stop? 24

9. At the movie theatre, 65 student tickets were sold for one performance.
a) The ratio of adult tickets sold to student tickets sold was 3:5. How many adult tickets were sold? 39
b) The ratio of adult tickets sold to child tickets sold was 3:2. How many child tickets were sold? 26
c) One adult ticket costs $13. One student ticket costs $7.50. One child ticket costs $4.50. How much money was made for that performance? $1111.50

10. Forty-five students take piano lessons.
The ratio of the numbers of students who take piano lessons to violin lessons is 15:8.
The ratio of the numbers of students who take violin lessons to clarinet lessons is 8:9.
a) How many students take violin lessons? 24
b) How many students take clarinet lessons? 27

Take It Further

11. Suppose you want to find the height of a flagpole. You know your height. You can measure the length of the shadow of the flagpole. Your friend can measure your shadow. How can you use ratios to find the height of the flagpole? Explain. Include a sketch in your explanation.

Reflect

Can you use a proportion to solve any ratio problem?
If your answer is yes, which ratio problem *would* you not use a proportion to solve?
If your answer is no, which ratio problem *could* you not use a proportion to solve?

56 UNIT 2: Applications of Ratio, Rate, and Percent

ASSESSMENT FOR LEARNING

What to Look For

Knowledge and Understanding
- ✔ Students understand how to write a proportion.
- ✔ Students understand how to solve a proportion.

Thinking
- ✔ Students can set up a proportion with an unknown term, then solve the proportion to solve the problem.

Communication
- ✔ Students can describe how to set up and solve a proportion.

What to Do

Extra Support: Many students solve proportional problems by using logical reasoning or even common sense. Do not discourage these methods. When students are comfortable with a reasoning method, have them use their answers and work backward to write a proportion.
Students can use Step-by-Step 1 (Master 2.9) to complete question 7.

Extra Practice: Have students repeat *Practice* question 1 with the second fraction inverted (parts a to c) and the terms of the second ratio transposed (parts d to f). (Answers: ***a)*** *9* ***b)*** *200* ***c)*** *22.5* ***d)*** $16\frac{1}{3}$ ***e)*** *135* ***f)*** *3.2*)
Students can complete Extra Practice 1 (Master 2.19).

Extension: Have students create a problem similar to *Practice* question 10, then trade problems with a classmate and solve their classmate's problem.

Recording and Reporting
Master 2.2 Ongoing Observations: Applications of Ratio, Rate, and Percent

2.2 Scale Drawings

Focus Solve problems involving scale drawings.

Explore

Work in a group.
You will need 1-cm grid paper and a metre stick, measuring tape, or trundle wheel.
Measure the perimeter of the classroom.
Make a scale drawing of the classroom floor.

What scale did you use?
Use your drawing to find the length of a diagonal of the classroom floor.

Reflect & Share

Compare your drawings with those of another group of classmates.
Justify your choice of scale to your classmates.
Compare your results for the length of a diagonal.
If the results are different, try to find out why.

Connect

A desktop is a rectangle with dimensions 1.06 m by 51 cm.
To make a scale drawing, we need to fit the rectangle on a piece of paper.
The paper measures 28 cm by 21.5 cm.
We need a margin around the drawing; so, we will use no more than 24 cm by 18 cm.
To choose a scale, find the ratios of the corresponding dimensions.

Multiply by 100 to convert metres to centimetres.

length of paper:length of desk	width of paper:width of desk
= 24 cm:1.06 m	= 18 cm:51 cm
= 24 cm:106 cm	= 18:51
= 24:106	$= \frac{18}{18}:\frac{51}{18}$
$= \frac{24}{24}:\frac{106}{24}$	= 1:2.83
= 1:4.416	
The desk is more than 4 times as long as the paper.	The desk is almost 3 times as wide as the paper.

2.2 Scale Drawings 57

Scale Drawings

LESSON ORGANIZER 80–100 min

Curriculum Focus: Solve problems involving scale drawings. (8m26, 8m27)

Student Materials
- 1-cm grid paper (PM 20)
- metre sticks, measuring tapes, or trundle wheels
- calculators

Optional
- atlases or maps
- Step-by-Step 2 (Master 2.10)
- Extra Practice 2 (Master 2.20)

Assessment: Master 2.2 Ongoing Observations: Applications of Ratio, Rate, and Percent

Key Math Learnings

1. A scale is a ratio of two measures in the same units.
2. A scale drawing can be used to draw a reduction or an enlargement of an object or a drawing.

Sample Solutions

2. 275 is a multiple of 25. Try 25 m to 1 cm; then 275 m to 11 cm. Scale is 1:2500.
3. For example, a fingernail approximates a square. My fingernail is approximately a square of side length 1.2 cm. A scale of 10:1 will give a 12-cm by 12-cm drawing.

BEFORE Get Started

Ask:
- What is a scale drawing?
(*It is a picture of an object where the lengths on the picture are greater than or less than the lengths on the object. When an object is drawn to scale, the lengths on the picture are directly proportional to the lengths on the object.*)
- Where are scale drawings used?
(*Architectural drawings, street plans, blueprints*)
- Why are scale drawings used?
(*You could not draw a life-size map of Ontario. You could not get a piece of paper big enough.*)

Present *Explore*.

DURING Explore

Ongoing Assessment: Observe and Listen

As students work, ask questions, such as:
- What do we mean by perimeter?
(*The distance around the outside edge of the room*)
- How will you measure the perimeter?
(*Since the room is rectangular, I can measure two different lengths of walls, add the measures, then double the answer.*)
- What is the length and width of the room?
(*10 m by 8 m*)
- What scale would be simple to use, and fit on the page?
(*One centimetre for each 1 m would be small. Two centimetres for each 1 m will fit the page.*)
- What are the dimensions of your drawing?
(*20 cm by 16 cm*)
- What is the length of the diagonal of your drawing?
(*25.6 cm*)
- How can you calculate the length of the diagonal of the room?
(*The length on my drawing in centimetres is double the length of the diagonal of the room in metres. So, the diagonal of the room is 25.6 m ÷ 2 = 12.8 m.*)

REACHING ALL LEARNERS

Early Finishers

Have students make a scale drawing of another room in the school, such as the library. Students could include furniture in the room, such as tables and bookcases.

Common Misconceptions

➤Students do not know when a given scale represents an enlargement or a reduction.

How to Help: Remind students that when the first term in the scale is greater than the second term, the scale represents an enlargement. Students could refer to an atlas. All maps are reductions, and all scales have the first term less than the second term.

➤Students forget to ensure that all dimensions are in the same units when calculating a scale.

How to Help: Students know they have to use the same units when calculating the area or perimeter of a figure. The same "rule" applies to scale drawings.

5. a) Let d represent the actual distance, in kilometres.

d:2.1 = 5 000 000:1

In fraction form: $\frac{d}{2.1} = \frac{5\,000\,000}{1}$

$\frac{d}{2.1} \times 2.1 = \frac{5\,000\,000}{1} \times 2.1 \rightarrow$

d = 10 500 000;

the distance is 10 500 000 cm = 105 km

b) Let d represent the map distance, in centimetres.

30 km = 30 000 m = 3 000 000 cm

Then, d:3 000 000 = 1:500 000

In fraction form: $\frac{d}{3\,000\,000} = \frac{1}{500\,000}$

So, we will choose a scale of 1:5, or 1 cm represents 5 cm.
The desktop has dimensions 106 cm by 51 cm.
So, the scale drawing has dimensions:
$\frac{106 \text{ cm}}{5}$ by $\frac{51 \text{ cm}}{5}$, or 21.2 cm by 10.2 cm
To illustrate the scale drawing in this textbook, we will use a smaller scale of 1:10, or 1 cm represents 10 cm.
Then, the scale drawing has dimensions:
$\frac{106 \text{ cm}}{10}$ by $\frac{51 \text{ cm}}{10}$, or 10.6 cm by 5.1 cm.

The scale drawing is labelled with the dimension of the desktop.

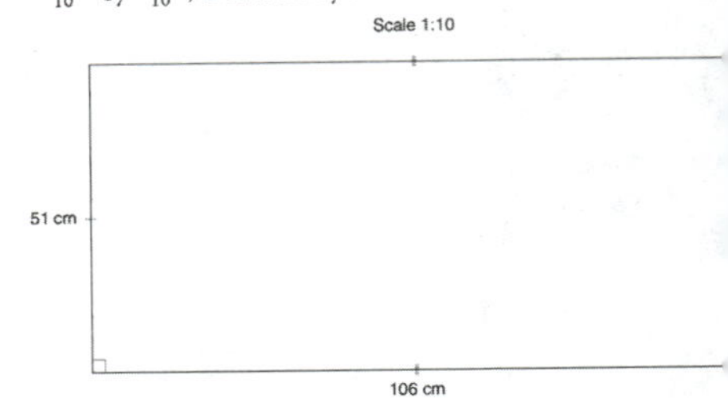

The straight-line distance is sometimes referred to "as the crow flies."

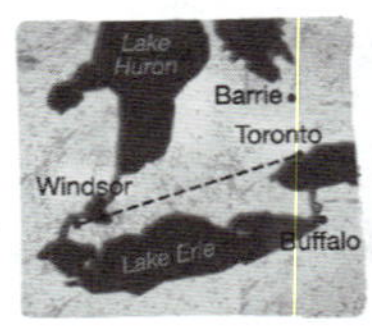

In a similar way:
We can use the scale on a map to calculate the distance between two towns on the map.
On a map of Ontario, the straight-line distance between Windsor and Toronto is 3.6 cm.
The scale on the map is written as the ratio of the map distance to the actual distance, 1:10 000 000.
This means that 1 cm on the map represents 10 000 000 cm actual distance.
So, the actual distance between Windsor and Toronto, as the crow flies, is:

3.6 cm × 10 000 000
= 36 000 000 cm — Divide by 100. (There are 100 cm in 1 m.)
= 360 000 m — Divide by 1000. (There are 1000 m in 1 km.)
= 360 km

The straight-line distance from Windsor to Toronto is 360 km.

We can write, then solve, a proportion to calculate a distance on a scale drawing.

58 UNIT 2: Applications of Ratio, Rate, and Percent

AFTER Connect

Invite students to share the scales they used and their reasons for selecting the scales.

Discuss methods for calculating scales and explain reasons for making scales simple to use. Point out that, to find a scale, the measures used must be in the same unit. In *Connect*, the units are centimetres.

Introduce *Connect* and describe the process for finding the appropriate scales.

Have students investigate why we did not choose a scale of 1:4 or 1:3.

With a scale of 1:4, the dimensions of the scale drawing would be $\frac{106}{4}$ cm by $\frac{51}{4}$ cm, or 26.5 cm by 12.75 cm.

The width, 12.75 cm, would fit on the page, but the length, 26.5 cm, is too long to allow for a margin.

It is not intuitive for some students that since a scale of 1:4 produces a drawing that is too large, a scale of 1:3 will produce a drawing that is even larger. So, repeat the investigation with this scale.

With a scale of 1:3, the dimensions of the scale drawing would be $\frac{106}{3}$ cm by $\frac{51}{3}$ cm, or $35.\overline{3}$ cm by 17 cm.

Again, the width, 17 cm, would fit on the page, but the length, $35.\overline{3}$ cm, is too long.

As a general rule, when calculating the scale, round up the ratio that produces the smaller scale.

Ask:

- Why write a scale as 1:500 000?
  (It removes any problems related to metric, Imperial or U.S. systems. 1:500 000 means 1 cm on a map represents 500 000 cm actual distance, or 1 inch on a map represents 500 000 inches actual distance.)

Example

Here is a scale drawing of a leaf-cutting ant. Calculate the actual length of the ant.

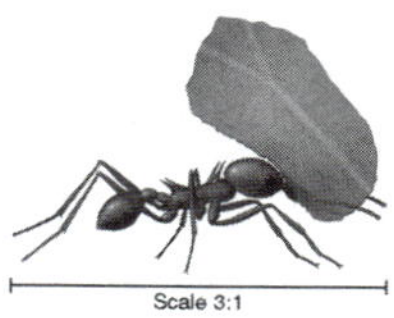

Solution

The scale is 3:1.
That is, length on drawing to actual length is 3:1.
Or, actual length to length on drawing is 1:3.
Let the actual length be l centimetres.
The length on the drawing is measured as 4.9 cm.
So, actual length to length on drawing is l:4.9.
The proportion is

$l:4.9 = 1:3$

Write these ratios in fraction form.

$\frac{l}{4.9} = \frac{1}{3}$

Multiply each side by 4.9.

$4.9 \times \frac{l}{4.9} = \frac{1}{3} \times 4.9$

$\frac{4.9l}{4.9} = \frac{4.9}{3}$

$l \doteq 1.63$

The actual length of the ant is about 1.6 cm.

In the *Example*, the first term of the scale is greater than the second term.
This indicates that the scale drawing is an enlargement.

Practice

1. Measure, then use the scale to find each actual measurement.
   a) Scale 1:90
   b) Scale 65:1

450 cm or 4.5 m

0.02 cm or 0.2 mm

$\frac{d}{3\ 000\ 000} = \frac{1}{500\ 000} \rightarrow \frac{d}{3\ 000\ 000} \times 3\ 000\ 000 = \frac{1}{500\ 000} \times 3\ 000\ 000 \rightarrow d = 6$; the map distance is 6 cm.

6. a) Let the width of the room be w centimetres. Let the length of the room be l centimetres.
   w:480 = 1:50
   In fraction form: $\frac{w}{480} = \frac{1}{50}$
   $\frac{w}{480} = \frac{1}{50} \rightarrow \frac{w}{480} \times 480 = \frac{1}{50} \times 480 \rightarrow w = 9.6$
   l:640 = 1:50
   In fraction form: $\frac{l}{640} = \frac{1}{50}$
   $\frac{l}{640} = \frac{1}{50} \rightarrow \frac{l}{640} \times 640 = \frac{1}{50} \times 640 \rightarrow l = 12.8$
   The dimensions are 9.6 cm by 12.8 cm.
7. I assumed the page is 25 cm long.
   Then, $25:5300 = \frac{25}{25} : \frac{5300}{25} = 1:212$
   The scale of the photo is 1:212.
9. I chose the family room. It has dimensions 4.8 m by 3.9 m.
   The length of the grid paper is about 20 cm. The width of the grid paper is about 16 cm.
   The ratio length of grid paper:length of room is: 20:480 = 1:24
   The ratio width of grid paper:width of room is: 16:390 ≐ 1:24
   I will use the scale 1:25.
   The length of the family room on the drawing is:
   $\frac{l}{480} = \frac{1}{25} \rightarrow l = 19.2$; the length is 19.2 cm.
   The width of the family room on the drawing is:
   $\frac{w}{390} = \frac{1}{25} \rightarrow w = 15.6$; the width is 15.6 cm.

(Sample Solutions continue on page 17.)

In the *Example*, remind students that a period above an equal sign shows the answer is approximate.

Practice

Encourage students to show the steps in their solutions.

Question 1: Students may write the proportions as $\frac{5}{l} = \frac{1}{90}$ or $\frac{1.3}{l} = \frac{65}{1}$, which they may have difficulty solving. Remind students that the fractions can be inverted without changing the values of the proportions. So, $\frac{5}{l} = \frac{1}{90}$ can be written as $\frac{l}{5} = \frac{90}{1}$ and $\frac{1.3}{l} = \frac{65}{1}$ can be written as $\frac{l}{1.3} = \frac{1}{65}$.

Question 2: A scale that is a multiple of 5 or a multiple of 11 probably works best.

Question 4: Before writing a proportion, the actual height in metres will have to be converted to centimetres to correspond to the measure of the height in the photograph.

Question 5: Remind students a ratio of 1:5 000 000 means 1 cm on the map represents 5 000 000 cm actual distance and answers will have to be converted to kilometres. Some students may find it easier to convert to actual measures before calculating.

Question 6: Since students are calculating dimensions on the blueprint, they might benefit from reversing the scale and use 50 cm in the house represents 1 cm on the blueprint.

Question 8: Remind students to use the same units when working with scales.

Assessment Focus: Question 9

Encourage students to pick a room that has at least 4 pieces of furniture.

Some useful dimensions are: sofa 216 cm by 100 cm; easy chair 75 cm by 65 cm; TV 65 cm by 55 cm; table 1.2 m by 90 cm; bed 2 m by 80 cm; bookcase 68 cm by 40 cm; coffee table: 115 cm by 58 cm; dressing table 1.4 m by 50 cm.

Number Strategies

Write 24 as products of 2 factors.
Write 48 as products of 2 factors.

Assignment Guidelines

If your students do not have time to complete all the *Practice* questions on pages 59 and 60, these questions provide minimum curriculum coverage: 2, 5, 6, 7, *Reflect*

To assess the 4 Achievement Chart categories listed in the curriculum document, have students complete these *Practice* questions:
Communication: 2
Knowledge and Understanding: 5
Application: 6
Thinking: 7

2. A square field has edge length 275 m.
Choose a scale. Make a scale drawing of the field.
Justify the scale you used.

3. Measure a fingernail.
Choose a scale. Make a scale drawing of your fingernail.
Justify the scale you used.

4. The Eiffel Tower in Paris, France, is 321 m tall, including the television antenna.
Measure the height of the tower in this picture.
What is the scale for this picture? About 1:8025

Number Strategies

How many different ways can 24 bottles of water be arranged in a rectangular array? 1 × 24, 2 × 12, 3 × 8, 4 × 6
What if the number of bottles is doubled. Which rectangular arrays are possible now?
1 × 48, 2 × 24, 3 × 16, 4 × 12, 6 × 8

5. a) The scale on a map of British Columbia is 1:5 000 000. The map distance between Kelowna and Salmon Arm is 2.1 cm. 105 km
What is the actual distance between these towns?
b) The scale on a map of Japan is 1:500 000.
The actual distance between Tokyo and Yokohama is 30 km.
What is the map distance between these cities? 6 cm

6. A blueprint for a new house has a scale of 1:50.
Here are the dimensions of two rooms.
Calculate the dimensions of each room on the blueprint.
a) 4.8 m by 6.4 m 9.6 cm by 12.8 cm
b) 3.1 m by 4.2 m 6.2 cm by 8.4 cm

7. The Horseshoe Falls at Niagara are 53 m high. A person takes a photo of the Falls. What if the photograph just fits on this pa[ge]
What is the scale of the photo?

8. A ladybug is 4 mm long.
A scale drawing of the bug is 5.6 cm long.
What is the scale of the drawing? 56:4 or 14:1

9. **Assessment Focus** Make a scale drawing of the floor of a room in your home. Include any furniture on the floor. Justify your choice of scale. Show your work.

Reflect

Describe two types of scale drawing.
Explain how the scale describes the actual measurements of an object and its measurements on the drawing.

60 UNIT 2: Applications of Ratio, Rate, and Percent

ASSESSMENT FOR LEARNING

What to Look For	What to Do
Knowledge and Understanding ✔ Students understand how scale drawings can be used to make enlargements and reductions of pictures and diagrams. ***Thinking*** ✔ Students can choose a suitable scale to fit a drawing on a page. ***Application*** ✔ Students can choose scales and make scale drawings.	***Extra Support:*** Students who have difficulty deciding on a scale could begin by using simple scales, such as 1:10 or 1:20. Students can use Step-by-Step 2 (Master 2.10) to complete question 9. ***Extra Practice:*** Students could repeat *Practice* question 6 using different scales; for example, 1:25; 1:75. Students can complete Extra Practice 2 (Master 2.20). ***Extension:*** Have students use an atlas with a map of Ontario or Canada. They measure, then use a scale to calculate the actual distances between various towns.

Recording and Reporting
Master 2.2 Ongoing Observations: Applications of Ratio, Rate, and Percent

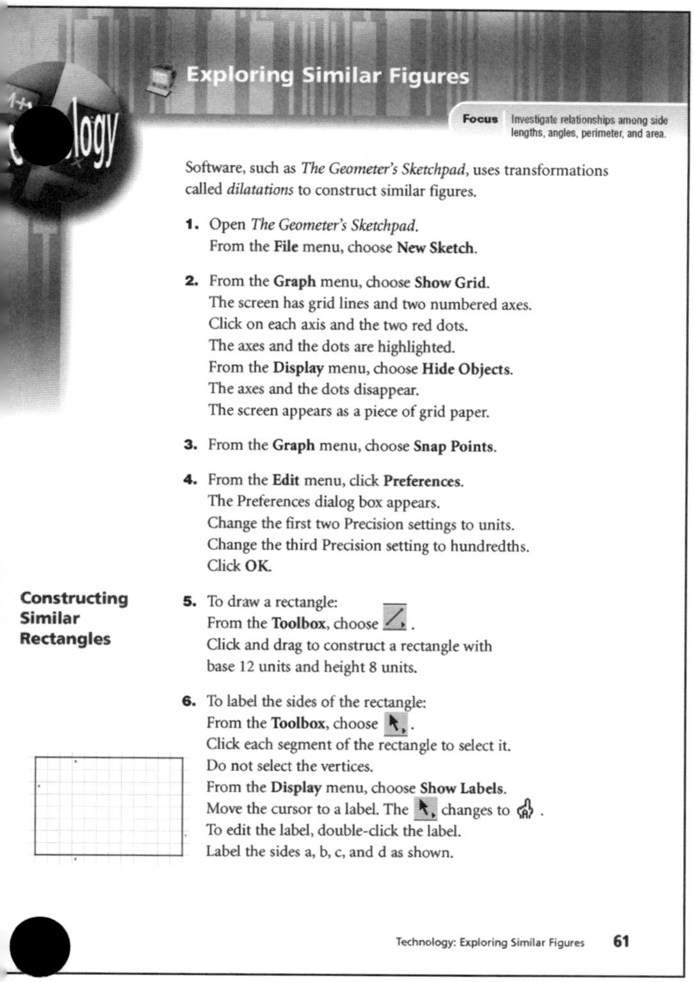
Technology

Exploring Similar Figures

Focus Investigate relationships among side lengths, angles, perimeter, and area.

Software, such as *The Geometer's Sketchpad*, uses transformations called *dilatations* to construct similar figures.

1. Open *The Geometer's Sketchpad*.
   From the **File** menu, choose **New Sketch**.
2. From the **Graph** menu, choose **Show Grid**.
   The screen has grid lines and two numbered axes.
   Click on each axis and the two red dots.
   The axes and the dots are highlighted.
   From the **Display** menu, choose **Hide Objects**.
   The axes and the dots disappear.
   The screen appears as a piece of grid paper.
3. From the **Graph** menu, choose **Snap Points**.
4. From the **Edit** menu, click **Preferences**.
   The Preferences dialog box appears.
   Change the first two Precision settings to units.
   Change the third Precision setting to hundredths.
   Click OK.

Constructing Similar Rectangles

5. To draw a rectangle:
   From the **Toolbox**, choose .
   Click and drag to construct a rectangle with base 12 units and height 8 units.
6. To label the sides of the rectangle:
   From the **Toolbox**, choose .
   Click each segment of the rectangle to select it.
   Do not select the vertices.
   From the **Display** menu, choose **Show Labels**.
   Move the cursor to a label. The changes to .
   To edit the label, double-click the label.
   Label the sides a, b, c, and d as shown.

Technology: Exploring Similar Figures 61

Exploring Similar Figures

LESSON ORGANIZER 80–100 min

Curriculum Focus: Investigate relationships among side lengths, angles, perimeter, and area. (8m46)

Student Materials

- Alternative Explore for Similar Figures (Master 2.18)
- 0.5-cm grid paper (PM 14)
- 1-cm grid paper (PM 20)
- square dot paper (PM 22)
- isometric dot paper (PM 23)
- 5-column chart (PM 29)

Assessment: Master 2.2 Ongoing Observations: Applications of Ratio, Rate, and Percent

Key Math Learning

In similar figures: corresponding angles are equal; the ratios of corresponding sides are equal; the ratio of perimeters is equal to the ratios of corresponding sides; the ratio of areas is equal to the square of the ratio of corresponding sides.

Teaching Note

These notes provide an alternative lesson for students to study similar figures, if you do not have access to *The Geometer's Sketchpad*.

BEFORE Get Started

Remind students of the work they did in Grade 7, where they used dilatations to produce similar figures. On the board, draw a triangle. Choose a dilatation centre outside the triangle, and draw two similar triangles: one triangle is a reduction, and one an enlargement.

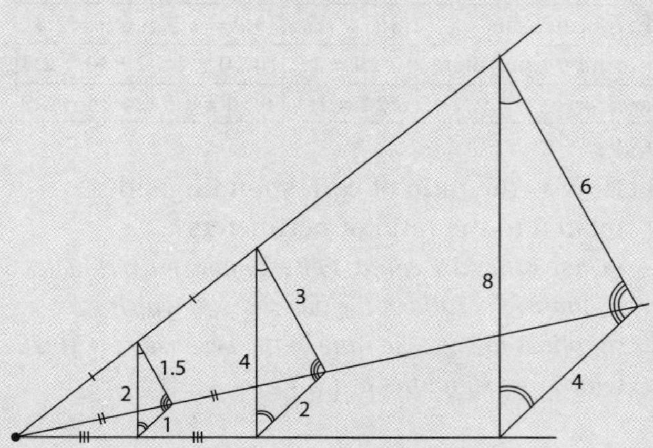

Remind students that corresponding angles are equal, and corresponding sides are in the same ratio; for example, for the two larger triangles 4:8 = 3:6 = 2:4.

Distribute copies of Master 2.18 Alternative Explore for Similar Figures. Make sure students understand what they have to do. Distribute 1-cm grid paper (PM 20) and 5-column charts (PM 29).

DURING Explore

Ongoing Assessment: Observe and Listen

As students work, ask questions, such as:

- How do you know your rectangles are similar?
  (When I look at each pair of rectangles in turn, the ratio of the bases is equal to the ratio of the heights.)

REACHING ALL LEARNERS

Alternative Explore

Materials: large (11 pin by 11 pin) geoboards, geobands, square dot paper (PM 22)

Have students complete the *Explore*, using geoboards and geobands. They record their rectangles on square dot paper.

Early Finishers

Have students repeat the *Explore*, but use square or isometric dot paper to draw 3 similar triangles. They may need to use the formula for the area of a triangle, or possibly count squares and half squares.

Common Misconceptions

➤ Students do not understand that when a figure is enlarged or reduced, its angle measures do not change.

How to Help: Have students use protractors to check the measures of the angles of these figures.

7. To construct a smaller similar rectangle:
From the **Toolbox**, choose ↖.
Double-click the lower left vertex.
Draw a box around the rectangle to select it.
From the **Transform** menu, choose **Dilate**.

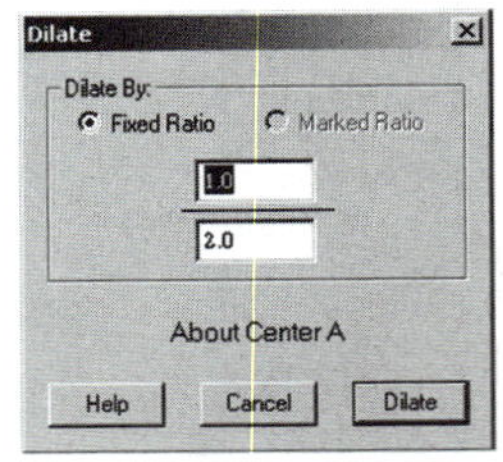

The Dilate dialog box should appear as shown.
If not, change the settings to match those shown.
The Fixed Ratio 1.0:2.0 is the ratio of correspondir
sides of the new rectangle and the original rectang
The new rectangle is a dilatation image of the original rectangle.
Click **Dilate.** The image rectangle is shown.
Click anywhere on the screen.
Click each side of the image rectangle to select it.
From the **Display** menu, choose **Show Labels.**
The sides are labelled a′, b′, c′, d′.

8. To construct another smaller, similar rectangle:
From the **Toolbox**, choose ↖.
Draw a box around the smaller rectangle to select it.
From the **Transform** menu, choose **Dilate.**
The dialog box is unchanged.
Click **Dilate.**
Click anywhere on the screen.
Click each side of the image rectangle to select it.
From the **Display** menu, choose **Show Labels.**
The sides are labelled a″, b″, c″, d″.

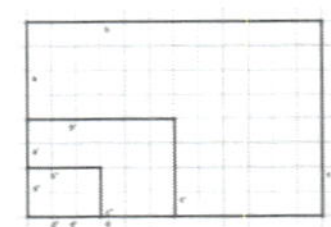

There are now 3 similar rectangles: the original rectangle, the first image, and the second image.

Exploring Side Lengths of Similar Rectangles

9. To measure the base and height of each rectangle:
From the Toolbox, choose ↖.
Click anywhere on the screen.
Click the base (side b) and height (side c) for all three rectangl
From the **Measure** menu, choose **Length.**
How do the bases and heights compare?
Click and drag a vertex of the original rectangle.
Observe the changing measures. Return to the original rectang

- How do you know the rectangles are not congruent?
  (*The bases are different and the heights are different.*)
- How do you write a ratio in simplest form?
  (*I divide the terms of the ratio by their greatest common factor.*)
- How do you know a ratio is in simplest form?
  (*The terms do not have any common factors other than 1.*)

AFTER Connect

What you might see:

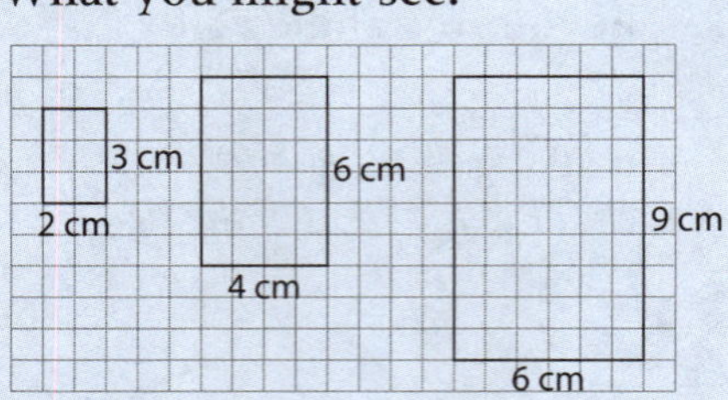

Rectangle	Base (cm)	Height (cm)	Perimeter (cm)	Area (cm²)
A	2	3	10	6
B	4	6	20	24
C	6	9	30	54

	A:B	A:C	B:C
base:base	2:4 = 1:2	2:6 = 1:3	4:6 = 2:3
height:height	3:6 = 1:2	3:9 = 1:3	6:9 = 2:3
perimeter:perimeter	10:20 = 1:2	10:30 = 1:3	20:30 = 2:3
area:area	6:24 = 1:4	6:54 = 1:9	24:54 = 4:9

Ask:

- How is the ratio of corresponding sides related to the ratio of perimeters?
  (*These ratios are equal. For example, for rectangles A and B, the ratio of the bases is 2:4, which simplifies to 1:2. The ratio of the perimeters is 10:20, which also simplifies to 1:2.*)

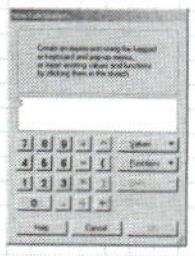

10. To calculate the base-to-height ratio of similar rectangles:
From the **Measure** menu, choose **Calculate.**
The *Sketchpad* calculator appears.
Calculate the base-to-height ratio of the original rectangle.
Select [b = 12 cm], then [÷], then [c = 8 cm]. Press [OK].
Record your findings.
Repeat this step to calculate the base-to-height ratio of each smaller rectangle.
What is true about the base-to-height ratios of similar rectangles?
What happens to the ratios when you drag a vertex?
Does the size of the rectangle change the ratio? Explain.
Does the type of quadrilateral change the ratio? Explain.

11. To compare the base-to-base and height-to-height ratios of two similar rectangles:
From the **Measure** menu, choose **Calculate.**
Calculate the base-to-base ratio for the original rectangle (b) and its image rectangle (b′).
Calculate the height-to-height ratio of the original rectangle (c) and its image rectangle (c′). Record your findings.
Compare b′:b″ with c′:c″. Compare b:b″ with c:c″.
What do you notice?

Comparing Corresponding Angles in Similar Figures

12. Click and drag a vertex of the original rectangle to get 3 similar quadrilaterals. To measure an angle:
Click on 3 vertices in order.
From the **Measure** menu, choose **Angle.**
The measure of the angle described by the 3 vertices is shown.
Measure all the angles of each quadrilateral.
What do you notice about the measures of angles in similar figures?

Exploring Perimeters of Similar Rectangles

13. A figure must have an *interior* to measure its perimeter or area.
To construct an interior:
From the **Toolbox,** choose [arrow tool].
Click anywhere on the screen.

Technology: Exploring Similar Figures 63

(Sample Solutions, continued from page 10)

10. a) Let the number of students who take violin lessons be *v*.
Then, $v{:}45 = 8{:}15$
In fraction form: $\frac{v}{45} = \frac{8}{15}$
$\frac{v}{45} \times 45 = \frac{8}{15} \times 45 \rightarrow v = 8 \times 3 \rightarrow v = 24;$
24 students take violin lessons.

b) Let the number of students who take clarinet lessons be *c*.
Then, $c{:}24 = 9{:}8$
In fraction form: $\frac{c}{24} = \frac{9}{8}$
$\frac{c}{24} \times 24 = \frac{9}{8} \times 24 \rightarrow c = 9 \times 3 \rightarrow c = 27;$
27 students take clarinet lessons.

11. I can use this proportion:

$$\frac{\text{height of flagpole}}{\text{length of its shadow}} = \frac{\text{my height}}{\text{length of my shadow}}$$

I can measure the length of the shadow of the flagpole. I know my height, and my friend can measure the length of my shadow. Then, I solve the proportion to find the height of the flagpole.

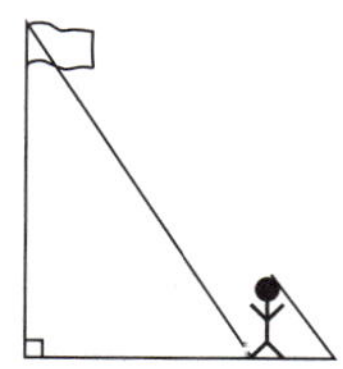

REFLECT: Yes, I can use a proportion to solve any ratio problem, if I know 3 terms out of the 4 terms in the proportion. I would not use a proportion to solve a simple problem like this: "The ratio of boys to girls is 2:3. There are 20 boys. How many girls are there?" I would use logical reasoning and equivalent ratios.
I multiply 2 by 10 to get 20.
So, I multiply 3 by 10 to get 30.
There are 30 girls.

- How is the ratio of corresponding sides related to the ratio of areas?
(The ratio of areas is the square of the ratio of corresponding sides. For example, for rectangles B and C, the ratio of the heights is 6:9, which simplifies to 2:3. The ratio of the areas is 24:54. These terms have a common factor of 6. The ratio is 4:9 in simplest form. This ratio is $2^2{:}3^2$, which is the square of the terms in the ratio of heights.)

Ensure students understand the relationships among the ratios.

(Sample Solutions, continued from page 13)

Actual dimensions of the furniture in the family room:
Bookcase: 68 cm by 40 cm
Sofa: 216 cm by 100 cm
Coffee table: 115 cm by 58 cm
Dimensions of furniture on scale drawing:
Bookcase: $\frac{l}{68} = \frac{1}{25} \rightarrow l = 2.72$ cm; $\frac{w}{40} = \frac{1}{25} \rightarrow w = 1.6$ cm
Sofa: $\frac{l}{216} = \frac{1}{25} \rightarrow l = 8.64$ cm; $\frac{w}{100} = \frac{1}{25} \rightarrow w = 4.0$ cm
Coffee table: $\frac{l}{115} = \frac{1}{25} \rightarrow l = 4.6$ cm; $\frac{w}{58} = \frac{1}{25} \rightarrow w = 2.32$ cm

(Sample Solutions continue on page 18.)

(Sample Solutions, continued from page 17)

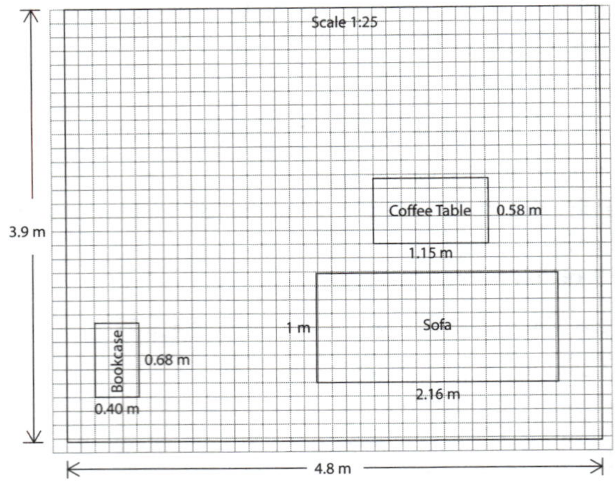

REFLECT: A scale drawing can be either an enlargement or a reduction of a picture or object.
A scale of 3:1 produces a drawing where each dimension is 3 times the actual dimension.
This drawing is an enlargement. If the actual drawing is 9 cm by 12 cm, the scale drawing will be 3 × 9 cm = 27 cm by 3 × 12 cm = 36 cm.
A scale of 1:3 produces a drawing where each dimension is $\frac{1}{3}$ the actual dimension. This drawing is a reduction. If the actual drawing is 9 cm by 12 cm, the scale drawing will be 9 cm ÷ 3 = 3 cm by 12 cm ÷ 3 = 4 cm.

If anything other than points is selected, this option will not appear.

Click the vertices of the original rectangle in order.
Do not click the segments.
From the **Construct** menu, choose **Quadrilateral In**

14. To measure the perimeter:
From the **Toolbox**, choose [arrow tool].
From the **Measure** menu, choose **Perimeter**.
The vertices of the original rectangle now appear labelled A, B

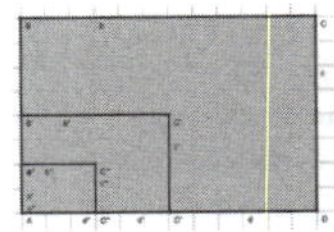

15. Repeat *Steps 13* and *14* for each of the smaller rectangles.

16. To compare the perimeters of two similar rectangles:
From the **Measure** menu, choose **Calculate**.
Calculate the perimeter-to-perimeter ratio for the original rectangle and its first image.
Compare the perimeter-to-perimeter ratio for the first and second image rectangles, and for the original rectangle and th second image. What do you notice?

17. For each rectangle, what is the ratio of perimeter:base? What do you notice?

Exploring Areas of Similar Rectangles

18. To measure the area:
Repeat *Step 13* to construct quadrilateral interior.
From the **Toolbox**, choose [arrow tool].
From the **Measure** menu, choose **Area**.

19. Repeat *Step 18* for each image rectangle.

20. For the original rectangle and the first image rectangle, comp ratio of the areas with the ratio of the bases.
Write each ratio in simplest form. What do you notice?

21. Repeat *Step 20* for the original rectangle and the second image rectangle.

Reflect

Use your observations to list some properties of similar rectangles. Are these properties true for other polygons? Use *The Geometer's Sketchpad* to find out.

64 UNIT 2: Applications of Ratio, Rate, and Percent

ASSESSMENT FOR LEARNING

What to Look For	What to Do
Knowledge and Understanding ✔ Students understand that, in similar figures, the ratios of corresponding sides are equal. ***Communication*** ✔ Students can explain how the ratio of corresponding sides is related to the ratio of areas.	***Extra Support:*** Have students use Pattern Blocks to produce similar figures; for example, 4 orange blocks form a square similar to 1 orange block, and 9 orange blocks form a square similar to both the smaller squares. ***Extra Practice:*** Have students repeat the *Explore* using square dot paper on which they draw 3 similar irregular quadrilaterals. To calculate the area of each quadrilateral, students can divide it into composite figures (triangle, parallelogram, trapezoid, and so on). ***Extension:*** Students can repeat the *Explore*, using 0.5-cm grid paper, and rectangles with dimensions that have a different ratio from that in *Explore*.

Recording and Reporting
Master 2.2 Ongoing Observations: Applications of Ratio, Rate, and Percent

2.3 Comparing Rates

Focus Use unit rates to compare rates.

Explore

Work on your own.
Use a calculator if it helps.

36 tea bags for $1.49 | 144 tea bags for $5.59

Which box of tea bags is the better buy?
What do you need to consider before you decide?

Reflect & Share

Compare your results with those of a classmate.
Did both of you choose the same box? If so, justify your choice.
If not, can both of you be correct? Explain.

Connect

Great Start cereal can be purchased in three different sizes and prices.

We want to find the least expensive cereal.
The smallest box costs the least, but that does not mean it is the least expensive.
We find the unit cost for each cereal.
The cost of 1 g is very small, so we calculate the cost of 100 g for each cereal.

2.3 Comparing Rates 65

Comparing Rates

LESSON ORGANIZER 80–100 min

Curriculum Focus: Use unit rates to compare rates. (8m14, 8m26, 8m29)

Student Materials
- calculators

Optional
- Step-by-Step 3 (Master 2.11)
- Extra Practice 3 (Master 2.21)

Assessment: Master 2.2 Ongoing Observations: Applications of Ratio, Rate, and Percent

Key Math Learning

We use unit rates to compare rates.

Math Link

Pricing of items in supermarkets must show unit costs. Costs may be given as costs per unit, costs per kilogram, or costs per 100 g. This allows customers to compare the costs of different quantities of the same or similar items.

Bar codes or UPCs (Universal Product Codes) are used to identify different products. The first 6 digits identify the producer and the next 5 digits give the item number. Every item has a different number. For example, a 2-L bottle of pop has a different number than a 1-L bottle of the same pop. The last number is a check number that ensures the correct code is punched into the till or computer.

BEFORE Get Started

Have students discuss situations in which they have come across special deals in stores. Examples might be: 1 carton of juice for $1.38 or 4 for $5.00; 1 loaf of bread for $1.24 or 4 loaves for $5.50; 1 can of soup for 62¢ or a case of 12 for $6.50.

Ask students why they think stores do this.

Present *Explore.*

DURING Explore

Ongoing Assessment: Observe and Listen

As students work, ask questions, such as:

- How can you compare the prices?
  (Find the cost of 1 tea bag in each box.)
- How will you find the costs for 1 tea bag?
  (Divide $1.49 by 36, and $5.59 by 144.)
- What are the costs of 1 tea bag?
  (Approximately 4.14¢ and 3.88¢)
- Which is the better price?
  (3.88¢ per tea bag or 144 tea bags for $5.59)
- Are there other ways you could compare the prices?
  (Yes, I could find the cost of 4 smaller boxes of tea bags by multiplying $1.49 by 4 to get $5.96. One box of 144 tea bags is a better buy than 4 boxes of 36 tea bags. I could find the cost of 36 tea bags by dividing $5.59, the cost of 144 tea bags, by 4 to get $1.40. This is less than $1.49 for a box of 36 tea bags. 144 tea bags for $5.59 is the better deal.)
- Is buying 144 tea bags always better?
  (Not if you do not drink tea very often. Some of the tea might get stale before you use it.)

AFTER Connect

Invite students to share their strategies for finding the better buy.

Introduce *Connect* and the methods of calculating unit costs and comparing rates.

REACHING ALL LEARNERS

Alternative Explore

Have students look through supermarket flyers to find two sizes and prices of the same product. Students calculate which is the better buy, and explain why.

Early Finishers

For each relevant *Practice* question, have students identify the measurements that are directly proportional, and write a sentence to describe the proportionality. For example, for question 8, the number of words typed is directly proportional to the time taken to type.

Common Misconceptions

➤ Students do not know which quantity to divide by when calculating a unit rate.

How to Help: Have students divide both ways, then decide which makes more sense. For example, in question 3, either $\frac{454\ \text{g}}{\$3.29} \doteq 138\ \text{g/\$}$ or $\frac{\$3.29}{454\ \text{g}} \doteq \$0.0072/\text{g}$

The first way is a rate in grams per dollar. The second way is a rate in dollars per gram. Do we want to know how many grams we can buy for \$1, or the cost of 1 g? Both rates are correct, but the latter makes more sense in the context of this problem.

Math Link

Your World

In a supermarket, the tag on the shelf with the bar code of an item often shows the cost of 1 g of the item.

With this information, you can compare the costs of different-size packages of the item.

Box A has mass 450 g and costs \$4.69.
450 g is 4.5 × 100 g; so, the cost of 100 g of Box A is: $\frac{\$4.69}{4.5} \doteq \$1.042$

Box B has mass 600 g and costs \$6.49.
The cost of 100 g of Box B is: $\frac{\$6.49}{6} \doteq \$1.082$

Box C has mass 1000 g and costs \$7.89.
The cost of 100 g of Box C is: $\frac{\$7.89}{10} = \$0.789$

Each unit cost can be written as a unit rate.
The least unit rate is \$0.789/100 g, for Box C.
The greatest unit rate is \$1.082/100 g, for Box B.
If you are buying cereal for a family, then the best buy is Box C.
If you do not eat much cereal, the best buy is probably Box A.
If you buy Box C because it has the least unit price, you might have to throw some of it away if it gets stale.

Example

Mariah is looking for a part-time job for 15 h a week.
She has been offered three positions.

Day Camp Counsellor	Cashier	Library Assistant
\$7.50 per hour	\$25.00 for 3 h	\$44.00 for 5 h

a) Which job should Mariah accept?
b) How much will Mariah earn in a week?

Solution

a) Calculate the unit rate for each job.
The unit rate is the hourly rate of pay.
For day camp counsellor, the unit rate is \$7.50/h.
For cashier, the unit rate is: $\frac{\$25.00}{3\ \text{h}} \doteq \$8.33/\text{h}$
For library assistant, the unit rate is: $\frac{\$44.00}{5\ \text{h}} = \$8.80/\text{h}$
The library assistant job pays the most.
So, if Mariah likes books, she should take the job in the library.

b) Mariah works 15 h a week, at a rate of \$8.80/h.
She will earn: 15 × \$8.80 = \$132.00
Mariah will earn \$132.00 a week as a part-time library assistant.

Unit rates occur in situations other than costs of items and rates of pay.

Ask students for examples of other unit rates and explain what they mean.

(*Possible answers: heart rate, number of beats per minute; average speed, distance covered each hour; keyboard skills, number of words typed per minute; rate of growth of plants, people, money; exchange rates for money, the amount of foreign money you will get for each Canadian dollar; scales for blueprints, 1:50 means 1 cm on the blueprint represents 50 cm in actual measurements*)

Remind students that a unit rate illustrates two measurements that are directly proportional. For each box, the cost of tea bags is directly proportional to the number of boxes. If I double the number of boxes I buy, I double the price I pay.

In the *Example*, the money earned is directly proportional to the time worked. If Mariah works for 5 h, she earns an amount that is equal to 5 times the hourly rate.

From a financial point of view, Mariah should select the library assistant job but, although money is an important factor, personal enjoyment, job satisfaction, and career plans should also be considered.

Practice

Students should be encouraged to show the steps in their solutions.

Question 2: For part b, students could either find the cost of 100 g of yogurt or 500 g of yogurt. For part c, students could find the cost of 50 mL, 100 mL, or 300 mL of toothpaste.

Practice

1. Write a unit rate for each statement.
   a) \$399 earned in 3 weeks \$133/week
   b) 680 km travelled in 8 h 85 km/h
   c) 12 bottles of juice for \$3.49 About \$0.29/bottle
   d) 3 cans of soup for \$0.99 \$0.33/can

2. Which is the better buy?
   a) 5 grapefruit for \$1.99 or (8 grapefruit for \$2.99)
   b) 500 g of yogurt for \$3.49 or (125 g for \$0.79)
   c) 100 mL of toothpaste for \$1.79 or (150 mL of toothpaste for \$2.19)
   d) (2 L of orange juice for \$4.49) or 1 L for \$2.89

3. How much does 1 kg of butter cost at the rate shown in the picture at the left? About \$7.25

4. Mr. Gomez travelled 525 km in 6 h.
   a) What was the mean distance travelled in 1 h? 87.5 km
   b) How is the mean distance related to average speed?
   c) At this rate, how long will it take Mr. Gomez to travel 700 km? 8 h

5. a) Which is the greatest average speed?
   i) (60 km in 3 h) ii) 68 km in 4 h iii) 70 km in 5 h
   b) Draw a graph to illustrate your answers in part a.

6. In the first 9 basketball games of the season, Lashonda scored 114 points.
   a) On average, how many points does Lashonda score per game? $12.\overline{6}$ points
   b) At this rate, how many points will Lashonda have after 24 games? 304 points

7. Lakelse Lake, B.C., had the most snow for one day in Canada, which was 118.1 cm. Assume the snow fell at a constant rate. How much snow fell in 1 h? About 4.9 cm

8. Who has the greatest average typing speed?
   a) (Mei-Lin types 350 words in 6 min.)
   b) Nishant types 250 words in 5 min.
   c) Adam types 300 words in 5.5 min.

9. A 2.5-kg bag of grass seed covers an area of 1200 m^2. How much seed is needed to cover a square park with side length 500 m?

2.3 Comparing Rates 67

Sample Solutions

4. b) The average speed is the mean distance travelled in 1 h.

5. a) i) 60 km ÷ 3 h = 20 km/h
ii) 68 km ÷ 4 h = 17 km/h
iii) 70 km ÷ 5 h = 14 km/h
20 km/h is greatest, so 60 km in 3 h is the greatest average speed.

b)

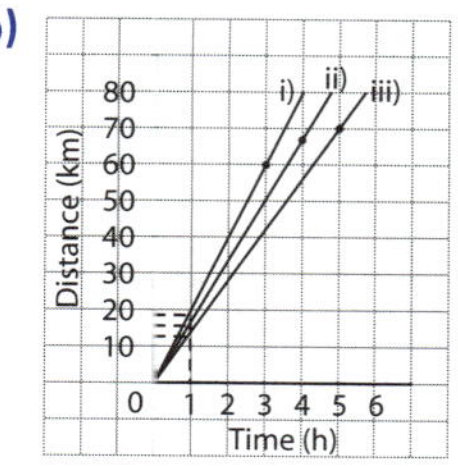

8. a) Mei-Lin: $\frac{350 \text{ words}}{6 \text{ min}} = 58.\overline{3}$ wpm
b) Nishant: $\frac{250 \text{ words}}{5 \text{ min}} = 50$ wpm
c) Adam: $\frac{300 \text{ words}}{5.5 \text{ min}} = 54.\overline{54}$ wpm

9. 2.5 kg cover 1200 m^2. So, 1 kg covers $\frac{1200 \text{ m}^2}{2.5} = 480$ m^2.
The park has area 500 m × 500 m = 250 000 m^2.
The seed, in kilograms, for 250 000 m^2 is $\frac{250\,000}{480} \doteq 520.8$
So, about 521 kg are needed. The number of bags is:
$\frac{520.8}{2.5} \doteq 208.3$
Round up. The number of bags is 209.

10. a) i) There are 60 Cal in an apple.
Cycling burns 216 Cal/h.
So, time taken is $\frac{60}{216}$ h = $\frac{60 \times 60}{216}$ min = $16.\overline{6}$ min.
It takes about 17 min to burn the calories in an apple.
ii) There are 140 Cal in 2 slices of bread. Walking burns 270 Cal/h.
So, time taken is $\frac{140}{270}$ h = $\frac{140 \times 60}{270}$ min = $31.\overline{1}$ min.
It takes about 31 min to burn the calories in 2 slices of bread.

Assessment Focus: Question 10

Students think about the different activities and what would be a reasonable time to spend on each one. For example, it is unlikely that a student could skip for an hour without a break, whereas it is possible a student could cycle or walk for more than an hour without a break.

For part a, students divide the number of calories by the calories burned per hour. They get an answer that is a decimal of an hour. Students multiply this by 60 to get the time in minutes. Some students may prefer to calculate the calories burned per minute, then divide the energy provided by that number.

Math Note

In Grade 9, students will learn that energy is measured in joules (J) or kilojoules (kJ). In question 10, the energy from food is measured in Calories. One Calorie is 4.19 J.

One Calorie (capital C) is actually 1000 calories (lowercase c). The statement that a medium apple provides 60 Calories means that 1 apple releases 60 × 1000 × 4.19 J of energy, which is 251 400 J, or 251.4 kJ.

Mental Math

To be divisible by 4 and 6, a number is a multiple of the lowest common multiple of 4 and 6, which is 12. Multiples of 12 less than 150 are 12, 24, 36, 48, 60, 72, 84, 96, 108, 120, 132, and 144, for a total of 12 numbers.

Assignment Guidelines

If your students do not have time to complete all the *Practice* questions on pages 67 and 68, these questions provide minimum curriculum coverage:
1, 2, 4, 5, 7, 9, 10, *Reflect*

To assess the 4 Achievement Chart categories listed in the curriculum document, have students complete these *Practice* questions:

Communication: 2
Knowledge and Understanding: 4
Application: 7
Thinking: 9

b) A vanilla fudge ice cream and a chocolate iced doughnut have (290 + 204) Cal = 494 Cal.

i) Swimming would burn the calories the quickest.
Time taken is: $\frac{494}{570}$ h = $\frac{494}{570} \times 60$ min = 52 min

ii) Cycling for 1 h, then walking for 1 h burns (216 + 270) Cal = 486 Cal.
This is approximately equal to the number of calories from the ice cream and doughnut.

c) For example: How long would a person have to do aerobics to burn the calories in a chocolate iced doughnut? (Answer: $\frac{204}{480}$ h = $\frac{204 \times 60}{480}$ min = 25.5 min)

11. a) Canada 30 007 094 people ÷ 9 984 670 km^2
≐ 3 people/km^2;
China 1 279 557 000 people ÷ 9 562 000 km^2
≐ 134 people/km^2;
Japan 127 538 000 people ÷ 377 727 km^2
≐ 338 people/km^2

b) Canada has very few people for the size of the country while Japan has a very large population in a small country. Although China has roughly the same area as Canada, it has far more people.

REFLECT: A rate compares two different things; for example, I cycle 30 km in 2 h is a rate. A unit rate compares one quantity to one unit of another quantity; for example, I cycle 15 km in 1 h, or I cycle 15 km/h. This is my average speed. I can use unit rates to solve problems, such as: which is the better or best buy for grocery items; and also problems that involve distance, time, and average speed.

---

10. **Assessment Focus** The food we eat provides energy in calories. When we exercise, we burn calories.
These tables illustrate these data for different foods a
different exercises.

These data are for a female with a mass of 56 kg. The data vary for men and women, and for different masses.

Food	Energy Provided (Calories)	Activity	Calories Burne per Hour
Medium apple	60	Skipping	492
Slice of white bread	70	Swimming	570
Medium peach	50	Cycling	216
Vanilla fudge ice cream	290	Aerobics	480
Chocolate iced doughnut	204	Walking	270

a) How long would a person have to:
i) cycle to burn the calories in an apple?
ii) walk to burn the calories in two slices of bread?
b) Suppose a person ate vanilla fudge ice cream and a chocola iced doughnut.
i) Which activity would burn the calories quickest? How long would it take?
ii) Which 2 activities would burn the calories in about 2 h?
c) Use the data in the tables to write your own problem. Solve your problem. Show your work.

Mental Math

How many numbers less than 150 are divisible by 4 and by 6?
Explain how you know.

12 numbers

Take It Further

11. Population density is a rate. It compares the number of people in a population with the area of the land where they live. Population density is measured in number of people per square kilometre.
a) Find the population density for each country.

These data are for 2002.

i) Canada: 30 007 094 people in 9 984 670 km^2
ii) China: 1 279 557 000 people in 9 562 000 km^2
iii) Japan: 127 538 000 people in 377 727 km^2
b) How do the population densities in part a compare?

Reflect

What is a unit rate?
Describe the types of problems you can solve using unit rates.

68 UNIT 2: Applications of Ratio, Rate, and Percent

ASSESSMENT FOR LEARNING

What to Look For	What to Do
Knowledge and Understanding ✔ Students understand the need to use unit rates to compare.	***Extra Support:*** Students can play the Additional Activity, *Rate It* (Master 2.8). Students can use Step-by-Step 3 (Master 2.11) to complete question 10.
Thinking ✔ Students can solve problems related to unit rates.	***Extra Practice:*** Have students create and solve problems similar to questions 1 and 5. Students can complete Extra Practice 3 (Master 2.21).
Communication ✔ Students can explain their methods of calculating and comparing unit rates.	***Extension:*** Have students draw graphs to illustrate the unit rates they found. Two or more unit rates for the same item can be graphed on the same grid.
Application ✔ Students can calculate unit rates. ✔ Students can compare unit rates.	

Recording and Reporting
Master 2.2 Ongoing Observations: Applications of Ratio, Rate, and Percent

Mid-Unit Review

LESSON

2.1 **1.** Find each missing term.
a) x:10 = 60:12 b) y:21 = 9:7
c) $\frac{z}{15} = \frac{20}{60}$ d) $\frac{a}{21} = \frac{4}{3}$

2. At the local high school, the ratio of boys to girls is 3 to 4.
There are 1200 boys in the school.
How many girls are there? 1600

3. The numbers of bass and pike in a lake are estimated to be in the ratio of 5:3. There are approximately 500 fish in the lake.
a) How many bass are there? About 310 bass
b) How many pike are there? About 190 pike

2.2 **4.** A boat is 26.5 m long.
A picture of the boat is drawn to the scale of 1:200.
What is the length of the boat in the picture? 13.25 cm

5. For each animal, its actual measurement is given. What scale would you use to draw each animal to fill a page of your notebook? Show your work.
a) The bee hummingbird is the smallest bird on Earth.
It measures 5.7 cm from beak tip to tail tip.
b) The blue whale is the largest animal on Earth.
Its length can be 33 m.

6. Use the scales you chose in question 5.
Draw a line segment to represent each length in question 5.

7. An amoeba is an organism with one cell. A picture of an amoeba is drawn to a scale of 250:1. The amoeba in the picture is 9 cm wide.
How wide is the actual amoeba? 0.36 mm

2.3 **8.** Find the unit cost of each item.
a) 4 L of milk for \$4.29
b) 2.4 kg of beef for \$10.72
c) 454 g of margarine for \$1.99

9. Which is the better buy?
Justify each answer.
a) 6.2 L of gas for \$5.39 or 8.5 L of gas for \$7.31 (circled)
b) 5 bagels for \$3.00 or 12 bagels for \$5.99 (circled)
c) 2 kg of potatoes for \$1.38 or 5 kg of potatoes for \$2.79 (circled)

10. Hisan can type 86 words in 2 min.
At this rate, how many words can Hisan type in each time?
a) 1 min b) 3 min c) 12.5 min

2.2 2.3 **11.** On a map, the distance between two cities is 5.6 cm. The scale on the map is 1:3 000 000.
A cyclist travels this distance in 4 h.
What is the cyclist's average speed? 42 km/h

Mid-Unit Review 69

LESSON ORGANIZER

Student Materials
- calculators

Assessment: Master 2.1 Unit Rubric: Applications of Ratio, Rate, and Percent; Master 2.4 Unit Summary: Applications of Ratio, Rate, and Percent

Sample Solutions

1. a) x:10 = 60:12
Write the second ratio in simplest form.
Divide each term by 12.
60:12 = 5:1
Then, x:10 = 5:1
For x:10 to equal 5:1, the first term x has to be 5 times as great as the second term 10.
That is, $x = 5 \times 10 = 50$

b) $\frac{y}{21} = \frac{9}{7} \rightarrow \frac{y}{21} \times 21 = \frac{9}{7} \times 21 \rightarrow y = 9 \times 3 \rightarrow y = 27$

c) $\frac{z}{15} = \frac{20}{60} \rightarrow \frac{z}{15} = \frac{1}{3} \rightarrow \frac{z}{15} \times 15 = \frac{1}{3} \times 15 \rightarrow z = 5$

d) $\frac{a}{21} = \frac{4}{3} \rightarrow \frac{a}{21} \times 21 = \frac{4}{3} \times 21 \rightarrow a = \frac{84}{3} \rightarrow a = 28$

2. The ratio of boys to girls is 3:4. Let x be the number of girls. Then the ratio of boys to girls is 1200:x. Look at the first terms in the ratios. To go to 1200 from 3, multiply by 400. So, to get the number of girls, multiply 4 by 400. That is, $x = 4 \times 400 = 1600$

4. The scale is 1:200. This means 1 cm on the drawing represents 200 cm on the boat.
The length of the boat is
26.5 m = 26.5 × 100 cm = 2650 cm
Divide by 200 to find the length on the picture.
$\frac{2650 \text{ cm}}{200} = 13.25$ cm
The length of the boat in the picture is 13.25 cm.

5. Sample answers:
a) The bee hummingbird is 5.7 cm.
The book page is 25 cm high.
The drawing will be an enlargement.
Leave a 1-cm margin.
So, the hummingbird picture is to be 23 cm long.
To find the scale, divide: $\frac{23}{5.7} \doteq 4.035$
Use a scale of 4:1. The drawing of the hummingbird will be 4 × 5.7 cm = 22.8 cm.
b) The blue whale is 33 m, or 3300 cm. The picture is to be 23 cm long.
The drawing will be a reduction.
To find the scale, divide: $\frac{3300}{23} \doteq 143.5$
A drawing to the scale of 1:140 will not quite fit.
So, use a scale of 1:150. The drawing of the whale will be $\frac{3300 \text{ cm}}{150} = 22$ cm.

6. a) Students should draw a line segment 22.8 cm long.
b) Students should draw a line segment 22 cm long.

7. 9 cm = 90 mm; $\frac{90}{250}$ mm = 0.36 mm; the amoeba is 0.36 mm wide.

8. a) \$4.29 ÷ 4 L ≐ \$1.07/L
b) \$10.72 ÷ 2.4 kg ≐ \$4.47/kg
c) 454 g of margarine for \$1.99
So, 1 g of margarine costs: $\frac{\$1.99}{454} \doteq \$0.00438$ = 0.438¢, or about 0.44¢
And, 100 g of margarine cost: \$0.00438 × 100 = \$0.438, or about 44¢
The unit cost is 0.44¢/g or 44¢/100 g.

10. a) 43 words **b)** 129 words **c)** About 538 words

11. On the map, 1 cm represents 3 000 000 cm, or 30 000 m, or 30 km.
So, a distance of 5.6 cm represents
5.6 × 30 km = 168 km.
A cyclist travels 168 km in 4 h.
So, the cyclist's average speed is:
168 km ÷ 4 h = 42 km/h

Calculating Percents

LESSON ORGANIZER

80–100 min

Curriculum Focus: Calculate percents from less than 1% to greater than 100%. (8m14, 8m17, 8m18, 8m28)

Student Materials
- calculators

Optional
- Step-by-Step 4 (Master 2.12)
- Extra Practice 4 (Master 2.22)

Assessment: Master 2.2 Ongoing Observations: Applications of Ratio, Rate, and Percent

Key Math Learnings

1. Fractions and decimals can be converted to percents.
2. Percent of a number, including percents less than 1% and greater than 100%, can be calculated.

2.4 Calculating Percents

Focus Calculate percents from less than 1% to greater than 100%.

Explore

Work with a partner.
Use a calculator if you need it.

There are 225 students in an elementary school.
- Eighteen students have no siblings.
  Estimate what fraction of the students in the school have no siblings.
  Write the fraction of students in the school who have no siblings.
  What percent of students in the school have no siblings?
- One-third of the students have two siblings.
  Estimate what percent of the students have two siblings.
  What fraction of the students do not have two siblings?
  What percent of the school is this?

Reflect & Share

What do you notice about the percents for one-third and two-thirds?
How are these different from other percents you have worked w

Connect

When the whole is 1.0, you know that:
100% = 1.0
10% = 0.10
1% = 0.01
We can extend this pattern to write percents less than 1% as decimals:
0.1% = 0.001
and 0.5% = 0.005

Some fractions have percents that are repeating decimals.
We can use a calculator to show that: $\frac{1}{3} = 0.3333333\ldots$
We write this decimal as $0.\overline{3}$.

70 UNIT 2: Applications of Ratio, Rate, and Percent

BEFORE Get Started

If you have not already done so, review *Skills You'll Need: Relating Fractions, Decimals, and Percents*, page 52.

Have students convert some simple fractions and decimals to percents.

Ask:
- What is $\frac{1}{2}$ as a percent? (*50%*)
  $\frac{3}{4}$? (*75%*) $\frac{4}{5}$? (*80%*) $\frac{17}{10}$? (*170%*)
- What is 0.4 as a percent? (*40%*)
  0.2? (*20%*) 0.6? (*60%*) 1.36? (*136%*)

Have students draw a number line labelled from 0 and 0% to 1 and 100%. Have them label the line with percents and their corresponding decimals, then extend the line to record percents greater than 100%, and their corresponding decimals.

Present *Explore*.

DURING Explore

Ongoing Assessment: Observe and Listen

As students work, ask questions, such as:
- What does *sibling* mean? (*Brother or sister*)
- How will you estimate the fraction of students who have no siblings?
  (*The fraction is $\frac{18}{225} \doteq \frac{20}{200} = \frac{1}{10}$.*)
- How will you find the exact fraction and percent of students who have no siblings?
  (*The fraction is $\frac{18}{225}$, which can be reduced to $\frac{2}{25}$. The percent is $\frac{2}{25} \times \frac{4}{4} = \frac{8}{100} = 8\%$.*)
- How will you estimate the percent of students who have 2 siblings?
  (*$\frac{1}{3} = 0.\overline{3} \doteq 0.3 = \frac{3}{10} = \frac{30}{100} = 30\%$*)
- What fraction of the students does not have 2 siblings? (*One-third of the students have 2 siblings, so $\frac{2}{3}$ do not have 2 siblings.*)
  What is this fraction as a percent?
  (*$\frac{2}{3} = 0.\overline{6}$; I used my calculator. $0.\overline{6}$ is 0.666... This is about $\frac{0.67}{100}$, or about 67%.*)

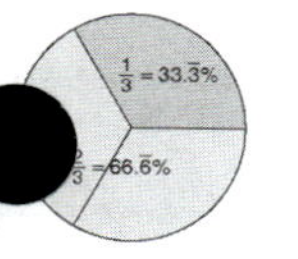

To write $\frac{1}{3}$ as a percent, we write $0.\overline{3}$ as $0.33\overline{3}$.

Then, $0.33\overline{3} = \frac{33.\overline{3}}{100}$

$= 33.\overline{3}\%$

And $\frac{2}{3} = 0.6666\ldots$

$= 0.66\overline{6}$

$= \frac{66.\overline{6}}{100}$

$= 66.\overline{6}\%$

Example 1

According to Statistics Canada, in 2001, the population of Ontario was about 11 410 000. About 0.35% of the population were aboriginal people living on reserves.

a) About how many aboriginal people lived on reserves?

b) Estimate to check the answer.

c) Illustrate the answer to part a with a diagram.

Solution

a) Find 0.35% of 11 410 000.

First write 0.35% as a decimal.

$0.35\% = \frac{0.35}{100}$

$= 0.0035$

Use a calculator.

Then, 0.35% of 11 410 000 $= 0.0035 \times 11\,410\,000$

$= 39\,935$

In 2001, about 40 000 people lived on reserves in Ontario.

b) 0.35% is approximately 0.33%.

0.33% is approximately $\frac{1}{3}$%, or $\frac{1}{3}$ of 1%.

1% of 11 410 000 is: $0.01 \times 11\,410\,000 = 114\,100$

114 100 is about 100 000.

$\frac{1}{3}$ of 100 000 is about 33 000.

This estimate is close to the calculated answer.

c) To illustrate 0.35%, first show 1% on a number line.

Then, 0.35% is about $\frac{1}{3}$ of 1%.

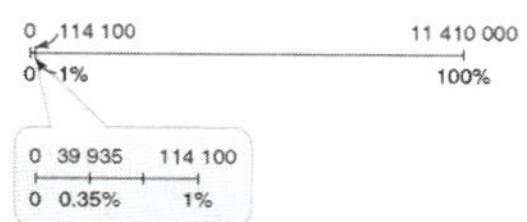

2.4 Calculating Percents 71

REACHING ALL LEARNERS

Early Finishers

Have students use a class list to estimate, then calculate, the fraction and percent of boys and the fraction and percent of girls in the class. If any students are absent, have students repeat these calculations for the students who are present.
Students share their results with others in the class.

Common Misconceptions

➤ Students have difficulty understanding/visualizing percents greater than 100%.

How to Help: To understand a percent such as 180%, students might prefer to think of it as 100% + 80%; that is, 1 whole + $\frac{8}{10}$ of that whole.

➤ Students have difficulty understanding percents less than 1%, and confuse a percent such as 0.1%, which is $\frac{1}{1000}$, with 0.1, which is $\frac{1}{10}$.

How to Help: Remind students that the percent (%) symbol following a number means that that number is the numerator of a fraction with denominator 100.
Have students write: $0.1\% = \frac{0.1}{100} = \frac{0.1 \times 10}{100 \times 10} = \frac{1}{1000}$;
$0.2\% = \frac{0.2}{100} = \frac{0.2 \times 10}{100 \times 10} = \frac{2}{1000}$; and so on, up to $0.9\% = \frac{0.9}{100} = \frac{9}{1000}$.
Students could make a chart with fraction and decimal equivalents for the percents above, as well as percents such as 2.5%, 7.5%, and so on.

AFTER Connect

Invite students to share their results and their methods of finding percents.

Students are familiar with converting a (natural number) percent to a decimal, such as 26% is 0.26. Some students may be confused if you ask them to convert a percent, such as 12.5% to its equivalent as a decimal, 0.125. Make sure students understand the difference between a percent written to one or two decimal places, and the same percent written as a decimal.

Review *Connect*, and the explanation for the fractions $\frac{1}{3}$ and $\frac{2}{3}$ written as percents.
Remind students that we place a bar above the 3 and 6 to show they repeat.

Have students draw a number line from 0% to 100%, and label every 10% from 10% to 90%. Students then mark and label $33.\overline{3}\%$ and $66.\overline{6}\%$.

After you review *Example 1*, have students draw a number line from 0% to 1%, and label every 0.1% up to 0.9%. On this number line, they can mark and label 0.35%.

Review *Example 2*. Have students draw another number line, or extend the first line they drew if they have room, for 0% to 200%. On this line, students mark and label 180%.

Practice

Question 2b: Students should see that as the fractions increase by $\frac{1}{3}$, the percents increase by $33.\overline{3}$.

Assessment Focus: Question 7

Students have to know that 0.75% is $\frac{0.75}{100}$, or $\frac{75}{10\,000}$. Some students may misinterpret this as 75% or $\frac{3}{4}$. Have them draw a number line from 0% to 1%, and label 0.25%, 0.5%, and 0.75%.

Mental Math

The least number is the least common multiple of 2, 3, 5, 9, and 10. 2 and 5 are factors of 10, and 3 is a factor of 9, so the least common multiple is $9 \times 10 = 90$. Students should check that each number is a factor of 90.

Assignment Guidelines

If your students do not have time to complete all the *Practice* questions on pages 72 and 73, these questions provide minimum curriculum coverage: 1, 3, 5, 6, 7, *Reflect*

To assess the 4 Achievement Chart categories listed in the curriculum document, have students complete these *Practice* questions:
Communication: 1
Knowledge and Understanding: 3
Application: 4
Thinking: 7

Example 2

According to Statistics Canada, the number of children in Canada between 10 and 14 years of age in 2001 was about 180% of the number in 1951.
In 1951, there were about 1 131 000 children in this age group.

a) In 2001, about how many children in this age group were there in Canada?
b) Estimate to check the answer.
c) Illustrate the answer to part a with a diagram.

Solution

a) Find 180% of 1 131 000.
First, write 180% as a decimal.
$180\% = \frac{180}{100}$
$= 1.80$
Then, 180% of 1 131 000 $= 1.80 \times 1\,131\,000$
$= 2\,035\,800$
In 2001, there were about 2 million children between the ages of 10 and 14 in Canada.

b) 180% is close to 200%.
1 131 000 is close to 1 000 000.
200% of 1 000 000 is: $2 \times 1\,000\,000 = 2\,000\,000$
This estimate is close to the calculated answer.

c) 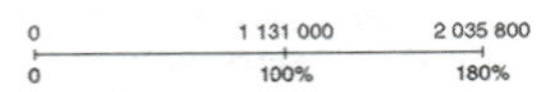

Practice

1. Write each percent as a decimal.
Draw a diagram to illustrate each percent.
a) 120% b) 250% c) 475% d) 0.3% e) 0.53% f) 0.75%
1.2 2.5 4.75 0.003 0.0053 0.007

2. a) Write each fraction as a percent.
i) $\frac{1}{3}$ ii) $\frac{2}{3}$ iii) $\frac{3}{3}$ iv) $\frac{4}{3}$ v) $\frac{5}{3}$ vi)
b) What patterns do you see in your answers in part a?
c) Use these patterns to write each fraction as a percent.
i) $\frac{7}{3}$ ii) $\frac{8}{3}$ iii) $\frac{9}{3}$

72 UNIT 2: Applications of Ratio, Rate, and Percent

Sample Solutions

1. a) $120\% = \frac{120}{100} = 1.2$ b) $250\% = \frac{250}{100} = 2.5$
c) $475\% = \frac{475}{100} = 4.75$ d) $0.3\% = \frac{0.3}{100} = 0.003$
e) $0.53\% = \frac{0.53}{100} = 0.0053$ f) $0.75\% = \frac{0.75}{100} = 0.0075$

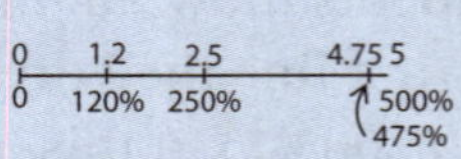

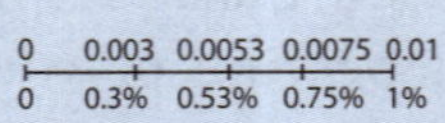

2. a) i) $\frac{1}{3} = 0.33\bar{3} = \frac{33.\bar{3}}{100} = 33.\bar{3}\%$
ii) $\frac{2}{3} = 0.66\bar{6} = \frac{66.\bar{6}}{100} = 66.\bar{6}\%$
iii) $\frac{3}{3} = 1 = 100\%$
iv) $\frac{4}{3} = 1\frac{1}{3} = 1.33\bar{3} = \frac{133.\bar{3}}{100} = 133.\bar{3}\%$
v) $\frac{5}{3} = 1\frac{2}{3} = 1.66\bar{6} = \frac{166.\bar{6}}{100} = 166.\bar{6}\%$
vi) $\frac{6}{3} = 2 = 200\%$
b) The percents start at $33.\bar{3}\%$ and increase by $33.\bar{3}\%$ each time. The numerator of each fraction is multiplied by $33.\bar{3}\%$.
c) i) $233.\bar{3}\%$ ii) $266.\bar{6}\%$ iii) 300%

3. a) i) 200% of 360 = $2 \times 360 = 720$
ii) 20% of 360 = $0.2 \times 360 = 72$
iii) 2% of 360 = $0.02 \times 360 = 7.2$
iv) 0.2% of 360 = $0.002 \times 360 = 0.72$
The decimal point in the answer moves 1 place to the left each time.

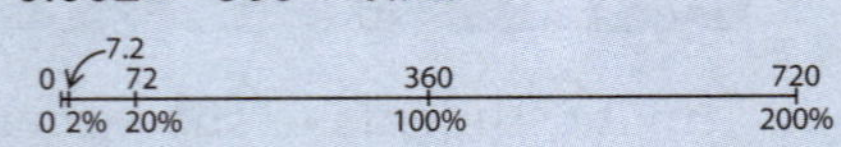

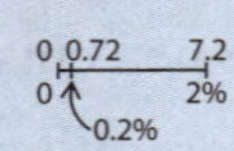

c) i) 2000% = $10 \times 200\%$; so, 2000% of 360 = $10 \times 720 = 7200$
ii) 0.02% = $\frac{1}{10} \times 0.2\%$; so, 0.02% of 360 = $\frac{1}{10} \times 0.72 = 0.072$

4. a) 0.8% of 618 = $0.008 \times 618 \doteq 5$; about 5 runners completed the race in this time.
b) 0.8% is about 1%; 1% of 600 = 6; this answer is close to the calculated answer.

5. a) 140% of 120 = $1.4 \times 120 = 168$; 168 people went to the theatre on Saturday.
b) 140% is about 150%; 150% of 120 = 100% of 120 + 50% of 120 = 120 + 60 = 180; this answer is close to the calculated answer.

6. Number of boys: 34% of 56 = $0.34 \times 56 \doteq 19$
Number of girls = 56 − 19 = 37
Percent of girls who attended = $\frac{31}{37} \times 100\% \doteq 84\%$

3. a) Find the percent of each number. Draw a diagram to illustrate.
i) 200% of 360 ii) 20% of 360 iii) 2% of 360 iv) 0.2% of 360
b) What patterns do you see in your answers in part a?
c) Use the patterns in part a to find each percent. Explain your work.
i) 2000% of 360 ii) 0.02% of 360
7200 0.072

4. Six hundred eighteen runners registered for the marathon. Of these runners, 0.8% completed the race in under 2 h 15 min.
a) How many runners completed the race in this time? About 5
b) Estimate to check your answer.

5. At the local theatre, 120 people attended the production of *Romeo and Juliet* on Friday. The attendance on Saturday was 140% of the attendance on Friday.
a) How many people went to the theatre on Saturday? 168 people
b) Estimate to check your answer.

ntal Math

at is the least whole ber that is divisible , by 3, by 5, by 9, by 10? 90

6. Fifty-six students signed up for the school play. About 34% of these students were boys. At the auditions, only 31 girls attended. What percent of the girls who signed up for the play attended the auditions? About 84%

7. **Assessment Focus** During the 1888 Gold Rush, a British Columbia town had a population of 2000. By 1910, the town had become a ghost town. The population was 0.75% of its population in 1888.
a) Estimate the population in 1910. Justify your estimate.
b) Calculate the population in 1910. 15 people
c) Find the decrease in population from 1888 to 1910. Show your work. 1985 people

Reflect

How do you find a percent of a number in each case?
- The percent is less than 1%.
- The percent is greater than 100%.

Use an example to explain each case. Include diagrams.

2.4 Calculating Percents 73

7. a) 0.75% is about 1%. The population in 1888 was 2000.
The population in 1910 was about 1% of 2000 =
$0.01 \times 2000 = 20$.
Since 0.75% is less than 1%, the population was less than 20.
b) The population in 1910 was 0.75% of 2000 =
$0.0075 \times 2000 = 15$.
The population in 1910 was 15 people.
c) The decrease in population is: $2000 - 15 = 1985$

REFLECT: I chose to find percent of 60.
To find 0.3% of 60, I write 0.3% as $\frac{0.3}{100} = \frac{3}{1000}$.
Then, 0.3% of 60 is $0.003 \times 60 = 0.18$.

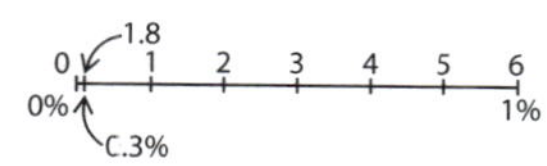

To find 130% of 60, I write 130% as $\frac{130}{100} = 1.3$.
Then, 130% of 60 = $1.3 \times 60 = 78$

ASSESSMENT FOR LEARNING

What to Look For	What to Do
Knowledge and Understanding ✔ Students understand percents less than 1% and greater than 100%. ***Communication*** ✔ Students can draw and label number lines to illustrate any percent from 0% to 200%. ***Application*** ✔ Students can convert percents less than 1% and greater than 100% to decimals. ✔ Students can calculate percents in problem-solving situations.	***Extra Support:*** Students could draw number lines on 0.5-cm grid paper. They could tape several pieces of grid paper in a row, and count squares. One square could represent 0.1%. Students can use Step-by-Step 4 (Master 2.12) to complete question 7. ***Extra Practice:*** Repeat *Practice* question 2 for $\frac{1}{6}, \frac{2}{6}, \ldots \frac{12}{6}$. Repeat *Practice* question 3 but change 360 to 180. Students can complete Extra Practice 4 (Master 2.22). ***Extension:*** Have students read newspapers or magazines to find situations involving percents. Students could write and solve a problem, then trade problems with a classmate and solve the classmate's problem.

Recording and Reporting
Master 2.2 Ongoing Observations: Applications of Ratio, Rate, and Percent

Solving Percent Problems

LESSON ORGANIZER 80–100 min

Curriculum Focus: Find the whole, when given a percent, and find percent increase and decrease. (8m17, 8m28)

Student Materials
- calculators

Optional
- Step-by-Step 5 (Master 2.13)
- Extra Practice 5 (Master 2.23)

Assessment: Master 2.2 Ongoing Observations: Applications of Ratio, Rate, and Percent

Key Math Learning

There are 3 types of percent problems:
- Given the whole and a percent, find that percent of the whole.
- Given part of the whole and its equivalent percent, find the whole.
- Given part of the whole and the whole, write the part as a percent of the whole.

Calculator Skills

The numbers can be arranged 6 ways:
$35 \times 10^7 = 350\ 000\ 000$; $53 \times 10^7 = 530\ 000\ 000$;
$57 \times 10^3 = 57\ 000$; $75 \times 10^3 = 75\ 000$;
$37 \times 10^5 = 3\ 700\ 000$; $73 \times 10^5 = 7\ 300\ 000$

2.5 Solving Percent Problems

Focus Find the whole, when given a perce and find percent increase and decr

Explore

Work with a partner.
Tasha conducted a survey of the students in her school.
- From the results, Tasha calculated that 60% of the students go to school by bus.
  Liam knows that 438 students go to school by bus.
  How can Liam use these data to find how many students are in the school?
- Tasha also found that 50% more students go by bus than walk or drive.
  About how many students walk or drive to school?

Sketch number lines to illustrate your work.

Reflect & Share

Compare your results with those of another pair of students.
Discuss the strategies you used to solve the problems.

Connect

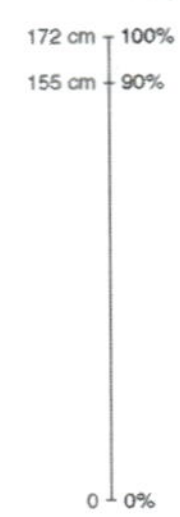

Grady is 13 years old and 155 cm tall. His height at this age is abou 90% of his height when he stops growing.

To estimate Grady's height when he stops growing:
90% of Grady's height is 155 cm.
So, 1% of his height is: $\frac{155\text{ cm}}{90}$
And, 100% of his height is: $\frac{155\text{ cm}}{90} \times 100 \doteq 172.2$ cm
So, when Grady stops growing, his height will be about 172 cm.

When we know a percent of the whole, we divide to find 1%, then multiply by 100 to find 100%, which is the whole.

Another type of problem involving percents is to find the percent increase or decrease. This is illustrated in *Example 1*.

74 UNIT 2: Applications of Ratio, Rate, and Percent

BEFORE Get Started

Have students do some mental calculations of fractions, decimals, and percents. Pose the situation that 9 out of 25 people prefer Brand A.

Ask questions, such as:
- What fraction of people prefer Brand A? ($\frac{9}{25}$)
- What percent of people prefer Brand A? (*36%*)
  How do you know?
  ($\frac{9}{25} = \frac{9 \times 4}{25 \times 4} = \frac{36}{100} = 36\%$)
- What percent of people prefer different brands? (*64%*)
  How do you know?
  (*100% is the whole, so 100% – 36% = 64%.*)
- Forty percent prefer Brand B. How many is this? (*10*) How do you know?
  (*40% is* $\frac{40}{100} = 0.4$. *So 40% of 25 is* $0.4 \times 25 = 10$.)

Present *Explore.* Encourage students to take time to read and understand the questions.

DURING Explore

Ongoing Assessment: Observe and Listen

As students work, ask questions, such as:
- What does it mean when it says 60% of the students go to school by bus?
  (*60% or 6 tenths of all the students go to school by bus.*)
- How are 60% and 438 related?
  (*438 is 60% of the student population.*)
- How can you find the total number of students in the school?
  (*60% is 438, so 10% is* $438 \div 6 = 73$, *and 100% is* $73 \times 10 = 730$.)
- How did you solve the problem?
  (*I set up a proportion. I let the total number of students be x. Then,* $\frac{x}{438} = \frac{100}{60}$; *I solved this by multiplying each side by 438, then dividing by 60. I got the answer x = 730, so there are 730 students in all.*)

Example 1

a) The price of a carton of milk in the school cafeteria increased from 95¢ to $1.25.
What was the increase as a percent?

b) At the same time, to encourage students to eat healthy food, the price of green salad decreased from $2.50 to $1.95.
What was this decrease as a percent?

Solution

a) The increase was: $\$1.25 - 95¢ = 125¢ - 95¢$
$= 30¢$

To find the percent increase, write the increase as a fraction of the original price: $\frac{30¢}{95¢}$

Use a calculator.

To write this fraction as a percent: $\frac{30}{95} \doteq 0.32$
$= \frac{32}{100}$
$= 32\%$

The price of a carton of milk increased by about 32%.

b) The decrease is: $\$2.50 - \$1.95 = 55¢$
To find the percent decrease, write the decrease as a fraction of the original price: $\frac{55¢}{\$2.50} = \frac{55}{250}$

Use a calculator.

To write this fraction as a percent: $\frac{55}{250} = 0.22$
$= \frac{22}{100}$
$= 22\%$

The price of a green salad decreased by 22%.

Example 2

In 2004, the cost to join a gym was $169.00.
In 2005, the cost was 7% more.
How much did it cost to join in 2005?

Solution

Here are two methods to find the cost in 2005.

REACHING ALL LEARNERS

Alternative Explore

Before the lesson, collect relevant data for the students in your school. Rewrite the *Explore* problem so that it relates to your school.

Early Finishers

Have students write, then solve, one each of the three types of percent problems.

Common Misconceptions

➤ Students have difficulty understanding how to find the whole, given a percent of it.

How to Help: Encourage students to use a 3-step process.

Step 1: Write the information given. For example: 4% of a number is 32.

Step 2: Divide the number by the given percent to find 1% of the number.
1% of the number is $\frac{32}{4} = 8$.

Step 3: Multiply the result by 100, to get 100% of the number.
100% of the number is $8 \times 100 = 800$

- What does "50% more students go by bus than walk or drive" mean?
(For example, if 100 students walk or drive, then 150 students go by bus. The number of students who go by bus is $1\frac{1}{2}$, or 1.5 times as many as those students who walk or drive.)
- When you know the number of students who take the bus, how can you find how many walk or drive?
(I know 438 students take the bus. This is 150% of those who walk or drive. Since 150% is 438, then 50% is $\frac{438}{3} = 146$; so, $100\% = 2 \times 50\% = 2 \times 146 = 292$. So, 292 students walk or drive to school.)
- How can you show the results on number lines?
(I draw one line for all the students. I label the line from 0, 0% to 730, 100%. I mark 50%, then 60% and 438. I draw another number line for the students who go by bus, and those who walk or drive. I label the line from 0, 0% to 150%, 438. I mark 50% and 100%. At the 100% mark, I label 292.)

AFTER Connect

Have students share answers and strategies.

Use the example in *Connect* to review how to find the whole, when a percent of it is given.

After *Example 1*, have students write these relationships in their notebooks.

$$\text{Percent increase} = \frac{\text{increase in price}}{\text{original price}} \times 100\%$$

$$\text{Percent decrease} = \frac{\text{decrease in price}}{\text{original price}} \times 100\%$$

These relationships illustrate the "shortcut" to go from a fraction to a percent: multiply the fraction by 100%. After *Example 2*, suggest that students choose the method they prefer, and consistently use it.

Practice

Encourage students to clarify their understanding of the questions by rewriting them in a format that makes sense to them.

Sample Solutions

1. a) 25% of a number is 5. So, 1% of the number is: $\frac{5}{25}$
And, 100% of the number is: $\frac{5}{25} \times 100 = 20$

b) 75% of a number is 18. So, 1% of the number is: $\frac{18}{75}$
And, 100% of the number is: $\frac{18}{75} \times 100 = 24$

c) 4% of a number is 32. So, 1% of the number is: $\frac{32}{4}$
And, 100% of the number is: $\frac{32}{4} \times 100 = 800$

d) 120% of a number is 48. So, 1% of the number is: $\frac{48}{120}$
And, 100% of the number is: $\frac{48}{120} \times 100 = 40$

3. a)

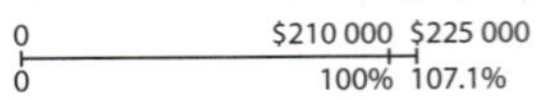

b)

5. a)

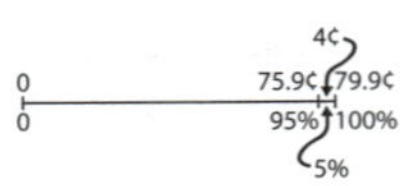

b)

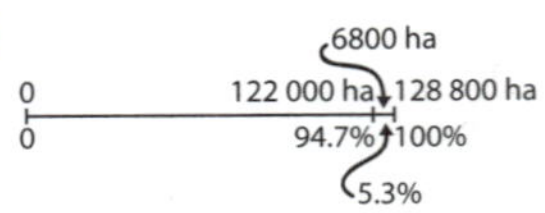

(Sample Solutions continue below, right.)

Method 1

The cost in 2004 was \$169.00.
This is 100%.
The cost in 2005 was 7% more.
7% of \$169.00
= 0.07 × \$169.00
= \$11.83
So, the cost in 2005 is:
\$169.00 + \$11.83 = \$180.83
It cost \$180.83 to join the gym in 2005.

Method 2

The cost in 2004 was \$169.00.
This is 100%.
The cost in 2005 was 7% more.
This is 100% + 7%,
or 107% of \$169.00.
107% of \$169.00
= 1.07 × \$169.00
= \$180.83

Practice

1. Find the number in each case.
Illustrate each answer with a number line.
a) 25% of a number is 5. b) 75% of a number is 18.
c) 4% of a number is 32. d) 120% of a number is 48.

2. Find the amount in each case.
a) 15% is 125 g. 833.$\overline{3}$ g b) 9% is 45 cm. 500 cm c) 0.8% is 12 g. 1500 g

3. Write each increase as a percent.
Illustrate each answer with a number line.
a) The price of a house increased from \$210 000 to \$225 000. About 7.1%
b) The elastic stretched from 10 cm to 13 cm. 30%

4. The volume of the gas in a container was 1500 cm³.
The gas was heated until its volume was 20% greater.
What was the new volume of the gas? 1800 cm³

One hectare (1 ha) is a unit of area, which is equal to 10 000 m².

5. Write each decrease as a percent.
Illustrate each answer with a number line.
a) The price of gasoline decreased from 79.9¢/L to 75.9¢/L. About 5%
b) The area of rain forest in Jamaica decreased from 128 800 ha in 1981 to 122 000 ha in 1990. About 5.3%

6. There were about 193 000 miners in Canada in 1986.
By 2001, the number of miners was 12% less.
How many miners were there in 2001? 169 840 miners

76 UNIT 2: Applications of Ratio, Rate, and Percent

Assessment Focus: Question 10

Students are solving a problem where they are given a percent of the whole, and they have to calculate the whole (their heights at age 21). The girls may know how tall they were at age 11; if not, have them estimate. The boys can probably use their current heights, even if they are already 14.

Assignment Guidelines

If your students do not have time to complete all the *Practice* questions on pages 76 and 77, these questions provide minimum curriculum coverage:
1, 2, 3, 5, 8, 9, *Reflect*

To assess the 4 Achievement Chart categories listed in the curriculum document, have students complete these *Practice* questions:
Knowledge and Understanding: 2
Communication: 3
Application: 8
Thinking: 9

(Sample Solutions continued)

9. a) Assume Anna has reached her final height by age 20.
90% of Anna's height is 150 cm.
So, 1% of her height is: $\frac{150}{90}$
100% of her height is: $\frac{150}{90} \times 100 \doteq 167$ cm

b) 98% of Raji's height is 176 cm.
So, 1% of her height is: $\frac{176}{98}$
100% of her height is: $\frac{176}{98} \times 100 \doteq 180$ cm

10. I am 14 years old and I am a girl. I am 160 cm tall now.
I don't know my height when I was 11, so I estimate that, at 14, my height is 93% of my final height.
93% is 160 cm.
So, 1% is $\frac{160}{93}$ cm and 100% = $\frac{160}{93}$ cm × 100 ≐ 172 cm
I shall be about 172 cm when I stop growing.
I assumed my height increases at a steady rate and that I am fully grown by age 21.

11. a) To find the space each person has, divide the country's area by its population.
Canada: 9 984 670 km² ÷ 32 507 874 people ≐ 0.31 km²/person
U.S.: 9 629 091 km² ÷ 293 027 571 people ≐ 0.03 km²/person
Mexico: 1 972 550 km² ÷ 104 959 594 people ≐ 0.02 km²/person

(Sample Solutions continue on next page.)

lculator Skills

... m.

$\square \times 10^{\square}$

ce the digits 3, 5, and 7 the boxes as many ferent ways as possible. ite each number you ke in standard form.

5 × 10⁷ = 350 000 000
3 × 10⁷ = 530 000 000
7 × 10³ = 57 000
5 × 10³ = 75 000
7 × 10⁵ = 3 700 000
3 × 10⁵ = 7 300 000

7. In a shipment of MP3 players, 2% are defective. There are 5 defective MP3 players. How many MP3 players are there in this shipment? 250

8. Scott delivers 14 newspapers in 10 min. This is 28% of his round.
a) How many more papers does Scott have to deliver? 36
b) Scott continues to deliver papers at the same rate. How long will it take him to deliver all his papers? About 36 min

9. On average, a girl reaches 90% of her final height by the time she is 11 years old, and 98% of her final height when she is 17 years old.
a) Anna is 11 years old. She is 150 cm tall. Estimate her height when she is 20 years old.
b) Raji is 17 years old. She is 176 cm tall. Estimate her height when she is 30 years old.

10. **Assessment Focus** On average, a boy reaches 90% of his final height by the time he is 13 years old, and 98% of his final height by the time he is 18 years old. Use these data or the data in question 9 to estimate your height when you are 21 years old. Explain any assumptions you made. Show your work.

Take It Further

11. Here are some data about countries in North America.

Country	Population in 2004	Area (km²)
Canada	32 507 874	9 984 670
U.S.	293 027 571	9 629 091
Mexico	104 959 594	1 972 550

a) How much space does each person have in each country?
b) By what percent does:
i) the population of Mexico exceed that of Canada?
ii) the area of Canada exceed that of Mexico?
c) Make up, then solve your own problem about these data.

Reflect

What is the difference between a percent increase and a percent decrease? Include examples in your explanation.

2.5 Solving Percent Problems 77

(Sample Solutions continued)

b) i) Difference in populations:
104 959 594 – 32 507 874 = 72 451 720
Percent by which population of Mexico exceeds that of Canada:
$\frac{72\ 451\ 720}{32\ 507\ 874} \times 100\% \doteq 223\%$

ii) Difference in areas:
9 984 670 – 1 972 550 = 8 012 120
Percent by which area of Canada exceeds that of Mexico: $\frac{8\ 012\ 120}{1\ 972\ 550} \times 100\% \doteq 406\%$

c) For example: What is the population density of the three countries combined?
Answer: Total population ÷ total area
= 430 495 039 ÷ 21 586 311
≐ 20 people/km²

REFLECT: Percent increase is calculated from the fraction: $\frac{\text{increase in value}}{\text{original value}}$
For example, the price of a cup of coffee increased from \$1.00 to \$1.25.
The increase is 25¢. The increase as a fraction is $\frac{25}{100}$ value.
As a percent, this is 25%.
Percent decrease is calculated from the fraction: $\frac{\text{decrease in value}}{\text{original value}}$
For example, the price of gasoline per litre decreased from 80¢ to 75¢.
The decrease is 5¢.
The decrease as a fraction is $\frac{5}{80} = 0.0625$.
As a percent, this is $\frac{6.25}{100}$, or 6.25%.

ASSESSMENT FOR LEARNING

What to Look For	What to Do
Knowledge and Understanding ✔ Students understand what percent increase and percent decrease are. ✔ Students understand how to find the whole given a percent of the whole. ***Thinking*** ✔ Students can apply their knowledge of percents to solve unfamiliar problems. ***Communication*** ✔ Students can explain how they solved percent problems. ***Application*** ✔ Students can solve the three types of percent problems.	***Extra Support:*** Encourage students to continue to sketch number lines or draw diagrams to illustrate what they are given, and what they need to find out. It may help students if they identify which of the 3 types of problems they are trying to solve. Students can use Step-by-Step 5 (Master 2.13) to complete question 10. ***Extra Practice:*** Have students draw number lines or diagrams to illustrate their answers for *Practice* questions 4, 6 to 10. Students can complete Extra Practice 5 (Master 2.23). ***Extension:*** Have students use an atlas to find data about other countries, similar to that in *Practice* question 11. Students could repeat question 11 with these new data.

Recording and Reporting
Master 2.2 Ongoing Observations: Applications of Ratio, Rate, and Percent

Sales Tax, Discount, and Commisson

LESSON ORGANIZER

80–100 min

Curriculum Focus: Investigate the uses of percent in consumer math. (8m28)

Student Materials
- calculators

Optional
- Step-by-Step 6 (Master 2.14)
- Extra Practice 6 (Master 2.24)

Vocabulary: discount, sales tax, commission, sliding scale

Assessment: Master 2.2 Ongoing Observations: Applications of Ratio, Rate, and Percent

Key Math Learning

Much consumer math (math outside the classroom) involves the calculation of percents.

Number Strategies

Students should find that 72 and 192 have the same prime factors, and that 210 and 1890 have the same prime factors.

The prime factors are:
72: 2, 3
192: 2, 3
210: 2, 3, 5, 7
1890: 2, 3, 5, 7

2.6 Sales Tax, Discount, and Commission

Focus Investigate the uses of percent in consumer math.

Explore

Work with a partner.

Estimate which racquet is the least expensive.
Then calculate the sale price of each racquet to check your estimate.

Reflect & Share

Compare your answers with those of another pair of classmates.
If you used the same method, think of a different way to find each sale price.

Connect

When an item is on sale for 20% off, we say that there is a **discount** of 20%.
A discount of 20% on an item for sale means that you pay:
100% − 20% = 80% of the regular price

A video game is marked with a discount of 30%.
Its regular price is $27.99.
The sale price of the video game is: 100% − 30%, or 70% of $27.99
70% of $27.99 = 0.7 × $27.99
= $19.59

This is the price before sales tax is added.
The provincial sales tax (PST) is 8%.
The goods and services tax (GST) is 7%.
So, the total sales tax is: 8% + 7% = 15%

78 UNIT 2: Applications of Ratio, Rate, and Percent

BEFORE Get Started

Ask:
- What is sales tax? (*Sales tax is the tax the provincial and federal governments add to the cost of an item.*) Discount? (*Discount is a reduction in the price of an item during a sale or special promotion.*) Commission? (*Commission is the percent of the price of an item that is paid to a salesperson. It is usually part of the salesperson's salary.*)
- Where do you see items on sale at a discount? (*Most stores have sales at different times of the year.*)
- What does a discount of 15% mean? (*15% of the regular price is calculated and subtracted from the original price. So, the sale price is 85% of the original price.*)

Present *Explore*. Remind students to estimate first.

DURING Explore

Ongoing Assessment: Observe and Listen

As students work, ask questions, such as:
- When you estimate the prices, what do you do to simplify the calculations? (*Change the prices to $130, $110, and $100.*)
- How will you estimate which racquet is the least expensive? (*Calculate 20% of $130, and 10% of $110, then subtract to get the sale prices.*)
- How else could you estimate? (*I subtract the percent first, then estimate. I calculate 80% of $130, and 90% of $110.*)
- Which racquet is least expensive? (*At Choice for Tennis, the sale price is about $104; at Live for Sport, the price is about $99; and at Essential Equipment, the price is about $100. Live for Sport is the least expensive.*)

So, the price you pay is: $19.59 + 15% of $19.59
We can calculate this directly as: 115% of $19.59 $= 1.15 \times \$19.59$
$= \$22.53$

Many salespeople earn commission.
A **commission** is a percent of the money received from the sale of the item.

Example

A real estate agent sells a home for $219 000.
She earns 2.5% commission.
How much does the agent earn on this sale?

Solution

The real estate agent earns 2.5% of $219 000.
This is: $0.025 \times \$219\,000 = \$5475$
The real estate agent earns $5475.

Practice

Use a calculator when you need to.

1. For each item below:

a) Estimate the PST and GST.
b) Calculate the PST and GST.
c) Calculate the cost, including taxes.

i)

ii)

REACHING ALL LEARNERS

Alternative Explore

An item is priced at $120. Calculate the sale price of the item if it is offered at:

i) 10% off ii) 12% off iii) 20% off

Explain how you calculated each sale price.
(Answer: i) $108 ii) $105.60 iii) $96)

In Store A, an item is on sale at 15% off the regular price of $100. In Store B, the same item is on sale at 10% off the regular price of $90. Which is the better deal? Explain.
(Answer: Store B, $81 instead of $85)

Early Finishers

Have students look through newspapers and flyers for items on sale. Students use the data to write, then solve, problems similar to those in *Practice*. Students share the problems and solutions with classmates.

Common Misconceptions

➤ When students calculate percents of amounts of money, they give the answer to the number of decimal places that show in the calculator, instead of rounding to the nearest cent.

How to Help: When students calculate the sale price in question 2c, part i, as 80% of $89.99, and write the answer as $71.992, ask them to say the amount in dollars and cents. They should realize that since there are 100¢ in $1, the greatest number of cents is 99¢, so the price is $71.99.

- How will you calculate the actual sale price of each racquet?
  (*Calculate 20% of $129.99 and 10% of $109.99, then subtract from each original price; or find the prices directly by calculating 80% of $129.99 and 90% of $109.99.*)
- What are the actual sale prices?
  (*At Choice for Tennis, the sale price is $103.99; at Live for Sport, the sale price is $98.99; and at Essential Equipment, the sale price is $99.99.*)
- Does this change your original estimate?
  (*No, Live for Sport is still the least expensive.*)

AFTER Connect

Invite students to share their conclusions and describe their estimates and calculations.

Ensure students understand PST and GST. Ask:

- What does GST stand for?
  (*GST is a government sales tax. It is calculated as a percent of the selling price of most items. The tax is 7% and the money goes to the federal government.*)
- What does PST stand for?
  (*PST is a provincial sales tax. It is charged by many, but not all, provincial governments. The tax can be as high as 15% in some provinces and as low as 0% in those provinces that do not apply PST. In Ontario, PST is 8%.*)

Use *Connect* to clarify the meanings of discount, sales tax, and commission.

Practice

Remind students that each of PST and GST are calculated on the selling price of the item. In Ontario, it is incorrect to add the GST and then calculate the PST on the new price.

Assignment Guidelines

If your students do not have time to complete all the *Practice* questions on pages 79, 80, and 81, these questions provide minimum curriculum coverage: 1, 2, 3, 4, 7, 8, 9, *Reflect*

To assess the 4 Achievement Chart categories listed in the curriculum document, have students complete these *Practice* questions:
Knowledge and Understanding: 2
Communication: 4
Application: 8
Thinking: 9

Sample Solutions

1\. a) i) PST: 1% of \$25.00 = \$0.25;
8% of \$25.00 = 8 × \$0.25 = \$2.00
GST: 7% of \$25.00 = 7 × \$0.25 = \$1.75
ii) PST: 1% of \$150 = \$15;
8% of \$150 = 8 × \$1.50 = \$12.00
GST: 7% of \$150 = 7 × \$1.50 = \$10.50
b) i) PST: 0.08 × \$25.99 ≐ \$2.08;
GST: 0.07 × \$25.99 ≐ \$1.82
ii) PST: 0.08 × \$152.45 ≐ \$12.20;
GST: 0.07 × \$152.45 ≐ \$10.67
c) i) \$25.99 + \$2.08 + \$1.82 = \$29.89
ii) \$152.45 + \$12.20 + \$10.67 = \$175.32
2\. i) a) 20% of \$100 = \$20; the discount is about \$20.
b) 0.20 × \$89.99 ≐ \$18.00

(Sample Solutions continue below, right.)

2. For each item below:
a) Estimate the discount.
b) Calculate the discount.
c) Calculate the sale price before taxes.
d) Calculate the sale price, including taxes.

i)
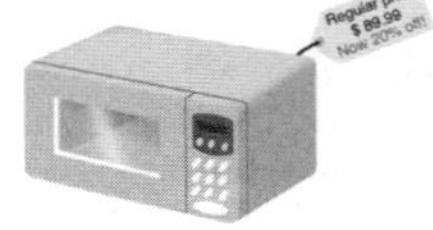

ii)

3. In a sale, a blow dryer is marked down from \$18.98 to \$11.39.
a) What is the percent decrease? About 40%
b) Calculate the sale price, including taxes. \$13.10

4. A car dealership offers two choices of discount on a car with a sticker price of \$25 000.
Choice A: \$4000 rebate
Choice B: 20% discount
Which is the better deal for the customer? Choice B
Justify your answer.

5. A video store offers these choices.
Choice A: 30% off each video with regular price \$25.00
Choice B: Buy two videos for \$40.00.
Which is the better deal for the customer? Choice A
Justify your answer.

6. A salesperson earns commission on a *sliding scale*: the more he sells, the greater his rate of commission. Jack earns 3% commission on sales up to and including \$75 000 per month, and 5% commission on sales over \$75 000.
How much commission does Jack earn on sales of \$90 000? \$3000

7. A new house was purchased for \$304 000.
After 3 years, its market value had increased by 28%.
What is the new market value of the house? \$389 120

Question 3: Remind students the percent decrease is calculated from the fraction $\frac{\text{decrease in price}}{\text{original price}}$.

Question 6: Review the meaning of *sliding scale.*

Assessment Focus: Question 9

Students need to understand that, in store A, the discount is calculated on the price from the previous week, not the original price. So, Store A does not give a discount of 25% in the third week, as the first 10% discount is calculated on 95% of the original price and the second 10% is calculated on the price for the second week. The "real" discount in week 3 is about 23% of the original price. Students may wish to start with an original price of, for example, \$100.

(Sample Solutions continued)

c) \$89.99 – \$18.00 = \$71.99
d) \$71.99 × 1.15 ≐ \$82.79
ii) a) About \$60 b) \$54.00 c) \$66.00 d) \$75.90
4\. Choice A: \$25 000 – \$4000 = \$21 000
Choice B: \$25 000 × 0.80 = \$20 000
5\. Choice A: \$25.00 × 0.70 = \$17.50; 17.50 × 2 = \$35.00; two videos cost \$35.00.
Choice B: \$40 for 2 videos
6\. 3% of \$75 000 = 0.03 × \$75 000 = \$2250
\$90 000 – \$75 000 = \$15 000;
5% of \$15 000 = 0.05 × \$15 000 = \$750
Total commission = \$2250 + \$750 = \$3000
8\. a) 0.20 × \$300 = \$60;
after 3 weeks the price is about \$300 – \$60 = \$240.
0.30 × \$240 ≐ \$70;
after 6 weeks the price is about \$240 – \$70 = \$170.
0.10 × \$170 ≐ \$20;
after 7 weeks the price is about \$170 – \$20 = \$150.
b) After 3 weeks: 0.8 × \$289.50 = \$231.60;
after 6 weeks: 0.7 × \$231.60 = \$162.12;
after 7 weeks: 0.9 × \$162.12 ≐ \$145.91
Sale price, including taxes is:
1.15 × \$145.91 ≐ \$167.80

Number Strategies

List the prime factors of each number.

72, 192, 210, 1890

72: 2, 3
192: 2, 3
210: 2, 3, 5, 7
1890: 2, 3, 5, 7

8. A clothing store reduces the price of an item by 20% if it is unsold after 3 weeks.
It reduces the price a further 30% if the item is still unsold after 6 weeks.
And, after 7 weeks if the item is unsold, a further 10% reduction is made.

a) Estimate the price, after 8 weeks, of a coat that had a regular price of $289.50.

b) Calculate the sale price, including the sales taxes. About $167.80

9. **Assessment Focus** Two stores have the same item for the same price.

- Store A offers successive discounts of 5% one week, 10% the next week, and 10% the third week.
- Store B offers one discount of 25% the third week.

Which offer results in the greater discount? Store B's offer
Justify your answer. Show your work.

10. During a 20% off sale, the sale price of a radio was $35.96. What was the regular price of the radio? $44.95

11. The price of a snowsuit is reduced by $28.38. This is a discount of 33%.

a) What is the regular price of the snowsuit? $86.00

b) What is the sale price of the snowsuit, including taxes? About $66.26

Take It Further

12. For a promotion, a store offers to pay the sales taxes on any item you buy. You are actually paying taxes but they are calculated on a lower price.
Suppose you buy an item for $100.
The sales taxes are 15%.

a) What is the true sale price of the item? About $86.96

b) How much tax are you really paying? $13.04

Reflect

Explain how percents are used in the world around you. Include examples in your explanation.

(Sample Solutions continued)

9. Assume an item costs $100.
Store A: after 1 week, the item costs 95% of $100 = 0.95 × $100 = $95; after 2 weeks, the item costs 90% of $95 = 0.90 × $95 = $85.50; and after 3 weeks, the item costs 90% of $85.50 = $76.95
Store B: after 3 weeks, the item costs 75% of $100 = 0.75 × $100 = $75
Store B offers the greater discount.

12. a) $100 is 115% of the sale price.
So, 1% of the sale price is: $\frac{\$100}{115}$
100% of the sale price is: $\frac{\$100}{115} \times 100\% \doteq \$86.96$

b) Tax paid: $100 – $86.96 = $13.04

REFLECT: I use percents when I calculate sales tax. For example, I buy a CD for $22.99. The sales tax is 15%.
So, I pay 115% of $22.99 = 1.15 × $22.99 = $26.44.
A real estate agent earns commission. When she sells a house for $225 000 and her commission is 2.5%, she earns 2.5% of $225 000 = 0.025 × $225 000 = $5625.

ASSESSMENT FOR LEARNING

What to Look For	What to Do
Knowledge and Understanding ✔ Students understand the meanings of sales tax, discount, and commission. ***Thinking*** ✔ Students can use percents to solve problems related to consumer math. ***Communication*** ✔ Students can explain their solutions to percent problems. ***Application*** ✔ Students can use percents to calculate sales tax, discount, and commission.	***Extra Support:*** Students who have difficulty with the variety of questions should work with a classmate who can break the problem into steps. Students can use Step-by-Step 6 (Master 2.14) to complete question 9. ***Extra Practice:*** Have students repeat *Practice* questions 1 and 2 but increase all regular prices by $15. (Answers: **1. b) i)** $3.28, $2.87 **ii)** $13.40, $11.72; **c) i)** $47.14 **ii)** $192.57; **2. b) i)** $21 **ii)** $60.75 **c) i)** $83.99 **ii)** $74.25; **d) i)** $96.59 **ii)** $85.39) Students can complete Extra Practice 6 (Master 2.24). ***Extension:*** Have students solve this problem: An article is on sale for 20% off. Which is the better deal for the customer? **a)** Deduct 20%, then add the tax. **b)** Add the tax, then deduct 20%. Explain.

Recording and Reporting
Master 2.2 Ongoing Observations: Applications of Ratio, Rate, and Percent

LESSON 2.7

Simple Interest

LESSON ORGANIZER 80–100 min

Curriculum Focus: Investigate simple interest. (8m28, 8m59)

Student Materials
- calculators

Optional
- Step-by-Step 7 (Master 2.15)
- Extra Practice 7 (Master 2.25)

Vocabulary: simple interest, principal, amount

Assessment: Master 2.2 Ongoing Observations: Applications of Ratio, Rate, and Percent

Key Math Learning

Simple interest is calculated on money invested or money borrowed.

2.7 Simple Interest

Focus Investigate simple interest.

When you buy a Canada Savings Bond (CSB), you are lending the Canadian government money. The government pays you for borrowing your money. It pays a percent of what you invested. In 2004, if you invested money for 1 year, the government paid you 1.55% of the amount you invested.

Explore

Work on your own.
You will need a calculator.
Suppose you bought a $500 CSB in 2004.
Estimate how much the government will pay you for 1 year.
Calculate how much the government will pay you for 1 year.
What if you bought a $1000 CSB? A $1500 CSB?
How much does the government pay in each case?

Reflect & Share

Compare your answers and solutions with those of a classmate.
What patterns do you see in your answers?

Connect

Interest is the "rent" you pay for borrowing money, or the "rent" paid to you when you save money.
You may pay interest when you buy something and pay for it later.

Mae bought a computer for college. It cost $1250.
Mae did not have to pay for 1 year.
The store charged her interest at a rate of 11.5% for that year.
The interest Mae paid at the end of the year was:
11.5% of $1250 = 0.115 × $1250
= $143.75

So, Mae paid a total of: $1250 + $143.75 = $1393.75

When the interest is calculated at the end of the period for which th
money is borrowed or invested, the interest is called **simple interest**

BEFORE Get Started

Review the introduction on page 82.

Ask students if any of them own Canada Savings Bonds, or if their parents have CSB accounts into which they pay monthly. Ask students what they think the federal government does with the money it borrows (*it funds government programs*).

Present *Explore*.

DURING Explore

Ongoing Assessment: Observe and Listen

As students work, ask questions, such as:

- Suppose you invested $100. What would the government pay you?
  (*1.55% of $100 = 0.0155 × $100 = $1.55*)
- What is a quick way to multiply by 100?
  (*Move the decimal point 2 places to the right.*)
- If the government pays you $1.55 for investing $100, about how much will it pay you for investing $500?
  (*I estimate: 5 × $1.50 = $7.50*)
- How did you estimate what the government would pay?
  (*I rounded 1.55% to 2%, then calculated 2% of $500 = 0.02 × $500 = $10.00.*)
- Is this estimate high or low? How do you know? (*Since I rounded 1.55% up to 2%, my estimate is high.*)
- How did you calculate what the government will pay?
  (*I found 1.55% of $500 = 0.0155 × $500 = $7.75.*)
- How did you calculate what the government will pay for a $1000 bond?
  (*I doubled the amount it pays for $500, because $1000 = 2 × $500. So, the government will pay $7.75 × 2 = $15.50.*)
  A $1500 bond? (*I tripled the amount it pays for $500; so, the government pays $7.75 × 3 = $23.25.*)

Example 1

Joe borrowed $7500 from his mother to buy a car.
His mother charged Joe 3.5% simple interest each year for 2 years.
Joe will pay back the money in equal monthly payments over 2 years.

a) What simple interest does Joe pay?
b) What is each monthly payment?

Solution

a) Joe pays 3.5% each year for 2 years.
Each year, Joe pays 3.5% of $7500 = 0.035 × $7500
= $262.50
So, for 2 years, the simple interest Joe pays is:
2 × $262.50 = $525.00

b) The total Joe pays is: $7500 + $525.00 = $8025
There are 12 months in 1 year, so there are 24 months in 2 years.
Joe makes 24 monthly payments.
Each monthly payment is: $8025 ÷ 24 = $334.38

In *Example 1*, we can calculate the simple interest directly.
The simple interest for 1 year is:
Money borrowed or invested × interest rate as a decimal
The simple interest for 2 years is double this:
Money borrowed or invested × interest rate as a decimal × 2

We write this formula for calculating simple interest: $I = Prt$
I is the simple interest.
P is the money borrowed, invested, or deposited;
it is called the **principal**.
r is the annual interest rate as a decimal.
t is the time in years.

Simple interest may be charged or paid for a time less than 1 year.

Example 2

Hannah borrows $1500 for 6 months.
The annual interest rate is 7%.

a) How much simple interest does Hannah pay?
b) How much does Hannah pay back?

2.7 Simple Interest 83

REACHING ALL LEARNERS

Early Finishers

Have students look through the financial sections of newspapers to find advertisements for lending rates. Have them use these rates to calculate the interest they would have to pay on a $5000 loan for 1 year.

Common Misconceptions

➤ Students do not know how to use a percent when it is given as a mixed number; for example, in *Practice* question 1f, g, h.

How to Help: Have students write the mixed number as a decimal. For example, $3\frac{1}{4}$ is 3.25. If students are not familiar with the decimal equivalents of benchmark fractions, they can use their calculators. Then, 3.25% is $\frac{3.25}{100}$ = 0.0325 as a decimal. Remind students to move the decimal point 2 places to the left to divide by 100.

AFTER Connect

Invite students to share their conclusions and describe their estimates and calculations.

Use the results of *Explore* to introduce the words *interest, principal,* and *amount*; where amount = principal + interest.

Have students calculate the amount after 1 year for a principal of $500 (*$500 + $7.75 = $507.75*), a principal of $1000 (*$1000 + $15.50 = $1015.50*), and a principal of $1500 (*$1500 + $23.25 = $1523.25*).

Review *Connect*. Students should not use the formula until they understand the process of calculating the interest on the principal for one year, then calculating the interest for several years.

For the formula, $I = Prt$, make sure students understand that the interest rate is a decimal, not a percent, and time is in years. So, for a period in months, the time is that number of months divided by 12; for example, 7 months is $\frac{7}{12}$ years.

Students should read the formula as "Interest equals principal times rate times time;" rather than just using the letters $I = Prt$.

The formula calculates the interest. The interest is added to the principal to get the amount.

Practice

Remind students to write the formula each time they use it, as this reinforces the learning.

Assessment Focus: Question 8

Students' problems could range from a one-step problem, such as, "How much interest did Marie earn in the first year?" to multi-step problems such as, "How long did it take for Marie's investment to amount to $1 360 000?"

Sample Solutions

2. a) $I = \$300 \times 0.03 \times 1 = \$9.00$
   b) $I = \$550 \times 0.04 \times 2 = \$44.00$
   c) $I = \$800 \times 0.02 \times 3 = \$48.00$
3. a) $I = \$4\ 000 \times 0.07 \times 3 = \$840.00$
   b) $I = \$10\ 000 \times 0.09 \times 2 = \$1800.00$
   c) $I = \$2960 \times 0.05 \times 5 = \$740.00$
4. a) 6 months = $\frac{1}{2}$ year, or 0.5;
   $I = \$2500 \times 0.06 \times 0.5 = \$75$
   Amount = $2500 + $75 = $2575
   b) $I = \$6000 \times 0.06 \times 3 = \$1080$;
   Amount = $6000 + $1080 = $7080
   c) 3 months = $\frac{1}{4}$ year, or 0.25;
   $I = \$700 \times 0.08 \times 0.25 = \$14$
   Amount = $700 + $14 = $714
5. a) $I = \$2000 \times 0.07 \times 4 = \$560$
   b) Amount = $2000 + $560 = $2560
   4 years = 48 months
   Each monthly payment = $2560 ÷ 48 ≐ $53.33
6. $I = \$500 \times 0.025 \times 1.5 = \$18.75$;
   Amount = $500 + $18.75 = $518.75
7. 8 months = $\frac{2}{3}$ years = $0.\bar{6}$ years
   $I = \$3350 \times 0.0625 \times 0.\bar{6} \doteq \$139.58$;
   Amount = $3350 + $139.58 = $3489.58

(Sample Solutions continue below.)

Solution

Remember that r is the interest rate as a decimal.

a) Use the formula: $I = Prt$
The principal, P, is $1500.
The annual interest rate, r, is 7%, or 0.07.
Since time, t, is measured in years,
write 6 months as a fraction of 1 year:
$\frac{6}{12} = \frac{1}{2} = 0.5$
Substitute: $P = 1500$, $r = 0.07$, and $t = 0.5$

Use a calculator.

So, $I = 1500 \times 0.07 \times 0.5$
$= 52.5$
Hannah pays $52.50 interest.

b) Hannah pays back principal and interest:
$1500 + $52.50 = $1552.50

In *Example 1b* and *2b*, the principal + interest is the **amount**.

Practice

Use a calculator when you need to.

1. Write each percent as a decimal.
   a) 5% 0.05 b) 7% 0.07 c) 3% 0.03 d) 1.25% 0.0125
   e) 3.5% 0.035 f) $3\frac{1}{4}$% 0.0325 g) $5\frac{3}{4}$% 0.0575 h) $2\frac{1}{2}$% 0.025
2. Calculate the simple interest paid on each deposit.

	Deposit ($)	Annual Interest Rate (%)	Time (years)	
a)	300	3	1	$9.00
b)	550	4	2	$44.00
c)	800	2	3	$48.00

3. Calculate the simple interest charged for each loan.

	Loan ($)	Annual Interest Rate (%)	Time (years)	
a)	4 000	7	3	$840.00
b)	10 000	9	2	$1800.00
c)	2 960	5	5	$740.00

(Sample Solutions continued)

8. For example: "How long did it take for Marie's investment to amount to $1 360 000?"
   Solution: Interest earned = $1 360 000 – $1 000 000 = $360 000
   $I = Prt$
   $\$360\ 000 = \$1\ 000\ 000 \times 0.04 \times t$
   $\$360\ 000 = \$40\ 000t$ Divide both sides by $40 000.
   $\frac{\$360\ 000}{\$40\ 000} = \frac{\$40\ 000t}{\$40\ 000}$
   $9 = t$
   It took Marie's investment 9 years to amount to $1 360 000.
9. 18 months = $1\frac{1}{2}$ years = 1.5 years
   $12\frac{1}{4}\% = 12.25\% = 0.1225$
   $I = \$2575 \times 0.1225 \times 1.5 \doteq \$473.16$;
   Amount = $2575 + 473.16 = $3048.16
10. Use guess and check.
   Guess rate of 5%; then the simple interest is
   0.05 × $600 = $30 – this is too small.
   Guess rate of 7%; then the simple interest is
   0.07 × $600 = $42 – this is too small, but close.
   Guess rate of 8%; then the simple interest is
   0.08 × $600 = $48 – this is too large, but close.
   Guess rate of 7.5%; then the simple interest is
   0.075 × $600 = $45 – this is correct.

REFLECT: Simple interest is the "fee" I pay to borrow money or the fee paid to me when I invest or lend money. If I deposit money in a bank or credit union, they pay me interest. If I deposit $500 for one year at 4% interest, I will get $500 × 0.04, or $20 interest at the end of a year. If I borrow $500 for one year at an interest rate of 8%, I will have to pay back the $500 plus interest of $500 × 0.08, or $40.

Calculator Skills

C[illegible] boxes.
Replace each box with the numbers 5, 6, 8, and 9 to make the product closest to 5000.

□□□
× □

986
× 5
4930

4. Calculate the simple interest and the amount.
   a) \$2500 invested at an annual interest rate of 6% for 6 months
   b) \$6000 invested at an annual interest rate of 6% for 3 years
   c) \$700 invested at an annual interest rate of 8% for 3 months

5. Mark borrows \$2000 at a rate of 7% per year for 4 years. Mark pays back the money in equal monthly payments over the years.
   a) What simple interest does Mark pay? \$560
   b) What is each monthly payment? About \$53.33

6. Shemaine has a \$500 savings bond. She has had the bond for 1.5 years. The bond paid 2.5% interest per year. Shemaine cashes her bond. What amount will she receive? \$518.75

7. Mumtaz borrows \$3350 from a friend. She will pay back the money after 8 months, including interest at a rate of 6.25% per year. What amount will Mumtaz pay after 8 months? \$3489.58

8. **Assessment Focus** Marie won \$1 000 000 on a lottery. She invested the money in her friend's business. Marie's friend paid Marie simple interest at a rate of 4% per year. Use this information to pose a problem. Solve your problem. Show your work.

9. Harpreet borrowed \$2575 to start a business. He will pay back the money in 18 months. He pays simple interest at a rate of $12\frac{1}{4}$% per year. What amount will Harpreet pay in 18 months? About \$3048.16

Take It Further

10. What is the interest rate when you borrow \$600 for 1 year and pay \$45.00 interest? 7.5%

Reflect

What is simple interest?
How is simple interest earned?
How is it paid?
Use examples in your explanation.

Calculator Skills

Choose 5 as the number to multiply by.

Divide 5000 by 5 to get 1000. Use the digits 6, 8, 9 to make the number closest to 1000.

986: 986 × 5 = 4930

Repeat the process using 6, then 8, and then 9 as the number to multiply by.

The product closest to 5000 is 986 × 5 = 4930

Assignment Guidelines

If your students do not have time to complete all the *Practice* questions on pages 84 and 85, these questions provide minimum curriculum coverage: 1, 3, 4, 5, 7, 8, *Reflect*

To assess the 4 Achievement Chart categories listed in the curriculum document, have students complete these *Practice* questions:
Knowledge and Understanding: 4
Application: 5
Thinking: 7
Communication: *Reflect*

ASSESSMENT FOR LEARNING

What to Look For

Knowledge and Understanding

✔ Students understand the meaning of simple interest.

Communication

✔ Students can explain the steps they use to solve problems related to simple interest.

Application

✔ Students can calculate simple interest and the amount.

What to Do

Extra Support: Students who have difficulty calculating simple interest should not use the formula. Have them continue to calculate the interest for 1 year, then multiply the answer by the number of years. These students should work with whole numbers of percents and years.
Students can use Step-by-Step 7 (Master 2.15) to complete question 8.

Extra Practice: Have students repeat *Practice* question 2 but change the interest rates to 4%, 5%, and 3%, then repeat question 3 with times of 4 years, 3 years, and 6 years.
(Answers: **2**. \$12, \$55, \$72; **3**. \$1120, \$2700, \$888)
Students can complete Extra Practice 7 (Master 2.25).

Extension: Have students make up problems similar to *Practice* question 10, where the interest rate is required, then trade problems with a classmate.

Recording and Reporting

Master 2.2 Ongoing Observations: Applications of Ratio, Rate, and Percent

Posing Math Problems

LESSON ORGANIZER

Student Materials
- calculators

Here are some sample problems (and their solutions) students may come up with. The object chosen is a calculator.

Problem 1

A calculator is sold in a cardboard box.
The box measures 16 cm by 8 cm by 3 cm.
How much cardboard is required to make each box?

Solution

Sketch and label the box.

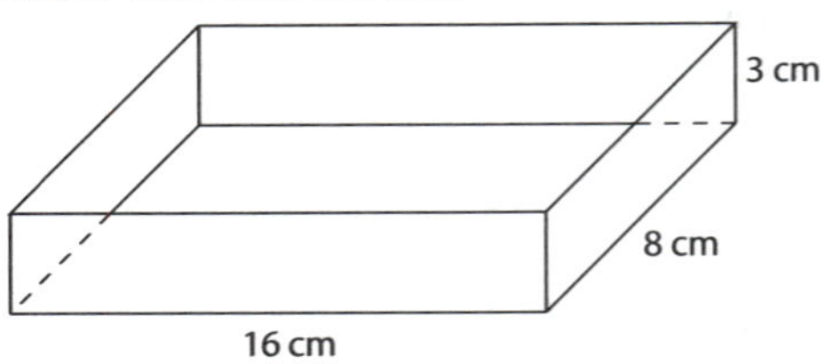

Posing Math Problems

People see the objects and events of everyday life differently.
They bring different perspectives, and ask different questions.
A person with an historical perspective might ask how the object was invented, by whom, where, and so on.
A person with a scientific perspective might ask how the object works, with what materials it is made, or how it could be improved.
Making sense of math often begins by seeing math in everyday experiences.
A mathematical perspective might ask questions about number, shape, patterns, and relationships.

Here are some questions or problems that you might pose about school desks, using the math strands as a guide:

Number

- How many desks are in the school?
- What is the ratio of desks to students in the school? Why?
- How many desks need replacing each year?
- What is the cost of replacing a student desk?

Geometry

- A desk manufacturer cuts many parts for the desk from flat sheets of material (metal or wood).
  Which figures are needed to create a desk?
- What is the best way to arrange and cut these figures from a flat sheet to save material?
- How can desks be stacked to take up the least space?
- How can desks be stacked differently if parts are disassembled and rearranged?
- How might you create a package to protect the desks during transportation?

86 UNIT 2: Applications of Ratio, Rate, and Percent

Draw a net.

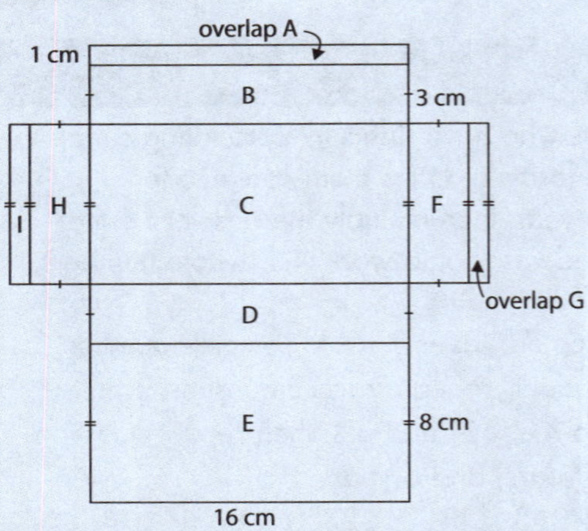

When the side faces and end faces of the boxes are joined, we need an overlap, so add 1 cm for overlap.
The area of the cardboard needed is the sum of the areas of rectangles A to I.
These rectangles are congruent: B and D, C and E, F and H, G and I
Areas of rectangles B and D: $2 \times 3 \times 16 = 96$
Areas of rectangles C and E: $2 \times 8 \times 16 = 256$
Areas of rectangles F and H: $2 \times 3 \times 8 = 48$
Areas of rectangles G and I: $2 \times 1 \times 8 = 16$
Area of rectangle A: $1 \times 16 = 16$
Total area: $96 + 256 + 48 + 16 + 16 = 432$
Each box needs 432 cm^2 of cardboard.

Problem 2

The net for each box is cut from a rectangular piece of cardboard.
What is the smallest rectangular piece that is needed?

Solution

Draw a rectangle to enclose the net.

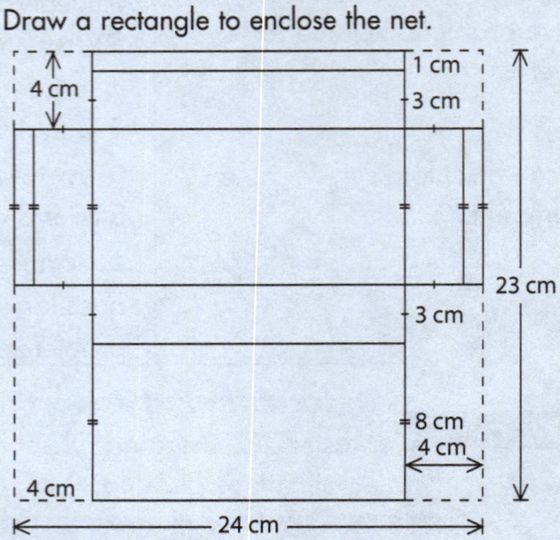

Reading and Writing in Math

Measurement

- What is the least shipping cost for delivering all the desks needed for a new school?
- How far do the desks travel from where they are made to the school?
- What is the operating cost for a transport truck?
- What is the volume of a desk?
- How much space is in a transport truck?
- How many trips would be necessary for a transport truck to deliver all the desks?

Patterning

- Based on the population growth of our school, how much money does the school need to set aside for purchasing desks in the next 10 years?
- How many desks will we need to purchase in the next 10 years?

Data Management

- A desk manufacturer needs to know how many desks to make in the next year. What would you suggest?
- What might be the typical costs for each year?
- How would you present this information in tables and graphs?

Many of these problems use information and skills from different math strands.

Choose an object or event.
Create a series of mathematical problems related to it.
Trade your problems with a classmate.
Solve your classmate's problems.

The dimensions of the cardboard are 23 cm by 24 cm.
The area of the cardboard is 23 cm × 24 cm = 552 cm².
The small piece of cardboard has area 552 cm².

Problem 3

a) How much cardboard is wasted when the net is cut?

b) Write the area of waste cardboard as a percent of the area of the rectangle from which the net is cut.

Solution

a) The cardboard that is wasted is:
$552\ \text{cm}^2 - 432\ \text{cm}^2 = 120\ \text{cm}^2$.

b) The percent wasted is $\frac{120}{552} \doteq 0.22 = \frac{22}{100}$
About 22% of the cardboard is wasted.

Problem 4

How many calculators in boxes can be packed in a carton that measures 48 cm by 40 cm by 16 cm?

Solution

Draw a diagram of a box and the carton.

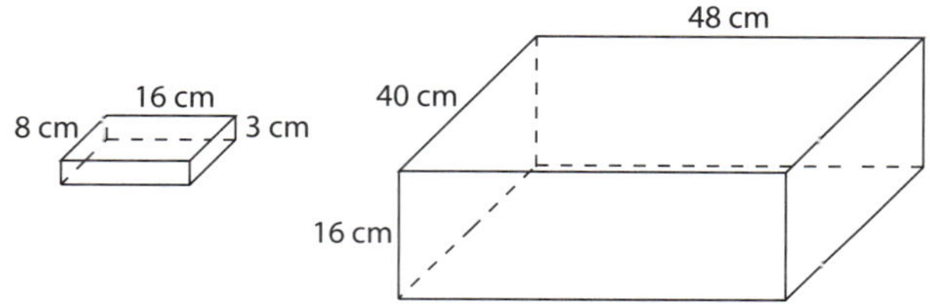

The number of boxes that fit across the length is: $\frac{48\ \text{cm}}{16\ \text{cm}} = 3$

The number of boxes that fit across the width is: $\frac{40\ \text{cm}}{8\ \text{cm}} = 5$

The number of boxes that fit in the height is: $\frac{16\ \text{cm}}{3\ \text{cm}} \doteq 5$

Total number that fit is 3 × 5 × 5 = 75.

Try to fit the boxes another way. Arrange them on end.

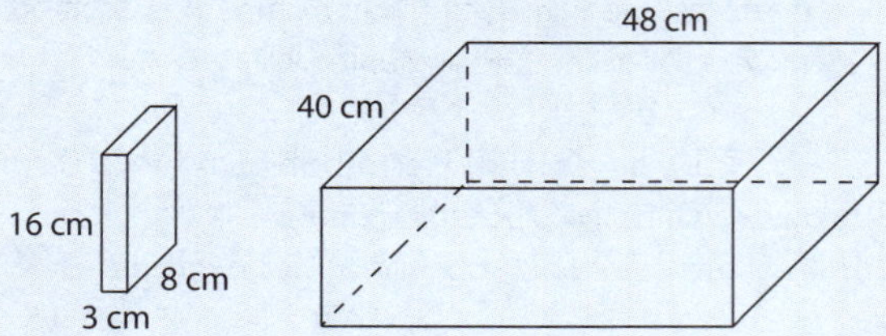

1 box fits in the height.

The number of boxes that fit across the length is: $\frac{48\ \text{cm}}{3\ \text{cm}} = 16$

The number of boxes that fit across the width is: $\frac{40\ \text{cm}}{8\ \text{cm}} = 5$

So, the total number that fit is 16 × 5 × 1 = 80.
With this arrangement, 80 boxes fit in the carton.

Problem 5

The store manager arranges a display of the calculators in a pile.
There is 1 box at the top, 3 on the next row, 5 on the next row, and so on.
There are 100 calculators in the display.
How many rows of calculators are there?

Solution

The pattern of boxes in the rows: 1, 3, 5, ...
These are the odd numbers.
We want to add the odd numbers until we reach 100.
Use a calculator.
1 + 3 + 5 + 7 + 9 + 11 + 13 + 15 + 17 + 19 = 100
So, there are 10 rows of calculators.

UNIT REVIEW

LESSON ORGANIZER

Student Materials
- calculators

Assessment: Master 2.1 Unit Rubric: Applications of Ratio, Rate, and Percent; Master 2.4 Unit Summary: Applications of Ratio, Rate, and Percent

Correlation of Extra Practice questions on page 489:

Lesson	Questions
2.1	1, 2, 3
2.2	4
2.3	5, 6
2.4	7
2.5	8, 10, 11, 12
2.6	9
2.7	13

Unit Review

Review any lesson wit[h] etext online

What Do I Need to Know?

✓ An *equivalent ratio* can be formed by multiplying or dividing the terms of a ratio by the same number.
For example:
10:16 = (10 × 2):(16 × 2) = 20:32
10:16 = (10 ÷ 2):(16 ÷ 2) = 5:8
5:8, 10:16, and 20:32 are equivalent ratios.

✓ A *proportion* is a statement that two ratios are equal.

✓ A *scale drawing* is a reduction or an enlargement of an object.
The scale may be written as a ratio.

✓ *Similar figures* have:
- corresponding angles equal
- corresponding sides in the same ratio

The ratio of the areas of similar figures is equal to the square of the ratio of corresponding sides. For example, if the ratio of sides is 1:2, the ratio of areas is 1:4.

✓ A *rate* is a comparison of two quantities with different units.
For example, 500 km in 4 h is a rate.
Divide 500 km by 4 h to get the unit rate of $\frac{500\text{ km}}{4\text{ h}}$, or 125 km/h.

✓ To calculate a *percent decrease*, divide the decrease by the original amount, then write the quotient as a percent.

✓ To calculate a *percent increase*, divide the increase by the original amount, then write the quotient as a percent.

✓ *Simple interest* is charged on money borrowed, or earned on money invested.
The formula for simple interest is: $I = Prt$, where P is the principal, r the annual interest rate as a decimal, and t the time in years.

88 UNIT 2: Applications of Ratio, Rate, and Percent

Sample Solutions

1. Let Renate's share be x dollars.
x:60 = 3:5 → $\frac{x}{60} = \frac{3}{5}$ → x = 36;
Renate received $36.00.

2. a) Canada's gold medals: Greece's gold medals = 1:2;
so, Canada's gold medals:(Canada's gold medals + Greece's gold medals) = 1:(1 + 2) = 1:3
Let x represent Canada's gold medals.
Then, x:9 = 1:3 → $\frac{x}{9} = \frac{1}{3}$ → x = 3;
Canada won 3 gold medals.
b) Greece won 9 – 3 = 6 gold medals.

3. Let the number of wins be w. Then, w:56 = 3:4 →
$\frac{w}{56} = \frac{3}{4}$ → w = 42; the team won 42 games.
So, the number of losses is 56 – 42 = 14.

4. a) Let the volume of orange juice needed be x millilitres. Then, x:1000 = 2:5 → $\frac{x}{1000} = \frac{2}{5}$ →
x = 400; 400 mL of orange juice are needed.
b) 15 people is about 7 people × 2, so about 2 times the quantities of pop and orange juice are needed. Pop: 1 L × 2 = 2 L; orange juice: 400 mL × 2 = 800 mL
20 people is about 7 people × 3, so about 3 times the quantities of pop and orange juice are needed. Pop: 1 L × 3 = 3 L; orange juice: 400 mL × 3 = 1200 mL, or 1.2 L

5. Let a represent the actual length of the bug, in millimetres.
a:25 = 1:15 → $\frac{a}{25} = \frac{1}{15}$ → $25 \times \frac{a}{25} = 25 \times \frac{1}{15}$ →
$a = \frac{5}{3}$ → $a \doteq 1.7$;
the actual length of the bug is about 1.7 mm.

6. 2.5 km is represented by 1 cm. So, 1 km is represented by $\frac{1}{2.5}$ cm. And, 45 km is represented by
$45 \times \frac{1}{2.5}$ cm = 18 cm.

7. $1155 ÷ $5.50/h = 210 h; Pierre baby-sat for 210 h.

8. a) 2.5 km ÷ 20 min = 0.125 km/min
b) 1 h = 60 min; 0.125 × 60 = 7.5; her average speed is 7.5 km/h.

9. Kieran: 8 laps ÷ 18 min = $0.\overline{4}$ laps/min
Jevon: 6 laps ÷ 10 min = 0.6 laps/min
Jevon has the greater average speed.

10. a) 40% of 73 kg = 0.4 × 73 kg = 29.2 kg; the mass of Ali's muscle is 29.2 kg.
b) For example, I have a mass of 50 kg. 40% of 50 kg = 0.4 × 50 kg = 20 kg;
the mass of my muscle is 20 kg.
c)

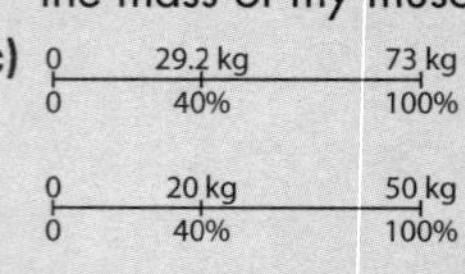

11. a) 0.85% is about 1%; 1% of 2000 is 20;
about 20 jars were broken.

What Should I Be Able to Do?

For extra practice, go to page 489.

1. Silva and Renate were given money in the ratio of 5 to 3. Silva's share was $60. How much did Renate receive? $36
2. At the 2004 Athens Olympics, the ratio of Canada's gold medals to Greece's gold medals was 1:2. Together, Canada and Greece won 9 gold medals.
   a) How many gold medals did Canada win? 3
   b) How many gold medals did Greece win? 6
3. The St. Croix junior hockey team won 3 out of every 4 games it played. The team played 56 games. How many games did it lose? 14
4. A punch recipe calls for orange juice and pop in the ratio of 2:5. The recipe requires 1 L of pop to serve 7 people.
   a) How much orange juice is needed for 7 people? 400 mL
   b) About how much orange juice and pop do you need to serve 15 people? 20 people? Justify your answers.

2.2 5. A picture of a bug has a scale of 15:1. The length of the bug in the picture is 2.5 cm. What is the actual length of the bug? About 1.7 mm

6. A scale on a map is 1 cm represents 2.5 km. Vivian drove 45 km. What is this distance on the map? 18 cm

2.3 7. Pierre baby-sits for $5.50/h. He earned $1155 during the summer. How many hours did Pierre baby-sit? 210 h

8. A speed walker walks 2.5 km in 20 min.
   a) What is her average speed in kilometres per minute? 0.125 km/min
   b) What is her average speed in kilometres per hour? 7.5 km/h
9. Kieran ran 8 laps of the track in 18 min. Jevon ran 6 laps of the track in 10 min. Who had the greater average speed? How do you know? Jevon

2.4 10. Forty percent of an average person's body is muscle.
   a) Ali has a mass of 73 kg. What is the mass of his muscle? 29.2 kg
   b) What mass of your body is muscle? How do you know?
   c) Draw a diagram to illustrate your answers.

11. In a shipment of 2000 tomato sauce jars, 0.85% were broken.
   a) Estimate how many jars were broken. About 20 jars

Unit Review 89

b) 0.85% of 2000 = 0.0085 × 2000 = 17
17 jars were broken.

c) 

12. 20% is 5 cards. So, 100% is 5 × 5 cards = 25 cards.

13. The new depth of water is 100% + 15% = 115% of the original depth.
115% of 15 m = 1.15 × 15 m = 17.25 m; the new depth of water is 17.25 m.

14. 60% of the total possible mark is 39. So, 1% of the total is: $\frac{39}{60}$
And, 100% of the total is: $\frac{39}{60} \times 100 = 65$; the total possible mark was 65.

15. The mass of cod caught was 100% − 87% = 13% of the original mass.
13% of 310 000 t = 0.13 × 310 000 t = 40 300 t; 40 300 t of cod were caught in 2001.

16. 64% of the distance is 72 cm. So, 1% of the distance is: $\frac{72\text{ cm}}{64}$
And, 100% of the distance is: $\frac{72\text{ cm}}{64} \times 100 = 112.5$ cm; the ball was dropped from a height of 112.5 cm.

17. a) The length and width will be 100% − 2% = 98% of the original dimensions.
Length: 0.98 × 210 cm = 205.8 cm;
Width: 0.98 × 240 cm = 235.2 cm
b) Original area: 210 cm × 240 cm = 50 400 cm^2
Area after washing:
205.8 cm × 235.2 cm = 48 404.16 cm^2
Percent decrease in area:
$\frac{50\,400 - 48\,404.16}{50\,400} \times 100\% = 3.96\%$

18. a) Regular price: $49.99 + $20.00 = $69.99
b) Percent discount: $\frac{20.00}{69.99} \times 100\% \doteq 28.6\%$

19. Sale price: 75% of $89.99 = 0.75 × $89.99 ≐ $67.49
Total price, including taxes:
115% of $67.49 = 1.15 × $67.49 = $77.61

20. a) Commission: 5% of $350 000 = 0.05 × $350 000 = $17 500
b) $350 000 − $17 500 = $332 500; the family received $332 500.
c) $2\frac{3}{4}$% of $350 000 = 2.75% of $350 000
= 0.0275 × $350 000 = $9625
The family would have saved $17 500 − $9625 = $7875.

21. $I = Prt$
= $7500 × 0.02 × 0.25 3 months = $\frac{1}{4}$ of a year, or 0.25
= $37.50

22. $7\frac{3}{4}$% = 7.75% = 0.0775
a) I = $1500 × 0.0775 × 1.5 ≐ $174.38
b) Total amount = $1500.00 + $174.38 = $1674.38
c) $1\frac{1}{2}$ years = 18 months
Each monthly payment: $1674.38 ÷ 18 ≐ $93.02

LESSON

b) Calculate how many jars were broken. 17 jars

c) Draw a diagram to illustrate your answer in part b.

2.5 **12.** Joline collects hockey cards. She needs 5 cards to complete a set. This is 20% of the set. How many cards are in the set? Justify your answer. 25 cards

13. The water in the dam was 15 m deep. After a storm, the depth of the water was 15% greater. What was the new depth of water? 17.25 m

14. Jehane had a mark of 39 on a test. This mark was 60%. What was the total possible mark? 65

15. About 310 000 t of Atlantic cod were caught in 1991. In 2001, the mass of cod caught was 87% less. How much cod was caught in 2001? 40 300 t

16. A ball bounced 64% of the distance through which it had fallen. The bounce was 72 cm high. From what height was the ball dropped? 112.5 cm

2.4 2.5 **17.** A new queen size bed sheet measures 210 cm by 240 cm. The length and width each shrinks by 2% after the first washing.

a) What are the dimensions of the sheet after washing? 205.8 cm by 235.2 cm

b) What is the percent decrease in the area of the sheet? 3.96%

2.6 **18.** A portable CD player is on sale. It is advertised as, "Save $20. You pay $49.99."

a) What is the regular price? $69.99

b) What is the percent discount? About 28.6%

19. A gym suit sells for $89.99 at Aerobics for All. For August, there is a 25% discount as a *Back to School* special. Calculate the total price, including taxes. $77.61

20. A family sold a home for $350 000 and paid 5% commission.

a) How much was the commission? $17 500

b) How much did the family receive for the house? $332 500

c) What if the family had sold its house through a realtor who charged only $2\frac{3}{4}$% commission. How much would the family have saved? $7875

2.7 **21.** Find the simple interest paid on an investment of $7500 at 2% per year for 3 months. $37.50

22. Jamie borrowed $1500 from her mother. She promised to repay the money in $1\frac{1}{2}$ years, with simple interest at $7\frac{3}{4}$% per year.

a) What simple interest does Jamie pay? About $174.38

b) What amount must Jamie pay in $1\frac{1}{2}$ years? $1674.38

c) What if Jamie repaid the money in monthly instalments. What would each monthly payment be? About $93.02

90 UNIT 2: Applications of Ratio, Rate, and Percent

ASSESSMENT FOR LEARNING

What to Look For

Knowledge and Understanding

✔ **Questions 12 and 14:** Student understands how to calculate the whole when given a percent.
✔ **Question 18:** Student understands how to calculate the regular price and percent discount.
✔ **Questions 21 and 22:** Student understands how to calculate simple interest.

Thinking

✔ **Questions 2 and 4:** Student can set up a proportion, then solve the proportion to solve the problem.
✔ **Questions 5 and 6:** Student can solve problems involving scale drawings.
✔ **Questions 16, 17, and 20:** Student can solve problems involving percent.

Communication

✔ **Questions 10 and 11:** Student can draw a diagram to illustrate an answer.

Application

✔ **Questions 8 and 9:** Student can calculate and compare unit rates.
✔ **Question 11:** Student can calculate a percent less than 1%.
✔ **Question 19:** Student can calculate sales tax.

Recording and Reporting

Master 2.1 Unit Rubric: Applications of Ratio, Rate, and Percent
Master 2.4 Unit Summary: Applications of Ratio, Rate, and Percent

Practice Test

1. Fuel for an outboard motor has a gas to oil ratio of 50:1. How much oil is needed for 25.5 L of gas? 0.51 L

2. Spyri travels from Edmonton to Grande Prairie. On the map, this distance is 9.1 cm. The scale on the map is 1:5 000 000.
   a) What is the actual distance between these two cities? 455 km
   b) Spyri's car uses 1 L of gas to travel 7.5 km. At this rate, how much gas will she need for this trip? $60.\overline{6}$ L
   c) Spyri estimates that her average speed will be 70 km/h. How long will it take her to complete the trip? 6.5 h
   d) What if Spyri's average speed was 10 km/h greater. How much time would she save? 49 min

3. Ben received 1 mark for every correct answer on a multiple-choice test.
   He answered 75 questions correctly out of a total of 135 questions.
   On the test, 55% is a pass. Did Ben pass the test? Yes
   Give reasons for your answer.

4. The Grade 8 class at Wheatly Middle School sold 77 boxes of almond chocolates.
   This is 22% of all the boxes of chocolates sold.
   a) Estimate the total number of boxes sold. About 400
   b) Calculate how many boxes were sold. 350

5. Joginder borrowed $3500 at an annual rate of simple interest of 12%.
   Calculate the amount Joginder repays after 2 years. $4340

6. The price of a house increased by 20% from 2002 to 2003.
   The price of the house decreased by 20% from 2003 to 2004.
   Will the price of the house at the beginning of 2002 be equal to its price at the end of 2004? No
   If your answer is yes, show how you know.
   If your answer is no, when is the house less expensive?
   At the end of 2004

Practice Test 91

LESSON ORGANIZER

Student Materials

- calculators

Assessment: Master 2.1 Unit Rubric: Applications of Ratio, Rate, and Percent
Master 2.4 Unit Summary: Applications of Ratio, Rate, and Percent

Assignment Guidelines

To assess the 4 Achievement Chart categories listed in the curriculum document, use these test questions:
Application: 2
Communication: 3
Knowledge and Understanding: 5
Thinking: 6

Sample Solutions

1. Let the volume of oil be x litres. Then, x:25.5 = 1:50
   In fraction form: $\frac{x}{25.5} = \frac{1}{50}$
   $\frac{x}{25.5} \times 25.5 = \frac{1}{50} \times 25.5 \rightarrow x = 0.51$;
   0.51 L of oil is needed.

2. a) Let d represent the actual distance, in centimetres.
   d:9.1 = 5 000 000:1
   In fraction form: $\frac{d}{9.1} = \frac{5\,000\,000}{1}$
   $\frac{d}{9.1} = \frac{5\,000\,000}{1} \rightarrow \frac{d}{9.1} \times 9.1 = \frac{5\,000\,000}{1} \times 9.1 \rightarrow$
   $d = 45\,500\,000$;
   the distance is 45 500 000 cm
   = (45 500 000 ÷ 100 000) km = 455 km
   b) 1 L of gas is needed for 7.5 km. So, for a trip of 455 km, $\frac{455}{7.5}$ L are needed.
   $\frac{455}{7.5}$ L ≐ $60.\overline{6}$ L
   c) Time = $\frac{\text{distance}}{\text{speed}} = \frac{455\text{ km}}{70\text{ km/h}}$ = 6.5 h, or 6 h 30 min
   d) Time = $\frac{\text{distance}}{\text{speed}} = \frac{455\text{ km}}{80\text{ km/h}}$ = 5.6875 h
   To write 0.6875 h in minutes, multiply by 60.
   0.6875 × 60 min = 41.25 min
   The time is about 5 h 41 min.
   Time saved = 6 h 30 min – 5 h 41 min
   = 390 min – 341 min = 49 min

3. Write $\frac{75}{135}$ as a decimal: $0.5\overline{5}$
   This is $\frac{55.\overline{5}}{100} = 55.\overline{5}\%$; Ben just passed the test.

4. a) Round 22% to 20%, and round 77 boxes to 80 boxes.
   20% is 80 boxes; so, 100% is 5 × 80 boxes = 400 boxes; about 400 boxes were sold.
   b) 22% is 77 boxes. So, 1% is: $\frac{77\text{ boxes}}{22}$
   And, 100% is: $\frac{77\text{ boxes}}{22} \times 100$ = 350 boxes;
   350 boxes were sold.

5. $I = Prt$ = $3500 × 0.12 × 2 = $840
   Amount = $3500 + $840 = $4340

6. Assume a price of $100 000.
   2003 price: (100% + 20%) of $100 000
   = 120% of $100 000
   = 1.2 × $100 000
   = $120 000
   2004 price: (100% – 20%) of $120 000
   = 80% of $120 000
   = 0.8 × $120 000
   = $96 000
   The price of the house at the end of 2004, $96 000, is less than the price at the beginning of 2002, $100 000.

Where to Live?

LESSON ORGANIZER 80–100 min

Student Grouping: 2–4
Student Materials
- calculators

Assessment: Master 2.3 Performance Assessment Rubric: Where to Live?; Master 2.4 Unit Summary: Applications of Ratio, Rate, and Percent

Unit Problem Where to Live?

Alison is 18 years old.
She plans to go to college for 4 years to study computer an[illegible]n.
Alison has two choices:
- Live at home and buy a car to travel 30 km each way to college every day.
- Live in residence and pay $15 000 room and board each year.

Here are the list prices of new and used cars.

Vehicles	New ($)	Used ($)	Gas Consumption in Cit[illegible] (L/100 km)
Hyundai Accent	12 895	10 495	8.0
Kia Spectra	14 995	9 995	10.0
Chevrolet Aveo	13 480	11 195	8.8

92 UNIT 2: Applications of Ratio, Rate, and Percent

Sample Response

If Alison buys a new Hyundai Accent, she will pay, including taxes: $12 895 × 1.15 = $14 829.25

Assume Alison borrows $15 000 for 4 years at an annual interest rate of 4.5%.

I = $15 000 × 4 × 0.045 = $2700

The amount is $15 000 + $2700 = $17 700

If Alison repays the money in equal monthly payments over 4 years, she will pay: $17 700 ÷ 48 = $368.75 per month

Because Alison is 18, insurance will be high: I found an estimate of $2000 on the Internet. This assumed Alison's parents added her to their existing automobile insurance policy.

Regular maintenance costs: An oil change should be done every 3 months. Assume an oil change costs about $35.00, plus taxes:

Students will require time to research and collect all the necessary information to solve the problem. Students could brainstorm to list the information they need (*purchase costs — pay cash, finance the purchase, borrow from bank, or lease; insurance costs — different types, deductibles, age factors; depreciation costs; maintenance costs — new car versus used car; vehicle plate fee; number of travel days to college; costs related to living on campus — trips home, other travel costs*).

Encourage groups to share their information to produce a class list of information required.

Groups should also list sources of information used, such as family, friends, car dealerships, insurance companies, car repair shops, Internet sites, and so on.

REFLECT ON THE UNIT

A ratio is a comparison of two quantities measured in the same unit. A ratio can be a part-to-part ratio, or a part-to-whole ratio. For example, the ratio of boys to girls is 14:21 or 2:3. The ratio of boys to boys and girls is 14:35 or 2:5.

A rate is a comparison of two quantities with different units. For example, 30 km in 5 h is a rate of $\frac{30 \text{ km}}{5 \text{ h}}$ or 6 km/h. This is called average speed.

A percent is the numerator of a fraction with denominator 100.

For example, $38\% = \frac{38}{100} = 0.38$

Ratios, rates, and percents can be written as fractions, but a part-to-part ratio is not a fraction.

Percent outside the classroom:

A weather forecast of an 80% chance of rain tomorrow means it is very likely it will rain tomorrow.

A sale price of 25% off means the price will be reduced by 25%, or one-quarter of the original price, and I pay 75% of the original price.

10% of the students are ill means that 1 of every 10 students is ill. So, if there are 30 students in the class, then 3 are ill.

If Alison buys a car, she will have to pay GST and PST.
She will also have to pay for regular maintenance, insurance, and a vehicle plate fee.
A new car should not need as many repairs as a used car.
Interview a family member or friend.
Find the approximate costs of car repairs, maintenance, and fuel.
Should Alison buy a car or live in residence?
Justify your answer.

Check List

Your work should show:

✓ the methods you used to calculate and compare costs of buying a new or used car, and living in residence

✓ correct calculations of unit rates, and all costs, including taxes

✓ your conclusions and justification for your decision

✓ clear explanations, with correct use of mathematical language

Reflect on the Unit

How are ratio, rate, and percent related?
How can you use your knowledge of percents outside the classroom?
Include examples in your explanation.

Unit Problem: Where to Live? **93**

$35.00 × 1.15 = $40.25
4 oil changes per year would cost $40.25 × 4 = $161.

With a new car, other maintenance fees will be minimal.

Vehicle plate fee: Assuming Alison lives in Southern Ontario, the fee is $74 for one year.

Fuel: Assume Alison goes to college 5 days a week for 9 months.
9 months × 4 weeks/month = 36 weeks
36 weeks × 5 days/week = 180 days
Alison drives 30 km × 2 = 60 km per day
60 km/day × 180 days = 10 800 km
The Hyundai Accents uses 8.0 L of fuel for every 100 km.
So, Alison will use 10 800 km ÷ 100 km × 8.0 L = 864 L of fuel.
Assume 1 L of gas costs 80¢. 864 L × $0.80/L = $691.20
Alison will pay about $691.20 for gas to go back and forth to college.

Total cost to own the car for 1 year: ($368.75 × 12) + $2000 + $161 + $74 + $691.20 = $7351.20

If Alison lives in residence, she will pay $15 000 per year, about double the cost of owning a car. Alison should buy a car.

I would not recommend Alison buy a used car as the maintenance fees would be greater, and it may not be reliable.

ASSESSMENT FOR LEARNING

What to Look For	What to Do
Thinking ✔ Students can apply their knowledge of ratio, rate, and percent to solve an unfamiliar problem. ***Communication*** ✔ Students can use correct mathematical terminology to describe the processes they used. ✔ Students present their work clearly. ***Application*** ✔ Students can correctly use ratio, rate, and percent to solve problems related to owning a car.	***Extra Support:*** Make the problem accessible. Provide a list of the minimum information to be collected for the problem. Provide resources from which students can obtain the necessary information. Provide a list of the costs to be calculated.

Recording and Reporting

Master 2.3 Performance Assessment Rubric: Where to Live?
Master 2.4 Unit Summary: Applications of Ratio, Rate, and Percent

Evaluating Student Learning: Preparing to Report: Unit 2 Applications of Ratio, Rate, and Percent

This unit provides an opportunity to report on the **Number Sense and Numeration** strand. *Master 2.4 Unit Summary: Applications of Ratio, Rate, and Percent* provides a comprehensive format for recording and summarizing evidence collected.

Here is an example of a completed summary chart for this Unit:

Strand: *Number Sense and Numeration*	**Knowledge and Understanding**	**Thinking**	**Communication**	**Application**	***Overall***
Ongoing Observations	4	4	3	4	4
Work samples or portfolios; conferences	4	3	4	4	4
Unit Review	4	4	4	4	4
Unit Test	4	4	3	4	4
Unit Problem Where to Live?	4	3	4	4	4
Achievement Level for reporting					4

Recording	How to Report
Ongoing Observations	Use *Master 2.2 Ongoing Observations: Applications of Ratio, Rate, and Percent* to determine the most consistent level achieved in each category. Enter it in the chart. Choose to summarize by achievement category, or simply to enter an overall level. Observations from late in the unit should be most heavily weighted.
Portfolios or collections of work samples; conferences or interviews	Use *Master 2.1 Unit Rubric: Applications of Ratio, Rate, and Percent* to guide evaluation of collections of work and information gathered in conferences. Teachers may choose to focus particular attention on the Assessment Focus questions. Work from late in the unit should be most heavily weighted.
Unit Review	*Master 2.1 Unit Rubric: Applications of Ratio, Rate, and Percent* may be helpful in determining levels of achievement. #1, 3, 6, 9, 11, 12, 18, and 21 provide evidence of Knowledge and Understanding; #2, 5, 7, 8, 10, 13, 14, 15, 16, 19, and 22 provide evidence of Application; #4, 17, and 20 provide evidence of Thinking; all questions provide evidence of Communication.
Unit Test	*Master 2.1 Unit Rubric: Applications of Ratio, Rate, and Percent* may be helpful in determining levels of achievement. #1 and 2 provide evidence of Knowledge and Understanding; #4 provides evidence of Application; #3 and 5 provide evidence of Thinking; all questions provide evidence of Communication.
Unit Problem	Use *Master 2.3 Performance Assessment Rubric: Where to Live?* The *Unit Problem* offers a snapshot of students' achievement. In particular, it shows their ability to synthesize and apply what they have learned.
Student Self-Assessment	Note students' perceptions of their own progress. This may take the form of an oral or written comment, or a self-rating.
Comments	Analyse the pattern of achievement to identify strengths and needs. In some cases, specific actions may need to be planned to support the learner.

Learning Skills	Ongoing Records
PM 4: Learning Skills Check List Use to record and report throughout a reporting period, rather than for each unit and/or strand.	*PM 10: Summary Class Record: Strands* *PM 11: Summary Class Record: Achievement Categories* *PM 12: Summary Record: Individual* Use to record and report evaluations of student achievement over several clusters, a reporting period, or a school year. These can also be used in place of the Unit Summary.

Name ____________________ Date ____________________

Master 2.1

Unit Rubric: Applications of Ratio, Rate, and Percent

	Level 1	Level 2	Level 3	Level 4
Knowledge and Understanding • Shows understanding by demonstrating or explaining: – direct proportionality – relationships among measures of similar figures – unit rates – conversions among fractions, decimals, and percents	shows limited understanding; may be unable to demonstrate or explain: – direct proportionality – relationships among measures of similar figures – unit rates – conversions among fractions, decimals, and percents	shows some understanding; partially able to demonstrate or explain: – direct proportionality – relationships among measures of similar figures – unit rates – conversions among fractions, decimals, and percents	shows considerable understanding; able to clearly and appropriately demonstrate or explain: – direct proportionality – relationships among measures of similar figures – unit rates – conversions among fractions, decimals, and percents	shows a high degree of understanding; able to accurately and effectively demonstrate or explain: – direct proportionality – relationships among measures of similar figures – unit rates – conversions among fractions, decimals, and percents
Thinking • Chooses and carries out a range of strategies to pose, solve, and check multi-step problems involving ratios, rates, and percents; justifies the strategies used to produce an accurate solution	with assistance, chooses, carries out, and justifies a limited range of appropriate strategies to pose, solve, and check multi-step problems; rarely produces an accurate solution	with limited assistance, chooses, carries out, and justifies some appropriate strategies to pose, solve, and check problems; frequently produces an accurate solution	chooses, carries out, and justifies many appropriate strategies to pose, solve, and check problems; usually produces an accurate solution	develops, carries out, and justifies effective, and often innovative, strategies to pose, solve, and check problems; always produces an accurate solution
Communication • Explains concepts, procedures, and reasoning clearly, using appropriate terms (for example, unit rate, direct proportionality, discount)	unable to explain concepts, procedures, and reasoning clearly	partially explains concepts, procedures, and reasoning	explains concepts, procedures, and reasoning clearly	explains concepts, procedures, and reasoning clearly, precisely, and confidently
• Presents work clearly	presents work with little clarity	presents work with some clarity and precision	presents work with considerable clarity and precision	presents work with a high degree of clarity and precision
Application • Accurately: – solves proportions – uses scales to calculate distance – calculates and compares rates – calculates percents – calculates discounts, sales tax, commission, and simple interest	limited accuracy; major errors or omissions in: – solving proportions – using scales to calculate distance – calculating and comparing rates – calculating percents – calculating discounts, sales tax, commission, and simple interest	somewhat accurate; several minor errors or omissions in: – solving proportions – using scales to calculate distance – calculating and comparing rates – calculating percents – calculating discounts, sales tax, commission, and simple interest	generally accurate; few minor errors or omissions in: – solving proportions – using scales to calculate distance – calculating and comparing rates – calculating percents – calculating discounts, sales tax, commission, and simple interest	accurate and precise; no errors in: – solving proportions – using scales to calculate distance – calculating and comparing rates – calculating percents – calculating discounts, sales tax, commission, and simple interest

Name ____________________ Date ________________

Master 2.2

Ongoing Observations: Applications of Ratio, Rate, and Percent

The behaviours described under each heading are examples; they are not intended to be an exhaustive list of all that might be observed. More detailed descriptions are provided in each lesson under *Assessment for Learning.*

STUDENT ACHIEVEMENT: Applications of Ratio, Rate, and Percent				
Student	**Knowledge and Understanding** • Demonstrates and explains: – direct proportionality – relationships among measures of similar figures – unit rates – conversions (fraction, decimal, and percent)	**Thinking** • Chooses and carries out a range of strategies to pose, solve, and check problems involving ratios, rates, and percents	**Communication** • Explains concepts, procedures, and reasoning clearly • Presents work clearly	**Application** • Accurately: – solves proportions – calculates ratios, rates, and percents – calculates simple interest, percent increase, and percent decrease

Level 1 – very limited; Level 2 – somewhat or limited; Level 3 – satisfactory; Level 4 – thorough

Name ____________________ Date ________________

Master 2.3

Performance Assessment Rubric: Where to Live?

	Level 1	Level 2	Level 3	Level 4
Knowledge and Understanding • Offers conclusions and justifications that show understanding of concepts of rate and percent	shows limited understanding; may be unable to justify decision	shows some understanding; gives appropriate but incomplete justification for decision	shows considerable understanding by giving appropriate and complete justification for decision	shows a high degree of understanding by giving appropriate and thorough justification for decision
Thinking • Successfully uses appropriate strategies to compare the costs of living at home (buying new or used car) and living in residence; verifies solution	uses a limited range of appropriate strategies to solve the problem (compare costs); little success	uses some appropriate strategies to solve the problem (compare costs); partially successful	uses many appropriate strategies to solve the problem (compare costs); generally successful	uses innovative and effective strategies to solve the problem (compare costs); high degree of success
Communication • Explains reasoning clearly using appropriate mathematical terminology (for example, unit rate)	explains reasoning unclearly and imprecisely using few mathematical terms	explains reasoning with some clarity using some appropriate mathematical terms	explains reasoning clearly and precisely using appropriate mathematical terms	explains reasoning clearly, precisely, and confidently using a range of appropriate mathematical terminology
• Presents work clearly	presents work with little clarity	presents work with some clarity	presents work clearly	presents work clearly and precisely
Application • Accurately calculates unit rates, and all costs, including taxes	limited accuracy; major errors or omissions in calculating unit rates, and costs, including taxes	somewhat accurate; several minor errors or omissions in calculating unit rates, and costs, including taxes	generally accurate; few minor errors or omissions in calculating unit rates, and costs, including taxes	accurate and precise; with no errors or omissions in calculating unit rates, and costs, including taxes

Name ____________________ Date ______________

Master 2.4

Unit Summary: Applications of Ratio, Rate, and Percent

Review assessment records to determine the most consistent achievement levels for the assessments conducted. Some cells may be blank. *Overall* achievement levels may be recorded in each row, rather than identifying levels for each achievement category.

	Most Consistent Level of Achievement*				
Strand: *Number Sense and Numeration*	**Knowledge and Understanding**	**Thinking**	**Communication**	**Application**	***Overall***
Ongoing Observations					
Work samples or portfolios; conferences					
Unit Review					
Unit Test					
Unit Problem Where to Live?					
Achievement Level for reporting					

*Use Ontario Achievement Levels 1, 2, 3, 4

Self-Assessment:

Comments: (Strengths, Needs, Next Steps)

Name ____________________ Date ______________

Master 2.5a

Additional Activity 1: Reductions

Play with a partner.

You will need a set of game cards.

How to Play:

1. Shuffle the cards. Place the cards face down in a pile.

2. Player A turns over 2 cards.
   She states the ratio of the number on the first card to the number on the second card.
   She then says the ratio in simplest form.
   One point is awarded for a correct statement.
   If the ratio is already in simplest form, the student gets a point for explaining why it is.
   Place the cards in a discard pile.

3. Player B has a turn.

4. Continue to take turns.
   The player with the higher score after 6 rounds wins.

Take It Further: Play the game again.
This time, use the numbers to form a fraction.
Then write the fraction as a percent.
Use a calculator if you need to.
You get 1 point for each percent you name.

Name ______________________ Date ________________

Master 2.5b

Reduction Cards

10	5	40	96
15	90	120	12
50	20	8	80
42	18	24	6
36	45	75	100
30	60	72	27
25	3	16	2

Name ____________________ Date ______________

Master 2.6a

Additional Activity 2: Triple Play

Play with a partner.

You will need a set of ratio game cards.

How to Play:

1. Shuffle the cards and place them face down in a pile.

2. Player A turns over 1 card.
He says the ratio in simplest form, then says 2 equivalent ratios.
One point is awarded for the ratio in simplest form, and 1 point for each equivalent ratio.
Place the card in a discard pile.

4. Player B has a turn.

5. Continue to take turns.
The player with the higher score after 6 rounds wins.

Take It Further: Create a set of cards with the ratios in simplest form.
Combine the cards you created with the game cards.
Shuffle the cards, then deal 8 cards to each player.
The goal of the game is to collect pairs of cards that show equivalent ratios.
Students pick and discard a card each round.
The player with more equivalent ratios after 8 rounds wins.

Name ____________________ Date ________________

Master 2.6b

Ratio Cards

10:15	28:35	24:8	12:16
8:14	35:28	15:21	27:33
40:35	9:21	14:18	24:18
7:14	33:45	15:6	10:25
7:35	42:30	6:18	24:15
56:32	27:81	22:99	21:6
12:42	30:18	27:15	18:30
21:36	33:21	14:49	13:91

Name ____________________ Date ______________

Master 2.7a

Additional Activity 3: Pair It Up

Play with a partner.

You will need a set of game cards.

How to Play:

1. Shuffle the cards. Place the cards face down in a rectangular array.

2. Player A turns over 2 cards.
   If the cards show equivalent numbers, she keeps the cards.
   If the numbers are not equivalent, Player A turns the cards face down.

3. Player B has a turn.

4. Play continues until all cards have been removed.
   The player with more pairs of cards wins.

Take It Further: Play the game again.
This time, deal 8 cards to each player.
Place the remaining cards face down.
The goal of the game is to collect equivalent pairs.
Players pick and discard a card each round.
The player with more equivalent pairs wins.

Name ____________________ Date ________________

Master 2.7b

Pair It Up Cards

$\frac{33}{100}$	25%	0.2	15%
$\frac{1}{4}$	10%	0.3	35%
$\frac{1}{10}$	20%	0.6	45%
$\frac{2}{5}$	30%	0.7	55%
$\frac{1}{2}$	40%	0.9	65%
$\frac{4}{5}$	50%	0.84	75%
$\frac{7}{20}$	60%	0.79	85%
$\frac{11}{20}$	70%	0.15	95%
$\frac{3}{4}$	80%	0.45	100%
$\frac{19}{20}$	90%	0.65	24%
$\frac{6}{25}$	84%	0.85	36%
$\frac{9}{25}$	79%	1	33%

Name ____________________ Date ______________

Master 2.8a

Additional Activity 4: Rate It

Play with a partner.

You will need a set of game cards.

How to Play:

1. Shuffle the cards. Place the cards face down in a pile.

2. Player A turns over a card.
He compares the quantities, and states them as a unit rate.
One point is awarded for a correct response.

3. Player B has a turn.

4. Continue to take turns.
The player with the higher score after 6 rounds wins.

Take It Further: Use index cards to write another set of game cards.
Play the game again with the new set of cards.

Name ____________________ Date ________________

Master 2.8b

Rate It Cards

Earn $62 in 4 h.	Earn $72 in 9 h.
Cycle 84 km in 7 h.	Drive 600 km in 8 h.
Run 200 m in 40 s.	Hike 115 km in 5 days.
36 pencils in 9 boxes	96 radios in 2 cartons
48 bottles in 3 crates	$3.28 for 8 cards
Type 126 words in 3 min.	Produce 30 labels in 2 h.
48 players on 6 teams	Cut out 27 figures in 9 min.
350 beats in 5 min	Fly 3750 km in 5 h.
6 m cost $45.	$8.40 for 12 tickets
Swim 300 m in 1 min 40 s.	Work 92 h in 4 weeks.

Name ____________________ Date ______________

Master 2.9

Step-by-Step 1

Lesson 2.1, Question 7

Step 1 Label this rectangle MNPQ.
Draw MP.

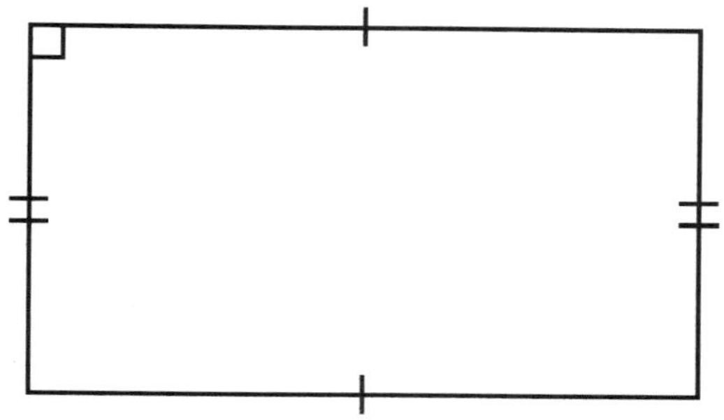

Step 2 Write this ratio. Length of MN:length of MP

____

Step 3 Does the ratio in *Step 2* tell you the length of MN? Explain.

____

Step 4 Use equivalent ratios. Write 3 sets of possible lengths for MN and MP.

MN = ______, MP = _______;

MN = ______, MP = _______;

MN = ______, MP = _______

Step 5 Suppose MN is 12 cm. How long is MP? How do you know?

____

____

Name ____________________ Date ________________

Master 2.10

Step-by-Step 2

Lesson 2.2, Question 9

You will need a sheet of grid paper.

Step 1 Choose a room in your home: ______________________________

What is the length of the room? __________

The width of the room? ____________

Step 2 What is the length of the grid paper? ______________

What is the width of the grid paper? _______________

Step 3 What is the ratio length of the grid paper: length of the room? __________

What is the ratio width of the grid paper: width of the room? __________

Step 4 What scale will you use for your drawing? Explain.

____

____

Step 5 What will be the length of your room on the drawing? _______________

What will be the width of your room on the drawing? ________________

Step 6 Draw a scale drawing of the room on grid paper.

Step 7 Name 3 pieces of furniture on the floor of your room.
Complete the table.

Item	Actual dimensions		Dimensions on scale drawing	
	$l =$	$w =$	$l =$	$w =$
	$l =$	$w =$	$l =$	$w =$
	$l =$	$w =$	$l =$	$w =$

Draw the items in the table on your scale drawing.

Name ____________________ Date ______________

Master 2.11

Step-by-Step 3

Lesson 2.3, Question 10

Step 1 How many calories are there in 1 apple? ______________________

How many calories are burned in 60 min of cycling? ______________

How many minutes of cycling will it take to burn the calories in 1 apple?

Step 2 How many calories are there in 2 slices of bread? ________________

How many calories are burned in 60 min of walking? ______________

How many minutes of walking will it take to burn the calories in 2 slices of bread?

Step 3 How many calories are in a vanilla fudge ice cream and a chocolate iced doughnut?

____

Which activity burns the most calories in 60 min? ________________

Step 4 Use your answers to *Step 3*. How long would it take to burn the calories in the ice cream and doughnut?

____

Step 5 Use the calories in *Step 3*. In 2 h, which 2 activities burn about the same number of calories as the ice cream and doughnut? ______________

____

Step 6 Use the data in the tables to write your own problem.
Solve your problem. Show your work.

Name ____________________ Date ________________

Master 2.12

Step-by-Step 4

Lesson 2.4, Question 7

Step 1 Round 0.75% to the nearest percent. ________________________
Use the rounded percent and the population in 1888.
Estimate the population in 1910.

____

Step 2 Write 0.75% as a decimal. ______________________________

Calculate 0.75% of 2000. ______________________________

What was the population in 1910? __________________________

Step 3 What was the population in 1888? __________________________

What was the population in 1910? __________________________
Subtract the populations:

What is the decrease in population?

____

Name ____________________ Date ________________

Master 2.13

Step-by-Step 5

Lesson 2.5, Question 10

Step 1 How old are you? ________

What is your height in centimetres? ___________

Step 2 If you are a boy, follow *Steps 3* and *6*.
If you are a girl, follow *Steps 4*, *5*, and *6*.

Step 3 Divide your height by 90: _________

Multiply the answer by 100: ______________

This is your approximate height at age 21.

Step 4 Estimate your height when you were 11. ____________

Step 5 Divide the height in *Step 4* by 90: _________

Multiply the answer by 100: ______________

This is your approximate height at age 21.

Step 6 What assumptions did you make? ______________________________

____

____

Name ____________________ Date ________________

Master 2.14

Step-by-Step 6

Lesson 2.6, Question 9

Assume the price of the item is $100.

Store A

Step 1 There is a 5% discount the first week.

What percent of the regular price do you pay? ____________________

Calculate the price after Week 1. ______________________________

Step 2 There is a 10% discount the second week.

What percent of the price in *Step 1* do you pay? __________________

Calculate the price after Week 2. ______________________________

Step 3 There is another 10% discount the third week.

What percent of the price in *Step 2* do you pay? __________________

Calculate the price after Week 3. ______________________________

Step 4 Calculate the total discount at Store A:

Original price – Final price = ___________________________________

Store B

Step 5 Store B offers one discount of 25% the third week.

What percent of the regular price do you pay? ____________________

Calculate the price after Week 3. ______________________________

What is the final price of the item in Store B? ____________________

Step 6 Calculate the total discount at Store B:

Original price – Final price = ___________________________________

Step 7 Which store gives the greater discount? Explain.

____

Name ______________________ Date ________________

Master 2.15

Step-by-Step 7

Lesson 2.7, Question 8

Marie has $1 000 000.
She earns interest at a rate of 4% per year.

Step 1 Write a problem using these data.

____

____

Step 2 Solve the problem you wrote.

Step 3 If you have difficulty writing a problem, solve this problem about the data.

Problem:
Marie invested her money for 5 years.
What was the simple interest she earned?

Solution:

Use the formula $I = Prt$

Write the rate as a decimal. _________________________________

Substitute $P =$ ________, $r =$ ________, $t =$ ________

$I =$ ________ × ________ × ________

$=$ __________

What is the simple interest earned? ___________________________

Name ____________________ Date ________________

Master 2.16a

Unit Test: Unit 2 Applications of Ratio, Rate, and Percent

1. Find each percent of 160.
Draw a number line to show the percents.

a) 300% of 160 **b)** 30% of 160

c) 3% of 160 **d)** 0.3% of 160

2. Solve each proportion. Use a calculator when you need to.

a) $\frac{x}{5} = \frac{36}{4}$ **b)** $\frac{x}{36} = \frac{5}{4}$

c) $\frac{x}{4} = \frac{36}{5}$ **d)** $\frac{x}{5} = \frac{4}{36}$

Name ____________________ Date ______________

Master 2.16b **Unit Test continued**

3. At the checkout, you hear a customer ask about a discount.
The customer says, "I would like you to take the 30% off the regular price before you calculate the 15% sales tax." The clerk says, "It doesn't make any difference.
If I calculate the sales tax, then take off 30%, you still pay the same."
Is the clerk correct? Explain.
Use an example in your explanation.

4. A student invests $500 in an account that pays simple interest.
The interest rate is 2% per year. The money is invested for 9 months.
What is the amount of the investment after 9 months?

Name ____________________ Date ______________

Master 2.16c

Unit Test continued

5. A 6-pack of juice boxes costs $3.99.
A 12-pack costs $5.99.
A 24-pack costs $9.99.
A person wants to buy 158 juice boxes.
What is the least expensive way to do this?
What do 158 juice boxes cost? Justify your answer.

Name ____________________ Date ____________

Master 2.17

Sample Answers

Unit Test – Master 2.16

1. a) 300% of 160 = 3 × 160 = 480
   b) 30% of 160 = 0.3 × 160 = 48
   c) 3% of 160 = 0.03 × 160 = 4.8
   d) 0.3% of 160 = 0.003 × 160 = 0.48

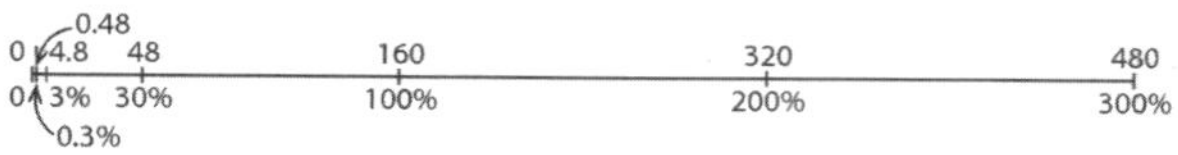

2. a) $\frac{x}{5} = \frac{36}{4} \Rightarrow \frac{x}{5} = 9 \Rightarrow 5 \times \frac{x}{5} = 9 \times 5 \Rightarrow x = 45$
   b) $\frac{x}{36} = \frac{5}{4} \Rightarrow 36 \times \frac{x}{36} = \frac{5}{4} \times 36 \Rightarrow x = 45$
   c) $\frac{x}{4} = \frac{36}{5} \Rightarrow 4 \times \frac{x}{4} = \frac{36}{5} \times 4 \Rightarrow x = 28.8$
   d) $\frac{x}{5} = \frac{4}{36} \Rightarrow 5 \times \frac{x}{5} = \frac{4}{36} \times 5 \Rightarrow x = 0.\overline{5}$

3. The clerk is correct.
   Assume the regular price of the item is $100.
   Method 1: Take 30% off, then pay 15% tax.
   30% off means I pay 70%.
   70% of $100 = $70
   Add 15% tax. The total paid is:
   115% of $70 = 1.15 × $70 = $80.50
   Method 2: Pay 15% tax, then take 30% off.
   Pay 15% tax means the item costs 115% of $100 = 1.15 × $100 = $115.
   Take 30% off, so I pay 70%.
   70% of $115 = 0.70 × $115 = $80.50

4. $500 for 9 months at 2% interest rate
   Use $I = Prt$, where $P = 500$, $r = 0.02$,
   and $t = \frac{9}{12} = \frac{3}{4}$
   Then, $I = 500 \times 0.02 \times \frac{3}{4}$
   $= 7.5$
   The amount after 9 months is:
   $500 + $7.50 = $507.50

5. 6-pack is $3.99. 12-pack is $5.99.
   24-pack is $9.99.
   Find each unit price.
   6-pack: $\frac{\$3.99}{6} = \$0.665$
   12-pack: $\frac{\$5.99}{12} \doteq \$0.50$
   24-pack: $\frac{\$9.99}{24} = \$0.42$
   The 24-pack has the lowest unit price, so I buy as many 24-packs as possible.
   Divide: $\frac{158}{24} = 6.58\overline{3}$
   So, I buy six 24-packs. That is
   6 × 24 boxes = 144 boxes
   and they cost $9.99 × 6 = $59.94.
   I need to buy 158 – 144 = 14 more boxes.
   This means I buy a 12-pack and a 6-pack for $5.99 + $3.99 = $9.98. This is 1¢ less than if I buy a 24-pack instead. So, I shall buy seven 24-packs for $9.99 × 7 = $69.93. I shall have a few boxes as spare.

Name ______________________ Date ________________

Master 2.18

Alternative Explore for Similar Figures

Work with a partner.

You will need 1-cm grid paper and a 5-column chart.

➢ Label the chart with these headings.

Rectangle	Base (cm)	Height (cm)	Perimeter (cm)	Area (cm^2)
A				
B				
C				

➢ Draw 3 similar rectangles.
Make sure that no two rectangles are congruent.
Label them A, B, and C.

➢ Measure the base and height of each rectangle.
Record these measurements in the chart.

➢ Calculate the perimeter and area of each rectangle.
Record these measurements in the chart.

➢ For each pair of rectangles, calculate these ratios.

	A:B	A:C	B:C
base:base			
height:height			
perimeter:perimeter			
area:area			

Write each ratio in simplest form.

➢ How are the ratios related?

Reflect and Share

Compare your results with those of another pair of classmates who drew different rectangles.
How is the ratio of corresponding sides related to the ratio of perimeters?
How is the ratio of corresponding sides related to the ratio of areas?

Extra Practice Masters 2.19–2.26

Go to the CD-ROM to access editable versions of these Extra Practice Masters.

Name ____________ Date ____________

Master 2.19 **Extra Practice 1**

Lesson 2.1: Using Proportions to Solve Ratio Problems

1. Find each missing term.
   a) $x:8 = 9:24$ b) $y:15 = 7:3$
   c) $a:8 = 9:4$ d) $\frac{p}{12} = \frac{15}{10}$
   e) $\frac{b}{5} = \frac{18}{6}$ f) $\frac{t}{11} = \frac{6}{33}$
2. Belinda jogged 1.5 km, then walked 500 m.
   Write the ratio of distance jogged to distance walked in simplest form.
3. An advertisement claims that 7 out of 8 people prefer Brand X.
   Suppose 216 people were interviewed.
   Find the number of people who prefer Brand X.
4. The Grade 8 students held a graduation dance.
   Four out of 7 students attended.
   There are 112 Grade 8 students.
   How many students attended the dance?
5. A ski shop rents 5 snowboards for every 3 sets of skis it rents.
   Suppose 126 sets of skis were rented.
   How many snowboards were rented?
6. For a painting, the ratio of the length to the width is 5:3.
   The painting is 45 cm wide.
   How long is the painting?
7. The ratio of the number of students who take trumpet lessons to clarinet lessons is 6:5.
   The ratio of the number of students who take piano lessons to trumpet lessons is 8:3.
   Ten students take clarinet lessons.
   a) How many students take trumpet lessons?
   b) How many students take piano lessons?

Name ____________ Date ____________

Master 2.20 **Extra Practice 2**

Lesson 2.2: Scale Drawings

1. A model airplane was made using a scale of 1:150.
   The model is 48 cm long.
   What is the actual length of the plane?
2. A blueprint for a cottage has a scale of 1:40.
   One room measures 3.4 m by 4.8 m.
   Calculate the dimensions of the room on the blueprint.
3. a) The scale on a map of Ontario is 1:3 000 000.
   The map distance between London and Timmins is 28 cm.
   What is the actual distance between the cities?
   b) The scale on a large map of Canada is 1:10 000 000.
   The actual distance between Fredericton, New Brunswick, and Vancouver, British Columbia, is 5650 km.
   What is the map distance between Fredericton and Vancouver?
4. A bug is 6 mm long.
   A scale drawing of the bug is 7.8 cm long.
   What is the scale of the drawing?
5. A rectangular garden measures 24 m by 18 m.
   Choose a suitable scale.
   Make a scale drawing of the garden.
6. An ant is 1.4 cm long.
   Which scale would you use to draw the ant in your notebook? Explain.
   a) 10:1 b) 1:10 c) 100:1
   d) 1:100 e) 1000:1 f) 1:1000
7. Brock's Monument on Queenston Heights is about 56 m tall.
   A drawing of the monument just fits on this page.
   What is the scale of the drawing?

Name ____________ Date ____________

Master 2.21 **Extra Practice 3**

Lesson 2.3: Comparing Rates

1. Write a unit rate for each statement.
   a) 560 km travelled in 7 h
   b) 4 cans of beans for $1.76
   c) 280 words typed in 7 min
   d) $786 earned in 6 weeks
2. Banana chips sell for 44¢ per 100 g.
   How much would 450 g of banana chips cost?
3. Which is the greatest average speed?
   a) 78 km in 3 h
   b) 96 km in 4 h
   c) 125 km in 5 h
4. Which is the better buy?
   a) 5 oranges for $1.65 or 8 oranges for $2.77
   b) 2 L of lemonade for $2.56 or 1 L for $1.32
   c) 3 kg of apples for $5.70 or 2 kg for $3.90
5. A 2.5-kg bag of flour contains enough flour to make 4 cakes.
   a) How much flour is needed to make 50 cakes?
   b) How many bags of flour do you need?
6. Ned types 360 words in 6 min.
   Nate types 220 words in 4 min.
   Who would type more words in 10 min?
   What assumptions do you make?
7. In the first 8 games of the hockey season, Moira scored 26 goals.
   a) On average, how many goals did Moira score per game?
   b) At this rate, how many goals will Moira score in 20 games?
8. The courier travelled 508 km in 8 h.
   a) What was the average speed?
   b) At this rate, how long will it take the courier to travel 889 km?

Name ____________ Date ____________

Master 2.22 **Extra Practice 4**

Lesson 2.4: Calculating Percents

1. Write each percent as a decimal.
   Draw diagrams to illustrate your answers.
   a) 275% b) 56%
   c) 0.8% d) 0.25%
   e) 9% f) 105%
2. Write each fraction as a percent.
   Draw diagrams to illustrate your answers.
   a) $\frac{3}{5}$ b) $\frac{1}{40}$
   c) $\frac{15}{3}$ d) $\frac{5}{6}$
   e) $\frac{7}{25}$ f) $\frac{9}{2}$
3. Find the percent of each number.
   Draw diagrams to illustrate your answers.
   a) 40% of 240 b) 7% of 320
   c) 200% of 64 d) 0.5% of 600
4. One hundred sixty students attended Music Night on Thursday night.
   The attendance on Friday night was 120% of the attendance on Thursday night.
   The attendance on Saturday night was 75% of the attendance on Friday night.
   a) How many people attended Music Night on Friday night?
   b) How many people attended on Saturday night?
   c) What was the total attendance for the 3 nights?
5. Thirty girls and 20 boys signed up for the trip to the museum.
   On the day of the trip, 4 boys and 2 girls were absent.
   a) What percent of the girls who signed up were absent?
   b) What percent of the boys who signed up were absent?
   c) What percent of the students who signed up were absent?
6. In a 500-word assignment, the teacher noted that 1.2% of the words were incorrectly spelled.
   a) How many words were correctly spelled?
   b) Estimate to check your answer.

Name ____________ Date ____________

Master 2.23 **Extra Practice 5**

Lesson 2.5: Solving Percent Problems

1. Find the number in each case.
   a) 30% of a number is 12.
   b) 2% of a number is 9.
   c) 150% of a number is 60.
   d) 55% of a number is 11.
2. Find the amount in each case.
   a) 8% is 72 cm.
   b) 0.6% is 18 g.
   c) 120% is 24 m.
   d) 32% is 64 mL.
3. Write each increase as a percent.
   a) The price of gasoline increased from 93.9¢ to 99.9¢.
   b) The price of a car increased from $32 000 to $36 000.
   c) The price of a loaf of bread increased from $1.99 to $2.49.
4. Write each decrease as a percent.
   a) The number of employees decreased from 6800 to 5200.
   b) The area of a park decreased from 840 ha to 672 ha.
   c) The price of a computer decreased from $3000 to $2400.
5. A printing machine produces labels.
   Four percent of the labels produced are defective.
   Suppose 372 labels were defective.
   How many labels are not defective?
6. A field goal kicker was successful 75% of the time.
   He made 51 field goals.
   How many kicks did he make in total?
7. Lesley and Enid left their waitress a 15% tip.
   The tip was $10.25.
   What was their total bill, not including the tip?

Name ____________ Date ____________

Master 2.24 **Extra Practice 6**

Lesson 2.6: Sales Tax, Discount, and Commission

1. For each item below:
   a) Calculate the PST and GST.
   b) Calculate the cost, including taxes.
      i) A pair of running shoes priced at $89.60
      ii) A DVD priced at $24.86
2. For each item below:
   a) Calculate the discount.
   b) Calculate the sale price, before taxes.
   c) Calculate the sale price, including taxes.
      i) Notebook: Regular price $1598, now 20% off
      ii) Digital camera phone: Regular price $158, now 15% off
3. For each item below, calculate:
   i) the percent decrease in price
   ii) the sale price, including taxes
      a) A television marked down from $1488 to $1100
      b) An electronic game marked down from $56.84 to $49.99
4. A camera shop reduced the price of a digital camera by 10% at the end of the first week, by 20% at the end of the second week, and by a further 20% at the end of the third week.
   The original price of the camera was $625.
   a) Calculate the sale price after 3 weeks.
   b) Calculate the sale price, including the sales taxes.
5. During a 15% off sale, the sale price of a garden bench was $84.99.
   What was the regular price of the bench?
6. A family sold a home for $425 000 and paid 6% commission.
   a) How much was the commission?
   b) How much did the family receive for the house?
   c) What if the family had been able to pay only 5% commission.
   How much would the family have saved?
7. A furniture store offers two choices of discount on a sofa with a price of $1250.
   Choice A: 15% discount
   Choice B: $200 rebate
   Which is the better deal for the customer?
   Justify your answer.

Name ____________ Date ____________

Master 2.25 **Extra Practice 7**

Lesson 2.7: Simple Interest

1. Calculate the simple interest paid on each deposit.
   a) $600 invested at an annual interest rate of 3% for 2 years
   b) $1800 invested at an annual interest rate of 4% for 5 years
   c) $380 invested at an annual interest rate of 6% for 3 years
   d) $15 000 invested at an annual interest rate of 8% for 2 years
2. Calculate the simple interest and the amount.
   a) $1200 invested at an annual interest rate of 8% for 6 months
   b) $800 invested at an annual interest rate of 5% for 9 months
   c) $7500 invested at an annual interest rate of 6% for 18 months
   d) $50 000 invested at an annual interest rate of 2% for 8 months
3. Janine borrows $8000 at a rate of 6% per year for 5 years.
   She pays back the money in equal monthly payments over the 5 years.
   a) What simple interest does Janine pay?
   b) What is each monthly payment?
4. Karl invested $40 000 at a simple interest rate of 6.5% per year.
   How much will Karl earn in 1 year?
5. Clarissa borrowed $3600 to buy a car.
   She will pay back the money after 15 months.
   She pays simple interest at a rate of $8\frac{1}{4}$% per year.
   What amount will Clarissa pay after 15 months?
6. Justin has a $3000 savings bond.
   He has had the bond for 5 years.
   The bond paid 2% interest per year.
   Justin cashes the bond.
   a) What simple interest does Justin receive?
   b) What amount will Justin receive?

Name ____________ Date ____________

Master 2.26 **Sample Answers**

Extra Practice 1 – Master 2.19
Lesson 2.1

1. a) $x = 3$ b) $y = 35$ c) $a = 18$
   d) $p = 18$ e) $b = 15$ f) $t = 2$
2. 3:1
3. 189 people
4. 64 students
5. 210 snowboards
6. 75 cm
7. a) 12 students b) 32 students

Extra Practice 2 – Master 2.20
Lesson 2.2

1. 7200 cm or 72 m
2. 8.5 cm by 12 cm
3. a) 840 km b) 56.5 cm
4. 13:1
5. For example, a scale of 1:120 will give a drawing of dimensions 20 cm by 15 cm.
6. 10:1; the drawing of the ant will be 14 cm long. The other scales will produce drawings that will not fit on a page of any notebook.
7. For example, I assumed the page is 25 cm long. Then, the scale of the drawing is 1:224.

Extra Practice 3 – Master 2.21
Lesson 2.3

1. a) 80 km/h b) $0.44/can
   c) 40 words/min d) $131/week
2. $1.98
3. 78 km in 3 h
4. a) 5 oranges for $1.65 b) 2 L for $2.56
   c) 3 kg for $5.70
5. a) 31.25 kg b) 13 bags
6. Ned; I assume he can maintain his unit rate for 10 min.
7. a) 3.25 goals per game b) 65 goals
8. a) 63.5 km/h b) 14 h

Extra Practice 4 – Master 2.22
Lesson 2.4

1. a) 2.75 b) 0.56
   c) 0.008 d) 0.0025
   e) 0.09 f) 1.05
2. a) 60%
   b) 2.5%
   c) 500%
   d) $83.\overline{3}$%
   e) 28%
   f) 450%
3. a) 96
   b) 22.4
   c) 128
   d) 3
4. a) 192 b) 144 c) 496
5. a) $6.\overline{6}$% b) 20% c) 12%
6. a) 494 words
   b) 1% of 500 is 5; about 500 – 5 = 495 words were spelled correctly.

Extra Practice 5 – Master 2.23
Lesson 2.5

1. a) 40 b) 450 c) 40 d) 20
2. a) 9 m b) 3 kg
   c) 20 m d) 200 mL
3. a) About 6.4% b) 12.5% c) About 25.1%
4. a) About 23.5% b) 20% c) 20%
5. 9300 labels
6. 68 kicks
7. $68.33

Extra Practice 6 – Master 2.24
Lesson 2.6

1. i) a) $7.17, $6.27 b) $103.04
   ii) a) $1.99, $1.74 b) $28.59
2. i) a) $319.60 b) $1278.40 c) $1470.16
   ii) a) $23.70 b) $134.30 c) $154.45

3. a) About 26%; $1265.00
   b) About 12%; $57.49
4. a) $360.00 b) $414.00
5. $99.99
6. a) $25 500 b) $399 500 c) $4250
7. Choice A: $1062.50 before taxes
   Choice B: $1050 before taxes
   Choice B is the better deal.

Extra Practice 7 – Master 2.25
Lesson 2.7

1. a) $36.00 b) $360.00
   c) $68.40 d) $2400.00
2. a) $48; $1248 b) $30; $830
   c) $675; $8175 d) $666.67; $50 666.67
3. a) $2400 b) $173.33
4. $2600
5. $3971.25
6. a) $300 b) $3300

Addison Wesley Mathematics Makes Sense

Program Authors

Trevor Brown
Antonietta Lenjosek
Cathy Heideman
Jim Mennie
Georgia Konis-Chatzis
A.J. Keene
Margaret Sinclair
Craig Featherstone
Jason Johnston
Bryn Keyes
Elizabeth Wood
Elizabeth Milne
David Sufrin
Don Jones
Sharon Jeroski
Lynn Strangway

Printed and bound in Canada

2 3 4 5 – TC – 09 08 07 06

PEARSON Education Canada

ADDISON WESLEY

Ontario

Math Makes Sense 8

Ontario

Teacher Guide

Unit 3: Geometry and Measurement

PEARSON
Education Canada

UNIT 3

Geometry and Measurement

"Spatial sense includes the ability to visualize mentally objects and spatial relationships — to turn things around in your mind. It includes a comfort with geometric descriptions of objects and position. People with spatial sense appreciate geometric form in art, nature, and architecture."
– John A. Van de Walle

FOCUS STRANDS
Geometry and Spatial Sense
Measurement

SUPPORTING STRANDS
Patterning and Algebra
Number Sense and Numeration

TIPS
Have technological tools and manipulatives available at assessment time so that students have a choice of tools for problem solving.

Mathematics Background

What Are the Big Ideas?

- The volume of any prism is given by base area × height.
- The use of area and volume formulas is an application of the evaluation of algebraic expressions.

How Will the Concepts Develop?

Students review the formulas for the surface area and volume of a triangular prism. This review provides students with practice in evaluating algebraic expressions in context, and in converting among metric units of area, volume, and capacity.

Why Are These Concepts Important?

Students should be able to represent the solution to a problem in a variety of ways. For example, an accurate, well-presented diagram is often a good starting point for solutions to many problems a student will encounter, both in mathematics and other disciplines, as well as everyday activities.

Presenting students with realistic uses for the application of their algebra skills, in the form of appropriate measurement formulas, should aid students' understanding of more abstract algebra concepts.

Both measurement and geometry are involved in the development of surface area and volume formulas and in how surface area and volume are related. Formulas allow us to use measures that are easily found to determine another measure that is not so easily found; for example, the volume of a prism.

Curriculum Overview

The codes refer to the 2005 revised curriculum.

Overall Expectations
- Research, describe, and report on applications of volume and capacity measurement. (8m30)
- Determine the relationships among units and measurable attributes … (8m31)
- Develop geometric relationships involving … polyhedra, … (8m41)
- Solve problems involving whole numbers, decimal numbers … using a variety of computational strategies. (8m9)
- … solve and verify algebraic equations, using a variety of strategies, … (8m55)

Specific Expectations
- Research, describe, and report on applications of volume and capacity measurement. (8m32)
- Solve problems that require conversions involving metric units of area, volume, and capacity. (8m33)
- Determine, through investigation using concrete materials, the relationship among the number of faces, edges, and vertices of a polyhedron. (8m51)
- Translate statements describing mathematical relationships into algebraic expressions and equations. (8m61)
- Evaluate algebraic expressions with up to three terms, by substituting … decimals, … for the variables. (8m62)
- Solve multi-step problems arising from real-life contexts and involving whole numbers and decimals, using a variety of tools and strategies. (8m16)
- Multiply and divide decimal numbers by various powers of ten. (8m24)

Launch

Lesson 3.1: Building and Sketching Objects

Lesson 3.2: Sketching and Folding Nets

Mid-Unit Review

Lesson 3.3: Surface Area of a Triangular Prism

Lesson 3.4: Volume of a Triangular Prism

Unit Review
Practice Test

Unit Problem
Under the Big Top

Curriculum across the Grades

Grade 7	Grade 8
Students investigate the angles between the faces of a prism, and identify right prisms. Students develop the formula for the volume of right prisms. They sketch different polygonal prisms that share the same volume. Students determine the surface area of right prisms. They solve problems involving the surface area and volume of right prisms that involve converting between metric units of area, capacity, and volume. Students evaluate algebraic expressions by substituting natural numbers for the variables. Students solve multi-step problems involving whole numbers and decimals in real-life situations.	Students investigate applications of volume and capacity measurement. They solve problems that require conversions involving metric units of area, volume, and capacity. Students determine the relationship among the numbers of faces, edges, and vertices of a polyhedron. Students solve multi-step problems involving whole numbers and decimals in real-life situations. Students translate statements into algebraic expressions and equations. They evaluate algebraic expressions with up to three terms, by substituting decimals for the variables.

Materials for This Unit

You will need a variety of solids and linking cubes. For Lesson 3.3 *Connect,* a large net of the triangular prism shown, made from stiff cardboard that will fold and unfold, will help present the concept. For Lesson 3.4 *Explore,* you will need 4 identical empty cereal boxes for each group of four students.

Additional Activities

Spin, Build, Draw

For Extra Practice (Appropriate for use after Lesson 3.1)

Materials: *Spin, Build, Draw* (Master 3.5a), *Spin, Build, Draw Spinner* (Master 3.5b), number cubes, linking cubes, 1-cm grid paper (PM 20) or square dot paper (PM 22), open paper clip

Playing this game reinforces the skills of building an object and drawing its views.

The work students do: Students play in pairs. Each student spins the pointer to find how many different views she must draw, then rolls the number cube to find how many linking cubes she must use (students roll again if they roll 1 or 2). Each student uses her linking cubes to build an object, then draws the number of views required. Students trade views and build each other's object. Students get 1 point for each correct view, and 1 point if the object matches her opponent's object. The student with more points after 4 rounds wins.

Take It Further: Students roll the number cube twice, and use the sum of the numbers as the number of linking cubes to use.

Spatial/Social/Kinesthetic
Partner Activity

The Platonic Solids

For Extra Practice (Appropriate for use after Lesson 3.2)

Materials: *The Platonic Solids* (Master 3.6a), nets for tetrahedron, cube, octahedron, dodecahedron, icosahedron (Masters 3.6b to 3.6f), scissors, and tape

Conducting this activity illustrates how the 5 Platonic solids satisfy Euler's theorem.

The work students do: Students work in groups. They use nets to construct the 5 Platonic solids, then count the numbers of edges, faces, and vertices on each solid. They confirm that each solid obeys Euler's theorem.

Take It Further: Students identify the attributes of a Platonic solid (that is: all faces are congruent polygons; the same number of faces meet at a vertex; and the same number of edges meet at a vertex).

Spatial/Social/Kinesthetic
Group Activity

Measurement Bingo

For Extra Practice (Appropriate for use after Lesson 3.4)

Materials: *Measurement Bingo* (Master 3.7a), *Measurement Bingo Game Pieces* (Master 3.7b), 3 number cubes, paper bag, scissors, 4-column chart (PM 19)

Playing this game reinforces the skills of calculating perimeter, area, surface area, and volume.

The work students do: Students play in groups of 4. Students complete each column of their game cards using numbers from 0 to 9 (numbers may be used more than once). Students cut out the game pieces and place them in a paper bag. Students take turns to draw a game piece from the bag, then roll the number cubes to find the dimensions of the figure or object on the game piece. Students calculate the required measurement, then cross off any digits in their answers that are found in the corresponding column of their bingo cards. The first student to cross off all the numbers in a row, column, or diagonal wins.

Take It Further: Students write a possible measurement in each column of the bingo cards by considering the possible combinations of numbers that could be rolled and their probabilities. Students cross off measurements, rather than digits.

Mathematical/Social
Group Activity

Planning for Unit 3

Planning for Instruction

Suggested Unit time: 1–2 weeks

Lesson	Time	Materials	Program Support
Launch, page 2	15–20 min		
Skills You'll Need, page 4	optional but recommended	large rectangular prism and corresponding net 1-cm grid transparency isometric dot paper and transparency linking cubes metre stick calculators	PM 20: 1-cm Grid Paper PM 23: Isometric Dot Paper
3.1: Building and Sketching Objects, page 10 Recognize, build, and sketch an object given different views of the object.	optional but recommended	square dot paper and transparency 1-cm grid paper isometric dot paper and transparency linking cubes	PM 20: 1-cm Grid Paper PM 22: Square Dot Paper PM 23: Isometric Dot Paper Master 3.8: Step-by-Step 1 Master 3.14: Extra Practice 1
3.2: Sketching and Folding Nets, page 14 Sketch nets and use them to build objects.	optional	scissors tape square dot paper 1-cm grid paper and transparency 0.5-cm grid paper cube	PM 14: 0.5-cm Grid Paper PM 20: 1-cm Grid Paper PM 22: Square Dot Paper Master 3.9: Step-by-Step 2 Master 3.15: Extra Practice 2
Mid-Unit Review, page 19		linking cubes isometric dot paper square dot paper 1-cm grid paper scissors, tape	PM 20: 1-cm Grid Paper PM 22: Square Dot Paper PM 23: Isometric Dot Paper
3.3: Surface Area of a Triangular Prism, page 20 Develop a formula for finding the surface area of a triangular prism.	optional but recommended	1-cm grid paper square dot paper calculators	PM 20: 1-cm Grid Paper PM 22: Square Dot Paper Master 3.10: Step-by-Step 3 Master 3.16: Extra Practice 3
3.4: Volume of a Triangular Prism, page 25 Develop and use a formula for finding the volume of a triangular prism.	optional but recommended	4 identical empty cereal boxes for each group scissors markers calculators	Master 3.11: Step-by-Step 4 Master 3.17: Extra Practice 4
Reading and Writing in Math: Features of Word Problems, page 30		calculators	
Unit Review, page 32		linking cubes isometric dot paper scissors, tape, compasses 1-cm grid paper calculators	PM 20: 1-cm Grid Paper PM 23: Isometric Dot Paper Extra Practice: Student Book page 490

Lesson	Time	Materials	Program Support
Practice Test, page 35		linking cubes isometric dot paper scissors, tape, compasses 1-cm grid paper calculators	PM 20: 1-cm Grid Paper PM 23: Isometric Dot Paper
Unit Problem: Under the Big Top, page 36	optional but recommended	isometric dot paper scissors, tape, compasses 1-cm grid paper square dot paper	PM 20: 1-cm Grid Paper PM 22: Square Dot Paper PM 23: Isometric Dot Paper

Planning for Assessment

Purpose	Tools and Process	Recording and Reporting
Diagnostic	*Unit Launch* Question; conference; scaffold problems throughout the unit	PM 8: Conference Prompts
Formative	*Explore* – Ongoing Assessment: Observe and Listen	Master 3.2 Ongoing Observations: Geometry and Measurement PM 1: Inquiry Process Check List PM 6: Observation Record 1 PM 7: Observation Record 2 PM 8: Conference Prompts PM 2: Self-Assessment PM 3: Self-Assessment: Problem Solving PM 9: Work Sample Records
Summative	*Unit Review* *Unit Problem* – Performance Assessment Unit Test Review assessment records; add unit results to ongoing records	Master 3.1 Geometry and Measurement Master 3.3 Performance Assessment Rubric: Under the Big Top Master 3.4 Unit Summary: Geometry and Measurement PM 10: Summary Class Records: Strands PM 11: Summary Class Records: Achievement Categories PM 12: Summary Record: Individual
Learning Skills/Mathematical Disposition	Observe and record throughout unit	PM 4: Learning Skills Check List PM 5: Mathematical Dispositions and Learning Skills

Program Masters (PM) are in the *Grade 8 Planning and Program Masters* module.
Extra Practice Masters are on the CD-ROM and printed in reduced format on page 60 of this module.

LESSON ORGANIZER

15–20 min

Curriculum Focus: Activate prior learning about two- and three-dimensional geometry, surface area, and volume.

ASSUMED PRIOR KNOWLEDGE

- ✓ Students can calculate the area of a triangle and the area of a rectangle.
- ✓ Students can calculate the surface area and volume of a rectangular prism.

Teaching notes for Cross Strand Investigation *Golden Rectangles* are in the *Additional Assessment Support* module.

UNIT 3

Geometry and Measurement

These students are setting up a tent.
How do the students know how to set up the tent?
How is the shape of the tent created?
How could students find the amount of material needed to make the tent?
Why might students want to know the volume of the tent?

What You'll Learn

- Recognize and sketch objects.
- Use nets to build objects.
- Develop and use a formula for the surface area of a triangular prism.
- Develop and use a formula for the volume of a triangular prism.
- Solve problems involving prisms.

Why It's Important

- We find out about our environment by looking at objects from different views. When we combine these views, we have a better understanding of these objects.
- We need measurement and calculation skills to design and build objects, such as homes and parks.

94

ACTIVATE PRIOR LEARNING

Engage students in a discussion about setting up a tent. Students may want to discuss the types of tents they have. Encourage them to discuss the shapes of tents and how they are supported.

Discuss each question on page 94. Make a list of any mathematical words or formulas students use in their answers. Ask:

- How do the students know how to set up the tent? (*They may look at the parts and try to find out how they are put together. They may use a finished picture that shows how the parts are put together. They may read the instructions, or follow step-by-step pictures.*)
- How is the shape of the tent created? (*A tent is supported with poles, and by ropes secured to the ground with pegs.*) (Students may use the word "frame" to describe a supporting structure over which the canvas is stretched to create the shape.)
- How could you find the amount of material needed to make the tent? (*I could find the area of each part of the tent. The tent has 2 triangular faces and 3 rectangular faces. I could measure to find the dimensions of each face, calculate the area of each face, then add to find the total area. I would have to add extra material for seams or overlap.*)

Remind students that this area is called the surface area of the tent. Ask:

- Why might you want to know the volume of the tent? (*The volume of the tent is the amount of space occupied by the tent. The volume may help determine how many people the tent can sleep comfortably, or the amount of space available if the tent is used for storage.*)

Tell students that in this unit, they will learn more about sketching and building three-dimensional objects, and finding the surface area and volume of a triangular prism. Students will demonstrate what they have learned by building a circus tent and designing a prop for a circus act.

Key Words
- isometric diagram
- pictorial diagram
- triangular prism
- surface area
- volume

95

FROM THE LIBRARY

Daily Warm-Ups: Geometry by Thomas Campbell.
J. Weston Walch Publishing, 2004.
ISBN: 0825144981
These daily warm-ups in geometry give students the opportunity to strengthen their problem-solving skills. This book uses math riddles and real-life examples to make lessons fun.

REACHING ALL LEARNERS

e-tools Some students may benefit from using the virtual manipulatives on the e-Tools CD-ROM. The e-Tools appropriate for this unit are *Geometry Shapes* and *Geometry Drawing*.

DIAGNOSTIC ASSESSMENT

What to Look For	What to Do
✔ Students can calculate the area of a triangle and the area of a rectangle. ✔ Students can calculate the surface area and volume of a rectangular prism.	***Extra Support:*** Students who have difficulty calculating the area of a triangle or a rectangle should begin by drawing the figure on grid paper, then counting grid squares to estimate the area. *Work on this skill during Skills You'll Need.* Students who have difficulty calculating the surface area of a rectangular prism should draw a net on grid paper and calculate the sum of the areas of the faces, before they use the formula to check. Students relate each area calculation to its place in the formula. *Work on this skill during Skills You'll Need.*

LESSON ORGANIZER (optional but recommended)

Skills in Review
- Drawing isometric and pictorial diagrams
- Calculating the surface area and volume of a rectangular prism
- Calculating the area of a triangle
- Converting among units of measure

Teacher Materials
- large rectangular prism (box) and corresponding net
- 1-cm grid transparency (PM 20)
- metre stick

Optional
- isometric dot paper transparency (PM 23)

Student Materials
- linking cubes
- isometric dot paper (PM 23)
- calculators

Vocabulary: isometric diagram, pictorial diagram, regular polyhedron

UNIT 3

Skills You'll Need

Drawing Isometric and Pictorial Diagrams

An **isometric diagram** shows three dimensions of an object. It is drawn on isometric (triangular) dot paper. Vertical edges of an object are drawn as vertical line segments. Parallel edges of an object are drawn as parallel line segments.

Example 1

Make an isometric diagram of this object.

Solution

On isometric paper, join a pair of dots for each vertical edge.

Join a pair of dots diagonally for each horizontal edge that goes up to the right.

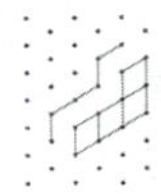

Join a pair of dots diagonally for each horizontal edge that goes up to the left.
Shade the faces so the object appears three-dimensional.

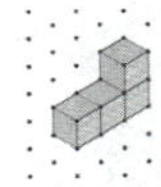

In a **pictorial diagram**, the depth of an object is drawn to a smaller scale than the length and width. This gives the object a three-dimensional appearance.

Example 2

Make a pictorial diagram of this cylinder.

96 UNIT 3: Geometry and Measurement

Alternative Example 1

Make an isometric diagram of a cube with edge length 3 units.

Solution

On isometric paper, join a pair of dots 3 units apart for each vertical edge.

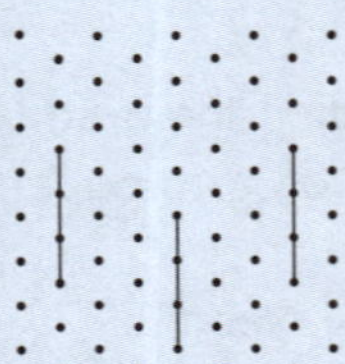

Join a pair of dots diagonally 3 units apart for each horizontal edge that goes up to the right.

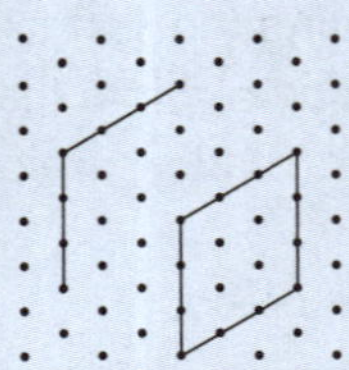

Join a pair of dots diagonally 3 units apart for each horizontal edge that goes up to the left.

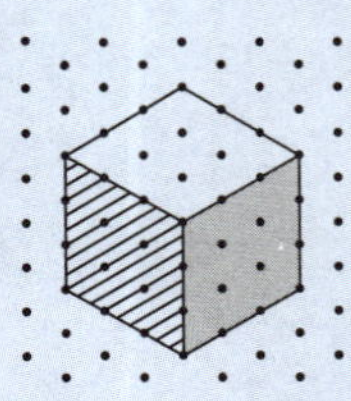

Shade visible faces differently to get a three-dimensional look.

Drawing Isometric and Pictorial Diagrams

Isometric and pictorial diagrams are review from Grade 6. The way the faces of the object in a diagram are shaded may cause some perspective differences. Discuss this "optical illusion."

Tell students that they can use ideas similar to those in *Example 1* to sketch a 3-D picture of an object, or a *pictorial diagram*. Review *Example 2*.

Circulate while students complete the questions in *Check*. Ensure students use rulers for straight line segments and that the dimensions clearly illustrate those given; for example, the 5-unit edge should appear longer than the 3-unit edge. However, in a pictorial diagram, allowance has to be made for perspective. If the horizontal edge is 3 units, and the edge that goes up to the right is 5 units, then these two edges should be drawn approximately the same length.

Solution

The top and bottom of a cylinder are circles.
...ictorial diagram, a circular face is an oval.
...half of the bottom circular face is
drawn as a broken curve. This indicates that
this half cannot be seen.
Draw vertical line segments to join the
top and bottom ovals.

✓ Check

1. Make an isometric diagram of each object.
   a) a rectangular prism with dimensions 3 units by 4 units by 5 units
   b) a square pyramid

Remember to look up any terms that you are unsure of in the *Glossary*.

2. Make a pictorial diagram of each object.
   a) a rectangular prism with dimensions 3 units by 4 units by 5 units
   b) a regular tetrahedron

Calculating the Surface Area and Volume of a Rectangular Prism

The surface area of a rectangular prism is the sum of the areas of all its faces.
Since opposite faces are congruent,
this formula can be used to find the surface area:
Surface area = 2 × area of base + 2 × area of side face + 2 × area of front face
Using symbols, we write: $SA = 2lw + 2hw + 2lh$
Since the congruent faces occur in pairs, this formula can be written as:
$SA = 2(lw + hw + lh)$
In this formula,
l represents length,
w represents width,
and h represents height.

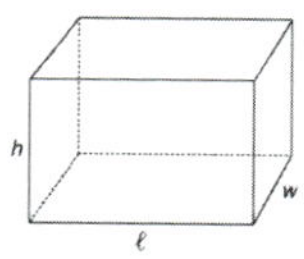

The volume of a rectangular prism is the space occupied by the prism.
One formula for the volume is: Volume = area of base × height
Using symbols, we write: $V = lwh$

Skills You'll Need 97

Alternative Example 2

Make a pictorial diagram of this square pyramid.

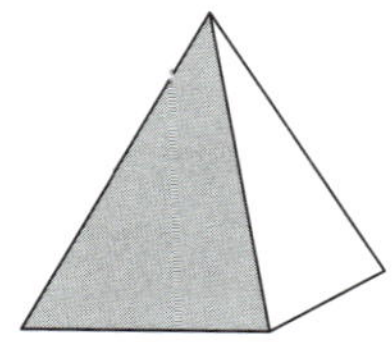

Solution

The base of the pyramid is a square.

In a pictorial diagram, a square is a parallelogram.

Draw a parallelogram.

Find the midpoint of the base by drawing diagonals and finding where they meet.

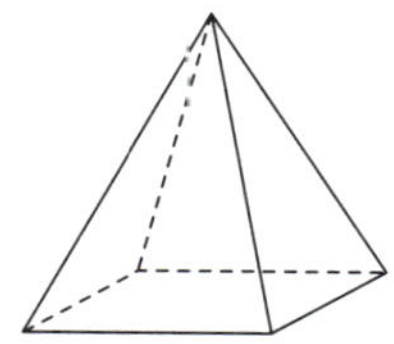

Draw a vertex vertically above the point, then join each vertex of the base to the top vertex for edges.

As students work, observe their methods of drawing and note any students who use a different method to produce the correct isometric diagram. Have these students share their methods with the class. Some students may draw an object from a different perspective. Discuss these differences and how the isometric diagram changes when the object is turned around or drawn from a different angle. In the Student Book, diagrams are drawn from a front/right/top perspective. Students are not wrong if they draw a diagram from a different perspective.

Common Misconceptions

➤ Students do not know how to start their drawings.
How to Help: Have a student work with a partner who has good spatial sense. As the partner *slowly* completes each part of the diagram, the student sees how the diagram relates to the object. Depth perception can be a difficult concept for some students, and these students may become frustrated. A simple test about 3-D vision can be found at *http://www.vision3d.com/stereo.html* (accessed June, 2005).

Alternative Example 3

A rectangular prism has dimensions 4.2 cm by 1.8 cm by 2.5 cm.

a) Calculate the surface area.
b) Calculate the volume.

Solution

Draw and label a pictorial diagram.

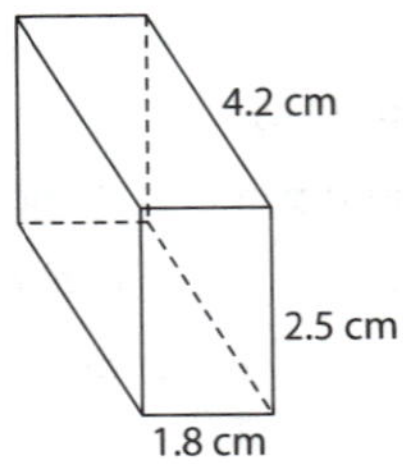

a) $SA = 2(lw + hw + lh)$

Substitute: $l = 4.2$, $w = 1.8$, and $h = 2.5$

$SA = 2(4.2 \times 1.8 + 2.5 \times 1.8 + 4.2 \times 2.5)$
$= 2(7.56 + 4.5 + 10.5)$
$= 2(22.56)$
$= 45.12$

The surface area is 45.12 cm^2.

b) $V = lwh$

Substitute: $l = 4.2$, $w = 1.8$, and $h = 2.5$

$V = 4.2 \times 1.8 \times 2.5$
$= 18.9$

The volume is 18.9 cm^3.

Example 3

A rectangular prism has dimensions 4 m by 6 m by 3 m.
a) Calculate the surface area. **b)** Calculate the volume.

Solution

Draw and label a pictorial diagram.

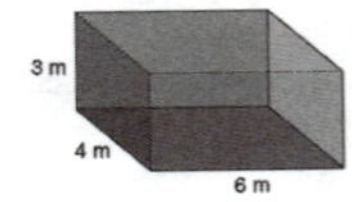

a) Use the formula for the surface area of a rectangular prism:
$SA = 2(lw + hw + lh)$
Substitute: $l = 6$, $w = 4$, and $h = 3$
$SA = 2(6 \times 4 + 3 \times 4 + 6 \times 3)$ In the brackets, multiply then add.
$= 2(24 + 12 + 18)$
$= 2(54)$
$= 108$
The surface area is 108 m^2.

Area and surface area are measured in square units (m^2).

b) Use the formula for the volume of a rectangular prism:
$V = lwh$
Substitute: $l = 6$, $w = 4$, and $h = 3$
$V = 6 \times 4 \times 3$
$= 72$
The volume is 72 m^3.

Volume is measured in cubic units (m^3).

A cube is a regular polyhedron with 6 square faces. Since all the faces of a cube are congruent, we can simplify the formulas for surface area and volume. Each edge length is *s*.
The area of each square face is: $s \times s = s^2$
So, the surface area of a cube is: $SA = 6s^2$
The volume of a cube is: $V = s \times s \times s = s^3$

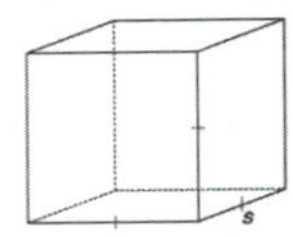

✓ Check

3. Find the surface area and volume of each rectangular prism. Include a labelled pictorial diagram for each rectangular prism.
a) 12 cm by 6 cm by 8 cm **b)** 7 mm by 7 mm by 4 mm
c) 2.50 m by 3.25 m by 3.25 m **d)** 5 cm by 5 cm by 5 cm

98 UNIT 3: Geometry and Measurement

Calculating the Surface Area and Volume of a Rectangular Prism

Use a large rectangular prism and its corresponding net to illustrate the concepts on page 97. As with the matching of measurements to variables, it does not matter which face is designated *base*, *side*, or *front*. When the prism is rotated, the front face (as well as the other faces) changes.

When you review the two formulas for surface area, ensure students understand that both formulas represent the same area. In the first formula, the area of each different face is doubled and the areas are added. In the second formula, the area of each different face is calculated, then the areas are added, and their sum is doubled. Use the formula $SA = 2lw + 2hw + 2lh$ to verify the answer to *Example 3*, part a.

$SA = 2lw + 2hw + 2lh$

Substitute: $l = 6$, $w = 4$, $h = 3$

$SA = 2(6 \times 4) + 2(3 \times 4) + 2(6 \times 3)$
$= 2(24) + 2(12) + 2(18)$
$= 48 + 24 + 36$
$= 108$

The surface area is 108 m^2.

Remind students that the 2s in the formulas for surface area are *constant*; that is, their values do not change, while *l*, *w*, and *h* are *variables*, so their values do change.

Review the formula for the volume of a rectangular prism. Remind students that the volume of a prism is the amount of space it occupies. Ensure students understand how Volume = base area × height is $V = (l \times w) \times h$, or $V = lwh$. Remind students that we do not need to use multiplication signs with the product of variables.

Calculating the Area of a Triangle

... of a triangle is calculated with either of these formulas:
...ase × height ÷ 2, or
... one-half × base × height
Using symbols,
we write: $A = \frac{bh}{2}$ or $A = \frac{1}{2}bh$
where b is the length of the base and h is the corresponding height.

These formulas are equivalent. Dividing bh by 2 is the same as multiplying bh by $\frac{1}{2}$.

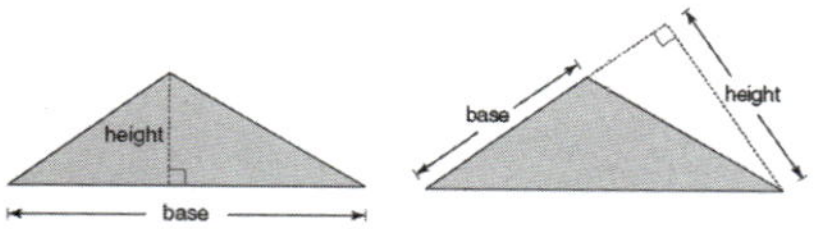

Example 4

The side lengths of △PQR are 12 cm, 5 cm, and 13 cm.

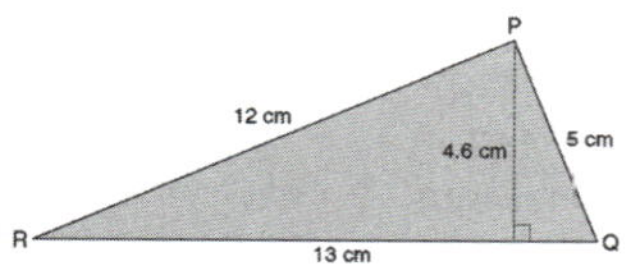

a) The height from P to QR is about 4.6 cm.
Use this to calculate the area of △PQR.

b) Triangle PQR is a right triangle with ∠P = 90°.
Use this to calculate the area of △PQR a different way.

Solution

a) Use the formula: $A = \frac{bh}{2}$
Substitute: $b = 13$ and $h = 4.6$

$A = \frac{13 \times 4.6}{2}$
$= \frac{59.8}{2}$
$= 29.9$

The area is 30 cm² to the nearest square centimetre.

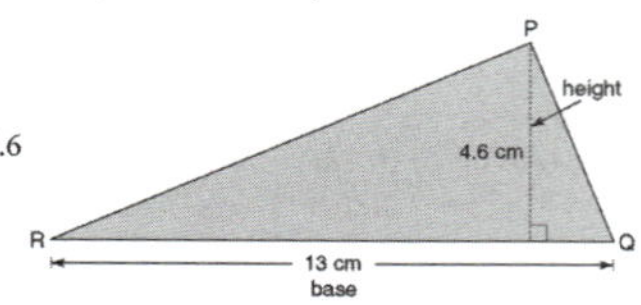

Skills You'll Need 99

Alternative Example 4

Calculate the area of △ABC.

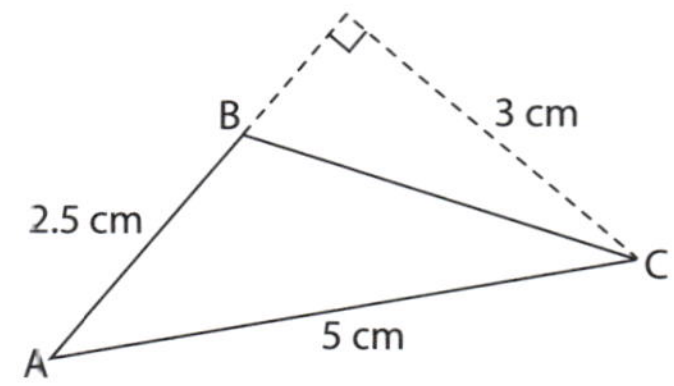

Solution

Use the formula: $A = \frac{bh}{2}$
△ABC is an obtuse triangle, so one height is outside the triangle.
Substitute: $b = 2.5$ and $h = 3$

$A = \frac{2.5 \times 3}{2}$
$= \frac{7.5}{2}$
$= 3.75$

The area is 3.75 cm².

Common Misconceptions

➤ Students do not know how to relate a measurement to each variable.

How to Help: Ensure students understand that it does not matter which of the 3 given dimensions is labelled as l, w, or h. For the volume formula, three numbers are multiplied, and their product is the same regardless of the order in which they were multiplied. For the surface area formula, the three measurements are multiplied in pairs, then added. Again, the order does not matter.

Calculating the Area of a Triangle

Students developed the formula for the area of a triangle in Grade 6. If necessary, remind students of the relationship between the area of a triangle and the area of a parallelogram with the same base and height. Use a 1-cm grid transparency on the overhead projector. Draw a parallelogram with base 6 cm and height 4 cm. Draw a diagonal in the parallelogram. Ask:

- What do we get when a diagonal is drawn?
  (*The diagonal divides the parallelogram into 2 congruent triangles.*)
- What is the formula for the area of a parallelogram?
  (*$A = bh$*)
- What is the area of this parallelogram?
  (*$A = 6 \times 4 = 24$; 24 cm²*)
- What is the area of each triangle?
  (*The area of each triangle is one-half the area of the parallelogram: $\frac{1}{2}$ of 24 cm² = 12 cm².*)

Sample Solutions

1. a)

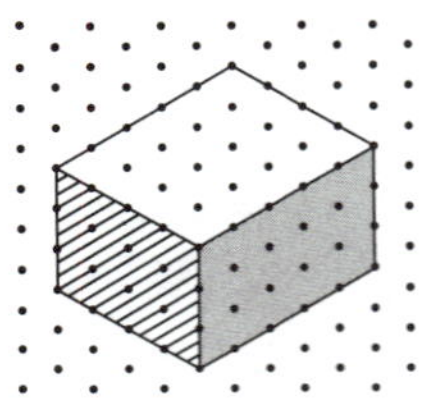

b)

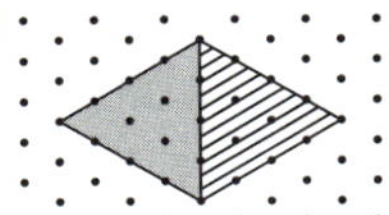

2. a)

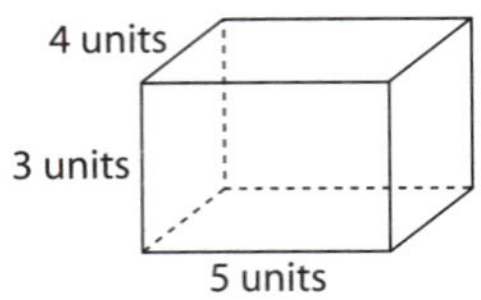

b)

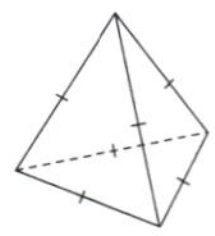

3. a) $SA = 432\ \text{cm}^2;\ V = 576\ \text{cm}^3$
   b) $SA = 210\ \text{mm}^2;\ V = 196\ \text{mm}^3$
   c) $SA = 53.625\ \text{m}^2;\ V \doteq 26.41\ \text{m}^3$
   d) $SA = 150\ \text{cm}^2;\ V = 125\ \text{cm}^3$
   Students' responses should include a labelled pictorial diagram.

b) Since $\triangle PQR$ is a right triangle, the two sides that form the right angle are the base and height.
$\angle QPR = 90°$, so $QP = 5$ cm is the height; and $PR = 12$ cm is the base.
Use the formula: $A = \frac{bh}{2}$
Substitute: $b = 12$ and $h = 5$

$A = \frac{12 \times 5}{2}$
$= \frac{60}{2}$
$= 30$

The area is 30 cm².

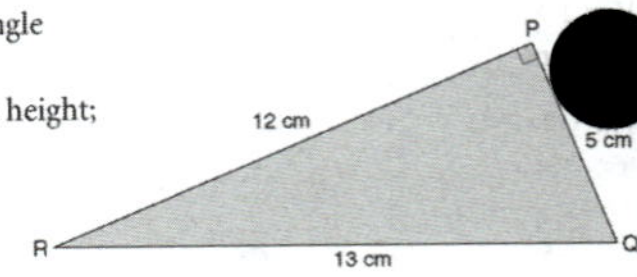

Any triangle has 3 sets of base and height. All sets produce the same area.

✓ Check

4. Calculate the area of each triangle.

a)

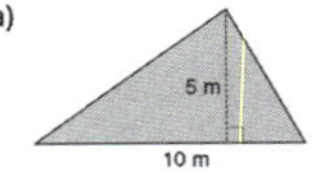

25 m²

b)

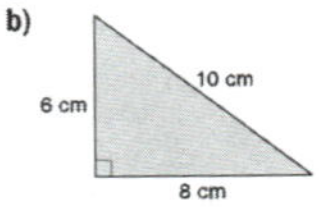

24 cm²

c)

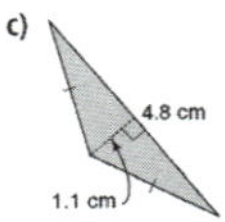

2.64 cm²

Converting among Units of Measure

1 m = 100 cm

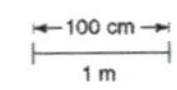

The area of a square with side length 1 m is:
$A = 1\ \text{m} \times 1\ \text{m}$
$= 1\ \text{m}^2$

The area of a square with side length 100 cm is:
$A = 100\ \text{cm} \times 100\ \text{cm}$
$= 10\ 000\ \text{cm}^2$
So, $1\ \text{m}^2 = 10\ 000\ \text{cm}^2$, or $10^4\ \text{cm}^2$

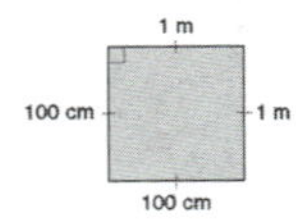

- How can we use the formula for the area of a parallelogram to get a formula for the area of a triangle? (*The area of a triangle is one-half the area of a parallelogram with the same base and height. So, the area of a triangle is* $A = \frac{bh}{2}$, *or* $A = \frac{1}{2}bh$.)

Students might need help to recognize the three different bases and corresponding heights of a triangle. Remind students that the height and base of a triangle must always be at right angles.

Common Misconceptions

➤ Students have difficulty evaluating the fraction in the formula.

How to Help: Remind students that $\frac{1}{2} = 0.5$, so $\frac{1}{2}bh = 0.5bh = 0.5 \times b \times h$. When students use the formula in this form, they do not need to divide.

Converting among Units of Measure

Use a metre stick to remind students of the relationship between metres and centimetres. Draw a 1-m by 1-m square on the board. Place a 1-cm cube inside it.

Hold the metre stick at one vertex of the square, and at right angles to the board, to illustrate one cubic metre.

Example 5 shows students how to convert from larger units to smaller units by multiplying by a power of 10. This is a curriculum requirement. Students are also required to divide by powers of 10; question 5a, b, and c review this concept. Use *Alternative Example 5* part b, to illustrate how to convert from smaller units to larger units.

The volume of a cube with edge length 1 m is:
$V = 1 \text{ m} \times 1 \text{ m} \times 1 \text{ m}$
m^3

The volume of a cube with edge length 100 cm is:
$V = 100 \text{ cm} \times 100 \text{ cm} \times 100 \text{ cm}$
$= 1\ 000\ 000 \text{ cm}^3$
So, $1 \text{ m}^3 = 1\ 000\ 000 \text{ cm}^3$, or 10^6 cm^3

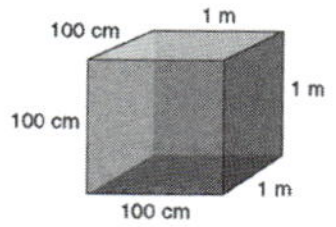

The volume of a cube with edge length 10 cm is:
$V = 10 \text{ cm} \times 10 \text{ cm} \times 10 \text{ cm}$
$= 1000 \text{ cm}^3$
Since $1 \text{ cm}^3 = 1 \text{ mL}$,
then $1000 \text{ cm}^3 = 1000 \text{ mL}$
$= 1 \text{ L}$

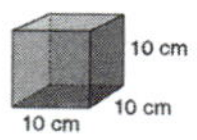

Example 5

Convert.

a) 0.72 m^2 to square centimetres

b) 1.05 m^3 to cubic centimetres

Solution

a) 0.72 m^2 to square centimetres
$1 \text{ m}^2 = 10\ 000 \text{ cm}^2$
So, $0.72 \text{ m}^2 = 0.72 \times 10\ 000 \text{ cm}^2$
$= 7200 \text{ cm}^2$

To multiply by 10 000, move the decimal point 4 places to the right.

b) 1.05 m^3 to cubic centimetres
$1 \text{ m}^3 = 1\ 000\ 000 \text{ cm}^3$, or 10^6 cm^3
So, $1.05 \text{ m}^3 = 1.05 \times 10^6 \text{ cm}^3$ ← This answer is in scientific notation.
$= 1\ 050\ 000 \text{ cm}^3$ ← This answer is in standard form.

Check

Convert. Write your answers in standard form and in scientific notation, where appropriate.

a) 726.5 cm to metres 7.265 m

b) 4300 cm^2 to square metres 0.43 m^2

c) $980\ 000 \text{ cm}^3$ to cubic metres 0.98 m^3

d) $4\ 280\ 000 \text{ cm}^3$ to litres 4280 L or 4.28×10^3 L

e) 8.75 m to centimetres 875 cm 8.75×10^2 cm

f) 1.36 m^2 to square centimetres $13\ 600 \text{ cm}^2$ or $1.36 \times 10^4 \text{ cm}^2$

g) 14.98 m^3 to cubic centimetres $14\ 980\ 000 \text{ cm}^3$ or $1.498 \times 10^7 \text{ cm}^3$

h) 9.87 L to cubic centimetres 9870 cm^3 or $9.87 \times 10^3 \text{ cm}^3$

Alternative Example 5

Convert.

a) 3.4 m^3 to cubic centimetres

b) $27\ 500 \text{ cm}^2$ to square metres

Solution

a) 3.4 m^3 to cubic centimetres
$1 \text{ m}^3 = 1\ 000\ 000 \text{ cm}^3$
So, $3.4 \text{ m}^3 = 3.4 \times 1\ 000\ 000 \text{ cm}^3$
$= 3\ 400\ 000 \text{ cm}^3$
$= 3.4 \times 10^6 \text{ cm}^3$

b) $27\ 500 \text{ cm}^2$ to square metres
$1 \text{ m}^2 = 10\ 000 \text{ cm}^2$
So, $27\ 500 \text{ cm}^2 = \frac{27\ 500}{10\ 000} \text{ m}^2$
$= 2.75 \text{ m}^2$

Remind students that dividing by 10 000 is the same as multiplying by $\frac{1}{10\ 000}$, or 0.0001.

So, an alternative way to convert square centimetres to square metres is to multiply by 0.0001; that is,
$27\ 500 \text{ cm}^2 = 27\ 500 \times 0.0001 \text{ m}^2$
$= 2.75 \text{ m}^2$

Similarly, to convert cubic centimetres to cubic metres, multiply by $\frac{1}{1\ 000\ 000}$, or 0.000 001.

Common Misconceptions

➤ Students have difficulty deciding whether to multiply or divide when converting units.

How to Help: Have students think about the result. If they convert from a large unit to a smaller unit, there will be more smaller units than large units, and the way to get more is to multiply.

Similarly, if they convert from a small unit to a larger unit, there will be fewer larger units, and the way to get fewer units is to divide. Suggest students write this aid on an index card as a reference:

Divide: cm → m; cm^2 → m^2; cm^3 → m^3; cm^3 → L

Multiply: m → cm; m^2 → cm^2; m^3 → cm^3; L → cm^3

Building and Sketching Objects

LESSON ORGANIZER (optional but recommended)

Curriculum Focus: Recognize, build, and sketch an object given different views of the object.

Teacher Materials
- linking cubes
- square dot paper transparency (PM 22)
- isometric dot paper transparency (PM 23)

Optional
- hexagonal prism

Student Materials
- linking cubes
- 1-cm grid paper (PM 20)
- square dot paper (PM 22)
- isometric dot paper (PM 23)

Optional
- Step-by-Step 1 (Master 3.8)
- Extra Practice 1 (Master 3.14)

Assessment: Master 3.2 Ongoing Observations: Geometry and Measurement

Key Math Learnings

1. Two-dimensional views of an object can be used to build and sketch the object.
2. Each view of an object provides information about the shape of the object.

3.1 Building and Sketching Objects

Focus Recognize, build, and sketch an obje given different views of the

When we draw a view of an object, we show internal line segments only where the depth or thickness of the object changes.
Here is an object made with 7 linking cubes.

Here are the views:

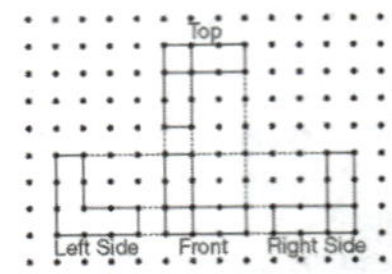

The broken lines show how the views are aligned.

Explore

Work in a group of 3.
Each student needs 8 linking cubes and isometric dot paper.
Each student chooses *one* of these views.

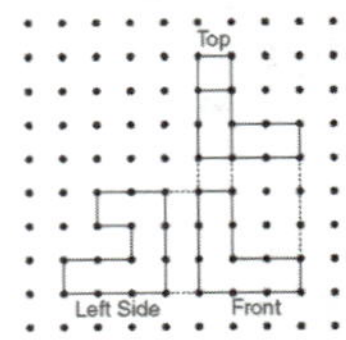

You use 8 cubes to build an object that matches the view you chose.
Sketch your object on isometric paper.
Use your cubes to build, then sketch, a different object with the view you chose.

Reflect & Share

Compare your objects with those of other members of your group.
Does any object match all 3 views?
If not, build and sketch one that does.
What helped you decide the shape of the object?
Are any other views needed to identify the object? Explain.

102 UNIT 3: Geometry and Measurement

Curriculum Note

In this lesson, students recognize, build, and sketch an object given different views of the object. While this material is not a Grade 8 curriculum expectation, *Practice* question 5 addresses the curriculum outcome:

- Determine, through investigation using concrete materials, the relationship among the number of faces, edges, and vertices of a polyhedron. (8m51)

Have students complete this question.
The Additional Activity, *The Platonic Solids* (Master 3.6a) also addresses this outcome. Have students complete this activity.

BEFORE Get Started

Use 7 linking cubes to build the object shown in the introduction to the lesson.

Show the class one view of the object at a time. Have students relate each view to the views drawn in the Student Book. Ensure students understand why internal line segments are drawn in some views, and what they represent. Tell students that many different objects may share one or more of these views, but that when 3 or 4 views of an object are given, only one object usually fits all the views.

If you have not already done so, review *Skills You'll Need*, page 96, *Drawing Isometric and Pictorial Diagrams.*

Present *Explore*. Distribute 24 linking cubes to each group of students.

DURING Explore

Ongoing Assessment: Observe and Listen

As students work, ask questions, such as:
- How did you make an object that matched your view?
  (*I put 5 linking cubes together to make the front view, then placed the other 3 cubes behind the front view, so that the front view was not affected.*)

Connect

Each view of an object provides information about the shape of the object. When an object is built with linking cubes, the top, front, and side views are often enough to identify and build the object. These views are drawn with the top view above the front view, and the side views beside the front view, as they were at the top of page 102. In this way, matching edges are adjacent.

Example Which object has these views?

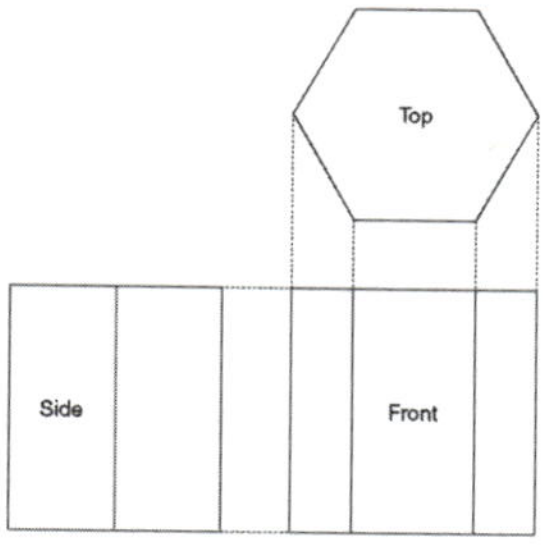

Solution The top view is a regular hexagon.
The side view is 2 congruent rectangles.
The front view is 3 rectangles, 2 of which are congruent.
This object is a hexagonal prism.

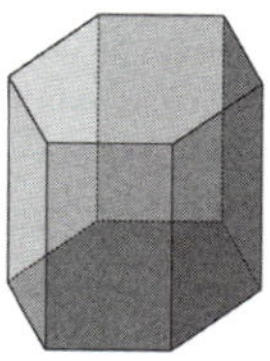

REACHING ALL LEARNERS

Early Finishers

Have students add one cube to the object they built in *Practice* questions 4, 6, or 7, then draw the views of the new object.

Common Misconceptions

➤ Students have difficulty building an object to match a given set of views.

How to Help: Have students use the views to find the overall dimensions of the object: the length and width can be determined from the top view, and the height can be determined from the front view. Have students build a rectangular prism with these dimensions, then take away cubes as they try to match each view.

Sample Solutions

1.

Object/View	Top	Bottom	Front	Left	Right
H	A	A	B	B*	B*
I	C	C	B	B	B
J	B	B		D	D
K		A	A	A*	A*
L				D	B*

* These rectangles and triangles will not look exactly as shown because of perspective.

2. Front View of Object J Top View of Object K

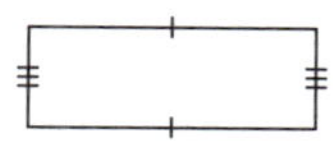

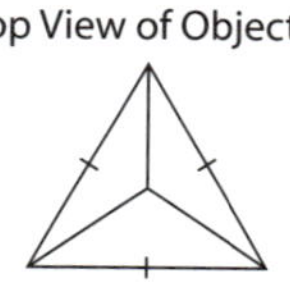

- Did you find an object that matched all 3 views? (*Not at first; we had several objects that matched the front and left side views, but the change in depth in the top view was not found in the objects we had drawn.*)
- Which view helped you decide the shape of the object?
(*The top view was the only view with a change in depth, so it helped us decide on the shape.*)
- Would another view have helped identify the object? (*Yes, if we'd had the right side view, we could more easily have made the object.*)

Have students who finish early try to build an object that would require more than 3 views to identify.

AFTER Connect

What you might see:

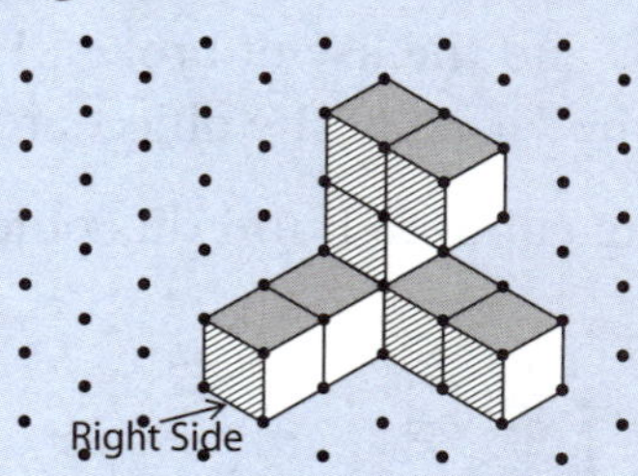

The top view shows three depth changes, but none of these changes is visible on the left side view or front view. Six cubes are needed to make the left side view. Adding 2 more cubes to the side view to make the front view creates the necessary depth changes in the top view, and uses all 8 cubes. So, no other views are needed to identify the object.

3. The hidden cube is green.

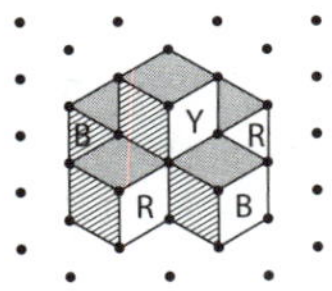

4. b)

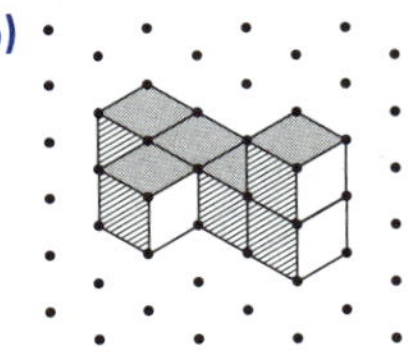

5. a) i)

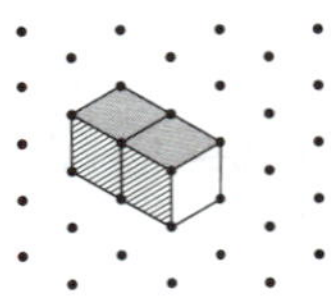

ii)

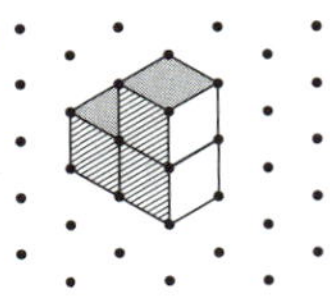

iii)

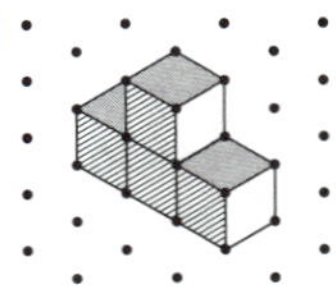

iv)

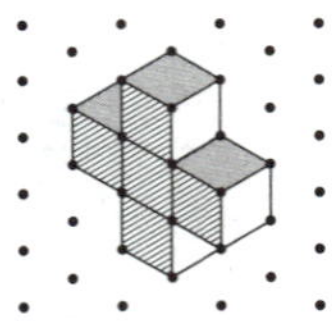

v)

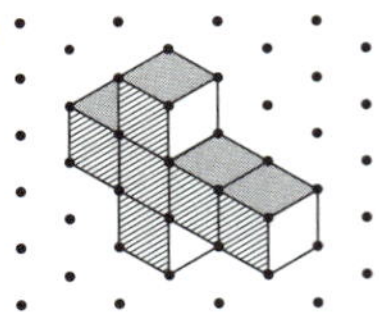

b)

Number of Cubes	Faces	Vertices	Edges
2	6	8	12
3	8	12	18
4	12	14	24
5	14	24	36
6	14	24	36

6. b)

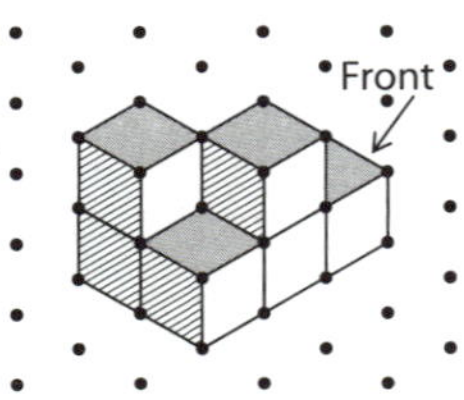

c)

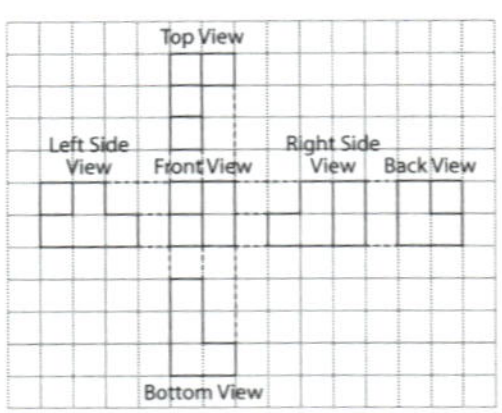

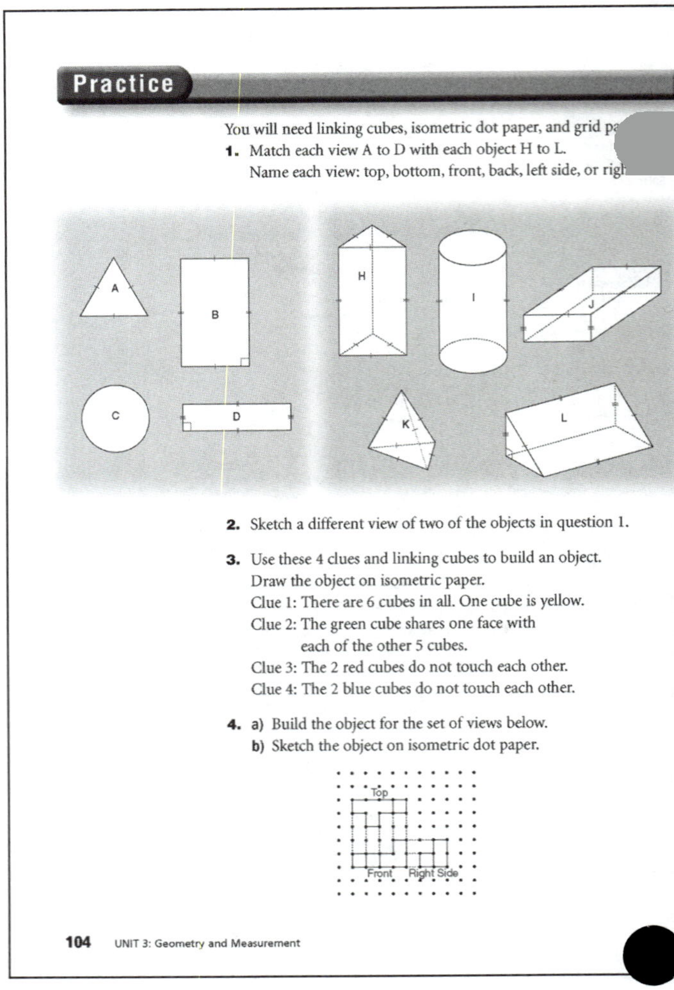

Practice

You will need linking cubes, isometric dot paper, and grid pa

1. Match each view A to D with each object H to L.
Name each view: top, bottom, front, back, left side, or righ

2. Sketch a different view of two of the objects in question 1.
3. Use these 4 clues and linking cubes to build an object.
Draw the object on isometric paper.
Clue 1: There are 6 cubes in all. One cube is yellow.
Clue 2: The green cube shares one face with each of the other 5 cubes.
Clue 3: The 2 red cubes do not touch each other.
Clue 4: The 2 blue cubes do not touch each other.
4. a) Build the object for the set of views below.
b) Sketch the object on isometric dot paper.

104 UNIT 3: Geometry and Measurement

Have groups show the object they decided matched all three views. Discuss any differences. Reinforce the standard arrangement of the views, and the use of broken lines to show how the views of the object are aligned.

Use 8 linking cubes to build this object.

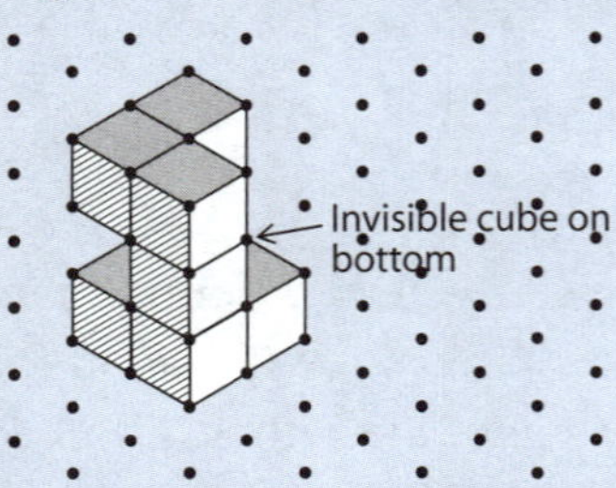

Discuss with students why the top view, front view, and left side view are not enough to identify this object. Without the right side or bottom view, it is impossible to tell if the bottom layer has 3 or 4 cubes.

Review the *Example*. Use a hexagonal prism to show students the different views.

Practice

In question 5, many different objects can be built. Care must be taken when counting the faces (F), edges (E), and vertices (V) to find the relationship $F + V - E = 2$. Two connected cubes make a rectangular prism, with 6 faces, 12 edges, and 8 vertices. Make sure students do not count the adjacent edges (and faces) of 2 cubes as 2 edges (or 2 faces) instead of 1.

Assessment Focus: Question 6

The side view shows that the object is 2 cubes high and 3 cubes wide. Some students may build objects that match one view, then check to see if any object matches the other view. Other students may make an object that fits one view, then add cubes to try to match the other view. Students should find that the object has 6 cubes. The isometric diagram of the object shows the back view, to include the cube that is not visible from the front or right side.

The relationship in part c [...] Euler's formula. It [...] for a Swiss [...]matician, Leonhard Euler, who lived in the 18th century.

5. a) Build an object with each number of linking cubes.
For 3 or more cubes, do *not* make a rectangular prism.
i) 2 ii) 3 iii) 4 iv) 5 v) 6
b) For each object you build, count the number of its faces, edges, and vertices. Record your results in a table.
c) Look for a pattern in the table in part b.
For any object, how are the numbers of faces, edges, and vertices related? Vertices + Faces − Edges = 2
d) Build an object with 7 linking cubes.
Check that the relationship in part c is true.

[Nu]mber Strategies

[Writ]e each number in [scie]ntific notation.

[...]590 000 $3.59 \times 10^{[...]}$
[...]0 400 000 4.04×10^{7}
[...]98 759 $3.987\ 59 \times 10^{5}$

6. Assessment Focus
a) Use these views to build an object.

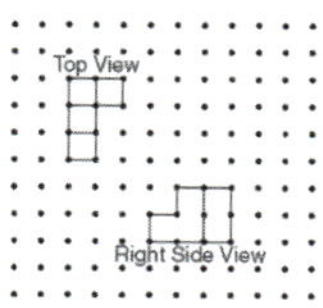

b) Sketch the object on isometric dot paper.
c) Draw the other views of the object.

7. a) Use these views to build an object. A shaded region has no cubes.
b) Sketch the object. Explain your work.

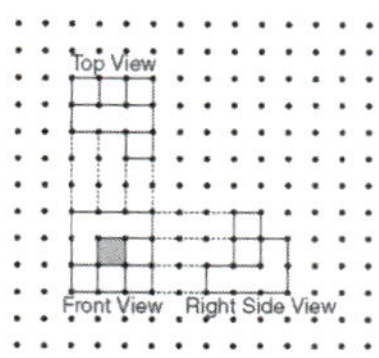

Reflect

How do views help to show a three-dimensional object? Use an example to explain.

7. b)

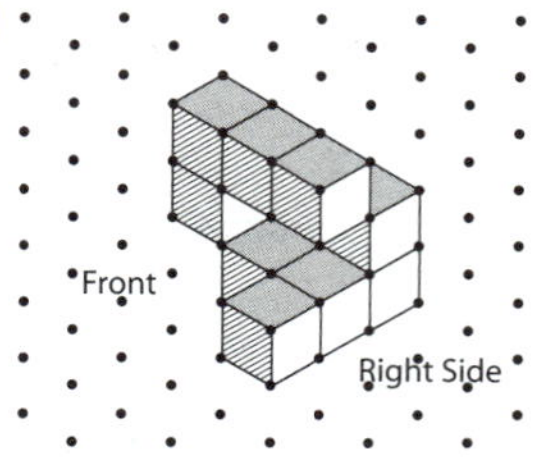

REFLECT: I used the set of views in question 4. Each view tells me about the shape of the object and its dimensions; for example, the object is 4 cubes long, 2 cubes wide, and 2 cubes high. The internal line segments show where the depth of the object changes. The broken lines show how the views are aligned. I can use these views to build the object, then sketch the object on isometric paper.

Assignment Guidelines

If your students do not have time to complete all the *Practice* questions on pages 104 and 105, these questions provide minimum curriculum coverage: 1, 4, 5, 6, 7, *Reflect*

To assess the 4 Achievement Chart categories listed in the curriculum document, have students complete these *Practice* questions:

Knowledge and Understanding: 1 Thinking: 7
Application: 6 Communication: *Reflect*

Number Strategies

Remind students that a number in scientific notation is written as a product of two factors: one factor is greater than or equal to 1 and less than 10, and the other factor is a power of 10.

ASSESSMENT FOR LEARNING

What to Look For	What to Do
Knowledge and Understanding ✔ Students recognize the changes in depth on views of an object. ✔ Students understand that each view of an object provides information about the shape of the object. ***Communication*** ✔ Students can explain how they use views to draw a 3-D diagram of the object. ***Application*** ✔ Students can draw an isometric diagram of an object, given its views.	***Extra Support:*** Students who have difficulty building an object for a given set of views may benefit from working with a partner so they can discuss their reasons for combining cubes in certain ways. Students can use Step-by-Step 1 (Master 3.8) to complete question 6. ***Extra Practice:*** Students can play the Additional Activity *Spin, Build, Draw* (Master 3.5a). Students can complete Extra Practice 1 (Master 3.14). ***Extension:*** Students can build their own object, create a set of views for the object, then trade views with a classmate and build their classmate's object. Encourage students to build an object where more than three views are needed to identify the object.

Recording and Reporting
Master 3.2 Ongoing Observations: Geometry and Measurement

Sketching and Folding Nets

LESSON ORGANIZER (optional)

Curriculum Focus: Sketch nets and use them to build objects.

Teacher Materials
- 1-cm grid transparency (PM 20)
- cube

Optional
- nets and corresponding polyhedra of objects in *Connect*
- triangular prism

Student Materials
- scissors
- tape
- 0.5-cm grid paper (PM 14)
- 1-cm grid paper (PM 20)
- square dot paper (PM 22)

Optional
- protractors
- compasses
- Step-by-Step 2 (Master 3.9)
- Extra Practice 2 (Master 3.15)

Assessment: Master 3.2 Ongoing Observations: Geometry and Measurement

Key Math Learnings

1. A net of a three-dimensional object can be drawn, then used to build the object.
2. Many views of an object are needed to create its net.

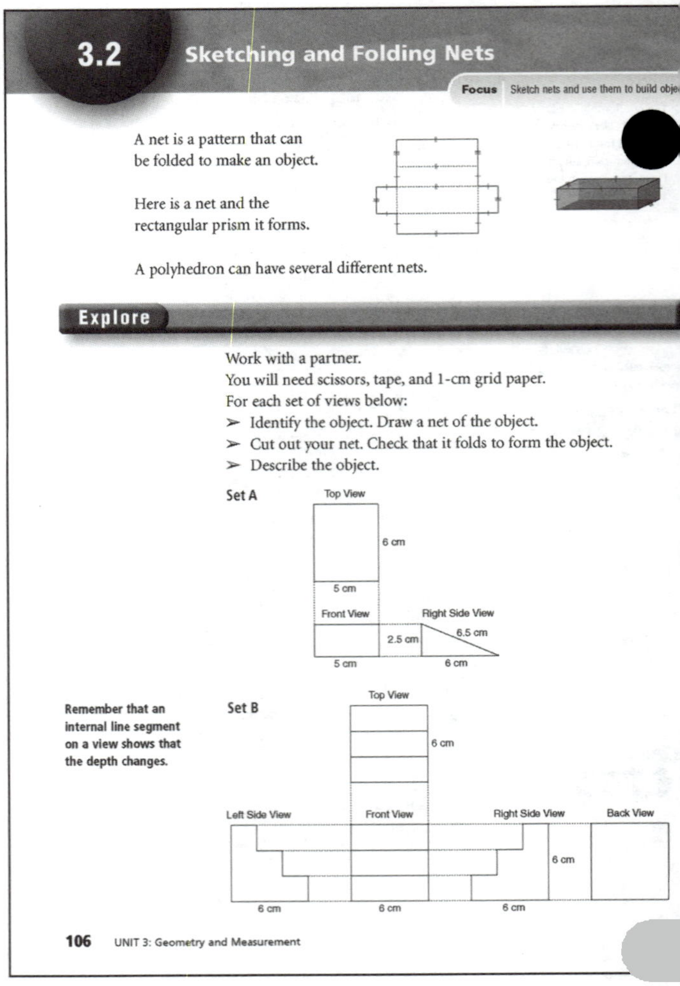

3.2 Sketching and Folding Nets

Focus Sketch nets and use them to build obje...

A net is a pattern that can be folded to make an object.

Here is a net and the rectangular prism it forms.

A polyhedron can have several different nets.

Explore

Work with a partner.
You will need scissors, tape, and 1-cm grid paper.
For each set of views below:
- ➢ Identify the object. Draw a net of the object.
- ➢ Cut out your net. Check that it folds to form the object.
- ➢ Describe the object.

106 UNIT 3: Geometry and Measurement

Curriculum Note

In this lesson, students sketch nets and use them to build objects. This material is not required by the Grade 8 curriculum.

BEFORE Get Started

Show students a cube. Use a 1-cm grid transparency to show students that there are 11 possible nets for a cube.

Have students sketch different nets on the board for the rectangular prism shown in the introduction.

Remind students that when a net is drawn, care must be taken to ensure that the measures of the side lengths are accurate, edges are drawn with a ruler, compasses are used for accurate constructions, and cutting is done neatly and precisely.

Present *Explore*. Encourage students to include the numbers of faces, edges, and vertices in the descriptions of their objects, and to ensure that Euler's formula ($F + V - E = 2$) applies.

DURING Explore

Ongoing Assessment: Observe and Listen

Watch as students measure, cut, and fold. Allow students to attempt to join edges that do not match. It is in the folding that they will

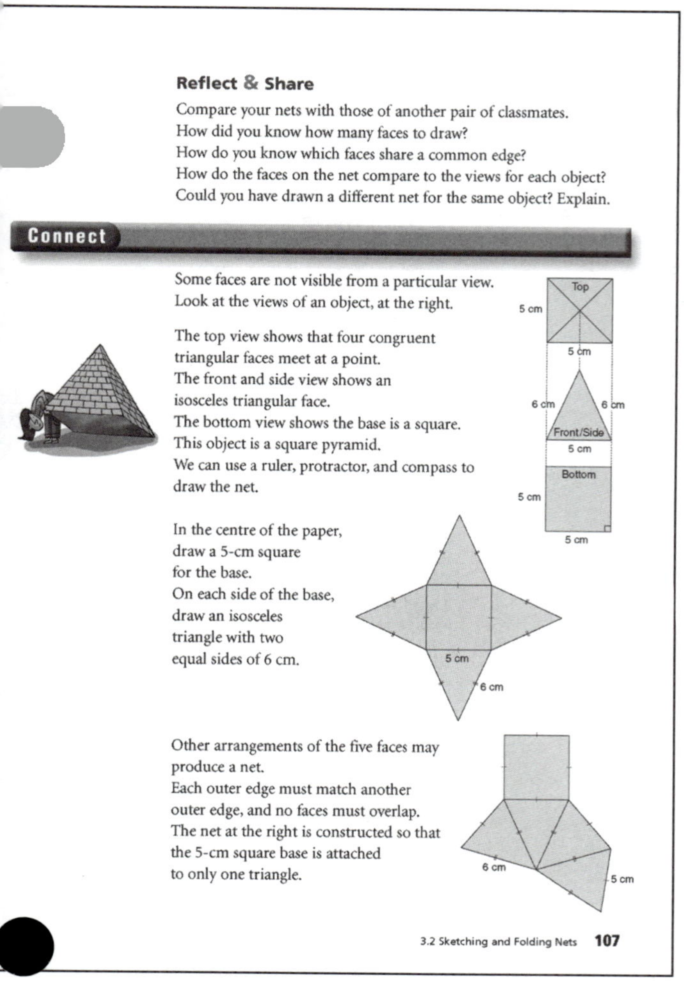

Reflect & Share

Compare your nets with those of another pair of classmates.
How did you know how many faces to draw?
How do you know which faces share a common edge?
How do the faces on the net compare to the views for each object?
Could you have drawn a different net for the same object? Explain.

Connect

Some faces are not visible from a particular view.
Look at the views of an object, at the right.

The top view shows that four congruent triangular faces meet at a point.
The front and side view shows an isosceles triangular face.
The bottom view shows the base is a square.
This object is a square pyramid.
We can use a ruler, protractor, and compass to draw the net.

In the centre of the paper, draw a 5-cm square for the base.
On each side of the base, draw an isosceles triangle with two equal sides of 6 cm.

Other arrangements of the five faces may produce a net.
Each outer edge must match another outer edge, and no faces must overlap.
The net at the right is constructed so that the 5-cm square base is attached to only one triangle.

3.2 Sketching and Folding Nets 107

REACHING ALL LEARNERS

Early Finishers

Challenge students to make a net for an object in the classroom, then cut out the net and build the object. Students compare their object to the original object to check for accuracy.

Common Misconceptions

➤ Students confuse "side view" with "side face."

How to Help: Use a triangular prism to demonstrate the difference in *Practice* question 1 part ii. The side face is a rectangle that measures 2 cm by 3 cm. The side view is a rectangle that has the same height, but shorter width. Show students the prism — place it so they look directly at the front view. Then, have the students move to see the prism from the side view. Because the side face is viewed at an angle, the view is a rectangle with a shorter width.

ESL Strategies

Students for whom English is a second language should make a list of the terms used in this unit, and draw a visual reminder of the meaning of each term. These terms may include isometric diagram, pictorial diagram, and net.

Number Strategies

Remind students that the perimeter is the distance around a figure. Students should round each answer up to the nearest can.

learn how to create the object correctly. Permit students to cut out faces and rejoin them with tape until they get a correct arrangement. Students can then unfold the object to see how the faces could be arranged to form a net.

As students work, ask questions, such as:

- How did you know how many faces to draw? (*Each change in depth represents a face of the object. All polygons in each face must be identified and any faces not shown must be included to find out the number of faces to draw.*)
- Which object does each set of views form? (*Set A is a right triangular prism and Set B is a set of stairs.*)
- Do the views show all the faces of each object? (*No, in Set A, the left side view and the bottom view are missing. I know a triangular prism has 2 congruent triangular faces and 3 rectangular faces. So, the left side view is a triangle congruent to the triangle in the right side view, and the bottom view is a rectangle. In Set B, the bottom view is missing. Because all views have dimensions 6 cm by 6 cm, the bottom view is a square with side length 6 cm.*)
- How do you know which faces share a common edge? (*Where the broken line segments meet the solid line segments in the views, there is a common vertex. The solid line segments inside the top view and the front view are fold lines.*)

AFTER — Connect

What you might see: Set A

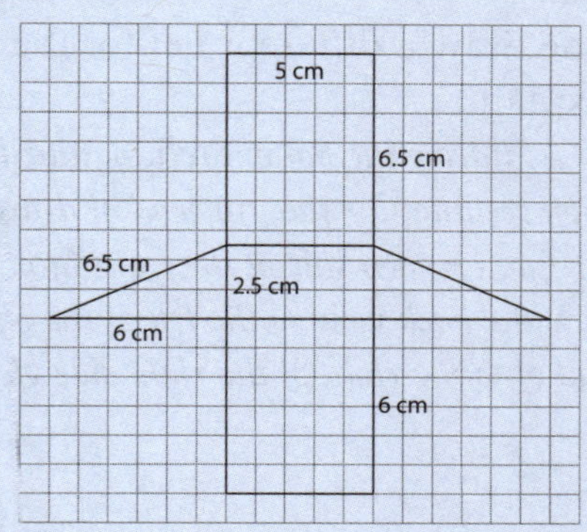

Sample Solutions

1. b) i)

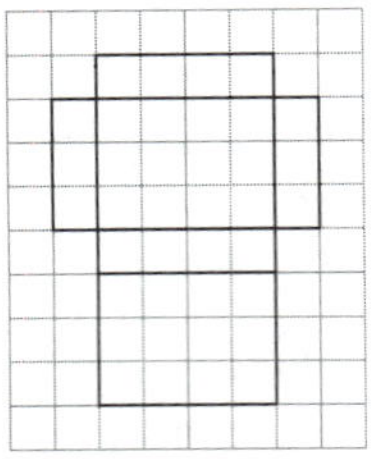

ii)

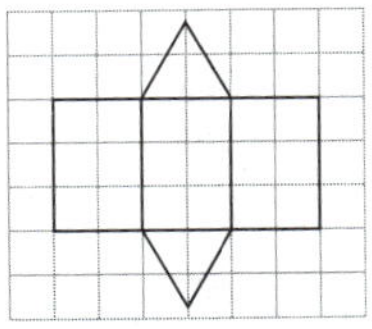

d) i) The rectangular prism has 6 faces, 8 vertices, and 12 edges. The front and back faces are congruent 6-cm by 8-cm rectangles. The top and bottom faces are congruent 2-cm by 8-cm rectangles. The side faces are congruent 2-cm by 6-cm rectangles.

ii) The triangular prism has 5 faces, 6 vertices, and 9 edges. The 3 rectangular faces are 2-cm by 3-cm rectangles. The two bases are congruent equilateral triangles with side length 2 cm.

2. a)

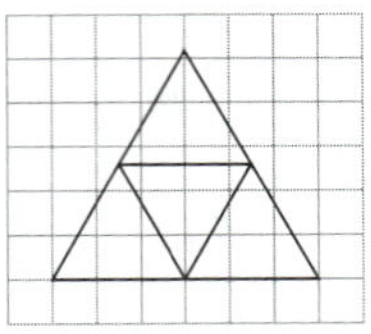

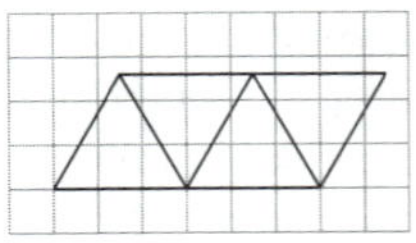

Each net folds to form a square pyramid.

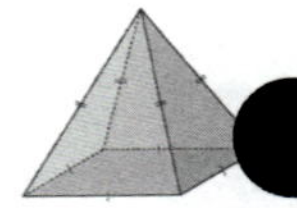

Many views of an object are needed to create its net, especially if the object is made with linking cubes.

Example

These four views show an object made with linking cubes. Use the views to draw a net for the object.

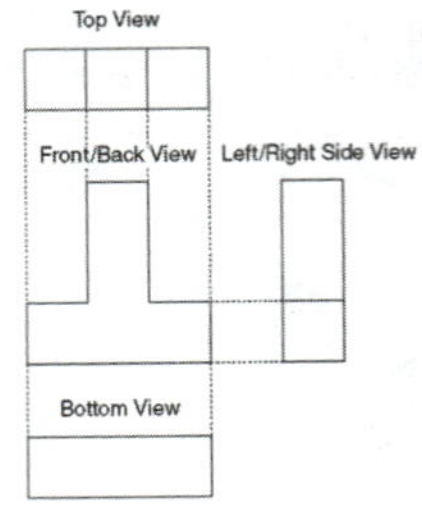

Solution

Use 1-cm dot paper.
Start with the simplest view, which is the bottom view.
Draw the bottom face.
Draw the front face and back face above and below the bottom face.
The top view and side views show a change in depth.
A new face is drawn for each depth change.
A side square is drawn for each depth change.

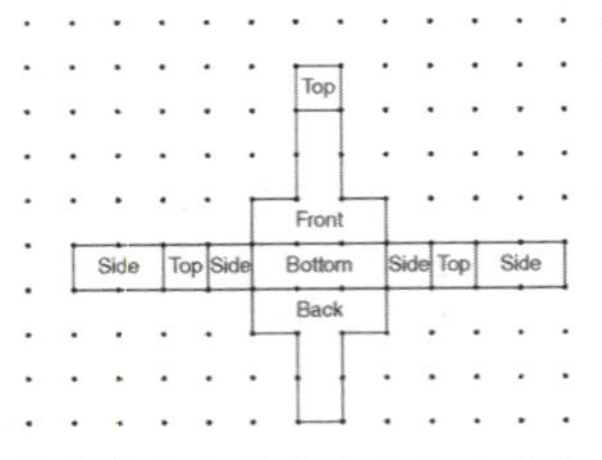

Each side view is drawn to touch the square that shows the change in depth.

108 UNIT 3: Geometry and Measurement

Set B

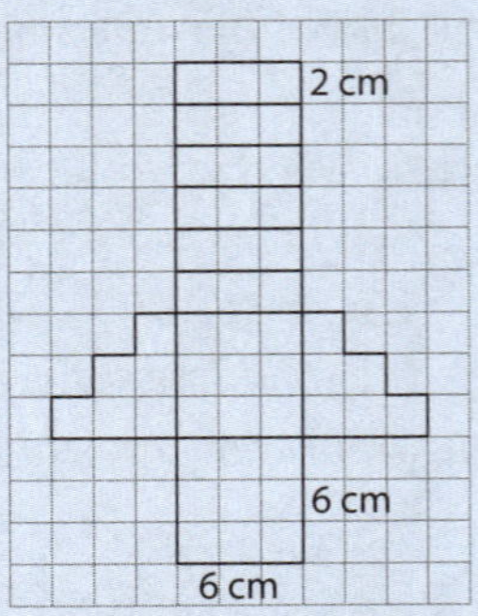

Have one pair of students share their nets with the class. Ask:

- Did anyone draw a different net for the same object? Explain.
(Yes, in Set A, I drew the bottom rectangular face above the top rectangular face, instead of drawing a rectangular face on each side of the front face. In Set B, I drew the back view to the left of the left side view instead of to the right of the right side view.)
- How do the faces on the net compare to the views for each object?
(When I draw a net, the dimensions of the faces must be exact to make sure the net fits together to form the object. When I draw the views, the dimensions may be different because of perspective.)
- How could you decide which net was the "best" net? (*By choosing the net that uses the least amount of materials, or that has the fewest joins*)

Introduce *Connect*. Use the square pyramid to show students another example where more than one net is possible for the same object. Initiate a discussion about which net students think is "better." There is no correct answer but their choices should be based on some criteria; for example, the second net is more compact and there is less wasted paper.

The net in the *Example* folds to form this object with 10 faces, including the bottom face.

The symmetry of the object made it easier to draw a net. Other arrangements of the 10 faces may be folded to form the object.

Practice

1. Each set of views below represents an object.

a) Identify each object.
b) Draw a net for the object.
c) Cut out the net. Build the object.
d) Describe the object.

i) Rectangular prism
ii) Equilateral triangular prism

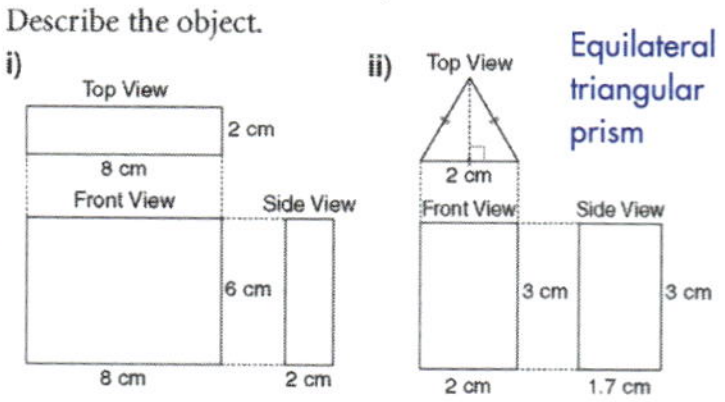

2. Each set of views represents an object. Draw 2 different nets for each object. Build the object.

a) Regular tetrahedron
b) Frustum of a square-based pyramid

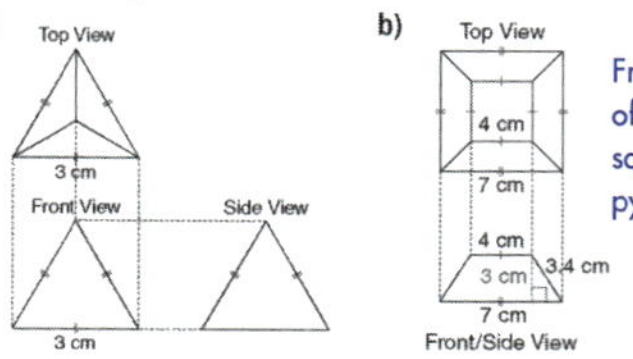

3. Choose one set of views from question 2. Describe the steps you used to draw the net.

b)

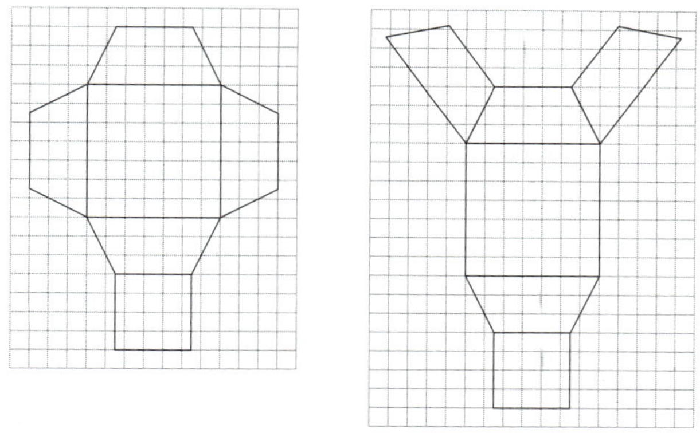

3. For the set of views in question 2a, I drew an equilateral triangle with side length 3 cm as the base of the tetrahedron. I then drew a congruent equilateral triangle on each side of the base triangle to make the other 3 faces. Each face shares one side with the base triangle.
For the set of views in question 2b, I drew a square with side length 7 cm as the base. I drew 4 congruent trapezoids of height 3 cm and parallel sides of lengths 4 cm and 7 cm to make the sloping faces. Each trapezoid shares one side with the square base. I drew a square with side length 4 cm on one trapezoid to make the top face.

4. a)

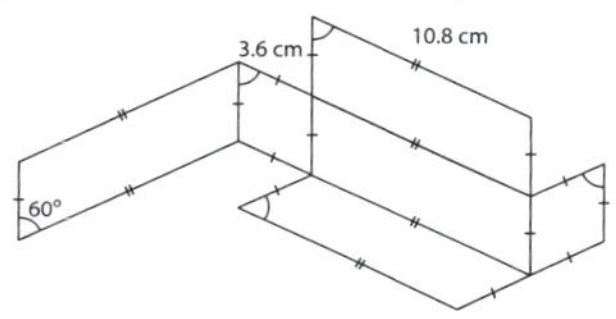

(Sample Solutions continue below, right.)

Practice

The drawing, cutting, and folding of nets is very time consuming. Have students work in pairs to share the work.

Some students may want to include tabs on the outside edges of their nets to help hold the nets together. Encourage students to make the "best" net by using the least amount of grid paper. Remind students to work with accuracy to ensure edges meet and objects can be built.

Assessment Focus: Question 6

Students could draw one net and then build the object, before attempting a second net. This way, the first net may give students insight into strategies that will help them build a better net the second time.

(Sample Solutions continued)

b) The cardboard net has tabs and other parts attached to it to allow the box to be glued together.

5. This net is for a hexagonal prism with two faces missing. Some students may assume only one face is missing.

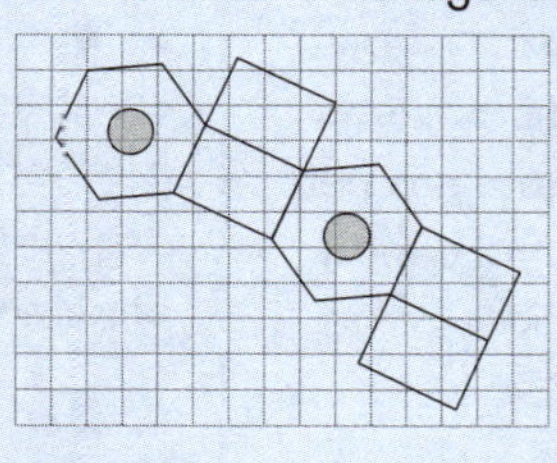

6. a) Irregular hexagonal prism; the base of the prism is the front view.

b) For example,

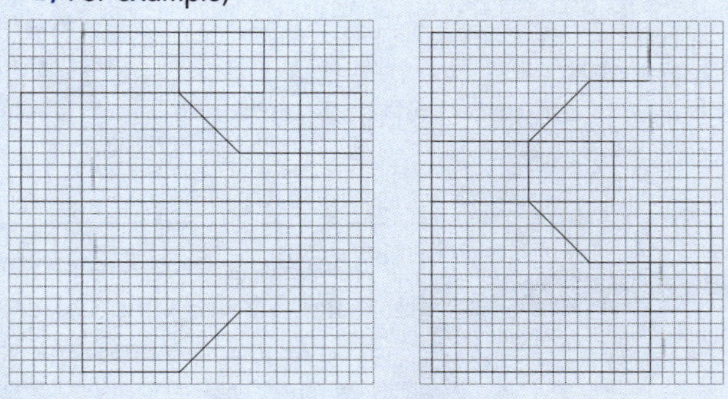

d) Some nets make better use of the grid paper. Some arrangements of the faces extend beyond the edge of the paper, so 2 sheets of paper have to be taped together. It is easier to fold the net if the longer line segments are fold lines and the shorter line segments are outside lines.

REFLECT: I used the set of views in question 6. The views show some faces of the object. The front view shows an irregular hexagon with no depth changes, so it is a good face to draw on the net first. Since the other views are rectangular faces, the object is a prism. I know that some faces are not visible from a particular view, but because the object is a prism, I know that a second congruent hexagon and more rectangular faces are needed. The dimensions of the figures on a net are accurate to ensure the net fits together. The dimensions of some figures in a set of views are different from the actual dimensions of the faces they represent because of the angle of view.

More than one correct net can be drawn for a set of views. In question 6, I created another net by arranging the faces differently. I had to make sure the faces still folded to make the object.

Assignment Guidelines

If your students do not have time to complete all the *Practice* questions on pages 109 and 110, these questions provide minimum curriculum coverage: 1 part i, 2 part ii, 5, 6, *Reflect*

To assess the 4 Achievement Chart categories listed in the curriculum document, have students complete these *Practice* questions:

Knowledge and Understanding: 1
Application: 2
Thinking: 5
Communication: *Reflect*

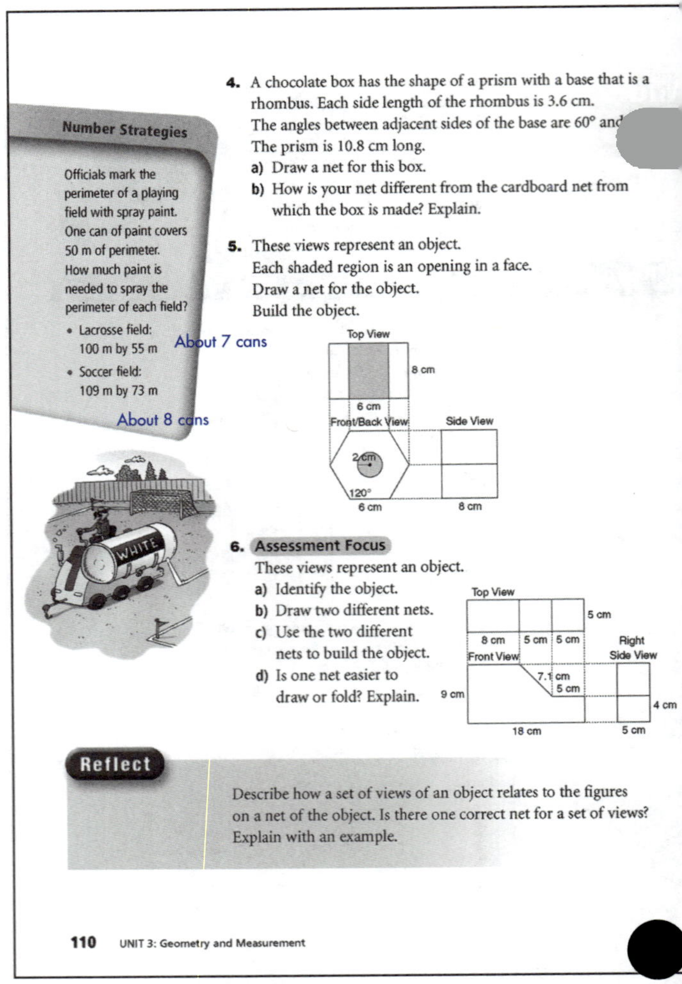

Number Strategies

Officials mark the perimeter of a playing field with spray paint. One can of paint covers 50 m of perimeter. How much paint is needed to spray the perimeter of each field?

- Lacrosse field: 100 m by 55 m — About 7 cans
- Soccer field: 109 m by 73 m — About 8 cans

4. A chocolate box has the shape of a prism with a base that is a rhombus. Each side length of the rhombus is 3.6 cm. The angles between adjacent sides of the base are 60° and [illegible]
The prism is 10.8 cm long.
a) Draw a net for this box.
b) How is your net different from the cardboard net from which the box is made? Explain.

5. These views represent an object.
Each shaded region is an opening in a face.
Draw a net for the object.
Build the object.

6. Assessment Focus
These views represent an object.
a) Identify the object.
b) Draw two different nets.
c) Use the two different nets to build the object.
d) Is one net easier to draw or fold? Explain.

Reflect

Describe how a set of views of an object relates to the figures on a net of the object. Is there one correct net for a set of views? Explain with an example.

110 UNIT 3: Geometry and Measurement

ASSESSMENT FOR LEARNING

What to Look For	What to Do
Knowledge and Understanding ✔ Students understand that many views of an object are needed to create its net. ✔ Students understand that more than one arrangement of the faces of an object may produce a net. ***Communication*** ✔ Students can explain the steps they used to draw a net. ***Application*** ✔ Students can draw, cut, and fold a net accurately.	***Extra Support:*** Students with fine motor problems will find the construction of nets difficult. Have them work with a supportive partner or allow them to use *The Geometer's Sketchpad* or other drawing programs to draw the nets. Students can use Step-by-Step 2 (Master 3.9) to complete question 6. ***Extra Practice:*** If they have not already done so, students can complete the Additional Activity *The Platonic Solids* (Master 3.6a). Students can complete Extra Practice 2 (Master 3.15). ***Extension:*** Have students draw a different net for the object in the *Example*.

Recording and Reporting
Master 3.2 Ongoing Observations: Geometry and Measurement

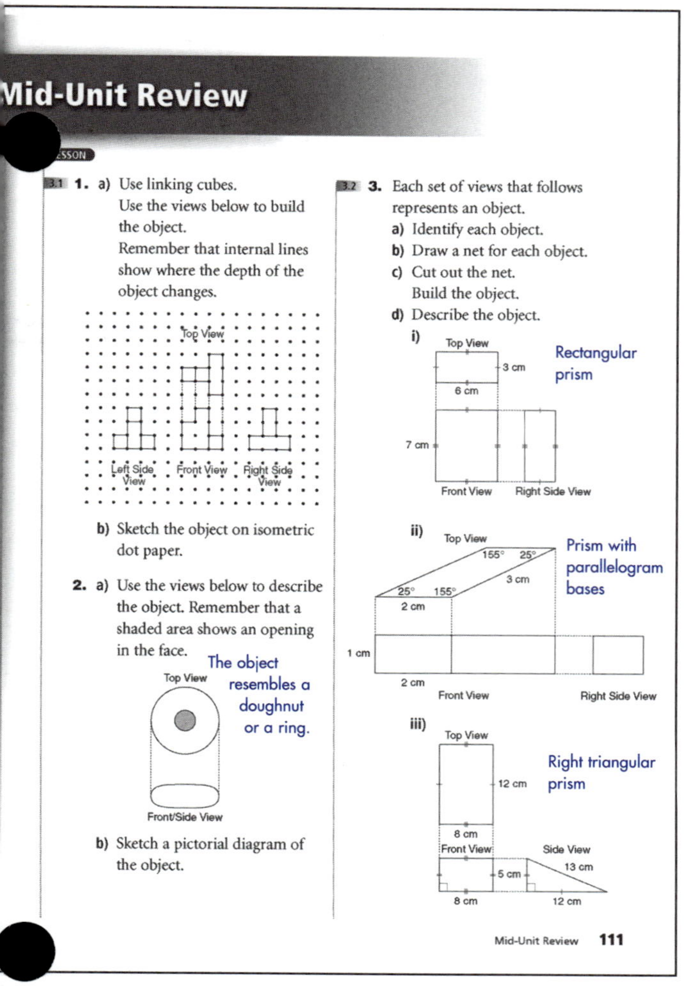

Mid-Unit Review

LESSON

3.1 **1. a)** Use linking cubes.
Use the views below to build the object.
Remember that internal lines show where the depth of the object changes.

Top View

Left Side View   Front View   Right Side View

b) Sketch the object on isometric dot paper.

2. a) Use the views below to describe the object. Remember that a shaded area shows an opening in the face. *The object resembles a doughnut or a ring.*

Top View

Front/Side View

b) Sketch a pictorial diagram of the object.

3.2 **3.** Each set of views that follows represents an object.
a) Identify each object.
b) Draw a net for each object.
c) Cut out the net.
Build the object.
d) Describe the object.

i) Top View, 3 cm, 6 cm, 7 cm, Front View, Right Side View — *Rectangular prism*

ii) Top View, 155°, 25°, 3 cm, 25°, 155°, 2 cm, 1 cm, 2 cm, Front View, Right Side View — *Prism with parallelogram bases*

iii) Top View, 12 cm, 8 cm, Front View, Side View, 5 cm, 13 cm, 8 cm, 12 cm — *Right triangular prism*

Mid-Unit Review 111

LESSON ORGANIZER

Student Materials
- linking cubes
- 1-cm grid paper (PM 20)
- scissors
- tape
- square dot paper (PM 22)
- isometric dot paper (PM 23)

Optional
- protractors
- compasses

Assessment: Masters 3.1 Unit Rubric: Geometry and Measurement, 3.4 Unit Summary: Geometry and Measurement

Sample Solutions

1. b)

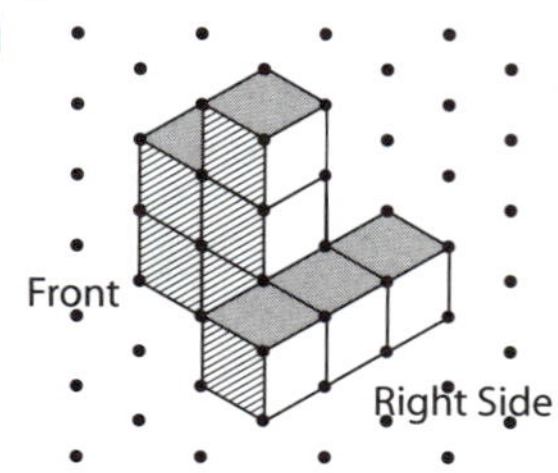

2. b)

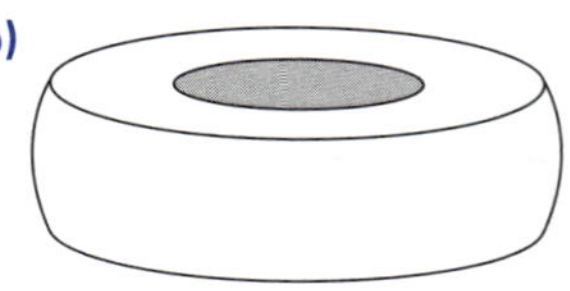

3. b) i)

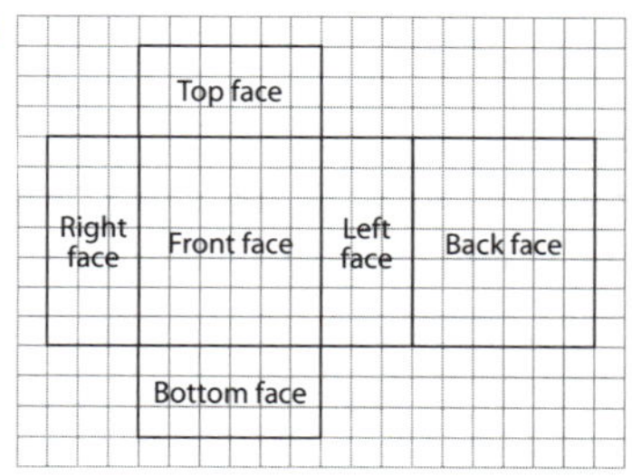

ii)

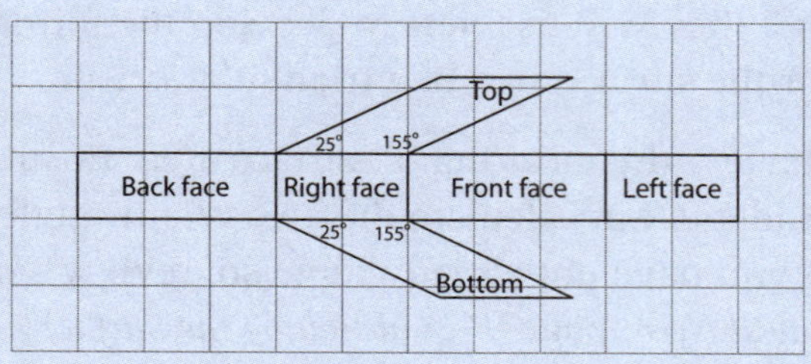

iii)

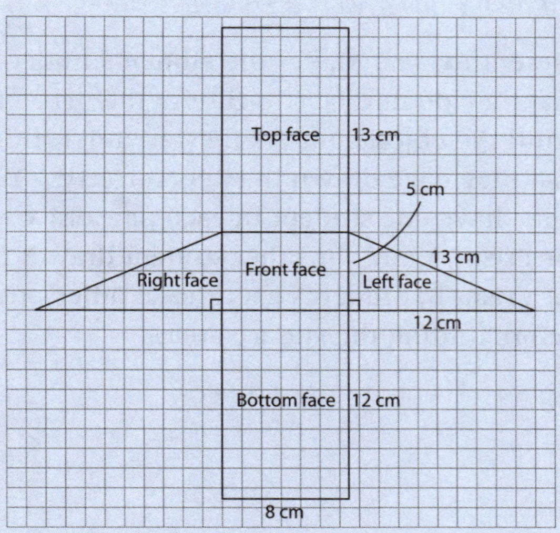

d) i) The prism has 6 faces, 8 vertices, and 12 edges. All faces are rectangles. The front and back faces are congruent 6-cm by 7-cm rectangles. The top and bottom faces are congruent 3-cm by 6-cm rectangles. The side faces are congruent 3-cm by 7-cm rectangles.

ii) The prism has 6 faces, 8 vertices, and 12 edges. The front and back faces are congruent 2-cm by 1-cm rectangles. The bases are congruent 2-cm by 3-cm parallelograms. The side faces are congruent 3-cm by 1-cm rectangles.

iii) The prism has 5 faces, 6 vertices, and 9 edges. The front face is a 5-cm by 8-cm rectangle. The top face is an 8-cm by 13-cm rectangle. The bottom face is an 8-cm by 12-cm rectangle. The bases are congruent right triangles with height 5 cm and base 12 cm. The object resembles a ramp.

Assignment Guidelines

To assess the 4 Achievement Chart categories listed in the curriculum document, have students complete these questions:

Knowledge and Understanding: 1
Application: 2
Thinking: 3
Communication: 3

Surface Area of a Triangular Prism

LESSON ORGANIZER (optional but recommended)

Curriculum Focus: Develop a formula for finding the surface area of a triangular prism. (8m16, 8m24, 8m33, 8m62)

Student Materials
- 1-cm grid paper (PM 20)
- square dot paper (PM 22)
- calculators

Optional
- compasses
- protractors
- scissors
- Step-by-Step 3 (Master 3.10)
- Extra Practice 3 (Master 3.16)

Assessment: Master 3.2 Ongoing Observations: Geometry and Measurement

Key Math Learning

A formula for the surface area of a triangular prism can be developed from its net.

Number Strategies

Ensure students understand that they do not have to use four 3s each time. Remind students of the order of operations.

3.3 Surface Area of a Triangular Prism

Focus Develop a formula for finding the surface area of a triangular prism.

A triangular prism is formed when a triangle is translated in the air so that each side of the triangle is always parallel to its original position.

The two triangular faces are the bases of the prism.

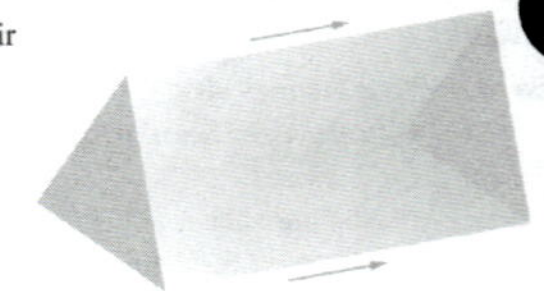

Explore

Work with a partner.
You will need 1-cm grid paper.
➢ For each triangular prism below:
Draw a net.
Find the surface area of the prism.

The surface area of an object is the sum of the areas of its faces.

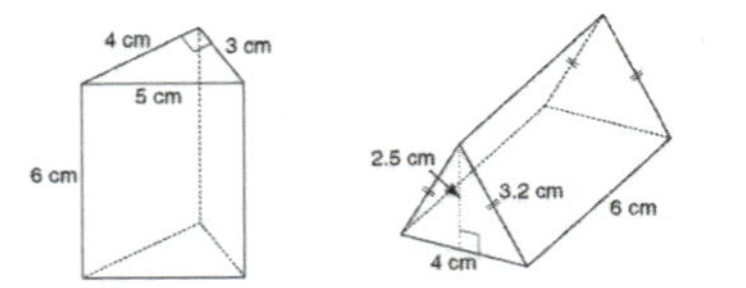

Prism A 84 cm² Prism B 72.4 cm²

➢ Write a formula you can use to find the surface area of any triangular prism.

Reflect & Share

Compare your nets and formula with those of another pair of classmates.
Did you write the same formula?
If not, do both formulas work? Explain.
Did you write a word formula or use variables? Explain.

112 UNIT 3: Geometry and Measurement

Curriculum Note

In this lesson, students develop a formula for finding the surface area of a triangular prism. If your students followed the 1997 curriculum in Grade 6, this lesson should be completed.
This lesson is recommended as it does address several outcomes in the Grade 8 curriculum.

BEFORE Get Started

Have students look at the triangular prism at the top of page 112 in the Student Book. Another way to think about a triangular prism is to imagine that the prism is made of an endless number of triangular slices, all parallel to the original triangle.

Remind students that, in an earlier grade, they used cereal boxes to develop a formula for the surface area of a rectangular prism. Tell students that they will use nets to develop the formula for the surface area of a triangular prism.

Review the meaning of surface area. Ensure students can calculate the area of a triangle. If you have not already done so, review *Skills You'll Need*, page 97, *Calculating the Surface Area and Volume of a Rectangular Prism*, and page 99, *Calculating the Area of a Triangle*.

Present *Explore*. Make sure students understand that they do not have to cut out the nets and build the objects, unless they are not confident that they have drawn the nets correctly. To save time, have one student in each pair draw a net for Prism A and the other student draw a net for Prism B. Students check each other's net before finding the surface areas.

Connect

Here is a triangular prism and its net.
Both the prism and net are drawn to scale.

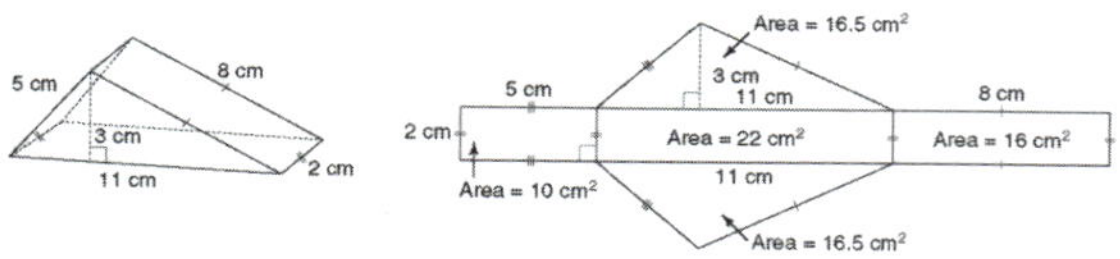

The two triangular faces of the prism are congruent.
Each triangular face has base 11 cm and height 3 cm.
So, the area of one triangular face is: $\frac{1}{2} \times 11 \times 3$
The surface area of a triangular prism can be expressed using a word formula:

SA = sum of the areas of three rectangular faces + 2 × area of one triangular face

The area of a rectangle is base × height.

Use this formula to find the surface area of the prism above.

$SA = (5 \times 2) + (11 \times 2) + (8 \times 2) + 2 \times \frac{1}{2} \times 11 \times 3$
$= 10 + 22 + 16 + 33$
$= 81$

Use the order of operations. Multiply before adding.

The surface area of the prism is 81 cm².

We can use variables to write a formula for the surface area of a triangular prism.

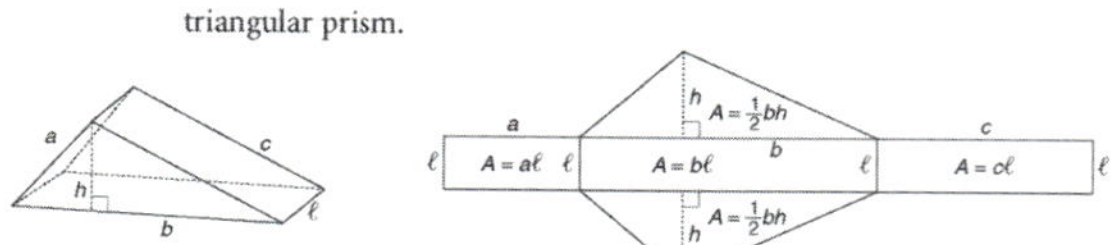

To avoid confusion between the height of a triangle and the height of the prism, we now use *length* instead of *height* to describe the edge that is perpendicular to the base.
For the triangular prism above:
The length of the prism is *l*.
Each triangular face has side lengths *a*, *b*, and *c*.
The height of a triangular face is *h* and its base is *b*.

a, b, c, h, and l are variables.

3.3 Surface Area of a Triangular Prism **113**

REACHING ALL LEARNERS

Alternative Explore

Materials: 1-cm grid paper (PM 20), scissors, tape
Have students draw nets of 2 different triangular prisms on 1-cm grid paper. Students cut out the nets to be sure they form triangular prisms, then calculate the surface area of each net. Students write a formula they could use to find the surface area of any triangular prism. Students compare nets and formulas with other classmates, then report on their findings.

Early Finishers

Have students find triangular prisms in the classroom, measure the dimensions, and calculate their surface areas.

Common Misconceptions

➤ Students have difficulty converting square centimetres to square metres, and vice versa.

How to Help: Have students convert each linear measure from centimetres to metres (divide by 100), or from metres to centimetres (multiply by 100) before substituting for the variables in the equation. This will ensure that the answers are given in the required units.

Sample Solutions

5. a) The piece of pie is 5 cm deep, so I chose 6 cm for the depth of my container. I drew a circle to represent the top of the pie. I divided the circle into 6 congruent sectors. Each sector is approximately an equilateral triangle with side length about 12 cm. I added 2 cm to each side, for my

DURING Explore

Ongoing Assessment: Observe and Listen

As students work on *Explore*, watch and listen for students:

- constructing the correct nets
- calculating the area of each face
- using word formulas and variable formulas
- recognizing that the different dimensions of the prism require a clear assignment of words or variables

Encourage pairs of students to cut and fold their net if it appears that the net has been drawn incorrectly and will not form the required prism.

Ask questions, such as:

- Do the prisms have any congruent faces? Explain.
  (Prism A has two congruent triangular faces. Prism B has two congruent triangular faces and two congruent rectangular faces.)
- How did you use the net to find the surface area of the prism?
  (I calculated the area of each face in the net, then found the sum of these areas.)
- How can congruent faces make your calculations easier?
  (I can find the area of one of the congruent faces, then multiply its area by the number of times the face appears.)
- How did you write the surface area as a formula?
  (I labelled the triangles and rectangles A, B, C, D, E, then wrote the formula as: Surface area = the areas of rectangles A, B, and C + the area of triangles D and E.)
- Can your formula be simplified?
  (Yes, a triangular prism has 2 congruent triangular faces. So, I can write the formula as: Surface area = the areas of rectangles A, B, and C + 2 × the area of triangle D.)

container. My container is a triangular prism, with an equilateral triangle base, with side length 14 cm, and the prism is 6 cm high. I measured the height of the triangular base. It was about 12.1 cm.

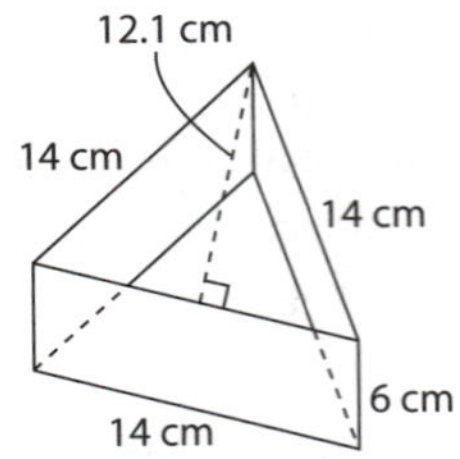

b) $SA = al + bl + cl + bh$

Substitute $a = b = c = 14$, $l = 6$, $h = 12.1$

$SA = (14 \times 6) + (14 \times 6) + (14 \times 6) + (14 \times 12.1)$

$= 421.4$

The area of plastic in my design is about 420 cm^2.

This does not consider the thickness of the container or the overlap for the lid. So, I estimate about 500 cm^2 of plastic is needed.

6. a) The possible dimensions are:

Edge length of triangular base (cm)	Length of prism (cm)
2	12
3	8
4	6
6	4
8	3
12	2

When you use this formula, you must identify what each variable represents.

The surface area of the prism is:

SA = sum of the areas of the 3 rectangular faces + 2 × area of one triangular face

$SA = al + bl + cl + 2 \times \frac{1}{2}bh$

$SA = al + bl + cl + bh$

Example

Find the surface area of the prism below.

Each dimension has been rounded to the nearest whole number.

Write the surface area in square centimetres and in square metres.

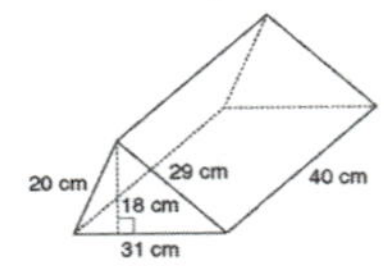

Solution

Identify the variable that represents each dimension.

Sketch, then label the prism with these variables.

The length of the prism is:

$l = 40$

The 3 sides of a triangular face are:

$a = 20, b = 31, c = 29$

The height of a triangular face is:

$h = 18$

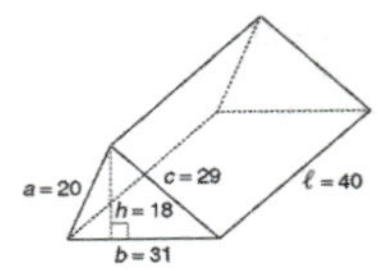

Substitute for each variable in the formula for surface area.

$SA = al + bl + cl + bh$

$= (20 \times 40) + (31 \times 40) + (29 \times 40) + (31 \times 18)$

$= 800 + 1240 + 1160 + 558$

$= 3758$

The surface area of the prism is 3758 cm^2.

There are 10 000 cm^2 in 1 m^2.

To convert square centimetres to square metres, divide by 10 000.

$3758 \text{ cm}^2 = \frac{3758}{10\,000} \text{ m}^2$

$= 0.3758 \text{ m}^2$

The surface area of the prism is 0.3758 m^2.

114 UNIT 3: Geometry and Measurement

AFTER Connect

Have students share their nets and formulas with the class. Ask:

- Did you write the same formula as your classmate? Explain.
  (No, I used variables instead of words. I assigned 3 variables to the side lengths of the triangular face, a variable to the height of the triangular face, and a variable to the length of the prism.)
- Do both your formula and your classmate's formula work? Explain.
  (Yes, we both wrote word formulas, but the order in which we calculated the areas was different. Since the order of addition does not matter, both formulas work.)

Remind students that a formula that uses variables is more compact, both to write and to use. It is a short form of the steps used to find the surface area, with variables replacing the words.

Introduce *Connect*. Point out that when the area of one triangular face is doubled ($2 \times \frac{1}{2}bh$), $2 \times \frac{1}{2}$ is 1, so the area of the 2 triangular faces is bh. This means that the area of the two congruent triangular faces is the same as the area of a rectangle or a parallelogram with the same dimensions. This concept can be used when presenting the variable formula.

Some students who have strong algebra skills may visualize the surface area as the sum of the areas of the two congruent triangles, and the area of a large rectangle with length l and width equal to the perimeter of the triangular face.

The variable formula is: $SA = bh + l(a + b + c)$

Students should understand what each part of the formula represents so that when parts of the surface area are not required, the formula can be adjusted. This occurs in some *Practice* questions.

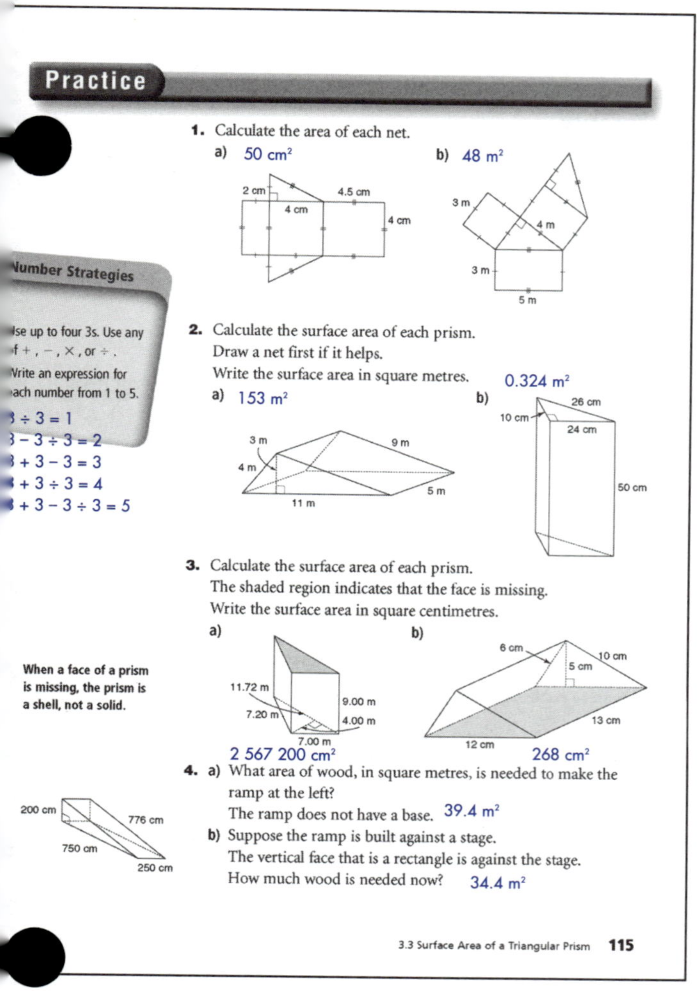

Practice

1. Calculate the area of each net.
   a) 50 cm^2 b) 48 m^2

2. Calculate the surface area of each prism.
   Draw a net first if it helps.
   Write the surface area in square metres.
   a) 153 m^2 b) 0.324 m^2

3. Calculate the surface area of each prism.
   The shaded region indicates that the face is missing.
   Write the surface area in square centimetres.
   a) 2 567 200 cm^2 b) 268 cm^2

4. a) What area of wood, in square metres, is needed to make the ramp at the left?
   The ramp does not have a base. 39.4 m^2
   b) Suppose the ramp is built against a stage.
   The vertical face that is a rectangle is against the stage.
   How much wood is needed now? 34.4 m^2

Number Strategies

Use up to four 3s. Use any of +, −, ×, or ÷.
Write an expression for each number from 1 to 5.

$3 \div 3 = 1$
$3 - 3 \div 3 = 2$
$3 + 3 - 3 = 3$
$3 + 3 \div 3 = 4$
$3 + 3 - 3 \div 3 = 5$

When a face of a prism is missing, the prism is a shell, not a solid.

3.3 Surface Area of a Triangular Prism 115

b) The greatest length is 12 cm, so the equilateral triangular faces will have edge length 2 cm.

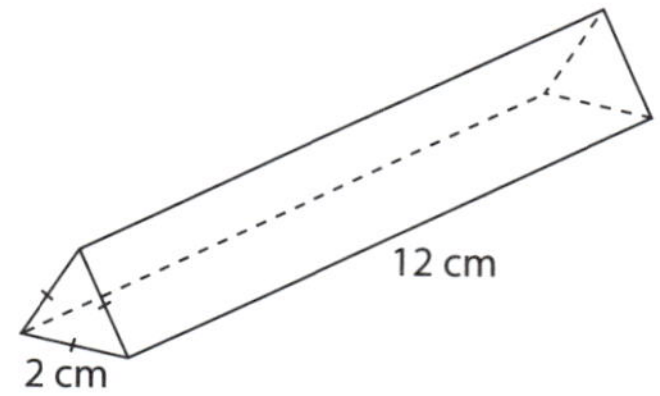

7. Because one rectangular face is missing, the formula for surface area becomes $SA = al + cl + bh$.
Substitute $a = 50$, $b = 60$, $c = 50$, $l = 120$, $h = 40$
$SA = (50 \times 120) + (50 \times 120) + (60 \times 40)$
$= 14\ 400$
The surface area is 14 400 cm^2.
To convert square centimetres to square metres, divide by 10 000.
$14\ 400\ cm^2 = \frac{14\ 400}{10\ 000}\ m^2 = 1.44\ m^2$
To build the water trough, 1.44 m^2 of metal is needed.

8. c)

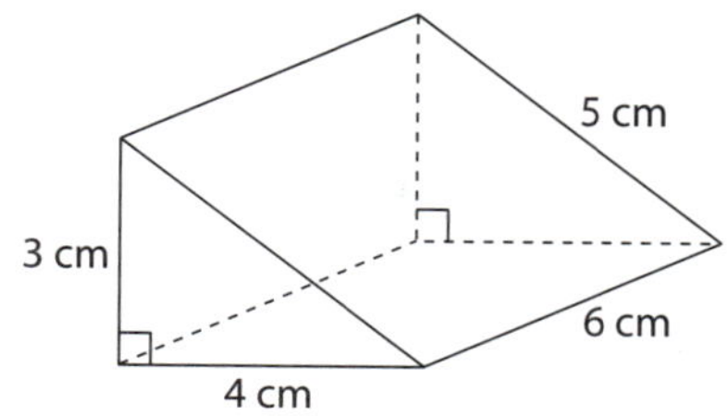

Have students suggest how the formula could be adjusted when the triangular face is an isosceles triangle (for example, if $a = c$, $SA = 2al + bl + bh$, or an equilateral triangle, $SA = 3al + bh$).

The *Example* requires the concept of dividing by a power of 10, as does any *Practice* question that necessitates converting from a smaller unit to a larger unit; for example, questions 2b and 7.

If students have difficulty converting from square centimetres to square metres, and vice versa, have them review *Skills You'll Need*, page 100, *Converting among Units of Measure.*

Practice

Some students may need to use nets and word formulas to calculate the surface area when a diagram of a prism is given.

Questions 3, 4, and 7 require students to adjust the surface area formula because one face of the prism is missing.

Assessment Focus: Question 7

Students should realize that one face of the triangular prism is missing, and that, because the triangular faces are isosceles triangles, the two rectangular faces are congruent. So, students may write this formula for surface area: $SA = 2al + bh$. The dimensions of the prism are given in centimetres. To give the answer in square metres, students could convert the dimensions to metres before calculating, or they could convert the area to square metres after calculating.

Assignment Guidelines

If your students do not have time to complete all the *Practice* questions on pages 115 and 116, these questions provide minimum curriculum coverage: 2, 4, 6, 7, 8, *Reflect*

To assess the 4 Achievement Chart categories listed in the curriculum document, have students complete these *Practice* questions:

Knowledge and Understanding: 2	Communication: 6
Application: 4	Thinking: 7

9. Here is a sketch.

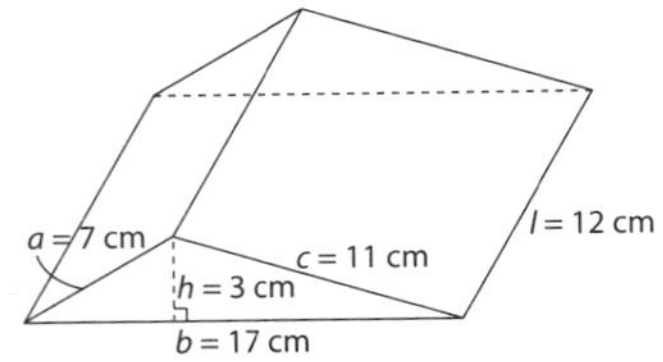

$SA = al + bl + cl + bh$

Substitute $a = 7$, $b = 17$, $c = 11$, $l = 12$, $h = 3$

$SA = (7 \times 12) + (17 \times 12) + (11 \times 12) + (17 \times 3)$

$= 84 + 204 + 132 + 51$

$= 471$

REFLECT: To find the surface area of a triangular prism, I find the sum of the areas of three rectangular faces plus 2 times the area of one triangular face. I label the side lengths of a triangular face *a*, *b*, and *c*, the height of the triangular face *h*, and the length of the prism *l*.
I can use the formula $SA = al + bl + cl + bh$.

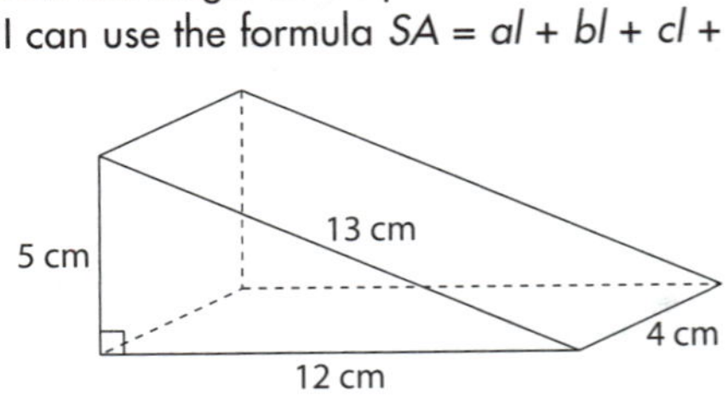

Substitute $a = 5$, $b = 12$, $c = 13$, $l = 4$, $h = 5$

$SA = (5 \times 4) + (12 \times 4) + (13 \times 4) + (12 \times 5)$

$= 20 + 48 + 52 + 60$

$= 180$

The surface area is 180 cm^2.

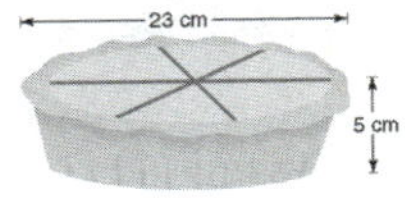

5. A plastic container company designs a container with a lid to hold one piece of pie.

a) Design the container as a triangular prism. Explain your choice of dimensions.

b) Calculate the area of plastic in your design.

6. The total area of the 3 rectangular faces of an equilateral triangular prism is 72 cm^2.

a) No dimension can be 1 cm. What are the possible whole-number dimensions of the edges?

b) Sketch the prism with the greatest length. Include dimensions. Explain your choice.

7. **Assessment Focus** How much metal, in square metres, is needed to build this water trough?

144 m^2

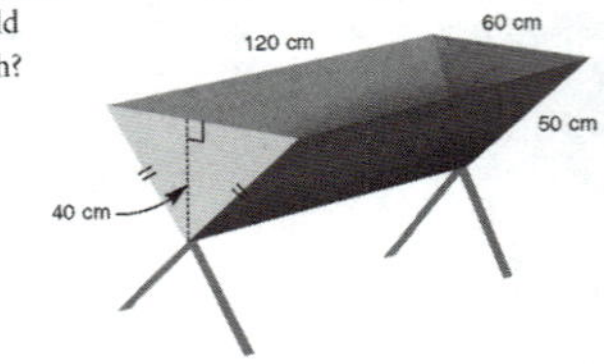

8. A right triangular prism has a base with perimeter 12 cm and area 6 cm^2.

a) Find the whole-number dimensions of the base. 3 cm by 4 cm by 5 cm

b) The length of the prism is 6 cm. Calculate the surface area of the prism. 84 cm^2

c) Sketch the prism. Include its dimensions.

Take It Further

9. Use the variables below to sketch and label a triangular prism. The lengths have been rounded to the nearest whole number. Calculate the surface area of the prism. 471 cm^2

$a = 7$ cm, $b = 17$ cm, $c = 11$ cm, $h = 3$ cm, $l = 12$ cm

Reflect

Write to explain how to find the surface area of a triangular prism. Include an example and a diagram.

116 UNIT 3: Geometry and Measurement

ASSESSMENT FOR LEARNING

What to Look For	What to Do
Knowledge and Understanding ✔ Students understand how a formula for the surface area of a triangular prism is developed. ***Thinking*** ✔ Students can solve surface area problems that involve changes in units or missing faces. ***Application*** ✔ Students can use the formula for the surface area of a triangular prism by substituting the dimensions for the variables.	***Extra Support:*** Have students draw a net on grid paper for each triangular prism before they use the formula, so they can see all the areas to be calculated. Students can use Step-by-Step 3 (Master 3.10) to complete question 7. ***Extra Practice:*** Have students calculate the surface area of the triangular prism in Lesson 3.2, *Practice* question 1, part ii, and in the Mid-Unit Review, question 3, part iii. In the first question, the height is not given. Students can construct an equilateral triangle with side length 2 cm, then measure the height to the nearest millimetre. Students can complete Extra Practice 3 (Master 3.16). ***Extension:*** Students can extend their work to calculate the surface areas of other prisms for which they created nets in Lesson 3.2; for example, *Practice* questions 4, 5, and 6.

Recording and Reporting

Master 3.2 Ongoing Observations: Geometry and Measurement

3.4 Volume of a Triangular Prism

Focus Develop and use a formula for finding the volume of a triangular prism.

Recall that the area of a triangle is one-half the area of a rectangle that has the same base and height.
That is,
the area of $\triangle DEC = \frac{1}{2}$ the area of rectangle ABCD

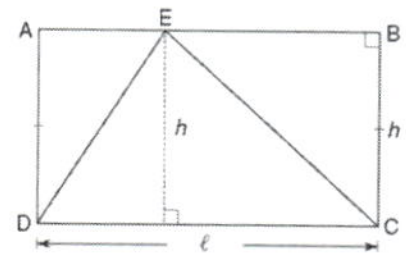

Explore

Work in a group of 4.
You will need 4 identical cereal boxes, one for each group member, and markers.

- ➢ Find the volume of your cereal box, which is a rectangular prism.
- ➢ Use a ruler to draw a triangle on one end of the cereal box.
  The base of each triangle should be along one edge of the box.
  The third vertex of the triangle should be on the opposite edge.
  Make sure you draw different triangles.
  What is the volume of a triangular prism with this triangle as its base, and with length equal to the length of the cereal box?
- ➢ Compare your answer with those of other members of your group. What do you notice?
- ➢ Work together to write a formula for the volume of a triangular prism.

Reflect & Share

How is the volume of a triangular prism related to the volume of a rectangular prism?
Compare your formula for the volume of a triangular prism with that of another group.
Did you use variables in your formula?
If not, work together to write a formula that uses variables.

Connect

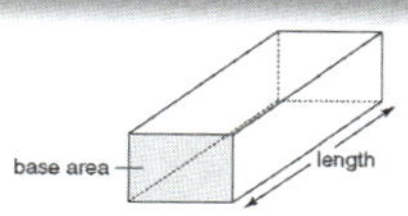

The volume of a rectangular prism is:
V = base area × length

3.4 Volume of a Triangular Prism **117**

LESSON 3.4

Volume of a Triangular Prism

LESSON ORGANIZER (optional but recommended)

Curriculum Focus: Develop and use a formula for finding the volume of a triangular prism. (8m16, 8m24, 8m33, 8m62)

Teacher Materials
Optional
- cereal box
- rice

Student Materials
- 4 identical cereal boxes for each group of 4 students
- markers
- scissors
- calculators

Optional
- Step-by-Step 4 (Master 3.11)
- Extra Practice 4 (Master 3.17)

Assessment: Master 3.2 Ongoing Observations: Geometry and Measurement

Key Math Learning

The formula for the volume of a triangular prism is the same as the formula for the volume of any prism: the area of its base multiplied by its height.

Curriculum Note

In this lesson, students develop and use a formula for finding the volume of a triangular prism. If your students followed the 1997 curriculum in Grade 6, this lesson should be completed.
This lesson is recommended as it does address several outcomes in the Grade 8 curriculum.

BEFORE Get Started

Remind students that the volume of all prisms is: V = base area × length.

Ensure students understand that volume is the amount of space an object takes up, measured in cubic units.

If you have not already done so, review *Skills You'll Need*, page 97, *Calculating the Surface Area and Volume of a Rectangular Prism*, and page 99, *Calculating the Area of a Triangle*.

Have students look at the diagram at the top of page 117 of the Student Book. Ensure students understand that the base and height of the rectangle are, respectively, equal to the base and height of the triangle.

Use a cereal box to demonstrate one side face as rectangle ABCD. Point out that CD is the base of $\triangle CDE$, and vertex E can be any point on side AB.

DURING Explore

Ongoing Assessment: Observe and Listen

As students work, watch for students who begin by measuring the dimensions required to find the volume of the cereal box. Be sure each group member is using the same face to draw the triangular base and the same edge for the opposite vertex. If students use a different face or edge, the volume will still be one-half the volume of the rectangular prism,

REACHING ALL LEARNERS

Alternative Explore

Materials: open rectangular prism (cereal box), cardboard, tape, scissors, rulers

Students could bring in a cereal box, then build a triangular prism whose triangular faces have the same base and height as the rectangular base, and whose length is the same length as the rectangular prism.

Have students pour rice from the rectangular prism into the triangular prism to discover how the volume of a triangular prism is related to the volume of a rectangular prism.

Early Finishers

Have students find the surface area of each triangular prism they visualized in *Explore*.

Common Misconceptions

➤ Students confuse the base of a triangular prism, with the base of a triangular face.

How to Help: Have students draw, shade, and label a diagram to illustrate that the base of the prism is a triangle; and the base of the triangle, *b*, is a line segment.

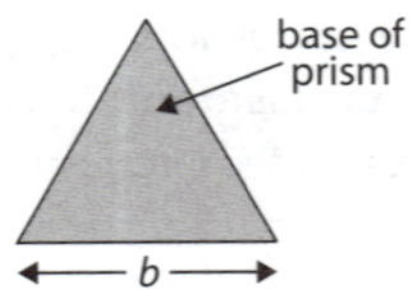

Number Strategies

Students should recall their multiplication and division facts. They can use guess and check, beginning with 49 and working backward. They may need to check other numbers such as 36, to find out it has 9 factors.

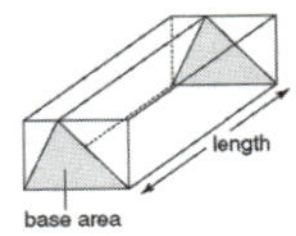

Suppose we draw a triangle on the base of the prism so that the base of the triangle is one edge, and the third vertex of the triangle is on the opposite edge.

The volume of a triangular prism with this base, and with len equal to the length of the rectangular prism, is one-half the volume of the rectangular prism.

Since the base area of the triangular prism is one-half the base area of the rectangular prism, the volume of a triangular prism is also: V = base area × length

The base is a triangle, so the base area is the area of a triangle.

We can use variables to write a formula for the volume of a triangular prism.

For the triangular prism below:

The length of the prism is l.

Each triangular face has base b and height h.

The volume of the prism is:

When we use this formula, we must identify what each variable represents.

V = base area × length

$V = \frac{1}{2}bh \times l$

$V = \frac{1}{2}bhl$

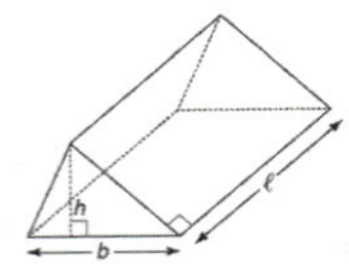

Example

How much water can the water trough hold?
Give the answer in litres.

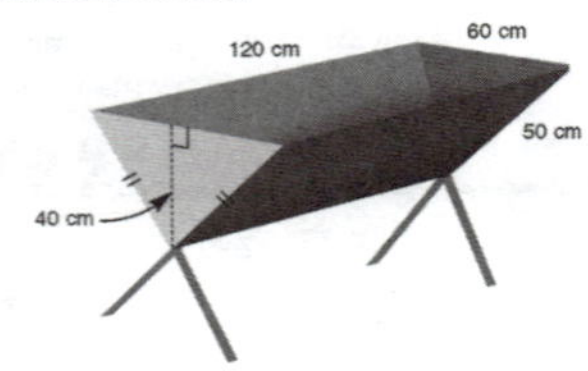

but developing the variable formula may be more difficult for students to visualize.

Ask questions, such as:

- How many dimensions are needed to find the volume of the cereal box?
  (*Three: length, width, and height*)
- How do the areas of the triangles compare?
  (*The areas of the triangles are equal because they have the same base and height.*)
- If layers of congruent triangles were placed inside the box, how much space would they occupy?
  (*They would occupy one-half of the cereal box.*)
- Does your formula for the volume of a triangular prism use the same variables as your formula for the surface area of a triangular prism? Explain.
  (*No, we do not need to know the length of all 3 sides of a triangular face to find the volume. We only use the variables for the base and height of the triangle, and the length of the prism.*)
- How would the surface areas of the 4 triangular prisms compare?
  (*The surface areas would be different because the lengths of the other two sides of the triangular faces would be different.*)

If students have difficulty visualizing the triangular prism inside the cereal box, have students insert rectangular cardboard pieces inside the box to represent the other rectangular faces of the prism.

AFTER Connect

Have students share their formulas with the class. Ask:

- How is the volume of a triangular prism related to the volume of a rectangular prism?
  (*The volume of a triangular prism is one-half the volume of the related rectangular prism.*)

Solution

...ity is the ...nt a container ...hold, commonly measured in litres (L) or millilitres (mL). Volume is the amount of space an object occupies, commonly measured in cubic units.

The amount of water the trough can hold is the capacity of the triangular prism.

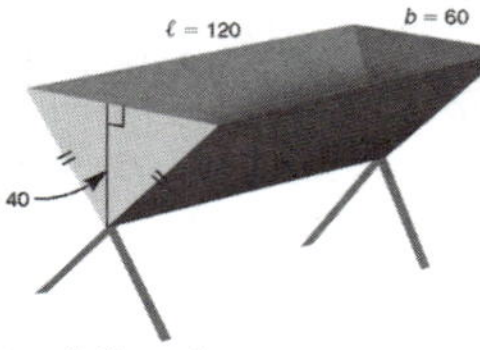

Sketch the prism.
Identify the variable that represents each dimension.
The base of the triangle is: $b = 60$
The height of the triangle is: $h = 40$
The length of the prism is: $l = 120$
Substitute for each variable into the formula for volume.

$V = \frac{1}{2}bhl$

$V = \frac{1}{2} \times 60 \times 40 \times 120$

$V = 144\,000$

The volume of the trough is 144 000 cm^3.
1000 cm^3 = 1 L
So, 144 000 cm^3 = 144 L
The trough can hold 144 L of water.

Practice

1. The base area and length for each triangular prism are given. Find the volume of each prism.

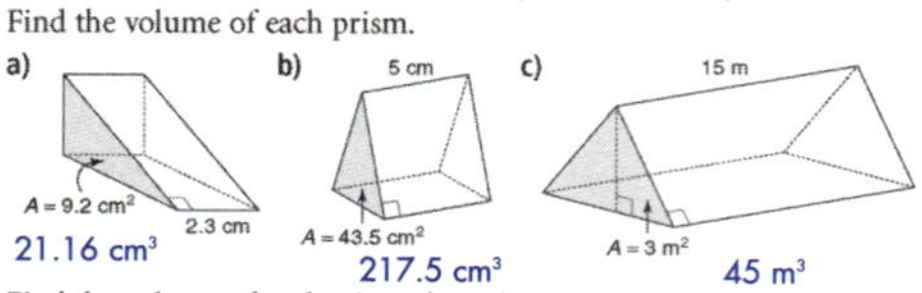

2. Find the volume of each triangular prism.

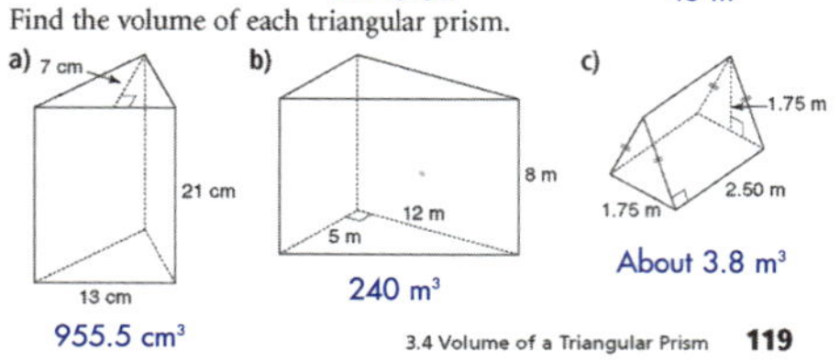

3.4 Volume of a Triangular Prism 119

Sample Solutions

4. a) $\frac{1}{2}bhl = 5$, so $bhl = 10$

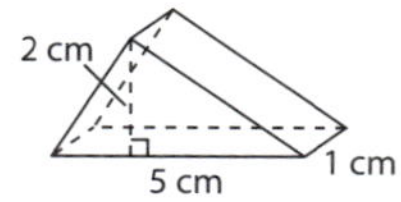

b) $\frac{1}{2}bhl = 9$, so $bhl = 18$

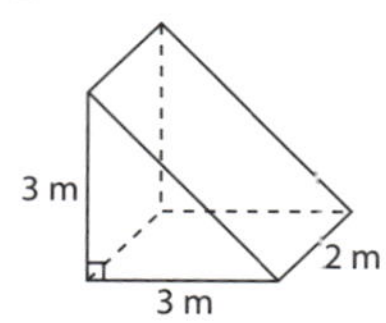

c) $\frac{1}{2}bhl = 8$, so $bhl = 16$

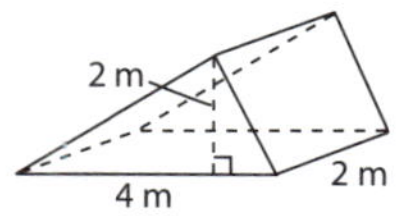

d) $\frac{1}{2}bhl = 18$, so $bhl = 36$

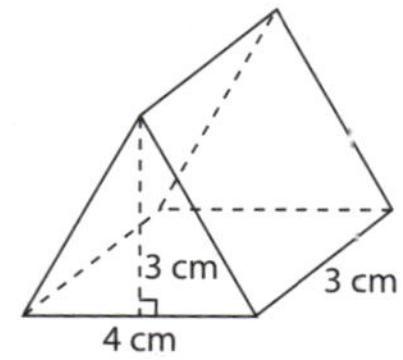

6. No, only a triangular face can be used as the base of a triangular prism. It is the triangular faces that are parallel and give the prism its name.

8. b) Since the length is twice as long, the surface area increases but does not double. Only the rectangular faces double in length. The lengths of the sides of the triangular faces do not change.
The volume doubles because we can think of doubling the length as placing 2 congruent prisms side by side.

c) The area of the triangular faces is 4 times as great when the base and height are doubled. The area of the rectangular faces doubles, so the surface area more than doubles. The volume is 4 times as great.

- How did you find the volume of the triangular prism?
(*We found the volume of the rectangular prism and divided it by 2.*)
- What variable formula did you write for the volume of a triangular prism?
(*We used b for the base of a triangular face; h for the height of the triangular face, so the area of the triangular face is bh ÷ 2. We then multiplied the area of the base by l, the length of the prism, so our formula for the volume of the prism is* $V = bh \div 2 \times l$.)

To reinforce the concept that the volume of a triangular prism is one-half the volume of the related rectangular prism, use a model of an open rectangular prism and its related triangular prism. (Construct the related triangular prism from strong cardboard.) Fill the cereal box with rice, then ask how many times the triangular prism can be filled from the contents of the cereal box. If students have understood *Explore*, they should predict that the triangular prism can be filled twice. Have a volunteer pour the rice into the triangular prism to check.

As you review *Connect*, and explain how the volume of a triangular prism is related to the volume of a rectangular prism, ensure students understand that since the area of a triangle is $A = \frac{1}{2}bh$, we use the variable b to represent the length of one side of the rectangle. Because h represents the height of the triangular base, we use l to represent the length (or height) of the prism.

In the *Example*, the triangular prism is missing a rectangular face. Ensure students understand that the missing face affects the surface area of the prism but that it does not affect its volume. When we convert from cubic centimetres to litres, we divide by 10^3. If you think your students require further practice, have them

d) The surface area is 4 times as great and the volume is 8 times as great.

9. a) $V = \frac{1}{2}bhl$
Substitute $b = 3$, $h = 3$, $l = 0.25$.
$V = \frac{1}{2} \times 3 \times 3 \times 0.25$
$= 1.125$
Jackie will need to mix 1.125 m^3 of cement to fill the form.

b) Since Jackie doubles two of the dimensions, she will need to mix four times the volume of cement. She will need to mix 4×1.125 m^3 = 4.5 m^3 of cement.

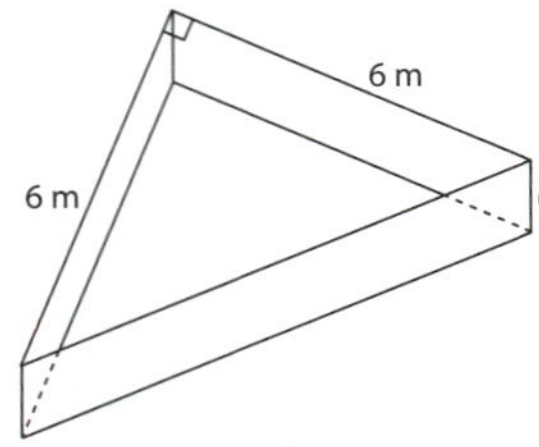

Check: $V = \frac{1}{2}bhl$ Substitute $b = 6$, $h = 6$, $l = 0.25$.
$= \frac{1}{2} \times 6 \times 6 \times 0.25$
$= 4.5$

10. b) i) The mass is 4 times as great, so the volume is also 4 times as great. One way to do this is to double the base and height of the triangular faces. The equilateral triangles have side length 7 cm and height about 6.2 cm, and the prism is 21 cm long. It is also possible to leave the dimensions of the equilateral triangles as they were in the 100-g box, and make the length of the box 4 times

3. Calculate the volume of each prism.

a)

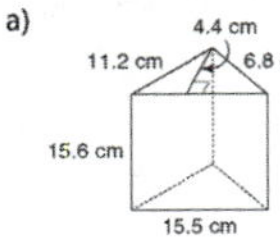

531.96 cm^3

b)

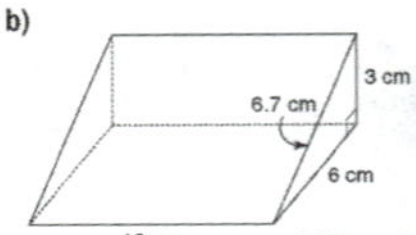

108 cm^3

Use an isometric diagram or a pictorial diagram for the sketch of the prism.

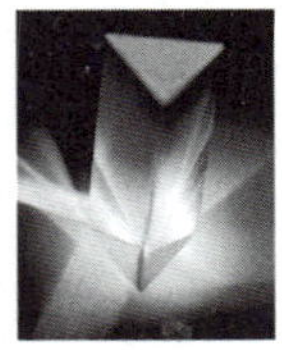

4. Find possible values for *b*, *h*, and *l* for each volume of a triangular prism. Sketch one possible prism for each volume.
a) 5 cm^3 b) 9 m^3 c) 8 m^3 d) 18 cm^3

5. What is the volume of glass in this prism? 18 cm^3

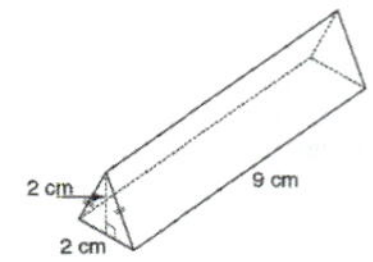

6. Any face can be used as the base of a rectangular prism.
Can any face be used as the base of a triangular prism? Explain.

7. The volume of a triangular prism is 30 cm^3.
Each triangular face has an area of 4 cm^2.
How long is the prism? 7.5 cm

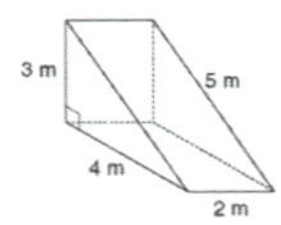

8. a) Calculate the surface area and volume of this triangular prism. $SA = 36$ m^2; $V = 12$ m^3
b) What do you think happens to the surface area and volume when the length of the prism is doubled? Justify your answer.
Calculate the surface area and volume to check your ideas. $SA = 60$ m^2; $V = 24$ m^3
c) What do you think happens to the surface area and volume when the base and height of the triangular faces are doubled?
Justify your answer. $SA = 96$ m^2; $V = 48$ m^3
Calculate the surface area and volume to check your ideas.
d) What do you think happens to surface area and volume when all the dimensions are doubled?
Justify your answer.
Calculate the surface area and volume to check your ideas.
$SA = 144$ m^2; $V = 96$ m^3

120 UNIT 3: Geometry and Measurement

convert cubic centimetres to cubic metres in questions 1b, 2a, and 3a. For conversions from cubic metres to cubic centimetres, use questions 1c, 2c, and 8a.

Practice

Questions 1, 2, and 3 allow students to practise using the volume formula with triangular prisms in a variety of orientations.
In question 4, students may recognize that, since the volume of a triangular prism is one-half the volume of a rectangular prism, they can find the dimensions of a rectangular prism (3 factors) that have a product equal to twice the given volume. The factors can be assigned in a variety of ways for *b*, *h*, and *l*.
Questions 8, 9, and 10 challenge students to discover how changing one or more dimensions of a triangular prism affects its volume and surface area.

Assessment Focus: Question 9

Students should be able to use the formula for the volume of a triangular prism to find the amount of cement needed to fill the form. From question 8, students should realize that four times as much cement will be needed to fill the form when two dimensions are doubled. Students should calculate the volume of the new form to verify the new amount and include a labelled diagram.

Assignment Guidelines

If your students do not have time to complete all the *Practice* questions on pages 119, 120, and 121, these questions provide minimum curriculum coverage:
2, 4, 6, 8, 9, 10, *Reflect*

To assess the 4 Achievement Chart categories listed in the curriculum document, have students complete these *Practice* questions:

Knowledge and Understanding: 2
Application: 4
Communication: 6
Thinking: 10

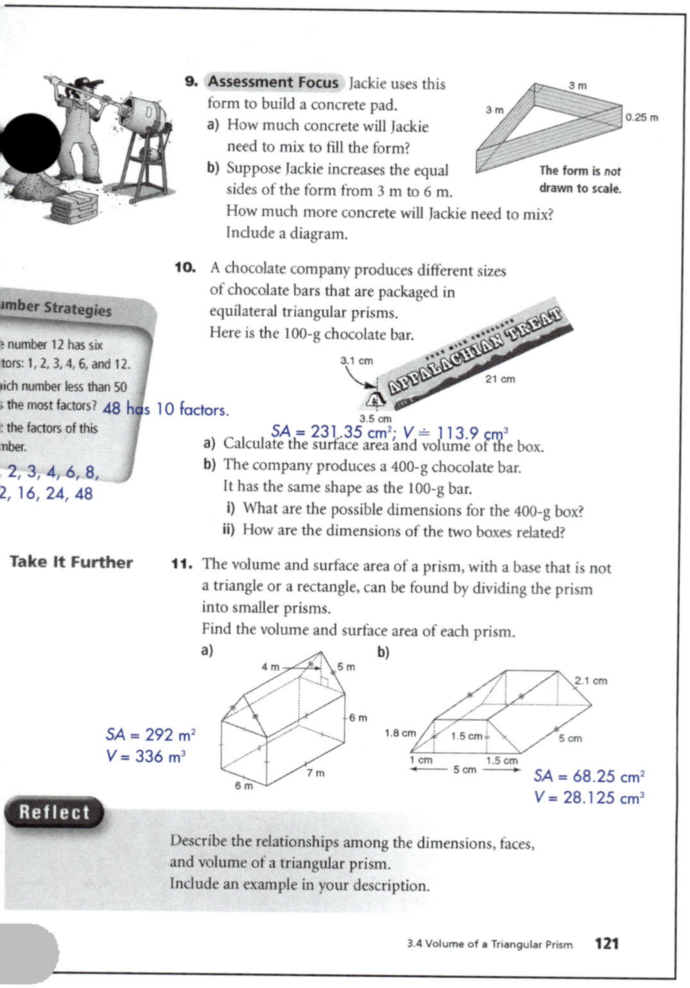

9. **Assessment Focus** Jackie uses this form to build a concrete pad.
a) How much concrete will Jackie need to mix to fill the form?
b) Suppose Jackie increases the equal sides of the form from 3 m to 6 m. How much more concrete will Jackie need to mix? Include a diagram.

10. A chocolate company produces different sizes of chocolate bars that are packaged in equilateral triangular prisms. Here is the 100-g chocolate bar.

a) Calculate the surface area and volume of the box.
$SA = 231.35$ cm²; $V \doteq 113.9$ cm³
b) The company produces a 400-g chocolate bar. It has the same shape as the 100-g bar.
i) What are the possible dimensions for the 400-g box?
ii) How are the dimensions of the two boxes related?

Number Strategies

The number 12 has six factors: 1, 2, 3, 4, 6, and 12.
Which number less than 50 has the most factors? 48 has 10 factors.
List the factors of this number.
1, 2, 3, 4, 6, 8, 12, 16, 24, 48

Take It Further

11. The volume and surface area of a prism, with a base that is not a triangle or a rectangle, can be found by dividing the prism into smaller prisms. Find the volume and surface area of each prism.
a)

$SA = 292$ m²
$V = 336$ m³

b)

$SA = 68.25$ cm²
$V = 28.125$ cm³

Reflect

Describe the relationships among the dimensions, faces, and volume of a triangular prism. Include an example in your description.

3.4 Volume of a Triangular Prism 121

as great; that is, 84 cm. This would not be practical because the box would be almost 1 m long.

ii) To maintain the shape of the box, the base and height of the original triangular faces are doubled, or the length of the box is quadrupled, or each dimension is multiplied by the same factor.

REFLECT: A triangular prism has three dimensions that are used to calculate its volume: the base and height of a triangular face and the length of the prism.
The volume of the prism is the area of a triangular face multiplied by the length of the prism.

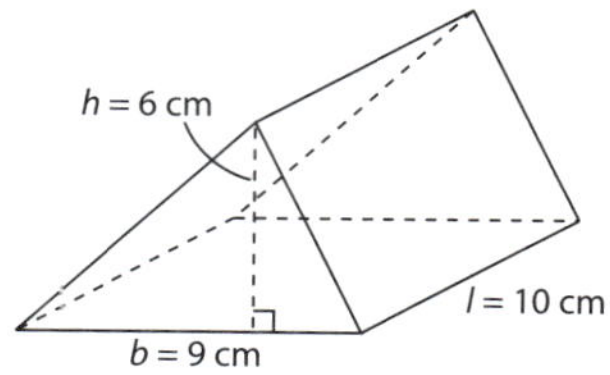

To find the volume of the prism above, I can use a word formula: Volume = area of base × length
or a variable formula, where *b* represents the base of the triangular face, *h* represents the height of the triangular face, and *l* represents the length of the prism.

$V = \frac{1}{2}bhl$ Substitute $b = 9$, $h = 6$, $l = 10$.

$= \frac{1}{2} \times 9 \times 6 \times 10$

$= 270$

The volume of the prism is 270 cm³.

ASSESSMENT FOR LEARNING

What to Look For	What to Do
Knowledge and Understanding ✔ Students understand that the volume of a triangular prism is the product of the base area and its length. ***Thinking*** ✔ Students can investigate how changing dimensions affects the volume of a triangular prism. ***Communication*** ✔ Students present organized solutions, including well-labelled diagrams. ***Application*** ✔ Students can use the formula to solve problems involving the volume of a triangular prism.	***Extra Support:*** Students who have difficulty identifying the base of a triangular prism could sketch the prism, then shade the triangular face, as in *Practice* question 1. Students can use Step-by-Step 4 (Master 3.11) to complete question 9. ***Extra Practice:*** Students can play the Additional Activity *Measurement Bingo* (Master 3.7a). Students can complete Extra Practice 4 (Master 3.17). ***Extension:*** Have students draw a regular hexagon, and use that as the base of a hexagonal prism. Students choose the length of the prism, then measure to find the required lengths to calculate the volume of the prism.

Recording and Reporting
Master 3.2 Ongoing Observations: Geometry and Measurement

Features of World Problems

LESSON ORGANIZER

Student Materials
- calculators

ESL Strategies

Solving word problems can be difficult for students for whom English is a second language. These students may need the problems explained in greater detail. In the example, "refrigerator" and "fridge" refer to the same appliance, but this may confuse ESL students. In questions 3 and 4, some students may not have any experience with games or contests.

Have ESL students work with a partner. Have the partner read and explain important words in each problem. Have the ESL student read the problem back to the partner to reinforce the vocabulary.

Features of Word Problems

In *Unit 2*, you wrote problem statements as questions.
Math problems include information to help you understand and solve the problem.
Here are some features of math word problems.

Context – may describe who, what, when, where, and why, like the setting of a story.

Math Information – may include words, numbers, figures, drawings, tables, graphs, and/or models.

Problem Statement – tells you to do something with the information. It may be a question or an instruction. Key words are sometimes used to suggest how the response is to be communicated.

Context: Suppose you have an old refrigerator and are thinking about buying a new one.

Math Information: The new refrigerator costs $900. It costs $126 a year to run your old fridge, and $66 a year to run the new, more energy-efficient fridge.

Problem Statement: Is it more economical to buy the new fridge? Justify your answer.

To solve the problem, we need to compare the costs of buying the new fridge and running it with the costs of running the old fridge.
We can use a table and a graph.
In the second column of the table, add $126 each year.
In the third column of the table, add $66 each year.

Cumulative Costs		
Year	Old Fridge Cost ($)	New Fridge Cost ($)
1	126	900 + 66 = 966
2	252	1032
3	378	1098
4	504	1164
5	630	1230
6	756	1296
7	882	1362

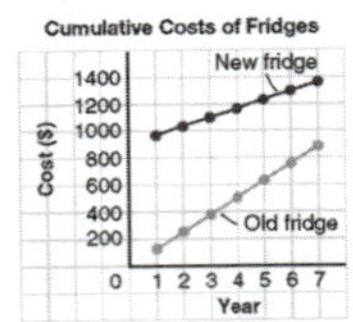

Here is part of the table and a graph.
Continue the table until the costs are equal.
Draw a graph for the data.
Use the table and graph to solve the problem.

122 UNIT 3: Geometry and Measurement

Answer to Example Problem

The costs are equal after 15 years. The graphs intersect at 15 years and $1890. Students should consider changing energy costs, the possible break down of the old fridge, the cost of a loan to buy the new fridge, environmental issues of using appliances that are more energy efficient, and so on, when trying to decide whether it is more economical to buy the new fridge.

Sample Solutions

1. Context: Hori is buying carpet for his living room.
   Math Information: Room is rectangular with dimensions 4 m by 5 m.
   Regular price is $9.99 per square metre.
   The carpet is on sale for 20% off.
   Problem: How much will Hori save if he buys the carpet at the sale price?
   Solution: $A = l \times w$
   $= 5 \times 4$
   $= 20$
   Hori needs 20 m^2 of carpet.
   Total regular price: $9.99 × 20 = $199.80
   20% discount: 0.20 × $199.80 = $39.96
   Hori saves $39.96 if he buys the carpet at the sale price.

2. Context: Possible table arrangements at a graduation dinner
   Math Information: 122 people are to be seated.
   Tables seat 8 or 10 people.
   Problem: Find all possible table arrangements so there are no empty seats.
   Solution: Use guess and check.
   Use enough tables of 8 so the remainder is divisible by 10.
   $122 - (8 \times 4) = 122 - 32 = 90$
   90 people can be seated at 9 tables of 10.
   So, one arrangement is 4 tables of 8 and 9 tables of 10.
   $122 - (8 \times 9) = 122 - 72 = 50$
   50 people can be seated at 5 tables of 10.
   So, another arrangement is 9 tables of 8 and 5 tables of 10.
   $122 - (8 \times 14) = 122 - 112 = 10$
   Another arrangement is 14 tables of 8 and 1 table of 10.

3. Context: Winning a contest by identifying the mystery number
   Math Information: $\frac{2}{3}$ of a number plus 16 equals 2 times the number.
   Problem: Find the mystery number.

Reading and Writing in Math

Check

With a partner, identify the context, math information, and problem statement for each of questions 1 to 4. Then solve the problem.

CARPET SALE
Regular $9.99 per square metre
Now on Sale For 20% off

1. Hori is buying carpet for his living room. It is rectangular with dimensions 4 m by 5 m. How much will Hori save if he buys the carpet at the sale price shown at the left? $39.96
2. Suppose you are in charge of setting up the cafeteria for a graduation dinner. One hundred twenty-two people will attend. The tables seat either 8 or 10 people. You do not want empty seats. How many of each size table will you need to use to make sure everyone has a seat? List all the combinations.
3. To win a contest, you have to find a mystery number. The mystery number is described this way: Sixteen more than $\frac{2}{3}$ of the mystery number is equal to two times the mystery number. What is the mystery number? 12

4. Alicia and Chantelle are playing a game. There are six tiles in a box: three red and three blue. A player picks two tiles without looking. Alicia gets a point if the tiles do not match; Chantelle gets a point if they do match. The tiles are returned to the box each time. What is the probability that both tiles have the same colour? Is this a fair game? Explain. No
5. Write a word problem using the numbers 48, 149, and 600. Remember to include a context, math information, and a problem statement. Trade problems with a classmate. Identify the features of your classmate's problem. Solve the problem.

Reading and Writing in Math: Features of Word Problems 123

Solution: Use guess and check and logical reasoning.
Since 16 is added to $\frac{2}{3}$ of a number to get 2 times the number, the number must be greater than 8 (because $2 \times 8 = 16$).
Guess a number divisible by 3.
Try 9: $\frac{2}{3} \times 9 + 16 = 6 + 9 = 15$
and $2 \times 9 = 18$ too low
Try 12: $\frac{2}{3} \times 12 + 16 = 8 + 16 = 24$
and $2 \times 12 = 24$ correct
The mystery number is 12.

4. Context: Alicia and Chantelle are playing a game of chance.
Math Information: 3 red tiles and 3 blue tiles
Two tiles are drawn.
Alicia gets a point if the tiles do not match.
Chantelle gets a point if the tiles match.
Problem: What is the probability that both tiles have the same colour? Is it a fair game?
Solution:

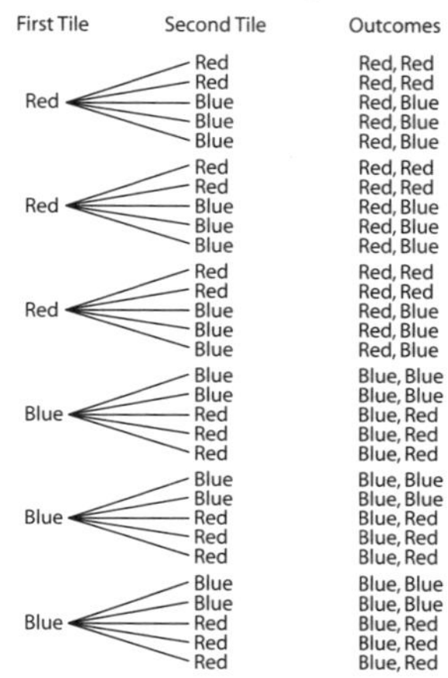

The probability of the tiles matching is: $\frac{12}{30} = \frac{2}{5}$
The probability of the tiles not matching is: $\frac{18}{30} = \frac{3}{5}$
Since these probabilities are different, the game is not fair.

5. Sample problem: Jenna's class is collecting grocery tapes to raise funds for the school library. The students receive 0.5% of the total on each grocery tape. Jenna brings in grocery tapes for $48, $149, and $600. How much will her contribution be? There are 30 students in the class. Suppose each student raised as much money as Jenna. How much money would the class raise?
Context: Jenna's class is collecting grocery tapes to raise money for the school library.
Math Information: The students receive 0.5% of the total on each grocery tape.
Jenna brings in grocery tapes for $48, $149, and $600.
Each of 30 students raises the same amount as Jenna.
Problem: What is Jenna's contribution? How much money would the class raise?
Solution: Total of Jenna's grocery tapes:
$48 + $149 + $600 = $797
Jenna's contribution:
0.5% of $797 = 0.005 × $797
= $3.99
Funds raised by the class:
$3.99 × 30 = $119.70

LESSON ORGANIZER

Student Materials
- linking cubes
- 1-cm grid paper (PM 20)
- isometric dot paper (PM 23)
- calculators
- scissors, tape
- compasses

Assessment: Masters 3.1 Unit Rubric: Geometry and Measurement, 3.4 Unit Summary: Geometry and Measurement

Correlation of Extra Practice questions on page 490:

Lesson	Questions
3.1	1
3.2	2
3.3	3
3.4	4, 5, 6, 7, 8

Unit Review

Review any lesson with etext online tutorial

What Do I Need to Know?

✓ **Euler's Formula**
For any polyhedron, the numbers of faces, edges, and vertices are related by this formula:
vertices + faces − edges = 2

✓ **Surface Area of a Triangular Prism**
Surface area = sum of the areas of 3 rectangular faces + 2 × area of one triangular face
$SA = al + bl + cl + bh$
The side lengths of a triangular face are *a*, *b*, and *c*.
The height of a triangular face is *h*.
The length of the prism is *l*.

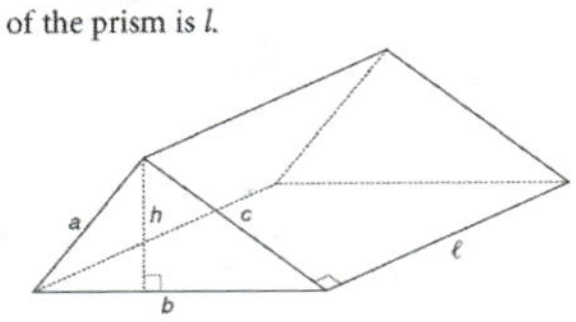

✓ **Volume of a Triangular Prism**
Volume = area of triangular base × length of prism
$V = \frac{1}{2}bhl$
The base and height of a triangular face are *b* and *h*, respectively.
The length of the prism is *l*.

124 UNIT 3: Geometry and Measurement

Sample Solutions

1. b)

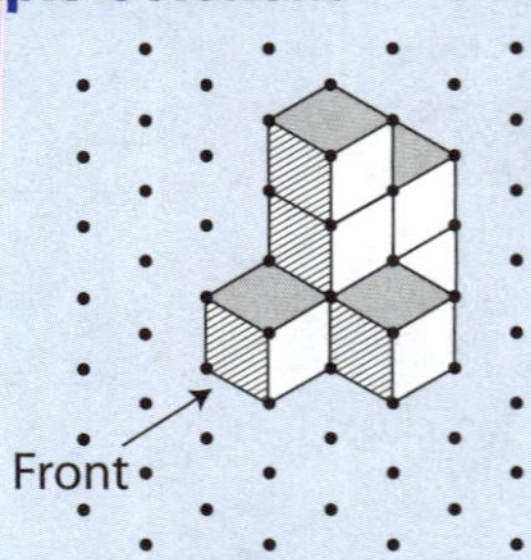

2. For example, students could sketch a triangular prism, a rectangular prism, a trapezoidal prism, and an irregular hexagonal prism.

3. b)

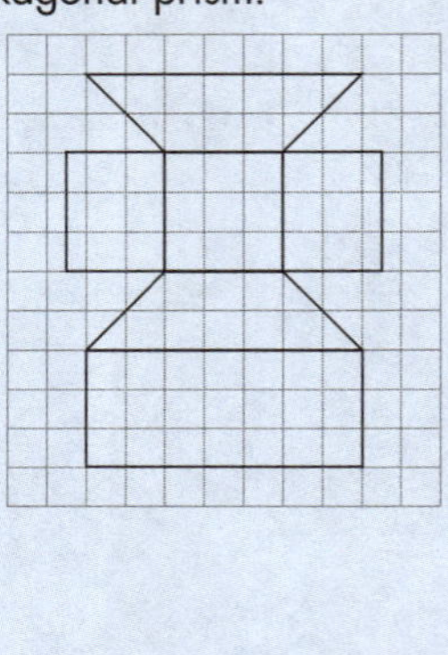

d) The prism has 6 faces, 12 edges, and 8 vertices. The bases are congruent trapezoids. The rectangular faces are: two congruent 5.7-cm by 6-cm rectangles; a 6-cm square; and a 14-cm by 6-cm rectangle.

6. The amount of soil needed is the volume of a triangular prism with dimensions:
$b = 6$ m, $h = 8$ m, $l = 0.25$ m
$V = \frac{1}{2}bhl = \frac{1}{2} \times 6 \times 8 \times 0.25 = 6$

7. Since 21 m^3 is the volume of the triangular prism, then 2×21 m^3 = 42 m^3 is the volume of the related rectangular prism.
Assume the triangular prism has a right triangular base. Then the dimensions, in metres, of the triangular prism are 3 numbers with a product of 42.
b is the base of a triangular face.
h is the height of a triangular face.
l is the length of the prism.
Find whole-number values for *b*, *h*, and *l* that have a product of 42.
For example, $b = 1$ m, $h = 2$ m, $l = 21$ m; $b = 7$ m, $h = 6$ m, $l = 1$ m; $b = 3$ m, $h = 7$ m, $l = 2$ m; $b = 14$ m, $h = 3$ m, $l = 1$ m; $b = 2$ m, $h = 7$ m, $l = 3$ m
There are many different possible combinations for each set of dimensions.

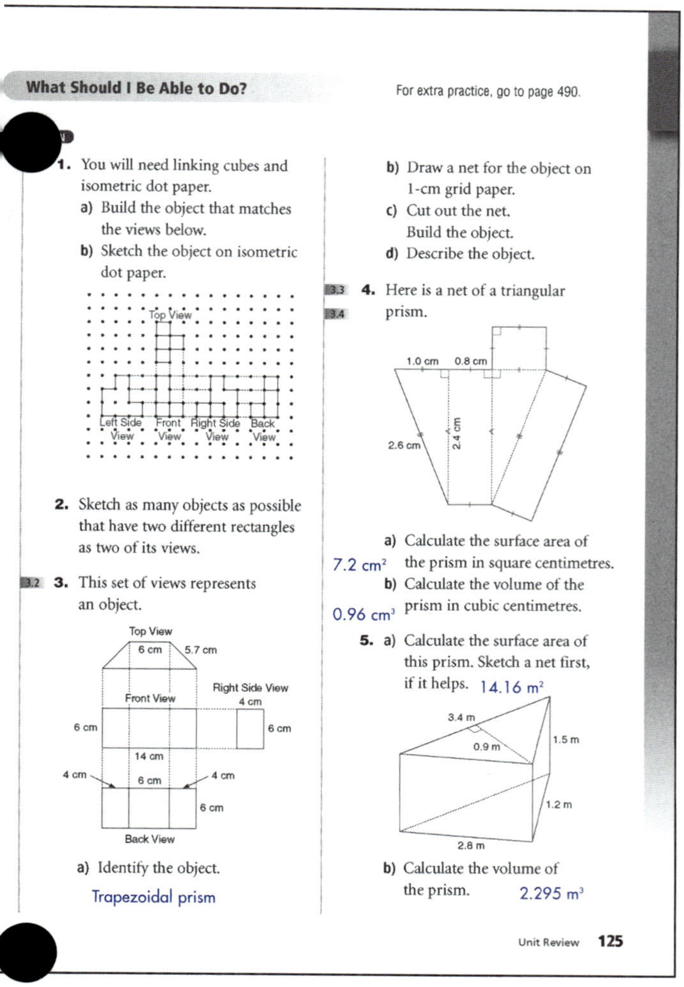

What Should I Be Able to Do?

For extra practice, go to page 490.

1. You will need linking cubes and isometric dot paper.
   a) Build the object that matches the views below.
   b) Sketch the object on isometric dot paper.

2. Sketch as many objects as possible that have two different rectangles as two of its views.

3.2 3. This set of views represents an object.

a) Identify the object.

Trapezoidal prism

b) Draw a net for the object on 1-cm grid paper.
c) Cut out the net. Build the object.
d) Describe the object.

3.3 3.4 4. Here is a net of a triangular prism.

a) Calculate the surface area of the prism in square centimetres. 7.2 cm²
b) Calculate the volume of the prism in cubic centimetres. 0.96 cm³

5. a) Calculate the surface area of this prism. Sketch a net first, if it helps. 14.16 m²

b) Calculate the volume of the prism. 2.295 m³

Unit Review 125

For example:

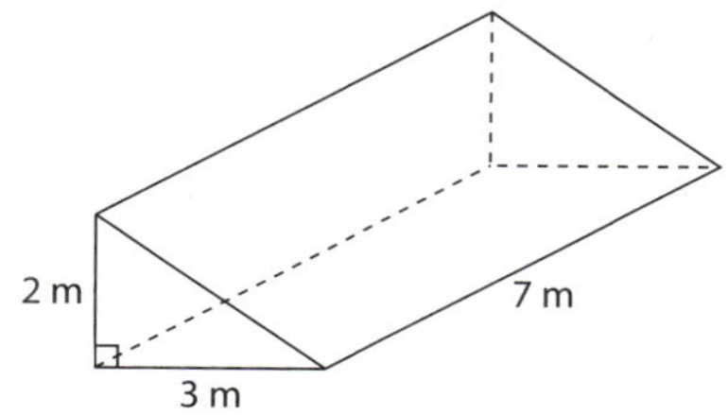

8. a) Alijah can double the length of one side of the bed that is parallel to the street.

b)

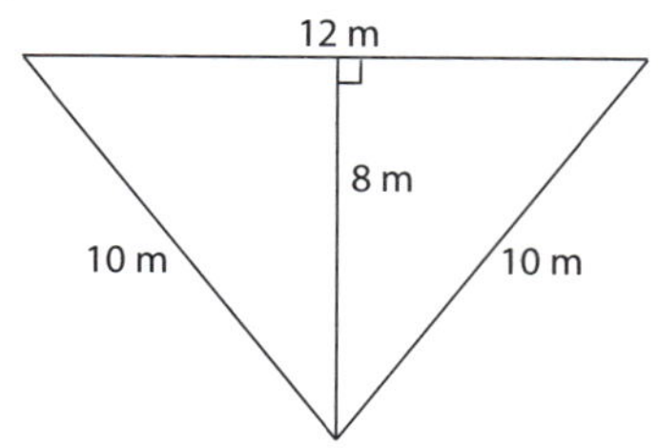

c) When one side length doubles from 6 m to 12 m, the triangle becomes an isosceles triangle, with the same height as before.

Volume of new soil: $V = \frac{1}{2} \times 12 \times 8 \times 0.25$

$= 12$

The new volume of soil is 12 m³.

This is double the soil needed before.

9. a) I assumed the soil in the bucket was not piled higher than the edges of the bucket. I assumed that the bucket was tilted up, and that soil would not fall out as the tractor was moving.

b) When the dimensions of the triangular faces are doubled, the height of the triangle also doubles. Since the base and height are doubled, the volume is 4 times as great. The extra soil would be 3 times as great as the original volume of soil.

c) $h = 80 \text{ cm} \times 2 = 160 \text{ cm}$

$b = 48 \text{ cm} \times 2 = 96 \text{ cm}$

$l = 178 \text{ cm}$

Substitute into $V = \frac{1}{2}bhl$.

$V = \frac{1}{2} \times 96 \times 160 \times 178 = 1\ 367\ 040 \text{ cm}^3$

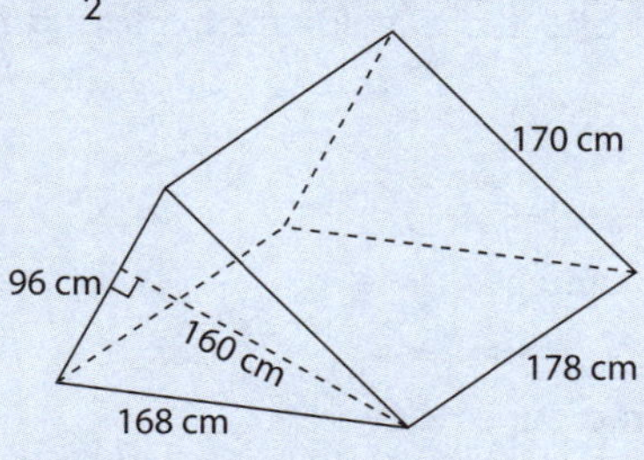

The extra soil is:

$1\ 367\ 040 \text{ cm}^3 - 341\ 760 \text{ cm}^3 = 1\ 025\ 280 \text{ cm}^3$

1 025 280 is 3 × 341 760, so the extra soil is 3 times as great as the original volume.

10. a) The volume of the triangular prism is 25 m³.

The related rectangular prism has volume $2 \times 25 \text{ m}^3 = 50 \text{ m}^3$.

The base of a triangular face is b.

The height of a triangular face is h.

The length of the prism is l.

Find whole-number values for b, h, and l that have a product of 50.

For example, $b = 5$ m, $h = 2$ m, $l = 5$ m; $b = 5$ m, $h = 10$ m, $l = 1$ m; $b = 1$ m, $h = 2$ m, $l = 25$ m; $b = 50$ m, $h = 1$ m, $l = 1$ m

There are many different possible combinations for each set of dimensions.

The most likely dimensions are 5 m by 2 m by 5 m.

b)

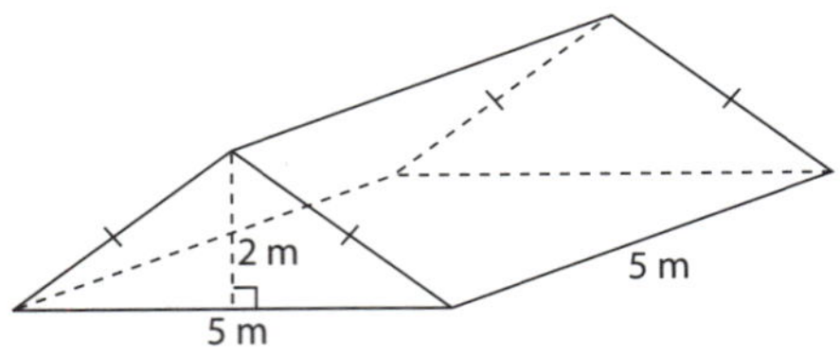

c) i) The volume of the larger tent is 4 times as great as the volume of the smaller tent. So, two of the three dimensions of the prism could have been doubled. The tent could be 10 m by 4 m by 5 m; 10 m by 20 m by 1 m; 2 m by 4 m by 25 m; 100 m by 2 m by 1 m, and so on. The most likely dimensions are 10 m by 4 m by 5 m. A tent is unlikely to be 20 m, 25 m, or 100 m long.

ii) The lengths of the base and height of the larger tent are double what they were in the smaller tent.

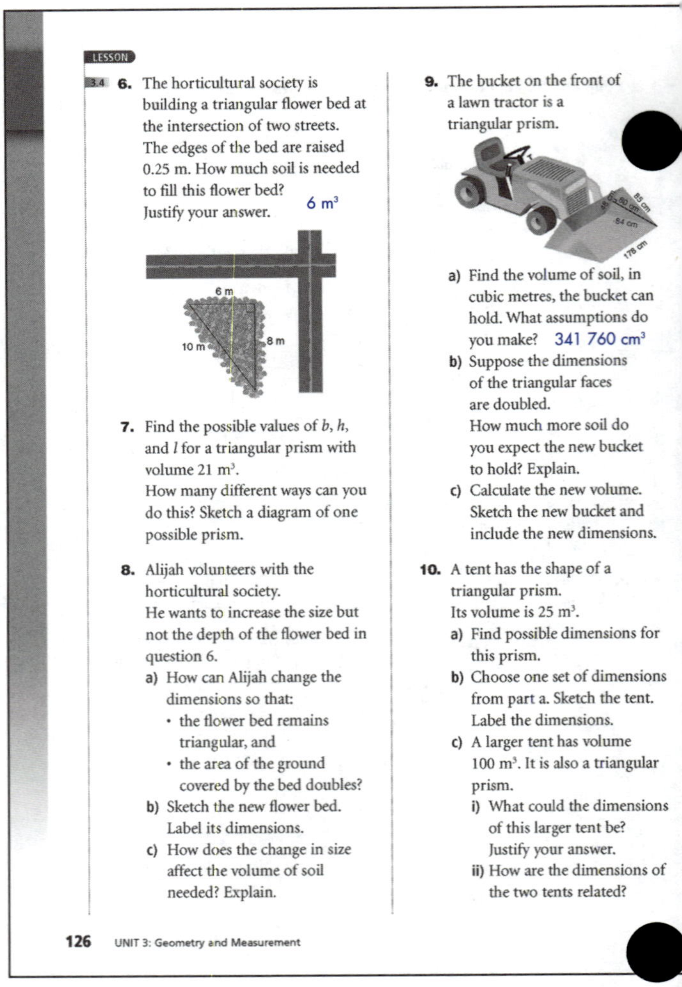

LESSON 3.4

6. The horticultural society is building a triangular flower bed at the intersection of two streets. The edges of the bed are raised 0.25 m. How much soil is needed to fill this flower bed? Justify your answer. 6 m^3

7. Find the possible values of b, h, and l for a triangular prism with volume 21 m^3. How many different ways can you do this? Sketch a diagram of one possible prism.

8. Alijah volunteers with the horticultural society. He wants to increase the size but not the depth of the flower bed in question 6.

a) How can Alijah change the dimensions so that:
- the flower bed remains triangular, and
- the area of the ground covered by the bed doubles?

b) Sketch the new flower bed. Label its dimensions.

c) How does the change in size affect the volume of soil needed? Explain.

9. The bucket on the front of a lawn tractor is a triangular prism.

a) Find the volume of soil, in cubic metres, the bucket can hold. What assumptions do you make? 341 760 cm^3

b) Suppose the dimensions of the triangular faces are doubled. How much more soil do you expect the new bucket to hold? Explain.

c) Calculate the new volume. Sketch the new bucket and include the new dimensions.

10. A tent has the shape of a triangular prism. Its volume is 25 m^3.

a) Find possible dimensions for this prism.

b) Choose one set of dimensions from part a. Sketch the tent. Label the dimensions.

c) A larger tent has volume 100 m^3. It is also a triangular prism.

i) What could the dimensions of this larger tent be? Justify your answer.

ii) How are the dimensions of the two tents related?

126 UNIT 3: Geometry and Measurement

ASSESSMENT FOR LEARNING

What to Look For

Knowledge and Understanding

✔ **Question 1:** Student understands that each view of an object provides information about the shape of the object.

✔ **Question 5:** Student understands that the volume of a triangular prism is the product of the base area and its length.

Thinking

✔ **Questions 8, 9, and 10**: Student can investigate how changing dimensions affects the volume of a triangular prism.

Communication

✔ **Question 3**: Student can describe an object built from a net created from a set of views.

✔ **Question 7**: Student can describe different triangular prisms for a given volume.

Application

✔ **Question 1:** Student can make an isometric diagram of an object built from a set of views.

✔ **Questions 4, 5, and 9:** Student can use the formulas for surface area and volume of a triangular prism by substituting the dimensions for the variables.

Recording and Reporting

Master 3.1 Unit Rubric: Geometry and Measurement
Master 3.4 Unit Summary: Geometry and Measurement

Practice Test

1. You will need linking cubes and isometric dot paper.
   a) Build the object that has these views.
   b) Sketch the object on isometric dot paper.
   c) Draw a net for the object. Cut out and fold the net to make the object.

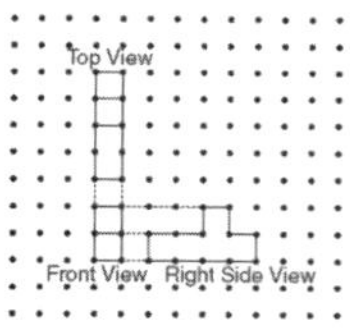

2. Calculate the surface area and volume of this prism.
   $SA = 17.99\ m^2$

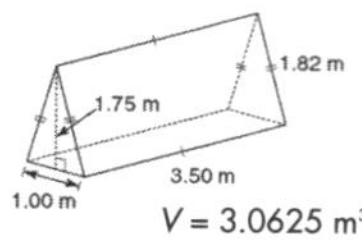

   $V = 3.0625\ m^3$

3. Look at the triangular prism in question 2.
   Suppose the base and height of the triangular faces are tripled.
   a) How does this affect the volume of the prism? Explain. 9 times as great
   b) Sketch the larger prism.
   c) Calculate the volume of the larger prism. $V = 27.5625\ m^3$

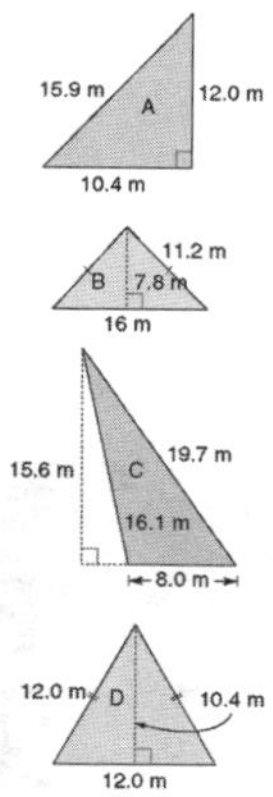

4. The triangular faces at the left are the bases of four triangular prisms. All the prisms have the same length.
   a) Which prism has the greatest volume? Explain. All have the same volume.
   b) Which prism has the least surface area? Explain.
   The prism with Triangle D as its base
5. The volume of a triangular prism is 210 cm^3.
   a) The length of the prism is 7 cm.
   What are the possible base and height of the triangular faces?
   b) On 1-cm grid paper, draw two possible triangular faces for this prism. Measure to find the lengths of any sides you do not know.
   c) Calculate the surface area of each prism whose face you drew in part b.

Practice Test 127

LESSON ORGANIZER

Student Materials

- linking cubes
- 1-cm grid paper (PM 20)
- isometric dot paper (PM 23)
- calculators
- scissors, tape
- compasses

Assessment: Masters 3.1 Unit Rubric: Geometry and Measurement, 3.4 Unit Summary: Geometry and Measurement

Assignment Guidelines

To assess the 4 Achievement Chart categories listed in the curriculum document, use these test questions:
Knowledge and Understanding: 1
Communication: 3
Thinking: 4
Application: 5

Sample Solutions

1. b)

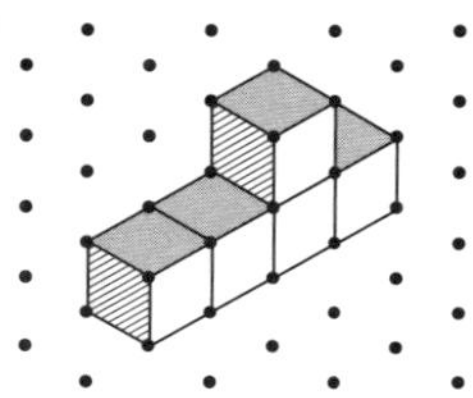

c)

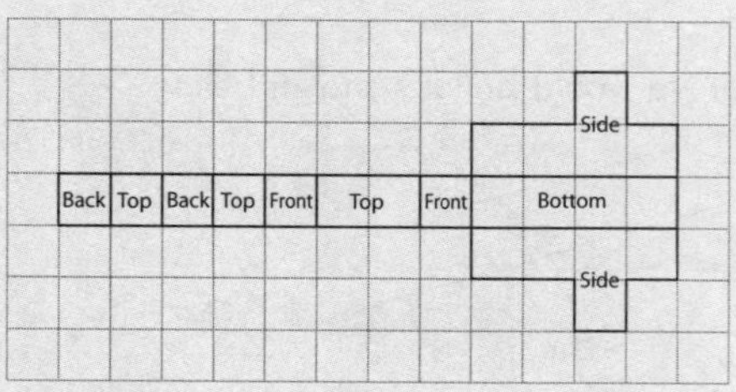

3. b)

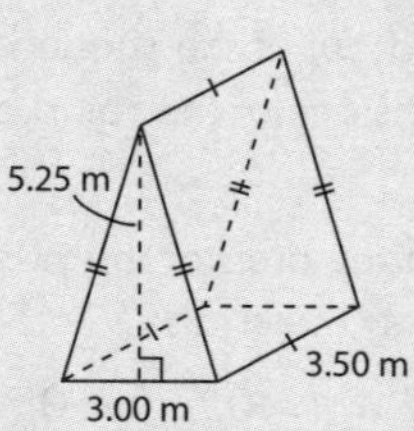

4. a) Since each triangle has area 62.4 m^2, all the prisms have the same volume.

b) The triangular faces in each prism have the same area. So, the triangular face with the least perimeter will give rectangular faces with the least total area.
Triangle A: $P = 38.3$ m; Triangle B: $P = 38.4$ m;
Triangle C: $P = 43.8$ m; Triangle D: $P = 36$ m

5. a) For example: 1 cm by 60 cm, 2 cm by 30 cm, 3 cm by 20 cm, 4 cm by 15 cm, 5 cm by 12 cm, 6 cm by 10 cm, 10 cm by 6 cm, 12 cm by 5 cm, 15 cm by 4 cm, 20 cm by 3 cm, 30 cm by 2 cm, 60 cm by 1 cm

b)

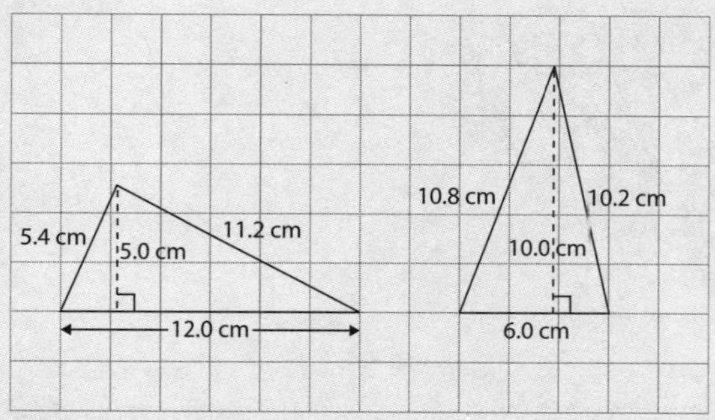

c) Possible surface areas:
$SA = (5.4 \times 7) + (12 \times 7) + (11.2 \times 7) + (12 \times 5)$
$= 260.2$; the prism has surface area 260.2 cm^2.
$SA = (10.8 \times 7) + (6 \times 7) + (10.2 \times 7) + (6 \times 10)$
$= 249$; the prism has surface area 249 cm^2.
Answers will vary depending on how students draw each triangular base.

UNIT PROBLEM

Under the Big Top

LESSON ORGANIZER (optional but recommended)

Student Grouping: 3 or 4
Student Materials
- 1-cm grid paper (PM 20)
- square dot paper (PM 22)
- isometric dot paper (PM 23)
- scissors, tape, and compasses

Assessment: Masters 3.3 Performance Assessment Rubric: Under the Big Top, 3.4 Unit Summary: Geometry and Measurement

Curriculum Note

While most of the material in the *Unit Problem* is not required by the Grade 8 curriculum, Part 3 of the *Unit Problem* does address the expectation:
- Research, describe, and report on applications of volume and capacity measurement. (8m32)

Have students complete Part 3 of the *Unit Problem*.

Present the *Unit Problem*. Encourage students to divide the tasks to be sure the activity can be completed in a reasonable time. Ensure students understand that although the dimensions on the views are given in metres, they are to produce a model. Students may choose their own scale, but the same scale should be used for related parts.

Unit Problem Under the Big Top

Suppose your class is responsible for building a circus tent. The organizers have given you the views below.

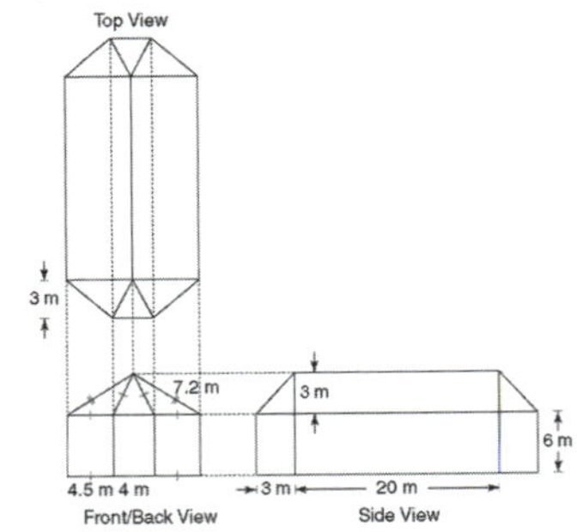

Work in a group.

Part 1

Prepare a presentation for the organizers.
Your presentation must include:
- a 3-D sketch
- a net for the tent
- a list of steps for building the net
- a model of the tent

Sample Response

Part 1

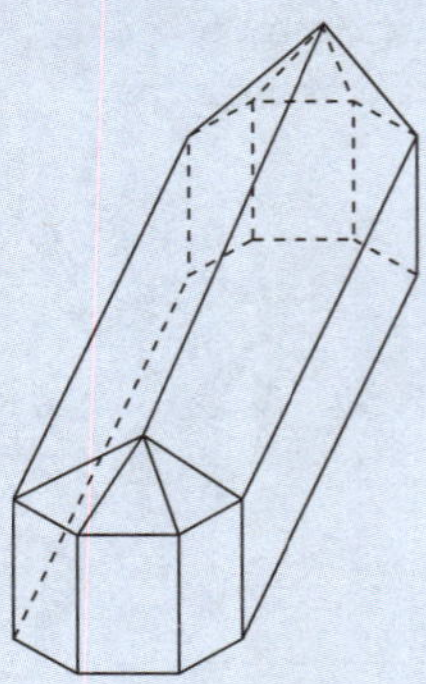

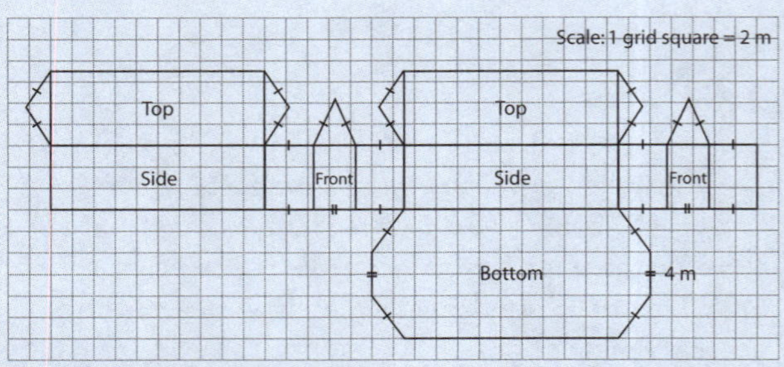

Students' work should include a list of steps they used to draw the net and a model of the tent.

Part 2

The ramp that we would build is shown below.

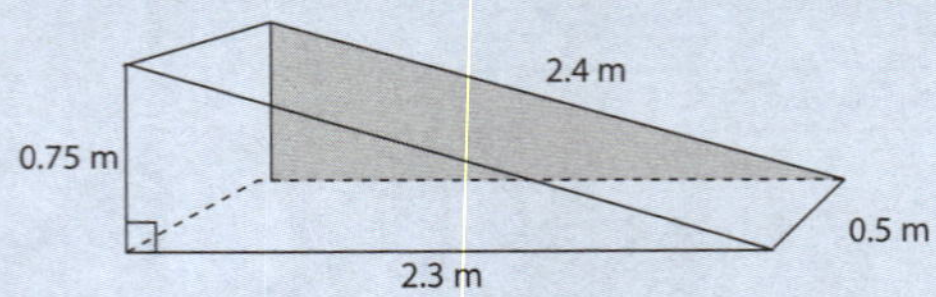

The ramp needs to be large enough to hide a person. A person could crawl or roll in and out of the shaded face, which would be hinged. The dimensions of the ramp allow a person to easily hide in it.

The cost of the materials is the surface area of the prism multiplied by the cost of the building materials, $16.50/m^2.

Substitute $a = 0.75$, $b = 2.3$, $c = 2.4$, $l = 0.5$, $h = 0.75$ into the surface area formula, then multiply by 16.50.

Costs $= (al + bl + cl + bh) \times 16.50$
$= (0.75 \times 0.5 + 2.3 \times 0.5 + 2.4 \times 0.5 + 2.3 \times 0.75) \times 16.50$
$= 4.45 \times 16.50$
$\doteq 73.43$

The cost of materials is about $73.43.
Since the materials may need to be purchased to the nearest square metre, we would purchase 5 m^2 of materials and the cost would be 5 × $16.50 = $82.50.

Part 2

Some members of a local service club will perform in the circus. They need a prop built for their act. It is a triangular prism in which one performer can hide, and which can also be used as a ramp for a bicycle jump. Prepare an estimated cost to build this prop.

Your estimate must include:

- a diagram of the prop with appropriate dimensions
- an explanation of the dimensions you chose
- calculations for the amount of materials used
- cost of materials if the building material is $\$16.50/m^2$

Check List

Your work should show:

✓ a correctly constructed model

✓ all diagrams, sketches, and calculations in detail

✓ clear explanations of your choices, procedures, and results

✓ a description of situations at home where volume and capacity are used

Part 3

The volume or capacity of the tent depends on its dimensions. Research situations where volume and capacity are used in your home.

Write a report on your findings.

Reflect on the Unit

Write a paragraph on what you have learned about representing three-dimensional objects and triangular prisms.

Try to include something from each lesson in the unit.

Unit Problem: Under the Big Top 129

Part 3

Situations where volume and capacity are used in my home:

- When I measure ingredients using a measuring cup, I use capacity. When I measure ingredients using kitchen scales, I use mass.
- When my sister fills the gas tank in her car, she is using capacity. Both the amount a gas tank holds and the amount of gas she buys are measured in litres.

Students could also report on:

- Filling the swimming pool
- Mixing rug cleaner, using concentrate and water
- Making juice from concentrate
- Doing the laundry and deciding on load size and amount of detergent

REFLECT ON THE UNIT: Three-dimensional objects can be represented using two-dimensional views from different perspectives. They can also be represented using isometric or pictorial diagrams, both of which show three dimensions. The objects can be built from linking cubes and nets. When I represent a triangular prism, the triangular face does not have to be on the bottom. No matter how a triangular prism is presented, the surface area and volume formulas can be used as long as I know the dimensions I need for the formulas.

ASSESSMENT FOR LEARNING

What to Look For	What to Do
Knowledge and Understanding ✔ Students understand how to calculate the surface area and volume of a triangular prism. ***Thinking*** ✔ Students can design an appropriate prop and find cost of materials. ***Communication*** ✔ Students can justify the dimensions of the ramp. ***Application*** ✔ Students can create an isometric or pictorial drawing of the tent.	***Extra Support:*** Make the problem accessible. Students may need some scaffolding of the steps. Use questions, such as: • What scale could you use for this model? • Which kind of representation of an object are you most comfortable with? Begin with this one. • Have you assigned a task to each person in your group? • How can you find appropriate dimensions for the prop?

Recording and Reporting

Master 3.3 Performance Assessment Rubric: Under the Big Top

Master 3.4 Unit Summary: Geometry and Measurement

Evaluating Student Learning: Preparing to Report: Unit 3 Geometry and Measurement

This unit provides an opportunity to report on the **Geometry and Spatial Sense** and **Measurement** strands.

Master 3.4: Unit Summary: Geometry and Measurement provides a comprehensive format for recording and summarizing evidence collected.

Here is an example of a completed summary chart for this Unit:

Strand: *Geometry and Spatial Sense/Measurement*	**Knowledge and Understanding**	**Thinking**	**Communication**	**Application**	***Overall***
Ongoing Observations	4	3	3	4	3/4
Work samples or portfolios; conferences	3	2	3	3	3
Unit Review	4	3	4	4	4
Unit Test	4	3	3	4	3/4
Unit Problem Under the Big Top	3	3	3	3	3
Achievement Level for reporting					3

Recording	How to Report
Ongoing Observations	Use *Master 3.2 Ongoing Observations: Geometry and Measurement* to determine the most consistent level achieved in each category. Enter it in the chart. Choose to summarize by achievement category, or simply to enter an overall level. Observations from late in the unit should be most heavily weighted.
Portfolios or collections of work samples; conferences or interviews	Use *Master 3.1 Unit Rubric: Geometry and Measurement* to guide evaluation of collections of work and information gathered in conferences. Teachers may choose to focus particular attention on the Assessment Focus questions. Work from late in the unit should be most heavily weighted.
Unit Review	*Master 3.1 Unit Rubric: Geometry and Measurement* may be helpful in determining levels of achievement. #1 and 5 provide evidence of Knowledge and Understanding; #2, 3, 4, 6, and 7 provide evidence of Application; #8, 9, and 10 provide evidence of Thinking; all questions provide evidence of Communication.
Unit Test	*Master 3.1 Unit Rubric: Geometry and Measurement* may be helpful in determining levels of achievement. #1 provides evidence of Knowledge and Understanding; #3 provides evidence of Application; #2 provides evidence of Thinking; all questions provide evidence of Communication.
Unit Problem	Use *Master 3.3 Performance Assessment Rubric: Under the Big Top*. The *Unit Problem* offers a snapshot of students' achievement. In particular, it shows their ability to synthesize and apply what they have learned.
Student Self-Assessment	Note students' perceptions of their own progress. This may take the form of an oral or written comment, or a self-rating.
Comments	Analyse the pattern of achievement to identify strengths and needs. In some cases, specific actions may need to be planned to support the learner.

Learning Skills	Ongoing Records
PM 4: Learning Skills Check List Use to record and report throughout a reporting period, rather than for each unit and/or strand.	*PM 10: Summary Class Records: Strands* *PM 11: Summary Class Records: Achievement Categories* *PM 12: Summary Record: Individual* Use to record and report evaluations of student achievement over several clusters, a reporting period, or a school year. These can also be used in place of the Unit Summary.

Name ____________________ Date ____________________

Master 3.1

Unit Rubric: Geometry and Measurement

	Level 1	Level 2	Level 3	Level 4
Knowledge and Understanding • Shows understanding by demonstrating and explaining: – relationship among the number of faces, edges, and vertices of a polyhedron – formulas for finding surface area and volume of a triangular prism – relationships between dimensions and volume of a triangular prism	shows limited understanding; may be unable to demonstrate or explain: – relationship among the number of faces, edges, and vertices – formulas for finding surface area and volume of a triangular prism – relationships between dimensions and volume of a triangular prism	shows some understanding; partially able to demonstrate or explain: – relationship among the number of faces, edges, and vertices – formulas for finding surface area and volume of a triangular prism – relationships between dimensions and volume of a triangular prism	shows considerable understanding; able to clearly and appropriately demonstrate or explain: – relationship among the number of faces, edges, and vertices – formulas for finding surface area and volume of a triangular prism – relationships between dimensions and volume of a triangular prism	shows a high degree of understanding; able to accurately and effectively demonstrate or explain: – relationship among the number of faces, edges, and vertices – formulas for finding surface area and volume of a triangular prism – relationships between dimensions and volume of a triangular prism
Thinking • Chooses, carries out, and justifies a range of strategies to pose and solve problems involving triangular prisms	with assistance, chooses, carries out, and justifies a limited range of appropriate strategies to pose, solve, and check problems; rarely produces an accurate solution	with limited assistance, chooses, carries out, and justifies some appropriate strategies to pose, solve, and check problems; frequently produces an accurate solution	chooses, carries out, and justifies many appropriate strategies to pose, solve, and check problems; usually produces an accurate solution	develops, carries out, and justifies effective, and often innovative, strategies to pose, solve, and check problems; always produces an accurate solution
Communication • Explains concepts, procedures, and reasoning clearly, using appropriate terms	unable to explain concepts, procedures, and reasoning clearly	partially explains concepts, procedures, and reasoning	explains concepts, procedures, and reasoning clearly	explains concepts, procedures, and reasoning clearly, precisely, and confidently
• Presents work, including sketches and diagrams, clearly	presents work with little clarity	presents work with some clarity	presents work with considerable clarity	presents work with a high degree of clarity
Application • Accurately: – uses formulas to calculate the surface area and volume of triangular prisms – converts between metric units of area, volume, and capacity	limited accuracy; major errors or omissions in: – calculating surface area and volume of triangular prisms – converting between metric units	somewhat accurate; several minor errors or omissions in: – calculating surface area and volume of triangular prisms – converting between metric units	generally accurate; few minor errors or omissions in: – calculating surface area and volume of triangular prisms – converting between metric units	accurate and precise; no errors in: – calculating surface area and volume of triangular prisms – converting between metric units

Name ____________________ Date ______________

Master 3.2

Ongoing Observations: Geometry and Measurement

The behaviours described under each heading are examples; they are not intended to be an exhaustive list of all that might be observed. More detailed descriptions are provided in each lesson under *Assessment for Learning*.

STUDENT ACHIEVEMENT: Geometry and Measurement

Student	**Knowledge and Understanding** • Demonstrates and explains formulas for surface area and volume (triangular prism)	**Thinking** • Chooses and carries out appropriate strategies to solve problems involving the surface area and volume of triangular prisms	**Communication** • Explains concepts, procedures, and reasoning clearly • Presents work clearly, including sketches and diagrams	**Application** • Calculates surface area and volume of triangular prisms • Converts between metric units of area, volume, and capacity

Level 1 – very limited; Level 2 – somewhat or limited; Level 3 – satisfactory; Level 4 – thorough

Name ____________________ Date ____________________

Master 3.3

Performance Assessment Rubric: Under the Big Top

	Level 1	Level 2	Level 3	Level 4
Knowledge and Understanding • Shows understanding by explaining and justifying: – steps for building the net – the dimensions chosen for the prop – how the amount of materials needed was calculated	shows limited understanding; may be unable to explain or justify: – how to build the net – dimensions chosen for the prop – calculations for the amount of materials needed	shows some understanding; partially able to explain or justify: – how to build the net – dimensions chosen for the prop – calculations for the amount of materials needed	shows considerable understanding; able to explain or justify: – how to build the net – dimensions chosen for the prop – calculations for the amount of materials needed	shows a high degree of understanding; able to accurately and effectively explain or justify: – how to build the net – dimensions chosen for the prop – calculations for the amount of materials needed
Thinking • Successfully uses appropriate strategies to: – construct a model of the tent (Part 1) – design an appropriate prop and determine cost of materials (Part 2)	uses a limited range of appropriate strategies to solve the problems; little success	uses some appropriate strategies to solve the problems; partially successful	uses many appropriate strategies to solve the problems; generally successful	uses innovative and effective strategies to solve the problems; highly successful
Communication • Explains reasoning clearly using appropriate mathematical terminology	explains reasoning unclearly and imprecisely using few mathematical terms	explains reasoning with some clarity using some appropriate mathematical terms	explains reasoning clearly and precisely using appropriate mathematical terms	explains reasoning clearly, precisely, and confidently using a range of appropriate mathematical terminology
• Presents work clearly, including sketches, diagrams, formulas, calculations, and research	presents work with little clarity	presents work with some clarity	presents work clearly	presents work clearly and precisely
Application • Accurately: – produces a 3-D sketch, a net, and a model of the tent – calculates the amount of materials used for the prop – calculates the cost of materials for the prop	limited accuracy; major errors or omissions in: – producing a 3-D sketch, a net, and a model – calculating the amount of materials used for the prop – calculating the cost of materials for the prop	somewhat accurate; several minor errors or omissions in: – producing a 3-D sketch, a net, and a model – calculating the amount of materials used for the prop – calculating the cost of materials for the prop	generally accurate; few minor errors or omissions in: – producing a 3-D sketch, a net, and a model – calculating the amount of materials used for the prop – calculating the cost of materials for the prop	accurate and precise; no errors or omissions in: – producing a 3-D sketch, a net, and a model – calculating the amount of materials used for the prop – calculating the cost of materials for the prop

Name ______________________ Date ________________

Master 3.4

Unit Summary: Geometry and Measurement

Review assessment records to determine the most consistent achievement levels for the assessments conducted. Some cells may be blank. *Overall* achievement levels may be recorded in each row, rather than identifying levels for each achievement category.

	Most Consistent Level of Achievement*				
Strand: *Geometry and Spatial Sense/Measurement*	**Knowledge and Understanding**	**Thinking**	**Communication**	**Application**	***Overall***
Ongoing Observations					
Work samples or portfolios; conferences					
Unit Review					
Unit Test					
Unit Problem Under the Big Top					
Achievement Level for reporting					

*Use Ontario Achievement Levels 1, 2, 3, 4

Self-Assessment:

Comments: (Strengths, Needs, Next Steps)

Name ____________________ Date ______________

Master 3.5a

Additional Activity 1: Spin, Build, Draw

Play with a partner.

Materials: *Spin, Build, Draw Spinner* (Master 3.5b), number cube labelled 1 to 6, linking cubes, 1-cm grid paper (PM 20) or square dot paper (PM 22), open paper clip

How to Play:

1. Use a pencil to hold the open paper clip in place in the centre of the spinner.
   Each player spins the paper clip to find how many views she must draw.
   Each player rolls the number cube to find how many linking cubes she must use.
   If you roll a 1 or 2, roll again.

2. Each player uses her linking cubes to build an object.
   Use square dot paper or grid paper.
   Draw the number of different views spun.

3. Trade views with your partner. Build your partner's object.

4. A player gets 1 point for each view that matches the views drawn.
   A player gets 1 point if the object matches her opponent's object.

5. Play another round. The winner is the player with more points after 4 rounds.

Take It Further: Play the game again.
This time, roll the number cube twice and add the numbers.
This is now the number of linking cubes to use.

Name ____________________ Date ________________

Master 3.5b

Spin, Build, Draw Spinner

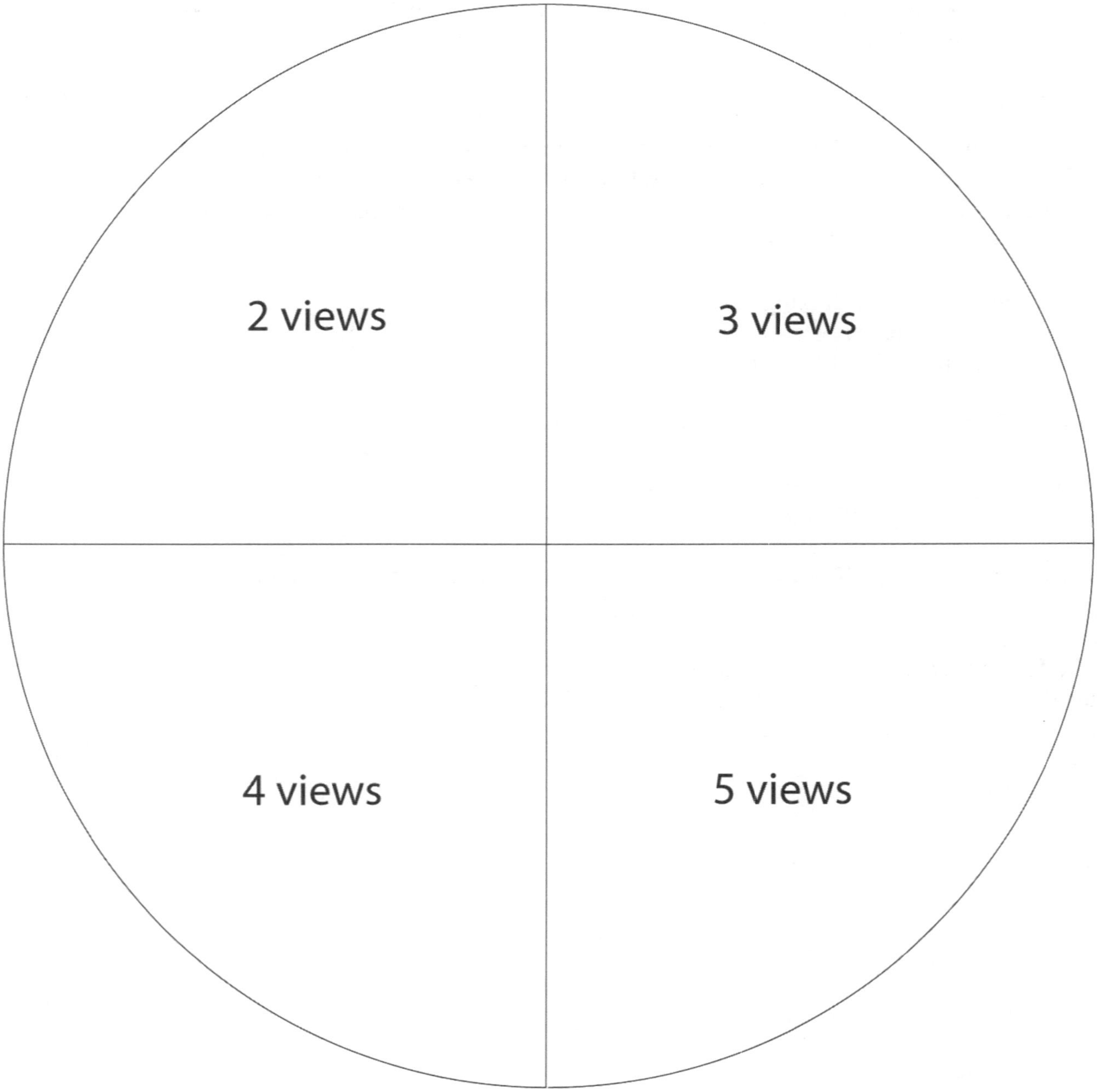

Name ____________________ Date ______________

Master 3.6a

Additional Activity 2: The Platonic Solids

Work in a group.

Materials: Nets for a tetrahedron, cube, octahedron, dodecahedron, icosahedron (Masters 3.6b to 3.6f), scissors, tape

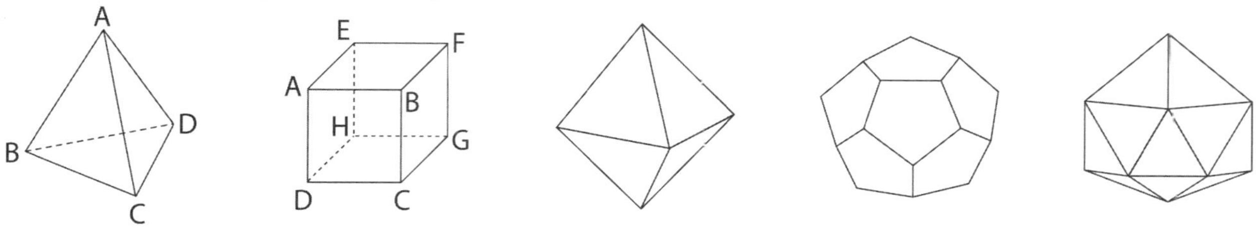

Tetrahedron | Cube | Octahedron | Dodecahedron | Icosahedron

What to Do:

Share the work.
For the octahedron, use 2 copies of Master 3.6d.
For the dodecahedron, use 2 copies of Master 3.6e.
For the icosahedron, use 2 copies of Master 3.6f.

1. Cut out each net.
Fold, then tape, the net to make the solid named.

2. What do you notice about the faces on each solid?

3. Count the numbers of faces, edges, and vertices on each solid.
Copy and complete this table.

Object	Number of Faces	Number of Edges	Number of Vertices
Tetrahedron			
Cube			
Octahedron			
Dodecahedron			
Icosahedron			

4. Do the solids obey Euler's formula? Explain.

Take It Further: The 5 solids you constructed are the Platonic solids.
How are they different from other solids such as a square pyramid or a triangular prism?

Name ______________________ Date ________________

Master 3.6b

Net of a Tetrahedron

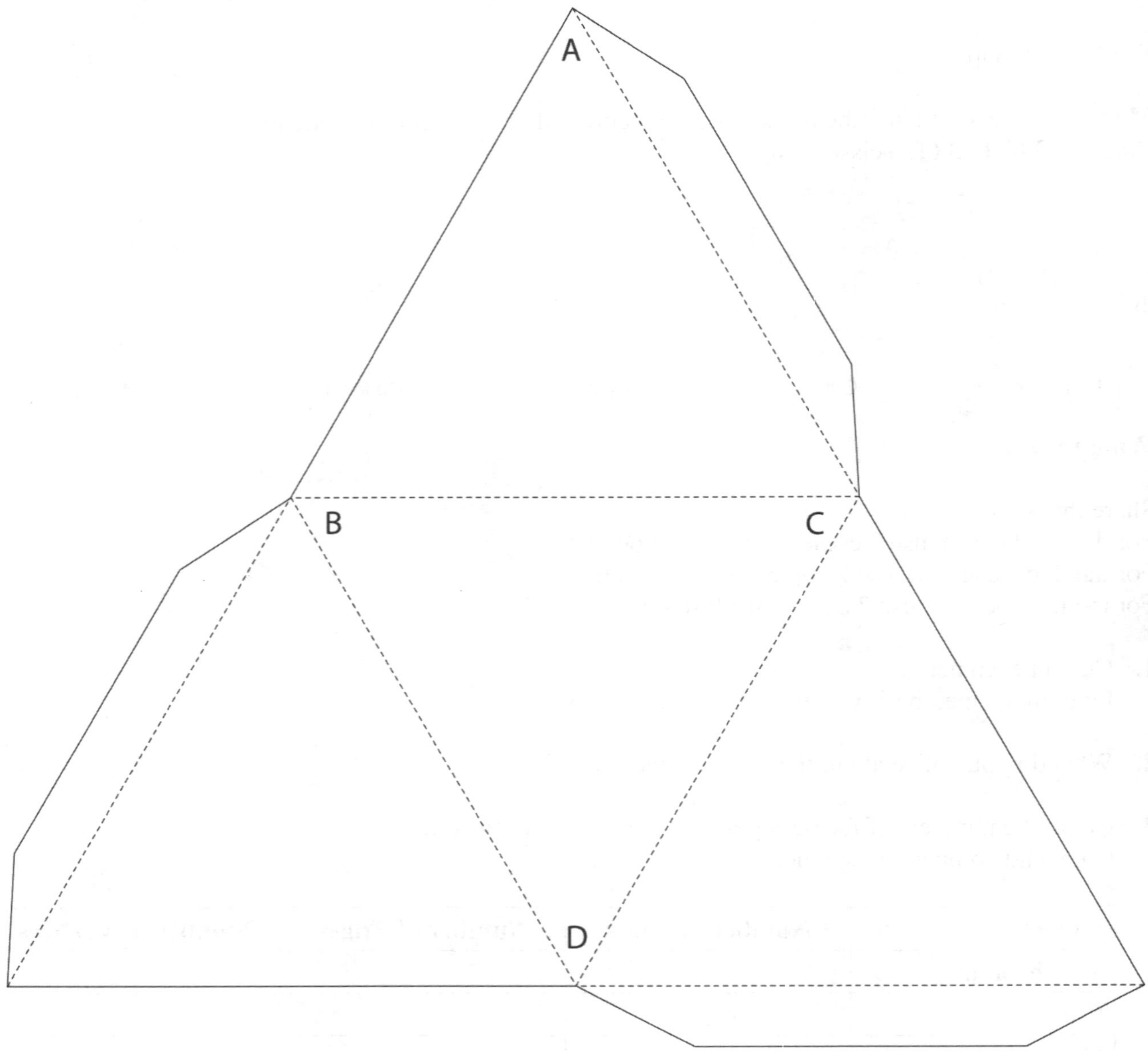

Name ____________________ Date ________________

Master 3.6c

Net of a Cube

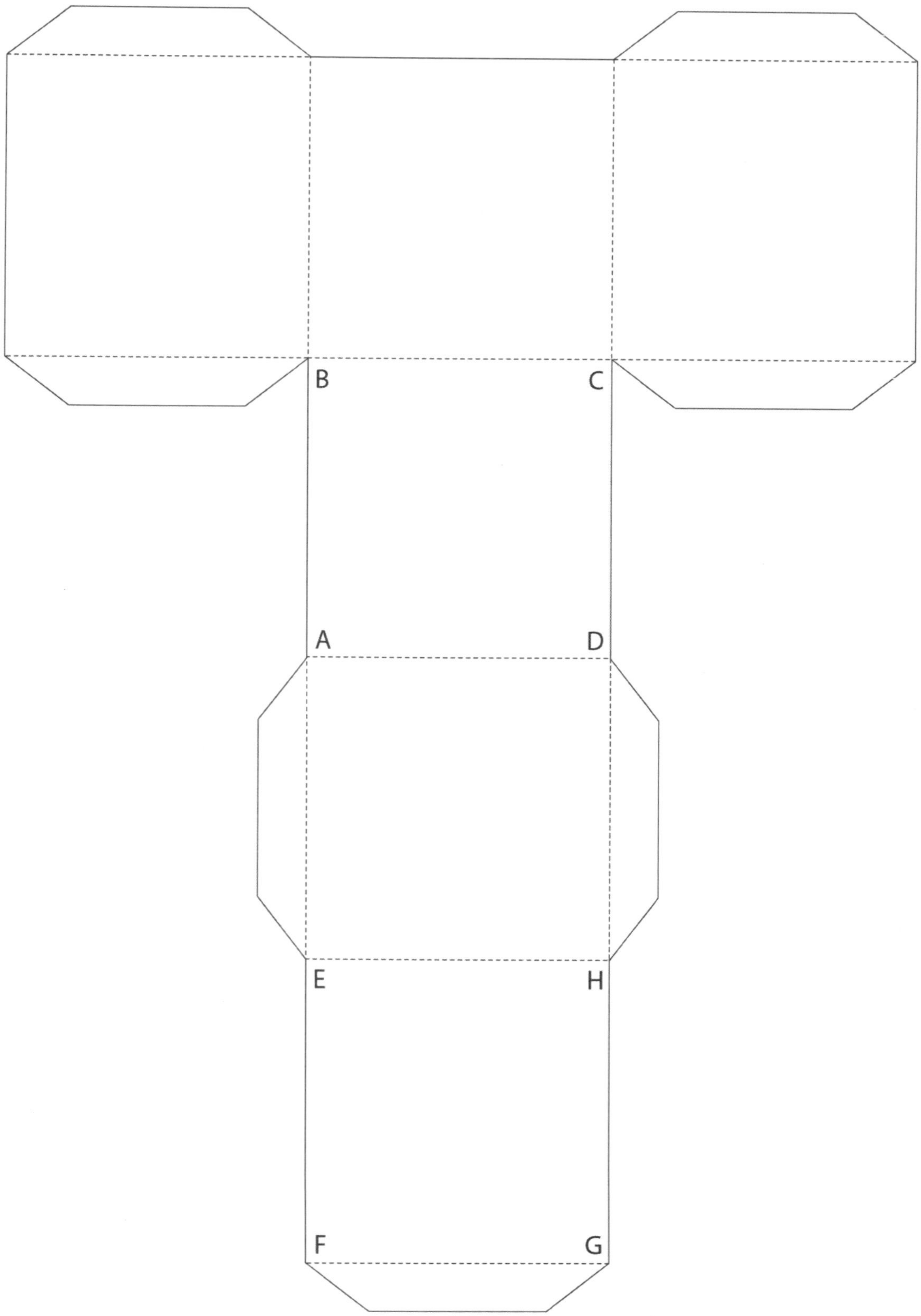

Name ____________________ Date ________________

Master 3.6d

Net for an Octahedron

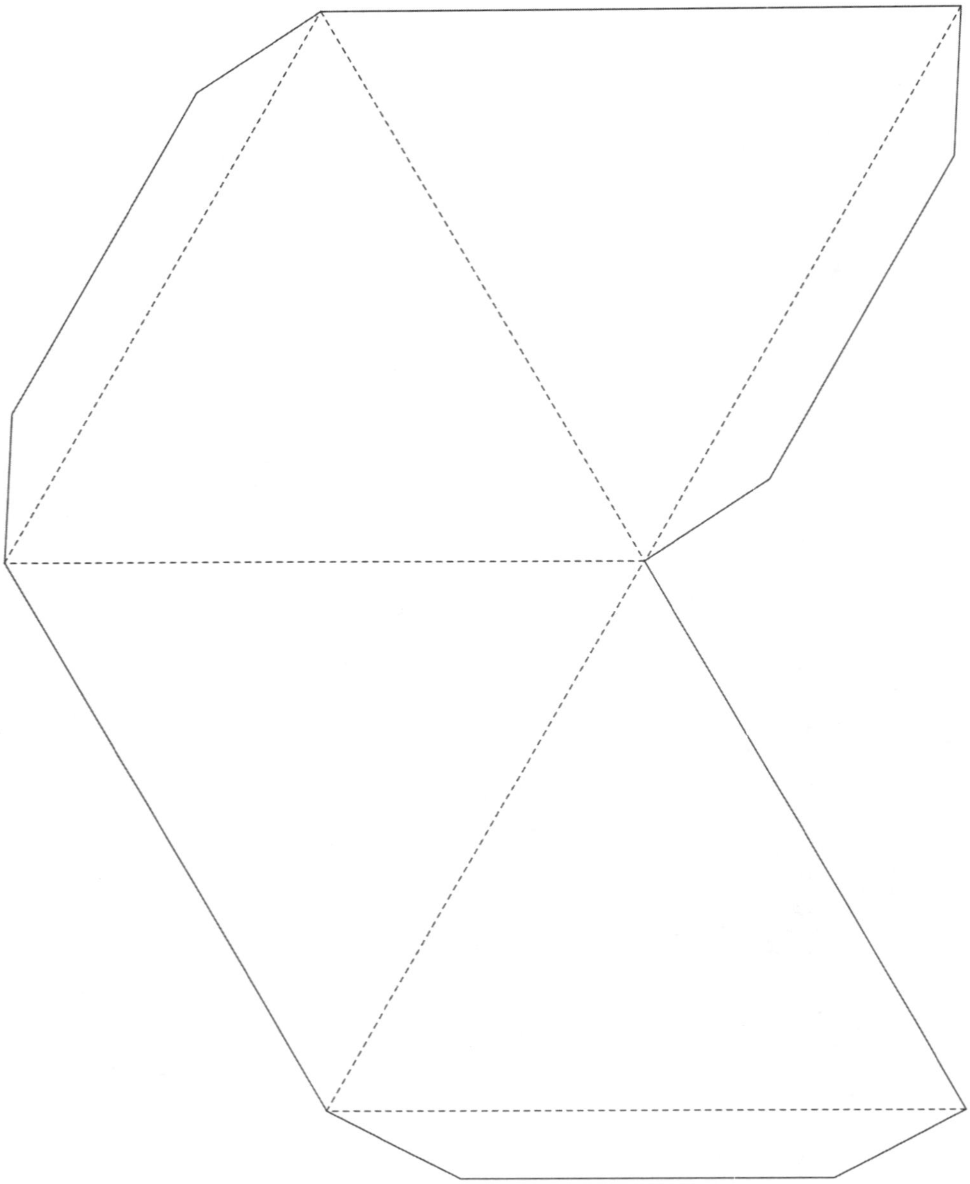

Name ____________________ Date ________________

Master 3.6e

Net for a Dodecahedron

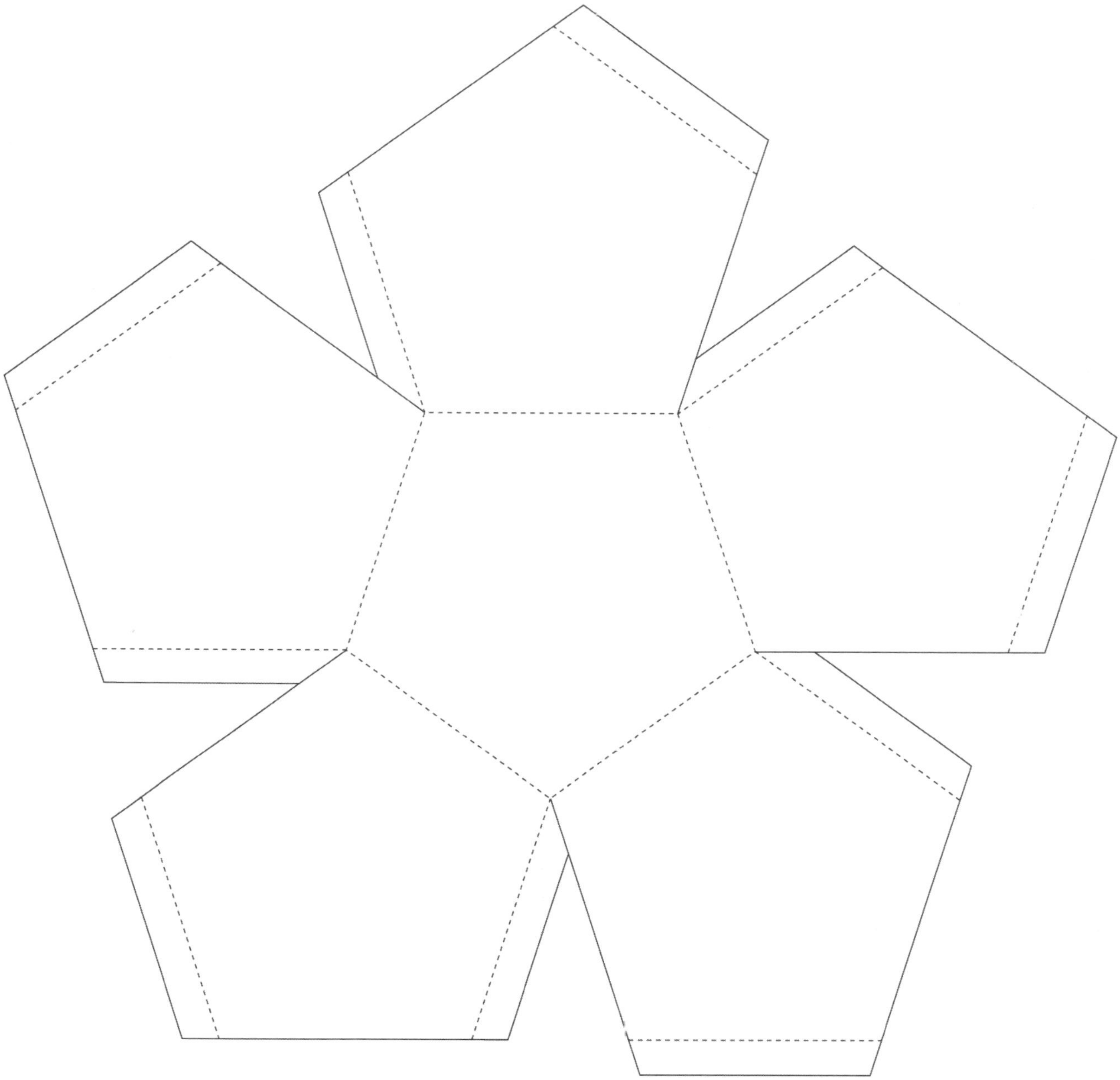

Name ____________________ Date ________________

Master 3.6f

Net for an Icosahedron

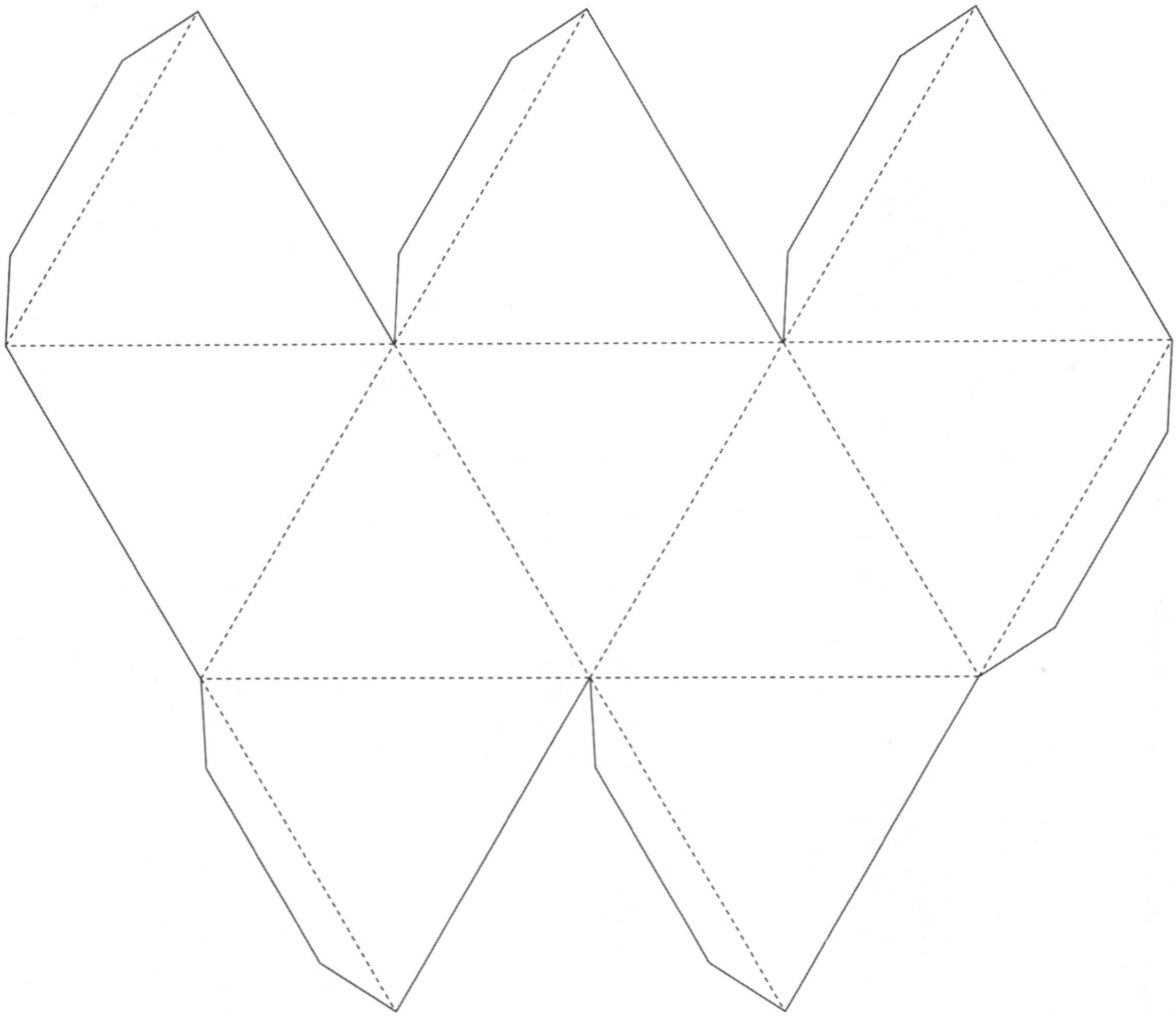

Name ____________________ Date ______________

Master 3.7a

Additional Activity 3: Measurement Bingo

Play in groups of 4.

Materials: *Measurement Bingo Game Pieces* (Master 3.7b), scissors, 3 number cubes labelled from 1 to 6, paper bag, 4-column charts (PM 19)

How to Play:

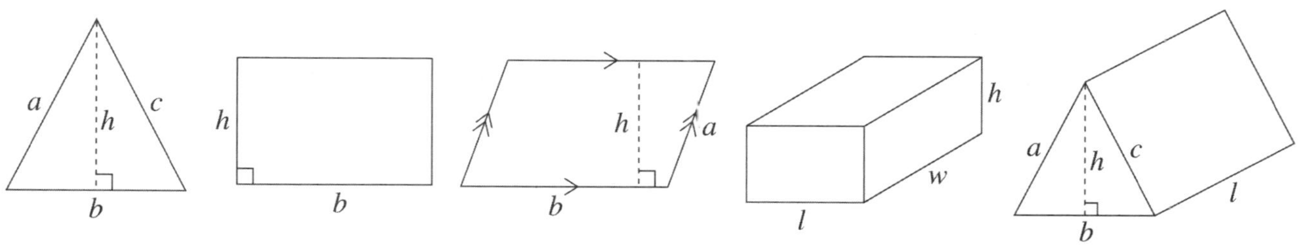

1. Each player uses a 4-column chart to make a bingo card with column headings:
   P Perimeter (cm), *A* Area (cm^2), *SA* Surface Area (cm^2), and *V* Volume (cm^3).
   Divide the columns into 4 rows.
   Complete each column by placing one number from 0 to 9 in each cell.
   A number may be used more than once.

2. Cut out the game pieces. Place them in a paper bag.

3. Player A draws a game piece from the bag.
   He rolls 2 or 3 number cubes depending on the game piece drawn.
   The numbers rolled are the dimensions of the figure or object in centimetres.
   He uses these dimensions to calculate the indicated measurement.
   The other players must agree that the calculation is correct.

4. Player A crosses off any digits in his answer that are in the corresponding column of his bingo card. For example, for the game piece "*P* Triangle Roll 3 cubes for *a*, *b*, *c*:"
   2, 5, and 6 are rolled so the perimeter is 2 cm + 5 cm + 6 cm = 13 cm.
   Then, 1 and 3 can be crossed off in the column *P* Perimeter.
   The game piece is returned to the bag.

5. Players take turns. The first player to cross off all the numbers in a row, column, or diagonal wins.

Take It Further: Play the game again.
This time, write a possible measurement in each cell by considering the possible combinations of numbers that can be rolled and their probabilities. Players cross off measurements rather than digits.

Name ____________________ Date ____________________

Master 3.7b

Measurement Bingo Game Pieces

P Triangle Roll 3 cubes for *a*, *b*, and *c*	*P* Triangle Roll 3 cubes for *a*, *b*, and *c*	*P* Rectangle Roll 2 cubes for *b* and *h*	*P* Rectangle Roll 2 cubes for *b* and *h*	*P* Parallelogram Roll 2 cubes for *a* and *b*	*P* Parallelogram Roll 2 cubes for *a* and *b*
A Triangle Roll 2 cubes for *b* and *h*	*A* Triangle Roll 2 cubes for *b* and *h*	*A* Rectangle Roll 2 cubes for *b* and *h*	*A* Rectangle Roll 2 cubes for *b* and *h*	*A* Parallelogram Roll 2 cubes for *b* and *h*	*A* Parallelogram Roll 2 cubes for *b* and *h*
SA Rectangular Prism Roll 3 cubes for *l*, *w*, and *h*	*SA* Rectangular Prism Roll 3 cubes for *l*, *w*, and *h*	*SA* Rectangular Prism Roll 3 cubes for *l*, *w*, and *h*	*SA* Rectangular Prism Roll 3 cubes for *l*, *w*, and *h*	*SA* Rectangular Prism Roll 3 cubes for *l*, *w*, and *h*	*SA* Rectangular Prism Roll 3 cubes for *l*, *w*, and *h*
V Rectangular Prism Roll 3 cubes for *l*, *w*, and *h*	*V* Rectangular Prism Roll 3 cubes for *l*, *w*, and *h*	*V* Rectangular Prism Roll 3 cubes for *l*, *w*, and *h*	*V* Rectangular Prism Roll 3 cubes for *l*, *w*, and *h*	*V* Rectangular Prism Roll 3 cubes for *l*, *w*, and *h*	*V* Rectangular Prism Roll 3 cubes for *l*, *w*, and *h*
SA Rectangular Faces of the Triangular Prism, $l = 3$ Roll 3 cubes for *a*, *b*, and *c*	*SA* Rectangular Faces of the Triangular Prism, $l = 3$ Roll 3 cubes for *a*, *b*, and *c*	*SA* Rectangular Faces of the Triangular Prism, $l = 7$ Roll 3 cubes for *a*, *b*, and *c*	*SA* Rectangular Faces of the Triangular Prism, $l = 7$ Roll 3 cubes for *a*, *b*, and *c*	*SA* Rectangular Faces of the Triangular Prism, $l = 1$ Roll 3 cubes for *a*, *b*, and *c*	*SA* Rectangular Faces of the Triangular Prism, $l = 1$ Roll 3 cubes for *a*, *b*, and *c*
V Triangular Prism Roll 3 cubes for *b*, *h*, and *l*	*V* Triangular Prism Roll 3 cubes for *b*, *h*, and *l*	*V* Triangular Prism Roll 3 cubes for *b*, *h*, and *l*	*V* Triangular Prism Roll 3 cubes for *b*, *h*, and *l*	*V* Triangular Prism Roll 3 cubes for *b*, *h*, and *l*	*V* Triangular Prism Roll 3 cubes for *b*, *h*, and *l*

Name ______________________ Date ________________

Master 3.8

Step-by-Step 1

Lesson 3.1, Question 6

You will need 6 linking cubes, isometric dot paper, and square dot paper.

Step 1 How wide is the top view? _______ How long is the top view? _______

Look at the side view. How high is the object? _______

Step 2 Use linking cubes to make the top view.
Remember that an internal line segment shows a depth change.
Think about the height you found in *Step 1*.

Step 3 Check to see that the right side view of your object matches.
If not, try again.

Step 4 Place the object so the back/left side is facing you.
To make an isometric drawing of your object:
Draw the vertical edges on isometric dot paper.
Draw the horizontal edges that appear to go down to the right.
Draw the vertical edges that appear to go up to the right.

Step 5 Which other views of the object could you draw?

____

Draw these views on square dot paper.
Use internal line segments to show changes in depth.

Name ____________________ Date ______________

Master 3.9

Step-by-Step 2

Lesson 3.2, Question 6

You will need 0.5-cm grid paper, scissors, and tape.

Step 1 Look at the views. Which figures are the faces of the object?

____

Step 2 Is the object a prism or a pyramid? ______________

How many faces does this object have? _________
Remember there are more views than are given.

Step 3 Look at your answers in *Steps 1* and *2*.
Which object do the views represent? ______________________________

Drawing a Net

Step 4 Which view shows no changes in depth? ____________
Draw this view on grid paper. Let the length of 1 grid square represent 1 cm.

Step 5 Use the other views to draw the top face and right side face.
Remember that both views show a change in depth.
Draw faces at common edges for the missing views.
Consider the edges the faces join to help with dimensions.

Step 6 Cut out the net. Build the object.
Does the net form the object? _____
If your answer is no, are there edges that do not match? Are faces missing?
Can you rearrange or cut out some of the faces to form the object?
Make corrections to your net.
If your answer is yes, did you build the object you named in *Step 3*? Explain.

____

Step 7 Use the net from *Step 6*. Rearrange the faces to make a different net for the object.

Step 8 Which net is easier to draw or fold? Explain.

____

____

Name ____________ Date ____________

Master 3.10

Step-by-Step 3

Lesson 3.3, Question 7

This triangular prism represents the water trough.

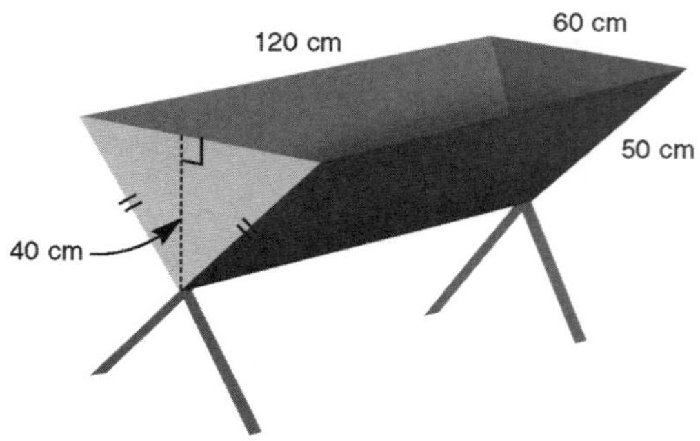

Step 1 Identify the variable that represents each dimension.

The length of the prism is l = _____

The 3 sides of a triangular face are: a = ____________

b = ____________

c = ____________

The height of a triangular face is: h = ____________

Step 2 Which face of the trough is missing? ______________________________

Step 3 Write the area of each face.

One rectangular face: _______

Other rectangular face: _______

One triangular face: _______

Other triangular face: _______

What is the surface area of the trough? _______ cm^2

Step 4 To convert square centimetres to square metres, divide the surface area from *Step 3* by 10 000.

How much metal is needed to build the water trough? ____________________ m^2

Name ____________________ Date ________________

Master 3.11

Step-by-Step 4

Lesson 3.4, Question 9

The amount of concrete needed to fill the form is the volume of this triangular prism.

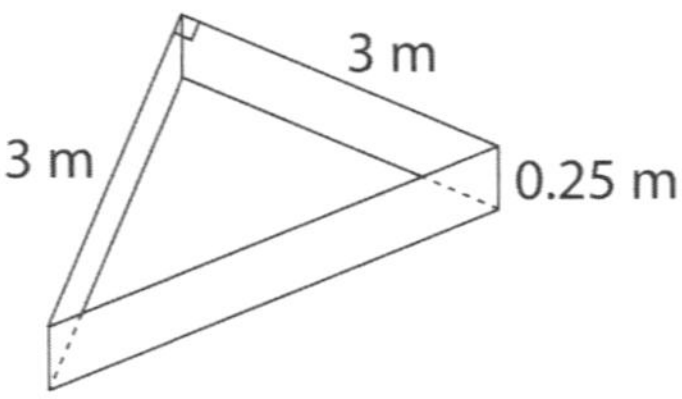

Step 1 Identify the variable that represents each dimension.

The base of the triangle is: b = _____

The height of the triangle is: h = _____

The length of the prism is: l = _____

Step 2 Use the formula $V = \frac{1}{2}bhl$. Find the volume of the form.

Step 3 How much concrete will Jackie need to mix to fill the form? ____________

Step 4 Jackie increases the equal sides of the form from 3 m to 6 m.
Here is a sketch of the larger form.
Label it with the variables and new dimensions.

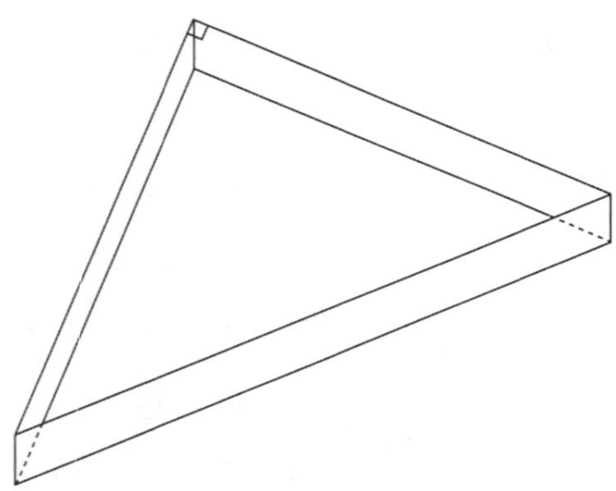

Step 5 Repeat *Steps 1* and *2* to find how much concrete Jackie needs to fill the larger form.

Step 6 Compare your answers in *Steps 3* and *5*.
How much more concrete will Jackie need to mix to fill the larger form?

__________ – __________ = __________

Name ____________________ Date ______________

Master 3.12a

Unit Test: Unit 3
Geometry and Measurement

1. Calculate the surface area and volume of this prism.
Write the surface area in square centimetres and square metres.
Write the volume in cubic centimetres and cubic metres.

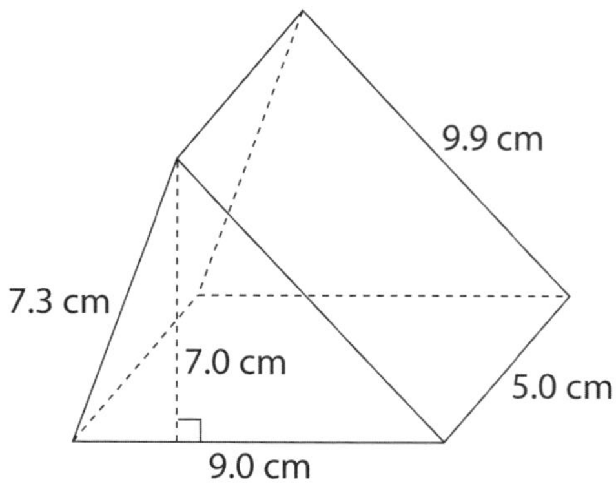

2. Look at the triangular prism in question 1.

a) Suppose the length of the prism is doubled.
How does this affect the volume of the prism? Explain.

b) Suppose all the dimensions of the prism are tripled.
How does this affect the surface area of the prism? Explain.

Name ______________________ Date ________________

Master 3.12b

Unit Test continued

3. A landscaping company digs a drainage ditch 5 m long. The ditch holds 30 m^3 of gravel.

a) The ditch has the shape of a triangular prism. What could the dimensions of this ditch be?

b) The ditch has a depth greater than 1 m. Sketch a possible ditch.

Name ____________________ Date ________________

Master 3.13

Sample Answers

Unit Test – Master 3.12

1. $SA = 194 \text{ cm}^2$, 0.0194 m^2;
   $V = 157.5 \text{ cm}^3$, $0.000\,157\,5 \text{ m}^3$

2. **a)** The volume of the prism will double because only one of the three dimensions has been doubled.

   b) Each dimension has tripled. So, the area of each face will be 9 times as great. When the areas are added, the surface area will be about 9 times as great as in question 1.

3. **a)** The volume of gravel in the ditch is 30 m^3 and the length of the ditch is 5 m. So, the area of a triangular face, in square metres, is $30 \div 5 = 6$.
   Let the base of the triangular face be b and its height h. The area is $\frac{1}{2}bh$, which is 6.
   So, $bh = 12$
   Find whole-number values of b and h that have a product of 12.
   Possible values are:
   $b = 1$ m, $h = 12$ m; $b = 2$ m, $h = 6$ m;
   $b = 3$ m, $h = 4$ m; $b = 12$ m, $h = 1$ m;
   $b = 6$ m, $h = 2$ m; $b = 4$ m, $h = 3$ m
   The dimensions of the ditch are any of the pairs of b and h values above, and length 5 m.

   b) For example, since the depth has to be greater than 1 m, the ditch could be 2 m deep, 6 m wide, and 5 m long.

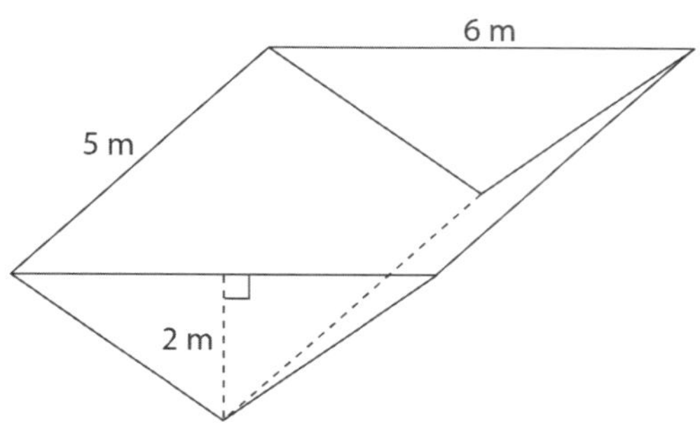

Extra Practice Masters 3.14–3.18

Go to the CD-ROM to access editable versions of these Extra Practice Masters

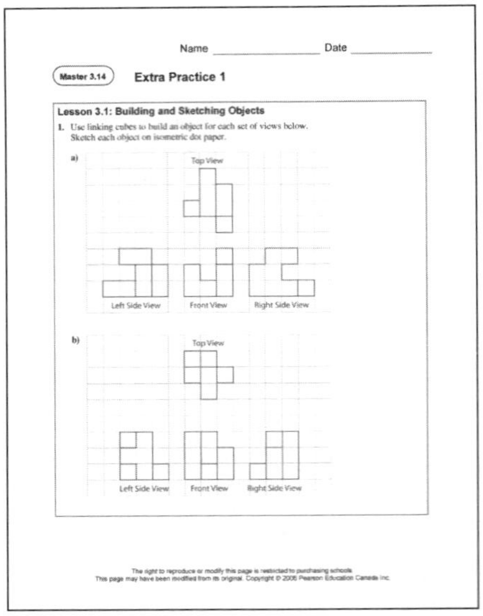

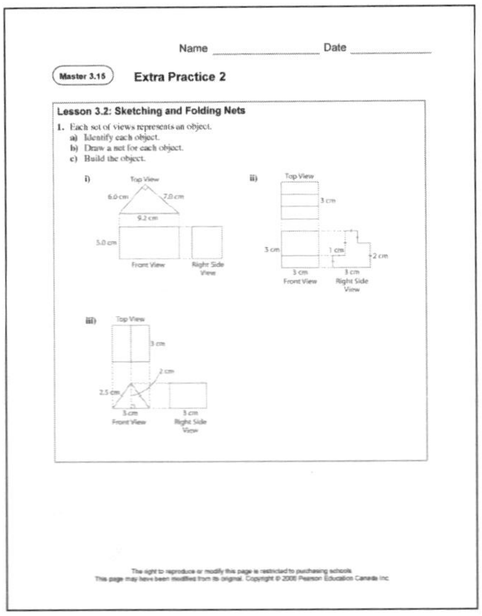

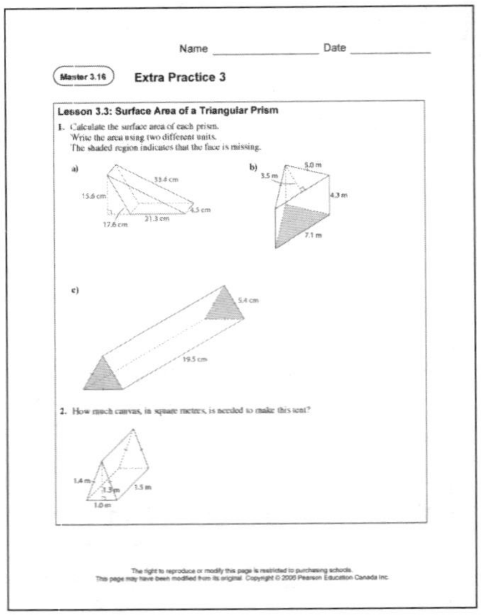

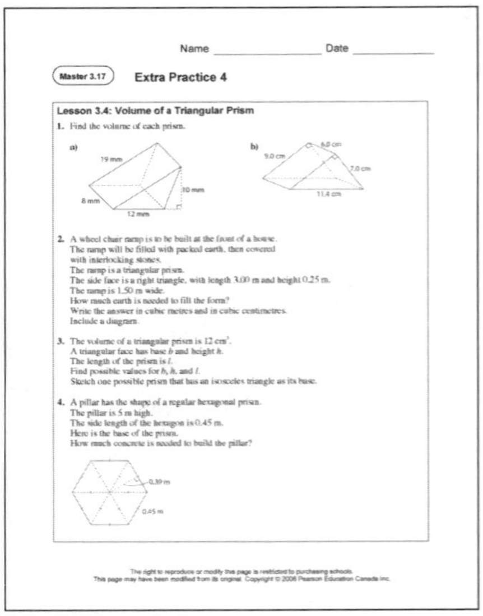

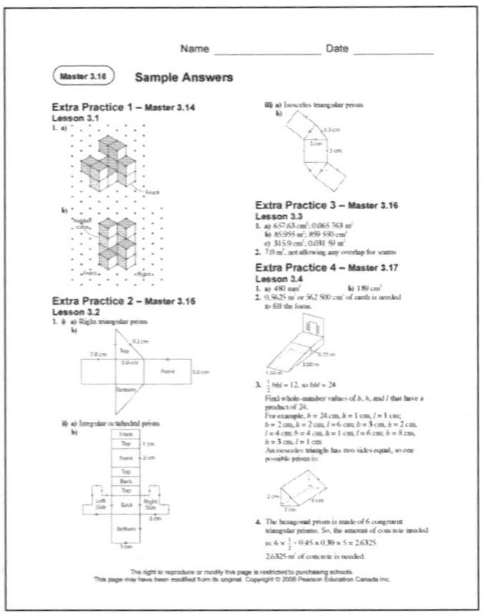

Addison Wesley
Mathematics Makes Sense

Program Authors

Trevor Brown
Antonietta Lenjosek
Cathy Heideman
Jim Mennie
Georgia Konis-Chatzis
A.J. Keene
Margaret Sinclair
Craig Featherstone
Jason Johnston
Bryn Keyes
Elizabeth Wood
Elizabeth Milne
David Sufrin
Don Jones
Sharon Jeroski
Lynn Strangway

Printed and bound in Canada

2 3 4 5 – TC – 09 08 07 06

PEARSON
Education Canada

ADDISON WESLEY

Ontario

Math Makes Sense 8

Ontario

Teacher Guide

Unit 4: Fractions and Decimals

PEARSON
Education Canada

UNIT 4

Fractions and Decimals

"Learning fractions need not be the 'hard stuff' of the mathematics program. Concepts should be developed at a judicious pace and in a comprehensible manner. The study of fractions should be approached from a discovery orientation."

– Cathcart, Pothier, and Vance (2004), *Learning Mathematics in Elementary and Middle Schools*, Pearson Prentice Hall, p. 270

FOCUS STRAND
Number Sense and Numeration

SUPPORTING STRANDS
Measurement
Patterning and Algebra

TIPS
Adolescent learners benefit from kinesthetic activities that allow them to be physically active. This can be achieved simply through using manipulatives like dice, counters, and Pattern Blocks, but also through activities that require them to move about.

Mathematics Background

What Are the Big Ideas?

- Equivalent fractions name the same quantity.
- Multiplication and division are related and this relationship is used to develop the algorithms for division of fractions.
- A fraction is an indicated division, and this can be used to find a decimal representation.

How Will the Concepts Develop?

Students use prior knowledge to compare and order fractions using equivalence. They consolidate their knowledge of algorithms for adding and subtracting fractions.

Students use models and concrete materials to develop the concepts of multiplying and dividing fractions. Students develop algorithms from area models for multiplication and patterns. In previous grades, division was conceptualized as grouping or sharing. These ideas help students use the number line to divide fractions and whole numbers, and patterning to develop algorithms for dividing fractions.

Students use calculators to convert between fractions and decimals. Strategies for mental computations with 0.1, 0.01, and 0.001 develop from prior knowledge of operations with powers of 10.

Why Are These Concepts Important?

Understanding fractions helps reinforce student understanding of number and quantity. Being able to work flexibly with fractions is important in future work with algebra and geometry, especially where this work relates to proportional reasoning.

Students encounter fraction and decimal equivalence daily, in the form of money, retail experiences, and the metric system. The ability to convert easily between different fraction representations enables students to make sense of the math in their world.

Curriculum Overview

The codes refer to the 2005 revised curriculum.

Cluster 1: Adding and Subtracting Fractions

Overall Expectations
- Represent, compare, and order equivalent representations of numbers, ... (8m8)
- Solve problems involving ... fractions, ... using a variety of computational strategies. (8m9)

Specific Expectations
- Represent, compare, and order rational numbers. (8m13)
- Use estimation when solving problems involving operations with ... fractions, to help judge the reasonableness of a solution. (8m18)
- Solve problems involving addition, subtraction, ... with simple fractions. (8m20)

Cluster 2: Multiplying and Dividing Fractions

Overall Expectations
- Solve problems involving ... fractions, ... using a variety of computational strategies. (8m9)

Specific Expectations
- Use estimation when solving problems involving operations with ... fractions, to help judge the reasonableness of a solution. (8m18)
- Represent the multiplication and division of fractions, using a variety of tools and strategies. (8m19)
- Solve problems involving ... multiplication and division with simple fractions. (8m20)

Cluster 3: Fractions and Decimals

Overall Expectations
- Represent, compare, and order equivalent representations of numbers, ... (8m8)
- Solve problems involving ... decimal numbers, fractions, ... using a variety of computational strategies. (8m9)

Specific Expectations
- Represent, compare, and order rational numbers. (8m13)
- Translate between equivalent forms of a number. (8m14)
- Solve multi-step problems ... involving ... decimals, using a variety of tools and strategies. (8m16)
- Multiply and divide decimal numbers by various powers of ten. (8m24)

Launch

↓

Lesson 4.1: Comparing and Ordering Fractions
Lesson 4.2: Adding Fractions
Lesson 4.3: Subtracting Fractions

↓

Lesson 4.4: Using Models to Multiply Fractions
Lesson 4.5: Multiplying Fractions
Mid-Unit Review
Lesson 4.6: Using Models to Divide Fractions and Whole Numbers
Lesson 4.7: Dividing Fractions

↓

Lesson 4.8: Converting between Decimals and Fractions
Lesson 4.9: Dividing by 0.1, 0.01, and 0.001

↓

Unit Review
Practice Test

Unit Problem
Dividing a Square

Curriculum across the Grades

Grade 7	Grade 8
Students represent, compare, and order decimals to hundredths and fractions. Students add and subtract fractions with simple like and unlike denominators. They demonstrate the relationship between the repeated addition of fractions and the multiplication of that fraction by a whole number. Students divide whole numbers by simple fractions and by decimal numbers to hundredths. Students solve problems involving the addition and subtraction of fractions and decimals, and involving the multiplication and division of decimal numbers to thousandths by one-digit whole numbers. Students use estimation when solving problems involving operations with decimals to help judge the reasonableness of a solution.	Students represent, compare, and order rational numbers. They translate between equivalent forms of a number. Students represent the multiplication and division of fractions. They multiply and divide decimal numbers by various powers of ten. Students solve problems involving addition, subtraction, multiplication, and division with simple fractions. They use estimation when solving problems involving operations with fractions and decimals to help judge the reasonableness of a solution.

Materials for This Unit

Cut out and laminate number lines (Master 4.24). Some students may require fraction strips or fraction circles for use throughout the unit.

Additional Activities

Fraction 50

For Extra Practice (Appropriate for use after Skills You'll Need)

Materials: *Fraction 50* (Master 4.5), *Fraction 50 Game Board* (Master 4.5b), 15 counters for each player

Playing this game reinforces the skills of finding a fraction of a whole, and multiplying a fraction and a whole number.

The work students do: Students play in pairs. Players alternately take a turn putting a counter on one of the squares of the game board. Students evaluate the expression in the square, and keep a running total. The first player to reach 50 points wins. The game can be more thought provoking for students if they have to get *exactly* 50 points.

Take It Further: Students attempt to get the squares in a row, column, or diagonal covered with their counters.

Mathematical/Social/Logical

Partner Activity

Fraction-Part-Whole Concentration

For Extra Practice (Appropriate for use after Skills You'll Need)

Materials: *Fraction-Part-Whole Concentration* (Master 4.6), *Fraction-Part-Whole Concentration* Game Cards (Master 4.6b)

This game is played like Concentration, and encourages mental strategies for finding a fraction of a whole number.

The work students do: Students play in pairs or groups of three. Students arrange each set of cards face down in a horizontal line. Students take turns to turn over 3 cards, and try to match the part, the whole, and the fraction. For example: $\frac{3}{4}$, 36, and 48 would be a match because 36 is $\frac{3}{4}$ of 48.

Take It Further: Students can make up their own game cards to allow more people to play or to challenge their memories further.

Mathematical/Social/Logical

Partner Activity

Planning for Unit 4

Planning for Instruction

Suggested Unit time: About 4 weeks

Lesson	Time	Materials	Program Support
Launch, page 2	15–20 min		Master 4.18: Unit Launch, Step 4
Skills You'll Need, page 4	20–25 min		
4.1: Comparing and Ordering Fractions, page 5 Use equivalent fractions to compare fractions.	80–100 min	1-cm grid paper 12-section square transparency 12-section squares fraction strips and transparency (optional)	PM 20: 1-cm Grid Paper Master 4.19: Lesson 4.1 *Explore* Master 4.20: Fraction Strips Master 4.7: Step-by-Step 1 Master 4.26: Extra Practice 1
4.2: Adding Fractions, page 9 Use common denominators to add fractions.	80–100 min	fraction circles and transparency (optional) fraction rings (optional)	Master 4.21: Fraction Circles Master 4.8: Step-by-Step 2 Master 4.27: Extra Practice 2
4.3: Subtracting Fractions, page 13 Use common denominators to subtract fractions.	80–100 min	1-cm grid paper coloured pencils fraction circles (optional) symmetrical designs and transparency	Master 4.22: Symmetrical Designs Master 4.21: Fraction Circles PM 20: 1-cm Grid Paper Master 4.9: Step-by-Step 3 Master 4.28: Extra Practice 3
4.4: Using Models to Multiply Fractions, page 18 Use an area model to multiply fractions.	80–100 min	0.5-cm grid paper 1-cm grid paper coloured pencils	PM 14: 0.5-cm Grid Paper PM 20: 1-cm Grid Paper Master 4.10: Step-by-Step 4 Master 4.29: Extra Practice 4
4.5: Multiplying Fractions, page 21 Develop an algorithm to multiply fractions.	80–100 min	2-cm grid transparency (optional) 0.5-cm grid paper 1-cm grid paper coloured pencils spinners	PM 14: 0.5-cm Grid Paper PM 20: 1-cm Grid Paper PM 21: 2-cm Grid Paper Master 4.23: Fraction Product Spinner Master 4.11: Step-by-Step 5 Master 4.30: Extra Practice 5
Mid-Unit Review, page 26		0.5-cm grid paper 1-cm grid paper	PM 14: 0.5-cm Grid Paper PM 20: 1-cm Grid Paper
4.6: Using Models to Divide Fractions and Whole Numbers, page 27 Use a number line to divide fractions and whole numbers.	80–100 min	overhead counters (optional) fraction circles and transparency (optional) number lines 1-cm grid paper (optional)	PM 20: 1-cm Grid Paper Master 4.21: Fraction Circles Master 4.24: Number Lines Master 4.12: Step-by-Step 6 Master 4.31: Extra Practice 6
4.7: Dividing Fractions, page 31 Develop algorithms to divide fractions.	80–100 min	number lines transparency (optional) number lines	Master 4.24: Number Lines Master 4.13: Step-by-Step 7 Master 4.32: Extra Practice 7
4.8: Converting between Decimals and Fractions, page 35 Use a calculator and patterns to convert between decimals and fractions.	80–100 min	hundredths squares and transparency calculators	Master 4.25: Hundredths Square Master 4.14: Step-by-Step 8 Master 4.33: Extra Practice 8
4.9: Dividing by 0.1, 0.01, and 0.001, page 39 Relate division by 0.1, 0.01, and 0.001 to multiplication by powers of 10.	80–100 min	calculators 0.5-cm grid paper	PM 14: 0.5-cm Grid Paper Master 4.15: Step-by-Step 9 Master 4.34: Extra Practice 9
Reading and Writing in Math: Providing Math Information, page 42		calculators	

Lesson	Time	Materials	Program Support
Unit Review, page 44		calculators number lines 0.5-cm grid paper 1-cm grid paper	PM 14: 0.5-cm Grid Paper PM 20: 1-cm Grid Paper Master 4.24: Number Lines Extra Practice: Student Book page 491
Practice Test, page 47		1-cm grid paper	PM 20: 1-cm Grid Paper
Unit Problem: Dividing a Square, page 48	80–100 min	0.5-cm grid paper 1-cm grid paper coloured pencils	PM 14: 0.5-cm Grid Paper PM 20: 1-cm Grid Paper

Planning for Assessment

Purpose	Tools and Process	Recording and Reporting
Diagnostic	*Unit Launch* Question; conference; scaffold problems throughout the unit	PM 8: Conference Prompts
Formative	*Explore* – Ongoing Assessment: Observe and Listen	Master 4.2 Ongoing Observations: Fractions and Decimals PM 1: Inquiry Process Check List PM 6: Observation Record 1 PM 7: Observation Record 2 PM 8: Conference Prompts PM 2: Self-Assessment PM 3: Self-Assessment: Problem Solving PM 9: Work Sample Records
Summative	*Unit Review* *Unit Problem* – Performance Assessment *Unit Test* Review assessment records; add unit results to ongoing records	Master 4.1 Unit Rubric: Fractions and Decimals Master 4.3 Performance Assessment Rubric: Dividing a Square Master 4.4 Unit Summary: Fractions and Decimals PM 10: Summary Class Records: Strands PM 11: Summary Class Records: Achievement Categories PM 12: Summary Record: Individual
Learning Skills/Mathematical Disposition	Observe and record throughout unit	PM 4: Learning Skills Check List PM 5: Mathematical Dispositions and Learning Skills

Program Masters (PM) are in the *Grade 8 Planning and Program Masters* module.
Extra Practice Masters are on the CD-ROM and printed in reduced format on page 82 of this module.

LESSON ORGANIZER

15–20 min

Curriculum Focus: Activate prior learning about comparing and adding fractions.

Teacher Materials

- Unit Launch, Step 4 (Master 4.18)

Vocabulary: perimeter, fraction

ASSUMED PRIOR KNOWLEDGE

- ✓ Students can find and recognize equivalent fractions.
- ✓ Students can add fractions using models or algorithms.
- ✓ Students can multiply to find a fraction of a whole number.

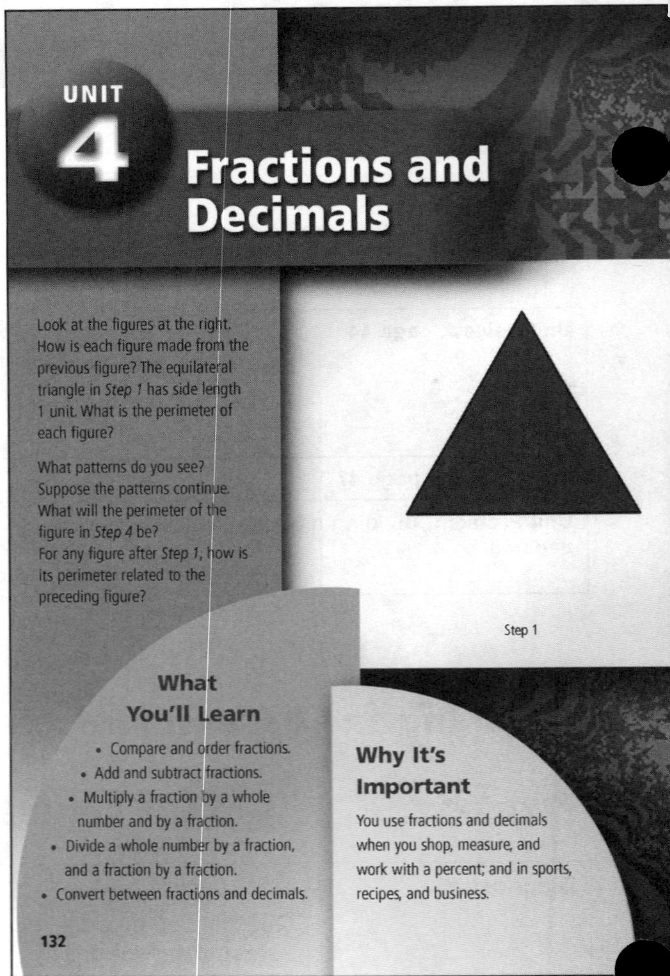

UNIT 4

Fractions and Decimals

Look at the figures at the right. How is each figure made from the previous figure? The equilateral triangle in *Step 1* has side length 1 unit. What is the perimeter of each figure?

What patterns do you see? Suppose the patterns continue. What will the perimeter of the figure in *Step 4* be? For any figure after *Step 1*, how is its perimeter related to the preceding figure?

Step 1

What You'll Learn

- Compare and order fractions.
- Add and subtract fractions.
- Multiply a fraction by a whole number and by a fraction.
- Divide a whole number by a fraction, and a fraction by a fraction.
- Convert between fractions and decimals.

Why It's Important

You use fractions and decimals when you shop, measure, and work with a percent; and in sports, recipes, and business.

132

ACTIVATE PRIOR LEARNING

Read the text on page 132 of the Student Book together. Talk about how each figure is made from the previous one. (The centre $\frac{1}{3}$ of each side of the triangle in *Step 1* is the base of an equilateral triangle in *Step 2*. Similarly, the centre $\frac{1}{3}$ of each side of each of the 6 small triangles in *Step 2* is the base of an equilateral triangle in *Step 3*.)

Ask:

- How can we find the perimeter of the second figure? (*The side length of the first triangle is 1 unit, so each side length of the new triangles is $\frac{1}{3}$ of a unit. There are 12 sides, each with length $\frac{1}{3}$, so we can add and get $\frac{12}{3}$, or 4 units; or we can multiply $12 \times \frac{1}{3}$ unit = 4 units.*)
- How else could we find the perimeter? (*There are 12 sides. Each time we count 3 sides, we get a length of 1 unit, so that is 4 units altogether.*)
- How many sides does the third figure have? (*48*)
- How long is each side of the third figure? (*$\frac{1}{9}$ of a unit; the pattern continues. Each side of a small triangle in Step 3 is $\frac{1}{3}$ of a side of a small triangle in Step 2.*)
- How could you calculate the perimeter of the third figure? (*There are 48 sides. Each time we count 9 sides, we get a length of 1 unit. We could add: 9, 18, 27, 36, 45 with 3 left over. The perimeter is 5 and $\frac{3}{9}$, or $5\frac{1}{3}$ units.*)

For the pattern in the perimeters: Each successive figure has side length $\frac{1}{3}$ of the preceding figure, and the number of sides is 4 times the number for the preceding figure. So, each perimeter is: preceding perimeter $\times 4 \div 3$. So, the figure in *Step 4* has perimeter $\frac{16}{3} \times 4 \div 3 = \frac{64}{9}$.

Ask students to describe what *Step 4* would look like, and then show them *Unit Launch, Step 4*, Master 4.18.

These figures illustrate *fractals*. For more information about fractals, visit http://math.rice.edu/~lanius/frac/ (accessed August, 2005).

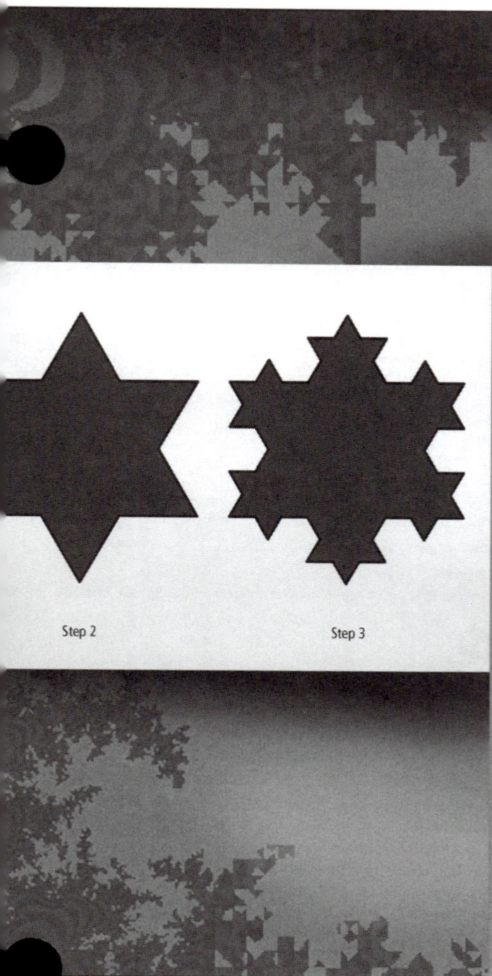

Key Words

- reciprocals
- terminating decimal
- repeating decimal

133

FROM THE LIBRARY

5-Minute Math Problem of the Day by Martin Lee and Marcia Miller. Scholastic Publishing, 2000.
ISBN: 0439175399
This book is full of problems to help students practise essential problem-solving skills throughout the year. These problems address whole number concepts and operations, decimals, fractions, measurement, geometry, and more. The problems are designed to meet a range of abilities and are fully reproducible.

Lessons for Multiplying and Dividing Fractions: Grades 5–6 by Marilyn Burns.
Math Solutions Publications, 2003.
ISBN: 0941355640
Although this book is identified for grades 5–6, the author has rich descriptions of concept-building lessons that many students, particularly struggling students, may benefit from.

REACHING ALL LEARNERS

e-tools Some students may benefit from using the virtual manipulatives on the e-Tools CD-ROM. The e-Tools appropriate for this unit are *Fractions* and *Place-Value Blocks*.

DIAGNOSTIC ASSESSMENT

What to Look For	What to Do
✔ Students can find and recognize equivalent fractions. ✔ Students can add fractions using models or algorithms. ✔ Students can multiply to find a fraction of a whole number.	***Extra Support:*** Students who have difficulty with equivalent fractions should use concrete materials, such as Cuisenaire rods, Pattern Blocks, and/or grid paper. *Work on this skill during Lesson 4.1.* Students who have difficulty adding fractions should use concrete materials, such as Cuisenaire rods, Pattern Blocks, fraction circles, and/or number lines. Remind students of the work they did in Grade 7 with fraction strips and number lines. Reinforce the use of estimates and benchmark fractions. *Work on this skill during Lesson 4.2.* Students who have difficulty multiplying a fraction by a whole number should first use repeated addition to get the product. Begin with unit fractions, and have students say aloud the fraction part followed by the whole number; for example, $\frac{1}{3}$ of 27 is 27 thirds. Students can count up (*3 thirds is 1, 6 thirds is 2, and so on*) until they reach the required number. *Work on this skill during Lesson 4.4.*

LESSON ORGANIZER 20–25 min

Skills in Review

- Multiplying a fraction by a whole number

Vocabulary: unit fraction, reciprocals

Alternative Example

a) Find $\frac{1}{4}$ of 32. **b)** Multiply. $9 \times \frac{5}{6}$

Solution

a) $\frac{1}{4}$ of 32 is

$\frac{1}{4} \times 32 = 32 \times \frac{1}{4}$

Think: 32 times $\frac{1}{4}$ is 32 fourths.

$\frac{1}{4} \times 32 = \frac{32}{4}$

$= 8$

b) $9 \times \frac{5}{6} = \frac{45}{6}$

$= \frac{15}{2}$

UNIT 4

Skills You'll Need

Multiply a Fraction by a Whole Number

We multiply a fraction by a whole number to find that fraction of the whole number.

Example

a) Find $\frac{1}{3}$ of 27.

b) Multiply. $\frac{3}{4} \times 6$

Solution

a) $\frac{1}{3}$ of 27 is

$\frac{1}{3} \times 27 = 27 \times \frac{1}{3}$

Think: 27 times $\frac{1}{3}$ is 27 thirds.

$\frac{1}{3} \times 27 = \frac{27}{3}$

$= 9$

b) $\frac{3}{4} \times 6 = \frac{18}{4}$

$= \frac{9}{2}$

In *Example* part a, note that $27 \times \frac{1}{3}$ is the same as $27 \div 3$.
To find $\frac{1}{3}$ of a number, we multiply by $\frac{1}{3}$ or divide by 3.
$\frac{1}{3}$ and 3 are **reciprocals**.
To multiply a number by a unit fraction, we can divide by the reciprocal instead.

A unit fraction has numerator 1.

✓ Check

1. Find.
a) $\frac{1}{5}$ of 25 5 **b)** $\frac{1}{4}$ of 64 16 **c)** $\frac{1}{8}$ of 40 5

2. Multiply.
a) $\frac{3}{2} \times 20$ 30 **b)** $\frac{5}{3} \times 5$ $\frac{25}{3}$ **c)** $\frac{7}{9} \times 4$ $\frac{28}{9}$

3. There are 660 students in Parkside School from Kindergarten to Grade 8.
a) Three-quarters of the students are boys. How many boys attend the school? 495 boys
b) One-third of the students are in K to Grade 4. How many students are in Grades 5 to 8? 440 students

134 UNIT 4: Fractions and Decimals

Multiply a Fraction by a Whole Number

On the board, draw a rectangular strip, length 24 cm and width 1 cm.
Ask students how they can find $\frac{3}{4}$ of this strip. Give students a chance to think about their strategies for solving the problem.
Ask:

- How can you find $\frac{3}{4}$ of this strip? (*The strip is 24 cm long. One-half of the strip is 12 cm long. One-half of one-half, or $\frac{1}{4}$ of the strip, is 6 cm long. $\frac{3}{4} = \frac{1}{2} + \frac{1}{4}$ = 12 cm + 6 cm = 18 cm; $\frac{3}{4}$ of the strip is 18 cm long.*)
- How else did you find $\frac{3}{4}$ of the strip? (*I divided 24 cm by 4 as we are finding fourths; 24 cm ÷ 4 = 6 cm. So, 6 cm is $\frac{1}{4}$ of the strip and 6 cm × 3 = 18 cm, which is $\frac{3}{4}$ of the strip.*)

Model dividing the strip into fourths, then shading 3 fourths.

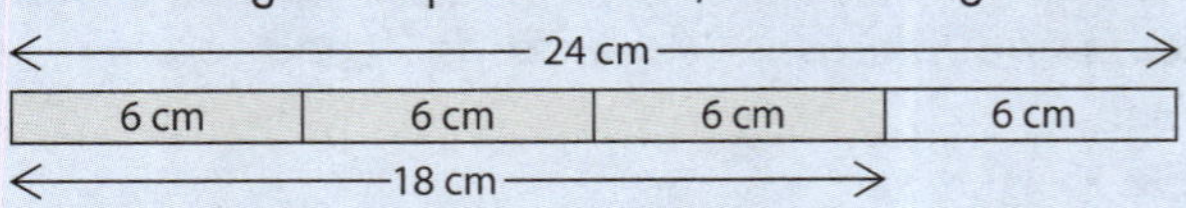

Tell students that a strip is a model that can be used to help find a fraction of a whole. The length of the strip is the whole, and the denominator of the fraction tells how many parts the strip is to be divided into. Divide the total length by the number of parts to get the length of each part. The numerator tells how many parts you are trying to find. Multiply the number of parts by the length of each part to find the fraction of the whole. Connect this representation to the *Examples*. This model works best if students think of a fraction such as $\frac{3}{4}$ as $3 \times \frac{1}{4}$.

Encourage students to check their answers to question 1 by using a different strategy: either multiplying by the fraction, or dividing by the reciprocal.

For extra practice, students can play *Fraction 50* (Master 4.5) or *Fraction-Part-Whole Concentration* (Master 4.6).

Common Misconceptions

➤ Students multiply both the numerator and denominator of the fraction by the whole number.

How to Help: These students have learned a rule, and applied it incorrectly. Students should not use a rule until they understand the math behind it. Encourage students to think about the question before attempting any calculations. Look at the fraction and decide if the answer should be less than or greater than 1 (if the fraction is less than 1, the product will be less than the whole number; if the fraction is greater than 1, the product will be greater than the whole number). For the calculation, suggest that students use the model described in the lesson; that is, $\frac{3}{4}$ of 6 is $\frac{3}{4} \times 6 = 18$ quarters, which is $\frac{18}{4} = 4\frac{1}{2}$.

4.1 Comparing and Ordering Fractions

Focus Use equivalent fractions to compare fractions.

Some photographers use a manual camera with a shutter speed dial. The numbers on the dial show how long the shutter stays open when a person takes a picture.

This setting opens the shutter for 2 s.

This setting opens the shutter for $\frac{1}{2}$ of 1 s.

This setting opens the shutter for $\frac{1}{4}$ of 1 s.

This pattern continues.
How long is the shutter open when the setting is 8? 15? 30?
Does a setting of 8 allow more or less light than a setting of 15?
Suppose a setting of 125 does not allow enough light.
Which setting might allow enough light?

Explore

Work in a group.

This square has side length 1 unit.

Your teacher will give you a copy of this square.
What fraction of the whole square is each piece?
Order the fractions from least to greatest.

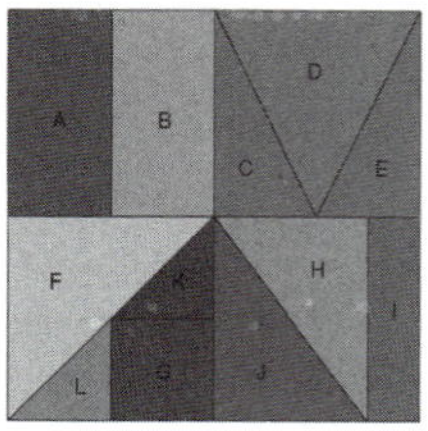

$A = \frac{1}{8}$ $G = \frac{1}{16}$
$B = \frac{1}{8}$ $H = \frac{3}{32}$
$C = \frac{1}{16}$ $I = \frac{1}{16}$
$D = \frac{1}{8}$ $J = \frac{3}{32}$
$E = \frac{1}{16}$ $K = \frac{1}{32}$
$F = \frac{1}{8}$ $L = \frac{1}{32}$

Reflect & Share

Share your results with those of another group of classmates.
How did you write each piece as a fraction of the whole?
What strategies did you use to order the fractions?
Could you use these strategies to order any set of fractions? Explain.

4.1 Comparing and Ordering Fractions 135

LESSON 4.1

Comparing and Ordering Fractions

LESSON ORGANIZER

80–100 min

Curriculum Focus: Use equivalent fractions to compare fractions. (8m13)

Teacher Materials

Optional
- Lesson 4.1 *Explore* transparency (Master 4.19)
- fraction strips transparency (Master 4.20)

Student Materials
- Lesson 4.1 *Explore* (Master 4.19)
- 1-cm grid paper (PM 20)

Optional
- fraction strips (Master 4.20)
- Step-by-Step 1 (Master 4.7)
- Extra Practice 1 (Master 4.26)

Vocabulary: improper fraction, equivalent fraction

Assessment: Master 4.2 Ongoing Observations: Fractions and Decimals

Key Math Learnings

1. One way to compare fractions is to use equivalent fractions. Write each fraction with the same denominator, then compare the numerators.
2. One way to find a common denominator is to find the lowest common multiple of the denominators of the fractions.

BEFORE Get Started

Place a transparency of fraction strips (Master 4.20) on the overhead projector. Cover all the strips except the longest. Tell students that the strip is 1 unit long. Write the number 1 below the first strip. Uncover the second strip. Ask:

- What fraction of the first strip is this strip? How do you know? (*$\frac{1}{2}$; it looks as if two of these strips would fill the longer one.*)

Write the number $\frac{1}{2}$ below the second strip. Continue uncovering strips, and asking students to identify the fraction each represents. Be sure to record the fractions below the strips. When you have finished, ask:

- What patterns do you see? (*As the strips get smaller, the denominators get larger; each denominator represents the number of shorter strips that fit on the longest strip.*)

As a class, read the introduction to the lesson. Have students relate the ideas presented with the fraction strips to the questions in the introduction. When the setting is 8, the shutter is open for $\frac{1}{8}$ s. Similarly, a setting of 15 is $\frac{1}{15}$ s, and a setting of 30 is $\frac{1}{30}$ s. Since $\frac{1}{8}$ is greater than $\frac{1}{15}$, a setting of 8 allows more light than a setting of 15. If a setting of 125 (which is $\frac{1}{125}$ s) does not allow enough light, we want a lesser number because its reciprocal will be greater. So, we want a setting of 60, which allows light in for $\frac{1}{60}$ s.

Remind students that a unit fraction is a fraction with a numerator of 1. With unit fractions, as the denominator increases, the number decreases.

Distribute copies of Lesson 4.1 *Explore* (Master 4.19). Read *Explore* together.

Ensure students understand what they have to do.

REACHING ALL LEARNERS

Early Finishers

Challenge students to find a way to order fractions by finding common numerators instead of common denominators. For example, $\frac{5}{8}, \frac{4}{5}, \frac{3}{4}$ have a common numerator of 60 $\rightarrow \frac{60}{96}, \frac{60}{75}$, and $\frac{60}{80}$; since $\frac{1}{96} < \frac{1}{80} < \frac{1}{75}$, the order is $\frac{60}{96}, \frac{60}{80}, \frac{60}{75}$, or $\frac{5}{8}, \frac{3}{4}, \frac{4}{5}$.

Common Misconceptions

➤ Students think that, when comparing fractions, only the lowest common denominator can be used.

How to Help: Compare $\frac{7}{9}$ and $\frac{5}{6}$ by finding the lowest common denominator.

Multiples of 9: 9, **18**, 27, ... Multiples of 6: 6, 12, **18**, 24, ...

The lowest common denominator of 6 and 9 is 18.

$\frac{7}{9} = \frac{14}{18}$ and $\frac{5}{6} = \frac{15}{18}$ so, $\frac{15}{18} > \frac{14}{18}$ and $\frac{5}{6} > \frac{7}{9}$

Compare $\frac{7}{9}$ and $\frac{5}{6}$ by multiplying the denominators to find a common denominator.

$9 \times 6 = 54$, so 54 is a common denominator.

$\frac{7}{9} = \frac{42}{54}$ and $\frac{5}{6} = \frac{45}{54}$ so, $\frac{45}{54} > \frac{42}{54}$ and $\frac{5}{6} > \frac{7}{9}$

Any common denominator can be used to compare fractions, but the lowest common denominator is the most efficient.

Mental Math

The volume of a rectangular prism is length × width × height. To find the dimensions of a rectangular prism with volume 72 cm^3, find 3 numbers whose product is 72. One strategy might be to list pairs of factors of 72, then factor one of the 2 numbers again. Alternatively, start with 1, and systematically work through all possible dimensions.

Connect

One way to compare fractions is to use equivalent fractions.
Write each fraction with the same denominator,
then compare the numerators.

For example, to order $\frac{5}{8}, \frac{4}{5}$, and $\frac{3}{4}$:
Write equivalent fractions for each fraction until all the fractions have the same denominator:

These are proper fractions. In a proper fraction, the numerator is less than the denominator.

$$\frac{5}{8} = \frac{10}{16} = \frac{15}{24} = \frac{20}{32} = \frac{25}{40}$$

(×2, ×3, ×4, ×5)

$$\frac{4}{5} = \frac{8}{10} = \frac{12}{15} = \frac{16}{20} = \frac{20}{25} = \frac{24}{30} = \frac{28}{35} = \frac{32}{40}$$

$$\frac{3}{4} = \frac{6}{8} = \frac{9}{12} = \frac{12}{16} = \frac{15}{20} = \frac{18}{24} = \frac{21}{28} = \frac{24}{32} = \frac{27}{36} = \frac{30}{40}$$

Now, each fraction has denominator 40.
Compare the numerators: $25 < 30 < 32$
So, $\frac{25}{40} < \frac{30}{40} < \frac{32}{40}$
So, $\frac{5}{8} < \frac{3}{4} < \frac{4}{5}$
In order from least to greatest: $\frac{5}{8}, \frac{3}{4}, \frac{4}{5}$
A simpler way to find the common denominator is to find the lowest common multiple of the denominators.
We can use this method to order improper fractions.

Example

Write these fractions in order from least to greatest:
$\frac{5}{3}, \frac{3}{2}, \frac{8}{5}$

Solution

$\frac{5}{3}, \frac{3}{2}, \frac{8}{5}$
Find the lowest common denominator.
Since the denominators have no common factors,
list the multiples of 3, 2, and 5.

In an improper fraction, the numerator is greater than the denominator.

3: 3, 6, 9, 12, 15, 18, 21, 24, 27, **30**, …
2: 2, 4, 6, 8, 10, 12, 14, 16, 18, 20, 22, 24, 26, 28, **30**, …
5: 5, 10, 15, 20, 25, **30**, …

136 UNIT 4: Fractions and Decimals

DURING Explore

Ongoing Assessment: Observe and Listen

As students work, ask questions, such as:

- Which figures are easiest to describe as fractions? (*A and B are rectangles and together make up $\frac{1}{4}$ of the square. Each must be $\frac{1}{8}$. G is $\frac{1}{4}$ of $\frac{1}{4}$ of the square. It would take 16 G squares to fill the whole square, so G must be $\frac{1}{16}$.*)
- Which figures are more difficult to describe as fractions? (*The triangular pieces, such as C and E, aren't easy to describe. H and J are difficult because together they don't even make $\frac{1}{4}$ of the square.*)
- What strategies can you use? (*I can use a ruler to measure the dimensions; I can visually move pieces around; I can cut pieces out to see how they compare to other pieces.*)

Provide struggling students with 1-cm grid paper on which they can copy the square, and count grid squares to find the area of each figure. They can then write the area of each figure as a fraction of the total area.

As students begin to order the fractions, ask:

- What strategies are you using to order the fractions? (*I look for congruent figures; I know which figures are largest and list them last.*)

Look for students to use their prior knowledge of geometry and area to help determine the fractional pieces that are equivalent. (*Figures can be composed and decomposed to form other figures; for example, two congruent triangles form a parallelogram.*)

AFTER Connect

What you might see:
From least to greatest: K, L ($\frac{1}{32}$), C, E, G, I ($\frac{1}{16}$), H, J ($\frac{3}{32}$), A, B, D, F ($\frac{1}{8}$)

Invite students to share their strategies for finding the fractions and for ordering the fractional parts.

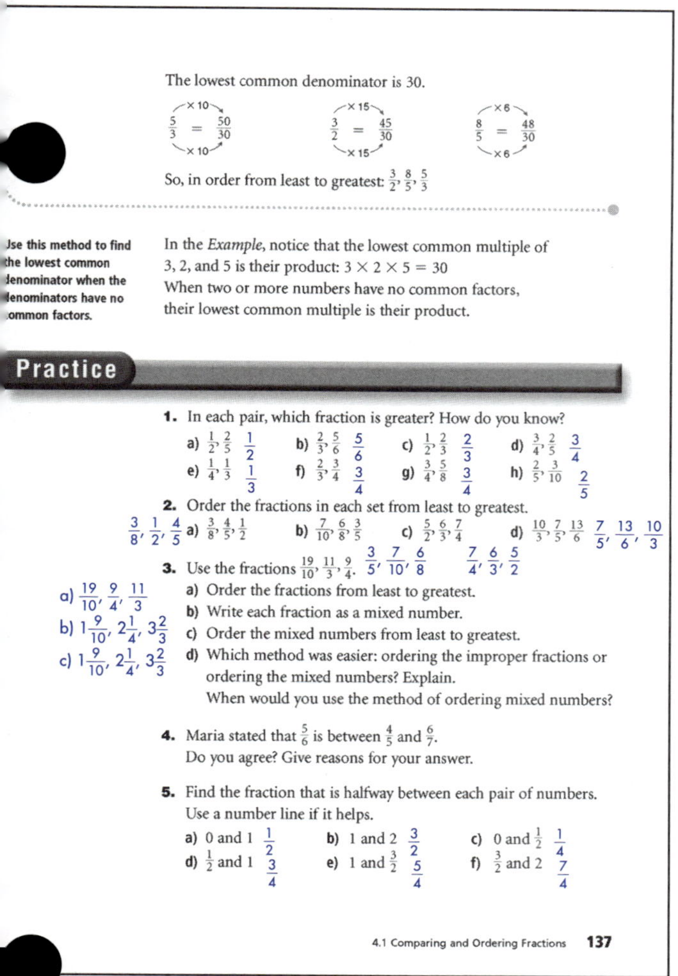

The lowest common denominator is 30.

$\frac{5}{3} = \frac{50}{30}$ (×10) $\frac{3}{2} = \frac{45}{30}$ (×15) $\frac{8}{5} = \frac{48}{30}$ (×6)

So, in order from least to greatest: $\frac{3}{2}, \frac{8}{5}, \frac{5}{3}$

Use this method to find the lowest common denominator when the denominators have no common factors.

In the *Example*, notice that the lowest common multiple of 3, 2, and 5 is their product: $3 \times 2 \times 5 = 30$
When two or more numbers have no common factors, their lowest common multiple is their product.

Practice

1. In each pair, which fraction is greater? How do you know?
   a) $\frac{1}{2}, \frac{2}{5}$ $\frac{1}{2}$ b) $\frac{2}{3}, \frac{5}{6}$ $\frac{5}{6}$ c) $\frac{1}{2}, \frac{2}{3}$ $\frac{2}{3}$ d) $\frac{3}{4}, \frac{2}{5}$ $\frac{3}{4}$
   e) $\frac{1}{4}, \frac{1}{3}$ $\frac{1}{3}$ f) $\frac{2}{3}, \frac{3}{4}$ $\frac{3}{4}$ g) $\frac{3}{4}, \frac{5}{8}$ $\frac{3}{4}$ h) $\frac{2}{5}, \frac{3}{10}$ $\frac{2}{5}$
2. Order the fractions in each set from least to greatest.
   $\frac{3}{8}, \frac{1}{2}, \frac{4}{5}$ a) $\frac{3}{8}, \frac{4}{5}, \frac{1}{2}$ b) $\frac{7}{10}, \frac{6}{8}, \frac{3}{5}$ $\frac{3}{5}, \frac{7}{10}, \frac{6}{8}$ c) $\frac{5}{2}, \frac{6}{3}, \frac{7}{4}$ $\frac{7}{4}, \frac{6}{3}, \frac{5}{2}$ d) $\frac{10}{3}, \frac{7}{5}, \frac{13}{6}$ $\frac{7}{5}, \frac{13}{6}, \frac{10}{3}$
3. Use the fractions $\frac{19}{10}, \frac{11}{3}, \frac{9}{4}$.
   a) Order the fractions from least to greatest. a) $\frac{19}{10}, \frac{9}{4}, \frac{11}{3}$
   b) Write each fraction as a mixed number. b) $1\frac{9}{10}, 2\frac{1}{4}, 3\frac{2}{3}$
   c) Order the mixed numbers from least to greatest. c) $1\frac{9}{10}, 2\frac{1}{4}, 3\frac{2}{3}$
   d) Which method was easier: ordering the improper fractions or ordering the mixed numbers? Explain.
   When would you use the method of ordering mixed numbers?
4. Maria stated that $\frac{5}{6}$ is between $\frac{4}{5}$ and $\frac{6}{7}$.
   Do you agree? Give reasons for your answer.
5. Find the fraction that is halfway between each pair of numbers.
   Use a number line if it helps.
   a) 0 and 1 $\frac{1}{2}$ b) 1 and 2 $\frac{3}{2}$ c) 0 and $\frac{1}{2}$ $\frac{1}{4}$
   d) $\frac{1}{2}$ and 1 $\frac{3}{4}$ e) 1 and $\frac{3}{2}$ $\frac{5}{4}$ f) $\frac{3}{2}$ and 2 $\frac{7}{4}$

4.1 Comparing and Ordering Fractions 137

Assignment Guidelines

If your students do not have time to complete all the *Practice* questions on pages 137 and 138, these questions provide minimum curriculum coverage:
1, 2, 5, 7, 8, *Reflect*
To assess the 4 Achievement Chart categories listed in the curriculum document, have students complete these *Practice* questions:
Communication: 1
Knowledge and Understanding: 2
Thinking: 7
Application: 8

Sample Solutions

1. a) Write each fraction with the same denominator: $\frac{1}{2} = \frac{5}{10}$ and $\frac{2}{5} = \frac{4}{10}$
Compare the numerators: 5 > 4
So, $\frac{5}{10} > \frac{4}{10}$
So, $\frac{1}{2} > \frac{2}{5}$

3. d) Ordering the mixed numbers was easier. You need only to look at the whole numbers and ignore the fractions. It is the better strategy to use when the whole numbers are different.

4. Yes; $\frac{4}{5}$ is one-fifth less than 1 whole, $\frac{5}{6}$ is one-sixth less than 1 whole, and $\frac{6}{7}$ is one-seventh less than 1 whole. A diagram helps:

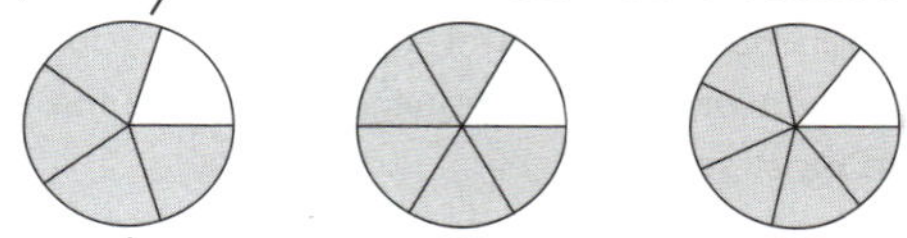

$\frac{4}{5}$ $\frac{5}{6}$ $\frac{6}{7}$

Use the examples in *Connect* to illustrate ordering fractions that are not easily compared by inspection or by using benchmarks (such as 0, $\frac{1}{2}$, 1). Illustrate the two methods for finding common denominators using the examples in *Connect*. Discuss which strategy is easier or more efficient to use in different situations.

Ask:

- If the denominators have a common factor, will the lowest common multiple be greater or less than their product? (*Less*) How do you know? (*I tried it with different examples — the lowest common multiple of 12 and 8 is 24, but their product is 96. The lowest common multiple of 6 and 9 is 18, but their product is 54.*)

Discuss when it is most appropriate to use common denominators to compare fractions. (*When the fractions are not related; when you have many different fractions to compare*)

Here are two examples where finding common denominators may not be the most efficient strategy:

- Which is greater: $\frac{3}{7}$ or $\frac{3}{8}$? ($\frac{1}{7}$ is greater than $\frac{1}{8}$, so $\frac{3}{7}$ is greater than $\frac{3}{8}$.)
- Which is greater: $\frac{4}{9}$ or $\frac{3}{5}$? ($\frac{4}{9}$ is less than $\frac{1}{2}$, $\frac{3}{5}$ is greater than $\frac{1}{2}$, so $\frac{3}{5}$ is greater.)

Have students post their own rules for finding lowest common denominators in the classroom.

Practice

Encourage students to look at the fractions and decide which strategy would be most effective before answering the questions.

Assessment Focus: Question 7

Students show 5 and 6 as improper fractions with a common denominator; for example, $\frac{15}{3}$ and $\frac{18}{3}$. Students then look at the numerators to find a fraction between the two; for example, $\frac{16}{3}$.

7. a) I can write 5 and 6 as improper fractions, using a different denominator each time, then list all the fractions between these two fractions. I can increase the denominator by 1 each time.
For example, $5 = \frac{15}{3}$ and $6 = \frac{18}{3}$: fractions between 5 and 6 are $\frac{16}{3}$ and $\frac{17}{3}$.
$5 = \frac{20}{4}$ and $6 = \frac{24}{4}$: fractions between 5 and 6 are $\frac{21}{4}$, $\frac{22}{4}$, and $\frac{23}{4}$.
$5 = \frac{25}{5}$ and $6 = \frac{30}{5}$: fractions between 5 and 6 are $\frac{26}{5}$, $\frac{27}{5}$, $\frac{28}{5}$, and $\frac{29}{5}$.
b) I have not found all the fractions between 5 and 6 because there are more than anyone could write. I could continue to increase the denominator forever.

8. a) $\frac{3}{3}, \frac{3}{4}, \frac{3}{5}, \frac{3}{6}, \frac{4}{3}, \frac{4}{4}, \frac{4}{5}, \frac{4}{6}, \frac{5}{3}, \frac{5}{4}, \frac{5}{5}, \frac{5}{6}, \frac{6}{3}, \frac{6}{4}, \frac{6}{5}, \frac{6}{6}$
b) $\frac{3}{6}, \frac{3}{5}, \frac{4}{6}, \frac{3}{4}, \frac{4}{5}, \frac{5}{6}, \frac{3}{3}, \frac{4}{4}, \frac{5}{5}, \frac{6}{6}, \frac{6}{5}, \frac{5}{4}, \frac{4}{3}, \frac{6}{4}, \frac{5}{3}, \frac{6}{3}$

9. a) $\frac{22}{32}$: An equivalent fraction is $\frac{44}{64}$. Sixty-fourths are greater than sixty-fifths, and you have one more sixty-fourth.
b) $\frac{919}{999}$: You could use a calculator to write each fraction as a decimal, then compare the resulting decimals. $\frac{919}{999} = 0.\overline{919}$ and $\frac{91\,919}{99\,999} = 0.\overline{91919}$; $0.\overline{919} > 0.\overline{91919}$

REFLECT: You can compare and order fractions by finding a common denominator. You can also compare and order fractions by using benchmarks of 0, $\frac{1}{2}$, and 1.
Each strategy can be used in different situations. You should look at the question and the fractions, and choose the strategy that makes the most sense.

The Farey sequence is named for the British geologist and mathematician, John Farey, who lived from 1766 to 1826.

6. A Farey sequence is a list of certain fractions that follow a pattern.
1st Farey sequence: $\frac{0}{1}, \frac{1}{1}$
2nd Farey sequence: $\frac{0}{1}, \frac{1}{1}, \frac{1}{2}$
3rd Farey sequence: $\frac{0}{1}, \frac{1}{1}, \frac{1}{2}, \frac{1}{3}, \frac{2}{3}$
4th Farey sequence: $\frac{0}{1}, \frac{1}{1}, \frac{1}{2}, \frac{1}{3}, \frac{2}{3}, \frac{1}{4}, \frac{3}{4}$
a) Look at the lists above. Extend the pattern. Write the 5th Farey sequence. $\frac{0}{1}, \frac{1}{1}, \frac{1}{2}, \frac{1}{3}, \frac{2}{3}, \frac{1}{4}, \frac{3}{4}, \frac{1}{5}, \frac{2}{5}, \frac{3}{5}, \frac{4}{5}$
b) Order the fractions in the 5th Farey sequence from least to greatest. $\frac{0}{1}, \frac{1}{5}, \frac{1}{4}, \frac{1}{3}, \frac{2}{5}, \frac{1}{2}, \frac{3}{5}, \frac{2}{3}, \frac{3}{4}, \frac{4}{5}, \frac{1}{1}$

Mental Math

Use whole numbers. List all the possible dimensions of a rectangular prism with volume 72 cm³.

1 × 1 × 72
1 × 2 × 36
1 × 3 × 24
1 × 4 × 18
1 × 6 × 12
1 × 8 × 9
2 × 2 × 18
2 × 3 × 12
2 × 4 × 9
2 × 6 × 6
3 × 3 × 8
3 × 4 × 6

7. **Assessment Focus** The fraction $\frac{11}{2}$ is halfway between 5 and 6. The fraction $\frac{23}{4}$ is halfway between $\frac{11}{2}$ and 6.
a) How many more fractions can you find between 5 and 6? List all the fractions you find.
b) Have you found *all* the fractions between 5 and 6? How do you know?
Show your work.

8. a) Use the digits 3, 4, 5, and 6 to write as many proper and improper fractions as you can. Each numerator and denominator is a single digit.
b) Order the fractions in part a from least to greatest.
c) Which fractions in part a are:
i) less than $\frac{1}{2}$? none
ii) between $\frac{1}{2}$ and 1? $\frac{3}{5}, \frac{4}{6}, \frac{3}{4}, \frac{4}{5}, \frac{5}{6}$
iii) greater than 1? $\frac{6}{5}, \frac{5}{4}, \frac{4}{3}, \frac{6}{4}, \frac{5}{3}, \frac{6}{3}$

Take It Further

9. In each pair, which fraction is greater? How do you know?
a) $\frac{22}{32}$ or $\frac{43}{65}$ b) $\frac{91\,919}{99\,999}$ or $\frac{919}{999}$

Reflect

Name two ways you can compare and order fractions. Which way do you prefer? Explain.

ASSESSMENT FOR LEARNING

What to Look For	What to Do
Knowledge and Understanding ✔ Students understand that common denominators can be used to compare fractions. ✔ Students know different strategies for finding common denominators. ***Thinking*** ✔ Students use critical thinking skills to select a strategy to compare fractions. ***Communication*** ✔ Students can explain how to compare and order fractions, and justify their strategy.	***Extra Support:*** Students who have difficulty finding common denominators could use two number lines to visualize skip counting to list multiples. Students can use Step-by-Step 1 (Master 4.7) to complete question 7. ***Extra Practice:*** For *Practice* questions 1 and 2, have students interchange the denominators for each set of fractions, then compare the new fractions. Students can complete Extra Practice 1 (Master 4.26). ***Extension:*** Students can complete the 6th Farey sequence and order the fractions from least to greatest. Explain that the fractions in a Farey sequence are usually written in order. Challenge students to find a strategy for writing the fractions in the 6th sequence, in order, as they work.

Recording and Reporting
Master 4.2 Ongoing Observations: Fractions and Decimals

4.2 Adding Fractions

Focus Use common denominators to add fractions.

Explore

Work on your own.
Copy these diagrams.

$\frac{\square}{\square} + \frac{\square}{\square} =$ (greatest sum) $\qquad \frac{\square}{\square} + \frac{\square}{\square} =$ (least sum)

Use the numbers 1, 2, 4, and 8 to make the greatest sum and the least sum.
In each case, use each number once.

Reflect & Share

Share your results with a classmate.
Do both of you have the same answers?
If not, which is the greatest sum? The least sum?
What strategies did you use to add?

Connect

Recall how to add fractions with the same denominator.
For example, to add $\frac{3}{12}$ and $\frac{4}{12}$,
add the numerators: $\frac{3}{12} + \frac{4}{12} = \frac{7}{12}$
We can illustrate this sum with a diagram.

$\frac{3}{12}$

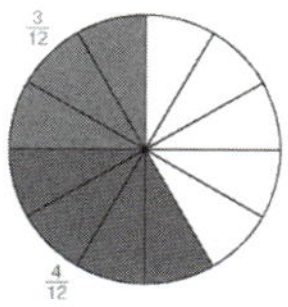

$\frac{4}{12}$

To add fractions that do not have the same denominator, we find and use a common denominator.

Adding Fractions

LESSON ORGANIZER (80–100 min)

Curriculum Focus: Use common denominators to add fractions. (8m20)

Teacher Materials *Optional*
- fraction circles transparency (Master 4.21)
- fraction rings

Student Materials *Optional*
- fraction circles (Master 4.21)
- Step-by-Step 2 (Master 4.8)
- Extra Practice 2 (Master 4.27)

Vocabulary: unit fraction

Assessment: Master 4.2 Ongoing Observations: Fractions and Decimals

Key Math Learning

Fractions can be added using equivalent fractions with common denominators.

Calculator Skills

Students will probably use guess and check. There are 6 ways to arrange the 3 numbers: 23^4, 32^4, 34^2, 43^2, 24^3, 42^3. The greatest number is 32^4 = 1 048 576.

BEFORE Get Started

Draw 4 blank fractions on the board, similar to those in *Explore*. Separate the fractions with a comma rather than an addition sign. Write the numbers 1 to 8 below the blank fractions. Initiate a class discussion.

Ask:
- How can you write these numbers in the boxes so the fractions are in order from least to greatest?

Allow students to think about the problem and to try placing the numbers. After several minutes, ask students for some sample solutions. ($\frac{1}{8}, \frac{2}{7}, \frac{3}{6}, \frac{4}{5}$; $\frac{1}{7}, \frac{2}{8}, \frac{3}{5}, \frac{4}{6}$; $\frac{5}{4}, \frac{6}{3}, \frac{7}{2}, \frac{8}{1}$)

Ask students to describe their strategies for placing the numbers, and how they know the placements were correct.

Present *Explore*. Explain that students will be doing a similar activity, only this time they will be adding fractions instead of ordering them.

DURING Explore

Ongoing Assessment: Observe and Listen

As students work, ask questions, such as:
- How are you trying to find the greatest sum?
  (I use guess and check. I put 1 and 2 in the numerators and 4 and 8 in the denominators, find each sum, then swap the numbers in the numerators, and swap them from numerator to denominator, finding each sum each time.)
- What method are you using to find the greatest sum?
  (I put the greatest numbers in the numerators, because that way I get the greatest fractions.)
- How do you add $\frac{8}{1} + \frac{4}{2}$?
  ($\frac{8}{1}$ is 8; $\frac{4}{2}$ is 2; then 8 + 2 = 10.)

REACHING ALL LEARNERS

Alternative Explore

Materials: number cube labelled 1 to 6

Students work in pairs. Set up the two fractions, as in *Explore*. The goal is to get the greatest sum.

One student rolls the number cube. Each student writes that number in the fraction. Students take turns to roll the cube, with both students writing the number. After 4 rolls, students add their fractions. The person with the greater sum gets a point. Students repeat the game as long as time permits. Students then play a similar game, with the goal to get the least sum.

Early Finishers

Have students find as many different pairs of fractions as possible that have a sum of $3\frac{1}{2}$.

Common Misconceptions

➤ Students cannot recognize when the sum of 2 fractions is in simplest form.

How to Help: Have students use divisibility rules to check that the numerator and denominator have no common factors. For example, if both the numerator and denominator are even, then they can be simplified because 2 is a common factor.

Example 1 Add. $\frac{5}{12} + \frac{5}{6}$

Solution $\frac{5}{12} + \frac{5}{6}$

Use equivalent fractions to write the fractions with a common denominator.
Since 6 is a factor of 12, the lowest common multiple of 12 and 6 is 12.

Use 12 as the common denominator.

$$\frac{5}{6} \overset{\times 2}{=} \frac{10}{12}$$

$$\frac{5}{12} + \frac{5}{6} = \frac{5}{12} + \frac{10}{12}$$ Add the numerators.

$$= \frac{15}{12}$$ To reduce to simplest form, divide the numerator and denominator by their greatest common factor, 3.

$$= \frac{15 \div 3}{12 \div 3}$$

$$= \frac{5}{4}$$ Since 5 > 4, this is an improper fraction.

A fraction is in simplest form when the numerator and denominator have no common factors.

To write the fraction as a mixed number:

$\frac{5}{4} = \frac{4}{4} + \frac{1}{4}$

$= 1 + \frac{1}{4}$

$= 1\frac{1}{4}$ ← This is a mixed number.

We can also use common denominators to add more than two fractions.

Example 2 Add. $\frac{2}{3} + \frac{4}{5} + \frac{3}{4}$

Solution $\frac{2}{3} + \frac{4}{5} + \frac{3}{4}$

Use equivalent fractions to write the fractions with a common denominator.

140 UNIT 4: Fractions and Decimals

- How did you find a lesser sum? (*I turned my fractions for the greatest sum upside down to get $\frac{1}{8}$ and $\frac{2}{4}$.*)
- How do you add $\frac{1}{8} + \frac{2}{4}$? (*I change $\frac{2}{4}$ to $\frac{4}{8}$, then $\frac{1}{8} + \frac{2}{4} = \frac{1}{8} + \frac{4}{8} = \frac{5}{8}$.*)
- Is $\frac{1}{8} + \frac{2}{4}$ the least sum? (*I thought it was, but then I tried $\frac{2}{8} + \frac{1}{4}$, which is $\frac{2}{8} + \frac{2}{8} = \frac{4}{8}$, and found that $\frac{2}{8} + \frac{1}{4}$ is the least sum.*)

Provide struggling students with fraction circles (Master 4.21) to help add fractions such as $\frac{1}{4} + \frac{2}{8}$.

Have students who added fractions by finding a common denominator share their strategies with the class.

AFTER Connect

If you have overhead fraction circles and rings, model the sum at the bottom of page 139.

Remind students of the strategies they used in Grade 7 to estimate the sums of fractions. Use the benchmarks 0, $\frac{1}{2}$, and 1 to illustrate. In *Example 1*, $\frac{5}{12}$ is about $\frac{1}{2}$, and $\frac{5}{6}$ is about 1, so $\frac{5}{12} + \frac{5}{6}$ is about $1\frac{1}{2}$. Since each fraction is less than its benchmark, the sum will be less than $1\frac{1}{2}$.

Use *Example 1* to review the two methods from the previous lesson for finding common denominators. Ask:

- Why do we multiply both the numerator and the denominator? (*To make sure the value of the fraction does not change*)

For *Example 2*, estimate the sum first. $\frac{2}{3}$ is about $\frac{1}{2}$, but greater than $\frac{1}{2}$. $\frac{4}{5}$ is close to 1. $\frac{3}{4}$ is between $\frac{1}{2}$ and 1. So, the sum will be about 2, but greater than 2.

Review the method for writing an improper fraction as a mixed number: we write the mixed number as a sum of two fractions, one of

The denominators 3, 5, and 4 have no common factors.
So, their lowest common multiple is their product: 3 × 5 × 4 = 60
Write each fraction with denominator 60.

$\frac{2}{3} = \frac{40}{60}$ (× 20) $\frac{4}{5} = \frac{48}{60}$ (× 12) $\frac{3}{4} = \frac{45}{60}$ (× 15)

$$\frac{2}{3} + \frac{4}{5} + \frac{3}{4} = \frac{40}{60} + \frac{48}{60} + \frac{45}{60}$$

$= \frac{133}{60}$ Since 133 > 60, this is an improper fraction. It can be written as a mixed number.

$= \frac{120}{60} + \frac{13}{60}$

$= 2 + \frac{13}{60}$

$= 2\frac{13}{60}$

Practice

Write all sums in simplest form.

1. Add.
   a) $\frac{4}{9} + \frac{1}{3}$ $\frac{7}{9}$ b) $\frac{1}{2} + \frac{1}{3}$ $\frac{5}{6}$ c) $\frac{2}{3} + \frac{1}{6}$ $\frac{5}{6}$ d) $\frac{3}{4} + \frac{1}{6}$ $\frac{11}{12}$
   e) $\frac{2}{5} + \frac{1}{3}$ $\frac{11}{15}$ f) $\frac{2}{5} + \frac{1}{10}$ $\frac{1}{2}$ g) $\frac{1}{12} + \frac{1}{4}$ $\frac{1}{3}$ h) $\frac{3}{8} + \frac{1}{4}$ $\frac{5}{8}$
2. Add.
   a) $\frac{3}{8} + \frac{3}{2}$ $1\frac{7}{8}$ b) $\frac{7}{4} + \frac{4}{5}$ $2\frac{11}{20}$ c) $\frac{7}{6} + \frac{5}{7}$ $1\frac{37}{42}$ d) $\frac{13}{10} + \frac{4}{3}$ $2\frac{19}{30}$
   e) $\frac{5}{8} + \frac{2}{3}$ $1\frac{7}{24}$ f) $\frac{4}{5} + \frac{4}{7}$ $1\frac{13}{35}$ g) $\frac{9}{4} + \frac{4}{9}$ $2\frac{25}{36}$ h) $\frac{8}{5} + \frac{11}{6}$ $3\frac{13}{30}$
3. Damara and Baldwin had to shovel snow from their driveway.
   Damara shovelled about $\frac{3}{10}$ of the driveway.
   Baldwin shovelled about $\frac{2}{3}$ of the driveway. About $\frac{29}{30}$ of the driveway
   About what fraction of the driveway was cleared of snow?
4. a) Write each fraction as the sum of two fractions with the same denominator.
   i) $\frac{1}{2}$ ii) $\frac{3}{4}$ iii) $\frac{9}{10}$
   b) Write each fraction in part a as the sum of two fractions with different denominators.

Calculator Skills

Copy the boxes below. Write the digits 2, 3, and 4 in the boxes to make the greatest number.

3 2 4

4.2 Adding Fractions 141

Assignment Guidelines

If your students do not have time to complete all the *Practice* questions on pages 141 and 142, these questions provide minimum curriculum coverage:
2, 4, 5, 6, 7, 8, *Reflect*

To assess the 4 Achievement Chart categories listed in the curriculum document, have students complete these *Practice* questions:
Knowledge and Understanding: 2
Thinking: 5
Application: 7
Communication: *Reflect*

Sample Solutions

4. Answers may vary.
   a) i) $\frac{5}{16} + \frac{3}{16} = \frac{8}{16} = \frac{1}{2}$ ii) $\frac{5}{8} + \frac{1}{8} = \frac{6}{8} = \frac{3}{4}$ iii) $\frac{4}{10} + \frac{5}{10} = \frac{9}{10}$
   b) i) $\frac{1}{6} + \frac{1}{3} = \frac{1}{6} + \frac{2}{6} = \frac{3}{6} = \frac{1}{2}$
   ii) $\frac{1}{4} + \frac{4}{8} = \frac{2}{8} + \frac{4}{8} = \frac{6}{8} = \frac{3}{4}$ iii) $\frac{2}{5} + \frac{5}{10} = \frac{4}{10} + \frac{5}{10} = \frac{9}{10}$
5. a) Start with fractions with denominator 5: $\frac{1}{5} + \frac{3}{5} = \frac{4}{5}$; $\frac{2}{5} + \frac{2}{5} = \frac{4}{5}$
   Find an equivalent fraction for one of the fractions with denominator 5 in each of the statements: $\frac{1}{5} + \frac{6}{10} = \frac{4}{5}$; $\frac{2}{5} + \frac{4}{10} = \frac{4}{5}$
   Find an equivalent fraction for both of the fractions with denominator 5 in each of the statements: $\frac{6}{30} + \frac{6}{10} = \frac{4}{5}$; $\frac{20}{50} + \frac{4}{10} = \frac{4}{5}$

which is an expression for a whole number.
Ask:

- Why do you think $\frac{133}{60}$ was written as $\frac{120}{60} + \frac{13}{60}$? (*60 sixtieths make 1 whole, 120 sixtieths are 2 wholes. We write as many sixtieths as we can to make a whole number.*)

You may want to teach your students this method for writing an improper fraction as a mixed number. For $\frac{133}{60}$, divide 133 by 60 to get 2 remainder 13; that is, 2 wholes and $\frac{13}{60}$, or $2\frac{13}{60}$. In general, divide the numerator by the denominator, then write the remainder as a fraction of the denominator.

Practice

Encourage students to look at the fractions and decide which strategy for finding common denominators would be most effective before answering the questions.

Have students estimate each sum before they calculate it.

For question 6, you may need to review how to add mixed numbers. Use a simple problem, such as:

$$1\frac{1}{4} + 2\frac{1}{2} \rightarrow 1 + 2 + \frac{1}{4} + \frac{1}{2} = 3 + \frac{1}{4} + \frac{1}{2} = 3 + \frac{3}{4} = 3\frac{3}{4}$$

Assessment Focus: Question 5

Students will probably show the sum of the fractions initially using 2 fractions with the same denominator (*for example,* $\frac{3}{5} + \frac{1}{5} = \frac{4}{5}$). Students may use diagrams to find fractions with different denominators, or may recognize that finding a fraction equivalent to one of the added fractions gives the same result (*for example,* $\frac{3}{5} + \frac{2}{10} = \frac{4}{5}$). There are many possible answers.

I can continue to write each of the fractions being added as equivalent fractions with different denominators. There are many possibilities.

b) For example: $\frac{1}{5} + \frac{1}{2} = \frac{7}{10}$; $\frac{1}{5} + \frac{4}{20} + \frac{3}{10} = \frac{7}{10}$

c) For example: $\frac{1}{6} + \frac{1}{18} = \frac{2}{9}$; $\frac{1}{9} + \frac{1}{9} = \frac{2}{9}$; $\frac{5}{30} + \frac{2}{36} = \frac{2}{9}$

8. a) $1\frac{11}{12}$ **b)** $1\frac{29}{60}$ **c)** $2\frac{29}{30}$ **d)** $2\frac{1}{60}$ **e)** $5\frac{3}{5}$ **f)** $2\frac{11}{30}$

9. The sums in parts a, f, h, and i are correct. I used equivalent fractions to write the fractions with a common denominator. I added the numerators, and got the indicated sum.

a) $\frac{1}{5} + \frac{1}{2} = \frac{2}{10} + \frac{5}{10} = \frac{7}{10}$ **f)** $\frac{1}{10} + \frac{1}{30} = \frac{3}{30} + \frac{1}{30} = \frac{4}{30} = \frac{2}{15}$

h) $\frac{1}{3} + \frac{1}{15} = \frac{5}{15} + \frac{1}{15} = \frac{6}{15} = \frac{2}{5}$ **i)** $\frac{1}{5} + \frac{1}{15} = \frac{3}{15} + \frac{1}{15} = \frac{4}{15}$

10. a) $\frac{1}{4} + \frac{1}{2} = \frac{1}{4} + \frac{2}{4} = \frac{3}{4}$ **b)** $\frac{1}{12} + \frac{1}{3} = \frac{1}{12} + \frac{4}{12} = \frac{5}{12}$

c) $\frac{1}{5} + \frac{1}{2} = \frac{2}{10} + \frac{5}{10} = \frac{7}{10}$

11. I started by finding pairs of fractions whose sum was 1.

There were 7 pairs: $\frac{1}{2} + \frac{2}{4}$; $\frac{1}{3} + \frac{4}{6}$; $\frac{1}{4} + \frac{3}{4}$; $\frac{1}{5} + \frac{4}{5}$; $\frac{1}{6} + \frac{5}{6}$; $\frac{2}{3} + \frac{2}{6}$; $\frac{2}{5} + \frac{3}{5}$; $\frac{3}{6}$ was left.

$7 \times 1 + \frac{3}{6} = 7 + \frac{3}{6} = 7\frac{1}{2}$; the sum is $7\frac{1}{2}$.

REFLECT: It is more efficient to add fractions when they are mixed numbers. Whole numbers are easy to add, and the fraction part of a mixed number has lesser numbers than the improper fraction, so the numbers are easier to work with.

For example, $\frac{23}{4} + \frac{8}{3} = \frac{69}{12} + \frac{32}{12} = \frac{101}{12} = 8\frac{5}{12}$

When the fractions are converted to mixed numbers, the question becomes:

$5\frac{3}{4} + 2\frac{2}{3} = 5 + 2 + \frac{3}{4} + \frac{2}{3} = 7 + \frac{9}{12} + \frac{8}{12} = 7 + \frac{17}{12}$

$= 7 + 1 + \frac{5}{12} = 8\frac{5}{12}$

---

5. **Assessment Focus** Write each fraction as the sum of two or more fractions in as many different ways as you can.

a) $\frac{4}{5}$ b) $\frac{7}{10}$ c) $\frac{2}{9}$

Show your work.

To add mixed numbers, add the fractions, then add the whole numbers.

6. Add.

a) $3\frac{1}{3} + 4\frac{1}{4}$ $7\frac{7}{12}$ b) $2\frac{1}{2} + 1\frac{9}{10}$ $4\frac{2}{5}$ c) $1\frac{3}{4} + 2\frac{3}{5}$ $4\frac{7}{20}$

d) $\frac{7}{8} + 1\frac{2}{3}$ $2\frac{13}{24}$ e) $2\frac{3}{5} + \frac{2}{3}$ $3\frac{4}{15}$ f) $5\frac{2}{5} + 1\frac{7}{8}$ $7\frac{11}{40}$

7. Two students, Galen and Mai, worked on a project.
Galen worked for $3\frac{2}{3}$ h.
Mai worked for $2\frac{4}{5}$ h.
What was the total time spent on the project? $6\frac{7}{15}$ h

8. Add.

a) $\frac{1}{2} + \frac{2}{3} + \frac{3}{4}$ b) $\frac{1}{3} + \frac{3}{4} + \frac{2}{5}$ c) $\frac{5}{6} + \frac{4}{5} + \frac{4}{3}$

d) $\frac{5}{4} + \frac{3}{5} + \frac{1}{6}$ e) $\frac{7}{10} + \frac{7}{5} + \frac{7}{2}$ f) $\frac{5}{12} + \frac{6}{5} + \frac{3}{4}$

Math Link

History
Unit fractions are often called Egyptian fractions because the ancient Egyptians investigated fractions in this form.

9. Each fraction below is written as the sum of two unit fractions. Which sums are correct? How do you know?

a) $\frac{7}{10} = \frac{1}{5} + \frac{1}{2}$ b) $\frac{5}{12} = \frac{1}{3} + \frac{1}{4}$ c) $\frac{5}{6} = \frac{1}{3} + \frac{1}{3}$

d) $\frac{7}{12} = \frac{1}{2} + \frac{1}{6}$ e) $\frac{11}{8} = \frac{1}{2} + \frac{1}{9}$ f) $\frac{2}{15} = \frac{1}{10} + \frac{1}{30}$

g) $\frac{7}{15} = \frac{1}{5} + \frac{1}{3}$ h) $\frac{2}{5} = \frac{1}{3} + \frac{1}{15}$ i) $\frac{4}{15} = \frac{1}{5} + \frac{1}{15}$

10. Write each fraction as the sum of two different unit fractions.

a) $\frac{3}{4}$ b) $\frac{5}{12}$ c) $\frac{7}{10}$

Take It Further

11. Find this sum. Explain your method.

$\frac{1}{2} + \frac{1}{3} + \frac{1}{4} + \frac{1}{5} + \frac{1}{6} + \frac{2}{3} + \frac{2}{4} + \frac{2}{5} + \frac{2}{6} + \frac{3}{4} + \frac{3}{5} + \frac{3}{6} + \frac{4}{5} + \frac{4}{6} + \frac{5}{6}$

Reflect

Choose two improper fractions. Add them.
Write each improper fraction as a mixed number.
Add the mixed numbers.
Which method is more efficient for finding the sum of two improper fractions? Why?

142 UNIT 4: Fractions and Decimals

ASSESSMENT FOR LEARNING

What to Look For	What to Do
Knowledge and Understanding ✔ Students understand that common denominators can be used to add fractions.	***Extra Support:*** Students who have difficulty may still require models to add fractions. Use models to help students see the equivalency of fractions with common denominators. Students can use Step-by-Step 2 (Master 4.8) to complete question 5.
Communication ✔ Students can explain their own rules for adding fractions.	***Extra Practice:*** Students generate extra questions by choosing one fraction from each of questions 1 and 2, part a; for example, $\frac{4}{9} + \frac{3}{8}$. Students repeat this for each of parts b to h. Students can complete Extra Practice 2 (Master 4.27).
Application ✔ Students can find a common denominator to add fractions.	***Extension:*** Students could use 2 number cubes labelled 1 to 6 to play a version of Nim. Each player takes a turn and rolls the cubes. The 2 numbers are used to make a fraction, which Player 1 records. On her second turn, Player 1 rolls again, and this time adds or subtracts the fraction from the first one. After 5 rolls, the player closer to 1 wins.

Recording and Reporting
Master 4.2 Ongoing Observations: Fractions and Decimals

4.3 Subtracting Fractions

Focus Use common denominators to subtract fractions.

Explore

Work with a partner.
You will need 1-cm grid paper and coloured pencils.

Use these rules to create a rectangular design on grid paper:

- The design must have line symmetry or rotational symmetry.
- One-half of the grid squares must be red. One-third of the grid squares must be blue. The remaining grid squares must be green.
- The rectangle must have the fewest squares possible.

What fraction of the squares are green? How do you know?
How many squares did you use? Explain.
Describe your design.

Reflect & Share

Compare your design with that of another pair of classmates.
If the designs are different, do both of them obey the rules? Explain.
Compare your designs with those of other classmates.
How many different designs are possible?

Connect

To subtract fractions, we use a strategy similar to that for adding fractions.
When the denominators are different, we find a common denominator first.

4.3 Subtracting Fractions 143

LESSON 4.3

Subtracting Fractions

LESSON ORGANIZER (80–100 min)

Curriculum Focus: Use common denominators to subtract fractions. (8m18, 8m20)

Teacher Materials

- Symmetrical Designs transparency (Master 4.22)

Student Materials

- Symmetrical Designs (Master 4.22)
- 1-cm grid paper (PM 20)
- coloured pencils

Optional

- fraction circles (Master 4.21)
- Step-by-Step 3 (Master 4.9)
- Extra Practice 3 (Master 4.28)

Assessment: Master 4.2 Ongoing Observations: Fractions and Decimals

Key Math Learning

Fractions can be subtracted using equivalent fractions with common denominators.

Number Strategies

Rounded to the nearest dime: \$198.90 + \$201.80 = \$400.70
Rounded to the nearest dollar: \$199 + \$202 = \$401

BEFORE Get Started

On an overhead projector, display a transparency of Symmetrical Designs (Master 4.22).

Ask:

- What types of symmetry do you see? (*Rotational symmetry and line symmetry*)
- Which figures have line symmetry? (*Figure A: 6 lines of symmetry; Figure C: 2 lines of symmetry; Figure D: 3 lines of symmetry*)
- Which figures have rotational symmetry? (*Figure A: order 6; Figure B: order 2; Figure C: order 2; Figure D: order 3*)

Draw lines of symmetry as students explain where they are. Discuss how the shadings in the design must also be symmetrical. Ensure students understand line symmetry and rotational symmetry.

Present *Explore*.

DURING Explore

Ongoing Assessment: Observe and Listen

As students work, ask questions, such as:

- How did you find out what fraction of the grid squares is green? (*I started with 6 squares. If $\frac{1}{2}$ are red, then that is 3 squares. $\frac{1}{3}$ are blue, which means 2 squares are blue. That leaves 1 green square, so it is $\frac{1}{6}$.*)
- What other way is there to find out what fraction of the squares is green? (*The whole rectangle is 1. $1 - \frac{1}{2}$ is red, so there is $\frac{1}{2}$ the rectangle left. I now have to take away the blue: $\frac{1}{2} - \frac{1}{3}$. I used a common denominator to get $\frac{1}{6}$.*)
- How did you know you had the fewest squares possible? (*Once I knew I needed at least 6 squares for the design to meet the fraction rules, I tried to make designs with multiples of 6. The smallest I could make was a design with 6 squares.*)

REACHING ALL LEARNERS

Alternative Explore

Materials: coloured tiles, 1-cm grid paper

Have students use coloured tiles to complete the task, then record their designs on grid paper. Instead of finding rectangular designs, students may create any design that meets the criteria. Using the fewest number of squares is not required.

Early Finishers

Have students find as many pairs of fractions as they can, with a difference of $\frac{5}{6}$. The fractions must have different denominators.

Common Misconceptions

➤ Students subtract numerators and subtract denominators without finding a common denominator.

How to Help: Use an illustration to discuss this misconception. Write the equation, $\frac{3}{4} - \frac{1}{2} = \frac{2}{2} = 1$. Ask, "Does this make sense? (*No*) "Why not?" (*You started with less than one whole, and took one-half away. You can't end up with a whole.*)

Illustrate that subtracting numerators and denominators does not result in a fraction equivalent to the difference of the two fractions. Use a number line to model subtracting fractions and to identify equivalent fractions.

Example 1

Subtract. $\frac{4}{5} - \frac{3}{10}$

Solution

$\frac{4}{5} - \frac{3}{10}$

Since 5 is a factor of 10, the lowest common denominator is 10.

$\frac{4}{5} = \frac{8}{10}$ (×2 numerator and denominator)

$\frac{4}{5} - \frac{3}{10} = \frac{8}{10} - \frac{3}{10}$

$= \frac{5}{10}$ This is not in simplest form.

$= \frac{5 \div 5}{10 \div 5}$ 5 is a factor of the numerator and denominator.

$= \frac{1}{2}$

To subtract mixed numbers, we subtract the fractions, then subtract the whole numbers. We must check the fractions to see which is greater. When the second fraction is greater than the first fraction, we cannot subtract directly.

Example 2

Subtract. $3\frac{1}{5} - 1\frac{3}{4}$

Solution

Method 1

Subtract the whole numbers and the fractions separately.

$3\frac{1}{5} - 1\frac{3}{4}$

Subtract the fractions: $\frac{1}{5} - \frac{3}{4}$

But $\frac{1}{5} < \frac{3}{4}$, so we cannot subtract $\frac{3}{4}$ from $\frac{1}{5}$.

Write $3\frac{1}{5}$ as $2 + 1\frac{1}{5}$, or $2 + \frac{6}{5}$.

The problem can be written $2\frac{6}{5} - 1\frac{3}{4}$.

Then, subtract the fractions.

$\frac{6}{5} - \frac{3}{4}$

The denominators 5 and 4 have no common factors.

Estimate: Since $\frac{1}{5} < \frac{1}{2}$ and $\frac{3}{4} > \frac{1}{2}$; $\frac{1}{5} < \frac{3}{4}$

144 UNIT 4: Fractions and Decimals

AFTER Connect

What you might see:

Arrangements with line symmetry:

B	G	B
R	R	R

B	R	B
R	G	R

It is not possible for a rectangle with 6 squares and the colours indicated to have rotational symmetry.

Bring students together to discuss *Explore*. After students have described how they calculated that $\frac{1}{6}$ is green, ask:

- Did anyone use a different strategy?
  (*I drew rectangles with a certain number of squares until I found one that could be cut into halves and thirds. Then I thought about how I could colour the squares to get symmetry.*)
- Why is finding the least number of squares significant?
  (*It represents the lowest common multiple of 2 and 3.*)

Before you subtract in *Example 1*, remind students how to estimate the difference: $\frac{4}{5} - \frac{3}{10}$

$\frac{4}{5}$ is a bit less than 1.

$\frac{3}{10}$ is a bit less than $\frac{1}{2}$.

So, an estimate is $1 - \frac{1}{2} = \frac{1}{2}$.

Provide one or two more examples using simple denominators, if you think it is necessary, before subtracting mixed numbers in *Example 2*.

Before you subtract in *Example 2*, estimate first.

$3\frac{1}{5}$ is a bit more than 3.

$1\frac{3}{4}$ is a bit less than 2.

$3 - 2 = 1$

So, their lowest common denominator is $4 \times 5 = 20$.

$\frac{6}{5} = \frac{24}{20}$ (×4) $\qquad \frac{3}{4} = \frac{15}{20}$ (×5)

$\frac{6}{5} - \frac{3}{4} = \frac{24}{20} - \frac{15}{20}$
$= \frac{9}{20}$

Now, subtract the whole numbers that remain: $2 - 1 = 1$
So, $3\frac{1}{5} - 1\frac{3}{4} = 1\frac{9}{20}$

Method 2
Change both fractions to improper fractions, then subtract.

$3\frac{1}{5} = 3 + \frac{1}{5}$ $\qquad 1\frac{3}{4} = 1 + \frac{3}{4}$
$= \frac{15}{5} + \frac{1}{5}$ $\qquad = \frac{4}{4} + \frac{3}{4}$
$= \frac{16}{5}$ $\qquad = \frac{7}{4}$

The denominators have no common factors.
So, their lowest common denominator is $4 \times 5 = 20$.

$\frac{16}{5} = \frac{64}{20}$ (×4) $\qquad \frac{7}{4} = \frac{35}{20}$ (×5)

$\frac{16}{5} - \frac{7}{4} = \frac{64}{20} - \frac{35}{20}$
$= \frac{29}{20}$

To write the fraction as a mixed number:
$\frac{29}{20} = \frac{20}{20} + \frac{9}{20}$
$= 1 + \frac{9}{20}$
$= 1\frac{9}{20}$
So, $3\frac{1}{5} - 1\frac{3}{4} = 1\frac{9}{20}$

In *Example 2*, the answer was written as a mixed number because the question was written with mixed numbers.
In general, the answer should be written in the same form as the question.

4.3 Subtracting Fractions **145**

Assignment Guidelines

If your students do not have time to complete all the *Practice* questions on pages 146 and 147, these questions provide minimum curriculum coverage:
1, 3, 4, 5, 6, 7, 9, *Reflect*

To assess the 4 Achievement Chart categories listed in the curriculum document, have students complete these *Practice* questions:
Application: 3
Knowledge and Understanding: 4
Thinking: 5
Communication: 7

Sample Solutions

3. $\frac{3}{8} + \frac{1}{4} = \frac{3}{8} + \frac{2}{8} = \frac{5}{8}$; $\frac{5}{8}$ of the shoes were basketball shoes or running shoes.
The rest of the shoes were golf shoes. So, $1 - \frac{5}{8} = \frac{8}{8} - \frac{5}{8} = \frac{3}{8}$;
$\frac{3}{8}$ of the order was golf shoes.

4. a) $\frac{10}{3} - \frac{3}{4} = \frac{40}{12} - \frac{9}{12} = \frac{31}{12}$ **b)** $\frac{14}{15}$
c) $\frac{23}{20}$ **d)** $\frac{17}{10} - \frac{5}{6} = \frac{102}{60} - \frac{50}{60} = \frac{52}{60} = \frac{13}{15}$
e) $\frac{29}{10}$ **f)** $\frac{53}{30}$ **g)** $\frac{5}{6}$ **h)** $\frac{41}{24}$

5. a) $\frac{5}{2} - \frac{4}{3} = \frac{7}{6}$; $\frac{5}{2} - \frac{3}{4} = \frac{7}{4}$; $\frac{5}{4} - \frac{2}{3} = \frac{7}{12}$; $\frac{5}{3} - \frac{2}{4} = \frac{7}{6}$; $\frac{4}{2} - \frac{3}{5} = \frac{7}{5}$;
$\frac{4}{2} - \frac{5}{3} = \frac{1}{3}$; $\frac{4}{3} - \frac{2}{5} = \frac{14}{15}$; $\frac{4}{5} - \frac{2}{3} = \frac{2}{15}$; $\frac{3}{5} - \frac{2}{4} = \frac{1}{10}$;
$\frac{3}{4} - \frac{2}{5} = \frac{7}{20}$; $\frac{3}{2} - \frac{4}{5} = \frac{7}{10}$; $\frac{3}{2} - \frac{5}{4} = \frac{1}{4}$

But we subtract a number less than 2 from a number greater than 3, so the answer will be greater than 1.

As you work through *Example 2*, ask:

- When we subtract mixed numbers, why do we subtract the fractions before the whole numbers?
  (If the second fraction is greater, you have to regroup first to subtract.)
- Why didn't this matter when we added mixed numbers?
  (We can add 2 fractions in any order. We can only subtract a lesser fraction from a greater fraction.)

Review methods for finding a common denominator. Ask students to suggest subtraction questions where:

- the fractions share no common factors
- the fractions have a common factor
- one fraction is a multiple of the other

Ask students to explain the methods they would use in each situation.

Review subtracting a fraction from a whole number.

Write a question, such as $1 - \frac{1}{8}$, on the board.

Have students suggest strategies for finding the difference. One mental math strategy is to know that $1 = \frac{8}{8}$, so $\frac{8}{8} - \frac{1}{8} = \frac{7}{8}$.

Then write $2 - \frac{3}{8}$. Students could repeat the mental math strategy, knowing that 2 wholes is $\frac{16}{8}$, and $\frac{16}{8} - \frac{3}{8} = \frac{13}{8}$, or, they could think of $2 - \frac{3}{8}$ as $1 + 1 - \frac{3}{8} = 1 + \frac{5}{8}$, or $1\frac{5}{8}$.

Practice

Remind students of the two methods for subtracting mixed numbers, and to think about which one they find more useful.

Other subtraction statements that I was able to write I could not find an answer to, because I cannot subtract a greater fraction from a lesser fraction; for example, $\frac{5}{4} - \frac{3}{2}$.
For parts b and c, I ordered the differences from least to greatest:
$\frac{1}{10}, \frac{2}{15}, \frac{1}{4}, \frac{1}{3}, \frac{7}{20}, \frac{7}{12}, \frac{7}{10}, \frac{14}{15}, \frac{7}{6}, \frac{7}{6}, \frac{7}{5}, \frac{7}{4}$

b) The statement with the greatest difference is $\frac{5}{2} - \frac{3}{4} = \frac{7}{4}$.

c) The statement with the least difference is $\frac{3}{5} - \frac{2}{4} = \frac{1}{10}$.

6. a) $3\frac{3}{4} - 1\frac{1}{5}$
Subtract the whole numbers and the fractions separately.
Subtract the fractions: $\frac{3}{4} - \frac{1}{5} = \frac{15}{20} - \frac{4}{20} = \frac{11}{20}$
Now subtract the whole numbers: $3 - 1 = 2$
So, $3\frac{3}{4} - 1\frac{1}{5} = 2\frac{11}{20}$

b) $3\frac{2}{5} - 1\frac{5}{8}$
Subtract the whole numbers and the fractions separately.
Subtract the fractions: $\frac{2}{5} - \frac{5}{8}$
But, $\frac{2}{5} < \frac{5}{8}$, so I cannot subtract $\frac{2}{5} - \frac{5}{8}$.
I write $3\frac{2}{5}$ as $2 + 1\frac{2}{5}$, or $2 + \frac{7}{5}$
The problem can be written $2\frac{7}{5} - 1\frac{5}{8}$.
Subtract the fractions: $\frac{7}{5} - \frac{5}{8} = \frac{56}{40} - \frac{25}{40} = \frac{31}{40}$
Now subtract the whole numbers: $2 - 1 = 1$
So, $3\frac{2}{5} - 1\frac{5}{8} = 1\frac{31}{40}$

7. a) i) $3 - \frac{4}{5} = 2 + \frac{5}{5} - \frac{4}{5} = 2 + \frac{1}{5} = 2\frac{1}{5}$ **ii)** $3\frac{4}{7}$ **iii)** $4\frac{1}{6}$

b) I rewrote 1 whole as an improper fraction, then subtracted the proper fraction from the improper fraction, and added this difference to the remaining wholes.

(Sample Solutions continue below, right.)

Practice

1. Subtract.
a) $\frac{7}{2} - \frac{5}{4}$ $\frac{9}{4}$ b) $\frac{7}{8} - \frac{3}{4}$ $\frac{1}{8}$ c) $\frac{13}{6} - \frac{8}{12}$ $\frac{3}{2}$ d) $\frac{5}{3} - \frac{2}{6}$ $\frac{4}{3}$
e) $\frac{7}{5} - \frac{4}{10}$ 1 f) $\frac{5}{3} - \frac{2}{9}$ $\frac{13}{9}$ g) $\frac{7}{2} - \frac{2}{4}$ 3 h) $\frac{3}{2} - \frac{9}{7}$ $\frac{3}{14}$

2. Subtract.
a) $\frac{11}{12} - \frac{5}{6}$ $\frac{1}{12}$ b) $\frac{7}{10} - \frac{1}{2}$ $\frac{1}{5}$ c) $\frac{3}{4} - \frac{3}{5}$ $\frac{3}{20}$ d) $\frac{7}{8} - \frac{1}{3}$ $\frac{13}{24}$
e) $\frac{2}{3} - \frac{7}{12}$ $\frac{1}{12}$ f) $\frac{7}{5} - \frac{2}{3}$ $\frac{11}{15}$ g) $\frac{9}{5} - \frac{1}{2}$ $\frac{13}{10}$ h) $\frac{4}{5} - \frac{1}{3}$ $\frac{7}{15}$

Number Strategies

Round each amount to the nearest dime, then add. $400.70
Round each amount to the nearest dollar, then add.
- $198.85 $401
- $201.79

3. A sports store placed an order for shoes.
Three-eighths of the order was basketball shoes;
one-quarter was running shoes; and the rest were golf shoes.
What fraction of the order was golf shoes?

4. Subtract.
a) $\frac{10}{3} - \frac{3}{4}$ b) $\frac{8}{5} - \frac{2}{3}$ c) $\frac{7}{4} - \frac{3}{5}$ d) $\frac{17}{10} - \frac{5}{6}$
e) $\frac{7}{2} - \frac{3}{5}$ f) $\frac{13}{6} - \frac{2}{5}$ g) $\frac{7}{3} - \frac{3}{2}$ h) $\frac{7}{3} - \frac{5}{8}$

Make sure the first fraction is greater than the second.

5. **Assessment Focus** Copy this diagram.
Use the numbers 2, 3, 4, and 5 as numerators or denominators.

$$\frac{\square}{\square} - \frac{\square}{\square} =$$

a) Write as many different subtraction statements as possible.
Use each number once each time.
b) Which statement has the greatest difference?
c) Which statement has the least difference?
Show your work.

6. Subtract.
a) $3\frac{3}{4} - 1\frac{1}{5}$ $2\frac{11}{20}$ b) $3\frac{2}{5} - 1\frac{5}{8}$ $1\frac{31}{40}$ c) $3\frac{7}{10} - 2\frac{1}{3}$ $1\frac{11}{30}$
d) $3\frac{1}{3} - 2\frac{7}{10}$ $\frac{19}{30}$ e) $4\frac{2}{9} - 1\frac{1}{6}$ $3\frac{1}{18}$ f) $4\frac{1}{6} - 1\frac{2}{9}$ $2\frac{17}{18}$

7. a) Subtract.
i) $3 - \frac{4}{5}$ ii) $4 - \frac{3}{7}$ iii) $5 - \frac{5}{6}$
b) Which methods did you use in part a? Explain your choice.

146 UNIT 4: Fractions and Decimals

Assessment Focus: Question 5

Students may use guess and check. There are 12 possible fractions. There are only 12 possible subtraction statements that result in a positive difference. Students might communicate this as they "play" with the numbers.

(Sample Solutions continued)

8. Answers may vary.
a) $\frac{11}{14} - \frac{2}{7} = \frac{1}{2}$ **b)** $\frac{19}{20} - \frac{1}{5} = \frac{3}{4}$ **c)** $\frac{3}{5} - \frac{1}{2} = \frac{1}{10}$
d) $\frac{1}{2} - \frac{1}{3} = \frac{1}{6}$ **e)** $\frac{11}{12} - \frac{2}{3} = \frac{1}{4}$

9. a) $3 + 2 + 1 = 6$; $\frac{1}{2}$ is 6 books. So, $\frac{2}{2} = 2 \times 6$ books $= 12$ books
b) $2 + 3 + 1 = 6$; $\frac{1}{3}$ is 6 books. So, $\frac{3}{3} = 3 \times 6$ books $= 18$ books

10. a) $\frac{1}{2}, \frac{1}{6}, \frac{1}{12}, \frac{1}{20}$
b) For example, $\frac{1}{5} - \frac{1}{6} = \frac{1}{30}, \frac{1}{6} - \frac{1}{7} = \frac{1}{42}, \frac{1}{7} - \frac{1}{8} = \frac{1}{56}$
c) The product of the denominators in the fractions that are subtracted is equal to the denominator of the difference, whose numerator is also 1.
(Teacher note: After students have multiplied fractions, yo could point out that the product and difference of each pc fractions are equal.)

11. The difference between $\frac{1}{3}$ of the pennies and $\frac{1}{4}$ of the pennie 2 pennies.
The difference: $\frac{1}{3} - \frac{1}{4} = \frac{4}{12} - \frac{3}{12} = \frac{1}{12}$
So, $\frac{1}{12}$ is 2 pennies, and $\frac{12}{12} = 12 \times 2$ pennies $= 24$ pe

8. Write each fraction as the difference of two proper fractions with different denominators.
a) $\frac{1}{2}$ b) $\frac{3}{4}$ c) $\frac{1}{10}$ d) $\frac{1}{6}$ e) $\frac{1}{4}$

9. a) One-half of the books in Kevin's backpack are novels.
He also has 3 science books, 2 history books, and 1 geography book.
How many books are in Kevin's backpack? 12 books

b) In Raji's locker, one-third of the books are novels and one-third are science books. She also has 2 geography books, 3 history books, and 1 social studies book.
How many books are in Raji's locker? 18 books

10. Here are some subtraction statements with unit fractions having denominators that are consecutive whole numbers:

$\frac{1}{1} - \frac{1}{2}$; $\frac{1}{2} - \frac{1}{3}$; $\frac{1}{3} - \frac{1}{4}$; $\frac{1}{4} - \frac{1}{5}$

a) Find the difference of the fractions in each pair above.
b) Write more pairs of fractions like these.
Find each difference.
c) What patterns do you see?

Take It Further

11. There are some pennies on a table.
One-quarter of the pennies show heads.
Two pennies are turned over.
Now, one-third of the pennies show heads.
How many pennies are on the table? 24 pennies
How do you know?

12. Two matching pitchers contain grapefruit juice.
Pitcher A is $\frac{1}{3}$ full. Pitcher B is $\frac{2}{5}$ full.
Each pitcher is then filled with water.
The contents of both pitchers are poured into one large bowl.
What fraction of the liquid is grapefruit juice? $\frac{11}{30}$

Reflect

Which fractions or mixed numbers are easy to subtract?
Which are more difficult?
Give an example in each case.

12. The bowl contains twice what each pitcher contains. So, $\frac{1}{3}$ of the pitcher is $\frac{1}{6}$ of the bowl.
And, $\frac{2}{5}$ of the pitcher is $\frac{2}{10}$ of the bowl.
$\frac{1}{6} + \frac{2}{10} = \frac{5}{30} + \frac{6}{30} = \frac{11}{30}$
There is $\frac{11}{30}$ grapefruit juice in the bowl.

REFLECT: The easiest fractions to subtract are those that have the same denominators; for example, $\frac{9}{10} - \frac{4}{10} = \frac{5}{10} = \frac{1}{2}$.
The next easiest is when the denominator of one fraction is a multiple of the other denominator. I only have to change one denominator.
For example, $\frac{4}{5} - \frac{3}{10} = \frac{8}{10} - \frac{3}{10} = \frac{5}{10} = \frac{1}{2}$
The next easiest is when the denominators have no common factors, so the common denominator is the product of the denominators.
For example, $\frac{8}{9} - \frac{3}{5} = \frac{40}{45} - \frac{27}{45} = \frac{13}{45}$
The fractions that require the most work are those where the denominators have a common factor. Then, I have to find the lowest common denominator first. For example, $\frac{7}{6} - \frac{2}{9}$; I have to find the least number that 6 and 9 goes into — it is 18.
Then $\frac{7}{6} - \frac{2}{9} = \frac{21}{18} - \frac{4}{18} = \frac{17}{18}$

ASSESSMENT FOR LEARNING

What to Look For

Knowledge and Understanding

✔ Students understand that common denominators can be used to subtract fractions.

Thinking

✔ Students can solve problems that require subtracting two fractions.

Communication

✔ Students can explain their own rules for subtracting fractions.

Application

✔ Students can find a common denominator to subtract fractions.

What to Do

Extra Support: Students who have difficulty could use fraction strips or Cuisenaire rods to model the questions.
Students can use Step-by-Step 3 (Master 4.9) to complete question 5.

Extra Practice: Students can repeat *Explore*, using 4 colours. They must create a rectangular design that is $\frac{1}{2}$ red, $\frac{1}{3}$ blue, and $\frac{1}{4}$ green. The remaining squares are yellow.
Students can complete Extra Practice 3 (Master 4.28).

Extension: Students play in pairs with a number cube labelled 1 to 6. Each player starts at 5, and takes a turn to roll the cube. Player A rolls the cube twice, and uses the numbers to make a fraction that she subtracts from 5. The next time she rolls, she subtracts another fraction from the new total. The winner is the student who is closer to 0 after 5 or fewer rolls.

Recording and Reporting

Master 4.2 Ongoing Observations: Fractions and Decimals

Using Models to Multiply Fractions

LESSON ORGANIZER (80–100 min)

Curriculum Focus: Use an area model to multiply fractions. (8m19, 8m20)

Student Materials
- 0.5-cm grid paper (PM 14)
- 1-cm grid paper (PM 20)
- coloured pencils

Optional
- Step-by-Step 4 (Master 4.10)
- Extra Practice 4 (Master 4.29)

Vocabulary: area model

Assessment: Master 4.2 Ongoing Observations: Fractions and Decimals

Key Math Learning

An area model can be used to understand the process of multiplying two fractions.

Calculator Skills

Students could list all the perfect squares from 1 to 100 (1, 4, 9, 16, 25, 36, 49, 64, 81, 100), then use guess and check to solve the problem.

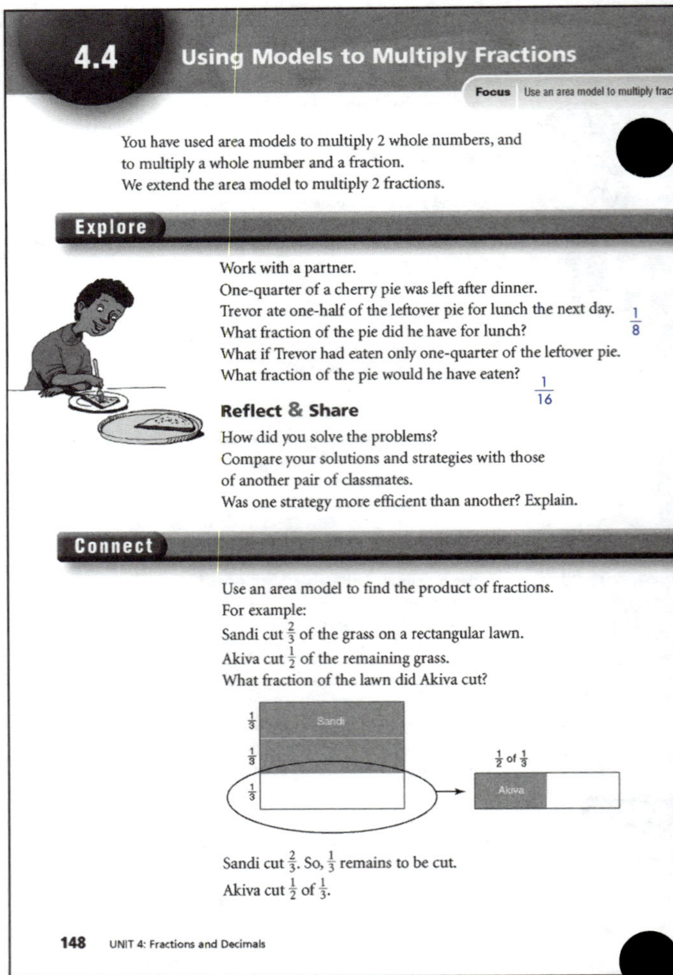

4.4 Using Models to Multiply Fractions

Focus Use an area model to multiply fract

You have used area models to multiply 2 whole numbers, and to multiply a whole number and a fraction.
We extend the area model to multiply 2 fractions.

Explore

Work with a partner.
One-quarter of a cherry pie was left after dinner.
Trevor ate one-half of the leftover pie for lunch the next day.
What fraction of the pie did he have for lunch? $\frac{1}{8}$
What if Trevor had eaten only one-quarter of the leftover pie.
What fraction of the pie would he have eaten? $\frac{1}{16}$

Reflect & Share

How did you solve the problems?
Compare your solutions and strategies with those of another pair of classmates.
Was one strategy more efficient than another? Explain.

Connect

Use an area model to find the product of fractions.
For example:
Sandi cut $\frac{2}{3}$ of the grass on a rectangular lawn.
Akiva cut $\frac{1}{2}$ of the remaining grass.
What fraction of the lawn did Akiva cut?

Sandi cut $\frac{2}{3}$. So, $\frac{1}{3}$ remains to be cut.
Akiva cut $\frac{1}{2}$ of $\frac{1}{3}$.

148 UNIT 4: Fractions and Decimals

BEFORE Get Started

Show students an area model to represent $3 \times 4 = 12$. Draw a 3 by 4 rectangle on the board, and have students say its area (12 square units).

Present *Explore*. Students may need to be reminded that they are finding the fraction of the original (whole) pie.

DURING Explore

Ongoing Assessment: Observe and Listen

As students work, ask:

- What strategy are you using?
  (I am drawing a picture of a pie. I need to find $\frac{1}{2}$ of $\frac{1}{4}$, so I am using what I know about adding fractions. I know that $\frac{1}{8} + \frac{1}{8}$ is $\frac{1}{4}$, so $\frac{1}{2}$ of $\frac{1}{4}$ is $\frac{1}{8}$.)
- How does drawing a picture help?
  (I can see the fractional parts, and I can cut the pie into small enough pieces to identify what fraction has been eaten.)

AFTER Connect

What you might see:
For the 1st question:

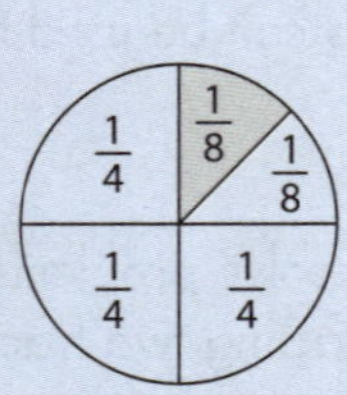

Trevor ate $\frac{1}{8}$ of the pie.

For the 2nd question:

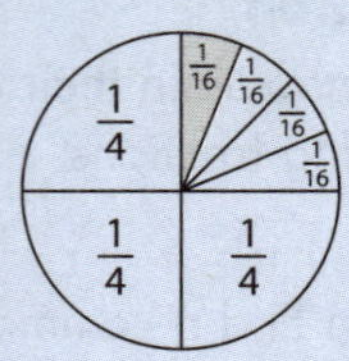

Trevor ate $\frac{1}{16}$ of the pie.

Have students share their solutions for *Explore*.

Look for students who used a circle or a rectangle model. If no group drew a diagram, show each model above.

From the rectangle, $\frac{1}{2}$ of $\frac{1}{3} = \frac{1}{6}$
$\frac{1}{6}$ is the area of part of a rectangle,
with one side length $\frac{1}{2}$ of the original length
and the other side length $\frac{1}{3}$ of the original length.
Since the area of a rectangle is length × width, we can write
$\frac{1}{2}$ of $\frac{1}{3}$ as the multiplication statement: $\frac{1}{2} \times \frac{1}{3} = \frac{1}{6}$
So, Akiva cut $\frac{1}{6}$ of the lawn.

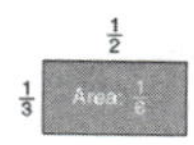

Example

One-half of the Grade 8 students tried out for the school's volleyball team. Three-quarters of the students were successful.

a) What fraction of the Grade 8 students are on the team?

b) Draw an area model and write a multiplication statement to show your answer.

Solution

a) Three-quarters of one-half of the Grade 8 students are on the team.
Draw a rectangle.
Show $\frac{1}{2}$ of the rectangle.

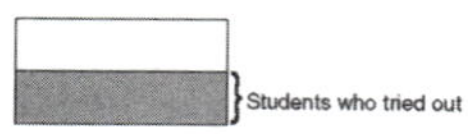

Divide $\frac{1}{2}$ of the rectangle into quarters.
Shade $\frac{3}{4}$.

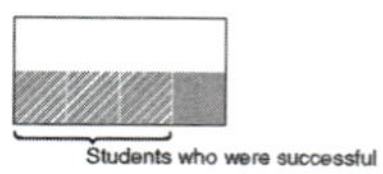

Use broken lines to divide the whole rectangle into equal parts.
There are 8 equal parts.
Three parts are shaded.
So, $\frac{3}{8}$ of the Grade 8 students are on the team.

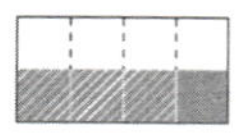

b) $\frac{3}{4}$ of $\frac{1}{2}$ is $\frac{3}{8}$.
So, $\frac{3}{4} \times \frac{1}{2} = \frac{3}{8}$

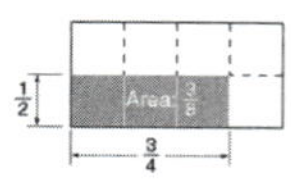

4.4 Using Models to Multiply Fractions **149**

REACHING ALL LEARNERS

Early Finishers

Have students write a scenario, similar to that in *Explore*, that would result in a product of $\frac{3}{8}$.

Common Misconceptions

➤ When students draw an area model, they do not know what the dimensions of the rectangle should be.

How to Help: Have students use the models in question 1 and look for patterns in the dimensions and the fractions. They should notice that the number of squares in the length and the width are equal to the denominators. For example, for $\frac{6}{7} \times \frac{2}{3}$, we need $\frac{7}{7}$ to be able to show $\frac{6}{7}$, and we need $\frac{3}{3}$ to be able to show $\frac{2}{3}$. That is, each dimension represents 1 whole, and these wholes are different.

Sample Solutions

3. For example: $\frac{3}{8} \times \frac{2}{3} = \frac{6}{24} = \frac{1}{4}$, $\frac{2}{9} \times \frac{3}{8} = \frac{6}{72} = \frac{1}{12}$, $\frac{2}{7} \times \frac{3}{4} = \frac{6}{28} = \frac{3}{14}$

4. b) When I swap the numerators or swap the denominators in a pair of fractions, their product does not change. I notice that pairs of rectangles that represent the same product are congruent and have the same area, but are oriented differently. This is similar to what I learned about the multiplication of whole numbers: the order of the factors does not matter.
Other products similar to those above are:
$\frac{4}{7} \times \frac{2}{9} = \frac{8}{63}$ and $\frac{4}{9} \times \frac{2}{7} = \frac{8}{63}$; $\frac{3}{7} \times \frac{2}{4} = \frac{3}{14}$ and $\frac{2}{7} \times \frac{3}{4} = \frac{3}{14}$; $\frac{5}{7} \times \frac{4}{8} = \frac{5}{14}$ and $\frac{4}{7} \times \frac{5}{8} = \frac{5}{14}$

Review the lawn cutting example in *Connect*. Draw the rectangle on the board as you explain. Reinforce that the area model for multiplying fractions is based on prior knowledge of the area of a rectangle: length × width

When you write: $\frac{1}{2} \times \frac{1}{3}$, show students how to estimate the product. One-half of any number is less than that number, so $\frac{1}{2}$ of $\frac{1}{3}$ will be less than $\frac{1}{3}$.

In mathematics, the word "of" indicates multiplication.

Use another rectangle on the board to model the *Example*. As before, show students how to estimate $\frac{3}{4}$ of $\frac{1}{2}$. One benchmark is $\frac{1}{2} \times \frac{1}{2} = \frac{1}{4}$. Students know that $1 \times \frac{1}{2} = \frac{1}{2}$; that is, multiplying a number by 1 does not change the number.

Since $\frac{3}{4}$ is between $\frac{1}{2}$ and 1, the product $\frac{3}{4} \times \frac{1}{2}$ is between $\frac{1}{4}$ and $\frac{1}{2}$.

Practice

Provide grid paper for students to record their solutions. Encourage students to estimate each product before they calculate. Since all products in this lesson involve proper fractions (that is, fractions less than 1), each product will be less than either fraction in the multiplication statement. For example, the product $\frac{4}{5} \times \frac{3}{4}$ is less than both $\frac{4}{5}$ and $\frac{3}{4}$.

Assessment Focus: Question 4

As students draw models for the products of fractions, they should notice that pairs of rectangles are congruent. The rectangles that represent the same products have the same area, but different orientations.

Students demonstrate their understanding of the commutative property; that is, the order of the factors does not affect the product.

5. I draw the first rectangle with length $\frac{12}{12}$ and height $\frac{8}{8}$.
I label $\frac{3}{12}$, then shade $\frac{5}{8}$ of those $\frac{3}{12}$.
I draw a second rectangle with length $\frac{8}{8}$ and height $\frac{12}{12}$.
I label $\frac{5}{12}$, then shade $\frac{3}{8}$ of those $\frac{5}{12}$.
I end up with matching shaded areas on both rectangles; 15 of 96 squares are shaded.

REFLECT: I use the denominators as the dimensions of the rectangle. For example, for the question $\frac{3}{4} \times \frac{2}{5}$, I would draw a 4 × 5 rectangle. This represents $\frac{4}{4}$ by $\frac{5}{5}$. Then $\frac{3}{4} \times \frac{2}{5} = \frac{6}{20}$, which I write as $\frac{3}{10}$.

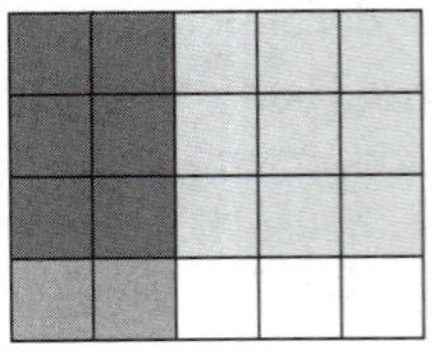

Assignment Guidelines

If your students do not have time to complete all the *Practice* questions on page 150, these questions provide minimum curriculum coverage:
2, 4, 5, *Reflect*

To assess the 4 Achievement Chart categories listed in the curriculum document, have students complete these *Practice* questions:
Knowledge and Understanding: 2
Application: 4
Thinking: 5
Communication: *Reflect*

Practice

1. Draw each rectangle on grid paper.
Use the rectangle to find each product.
a) $\frac{1}{2} \times \frac{3}{4} = \frac{3}{8}$ b) $\frac{3}{4} \times \frac{2}{3} = \frac{6}{12} = \frac{1}{2}$ c) $\frac{2}{5} \times \frac{1}{2} = \frac{2}{10} = \frac{1}{5}$
d) $\frac{5}{6} \times \frac{1}{2} = \frac{5}{12}$ e) $\frac{3}{5} \times \frac{7}{8} = \frac{21}{40}$ f) $\frac{4}{5} \times \frac{3}{4} = \frac{12}{20} = \frac{3}{5}$

2. Draw a rectangle on grid paper to find each product.
a) $\frac{3}{4} \times \frac{5}{8} = \frac{15}{32}$ b) $\frac{4}{9} \times \frac{2}{5} = \frac{8}{45}$ c) $\frac{3}{4} \times \frac{2}{3} = \frac{6}{12} = \frac{1}{2}$
d) $\frac{6}{7} \times \frac{2}{3} = \frac{12}{21} = \frac{4}{7}$ e) $\frac{2}{3} \times \frac{1}{3} = \frac{2}{9}$ f) $\frac{4}{5} \times \frac{4}{5} = \frac{16}{25}$

3. Write 3 multiplication statements using proper fractions. Make sure they are different from any products you have found so far. Draw a rectangle to illustrate each product.

4. **Assessment Focus**
a) Draw an area model to find each product.
i) $\frac{3}{4} \times \frac{2}{5}$ ii) $\frac{2}{4} \times \frac{3}{5}$ iii) $\frac{1}{4} \times \frac{3}{8}$
iv) $\frac{3}{4} \times \frac{1}{8}$ v) $\frac{3}{5} \times \frac{4}{6}$ vi) $\frac{3}{6} \times \frac{4}{5}$
b) Compare the area models. What patterns do you see? Write some other products similar to those in part a. Show your work.

4. a i) $= \frac{6}{20} = \frac{3}{10}$
ii) $= \frac{6}{20} = \frac{3}{10}$
iii) $= \frac{3}{32}$
iv) $= \frac{3}{32}$
v) $= \frac{12}{30} = \frac{2}{5}$
vi) $= \frac{12}{30} = \frac{2}{5}$

5. Why is $\frac{5}{8}$ of $\frac{3}{12}$ equal to $\frac{3}{8}$ of $\frac{5}{12}$?
Draw area models to explain your answer.

Calculator Skills

Find a perfect square that is the sum of a two-digit perfect square and a one-digit perfect square. How many can you find?
25 = 16 + 9

Reflect

When you use an area model to multiply two fractions, how do you decide how to draw the rectangle? Include an example in your explanation.

150 UNIT 4: Fractions and Decimals

ASSESSMENT FOR LEARNING

What to Look For	What to Do
Knowledge and Understanding ✔ Students understand that the product of two fractions can be modelled using a rectangle. ***Communication*** ✔ Students can explain their choice of dimensions for the rectangles they draw. ***Application*** ✔ Students can apply the area model to find the product of two fractions.	***Extra Support:*** Students who have difficulty using an area model could complete the questions with a partner. Alternatively, provide students with the rectangles representing the multiplication statement already drawn on grid paper. Students would then have to shade the product in the rectangle. Students can use Step-by-Step 4 (Master 4.10) to complete question 4. ***Extra Practice:*** Have students interchange the fractions in question 2a, b; c, d; and e, f to make 6 new products that they can calculate. For example, for question 2a, b, find: $\frac{3}{4} \times \frac{2}{5}$ and $\frac{5}{8} \times \frac{4}{9}$. Students can complete Extra Practice 4 (Master 4.29). ***Extension:*** Have students find as many multiplication statements as they can that have the product $\frac{2}{3}$.

Recording and Reporting
Master 4.2 Ongoing Observations: Fractions and Decimals

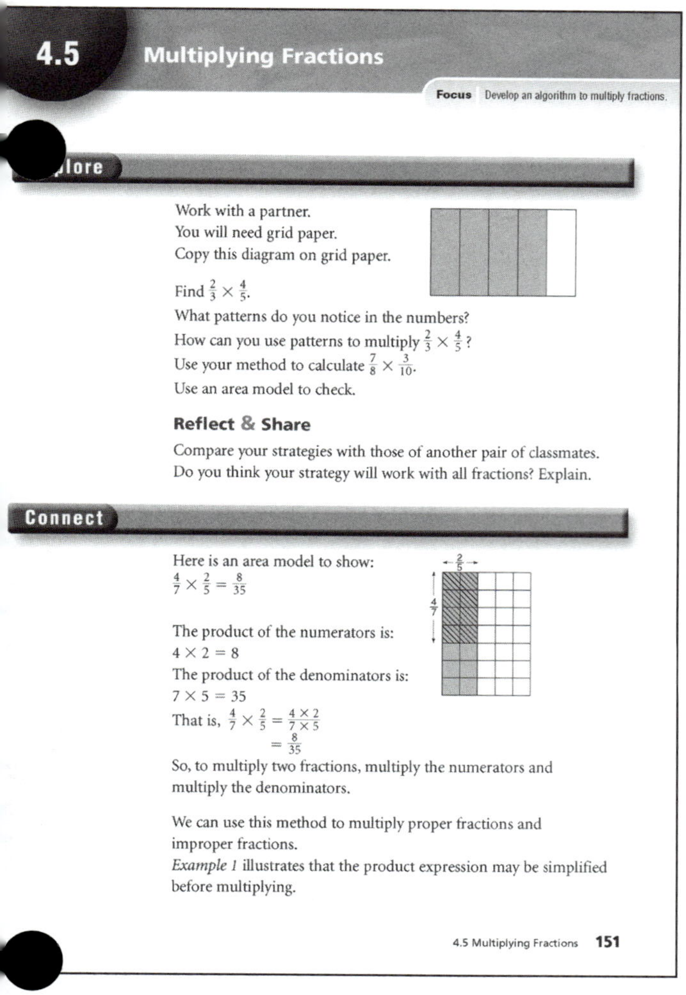

4.5 Multiplying Fractions

Focus Develop an algorithm to multiply fractions.

Explore

Work with a partner.
You will need grid paper.
Copy this diagram on grid paper.

Find $\frac{2}{3} \times \frac{4}{5}$.
What patterns do you notice in the numbers?
How can you use patterns to multiply $\frac{2}{3} \times \frac{4}{5}$?
Use your method to calculate $\frac{7}{8} \times \frac{3}{10}$.
Use an area model to check.

Reflect & Share

Compare your strategies with those of another pair of classmates.
Do you think your strategy will work with all fractions? Explain.

Connect

Here is an area model to show:
$\frac{4}{7} \times \frac{2}{5} = \frac{8}{35}$

The product of the numerators is:
$4 \times 2 = 8$
The product of the denominators is:
$7 \times 5 = 35$
That is, $\frac{4}{7} \times \frac{2}{5} = \frac{4 \times 2}{7 \times 5}$
$= \frac{8}{35}$
So, to multiply two fractions, multiply the numerators and multiply the denominators.

We can use this method to multiply proper fractions and improper fractions.
Example 1 illustrates that the product expression may be simplified before multiplying.

4.5 Multiplying Fractions 151

Multiplying Fractions

LESSON ORGANIZER 80–100 min

Curriculum Focus: Develop an algorithm to multiply fractions. (8m18, 8m19, 8m20)

Teacher Materials
Optional
- 2-cm grid transparency (PM 21)

Student Materials
- 0.5-cm grid paper (PM 14)
- 1-cm grid paper (PM 20)
- coloured pencils
- Fraction Product Spinner (for question 6) (Master 4.23)

Optional
- Step-by-Step 5 (Master 4.11)
- Extra Practice 5 (Master 4.30)

Assessment: Master 4.2 Ongoing Observations: Fractions and Decimals

Key Math Learnings

1. To multiply two fractions, multiply the numerators and multiply the denominators.
2. If two fractions share common factors in their numerators and denominators, the fractions should be simplified before multiplying.

Number Strategies

There are 24 different combinations. Students may use tree diagrams or other models to solve the problem.

BEFORE Get Started

Review using an area model to find the product of two fractions. Present *Explore*. Explain that students are to make up their own rule for multiplying two fractions.

DURING Explore

Ongoing Assessment: Observe and Listen

As students work, ask questions, such as:

- What patterns do you notice?
(*The numerator of the product is equal to the product of the numerators of the fractions I am multiplying. The same pattern is true for the denominators.*)
- What is your strategy for multiplying two fractions?
(*Multiply the numerators and multiply the denominators.*)
- Will this work for all fractions?
(*It should*) How can you find out? (*I could try it with 3 or 4 different multiplication statements, including improper fractions, to see if it works.*)

AFTER Connect

What you should see:

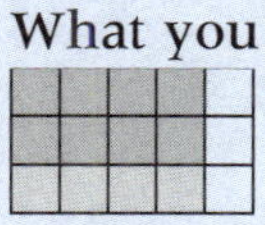

$\frac{2}{3} \times \frac{4}{5} = \frac{8}{15}$

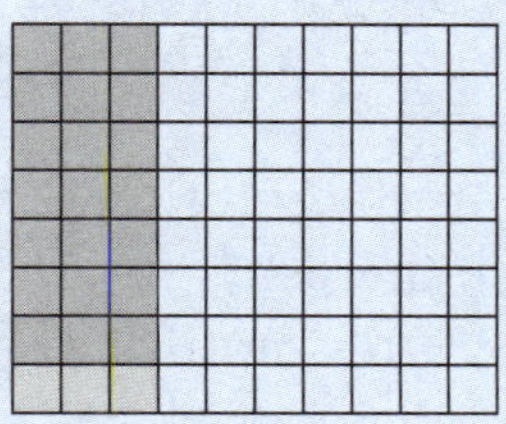

$\frac{7}{8} \times \frac{3}{10} = \frac{21}{80}$

Have students share their strategies for multiplying fractions. Ask students to come to the overhead projector to use area models to check their solutions.

REACHING ALL LEARNERS

Alternative Explore

Materials: grid paper

Have students use grid paper to solve this question:

Two-fifths of a park houses a petting zoo. Three-quarters of the petting zoo houses farm animals. What fraction of the whole park houses farm animals? What if only one-half of the petting zoo was used for farm animals. What fraction of the whole park would be needed?

Early Finishers

One method for multiplying fractions is to interchange numerators or trade denominators to make the statement easier to solve. Have students write multiplication statements where this strategy is most effective. For example, the numerators in $\frac{3}{5} \times \frac{5}{8}$ can be interchanged to be $\frac{5}{5} \times \frac{3}{8}$ without affecting the product. $\frac{5}{5}$ is 1, and $1 \times \frac{3}{8} = \frac{3}{8}$. Another example is $\frac{6}{2} \times \frac{1}{10}$. Written as $\frac{1}{2} \times \frac{6}{10}$, one-half of six-tenths is three-tenths.

Common Misconceptions

➤ Students forget to write the product in simplest form, or they do not recognize when the product is *not* in simplest form.

How to Help: Encourage students to look for factors that are common to numerators and denominators before multiplying. When any factors have been identified, divide both numerator and denominator by these factors, before multiplying the fractions. For students who struggle with this concept, ensure that once a product has been calculated, they look for a common factor. It may be helpful to review the divisibility rules.

Example 1

Multiply.

a) $\frac{4}{9} \times \frac{3}{8}$ b) $\frac{7}{5} \times \frac{8}{3}$

Solution

a) $\frac{4}{9} \times \frac{3}{8} = \frac{4 \times 3}{9 \times 8}$

Notice that the numerator and denominator have common factors 3 and 4.

Divide the numerator and denominator by these factors.

$$\frac{4}{9} \times \frac{3}{8} = \frac{\overset{1}{\cancel{4}} \times \overset{1}{\cancel{3}}}{\underset{3}{\cancel{9}} \times \underset{2}{\cancel{8}}} = \frac{1 \times 1}{3 \times 2} = \frac{1}{6}$$

$4 \div 4 = 1$ $3 \div 3 = 1$
$9 \div 3 = 3$ $8 \div 4 = 2$

b) $\frac{7}{5} \times \frac{8}{3}$

There are no common factors in the numerators and denominators.

So, $\frac{7}{5} \times \frac{8}{3} = \frac{56}{15}$

Here is an area model to illustrate the product of the improper fractions in *Example 1b*.

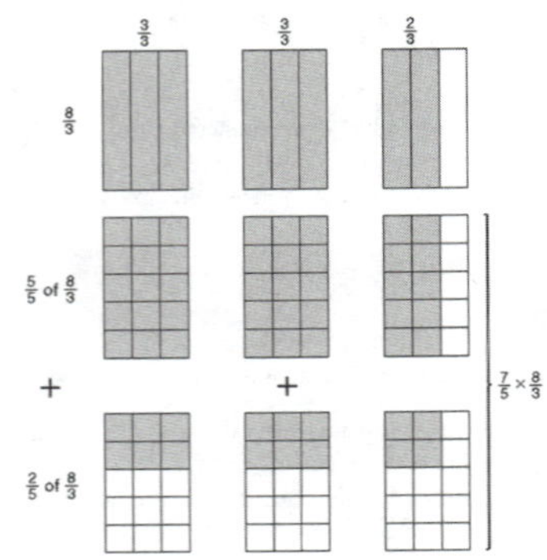

As you review the area model at the bottom of page 151, remind students that each dimension is 1 whole. The length is 1 whole, divided into $\frac{5}{5}$. The height is 1 whole, divided into $\frac{7}{7}$.

Show students how to estimate the product of $\frac{4}{7} \times \frac{2}{5}$.

$\frac{4}{7}$ is a bit more than $\frac{1}{2}$.

$\frac{2}{5}$ is a bit less than $\frac{1}{2}$.

Students know that $\frac{1}{2} \times \frac{1}{2} = \frac{1}{4}$.

So, $\frac{4}{7} \times \frac{2}{5}$ will be about $\frac{1}{4}$.

After *Example 1a*, show students the solution when we do not simplify first; that is, $\frac{4}{9} \times \frac{3}{8} = \frac{12}{72}$. The product is not as easy to simplify as the original fractions were. Students may recognize that 12 is a common factor of the numerator and denominator, and get $\frac{1}{6}$ directly, or they may divide by 2 twice, then by 3, before they get the simplest form.

After you have reviewed the area model for *Example 1b*, ask:

- How is this model different from the models in *Explore*?
  (*The fractions are improper. We think of $\frac{8}{3}$ as $2\frac{2}{3}$, then draw and shade 1 rectangle for each whole number. We shade $\frac{2}{3}$ of another rectangle for the fraction part of the mixed number.*)
- How do we show $\frac{7}{5}$ of $\frac{8}{3}$?
  (*We repeat the 3 rectangles. We shade all of the first 2 rectangles and $\frac{2}{3}$ of the third rectangle to represent $\frac{5}{5}$ of $\frac{8}{3}$. We repeat the 3 rectangles again. We shade $\frac{2}{5}$ of the first 2 rectangles and for the third rectangle we shade an area equal to $\frac{2}{5}$ of the area shaded in the rectangle above it. This represents $\frac{2}{5}$ of $\frac{8}{3}$.*)

Show students how we use the distributive property here:

$$\frac{7}{5} \times \frac{8}{3} = \frac{5}{5} \times \frac{8}{3} + \frac{2}{5} \times \frac{8}{3}$$

Before multiplying in *Example 2*, show students how to estimate.

Each small square is $\frac{1}{15}$.
The number of shaded squares is: 15 + 15 + 10 + 6 + 6 + 4 = 56
So, $\frac{56}{15}$ are shaded.
$\frac{7}{5} \times \frac{8}{3} = \frac{56}{15}$

To multiply two mixed numbers, change them to improper fractions first.

Example 2

Multiply. $2\frac{1}{4} \times 3\frac{2}{5}$

Solution

$2\frac{1}{4} \times 3\frac{2}{5}$

$2\frac{1}{4} = 2 + \frac{1}{4} = \frac{8}{4} + \frac{1}{4} = \frac{9}{4}$

$3\frac{2}{5} = 3 + \frac{2}{5} = \frac{15}{5} + \frac{2}{5} = \frac{17}{5}$

$2\frac{1}{4} \times 3\frac{2}{5} = \frac{9}{4} \times \frac{17}{5} = \frac{153}{20}$

As a mixed number: $\frac{153}{20} = 7\frac{13}{20}$

So, $2\frac{1}{4} \times 3\frac{2}{5} = \frac{153}{20}$, or $7\frac{13}{20}$

We can apply the rules for multiplying two fractions to multiply three or more fractions.
You will do this in *Practice* question 7.

Practice

1. Multiply. Check each product by drawing an area model.
   a) $\frac{3}{8} \times \frac{5}{6} = \frac{5}{16}$ b) $\frac{4}{5} \times \frac{1}{2} = \frac{2}{5}$ c) $\frac{3}{10} \times \frac{3}{4} = \frac{9}{40}$
2. Multiply.
   a) $\frac{3}{5} \times \frac{2}{3} = \frac{2}{5}$ b) $\frac{1}{2} \times \frac{5}{10} = \frac{1}{4}$ c) $\frac{1}{6} \times \frac{1}{4} = \frac{1}{24}$
   d) $\frac{13}{8} \times \frac{3}{2} = \frac{39}{16}$ e) $\frac{5}{4} \times \frac{11}{10} = \frac{11}{8}$ f) $\frac{7}{3} \times \frac{7}{8} = \frac{49}{24}$

4.5 Multiplying Fractions 153

Sample Solutions

1. a) $\frac{3}{8} \times \frac{5}{6} = \frac{15}{48} = \frac{5}{16}$ **b)** $\frac{4}{5} \times \frac{1}{2} = \frac{4}{10} = \frac{2}{5}$ **c)** $\frac{3}{10} \times \frac{3}{4} = \frac{9}{40}$

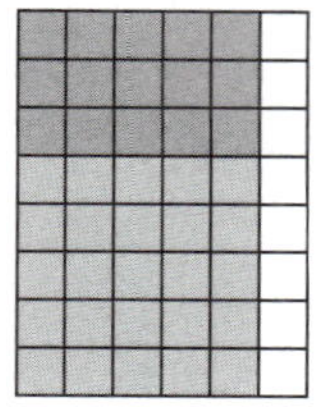
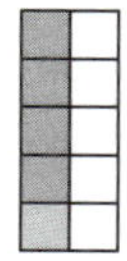
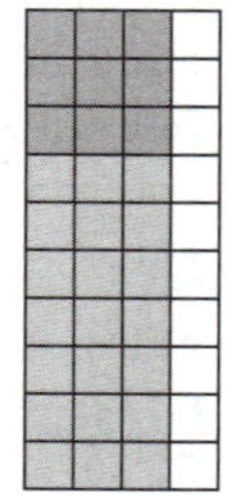

3. $\frac{7}{8} \times \frac{2}{3} = \frac{7}{\cancel{8}_4} \times \frac{\cancel{2}^1}{3} = \frac{7}{12}$; she uses $\frac{7}{12}$ of a tank of gas.

4. b) All the products have matching numerators and denominators.
All the products are 1.
Three more pairs of fractions that have the same product are: $\frac{2}{5} \times \frac{5}{2}$, $\frac{3}{11} \times \frac{11}{3}$, and $\frac{7}{8} \times \frac{8}{7}$
In each pair, the first fraction is the reciprocal of the second fraction, and vice versa.

5. a) $1\frac{3}{4} \times 2\frac{1}{2} = \frac{7}{4} \times \frac{5}{2} = \frac{35}{8} = \frac{32}{8} + \frac{3}{8} = 4\frac{3}{8}$ **b)** $8\frac{1}{15}$ **c)** $5\frac{15}{32}$ **d)** $14\frac{1}{16}$

e) $4\frac{3}{10} \times \frac{4}{5} = \frac{43}{10} \times \frac{4}{5} = \frac{43}{\cancel{10}_5} \times \frac{\cancel{4}^2}{5} = \frac{86}{25} = \frac{75}{25} + \frac{11}{25} = 3\frac{11}{25}$ **f)** $2\frac{11}{40}$

$2\frac{1}{4}$ is a bit more than 2.
$3\frac{2}{5}$ is a bit more than 3.
So, $2\frac{1}{4} \times 3\frac{2}{5}$ will be a bit more than $2 \times 3 = 6$.
As a supplement to *Example 2*, show students a strategy based on the distributive property.

$$\begin{aligned} 2\tfrac{1}{4} \times 3\tfrac{2}{5} &= (2 + \tfrac{1}{4}) \times (3 + \tfrac{2}{5}) \\ &= (2 \times 3) + (2 \times \tfrac{2}{5}) + (\tfrac{1}{4} \times 3) + (\tfrac{1}{4} \times \tfrac{2}{5}) \\ &= 6 + \tfrac{4}{5} + \tfrac{3}{4} + \tfrac{2}{20} \\ &= 6 + \tfrac{16}{20} + \tfrac{15}{20} + \tfrac{2}{20} \\ &= 6 + \tfrac{33}{20} \\ &= 6 + \tfrac{20}{20} + \tfrac{13}{20} \\ &= 6 + 1 + \tfrac{13}{20} \\ &= 7\tfrac{13}{20} \end{aligned}$$

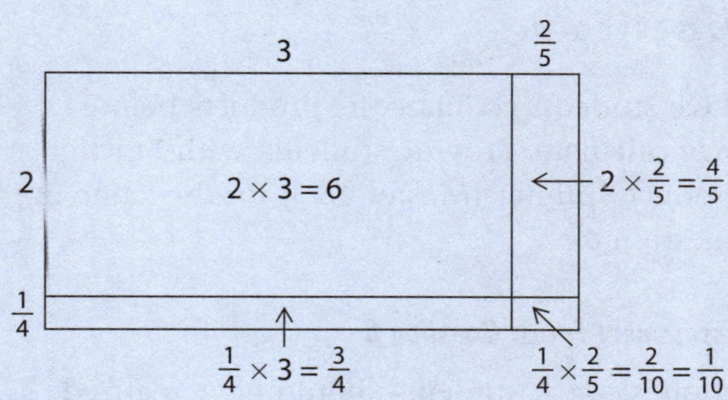

6. No, the game is not fair. The player who has to multiply has a disadvantage, as 4 of the 6 fractions are less than 1. When you multiply by a fraction less than 1, the number decreases. It is unlikely that the person who multiplies has the greater result. It would be a fair game if players alternated multiplying and adding.

7. a) $(\frac{2}{9})^2 = \frac{2}{9} \times \frac{2}{9} = \frac{4}{81}$

b) $(\frac{6}{5})^3 = \frac{6}{5} \times \frac{6}{5} \times \frac{6}{5} = \frac{6 \times 6 \times 6}{5 \times 5 \times 5} = \frac{216}{125}$

c) $(\frac{3}{10})^4 = \frac{3}{10} \times \frac{3}{10} \times \frac{3}{10} \times \frac{3}{10} = \frac{3 \times 3 \times 3 \times 3}{10 \times 10 \times 10 \times 10} = \frac{81}{10\,000}$

d) $(\frac{5}{2})^4 = \frac{5}{2} \times \frac{5}{2} \times \frac{5}{2} \times \frac{5}{2} = \frac{5 \times 5 \times 5 \times 5}{2 \times 2 \times 2 \times 2} = \frac{625}{16}$

8. a) i) $\frac{3}{4} \times \frac{8}{3} = 2$ ii) $\frac{3}{8} \times \frac{24}{3} = 3$ iii) $\frac{4}{5} \times \frac{20}{4} = 4$ iv) $\frac{3}{5} \times \frac{25}{3} = 5$

b) i) I know from question 4 that $\frac{2}{3} \times \frac{3}{2} = 1$, so to get a product of 2, I can multiply one of the numerators by 2: $\frac{4}{3} \times \frac{3}{2} = 2$

ii) Similarly, $\frac{6}{3} \times \frac{3}{2} = 3$ iii) $\frac{8}{3} \times \frac{3}{2} = 4$ iv) $\frac{10}{3} \times \frac{3}{2} = 5$

c) I start with a pair of fractions that has a product of 1: $\frac{1}{2} \times \frac{2}{1}$.
I then multiply the numerator of one fraction by 10.
The fraction pair then becomes $\frac{1}{2} \times \frac{20}{1} = 10$.
I could also have multiplied the other numerator by 10.
The fraction pair would then become $\frac{10}{2} \times \frac{2}{1} = 10$.

(Sample Solutions continue below, right.)

3. Paula has $\frac{7}{8}$ of a tank of gas.
She estimates she will use $\frac{2}{3}$ of the gas to get home.
What fraction of a tank of gas does she use?

4. a) Find each product.

i) $\frac{3}{4} \times \frac{4}{3} = 1$ ii) $\frac{1}{5} \times \frac{5}{1} = 1$
iii) $\frac{7}{2} \times \frac{2}{7} = 1$ iv) $\frac{5}{6} \times \frac{6}{5} = 1$
v) $\frac{8}{3} \times \frac{3}{8} = 1$ vi) $\frac{12}{11} \times \frac{11}{12} = 1$

b) What do you notice about the products in part a?
Write 3 more pairs of fractions that have the same product.
What is special about these fractions?

5. Multiply.

a) $1\frac{3}{4} \times 2\frac{1}{2}$ b) $3\frac{2}{3} \times 2\frac{1}{5}$ c) $4\frac{3}{8} \times 1\frac{1}{4}$
d) $3\frac{3}{4} \times 3\frac{3}{4}$ e) $4\frac{3}{10} \times \frac{4}{5}$ f) $\frac{7}{8} \times 2\frac{3}{5}$

6. Play this game with a partner.
Your teacher will give you a copy of this spinner.

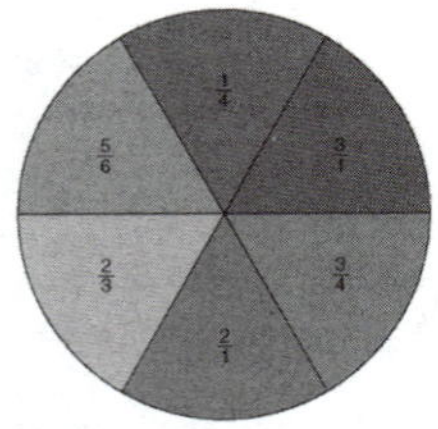

You will need an open paperclip as a pointer and a sharp pencil to keep the pointer in place.
For each turn, players spin twice.
Player A adds the fractions.
Player B multiplies the same two fractions.
The player with the greater result gets one point.
The first person to get 12 points wins.
Is this game fair?
Give reasons for your answer.

Practice

Have students estimate the products before they calculate. Provide students with Fraction Product Spinner (Master 4.23) for the game in question 6.

Assessment Focus: Question 8

In question 4, students should have realized that the product is 1 when the numerators and denominators have equal numbers. So, for a product of 2, they can start with one fraction, multiply by its reciprocal, then multiply one numerator by 2.

Similarly, for a product of 3, write a fraction, write its reciprocal, then multiply one numerator by 3.

(Sample Solutions continued)

9. $\frac{10}{9}$; I wrote $\frac{3}{5} \times \frac{?}{?} = \frac{2}{3}$
The denominator of the product is 3, so I replace the question mark in the denominator with 9. Then I have a common factor of 3 that I can divide by: $\frac{\cancel{3}^1}{5} \times \frac{?}{\cancel{9}_3} = \frac{2}{3}$.
I have to get rid of a 5 in the denominator and I need a 2 in the numerator.
So, I replace the question mark in the numerator with 10.
$\frac{\cancel{3}^1}{\cancel{5}_2} \times \frac{\cancel{10}^1}{\cancel{9}_3} = \frac{2}{3}$
The fraction I multiply by is $\frac{10}{9}$.

10. John ate $\frac{1}{6}$, so $\frac{5}{6}$ remains.
Susan ate $\frac{1}{5}$ of $\frac{5}{6}$, so $\frac{4}{5} \times \frac{5}{6}$ remains $= \frac{2}{3}$ remains.
Chan ate $\frac{1}{4}$ of $\frac{2}{3}$, so $\frac{3}{4} \times \frac{2}{3}$ remains $= \frac{1}{2}$ remains.
Cindy ate $\frac{1}{3}$ of $\frac{1}{2}$, so $\frac{2}{3} \times \frac{1}{2}$ remains $= \frac{1}{3}$ remains.
Luigi ate $\frac{1}{2}$ of $\frac{1}{3}$, so $\frac{1}{2} \times \frac{1}{3}$ remains $= \frac{1}{6}$ remains.

7. Use your knowledge of exponents and multiplying fractions to evaluate each power.

a) $\left(\frac{2}{9}\right)^2$ b) $\left(\frac{6}{5}\right)^3$ c) $\left(\frac{3}{10}\right)^4$ d) $\left(\frac{5}{2}\right)^4$

Number Strategies

A lunch counter offers 2 soups, 4 sandwiches, and 3 drinks.

How many different possible combinations are there for a person who wants a soup, a sandwich, and a drink?

So1Sa1D1; So1Sa1D2; So1Sa1D3; So1Sa2D1; So1Sa2D2; So1Sa2D3; So1Sa3D1; So1Sa3D2; So1Sa3D3; So1Sa4D1; So1Sa4D2; So1Sa4D3;
Take It Further
So2Sa1D1; So2Sa1D2; So2Sa1D3; So2Sa2D1; So2Sa2D2; So2Sa2D3; So2Sa3D1; So2Sa3D2; So2Sa3D3; So2Sa4D1; So2Sa4D2; So2Sa4D3

8. **Assessment Focus** In question 4, each product is 1.
   a) Write a pair of fractions that has each product.
      i) 2 ii) 3 iii) 4 iv) 5
   b) Write a pair of fractions that has the product 1. Change only one numerator or denominator each time to write a pair of fractions that has each product.
      i) 2 ii) 3 iii) 4 iv) 5
   c) How could you write a pair of fractions that has the product 10?
   Show your work.

9. The product of two fractions is $\frac{2}{3}$.
   One fraction is $\frac{3}{5}$.
   What is the other fraction?
   How do you know?

10. Amar baked a cake. John ate $\frac{1}{6}$ of the cake.
    Susan ate $\frac{1}{5}$ of what was left.
    Chan ate $\frac{1}{4}$ of what was left after that.
    Cindy ate $\frac{1}{3}$ of what was left after that.
    Luigi ate $\frac{1}{2}$ of what was left after that.
    How much of the original cake was left?

Reflect

Look at your answers to all the questions.
Some products were in simplest form after you multiplied.
Some products were not in simplest form.
How can you tell if a product of two fractions will be in simplest form after you multiply? Use examples in your explanation.

REFLECT: The product of two fractions will be in simplest form after I have multiplied, if the numerators of the two fractions I multiply have no common factors with the denominators.
For example, $\frac{1}{2} \times \frac{3}{5}$; the numerators 1 and 3 have no factor in common with the denominators 2 and 5.
The product $\frac{2}{5} \times \frac{5}{6}$ will not be in simplest form after I have multiplied, because the numerators and denominators have the common factors 5 and 2. The product is $\frac{10}{30}$, which simplifies to $\frac{1}{3}$.
I can simplify before I multiply: $\frac{\cancel{2}^{1}}{\cancel{5}_{1}} \times \frac{\cancel{5}^{1}}{\cancel{6}_{3}} = \frac{1 \times 1}{1 \times 3} = \frac{1}{3}$.

Assignment Guidelines

If your students do not have time to complete all the *Practice* questions on pages 153, 154, and 155, these questions provide minimum curriculum coverage:
1, 2, 3, 4, 5, 7, 8, *Reflect*

To assess the 4 Achievement Chart categories listed in the curriculum document, have students complete these *Practice* questions:
Knowledge and Understanding: 2
Thinking: 3
Communication: 4
Application: 7

ASSESSMENT FOR LEARNING

What to Look For

Knowledge and Understanding

✔ Students understand the algorithm for multiplying fractions.

Thinking

✔ Students can apply the algorithm to solve problems related to the product of fractions and mixed numbers.

Application

✔ Students can apply the algorithm to a variety of product statements, including improper fractions and mixed numbers.

What to Do

Extra Support: Most students do not have difficulty using the algorithm, but they may not understand why it works. Have these students continue to use an area model to illustrate each product. Students can use Step-by-Step 5 (Master 4.11) to complete question 8.

Extra Practice: Students can play the game in question 6 with different rules. This time, Player A spins twice, and multiplies the two fractions. On her second turn, Player A spins once, and multiplies her previous product by the new fraction. After 5 turns, the player closer to 0 wins.
Students can complete Extra Practice 5 (Master 4.30).

Extension: Students use 3 fractions to write a multiplication statement with a product of $\frac{3}{5}$. Students try to write as many statements as they can.

Recording and Reporting

Master 4.2 Ongoing Observations: Fractions and Decimals

LESSON ORGANIZER

Student Materials
- 0.5-cm grid paper (PM 14)
- 1-cm grid paper (PM 20)

Assessment:
Master 4.1 Unit Rubric: Fractions and Decimals
Master 4.4 Unit Summary: Fractions and Decimals

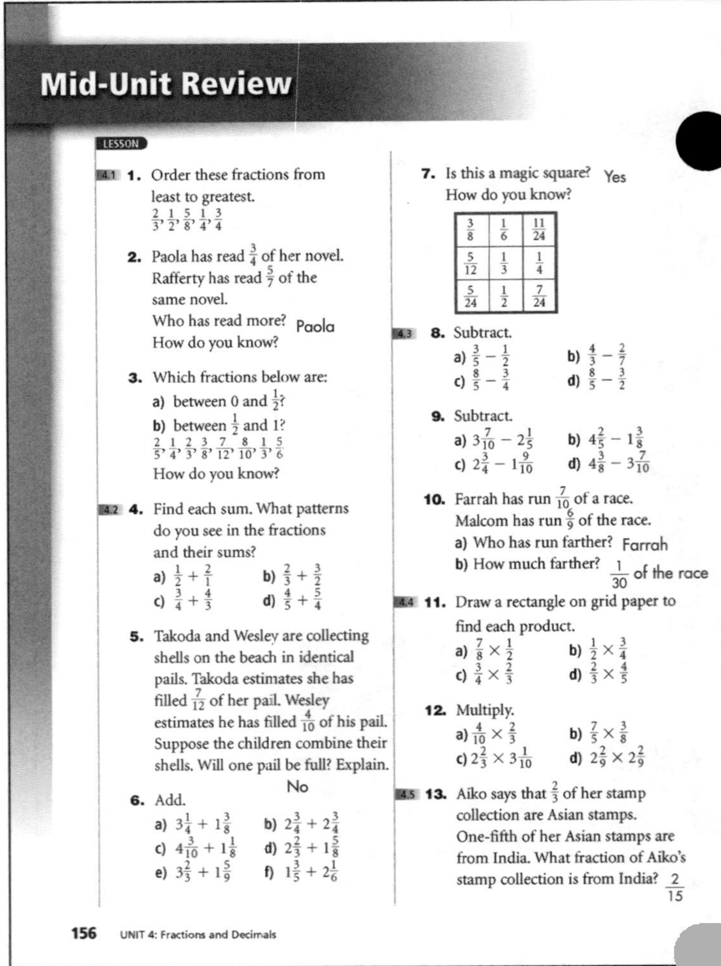

Mid-Unit Review

LESSON

4.1 **1.** Order these fractions from least to greatest.
$\frac{2}{3}, \frac{1}{2}, \frac{5}{8}, \frac{1}{4}, \frac{3}{4}$

2. Paola has read $\frac{3}{4}$ of her novel. Rafferty has read $\frac{5}{7}$ of the same novel.
Who has read more? Paola
How do you know?

3. Which fractions below are:
a) between 0 and $\frac{1}{2}$?
b) between $\frac{1}{2}$ and 1?
$\frac{2}{5}, \frac{1}{4}, \frac{2}{3}, \frac{3}{8}, \frac{7}{12}, \frac{8}{10}, \frac{1}{3}, \frac{5}{6}$
How do you know?

4.2 **4.** Find each sum. What patterns do you see in the fractions and their sums?
a) $\frac{1}{2} + \frac{2}{1}$ b) $\frac{2}{3} + \frac{3}{2}$
c) $\frac{3}{4} + \frac{4}{3}$ d) $\frac{4}{5} + \frac{5}{4}$

5. Takoda and Wesley are collecting shells on the beach in identical pails. Takoda estimates she has filled $\frac{7}{12}$ of her pail. Wesley estimates he has filled $\frac{4}{10}$ of his pail. Suppose the children combine their shells. Will one pail be full? Explain.
No

6. Add.
a) $3\frac{1}{4} + 1\frac{3}{8}$ b) $2\frac{3}{4} + 2\frac{3}{4}$
c) $4\frac{3}{10} + 1\frac{1}{8}$ d) $2\frac{2}{3} + 1\frac{5}{8}$
e) $3\frac{2}{3} + 1\frac{5}{9}$ f) $1\frac{3}{5} + 2\frac{1}{6}$

7. Is this a magic square? Yes
How do you know?

$\frac{3}{8}$	$\frac{1}{6}$	$\frac{11}{24}$
$\frac{5}{12}$	$\frac{1}{3}$	$\frac{1}{4}$
$\frac{5}{24}$	$\frac{1}{2}$	$\frac{7}{24}$

4.3 **8.** Subtract.
a) $\frac{3}{5} - \frac{1}{2}$ b) $\frac{4}{3} - \frac{2}{7}$
c) $\frac{8}{5} - \frac{3}{4}$ d) $\frac{8}{5} - \frac{3}{2}$

9. Subtract.
a) $3\frac{7}{10} - 2\frac{1}{5}$ b) $4\frac{2}{5} - 1\frac{3}{8}$
c) $2\frac{3}{4} - 1\frac{9}{10}$ d) $4\frac{3}{8} - 3\frac{7}{10}$

10. Farrah has run $\frac{7}{10}$ of a race. Malcom has run $\frac{6}{9}$ of the race.
a) Who has run farther? Farrah
b) How much farther? $\frac{1}{30}$ of the race

4.4 **11.** Draw a rectangle on grid paper to find each product.
a) $\frac{7}{8} \times \frac{1}{2}$ b) $\frac{1}{2} \times \frac{3}{4}$
c) $\frac{3}{4} \times \frac{2}{3}$ d) $\frac{2}{3} \times \frac{4}{5}$

12. Multiply.
a) $\frac{4}{10} \times \frac{2}{3}$ b) $\frac{7}{5} \times \frac{3}{8}$
c) $2\frac{2}{3} \times 3\frac{1}{10}$ d) $2\frac{2}{9} \times 2\frac{2}{9}$

4.5 **13.** Aiko says that $\frac{2}{3}$ of her stamp collection are Asian stamps. One-fifth of her Asian stamps are from India. What fraction of Aiko's stamp collection is from India? $\frac{2}{15}$

156 UNIT 4: Fractions and Decimals

Assignment Guidelines

To assess the 4 Achievement Chart categories listed in the curriculum document, have students complete these *Practice* questions:
Knowledge and Understanding: 1, 6, 8, 9, 11, 12
Application: 3, 5
Thinking: 10, 13
Communication: 2, 4, 7

Sample Solutions

1. In order from least to greatest: $\frac{1}{4}, \frac{1}{2}, \frac{5}{8}, \frac{2}{3}, \frac{3}{4}$
2. $\frac{3}{4} = \frac{21}{28}$ and $\frac{5}{7} = \frac{20}{28}$
   Since 21 > 20, $\frac{21}{28} > \frac{20}{28}$ and $\frac{3}{4} > \frac{5}{7}$; Paola has read more.
3. I looked at the denominator of each fraction, and found a fraction equivalent to one-half with that denominator. For example, for the fraction $\frac{7}{12}$, 6 is one-half of 12, so $\frac{1}{2}$ would be $\frac{6}{12}$. I then looked at the numerator of the fraction to see if the fraction is less than or more than one-half.
   a) $\frac{2}{5}, \frac{1}{4}, \frac{3}{8}$, and $\frac{1}{3}$ are between 0 and $\frac{1}{2}$.
   b) $\frac{2}{3}, \frac{7}{12}, \frac{8}{10}$, and $\frac{5}{6}$ are between $\frac{1}{2}$ and 1.
4. a) $\frac{5}{2}$ or $2\frac{1}{2}$ b) $\frac{13}{6}$ or $2\frac{1}{6}$ c) $\frac{25}{12}$ or $2\frac{1}{12}$ d) $\frac{41}{20}$ or $2\frac{1}{20}$
   The fractions that are added are reciprocals. Each sum is a mixed number. The whole number is always 2. The fraction is a unit fraction whose denominator is the product of the denominators of the two fractions being added.
5. $\frac{7}{12} + \frac{4}{10} = \frac{35}{60} + \frac{24}{60} = \frac{59}{60}$; the children will have $\frac{59}{60}$ of a pail. The pail will not be full.
6. a) $4\frac{5}{8}$ b) $5\frac{1}{2}$ c) $5\frac{17}{40}$
   d) $4\frac{7}{24}$ e) $5\frac{2}{9}$ f) $3\frac{23}{30}$
7. The sum of the fractions in any row, column, or diagonal is 1.
8. a) $\frac{1}{10}$ b) $\frac{22}{21}$ c) $\frac{17}{20}$ d) $\frac{1}{10}$
9. a) $1\frac{1}{2}$ b) $3\frac{1}{40}$ c) $\frac{17}{20}$ d) $\frac{27}{40}$
10. a) $\frac{7}{10} = \frac{63}{90}$ and $\frac{6}{9} = \frac{60}{90}$
    Since 63 > 60, $\frac{63}{90} > \frac{60}{90}$ and $\frac{7}{10} > \frac{6}{9}$;
    Farrah has run farther.
    b) $\frac{63}{90} - \frac{60}{90} = \frac{3}{90} = \frac{1}{30}$
11. a) $\frac{7}{8} \times \frac{1}{2} = \frac{7}{16}$

    b) $\frac{1}{2} \times \frac{3}{4} = \frac{3}{8}$

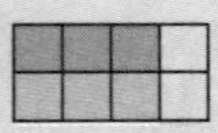

    c) $\frac{3}{4} \times \frac{2}{3} = \frac{1}{2}$

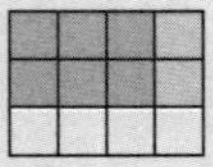

    d) $\frac{2}{3} \times \frac{4}{5} = \frac{8}{15}$

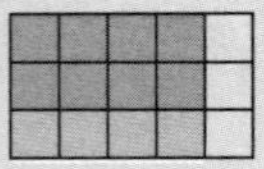

12. a) $\frac{4}{15}$ b) $\frac{21}{40}$ c) $8\frac{4}{15}$ d) $4\frac{76}{81}$
13. $\frac{1}{5}$ of $\frac{2}{3} = \frac{1}{5} \times \frac{2}{3} = \frac{2}{15}$

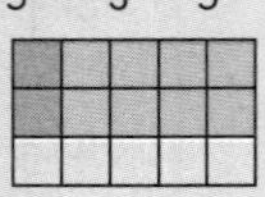

4.6 Using Models to Divide Fractions and Whole Numbers

Focus Use a number line to divide fractions and whole numbers.

When you first studied division, you learned two ways: sharing and grouping.
For example, $20 \div 5$ can be thought of as:

- Sharing 20 items equally among 5 sets
- Grouping 20 items into sets of 5

Recall that multiplication and division are inverse operations.
We know: $20 \div 5 = 4$
So, we also know: $4 \times 5 = 20$

Explore

Work with a partner.
Suppose you have 5 cups of concentrate.

➢ A recipe for a bowl of punch calls for $\frac{1}{4}$ cup of concentrate.
How many bowls of punch can you make?

➢ A different recipe calls for $\frac{3}{4}$ cup of concentrate for one bowl of punch.
How many bowls of punch could you make if you used this recipe?
Draw a diagram to illustrate your answers.

Reflect & Share

Compare your answers with those of another pair of classmates.
Did you solve the problems the same way?
If not, explain your method to your classmates.

Connect

Before we divide a whole number by a fraction, think about how we divide whole numbers.

➢ To find how many 3s are in 6, group 6 into 3s.
We can show this on a number line.
There are 2 groups of 3 in 6.

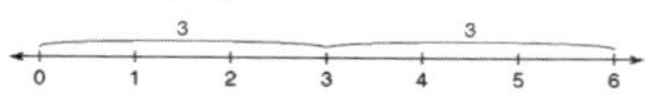

$6 \div 3 = 2$

Using Models to Divide Fractions and Whole Numbers

LESSON ORGANIZER 80–100 min

Curriculum Focus: Use a number line to divide fractions and whole numbers. (8m19, 8m20)

Teacher Materials
Optional
- fraction circles transparency (Master 4.21)
- overhead counters

Student Materials
- number lines (Master 4.24)

Optional
- fraction circles (Master 4.21)
- 1-cm grid paper (PM 20)
- Step-by-Step 6 (Master 4.12)
- Extra Practice 6 (Master 4.31)

Vocabulary: quotient

Assessment: Master 4.2 Ongoing Observations: Fractions and Decimals

Key Math Learning

A number line can be used to divide fractions.

BEFORE Get Started

Place 20 counters in a pile on the overhead projector. Ask:

- How can we share these 20 counters among five people?
(*We can give one counter to each person until we have no counters left. Each person gets 4 counters.*)

Model sharing by sliding the counters, one at a time, into 5 equal groups. Remind students that this is *division by sharing*.

Put the counters back into a pile. Ask:

- How many groups of 5 counters can we make with the 20 counters? (*4 groups*) How is this different from the earlier division by sharing? (*In division by sharing, we knew how many groups were needed. We did not know how many counters were in each group. In this case, we know how many counters are in each group, but we do not know how many groups we have.*)

Model grouping by putting 5 counters in each group until all counters have been used.

Remind students that this is *division by grouping*.

Present *Explore*.

DURING Explore

Ongoing Assessment: Observe and Listen

As students work, ask questions, such as:

- What are you being asked to find in the first problem? (*How many $\frac{1}{4}$s there are in 5*)
- How did you use a diagram to help you solve the first problem? (*I drew 5 squares to represent 5 cups. I divided each square into 4 equal parts. Each part represents $\frac{1}{4}$. So, I had 20 quarters. I can make 20 bowls of punch.*)
- How did you solve the second problem? (*I drew 5 squares and divided them into quarters, again. I shaded groups of $\frac{3}{4}$, and then counted how many $\frac{3}{4}$ I had. There were 20 quarters, so that was 6 groups of $\frac{3}{4}$, with $\frac{2}{4}$ left over. I can make 6 bowls of punch, and have some concentrate left over.*)

REACHING ALL LEARNERS

Alternative Explore

Materials: Cuisenaire rods, 1-cm grid paper (PM 20)

Have students use Cuisenaire rods to explore division with fractions.

- Let the brown rod represent 1 whole. Model and find $2 \div \frac{1}{4}$.
- Model and find $2 \div \frac{3}{4}$.

Students can copy their models onto 1-cm grid paper, then explain how they found the answers.

Early Finishers

Have students write problems similar to *Practice* question 5 where students have to:

- divide a fraction by a whole number
- divide a whole number by a fraction

Students exchange problems with a classmate, then solve their classmate's problems.

Common Misconceptions

➤ When a fraction does not divide exactly into a whole number, students write the fraction part of the quotient with the same denominator as the divisor. For example, students think $2 \div \frac{3}{4}$ is $2\frac{2}{4}$ instead of $2\frac{2}{3}$, because the divisor has denominator 4.

How to Help: Use fraction circles or a number line to model the solution to $2 \div \frac{3}{4}$. There are 2 groups of three-fourths, with 2 fourths left over. One more fourth is needed to make $\frac{3}{4}$. We have 2 of the 3 parts needed, so we have $\frac{2}{3}$ of $\frac{3}{4}$. So, $2 \div \frac{3}{4} = 2\frac{2}{3}$. Ensure students understand that the remainder is written as a fraction of the divisor, not as a fraction of the denominator of the divisor.

➢ To find how many thirds are in 6, divide 6 into thirds.

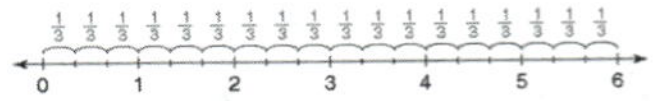

There are 18 thirds in 6.
Write this as a division statement.
$6 \div \frac{1}{3} = 18$ Notice: $6 \times 3 = 18$

➢ Use the same number line to find how many two-thirds are in 6.

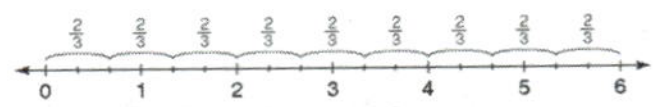

Arrange 18 thirds into groups of two-thirds.
There are 9 groups of two-thirds.
We write: $6 \div \frac{2}{3} = 9$

➢ Use the number line again to find how many five-thirds are in 6; that is, $6 \div \frac{5}{3}$.
Arrange 18 thirds into groups of five-thirds.

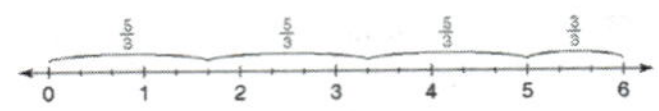

There are 3 groups of five-thirds.
There are 3 thirds left over.
Think: What fraction of $\frac{5}{3}$ is $\frac{3}{3}$?

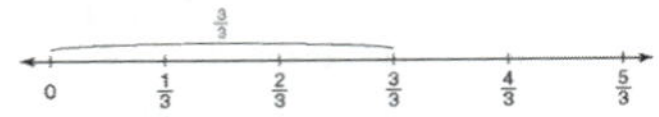

From the number line, $\frac{3}{3}$ is $\frac{3}{5}$ of $\frac{5}{3}$.
So, $6 \div \frac{5}{3} = 3\frac{3}{5}$

We can also use a number line to divide a fraction by a whole number. This is illustrated in the *Example* that follows.

- What division statement can you write for the first problem? *($5 \div \frac{1}{4} = 20$)*
- What division statement can you write for the second problem? *($5 \div \frac{3}{4} = 6\ R\frac{2}{4}$)*

As students work through the problems, look for students who use other methods that illustrate sharing and grouping (for example, students who draw 5 cups divided into fourths, then circle groups of three-fourths to represent bowls of punch). Have these students share their solutions with the class.

AFTER Connect

What you might see for the first problem:

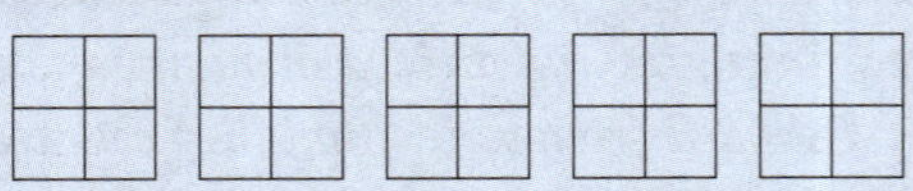

Since there are 20 fourths in 5 cups, 20 bowls of punch could be made.

What you might see for the second problem:

Since 6 groups of three-fourths are circled, 6 bowls of punch could be made. To make a seventh bowl of punch, you would need another one-fourth of concentrate.

Use the diagram to show that in this problem the quotient $6\ R\frac{2}{4}$ can be written as $6\frac{2}{3}$.

Each group has $\frac{3}{4}$:

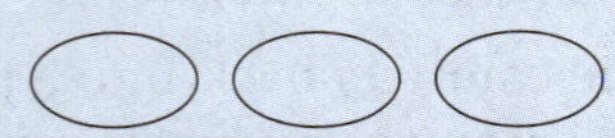

Shade 2 of the quarters to represent the remainder:

We have shaded $\frac{2}{3}$ of the group.

So, $5 \div \frac{3}{4} = 6\ R\frac{2}{4}$ is the same as $5 \div \frac{3}{4} = 6\frac{2}{3}$.

Model grouping using a number line as in *Connect*. You may wish to provide additional

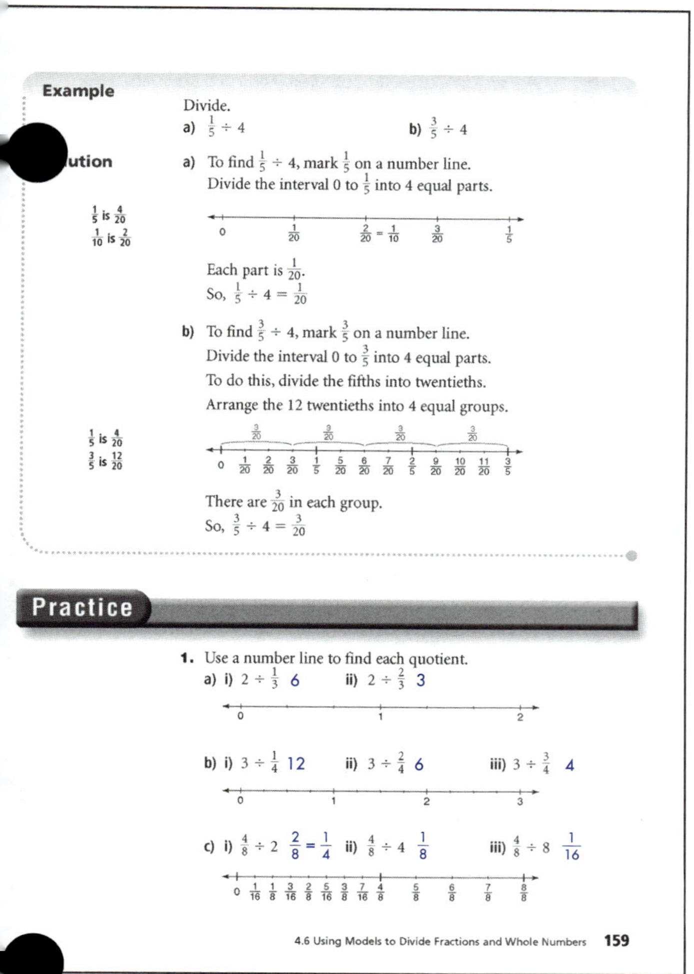
Example

Divide.
a) $\frac{1}{5} \div 4$ b) $\frac{3}{5} \div 4$

Solution

a) To find $\frac{1}{5} \div 4$, mark $\frac{1}{5}$ on a number line.
Divide the interval 0 to $\frac{1}{5}$ into 4 equal parts.

$\frac{1}{5}$ is $\frac{4}{20}$
$\frac{1}{10}$ is $\frac{2}{20}$

Each part is $\frac{1}{20}$.
So, $\frac{1}{5} \div 4 = \frac{1}{20}$

b) To find $\frac{3}{5} \div 4$, mark $\frac{3}{5}$ on a number line.
Divide the interval 0 to $\frac{3}{5}$ into 4 equal parts.
To do this, divide the fifths into twentieths.
Arrange the 12 twentieths into 4 equal groups.

$\frac{1}{5}$ is $\frac{4}{20}$
$\frac{3}{5}$ is $\frac{12}{20}$

There are $\frac{3}{20}$ in each group.
So, $\frac{3}{5} \div 4 = \frac{3}{20}$

Practice

1. Use a number line to find each quotient.
a) i) $2 \div \frac{1}{3}$ 6 ii) $2 \div \frac{2}{3}$ 3
b) i) $3 \div \frac{1}{4}$ 12 ii) $3 \div \frac{2}{4}$ 6 iii) $3 \div \frac{3}{4}$ 4
c) i) $\frac{4}{8} \div 2$ $\frac{2}{8} = \frac{1}{4}$ ii) $\frac{4}{8} \div 4$ $\frac{1}{8}$ iii) $\frac{4}{8} \div 8$ $\frac{1}{16}$

4.6 Using Models to Divide Fractions and Whole Numbers 159

Sample Solutions

6. To find $\frac{2}{3} \div 4$, mark $\frac{2}{3}$ on a number line. Divide the interval 0 to $\frac{2}{3}$ into 4 equal parts.

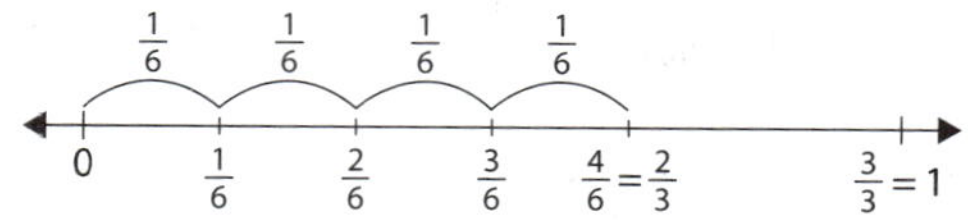

Each part is $\frac{1}{6}$. So, $\frac{2}{3} \div 4 = \frac{1}{6}$
To find $4 \div \frac{2}{3}$, mark 4, or $\frac{12}{3}$, on a number line. Arrange the 12 thirds into groups of two-thirds.

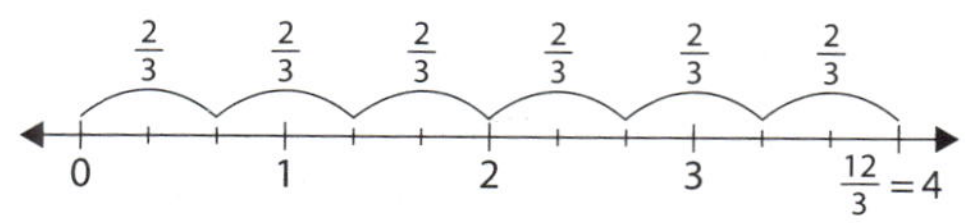

There are 6 groups of two-thirds. So, $4 \div \frac{2}{3} = 6$

7. a) Possible division statements:
$2 \div \frac{4}{6}$; $2 \div \frac{6}{4}$; $4 \div \frac{2}{6}$; $4 \div \frac{6}{2}$; $6 \div \frac{2}{4}$; $6 \div \frac{4}{2}$

b) $2 \div \frac{4}{6} = 3$; $2 \div \frac{6}{4} = 1\frac{1}{3}$; $4 \div \frac{2}{6} = 12$; $4 \div \frac{6}{2} = 1\frac{1}{3}$;
$6 \div \frac{2}{4} = 12$; $6 \div \frac{4}{2} = 3$
I notice that the division statement with the greatest quotient has a greater whole number divided by a lesser fraction. So, both $4 \div \frac{2}{6}$ and $6 \div \frac{2}{4}$ have the greatest quotient, 12.
I notice that the division statement with the least quotient has a lesser whole number divided by a greater fraction. So, both $2 \div \frac{6}{4}$ and $4 \div \frac{6}{2}$ have the least quotient, $1\frac{1}{3}$.

whole number examples before dividing 6 by $\frac{1}{3}$ and 6 by $\frac{2}{3}$.

Use fraction circles to model: $3 \div \frac{2}{3}$. Place 3 whole circles on the overhead projector. Replace each whole circle with a circle divided into thirds. Ask:

- How can you use this model to find how many two-thirds are in 3?
(*I can place the circles into groups of two-thirds.*)
- How many groups of $\frac{2}{3}$ are there? (4)
- How many thirds are left over? (*One-third*)
- What fraction of $\frac{2}{3}$ is $\frac{1}{3}$? (*$\frac{1}{3}$ is one-half of $\frac{2}{3}$.*)
- What is $3 \div \frac{2}{3}$?
(*4 whole ones and one-half of $\frac{2}{3}$, so $4\frac{1}{2}$*)

Continue working through *Connect*, to show students the division of a whole number by an improper fraction.

Use the *Example* to model how fractions can be divided by whole numbers.

Practice

Distribute copies of number lines (Master 4.24) for students to complete questions 1 to 4. Encourage students to use benchmarks when dividing fractions by whole numbers.

Assessment Focus: Question 7

Students should find that there are 6 possible division statements.

Students should realize that the statement that has the greatest quotient is a large number divided by a small fraction (the smaller the fraction, the more parts it takes to make a whole). Both $6 \div \frac{2}{4}$ and $4 \div \frac{2}{6}$ have the quotient 12.

Students should also realize that the statement that has the least quotient is a small number divided by a large fraction. Both $2 \div \frac{6}{4}$ and $4 \div \frac{6}{2}$ have the quotient $\frac{4}{3}$.

8. For example, $\frac{25}{4}$ and 5: $\frac{25}{4} - 5 = \frac{5}{4}$ and $\frac{25}{4} \div 5 = \frac{5}{4}$

$\frac{36}{5}$ and 6: $\frac{36}{5} - 6 = \frac{6}{5}$ and $\frac{36}{5} \div 6 = \frac{6}{5}$

The numerator of the fraction is the square of the whole number. The denominator of the fraction is 1 less than the whole number.

REFLECT: When I divide a whole number by a proper fraction, the quotient is always greater than the whole number because I am dividing the whole into groups of less than 1; for example, $3 \div \frac{1}{2} = 6$.

Assignment Guidelines

If your students do not have time to complete all the *Practice* questions on pages 159 and 160, these questions provide minimum curriculum coverage: 1, 2, 3, 5, 7, *Reflect*

To assess the 4 Achievement Chart categories listed in the curriculum document, have students complete these *Practice* questions:

Knowledge and Understanding: 1

Application: 5

Thinking: 7

Communication: *Reflect*

Number Strategies

For the first set, students could write each number as a decimal, then order the numbers. For the second set, students could look at the exponents and use estimation. For example, students should recognize that 22^1 has the least value, and that 20^4 has the greatest value because $10^4 = 10\ 000$.

Number Strategies

Order the numbers in each set from least to greatest.

- $1.2, \frac{11}{2}, 2.12, 125\%$
- $2^7, 22^1, 20^4, 40^2, 7^2$

$1.2, 125\%, 2.12, \frac{11}{2}$; $22^1, 7^2, 2^7, 40^2, 20^4$

2. Find each quotient. Use number lines to illustrate the answers.

a) $2 \div \frac{1}{2}$ 4 b) $3 \div \frac{1}{3}$ 9 c) $3 \div \frac{2}{3}$ $4\frac{1}{2}$

d) $4 \div \frac{1}{4}$ 16 e) $4 \div \frac{2}{4}$ 8 f) $4 \div \frac{3}{4}$ $5\frac{1}{3}$

3. Find each quotient. Use number lines to illustrate the answers.

a) $\frac{1}{2} \div 2$ $\frac{1}{4}$ b) $\frac{1}{3} \div 3$ $\frac{1}{9}$ c) $\frac{2}{3} \div 3$ $\frac{2}{9}$

d) $\frac{1}{4} \div 4$ $\frac{1}{16}$ e) $\frac{2}{4} \div 4$ $\frac{1}{8}$ f) $\frac{3}{4} \div 4$ $\frac{3}{16}$

4. Use a number line to find each quotient.

a) $\frac{4}{5} \div 3$ $\frac{4}{15}$ b) $2 \div \frac{3}{8}$ $5\frac{1}{3}$ c) $\frac{1}{2} \div 5$ $\frac{1}{10}$

d) $6 \div \frac{3}{4}$ 8 e) $4 \div \frac{2}{3}$ 6 f) $\frac{5}{8} \div 2$ $\frac{5}{16}$

5. Ioana wants to spend $\frac{3}{4}$ of an hour studying each subject. She has 3 h to study. How many subjects can she study? 4

6. Why is $\frac{2}{3} \div 4$ not the same as $4 \div \frac{2}{3}$? Use number lines in your explanation.

7. **Assessment Focus** Copy these boxes.

$\square \div \frac{\square}{\square}$

a) Write the digits 2, 4, and 6 in the boxes to find as many division statements as possible.

b) Which statement in part a has the greatest quotient? The least quotient? How do you know?

Show your work.

Take It Further

8. The numbers $\frac{9}{2}$ and 3 share this property: their difference is equal to their quotient. That is, $\frac{9}{2} - 3 = \frac{3}{2}$ and $\frac{9}{2} \div 3 = \frac{3}{2}$

Find other pairs of numbers with this property. Describe any patterns you see.

Reflect

When you divide a whole number by a proper fraction, is the quotient greater than or less than the whole number? Include an example in your explanation.

ASSESSMENT FOR LEARNING

What to Look For	What to Do
Knowledge and Understanding ✔ Students understand that a number line can be used to divide fractions and whole numbers. ***Communication*** ✔ Students can use diagrams and grouping or sharing to explain the division of fractions and whole numbers. ***Application*** ✔ Students can use a number line to model the division of fractions and whole numbers.	***Extra Support:*** Students who have difficulty using a number line may benefit from using fraction circles instead. When students can successfully model division with fraction circles, connect the model to using a number line (*each piece of a circle can be represented by a "jump" on a number line; each third is one jump on a number line that is divided into thirds, from 0 to 1*). Students can use Step-by-Step 6 (Master 4.12) to complete question 7. ***Extra Practice:*** Have students use Cuisenaire rods or fraction circles to model their answers to some of the *Practice* questions. Students can complete Extra Practice 6 (Master 4.31). ***Extension:*** Have students use a number line to find: $5 \div \frac{2}{3}$ and $5 \div \frac{4}{3}$; $\frac{3}{4} \div 2$ and $\frac{3}{4} \div 4$. Students write about their findings.

Recording and Reporting

Master 4.2 Ongoing Observations: Fractions and Decimals

4.7 Dividing Fractions

Focus Develop algorithms to divide fractions.

You have used grouping to divide 4 by $\frac{2}{3}$: $4 \div \frac{2}{3}$
You have used sharing to divide $\frac{2}{3}$ by 4: $\frac{2}{3} \div 4$
You will now investigate dividing a fraction by a fraction: $\frac{2}{3} \div \frac{1}{4}$

Explore

Work with a partner.
Use this number line to find how many quarters are in $\frac{2}{3}$;
that is, find $\frac{2}{3} \div \frac{1}{4}$.

0 $\frac{1}{12}$ $\frac{2}{12}$ $\frac{3}{12}$ $\frac{1}{3}$ $\frac{5}{12}$ $\frac{6}{12}$ $\frac{7}{12}$ $\frac{2}{3}$ $\frac{9}{12}$ $\frac{10}{12}$ $\frac{11}{12}$ 1

Look at the quotient.
Try to find a method to calculate the quotient without using a number line.
Use a different division problem to check your method.

Reflect & Share

Compare your method with that of another pair of classmates.
Does your method work with their problem? Explain.
Does their method work with your problem? Explain.

Connect

Here are two ways to divide fractions.

➢ Use common denominators.
To divide: $\frac{3}{5} \div \frac{1}{4}$
Write each fraction with a common denominator.
Since 5 and 4 have no common factors,
their common denominator is $5 \times 4 = 20$.

$\frac{3}{5} = \frac{12}{20}$ (×4) $\frac{1}{4} = \frac{5}{20}$ (×5)

4.7 Dividing Fractions 161

LESSON 4.7

Dividing Fractions

LESSON ORGANIZER 80–100 min

Curriculum Focus: Develop algorithms to divide fractions. (8m18, 8m19, 8m20)

Teacher Materials
Optional
- number lines transparency (Master 4.24)

Student Materials
- number lines (Master 4.24)

Optional
- Step-by-Step 7 (Master 4.13)
- Extra Practice 7 (Master 4.32)

Vocabulary: reciprocals

Assessment: Master 4.2 Ongoing Observations: Fractions and Decimals

Key Math Learnings

1. Fractions can be divided using algorithms.
2. Two ways to divide fractions are:
   - use common denominators and divide the numerators
   - convert the division statement to a multiplication statement

Number Strategies

Remind students of the order of operations.

BEFORE — Get Started

Review division with whole numbers and fractions. Write $2 \div \frac{4}{5}$ on the board. Have a student use a number line on the board to model the solution. Ask:

- Does $\frac{4}{5}$ divide into 2 exactly? (*No*)
- How many groups of four-fifths are in 2? (*2, with 2 fifths left over*)
- What fraction of $\frac{4}{5}$ is $\frac{2}{5}$? Explain. (*We have 2 fifths. We need 2 more fifths to make $\frac{4}{5}$. So, we have 2 of the 4 parts needed; $\frac{2}{5}$ is $\frac{1}{2}$ of $\frac{4}{5}$.*)
- What is $2 \div \frac{4}{5}$? ($2\frac{1}{2}$)

Present *Explore*. Encourage students to estimate the quotient first.

DURING — Explore

Ongoing Assessment: Observe and Listen

As students work, ask questions, such as:

- How did you estimate $\frac{2}{3} \div \frac{1}{4}$? (*$\frac{2}{3}$ is a bit more than $\frac{1}{2}$; and I know that there are two quarters in $\frac{1}{2}$. So, $\frac{2}{3} \div \frac{1}{4}$ is a bit more than 2.*)
- How did you use a number line to find $\frac{2}{3} \div \frac{1}{4}$? (*I know that $\frac{1}{4}$ is equivalent to $\frac{3}{12}$. I used the number line to find how many groups of three-twelfths are in $\frac{2}{3}$. There are 2 groups of three-twelfths, with 2 twelfths left over.*)
- How did you deal with the leftovers? (*There are 2 twelfths left over. I need one more twelfth to make $\frac{3}{12}$. I have 2 of the 3 parts needed. So, $\frac{2}{12}$ is $\frac{2}{3}$ of $\frac{3}{12}$.*)
- What is $\frac{2}{3} \div \frac{1}{4}$? ($2\frac{2}{3}$)
- What is $2\frac{2}{3}$ as an improper fraction? ($\frac{6}{3} + \frac{2}{3} = \frac{8}{3}$)
- Look at the division statement $\frac{2}{3} \div \frac{1}{4} = \frac{8}{3}$. How can you find the quotient without using a number line? (*I used a common denominator. $\frac{2}{3}$ is $\frac{8}{12}$ and $\frac{1}{4}$ is $\frac{3}{12}$, so I changed the question to $\frac{8}{12} \div \frac{3}{12}$. There are two*

REACHING ALL LEARNERS

Alternative Explore

Have students work with a partner to find:

$\frac{1}{2} \div \frac{1}{3}$; $\frac{1}{2} \div \frac{1}{4}$; $\frac{1}{2} \div \frac{1}{5}$; $\frac{1}{2} \div \frac{1}{6}$

Students use models to find the quotients, then look for patterns to find a method for finding the quotients without using models. Students use their methods to check other division problems.

Early Finishers

Have students use number lines to find the quotients in *Practice* questions 2 and 3.

Common Misconceptions

➤ Students do not know if the quotient is reasonable once they have used the algorithm to divide.

How to Help: Begin with whole numbers. Show students that, for a given dividend, as the divisor decreases, the quotient increases; for example, $24 \div 8 = 3$ and $24 \div 2 = 12$. Proper fractions are less than 1, so when a whole number is divided by a proper fraction, the quotient is greater than the whole number; for example, $3 \div \frac{1}{2} = 6$.

When students divide a fraction by another fraction, encourage them to use benchmarks to estimate, as described earlier.

ESL Strategies

Students for whom English is a second language may have difficulty interpreting fractions written in words. Encourage these students to write the fractions in fraction form, then check with a classmate if they need verification.

When the denominators are the same, divide the numerators.

$\frac{3}{5} \div \frac{1}{4} = \frac{12}{20} \div \frac{5}{20}$

This means: How many five-twentieths are in $\frac{12}{20}$?

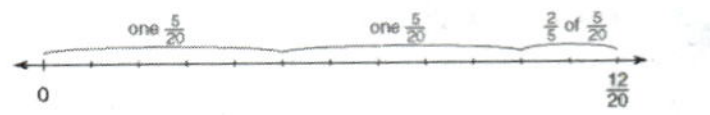

From the number line, this is: $12 \div 5 = 2\frac{2}{5}$

So, $\frac{3}{5} \div \frac{1}{4} = 2\frac{2}{5}$

➤ Use multiplication.

Recall that another way to divide by 4 is to multiply by $\frac{1}{4}$.

$12 \div 4 = 3$ and $12 \times \frac{1}{4} = 3$

Since 4 can be written as $\frac{4}{1}$,

dividing by 4 is the same as dividing by $\frac{4}{1}$.

So, we can write $12 \div \frac{4}{1} = 3$ and $12 \times \frac{1}{4} = 3$.

Similarly, another way to divide by $\frac{1}{4}$ is to multiply by 4.

$3 \div \frac{1}{4} = 12$ and $3 \times \frac{4}{1} = 12$

We can use the same pattern to divide two fractions.

The fraction $\frac{1}{4}$ is the reciprocal of the fraction $\frac{4}{1}$.

That is, $\frac{3}{5} \div \frac{1}{4} = \frac{3}{5} \times \frac{4}{1}$
$= \frac{12}{5}$

Up until now, we have divided a fraction by a lesser fraction. We can use the same methods when we divide a fraction by a greater fraction or when we divide mixed numbers.

Example

Divide.

a) $\frac{3}{4} \div \frac{5}{6}$ b) $1\frac{7}{8} \div 1\frac{1}{4}$

Solution

a) $\frac{3}{4} \div \frac{5}{6}$

Use multiplication.

Dividing by $\frac{5}{6}$ is the same as multiplying by $\frac{6}{5}$.

$\frac{3}{4} \div \frac{5}{6}$ can be written as

$$\frac{3}{4} \times \frac{6}{5} = \frac{3 \times \overset{3}{\cancel{6}}}{\underset{2}{\cancel{4}} \times 5} = \frac{3 \times 3}{2 \times 5} = \frac{9}{10}$$

$\frac{3}{12}$ in $\frac{8}{12}$, with $\frac{2}{12}$ left over. Two-twelfths is $\frac{2}{3}$ of $\frac{3}{12}$, so the quotient is $2\frac{2}{3}$.)

- What other division problem did you use to check your method? ($\frac{3}{5} \div \frac{1}{2}$)
- Did your method work? Explain. (*Yes. I used a number line to find that $\frac{3}{5} \div \frac{1}{2} = \frac{6}{5}$. When I used my other method, I got the same quotient.*)

AFTER — Connect

Have students share their problems, and methods for dividing fractions. Have volunteers use models or diagrams to explain their methods to the class. Relate students' methods to the two strategies shown in the *Example*, where possible.

Remind students that in the previous lesson, it was sometimes necessary to write a fraction as an equivalent fraction before dividing by a whole number (for example, when students divided $\frac{5}{8}$ by 2, they wrote $\frac{5}{8}$ as the equivalent fraction $\frac{10}{16}$ so they could divide the numerator into 2 equal parts.)

Use the examples in *Connect* to show students how to estimate quotients, using benchmark quotients.

For $\frac{3}{5} \div \frac{1}{4}$; $\frac{3}{5}$ is greater than $\frac{1}{2}$, and there are 2 quarters in $\frac{1}{2}$, so there are more than 2 quarters in $\frac{3}{5}$. So, the quotient will be greater than 2.

Use *Connect* to introduce the strategy of using common denominators to find equivalent fractions to divide fractions. Before reviewing the *Example*, have students estimate each quotient.

After reviewing the *Example*, part a, use the common denominator strategy to verify the solution. Ask:

- What is the lowest common denominator of 4 and 6? (*12*)

b) $1\frac{7}{8} \div 1\frac{1}{4}$

Change the mixed numbers to improper fractions.

$1\frac{7}{8} = \frac{8}{8} + \frac{7}{8} = \frac{15}{8}$ $\qquad$ $1\frac{1}{4} = \frac{4}{4} + \frac{1}{4} = \frac{5}{4}$

So, $1\frac{7}{8} \div 1\frac{1}{4} = \frac{15}{8} \div \frac{5}{4}$

Use common denominators.

Since 4 is a factor of 8, the lowest common denominator is 8.

Multiply the numerator and denominator by 2: $\frac{5}{4} = \frac{10}{8}$

$\frac{15}{8} \div \frac{5}{4} = \frac{15}{8} \div \frac{10}{8}$ Since the denominators are the same, divide the numerators.

$= \frac{15}{10}$ Reduce to simplest form.

$= \frac{15 \div 5}{10 \div 5}$

$= \frac{3}{2}$, or $1\frac{1}{2}$

Practice

1. Use a copy of each number line to illustrate each quotient.

a) $\frac{5}{6} \div \frac{1}{3}$ $2\frac{1}{2}$

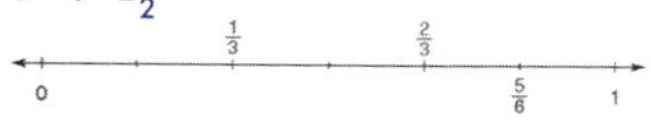

b) $\frac{3}{4} \div \frac{1}{3}$ $2\frac{1}{4}$

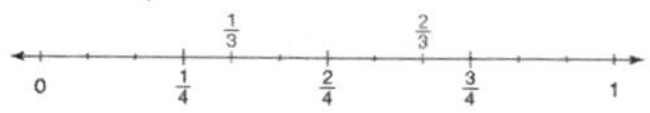

2. Use multiplication to find each quotient.

a) $\frac{8}{5} \div \frac{3}{4}$ $2\frac{2}{15}$ b) $\frac{9}{10} \div \frac{5}{3}$ $\frac{27}{50}$ c) $\frac{7}{2} \div \frac{4}{3}$ $\frac{21}{8}$ d) $\frac{1}{2} \div \frac{7}{6}$ $\frac{3}{7}$

3. Use common denominators to find each quotient.

a) $\frac{7}{12} \div \frac{1}{4}$ $\frac{7}{3}$ b) $\frac{3}{5} \div \frac{11}{10}$ $\frac{6}{11}$ c) $\frac{5}{2} \div \frac{1}{3}$ $\frac{15}{2}$ d) $\frac{5}{6} \div \frac{9}{8}$ $\frac{20}{27}$

4. Divide.

a) $1\frac{9}{10} \div 2\frac{2}{3}$ $\frac{57}{80}$ b) $2\frac{3}{4} \div 2\frac{1}{3}$ $1\frac{5}{28}$ c) $3\frac{1}{2} \div 1\frac{4}{5}$ $1\frac{17}{18}$ d) $1\frac{3}{8} \div 1\frac{3}{8}$ 1

4.7 Dividing Fractions 163

Sample Solutions

6. b) In each pair, the fractions are the same, but in a different order. The dividend in the first statement is the divisor in the second statement, and vice versa. The quotient of the first statement is the reciprocal of the quotient of the second statement, and vice versa.

$\frac{1}{3} \div \frac{3}{4} = \frac{4}{9}$ and $\frac{3}{4} \div \frac{1}{3} = \frac{9}{4}$, or $2\frac{1}{4}$; $\frac{4}{7} \div \frac{5}{8} = \frac{32}{35}$ and $\frac{5}{8} \div \frac{4}{7} = \frac{35}{32}$, or $1\frac{3}{32}$

7. a) There are 24 different division statements:

$\frac{2}{3} \div \frac{4}{5}$; $\frac{2}{3} \div \frac{5}{4}$; $\frac{3}{2} \div \frac{4}{5}$; $\frac{3}{2} \div \frac{5}{4}$; $\frac{4}{5} \div \frac{2}{3}$; $\frac{4}{5} \div \frac{3}{2}$; $\frac{5}{4} \div \frac{2}{3}$; $\frac{5}{4} \div \frac{3}{2}$;
$\frac{3}{4} \div \frac{2}{5}$; $\frac{3}{4} \div \frac{5}{2}$; $\frac{4}{3} \div \frac{2}{5}$; $\frac{4}{3} \div \frac{5}{2}$; $\frac{5}{2} \div \frac{3}{4}$; $\frac{5}{2} \div \frac{4}{3}$; $\frac{2}{5} \div \frac{3}{4}$; $\frac{2}{5} \div \frac{4}{3}$;
$\frac{2}{4} \div \frac{3}{5}$; $\frac{2}{4} \div \frac{5}{3}$; $\frac{4}{2} \div \frac{3}{5}$; $\frac{4}{2} \div \frac{5}{3}$; $\frac{5}{3} \div \frac{2}{4}$; $\frac{5}{3} \div \frac{4}{2}$; $\frac{3}{5} \div \frac{2}{4}$; $\frac{3}{5} \div \frac{4}{2}$

b) The division statement that has the greatest quotient is such that the product of the numerator of the dividend and the denominator of the divisor is the greatest possible product ($4 \times 5 = 20$), and the product of the numerator of the divisor and the denominator of the dividend is the least possible product ($2 \times 3 = 6$). The division statements are:
$\frac{4}{3} \div \frac{2}{5} = \frac{10}{3}$, $\frac{4}{2} \div \frac{3}{5} = \frac{10}{3}$, $\frac{5}{3} \div \frac{2}{4} = \frac{10}{3}$, and $\frac{5}{2} \div \frac{3}{4} = \frac{10}{3}$
The opposite is true for the division statement with the least quotient. The product of the numerator of the dividend and the denominator of the divisor is the least possible product ($2 \times 3 = 6$), and the product of the numerator of the divisor and the denominator of the dividend is the greatest possible product ($4 \times 5 = 20$). The division statements are:
$\frac{3}{4} \div \frac{5}{2} = \frac{3}{10}$, $\frac{3}{5} \div \frac{4}{2} = \frac{3}{10}$, $\frac{2}{4} \div \frac{5}{3} = \frac{3}{10}$, and $\frac{2}{5} \div \frac{4}{3} = \frac{3}{10}$

- What is $\frac{3}{4}$ as a fraction with denominator 12? *($\frac{9}{12}$)* $\frac{5}{6}$? *($\frac{10}{12}$)*
- What is $\frac{3}{4} \div \frac{5}{6}$? *($\frac{3}{4} \div \frac{5}{6} = \frac{9}{12} \div \frac{10}{12} = \frac{9}{10}$)*

Use a number line to show how multiplying by the reciprocal relates to dividing fractions.

Draw a number line from 0 to 12. Divide this interval into 4 equal segments. Each segment is 3 units long. Above the number line, write $12 \div 4 = 3$.

$12 \div 4 = 3$

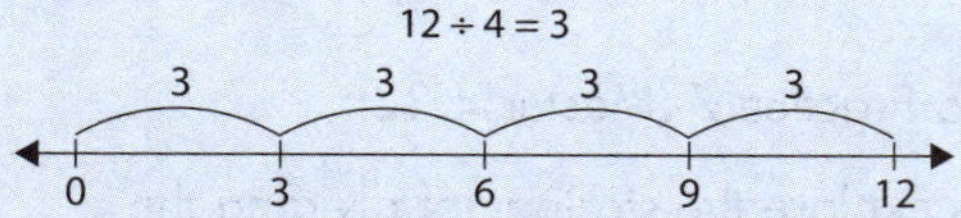

Draw a second number line.

"Jump" 12 one-fourths to show $12 \times \frac{1}{4}$.

$12 \times \frac{1}{4} = 3$

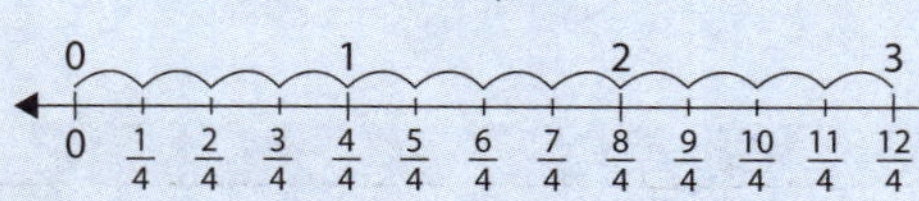

Have students look at the last fraction ($\frac{12}{4}$). Ask:

- How else can we read this fraction? *(12 divided by 4)*

Connect this interpretation to the previous number line, reinforcing the idea that $12 \div 4 = 3$ is equivalent to $12 \times \frac{1}{4} = 3$.

The *Example*, part b, illustrates that, to divide mixed numbers, change the mixed numbers to improper fractions first.

Practice

Use a copy of Number Lines (Master 4.24). Mark it up as in *Practice* question 1, then photocopy and distribute for students to complete question 1.

Assessment Focus: Question 7

Students may notice patterns in the products of the numerator of the dividend and the denominator of the divisor. When this product is greatest, the quotient is greatest. When this product is least, the quotient is least.

8. In parts a and b, $3\frac{1}{5}$ is multiplied by a number less than 1, so the quotient will be less than $3\frac{1}{5}$. In part d, $3\frac{1}{5}$ is divided by a number greater than 1, so the quotient will be less than $3\frac{1}{5}$. In part f, the sum is greater than that in part e because the fraction added to $3\frac{1}{5}$ is greater.
I look at parts c and f more closely. In part f, $\frac{3}{2}$ is added to $3\frac{1}{5}$. In part c, $3\frac{1}{5} \div \frac{2}{3} = 3\frac{1}{5} \times \frac{3}{2}$; $3\frac{1}{5}$ is multiplied by $\frac{3}{2}$. Since $\frac{3}{2}$ is greater than 1, the product is greater than the sum. So, the statement with the greatest value is: $3\frac{1}{5} \div \frac{2}{3} = 4\frac{4}{5}$.

REFLECT: The quotient is greater than 1 when the divisor is less than the dividend; for example, $\frac{3}{5} \div \frac{1}{2} = \frac{6}{5}$, or $1\frac{1}{5}$; $\frac{7}{2} \div \frac{5}{3} = \frac{21}{10}$, or $2\frac{1}{10}$

The quotient is less than 1 when the divisor is greater than the dividend; for example, $\frac{1}{2} \div \frac{3}{5} = \frac{5}{6}$; $\frac{5}{3} \div \frac{7}{2} = \frac{10}{21}$

The quotient is equal to 1 when the divisor and the dividend are equal; for example, $\frac{3}{5} \div \frac{6}{10} = 1$

Assignment Guidelines

If your students do not have time to complete all the *Practice* questions on pages 163 and 164, these questions provide minimum curriculum coverage: 2, 3, 4, 6, 7, *Reflect*

To assess the 4 Achievement Chart categories listed in the curriculum document, have students complete these *Practice* questions:

Knowledge and Understanding: 2	Thinking: 6
Application: 4	Communication: 7

Number Strategies

Evaluate. Use the order of operations.

- $4 \times 5^2 - 3^2 + 33$ 124
- $6 \times 7 - 8.1 \div 9 + 12.7$ 53.8

5. Divide.

a) $\frac{5}{3} \div \frac{3}{5}$ $\frac{25}{9}$ b) $\frac{4}{9} \div \frac{4}{9}$ 1 c) $\frac{1}{6} \div \frac{5}{2}$ $\frac{1}{15}$ d) $1\frac{3}{4} \div 2\frac{9}{10}$ $\frac{35}{58}$

6. a) Find each quotient.

i) $\frac{3}{4} \div \frac{5}{8}$ $\frac{6}{5} = 1\frac{1}{5}$ ii) $\frac{5}{8} \div \frac{3}{4}$ $\frac{5}{6}$ iii) $\frac{7}{12} \div \frac{2}{5}$ $\frac{35}{24} = 1\frac{11}{24}$

iv) $\frac{2}{5} \div \frac{7}{12}$ $\frac{24}{35}$ v) $\frac{5}{3} \div \frac{4}{5}$ $\frac{25}{12} = 2\frac{1}{12}$ vi) $\frac{4}{5} \div \frac{5}{3}$ $\frac{12}{25}$

b) In part a, what patterns do you see in the division statements and their quotients?
Write two more pairs of division statements that follow the same pattern.

7. **Assessment Focus**

a) Copy the boxes below.
Write the digits 2, 3, 4, and 5 in the boxes to make as many different division statements as you can.

$\frac{\square}{\square} \div \frac{\square}{\square}$

b) Which division statement in part a has the greatest quotient? The least quotient? How do you know?
Show your work.

8. Which statement has the greatest value?
Give reasons for your answer.

a) $3\frac{1}{5} \times \frac{1}{2}$ b) $3\frac{1}{5} \times \frac{2}{3}$ c) $3\frac{1}{5} \div \frac{2}{3}$

d) $3\frac{1}{5} \div \frac{2}{1}$ e) $3\frac{1}{5} + \frac{2}{3}$ f) $3\frac{1}{5} + \frac{3}{2}$

9. Write as many division questions as you can that have $\frac{5}{6}$ as their quotient.
For example, $\frac{4}{8} \div \frac{3}{5} = \frac{5}{6}$; $\frac{5}{4} \div \frac{6}{4} = \frac{5}{6}$; $\frac{5}{8} \div \frac{3}{4} = \frac{5}{6}$; $\frac{8}{16} \div \frac{3}{5} = \frac{5}{6}$

Reflect

When you divide two fractions, how can you tell, before you divide, if the quotient will be:
- greater than 1?
- less than 1?
- equal to 1?

Use examples in your explanation.

164 UNIT 4: Fractions and Decimals

ASSESSMENT FOR LEARNING

What to Look For	What to Do
Knowledge and Understanding ✔ Students understand the different strategies for dividing fractions. ***Communication*** ✔ Students can explain different strategies for dividing fractions, and when each is more effective. ***Application*** ✔ Students can apply an appropriate strategy to divide fractions.	***Extra Support:*** Students who have difficulty understanding the algorithms should continue to model the division of fractions with number lines, fraction circles, or Cuisenaire rods. Students can use Step-by-Step 7 (Master 4.13) to complete question 7. ***Extra Practice:*** Have students write their own division statements, then trade statements with a classmate and solve their classmate's statements. Students can complete Extra Practice 7 (Master 4.32). ***Extension:*** Have students explore the strategy of dividing the numerators and dividing the denominators. Students can create division statements where this strategy is effective.

Recording and Reporting

Master 4.2 Ongoing Observations: Fractions and Decimals

Converting between Decimals and Fractions

4.8 **Converting between Decimals and Fractions**

Focus Use a calculator and patterns to convert between decimals and fractions.

Recall that we can write a fraction as a division.
For example, $\frac{5}{2}$ can be written as $5 \div 2$.

Explore

Use the *Glossary* if you have forgotten what a unit fraction is.

Work with a partner.
You will need a calculator.

➢ Write all the unit fractions with denominators from 1 to 10.
Write each fraction as a decimal.
Use a calculator to check your answers.

➢ Choose 3 different proper fractions.
Write each fraction as a decimal.
Trade decimals with your partner.
Order the decimals from least to greatest.

Reflect & Share

Compare your fractions and decimals with those of another pair of classmates.
Sort the decimals into two sets. Which attributes did you use?

Connect

Recall these two types of decimals.

- These are **terminating decimals:** 0.5, 0.76, 0.435
  Each decimal has a definite number of decimal places.
- These are **repeating decimals:**
  0.333…; 0.454 545…; 0.811 111…
  Some digits in each decimal repeat forever.

➢ To write a fraction as a decimal, divide the numerator by the denominator.
For example, $\frac{4}{11} = 4 \div 11 = 0.363\,636\,36\ldots$

This is a repeating decimal.

We write $\frac{4}{11} = 0.\overline{36}$, with a bar over the digits that repeat.
When we use a calculator to divide, the calculator may round the last digit and display 0.363 636 364.

4.8 Converting between Decimals and Fractions 165

LESSON ORGANIZER 80–100 min

Curriculum Focus: Use a calculator and patterns to convert between decimals and fractions. (8m13, 8m14)

Teacher Materials
- overhead transparency of hundredths square (Master 4.25)

Student Materials
- calculators

Optional
- hundredths squares (Master 4.25)
- Step-by-Step 8 (Master 4.14)
- Extra Practice 8 (Master 4.33)

Vocabulary: terminating decimals, repeating decimals

Assessment: Master 4.2 Ongoing Observations: Fractions and Decimals

Key Math Learnings

1. A fraction is a division statement. To write a fraction as a decimal, divide the numerator by the denominator.
2. For a terminating decimal, the number of digits after the decimal point tells the power of 10 in the denominator of an equivalent fraction.

BEFORE Get Started

Review how to write a fraction as a division. Ask:

- What is the division statement for $\frac{1}{2}$? (*1 ÷ 2*) What is the quotient? (*0.5*)
- What other fractions can you write a decimal for? (*$\frac{3}{4}$; 3 ÷ 4 = 0.75, $\frac{1}{4}$; 1 ÷ 4 = 0.25*)

Place the transparency of a hundredths square on the overhead projector. Ask:

- What does each row in the square represent? (*One-tenth*) Each small square? (*One-hundredth*)
- How can you use the hundredths square to show $\frac{3}{4}$?
  (*I can draw a horizontal and a vertical line to divide the square into four parts, then shade 3 parts.*)
- How much of the square is shaded? (*Seventy-five hundredths*) How do you know? (*7 rows of 10 hundredths plus 5 hundredths is 75 hundredths.*)
- How can you check your answer? (*I can use a calculator; 3 ÷ 4 = 0.75.*)

Present *Explore*. Students may use hundredths squares if they need them.

DURING Explore

Ongoing Assessment: Observe and Listen

As students work, ask:

- What is a unit fraction? (*A fraction with a numerator of 1*)
- Which unit fractions did you write? (*$\frac{1}{1}, \frac{1}{2}, \frac{1}{3}, \frac{1}{4}, \frac{1}{5}, \frac{1}{6}, \frac{1}{7}, \frac{1}{8}, \frac{1}{9}, \frac{1}{10}$*)
- Which unit fractions are easiest to represent as decimals? Explain.
  (*$\frac{1}{1}, \frac{1}{2}, \frac{1}{4}, \frac{1}{5}, \frac{1}{10}$; each of these fractions can be written as a fraction with denominator 100.*)
- Why are some of the unit fractions more difficult to represent as decimals?
  (*Some of the fractions have denominators that do not divide into 100 exactly. I cannot write equivalent fractions with denominator 100.*)

REACHING ALL LEARNERS

Alternative Explore

Materials: hundredths squares (Master 4.25)

Tell students that the hundredths square represents 1 whole. Have students use the hundredths square to find the decimal equivalents for $\frac{1}{2}$, $\frac{1}{4}$, $\frac{3}{4}$, $\frac{1}{5}$, $\frac{1}{8}$, $\frac{3}{8}$, and $\frac{4}{10}$. Have students find other fractions they could convert to decimals using the hundredths square.

Early Finishers

Students use the patterns in *Practice* question 9 to extend the conversion of fractions to decimals beyond 1 whole; for example, what is the decimal equivalent of $\frac{12}{11}$?

Common Misconceptions

➤ Students ignore the zeros before the digits in a decimal when converting a decimal to a fraction; for example, students write 0.0062 as $\frac{62}{100}$.

How to Help: Have students use patterning to connect fractions to the place-value system. Write $\frac{1}{10}$, $\frac{1}{100}$, and $\frac{1}{1000}$ on the board. Use a place-value chart to show students that $\frac{1}{10} = 0.1$, $\frac{1}{100} = 0.01$, and $\frac{1}{1000} = 0.001$. Use the place-value chart to extend this concept to fractions such as $\frac{17}{1000}$. Have students write the decimal in a place-value chart before they write it as a fraction.

Sample Solutions

1. b) The fractions that terminate do not fill the calculator screen.

5. I could use long division to show that $\frac{5}{17} = 0.294\ 117\ 647\ 058\ 823\ 5$.

➤ To write a terminating decimal as a fraction, look at these patterns.

$0.3 = \frac{3}{10}$

$0.03 = \frac{3}{100}$ $\qquad$ $0.33 = \frac{33}{100}$

$0.003 = \frac{3}{1000}$ $\qquad$ $0.333 = \frac{333}{1000}$

The number of digits after the decimal point tells the power of 10 in the denominator:

0.333 is 333 thousandths.

$0.333 = \frac{333}{1000}$ ← 10^3 in the denominator; ↑ 3 digits after the decimal point

0.4567 is 4567 ten-thousandths.

$0.4567 = \frac{4567}{10\,000}$ ← 10^4 in the denominator; ↑ 4 digits after the decimal point

Example 1

Write each decimal as a fraction in simplest form.

a) 0.365 $\qquad$ b) 0.0054

Solution

a) 0.365

There are 3 digits after the decimal point.

In fraction form, the denominator is 10^3, or 1000.

0.365 is 365 thousandths.

$0.365 = \frac{365}{1000}$

Write in simplest form.

5 is a common factor of 365 and 1000.

So, divide numerator and denominator by 5.

$\frac{365}{1000} = \frac{365 \div 5}{1000 \div 5} = \frac{73}{200}$

$0.365 = \frac{73}{200}$

b) 0.0054

There are 4 digits after the decimal point.

In fraction form, the denominator is 10^4, or 10 000.

0.0054 is 54 ten-thousandths.

$0.0054 = \frac{54}{10\,000}$ $\quad$ 2 is a common factor of 54 and 10 000.

$= \frac{27}{5000}$ $\quad$ Divide numerator and denominator by 2.

166 UNIT 4: Fractions and Decimals

- How did you write $\frac{1}{7}$ as a decimal? *(I used pencil and paper. I divided 7 into 1 to get 0.142 857 142 857 . . .)*
- How did you write the 3 proper fractions as decimals? *(I used my calculator to divide the numerator by the denominator.)*
- How did you order your partner's decimals? *(I used place value; I found which one had the greatest number of tenths; then hundredths, and so on.)*
- How did you sort the decimals? *(I put all those that had digits that repeated in one set, and all those that had digits that didn't repeat in the other set.)*

AFTER Connect

Have students share and model their strategies for converting fractions to decimals. Begin with the unit fractions $\frac{1}{1}$, $\frac{1}{2}$, $\frac{1}{4}$, $\frac{1}{5}$, and $\frac{1}{10}$. Ask:

- How did you find the decimal value of $\frac{1}{8}$? *(I know $\frac{1}{4}$ is 0.25. I know $\frac{1}{8}$ is one-half of $\frac{1}{4}$, which is $0.25 \div 2 = 0.125$.)*
- Did anyone use a different strategy? Explain. *(I used the hundredths square. I divided the square into 8 parts. There were 12.5 small squares, or hundredths, in each part. So, $\frac{1}{8} = 0.125$)*
- Which strategy did you use to write your proper fraction as a decimal? *(I used the fraction $\frac{3}{5}$. I know that $\frac{1}{5}$ is 0.2. So, $\frac{3}{5} = \frac{1}{5} \times 3 = 0.2 \times 3 = 0.6$)*

When you illustrate $\frac{4}{11}$ as a decimal, have a volunteer use short or long division on the board to write the fraction as a decimal.

Model how to write a repeating decimal when not all the digits repeat; for example, $\frac{1}{6} = 0.16666...$ The bar is written only over the 6, to show it repeats: $\frac{1}{6} = 0.1\overline{6}$

We use place value to order decimals.

Example 2

Order these decimals from least to greatest.
$0.\overline{45}, 0.4\overline{5}, 0.4, 0.45$

Solution

All the decimals have 0 in the ones place and 4 in the tenths place.
Compare digits in the hundredths place and beyond.

$0.\overline{45}$ can be written 0.454 545…
$0.4\overline{5}$ can be written 0.455 555…
0.4 can be written 0.400 000
0.45 can be written 0.450 000

0.4 has 0 in the hundredths place. It is the least.
0.45 has 0 in the thousandths place.
$0.\overline{45}$ has 4 in the thousandths place.
$0.4\overline{5}$ has 5 in the thousandths place. It is the greatest.

In order from least to greatest: $0.4, 0.45, 0.\overline{45}, 0.4\overline{5}$

Practice

1. a) Write each fraction as a decimal.
   i) $\frac{2}{3}$ $0.\overline{6}$ ii) $\frac{3}{4}$ 0.75 iii) $\frac{4}{5}$ 0.8 iv) $\frac{5}{6}$ $0.8\overline{3}$ v) $\frac{6}{7}$ $0.\overline{857\,142}$
   b) How can you tell which fractions in part a repeat and which terminate?

2. Write each decimal as a fraction, in simplest form.
   a) 0.73 $\frac{73}{100}$ b) 0.765 $\frac{153}{200}$ c) 0.8765 $\frac{1753}{2000}$ d) 0.0006 $\frac{3}{5000}$

3. For each fraction, write an equivalent fraction with a denominator that is a power of 10.
   Then, write the fraction as a decimal.
   a) $\frac{1}{2}$ $\frac{5}{10} = 0.5$ b) $\frac{2}{5}$ $\frac{4}{10} = 0.4$ c) $\frac{3}{4}$ $\frac{75}{100} = 0.75$ d) $\frac{13}{25}$ $\frac{52}{100} = 0.52$ e) $\frac{19}{50}$ $\frac{38}{100} = 0.38$

4. Write each fraction as a decimal.
   a) $\frac{2}{7}$ $0.\overline{285\,714}$ b) $\frac{3}{11}$ $0.\overline{27}$ c) $\frac{2}{9}$ $0.\overline{2}$ d) $\frac{5}{17}$ 0.294 117 647… e) $\frac{5}{13}$ $0.\overline{384\,615}$

4.8 Converting between Decimals and Fractions **167**

7. a) $0.76 = \frac{76}{100} = \frac{76 \div 4}{100 \div 4} = \frac{19}{25}$
To find equivalent fractions, I can multiply the numerator and denominator of $\frac{19}{25}$ by any natural number. For example, $\frac{19}{25} = \frac{19 \times 2}{25 \times 2} = \frac{38}{50}$; $\frac{19}{25} = \frac{19 \times 3}{25 \times 3} = \frac{57}{75}$; $\frac{19}{25} = \frac{19 \times 4}{25 \times 4} = \frac{76}{100}$; $\frac{19}{25} = \frac{19 \times 5}{25 \times 5} = \frac{95}{125}$; $\frac{19}{25} = \frac{19 \times 6}{25 \times 6} = \frac{114}{150}$; …

b) No, I can continue to multiply the numerator and denominator by increasingly larger numbers. As long as I multiply both the numerator and the denominator by the same number, the fractions will be equivalent.

8. a) I used a calculator to write each fraction as a decimal: 1.0, 2.0, 1.5, $1.\overline{6}$, 1.6, 1.625. The decimals are greater than or equal to 1 and less than or equal to 2. The decimals alternate between a number less than 1.62 and a number greater than 1.62. The difference between consecutive decimals decreases each time.

b) $\frac{21}{13} = 1.\overline{615\,384}$; $\frac{34}{21} = 1.\overline{619\,047}$;
$\frac{55}{34} = 1.6\overline{17\,647\,059}$; $\frac{89}{55} = 1.6\overline{18}$
As the pattern continues, the decimals continue to alternate between a number less than 1.618 and a number greater than 1.618. The decimals get closer to 1.618 each time.

9. a) $0.\overline{142\,857}, 0.\overline{285\,714}, 0.\overline{428\,571}, 0.\overline{571\,428}, 0.\overline{714\,285}, 0.\overline{857\,142}$
All of the decimals contain the same digits. The tenth digits increase from least to greatest, and the other digits follow the same sequence.

b) $0.\overline{1}, 0.\overline{2}, 0.\overline{3}, 0.\overline{4}, 0.\overline{5}, 0.\overline{6}, 0.\overline{7}, 0.\overline{8}$; the tenth digit increases by 1 each time, and always repeats.

Ask:

- Which of the unit fractions in *Explore* are repeating decimals?
  ($\frac{1}{3} = 0.\overline{3}, \frac{1}{6} = 0.1\overline{6}, \frac{1}{7} = 0.\overline{142\,857}, \frac{1}{9} = 0.\overline{1}$)

After you review *Example 1*, encourage students to say the fractions; for example, 0.365 is three hundred sixty-five thousandths; and 0.0054 is fifty-four ten-thousandths.

Remind students to reduce the fraction to simplest form after writing a decimal as a fraction.

As you review *Example 2*, you could illustrate the decimals on a place-value chart:

Ones	Tenths	Hundredths	Thousandths	Ten-thousandths
0	4	5	4	5 . . .
0	4	5	5	5 . . .
0	4			
0	4	5		

Students may more easily compare the decimals with this chart.

Practice

Encourage students to check that the answers make sense, and to use mental strategies where possible.

In question 4, the fraction $\frac{5}{17}$ produces a repeating decimal, but students' calculator displays are too small to show all the digits. Similarly, students may not realize that $\frac{5}{13}$ is a repeating decimal, because some calculators round the final digit in the display.

Assessment Focus: Question 8

Students may notice that the decimal equivalents get closer and closer to 1.618 033. . . Students may also notice that the decimals become too long to determine whether they repeat. As students write about their findings, encourage them to speculate whether each decimal will repeat.

c) $0.\overline{09}$, $0.\overline{18}$, $0.\overline{27}$, $0.\overline{36}$, $0.\overline{45}$, $0.\overline{54}$, $0.\overline{63}$, $0.\overline{72}$, $0.\overline{81}$, $0.\overline{90}$; the repeating digits are multiples of 9, in increasing order.

REFLECT: A decimal terminates if there is a definite number of decimal places. For example, 0.65, 0.2, and 0.886 54 all terminate. A terminating decimal often does not fill the calculator screen. A decimal repeats if one or more of the digits repeat forever. I might see a pattern in the digits that repeat. For example, 0.111 11. . . and 0.285 714 285 714. . . are repeating decimals. Repeating decimals have a bar over the digits that repeat; for example, $0.\overline{1}$ and $0.\overline{285\ 714}$.
A repeating decimal always fills the calculator screen.

Calculator Skills

Students should attempt the problem systematically and record their trials. Students could estimate before trying to solve the problem with a calculator.

Assignment Guidelines

If your students do not have time to complete all the *Practice* questions on pages 167 and 168, these questions provide minimum curriculum coverage:
1, 2, 3, 6, 8, 10, *Reflect*

To assess the 4 Achievement Chart categories listed in the curriculum document, have students complete these *Practice* questions:

Knowledge and Understanding: 2
Application: 8
Thinking: 6
Communication: *Reflect*

Calculator Skills

Replace each ☐ with + or − to get the answer indicated.
0.1 ⊞ 0.55 ⊞ 0.026
⊟ 0.076 ⊞ 0.4 = 1

5. In question 4d, the calculator display is not long enough to show the repeating digits. How could you find the repeating digits?

6. Write $\frac{1}{5}$ as a decimal. 0.2
Use this decimal to write each number below as a decimal.
a) $\frac{4}{5}$ 0.8 b) $\frac{7}{5}$ 1.4 c) $1\frac{4}{5}$ 1.8 d) $2\frac{1}{5}$ 2.2

7. a) How many fractions can you write that are equivalent to the decimal 0.76?
b) Have you written all possible fractions? Explain.

8. **Assessment Focus** Here is the Fibonacci sequence:
1, 1, 2, 3, 5, 8, 13, 21, 34, 55, 89, …
We can write consecutive terms as fractions:
$\frac{1}{1}, \frac{2}{1}, \frac{3}{2}, \frac{5}{3}, \frac{8}{5}, \frac{13}{8}$, and so on
a) Write each fraction above as a decimal.
What patterns do you see?
b) Continue to write consecutive terms as decimals.
Write about what you find out.

9. In each set, write the first three fractions as decimals.
Look for a pattern.
Use the pattern to write the remaining fractions as decimals.
a) $\frac{1}{7}, \frac{2}{7}, \frac{3}{7}, \frac{4}{7}, \frac{5}{7}, \frac{6}{7}$
b) $\frac{1}{9}, \frac{2}{9}, \frac{3}{9}, \frac{4}{9}, \frac{5}{9}, \frac{6}{9}, \frac{7}{9}, \frac{8}{9}$
c) $\frac{1}{11}, \frac{2}{11}, \frac{3}{11}, \frac{4}{11}, \frac{5}{11}, \frac{6}{11}, \frac{7}{11}, \frac{8}{11}, \frac{9}{11}, \frac{10}{11}$

10. Order the decimals in each set from least to greatest.
a) 1.01, 0.1, 0.01, $0.\overline{1}$ 0.01, 0.1, $0.\overline{1}$, 1.01
b) $1.\overline{3}$, $0.\overline{3}$, 2.3, 0.3, 0.35 0.3, $0.\overline{3}$, 0.35, $1.\overline{3}$, 2.3
c) 0.46, 0.64, $1.4\overline{6}$, $1.0\overline{6}$, $0.\overline{6}$ 0.46, 0.64, $0.\overline{6}$, $1.0\overline{6}$, $1.4\overline{6}$

Reflect

When you look at a decimal, how can you tell if it repeats or terminates?
Use examples in your explanation.

168 UNIT 4: Fractions and Decimals

ASSESSMENT FOR LEARNING

What to Look For	What to Do
Knowledge and Understanding ✔ Students understand how to use a calculator and mental math strategies to convert between fractions and decimals.	***Extra Support:*** Students who have difficulty understanding that a fraction and its equivalent decimal represent the same number should work with concrete materials, such as Base Ten Blocks and hundredths squares. For example, have students use Base Ten Blocks to show that 0.35 is the same as $\frac{35}{100}$. Students can use Step-by-Step 8 (Master 4.14) to complete question 8.
Thinking ✔ Students can use their knowledge of repeating and terminating decimals to solve problems involving comparing and ordering decimals.	***Extra Practice:*** Have students find other sets of fractions similar to those in *Practice* question 9 that contain a pattern when converting the fractions to decimals. Students should explain the patterns. Students can complete Extra Practice 8 (Master 4.33).
Application ✔ Students can apply their knowledge of unit fractions to convert more complex fractions to decimals.	***Extension:*** Have students use short or long division and a whole sheet of paper to show that $\frac{5}{17}$ is a repeating decimal.

Recording and Reporting
Master 4.2 Ongoing Observations: Fractions and Decimals

4.9 Dividing by 0.1, 0.01, and 0.001

Focus Relate division by 0.1, 0.01, and 0.001 to multiplication by powers of 10.

Recall that when you multiply a decimal by 10, the digits move 1 place to the left on a place-value chart, or the decimal point shifts 1 place to the right.
What happens when you multiply a decimal by 100? By 1000?

Explore

Work on your own.
Use a calculator.

➢ Choose a 4-digit decimal.
Divide it by 0.1, 0.01, and 0.001.
What patterns do you notice?

➢ Choose a different 4-digit decimal.
Use patterns to divide it by 0.1, 0.01, and 0.001.
Check your answers with a calculator.

Reflect & Share

Compare your strategies for dividing with those of a classmate.
How could you use multiplication to divide by 0.1, 0.01, and 0.001?

Connect

$0.1 = \frac{1}{10}$

➢ Dividing by $\frac{1}{10}$ is the same as multiplying by 10.
So, $1.35 \div 0.1 = 1.35 \div \frac{1}{10}$
$= 1.35 \times 10$
$= 13.5$

$0.01 = \frac{1}{100}$

➢ Dividing by $\frac{1}{100}$ is the same as multiplying by 100.
So, $1.35 \div 0.01 = 1.35 \div \frac{1}{100}$
$= 1.35 \times 100$
$= 135$

4.9 Dividing by 0.1, 0.01, and 0.001 169

Dividing by 0.1, 0.01, and 0.001

LESSON ORGANIZER (80–100 min)

Curriculum Focus: Relate division by 0.1, 0.01, and 0.001 to multiplication by powers of 10. (8m14, 8m16, 8m24)

Student Materials
- 0.5-cm grid paper (PM 14)
- calculators

Optional
- Step-by-Step 9 (Master 4.15)
- Extra Practice 9 (Master 4.34)

Vocabulary: dividend, divisor, quotient

Assessment: Master 4.2 Ongoing Observations: Fractions and Decimals

Key Math Learning

Dividing by 0.1, 0.01, and 0.001 is the same as multiplying by 10, 100, and 1000.

Math Note

The curriculum suggests that the powers of 10 be written as powers. Review this with students; for example, $1\ 000\ 000 = 10^6$
There is a curriculum requirement to also divide by powers of 10 up to 1 000 000. Both multiplication and division by powers of 10 are review from Grade 6.
Both these operations were reviewed in Unit 3, when students converted among measurement units.

BEFORE — Get Started

Review the multiplication of decimals by powers of 10. Write 2.5×10 on the board. Ask:

- How can you use mental math to find this product?
(*When you multiply a decimal by 10, the digits shift 1 place to the left. So, 2.5 × 10 = 25*)
- What happens when you multiply a decimal by 100? (*The digits shift 2 places to the left.*)
When you multiply a decimal by 1000?
(*The digits shift 3 places to the left.*)

It is important for students to see that the digits shift left, rather than that the decimal point moves right. Illustrate this on a place-value chart.

Present *Explore*. Ensure students understand that when they work with their second 4-digit decimals, they should only use calculators to check their answers.

DURING — Explore

Ongoing Assessment: Observe and Listen

As students work, ensure they record their work so that the patterns are noticeable. Ask:

- What patterns did you see when you divided your decimal by 0.1, 0.01, and 0.001?
(*The digits in my answer shifted 1 place to the left each time, or the decimal point moved 1 place to the right. My answers increased by a power of 10 each time.*)
- How can you describe your pattern?
(*When you multiply by 0.1, the digits shift 1 place to the left. When you multiply by 0.01, the digits shift 2 places to the left. When you multiply by 0.001, the digits shift 3 places to the left.*)
- How can you relate dividing by 0.1 to multiplication? (*Dividing by 0.1 is the same as multiplying by 10; for example, 3.456 ÷ 0.1 = 34.56, and 3.456 × 10 = 34.56.*)

REACHING ALL LEARNERS

Early Finishers

Have students repeat *Practice* question 7 for a rectangle with area 127.4 cm^2, and widths of 20 cm, 2 cm, 0.2 cm, 0.02 cm, and 0.002 cm.

Common Misconceptions

➤ Students confuse dividing by 0.1, 0.01, and 0.001 with dividing by 10, 100, and 1000.

How to Help: Encourage students to think about their answers. For example, when dividing 2.87 by 0.001, students should realize that 0.001, or $\frac{1}{1000}$, is a very small number. They should expect the quotient to be much greater than the dividend, 2.87. If students divide 2.87 by 1000, they get 0.002 87, which is much less than 2.87.

Sample Solutions

1. a) 5.47, 54.7, 547, 5470, 54 700, 547 000
   b) 8.79, 87.9, 879, 8790, 87 900, 879 000
   c) 0.345, 3.45, 34.5, 345, 3450, 34 500
   d) 0.0652, 0.652, 6.52, 65.2, 652, 6520
   e) 65.4212, 654.212, 6542.12, 65 421.2, 654 212, 6 542 120
   f) 0.002 34, 0.0234, 0.234, 2.34, 23.4, 234
   g) 0.089, 0.89, 8.9, 89, 890, 8900
   h) 0.1001, 1.001, 10.01, 100.1, 1001, 10 010

5. I investigated 3 different situations.
   The divisor is 1: For example, 36.2 ÷ 1 = 36.2; the quotient is equal to the dividend.
   The divisor is less than 1: For example, 36.2 ÷ 0.01 = 36.2 × 100 = 3620; the quotient is greater than the dividend.

$0.001 = \frac{1}{1000}$

➤ Dividing by $\frac{1}{1000}$ is the same as multiplying by 1000.

So, $1.35 \div 0.001 = 1.35 \div \frac{1}{1000}$
$= 1.35 \times 1000$
$= 1350$

➤ Recall how to divide by powers of 10, such as 10 and 100.

$1.35 \div 10 = 0.135$
$1.35 \div 100 = 0.0135$

We can think of dividing by 10 as multiplying by $\frac{1}{10} = 0.1$.

So, $1.35 \div 10 = 1.35 \times 0.1$
$= 0.135$

And, dividing by 100 is the same as multiplying by $\frac{1}{100} = 0.01$.

So, $135 \div 100 = 1.35 \times 0.01$
$= 0.0135$

We can use these patterns to mentally divide by multiples of 0.1, 0.01, and 0.001.

Example

Divide.

a) 0.275 ÷ 0.2 b) 1.863 ÷ 0.03

Solution

a) $0.275 \div 0.2 = 0.275 \div \frac{2}{10} = 0.275 \times \frac{10}{2} = \frac{2.75}{2} = 1.375$

b) $1.863 \div 0.03 = 1.863 \div \frac{3}{100} = 1.863 \times \frac{100}{3} = \frac{186.3}{3} = 62.1$

Practice

Use mental math.

1. Predict the quotient when you divide each number by 100, 10, 1, 0.1, 0.01, and 0.001.
   a) 547 b) 879 c) 34.5 d) 6.52
   e) 6542.12 f) 0.234 g) 8.9 h) 10.01

170 UNIT 4: Fractions and Decimals

AFTER Connect

Have students share their patterns and strategies for dividing by 0.1, 0.01, and 0.001.

Draw a number line from 0 to 1 on the board. Have a volunteer use the number line to model $1 \div \frac{1}{10}$. Ensure students understand that $\frac{1}{10} = 0.1$.

Ask:

- How many tenths are there in 1?
  (10; $1 = \frac{10}{10}$, and there are 10 groups of one-tenth in 10 tenths.)

Write 1 × 10 on the board. Ask:

- What is 1 × 10? *(10)*
- How can you relate 1 × 10 and $1 \div \frac{1}{10}$?
  (Dividing by $\frac{1}{10}$, or 0.1, is the same as multiplying by 10.)

Use the examples in *Connect* to illustrate this concept with hundredths and thousandths. Ask:

- How can you use mental math to find 3.75 ÷ 0.3? *(I divide 3.75 by 0.1 to get 37.5, then divide 37.5 by 3 to get 12.5.)*

Encourage students to summarize their strategies for dividing by 0.1, 0.01, and 0.001, and multiples of them.

Practice

Assessment Focus: Question 5

Students should investigate different scenarios and include examples of each:

- a divisor greater than 1
- a divisor that equals 1
- a divisor less than 1

Assignment Guidelines

If your students do not have time to complete all the *Practice* questions on pages 170 and 171, these questions provide minimum curriculum coverage:
1, 3, 4, 5, 6, 7, *Reflect*

To assess the 4 Achievement Chart categories listed in the curriculum document, have students complete these *Practice* questions:

Knowledge and Understanding: 2 Application: 6
Communication: 5 Thinking: 7

2. Write each quotient.

a) $\frac{147}{1000}$ 0.147 b) $\frac{147}{0.01}$ 14 700 c) $\frac{9.64}{0.1}$ 96.4 d) $\frac{12.30}{0.001}$ 12 300
e) $\frac{0.345}{0.01}$ 34.5 f) $\frac{12.3}{10}$ 1.23 g) $\frac{23.45}{0.01}$ 2345 h) $\frac{0.123}{0.001}$ 123

3. Find the missing divisor in each division statement.

a) $\frac{4.3}{?} = 4.3$ 1 b) $\frac{54}{?} = 5.4$ 10 c) $\frac{65.4}{?} = 6540$ 0.01
d) $\frac{43.45}{?} = 434.5$ 0.1 e) $\frac{785.03}{?} = 7850.3$ 0.1 f) $\frac{0.0345}{?} = 3.45$ 0.01
g) $\frac{0.003\ 45}{?} = 0.345$ 0.01 h) $\frac{345.6}{?} = 3456$ 0.1 i) $\frac{0.593}{?} = 59.3$ 0.01

4. Find the missing dividend in each division statement.

a) $\frac{?}{10} = 234$ 2340 b) $\frac{?}{0.1} = 34.5$ 3.45 c) $\frac{?}{0.01} = 12.23$ 0.1223
d) $\frac{?}{0.001} = 12\ 000$ 12 e) $\frac{?}{0.01} = 1320$ 13.2 f) $\frac{?}{0.001} = 50$ 0.05
g) $\frac{?}{0.1} = 0.725$ 0.0725 h) $\frac{?}{0.1} = 72.5$ 7.25 i) $\frac{?}{100} = 0.1456$ 14.56

Mental Math

Copy this statement.
$15 + 15 \div 3 + 2 \times 2 - 13$
Insert one pair of brackets to make the answer 8.
$15 + 15 \div (3 + 2) \times 2 - 13 = 8$

5. **Assessment Focus** A student says that when you divide two numbers, the quotient is always less than the dividend.
Is this true? Use examples to explain your answer.

6. Find each quotient.

a) $356.2 \div 0.2$ 1781 b) $127.5 \div 0.03$ 4250 c) $0.448 \div 0.4$ 1.12
d) $0.0525 \div 0.005$ 10.5 e) $63.6 \div 0.06$ 1060 f) $211.4 \div 0.007$ 30 200

7. A rectangle has an area of 15.5 cm^2.
Find the length and perimeter of the rectangle for each width.
a) 10 cm b) 1 cm c) 0.1 cm d) 0.01 cm e) 0.001 cm

Take It Further

Similar figures have corresponding sides in the same ratio.

8. a) Draw each rectangle on grid paper.
i) 4 cm by 4 cm ii) 6 cm by 4.4 cm iii) 8.6 cm by 4.8 cm
b) Calculate the area of each rectangle. i) 16 cm^2 ii) 26.4 cm^2 iii) 41.28 cm^2
c) What if you divide the area of the first rectangle by 0.1; the second by 0.01; the third by 0.001. Would each new rectangle be larger or smaller than the original rectangle? Explain. Larger
d) Find the area of each new rectangle in part c.
Is each new rectangle similar to the original rectangle? Only part ii
Give reasons for your answer.
i) 160 cm^2 ii) 2640 cm^2 iii) 41 280 cm^2

Reflect

Explain how you divide by 0.1, 0.01, and 0.001 mentally.
Use examples in your explanation.

4.9 Dividing by 0.1, 0.01, and 0.001 171

The divisor is greater than 1: For example, $36.2 \div 10 = 3.62$; the quotient is less than the dividend.
So, the student's statement is only true when the divisor is greater than 1.

7. a) $l = 1.55$ cm, $P = 23.1$ cm **b)** $l = 15.5$ cm, $P = 33$ cm
c) $l = 155$ cm, $P = 310.2$ cm **d)** $l = 1550$ cm, $P = 3100.02$ cm
e) $l = 15\ 500$ cm, $P = 31\ 000.002$ cm

8. c) Each area is divided by a decimal less than 1.
d) Dividing the area of the rectangle by 0.01 is the same as dividing the length and width of the rectangle by 0.1 ($0.1 \times 0.1 = 0.01$), to get a 60-cm by 44-cm rectangle. The area of this rectangle is 60 cm $\times$ 44 cm = 2640 cm^2, and the ratios of the sides of each rectangle (6:4.4 and 60:44) are the same. The rectangles are similar because 0.01 is a perfect square. In the other cases, 0.1 and 0.001 are not perfect squares, so the new rectangles will not be similar to the original rectangles.

REFLECT: When I divide by 0.1, 0.01, and 0.001 mentally, I shift the digits to the left according to the number of decimal places in the divisor. Example: $32.6 \div 0.01$
There are 2 decimal places in 0.01, so I shift the digits 2 places to the left.
Because there are no digits in the ones place, I write a zero.
So, $32.6 \div 0.01 = 3260$
When I divide by 0.1, I shift the digits 1 place to the left, and when I divide by 0.001, I shift the digits 3 places to the left.

Mental Math

Students can use guess and check or logical reasoning.

ASSESSMENT FOR LEARNING

What to Look For

Knowledge and Understanding

✔ Students understand that dividing by 0.1, 0.01, and 0.001 is the same as multiplying by 10, 100, and 1000.

Communication

✔ Students can use words and diagrams to describe strategies for dividing by 0.1, 0.01, and 0.001.

Application

✔ Students can apply mental math strategies to divide by multiples of 0.1, 0.01, and 0.001.

What to Do

Extra Support: Students who have difficulty dividing by 0.1, 0.01, and 0.001 should make a table of strategies, then refer to the table as they work. Alternatively, these students could use a place-value chart. Students can use Step-by-Step 9 (Master 4.15) to complete question 5.

Divide by	Multiply by	Strategy
0.1	10	Shift digits 1 place to the left
0.01	100	Shift digits 2 places to the left
0.001	1000	Shift digits 3 places to the left

Extra Practice: Students can write problems similar to *Practice* questions 3 and 4, trade problems with a classmate, and solve their classmate's problems.
Students can complete Extra Practice 9 (Master 4.34).

Extension: Have students write as many multiplication and division statements involving powers of 10 as they can that result in 58.6.

Recording and Reporting

Master 4.2 Ongoing Observations: Fractions and Decimals

Providing Math Information

LESSON ORGANIZER

Student Materials
- calculators

Providing Math Information

When you designed your own math problem, you wrote a problem statement in the form of a question. You need to include the math information required to solve the problem. To know what information is needed, it is helpful to work backward from the problem statement.

Problem Statement → Math Information

Start with the problem statement.
For example, here is a problem from *Unit 2*:
How many desks are in the school?

To answer this, you might need to know this information:
- How many classrooms are in the school?
- How many desks are in each classroom?
- How many other desks are in the school?

You can investigate to find the information or you can make up your own information.
The problem might be written this way:
There are 12 classrooms.
There are 30 desks in each classroom.
There are 25 more desks in the library resource room.
How many desks are in the school?

Strategies
- Make a table.
- Use a model.
- Draw a diagram.
- Solve a simpler problem.
- Work backward.
- Guess and check.
- Make an organized list.
- Use a pattern.
- Draw a graph.
- Use logical reasoning.

Some problems give more information than is needed.
It is helpful to highlight the math information needed to solve the problem and to ~~cross out~~ information that is not needed.
Ensure that all information needed to solve the problem is provided. Keep in mind the strategies at the left that can be used to solve a problem.

172 UNIT 4: Fractions and Decimals

Writing a math problem is an excellent way for students to consolidate their knowledge and skills. Students who create their own problems are often more engaged, as they get to choose the context of the math involved. This strategy not only encourages the development and consolidation of math skills and concepts, but it also allows for language development.

Initially, students who create their own word problems tend to copy existing problems, and change them by substituting their own numbers. Students do not have to consider the information needed in these cases.

As students begin to develop their own problems without using examples from other sources, they often design problems that do not contain enough information to solve. Encourage students to think about the math information needed to solve the problem as well as the strategies they might use to solve it.

Point out to students that one problem statement can lead to many different problems, depending on the information that is given.

Reading and Writing in Math

Check

1. a) In this problem, what extra information is needed to solve the problem?
Shazi bought some 30¢ candy bars and some 60¢ candy bars. She bought 10 candy bars in total. How many candy bars did she buy at each price?
b) Make up the information you need to solve the problem in part a.
Then solve the problem.

2. a) In this problem, what information is not needed to solve the problem?
A bicycle dealer put together a shipment of bicycles and tricycles.
Tricycles cost $25 more than bicycles.
The dealer used 50 seats and 130 wheels.
How many bicycles and how many tricycles did she put together?
b) Solve the problem in part a.

3. a) In this problem, what extra information is needed to solve the problem?
The local hockey league has two divisions.
Each division has 6 teams.
How many games are played during the season?
b) Try to find out about a local hockey league in your area.
Write a problem about the league.
Solve the problem.

4. Write your own word problem.
Identify what math information is needed to solve it.
Write the information needed to answer the problem, either by investigating to find the information or by making up your own information.
Solve the problem.
Trade problems with a classmate.
Solve your classmate's problem.

To write a word problem:
- Start with a problem statement. Work backward.
- Think about what is needed to solve the problem.
- Think about what math information is required.
- Write the word problem.

Reading and Writing in Math: Providing Math Information 173

Sample Solutions

1. a) To answer this, you need to know the total amount of money Shazi spent on candy bars.

b) I chose $5.10.
I use guess and check to solve the problem.
Try: one 30¢ bar and nine 60¢ bars
$0.30 + (9 × $0.60) = $5.70 too high
Try: four 30¢ bars and six 60¢ bars
(4 × $0.30) + (6 × $0.60) = $4.80.
too low
Try: three 30¢ bars and seven 60¢ bars
(3 × $0.30) + (7 × $0.60) = $5.10 correct
So, Shazi bought three 30¢ candy bars and seven 60¢ candy bars.

2. a) We do not need to know that tricycles cost $25 more than bicycles.

b) There are 50 seats. Since each bicycle has 1 seat, we know 50 bicycles were put together.
There are 130 wheels. A bicycle has 2 wheels and a tricycle has 3 wheels.
Use guess and check.
Try: 10 bicycles and 40 tricycles
10 × 2 + 40 × 3 = 140 too high
Try: 15 bicycles and 35 tricycles
15 × 2 + 35 × 3 = 135 close, but too high
Try: 20 bicycles and 30 tricycles
20 × 2 + 30 × 3 = 130 correct
So, 20 bicycles and 30 tricycles were put together.

3. a) You might need to know:
How many times does each team play each other?
Does the season include playoff games?
If so, is it a round-robin playoff?
How many teams in each division make the playoffs?

b) For example:
A local hockey league has 8 teams.
In the regular season, each team plays every other team 3 times.
How many games does each team play?
How many games are played during the regular season?
Solution:
Each team plays every other team 3 times.
There are 7 other teams.
So, each team plays: 3 × 7 = 21 games
There are 8 teams in the league.
So, there are (8 × 21) ÷ 2 = 84 games played in the regular season.
I divided by 2 because the order of the teams does not matter.
Team 1 vs. Team 2 is the same as Team 2 vs. Team 1.

4. For example:
How many students in the classroom are not wearing a watch or a ring?
I need to know:
How many students are in the classroom?
How many students are wearing a watch?
How many students are wearing a ring?
How many students are wearing both a watch and a ring?

Math information:
There are 28 students in the classroom.
18 students are wearing a watch.
11 students are wearing a ring.
7 students are wearing both a watch and a ring.
Solution:
Number of students wearing a watch, but not a ring:
18 – 7 = 11
Number of students wearing a ring, but not a watch:
11 – 7 = 4
Number of students wearing both a watch and a ring: 7
Number of students not wearing a watch or a ring:
28 – 11 – 4 – 7 = 6

LESSON ORGANIZER

Student Materials
- number lines (Master 4.24)
- 1-cm grid paper (PM 20)
- 0.5-cm grid paper (PM 14)
- calculators

Assessment: Master 4.1 Unit Rubric: Fractions and Decimals
Master 4.4 Unit Summary: Fractions and Decimals

Assignment Guidelines

To assess the 4 Achievement Chart categories listed in the curriculum document, use these questions:
Knowledge and Understanding: 9
Application: 12
Thinking: 15
Communication: 20

Correlation of Extra Practice questions on page 491:

Lesson	Questions
4.1	1, 8
4.2	2, 3, 6
4.3	3, 6
4.4	4, 6
4.5	4, 6
4.6	5, 6
4.7	5, 6
4.8	7
4.9	–

Unit Review

Review any lesson with etext online tutorial

What Do I Need to Know?

✓ **To add or subtract two fractions:**
Use equivalent fractions to make the denominators the same, then add or subtract the numerators. For example,

$\frac{5}{4}+\frac{3}{5}$
$=\frac{25}{20}+\frac{12}{20}$
$=\frac{37}{20}$, or $1\frac{17}{20}$

$\frac{7}{3}-\frac{3}{8}$
$=\frac{56}{24}-\frac{9}{24}$
$=\frac{47}{24}$, or $1\frac{23}{24}$

✓ **To multiply two fractions:**
Multiply the numerators and multiply the denominators.
$\frac{2}{3}\times\frac{1}{5}=\frac{2\times1}{3\times5}=\frac{2}{15}$

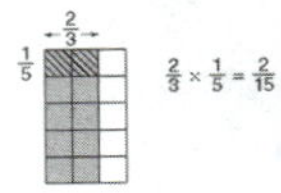

✓ **To divide a whole number by a fraction:**
Write the whole number as a fraction, then multiply.
For $4\div\frac{2}{3}$, write: $\frac{4}{1}\div\frac{2}{3}$ as $\frac{4}{1}\times\frac{3}{2}=\frac{12}{2}=6$

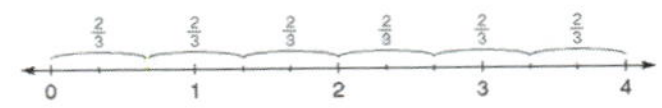

✓ **To divide a fraction by a whole number:**
Write the whole number as a fraction, then use common denominators.

$\frac{2}{3}\div4=\frac{2}{3}\div\frac{12}{3}$
$=\frac{2}{12}$
$=\frac{1}{6}$

Since the denominators are the same, divide the numerators.

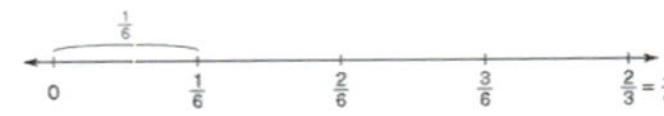

✓ **To divide two fractions:**

Method 1:
Use common denominators.
$\frac{4}{5}\div\frac{3}{2}=\frac{8}{10}\div\frac{15}{10}$
$=\frac{8}{15}$

Method 2:
Use multiplication.
$\frac{4}{5}\div\frac{3}{2}$ is the same as $\frac{4}{5}\times\frac{2}{3}=\frac{8}{15}$

174 UNIT 4: Fractions and Decimals

Sample Solutions

1. Write equivalent fractions with a common denominator that is greater than both denominators.
   a) $\frac{3}{8}$ b) $\frac{5}{8}$ c) $\frac{5}{12}$ d) $\frac{3}{4}$
2. a) $\frac{3}{5}=\frac{9}{15}$ and $\frac{2}{3}=\frac{10}{15}$; since $\frac{10}{15}>\frac{9}{15}$, $\frac{2}{3}>\frac{3}{5}$
   Lalo completed more questions.
   b) The number of questions on the test must be a multiple of both 3 and 5; for example, there might have been 15, 30, 45, . . . questions on the test.
3. a) $\frac{1}{4}, \frac{2}{3}, \frac{3}{4}, \frac{4}{5}, \frac{5}{6}$ b) $\frac{1}{3}, \frac{3}{8}, \frac{2}{5}, \frac{3}{7}, \frac{7}{10}$
4. a) $\frac{7}{6}, \frac{7}{8}, \frac{3}{4}, \frac{1}{2}$ b) $\frac{4}{3}, \frac{3}{4}, \frac{4}{10}, \frac{3}{12}, \frac{1}{6}$ c) $\frac{4}{5}, \frac{2}{3}$ and $\frac{4}{6}, \frac{2}{4}, \frac{4}{10}$
7. a) $2\frac{2}{3}+1\frac{1}{2}=2+1+\frac{2}{3}+\frac{1}{2}=2+1+\frac{4}{6}+\frac{3}{6}=3+\frac{7}{6}=$
   $3+\frac{6}{6}+\frac{1}{6}=4\frac{1}{6}$
8. Subtract the juice Ping and Preston drank from the amount in the flask:
   $2\frac{1}{2}-\frac{3}{8}-\frac{7}{10}=\frac{5}{2}-\frac{3}{8}-\frac{7}{10}=\frac{100}{40}-\frac{15}{40}-\frac{28}{40}=\frac{57}{40}$
   $=\frac{40}{40}+\frac{17}{40}=1\frac{17}{40}$
9. a) 10

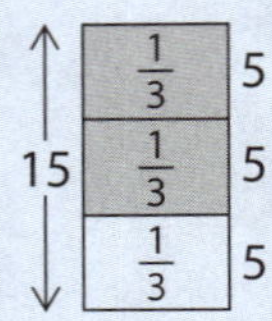

b) $\frac{7}{10}\times\frac{5}{8}=\frac{7}{16}$

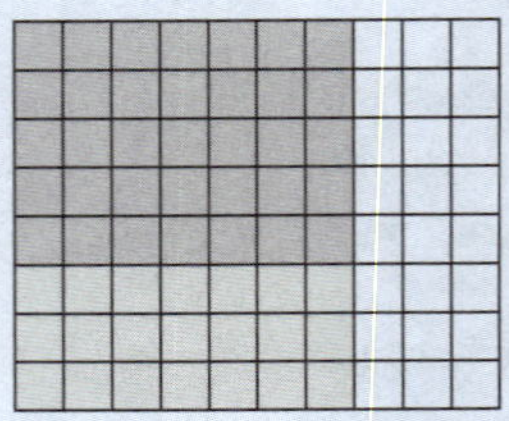

c) $5\times\frac{3}{2}=(5\times1)+(5\times\frac{1}{2})$; $\frac{15}{2}$, or $7\frac{1}{2}$

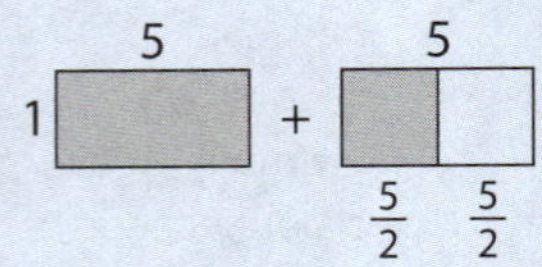

What Should I Be Able to Do?

For extra practice, go to page 491.

LESSON

1. Name a fraction between each pair of fractions.
   a) $\frac{1}{4}$ and $\frac{1}{2}$ b) $\frac{1}{2}$ and $\frac{3}{4}$
   c) $\frac{1}{3}$ and $\frac{3}{4}$ d) $\frac{3}{5}$ and $\frac{7}{8}$

2. Fletcher completed $\frac{3}{5}$ of the test questions. Lalo completed $\frac{2}{3}$ of the test questions.
   a) Who completed more questions? Lalo
   b) How many questions might have been on the test? Explain.

3. Order the fractions in each set from least to greatest.
   a) $\frac{2}{3}, \frac{4}{5}, \frac{5}{6}, \frac{3}{4}, \frac{1}{4}$ b) $\frac{7}{10}, \frac{1}{3}, \frac{3}{7}, \frac{3}{8}, \frac{2}{5}$

4. Order the fractions in each set from greatest to least.
   a) $\frac{1}{2}, \frac{3}{4}, \frac{7}{6}, \frac{7}{8}$
   b) $\frac{4}{3}, \frac{3}{4}, \frac{1}{6}, \frac{4}{10}, \frac{3}{12}$
   c) $\frac{4}{5}, \frac{4}{6}, \frac{4}{10}, \frac{2}{3}, \frac{2}{4}$

4.2 5. Add.
   a) $\frac{3}{8} + \frac{3}{4}$ $\frac{9}{8}$
   b) $\frac{5}{6} + \frac{2}{7}$ $\frac{47}{42}$
   c) $\frac{3}{2} + \frac{5}{3} + \frac{9}{10}$ $\frac{61}{15}$

4.3 6. Subtract.
   a) $\frac{9}{10} - \frac{3}{4}$ $\frac{3}{20}$ b) $\frac{19}{12} - \frac{1}{2}$ $\frac{13}{12}$
   c) $\frac{8}{9} - \frac{1}{8}$ $\frac{55}{72}$ d) $\frac{7}{5} - \frac{7}{6}$ $\frac{7}{30}$

4.2 4.3 7. Add or subtract as indicated.
   a) $2\frac{2}{3} + 1\frac{1}{2}$ $4\frac{1}{6}$ b) $3\frac{1}{3} - 1\frac{7}{10}$ $1\frac{19}{30}$
   c) $2\frac{1}{6} + 4\frac{7}{8}$ $7\frac{1}{24}$ d) $3\frac{1}{2} - 2\frac{3}{4}$ $\frac{3}{4}$

8. A flask contains $2\frac{1}{2}$ cups of juice. Ping drinks $\frac{3}{8}$ cup of juice. Preston drinks $\frac{7}{10}$ cup of juice. How much juice is in the flask now? $1\frac{17}{40}$ cups

4.4 4.5 9. Multiply. Use an area model to illustrate each product.
   a) $\frac{2}{3} \times 15$ b) $\frac{7}{10} \times \frac{5}{8}$
   c) $5 \times \frac{3}{2}$ d) $\frac{2}{3} \times \frac{3}{8}$
   e) $\frac{4}{5} \times \frac{3}{10}$ f) $\frac{9}{8} \times \frac{1}{5}$
   g) $\frac{10}{3} \times \frac{5}{2}$ h) $\frac{11}{6} \times \frac{7}{4}$

10. Twenty-five Grade 8 students are going on a school trip. They pre-order sandwiches. Three-quarters of the students order a turkey sandwich, while $\frac{1}{4}$ of the students order a roasted vegetable sandwich. Of the $\frac{3}{4}$ who want turkey, $\frac{2}{5}$ do not want mayonnaise. What fraction of the students do not want mayonnaise? $\frac{3}{10}$

4.6 11. Divide. Sketch a number line to show each quotient.
   a) $1 \div \frac{1}{3}$ b) $2 \div \frac{3}{4}$
   c) $3 \div \frac{4}{5}$ d) $4 \div \frac{5}{6}$

12. A glass holds $\frac{2}{3}$ cup of milk. A jug holds 8 cups of milk. How many glasses can be filled from the milk in the jug? 12 glasses

Unit Review 175

d) $\frac{2}{3} \times \frac{3}{8} = \frac{1}{4}$

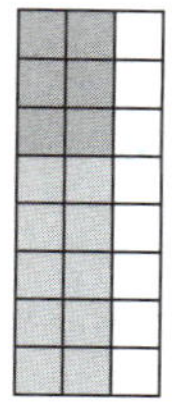

e) $\frac{4}{5} \times \frac{3}{10} = \frac{6}{25}$

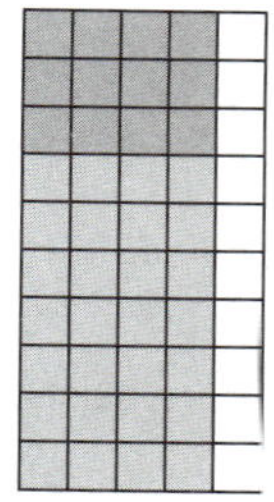

f) $\frac{9}{40}$

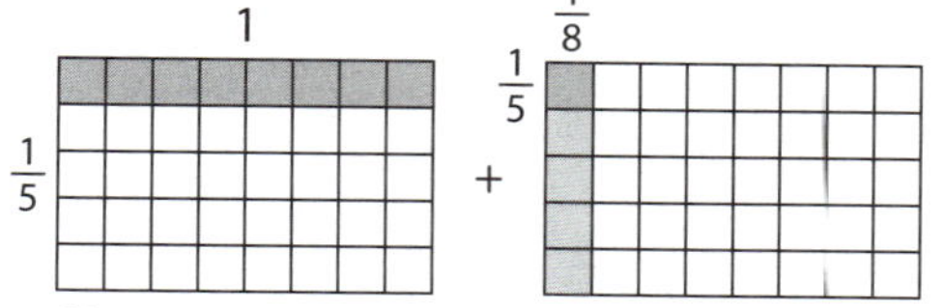

g) $\frac{25}{3}$ or $\frac{81}{3}$

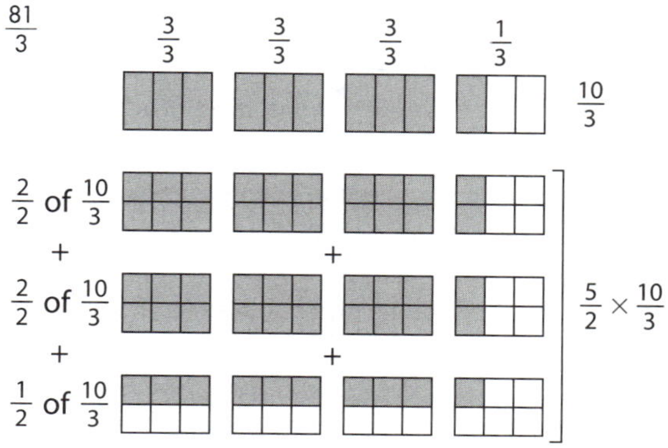

h) $\frac{77}{24}$, or $3\frac{5}{24}$

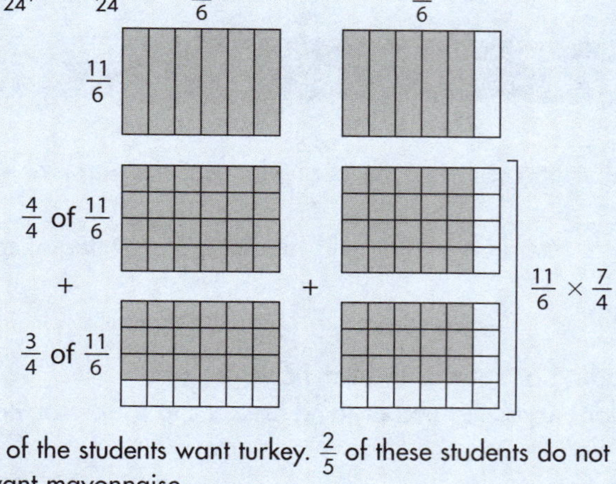

10. $\frac{3}{4}$ of the students want turkey. $\frac{2}{5}$ of these students do not want mayonnaise.
$\frac{2}{5}$ of $\frac{3}{4} = \frac{2}{5} \times \frac{3}{4} = \frac{3}{10}$

11. a) $1 \div \frac{1}{3} = 3$

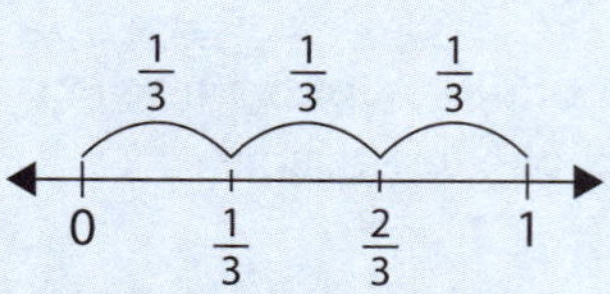

b) $2 \div \frac{3}{4} = 2\frac{2}{3}$

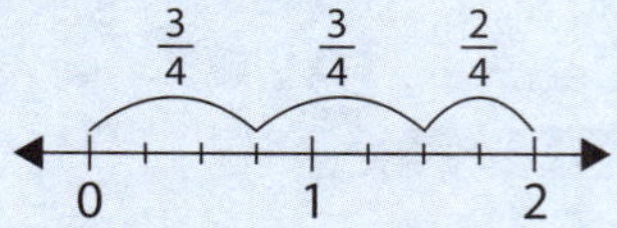

c) $3 \div \frac{4}{5} = 3\frac{3}{4}$

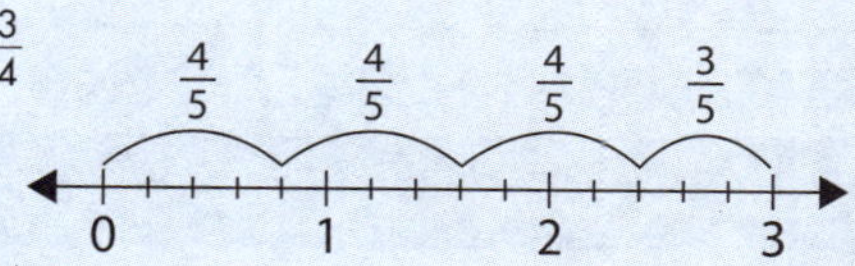

d) $4 \div \frac{5}{6} = 4\frac{4}{5}$

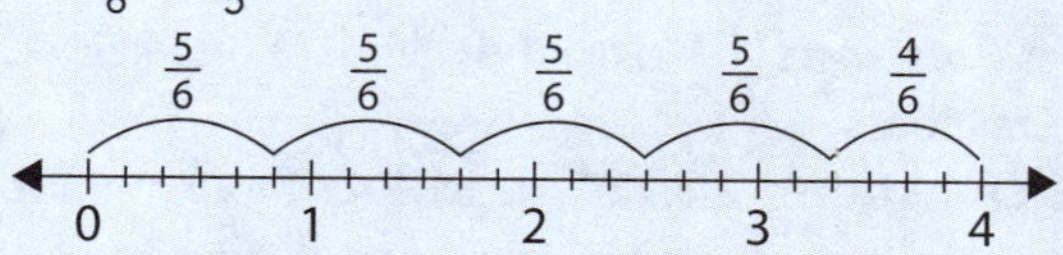

12. $8 \div \frac{2}{3} = \frac{24}{3} \div \frac{2}{3} = \frac{24}{2} = 12$

13. a) $\frac{3}{10} \div 2 = \frac{3}{20}$

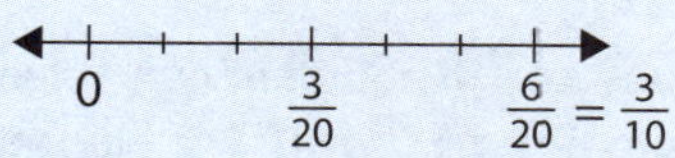

b) $\frac{8}{5} \div 3 = \frac{8}{15}$

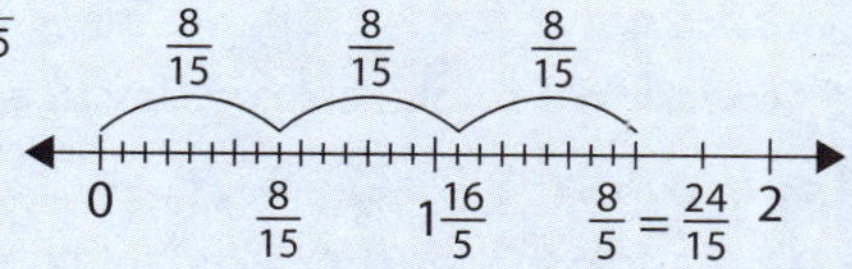

c) $\frac{13}{2} \div 4 = 1\frac{5}{8}$

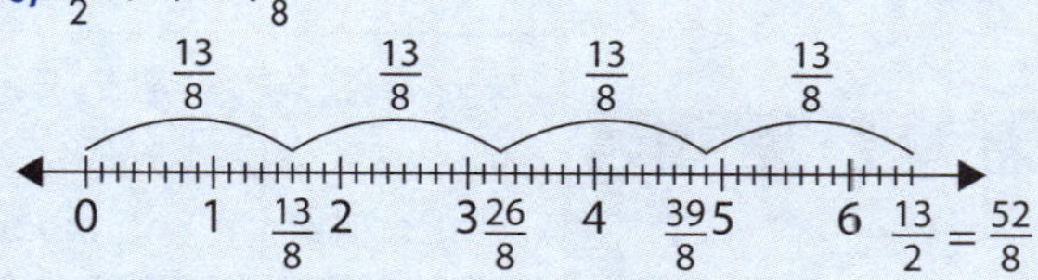

d) $\frac{5}{4} \div 3 = \frac{5}{12}$

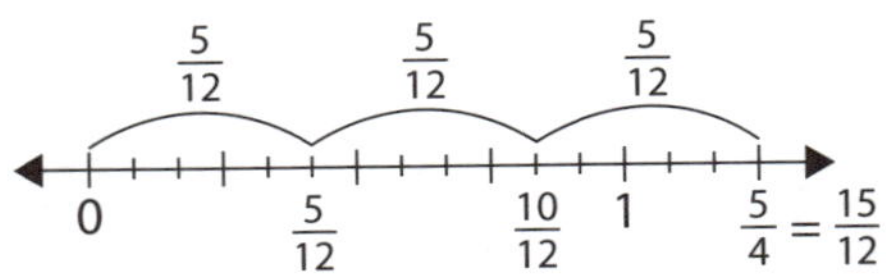

15. When you divide a proper fraction by a whole number, the quotient is less than 1; for example, $\frac{2}{5} \div 3 = \frac{2}{15}$. When you divide an improper fraction by a whole number, the quotient is greater than 1 if the whole number is less than the improper fraction (for example, $\frac{8}{2} \div 2 = 2$), and the quotient is less than 1 if the whole number is greater than the improper fraction (for example, $\frac{8}{2} \div 10 = \frac{2}{5}$).

19. The quotient is less than 1 if the initial fraction is less than 1; for example, $\frac{2}{3} \div \frac{3}{2} = \frac{4}{9}$.
The quotient is greater than 1 if the initial fraction is greater than 1; for example, $\frac{5}{2} \div \frac{2}{5} = \frac{25}{4} = 6\frac{1}{4}$.
The quotient is equal to 1 if the initial fraction is equal to 1; for example, $\frac{2}{2} \div \frac{2}{2} = 1$.

20. The product and quotient in each pair are equal.
The second fractions in each pair are reciprocals.

25. **a), b)** $\frac{1}{3} = 0.\overline{3}$ and $\frac{3}{4} = 0.75$
The decimal has tenths and hundredths. Possible decimals, in order from least to greatest, are: 0.34, 0.35, 0.36, 0.37, 0.38, 0.39, 0.40, 0.41, 0.42, . . ., 0.69, 0.70, 0.71, 0.72, 0.73, and 0.74

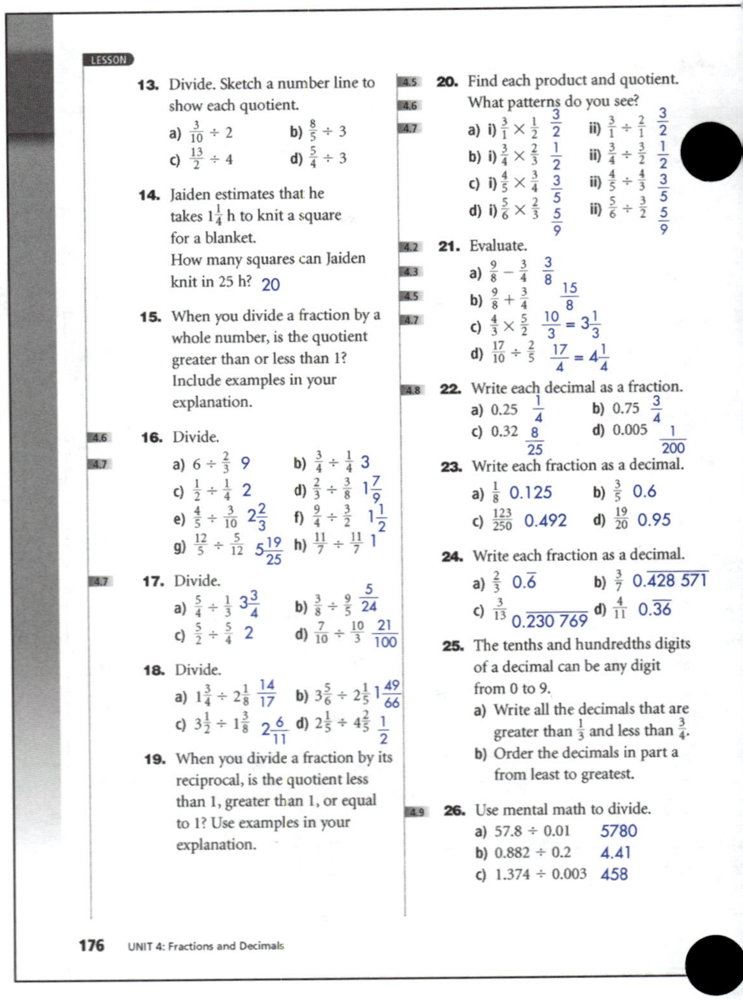

LESSON

13. Divide. Sketch a number line to show each quotient.
a) $\frac{3}{10} \div 2$ b) $\frac{8}{5} \div 3$
c) $\frac{13}{2} \div 4$ d) $\frac{5}{4} \div 3$

14. Jaiden estimates that he takes $1\frac{1}{4}$ h to knit a square for a blanket.
How many squares can Jaiden knit in 25 h? 20

15. When you divide a fraction by a whole number, is the quotient greater than or less than 1? Include examples in your explanation.

4.6 4.7 **16.** Divide.
a) $6 \div \frac{2}{3}$ 9 b) $\frac{3}{4} \div \frac{1}{4}$ 3
c) $\frac{1}{2} \div \frac{1}{4}$ 2 d) $\frac{2}{3} \div \frac{3}{8}$ $1\frac{7}{9}$
e) $\frac{4}{5} \div \frac{3}{10}$ $2\frac{2}{3}$ f) $\frac{9}{4} \div \frac{3}{2}$ $1\frac{1}{2}$
g) $\frac{12}{5} \div \frac{5}{12}$ $5\frac{19}{25}$ h) $\frac{11}{7} \div \frac{11}{7}$ 1

4.7 **17.** Divide.
a) $\frac{5}{4} \div \frac{1}{3}$ $3\frac{3}{4}$ b) $\frac{3}{8} \div \frac{9}{5}$ $\frac{5}{24}$
c) $\frac{5}{2} \div \frac{5}{4}$ 2 d) $\frac{7}{10} \div \frac{10}{3}$ $\frac{21}{100}$

18. Divide.
a) $1\frac{3}{4} \div 2\frac{1}{8}$ $\frac{14}{17}$ b) $3\frac{5}{6} \div 2\frac{1}{5}$ $1\frac{49}{66}$
c) $3\frac{1}{2} \div 1\frac{3}{8}$ $2\frac{6}{11}$ d) $2\frac{1}{5} \div 4\frac{2}{5}$ $\frac{1}{2}$

19. When you divide a fraction by its reciprocal, is the quotient less than 1, greater than 1, or equal to 1? Use examples in your explanation.

4.5 4.6 4.7 **20.** Find each product and quotient. What patterns do you see?
a) i) $\frac{3}{1} \times \frac{1}{2}$ $\frac{3}{2}$ ii) $\frac{3}{1} \div \frac{2}{1}$ $\frac{3}{2}$
b) i) $\frac{3}{4} \times \frac{2}{3}$ $\frac{1}{2}$ ii) $\frac{3}{4} \div \frac{3}{2}$ $\frac{1}{2}$
c) i) $\frac{4}{5} \times \frac{3}{4}$ $\frac{3}{5}$ ii) $\frac{4}{5} \div \frac{4}{3}$ $\frac{3}{5}$
d) i) $\frac{5}{6} \times \frac{2}{3}$ $\frac{5}{9}$ ii) $\frac{5}{6} \div \frac{3}{2}$ $\frac{5}{9}$

4.2 4.3 4.5 4.7 **21.** Evaluate.
a) $\frac{9}{8} - \frac{3}{4}$ $\frac{3}{8}$
b) $\frac{9}{8} + \frac{3}{4}$ $\frac{15}{8}$
c) $\frac{4}{3} \times \frac{5}{2}$ $\frac{10}{3} = 3\frac{1}{3}$
d) $\frac{17}{10} \div \frac{2}{5}$ $\frac{17}{4} = 4\frac{1}{4}$

4.8 **22.** Write each decimal as a fraction.
a) 0.25 $\frac{1}{4}$ b) 0.75 $\frac{3}{4}$
c) 0.32 $\frac{8}{25}$ d) 0.005 $\frac{1}{200}$

23. Write each fraction as a decimal.
a) $\frac{1}{8}$ 0.125 b) $\frac{3}{5}$ 0.6
c) $\frac{123}{250}$ 0.492 d) $\frac{19}{20}$ 0.95

24. Write each fraction as a decimal.
a) $\frac{2}{3}$ $0.\overline{6}$ b) $\frac{3}{7}$ $0.\overline{428\,571}$
c) $\frac{3}{13}$ $0.\overline{230\,769}$ d) $\frac{4}{11}$ $0.\overline{36}$

25. The tenths and hundredths digits of a decimal can be any digit from 0 to 9.
a) Write all the decimals that are greater than $\frac{1}{3}$ and less than $\frac{3}{4}$.
b) Order the decimals in part a from least to greatest.

4.9 **26.** Use mental math to divide.
a) $57.8 \div 0.01$ 5780
b) $0.882 \div 0.2$ 4.41
c) $1.374 \div 0.003$ 458

176 UNIT 4: Fractions and Decimals

ASSESSMENT FOR LEARNING

What to Look For

Knowledge and Understanding

✔ **Questions 11 and 13:** Student understands that a number line can be used to divide fractions and whole numbers.

✔ **Questions 22, 23, and 24:** Student understands how to use a calculator and mental math strategies to convert between fractions and decimals.

Thinking

✔ **Question 8:** Student can solve problems that require adding or subtracting fractions.

✔ **Questions 10 and 14:** Student can apply the algorithms for multiplying and dividing fractions to solve problems.

Communication

✔ **Question 15:** Student can describe the different possible quotients when a fraction is divided by a whole number.

Application

✔ **Questions 5 and 6:** Student can find a common denominator to add or subtract fractions.

✔ **Question 9:** Student can apply the area model to find the product of two fractions.

Recording and Reporting

Master 4.1 Unit Rubric: Fractions and Decimals
Master 4.4 Unit Summary: Fractions and Decimals

Practice Test

1. Evaluate.
   a) $\frac{7}{5}+\frac{3}{4}$ $\frac{43}{20}$ b) $\frac{13}{10}-\frac{2}{3}$ $\frac{19}{30}$
   c) $\frac{3}{7}\times\frac{4}{9}$ $\frac{4}{21}$ d) $\frac{5}{2}\div\frac{7}{6}$ $2\frac{1}{7}$
2. Which statement has the greatest value? How do you know?
   a) $\frac{7}{3}\times\frac{3}{4}$ b) $\frac{7}{3}-\frac{3}{4}$
   c) $\frac{7}{3}\div\frac{3}{4}$ d) $\frac{7}{3}+\frac{3}{4}$
3. Multiply a fraction by its reciprocal. What is the product? Use an example and an area model to explain.
4. a) Write $\frac{1}{7}$ as a decimal. $0.\overline{142\ 857}$
   b) What is the 2001st digit in the repeating decimal for $\frac{1}{7}$? Explain how you know.
5. Which number is added to the numerator and denominator of $\frac{2}{7}$ to get a fraction that is equivalent to $\frac{1}{2}$? Show your work. 3
6. Three-fifths of the Grade 8 class are in the band.
   a) On Tuesday, only $\frac{1}{3}$ of these students went to band practice. What fraction of the class went to band practice on Tuesday? $\frac{1}{5}$
   b) How many students might be in the class? How do you know?
7. Write each decimal as a fraction and each fraction as a decimal.
   a) $\frac{7}{8}$ 0.875 b) 0.64 $\frac{64}{100}=\frac{16}{25}$
   c) $\frac{5}{11}$ $0.\overline{45}$ d) 0.004 $\frac{4}{1000}=\frac{1}{250}$
8. a) Choose a proper fraction. Add 1 to the numerator and to the denominator. Write the new fraction. Which fraction is greater?
   b) Repeat part a for 3 more different fractions. Is your answer about the greater fraction always the same? Explain.

Practice Test 177

LESSON ORGANIZER

Student Materials

- 1-cm grid paper (PM 20)

Assessment: Master 4.1 Unit Rubric: Fractions and Decimals
Master 4.4 Unit Summary: Fractions and Decimals

Assignment Guidelines

To assess the 4 Achievement Chart categories listed in the curriculum document, use these test questions:
Knowledge and Understanding: 1
Communication: 3
Thinking: 5
Application: 8

Sample Solutions

2. a) The value is less than $\frac{7}{3}$ because $\frac{7}{3}$ is multiplied by a fraction less than 1.
   b) The value is less than $\frac{7}{3}$ because $\frac{3}{4}$ is subtracted from $\frac{7}{3}$.
   c) The value is greater than $\frac{7}{3}$ because $\frac{7}{3}$ is divided by a fraction less than 1.
   d) The value is greater than $\frac{7}{3}$ because $\frac{3}{4}$ is added to it.
   I calculated parts c and d:
   $\frac{7}{3}\div\frac{3}{4}=\frac{7}{3}\times\frac{4}{3}=\frac{28}{9}=3\frac{1}{9}$ $\frac{7}{3}+\frac{3}{4}=\frac{28}{12}+\frac{9}{12}=\frac{37}{12}=3\frac{1}{12}$
   $3\frac{1}{9}>3\frac{1}{12}$, so $\frac{7}{3}\div\frac{3}{4}$ has the greatest value.

3. The product is always 1. The product of the numerators is equal to the product of the denominators, so the product of a fraction and its reciprocal is equal to 1.
   For example: $\frac{2}{5}\times\frac{5}{2}=\frac{10}{10}=1$
   This can be illustrated using an area model:
   $\frac{2}{5}\times\frac{5}{2}=\frac{2}{5}\times 2\frac{1}{2}=\frac{10}{10}=1$

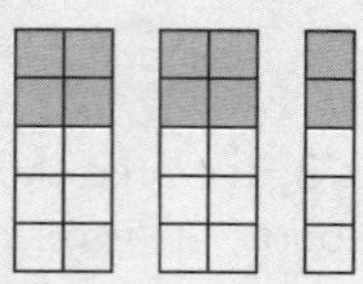

4. b) $\frac{1}{7}=0.142\ 857\ 142\ 857\ 142\ 857\ldots$
   (arrows marking the 6th, 12th, 18th digits)
   Every 6th digit is 7.
   Find the multiple of 6 closest to 2001.
   Divide: 2001 ÷ 6 = 333 R3
   So, the closest multiple is 6 × 333 = 1998.
   So, the 1998th term is 7, the 1999th term is 1, the 2000th term is 4, and the 2001st term is 2.

5. Use guess and check.
   Add 1: $\frac{2+1}{7+1}=\frac{3}{8}$
   Add 2: $\frac{2+2}{7+2}=\frac{4}{9}$
   Add 3: $\frac{2+3}{7+3}=\frac{5}{10}$, or $\frac{1}{2}$

6. a) $\frac{1}{3}$ of $\frac{3}{5}=\frac{1}{3}\times\frac{3}{5}=\frac{1}{5}$
   b) The number of students in the class must be a multiple of 3 and 5; for example, 15, 30, 45, 60, Thirty is the most reasonable class size.

8. a) For example: $\frac{2}{3}$
   $\frac{2+1}{3+1}=\frac{3}{4}$; $\frac{2}{3}=\frac{8}{12}$ and $\frac{3}{4}=\frac{9}{12}$
   $\frac{9}{12}>\frac{8}{12}$, so $\frac{3}{4}>\frac{2}{3}$; the new fraction is greater.
   b) For example: $\frac{4}{8}$ becomes $\frac{5}{9}$; $\frac{5}{7}$ becomes $\frac{6}{8}$; and $\frac{11}{12}$ becomes $\frac{12}{13}$
   The new fraction is always greater. In a proper fraction, the numerator is less than the denominator. So, adding 1 to each has a greater effect on the numerator than the denominator.

UNIT PROBLEM

Dividing a Square

LESSON ORGANIZER 80–100 min

Student Grouping: 2 or 3

Student Materials
- 1-cm grid paper (PM 20)
- 0.5-cm grid paper (PM 14)
- coloured pencils

Optional
- geoboards and geobands

Assessment: Master 4.3 Performance Assessment Rubric: Dividing a Square
Master 4.4 Unit Summary: Fractions and Decimals

Have students turn to pages 132 and 133 of the Student Book. Review *What You'll Learn,* the learning goals of the unit, and discuss the meanings of the Key Words. Tell students they will use the skills and concepts they learned in this unit to complete the *Unit Problem.*

Present the *Unit Problem.* Have one student read the *Check List* aloud. Remind students that they should use the *Check List* to assess their work before handing it in. You may also wish to provide students with copies of Master 4.3 Performance Assessment Rubric: Dividing a Square so they will know how their work will be assessed.

Unit Problem Dividing a Square

Part 1

Recall that hatch marks show equal line segments.

The side length of this square is 1 unit. Write the area of each of the 4 figures as a fraction of the area of the square.

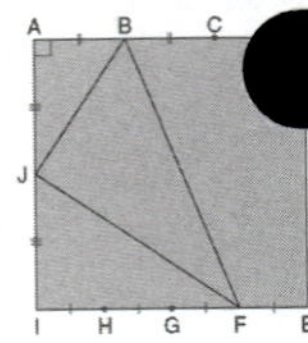

Show how you used multiplication of fractions to find the areas. Order the fractions from least to greatest.

Part 2

What fraction of each square is shaded green?

Square A

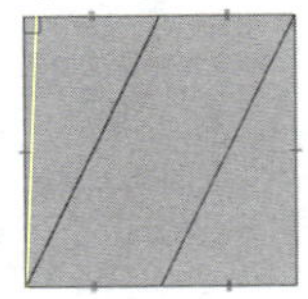

Square B

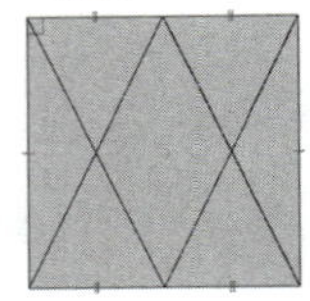

Square C

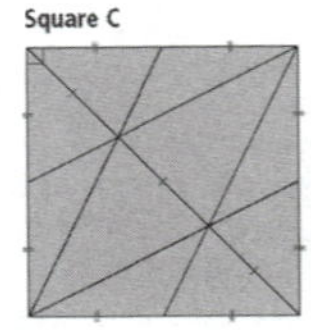

Square D

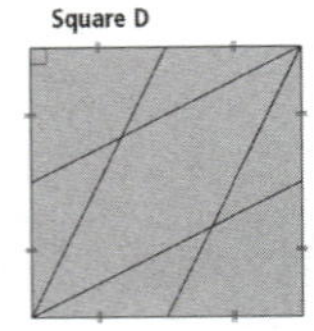

How did you use the addition or subtraction of fractions to find each fraction?

178 UNIT 4: Fractions and Decimals

Sample Response

Part 1

$\triangle$AJB has base $\frac{1}{3}$ and height $\frac{1}{2}$.
So, area $\triangle AJB = \frac{1}{2} \times \frac{1}{3} \times \frac{1}{2} = \frac{1}{12}$

$\triangle$JIF has base $\frac{3}{4}$ and height $\frac{1}{2}$.
So, area $\triangle JIF = \frac{1}{2} \times \frac{3}{4} \times \frac{1}{2} = \frac{3}{16}$

Trapezoid BDEF has parallel sides $\frac{2}{3}$ and $\frac{1}{4}$, and the distance between them is 1.

So, area of trapezoid BDEF $= \frac{1}{2}(\frac{2}{3} + \frac{1}{4}) \times 1$
$= \frac{1}{2}(\frac{11}{12})$
$= \frac{11}{24}$

The area of the square is 1.
The area of BFJ is the area of the square minus the areas of the other 3 figures:
$1 - \frac{1}{12} - \frac{3}{16} - \frac{11}{24} = 1 - \frac{4}{48} - \frac{9}{48} - \frac{22}{48} = \frac{13}{48}$ of the square
From least to greatest, the fractions representing the 4 areas are: $\frac{1}{12}, \frac{3}{16}, \frac{13}{48}, \frac{11}{24}$

Part 2

Square A: Shaded area = area of square − area of triangle on left − area of triangle on right
$= 1 - (\frac{1}{2} \times \frac{1}{2} \times 1) - (\frac{1}{2} \times \frac{1}{2} \times 1)$
$= 1 - \frac{1}{4} - \frac{1}{4}$
$= \frac{1}{2}$ of the square

Square B: The area shaded in Square A has been divided into 3 parts: the two smaller parts are congruent and not shaded; the large part is shaded and equal to $\frac{1}{2}$ the area of the shaded part in square A.
Shaded area = $\frac{1}{4}$ of the square
Square C: There are 6 triangles with a base on the diagonal.
Each triangle has base $\frac{1}{3}$ the length of the diagonal.
All triangles have the same height.
So, each triangle is $\frac{1}{6}$ the area of the square.
So, 2 triangles have area $\frac{1}{6} + \frac{1}{6} = \frac{1}{3}$ the area of the square.
Square D: Area shaded green = 1 − area shaded in square C
$= 1 - \frac{1}{3}$
$= \frac{2}{3}$ the area of the square

Part 3

Draw a large square with side length 1 unit.
Draw line segments to divide the square into different figures.
Find the area of each figure as a fraction of the area of the square.
Copy the square without the fractions.
Trade squares with a classmate.
For your classmate's square, write the area of each figure as a fraction of the area of the square.

Check List

Your work should show:

- ✓ how you used operations with fractions to solve the problems
- ✓ correct calculations and ordering of fractions
- ✓ an appropriate diagram of your problem
- ✓ clear explanations, with correct use of mathematical language

Reflect on the Unit

What do you know about fractions and decimals that you did not know before this unit? Use examples in your explanation.

Part 3

Students' responses may vary. Their reports should show how they divided a square, and calculated the areas.

REFLECT ON THE UNIT: I have learned several concepts about fractions and decimals that I did not know before:

- I learned how to use a number line to divide fractions.
- I learned two algorithms for dividing fractions:
  - find a common denominator, then divide the numerators; for example, $\frac{3}{8} \div \frac{3}{4} = \frac{3}{8} \div \frac{6}{8} = \frac{3}{6} = \frac{1}{2}$
  - multiply by the reciprocal; for example, $\frac{3}{8} \div \frac{3}{4} = \frac{3}{8} \times \frac{4}{3} = \frac{\cancel{3}^{1}}{\cancel{8}_{2}} \times \frac{\cancel{4}^{1}}{\cancel{3}_{1}} = \frac{1}{2}$

I also learned to think of dividing by 0.1, 0.01, and 0.001 as multiplying by 10, 100, and 1000; for example, $0.825 \div 0.01 = 0.825 \times 100 = 82.5$

ASSESSMENT FOR LEARNING

What to Look For

Knowledge and Understanding

✔ Students understand how to use operations with fractions to find a fraction of a square.

Thinking

✔ Students can develop strategies for determining the areas of the shaded sections.

Application

✔ Students can use prior knowledge of area formulas and substitute fractions for lengths.

What to Do

Extra Support: Make the problem accessible.

Some students may need to review the formulas for the areas of a triangle and a parallelogram.

Students could copy each square on grid paper, count squares to estimate or calculate the area, then write the area as a fraction of the square.

Recording and Reporting

Master 4.3 Performance Assessment Rubric: Dividing a Square
Master 4.4 Unit Summary: Fractions and Decimals

Units 1–4

LESSON ORGANIZER

Student Materials
- calculators
- linking cubes

Assessment: PM 9 Work Sample Records

Students can use this review to evaluate their progress in the mathematical content of Units 1 through 4.

Remind students that the unit containing the content required to answer each question is listed in red beside the question.

Encourage students to refer to the *Connect* sections of the relevant units.

Encourage students to draw on each other's skills as they work through the review.

Students who have identified areas in which they are strong may wish to act as volunteer tutors for students who require assistance.

Units 1–4 Cumulative Review

UNIT

1 **1.** The bird with the most feathers is the whistling swan.
It has 25 216 feathers.
The ruby-throated hummingbird has the fewest feathers.
It has 940 feathers.
a) How many more feathers does the whistling swan have than the ruby-throated hummingbird?
b) About how many hummingbirds together would have the same number of feathers as one whistling swan? Explain.

2. Write each number as a product of prime factors.
Use exponents where possible.
a) 38 2×19 b) 15 3×5
c) 252 $2^2 \times 3^2 \times 7$ d) 105 $3 \times 5 \times 7$

3. According to *Guinness World Records 2005*, the greatest number of dominoes set up single-handed and toppled is 303 621 out of 303 628 by Ma Li Hua, in 2003.
a) Write the number toppled in scientific notation. $3.036\ 21 \times 10^5$
b) Write the number set up in scientific notation. $3.036\ 28 \times 10^5$
c) What is the difference between the two numbers? 7
Why can we not write this difference in scientific notation?

4. Copy each statement.
Insert brackets to make each statement true.
a) $40 \div 5 + 3 \times (2^2 - 1) = 17$
b) $40 \div (5 + 3) \times 2^2 - 1 = 19$
c) $40 \div 5 + (3 \times 2)^2 - 1 = 43$
d) $40 \div (5 + 3) \times (2^2 - 1) = 15$

5. Twelve less than a number is 13.
Let x represent the number.
Then an equation is $x - 12 = 13$.
Solve the equation.
What is the number? 25

2 **6.** A primary class is going to the zoo. The ratio of adults to children must be 2:7. Twenty-eight children go on the zoo trip. How many adults are needed for supervision? 8 adults

7. The ostrich runs at 65 km/h.
At this rate, how far can the ostrich run in 90 s? About 1.625 km

8. There are 429 students registered at Woodside Public School.
On Wednesday, about 0.7% of the students were absent. About 3 students
a) How many students were absent?
b) What percent of students were at school? 99.3%

9. A salesperson earns commission at a rate of 8%. Last week, she earned \$450 commission. What were her total sales for the week? \$5625

180 Units 1–4

Sample Solutions

1. a) 24 276
b) $25\ 216 \div 940 \doteq 25\ 000 \div 1000 = 25$
About 25 hummingbirds together would have the same number of feathers as one whistling swan.

3. c) We cannot write this difference in scientific notation because we cannot write 7 as a product of two factors, with one factor a power of 10. The least number we can write in scientific notation is 10: 1.0×10^1.

5. $x - 12 = 13 \rightarrow x - 12 + 12 = 13 + 12 \rightarrow x = 25$

6. Let the number of adults needed for supervision be n.
Then, n:28 = 2:7
In fraction form: $\frac{n}{28} = \frac{2}{7}$
$\frac{n}{28} \times 28 = \frac{2}{7} \times 28 \rightarrow n = 2 \times 4 \rightarrow n = 8$

7. 1 h = 60 min
65 km/h = 65 km/60 min ≐ 1.083 km/min
90 s = 1.5 min
So, in 90 s, the ostrich can run about
1.083 km × 1.5 = 1.625 km

8. a) Number of students absent:
0.7% of 429 = 0.007 × 429 ≐ 3
b) Percent of students who were at school is:
100% – 0.7% = 99.3%

9. 8% of her total sales is \$450.
So, 1% of her total sales is: $\frac{\$450}{8}$
And, 100% of her total sales is: $\frac{\$450}{8} \times 100 = \$5625$

10. a) $I = \$500 \times 0.02 \times 1 = \$10$;
Amount = \$500 + \$10 = \$510
b) $I = \$2750 \times 0.035 \times 4 = \$385$;
Amount = \$2750 + \$385 = \$3135
c) 18 months = $1\frac{1}{2}$ years, or 1.5;
$I = \$4500 \times 0.0625 \times 1.5 \doteq \$421.88$
Amount = \$4500 + \$421.88 = \$4921.88

11.

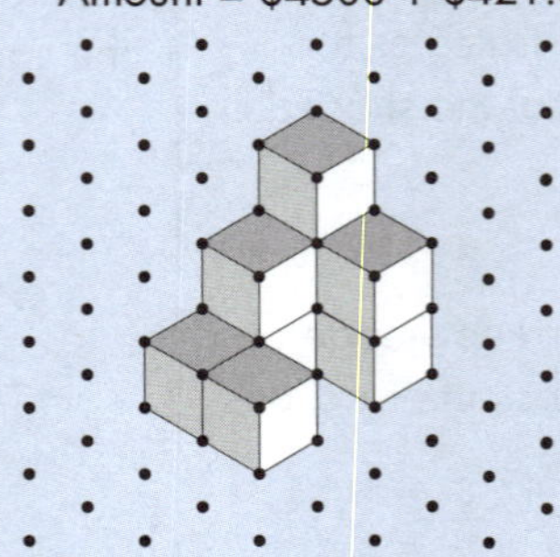

UNIT

Calculate the simple interest and the amount. $10; $510

a) $500 invested at an annual interest rate of 2% for 1 year

$385; $3135 b) $2750 invested at an annual interest rate of 3.5% for 4 years

c) $4500 invested at an annual interest rate of 6.25% for 18 months $421.88; $4921.88

11. Use 9 linking cubes.
Build an object.
Draw as many views as a classmate would need to build the object.
Trade views with a classmate.
Build your classmate's object.
Compare the object your classmate built from your views with the object you built.
Explain any differences.

12. Here is the net of a triangular prism.

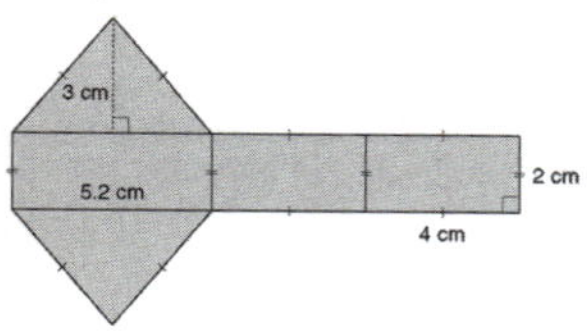

a) Calculate the surface area of the prism. 42 cm²

b) Calculate the volume of the prism. 15.6 cm³

13. The base of a triangular prism has base *b* and height *h*. The length of the prism is *l*.
What are the possible values of *b*, *h*, and *l* for a triangular prism:

a) with volume 12 cm³?

b) with volume 24 cm³?

14. Copy each pair of fractions.
Use <, >, or = to compare the fractions.

a) $\frac{2}{5} = \frac{6}{15}$ b) $\frac{1}{9} = \frac{2}{18}$

c) $\frac{8}{10} > \frac{3}{8}$ d) $\frac{2}{3} < \frac{4}{5}$

e) $\frac{3}{8} < \frac{2}{5}$ f) $\frac{5}{6} < \frac{6}{7}$

15. Add or subtract.

a) $\frac{2}{5} + \frac{1}{4}$ $\frac{13}{20}$ b) $\frac{3}{8} + \frac{1}{2}$ $\frac{7}{8}$

$\frac{5}{8}$ c) $\frac{7}{8} - \frac{1}{4}$ d) $\frac{1}{2} - \frac{1}{10}$ $\frac{2}{5}$

e) $5\frac{7}{9} - 2\frac{1}{4}$ $3\frac{19}{36}$ f) $3\frac{1}{3} + 1\frac{1}{8}$ $4\frac{11}{24}$

16. Which statement has the least value? c and f

a) $\frac{2}{3} + \frac{1}{6}$ $\frac{5}{6}$ b) $\frac{2}{3} - \frac{1}{6}$ $\frac{1}{2}$

$\frac{1}{9}$ c) $\frac{2}{3} \times \frac{1}{6}$ d) $\frac{2}{3} \div \frac{1}{6}$ 4

e) $\frac{1}{6} \div \frac{2}{3}$ $\frac{1}{4}$ f) $\frac{1}{6} \times \frac{2}{3}$ $\frac{1}{9}$

17. Write each fraction as a decimal.
Then order the decimals from least to greatest.

a) $\frac{13}{50}$ 0.26 b) $\frac{1}{4}$ 0.25 c) $\frac{51}{200}$ 0.255 d) $\frac{3}{11}$ $0.\overline{27}$

18. Find each quotient.

a) $\frac{3275}{0.1}$ 32 750 b) $\frac{3275}{0.01}$ 327 500

3 275 000 c) $\frac{3275}{0.001}$ d) $\frac{3275}{0.5}$ 6550

e) $\frac{3275}{0.05}$ 65 500 f) $\frac{3275}{0.005}$ 655 000

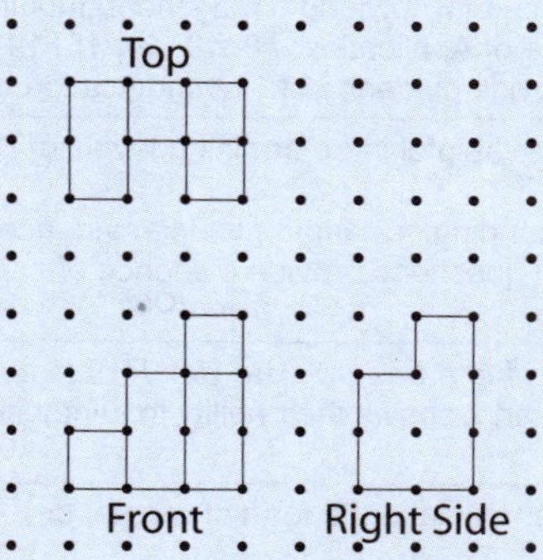

12. a) $SA = al + bl + cl + bh$
Substitute $a = 4$, $b = 5.2$, $c = 4$, $l = 2$, $h = 3$
$SA = (4 \times 2) + (5.2 \times 2) + (4 \times 2) + (5.2 \times 3)$
$= 42$
The surface area of the prism is 42 cm².

b) $V = \frac{1}{2}bhl = \frac{1}{2} \times 5.2 \times 3 \times 2$
$= 15.6$
The volume of the prism is 15.6 cm³.

13. a) $\frac{1}{2}bhl = 12$, so $bhl = 24$
Find whole-number values of *b*, *h*, and *l* that have a product of 24.
For example, $b = 4$ cm, $h = 3$ cm, $l = 2$ cm or $b = 6$ cm, $h = 2$ cm, $l = 2$ cm

b) $\frac{1}{2}bhl = 24$, so $bhl = 48$
Find whole-number values of *b*, *h*, and *l* that have a product of 48.
For example, $b = 4$ cm, $h = 4$ cm, $l = 3$ cm or $b = 8$ cm, $h = 2$ cm, $l = 3$ cm

17. From least to greatest: 0.25, 0.255, 0.26, $0.\overline{27}$

Evaluating Student Learning: Preparing to Report: Unit 4 Fractions and Decimals

This unit provides an opportunity to report on the **Number Sense and Numeration** strand.

Master 4.4: Unit Summary: Fractions and Decimals provides a comprehensive format for recording and summarizing evidence collected.

Here is an example of a completed summary chart for this Unit:

Strand: *Number Sense and Numeration*	**Knowledge and Understanding**	**Thinking**	**Communication**	**Application**	***Overall***
Ongoing Observations	3	3	3	4	3
Work samples or portfolios; conferences	3	2	3	3	3
Unit Review	3	3	2	3	3
Unit Test	2	3	3	2	2/3
Unit Problem Dividing a Square	3	3	3	3	3
Achievement Level for reporting					3

Recording	**How to Report**
Ongoing Observations	Use *Master 4.2 Ongoing Observations: Fractions and Decimals* to determine the most consistent level achieved in each category. Enter it in the chart. Choose to summarize by achievement category, or simply to enter an overall level. Observations from late in the unit should be most heavily weighted.
Portfolios or collections of work samples; conferences or interviews	Use *Master 4.1 Unit Rubric: Fractions and Decimals* to guide evaluation of collections of work and information gathered in conferences. Teachers may choose to focus particular attention on the Assessment Focus questions. Work from late in the unit should be most heavily weighted.
Unit Review	*Master 4.1 Unit Rubric: Fractions and Decimals* may be helpful in determining levels of achievement. #1, 3, 4, 5, 6, 7, 11, 13, 22, 23, and 24 provide evidence of Knowledge and Understanding; #2, 5, 6, 9, 12, 16, 17, 18, 20, and 21 provide evidence of Application; #8, 10, 14, 15, 19, and 25 provide evidence of Thinking; all questions provide evidence of Communication.
Unit Test	*Master 4.1 Unit Rubric: Fractions and Decimals* may be helpful in determining levels of achievement. #1 and 4 provide evidence of Knowledge and Understanding; #2 and 3 provide evidence of Application; #6 and 8 provide evidence of Thinking; all questions provide evidence of Communication.
Unit performance task	Use *Master 4.3 Performance Assessment Rubric: Dividing a Square*. The *Unit Problem* offers a snapshot of students' achievement. In particular, it shows their ability to synthesize and apply what they have learned.
Student Self-Assessment	Note students' perceptions of their own progress. This may take the form of an oral or written comment, or a self-rating.
Comments	Analyse the pattern of achievement to identify strengths and needs. In some cases, specific actions may need to be planned to support the learner.

Learning Skills	**Ongoing Records**
PM 4: Learning Skills Check List Use to record and report throughout a reporting period, rather than for each unit and/or strand.	*PM 10: Summary Class Records: Strands* *PM 11: Summary Class Records: Achievement Categories* *PM 12: Summary Record: Individual* Use to record and report evaluations of student achievement over several clusters, a reporting period, or a school year. These can also be used in place of the Unit Summary.

Name ____________________ Date ____________

Master 4.1

Unit Rubric: Fractions and Decimals

	Level 1	Level 2	Level 3	Level 4
Knowledge and Understanding • Shows understanding by demonstrating and explaining: – use of equivalent fractions to compare, order, add, and subtract – use of models to multiply and divide fractions	shows limited understanding; may be unable to demonstrate or explain: – use of equivalent fractions to compare, order, add, and subtract – use of models to multiply and divide fractions	shows some understanding; partially able to demonstrate or explain: – use of equivalent fractions to compare, order, add, and subtract – use of models to multiply and divide fractions	shows considerable understanding; able to clearly and appropriately demonstrate or explain: – use of equivalent fractions to compare, order, add, and subtract – use of models to multiply and divide fractions	shows a high degree of understanding; able to accurately and effectively demonstrate or explain: – use of equivalent fractions to compare, order, add, and subtract – use of models to multiply and divide fractions
Thinking • Chooses and carries out a range of appropriate strategies to pose, solve, and check problems involving fractions and decimals	with assistance, chooses, carries out, and justifies a limited range of appropriate strategies to pose, solve, and check problems; rarely produces an accurate solution	with limited assistance, chooses, carries out, and justifies some appropriate strategies to pose, solve, and check problems; frequently produces an accurate solution	chooses, carries out, and justifies many appropriate strategies to pose, solve, and check problems; usually produces an accurate solution	develops, carries out, and justifies effective, and often innovative, strategies to pose, solve, and check problems; always produces an accurate solution
Communication • Explains concepts, procedures, and reasoning clearly, using appropriate terms • Presents work clearly	unable to explain concepts, procedures, and reasoning clearly presents work with little clarity	partially explains concepts, procedures, and reasoning presents work with some clarity and precision	explains concepts, procedures, and reasoning clearly presents work with considerable clarity and precision	explains concepts, procedures, and reasoning clearly, precisely, and confidently presents work with a high degree of clarity and precision
Application • Accurately: – compares and orders fractions – adds and subtracts fractions – multiplies and divides fractions by a whole number, and by a fraction – converts between fractions and decimals – divides by 0.1, 0.01, 0.001	limited accuracy; major errors or omissions in: – comparing and ordering fractions – adding, subtracting, multiplying, and dividing fractions – converting between fractions and decimals – dividing by 0.1, 0.01, 0.001	somewhat accurate; several minor errors or omissions in: – comparing and ordering fractions – adding, subtracting, multiplying, and dividing fractions – converting between fractions and decimals – dividing by 0.1 0.01, 0.001	generally accurate; few minor errors or omissions in: – comparing and ordering fractions – adding, subtracting, multiplying, and dividing fractions – converting between fractions and decimals – dividing by 0.1, 0.01, 0.001	accurate and precise; no errors in: – comparing and ordering fractions – adding, subtracting, multiplying, and dividing fractions – converting between fractions and decimals – dividing by 0.1, 0.01, 0.001

Name ____________________ Date ________________

Master 4.2

Ongoing Observations: Fractions and Decimals

The behaviours described under each heading are examples; they are not intended to be an exhaustive list of all that might be observed. More detailed descriptions are provided in each lesson under *Assessment for Learning*.

STUDENT ACHIEVEMENT: Fractions and Decimals				
Student	**Knowledge and Understanding** • Demonstrates and explains: – use of equivalent fractions – use of models to multiply and divide	**Thinking** • Chooses, carries out, and justifies a range of appropriate strategies to pose, solve, and check problems; usually results in accurate solution	**Communication** • Explains concepts, procedures, and reasoning clearly • Presents work clearly	**Application** • Accurately: – compares, orders, adds, subtracts, multiplies, and divides fractions – converts between fractions and decimals – divides by 0.1, 0.01, 0.001

Level 1 – very limited; Level 2 – somewhat or limited; Level 3 – satisfactory; Level 4 – thorough

Name ____________________ Date ________________

Master 4.3

Performance Assessment Rubric: Dividing a Square

	Level 1	Level 2	Level 3	Level 4
Knowledge and Understanding • Shows understanding of fractions by demonstrating or explaining the procedures used, and justifying choice of procedures	shows limited understanding; may be unable to explain or justify procedures	shows some understanding; gives appropriate but incomplete explanations and justifications of procedures	shows considerable understanding by giving appropriate and complete explanations and justifications of procedures	shows a high degree of understanding by giving appropriate and thorough explanations and justifications of procedures
Thinking • Successfully uses appropriate strategies to solve and create the required problems involving fractions	uses a limited range of appropriate strategies to solve and create the required problems; little success	uses some appropriate strategies to solve and create the required problems; partially successful	uses many appropriate strategies to solve and create the required problems; considerable success	uses innovative and effective strategies to solve and create the required problems; highly successful
Communication • Explains reasoning clearly using appropriate mathematical terminology • Presents work clearly, including diagrams	explains reasoning unclearly and imprecisely using few mathematical terms presents work with little clarity	explains reasoning with some clarity using some appropriate mathematical terms presents work with some clarity	explains reasoning clearly and precisely using appropriate mathematical terms presents work clearly	explains reasoning clearly, precisely, and confidently using a range of appropriate mathematical terminology presents work clearly and precisely
Application • Accurately: – adds and subtracts fractions – multiplies a fraction by a whole number	limited accuracy; major errors or omissions in: – adding and subtracting fractions – multiplying a fraction by a whole number	somewhat accurate; several minor errors or omissions in: – adding and subtracting fractions – multiplying a fraction by a whole number	generally accurate; few minor errors or omissions in: – adding and subtracting fractions – multiplying a fraction by a whole number	accurate and precise; with no errors or omissions in: – adding and subtracting fractions – multiplying a fraction by a whole number

Name ____________________ Date ________________

Master 4.4

Unit Summary: Fractions and Decimals

Review assessment records to determine the most consistent achievement levels for the assessments conducted. Some cells may be blank. *Overall* achievement levels may be recorded in each row, rather than identifying levels for each achievement category.

	Most Consistent Level of Achievement*				
Strand: *Number Sense and Numeration*	**Knowledge and Understanding**	**Thinking**	**Communication**	**Application**	***Overall***
Ongoing Observations					
Work samples or portfolios; conferences					
Unit Review					
Unit Test					
Unit Problem Dividing a Square					
Achievement Level for reporting					

*Use Ontario Achievement Levels 1, 2, 3, 4

Self-Assessment:

Comments: (Strengths, Needs, Next Steps)

Name ______________________ Date ________________

Master 4.5

Additional Activity 1: Fraction 50

Play with a partner.

Materials: 15 counters per player (two different colours); *Fraction 50* game board (Master 4.5b); pencil and paper

How to Play:

Decide which player will go first.

1. Player A chooses a square on the board, and places a counter on that square.
   She calculates the answer and records it on paper.
2. Player B chooses a square, places his counter on that square, then calculates the answer.
3. Player A chooses another square. After calculating the answer, she adds the answer to her previous total.
4. Play continues until one player reaches 50.
5. Play another round, this time switching who plays first.

Variations:
The winner must get a score of exactly 50.
Choose a number greater than 50 as the goal.

Take It Further: Play the game again.
This time, players must correctly answer the question before placing a counter on a square.
The first player to get 4 counters in a row horizontally, vertically, or diagonally wins the game.

Name ____________________ Date ________________

Master 4.5b

Fraction 50 Game Board

$\frac{1}{2}$ of 20	$\frac{1}{3} \times 18$	$\frac{3}{4}$ of 12	$\frac{2}{10} \times 110$
$\frac{4}{5}$ of 5	$\frac{3}{2}$ of 6	$\frac{5}{6}$ of 12	$\frac{1}{12}$ of 60
$\frac{3}{8} \times 24$	$\frac{4}{3}$ of 3	$\frac{9}{10} \times 10$	$\frac{2}{5}$ of 15
$\frac{8}{3} \times 3$	$\frac{5}{10}$ of 16	$\frac{1}{9}$ of 36	$\frac{1}{20} \times 200$
$\frac{2}{3}$ of 9	$\frac{1}{50} \times 200$	$\frac{7}{8} \times 8$	$\frac{4}{10}$ of 20

Name ______________________ Date ________________

Master 4.6

Additional Activity 2: Fraction-Part-Whole Concentration

Play with a partner.

Materials: *Fraction-Part-Whole Concentration* game cards (Master 4.6b), pencil and paper

How to Play:

Cut out the cards. Separate them into fractions, parts, and wholes.
Decide which player will go first.

1. Shuffle each set of cards. Place each set of cards face down in a horizontal line.
2. Player A turns over 3 cards, one card from each row.
   He looks for a match of a fraction, a part, and a whole.
   For example, $\frac{1}{3}$, 7, and 21 is a match because $\frac{1}{3}$ of 21 is 7.
   ($\frac{1}{3}$ is the fraction, 7 is the part, and 21 is the whole.)
3. If no match is found, Player A turns all the cards back over.
4. Player B turns over 3 cards, looking for a match.
5. If a match is found, the player keeps those cards, and has another turn.
6. When all the matches have been found, the player with the most cards wins.

Take It Further: Create your own set of game cards, then play the game again.

Name ____________________ Date ________________

Master 4.6b

Fraction-Part-Whole Concentration Game Cards

$\frac{2}{3}$	$\frac{1}{6}$	$\frac{4}{3}$	$\frac{5}{8}$	$\frac{7}{5}$	$\frac{9}{10}$	$\frac{3}{5}$
40 Part	8 Part	144 Part	45 Part	49 Part	90 Part	12 Part
60 Whole	48 Whole	108 Whole	72 Whole	35 Whole	100 Whole	20 Whole

Name ______________ Date ______________

Master 4.7

Step-by-Step 1

Lesson 4.1, Question 7

Step 1 Divide this number line into thirds. Label the fractions.

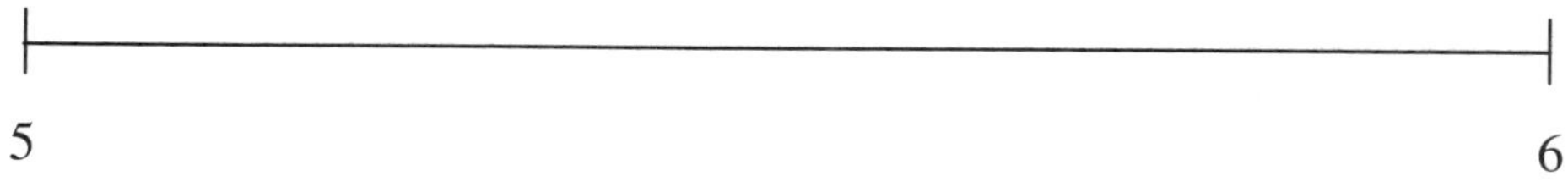

List fractions between 5 and 6: ______________________________

Step 2 Divide this number line into fifths. Label the fractions.

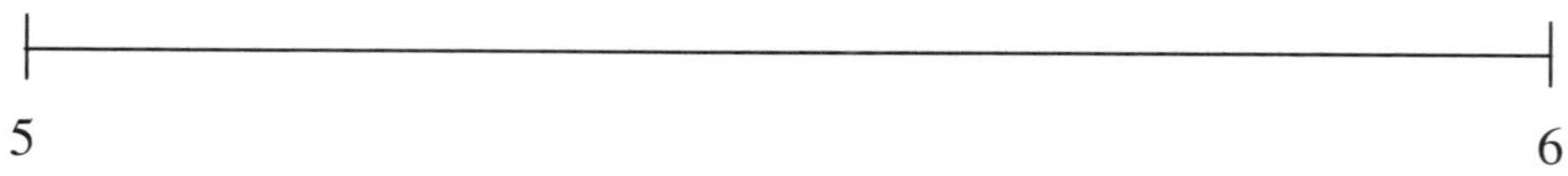

List fractions between 5 and 6: ______________________________

Step 3 Divide this number line into eighths. Label the fractions.

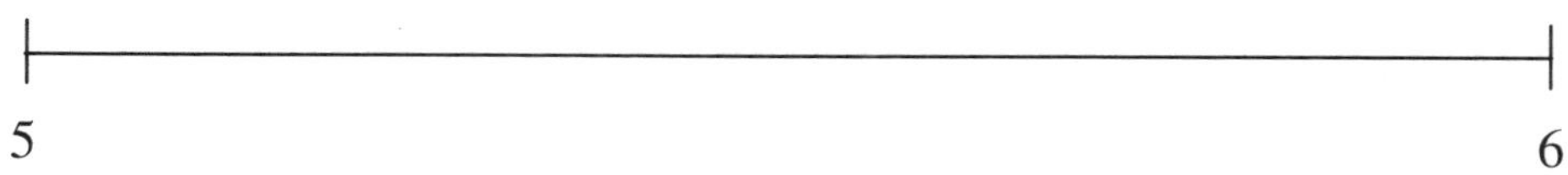

List fractions between 5 and 6: ______________________________

Step 4 How else could you divide the number line between 5 and 6?

____

____

Step 5 Have you found all the fractions between 5 and 6? ______________
How do you know?

____

____

Name ____________________ Date ________________

Master 4.8

Step-by-Step 2

Lesson 4.2, Question 5

Step 1 Fill in the numerators.

Find two different pairs of fractions that add to $\frac{4}{5}$.

$\frac{\quad}{5} + \frac{\quad}{5} = \frac{4}{5}$ $\qquad$ $\frac{\quad}{5} + \frac{\quad}{5} = \frac{4}{5}$

Step 2 Use one sum from *Step 1*.
Write an equivalent fraction for one fraction in the sum.
Write the new sum.

$\frac{\quad}{5} \overset{\times}{=} \frac{\quad}{\quad}$ $\qquad$ $\frac{\quad}{\quad} + \frac{\quad}{5} = \frac{4}{5}$

Step 3 Repeat *Step 2* to find more equivalent fractions.
This time, write equivalent fractions for both fractions that are added.

$\frac{\quad}{5} \overset{\times}{=} \frac{\quad}{\quad}$ $\qquad$ $\frac{\quad}{5} \overset{\times}{=} \frac{\quad}{\quad}$ $\qquad$ $\frac{\quad}{\quad} + \frac{\quad}{\quad} = \frac{4}{5}$

Step 4 Repeat *Steps 1–3* for each of parts b and c.

Name ____________________ Date ______________

Master 4.9

Step-by-Step 3

Lesson 4.3, Question 5

Step 1 The numerator of the first fraction is 2.
Write 3, 4, and 5 in the other boxes.
Do this as many different ways as you can.

$$\frac{2}{\square} - \frac{\square}{\square}; \quad \frac{2}{\square} - \frac{\square}{\square}; \quad \frac{2}{\square} - \frac{\square}{\square}$$

$$\frac{2}{\square} - \frac{\square}{\square}; \quad \frac{2}{\square} - \frac{\square}{\square}; \quad \frac{2}{\square} - \frac{\square}{\square}$$

Step 2 Draw 6 more sets of boxes like those in *Step 1*.
Write 3 as the numerator of the first fraction.
Write 2, 4, and 5 in the other boxes, as many different ways as you can.

Step 3 Repeat *Step 2* with 4 in the numerator of the first fraction.
Arrange 2, 3, and 5 in the other boxes.

Step 4 Repeat *Step 2* with 5 in the numerator of the first fraction.
Arrange 2, 3, and 4 in the other boxes.

Step 5 Look at the subtraction statements in *Steps 1* to *4*.
Identify where the first fraction is greater than the second.
Calculate each difference.

Step 6 Which statement has the greatest difference? ______________________________

Which statement has the least difference? ______________________________

Name ______________ Date ______________

Master 4.10

Step-by-Step 4

Lesson 4.4, Question 4

Step 1 Use the rectangle to show each product:

$\frac{3}{4} \times \frac{2}{5} =$ $\frac{2}{4} \times \frac{3}{5} =$

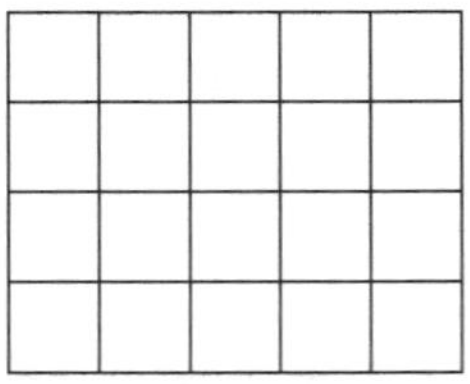

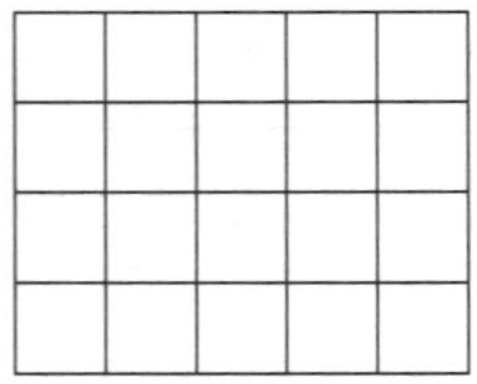

Step 2 Repeat *Step 1* for these products:

$\frac{1}{4} \times \frac{3}{8} =$ $\frac{3}{4} \times \frac{1}{8} =$

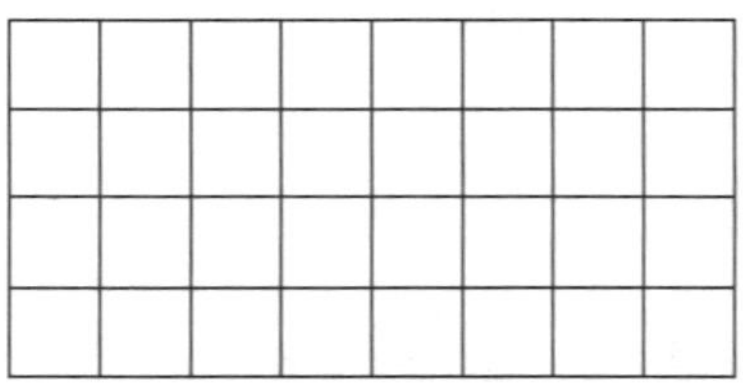

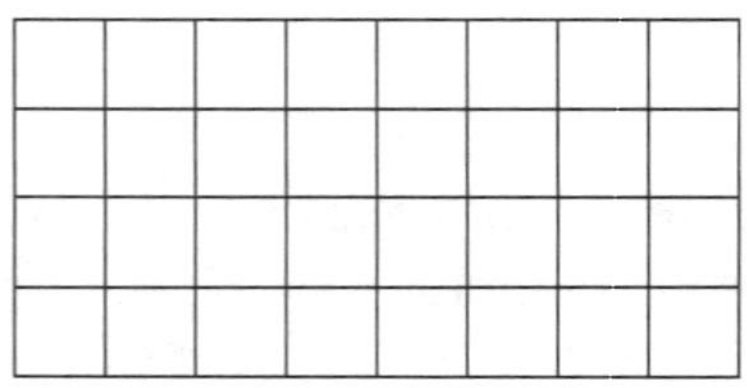

Step 3 Use grid paper. Draw a rectangle for each product:
$\frac{3}{5} \times \frac{4}{6}$ and $\frac{3}{6} \times \frac{4}{5}$
Look at all the rectangles you shaded.
What patterns do you see in the multiplication statements?

____

What patterns do you see when you compare the rectangles in each pair?

____

Step 4 Write two multiplication statements similar to those in *Steps 1* and *2*.
Use grid paper to check if you continued the pattern. How will you know?

____

____

Name ____________________ Date ________________

Master 4.11

Step-by-Step 5

Lesson 4.5, Question 8

Step 1 Find what you multiply $\frac{2}{3}$ by to get each product.

$\frac{2}{3} \times \frac{\square}{\square} = 1$; $\frac{2}{3} \times \frac{\square}{\square} = 2$; $\frac{2}{3} \times \frac{\square}{\square} = 3$; $\frac{2}{3} \times \frac{\square}{\square} = 4$; $\frac{2}{3} \times \frac{\square}{\square} = 5$

Step 2 Start with $\frac{3}{4} \times \frac{4}{3} = \frac{12}{12} = 1$.
Change a numerator to get:

$\frac{\square}{4} \times \frac{4}{3} = 2$; $\frac{\square}{4} \times \frac{4}{3} = 3$; $\frac{\square}{4} \times \frac{4}{3} = 4$; $\frac{\square}{4} \times \frac{4}{3} = 5$

Step 3 Start with $\frac{1}{60} \times \frac{60}{1} = \frac{60}{60} = 1$.
Change a denominator to get:

$\frac{1}{\square} \times \frac{60}{1} = 2$; $\frac{1}{\square} \times \frac{60}{1} = 3$; $\frac{1}{\square} \times \frac{60}{1} = 4$; $\frac{1}{\square} \times \frac{60}{1} = 5$

Step 4 Use the patterns in *Steps 2* or *3*.
Write a pair of fractions that has the product 10.

$\frac{\square}{\square} \times \frac{\square}{\square} = 10$

Name ____________________ Date ________________

Master 4.12

Step-by-Step 6

Lesson 4.6, Question 7

Step 1 Start with 2 as the dividend.
Write 4 and 6 in the other boxes, in as many different ways as you can.
Find each quotient.

$\boxed{2} \div \dfrac{\square}{\square} =$ _____ $\boxed{2} \div \dfrac{\square}{\square} =$ _____

Step 2 Repeat *Step 1* with 4 as the dividend.
Write 2 and 6 in the other boxes, in as many different ways as you can.

$\boxed{4} \div \dfrac{\square}{\square} =$ _____ $\boxed{4} \div \dfrac{\square}{\square} =$ _____

Step 3 Repeat *Step 1* with 6 as the dividend.
Write 2 and 4 in the other boxes, in as many different ways as you can.

$\boxed{6} \div \dfrac{\square}{\square} =$ _____ $\boxed{6} \div \dfrac{\square}{\square} =$ _____

Step 4 Which quotient above is the greatest? ______________________________

Step 5 Which quotient above is the least? ______________________________

Step 6 How could you have completed *Steps 4* and *5* without first completing *Steps 1* to *3*?

____

____

Name ____________________ Date ________________

Master 4.13

Step-by-Step 7

Lesson 4.7, Question 7

Step 1 The numerator of the first fraction is 2. Write 3, 4, and 5 in the other boxes. Do this as many different ways as you can.
Find each quotient.

$\frac{2}{\square} \div \frac{\square}{\square} =$; $\frac{2}{\square} \div \frac{\square}{\square} =$; $\frac{2}{\square} \div \frac{\square}{\square} =$

$\frac{2}{\square} \div \frac{\square}{\square} =$; $\frac{2}{\square} \div \frac{\square}{\square} =$; $\frac{2}{\square} \div \frac{\square}{\square} =$

Step 2 Draw 6 sets of boxes like those in *Step 1*. Write 3 as the numerator of the first fraction. Write 2, 4, and 5 in the other boxes, as many different ways as you can.
Find each quotient.

Step 3 Repeat *Step 2* with 4 in the numerator of the first fraction.
Arrange 2, 3, and 5 in the other boxes. Find the quotients.

Step 4 Repeat *Step 2* with 5 in the numerator of the first fraction.
Arrange 2, 3, and 4 in the other boxes. Find the quotients.

Step 5 Which quotient is greatest? ______________________________

What patterns do you see? ______________________________

____

Step 6 Which quotient is least? ______________________________

What patterns do you see? ______________________________

____

Name ____________________ Date ________________

Master 4.14

Step-by-Step 8

Lesson 4.8, Question 8

Here is the Fibonacci sequence: 1, 1, 2, 3, 5, 8, 13, 21, 34, 55, 89, …

Step 1 Write each fraction in the table as a decimal.

$\frac{1}{1}$	$\frac{2}{1}$	$\frac{3}{2}$	$\frac{5}{3}$	$\frac{8}{5}$	$\frac{13}{8}$

Step 2 Look at the decimals in the table.
What patterns do you see in the decimals?

____

____

Step 3 Extend the table using the Fibonacci sequence.
Continue to write consecutive terms as fractions.

$\frac{21}{13}$	$\frac{34}{21}$				

Step 4 Complete the tables. Write each fraction as a decimal.
Do the patterns in the table in *Step 1* continue? Explain.

____

____

What number do the decimals appear to get closer and closer to?

____

Name ____________________ Date ______________

Master 4.15

Step-by-Step 9

Lesson 4.9, Question 5

A student says that when you divide two numbers,
the quotient is always less than the dividend.
Is this true?
Use examples to explain your answer.

15	÷	3	=	5
↑		↑		↑
dividend		divisor		quotient

Use a calculator.

Step 1 Check whole numbers, where the dividend is greater than the divisor.
Find each quotient.

$100 \div 10 =$ ______ $50 \div 5 =$ ______ $144 \div 36 =$ ______

Is the quotient less than the dividend? __________

Step 2 Check whole numbers, where the dividend is less than the divisor.
Find each quotient.

$5 \div 10 =$ ______ $2 \div 3 =$ ______ $100 \div 1000 =$ ______

Is the quotient less than the dividend? ___________

Step 3 Check a whole number dividend, and a divisor less than 1.
Find each quotient.

$125 \div 0.1 =$ ______ $18 \div 0.5 =$ ______ $0.58 \div 0.01 =$ ______

Is the quotient less than the dividend? ___________

Step 4 Is the student's statement true? ______________________________________
Explain.

____

____

Name ____________________ Date ________________

Master 4.16a

Unit Test: Unit 4
Fractions and Decimals

1. Evaluate.

a) $\frac{7}{3} + \frac{2}{5}$

b) $\frac{8}{10} - \frac{1}{3}$

c) $\frac{4}{7} \times \frac{2}{3}$

d) $\frac{5}{2} \div \frac{3}{4}$

e) $2\frac{1}{4} + 3\frac{2}{5}$

f) $6\frac{3}{4} - 2\frac{5}{6}$

2. Antoine estimates he can read one chapter of a novel in $1\frac{1}{4}$ h.

Jenna estimates she can read three chapters of the same novel in $2\frac{5}{6}$ h.

Antoine read for 8 h. Jenna read for 6 h.
Who read more chapters? Show your work.

Name ______________________ Date ________________

Master 4.16b

Unit Test continued

3. There are 496 students in the school.
One-quarter of the students have green eyes.
Three-eighths of the students have blue eyes.
Five-sixteenths of the students have brown eyes.

a) How many students have brown eyes?

b) What is the most common eye colour among the students? How do you know?

c) What fraction of the students do not have brown, blue, or green eyes?

4. Write each fraction as a decimal, and each decimal as a fraction:

a) $\frac{3}{8}$ **b)** $\frac{6}{7}$ **c)** $\frac{1}{22}$

d) 0.063 **e)** 0.31 **f)** 0.0003

5. Which number is subtracted from the numerator and denominator of $\frac{11}{17}$ to get a fraction that is equivalent to $\frac{1}{4}$? Show your work.

Name ____________________ Date ________________

Master 4.16c

Unit Test continued

6. A small glass holds $\frac{3}{5}$ cup of water.

A jug holds 10 cups of water.

a) How many small glasses can be filled from the water in the jug?

b) A large glass holds $\frac{5}{6}$ cup of water.

Suppose you have 8 cups of water.
You want to fill both sizes of glasses.
How many of each size glass could you fill?
Show your work.

7. Evaluate.

a) $84.6 \div 0.002$ **b)** $1.422 \div 0.02$ **c)** 0.0036×20

8. When you divide a proper fraction by an improper fraction, is the quotient less than 1, greater than 1, or equal to 1? Use examples in your explanation.

Name ______________________ Date ________________

Master 4.17

Sample Answers

Unit Test – Master 4.16

1. **a)** $\frac{7}{3} + \frac{2}{5} = \frac{35}{15} + \frac{6}{15} = \frac{41}{15}$ **b)** $\frac{8}{10} - \frac{1}{3} = \frac{24}{30} - \frac{10}{30} = \frac{14}{30} = \frac{7}{15}$ **c)** $\frac{4}{7} \times \frac{2}{3} = \frac{8}{21}$

d) $\frac{5}{2} \div \frac{3}{4} = \frac{10}{4} \div \frac{3}{4} = \frac{10}{3}$ **e)** $2\frac{1}{4} + 3\frac{2}{5} = \frac{9}{4} + \frac{17}{5} = \frac{45}{20} + \frac{68}{20} = \frac{113}{20} = 5\frac{13}{20}$

f) $6\frac{3}{4} - 2\frac{5}{6} = \frac{27}{4} - \frac{17}{6} = \frac{81}{12} - \frac{34}{12} = \frac{47}{12} = 3\frac{11}{12}$

2. Antoine: $8 \div 1\frac{1}{4} = 8 \div \frac{5}{4} = 8 \times \frac{4}{5} = \frac{32}{5} = 6\frac{2}{5}$; Antoine read $6\frac{2}{5}$ chapters in 8 h.

Jenna: $6 \div 2\frac{5}{6} = 6 \div \frac{17}{6} = 6 \times \frac{6}{17} = \frac{36}{17} = 2\frac{2}{17}$; since Jenna reads 3 chapters in $2\frac{5}{6}$ h,

she read $2\frac{2}{17} \times 3 = 6\frac{6}{17}$ chapters in 6 h.

Compare $\frac{2}{5}$ and $\frac{6}{17}$: $\frac{2}{5} = \frac{34}{85}$ and $\frac{6}{17} = \frac{30}{85}$

$\frac{34}{85} > \frac{30}{85}$, so $\frac{2}{5} > \frac{6}{17}$

So, Antoine read more chapters.

3. **a)** $\frac{5}{16}$ of $496 = \frac{5}{16} \times 496 = 155$; 155 students have brown eyes.

b) Compare $\frac{1}{4}$, $\frac{3}{8}$, and $\frac{5}{16}$. The lowest common denominator is 16 because 4 and 8 are factors of 16. $\frac{1}{4} = \frac{4}{16}$; $\frac{3}{8} = \frac{6}{16}$; $\frac{5}{16}$

$\frac{3}{8}$ is the greatest fraction, so blue is the most common eye colour.

c) $1 - \frac{1}{4} - \frac{3}{8} - \frac{5}{16} = 1 - \frac{4}{16} - \frac{6}{16} - \frac{5}{16} = 1 - \frac{15}{16} = \frac{1}{16}$; $\frac{1}{16}$ of the students do not have brown, blue, or green eyes.

4. **a)** 0.375 **b)** $0.\overline{857\,142}$ **c)** $0.0\overline{45}$ **d)** $\frac{63}{1000}$ **e)** $\frac{31}{100}$ **f)** $\frac{3}{10\,000}$

5. $\frac{11-9}{17-9} = \frac{2}{8} = \frac{1}{4}$; 9 is subtracted from the numerator and denominator.

6. **a)** $10 \div \frac{3}{5} = 10 \times \frac{5}{3} = \frac{50}{3} = 16\frac{2}{3}$; $16\frac{2}{3}$ small glasses can be filled.

b) 5 small glasses and 6 large glasses can be filled with exactly 8 cups of water;

$5 \times \frac{3}{5} + 6 \times \frac{5}{6} = 3 + 5 = 8$

7. **a)** 42 300 **b)** 71.1 **c)** 0.072

8. The quotient will always be less than 1.
A proper fraction is less than 1. An improper fraction is greater than 1. A number less than 1, divided by a number greater than 1, will always be less than 1.

Name ____________________ Date ________________

Master 4.18

Unit Launch, Step 4

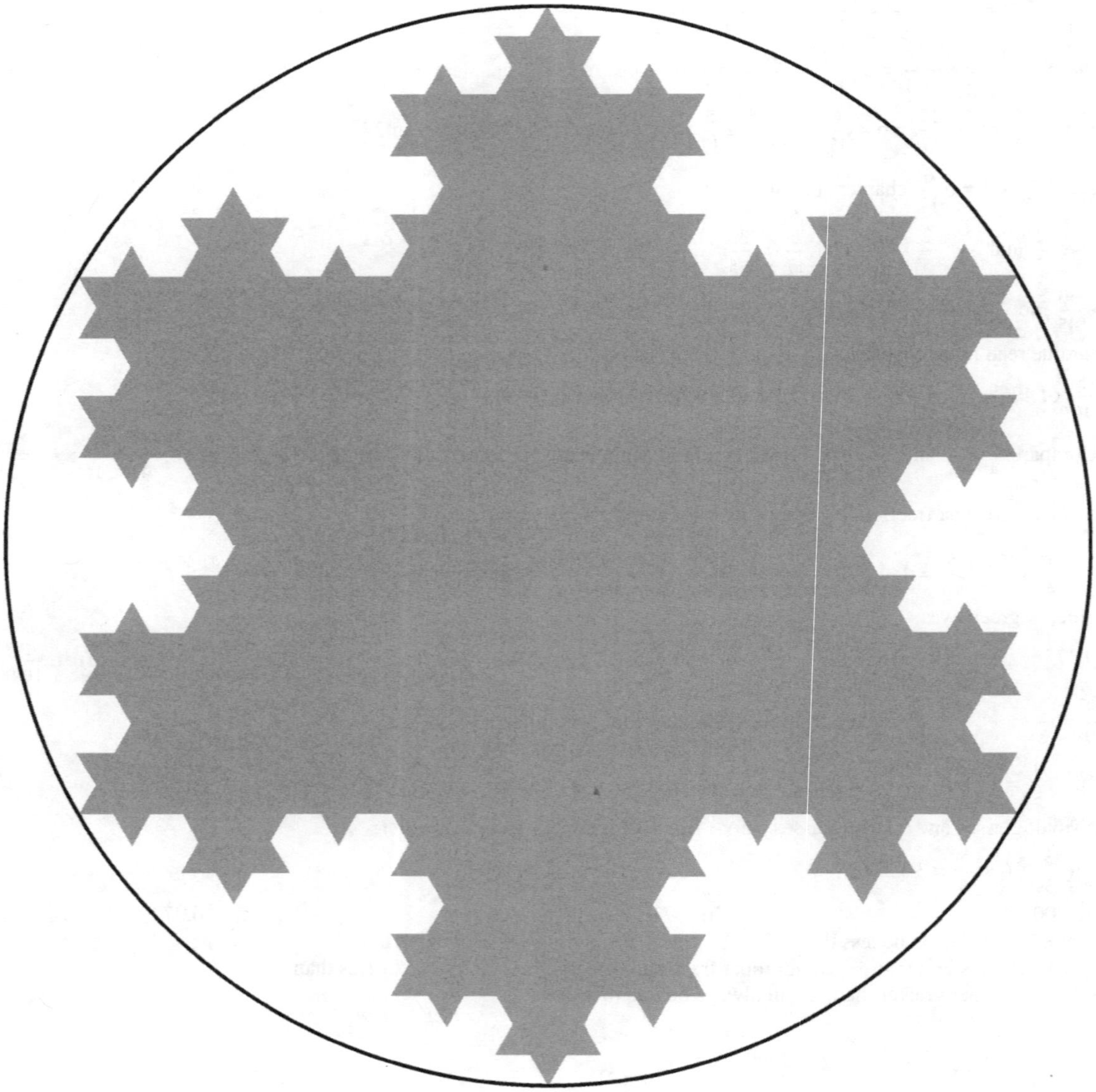

Name ______________________ Date ________________

Master 4.19

Lesson 4.1 *Explore*

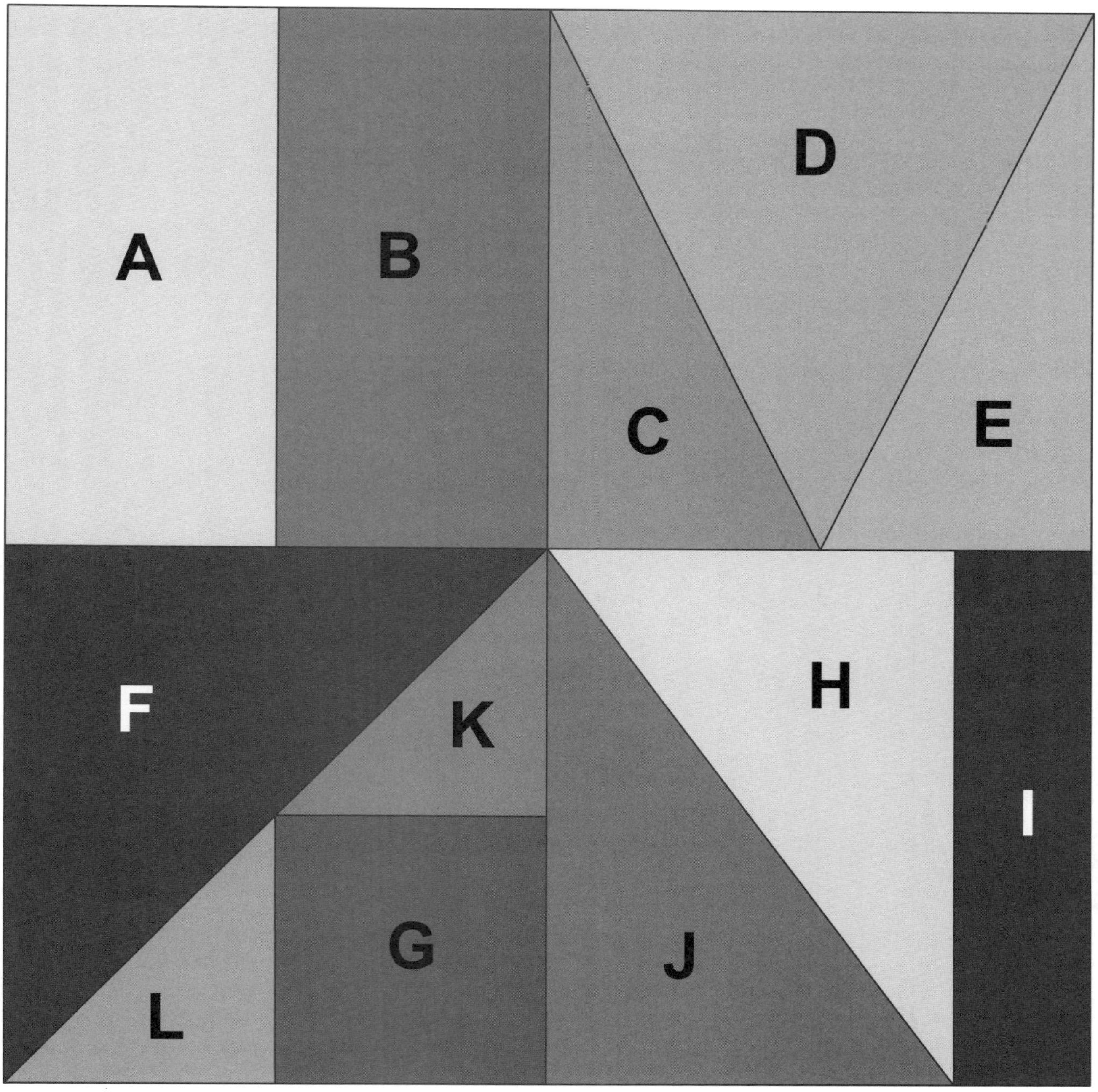

Name ____________________ Date ________________

Master 4.20

Fraction Strips

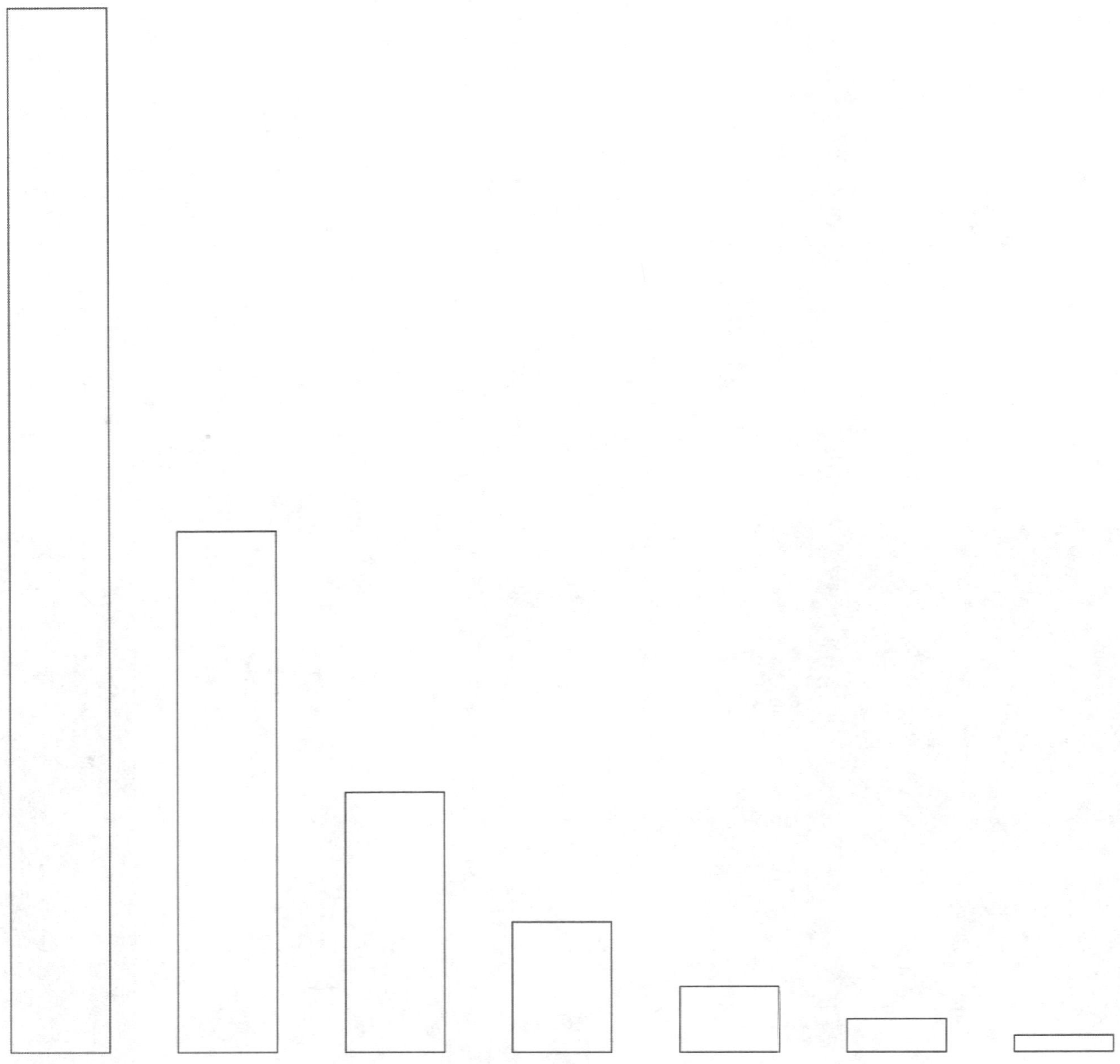

Name ______________________ Date ________________

Master 4.21

Fraction Circles (12ths, 8ths, 6ths, 4ths)

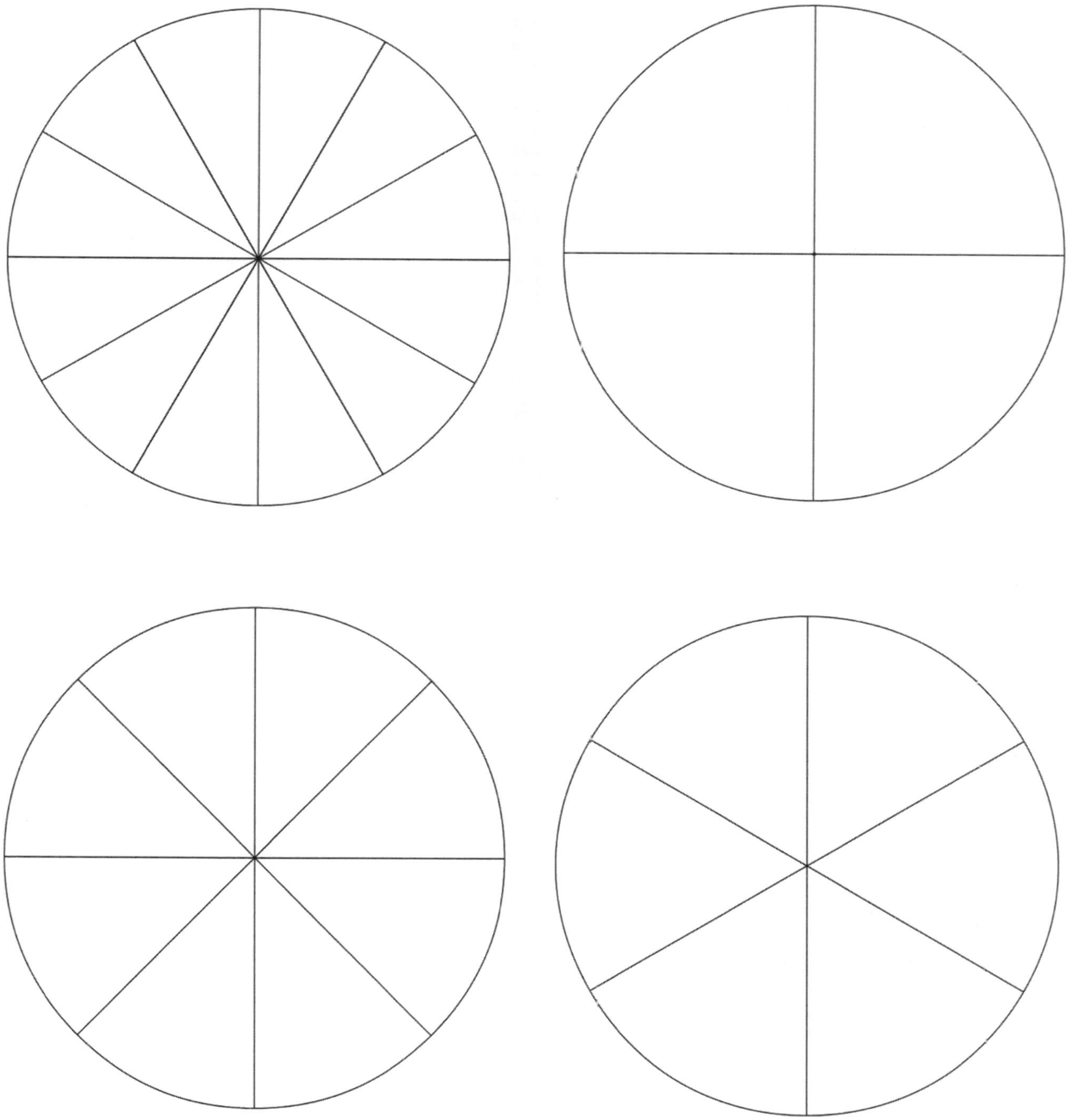

Name ____________________ Date ______________

Master 4.22

Symmetrical Designs

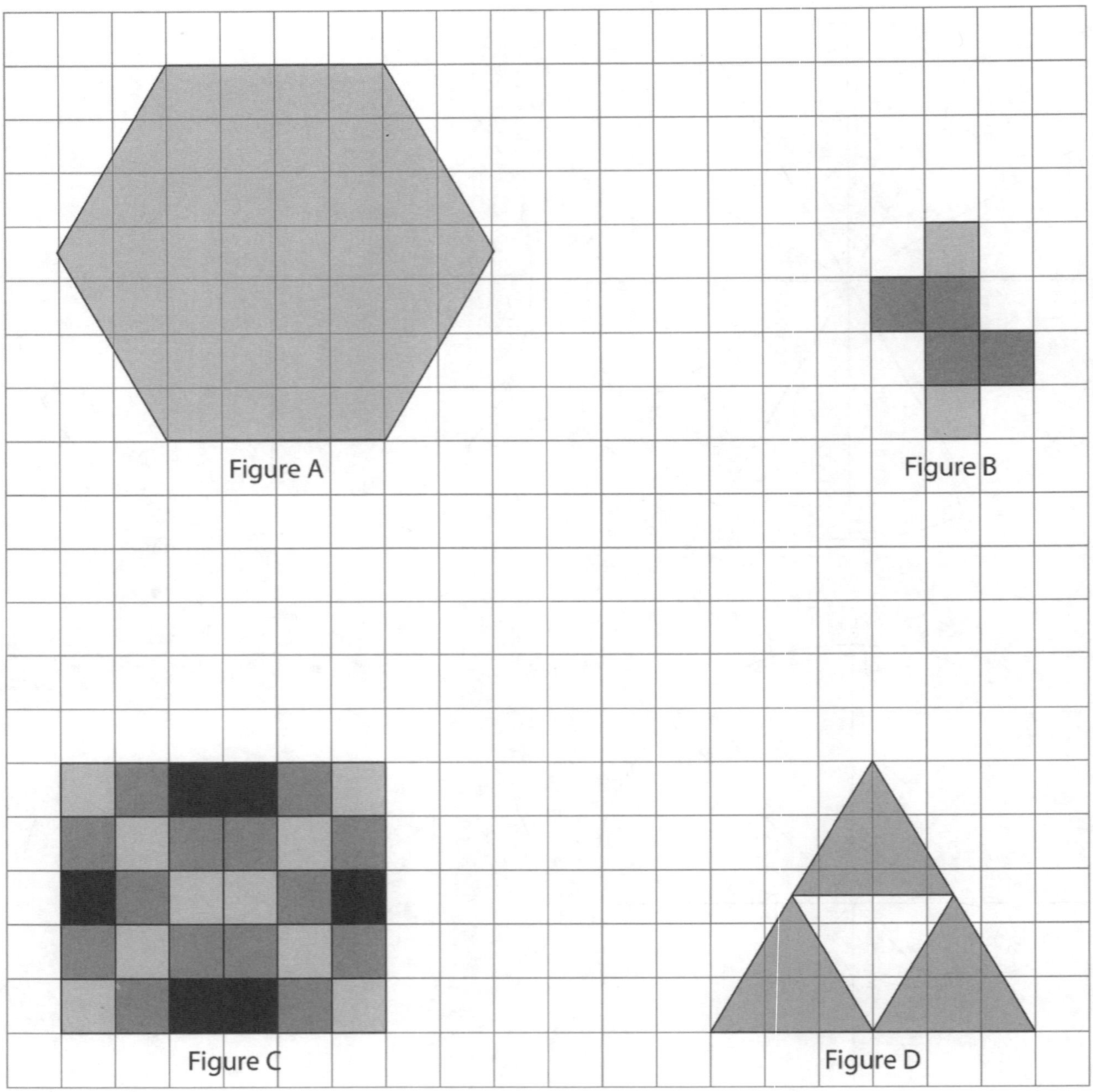

Name ____________________ Date ________________

Master 4.23

Fraction Product Spinner

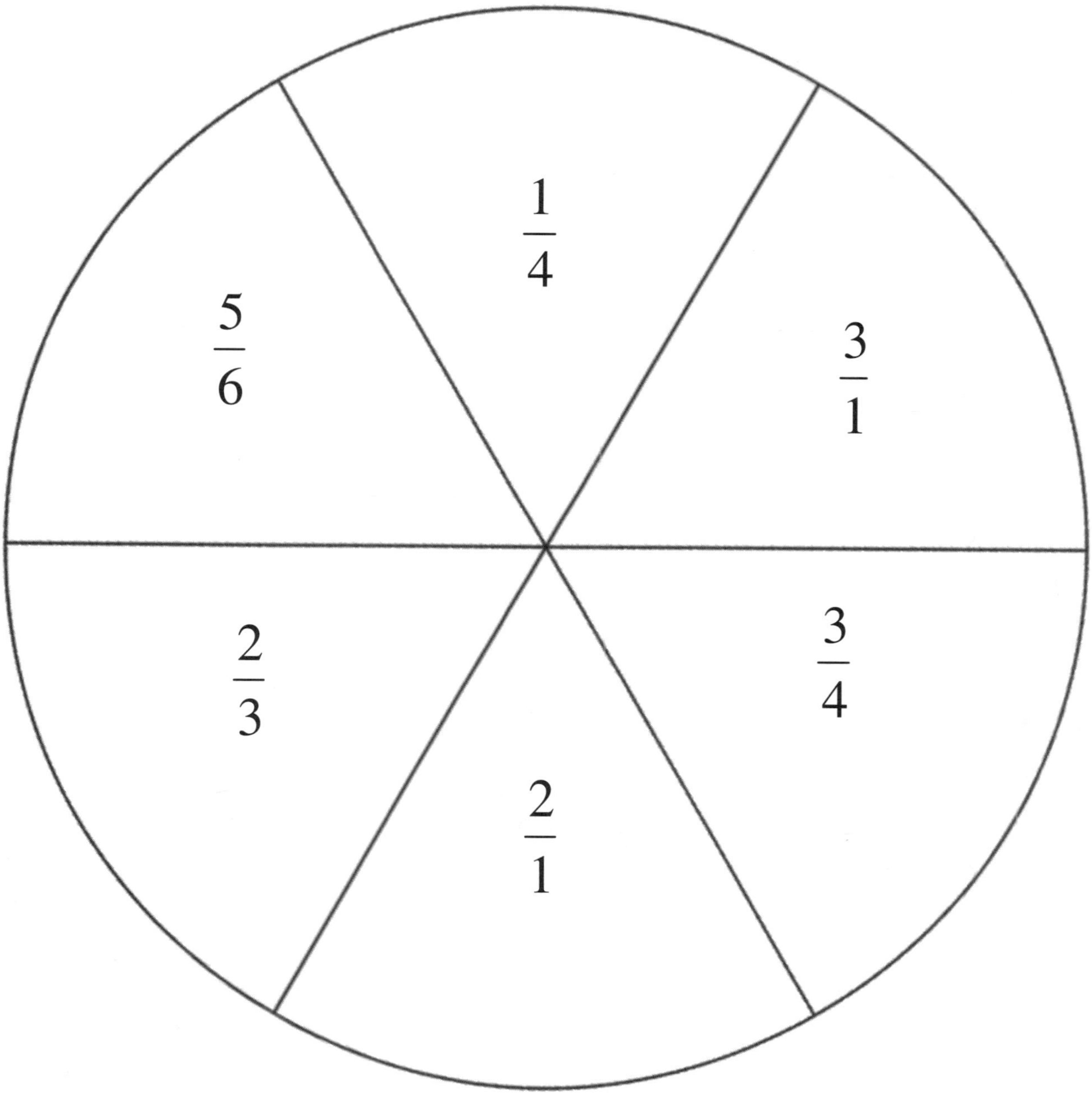

Name ____________________ Date ________________

Master 4.24

Number Lines

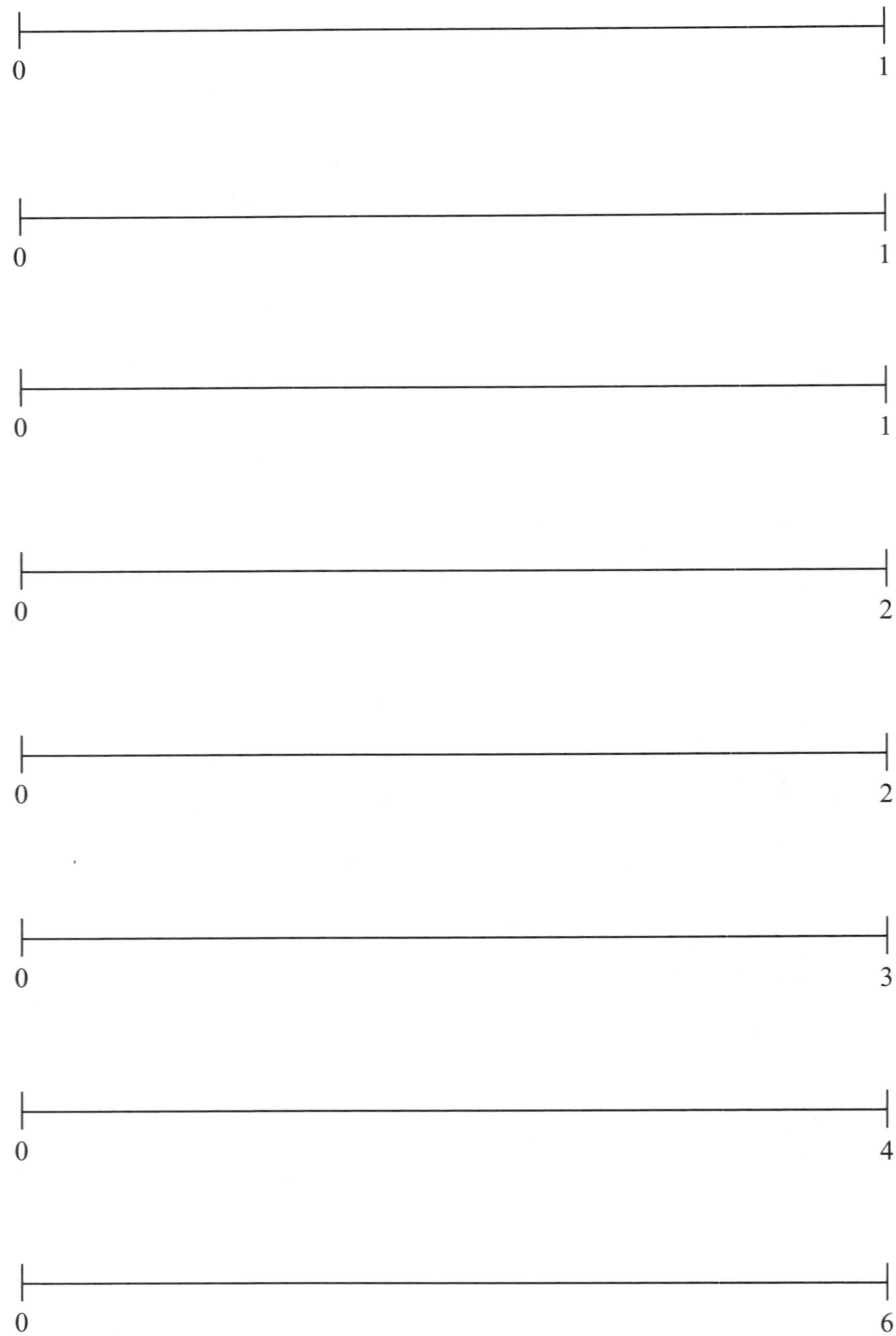

Name ____________________ Date ______________

Master 4.25

Hundredths Square

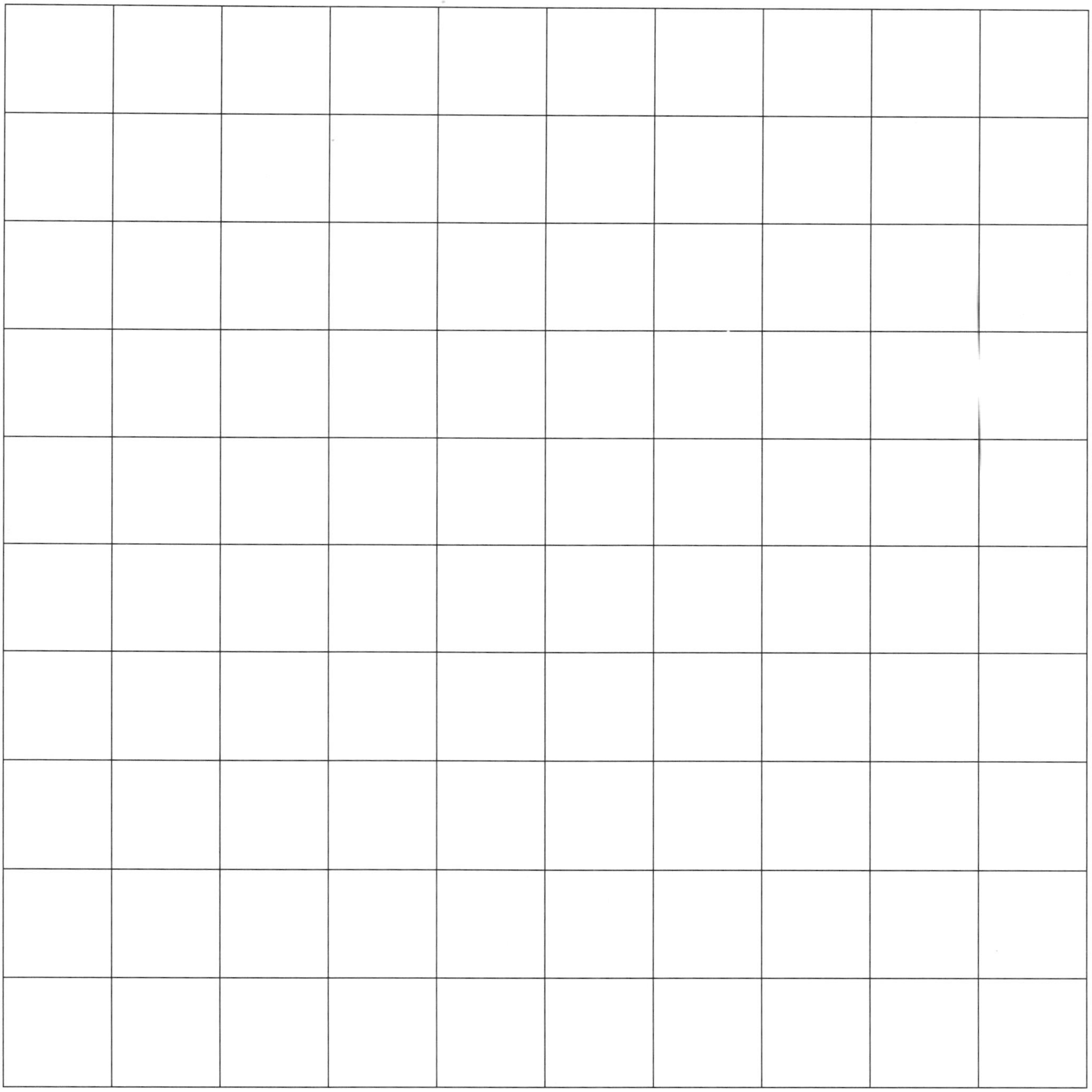

Extra Practice Masters 4.26–4.35

Go to the CD-ROM to access editable versions of these Extra Practice Masters

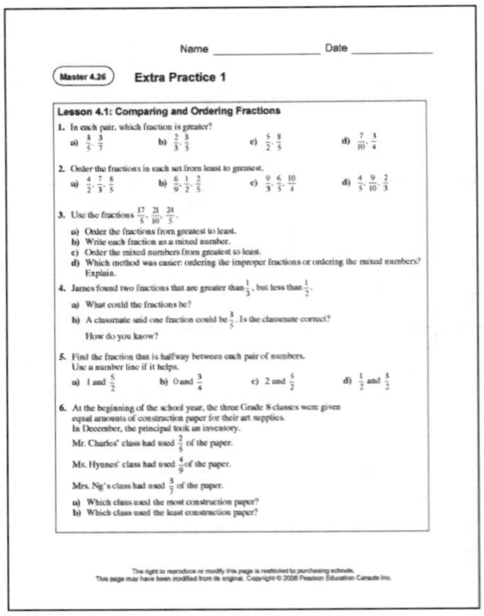
Master 4.26 Extra Practice 1
Lesson 4.1: Comparing and Ordering Fractions

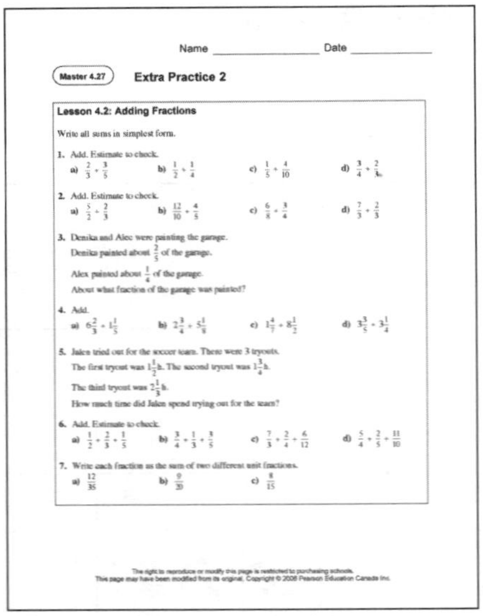
Master 4.27 Extra Practice 2
Lesson 4.2: Adding Fractions

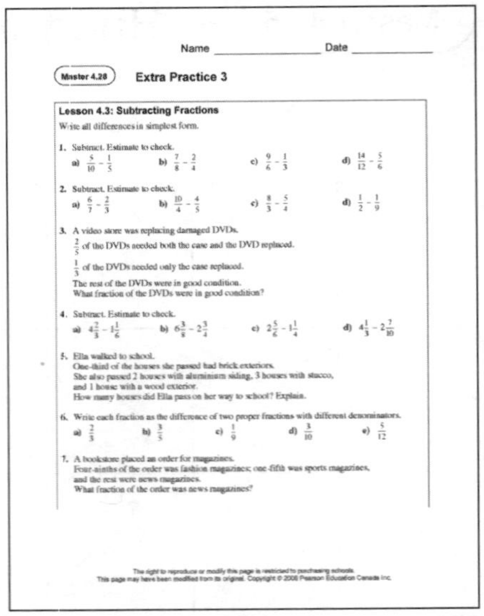
Master 4.28 Extra Practice 3
Lesson 4.3: Subtracting Fractions

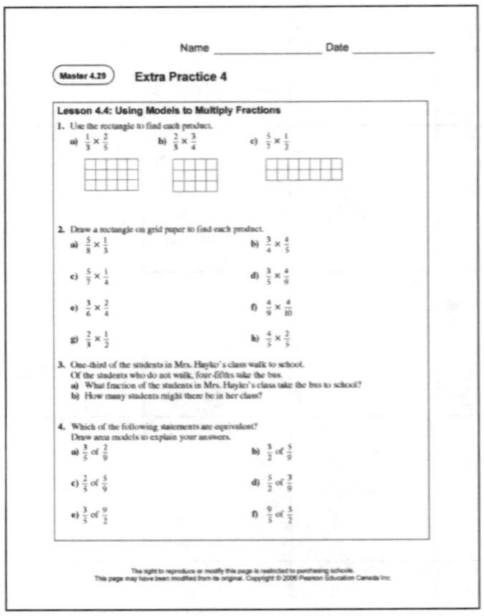
Master 4.29 Extra Practice 4
Lesson 4.4: Using Models to Multiply Fractions

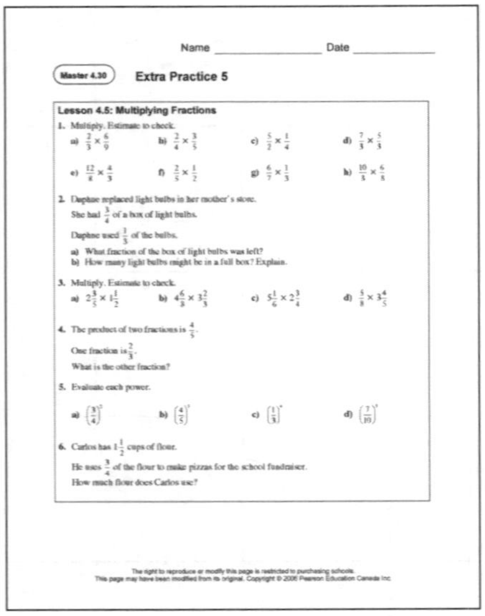
Master 4.30 Extra Practice 5
Lesson 4.5: Multiplying Fractions

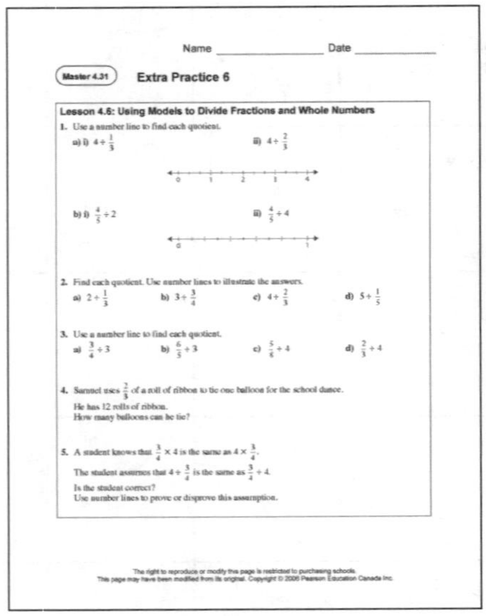
Master 4.31 Extra Practice 6
Lesson 4.6: Using Models to Divide Fractions and Whole Numbers

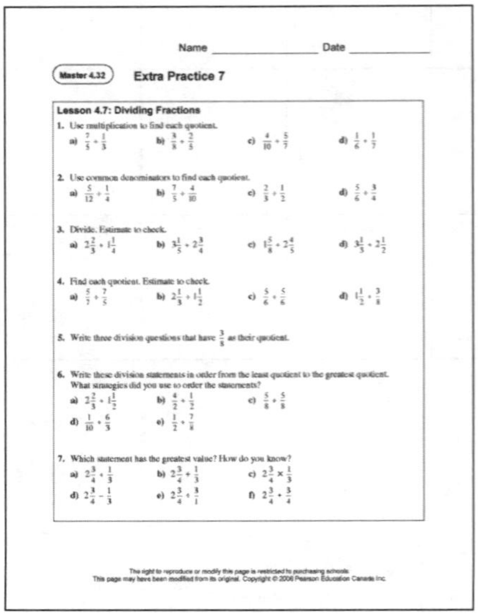
Master 4.32 Extra Practice 7
Lesson 4.7: Dividing Fractions

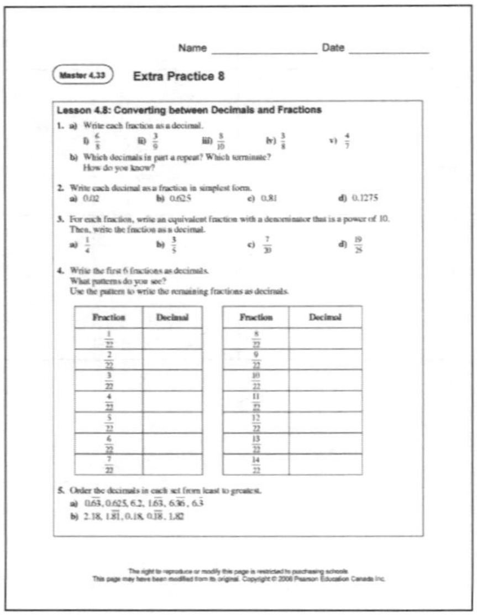
Master 4.33 Extra Practice 8
Lesson 4.8: Converting between Decimals and Fractions

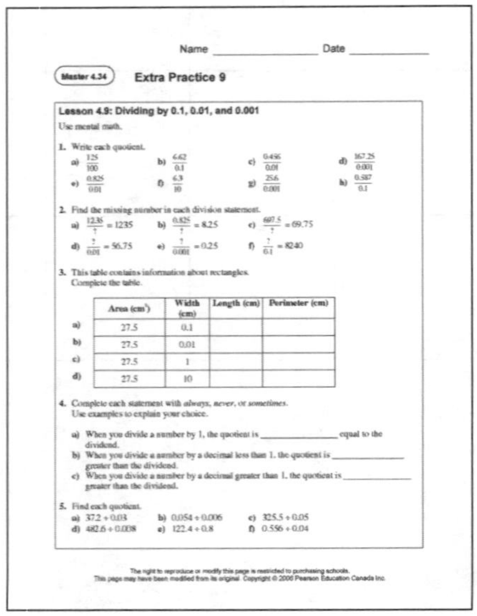
Master 4.34 Extra Practice 9
Lesson 4.9: Dividing by 0.1, 0.01, and 0.001

Name ______________ Date ______________

Master 4.35 Sample Answers

Extra Practice 1 – Master 4.26
Lesson 4.1

3\. d) Ordering the mixed numbers was easier because the whole numbers were different.

6\. a) Ms. Hymes' class b) Mr. Charles' class

Extra Practice 2 – Master 4.27
Lesson 4.2

Extra Practice 3 – Master 4.28
Lesson 4.3

Extra Practice 4 – Master 4.29
Lesson 4.4

Extra Practice 5 – Master 4.30
Lesson 4.5

Extra Practice 6 – Master 4.31
Lesson 4.6

Extra Practice 7 – Master 4.32
Lesson 4.7

Extra Practice 8 – Master 4.33
Lesson 4.8

Extra Practice 9 – Master 4.34
Lesson 4.9

Addison Wesley
Mathematics Makes Sense

Program Authors

Trevor Brown
Antonietta Lenjosek
Cathy Heideman
Jim Mennie
Georgia Konis-Chatzis
A.J. Keene
Margaret Sinclair
Craig Featherstone
Jason Johnston
Bryn Keyes
Elizabeth Wood
Elizabeth Milne
David Sufrin
Don Jones
Sharon Jeroski
Lynn Strangway

Printed and bound in Canada

2 3 4 5 – TC – 09 08 07 06

PEARSON
Education Canada

ADDISON WESLEY

Ontario

Math Makes Sense 8

Ontario

Teacher Guide

Unit 5: Data Management

PEARSON
Education Canada

UNIT 5 Data Management

"A big conceptual idea in data analysis can be referred to as the shape of data: a sense of how data are spread or grouped, what characteristics they have, and what they tell us in a global way about the population from which they are taken."

John A. Van de Walle

FOCUS STRAND
Data Management and Probability

SUPPORTING STRAND
Number Sense and Numeration

TIPS
Adolescent learners benefit from using graphic organizers and technology that depict relationships among key concepts.

Mathematics Background

What Are the Big Ideas?

- In a census survey, data are collected by surveying all the people in a population. In a sample survey, data are collected by surveying a portion of the population.
- Biased data are neither reliable nor valid.
- Data and graphs may be used to make inferences and to evaluate arguments.
- Data should be displayed in the most appropriate way so that trends may be identified and inferences can be made.
- The influence of outliers should be considered when determining measures of central tendency.
- Computer spreadsheet software can be used to record and graph data in a variety of ways.

How Will the Concepts Develop?

Students review the percent circle and trends in graphs.

Students collect data from a population and a sample. They learn the difference between census and sample surveys, and when a sample might produce biased results.

Students use *Census at School* to search for data, then use the data to solve problems. Students evaluate data and make predictions, or inferences.

Students use technology, such as *Appleworks* and *Fathom*, to create circle graphs, double-bar graphs, double-line graphs, and histograms. They investigate the effects of outliers on the measures of central tendency.

Students interpret and describe trends in graphs and solve related problems. They examine the impact this information has on decision making.

Why Are These Concepts Important?

Statistics Canada gathers information from one in five Canadian households every five years. Gathering, organizing, and analysing data from a large population is expensive, time-consuming, and not always possible. As a result, data are often gathered from a sample, or portion, of a population. Results based on the analysis of these data are then used to make predictions or draw conclusions about the entire population. It is necessary for students to understand how to collect data from a sample and then organize, represent, and analyse their findings to make predictions and draw conclusions.

Curriculum Overview

The codes refer to the 2005 revised curriculum.

Cluster 1: Collecting, Evaluating, and Analysing Data

Overall Expectations

- Collect and organize categorical, discrete, or continuous primary data and secondary data and display the data using charts and graphs, including frequency tables with intervals, histograms, and scatter plots. (8m65)
- Apply a variety of data management tools and strategies to make convincing arguments about data. (8m66)

Specific Expectations

- Collect data by conducting a survey or an experiment to do with themselves, their environment, issues in their school or community, or content from another subject, and record observations or measurements. (8m68)
- Collect and organize categorical, discrete, or continuous primary data and secondary data, and display the data in charts, tables, and graphs that have appropriate titles, labels, and scales that suit the range and distribution of the data, using a variety of tools. (8m70)
- Select an appropriate type of graph to represent a set of data, graph the data using technology, and justify the choice of graph. (8m71)
- Explain the relationship between a census, a representative sample, sample size, and a population. (8m72)
- Read, interpret, and draw conclusions from primary data and from secondary data, presented in charts, tables, and graphs. (8m73)
- Determine, through investigation, the appropriate measure of central tendency needed to compare sets of data. (8m74)
- Compare two attributes or characteristics, using a scatter plot, and determine whether or not the scatter plot suggests a relationship. (8m76)
- Identify and describe trends, based on the rate of change of data from tables and graphs, using informal language. (8m77)
- Make inferences and convincing arguments that are based on the analysis of charts, tables, and graphs. (8m78)
- Compare two attributes or characteristics, using a variety of data management tools and strategies. (8m79)

Launch

Lesson 5.1: Relating Census and Sample

Technology: Using *Census at School* to Get Secondary Data

Lesson 5.2: Inferring and Evaluating

Lesson 5.3: The Shape of Data

Technology: Using a Spreadsheet to Create Graphs

Mid-Unit Review

Lesson 5.4: Applying Measures of Central Tendency

Curriculum Overview

Cluster 2: Organizing and Representing Data

Overall Expectations

- Collect and organize categorical, discrete, or continuous primary data and secondary data and display the data using charts and graphs, including frequency tables with intervals, histograms, and scatter plots. (8m65)
- Apply a variety of data management tools and strategies to make convincing arguments about data. (8m66)

Specific Expectations

- Collect data by conducting a survey or an experiment to do with themselves, their environment, issues in their school or community, or content from another subject, and record observations or measurements. (8m68)
- Organize into intervals a set of data that is spread over a broad range. (8m69)
- Collect and organize categorical, discrete, or continuous primary data and secondary data, and display the data in charts, tables, and graphs that have appropriate titles, labels, and scales that suit the range and distribution of the data, using a variety of tools. (8m70)
- Select an appropriate type of graph to represent a set of data, graph the data using technology, and justify the choice of graph. (8m71)
- Read, interpret, and draw conclusions from primary data and from secondary data, presented in charts, tables, and graphs. (8m73)
- Demonstrate an understanding of the appropriate uses of bar graphs and histograms by comparing their characteristics. (8m75)

Lesson 5.5:
Drawing Histograms

Technology:
Using *Fathom* to Draw Histograms and Investigate Outliers

Lesson 5.6:
Drawing Circle Graphs

Unit Review
Practice Test

Unit Problem
Your Community

Curriculum across the Grades

Grade 7	Grade 8
Students collect data by conducting a survey or an experiment. They distinguish between a census and a sample from a population. Students collect and organize categorical, discrete, or continuous primary or secondary data and display the data in charts, tables, and graphs. They select an appropriate type of graph to represent a set of data, graph the data using technology, and justify the choice of graph. Students identify bias in data collection methods. They read, interpret, and draw conclusions from data presented in charts, tables, and graphs. Students identify graphs that present data in misleading ways. They determine the effect on a measure of central tendency of adding or removing a value or values. Students identify and describe trends in tables and graphs. They make inferences and convincing arguments based on the analysis of charts, tables, and graphs.	Students collect data by conducting a survey or an experiment and record observations or measurements. They organize into intervals a set of data that is spread over a broad range. Students collect and organize data and display the data in charts, tables, and graphs. They select an appropriate type of graph to represent a set of data, graph the data using technology, and justify the choice of graph. Students explain the relationship between a census, a representative sample, sample size, and a population. They read, interpret, and draw conclusions from primary data and from secondary data presented in charts, tables, and graphs. Students determine the appropriate measure of central tendency needed to compare sets of data. They demonstrate an understanding of the appropriate uses of bar graphs and histograms by comparing their characteristics. Students compare two attributes or characteristics using a scatter plot. They identify and describe trends, based on the rate of change of data from tables and graphs. Students make inferences and convincing arguments that are based on the analysis of charts, tables, and graphs. They compare two attributes or characteristics, using a variety of data management tools and strategies.

Additional Activities

Misleading Graphs

For Extra Practice (Appropriate for use after Lesson 5.2)
Materials: *Misleading Graphs* (Master 5.5), newspapers, magazines (or access to the Internet)

This activity reinforces the importance of carefully examining represented data.

The work students do: Students work with a partner. Students look through newspapers, magazines, or the Internet for examples of graphs, tables, or charts that show data in misleading ways. Students explain how the representation might mislead the reader, and why it may have been portrayed in that way. Students suggest how the presentation may be changed so that the data are shown accurately.

Take It Further: Students draw an accurate representation of the data.

Social/Visual
Partner Activity

Nutrition Circles

For Extra Practice (Appropriate for use after Lesson 5.6)
Materials: *Nutrition Circles* (Master 5.6), labels from packaged or canned food, compasses, and protractors (or percent circles (Master 5.15)), rulers, calculators, coloured pencils or markers

This activity provides practice in drawing circle graphs.

The work students do: Students work in groups of 3 or 4. Each group member brings in a label from a can of food, cereal box, or other packaged food. Each student calculates the mass of each nutritional ingredient in her or his label as a percent of the total mass. Students draw a circle graph to display the percent of each nutrient. Students compare graphs and decide which food item is the healthiest choice.

Take It Further: Students find the mass of each nutrient in 75 g of the food.

Social/Mathematical/Visual
Group Activity

Planning for Unit 5

Planning for Instruction

Suggested Unit time: About 3 weeks

Lesson	Time	Materials	Program Support
Launch, page 2	15–20 min		
Skills You'll Need, page 4	30–40 min	calculators percent circles	Master 5.15: Percent Circles
5.1: Relating Census and Sample, page 7 Collect data from a population and a sample.	80–100 min	2-column charts	PM 17: 2-Column Chart Master 5.7: Step-by-Step 1 Master 5.18: Extra Practice 1
Technology: Using *Census at School* to Get Secondary Data, page 12 Search databases for information and to solve problems.	40–50 min	computers (*Census at School* website)	
5.2: Inferring and Evaluating, page 14 Make inferences and evaluate arguments.	40–50 min		Master 5.8: Step-by-Step 2 Master 5.19: Extra Practice 2
5.3: The Shape of Data, page 20 Graph data, identify trends, and make inferences.	80–100 min	0.5-cm grid paper coloured pencils	Master 5.13: Graphs for 5.3 *Explore* Master 5.14: Graphs for 5.3 *Connect* PM 14: 0.5-cm Grid Paper Master 5.9: Step-by-Step 3 Master 5.20: Extra Practice 3
Technology: Using a Spreadsheet to Create Graphs, page 25 Display data on graphs using spreadsheets.	40–50 min	computers with *Appleworks*	
Mid-Unit Review, page 30		0.5-cm grid paper	PM 14: 0.5-cm Grid Paper
5.4: Applying Measures of Central Tendency, page 31 Understand how mean, median, and mode are affected by outliers.	80–100 min	calculators	Master 5.10: Step-by-Step 4 Master 5.21: Extra Practice 4
5.5: Drawing Histograms, page 36 Display and interpret data on histograms.	80–100 min	0.5-cm grid paper calculators coloured pencils	PM 14: 0.5-cm Grid Paper Master 5.11: Step-by-Step 5 Master 5.22: Extra Practice 5
Technology: Using *Fathom* to Draw Histograms and Investigate Outliers, page 41 Draw a histogram using *Fathom*.	40–50 min	computers with *Fathom*	
5.6: Drawing Circle Graphs, page 44 Display data on a circle graph.	80–100 min	0.5-cm grid paper protractors calculators compasses coloured pencils percent circles	PM 14: 0.5-cm Grid Paper Master 5.15: Percent Circles Master 5.12: Step-by-Step 6 Master 5.23: Extra Practice 6
Reading and Writing in Math: Identifying Key Verbs in Math Problems, page 48		construction paper tape scissors	
Unit Review, page 50		0.5-cm grid paper calculators compasses protractors coloured pencils percent circles	Master 5.15: Percent Circles PM 14: 0.5-cm Grid Paper Extra Practice: Student Book page 492
Practice Test, page 53		calculators protractors compasses 0.5-cm grid paper percent circles	PM 14: 0.5-cm Grid Paper Master 5.15: Percent Circles

Planning for Instruction

Lesson	Time	Materials	Program Support
Unit Problem: Your Community, page 54	80–100 min	calculators 0.5-cm grid paper coloured pencils protractors	PM 14: 0.5-cm Grid Paper

Planning for Assessment

Purpose	Tools and Process	Recording and Reporting
Diagnostic	*Unit Launch* Question; conference; scaffold problems throughout the unit	PM 8: Conference Prompts
Formative	*Explore* – Ongoing Assessment: Observe and Listen	Master 5.2 Ongoing Observations: Data Management PM 1: Inquiry Process Check List PM 6: Observation Record 1 PM 7: Observation Record 2 PM 8: Conference Prompts PM 2: Self-Assessment PM 3: Self-Assessment: Problem Solving PM 9: Work Sample Records
Summative	*Unit Review* *Unit Problem* – Performance Assessment Unit Test Review assessment records; add unit results to ongoing records	Master 5.1 Unit Rubric: Data Management Master 5.3 Performance Assessment Rubric: Your Community Master 5.4 Unit Summary: Data Management PM 10: Summary Class Records: Strands PM 11: Summary Class Records: Achievement Categories PM 12: Summary Record: Individual
Learning Skills/Mathematical Disposition	Observe and record throughout unit	PM 4: Learning Skills Check List PM 5: Mathematical Dispositions and Learning Skills

Program Masters (PM) are in the *Grade 8 Planning and Program Masters* module.
Extra Practice Masters are on the CD-ROM and printed in reduced format on page 76 of this module.

LESSON ORGANIZER

15–20 min

Curriculum Focus: Activate prior learning about collecting, organizing, representing, and interpreting data.
Vocabulary: Statistics Canada, data, survey

ASSUMED PRIOR KNOWLEDGE

- ✓ Students understand different ways of representing collected data.
- ✓ Students can suggest different ways to collect data.

UNIT 5

Data Management

What would you like to know about people in your community? Here are some questions to ask.

- What careers are your classmates interested in?
- How do people spend their leisure time?
- How many people speak two languages? Three languages?

What other questions could you ask?

What You'll Learn

- Relate a census and sample.
- Identify bias in data-collection methods.
- Use databases and spreadsheets.
- Collect, display, and evaluate data on charts and graphs.
- Identify and describe trends in graphs.
- Understand and apply the measures of central tendency.

Why It's Important

Statistics Canada is the federal government department that collects data from every household in Canada. Private companies conduct surveys and publish the results.
You need to understand how to interpret the data you read.

182

ACTIVATE PRIOR LEARNING

Engage students in a discussion about what they would like to ask people in their community. Then have them suggest possible ways of collecting this information. Invite students to discuss the role of Statistics Canada in gathering information about the Canadian community.

Ask:

- What questions could you ask children in your community?
  (*What is your favourite television show? How many siblings do you have? What is your favourite winter activity? What is your favourite colour?*)
- What questions could you ask adults in your community?
  (*What post-secondary education do you have? How many jobs have you had? Do you drive a car, van, SUV, or truck? In which country were you born?*)
- How could you collect these data?
  (*I could have people fill out a questionnaire. I could conduct a telephone survey. I could canvass door-to-door.*)
- What are Statistics Canada's two main databases?
  (*CANSIM II* and *E-STAT*)
- Why is it important to collect information about Canadians and Canada?
  (*To analyse trends, make predictions, and learn about our country and its people*)
- How are results of surveys represented?
  (*Circle graphs, bar graphs, stem-and-leaf plots, tally charts, pictographs, line graphs*)

Tell students that in this unit they will collect, display, and evaluate data with and without the use of technology. Students will also identify trends in graphs, and make arguments and inferences based on collected data. At the end of the unit, students will demonstrate what they have learned by designing and conducting a survey, and organizing and displaying their results.

Key Words

- population
- census
- sample
- *Census at School*
- inference
- histogram

FROM THE LIBRARY

Teaching Student-Centered Mathematics Grades 5–8,
by John A. Van de Walle and LouAnn H. Lovin.
Pearson Education Inc. (Allyn and Bacon), 2006.
ISBN: 0205417973
This book contains nearly 200 grade-appropriate activities for students. Teachers will find this book indispensable. The approach used will help students develop a strong understanding of different math topics, as well as build their confidence in mathematics.

REACHING ALL LEARNERS

Some students may benefit from using the virtual manipulatives on the e-Tools CD-ROM.
The e-Tool appropriate for this unit is *Spreadsheet/Data/Grapher*.

DIAGNOSTIC ASSESSMENT

What to Look For	What to Do
✔ Students understand different ways of representing collected data. ✔ Students can suggest different ways to collect data.	***Extra Support:*** Students who have difficulty remembering different ways of representing data should search newspapers or E-STAT to find examples of different types of graphs. *Work on this skill during Lesson 5.3.* Students who have difficulty suggesting different ways to collect data should identify the difference between primary and secondary data, then provide examples of each. *Work on this skill during Lesson 5.1.*

LESSON ORGANIZER 30–40 min

Skills in Review
- Using a percent circle to draw a circle graph
- Identifying trends in graphs

Student Materials
- Percent Circles (Master 5.15)
- calculators

Vocabulary: sector, trend

UNIT 5

Skills You'll Need

Using a Percent Circle to Draw a Circle Graph

The circle represents 100%.
A percent circle is divided into 10 congruent sectors.
Each large sector represents 10%.
Each sector is further divided into 10 parts.
Each part is 1% of the circle.

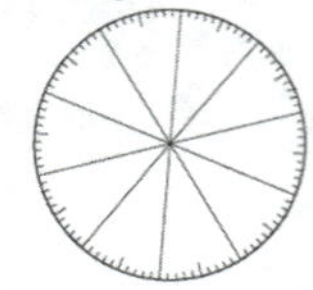

Example 1

Pitaq collected data about his classmates' favourite season.
He recorded the results in a table.

Classmates' Favourite Season

Season	Autumn	Winter	Spring	Summer
Number of Students	8	3	5	9

Use a percent circle to display the data on a circle graph.

Solution

Add the numbers in the table: 8 + 3 + 5 + 9 = 25. There are 25 students.
Write the number of students who chose each season as a fraction of 25, then as a percent.

Autumn: $\frac{8}{25} = \frac{32}{100} = 32\%$ (×4) Winter: $\frac{3}{25} = \frac{12}{100} = 12\%$ (×4)

Spring: $\frac{5}{25} = \frac{20}{100} = 20\%$ (×4) Summer: $\frac{9}{25} = \frac{36}{100} = 36\%$ (×4)

For autumn, 32% is three 10% sectors and two 1% parts.
For winter, 12% is one 10% sector and two 1% parts.
For spring, 20% is two 10% sectors.
For summer, 36% is three 10% sectors and six 1% parts.
Label each sector.
Write a title for the graph.

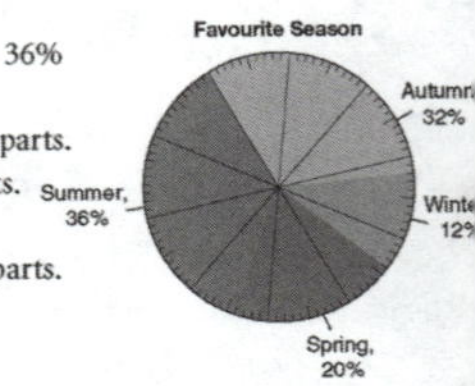

184 UNIT 5: Data Management

Using a Percent Circle to Draw a Circle Graph

Discuss with students why a percent circle is useful when drawing a circle graph.

Ask:
- Which numbers divide exactly into 100?
  (1, 2, 4, 5, 10, 20, 25, 50, 100)
- Why are these numbers important when drawing a circle graph?
  (Since these are factors of 100, they can be used to convert each fraction to one with denominator 100. Colour the portion of the circle that is represented by the numerator.)
- How do you find the size of the sector that represents $\frac{2}{5}$ of the circle?
  (Multiply the numerator and denominator by 20 to get $\frac{40}{100}$, then colour four 10% sectors.)

Common Misconceptions

➤ Students do not know how to write a fraction using the data from the table.

How to Help: Review the terms numerator and denominator. Tell students that the denominator represents the total amount of data collected and the numerator represents one entry in the data.

➤ Students have difficulty converting a fraction to a percent.

How to Help: Review multiplying fractions. Remind students that when a fraction has denominator 100, the numerator represents the percent. Students should multiply 5 by 20, 10 by 10, 20 by 5, 25 by 4, and 50 by 2, to get denominator 100.

✓ Check

1. For each set of data, use a percent circle to draw a circle graph.

a)

Coins in Laura's Piggy Bank

Coin	Pennies	Nickels	Dimes	Quarters
Number	12	15	9	14
	24%	30%	18%	28%

b)

Items in Lost and Found Box

Item	Hats	Socks	Sweaters	Gloves	Shoes
Number	8	16	6	8	2
	20%	40%	15%	20%	5%

Trends in Graphs

Data and graphs sometimes show a pattern or trend.

Example 2

Each line graph represents temperatures recorded in southern Ontario.

a) Describe any trends in each graph.

b) What were the temperatures on Sunday and Saturday?
How do you know?

Graph A

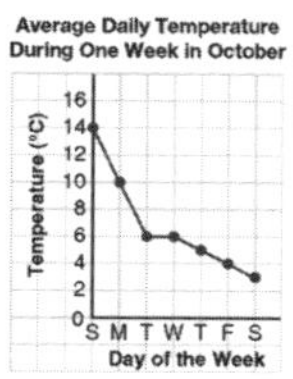

Graph B

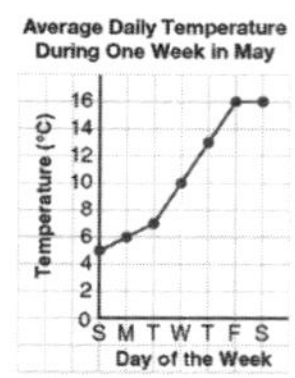

Solution

Graph A

a) The graph goes down to the right.
This means the temperature is decreasing.
The line segment from Tuesday to Wednesday is horizontal.
This means the temperature stayed the same during those two days.

Alternative Example 1

Selina collected data about the number of different types of trees on school property. She recorded the results.
Use a percent circle to display the data on a circle graph.

Trees on School Property			
Red Maple	Spruce	Pine	Poplar
4	3	6	7

Solution

Add the numbers in the table: 4 + 3 + 6 + 7 = 20
There are 20 trees.
Write the number of each type of tree as a fraction of 20, then as a percent.
Red Maple: $\frac{4}{20} = \frac{20}{100}$ = 20%; Spruce: $\frac{3}{20} = \frac{15}{100}$ = 15%;
Pine: $\frac{6}{20} = \frac{30}{100}$ = 30%; Poplar: $\frac{7}{20} = \frac{35}{100}$ = 35%

Trees on School Property

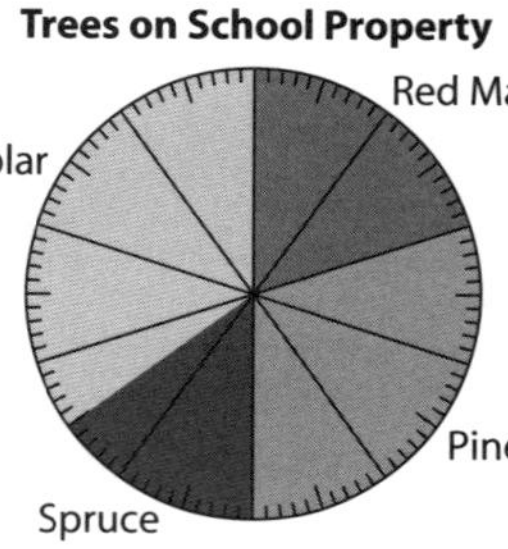

Red Maple has two 10% sectors. Spruce has one 10% sector and five 1% parts. Pine has three 10% sectors. Poplar has three 10% sectors and five 1% parts.

Sample Solutions

1. a) **Coins in Laura's Piggy Bank**

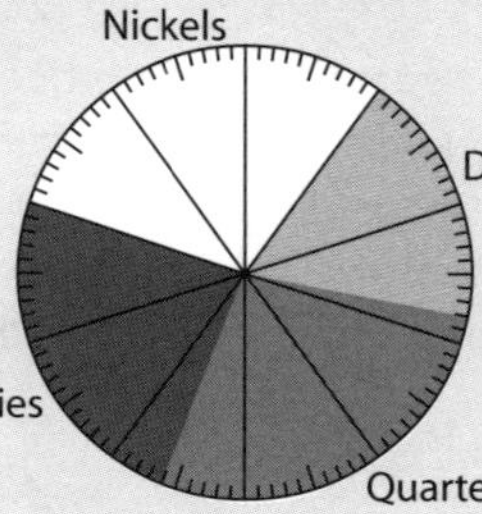

b) **Items in Lost and Found Box**

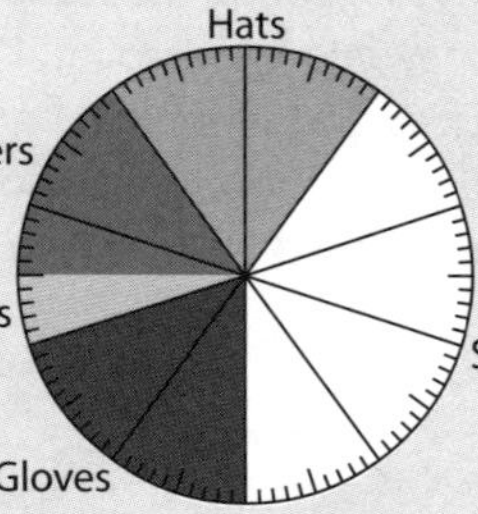

Alternative Example 2

Each line graph represents the population of a town.

a) Describe any trends in each graph.

b) Which town's population is greater?
How do you know?

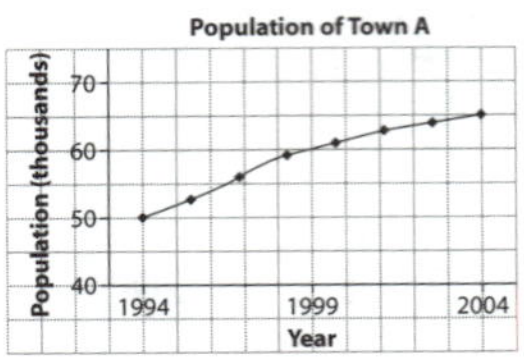

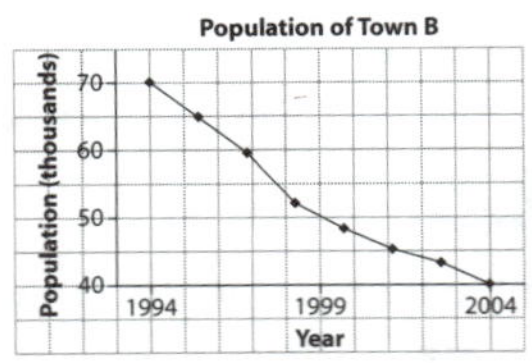

Solution

a) Town A: The line goes up to the right. This means the population is increasing.
Town B: The line goes down to the right. This means the population is decreasing.

b) The population in Town A is greater. In 2004, the population in Town A was about 65 000, while the population in Town B was about 40 000.

b) The first **S** on the horizontal axis represents Sunday.
The corresponding value on the vertical axis is 14°C.
The temperature on Sunday was 14°C.
To find the temperature on Saturday:
Draw a vertical line, from the last **S** on the horizontal axis, to meet the graph, as shown.
Then draw a horizontal line to meet the vertical axis.
The temperature was about 3°C on Saturday.

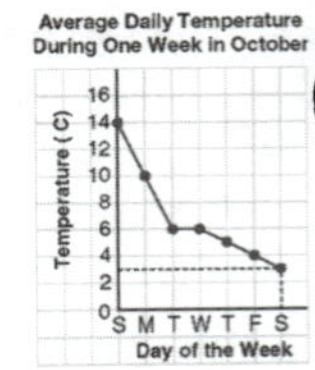

Graph B

a) The graph goes up to the right.
This means the temperature is increasing.
The line segment from Friday to Saturday is horizontal.
This means the temperature stayed the same during those two days.

b) The temperature on Sunday was 5°C.
The temperature on Saturday was 16°C.

✓ Check

2. Each of 3 people deposited $200 in a bank account at the beginning of January.
These graphs display the money in each account for the next 7 weeks.

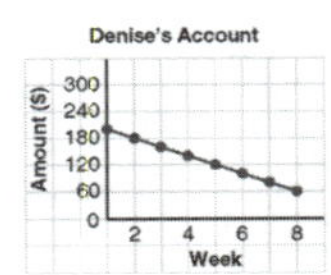

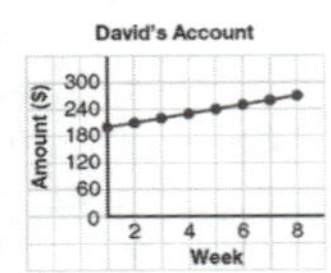

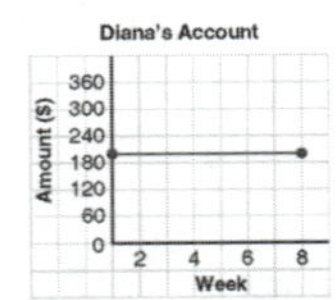

a) Who withdrew money from her or his account? How do you know? Denise

b) Who deposited money to her or his account? How do you know? David

c) Which account had no transactions? Explain. Diana's account

d) How much money did each person have at the end?
How do you know?
Denise: $60, David: $270, Diana: $200

Trends in Graphs

Discuss with students the meaning of the word *trend*. Remind students that the purpose of graphing data is to look for patterns or trends. Ask:

- What patterns might be seen in a line graph? What does each pattern tell us?
  (*The line might go up to the right. This tells us the values are increasing. The line might go down to the right. This tells us the values are decreasing. The line might be horizontal. This tells us the values stay the same.*)

Common Misconceptions

➤ Students do not read the graph from left to right.

How to Help: Tell students that the graph begins at the point closest to the vertical axis. Have them put their finger on this point, then move along the graph to the right. They should note whether their finger is moving up the line, down the line, or straight across.

➤ Students do not know how to locate a value on the vertical axis that corresponds to a value on the horizontal axis.

How to Help: Encourage students to place a finger on the horizontal axis, move it up to the graph, then move it left to its corresponding value on the vertical axis. Alternatively, students could use a ruler to draw a dotted line from the horizontal axis up to the graph, and then left to the vertical axis.

Sample Solutions

2. a) Denise withdrew money from her account. I know because the graph goes down to the right.

b) David deposited money into his account. I know because the graph goes up to the right.

c) Diana's account had no transactions. I know because the line is horizontal. This means there was no activity in the account.

5.1 Relating Census and Sample

Focus Collect data from a population and a sample.

Every five years, Statistics Canada (Stats Can) collects data from one in five households in Canada. It uses these data to help us better understand our country, including its people, natural resources, educational needs, society, and cultures.

Explore

Work in a group of 3.
Which kind of TV show is the most popular in your class?

- Have each student in your group name her or his favourite kind of TV show.
  Record the results in a tally chart.
  Make a conclusion based on these results.
- Combine your results with those of a second group of students.
  Make a conclusion.
- Combine results to get those of 3 groups of students.
  Make a conclusion.

Did your conclusions change after each additional group was included? Explain.
Would your conclusions likely change if you used the results for the whole class? Explain.

Reflect & Share

Record the results for your group on the board.
Compare them with the class results.
How did the results change as the number of responses increased?

Connect

One way to collect data is to survey all the people in a **population**.
This is called a **census** survey.
For example, Jared asked every student in each of the three Grade 8 classes in his school, "What is your favourite sport to play?"
Since Jared collected the data himself, the data are primary data.
Results from a census are accurate because the entire population provides input. For a large population, a census can be expensive and time-consuming.

5.1 Relating Census and Sample **187**

LESSON 5.1

Relating Census and Sample

LESSON ORGANIZER 80–100 min

Curriculum Focus: Collect data from a population and a sample. (8m68, 8m72)

Student Materials
- 2-column charts (PM 17)

Optional
- Step-by-Step 1 (Master 5.7)
- Extra Practice 1 (Master 5.18)

Vocabulary: population, census, sample, biased, reliable, valid, discrete data, continuous data, quantitative, qualitative

Assessment: Master 5.2 Ongoing Observations: Data Management

Key Math Learnings

1. In a census, survey data are collected from all the people in a population.
2. In a sample, survey data are collected from a portion of the population.
3. A biased survey does not accurately represent the population; a valid survey does.

BEFORE Get Started

Invite students to discuss their favourite kind of TV show. Ask:

- Is it enough to ask one student to find out the class's favourite kind of TV show? Why?
  (*No, that is one student's opinion. There are 27 students in the class.*)
- Is it enough to ask all the boys in the class, or all the girls in the class?
  (*No, boys might like different kinds of TV shows than girls.*)
- What is the best way to find out what the class's favourite kind of TV show is?
  (*Survey every student in the class.*)
- What is another way to find out what the class's favourite kind of TV show is?
  (*Ask a representative portion of the class.*)

Present *Explore*.

Ensure students understand that it is helpful to have a list of choices of different kinds of TV shows presented with the question, with the last choice being "other." This "other" category would include answers that are uncommon.

DURING Explore

Ongoing Assessment: Observe and Listen

As students work, ask questions, such as:

- What choices of TV shows did you list?
  (*Sitcom, drama, science fiction, soap opera, reality, game show, news, sports, cartoon, documentary, movie, talk show, music video, or other*)
- What conclusion did you make after surveying 3 students?
  (*Sitcom was the favourite kind of TV show.*)
- Did your conclusion stay the same or change after combining your results with another group? Two more groups?
  (*The conclusion changed each time. After combining with two more groups, reality shows were the favourite.*)

REACHING ALL LEARNERS

Early Finishers

Have students suggest what they would do to find the most popular kind of TV show among Grade 8 students in Canada and in North America. What survey methods would they use? How many Grade 8 students would they survey?

Common Misconceptions

➤ Students think that a sample survey produces the same results as a census.

How to Help: Choose every 5th student to tell her/his country of origin. Record the results. Have students conclude where most students come from and where fewest students come from. Then have every student record his/her country of origin on the board. Have students make the same conclusions as above. It is likely that the results from the sample and census will be different.

Number Strategies

Students should see that each percent is $\frac{1}{10}$ of the previous percent. Since the percent is divided by 10 each time, the pattern is: Start at 420. Divide by 10 each time. This corresponds to moving the decimal one place to the left.

Another way to collect data is to survey a portion or a **sample** of the population. For example, Alicia used the Internet to find the salaries of 10 professional basketball players. Since Alicia did not collect the data herself, the data are secondary data.

A sample survey is less costly and requires less time than a census. Results from a sample may not be as accurate as those from a census because not everyone in the population has input.

A sample is *biased* if it does not accurately represent the population. For example, if the population is 15 boys and 17 girls, a sample for this population should have approximately equal numbers of boys and girls. A sample of 8 boys is a biased sample.

A survey is *reliable* if the results can be duplicated in another survey. A biased sample may not produce reliable results. For example, suppose 100 people at a hockey game were asked to name their favourite sport. The results would be biased and probably different from asking 100 randomly-selected people to name their favourite sport.

A survey is *valid* if the results represent the population. Courtney surveys her friends in Grade 8 and finds that 75% have a DVD player at home. James surveys all the Grade 8 students in their school and finds that 38% have a DVD player at home. Courtney's survey is not valid because her sample results do not represent the Grade 8 population.

Example 1

For each survey, state if the sample is biased or reliable.

a) To find out if the school cafeteria should change its menu, all the teachers were surveyed.

b) *Rock Music* magazine asks its readers to reply to a question about the favourite music group of teenagers.

Solution

a) The sample is biased because the cafeteria is also used by students and they should be included in the survey.

b) The sample is biased because the readers are most likely fans of rock music, and not all teenagers prefer rock music.

- Do you think your conclusion would stay the same if the whole class was surveyed?
  (It might change because our three groups had more girls than boys.)

AFTER — Connect

Invite students to share their results with the class.

Ask questions, such as:

- Did any group of 9 have the same results?
  (Two groups of 9 had reality shows as their favourite; five out of 9 in one group and 6 out of 9 in another group.)
- What does this mean? How can the results of the third group influence the decision?
  (There are 27 students in the class. Eleven of 18 students chose reality shows. Depending on the results of the 3rd group, the overall class results may be different.)

Ensure students understand that the results in the tally charts can be combined to get the class results. Reinforce the idea that the larger the group, the more accurate the results.

Use *Connect* to introduce the terms *population, census, sample, biased, reliable,* and *valid.* Have students describe situations when a census survey should be used and when a sample survey should be used, and discuss the advantages and disadvantages of each. Ask:

- Would you use a census survey or a sample survey to determine the favourite kind of TV show of Grade 8 students in Ontario? In our school? Explain.
  (I would use a sample survey for Ontario because it is costly and time consuming to survey every Grade 8 student in Ontario. I would use a census survey in our school because there are only 72 Grade 8 students in our school and it would be easy to survey all students.)

Example 2

The owners of the City Mall want to find out if shoppers would like a video arcade to be opened in the mall.
How might the survey results be affected in each situation? Explain.

a) A survey of all shoppers is taken on a weekday morning.
b) A survey of all shoppers is taken on a Saturday afternoon.
c) A survey of teenage shoppers is taken.

Solution

a) On a weekday morning, most customers might be retired people or parents with small children. The sample is not representative of the population. The data collected from the survey would most likely indicate that a video arcade should not be opened.

b) On a Saturday afternoon, the mall would have a mixed population in age and gender. The data collected from the survey would probably be representative of the population.

c) When only teenagers are surveyed, the sample is biased. The data collected from the survey would most likely indicate that a video arcade should be opened.

Practice

1. In each case, are the data collected from a census or a sample? Justify your answer.
   a) To find the favourite TV show of Grade 8 students in a school, fifteen of the 40 Grade 8 students in the school are surveyed. Sample
   b) To find the favourite video game of Ontario 13-year-olds, all 13-year-old students in Ontario are surveyed. Census
   c) To find out if customers of a chain of coffee shops are happy with the service, some customers in every shop were surveyed. Sample

2. For each survey, state if the sample is biased or reliable. Justify your answer.
   a) To find out if the arena should offer more public skating times, a survey is posted on a bulletin board at the arena and left for patrons to complete and return. Biased

5.1 Relating Census and Sample **189**

Assignment Guidelines

If your students do not have time to complete all the *Practice* questions on pages 189, 190, and 191, these questions provide minimum curriculum coverage: 1, 2, 4, 6, 8, *Reflect*

To assess the 4 Achievement Chart categories listed in the curriculum document, have students complete these *Practice* questions:
Knowledge and Understanding: 2
Communication: 4
Application: 6
Thinking: 8

Sample Solutions

1. a) Only 15 of the 40 Grade 8 students were surveyed.
b) All 13-year-old students in Ontario were surveyed.
c) Only some, and not all, customers were surveyed.
2. a) Only those patrons who read it and respond have a say in the decision.
b) The students are randomly selected.
c) The readers who respond might be adults and not teenagers. Only those who read the fitness magazine will respond.
d) Only a small group of parents were asked. The players should also have been randomly selected and asked.

Ensure students can identify the difference between a reliable survey and a valid survey. Ask:

- Why is it important that a survey be reliable and valid?
  (When a survey is reliable, the results can be duplicated in another survey and the results are not biased. The results represent the population.)

Explain that data that cannot be measured numerically, such as opinions or hair colour, are called qualitative data. Data that can be measured using numbers, such as height or hours spent doing homework each day, are called quantitative data. Quantitative data can be divided into two types: *discrete* and *continuous*. Discrete data are based on counts. They cannot be subdivided and can only be represented by whole numbers, such as the number of people who visit the mall on a given day. Continuous data are measured on a continuum. They can be measured or broken down into smaller parts, such as the length of a room.

Ask:

- Are the data you collected on the class's favourite TV show an example of qualitative or quantitative data?
  (Since the favourite TV show cannot be expressed as a number, the data are qualitative.)
- What are some examples of discrete data? *(Population of my city, T-shirts sold, Snap Cubes in an object)* Continuous data? *(Perimeter, cost, temperature, time)*

Practice

Assessment Focus: Question 8

Have students work in pairs to discuss their ideas, but each student should write her or his own solution to the problem. If time permits, have students conduct the survey.

3. In each case the population is too large and a sample is the best means of collecting the data.
   a) It would be very costly and time consuming to collect information about all hockey equipment sold in Canada.
   b) It would be very costly and time consuming to collect information about every family in Canada.
   c) It would be too difficult to monitor how long every AAA battery lasts in every calculator.
4. Data may be collected using an Internet website or database—for example Statistics Canada. An advantage is that data are easy to obtain. The disadvantage is that there might not be data on the site on our topic of interest.
   Another method used to obtain data is to survey people you know. The advantage is that data are easy to obtain. The disadvantage is that the data may be biased because the sample may not be randomly selected.
6. i) b) Survey randomly selected students in each grade.
   ii) b) Survey every 10th customer regardless of the shoes they wear.
   iii) b) Survey randomly-selected city residents.
   iv) b) Survey all Canadians and not only those who read the paper.
7. a) The population is too large for a census.
   b) The population is too large for a census.
   c) The population is all Grades 6, 7, and 8 students in a school, and is manageable.
   d) The population is all your friends and is manageable.

b) To find out the favourite breakfast of Grades 7 and 8 students, a survey of 300 randomly-selected Grades 7 and 8 students was conducted. Reliable
c) To find out about the exercise habits of Canadian teenagers, a fitness magazine asks its readers to send in information about the exercise habits of teenagers. Biased
d) To find out if the soccer league should buy new uniforms for the players, 20 parents of the students in the soccer league were surveyed. Biased

3. For each situation, explain why data are collected from a sample and not a census.
   a) To find the mean cost of hockey equipment for teenagers in Canada
   b) To find the number of Canadian families with a cell phone
   c) To find the number of hours an AAA battery will last in a calculator
4. Name two methods used to collect data. Describe the advantages and disadvantages of each method.
5. Identify each population about which the data are to be collected.
   a) The management team of a shopping mall in Brantford wants to know how to attract more people between the ages of 13 and 25 to the mall. 13-to-25-year-olds in Brantford
   b) A juice company wants to find the actual volume of juice in a 1-L carton. Company-made 1-L juice cartons
   c) The board of education wants to find out which schools need renovations. All schools in the board

Number Strategies

Find each percent.
- 300% of 140 420
- 30% of 140 42
- 3% of 140 4.2
- 0.3% of 140 0.42

What patterns do you see in the answers?

Math Link

Your World
There are about 32 million Canadians, as of October, 2004. A company that conducts national surveys can make valid predictions based on the responses of a random sample of about 1000 Canadians.

190 UNIT 5: Data Management

Related Activities

Have students collect continuous data in one or more of the following ways.

1. At home, students bring water to a boil. They then take the temperature of the water every minute to determine how long it takes for the water to cool to room temperature.
2. Have students plant bean or corn seeds, then collect data about the height of the plant as it grows over a 3- or 4-week period. Begin this activity before the unit is taught so that students will have the data available for this lesson.
3. Have students bring in a record of their height and/or mass since birth. These data may be available through a doctor.
4. Students collect continuous data related to their community. Students research a topic related to weather. For example, they could research the amount of precipitation in their community for one season.
   Students use the newspaper to collect continuous data over a 2-week period. For example, some students may collect data about the bank rate or a particular stock. This might give students an opportunity to research an area they are interested in.
5. Have students provide their own idea of a topic about which they would like to collect continuous data, then present it to the class.

To follow these activities, students could graph their data using the most appropriate method. This is likely to be a line graph.

In small groups, have students discuss any trends that their graphs might show and what these trends indicate. For example, if students boiled water and took the temperature as it cooled, they could discuss when the temperature decreased the most or least.

6. For each situation below:
   a) Might the sampling method provide biased data?
   b) If your answer to part a is yes, how can the sampling method be changed so the data collected represent the population?
      i) The student council wants to know if students will attend another school dance this month.
      The student council members survey all their friends to find out. Yes

      ii) A sportswear store conducts a survey to find the most popular brands of athletic shoes.
      The first 300 people in the store who are wearing athletic shoes are surveyed. Yes
      iii) To find out the number of hours per week that people in her city spend exercising, a newspaper journalist interviews all the clients at five different fitness centres in the city. Yes
      iv) A company is hired to find out who Canadians think will win the next Grey Cup. To collect the data, the company puts an advertisement in the sports section of all major newspapers asking people to vote for their choice. Yes

7. Should a census or sample be used to collect data about each topic? Explain your choice.
   a) the effectiveness of a new suntan lotion Sample
   b) the popularity of a fruit-flavoured yogurt Sample
   c) the number of students in Grades 6, 7, and 8 in your school with braces Census
   d) the number of your friends who like to play computer games Census

8. **Assessment Focus** Suppose you are the manager of a high school cafeteria.
   You want to create a new breakfast and lunch menu for the students.
   Describe at least 2 different methods that could be used to collect data about food items to offer on the menu.
   How can you ensure that the results are reliable? Explain.

Reflect

Explain the difference between a census and a sample.
When is a sample biased?

8. **Method 1:** Use a census survey of all the students. This will ensure reliable results.
   Method 2: Survey a sample of randomly-selected students in each grade. The size of the sample should be dependent on the number of students in each grade. The more students in a particular grade, the greater the number in the sample from that grade. The larger the sample size, the more reliable the results.
   Another consideration: Students who do not normally purchase food should also be considered because they might purchase food if different items were made available.
   The survey should include a list of possible items to offer for breakfast and lunch, with an "other" category in which students can suggest additional items.

REFLECT: A census is collected by surveying all the people in a population. A sample is collected by surveying a portion of the population. A sample is biased when it does not accurately represent the population.

ASSESSMENT FOR LEARNING

What to Look For	What to Do
Knowledge and Understanding ✔ Students understand the difference between a census and a sample. ***Communication*** ✔ Students can explain when a survey is reliable, valid, or biased. ***Application*** ✔ Students can identify when a sampling method provides biased data and can change the method so the data collected represent the population.	***Extra Support:*** Students who have difficulty distinguishing between a census and a sample may benefit from asking themselves the question, "Are data being collected from the entire population or only from a portion of the population?" Students can use Step-by-Step 1 (Master 5.7) to complete question 8. ***Extra Practice:*** Students can complete Extra Practice 1 (Master 5.18). ***Extension:*** Students conduct a sample survey, then repeat the same survey using a census. Students compare the results of the two surveys.

Recording and Reporting
Master 5.2 Ongoing Observations: Data Management

Using *Census at School* to Get Secondary Data

LESSON ORGANIZER — 40–50 min

Curriculum Focus: Search databases for information and to solve problems. (8m73, 8m78)

Student Materials

- computers (*Census at School* website)

Vocabulary: database, *Census at School*

Assessment: Master 5.2 Ongoing Observations: Data Management

Key Math Learning

Databases can be used to find information.

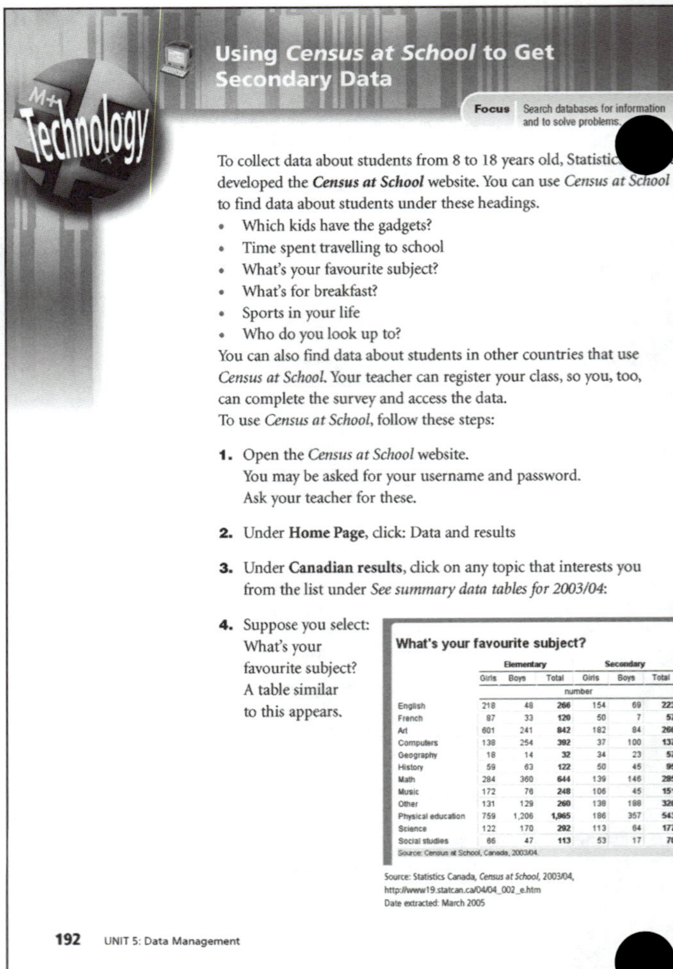

Using *Census at School* to Get Secondary Data

Focus: Search databases for information and to solve problems.

To collect data about students from 8 to 18 years old, Statistics Canada developed the ***Census at School*** website. You can use *Census at School* to find data about students under these headings.

- Which kids have the gadgets?
- Time spent travelling to school
- What's your favourite subject?
- What's for breakfast?
- Sports in your life
- Who do you look up to?

You can also find data about students in other countries that use *Census at School*. Your teacher can register your class, so you, too, can complete the survey and access the data.

To use *Census at School*, follow these steps:

1. Open the *Census at School* website. You may be asked for your username and password. Ask your teacher for these.
2. Under **Home Page**, click: Data and results
3. Under **Canadian results**, click on any topic that interests you from the list under *See summary data tables for 2003/04*:
4. Suppose you select: What's your favourite subject? A table similar to this appears.

What's your favourite subject?

	Elementary			Secondary		
	Girls	Boys	Total	Girls	Boys	Total
	number					
English	218	48	**266**	154	69	**223**
French	87	33	**120**	50	7	**57**
Art	601	241	**842**	182	84	**266**
Computers	138	254	**392**	37	100	**137**
Geography	18	14	**32**	34	23	**57**
History	59	63	**122**	50	45	**95**
Math	284	360	**644**	139	146	**285**
Music	172	76	**248**	106	45	**151**
Other	131	129	**260**	138	188	**326**
Physical education	759	1,206	**1,965**	186	357	**543**
Science	122	170	**292**	113	64	**177**
Social studies	66	47	**113**	53	17	**70**

Source: Census at School, Canada, 2003/04.

Source: Statistics Canada, *Census at School*, 2003/04, http://www19.statcan.ca/04/04_002_e.htm
Date extracted: March 2005

192 UNIT 5: Data Management

Information for Teachers

To access the *Census at School* website, enter www.censusatschool.ca and click on English.

To access class summary results, go to the Teachers page, click on *Register/Sign in* and enter your e-mail address and teacher password. Instructions are provided for either viewing the results or downloading them. For ideas on how to use your class data, click on *Learning activities* on the Teacher's page.

Using E-STAT to Search for Secondary Data

E-STAT is one of Statistics Canada's Internet databases. It is free for teachers and students. You may wish to have your students access this website to obtain information on a variety of topics.

To access E-STAT go to http://estat.statcan.ca.

The *Table of contents* page contains the following headings: *Preview, Articles, Data.*

The subheadings are: *Economy, Land and Resources, People, Nation, Censuses of Canada 1665 to 1871,* and *Elections Canada.* Each of these subheadings has a list of topics for which data are available.

You may wish to have students explore data under headings of their own choice. It may be helpful to guide them through one particular heading to show them how to access related data.

Print these data for later use on page 205.

To find data from students in other countries, follow these steps:

5. Return to *Step 3*. Under **International results**, click on Random data selector.

6. Under **Results and Data**, click: Phase 1 Results

7. Select any topic of interest listed on the page. Suppose you click: Month of Birth – What is the most popular month to be born in?

Month of Birth

All Data	Counts All pupils	Counts Males	Counts Females	Percentage of all pupils	Percentage of male pupils	Percentage of female pupils
Total	58,322	27,793	30,529	100.00	100.00	100.00
January	4,584	2,150	2,434	7.86	7.74	7.97
February	4,465	2,165	2,300	7.66	7.79	7.53
March	4,978	2,359	2,619	8.54	8.49	8.58
April	4,784	2,247	2,537	8.20	8.08	8.31
May	5,065	2,422	2,643	8.68	8.71	8.66
June	4,990	2,406	2,584	8.56	8.66	8.46
July	5,020	2,393	2,627	8.61	8.61	8.60
August	4,898	2,282	2,616	8.40	8.21	8.57
September	5,199	2,509	2,690	8.91	9.03	8.81
October	5,000	2,461	2,539	8.57	8.85	8.32
November	4,669	2,222	2,447	8.01	7.99	8.02
December	4,670	2,177	2,493	8.01	7.83	8.17

Excludes non responses

8. Suppose you select All Data. A table similar to this appears. The table shows data for the United Kingdom.

Source: *Census at School*–United Kingdom
http://www.censusatschool.ntu.ac.uk/table8-0.asp
Date extracted: March 2005

✓ Check

Use *Census at School* to solve each problem.
Remember to use the Random data selector to obtain data from the United Kingdom, South Africa, New Zealand, and parts of Australia. Print your data.

1. a) In which month are most students in the United Kingdom born? September
   b) Is this month the same for boys and girls? Explain. Yes

2. What percent of students in Canada take more than 1 h to get to school?

3. What is the difference in percents of people in Canada with blue eyes and with brown eyes?

REACHING ALL LEARNERS

Early Finishers

Have students obtain data on the same topic for different countries, then compare results for the same age groups, different age groups, same gender, and different gender.

Common Misconceptions

➤ Students think *Census at School* has the same information as E-STAT.

How to Help: Tell students that *Census at School* is designed for use by teachers and students. The website contains data based on questionnaires that teachers and students have completed. It is a growing database because as more classes register, more data are collected.

Sample Solutions

1. a) Most students in the United Kingdom are born in September; there are 5199 males and females. This accounts for 8.91% of the total.
   b) Yes, 2690 females or about 8.81% of females were born in September, and 2509 or about 9.03% of males were born in September.

2, 3. Answers may vary as data are updated regularly.

ASSESSMENT FOR LEARNING

What to Look For

Knowledge and Understanding

✔ Students understand what the *Census at School* website is about and how it is linked to Statistics Canada.

Communication

✔ Students can give examples of different types of databases and describe how they might be organized.

Application

✔ Students can follow the steps to search for data using the *Census at School* website.

What to Do

Extra Support: Encourage students to read the introductory notes in the *Census at School* website to learn that this website focuses on 8–18-year-olds. Students could also make a list of the topics and countries from which data are collected.

Extra Practice: Have students choose another topic listed on page 192, then make up and solve problems related to that topic.

Extension: Students search the same topic for all the available countries. Students search more than one topic of their choice for one or two countries. Students then compare the results between similar age groups in different countries; or between males and females in different countries; or between different age groups.

Recording and Reporting

Master 5.2 Ongoing Observations: Data Management

Inferring and Evaluating

LESSON ORGANIZER 40–50 min

Curriculum Focus: Make inferences and evaluate arguments. (8m70, 8m73, 8m76, 8m78, 8m79)

Student Materials *Optional*
- Step-by-Step 2 (Master 5.8)
- Extra Practice 2 (Master 5.19)

Vocabulary: inference, convincing argument, scatter plot

Assessment: Master 5.2 Ongoing Observations: Data Management

Key Math Learnings

1. Data and graphs may be used to make convincing arguments or conclusions.
2. Data and graphs may be used to make predictions.
3. A scatter plot can be used to compare two attributes.

5.2 Inferring and Evaluating

Focus Make inferences and evaluate arguments.

Explore

Work in a group of 3.
Suppose your group is responsible for selecting one of these students to be on an *Aim for the Top* quiz team for your school board:

Marks of Top Students

Student	Math	Language Arts	History	Science	Geography
Suresh	93	89	90	97	87
Marco	96	91	86	94	90
Nella	98	80	91	95	94
Yoko	90	92	91	91	92

Which student would you choose to be on the team?
Justify your choice.
What would you say to convince other groups about your choice?

Reflect & Share

Share your reasons with another group that picked the same student.
Are the reasons the same? Explain.
Share your choice with a group that picked a different student.
Discuss the reasons for your choices.

Connect

Data and graphs may be used to make convincing arguments.

The school cafeteria collected data on the numbers of cups of hot chocolate purchased by girls and boys during the first 15 days of school in September.

	Number of Cups of Hot Chocolate Purchased															Total
Girls	2	0	3	5	4	7	4	3	4	5	1	5	2	8	10	63
Boys	3	1	5	4	5	9	6	5	3	6	2	4	4	9	8	74

BEFORE **Get Started**

Invite students to discuss how they would choose schoolmates to be part of the city hockey team.

Ask:

- What criteria would you use to make the selections?
  (I would list all the students that have played competitive hockey, then narrow my search. For example, once I had a list of all students who played competitive hockey, I would look at the statistics for each player. I would look at their scoring averages, what position they play, their years of experience, and other relevant data before I make my decision.)
- What would you do to convince the coach to choose a particular student?
  (To convince the coach, I would gather the statistics and records of the students. I would need to present the statistics along with each student's history to present my case. It is not sufficient to simply show the statistics. It is important to look at the bigger picture.)

Present *Explore.* You may wish to pre-select groups of three students. To facilitate this process, make a list of the groups on a transparency and place it on the overhead projector so that students may organize themselves. Alternatively, let students choose their own groups.

DURING **Explore**

Ongoing Assessment: Observe and Listen

As students work, ask questions, such as:

- Why is it important to know the marks of the students in each subject area?
  (To be on the Aim for the Top quiz team, students need to have good academic marks in all subject areas so that they can answer questions in various subject areas.)
- What do you notice about the students' marks?
  (All students have excellent marks in most subjects.

Amy used the data in this table to argue that boys drink more hot chocolate than girls.
Alice said there were not enough data to make that argument.
The students collected more data to test Amy's argument.

Total Hot Chocolate Sales Per Month						
	Sept.	Oct.	Nov.	Dec.	Jan.	Total
Girls	85	128	197	201	252	863
Boys	92	130	190	207	249	868
Total	177	258	387	408	501	1731

Amy said that her conclusion was correct because the total number of hot chocolates purchased by girls was 863.
This is less than 868, which is the total for boys.
Alice looked at the data and made this argument:
More students drink hot chocolate when the weather is cold.
Alice said her argument was correct because the monthly sales increased for the colder months.
Alice's argument is more convincing than Amy's because, in 5 months, the total sales for boys was only 5 more than the total for girls. The numbers are too close for Amy's argument to be convincing.

When we use data to predict a value in the future, or to estimate a value between given data, we make an **inference**.
When we use data to make a conclusion, we *infer*.

Example

This double-bar graph shows the hourly wages of Canadians in 1997 and 2003.

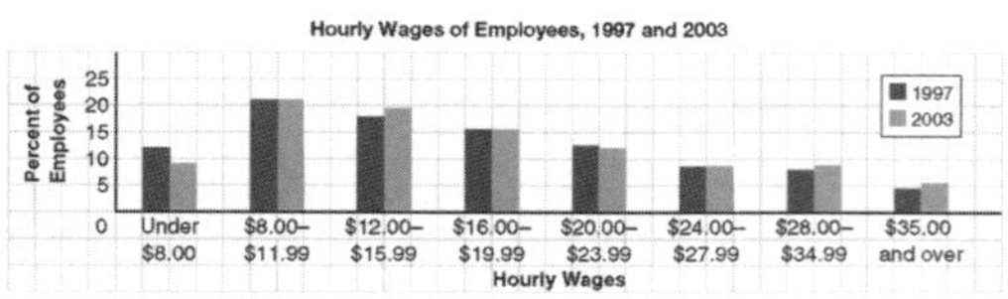

5.2 Inferring and Evaluating **195**

REACHING ALL LEARNERS

Alternative Explore

Work in a small group.

The following table provides the Goals (G), Assists (A), Total Points (P), +/− , and Penalty In Minutes (PIM) for three Ottawa Senators hockey players during the 2003–2004 NHL season. Suppose your group is going to start a new NHL team, and can choose one of these players. Which player would you choose to be on your team? Justify your choice.

Player	G	A	P	+/−	PIM
Radek Bonk	12	32	44	2	66
Wade Redden	17	26	43	21	65
Bryan Smolinski	19	27	46	22	49

Early Finishers

Have students collect data about a favourite personality. They use the data to make a convincing argument as to why that person is the best in her or his field.

Common Misconceptions

➤ Students think that the argument they make must be true.
How to Help: Tell students that the argument they make must be convincing based on the data and how they use them to put forth their statements.

Some students have extremely high marks in one or two subjects and a lower mark in another subject.)

- What would you consider to be most important in choosing the student to be on the team?
  (*The person who is chosen to be on the team should have consistently high marks in every subject so that he or she has the knowledge to answer questions in a variety of subject areas.*)
- What is the average mark for each student?
  (*The average mark for each student is: Suresh 91.2%, Marco 91.4%, Nella 91.6%, and Yoko 91.2%.*)
- What do you notice about the average mark for each student? (*The average mark for each student is about the same.*)
- Would you use the average mark to select the student? Explain.
  (*No, I would not use the average mark to select the student. For example, Nella has the highest average mark, but her Language Arts mark is low (80%) compared to the other students. This may mean that other students have more knowledge of Language Arts than Nella. I would choose the student with the most consistent marks in all subjects — Yoko.*)

AFTER Connect

Invite students to share their choices and reasons with the class.

Ask questions, such as:

- Why is the highest average mark not necessarily the most suitable?
  (*We cannot tell from the average if the student has a high mark in one subject and a low mark in another subject.*)
- What do you notice about Nella's marks?
  (*Her Language Arts mark is the lowest of the group. This could mean that others have greater knowledge and therefore more chance of answering questions correctly in Language Arts than Nella.*)
- Is there only one correct answer to *Explore*?
  (*No, it is possible that more than one student would*

Sample Solutions

1. I would choose Elise because her times are more consistent.
2. a) No, the claim is not true because the word "prefer" implies there was a choice of food. However, the cats were only given Purr-Fect cat food. Perhaps the cats who ate Purr-Fect cat food did so only because they were hungry.
   b) Seven out of 10 cats who were given Purr-Fect cat food ate it. Thirty percent of cats were either not hungry or disliked Purr-Fect cat food.
3. a) Government spending on water purification increased drastically in 1994 compared to the previous 2 years. Government spending on water purification from 1994 to 2002 averaged about $600 million.
   b) i) In 1998, spending was close to $800 million but in 2002, it was only $600 million; this is a drop of $200 million.
   ii) Between 1992 and 2002, government spending increased from less than $20 million to almost $800 million (40 times more than $20 million).
4. a) Liang could argue that compared to any other activity, the greatest number of students chose swimming as their favourite summer activity.
   b) Liang could argue that more than one-half of the students surveyed ($\frac{11}{20}$) chose land activities.
5. a) No, it is not a valid inference because not all students were surveyed, and of those surveyed, more than one-half had no opinion.
   b) A convincing argument could be that 40 of the 120 students surveyed, or one-third, wanted extended library hours.

a) How can the graph be used to justify each argument?
   i) The percent of employees who earned under $8.00/h decreased from 1997 to 2003.
   ii) Approximately 50% of employees earned $16.00/h or more in 2003.

b) What can be inferred about the percent of employees who will earn hourly wages over $24.00 in 2009? Explain.

Solution

a) i) The bar for the interval "Under $8.00" is shorter for 2003 than it is for 1997. This means that there was a decrease in the percent of employees who earned less than $8.00/h, from 1997 to 2003.
   ii) The percent of employees who earned $16.00/h or more in 2003 is given by the lengths of the bars for the intervals from $16.00, and up.
   Estimate the lengths: 16% + 12% + 9% + 9% + 6% = 52%
   Since about 52% of employees earned $16.00/h or more in 2003, the argument is valid.

b) The graph shows an increase, from 1997 to 2003, in the percent of employees earning hourly wages in these intervals: $24.00–$27.99, $28.00–$34.99, and $35.00 and over
If we assume this trend continues, we can infer that there will be an increase in the percent of employees who will earn hourly wages over $24.00 in 2009.

Practice

1. Elise, Mira, and Kim practised to compete in the 50-m butterfly stroke. Their practice times, in seconds, are given in the table. Which of the three swimmers would you choose to be on the competitive relay team to swim the butterfly stroke? Justify your choice.

Swimmer	1st Practice (s)	2nd Practice (s)	3rd Practice (s)	4th Practice (s)
Elise	45.4	45.3	45.8	46.2
Mira	47.9	43.2	44.7	45.0
Kim	45.2	48.3	43.1	44.3

196 UNIT 5: Data Management

be a good candidate for the team. There are factors, other than marks, that may make a student a better candidate. Some examples are: reflexes — for pressing the buzzer, experience playing trivia-type games, and so on.)

- How would your choice change if the selection was being made for a *Math for the Top* team?
  (*My choice would change because then only the math marks would need to be considered. The choice in that case would likely be Nella because she is the student with the highest math mark.*)

Review *Connect.* Inferences or arguments can be weak if there are few data values. A strong or convincing argument is one in which the data are consistent enough to support the inference made.

Inferences may be made from a scatter plot.

The following inferences were made from these scatter plots:

Ice Cream Sales against Temperature

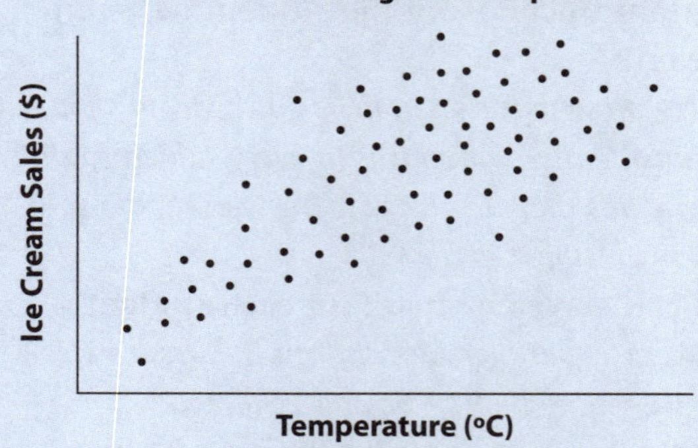

There is a relationship.
The dots go up to the right.
The scatter plot has an upward trend.
We can infer that as the temperature increased, ice cream sales increased.

2. Each of ten cats was given a bowl filled with Purr-Fect cat food. Seven cats ate the food in the bowl. Three cats did not.
Advertisers for Purr-Fect cat food claimed:
"70% of cats prefer Purr-Fect cat food."
  a) Is this claim true? Explain.
  b) What inferences would you make from the data? Explain.

3. a) What inferences can you make from this graph? Explain.

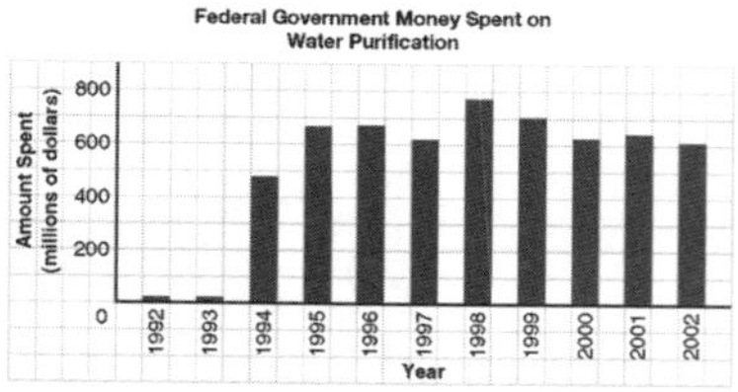

Source: Statistics Canada, Canada e-Book (11-404-XIE) based on the 2001 Canada Yearbook (11-402-XPE). http://142.206.72.67/01/01b/01b_graph/01b_graph_002d_1e.htm Date extracted: April 11, 2005

  b) How can the graph be used to justify each argument?
    i) The government has reduced its spending on water purification.
    ii) The government has increased its spending on water purification.

4. Liang asked 20 Grade 8 students:
"What is your favourite outdoor summer activity?"
He recorded these results:

Activity	Swimming	Biking	Canoeing	Skateboarding	Rollerblading
Number of Students	7	5	2	3	3

How could Liang use the results of his survey to make these arguments? Justify your answers.
  a) The majority of students surveyed chose swimming as their favourite outdoor activity.
  b) Land activities are preferred over water activities.

5.2 Inferring and Evaluating **197**

6. a) The reporter could use the data to convince readers that his statement is true by saying that 40 represents the greatest number of car accidents in one category.
  b) 60% of the car accidents did not occur within 3 km of the driver's home.
  c) Twice as many accidents occurred within 3 km of the driver's home, as those that occurred in parking lots. About 50% of accidents occurred on country roads or within 3 km of the driver's home.

7. a) The table shows the numbers of males and females between the ages of 12 and 34 who eat fruits and vegetables 5–10 times per day.
  b) i) More females eat 5–10 fruits and vegetables per day than males.
    ii) Almost twice as many men aged 25–34 eat 5 to 10 servings of fruits and vegetables per day than do men aged 20–24.
  c) i) Males aged 12–14 eat the least number of fruits and vegetables per day.
    ii) According to the table, about the same number of 15–19-year-old females and 20–24-year-old females eat 5–10 fruits and vegetables per day.
  d) i) Males and females between the ages of 12 and 34 who eat fruits and vegetables more than 10 times per day
    ii) No, the inferences I made in parts b and c do not hold for 12–14-year-olds and 15–19-year-olds because in this table, more males than females in these age groups eat over 10 fruits and vegetables per day.

Test Marks against Hours Spent Watching TV

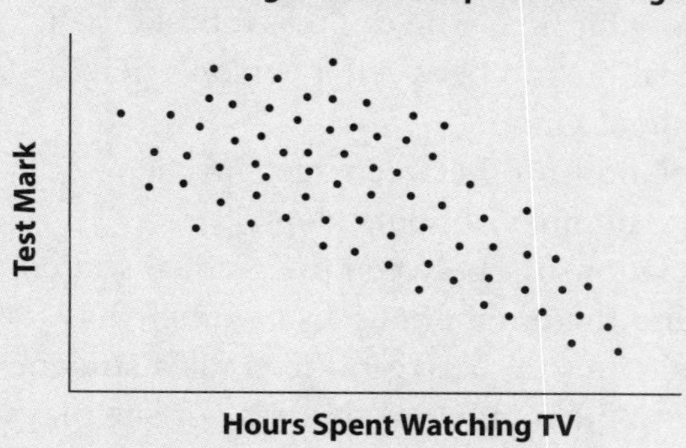

There is a relationship.
The dots go down to the right.
The scatter plot has a downward trend.
We can infer that the more hours spent watching TV, the lower the test mark.

Height against Test Marks

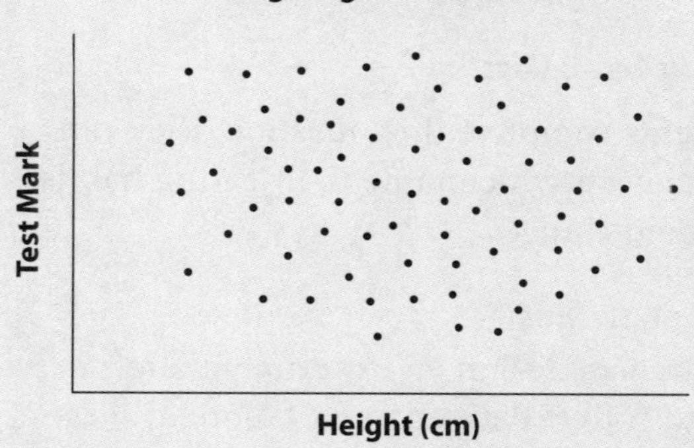

There is no pattern in the dots.
So, there is no relationship.
We can infer that height does not affect test marks.

REFLECT: When using data to make inferences or arguments, you should consider the following: the number of entries in the data set, whether the data are biased, whether the graph accurately represents the data or shows bias, and any trends or patterns that the graph may show. For example, suppose 30 randomly selected Grade 8 students in a school are asked how many books they read in a month. Suppose the data range from 0–3 books. A valid inference or argument may be that students in the school read less than 4 books per month. An invalid inference or argument would be that Grade 8 students in Ontario read less than 4 books per month. The sample and population need to be considered before the inference or argument is made.

Assignment Guidelines

If your students do not have time to complete all the *Practice* questions on pages 196, 197, 198, and 199, these questions provide minimum curriculum coverage: 1, 2, 5, 7, *Reflect*

To assess the 4 Achievement Chart categories listed in the curriculum document, have students complete these *Practice* questions:
Knowledge and Understanding: 1
Communication: 2
Application: 5
Thinking: 7

5. Fifteen hundred students attend Bishop Ryan High School.
One hundred twenty students were asked,
"Do you think the school library hours should be extended?"
Forty students agreed that library hours should be extended,
10 students said they were against extended hours,
and 70 students had no opinion.
The Bishop Ryan High School newspaper reported:

"Survey indicates 80% of the student body who had an opinion, agree that school library hours should be extended."

a) Is this a valid inference? Justify your answer.
b) Write a convincing argument that could be justified by the survey results.
Explain your reasoning.

6. Police recorded this information about 100 car accidents:
- 40 were within 3 km of the driver's home
- 30 were on the highway
- 20 were in parking lots
- 10 were on country roads

A newspaper reporter wrote the following headline:

Majority of Car Accidents Happen Close to Home

a) How could the reporter use the data to convince readers that his statement is true?
b) What statement could you make to prove the reporter is wrong? Justify your statement.
c) Write two inferences that can be made from the data. Justify your inferences.

198 UNIT 5: Data Management

Practice

Assessment Focus: Question 7

As students complete this question, they can think about in which table their eating habits would be included.

Related Activities

Have students design an experiment and/or survey to collect data on one or more of these topics:

1. The relationship between a person's height and foot length
2. The relationship between a person's foot length and hand length
3. The relationship between a person's height and arm span
4. The relationship between a person's height and how far he or she can toss a basketball
5. The relationship between a person's height and school grade
6. The relationship between age and the average number of hours slept
7. The relationship between the grade a student is in and the number of pets he or she has
8. The relationship between the grade a student is in and the number of sports he or she plays

Once a topic is chosen, tell students what to plot along the horizontal axis and what to plot along the vertical axis. Students compare their results with those of their classmates. Have students determine whether there is a relationship. Have them make inferences about the topic they have explored.

Number Strategies

brackets to make each statement true.

$24 \div (3 + 5) \times 2^2 + 4 = 16$

$24 \div 3 + 5 \times (2^2 + 4) = 48$

$24 \div 3 + (5 \times 2)^2 + 4 = 112$

$24 \div (3 + 5) \times (2^2 + 4) = 24$

7. Assessment Focus

a) What does the table show?

Eats Fruits and Vegetables 5 to 10 Times Per Day

Age Group (years)	Females	Males
12–14	250 238	231 755
15–19	391 589	326 369
20–24	393 640	307 997
25–34	841 078	572 224

Source: Statistics Canada, Canadian Community Health Survey, 2003, CANSIM table 01050249. http://www.statcan.ca/english/freepub/82-221-XIE/00604/tables/html/2187_03.htm Date extracted: March 18, 2005

b) What inferences can you make about the eating habits of each group?
   i) females ii) males
   Justify your answers.

c) What arguments can you make about the eating habits of each group?
   i) 12–14 year old males
   ii) 15–19 year old females compared to 20–24 year old females
   Justify your arguments.

These data come from a Stats Can Community Health Survey in 2003.

d) i) What does this table show?

Eats Fruits and Vegetables more than 10 Times Per Day

Age Group (years)	Females	Males
12–14	31 289	40 472
15–19	59 418	63 755
20–24	61 520	53 264
25–34	98 376	69 277

Source: Statistics Canada, Canadian Community Health Survey, 2003, CANSIM table 01050249. http://www.statcan.ca/english/freepub/82-221-XIE/00604/tables/html/2187_03.htm Date extracted: March 18, 2005

   ii) Do the inferences and arguments you made in parts b and c still hold? Explain.

Reflect

When you use a set of data to make an inference or a convincing argument, what sorts of things do you consider? Use an example in your explanation.

5.2 Inferring and Evaluating **199**

ASSESSMENT FOR LEARNING

What to Look For

Knowledge and Understanding

✔ Students can make a convincing argument based on given data.

Communication

✔ Students can identify an inference that is not valid and modify it to make a valid argument.

Application

✔ Students can identify if an inference is valid.

What to Do

Extra Support: Pair a student with strong math skills with a weaker student.
Students can use Step-by-Step 2 (Master 5.8) to complete question 7.

Extra Practice: Students can complete the Additional Activity *Misleading Graphs* (Master 5.5).
Students can complete Extra Practice 2 (Master 5.19).

Extension: Have students go to the Statistics Canada website to find out more about the Community Health Survey, 2003 used in question 7.

Recording and Reporting

Master 5.2 Ongoing Observations: Data Management

LESSON 5.3

The Shape of Data

LESSON ORGANIZER 80–100 min

Curriculum Focus: Graph data, identify trends, and make inferences. (8m70, 8m71, 8m73, 8m77)

Teacher Materials
- overhead transparency of Graphs for 5.3 *Connect* (Master 5.14)

Student Materials
- copies of Graphs for 5.3 *Explore* (Master 5.13)
- 0.5-cm grid paper (PM 14)
- coloured pencils

Optional
- Step-by-Step 3 (Master 5.9)
- Extra Practice 3 (Master 5.20)

Assessment: Master 5.2 Ongoing Observations: Data Management

Key Math Learnings

1. Different types of data are best represented by different types of graphs.
2. A circle graph displays data that represent part of one whole.
3. A line graph displays data that change over time.
4. A bar graph displays data that can be counted.
5. A scatter plot displays two related sets of data that are measured or counted.

5.3 The Shape of Data

Focus Graph data, identify trends, and make inferences.

Explore

Work in a small group.
Each graph is incomplete.
Identify each type of graph.
Match each graph with a table below. Explain your choice.
On a copy of the graphs, insert the title and labels for each graph.
Make a list of some information you know from each graph.

Table 4
Graph A

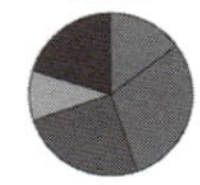

Table 2
Graph B

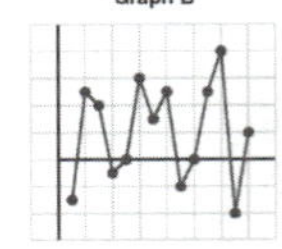

Table 1
Graph C

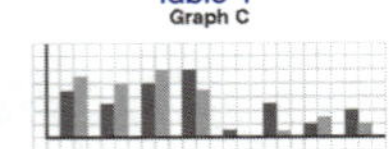

Table 3
Graph D

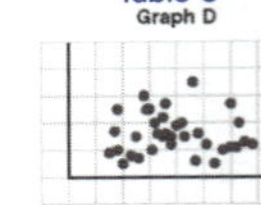

Table 1

Instruments Students Learn to Play

Instrument	Girls	Boys
Drums	7	9
Classical Guitar	5	8
Electric Guitar	8	10
Piano	10	7
Harp	1	0
Clarinet	5	1
Violin	2	3
Bagpipes	4	2

Table 2

Daily Maximum Temperatures for 2 Weeks in February

Feb.	1	2	3	4	5	6	7	8	9	10	11	12	13	14
Temp (°C)	−3	5	4	−1	0	6	3	5	−2	0	5	8	−4	2

Table 3

Fun Run Fundraiser – Participants' Age in Years and Distance Completed in Kilometres

Age	Distance	Age	Distance	Age	Distance	Age	Distance
28	30	23	8	36	27	42	20
63	20	60	11	35	22	62	11
46	35	47	6	36	16	15	9
37	15	48	16	65	13	35	15
38	12	51	12	60	27	25	15
29	25	40	19	57	10	18	10
33	16	31	10	68	12	17	17
54	5	20	5	32	20	18	25
43	15	30	25	38	15	26	7

Table 4

Homework Time Spent on Each Subject

Subject	Percent
French	15
Math	30
Spelling	25
History	10
Science	20

200 UNIT 5: Data Management

BEFORE Get Started

Use *Skills You'll Need,* pages 185 and 186, to review how data and graphs may show a pattern or a trend.

Present *Explore.* Remind students they are to work in a small group.

Give each student a copy of Graphs for Lesson 5.3 *Explore* (Master 5.13).

DURING Explore

Ongoing Assessment: Observe and Listen

As students work, ensure that they can match the data in the tables with each graph.

Ask questions, such as:
- How many sectors does the circle graph have? *(Five sectors)*
- Which table contains five items? *(Table 4)*
- What do you notice about the percents in the table? *(The percents add to 100%.)*
- Which table is represented by the line graph? *(Table 2)*
- Which table shows data over time? *(Table 2)*
- Which graph shows two sets of data? *(The double-bar graph)*
- Which table shows two sets of counted data? *(Table 1)*
- Which table does the scatter plot match? *(Table 3)* How do you know? *(There are 2 sets of related data that are counted or measured.)*
- How else could you display the data in Table 1? *(Table 1 could be displayed as two circle graphs.)*

AFTER Connect

Have each group share their findings with another group.

Reflect & Share

With your group, decide if the data could have been displayed another way. Draw each new display.

nnect

Here are some different types of graphs.

A circle graph displays data that represent parts of one whole.
Graph A in *Explore* is a circle graph.

A line graph displays data that change over time.
On a line graph, line segments join data points.
Graph B in *Explore* is a line graph.

A bar graph displays data that can be counted.
Two sets of data can be displayed on a double-bar graph.
Graph C in *Explore* is a double-bar graph.

A scatter plot displays two related sets of data that are measured or counted.
Graph D in *Explore* is a scatter plot.

Example

Life Expectancy at Birth

Birth Year	Females (years)	Males (years)
1920	61	59
1930	62	60
1940	66	63
1950	71	66
1960	74	68
1970	76	69
1980	79	72
1990	81	75

Source: Statistics Canada, *Canadian Statistics summary tables*. Last modified 2005-02-17.
http://www40.statcan.ca/l01/cst01/health26.htm
Date extracted: April 11, 2005

This table displays the life expectancy at birth for people born between 1920 and 1990.

a) A person is born in 1970.
How long can he or she expect to live?

b) Which types of graphs could be used to display the data? Explain.

c) Display the data using an appropriate graph.
Justify your choice.

d) What trends do you see in the data?
How does the graph show the trends?

e) How could the graph be used to predict the life expectancy of a female born in 2010?
What assumptions are made?

REACHING ALL LEARNERS

Early Finishers

Have students display the data in the two tables in *Practice* question 7 on page 199 of the Student Book, using the most appropriate graph.

Common Misconceptions

➤ Students think that all sets of data can be displayed using any type of graph.

How to Help: Have students try to draw a line graph and scatter plot for the data in Table 4. They will soon find out that neither of these are possible. Have them discuss why this is the case. They should notice that a line graph can only be drawn when the horizontal axis represents time, and that a scatter plot requires two related sets of measured or counted data.

Assignment Guidelines

If your students do not have time to complete all the *Practice* questions on pages 203 and 204, these questions provide minimum curriculum coverage: 1, 3, 4, 5, *Reflect*

To assess the 4 Achievement Chart categories listed in the curriculum document, have students complete these *Practice* questions:
Knowledge and Understanding: 1
Application: 3
Communication: 4
Thinking: 5

Review *Connect*. Explain to students that different types of graphs correspond to different types of data. Summarize with students when it is best to display data on a circle graph, line graph, double-line graph, bar graph, double-bar graph, and scatter plot.

Ask:

- Which type of data is best displayed by a circle graph?
  (Data that represent parts of one whole.)
- Which type of data is best displayed by a line graph? *(Data that change over time.)*
- Which type of data is best displayed by a bar graph? *(Data that can be counted.)* Double-bar graph? *(Two sets of data that can be counted.)*
- What type of data is best displayed by a scatter plot?
  (Two related sets of data that are measured or counted.)

Remind students that once data are displayed on a graph, patterns or trends may be more easily seen than when the data are organized in a table.

Ask:

- What does it mean when one line is above another line in a double-line graph, such as the one shown in the *Example*?
  (It means that the top line has data values that are consistently higher than the bottom line. In this case, female life expectancy is greater than male life expectancy for all ages.)
- Why is it easier to make predictions using a graph than a table?
  (The graph may be extended to find the value on the vertical axis that corresponds to a value that we want to predict on the horizontal axis.)

Have a short discussion with students as to why it is important to know how to interpret tables and graphs presented in the media. Students should understand that this is an

Sample Solutions

1. a)

Football Game Attendance

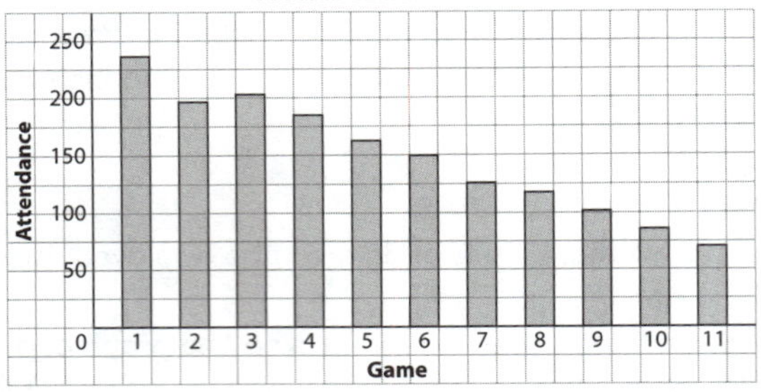

b) The trend is that attendance at after-school football games is decreasing.

c) Perhaps the football team was losing games, or the weather became colder, so attendance declined.

2. a) The data should be displayed on a double-bar graph because there are two sets of countable data.

Population of Some Canadian Cities

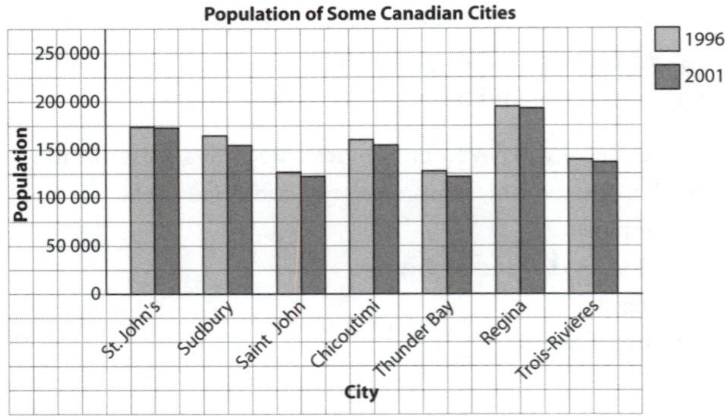

f) Simon extended the data in the table. The life expectancy for a male increased by 75 − 59, or 16 years from 1920 to 1990. So, Simon predicted that a male born in 2060 would have a life expectancy of 75 + 16, or 91 years. Is this a valid argument?

Solution

a) From the table, a female born in 1970 can expect to live for 76 years, and a male for 69 years.

b) There are two sets of data. They could be displayed using a double-bar graph or double-line graph.

c) Since the data represent change over time, a line graph is an appropriate graph.
Plot each set of data on the same grid.
Use a scale of 1 square for every 5 years.

Remember to label each axis and give the graph a title.

Life Expectancy at Birth

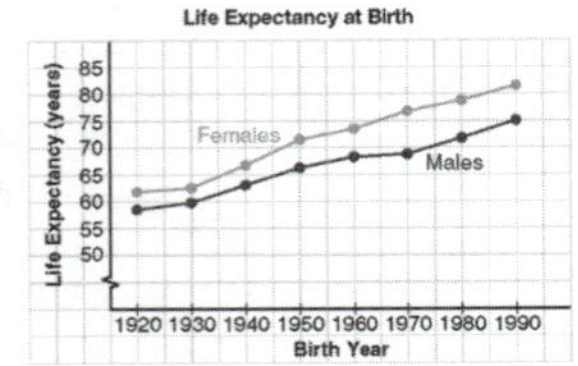

d) Both lines go up to the right, so life expectancy is increasing for both males and females.
The line representing females is above the line representing males, so females have a greater life expectancy than males.

e) To predict the life expectancy of a female born in 2010, extend the last line segment for female life expectancy to 2010.

Life Expectancy at Birth

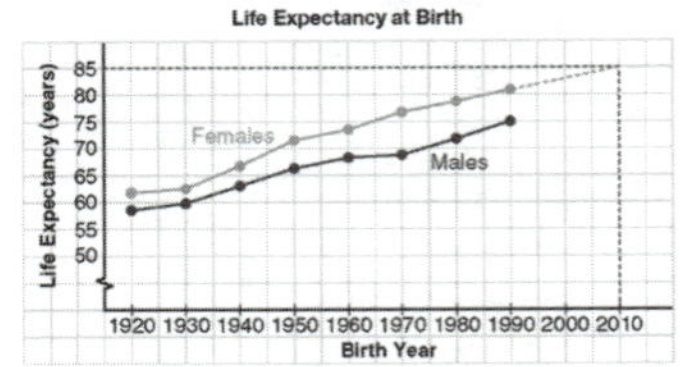

important skill, especially if the information is misrepresented. To determine how data could be misrepresented, place a transparency of Graphs for 5.3 *Connect* (Master 5.14) on an overhead projector.

Show students Graphs A and B.

Ask:

- How are the graphs similar?
  (*Both graphs represent the value of a car over 8 years. They both have the same scale on the horizontal axis.*)
- How are they different?
  (*The scale on the vertical axis is different for each graph.*)
- What impression does each graph give? Explain.
  (*Graph A gives the impression that the value of the car decreases gradually over 8 years. Graph B gives the impression that the value of the car decreases rapidly — especially in the first two years.*)
- Who might want to use Graph A? Explain.
  (*Graph A might be used by car dealers selling new cars who want to convince customers that buying a brand new car is the better option.*)
- Who might want to use Graph B? Explain.
  (*Graph B might be used by used car dealers who want to impress on customers that the value of a new car decreases very rapidly, and therefore buying a used car is the better option.*)

Students should know that information on graphs may sometimes be misrepresented to provide misleading or false impressions. Sometimes this is done on purpose to sway public opinion, or to increase ratings, or to influence people in making decisions.

Changing the scale on a graph is one way to misrepresent data.

A poorly worded survey question could also result in misleading data.

From the graph, the life expectancy of a female born in 2010 will be about 85 years. We assume that life expectancy will continue to increase at the same rate as it did from 1980 to 1990.
This may not happen.

f) The argument is not valid.
We cannot assume that life expectancy will continue to increase at the same rate for the next 70 years.
Certain diseases may be cured, but the human body wears out.
The life expectancy will probably reach an upper limit.

Practice

1. The table shows the attendance at after-school football games.

Game	1	2	3	4	5	6	7	8	9	10	11
Attendance	235	197	203	185	163	149	126	118	102	85	71

a) Display the data.
b) What trend does the graph show? Explain.
c) What are some possible reasons for this trend?

2. This table shows the populations of some Canadian cities in 1996 and in 2001.
a) Round the data to the nearest 1000.
Display the data using an appropriate graph.
Justify your choice.
b) What trends do you see in the data?
How does the graph show the trends?
c) Predict the population of each city in 2006.
Justify your numbers.

Populations of Some Canadian Cities

City	1996	2001
St. John's	174 051	172 918
Sudbury	165 336	155 219
Saint John	125 705	122 678
Chicoutimi	160 454	154 938
Thunder Bay	126 643	121 986
Regina	193 652	192 800
Trois-Rivières	139 956	137 507

3. a) What do the data in the table represent?

Average Daily Temperature (°C)

Month	J	F	M	A	M	J	J	A	S	O	N	D
Vancouver	2	3	5	9	12	15	18	17	13	9	5	2
Hawaii	22	22	21	18	15	13	12	13	15	18	19	21

5.3 The Shape of Data 203

b) The population of each city decreased over the 5 years.
The length of the bar for each city in 2001 is shorter than the length of the bar for each city in 1996.

c) To predict the population of each city in 2006, decrease each population in 2001 by the amount it decreased from 1996. So the population of each city in 2006 would be:

City	2006
St. John's	172 000 (decrease by 1000)
Sudbury	145 000 (decrease by 10 000)
Saint John	120 000 (decrease by 3000)
Chicoutimi	150 000 (decrease by 5000)
Thunder Bay	117 000 (decrease by 5000)
Regina	192 000 (decrease by 1000)
Trois-Rivières	136 000 (decrease by 2000)

3. a) The data in the table represent the average daily temperatures of Vancouver and Hawaii for one year.

b) A double-line graph is the most suitable way to display two sets of data that change over time.

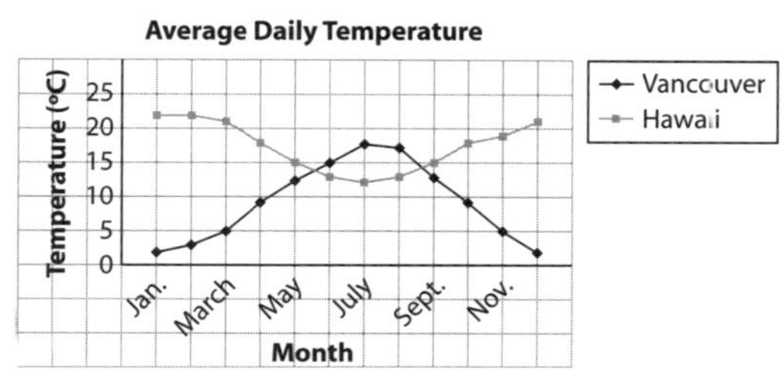

Collecting data from a sample that is too small or not representative of the population will also lead to incorrect or misleading information.

Show students Graphs C and D.

Ask:

- Compare the two graphs. Describe how one graph misrepresents the data and the other does not.
(*Graph C misrepresents the data. The vertical scale on Graph C begins at $600 million. This means the lengths of the bars represent amounts spent over $600 million. On Graph C there are no amounts shown for 1992, 1993, and 1994, so it appears that no money was spent in those years. However, Graph D shows that less than $50 million was spent in 1992 and 1993, and almost $500 million was spent in 1994. Graph D accurately displays the data. The vertical scale on Graph D begins at 0, so the length of each bar accurately represents the amount of money spent each year.*)
- Who might want to use the misleading graph and why?
(*Any group that wanted to show the government was not spending enough money on water purification might use Graph C.*)

Practice

All questions require 0.5-cm grid paper (PM 14).

Assessment Focus: Question 5

Students can display the data on a double-line graph or on a double-bar graph.

c) Trends for Vancouver: The average temperature increases from January to July, then decreases. The coldest months are November to March. The temperature range is 16°C.
Trends for Hawaii: The average temperature increases from August to March, then decreases from April to July.
The temperature range is 10°C.

d) The best time to visit Vancouver is from June to August, assuming you like the warmest months. The best time to visit Hawaii is from December to March, assuming you like the warmest months.

e) This information would be useful to tourists and to travel agents who suggest and book holidays.

4. a) A scatter plot is the most suitable way to display the data because the table shows two related sets of measured data.

Height against Age

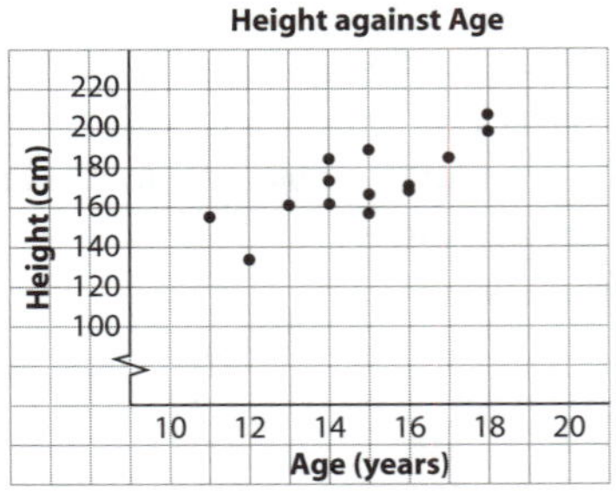

b) Yes, there does appear to be a relationship between age and height for this age group.
The points go up to the right. This means as age increases, height increases.

(Sample Solutions continue on page 28.)

Number Strategies

Evaluate.
- $\frac{4}{5} \div \frac{2}{3}$ $= \frac{6}{5}$
- $\frac{4}{5} \times \frac{2}{3}$ $= \frac{8}{15}$
- $\frac{4}{5} - \frac{2}{3}$ $= \frac{2}{15}$
- $\frac{4}{5} + \frac{2}{3}$ $= \frac{22}{15}$

b) Display the data using an appropriate graph.
c) Describe any trends in the graph.
d) When is the best time to visit Vancouver? Hawaii? Explain.
e) Who might be interested in these data? Why?

4. The table shows the ages in years and heights in centimetres of 15 students on a baseball team.

Age (years)	12	14	15	17	18	11	13	14
Height (cm)	134	161	158	185	199	157	161	183
Age (years)	18	16	15	16	14	15	17	
Height (cm)	207	172	189	169	175	166	185	

a) Display these data using an appropriate graph. Explain your choice.
b) Does there appear to be a relationship between age and height? Explain.

Average Annual Earnings of Canadians

Year	Females ($)	Males ($)
1993	22 300	34 700
1994	22 500	36 200
1995	23 000	35 400
1996	22 700	35 300
1997	22 900	36 200
1998	23 900	37 400
1999	24 200	37 800
2000	24 900	39 000
2001	25 100	39 100
2002	25 300	38 900

5. Assessment Focus
a) What do the data in the table represent?
b) Display the data using a suitable graph. Justify your choice.
c) Describe any trends. Justify your answers.
d) What do you think the average annual female earnings were in 1990? Explain. About $21 500
e) Predict the average annual male earnings for 2005. Explain. About $39 500
f) What inferences can you make from these data?
Show your work.

Reflect

Why do we need different types of graphs to display data? Give examples to support your answer.

204 UNIT 5: Data Management

ASSESSMENT FOR LEARNING

What to Look For	What to Do
Knowledge and Understanding ✔ Students understand how to choose a suitable graph to display data and how to analyse the graph. ***Communication*** ✔ Students can explain when each type of graph is best suited for given data. Students can interpret the graph to solve problems. ***Application*** ✔ Students can display data on bar graphs, circle graphs, line graphs, and scatter plots.	***Extra Support:*** Students who are having difficulty choosing a suitable graph to display data may benefit from writing a summary sheet of which type of graph is best suited for a particular set of data. They may refer to this summary sheet when they are required to draw a graph. Students can use Step-by-Step 3 (Master 5.9) to complete question 5. ***Extra Practice:*** Students can complete Extra Practice 3 (Master 5.20). ***Extension:*** Have students use the newspaper or Internet to find data that can be displayed using two types of graphs. Students graph the data, then write all they know from looking at the graphs.

Recording and Reporting
Master 5.2 Ongoing Observations: Data Management

Using a Spreadsheet to Create Graphs

Using a Spreadsheet to Create Graphs

Focus Display data on graphs using spreadsheets.

Spreadsheet software, such as *AppleWorks*, can be used to record, then graph, data.
Use these data for elementary students from *Census at School*.

What's your favourite subject?
Elementary Students

Subject	Girls	Boys
English	218	48
French	87	33
Art	601	241
Computers	138	254
Geography	18	14
History	59	63
Math	284	360
Music	172	76
Other	131	129
Phys-Ed	759	1206
Science	122	170
Social Studies	66	47

You found these data from *Census at School* on page 192.

To graph these data using *AppleWorks*, follow these steps.
Open *AppleWorks*. Choose Spreadsheet.
Enter the data into rows and columns in the spreadsheet.

To create a double-bar graph

1. Highlight the data. Include the column heads but do not include the table title.
2. Click the Make a Chart icon on the toolbar.
   A Chart Options dialogue box appears.
   Choose Bar, then click OK.
3. Right-click the graph. Choose Chart Options.
   Select the Labels tab.
   In the Title box, type **Favourite Subject, Elementary Students.**
   To insert labels, right-click the graph. Choose Chart Options.
   Click the Axes tab.

Technology: Using a Spreadsheet to Create Graphs 205

LESSON ORGANIZER 40–50 min

Curriculum Focus: Display data on graphs using spreadsheets.

Student Materials

- computers with *Appleworks*

Assessment: Master 5.2 Ongoing Observations: Data Management

Key Math Learning

Spreadsheet software, such as *Appleworks*, can be used to record and graph data.

Tell students they will use spreadsheet software to create double-bar graphs, double-line graphs, and circle graphs. They will enter the data into the computer, then use the computer to create a graph. Students can use the graph to look for patterns or trends in data, and to draw conclusions and make predictions.

Watch to ensure students understand and follow the directions carefully.

Invite volunteers to share their graphs and their findings.

Discuss using computers to make graphs. Elicit from students that a computer can create a graph quickly, especially when a set of data is large.

Suggestions for Alternative Software

Commercial spreadsheets, such as *Microsoft Excel* ™, allow you to enter a set of data and create graphs. The easiest way to create a graph from a set of data is to use the Chart Wizard.

1. Copy the data from the table on page 205 into a blank spreadsheet.
2. Select the cells that contain the data you want to graph.

Arial 10 B I U
A1 = Subject

	A	B	C	D
1	Subject	Girls	Boys	
2	English	218	48	
3	French	87	33	
4	Art	601	241	
5	Computers	138	254	
6	Geography	18	14	
7	History	59	63	
8	Math	284	360	
9	Music	172	76	
10	Other	131	129	
11	Phys-Ed	759	1206	
12	Science	122	170	
13	Social Stu	66	47	

3. Click the Chart Wizard icon on the toolbar.
   The Chart Wizard dialogue box appears.
4. Select the Chart type and Chart sub-type, then click Next. In this case, select Column and the first sub-type.

REACHING ALL LEARNERS

Early Finishers

Have students use spreadsheet software to graph the data in *Practice* questions 4 and 5, on page 204 of the Student Book. Students can then compare the computer graphs with the graphs they drew.

Select X axis. Type **Subject**. Ensure Grid Lines is not selected.
Select Y axis. Type **Number of Students**. Select Grid Lines.
Under Minimum: enter 0. Under Maximum: enter 1400.
Under Step Size: enter 200. Then click OK.
Your graph should look like the one below.

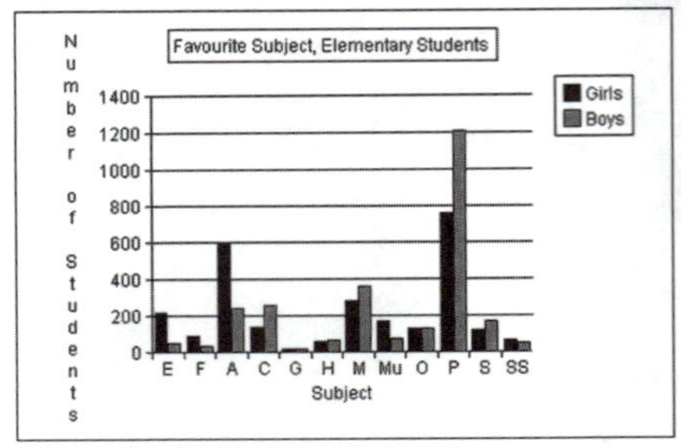

The double-bar graph shows a legend at the right. The legend shows what the two sets of bars represent.

To create a circle graph

This table shows how Stacy budgets her money each month.

Stacy's Monthly Budget

Category	Amount ($)
Food	160
Clothing	47
Transportation	92
Entertainment	78
Savings	35
Rent	87
Other	28

1. Enter the data into rows and columns in a spreadsheet. Highlight the data. Do not include the column heads or title.
2. Click the Make a Chart icon on the tool bar. A Chart Options dialogue box appears. Choose Pie, then click OK.

206 UNIT 5: Data Management

5. A Chart Wizard dialogue box appears, which gives you an idea of your chart's appearance. Click Next.

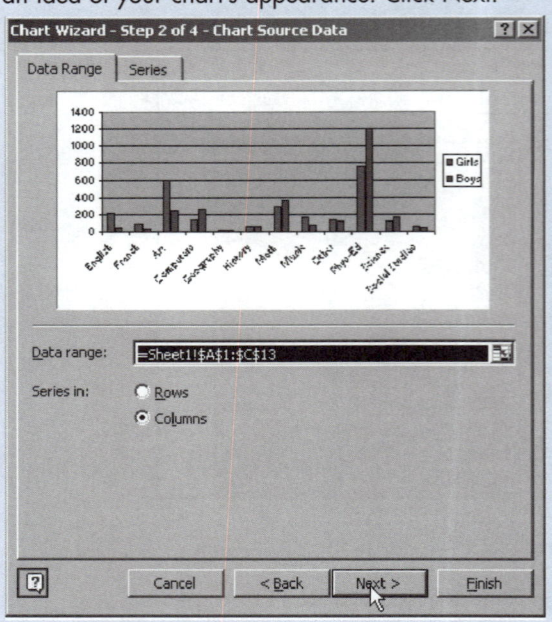

6. A Chart Wizard dialogue box appears. Enter the title of your chart, and labels for the axes, then press Next.

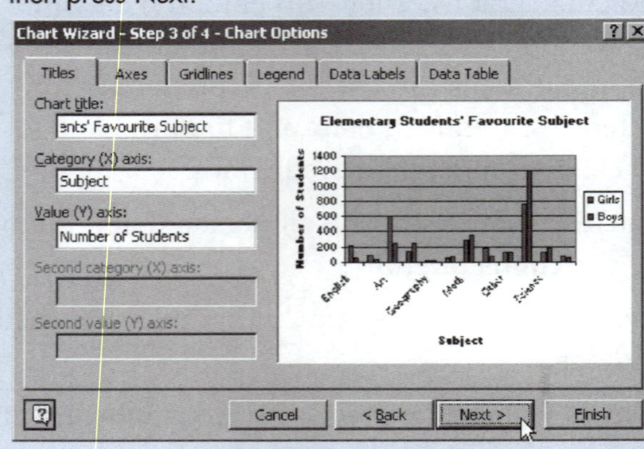

3. Right-click the graph. Choose Chart Options. Choose Series. Click Label Data. Click % in slice. Click OK.

4. To add a title, right-click the graph. Choose Chart Options. Select the Labels Tab. In the Title box, type **Stacy's Monthly Budget.** Then click OK. Your graph should look like the one below.

The circle graph shows a legend at the right. The legend shows what category each sector represents.

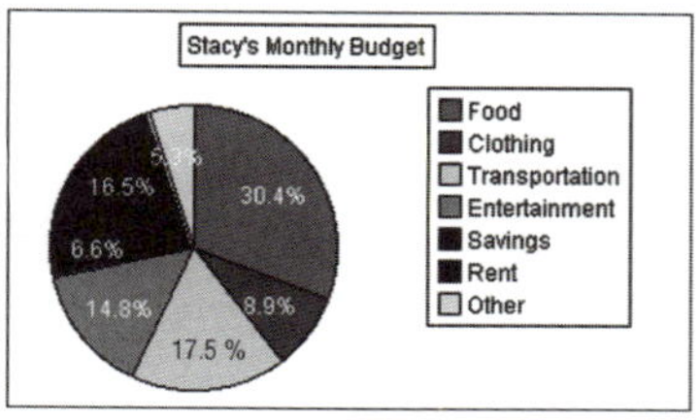

To create a double-line graph

Average Ticket Prices ($), Ontario

Year	Movie Theatres	Drive-Ins
1996–7	5.13	6.39
1997–8	5.38	6.79
1998–9	5.70	6.86
1999–0	6.14	6.92
2000–1	6.78	7.28
2001–2	—	—
2002–3	8.08	8.63

1. Enter the data into rows and columns in the spreadsheet.

2. Highlight the data. Include the column heads, but do not include the table title.

Sample Solutions

1. a) Phys-Ed is the subject liked most by boys. Phys-Ed has the greatest number in the table, 1206, and the highest bar on the graph for boys.
   b) Geography is the subject liked least by girls. It has the least number in the table, 18, and the shortest bar on the graph for girls.
   c) Geography and History; each subject has bars of almost equal height.
   d) The least favourite subject of girls and boys is Geography. It has the shortest bars on the graph. Math is the second favourite subject of boys. Phys-Ed is the favourite subject of girls.
2. The Food sector is about 3 times the size of the Clothing sector. The Transportation sector is about 3 times the size of the Other sector.
   It is easier to see the relative sizes of the sectors than to compare the numbers in the table.
3. a) Both lines go up to the right, so average ticket prices are increasing over time. The line for drive-ins is above the line for movie theatres, so this shows that the average ticket price for drive-ins is greater than the average ticket price for movie theatres.
   b) The 2001–2002 estimated average ticket price for movie theatres is about $7.50 and about $8.00 for drive-ins. The estimates are found by joining the points on the graph for 2000–1 with the points for 2002–3, then estimating the price by drawing a dotted line up to the graph from 2001–2 for each type of ticket, then across to the vertical axis.

7. A Chart Wizard dialogue box appears. Decide whether you want the graph to appear on a separate worksheet, or on the same worksheet as the data set. Click one of the options, then click Finish.
8. Excel draws your chart and places it on the chosen worksheet. You may choose to resize the graph by clicking and dragging a corner of the selected graph.

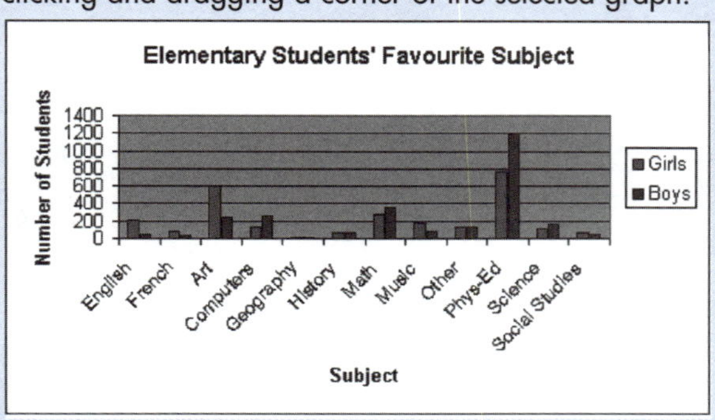

The same procedure is used to make a circle graph and a double-line graph. In Step 4, select "Pie" to obtain a circle graph, or select "Line" to obtain a double-line graph.
To show percents on a circle graph, right-click the graph, then select Chart Options.
Select Data Labels, then select Show percent.

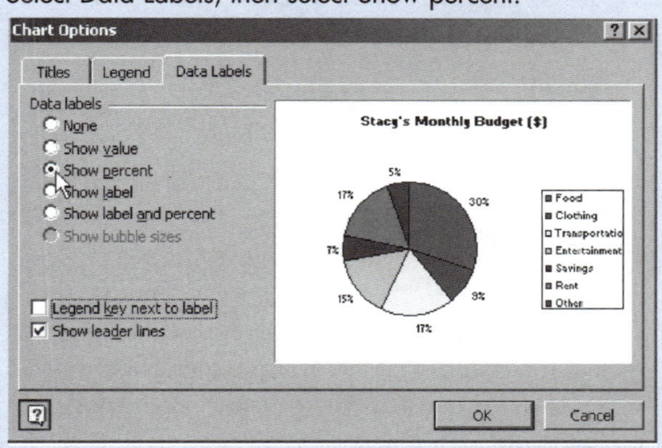

c) The 2004–2005 estimated average ticket price for movie theatres is about \$9.00 and about \$9.50 for drive-ins. Extend the horizontal axis to 2004–5. The estimates are found by extending the graph beyond 2002–3 to 2004–5, then estimating the price by drawing a dotted line up to the graph from 2004–5 for each ticket price, then across to the vertical axis.

d) Both lines are steepest from 2001–2 to 2002–3, so this is when movie tickets had the greatest increase in price. Drive-in tickets had the least increase in price from 1998–9 to 1999–0 because the graph is least steep during this period of time. Theatre tickets had the least increase in price from 1996–7 to 1997–8 because the graph is least steep during this period of time.

e) From 1996 to 2003, drive-ins were more expensive than movie theatres. However, the trend shows that the difference between the price of theatre tickets and drive-in tickets is decreasing. Movie theatre ticket prices are becoming closer to drive-in ticket prices.

3. Click the Make a Chart icon on the tool bar.
A Chart Options dialogue box appears.
Choose Lines, then click OK.

4. Right-click the graph. Choose Chart Options.
Select the Labels tab.
In the Title box, type **Average Ticket Prices (\$), Ontario.**
Then click OK. To insert labels, right-click the graph.
Choose Chart Options. Click the Axes tab.
Select X axis. Type **Year.** Ensure Grid Lines is not selected.
Select Y axis. Type **Amount (\$).** Select Grid Lines.
Then click OK.
Your graph should look like the one below.

The double-line graph shows a legend at the right. The legend shows what each line represents.

Note how *AppleWorks* draws the graph when data are missing. How would *you* draw this graph?

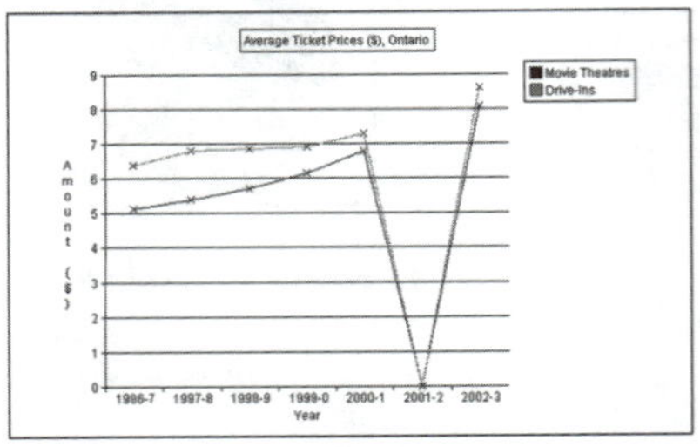

✓ Check

1. Use the data on page 205 or the double-bar graph on page 206.
a) Which subject is liked most by boys? How do you know?
b) Which subject is liked least by girls? How do you know?
c) Which subject is liked almost equally by boys and girls? How do you know?
d) Write 3 more things you know from looking at the table or the graph.

2. Use the circle graph on page 207.
One category is about 3 times as great as another.
How is it easier to identify these categories from the graph than the table?

208 UNIT 5: Data Management

(Sample Solutions for Lesson 5.3, page 24, continued)

5. a) The data in the table represent the average annual earnings of Canadian males and females from 1993 to 2002.

b) The table compares two sets of data over time and should be displayed using a double-line graph.

Average Annual Earnings of Canadians

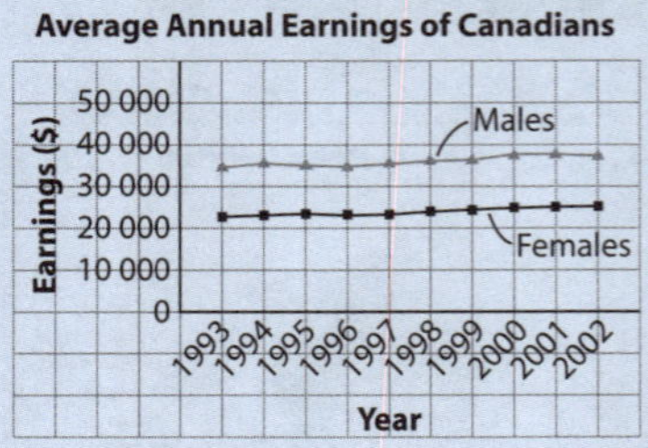

c) The line for females is consistently below the line for males. This means that the average annual earnings of females is lower than that of males. Both lines go up to the right. This means the average annual earnings are increasing for each gender.

f) Canadian males have higher average annual earnings than females. Average annual earnings have increased over the 10-year period.

REFLECT: Data that represent part of one whole are best displayed on a circle graph. Data that change over time are best displayed on a line graph. Data that can be counted are best displayed on a bar graph. Related sets of data that are measured or counted are best displayed on a scatter plot.

3. Use the data on page 207 or the double-line graph on page 208.
   a) What trends does the graph show? Explain.
   b) Estimate the average ticket prices for 2001–2002. Justify your answer.
   c) Estimate the average ticket prices for 2004–2005. Explain your reasoning.
   d) When did movie tickets have the greatest increase? The least increase? How do you know?
   e) What else can you infer from the table or the graph? Explain.

4. These data are from *Census at School.*

**What's for Breakfast?
Elementary Students (%)**

Item	Girls	Boys
Milk	51.0	57.8
Fruit juice	44.1	40.8
Hot drink	12.1	12.4
Hot cereal	11.8	12.9
Cold cereal	47.0	55.6
Eggs	23.9	32.0
Toast	50.0	52.0
Muffin	18.6	17.2
Bagel	30.9	27.8
Cereal bar	7.7	8.6
Cheese	10.3	13.1
Yogurt	18.5	14.8
No breakfast	16.7	11.2
Other	23.3	25.1

Source: Statistics Canada, *Census at School*, 2003/04
http://www19.statcan.ca/04/04_006_e.htm
Date extracted: March 2005

a) Use a spreadsheet to draw the most suitable graph for the data. Justify your choice of graph.
b) Write 3 questions about your graph. Answer your questions.
c) Compare your questions with those of a classmate. What else can you infer from the table or the graph?

Technology: Using a Spreadsheet to Create Graphs **209**

4. a) I chose a double-bar graph because there are two sets of countable data.

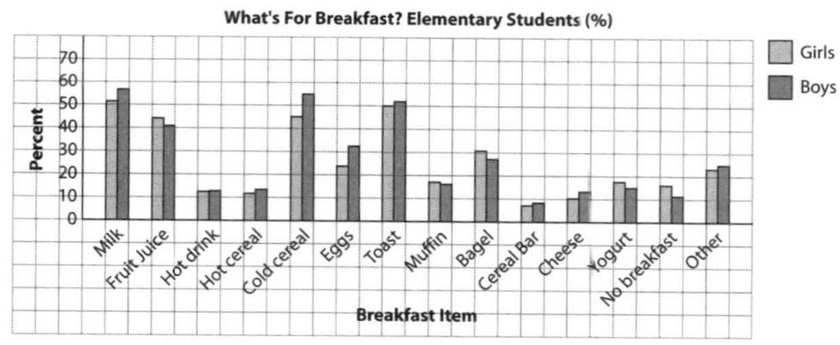

b) Three questions:
   i) What are the 3 most popular breakfast items?
   (Answer: *Milk, cold cereal, toast*)
   ii) What is the least popular breakfast item?
   (Answer: *Cereal bar*)
   iii) Compare the heights of the bars for boys and girls. What do you notice?
   (Answer: *In most cases, both bars are about the same height. This means that about the same percent of boys and girls eat the same types of breakfast items.*)

c) About 1 in 4 students (25%) eat a breakfast item not listed in the table.

LESSON ORGANIZER

Student Materials
- 0.5-cm grid paper (PM 14)

Assessment: Masters 5.1 Unit Rubric: Data Management; 5.4 Unit Summary: Data Management

Assignment Guidelines

To assess the 4 Achievement Chart categories listed in the curriculum document, have students complete these questions:
Knowledge and Understanding: 1
Communication: 2
Application: 3
Thinking: 4

Mid-Unit Review

LESSON

5.1 **1.** For each situation, explain why data are collected from a sample and not a census.
  a) To find the mean cost of ski equipment
  b) To find the number of Canadian families that have a DVD player

5.2 **2. a)** Write an inference based on this double-line graph. Justify your inference.

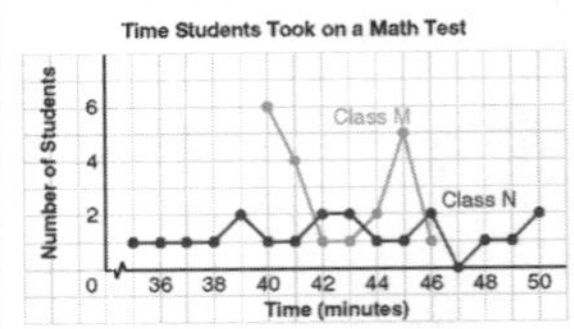

  b) Write a convincing argument based on the graph. Justify your argument.

3. This table shows the sales, in thousands of dollars, for 6 months for 2 employees of Electronics Warehouse.

Month	Jamar ($1000s)	Laura ($1000s)
Jan.	117	124
Feb.	118	125
Mar.	119	128
Apr.	120	126
May	121	124
June	137	126

  a) What do you infer from these data?
  b) Write a convincing argument each employee could use to persuade the manager that she should be named the better salesperson. Justify each argument.

5.3 **4.** This table, taken from *Census at School*, shows the days of the week students were born.

Day of Birth

Day	Males	Females
Monday	3369	3602
Tuesday	3973	4335
Wednesday	4235	4571
Thursday	4278	4486
Friday	4131	4756
Saturday	4128	4671
Sunday	3670	4108

Source: Statistics Canada, *Census at School*, 2003/04
http://www.censusatschool.ntu.ac.uk/table9-0.asp
Date extracted: March 2005

  a) Draw a double-bar graph to display the data.
  b) What can you infer from these data?
  c) What other type of graph could you draw to display these data? Justify your answer.
  d) Ask each student in the class for the day of the week he or she was born. How do these data compare with the data in the table?

210 UNIT 5: Data Management

Sample Solutions

1. a) It would be too difficult, time consuming, and expensive to find the cost of all ski equipment across Canada.
b) It would be too difficult, time consuming, and expensive to survey all Canadian families.

2. a) On average, students in each class took about the same amount of time to complete the test. The average time for students in Class M to complete the test was about 42 min. The average time for students in Class N to complete the test was about 43 min.
b) Students in Class M are more similar in their abilities and/or levels of efficiency in math. All students in Class M completed the test within a 6-min time period.

3. a) Laura's sales are more consistent; Jamar's sales are increasing.
b) Laura could argue that she is the better salesperson because in 5 out of 6 months, her sales were greater than Jamar's.
Jamar could argue that he is the better salesperson because his sales have increased over 6 months, and his greatest sales were $11 000 more than Laura's greatest sales.

4. a)

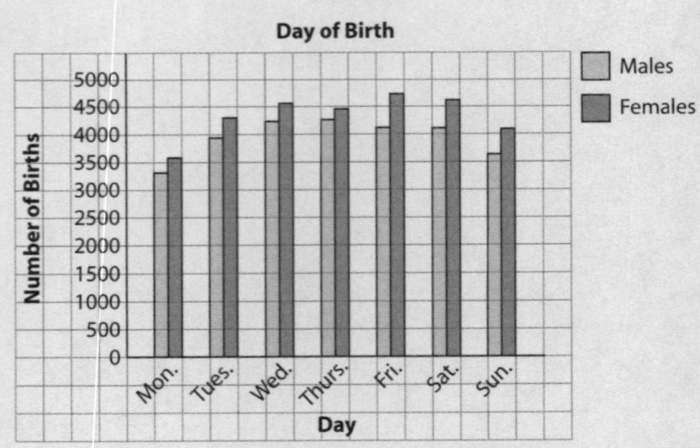

b) From the data, we can infer that more girls were born on a Friday than any other day of the week, and more boys were born on a Thursday. We can also infer that more girls than boys were born on any day of the week. Monday is the day when the least number of babies were born.
c) The data could also be displayed on a double-line graph or two circle graphs, one for males and one for females.

5.4 Applying Measures of Central Tendency

Focus Understand how mean, median, and mode are affected by outliers.

Explore

Work with a partner.
Students in a Grade 8 class measured their pulse rates.
Here are their results in beats per minute:
97, 69, 83, 66, 78, 8, 55, 82, 47, 52, 67, 76, 84,
64, 72, 80, 72, 70, 69, 80, 66, 60, 72, 88, 88

Recall that mean, median, and mode are measures of central tendency.

➢ Calculate the mean, median, and mode for these data. Which measure best represents the data? Explain.
➢ Remove any numbers that are significantly different from most of the data. Calculate the mean, median, and mode again. How are the three measures affected? Explain.

Reflect & Share

Compare your results with those of another pair of classmates. How did you decide which numbers were significantly different? Why do you think they are so different?

Connect

The *mean* of a set of data is the sum of the data values divided by the number of data values.
The mean is usually the best measure when no numbers in the data set are significantly different from the other numbers.

The *median* of a set of data is the middle number when the numbers are arranged in order. One-half the numbers are above the median and one-half are below the median. When there is an even number of data values, the median is the mean of the two middle values. The median is usually the best measure when there are numbers in the data set that are significantly different.

The *mode* of a set of data is the number that occurs most often. There may be no mode or there may be more than one mode.

5.4 Applying Measures of Central Tendency 211

Applying Measures of Central Tendency

LESSON ORGANIZER 80–100 min

Curriculum Focus: Understand how mean, median, and mode are affected by outliers. (8m74)

Student Materials
- calculators

Optional
- Step-by-Step 4 (Master 5.10)
- Extra Practice 4 (Master 5.21)

Vocabulary: mean, median, mode, outlier

Assessment: Master 5.2 Ongoing Observations: Data Management

Key Math Learnings

1. The mean of a set of data is the sum of the data values divided by the number of data values.
2. The median of a set of data is the middle number when the numbers are arranged in order.
3. The mode of a set of data is the number that occurs most often.
4. An outlier is a number in a data set that is significantly different from the others.

Mental Math

The decimal moves one place to the right each time.

BEFORE Get Started

Review the meanings of mean, median, and mode.

Ask:
- What are the mean, median, and mode?
  (They are measures of central tendency.)
- What is the mean of a set of numbers?
  (It is the sum of the data values divided by the number of data values.)
- What is the median of a set of numbers?
  (It is the middle number when the numbers are arranged in order.)
- What if there is an even number of numbers?
  (The median is the mean of the two middle numbers.)
- What is the mode of a set of numbers?
  (It is the number that occurs most often.)
- Is there always one mode?
  (No, there may be more than one mode or there may be no mode.)
- What is the range of a set of numbers?
  (It is the difference between the greatest number and the least number.)

Present *Explore.* Remind students they are to work with a partner.

DURING Explore

Ongoing Assessment: Observe and Listen

Students should arrange the data in order from least to greatest to make finding the median and mode easier.

Ask:
- What is the mean pulse rate? *(69.8)*
- What is the median pulse rate? *(72)*
- How did you find the median?
  (I arranged all the numbers in order, then counted them. There are 25 numbers. The middle number is the 13th number. The 13th number is 72.)
- What is the mode pulse rate? *(72)*

REACHING ALL LEARNERS

Alternative Explore

Have students collect their own set of data by measuring and recording their pulse rates. They can then use this data set to complete *Explore*.

Early Finishers

Have students organize the data from *Explore* in a frequency table, then graph the data, and justify their choice of graph. Students should describe how the frequency table and the graph show the numbers that are significantly different. Ask students to describe how the frequency table shows the mode.

Common Misconceptions

➤ Students think that the mean is the only "average."

How to Help: Remind students that the mean, median, and mode are averages, and that each provides valuable information in different situations.

Assignment Guidelines

If your students do not have time to complete all the *Practice* questions on pages 213, 214, and 215, these questions provide minimum curriculum coverage: 1, 3, 5, 7, 9, *Reflect*

To assess the 4 Achievement Chart categories listed in the curriculum document, have students complete these *Practice* questions:

Knowledge and Understanding: 1
Application: 7
Communication: 3
Thinking: 9

The mode is usually the best measure when the data represent measures such as shoe sizes or other clothing sizes.

A number in a set of data that is significantly different from the other numbers is called an **outlier**.

Example

Here are the marks for an English test for students in a Grade 8 class. They are shown in a stem-and-leaf plot.

English Test Marks

Stem	Leaf
2	1 3 4 4 7 9 9 9
3	2 7 7 8 9
4	0
5	0 0 1 4 6 7 8 9
6	1
7	1
8	0
9	9

a) How many students were in the class? How do you know?
b) What are the outliers? Explain.
c) Calculate the mean, median, and mode test marks.
d) Calculate the mean, median, and mode without the outliers. What do you notice? Explain.
e) Which measure of central tendency best describes the average test mark for the Grade 8 class? Explain.

Solution

a) Count the entries in the stem-and-leaf plot to find the number of students in the class. There are 26 students.
b) There is only one number, 99, that is significantly different. The outlier is 99.
c) There are 26 marks. The mean is:
$(21 + 23 + 2 \times 24 + 27 + 3 \times 29 + 32 + 2 \times 37 + 38 + 39 + 40 + 2 \times 50 + 51 + 54 + 56 + 57 + 58 + 59 + 61 + 71 + 80 + 99) \div 26$
$= 1175 \div 26 \doteq 45.2$
The median is the mean of the 13th and 14th marks.
The 13th mark is 39. The 14th mark is 40.
So, the median is: $\frac{39 + 40}{2} = \frac{79}{2} = 39.5$
The mode is the mark that occurs most often. This is 29.

- What is the range? *(89)*
- Which measure of central tendency best describes the average pulse rate?
(The median and the mode. They best describe the data set.)
- Which number in the data set is significantly different? *(8)*
- What do you think might have happened?
(A student may have counted her or his pulse rate incorrectly, or a student may have recorded her or his pulse rate incorrectly.)
- What are the measures of central tendency once this number is removed?
(Mean is 72.4; median is 72; mode is 72.)
- What do you notice when you compare these values with the original values?
(The mean is closer in value to the median and the mode. The median and mode have not changed.)

AFTER Connect

Invite students to share their findings with the class. Ask:

- How did you decide which numbers were significantly different?
(I arranged the numbers in order and examined them. Each value differed from the value before or after it by a maximum of 9. The exception was the value "8", which differed from the value after it by 39.)
- Which measure of central tendency was most affected by the number that was significantly different?
(The mean was the only measure that changed.)
- Which measure(s) of central tendency are more reliable when the data contain significantly different numbers?
(The median is more reliable. It is not greatly influenced by outliers because it is the middle number. The mode is the number that occurs most often.)

d) Without the outlier:
The mean is $\frac{1175 - 99}{25}$ = 43.04
The median is the 13th mark.
The median is 39.
The mode is 29.

e) Since the outlier has a greater effect on the mean, it is not the best measure to describe the average. The mode is too low to best describe the average. So, the median best describes the average mark.

Practice

1. For each set of data:
   i) Calculate the mean, median, and mode.
   ii) Identify the outliers.
   iii) Calculate the mean, median, and mode without the outliers.
   How is each measure of central tendency affected when the outliers are not included?
   a) marks on a set of exams:
   30, 66, 65, 72, 78, 93, 70, 68, 64, 90, 65, 68
   b) weekly income: \$625, \$750, \$800, \$650, \$725, \$850, \$625, \$650, \$625, \$1250, \$700, \$625
   c) waiting time, in minutes, at a fast-food restaurant:
   5, 5, 5, 6, 5, 7, 0, 5, 1, 7, 7, 5, 6, 5, 5, 5, 8, 5, 0, 5, 4, 5, 2, 7, 9
   d) number of baskets scored by a basketball player in 10 games: 15, 7, 8, 6, 2, 7, 5, 7, 1, 8

2. In each case:
   i) Calculate the mean, median, and mode of the new data set formed.
   ii) Explain how the mean, median, and mode are affected by the change.
   a) Add 5 to each number in question 1a.
   b) Subtract \$10 from each amount in question 1b.
   c) Multiply each time in question 1c by 3.
   d) Divide each number in question 1d by 2.

1. a) i) Mean ≐ 69.08, Median = 68, Mode = 65 and 68
ii) Outliers: 30, 90, 93 iii) Mean ≐ 68.4, Median = 68, Mode = 65 and 68
b) i) Mean ≐ \$739.58, Median = \$675, Mode = \$625
ii) Outlier: \$1250 iii) Mean ≐ \$693.18 Median = \$650, Mode = \$625
c) i) Mean = 4.96, Median = 5, Mode = 5
ii) Outliers: 0, 1, 2 iii) Mean ≐ 5.76, Median = 5, Mode = 5
d) i) Mean = 6.6, Median = 7, Mode = 7
ii) Outliers: 1, 2, 15
iii) Mean ≐ 6.86, Median = 7, Mode = 7
2. a) i) Mean ≐ 74.1, Median = 73, Mode = 70 and 73
b) i) Mean ≐ \$729.58, Median = \$665, Mode = \$615
c) i) Mean = 14.88 min, Median = 15 min, Mode = 15 min

5.4 Applying Measures of Central Tendency 213

Sample Solutions

1. a) iii) The mean decreased without the outliers; the median and modes remained the same.
   b) iii) The mean and the median decreased; the mode remained the same.
   c) iii) The mean increased; the median and mode did not change.
   d) iii) The mean increased. The median and mode did not change.
2. a) ii) The mean, median, and mode each increased by 5.
   b) ii) The mean, median, and mode each decreased by \$10.
   c) ii) The mean, median, and mode were each multiplied by 3.
   d) ii) The mean, median, and mode were each divided by 2.
3. a) The sum of the prices divided by 3 is \$10.
   b) About 150, because there is an average of 15 raisins per cookie.
4. The mean temperature was about 26.4°C. The median temperature was 27°C. The mode temperatures were 23°C and 28°C. The weather channel reported one of the mode temperatures.
5. c) The mean decreased. The median and mode remained the same.
   d) The median and mode best describe the data because they are not affected by the outliers.
6. The numbers in the data set are: 4, 4, 4, 7, a, b, c, where $a + b + c = 30$.
   The reason for this is that if 7 is the median of seven numbers, then 7 is the middle number; there are three numbers below 7 and three numbers above 7. Since the mode is 4 and it occurs

Review *Connect.* Explain to students that in a set of data, the significantly different values are called *outliers.*

Review with students that in data analysis, two sets of data are often compared. For example, a double-bar graph may show male and female data for various categories.

We may collect and examine the measures of central tendency for two sets of data, then compare the measures.

Juanita compared the heights of players on defence (including goalies) with the heights of forwards for the Ottawa Senators. She calculated the mean, median, and mode for each group.

Players on Defence	
Name	**Height (cm)**
Ray	188
Prusek	188
Hasek	180
Pothier	183
Chara	206
Phillips	191
de Vries	191
Redden	188
Volchenkov	185

Players on Forward	
Name	**Height (cm)**
Havlat	185
Alfredsson	180
Fisher	180
Schaefer	185
Hossa	180
Spezza	185
Vermette	188
Smolinski	185
Neil	183
Varada	178
White	191
Langfeld	183
Kelly	184

three times, then the first three numbers are 4s. The sum of 4, 4, 4, and 7 is 19. Since the mean is 7, then 19 plus the other three numbers, divided by 7, is 7.
That is: $\frac{19 + a + b + c}{7} = 7$. This means: $a + b + c = 30$
So, some possible data sets are: 4, 4, 4, 7, 8, 10, 12 or 4, 4, 4, 7, 7, 10, 13 or 4, 4, 4, 7, 9, 10, 11

7. b) No, he would need a math mark greater than 100% to get a mean of 84%.

8. No, Celia's reasoning is not correct. She should have multiplied 80% by 3 to get 240%, then added 94% to get 334%, and then divided by 4 to get 83.5%. This is the correct mean.

9. b) **i)** The data are best displayed in a stem-and-leaf plot so the mode and range are easily found. We can also see how many boxes have at least 460 raisins.

Number of Raisins in 15 Boxes of Cereal

Stem	Leaf
40	0
41	3 9
42	8
43	7
44	1
45	3
46	5 7
47	1 3 7
48	5 9
49	9

3. Is each conclusion correct? Explain.
a) The mean cost of a medium pizza is \$10. So, the prices of three medium pizzas could be \$9, \$10, and \$11. Yes
b) The number of raisins in each of 30 cookies was count[illegible]
The mean number of raisins was 15.
So, in 10 cookies, there would be 150 raisins. No

4. The daily high temperatures for one week at Clearwater Harbour were: 27°C, 31°C, 23°C, 25°C, 28°C, 23°C, 28°C.
The weather channel reported that the average temperature for Clearwater Harbour for that week was 23°C.
Is this correct? Explain. No

5. The masses, in tonnes, of household garbage collected in a municipality each weekday in April are:
285, 395, 270, 305, 320, 300, 290, 310, 315, 295, 310, 295, 305, 325, 315, 310, 305, 300, 325, 305, 305, 300
a) Organize the data in a stem-and-leaf plot.
b) Calculate the mean, median, and mode for the data.
c) What are the outliers? Outliers: 270, 395; Mean = 306 t
Calculate the mean without the outliers.
What do you notice? Explain.
d) Which measure of central tendency best describes the data? Explain.

Masses of Household Garbage Collected in April (tonnes)

Stem	Leaf
27	0
28	5
29	0 5 5
30	0 0 0 5 5 5 5 5
31	0 0 0 5 5
32	0 5 5
39	5

5. b) Mean = 308.4 t, Median = 305 t, Mode = 305 t

6. There are seven numbers in a set of data.
The mean and the median are 7.
The mode is 4 and occurs 3 times.
Find the numbers. Explain your method.

7. Andrew has these marks:
English 82%, French 75%, History 78%, Science 80%
a) What mark will Andrew need in math if he wants his mean mark to be each percent?
i) 80% ii) 81% iii) 82% i) 85% ii) 90% iii) 95%
b) Is it possible for Andrew to get a mean mark of 84% or higher?
Justify your answer.

214 UNIT 5: Data Management

Players on Defence

Median:
Arrange the heights in order:
180, 183, 185, 188, 188, 188, 191, 191, 206
The median is 188.

Mode: The mode is 188.

Mean: (180 + 183 + 185 + 188 + 188 + 188 + 191 + 191 + 206) ÷ 9 ≐ 189
The mean is about 189.

The median and mode are equal.
The median is the best measure of central tendency.

Players on Forward

Median:
Arrange the heights in order:
178, 180, 180, 180, 183, 183, 184, 185, 185, 185, 185, 188, 191
The median is 184.

Mode: The mode is 185.

Mean: (178 + 180 + 180 + 180 + 183 + 183 + 184 + 185 + 185 + 185 + 185 + 188 + 191) ÷ 13 ≐ 184
The mean is about 184.

The median and mean are equal. The median is the best measure of central tendency.

Comparing the median for players on defence with the median for players on forward, Juanita inferred that, in general, players on defence are taller than forwards.

Practice

Have calculators available for all questions.

Assessment Focus: Question 9

Students multiply the average number of raisins per cup of cereal by the number of cups of cereal in a box. They compare this number to the mean, both with and without the outliers.

8. Celia received a mean mark of 80% in her first three exams. She then had 94% on her next exam.
Celia stated that her overall mean mark was 87% because the mean of 80 and 94 is 87. Is Celia's reasoning correct? Explain.

Mental Math

Divide each number by 0.1, 0.01, and 0.001.

- 385 3850, 38 500, 385 000
- 3.84 38.4, 384, 3840
- 0.286 2.86, 28.6, 286
- 25.7 257, 2570, 25 700

What patterns do you see in the answers?

9. **Assessment Focus** A Grade 8 class wanted to find out if a TV advertisement was true. It claimed that *Full of Raisins* cereal guaranteed an average of 23 raisins per cup of cereal.
Each pair of students tested one box of cereal.
Each box contained 20 cups of cereal.
The number of raisins in each cup was counted.
   a) Assume the advertisement is true. 460 raisins
   How many raisins should there be in 1 box of cereal?
   b) Here are the results for the numbers of raisins in 15 boxes of cereal: 473, 485, 441, 437, 489, 471, 400, 453, 465, 413, 499, 428, 419, 477, 467
      i) Display the data. Justify your choice of display.
      ii) How do the outliers affect the mean?
      iii) Was the advertisement true? Justify your answer.

Take It Further

10. There are 20 students in a Grade 8 class.
Eighteen students wrote a Social Studies test.
Here are their marks: 75, 56, 83, 61, 91, 42, 57, 56, 60, 87, 32, 42, 57, 67, 89, 43, 49, 81
Two students who were absent wrote the test the next day.
The mean mark for the 20 students was 63.
The range was 63.
   a) What are the median mark and the mode mark for the 18 students?
   Median = 58.5, Modes = 42, 56 and 57
   b) What are possible marks for the two students who wrote the test late?
   c) Suppose the teacher gives each student 3 extra marks. How do the mean, median, mode, and range change?

Reflect

What is an outlier? How are measures of central tendency affected by outliers? Use examples in your explanation.

ii) The mean is 454.5. The mean without the outliers, 400 and 499, is 455.2. So, the mean increases.
iii) The advertisement is not true because the mean, with and without the outliers, is less than 460, the number stated in the advertisement.

10. b) The marks are 37 and 95. The sum of the marks of 18 students is 1128. This number plus 2 more marks, divided by 20 must equal the mean, 63. So, the two other marks must add to 132. However, the range of the first 18 marks is only 59. For the range to be 63, one of the two students had to get a mark of 95 (32 + 63). So, the other mark must be 37.

c) The mean, median, and mode would all increase by 3 marks; the range would not change.

REFLECT: An outlier is a number in a data set that is significantly different from the other numbers. An outlier has a greater effect on the mean, so the median usually best represents the data when there are outliers. The mode is usually not affected by an outlier. Suppose the following data are collected on the number of hours spent watching TV on the weekend by ten Grade 8 students: 5, 7, 6, 8, 7, 17, 6, 15, 6, 6. The mean is 8.3, the median is 6.5, and the mode is 6. The mean is most affected by the outliers, 17 and 15. The median and the mode are the same and best describe the number of hours spent watching TV.

ASSESSMENT FOR LEARNING

What to Look For

Knowledge and Understanding

✔ Students understand how to find the mean, median, mode, and range for a set of data with and without outliers.

Communication

✔ Students can identify outliers and explain how outliers affect the measures of central tendency.

Application

✔ Students can solve problems with outliers.

What to Do

Extra Support: Students having difficulty may benefit from working with data that are ordered from least to greatest. Students can use Step-by-Step 4 (Master 5.10) to complete question 9.

Extra Practice: Students can complete Extra Practice 4 (Master 5.21).

Extension: Have students collect data from the class (such as pulse rate, or height, or shoe size), identify the outliers, and explain how the outliers affect the measures of central tendency.

Recording and Reporting

Master 5.2 Ongoing Observations: Data Management

LESSON 5.5

Drawing Histograms

LESSON ORGANIZER (80–100 min)

Curriculum Focus: Display and interpret data on histograms. (8m69, 8m70, 8m71, 8m73, 8m75)

Student Materials
- 0.5-cm grid paper (PM 14)
- coloured pencils
- calculators

Optional
- Step-by-Step 5 (Master 5.11)
- Extra Practice 5 (Master 5.22)

Vocabulary: histogram, interval, frequency, continuous data

Assessment: Master 5.2 Ongoing Observations: Data Management

Key Math Learnings

1. A bar graph is used to represent measurements, or numbers, of different items. Adjacent bars are separated by a space.
2. In a histogram, the data are grouped into intervals with equal widths. The height of each bar represents the frequency of data in that interval. There is no space between the bars because the data are continuous.

5.5 Drawing Histograms

Focus Display and interpret data on histograms.

Explore

Work on your own.
Compare the two graphs below.
How are they similar? How are they different?

Graph A

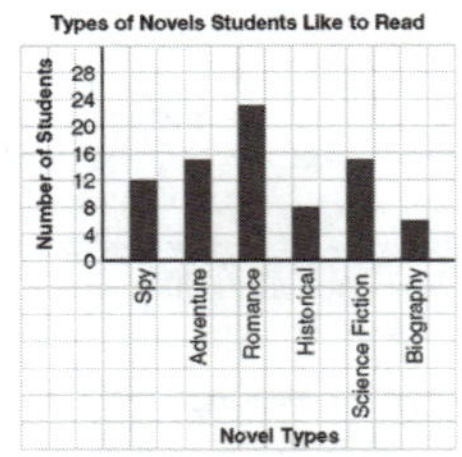

Graph B

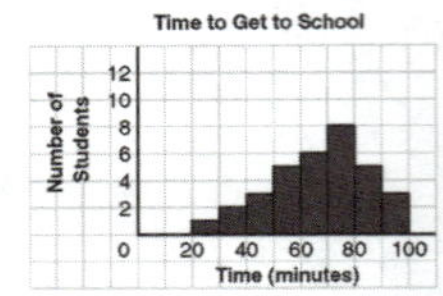

Reflect & Share

Compare your results with those of a classmate.
Why is there a space between the bars in Graph A but not in Graph B?
Why do you think each graph is drawn the way it is?

Connect

A bar graph is used to represent measurements, or numbers, of different items. Then, the items are compared.
Adjacent bars are separated by a space.
The length or height of each bar represents a number.

When we have a large amount of data where the numbers can be arranged in numerical order, then grouped, we use a **histogram** to graph the data.

216 UNIT 5: Data Management

BEFORE Get Started

Have students discuss what they know about bar graphs.

Ask:
- Which type of data does a bar graph represent?
  (A bar graph represents data that are counted.)
- What do the bars have in common? Explain.
  (The bars are of equal width; the heights are compared.)

Present *Explore*. Remind students they are to work on their own.

DURING Explore

Ongoing Assessment: Observe and Listen

Have students identify the facts that they can read from the graphs. For example, for Graph A, they may see that 12 students read Spy novels, 15 students read Adventure novels, and so on.

Ask questions, such as:
- What does each graph show?
  (Graph A shows the number of students who read different types of novels. Graph B shows the time it takes students to get to school.)
- What do you notice about the scale on each vertical axis?
  (The scales are both numerical.)
- What do you notice about the scale on each horizontal axis?
  (For Graph A, types of novels are listed on the horizontal axis. For Graph B, the horizontal scale is numerical and divided into intervals.)
- What do you notice about the bars on each graph?
  (Adjacent bars in Graph A are separated by a space. The bars in Graph B are beside each other, with no gaps.)

In a histogram, the data are usually grouped into intervals with equal widths. Each data value belongs in exactly 1 interval.
The height of each bar represents the *frequency* or number of pieces of data in that interval.
There is no space between the bars because the data are continuous.
That is, the end of one interval is the beginning of the next interval.

Example

Lucas recorded the heights, in centimetres, of all the Grade 8 students in his school. Here are his results:
147, 178, 161, 153, 130, 139, 159, 162, 151, 150, 133, 162, 147, 170, 153, 160, 174, 148, 155, 157, 163, 155, 138, 149, 152, 142, 163, 160, 155, 158, 181, 164, 158, 147, 164, 166, 177, 178, 162, 171, 169, 134, 180, 175, 140, 161, 149, 150, 187, 173, 156, 166, 164, 152, 183, 159, 137, 144, 145, 164

a) Display the data using a stem-and-leaf plot.
b) Make a frequency table.
c) What can you tell from the stem-and-leaf plot that you cannot tell from the frequency table?
d) Use the frequency table to draw a histogram.

Solution

a) In the stem-and-leaf plot, the hundreds and tens digits are the stems and the units digits are the leaves. Write the numbers in numerical order. Include repeated numbers.

Heights of Students in Centimetres

Stem	Leaf
13	0 3 4 7 8 9
14	0 2 4 5 7 7 7 8 9 9
15	0 0 1 2 2 3 3 5 5 5 6 7 8 8 9 9
16	0 0 1 1 2 2 2 3 3 4 4 4 4 6 6 9
17	0 1 3 4 5 7 8 8
18	0 1 3 7

Interval	Frequency
130–139	6
140–149	10
150–159	16
160–169	16
170–179	8
180–189	4

b) The least number is 130.
The greatest number is 187.
The range is: 187 − 130 = 57
A suitable interval to show a range of about 50 is 10.
Since the least number is 130,
the first interval in the frequency table is 130–139.
The next interval is 140–149, and so on, to 180–189.
Use the stem-and-leaf plot to make the frequency table at the left.

5.5 Drawing Histograms **217**

REACHING ALL LEARNERS

Early Finishers

Have students count and record the number of words in each sentence of one page of a novel they are reading. Have students organize and display their data.

Common Misconceptions

➤ Students do not understand which type of data can be graphed with spaces between the bars and which without spaces between the bars.

How to Help: Have students think about data related to the number of different coloured cars in a shopping mall parking lot. The horizontal axis would have the different colours, say red, blue, black, silver, and green, and each bar would represent the number of cars of each colour. Since the colours are not related, there would be a space between the bars. However, suppose students think about data collected about the heights of 100 Grade 8 students. The data would be organized by the number of students in an interval of heights, say 130 cm to 139 cm. The next bar would start at 140 cm and end at 149 cm. So, the bars are drawn adjacent to each other, without a gap.

ESL Strategies

Have students sketch Graph A and Graph B in their notebooks, then list the characteristics of each type of graph below the graphs.

- Why do you think the bars are drawn this way?
  (In Graph A, each bar represents a different type of novel, so the bars are separated. In Graph B, each bar represents an interval of time. The end of one interval is the beginning of the next interval. So, there is no space between the bars.)

AFTER Connect

Invite students to share their findings with the class.

- What do the heights of the bars in Graph A represent?
  (The heights of the bars in Graph A represent the number of students who read each type of novel.)
- What do the heights of the bars in Graph B represent?
  (The height of each bar in Graph B represents the number of students in that interval of time.)
- What do you notice about the intervals in Graph B? Why is that important?
  (The intervals in Graph B are equal. This is important because in order to make comparisons and note patterns, the intervals must be equal.)

Review information given about histograms and ensure students understand the meaning of the words *frequency* and *continuous*. Review the example in *Connect*. Involve students in a discussion of how to draw a stem-and-leaf plot and a frequency table.

Ask:

- Why is it helpful to construct a stem-and-leaf plot?
  (It is helpful to construct a stem-and-leaf plot to order and organize the data so that intervals can be made.)
- Why is it helpful to construct a frequency table?
  (It is helpful to construct a frequency table to count the data that belong in each interval.)

Sample Solutions

1. **a)** The most appropriate graph is a histogram because the data are grouped in intervals.

Photo Package Prices

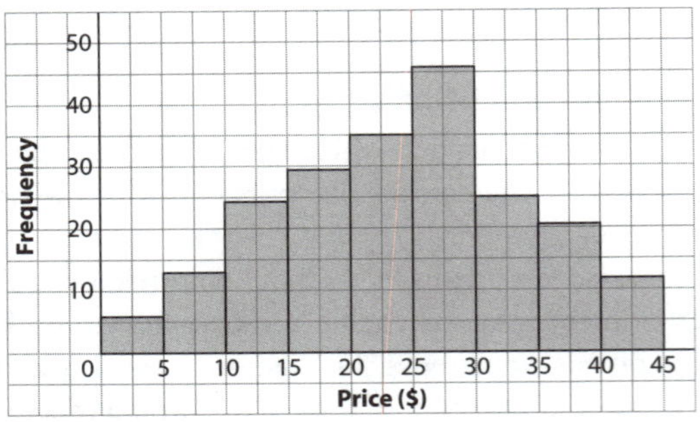

b) The most appropriate graph is a bar graph because the data represent numbers of different items.

Types of Flowers Ordered

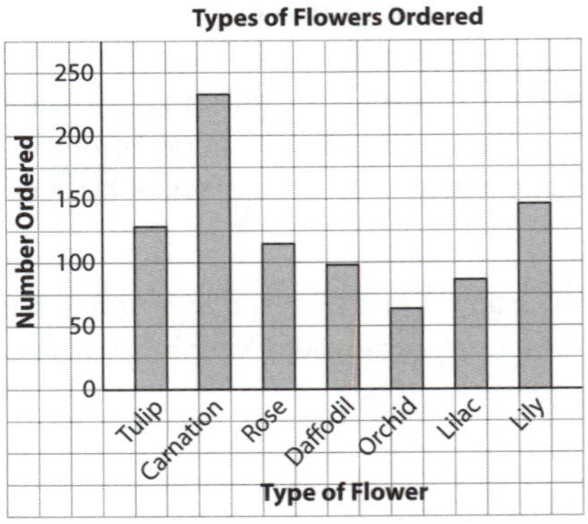

(Sample Solutions continue below, right.)

c) You can identify each piece of data from the stem-and-leaf plot. In the frequency table, you know only how many pieces of data are in each interval. You do not know the values of the data.

d) The horizontal axis represents the heights. Label it in intervals of 10, from 130 to 190. The vertical axis represents the frequency of each interval. Draw vertical bars whose lengths are the frequencies. Write a title for the graph. Label each axis.

Heights of Students in Grade 8

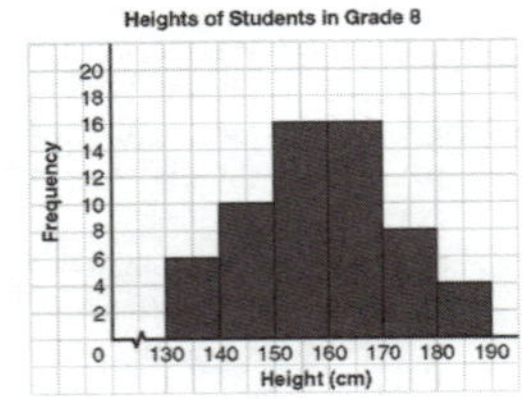

Practice

1. Draw the most appropriate graph to display each set of data. Explain your choice.

a)

Photo Package Price ($)	0–4	5–9	10–14	15–19	20–24	25–29	30–34	35–39	40–44
Frequency	6	13	24	29	35	46	25	21	12

b)

Type of Flower	Tulip	Carnation	Rose	Daffodil	Orchid	Lilac	Lily
Number Ordered	129	230	115	98	67	85	145

218 UNIT 5: Data Management

- Why is the range important?
  (The range is important to help decide what intervals should be used.)

Practice

Questions 1, 2, 4, 5, and 6 require 0.5-cm grid paper (PM 14).

Assessment Focus: Question 4

Most students will use intervals of 10 along the horizontal axis.

Assignment Guidelines

If your students do not have time to complete all the *Practice* questions on pages 218, 219, and 220, these questions provide minimum curriculum coverage: 1, 2, 4, 5, *Reflect*

To assess the 4 Achievement Chart categories listed in the curriculum document, have students complete these *Practice* questions:

Knowledge and Understanding: 1   Thinking: 4
Application: 2   Communication: 5

(Sample Solutions continued)

2. **a)** Hours per week that elementary school students participate in sports

   b) Assume 0–2 includes any time up to 3 h. Similarly, 3–6 includes any time from 3 h to 7 h, and so on.

Hours per Week Male Elementary Students Participate in Sports

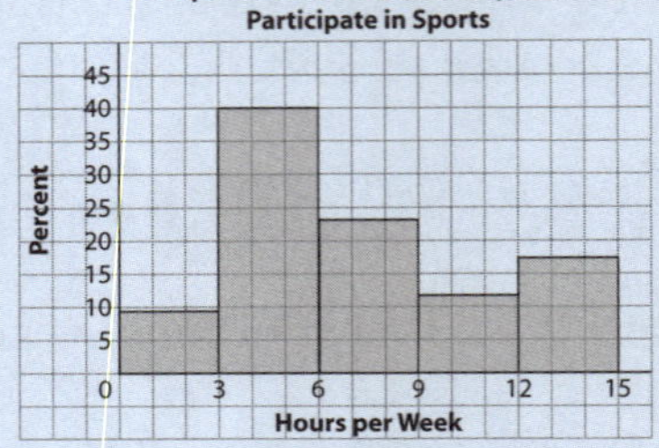

Hours per Week Female Elementary Students Participate in Sports

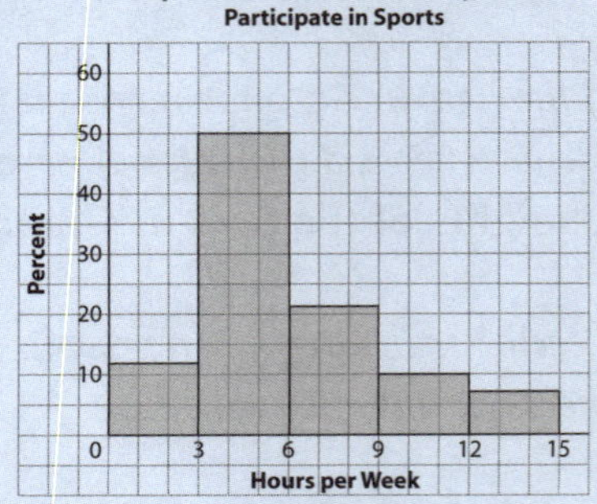

mber Strategies

te e...ction as a
imal.

6, 0.8$\overline{3}$, 0.1$\overline{6}$, 0.3

2. a) What information does this table provide?

Hours Per Week Students Participate in Sports
Elementary School

Hours Per Week	% Girls	% Boys
0–2	12	9
3–5	50	40
6–8	21	23
9–11	10	11
12–14	7	17

b) Draw appropriate graphs to display the data.
c) What can you infer from the table or the graphs?

3. For each set of data, would you use a bar graph or a histogram to display the data? Explain your choice.

a) Ravi recorded how many pairs of each shoe type were sold in his shoe store in April.
Sandals: 109; Dress Shoes: 46; Soccer Cleats: 65;
Athletic Shoes: 89; Rubber Boots: 77

b) Adriana recorded the times, in seconds, taken by 60 female swimmers to swim the 100-m backstroke.
120, 135, 98, 102, 87, 96, 145, 99, 77, 106, 113, 124, 126, 84, 95, 102, 128, 137, 111, 130, 122, 151, 117, 108, 129, 134, 133, 153, 148, 132, 126, 117, 119, 86, 133, 157, 140, 122, 107, 110, 139, 141, 140, 100, 155, 109, 114, 123, 133, 152, 135, 144, 133, 151, 128, 130, 145, 150, 111, 140

4. **Assessment Focus** Leah recorded the number of ice cream bars sold at the community centre each day in the month of July:
101, 112, 125, 96, 132, 125, 116, 97, 124, 136, 123, 119, 78, 105, 118, 130, 87, 108, 114, 99, 126, 86, 94, 117, 125, 107, 122, 119, 114, 105, 93

a) Display the data using a stem-and-leaf plot.
b) Find the median and the mode.
What does each measure tell you about the data?
c) Use the stem-and-leaf plot to make a frequency table.
d) What can you tell from the stem-and-leaf plot that you cannot tell from the frequency table?
e) Use the frequency table to draw a histogram.
f) What can you infer about the ice cream sales in July?

5.5 Drawing Histograms 219

c) From the data and the graphs, we can infer that most boys and girls spend 3–5 h per week participating in sports. Also, more boys than girls spend 12–14 h per week participating in sports.

3. a) I would choose a bar graph because the data are not continuous, and cannot be grouped into intervals.

b) I would choose a histogram because the data can be grouped into intervals, and the data are continuous.

4. a)

Number of Ice Cream Bars Sold in July

Stem	Leaf
7	8
8	6 7
9	3 4 6 7 9
10	1 5 5 7 8
11	2 4 4 6 7 8 9 9
12	2 3 4 5 5 5 6
13	0 2 6

b) The median is 114. The mode is 125. The median is the middle number of the data. This means that the middle number of ice cream bars sold was 114. So, there were as many days when fewer than 114 ice cream bars were sold as days when more than 114 ice cream bars were sold. The mode is the number of ice cream bars sold most often. This means that there were more days when 125 ice cream bars were sold than any other number of ice cream bars.

(Sample Solutions continue below, left.)

(Sample Solutions continued)

c) The least number of ice cream bars sold is 78, and the greatest number of ice cream bars sold is 136.
Subtract to find the range: 136 – 78 = 58
The range is 58. Use intervals of 10.

Interval	Frequency
70–79	1
80–89	2
90–99	5
100–109	5
110–119	8
120–129	7
130–139	3

d) You can identify each piece of data from the stem-and-leaf plot. In the frequency table, you know only how many pieces of data are in each interval. You do not know the values of the data.

e)

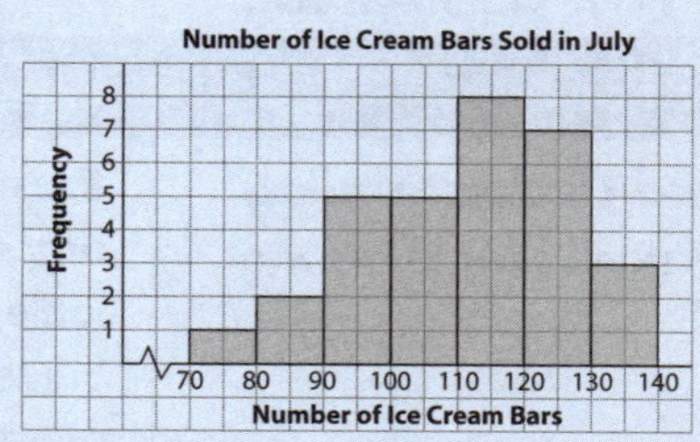

f) On most days in July, 100 or more ice cream bars were sold at the community centre.

5. a) i)

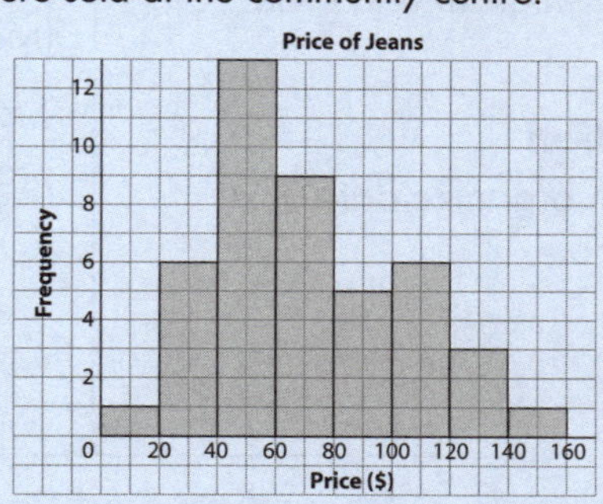

ii) From my graph, it is easy to see that more jeans are less than $100 than those priced at $100 or more.

iii) The graph can be used to estimate the median. Add the heights of the bars. The heights add to 44. So, there are 44 pieces of data. The median is the mean of the 22nd and 23rd pieces of data. I would start at the left-most bar and add the heights to see in which interval the 22nd and 23rd pieces of data lie. They fall in the 60–80 interval. So, I would estimate the median to be about $65.
The graph cannot be used to find the mode because it only shows intervals in which the data lie.

b) i)

Thickness of Library Books

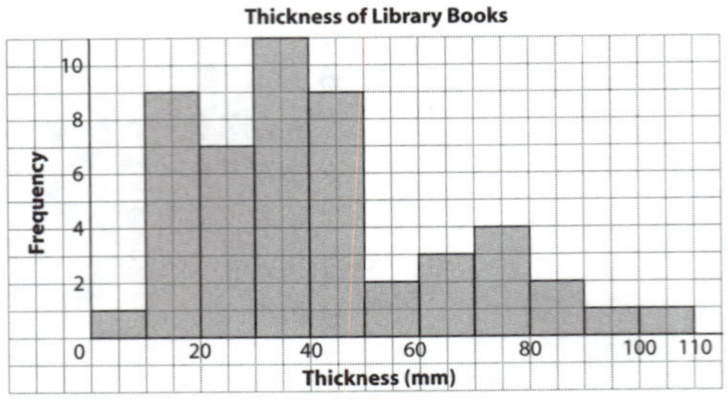

ii) It is easy to see that most books are from 10–49 mm thick.

iii) The graph can be used to estimate the median. Add the heights of the bars. The heights add to 50. So, there are 50 pieces of data. The median is the mean of the 25th and 26th pieces of data. I would start at the left-most bar and add the heights to see in which interval the 25th and 26th pieces of data lie. They fall in the 30–39 interval. So, I would estimate the median to be about 37 mm.
The graph cannot be used to find the mode because it only shows the intervals in which data lie.

(Sample Solutions continue on page 43.)

5. For each set of data below:
- **i)** Draw a histogram.
- **ii)** What do you know from the graph that you do not know from looking at the data?
- **iii)** Can the graphs be used to estimate the median? The mode? Explain your reasoning.

a) Data were collected on the prices, in dollars, of 44 different styles of jeans:
25, 59, 45, 120, 105, 100, 78, 45, 37, 49, 27, 19, 48, 39, 40, 55, 89, 95, 65, 40, 50, 33, 59, 62, 80, 74, 150, 78, 43, 35, 130, 75, 69, 105, 115, 110, 120, 80, 49, 40, 60, 109, 89, 72

b) Data were collected on the thickness, in millimetres, of 50 randomly chosen books from the library:
6, 15, 35, 12, 76, 80, 34, 22, 15, 17, 35, 40, 70, 25, 11, 45, 36, 28, 17, 20, 55, 63, 39, 47, 52, 60, 77, 81, 100, 39, 40, 75, 33, 92, 18, 22, 17, 30, 13, 44, 63, 28, 20, 31, 40, 34, 45, 40, 45, 38

Take It Further

6. Four hundred Grade 8 students in the Ottawa area participated in a math contest. The results are shown in the table.

Percent of Students	Range of Scores
8	91 to 100
21	81 to 90
29	71 to 80
22	61 to 70
9	51 to 60
7	41 to 50
3	31 to 40
1	21 to 30
0	11 to 20
0	1 to 10

Elias wanted to compare his school results, recorded below, to the city wide results.
67, 78, 93, 56, 68, 64, 98, 70, 59, 64, 83, 72, 75, 88, 69, 78, 76, 29, 55, 69, 77, 83, 88, 76, 48, 71, 60, 82, 80, 90, 55, 74, 73, 81, 58, 66, 81, 31, 47, 78, 99, 66, 64, 72, 80, 94, 75, 68

a) What type of graph would you use to display the city results? Justify your choice.
b) What type of graph would you use to display Elias' school results? Justify your choice.
c) Draw the graphs you chose in parts a and b.
d) Did Elias' school do better than all the other schools? How do you know?

Reflect

When would you group data before displaying them on a graph? When would you *not* group data? Include examples in your explanation.

220 UNIT 5: Data Management

ASSESSMENT FOR LEARNING

What to Look For

Knowledge and Understanding
- ✔ Students understand how to draw a histogram.

Thinking
- ✔ Students can explain the difference between a histogram and a bar graph.

Communication
- ✔ Students can organize data in a frequency table.

What to Do

Extra Support: Students having difficulty may benefit from organizing the data in a stem-and-leaf plot, making a frequency table, and then drawing a histogram.
Students can use Step-by-Step 5 (Master 5.11) to complete question 4.

Extra Practice: Students can complete Extra Practice 5 (Master 5.22).

Extension: Have students draw the graphs for the examples they provided in *Reflect.*

Recording and Reporting
Master 5.2 Ongoing Observations: Data Management

Technology

Using *Fathom* to Draw Histograms and Investigate Outliers

Focus Draw a histogram using *Fathom*.

You will use *Fathom* to draw a histogram, change an interval width, and find the mean and median of the data.

Here are the heights, in centimetres, of all the Grade 8 students who were on the school track team: 164, 131, 172, 137, 175, 168, 146, 176, 175, 173, 155, 170, 172, 160, 168, 178, 174, 184, 189

To use *Fathom* to draw a histogram for these data, follow these steps:

1. Open *Fathom*. From the File menu, select New.
2. To enter the title:
   Click the New Collection icon, then click the screen.
   Double-click Collection 1.
   Type **Heights of Grade 8 Students on the Track Team**, and click OK.
3. To enter the data:
   Click the New Case Table icon, then click the screen.
   Click <new>; type **Height**, then press Enter.
   Input the data under the heading Height. Press Enter each time.
4. To graph the data:
   Click the New Graph icon.
   Click the screen. Two axes appear.
   Click the column heading, *Height*, and drag it to the horizontal axis.
   Select *Histogram* from the drop-down menu in the top right.
   A histogram is created.

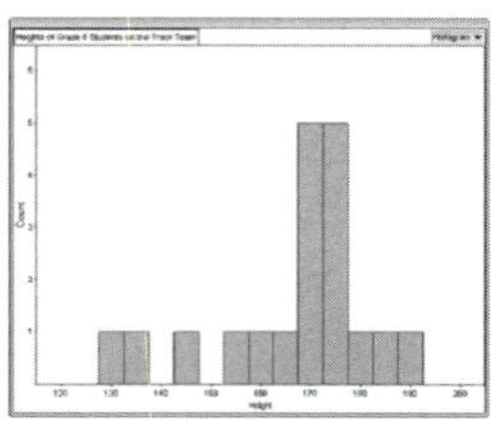

Technology: Using *Fathom* to Draw Histograms and Investigate Outliers **221**

Using *Fathom* to Draw Histograms and Investigate Outliers

LESSON ORGANIZER	40–50 min

Curriculum Focus: Draw a histogram using *Fathom*. (8m70)
Student Materials
- computers with *Fathom*

Assessment: Master 5.2 Ongoing Observations: Data Management

Key Math Learnings

1. Software, such as *Fathom*, can be used to draw histograms.
2. The width of the bars is automatically determined by the software.
3. The mean and median of the data set are easily found using *Fathom*.

Sample Solutions

1.

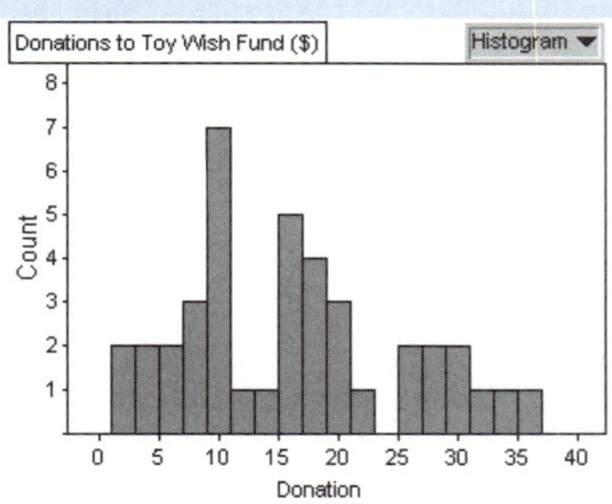

Information about this graph:
Histogram: Bin width: **2.0000** starting at: **1.0000**
The **Donation** axis is horizontal from **-2.5000** to **42.500**
The **Count** axis is vertical from 0 to **8.5000**

a) The bin width is: 2.0000 starting at 1.0000
Yes, these make sense because the lowest donation is 2 and the highest is 35, so the range of donations is 33.

b) The mean donation is about $15.68 and the median donation is $15.00.

c) I added donations of $100 and $150.

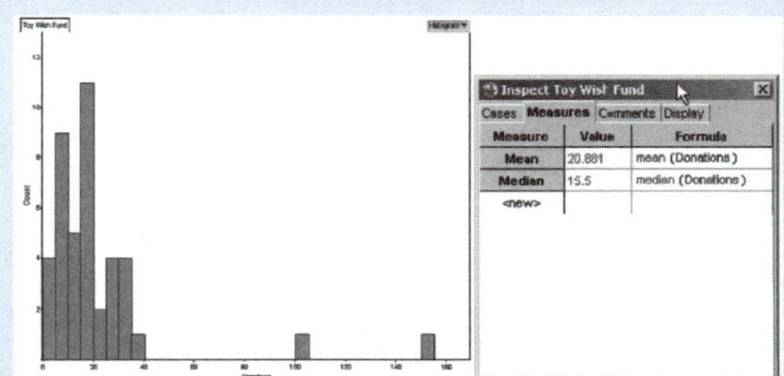

The mean and median increased.

REACHING ALL LEARNERS

Early Finishers

Have students research a topic of their choice using *Census at School, E-STAT,* or another database. Students then use *Fathom* to draw a histogram. Have them determine the mean and median of the data, and make observations about the interval widths.

Notes for the Teacher

1. Tell students that *Fathom* is a software that can be used to draw histograms. Students will use *Fathom* to create histograms, then use the software to make observations about the interval widths, and the mean and median of the data.
2. Pair students so that a computer-literate student works with a student whose computer knowledge is limited.
3. To adjust the horizontal axis so that the bars begin at 0, students can click on the horizontal axis (a hand will appear) and slide the scale so that 0 meets with the vertical axis. Also, to ensure that all the bars along the horizontal axis are easily viewed, students can click on the horizontal axis and slide to the left or right. This way, more or less of the axis can be viewed. The same is true for the vertical axis.

To view the heights that make up one bar, click on a bar.
It turns red.
In the table, the heights that correspond to that bar turn blue.

Fathom automatically selects a width for each bar.
To see the width, double-click the graph.
The text window for the graph appears.
You will see:

Information about this graph:
Histogram: Bin width: **5.0000** starting at: **127.50**
The **height** axis is horizontal from **115.00** to **205.00**
The **Count** axis is vertical from 0 to **6.5000**

The "Bin width" represents the width of the bars.
The "starting at" tells the starting value.

➢ To change the Bin width to 10, double-click the blue text that follows *Bin width*: and enter 10.
To change the starting number to 130, double-click the blue text that follows *starting at*: and enter 130.
To change the Count axis, double-click the blue text that currently shows 6.5 and enter 10.
The histogram changes.

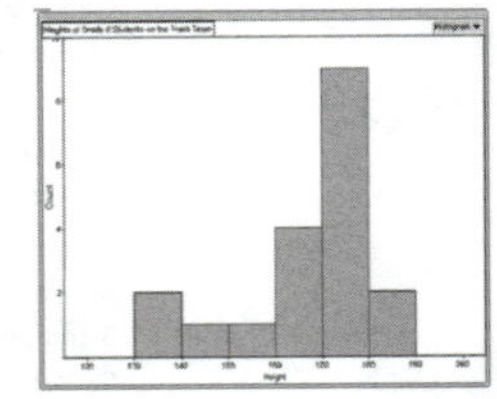

➢ To find the mean height, double-click the *Collection Box* to open the *Inspector* for the collection.
Select the *Measures tab*. Rename <new> to Mean. Press Enter.
Right-click the *Formula* column for the *Mean* measure, and select *Edit Formula*.
Double-click *Functions*, double-click *Statistical*, double-click *One Attribute*, and then double-click *mean*. Type **Height** in the brackets.
The word *mean* turns red and the word *Height* turns blue.
Press Enter. The mean is shown under *Value*.

222 UNIT 5: Data Management

2.

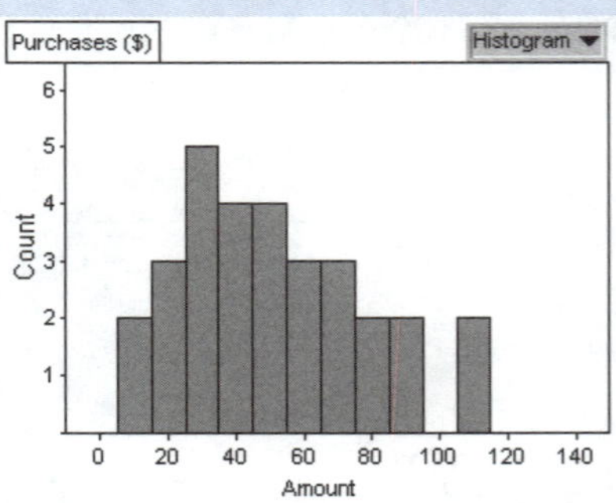

Information about this graph:
Histogram: Bin width: **10.000** starting at: **5.0000**
The **Amount** axis is horizontal from **-10.000** to **150.00**
The **Count** axis is vertical from 0 to **6.5000**

a) The bin width is: 10.0000 starting at 5.0000
Yes, these make sense because the lowest purchase is \$10.19 and the highest is \$112.48, so the range of donations is \$102.29.

b) The mean purchase is about \$51.23 and the median purchase is about \$46.44.

c) I added purchases of \$1.50 and \$2.00.

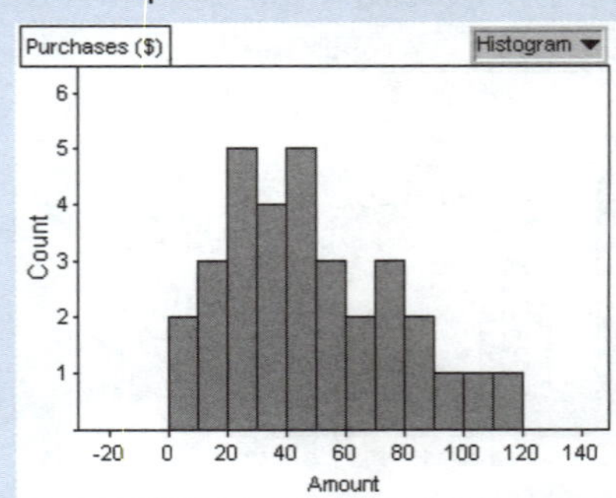

These outliers decreased the mean and median slightly.

➢ To find the median height, double-click the *Collection Box* to open the *Inspector* for the collection.
Select the *Measures* tab. Rename <new> to Median. Press Enter.
Right-click the *Formula* column for the *Median* measure, and select *Edit Formula*. Double-click *Functions*, double-click *Statistical*, double-click *One Attribute*, and then double-click *median*.
Type **Height** in the brackets.
The word *median* turns red and the word *Height* turns blue.
Press Enter. The median is shown below the mean, under *Value*.

➢ To find the effects of outliers on the mean and median, input these heights into the table: 125, 127
The histogram, the mean, and the median change to reflect the new heights.
How do these new heights affect the mean and median? Explain.

➢ Replace the heights added above with the heights 198 and 200.
How do these new heights affect the mean and median? Explain.

✓ **Check**

1. Use *Fathom* to draw a histogram for these data.
They are the donations, in dollars, that were made to a Toy Wish Fund.
5, 2, 3, 9, 10, 5, 2, 8, 7, 15, 14, 17, 28, 30, 16, 19, 4, 7, 9, 11, 25, 30, 32, 15, 27, 18, 9, 10, 16, 22, 34, 19, 25, 18, 20, 17, 9, 10, 15, 35
   a) What are the bin widths created by *Fathom*?
   Do these make sense? Explain.
   b) Use *Fathom* to find the mean and median.
   c) Add some outliers to your table.
   State the values you added.
   How do the new mean and median compare to their original values? Explain.

2. Repeat question 1 for these data.
They are the purchases, in dollars, made by customers at a grocery store.
55.40, 48.26, 28.31, 14.12, 88.90, 34.45, 51.02, 71.87, 105.12, 10.19, 74.44, 29.05, 43.56, 90.66, 23.00, 60.52, 43.17, 28.49, 67.03, 16.18, 76.05, 45.68, 22.76, 36.73, 39.92, 112.48, 81.21, 56.73, 47.19, 34.45

Technology: Using *Fathom* to Draw Histograms and Investigate Outliers **223**

(Sample Solutions for Lesson 5.5, page 40, continued.)

6. a) I would use a histogram since the data are grouped into intervals and the data are continuous.

b) I would use a histogram since the data can be grouped into intervals and the data are continuous.

c)

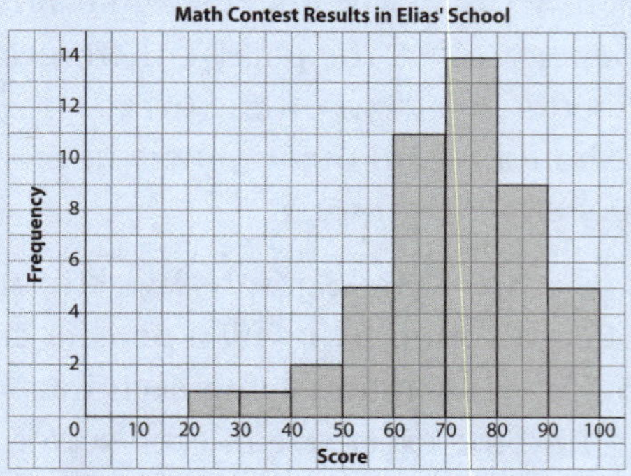

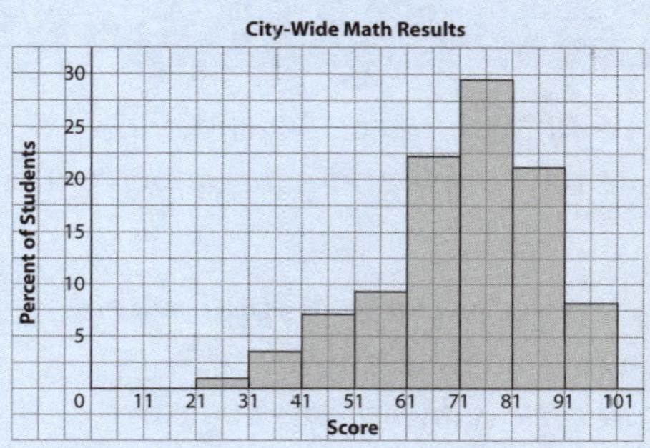

d) Yes, only 89% of students scored over 50% city wide, but 92% of students at Elias's school scored over 50%.

REFLECT: Certain types of graphs require data to be grouped, while other types of graphs do not have this requirement. Bar graphs, histograms, and pictographs, for example, require data to be grouped before they are displayed. Scatter plots and line graphs, for example, do not require data to be grouped before they are displayed.

Drawing Circle Graphs

LESSON ORGANIZER

80–100 min

Curriculum Focus: Display data on a circle graph. (8m68, 8m70, 8m71, 8m73)

Student Materials
- 0.5-cm grid paper (PM 14)
- protractors
- calculators
- compasses
- coloured pencils
- Percent Circles (Master 5.15)

Optional
- Step-by-Step 6 (Master 5.12)
- Extra Practice 6 (Master 5.23)

Vocabulary: sector angle, circle graph

Assessment: Master 5.2 Ongoing Observations: Data Management

Key Math Learnings

1. A circle graph is used to graph parts of one whole.
2. Each piece of data is written as a fraction of a whole and as a percent.

5.6 Drawing Circle Graphs

Focus Display data on a circle graph.

Explore

Work with a partner.
In a chart on the board, record the colour of your partner's eyes.
When you have the data for the whole class,
draw a circle graph to display the data.

Reflect & Share

Compare your graph with that of another pair of classmates.
Which is the most frequent eye colour in your class?
Suppose you drew a circle graph for the eye colours
of all the students in the school.
How would the graph compare to the graph you drew? Explain.

Connect

A circle graph is used to graph parts of one whole.
Each piece of data is written as a fraction of the whole.
This fraction is then used to find the sector angle in the circle graph.
Each fraction is also written as a percent.
The method is illustrated in the following example.

Example

All the students in two Grade 8 classes were asked how they get to school each day. Here are the results:
11 rode their bikes, 13 walked, 26 came by bus,
and 15 were driven by car.
Construct a circle graph to illustrate the data.

Solution

For each type of transport, write the number of students as a fraction of 65, the total number of students:
Bike: $\frac{11}{65}$; walk: $\frac{13}{65}$; bus: $\frac{26}{65}$; car: $\frac{15}{65}$
To calculate each sector angle, multiply each fraction by 360°.
To calculate each percent, multiply each fraction by 100%.
The results are shown in the following table.

224 UNIT 5: Data Management

BEFORE Get Started

Use *Skills You'll Need*, page 184, to review drawing a circle graph and using a percent circle.

Ask:

- Why is a percent circle helpful when constructing a circle graph?
  (A percent circle is divided into 100 parts, each part representing 1% of the circle. These parts are combined to form 10 congruent sectors. It is easy to shade the circle to display data.)
- How can we find the percent that corresponds with each part of the whole?
  (Express each part as a fraction. Convert each fraction to a percent. Then, colour that part of the circle.)

Present *Explore*.

DURING Explore

Ongoing Assessment: Observe and Listen

An alternative way to collect data is to have each student write her or his eye colour on a piece of paper. Collect the papers, then record the eye colours in a chart on the board. Students should record the numbers in their notebooks before beginning.

Students may draw circle graphs by estimating the size of each sector, by using a percent circle (Master 5.15), or by multiplying each fraction by 360° to find the exact size of each sector.

Ask:

- How many eye-colour categories did you use?
  (I used 4 categories: brown, blue, green, and other; other included any colour that did not fit into one of the categories mentioned.)
- What operation does the word *of* imply?
  (Multiplication)

d each sector
gle to the nearest degree. Round each percent to the nearest whole number.

How Students Get to School	Number of Students	Sector Angle (Using Fractions)	Percent
Bike	11	$\frac{11}{65} \times 360° \doteq 61°$	$\frac{11}{65} \times 100\% \doteq 17\%$
Walk	13	$\frac{13}{65} \times 360° = 72°$	$\frac{13}{65} \times 100\% = 20\%$
Bus	26	$\frac{26}{65} \times 360° = 144°$	$\frac{26}{65} \times 100\% = 40\%$
Car	15	$\frac{15}{65} \times 360° \doteq 83°$	$\frac{15}{65} \times 100\% \doteq 23\%$
Total	65	360°	100%

To graph the data, draw a large circle. Draw one radius.
Use a protractor to measure the greatest sector angle, 144°.
Draw the radius to make a sector with this angle.
Continue to make a sector for each of the other angles.
Label each sector with its percent.

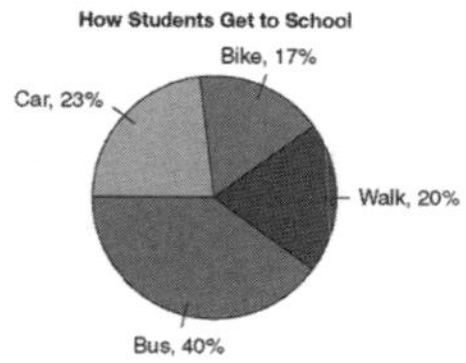

Practice

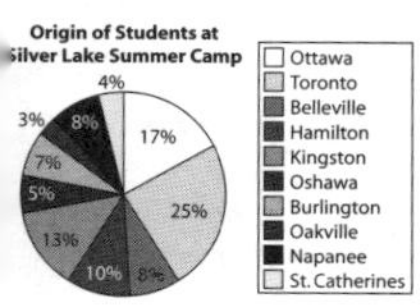

1. Liam asked students at Silver Lake Summer Camp, "Where are you from?" He recorded these results: Ottawa 60, Toronto 90, Belleville 30, Hamilton 36, Kingston 45, Oshawa 20, Burlington 24, Oakville 10, Napanee 30, St. Catharines 15
   a) Display the data in a circle graph.
   b) What can you tell from the graph that you cannot easily tell from the data?

2. a) Which of the sets of data on the next page could be represented by a circle graph? Explain.
   b) For each set of data that is not best represented by a circle graph, which graph is most appropriate? Explain.

5.6 Drawing Circle Graphs 225

REACHING ALL LEARNERS

Early Finishers

Students work in pairs. They collect data about eye colour from another Grade 8 class or from any other class in the school. They draw a circle graph and compare the data with the data obtained in *Explore*.

Common Misconceptions

➤ Students think that the frequency of each piece of data represents a percent.

How to Help: Remind students to write each frequency as a fraction of the whole, where the numerator represents each piece of data and the denominator represents the sum of the data.

Number Strategies

Students need to recall the formula for simple interest: $I = Prt$

Assignment Guidelines

If your students do not have time to complete all the *Practice* questions on pages 225, 226, and 227, these questions provide minimum curriculum coverage: 1, 2, 3, 4, *Reflect*

To assess the 4 Achievement Chart categories listed in the curriculum document, have students complete these *Practice* questions:

Knowledge and Understanding: 1 Application: 3
Communication: 2 Thinking: 4

- How can a fraction be converted to a percent?
  (Multiply the numerator by 100, then divide the product by the denominator.)
- How many degrees are there in a circle?
  (There are 360° in a circle.)
- How can a fraction be used to find the sector angle?
  (Multiply the numerator by 360°, then divide the product by the denominator.)
- How can the percent for each eye colour in the class be used to find the percent for each eye colour in the school?
  (The percents would be about the same.)
- How can the percent for each eye colour in the class be used to find the number of students with each eye colour in the school?
  (Multiply the total school population by the percent for each eye colour.)

AFTER Connect

Invite students to share their findings with the class.

Ask:

- What assumption do we make when we find the percent of each eye colour for the school?
  (We assume the eye colour of the school population will be approximately the same ratio or proportion as that of the class.)

Review *Connect*. Encourage students to organize their work in a chart so that no steps are missed, and they can see how they converted from fractions to sector angles to percents.

Ask:

- Why do the percents in the table sometimes add to more than 100% or less than 100%?
  (When rounding the values, it is possible to round up or down. So, the total may not always add to exactly 100%.)

Sample Solutions

1. **b)** It is easy to tell what percent of the population originates from each city.

2. **i) a)** Yes, each number of students can be written as a fraction of one whole.

c) **Eye Colours of Grades 7 and 8 Students**

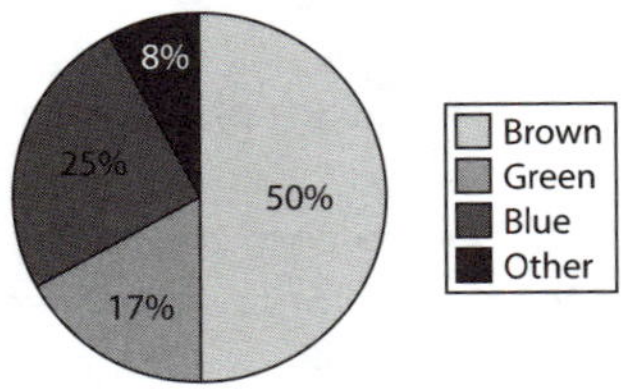

ii) a) No, there are two sets of data and the data are grouped in intervals.

b) I would use a histogram because the data are continuous and are grouped in intervals.

c) **Boys: Average Number of Hours per Week Spent Playing Video Games**

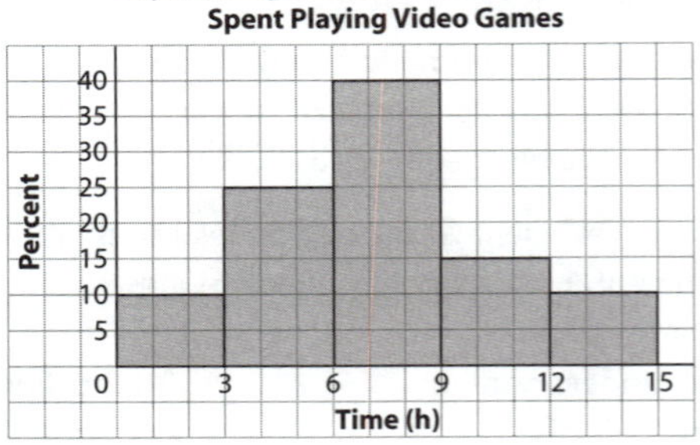

c) Display each set of data using the type of graph you chose.

i) Adam recorded the eye colours of all Grades 7 and 8 students in his school.

Eye Colour	Brown	Green	Blue	Other
Students	60	20	30	10

ii) Celine collected data on the average number of hours per week that Grade 8 girls and boys in her school played video games.

Number of Boys as a Percent	10	25	40	15	10
Number of Girls as a Percent	20	35	30	10	5
Hours Per Week Playing Video Games	0–2	3–5	6–8	9–11	12–14

iii) The table shows the area, in square kilometres, of some Canadian National Parks.

National Park	Banff	Nahanni	Pukaskwa	Prince Albert	Jasper
Area (km²)	6641	4766	1878	3874	10 878

iv) Tobias and Fabiana work evenings at Mamma Maria's restaurant. They recorded their tips for one week.

Day	Mon.	Tues.	Wed.	Thurs.	Fri.	Sat.	Sun.
Tips Tobias Earned ($)	20	12	28	15	32	35	38
Tips Fabiana Earned ($)	15	20	22	30	25	40	28

3. The school library budget to buy new books is $5000. The librarian has the following information about the types of books students borrowed in one month.

Type of Book Borrowed	Number of Students
History	125
Science	90
Biography	65
Geography	52
Fiction	110
Reference	88
French	70

a) Display the data in a circle graph.

b) How much money should be spent on each type of book? Explain.

226 UNIT 5: Data Management

(Sample Solutions continue below, right.)

- Why can the angles in the table sometimes add to more than 360° or less than 360°? *(When rounding the sector angles, it is possible to round up or down. So, the total may be more or less than 360°.)*

Remind students to use a protractor to make the correct angle measure.

Practice

All questions require protractors and compasses, or percent circles (Master 5.15). Have 0.5-cm grid paper available for question 2.

Assessment Focus: Question 4

Students might round to the nearest percent. As a result, those who entered by train will be rounded down to 0%.

(Sample Solutions continued)

Girls: Average Number of Hours per Week Spent Playing Video Games

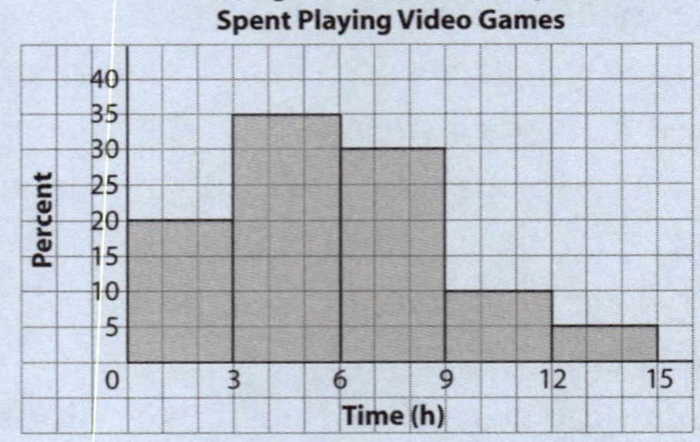

iii) a) No, the data do not represent part of a whole.

b) I would use a bar graph. The data are area measurements of different parks.

(Sample Solutions continue on top of next page.)

4. Assessment Focus This table shows the method of transport used by U.S. residents entering Canada in 2002.

United States Residents Entering Canada in 2002

Method of Transport	Number
Automobile	33 424 000
Plane	4 224 000
Train	121 000
Bus	1 582 000
Boat	886 000
Other	641 000

Source: Statistics Canada, Canadian Statistics, CANSIM table 427-0001. Last modified: 2005-05-18. http://www40.statcan.ca/l01/cst01/arts34.htm Date extracted: April 11, 2005

a) How many U.S. residents visited Canada in 2002? 40 878 000 residents
b) What percent of U.S. residents entered Canada by boat? About 2%
c) What fraction of U.S. residents entered Canada by plane? About $\frac{704}{6813}$
d) Display the data in a circle graph.
e) What else do you know from the table or circle graph? Write as much as you can.

Number Strategies

Calculate the simple interest paid on a loan of $2000 at an annual interest rate of 4% for 2 years. $160

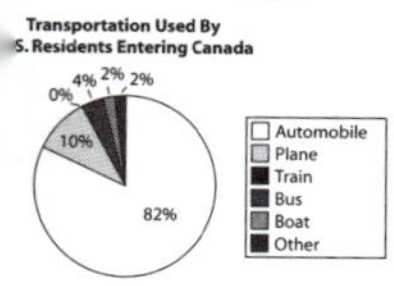

5. Here is the nutritional information on the wrapper of a roasted almond granola bar.

Protein	2.0 g
Fat	4.7 g
Sugar	6.4 g
Starch	7.3 g
Dietary Fibre	1.3 g

Use a circle graph to display these data.

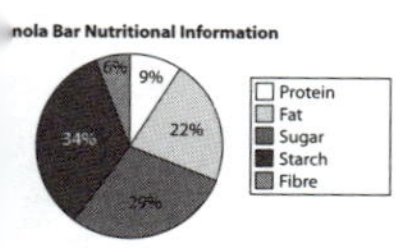

Reflect

Which type of data is best represented by a circle graph? Support your answer with an example.

5.6 Drawing Circle Graphs 227

(Sample Solutions continued from bottom of previous page)

c)

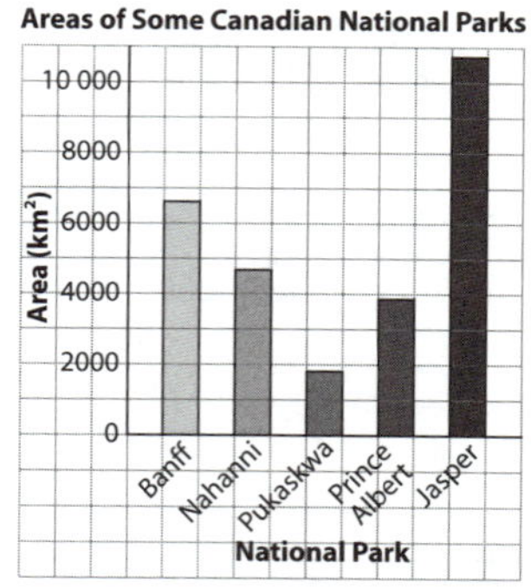

iv) a) No, there are two sets of data, and the data cannot be written as a fraction of one whole.

b) I would use a double-bar graph because it is easy to compare the tips for each day.

c)

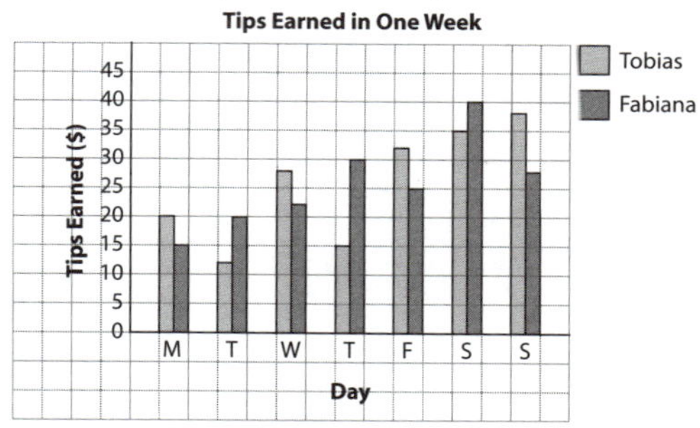

(Sample Solutions continue on page 49.)

ASSESSMENT FOR LEARNING

What to Look For

Knowledge and Understanding

✔ Students understand when data can be displayed on a circle graph.

Communication

✔ Students can use the circle graph to solve problems.

Application

✔ Students can construct a circle graph.

What to Do

Extra Support: Students having difficulty deciding when to use a circle graph should ask themselves if a set of data represents parts of one whole. If it does, it may be represented by a circle graph. Students can use Step-by-Step 6 (Master 5.12) to complete question 4.

Extra Practice: Students can complete the Additional Activity *Nutrition Circles* (Master 5.6).
Students can complete Extra Practice 6 (Master 5.23).

Extension: Students can research data from the *Census at School* website, use the data to draw a circle graph, and pose questions that can be answered from the graph.

Recording and Reporting

Master 5.2 Ongoing Observations: Data Management

Identifying Key Verbs in Math Problems

LESSON ORGANIZER

Student Materials
- construction paper
- tape
- scissors

Identifying Key Verbs in Math Problems

Many math problems are questions or puzzles presented without a context.
The question may ask you to do something with math information.
It may include a *key verb* to tell you what to do.
Here are some key verbs and their meanings.

Calculate, evaluate:	Find the answer to a question that uses any or all of the operations: add, subtract, multiply, and divide
Classify:	Sort objects into groups according to a rule. Tell the rule.
Compare:	Tell what is the same and what is different.
Construct:	Make a model. Draw accurately.
Describe, explain, represent:	Use numbers, words, pictures, diagrams, charts, and/or models to tell about your work and show your thinking.
Draw:	Create a picture or sketch.
Estimate:	Make a reasoned guess about what you know.
Justify:	Give reasons and evidence to show your answer makes sense.
Model:	Show with objects and/or pictures.
Predict:	Tell what you think will happen, based on what you know.
Relate:	Show and explain a connection between ideas, objects, drawings, numbers, and events.
Simplify:	Make simpler but equal.
Solve:	Develop a solution to a problem.
Show your work:	Record important calculations, numbers, words, pictures, diagrams, graphs, charts, and/or models. Include the steps you used to get your answer so that someone else could repeat it.

✓ Check

Identify the key verb, then solve each problem.

1. These figures can be used to construct different solids. You can use more than one of each figure.

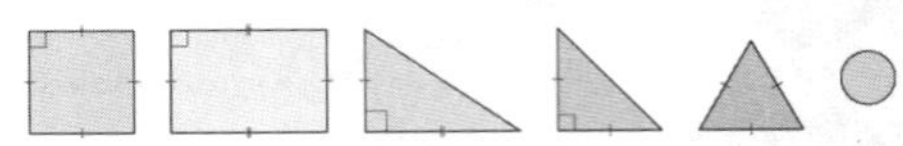

a) List the different solids that could be made. List
b) Construct one solid. Draw the others. Construct; Draw

228 UNIT 5: Data Management

1. a) For example: the following solids can be made with the figures shown: cube, rectangular prism, triangular prism, tetrahedron, square pyramid, cylinder, octahedron, icosahedron.

b) c) For example: cube:

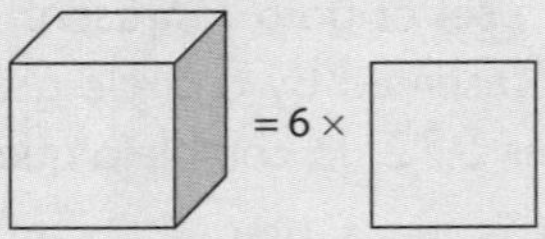

$= 6 \times 4\ units^2$
$= 24\ units^2$

square pyramid:

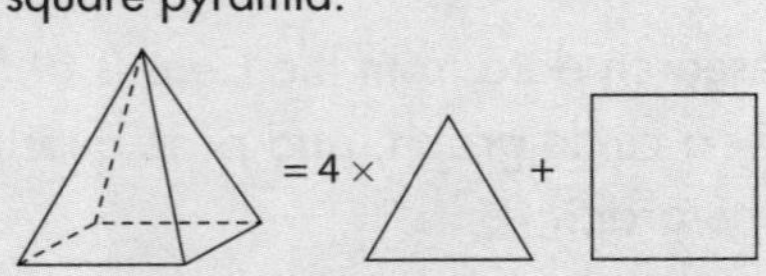

$= 4 \times 2\ units^2 + 4\ units^2$
$= 12\ units^2$

tetrahedron:

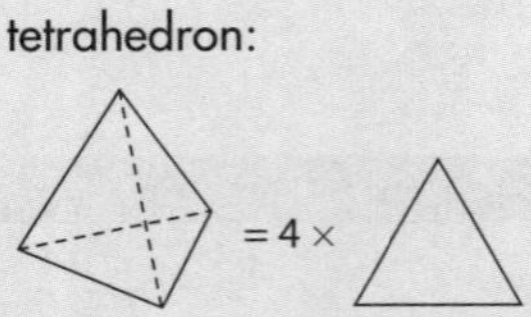

$= 4 \times 2\ units^2$
$= 8\ units^2$

rectangular prism:

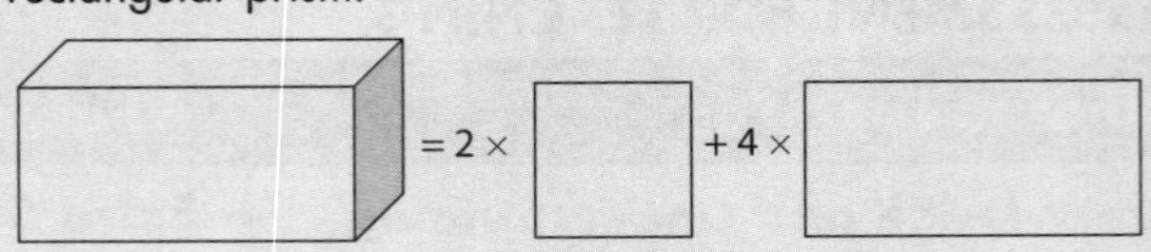

$= 2 \times 4\ units^2 + 4 \times 6\ units^2$
$= 32\ units^2$

triangular prism:

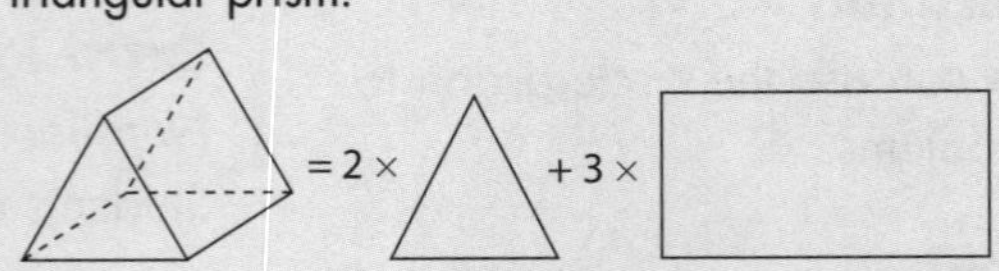

$= 2 \times 2\ units^2 + 3 \times 6\ units^2$
$= 22\ units^2$

cylinder:

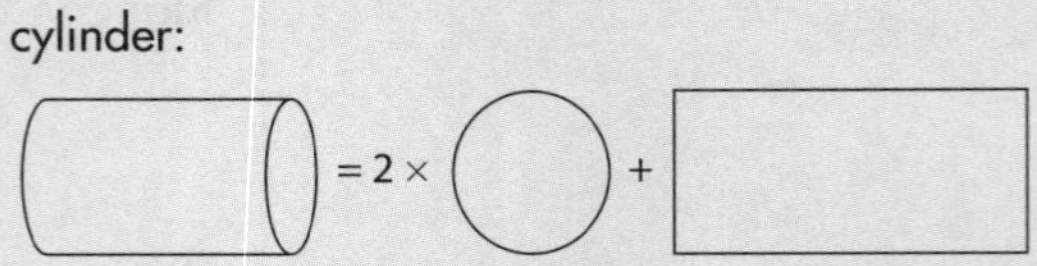

$= 2 \times 1\ unit^2 + 6\ units^2$
$= 8\ units^2$

c) The square has an area of 4 square units. The rectangle has an area of 6 square units. Four circles just fit inside the square. One triangle is one-half the rectangle. Another triangle is one-half the square. Estimate the surface area of each solid that is made from these figures. Estimate

Reading and Writing in Math

2. Here are some data from Statistics Canada for 2001.

Province or Territory	Median age (years)	Percent of population in each age group		
		0–19	65+	20–64
Newfoundland and Labrador	38.4	25.0	12.3	62.7
Prince Edward Island	37.7	27.3	13.7	59.0
Nova Scotia	38.8	25.0	13.9	61.1
New Brunswick	38.6	24.8	13.6	61.7
Quebec	38.8	24.2	13.3	62.5
Ontario	37.2	26.3	12.9	60.8
Manitoba	36.8	28.1	14.0	58.0
Saskatchewan	36.7	29.2	15.1	55.8
Alberta	35.0	28.3	10.4	61.4
British Columbia	38.4	25.0	13.6	61.4
Yukon Territory	36.1	29.0	6.0	64.9
Northwest Territories	30.1	35.0	4.4	60.7
Nunavut	22.1	46.5	2.2	51.2

Source: Statistics Canada, *2001 Census of Canada, analysis series*. Catalogue no. 96F0030XIE2001002. Last modified 2005-03-08. http://www12.statcan.ca/english/census01/Products/Analytic/companion/age/ewt1.cfm
Date extracted: April 11, 2005

a) For each province, relate the median age to the age groups. How do they compare? Explain. Relate; Compare; Explain

Represent; Draw b) Which different graphs could you draw to represent these data?

c) Suppose you need to decide where to spend health care dollars for an aging population. Justify where most money should be spent. Justify

d) Where might you increase money spent on education? Justify your answer. Justify

e) Write your own problem about these data. Solve your problem. Write; Solve

Reading and Writing in Math: Identifying Key Verbs in Math Problems 229

(Sample Solutions for Lesson 5.6, page 47, continued)

3. a) **Types of Books Borrowed**

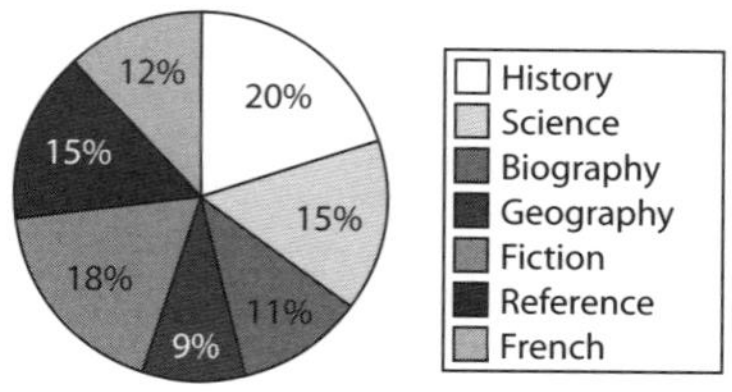

b) The amount that should be spent on each type of book should correspond to the percent in the circle graph.
French: $\frac{70}{600} \times \$5000 \doteq \$583$, Reference: $\frac{88}{600} \times \$5000 \doteq \$733$, Fiction: $\frac{110}{600} \times \$5000 \doteq \$917$, Geography: $\frac{52}{600} \times \$5000 \doteq \$433$, Biography: $\frac{65}{600} \times \$5000 \doteq \$542$, Science: $\frac{90}{600} \times \$5000 \doteq \$750$, History: $\frac{125}{600} \times \$5000 \doteq \$1042$

4. e) From the graph, we know that the greatest number entered by automobile and the least number entered by train. Approximately the same number entered by boat as by other methods of transport. More than 75% entered by automobile.

REFLECT: A circle graph best represents data that are part of one whole. For example, suppose there is a class barbecue. Each student can order a hot dog, hamburger, or veggie burger. If each student orders something, a circle graph can be used to display what portion of the class ordered each item at the barbecue. However, if only some students order barbecue items, a circle graph may not be appropriate because we are no longer measuring parts of the whole class.

2. a) In each province, the median age falls in the 20–64 age group.
This is not surprising as the 20–64 age group has the widest span of ages.

b) I could use a histogram or a circle graph and create a graph for each province. I could use a triple-bar graph to display all the data on one graph.

c) If I had to choose one province or territory in which to spend health-care dollars, I would choose Saskatchewan. I would make this choice because, compared to the other provinces and territories, Saskatchewan has the greatest percent of people aged 65+.

d) If I had to choose one province or territory in which to spend money on education, I would choose Nunavut. I would make this choice because, compared to the other provinces and territories, Nunavut has the greatest percent of people aged 0–19.

LESSON ORGANIZER

Student Materials

- compasses
- 0.5-cm grid paper (PM 14)
- coloured pencils
- calculators
- protractors
- Percent Circles (Master 5.15)

Assessment: Master 5.1 Unit Rubric: Data Management, Master 5.4 Unit Summary: Data Management

Correlation of Extra Practice questions on page 492:

Lesson	Questions
5.1	1, 2
5.2	3
5.3	3, 4, 5
5.4	—
5.5	—
5.6	5

Unit Review

Review any lesson with etext online tutorial

What Do I Need to Know?

A *census* collects data from all the people in a population.

A *sample* collects data from some of the people in a population.

A *double-bar graph* or a *double-line graph* displays two sets of data on the same grid.

A *histogram* displays data that can be grouped into intervals. There is no space between the bars in a histogram.

The *mean*, *median*, and *mode* are the three *measures of central tendency*.

An *outlier* is a number in a set of data that is much greater than or much less than most of the numbers in the data set.

What Should I Be Able to Do?

For extra practice, go to page 492.

LESSON

5.1 **1.** For each situation, explain why data are collected from a sample and not a census.

a) To test the quality of batteries

b) To find the number of hours a light bulb will burn

c) To find the percent of Grade 8 students who know the multiplication tables

2. In each case, identify the collected data as from a sample or a census. Justify your answer.

a) To find if the Grade 8 class should play soccer or basketball, each student in the class voted.

b) To find the percent of teenagers in Ontario who work part-time, all high school students in Hamilton were surveyed.

5.2 **3.** Rob researched accident statistics in his community. He learned that, in the past year, 20 people were injured in car accidents and 5 people were injured in motorcycle accidents. Rob inferred, "It is safer to ride a motorcycle than it is to drive a car." Is Rob's inference valid? Explain.

230 UNIT 5: Data Management

Sample Solutions

1. a) Too expensive to test every battery

b) Too expensive; no light bulbs left to sell

c) Too expensive and time consuming to test every Grade 8 student

2. a) Census; every student in the class voted.

b) Sample; only students in Hamilton were surveyed.

3. No, more people drive cars than ride motorcycles. It would have been better to relate the number of each type of accident to the number of people who use each type of transportation.

4. a) A double-bar graph could be used to display these data because the data compare items that are measured. Two circle graphs, one for Grade 7 students and one for Grade 8 students, could be used to display these data, because the data compare measurements that are part of one whole.

b)

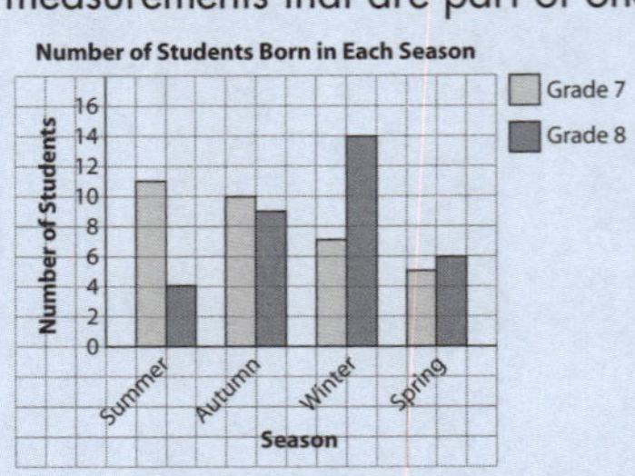

c) The least number of students are born in the spring. The two bars "added" together would produce the shortest bar (11 students).
The greatest number of students are born in the winter. The two bars "added" together would produce the tallest bar (21 students).

5. a) A double-line graph best displays these data because the data are continuous and are in two sets.

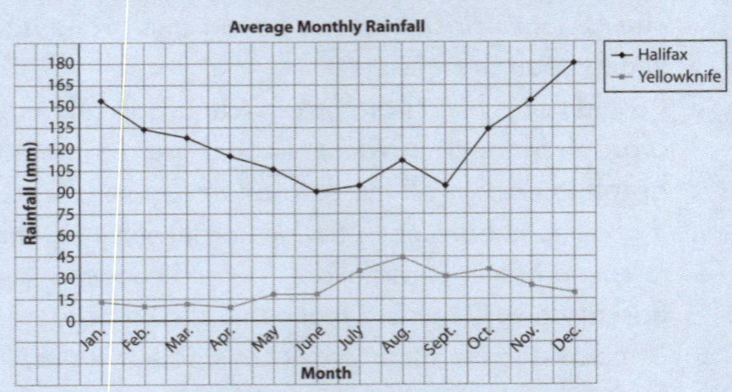

b) The graph shows that the rainfall in Yellowknife is consistently less than that in Halifax. In Halifax, it rains most in the winter months and least in the summer months. In Yellowknife, it rains most in the summer months and least in the winter months.

c) The average monthly rainfall for Halifax is much greater than that of Yellowknife.
The average monthly rainfall for Halifax is greatest from October to March. The average monthly rainfall for Yellowknife is greatest in July, August, and September. Yellowknife does not receive much rainfall.

LESSON

5.2 5.3 **4.** Odakota recorded the number of Grades 7 and 8 students born in each season.

Number of Students Born in Each Season

Season	Summer	Autumn	Winter	Spring
Grade 7	11	10	7	5
Grade 8	4	9	14	6

a) Which types of graphs could be used to display these data? Explain your choices.
b) Display the data using one of your choices from part a.
c) Write a convincing argument based on the graph. Justify your argument.

5. a) Display the data in the table using a suitable graph. Justify your choice.

Average Monthly Rainfall (mm)

Month	Halifax	Yellowknife
January	153	13
February	134	11
March	128	12
April	115	10
May	106	17
June	90	17
July	94	34
August	111	44
September	94	31
October	134	35
November	153	25
December	180	18

b) What trends does the graph show? Explain.
c) What inferences can you make from the graph? Explain.

6. This table shows the numbers of boys and girls who attended the school football games.

Game	1	2	3	4	5	6	7
Girls	35	67	71	69	56	63	65
Boys	52	58	60	78	67	61	63

a) Display the data using a suitable graph. Explain your choice.
b) Glenna looked at the data and inferred, "More girls than boys went to the games." Is Glenna's inference valid? If your answer is yes, explain how Glenna might have made the inference. If your answer is no, what inference would you make from the data? Explain.

5.4 **7.** The table shows the annual incomes of the employees of *Computers For You.*

Position	Salary ($)
1 owner	108 000
1 senior manager	81 500
2 managers	72 000
4 engineers	67 000
2 researchers	55 500
4 assistants	45 000
1 clerk	24 000

7. a) Mean: $61 100 Median: $67 000 Mode: $67 000 and $45 000

a) Find the measures of central tendency for these salaries.
b) Which measure best represents the salaries? Explain.
c) What inferences can you make from these data?

6. a) I chose a double-bar graph because there are 2 sets of data.

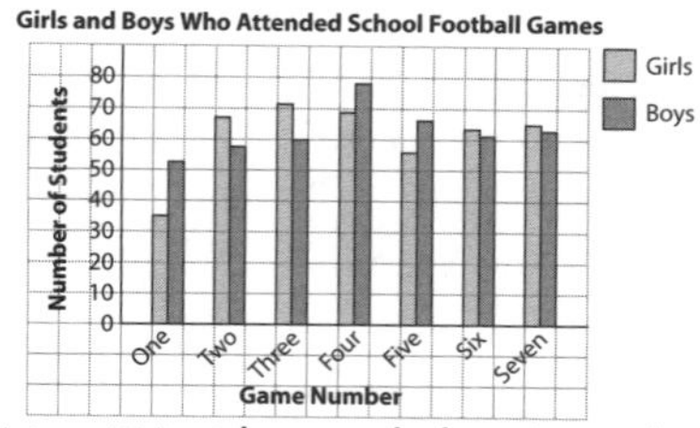

b) No, 426 girls attended and 439 boys attended, so more boys attended the games than girls. Glenna might have made the inference by counting the number of games where more girls attended: Games 2, 3, 6, 7. More than one-half of the games had more girls attending.
The inference I would make is that there were more games where more girls attended than boys, but overall more boys than girls attended the games.

7. b) The median best represents the salaries because the median is the middle salary and is less affected by high and low salaries.

c) Less than one-half of the staff earn less than $50 000. About 7% of the staff earn more than $100 000.

d) The outliers are $108 000 and $24 000. Only the mean is affected by the outliers. Without the outliers, the mean is $60 346.15. The median and mode remain the same.

8. a) The mean is the average of the scores. It is the median that is the middle score.

b) The mode is the colour that occurs most often, but the sum of the other colours could be greater than the mode.

c) The mean is the sum of the salaries divided by the total number of salaries. The mean only changes when the salaries being added change. To double the mean, the salaries would also have to double.

9. a) **Times for 400-m Race (s)**

Stem	Leaf
17	5 6
18	
19	
20	8 9
21	0
22	2 5 6
23	0 7 8
24	9
25	2 7
26	1 5 7 8 9
27	1
28	7
29	1 3 5 8
30	1 3 6
31	2
32	
33	3

c)

Interval	Frequency
170–189	2
190–209	2
210–229	4
230–249	4
250–269	7
270–289	2
290–309	7
310–329	2

d) The stem-and-leaf plot shows each piece of data. The frequency table only shows how many pieces of data are in each interval, not the values of the data.

e)

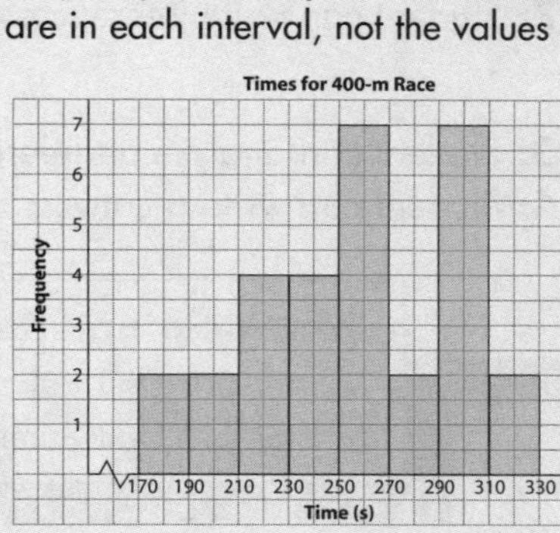

10. a) What Time People Wake Up

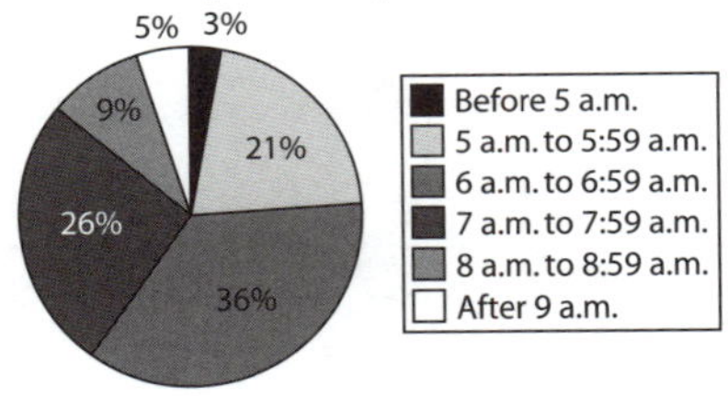

d) Most people wake up between 5 a.m. and 7:59 a.m. because the total percent for these times is 83%. Over one-third of people wake up between 6 a.m. and 6:59 a.m.

11. a) These data could be displayed using a histogram or a circle graph.

b) i) Histogram

Age of First Time Car Owners

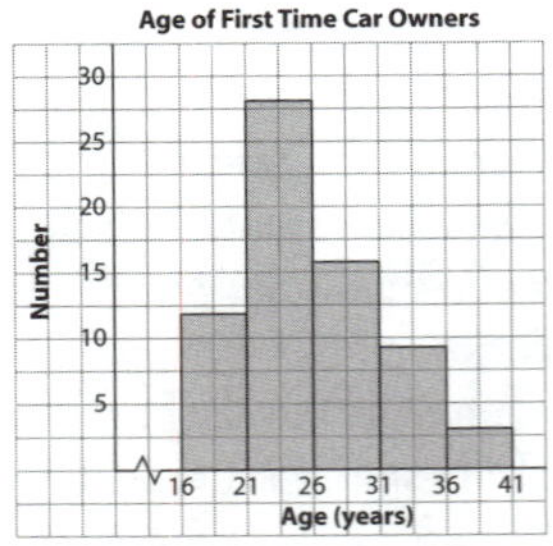

ii) Circle graph

Age of First Time Car Owners

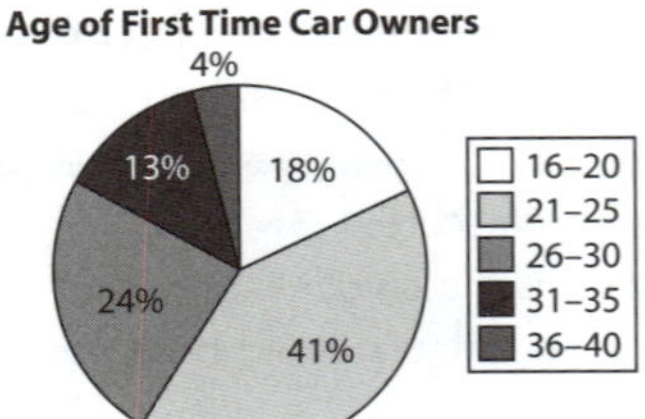

LESSON

d) What are the outliers? How do these affect the measures of central tendency? Explain.

8. Is each conclusion true or false? Explain.

a) The mean test score was 68%. Therefore, one-half the class scored above 68%. False

b) The mode colour of eyes in James' class is brown. Therefore, most of the students have brown eyes. False

c) A random sample of 100 people had a mean income of \$35 000. Therefore, a random sample of 200 people would have a mean income of \$70 000. False

5.5 **9.** The data show the times, in minutes and seconds, for swimmers to swim a 400-m freestyle race.
3:28, 2:56, 4:25, 3:42, 5:33, 3:57, 3:45, 4:29, 5:03, 4:55, 3:58, 2:55, 4:17, 3:29, 4:31, 3:30, 4:12, 4:21, 4:53, 5:06, 4:47, 3:50, 4:28, 4:09, 5:01, 3:46, 4:27, 4:51, 5:12, 4:58

a) Convert the data to seconds. Display the data using a stem-and-leaf plot.

b) State the range, median, and mode of the data.
Range: 158 s, Median: 263 s, Mode: none

c) Use the stem-and-leaf plot to set up a frequency table with intervals.

d) How does the frequency table differ from the stem-and-leaf plot?

e) Use the frequency table to draw a histogram.

5.2 5.6 **10.** Ester surveyed 120 people in her neighbourhood to find out what time people usually wake up on a weekday. She recorded her results in this table.

What Time People Wake Up

Time	Number of People
Before 5 a.m.	3
5 a.m. to 5:59 a.m.	25
6 a.m. to 6:59 a.m.	44
7 a.m. to 7:59 a.m.	31
8 a.m. to 8:59 a.m.	11
After 9 a.m.	6

a) Display the data in a circle graph.

b) What percent of people wake up after 6:59 a.m.? 40%

c) In which time interval do approximately 20% of the people wake up? 5 a.m. to 5:59 a.m.

d) What inferences could you make from these data? Explain.

11. A sample survey was conducted to find how old car owners were when they got their first car.

Age	16–20	21–25	26–30	31–35	36–4
Number of First Time Car Owners	12	28	16	9	3

a) What are two possible ways to display these data?

b) Display the data using both methods from part a.

c) In a group of 1000 car owners, about how many of them were over 30 when they got their first car? Explain. About 176 peopl

232 UNIT 5: Data Management

ASSESSMENT FOR LEARNING

What to Look For

Knowledge and Understanding

✔ **Question 1:** Student understands the difference between a census and a sample.

✔ **Question 4:** Student understands which type of graph best displays a set of data.

Thinking

✔ **Question 6:** Student can analyse conclusions to determine whether they are true.

Communication

✔ **Question 7:** Student can write inferences from a set of data.

Application

✔ **Question 3:** Student can analyse an inference to determine if it is valid.

✔ **Question 4:** Student can write a convincing argument based on a graph.

Recording and Reporting

Master 5.1 Unit Rubric: Data Management
Master 5.4 Unit Summary: Data Management

Practice Test

242, 225, 296, 352, 305, 260, 313, 220, 255, 236, 304, 220, 195, 215, 292, 281, 277, 310, 272, 219, 252, 311, 263, 252, 207, 283, 222, 245, 229, 278, 237, 400, 229, 201, 324, 335, 299, 356, 410, 348, 192, 355, 342, 324, 358, 369, 293, 347, 308, 317, 301, 220, 268, 415, 288

1. The lengths of the songs, in seconds, from a "Let's Dance" CD collection set are shown at the left.
- **a)** Use an appropriate graph to display the data. Explain your choice.
- **b)** Describe any trends the graph shows.
- **c)** An advertisement for the CD said, "The average song is no less than 5 minutes long." Is this true? Give reasons for your answer.
- **d)** Make a convincing argument based on the graph. Explain the reason for your argument.

2. The mean mark on a quiz was 7.
The median mark was 6 and the mode was 5.
Fifteen students wrote the quiz.
The lowest mark was 1 and the highest mark was 10.
- **a)** Write a possible set of marks.
- **b)** One student, who was absent, wrote the quiz later. Her mark was 20. How does this mark affect the mean, the median, and the mode? Explain.

2. a) 1, 5, 5, 5, 5, 5, 5, 6, 9, 9, 10, 10, 10, 10, 10

One Hour of Radio Time

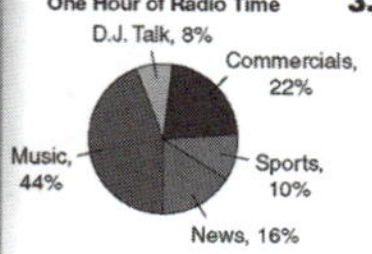

3. A radio station broadcasts 24 h a day, 7 days a week. The circle graph shows how one hour of a radio station's air-time is used. Suppose the radio station decided it wanted to allow more time for music. How do you think this could be achieved? Draw a new circle graph to show your answer. Explain your graph.

4. A random sample of 1200 Canadians were asked: "Overall, do you think Canada would benefit or lose out from having a common currency with the United States?" Here are the results:

Greatly Benefit	Somewhat Benefit	No Impact	Somewhat Lose Out	Greatly Lose Out
17%	27%	8%	22%	20%

A student claimed, "There are as many Canadians who would like a common currency with the U.S. as those who do not." Did the student interpret the results correctly? Explain.

Practice Test 233

LESSON ORGANIZER

Student Materials
- calculators
- protractors
- compasses
- Percent Circles (Master 5.15)
- 0.5-cm grid paper (PM 14)

Assessment: Masters 5.1 Unit Rubric: Data Management, 5.4 Unit Summary: Data Management

Assignment Guidelines

To assess the 4 Achievement Chart categories listed in the curriculum document, use these test questions:
Knowledge and Understanding: 1
Application: 2
Thinking: 3
Communication: 4

Sample Solutions

1. a) A histogram is an appropriate graph because the data can be grouped into intervals.

Lengths of Songs from a "Let's Dance" CD Collection Set

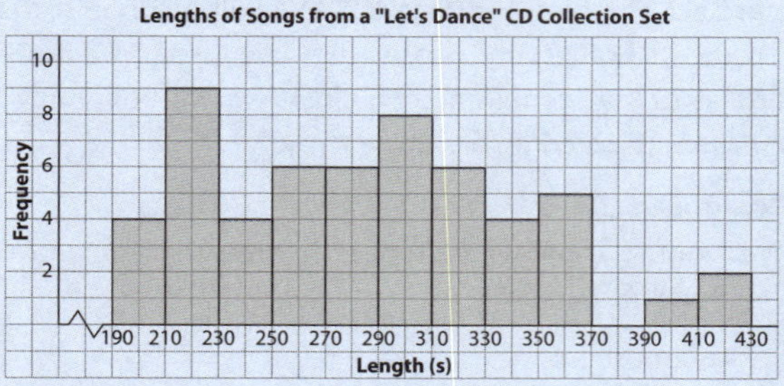

b) Very few songs are longer than 370 s. The greatest number of songs are between 210 s and 229 s long.

c) No, this is not true. Five minutes is 300 s. The median song length is 283 s. This means that one-half of the songs are shorter than 283 s and one-half of the songs are longer than 283 s. The mode is 220 s. The mean length is approximately 285 s. All of the measures of central tendency are less than 300 s.

d) A six-minute dance song is considered a long song in this CD collection. Only 4 out of 55 songs were longer than six minutes.

2. b) The mean increases; the median increases; the mode stays the same.

3. One way this could be achieved is to reduce the amount of time for each of the other 4 categories by 1%. This would increase music time to 48%.

One Hour of Radio Time

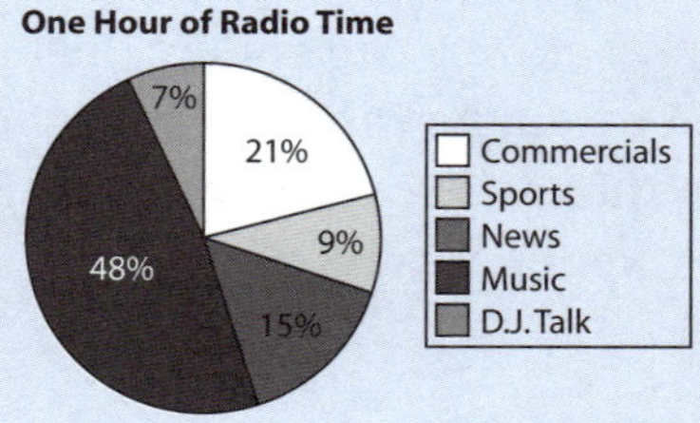

4. Answers may vary:
Yes, forty-four percent of Canadians feel they would benefit from a common currency, while 42% feel they would lose out. These results are quite close so the interpretation is correct.
OR
No, only 94% of Canadians are represented in the table. Since 6% of the population is missing, the student cannot conclude that there are as many Canadians who would like a common currency as those who do not.

Your Community

LESSON ORGANIZER 80–100 min

Student Grouping: 4 or 5
Student Materials
- calculators
- 0.5-cm grid paper (PM 14)
- coloured pencils
- protractors

Assessment: Masters 5.3 Performance Assessment Rubric: Your Community, 5.4 Unit Summary: Data Management

Unit Problem Your Community

What would you like to know about people in your commun
You will collect primary data on a topic that interests you.
You will design and conduct a survey.
You will display and analyse the data.

Work in a group.

Part 1

Choose a topic that interests you.
You may pick from this list or select one of your own.
- Careers that interest students
- Personal statistics such as age, height, heart rate, shoe size, and so on
- Which languages people speak
- Which professional sports people watch
- Which electronic games students play
- Which community activities people participate in
- How students spend their money

Design a survey. Think about:
- What information do you want to find out about the population?
- What data do you need to collect to get that information?
- Is the survey question clear, precise, and unbiased?

Test your survey on other classmates. Make changes if necessary.

Decide on the population you will sample. Be specific.
Decide on the sample size and the method you will use to pick your sample.

Conduct the survey. Collect data from males and females.
Record the results.

Part 2

Organize the data. Think about:
- Can a table be used to organize the data?
- What is the most suitable type of graph to display the data?
- What other types of graphs could be used to display the data?

234 UNIT 5: Data Management

Before students begin, have a discussion about how students will collect data. Ensure students know they will be doing this outside of the classroom. In some cases, they may need permission from their parents to visit people in their community so that they can collect the data they require. Encourage each group to pick a different topic so that different information is gathered about the community.

Sample Response

Part 1

Choosing a Topic

We are interested in finding out about careers that interest students in our community.

The population we will sample are the students at the local high school down the street.

We will sample 100 Grade 12 students and 100 Grade 11 students at the local high school. These are the students who will soon graduate and attend college or university. They should have a good idea of the career paths they would like to follow. We will compare the data for even numbers of males and females. We will arrange to visit five Grade 11 homeroom classes and five Grade 12 homeroom classes at the school. In each class, we will randomly select 20 students to complete our survey.

Designing the Survey

We want to know which types of careers students are interested in pursuing.

Survey question:

Which type of career are you interested in? (Please list three careers or three career areas.)

Part 2

We used a table to organize the data. We categorized the data into the most popular career areas. A double-bar graph best displays these data. They could also be displayed on two separate circle graphs, one for females and one for males.

Analyse the results.
Make inferences and convincing arguments based on your analysis.
Review your method of collecting data.
Were there any flaws or problems with the survey, or the way the data were collected?

Part 3

Write a report.
Present the results of your survey to your class.
Describe how you analysed the data and made inferences and arguments.
How do you know if your survey results are reliable and valid?

Check List

Your work should include:

- ✓ how you designed your survey and planned your data collection
- ✓ correctly constructed tables and graphs
- ✓ inferences and conclusions, based on reasonable arguments
- ✓ a clear explanation and analysis of the procedures you used

Reflect on the Unit

Describe the different graphs that can be used to display primary data.
How do you use tables and graphs to make inferences and convincing arguments?
Include examples in your explanation.

Unit Problem: Your Community 235

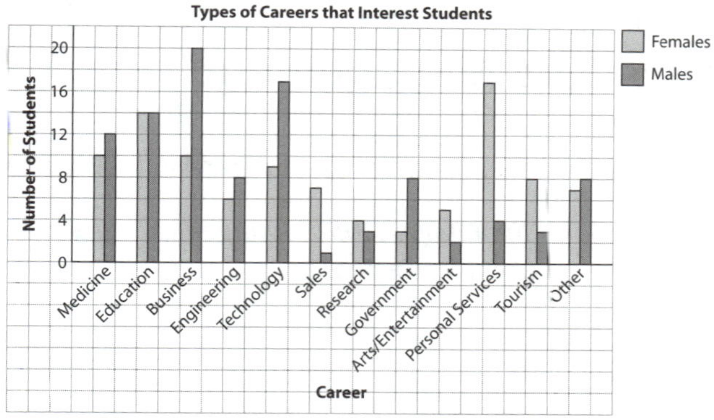

Possible Inferences: Most females are interested in a career in personal services because it has the highest female bar on the graph. Most males are interested in a career in business because it has the highest male bar on the graph.

REFLECT ON THE UNIT: Different graphs can be used to display primary data, including: line graphs, double-line graphs, bar graphs, double-bar graphs, circle graphs, scatter plots, and histograms. Tables and graphs can be used to make inferences and convincing arguments by describing any trends that they may show. For example, the largest sector in a circle graph corresponds to the highest percent or largest part of one whole. In a bar graph, the highest bar represents the greatest quantity while the shortest bar represents the least quantity. Inferences could be made about the items represented by these bars. In a line graph, a quantity increases when the line goes up to the right and decreases when it goes down to the right. The steeper the line, the faster the quantity is increasing. Inferences can be made about the item represented by the line.

ASSESSMENT FOR LEARNING

What to Look For

Knowledge and Understanding

✔ Students understand how to organize data on different plots and graphs.

Communication

✔ Students can describe, in their own words, which type of graph is most suitable to represent given data and justify their choice.

Application

✔ Students use data and graphs to make inferences and arguments and justify them.

What to Do

Extra Support: Make the problem accessible.

Some students may have problems deciding on a population and sample that is practical and suitable. (For example, they have a sample that is too large, or they have difficulty gathering data.) Ensure students select a sample that will be cooperative in completing the survey.

To prevent bias in their survey questions, tell students to avoid statements that might lead people to a particular answer.

Recording and Reporting

Master 5.3 Performance Assessment Rubric: Your Community
Master 5.4 Unit Summary: Data Management

Evaluating Student Learning: Preparing to Report: Unit 5 Data Management

This unit provides an opportunity to report on the **Data Management and Probability** strand.

Master 5.4: Unit Summary: Data Management provides a comprehensive format for recording and summarizing evidence collected.

Here is an example of a completed summary chart for this Unit:

Strand: *Data Management and Probability*	Knowledge and Understanding	Thinking	Communication	Application	*Overall*
Ongoing Observations	3	4	3	4	3/4
Work samples or portfolios; conferences	3	3	4	3	3
Unit Review	4	3	3	3	3
Unit Test	3	3	3	3	3
Unit Problem Your Community	3	3	4	4	3/4
Achievement Level for reporting					3

Recording	How to Report
Ongoing Observations	Use *Master 5.2 Ongoing Observations: Data Management* to determine the most consistent level achieved in each category. Enter it in the chart. Choose to summarize by achievement category, or simply to enter an overall level. Observations from late in the unit should be most heavily weighted.
Portfolios or collections of work samples; conferences or interviews	Use *Master 5.1 Unit Rubric: Data Management* to guide evaluation of collections of work and information gathered in conferences. Teachers may choose to focus particular attention on the Assessment Focus questions. Work from late in the unit should be most heavily weighted.
Unit Review	*Master 5.1 Unit Rubric: Data Management* may be helpful in determining levels of achievement. #1, 2, and 7 provide evidence of Knowledge and Understanding; #3, 4, 5, and 9 provide evidence of Application; #6 and 8 provide evidence of Thinking; all questions provide evidence of Communication.
Unit Test	*Master 5.1 Unit Rubric: Data Management* may be helpful in determining levels of achievement. #1 provides evidence of Knowledge and Understanding; #2 provides evidence of Application; #3 provides evidence of Thinking; all questions provide evidence of Communication.
Unit Problem	Use *Master 5.3 Performance Assessment Rubric: Your Community*. The *Unit Problem* offers a snapshot of students' achievement. In particular, it shows their ability to synthesize and apply what they have learned.
Student Self-Assessment	Note students' perceptions of their own progress. This may take the form of an oral or written comment, or a self-rating.
Comments	Analyse the pattern of achievement to identify strengths and needs. In some cases, specific actions may need to be planned to support the learner.

Learning Skills	Ongoing Records
PM 4: Learning Skills Check List Use to record and report throughout a reporting period, rather than for each unit and/or strand.	*PM 10: Summary Class Records: Strands* *PM 11: Summary Class Records: Achievement Categories* *PM 12: Summary Record: Individual* Use to record and report evaluations of student achievement over several clusters, a reporting period, or a school year. These can also be used in place of the Unit Summary.

Name ________________ Date ____________

Master 5.1

Unit Rubric: Data Management

	Level 1	Level 2	Level 3	Level 4
Knowledge and Understanding • Shows understanding by explaining and evaluating: – the relationship between a census and a sample – the structure of a database – trends and patterns on a graph – concepts of central tendency – bias in data-collection methods – inferences, arguments, and conclusions based on data – graphs and other presentations of data	shows limited understanding; may be unable to explain and evaluate: – the relationship between a census and a sample – the structure of a database – trends and patterns on a graph – concepts of central tendency – bias – inferences, arguments, and conclusions – graphs and other presentations of data	shows some understanding; partially able to explain and evaluate: – the relationship between a census and a sample – the structure of a database – trends and patterns on a graph – concepts of central tendency – bias – inferences, arguments, and conclusions – graphs and other presentations of data	shows considerable understanding; able to clearly and appropriately explain and evaluate: – the relationship between a census and a sample – the structure of a database – trends and patterns on a graph – concepts of central tendency – bias – inferences, arguments, and conclusions – graphs and other presentations of data	shows a high degree of understanding; able to accurately and effectively explain and evaluate: – the relationship between a census and a sample – the structure of a database – trends and patterns on a graph – concepts of central tendency – bias – inferences, arguments, and conclusions – graphs and other presentations of data
Thinking • Chooses and carries out a range of strategies for using quantitative data to solve problems including: – collection and analysis of primary data – manipulation of data using spreadsheets – database searches	with assistance, chooses and carries out a limited range of appropriate strategies to solve problems using quantitative data; rarely produces an accurate solution	with limited assistance, chooses and carries out some appropriate strategies to solve problems using quantitative data; frequently produces an accurate solution	chooses and carries out appropriate strategies to solve problems using quantitative data; usually produces an accurate solution	develops and carries out effective, and often innovative, strategies to solve problems using quantitative data; almost always produces an accurate solution
Communication • Explains concepts, reasoning, and conclusions clearly, using appropriate mathematical language	unable to explain concepts, reasoning, and conclusions clearly	partially explains concepts, reasoning, and conclusions	explains concepts, reasoning, and conclusions clearly	explains concepts, reasoning, and conclusions clearly, precisely, and confidently
• Presents work clearly, including labels and symbols	presents work with little clarity; rarely uses appropriate labels or symbols	presents work with some clarity; uses some appropriate labels and symbols	presents work clearly and precisely; uses appropriate labels and symbols	presents work clearly and precisely; uses a range of appropriate labels and symbols
Application • Accurately: – uses spreadsheets – applies measures of central tendency – interprets and constructs tally charts, stem-and-leaf plots, frequency tables, line graphs, comparative bar graphs, circle graphs, histograms	limited accuracy; major errors or omissions in: – using spreadsheets – applying measures of central tendency – interpreting and constructing data summaries and displays	somewhat accurate; several minor errors or omissions in: – using spreadsheets – applying measures of central tendency – interpreting and constructing data summaries and displays	generally accurate; few minor errors or omissions in: – using spreadsheets – applying measures of central tendency – interpreting and constructing data summaries and displays	accurate and precise; no errors in: – using spreadsheets – applying measures of central tendency – interpreting and constructing data summaries and displays

Name ____________________ Date ________________

Master 5.2

Ongoing Observations: Data Management

The behaviours described under each heading are examples; they are not intended to be an exhaustive list of all that might be observed. More detailed descriptions are provided in each lesson under *Assessment for Learning*.

STUDENT ACHIEVEMENT: Data Management				
Student	**Knowledge and Understanding** • Explains and evaluates: – data-collection methods – inferences, arguments, and conclusions – graphs and other presentations	**Thinking** • Chooses and carries out a range of strategies for using quantitative data to solve problems including primary data, spreadsheets, and databases	**Communication** • Explains concepts, reasoning, and conclusions clearly • Presents work clearly, including labels and symbols	**Application** • Uses spreadsheets • Applies measures of central tendency • Interprets and constructs data summaries and displays

Level 1 – very limited; Level 2 – somewhat or limited; Level 3 – satisfactory; Level 4 – thorough

Name ____________________ Date ____________________

Master 5.3

Performance Assessment Rubric: Your Community

	Level 1	Level 2	Level 3	Level 4
Knowledge and Understanding • Shows understanding of data by: – explaining why results are valid and unbiased – justifying choice of data displays – offering reasonable inferences, conclusions, and supporting arguments	shows limited understanding; may be unable to explain: – why results are valid and unbiased – choice of data displays – inferences, conclusions, and supporting arguments	shows some understanding; gives some appropriate but incomplete explanations for: – why results are valid and unbiased – choice of data displays – inferences, conclusions, and supporting arguments	shows considerable understanding by giving appropriate and complete explanations for: – why results are valid and unbiased – choice of data displays – inferences, conclusions, and supporting arguments	shows a high degree of understanding by giving insightful and complete explanations for: – why results are valid and unbiased – choice of data displays – inferences, conclusions, and supporting arguments
Thinking • Uses appropriate strategies to design and conduct a survey using primary data (valid and unbiased) to answer a question	uses a limited range of appropriate strategies to design and conduct a survey; does not produce valid, unbiased information	uses some appropriate strategies to design and conduct a survey; results are somewhat flawed in terms of validity and bias	uses appropriate strategies to design and conduct a survey; results are valid and unbiased	uses innovative and effective strategies to design and conduct a survey; results are valid, unbiased, and precise
Communication • Explains reasoning clearly, using appropriate mathematical terminology (e.g., sample, population, bias)	explains reasoning unclearly and imprecisely, using few mathematical terms	explains reasoning with some clarity, using some appropriate mathematical terms	explains reasoning clearly and precisely, using appropriate mathematical terms	explains reasoning clearly, precisely, and confidently, using a range of appropriate mathematical terminology
• Presents work clearly, including labels and symbols	presents work with little clarity	presents work with some clarity	presents work clearly	presents work clearly and precisely
Application • Constructs data displays correctly • Accurately identifies trends and patterns	limited accuracy; major errors or omissions in: – constructing data displays – identifying trends and patterns	somewhat accurate; several minor errors or omissions in: – constructing data displays – identifying trends and patterns	generally accurate; few minor errors or omissions in: – constructing data displays – identifying trends and patterns	accurate and precise; no errors or omissions in: – constructing data displays – identifying trends and patterns

Name ____________________ Date ________________

Master 5.4

Unit Summary: Data Management

Review assessment records to determine the most consistent achievement levels for the assessments conducted. Some cells may be blank. *Overall* achievement levels may be recorded in each row, rather than identifying levels for each achievement category.

	Most Consistent Level of Achievement*				
Strand: *Data Management and Probability*	**Knowledge and Understanding**	**Thinking**	**Communication**	**Application**	***Overall***
Ongoing Observations					
Work samples or portfolios; conferences					
Unit Review					
Unit Test					
Unit Problem Your Community					
Achievement Level for reporting					

*Use Ontario Achievement Levels 1, 2, 3, 4

Self-Assessment:

Comments: (Strengths, Needs, Next Steps)

Name ____________________ Date ______________

Master 5.5

Additional Activity 1: Misleading Graphs

Work with a partner.

You will need newspapers, magazines, or access to the Internet.

Instructions:

1. With your partner, look through newspapers, magazines or the Internet for examples of graphs, tables, or charts that show data in misleading ways.

2. Explain how the representation might mislead the reader.

3. Why might the graph, table, or chart have been presented this way?

4. How could you change the presentation so that the data are shown accurately?

Take It Further: Draw an accurate representation of the data.

Name ____________________ Date ______________

Master 5.6

Additional Activity 2: Nutrition Circles

Work in groups of 3 or 4.

You will need labels from packaged food or canned food, compasses, and protractors (or percent circles), rulers, calculators, and coloured pencils or markers.

Instructions:

1. Each group member chooses a food label.
   List each nutritional ingredient and its mass in grams.
   Add these masses.
   Subtract this total mass from the mass of one serving.
   Label this difference as "Other."
2. Write the mass of each nutrient and "Other" as a fraction of the mass of one serving.
3. Write each fraction as a percent.
4. Use the percents to draw a circle graph.
   Label each sector.
   Give the graph a title.
5. Compare graphs with other group members.
   Which food item is the healthiest choice?

Take It Further: Find the mass of each nutrient in 75 g of each food.

Name ____________________ Date ______________

Master 5.7

Step-by-Step 1

Lesson 5.1, Question 8

Step 1 Will you use a sample or a census? ________________

Step 2 Make a list of possible methods to gather data for the menu.
Look through the lesson for ideas.

Step 3 Which methods are reasonable? Explain.

____

____

Step 4 Describe how you could use one of the methods to collect data about food items on the menu.

____

____

____

Step 5 Would the results be duplicated if the data were collected again? If not, choose a method that, if repeated, may produce similar results.

____

____

____

Step 6 Repeat *Steps 4* and *5* for another method.

Name ____________________ Date ________________

Master 5.8

Step-by-Step 2

Lesson 5.2, Question 7

Step 1 Look at the title of the table and the headings for each column. What do these tell you about the data in the table?

Step 2 What do you notice about the numbers for each age group in the column for females?

Step 3 What do you notice about the number of years in each age group?

Step 4 Which age groups can be easily compared? Explain.

Step 5 Which age groups cannot be easily compared? Explain.

Step 6 What arguments can be made about the eating habits of females? Justify your answer.

Step 7 Repeat *Steps 2–6* for males.

Step 8 Compare the number of 12–14 year old males in the table with the number of 12–14 year old females in the table. What argument can you make about the eating habits of 12–14 year old males?

Step 9 Compare the number of 15–19 year old females in the table with the number of 20–24 year old females in the table. What do you notice? Explain.

Step 10 What does the second table show?

Step 11 Repeat *Steps 2–10* using this table.

Step 12 Compare your answers regarding the second table with the ones for the first table. Are they the same or different? Explain.

Name ____________________ Date ________________

Master 5.9

Step-by-Step 3

Lesson 5.3, Question 5

Materials: grid paper, ruler, coloured pencils

Step 1 Look at the title of the table and the column headings.
What do the data in the table represent?

____

Step 2 Which type of graph best displays two sets of data that change over time? __________
Display the data using this type of graph.
Ensure the horizontal axis goes from 1990 to 2005.

Step 3 Look at each line on the graph.

a) Describe any trends for females.

____

____

b) Describe any trends for males.

____

____

c) Compare the graphs for males and females.
Describe any overall trends you observe.

____

Step 4 Use the graph to estimate the average annual female earnings in 1990. ______________

Step 5 Use the graph to predict the average annual male earnings in 2005. ________________

Step 6 **a)** Make one inference about the average annual female earnings.

____

b) Make one inference about the average annual male earnings.

____

c) Make one inference about the average annual earnings of Canadians.

____

Name ____________________ Date ________________

Master 5.10

Step-by-Step 4

Lesson 5.4, Question 9

Step 1 **a)** What is the average number of raisins claimed to be in one cup of cereal? _______

b) How many cups of cereal are in one box? _______

c) Approximately how many raisins should be in one box? _______

Step 2 Use a stem-and-leaf plot to display the data. Why is this a good choice of display?

____

Step 3 To calculate the mean, find the sum of the entries in the stem-and-leaf plot, then divide the sum by the number of entries.

Step 4 An outlier is significantly different from the other entries in a set of data.

What are the outliers? ____

Step 5 Remove the outliers. Calculate the mean without the outliers. __________________

Step 6 Compare the values you found in *Steps 3* and *5*. What do you notice? Explain.

____

____

Step 7 Compare the means from *Steps 3* and *5* with the average number of raisins per box from *Step 1c*. What do you notice?

____

Was the advertisement true? __________________

Explain. ____

____

Name ____________________ Date ______________

Master 5.11

Step-by-Step 5

Lesson 5.5, Question 4

Materials: grid paper, coloured pencils, ruler

Step 1 Order the data from least to greatest.

Step 2 To find the median, count the number of values in *Step 1* and find the middle value. To find the mode, find the value that occurs most often.

Step 3 Present the ordered data from *Step 1* in a stem-and-leaf plot.
Create two columns: *Stem* and *Leaf.*
Under *Stem,* write: 7, 8, 9, 10, 11, 12, and 13. Under *Leaf,* write the last digit of each number in the data set that corresponds with each stem.
These should be in numerical order.

Step 4 Use the stem-and-leaf plot to complete the frequency table at the right.

Interval	Frequency
70–79	
80–89	
90–99	
100–109	
110–119	
120–129	
130–139	

Step 5 Describe the difference between the way data are presented in the stem-and-leaf plot and the frequency table. What do you not see in the frequency table?

Step 6 To draw a histogram:

- Draw a horizontal and a vertical axis.
- Use the intervals in the first column of the frequency table to make the horizontal scale.
- Use the numbers in the second column of the frequency table to create the heights of the bars.
- Label each axis.
- Give the graph a title.

Step 7 Look at the heights of the bars. What can you infer about ice creams sales in July?

Name ______________________ Date ________________

Master 5.12

Step-by-Step 6

Lesson 5.6, Question 4

Materials: protractor, calculator, ruler

Step 1 Find the sum of the numbers in the second column.
How many U.S. residents visited Canada in 2002? ____________________________

Step 2 Write a fraction by replacing the words with numbers:

$$\frac{\text{Number of residents who entered by boat}}{\text{Total number of U.S. visitors}} = \_\_\_\_\_\_\_\_$$

Convert this fraction to a percent by dividing the numerator by the denominator, then multiplying by 100.
What percent of U.S. residents entered Canada by boat? ______________________

Step 3 Write a fraction for the number of U.S. residents who entered Canada by plane.
Convert the fraction to a percent.

Step 4 Write fractions, similar to those in *Steps 2* and *3,* for the numbers of U.S. residents who entered by train, bus, boat, and other. Convert each fraction to a percent.

Step 5 Complete the table to determine the sector angle for each type of transportation.
Draw a circle graph.
Start from the radius shown.
Use a protractor to measure the sector angle for automobile.
Draw the radius to make a sector with this angle.
Continue to make a sector for each of the other angles.
Label each sector with its percent.

Method of Transport	Sector Angle Using Fractions
Automobile	________ × 360° = ______
Plane	________ × 360° = ______
Train	________ × 360° = ______
Bus	________ × 360° = ______
Boat	________ × 360° = ______
Other	________ × 360° = ______

Step 6 What do you know from the table or circle graph?

____

____

____

____

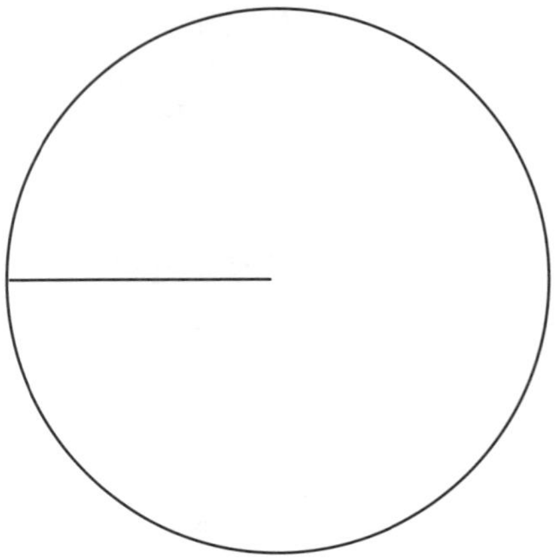

Name ____________________ Date ______________

Master 5.13

Graphs for 5.3 *Explore*

Graph A

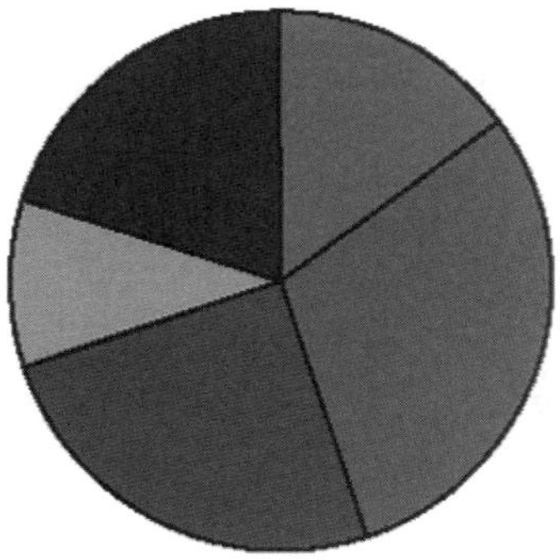

Graph B

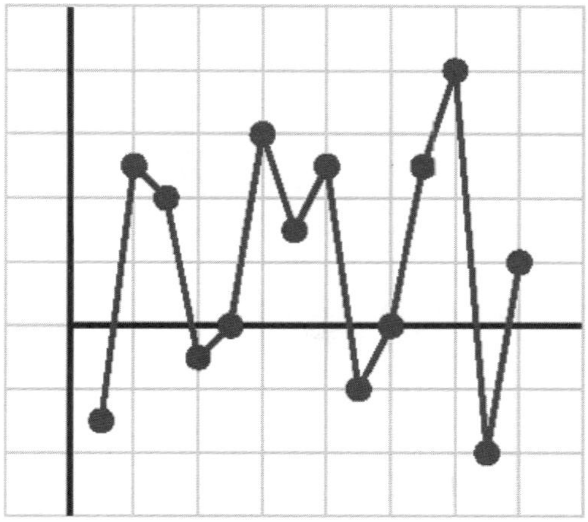

Graph C

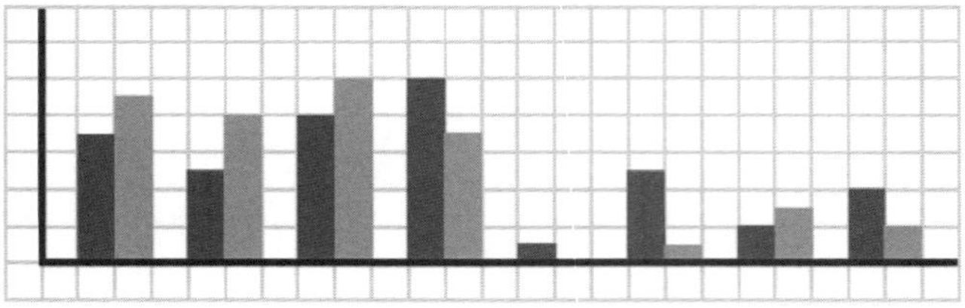

Graph D

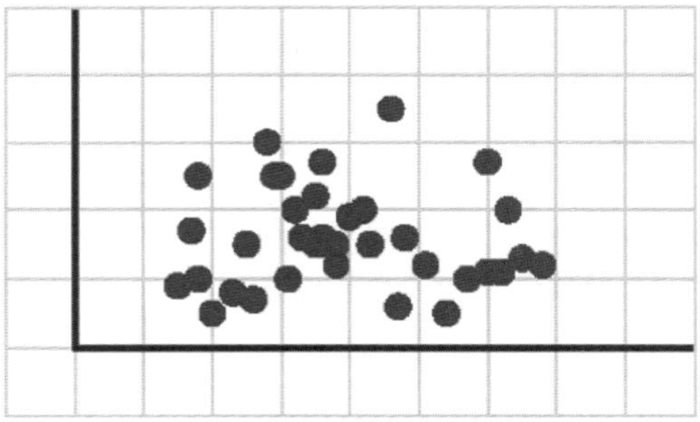

Name ____________________ Date ______________

Master 5.14

Graphs for 5.3 *Connect*

Graph A

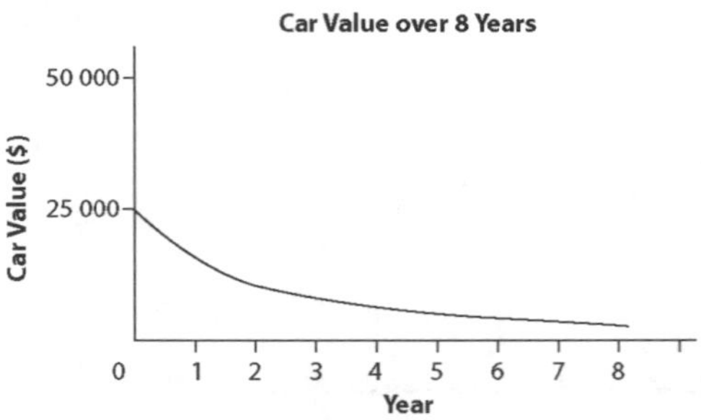

Graph B

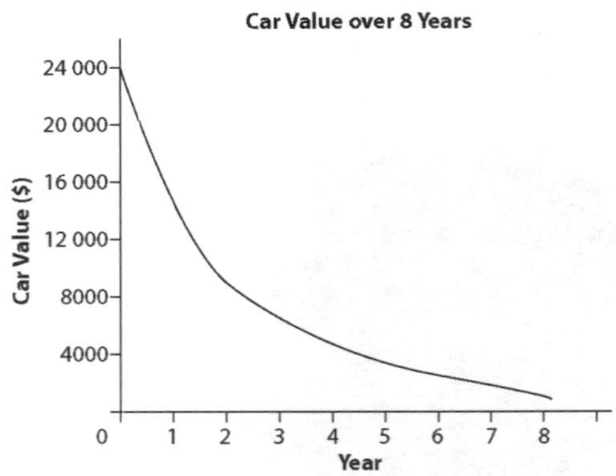

Graph C

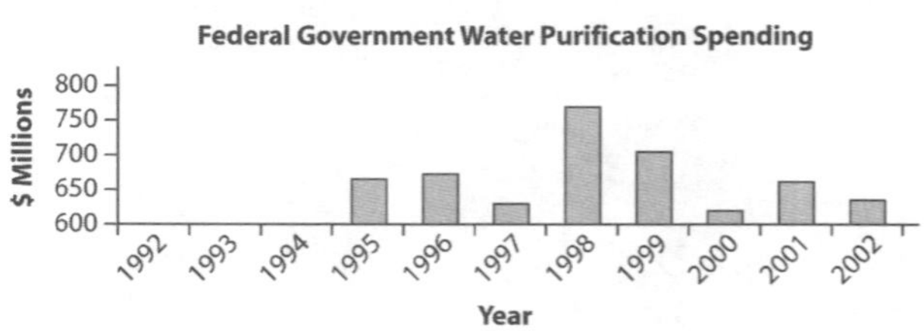

Graph D

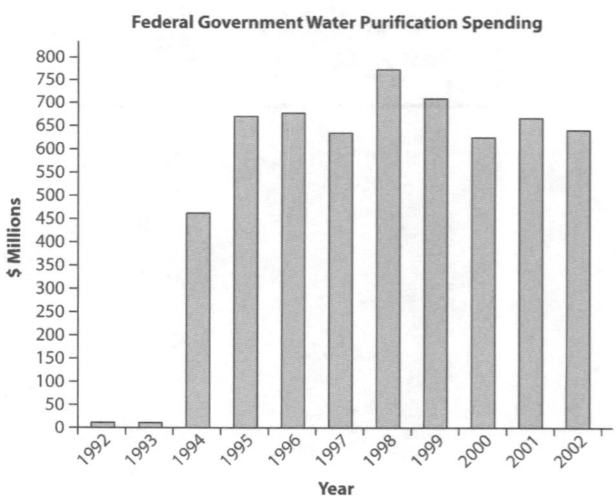

Name ____________________ Date ________________

Master 5.15

Percent Circles

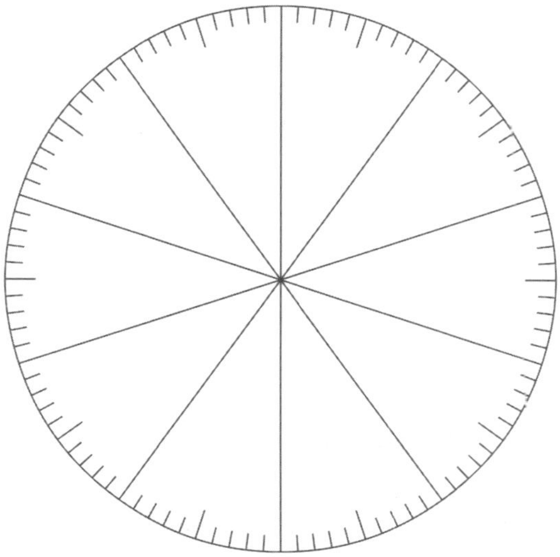

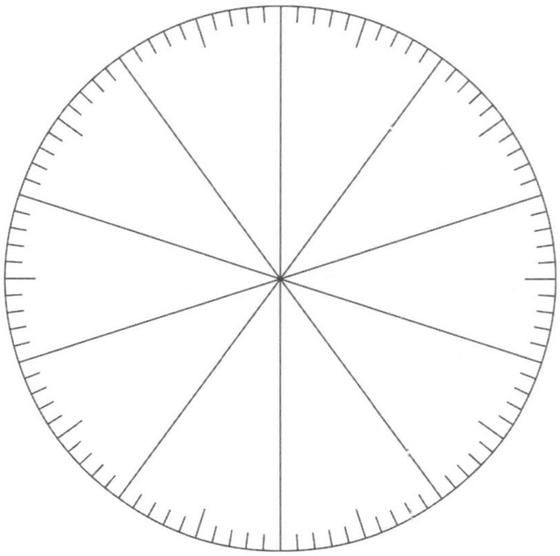

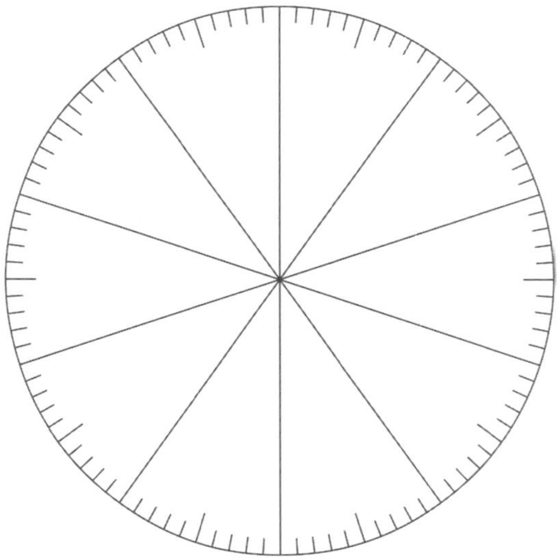

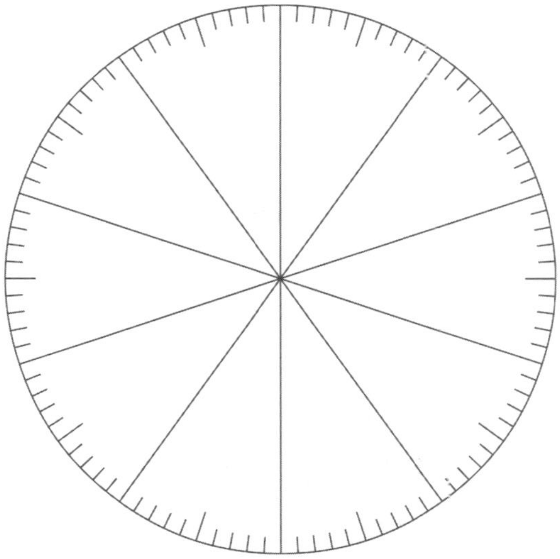

Name ____________________ Date ________________

Master 5.16a

Unit Test: Unit 5
Data Management

1. In each case, are the data collected from a sample or a census? Justify your answer.
   a) To find the favourite activity of children in a summer camp, each child was surveyed.

   b) To find the average annual salary of government workers, some employees in every branch of the government were surveyed.

2. Here are the math test marks for Grade 8 students at Grovsnor School: 78, 56, 73, 69, 82, 30, 55, 47, 60, 21, 73, 49, 89, 93, 59, 76, 70, 88, 100, 73, 97, 50, 65, 77, 53, 62, 80, 91, 76, 83, 51, 62, 73, 84, 99, 68, 81, 85, 74, 96, 82, 69, 72, 97, 54, 48, 61

   a) Complete the stem-and-leaf plot for these data.

   Math Test Marks

Stem	Leaf

   b) i) Identify any outliers.

   ii) Find the measures of central tendency for the data with *and* without the outliers.

   iii) How is each measure of central tendency affected when the outliers are not included?

   c) Complete the frequency table for these data.

Interval	Frequency

Name ______________________ Date ________________

Master 5.16b

Unit Test continued

d) What do you know from the stem-and-leaf plot that you do not know from the frequency table?

e) Which type of graph would best display the data? Justify your choice.

f) Draw the graph you selected in part e.

g) What inferences can you make from the graph? Explain.

3. a) For each set of data, draw the most suitable graph. Justify your choice.

i) **Minimum and Maximum Snowfalls for a City**

Month	**Nov.**	**Dec.**	**Jan.**	**Feb.**	**Mar.**	**April**
Maximum Snowfall (cm)	7	34	58	65	22	10
Minimum Snowfall (cm)	1	5	10	12	3	1

ii)

Favourite Sport to Play	**Girls**	**Boys**
Baseball	6	7
Volleyball	14	4
Hockey	3	18
Soccer	15	12
Basketball	9	7
Other	4	3

iii)

Fairlawn Carpentry March Budget	
Advertising	$420
Materials	$8500
Labour	$6400
Other	$900

b) What can you infer from the data? How does each graph show this?

Name ____________________ Date ________________

Master 5.17

Sample Answers

Unit Test – Master 5.16

1. a) Census; all the children were surveyed.

b) Sample; only some employees were surveyed.

2. a)

Math Test Marks

Stem	Leaf
2	1
3	0
4	7 8 9
5	0 1 3 4 5 6 9
6	0 1 2 2 5 8 9 9
7	0 2 3 3 3 3 4 6 6 7 8
8	0 1 2 2 3 4 5 8 9
9	1 3 6 7 7 9
10	0

b) i) 21 and 30

ii) With outliers: mean about 70.9, median 73, mode 73; without outliers:
mean about 72.9, median 73, mode 73

iii) The mean increases, while the median and mode stay the same.

c)

Interval	Frequency
21–30	2
31–40	0
41–50	4
51–60	7
61–70	8
71–80	11
81–90	8
91–100	7

d) In the frequency table, I know only how many pieces of data are in each interval. I do not know the values of the data.

e) A histogram best displays the data because there are many values in the data set and they can be grouped into intervals. The data are continuous.

f)

Math Test Marks

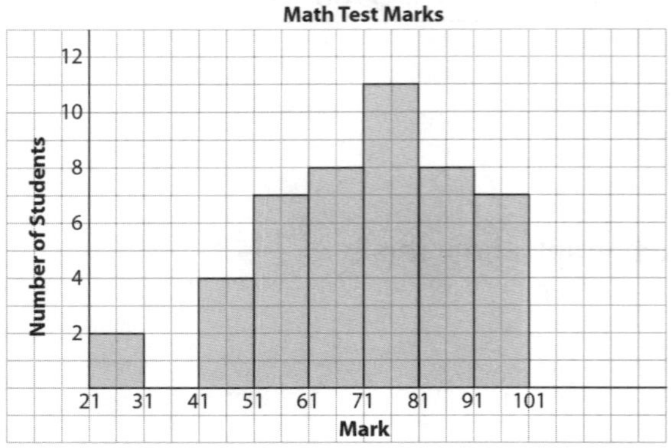

g) Most students passed the test. Very few students failed the test.

3. i) a) The most suitable graph to display the data is a double-line graph.

Minimum and Maximum Snowfalls

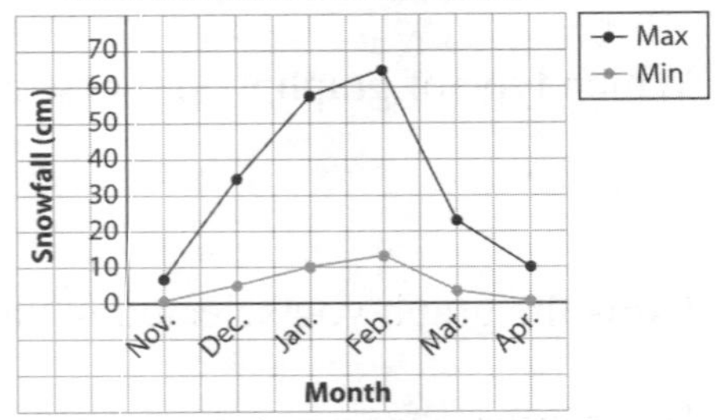

b) The difference between the maximum and minimum snowfalls is greatest in January and February because the gap between the two lines is greatest at this time. The minimum snowfall is fairly consistent — the line does not fluctuate significantly. The maximum snowfall varies significantly, and is highest in January and February.

ii) a) The most suitable graph to display counted data that are being compared is a double-bar graph.

Favourite Sport to Play

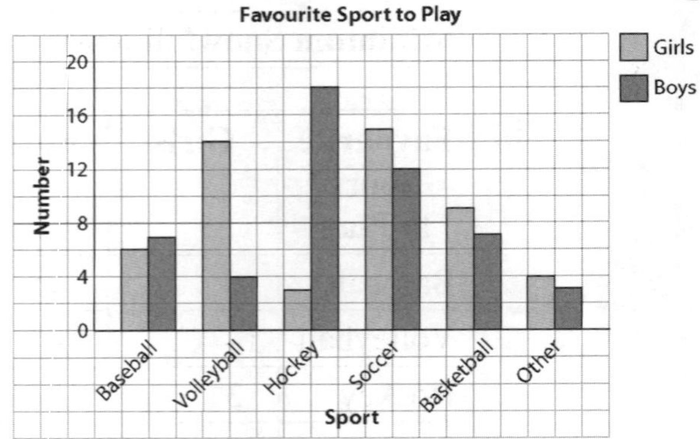

b) Most girls chose soccer and volleyball as their favourite sport; the least number of girls chose hockey. The bars for soccer and volleyball are the tallest; the bar for hockey is the shortest. Most boys chose hockey as their favourite sport.
The tallest bar on the graph for boys represents hockey.

iii) **a)** A circle graph is best to display a set of data that show part of one whole.

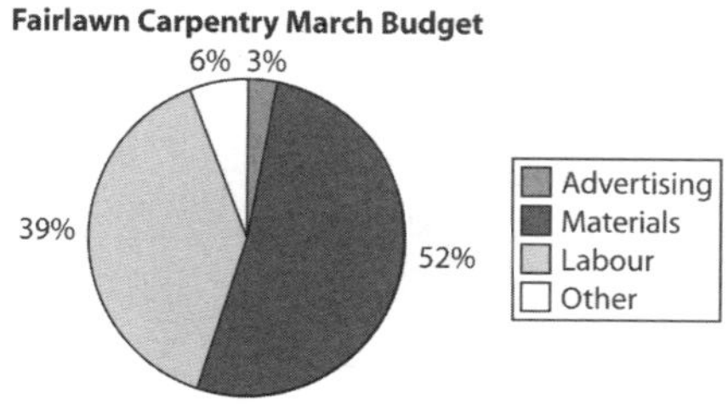

b) More than half of the budget is spent on materials.
About 90% of budget is spent on labour and materials.
From the circle graph, I can only tell what portion of the total budget is spent on each area. I cannot tell exactly how much was spent in each area, nor can I tell what the total monthly budget is.

Extra Practice Masters 5.18–5.24

Go to the CD-ROM to access editable versions of these Extra Practice Masters

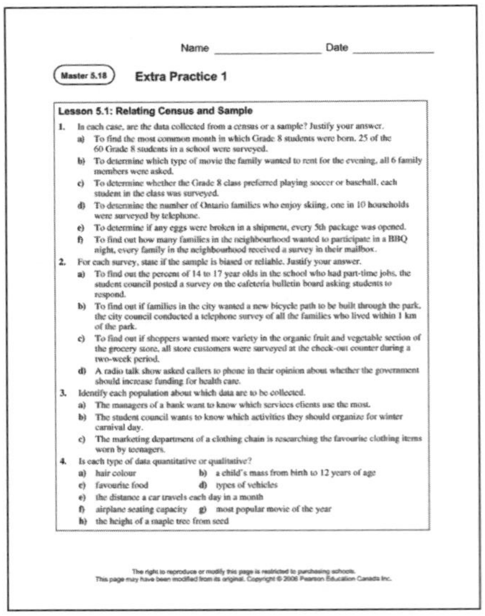
Master 5.18 Extra Practice 1 — Lesson 5.1: Relating Census and Sample

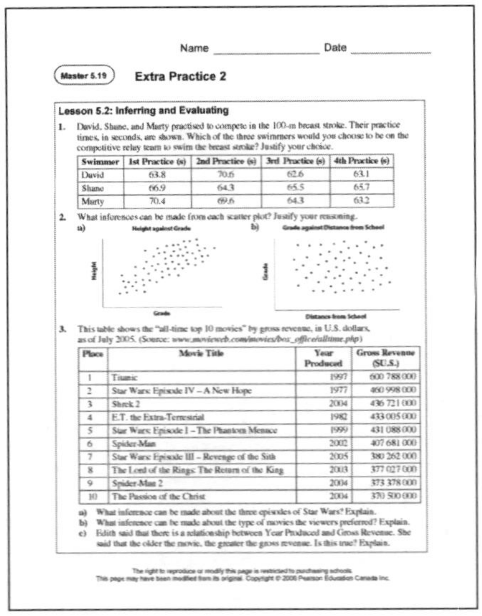
Master 5.19 Extra Practice 2 — Lesson 5.2: Inferring and Evaluating

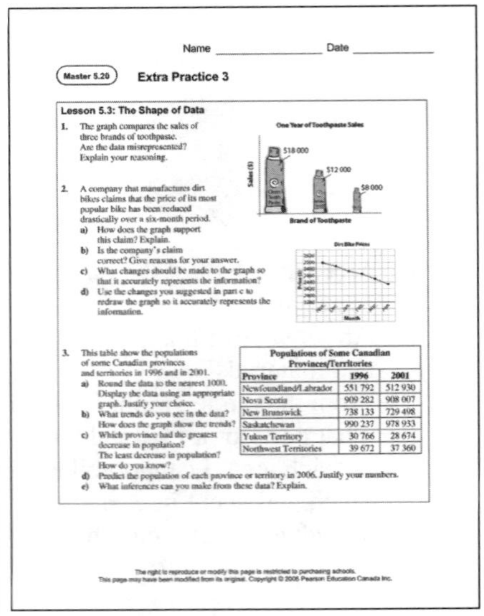
Master 5.20 Extra Practice 3 — Lesson 5.3: The Shape of Data

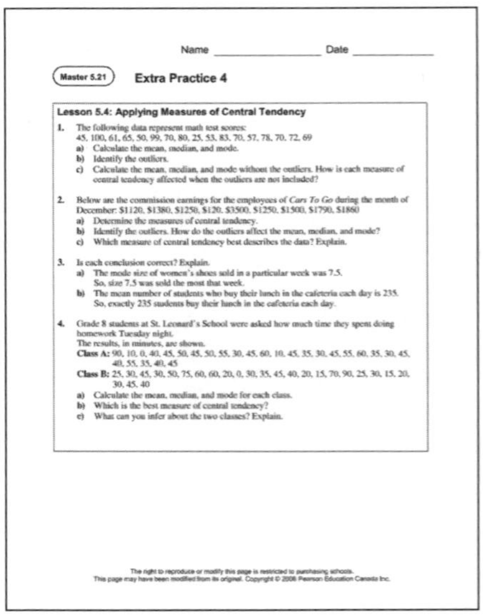
Master 5.21 Extra Practice 4 — Lesson 5.4: Applying Measures of Central Tendency

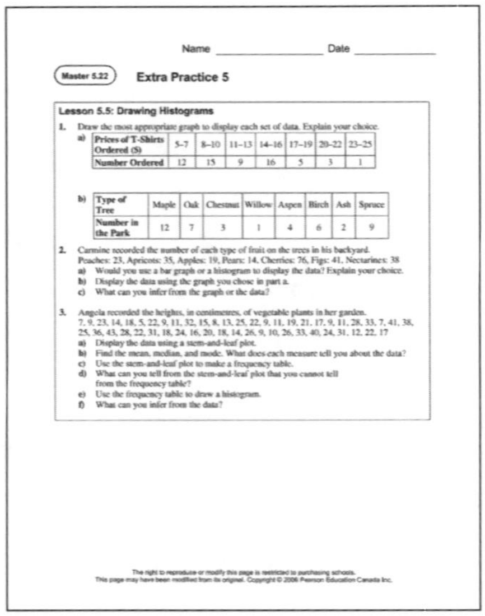
Master 5.22 Extra Practice 5 — Lesson 5.5: Drawing Histograms

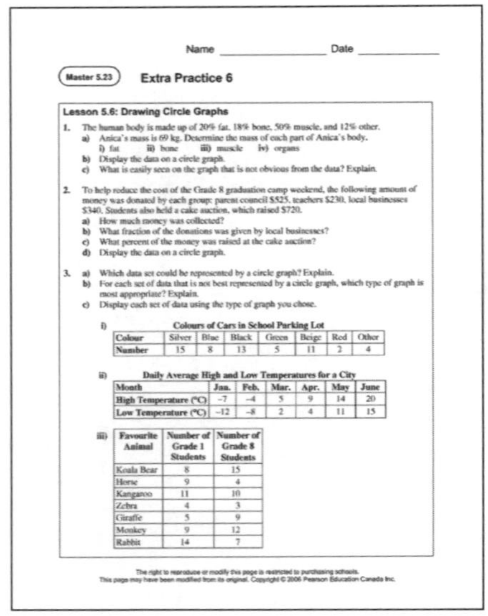
Master 5.23 Extra Practice 6 — Lesson 5.6: Drawing Circle Graphs

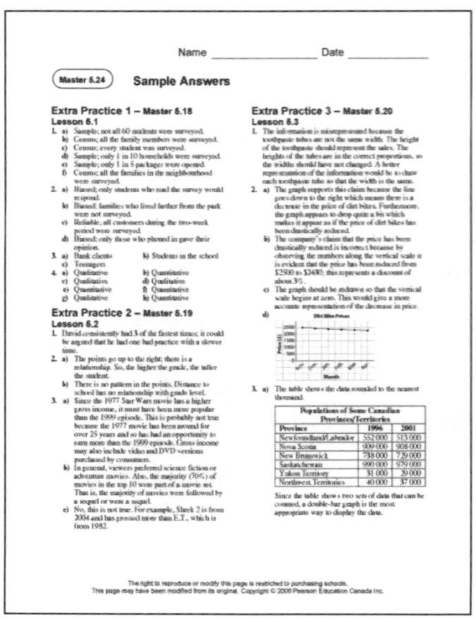
Master 5.24 Sample Answers

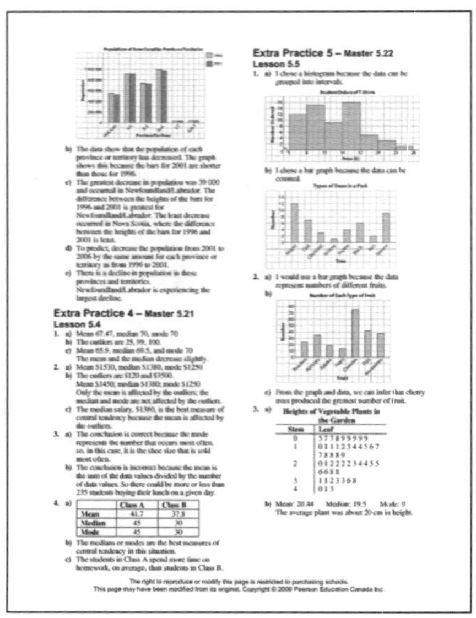

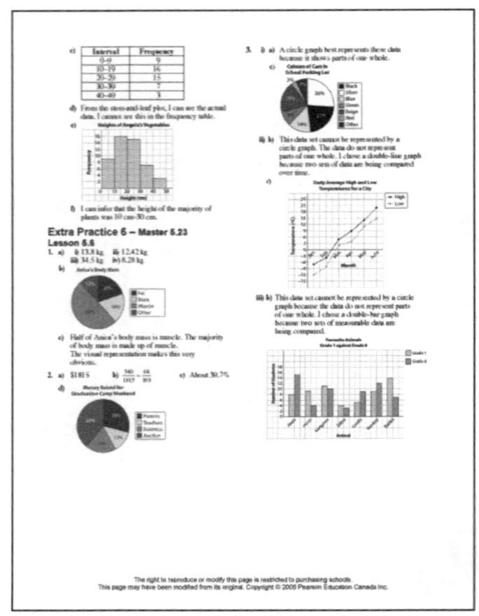

Addison Wesley Mathematics Makes Sense

Program Authors

Trevor Brown
Antonietta Lenjosek
Cathy Heideman
Jim Mennie
Georgia Konis-Chatzis
A.J. Keene
Margaret Sinclair
Craig Featherstone
Jason Johnston
Bryn Keyes
Elizabeth Wood
Elizabeth Milne
David Sufrin
Don Jones
Sharon Jeroski
Lynn Strangway

Printed and bound in Canada

2 3 4 5 – TC – 09 08 07 06

PEARSON Education Canada

ADDISON WESLEY

Ontario

Math Makes Sense 8

Ontario

Teacher Guide

Unit 6: Circles

PEARSON Education Canada

UNIT 6

Circles

"The universe cannot be read until we have learnt the language and become familiar with the characters in which it is written. It is written in mathematical language, and the letters are triangles, circles, and other geometrical figures, without which means it is humanly impossible to comprehend a single word."

From *Opere Il Saggiatore* by Galileo Galilei, 1564-1642.

FOCUS STRANDS
Measurement
Patterning and Algebra

SUPPORTING STRANDS
Number Sense and Numeration
Geometry and Spatial Sense

TIPS
Adolescent learners require opportunities to progress through different representations (concrete to diagrams). Use formulas only after students have developed them.

Mathematics Background

What Are the Big Ideas?

- The ratio of the circumference C to the diameter d of any circle equals π; that is, $\frac{C}{d} = \pi$. π is an irrational number.
- The ratio of the area A to the square of the radius r of any circle equals π; that is, $\frac{A}{r^2} = \pi$.
- A cylinder is a special type of prism, so the volume of a cylinder is base area times height.

How Will the Concepts Develop?

Students share their own methods for finding the centre of a circle. Students measure the circumference, radii, and diameters of circular objects and use these data to write a formula for the circumference of a circle.

Students approximate the area of a circle by cutting a circle into congruent sectors and then rearranging the sectors to form a parallelogram. Students conclude that, with many sectors, the circle will result in a rectangle with width r and length πr. From this, students develop the formula for the area of any circle.

Students use the fact that a cylinder is a special prism to develop formulas for the volume and surface area of a cylinder.

Why Are These Concepts Important?

Students measured polygons and prisms in earlier grades. The measurements of circles and cylinders are an extension of these concepts. They illustrate how knowledge and skills can be applied in other contexts.

Curriculum Overview

The codes refer to the 2005 revised curriculum.

Cluster 1: Measuring Circles

Overall Expectations
- Determine the relationships among units and measurable attributes, including the area of a circle ... (8m31)
- Demonstrate an understanding of the geometric properties of ... circles and the applications of geometric properties in the real world. (8m40)
- Solve problems by using proportional reasoning in a variety of meaningful contexts. (8m10)

Specific Expectations
- Solve problems that require conversions involving metric units of area ... (8m33)
- Measure the circumference, radius, and diameter of circular objects, using concrete materials. (8m34)
- Determine, through investigation using a variety of tools and strategies, the relationships for calculating the circumference and the area of a circle, and generalize to develop the formulas. (8m35)
- Solve problems involving the estimation and calculation of the circumference and the area of a circle. (8m36)
- Construct a circle, given its centre and radius, or its centre and a point on the circle, or three points on the circle. (8m44)
- Investigate and describe applications of geometric properties in the real world. (8m45)
- Identify and describe real-life situations involving two quantities that are directly proportional. (8m26)
- Solve problems involving proportions, using concrete materials, drawings, and variables. (8m27)
- Translate statements describing mathematical relationships into algebraic expressions and equations. (8m61)
- Evaluate algebraic expressions with up to three terms, by substituting ... decimals, ... for the variables. (8m62)

Launch

Lesson 6.1: Investigating Circles

Lesson 6.2: Circumference of a Circle

Lesson 6.3: Area of a Circle

Mid-Unit Review

Curriculum Overview

Cluster 2: Measuring Cylinders

Overall Expectations

- Research, describe, and report on applications of volume and capacity measurement. (8m30)
- Determine the relationships among units and measurable attributes, including . . . the volume of a cylinder. (8m31)

Specific Expectations

- Solve problems that require conversions involving metric units of area, volume, and capacity. (8m33)
- Determine, through investigation using a variety of tools and strategies, the relationship between the area of the base and height and the volume of a cylinder, and generalize to develop the formula. (8m37)
- Determine, through investigation using concrete materials, the surface area of a cylinder. (8m38)
- Solve problems involving the surface area and the volume of cylinders, using a variety of strategies. (8m39)
- Investigate and describe applications of geometric properties in the real world. (8m45)
- Translate statements describing mathematical relationships into algebraic expressions and equations. (8m61)
- Evaluate algebraic expressions with up to three terms, by substituting . . . decimals, . . . for the variables. (8m62)

Lesson 6.4:
Volume of a Cylinder

Lesson 6.5:
Surface Area of a Cylinder

Unit Review
Practice Test

Unit Problem
Circle Designs

Curriculum across the Grades

Grade 7	Grade 8
Students solve problems that require conversion between metric units of measure. Through investigation, students determine the formulas for finding the surface area and volume of a right prism.	Students solve problems that require measurement conversions. Students measure the circumference, radius, and diameter of circular objects, using concrete materials and develop formulas for finding the area and circumference of a circle. Students construct a circle, given its centre and radius, or its centre and a point on the circle, or three points on the circle. Through investigation, students determine the formulas for finding the volume and surface area of a cylinder. They solve problems involving the surface area and the volume of cylinders.

Additional Activities

Circle Mania

For Extra Practice (Appropriate for use after Lesson 6.2)
Materials: *Circle Mania* (Master 6.5), rulers, compasses, calculators

This activity provides practice in constructing a circle, given its centre and radius, or given its centre and a point on the circle.

The work students do: Students work in pairs. Player A marks a point on a piece of paper and says a radius. Player B draws the circle. Students switch roles.

In the next round, Player A marks two points on the paper. He labels one point the centre, and says the other point is on the circle. Player B draws the circle. Students switch roles.

Students score one point for a correct drawing. Players continue to alternate between the two types of constructions. The player with more points after 5 rounds wins.

Take It Further: Students calculate the circumference of each circle they draw.

Mathematical/Spatial/Kinesthetic
Partner Activity

Cylinder Comparison

For Extra Practice (Appropriate for use after Lesson 6.4)
Materials: *Cylinder Comparison* (Master 6.6), a variety of cylindrical objects, calculators, rulers

This activity introduces students to the relationship between the circumference and the height of a cylinder.

The work students do: Students work on their own. Students choose a cylindrical object. They estimate which is greater: circumference or height. Students measure the diameter of a cylindrical object, then use the diameter to calculate the circumference of the cylinder. Students measure the height of the cylinder. They record their measures in a table. Students repeat the activity for at least five different cylindrical objects. Students estimate, then compare, the circumference and height of each cylinder to determine which is the greater measure. Students report on their findings.

Take It Further: Students calculate the volume of each cylindrical object they use.

Spatial/Kinesthetic/Mathematical
Individual Activity

Planning for Unit 6

Planning for Instruction

Suggested Unit time: About 2–3 weeks

Lesson	Time	Materials	Program Support
Launch, page 2	15–20 min		
Skills You'll Need, page 4	10–15 min		
6.1: Investigating Circles, page 5 Measure radius and diameter, and discover their relationship.	80–100 min	objects with circular cross sections compasses, scissors, rulers, protractors, copies of logo, 3-column charts	PM 18: 3-Column Chart Master 6.12: Logo for 6.1 *Practice* Question 9 Master 6.7: Step-by-Step 1 Master 6.16: Extra Practice 1
6.2: Circumference of a Circle, page 8 Develop and use the formula for the circumference of a circle.	80–100 min	6 objects with circular cross sections dental floss, scissors, rulers, calculators, 4-column charts	PM 19: 4-Column Chart Master 6.8: Step-by-Step 2 Master 6.17: Extra Practice 2
6.3: Area of a Circle, page 13 Develop and use the formula for the area of a circle.	80–100 min	scissors, glue, compasses, protractors, rulers, calculators, 0.5-cm grid paper	PM 14: 0.5-cm Grid Paper Master 6.9: Step-by-Step 3 Master 6.18: Extra Practice 3
Mid-Unit Review, page 18		calculators, rulers, compasses, protractors	
6.4: Volume of a Cylinder, page 19 Develop and use the formula for the volume of a cylinder.	80–100 min	cylindrical objects rulers, calculators, dental floss	Master 6.10: Step-by-Step 4 Master 6.19: Extra Practice 4
Reading and Writing in Math: Explaining Solutions, page 22		calculators	
6.5: Surface Area of a Cylinder, page 24 Develop and use the formula for the surface area of a cylinder.	80–100 min	calculators, cardboard tubes, scissors, sticky tape, rulers	Master 6.13: Nets for 6.5 *Practice* Master 6.11: Step-by-Step 5 Master 6.20: Extra Practice 5
Unit Review, page 27		calculators, rulers, compasses, large circular objects	Extra Practice: Student Book page 493
Practice Test, page 29		rulers, compasses, calculators	
Unit Problem: Circle Designs, page 30	80–100 min	rulers, compasses, coloured pencils, calculators	

Planning for Assessment

Purpose	Tools and Process	Recording and Reporting
Diagnostic	*Unit Launch* Question; conference; scaffold problems throughout the unit	PM 8: Conference Prompts
Formative	*Explore* – Ongoing Assessment: Observe and Listen	Master 6.2: Ongoing Observations: Circles PM 1: Inquiry Process Check List PM 6: Observation Record 1 PM 7: Observation Record 2 PM 8: Conference Prompts PM 2: Self-Assessment PM 3: Self-Assessment: Problem Solving PM 9: Work Sample Records
Summative	*Unit Review* *Unit Problem* – Performance Assessment Unit Test Review assessment records; add unit results to ongoing records	Master 6.1: Unit Rubric: Circles Master 6.3: Performance Assessment Rubric: Circle Designs Master 6.4: Unit Summary: Circles PM 10: Summary Class Records: Strands PM 11: Summary Class Records: Achievement Categories PM 12: Summary Record: Individual
Learning Skills/Mathematical Disposition	Observe and record throughout the unit.	PM 4: Learning Skills Check List PM 5: Mathematical Dispositions and Learning Skills

Program Masters (PM) are in the *Grade 8 Planning and Program Masters* module.
Extra Practice Masters are on the CD-ROM and printed in reduced format on page 50 of this module.

LESSON ORGANIZER

15–20 min

Curriculum Focus: Activate prior learning about circles.
Vocabulary: circle

ASSUMED PRIOR KNOWLEDGE

- ✓ Students can recognize a circle.
- ✓ Students understand that perimeter is measured in linear units, area in square units, and volume in cubic units.
- ✓ Students can calculate the area of a parallelogram.

UNIT 6

Circles

- What is a circle?
- Where do you see circles?
- What do you know about a circle?
- What might be useful to know about a circle?

What You'll Learn

- Measure the radius, diameter, and circumference of a circle.
- Investigate and explain the relationships among the radius, diameter, and circumference of a circle.
- Develop formulas to find the circumference and area of a circle.
- Estimate the measures for a circle, then use the formulas to calculate these measures.
- Draw a circle, given its radius, area, or circumference.
- Develop formulas to find the surface area and volume of a cylinder.

Why It's Important

Measuring circles is an extension of measuring polygons in earlier grades.

236

ACTIVATE PRIOR LEARNING

All students should be able to recognize a circle, but many may not be able to explain what it is.

In response to the first and third questions, students may say a circle is a closed curve; it has too many lines of symmetry to count. A circle is a set of points, all of which are the same distance from another point, the centre of the circle.

In response to the second question, students may describe the circles on the student pages or any circles they see in the classroom or their environment.

In response to the fourth question, students may suggest the distance around the circle, the area of the circle, and the distance across the circle, through its centre.

Share with students that, in this unit, they will develop formulas for the distance around a circle, the area of a circle, the surface area of a cylinder, and the volume of a cylinder. Upon completion of the unit, students will use their understanding of the circumference of a circle and the area of a circle to create a design involving circles and lines.

FROM THE LIBRARY

Hands-On Math Projects with Real-Life Applications: Ready-to-Use Lessons and Materials for Grades 6–12 by Gary Robert Muschla and Judith A. Muschla.
Jossey-Bass, 1996.
ISBN: 0876283849
The projects are appropriate for grades 6–12 and are organized into six major sections: Math & Science; Math & Social Studies; Math & Language; Math & Art & Music; Math & Sports & Recreation; and Math & Life Skills.

Piece of Pi: Wit-Sharpening, Brain-Bruising, Number-Crunching Activities with Pi by Naila Bokhari.
Prufrock Press, 2001.
ISBN: 1883055431
This book shares the many ways that pi has been calculated. The activities have some fun real-world applications. The book is intended for students in Grades 6–8.

REACHING ALL LEARNERS

Some students may benefit from using the virtual manipulatives on the e-Tools CD-ROM.
The e-Tool appropriate for this unit is *Geometry Drawing*.

DIAGNOSTIC ASSESSMENT

What to Look For	What to Do
✔ Students can recognize a circle. ✔ Students understand that perimeter is measured in linear units, area in square units, and volume in cubic units. ✔ Students can calculate the area of a parallelogram.	***Extra Support:*** Students who have difficulty could draw around circular objects, or use a compass to draw a circle. *Work on this skill during the Launch.* Students who have difficulty remembering which units to use can think of a line segment 1 cm long; a square with area 1 cm^2, and a cube with volume 1 cm^3. *Work on this skill during Skills You'll Need.* Work with students who have difficulty calculating the area of a parallelogram to review and use the formula. *Work on this skill during Lesson 6.3.*

LESSON ORGANIZER

10–15 min

Skills in Review

- Rounding measurements

Alternative Example

Write each measurement to the nearest centimetre.

a) 12.7 mm **b)** 35.12 cm **c)** 76.458 m

Solution

a) 12.7 mm is 1.27 cm.
Since there are 2 tenths, round down.
12.7 mm is 1 cm to the nearest centimetre.

b) 35.12 cm
Since there is 1 tenth, round down.
35.12 cm is 35 cm to the nearest centimetre.

c) 76.458 m
To round a measure in metres to the nearest centimetre is to round to the nearest hundredth.
Since there are 8 thousandths, round up.
76.458 m is 76.46 m to the nearest centimetre.

UNIT 6

Skills You'll Need

Rounding Measurements

1 cm = 10 mm
and, 1.6 cm = 16 mm
When a measurement in centimetres has 1 decimal place, the measurement is given to the nearest millimetre.

1 cm
1.6 cm

1 m = 100 cm
1.3 m = 130 cm
1.37 m = 137 cm ← **When a measurement in metres has 2 decimal places, the measurement is given to the nearest centimetre.**

1 m = 1000 mm
1.4 m = 1400 mm
1.43 m = 1430 mm
1.437 m = 1437 mm ← **When a measurement in metres has 3 decimal places, the measurement is given to the nearest millimetre.**

Example

Write each measurement to the nearest millimetre.

a) 25.2 mm **b)** 3.58 cm

Solution

a) 25.2 mm
Since there are 2 tenths, round down.
25.2 mm is 25 mm to the nearest millimetre.

b) 3.58 cm
To round to the nearest millimetre, round to 1 decimal place.
Since there are 8 hundredths, round up.
3.58 cm is 3.6 cm to the nearest millimetre.

✓ Check

1. a) Round to the nearest metre.
i) 4.38 m 4 m **ii)** 57.298 m 57 m **iii)** 158.5 cm 2 m

b) Round to the nearest millimetre and nearest centimetre.
i) 47.2 mm **ii)** 47.235 cm **iii)** 1.0579 m

238 UNIT 6: Circles

Rounding Measurements

Students have rounded before but may need a reminder of place value. Begin by having students share their understanding of place value, as a class. Some students may find it easier to first convert all measurements to the units to which they are asked to round, round, then convert back to the original units of measure.

Common Misconceptions

➤ Rounding to the nearest unit may be interpreted as no digits after the decimal point.

How to Help: Make a comparison to money. For example, you have four hundred and thirty-two pennies. How is this written in dollars? ($4.32) How much money do you have to the nearest dime? ($4.30)

Sample Solutions

1. b) i) Since 47.2 mm is closer to 47 than to 48, round 47.2 mm to 47 mm.
47.2 mm = 4.72 cm
Since 4.72 is closer to 5 than to 4, round 4.72 cm to 5 cm.

ii) Rounding 47.235 cm to the nearest millimetre means rounding to the nearest tenth.
47.235 rounded to the nearest tenth is 47.2.
So, 47.235 cm rounded to the nearest millimetre is 47.2 cm.
Since 47.235 is closer to 47 than to 48, rounding 47.235 cm to the nearest centimetre is 47 cm.

iii) Rounding 1.0579 m to the nearest millimetre means rounding to the nearest thousandth.
1.0579 rounded to the nearest thousandth is 1.058.
So, 1.0579 m rounded to the nearest millimetre is 1.058 m.
Rounding 1.0579 m to the nearest centimetre means rounding to the nearest hundredth.
1.0579 rounded to the nearest hundredth is 1.06.
So, 1.0579 m rounded to the nearest centimetre is 1.06 m.

6.1 Investigating Circles

Focus Measure radius and diameter, and discover their relationship.

Which attribute do these objects share?

Explore

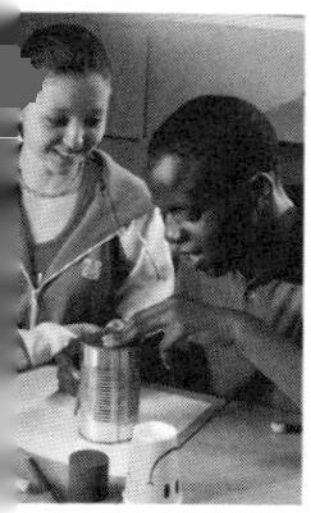

Work with a partner.
You will need circular objects, a compass, ruler, and scissors.

➢ Use a compass. Draw a large circle.
Use a ruler.
Draw a line segment that joins two points on the circle.
Measure the line segment. Label the line segment with its length.
Draw and measure other segments that join two points on the circle.
Find the longest segment in the circle.
Repeat the activity for other circles.

➢ Trace a circular object.
Find a way to locate the centre of the circle.
Measure the distance from the centre to the circle.
Measure the distance across the circle, through its centre.
Record the measurements in a table.
Repeat the activity with other circular objects.
What pattern do you see in your results?

Reflect & Share

Compare your results with those of another pair of classmates.
Where is the longest segment in any circle?
What relationship did you find between the distance across a circle through its centre, and the distance from the centre to the circle?

Investigating Circles

LESSON ORGANIZER 80–100 min

Curriculum Focus: Measure radius and diameter, and discover their relationship. (8m34, 8m44, 8m45)

Student Materials
- objects with circular cross sections
- compasses
- scissors
- rulers
- protractors
- copies of Logo for 6.1 *Practice* Question 9 (Master 6.12)
- 3-column charts (PM 18)

Optional
- Step-by-Step 1 (Master 6.7)
- Extra Practice 1 (Master 6.16)

Vocabulary: radius, diameter, cross section

Assessment: Master 6.2 Ongoing Observations: Circles

Key Math Learnings

1. The length of the radius of a circle is one-half of the diameter.
2. The length of the diameter of a circle is twice the length of the radius.
3. The diameter of a circle is the longest line segment that joins two points on the circle.

BEFORE Get Started

List on the board the student responses to the question on page 239. All the objects have circular cross sections. You may need to explain what a cross section is. Having a model (for example, a soup can, paper towel roll, orange, or Styrofoam ball that you can slice) that you can use to demonstrate is helpful for kinesthetic learners.

Present *Explore.*

Distribute copies of 3-Column Chart (PM 18) to pairs of students. Have students write these headings in the table: "Object," "Distance from the centre," and "Distance across the circle." Students use this table for the second activity in *Explore*.

DURING Explore

Some students may have difficulties using a compass. Be prepared to help with this.

Finding the centre of the circle may be difficult for some students. Have students share their technique with you before completing *Explore*.

As students work, ask questions, such as:

- How did you decide that you had found the longest segment?
  (*We drew many segments until we found three that were equal and the longest.*)
- How did you find the centre of the circle?
  (*We folded the circle in half, twice. The centre of the circle is where the fold lines intersect.*)
- Can you describe another way to find the centre of the circle?
  (*Find two line segments that are the longest and where they intersect is the centre of the circle.*)

REACHING ALL LEARNERS

Alternative Explore

Materials: compasses and rulers

Have students draw different circles, measure the diameter and radius of each circle, and determine the relationship between radius and diameter.

Common Misconceptions

➤ Students think the space enclosed by a circle and the centre of the circle are parts of the circle.

How to Help: Show students a hula-hoop. Ask one student to stand inside the hula-hoop. Explain that the hula-hoop is a circle and the student is standing inside the circle. The student is not part of the circle, but is *inside* the circle.

ESL Strategies

Have students create a card for each figure, solid, and formula in this unit. On the card, students sketch and name the figure, and write the relevant formula, where appropriate.

Number Strategies

Work backward. Since the mean is 30, the three numbers must add to 90 because $3 \times 30 = 90$. If the least number is 26, then the other two numbers add to 64 because $90 - 26 = 64$. Assuming all numbers are whole numbers, any two numbers that are greater than 26 and add to 64 are possible.

Connect

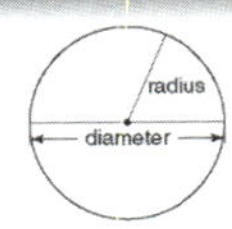

A circle is a closed curve.
All points on a circle are the same distance from the centre of the circle.
This distance is the **radius** of the circle.

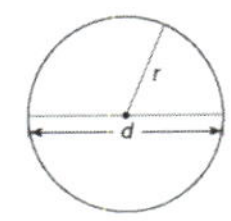

The distance across a circle through its centre is the **diameter** of the circle.
The radius is one-half the diameter.
Let r represent the radius, and d the diameter.
Then, $r = \frac{1}{2}d$, or $r = \frac{d}{2}$
The diameter is two times the length of the radius.
That is, $d = 2r$

Example

Draw a line segment.
Construct a circle for which this segment is:
a) the radius b) the diameter

Solution

a) Draw a line segment.
Place the compass point at one end.
Place the pencil point at the other end.
Draw a circle.

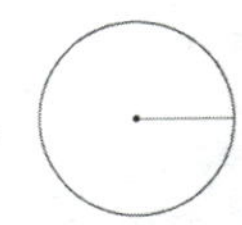

b) Measure the line segment in part a.
Draw a congruent segment.
Mark its midpoint.
Place the compass point at the midpoint.
Place the pencil point at one end of the segment.
Draw a circle.

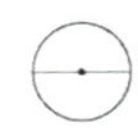

Practice

1. Draw a circle with radius 6 cm.
What is the diameter of the circle? Explain.
12 cm; the diameter is twice the radius.
2. Draw a circle with diameter 8 cm.
What is the radius of the circle? Explain.
4 cm; the radius is one-half the diameter.

240 UNIT 6: Circles

- What patterns do you see in your results? (*The distance from the centre of the circle to the circle is one-half the distance across the circle through its centre.*)

AFTER Connect

Use students' results or *Connect* to illustrate the relationship between diameter and radius.

Review the *Example* to illustrate how to draw a circle, given its radius or diameter.

Practice

Questions 1, 2, 8, and 10 require a ruler and compass. Question 9 requires Logo for 6.1 *Practice* Question 9 (Master 6.12).

Assessment Focus: Question 9

Students should be able to explain how to find the centre of a circle using a reliable, consistent method. Students should also be able to explain the relationship between the radius and the diameter of a circle. (*The radius is one-half the diameter.*)

Students who need extra support to complete the Assessment Focus questions may benefit from the Step-by-Step masters (Masters 6.7–6.11).

Assignment Guidelines

If your students do not have time to complete all the *Practice* questions on pages 240 and 241, these questions provide minimum curriculum coverage: 4, 5, 6, 7, *Reflect*

To assess the 4 Achievement Chart categories listed in the curriculum document, have students complete these *Practice* questions:

Knowledge and Understanding: 4
Thinking: 6
Application: 7
Communication: *Reflect*

The word *radii* is the plural of *radius*.

3. a) How many radii does a circle have?
b) How many diameters does a circle have?

4. A circle has diameter 3.8 cm. What is the radius? 1.9 cm

5. A circle has radius 7.5 cm. What is the diameter? 15 cm

6. A circular tabletop is to be cut from a rectangular piece of wood that measures 1.20 m by 1.80 m.
What is the radius of the largest tabletop that could be cut? 0.60 m
Justify your answer. Include a sketch.
The largest diameter is 1.20 m

7. A glass has a circular base with radius 3.5 cm.
A rectangular tray has dimensions 40 cm by 25 cm.
How many glasses will fit on the tray? 77 glasses
What assumptions do you make?

8. a) Draw a circle.
Draw a diameter. Label it AB.
Choose a point P on the circle.
Join AP and PB. Measure ∠APB. ∠APB = 90°
b) Choose another point Q on the circle.
Join AQ and QB. Measure ∠AQB. ∠AQB = 90°
c) Repeat parts a and b for a different circle.
What do you notice? The angle formed between a diameter and any point on the circle is always 90°.

9. **Assessment Focus** Your teacher will give you a large copy of this logo.
Find the radius and diameter of each circle in this logo.
Show your work.

This is the logo for the Aboriginal Health Department of the Vancouver Island Health Authority.

Number Strategies

The mean of 3 numbers is 30.
The least number is 26.
What might the other 2 numbers be?
Find as many answers as you can.

27 and 37,
28 and 36,
29 and 35,
30 and 34,
31 and 33,
32 and 32

Take It Further

10. A circular area of grass needs watering.
A sprinkler is to be placed at the centre of the circle.
Explain how you would locate the centre of the circle.
Include a diagram in your explanation.

Reflect

How are the diameter and radius of a circle related?
When you know the diameter, how can you find the radius?
When you know the radius, how can you find the diameter?
Include examples in your explanation.

Sample Solutions

3. The number of radii and diameters are not countable. However many I draw, I can always draw more.

7. I assumed that the tray did not have an edge, and that all glasses were cylindrical.

9. From largest to smallest circle:
$d = 12.5$ cm, $r = 6.25$ cm;
$d = 8.1$ cm, $r = 4.05$ cm;
$d = 7.4$ cm, $r = 3.7$ cm;
$d = 2.1$ cm, $r = 1.05$ cm;
$d = 1.6$ cm, $r = 0.8$ cm;
$d = 1.2$ cm, $r = 0.6$ cm;

10. I would use a long measuring tape to measure across the circle until I found the longest measure—the diameter.
I would use another measuring tape to find another diameter.
Where the two diameters intersect is the centre of the circle.

REFLECT: The diameter of a circle is twice the length of the radius. To find the radius, divide the diameter by 2. To find the diameter, multiply the radius by 2.
For example:
If the diameter of a circle is 8.36 m, then the radius is 8.36 m ÷ 2 = 4.18 m.
If the radius of a circle is 12.43 cm, then the diameter is 12.43 cm × 2 = 24.86 cm.

ASSESSMENT FOR LEARNING

What to Look For

Knowledge and Understanding

- ✔ Students understand the terms radius, diameter, line segment, and midpoint, and how these apply to circles.
- ✔ Students can find the centre of a circle.

Thinking

- ✔ Students can solve problems related to radii and diameters of circles.

Application

- ✔ Students can use the relationship between diameter and radius to find one measure when the other is given.

What to Do

Extra Support: As students complete *Practice* question 7, provide them with a cardboard cutout of a circle with radius 3.5 cm and a rectangle that measures 40 cm by 25 cm, so they can use these manipulatives to solve the problem.
Students can use Step-by-Step 1 (Master 6.7) to complete question 9.

Extra Practice: Have students make up and solve problems similar to *Practice* question 6.
Students can complete Extra Practice 1 (Master 6.16).

Extension: Have students estimate, then draw to check, how many circles with equal radii of a given measure will fill a page. Have them investigate if they can fit more circles if they are not arranged in an array.

Recording and Reporting
Master 6.2 Ongoing Observations: Circles

Circumference of a Circle

LESSON ORGANIZER

80–100 min

Curriculum Focus: Develop and use the formula for the circumference of a circle. (8m26, 8m27, 8m33, 8m34, 8m35, 8m36, 8m62)

Student Materials

- 6 objects with circular cross sections
- dental floss
- scissors
- rulers
- calculators
- 4-column charts (PM 19)

Optional

- compasses
- toonies
- bicycle tire and a small stone
- 3-column charts (PM18)
- Step-by-Step 2 (Master 6.8)
- Extra Practice 2 (Master 6.17)

Vocabulary: circumference, irrational number, pi

Assessment: Master 6.2 Ongoing Observations: Circles

Key Math Learning

The ratio of the circumference C of a circle to its diameter d is equal to π; that is $\frac{C}{d} = \pi$.

6.2 Circumference of a Circle

Focus Develop and use the formula for the circumference of a circle.

You know the relationship between the radius and diameter of a circle. You will now investigate how these two measures are related to the distance around a circle.

Explore

Work with a partner.
You will need 6 circular objects, dental floss, scissors, and a ruler.

Choose an object.
Use dental floss to measure the distance around it.
Measure the radius and diameter of the object.
Record these measures in a table.

Object	Distance Around (cm)	Radius (cm)	Diameter (cm)

Repeat the activity for the remaining objects.
What patterns can you see in the table?
How is the diameter related to the distance around?
How is the radius related to the distance around?
For each object, calculate:

- distance around ÷ diameter
- distance around ÷ radius

What do you notice?

Reflect & Share

Compare your results with those of another pair of classmates. Work together to write a formula for the distance around a circle, when you know its diameter.

Connect

The distance around a circle is its **circumference**.
For any circle, the circumference, C, divided by the diameter, d, is $\frac{C}{d}$, which is constant with value approximately 3.

242 UNIT 6: Circles

BEFORE — Get Started

Ensure students understand that the distance around a figure is its perimeter. For visual or kinesthetic learners, seeing a person walk around a circle helps them relate the distance around to perimeter.

Present *Explore.* Distribute copies of 4-Column Chart (PM 19) to pairs of students. If you decide to include the suggestion that follows, have students use a 3-column chart (PM 18) and draw vertical lines to divide each column.

DURING — Explore

Ongoing Assessment: Observe and Listen

Students could include two more columns on the table: "Distance around ÷ diameter" and "Distance around ÷ radius." If students do include the 2 extra columns, have them write each quotient to 1 decimal place.

Students may need a strategy to measure the distance around an object. Place the object with its circular face on the desk. Wrap the floss around, so the floss is also on the desk.

Students may need to be reminded that, to measure the radius or diameter, they may need to trace the object, then find the centre of the circle.

As students work, ask questions, such as:

- How did you find the distance around the object?
  (I placed the object so its circular face was on the desk. I wrapped floss around the object, keeping the floss horizontal and at the base of the object. I cut the floss, then measured its length with a ruler.)
- How did you find the centre of the circle?
  (I traced around the object, then folded the circle in half twice to find the centre of the circle. The folds intersect at the centre of the circle.)

So, the circumference is approximately 3 times the diameter.
And, the circumference C divided by the radius, r, is $\frac{C}{r}$, which is approximately 6.
So, the circumference is approximately 6 times the radius.

You will learn about other irrational numbers in Unit 8.

For any circle, the ratio $\frac{C}{d} = \pi$
We use the symbol π because the value of $\frac{C}{d}$ is an **irrational number**; that is, π represents a decimal that never repeats and never terminates.
The symbol π is a Greek letter that we read as "pi."
$\pi \doteq 3.14$
So, the circumference is π multiplied by d.
We write: $C = \pi d$

The circumference of a circle is also the perimeter of the circle.

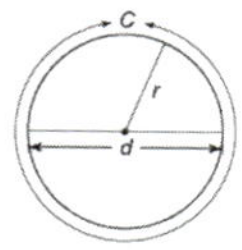

Since $d = 2r$, the circumference is also π multiplied by $2r$.
We write: $C = \pi \times 2r$, or $C = 2\pi r$
When we know the radius or diameter of a circle, we can use one of the formulas above to find the circumference of the circle.

Example 1

The face of a toonie has a radius of 1.4 cm.
a) What is the diameter of the face?
b) Estimate the circumference of the face.
c) Calculate the circumference.
Give the answer to the nearest millimetre.

Solution

a) The diameter $d = 2r$, where r is the radius.
Substitute: $r = 1.4$
$d = 2 \times 1.4$
$= 2.8$
The diameter is 2.8 cm.

The circumference is a length, so its units are units of length such as centimetres, metres, or millimetres.

b) The circumference is approximately 3 times the diameter:
$3 \times 2.8 \text{ cm} \doteq 3 \times 3 \text{ cm}$
$= 9 \text{ cm}$
The circumference is approximately 9 cm.

6.2 Circumference of a Circle **243**

REACHING ALL LEARNERS

Alternative Explore

Materials: computer with *The Geometer's Sketchpad*
Have students use *The Geometer's Sketchpad's* Compass Tool to construct several circles. Students use the Straightedge Tool to construct diameters for each circle and use the Measure function to determine the circumference and length of each diameter. Students then use the software calculator to divide the circumference by the diameter to determine the relationship. Students compare their findings with a classmate.

Early Finishers

Get a baseball from the Physical Education Department in your school. Have students measure the circumference of the baseball, then calculate the diameter of the baseball. Students measure the diameter of a basketball hoop, and calculate how many baseballs could fit through the hoop—side by side.
(Answer: for example, 40.64 cm ÷ 7.28 cm ≐ 5)

Common Misconceptions

➤ Students erroneously substitute the radius for d in the formula $C = \pi d$.

How to Help: Have students sketch and label a circle each time, with the given measurement. Then they can see whether it is r or d that is given.

- How are the distance around and diameter related?
(*It seems that the distance around is about 3 times the diameter.*)
- How are the distance around and the radius related?
(*It seems that the distance around is about 6 times the radius.*)

AFTER Connect

Put two headings "distance around ÷ diameter" and "distance around ÷ radius" on the board. Have one person from each group write her or his group's results under each heading. Have students calculate the mean of the numbers in each column to the nearest hundredth, then draw a conclusion. Ask students to share what they notice.

Use students' results to introduce the terms *circumference* and π, as described in the Student Book. Review *Example 1* to show how to estimate, then calculate the circumference of a circle when its diameter is given. For estimation, we approximate π as 3. The key sequence in the Solution may be different for students' calculators. Ensure each student knows the key sequence for her or his calculator.

Review how to calculate the diameter when the circumference is known and use *Example 2* to illustrate how and when this knowledge is applied.

Most students would be more comfortable thinking in terms of words rather than algebraic symbols. Students should think and say:
"The circumference is π times the diameter."
"The diameter is the circumference divided by π."

Number Strategies

Remind students of the formula for the area of a rectangle:
$A = b \times h$
Students find pairs of whole numbers that multiply to 256.

Assignment Guidelines

If your students do not have time to complete all the *Practice* questions on pages 245 and 246, these questions provide minimum curriculum coverage: 1, 2, 5, 7, 9

To assess the 4 Achievement Chart categories listed in the curriculum document, have students complete these *Practice* questions:
Knowledge and Understanding: 1
Communication: 5
Application: 7
Thinking: 9

Sample Solutions

1. a) The circumference is approximately 3 times the diameter:
3×10 cm = 30 cm
The circumference is approximately 30 cm.
   b) About 42 cm c) About 45 m
2. a) $C = \pi d$
$= \pi \times 10$
$\doteq 31.416$
$\doteq 31.4$
The circumference is about 31.4 cm.
   b) 44.0 cm c) 47.1 m

---

c) *Method 1*
The circumference is: $C = \pi d$
Substitute: $d = 2.8$
$C = \pi \times 2.8$
Key in: [π] [×] 2.8 [ENTER]
to display 8.79645943
So, $C \doteq 8.796$
$\doteq 8.8$

Method 2
The circumference is: $C = 2\pi r$
Substitute: $r = 1.4$
$C = 2 \times \pi \times 1.4$
Key in: 2 [×] [π] [×]
to display 8.79645943
So, $C \doteq 8.796$
$\doteq 8.8$

The circumference is 8.8 cm, to the nearest millimetre.

Use a calculator. If your calculator does not have a π key, use 3.14 instead.

When we know the circumference,
we can use a formula to find the diameter.
Use the formula $C = \pi d$. To isolate d, divide each side by π.

$$\frac{C}{\pi} = \frac{\pi d}{\pi}$$
$$\frac{C}{\pi} = d$$
$$\text{So, } d = \frac{C}{\pi}$$

Example 2

A circular pond has circumference 12 m.
a) Estimate the lengths of the diameter and radius of the pond.
b) Calculate the diameter and radius.
Give the answers to the nearest centimetre.

Solution

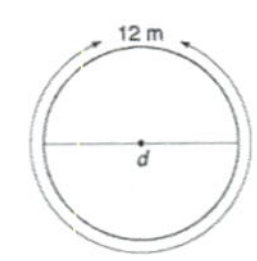

a) Since the circumference is approximately 3 times the diameter, then the diameter is about $\frac{1}{3}$ the circumference.
One-third of 12 m is 4 m. So, the diameter is about 4 m.
The radius is $\frac{1}{2}$ the diameter. One-half of 4 m is 2 m.
So, the radius of the pond is about 2 m.

b) The diameter is: $d = \frac{C}{\pi}$
Substitute: $C = 12$
$d = \frac{12}{\pi}$
$\doteq 3.8197$

Use a calculator.
Do not clear the calculator.

The radius is $\frac{1}{2}$ the diameter.
Divide the number in the calculator display by 2.
$r \doteq 1.9099$
The diameter is 3.82 m to the nearest centimetre.
The radius is 1.91 m to the nearest centimetre.

244 UNIT 6: Circles

Ask questions, such as:

- Now that you know a formula for the circumference of a circle, how could you use it to check the radius of an object you measured in *Explore*?
(I could use the circumference measure of the object, and divide that measure by π. That gives me the diameter of the circle. Then I divide the diameter by 2 to get the radius.)

Practice

Questions 2, 4, 6–11 require a calculator.

Question 9 requires a compass.

For question 6b, students may need to review unit rate.

For question 11b, students need to understand that the question requires the radius of the ring given its circumference.

Assessment Focus: Question 7

Visual and kinesthetic learners may need to see and use a bicycle wheel to understand this problem. Lodge a stone in the tire of the wheel, and have students roll the wheel along the ground to get a better sense of what measurement students require. Students need to understand that part a requires the circumference of the tire. To calculate the answer to part b, the distance of 1 km must first be converted into centimetres, the units used for the circumference in part a.

Students who need extra support to complete this Assessment Focus question may benefit from Step-by-Step 2 (Master 6.8).

Practice

1. Estimate the circumference of each circle.

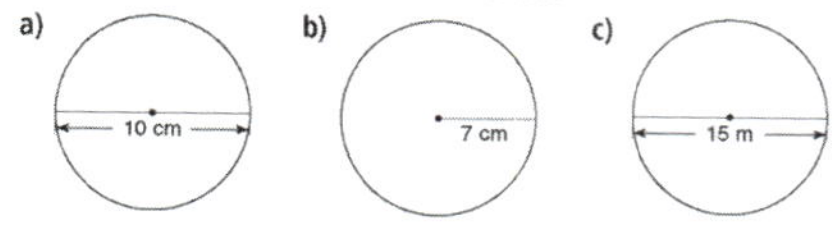

2. Calculate the circumference of each circle in question 1.
Give the answers to 1 decimal place.

3. Estimate the diameter and radius of each circle.

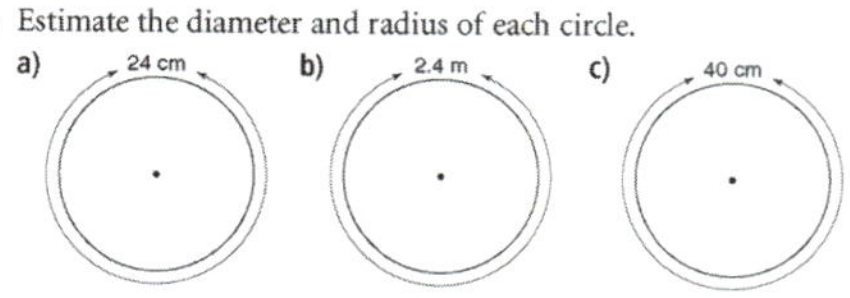

4. Calculate the diameter and radius of each circle in question 3.
Give the answers to the nearest millimetre.

5. When you estimate the circumference, you use 3 instead of π.
Is the estimated value greater than or less than the calculated value? Explain. Less than

6. A circular garden has diameter 2.4 m.
   a) The garden is to be enclosed with plastic edging.
   How much edging is needed? About 7.5 m
   b) The edging costs $4.53/m.
   What is the cost to edge the garden? About $33.98

Math Link

Science
The orbit of Earth around the sun is approximately a circle.
The radius of the orbit is about 1.5×10^8 km.
How could you calculate the circumference of the orbit?
The orbit of a communication satellite around Earth is approximately a circle.
The satellite is about 35 800 km above Earth's surface.
What would you need to know to be able to calculate the radius of the orbit?

6.2 Circumference of a Circle **245**

3. a) Since the circumference is approximately 3 times the diameter, then the diameter is about $\frac{1}{3}$ the circumference.
One-third of 24 cm is 8 cm.
So, the diameter is about 8 cm.
The radius is $\frac{1}{2}$ the diameter. One-half of 8 cm is 4 cm.
So, the radius is about 4 cm.

b) $d \doteq 0.8$ m; $r \doteq 0.4$ m **c)** $d \doteq 13$ cm; $r \doteq 6.5$ cm

4. a) The diameter is: $d = \frac{C}{\pi}$

$$= \frac{24}{\pi}$$

$$\doteq 7.639$$

The radius is $\frac{1}{2}$ the diameter.
Divide the diameter by 2.
$r \doteq 3.82$
The diameter is 7.6 cm to the nearest millimetre.
The radius is 3.8 cm to the nearest millimetre.

b) $d \doteq 0.764$ m; $r \doteq 0.382$ m **c)** $d \doteq 12.7$ cm; $r \doteq 6.4$ cm

5. The estimated value is less than the calculated value because 3 is less than π.

6. a) $C = \pi d$

$$= \pi \times 2.4 \text{ m}$$

$$\doteq 7.54 \text{ m}$$

The circumference is about 7.5 m. So, about 7.5 m of edging is needed.

b) The cost in dollars is: $7.5 \times \$4.53 = \$33.98$
It will cost about $33.98 to edge the garden, assuming the edging does not have to be bought in whole metres.

(Sample Solutions continue below, left.)

(Sample Solutions continued)

7. a) Use $C = \pi d$.
Substitute $d = 2 \times 46$ cm $= 92$ cm.
$C = \pi \times 92$ cm $\doteq 289.02$ cm
Round C to 290 cm.
The bicycle travels about 290 cm.

b) 1 km = 100 000 cm
The number of times the stone hits the ground is about $100\ 000 \div 290 \doteq 344.8$.
The stone hits the ground about 345 times.

8. 1 m = 100 cm
So, 4.5 m = 4.5×100 cm = 450 cm
The tabletop has circumference 450 cm.
The diameter is: $d = \frac{C}{\pi}$

$$= \frac{450}{\pi}$$

$$\doteq 143.24$$

The radius is $\frac{1}{2}$ the diameter.
Divide the diameter by 2.
$r \doteq 71.6$
The radius of the tabletop is about 71.6 cm.

9. No, it is not possible to draw a circle to an exact length because the calculation of the radius needed to draw the circle involves π, which is not exact.
However, it is possible to draw a circle with circumference about 33 cm. I used the formula to find the diameter of a circle with circumference 33 cm. The diameter is about 10.5 cm, so the radius is about 5.25 cm. I can set my compass to 5.25 cm and draw a circle.

10. a), b) The formula for the circumference of a circle is $C = \pi d$. If the diameter is doubled, the circumference is doubled, and if the diameter is tripled, the circumference is tripled.

11. b) You could drive in a school bus under the ring.
Add 1 km to the circumference from part a. The new circumference would be about 40 075.8 km.
Calculate the radius: $r = \frac{40\ 075.8}{2\pi}$, or about 6378.26 km
Calculate the difference between the radii:
$6378.26 - 6378.1 = 0.16$
So, the difference between the two radii is about 0.16 km.
0.16 km = 160 m
When the length of the ring is increased by 1 km, its radius increases by about 160 m, and you could drive a school bus (approximate height 2.44 m) under the ring.

REFLECT: When I know the circumference of a circle, I divide the circumference by π to get the diameter, and then divide the diameter by 2 to get the radius.

Suppose a circle has circumference 14 m.

Calculate its diameter and radius.

The diameter is $\frac{14 \text{ m}}{\pi} \doteq 4.46$ m.

The radius is about $\frac{4.46 \text{ m}}{2} = 2.23$ m.

The diameter is about 4.46 m.

The radius is about 2.23 m.

Math Link

The circumference of the orbit of the sun around Earth is:
$\pi \times 1.5 \times 10^8 \text{ km} \doteq 4.7 \times 10^8 \text{ km}$
The radius of the Earth is negligible compared to the radius of the orbit, so we do not include it. However, to calculate the radius of the orbit of the satellite, we would need to know that the radius of Earth is about 6378 km.
Then the radius of the orbit of the satellite is:
6378 km + 35 800 km = 42 178 km

Number Strategies

A rectangular plot of land has area 256 m^2.
List the possible whole-number dimensions of the plot.
1 m by 256 m,
2 m by 128 m,
4 m by 64 m,
8 m by 32 m,
16 m by 16 m

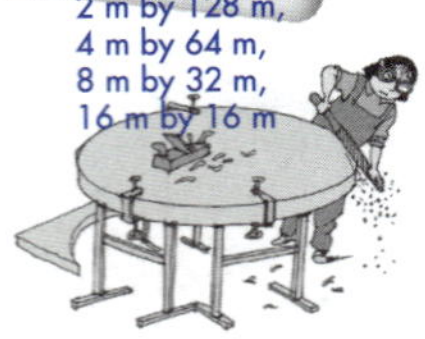

7. **Assessment Focus** A bicycle tire has a stone stuck in it.
The radius of the tire is 46 cm.
Every time the wheel turns, the stone hits the ground.
   a) How far will the bicycle travel between the stone hitting the ground for the first time and the second time? About 290 cm
   b) How many times will the stone hit the ground when the bicycle travels 1 km? About 345 times

   Show your work.

8. A carpenter is making a circular tabletop with circumference 4.5 m.
What is the radius of the tabletop in centimetres? About 71.6 cm

9. Can you draw a circle with circumference 33 cm? No
If you can, draw the circle and explain how you know its circumference is correct.
If you cannot, explain why it is not possible.

10. a) What if you double the diameter of a circle.
What happens to the circumference?
   b) What if you triple the diameter of a circle.
What happens to the circumference?

Take It Further

11. Suppose a metal ring could be placed around Earth at the equator.
   a) The radius of Earth is 6378.1 km.
How long is the metal ring? About 40 074.8 km
   b) Suppose the length of the metal ring is increased by 1 km.
Would you be able to crawl under the ring, walk under the ring, or drive in a school bus under the ring?
Explain how you know.

Reflect

When you know the circumference of a circle, how can you calculate its radius and diameter?
Include an example in your explanation.

246 UNIT 6: Circles

ASSESSMENT FOR LEARNING

What to Look For	What to Do
Knowledge and Understanding ✔ Students understand how diameter, radius, and π relate to the circumference of a circle. ***Communication*** ✔ Students can explain how to calculate the circumference of a circle, given its radius or diameter. ***Application*** ✔ Students can use the formulas $C = \pi d$ or $C = 2\pi r$ to calculate the circumference of a circle.	***Extra Support:*** Students who confuse the terms radius, diameter, and circumference, may benefit from making a reference card. Students draw a circular arrow around the outside of a circle and label it *C*, a line segment from the centre of a circle to a point on the circle and label it *r*, and a line across a circle through its centre and label it *d*. Students can use Step-by-Step 2 (Master 6.8) to complete question 7. ***Extra Practice:*** Have students complete the Additional Activity *Circle Mania* (Master 6.5). Students can complete Extra Practice 2 (Master 6.17). ***Extension:*** Have students use their data from *Explore* to graph *Circumference* against *Radius* and *Circumference* against *Diameter* on different grids, then compare the graphs and make inferences.

Recording and Reporting
Master 6.2 Ongoing Observations: Circles

6.3 Area of a Circle

Focus Develop and use the formula for the area of a circle.

ore

Work in a group of 4.
You will need scissors, glue, a compass, and protractor.

➢ Each of you draws a circle with radius 8 cm.
Each of you chooses one of these:
- 4 congruent sectors
- 8 congruent sectors
- 10 congruent sectors
- 12 congruent sectors

The angle at the centre of the circle is 360°. Divide this angle by the number of sectors. The quotient is the sector angle.

➢ Use a protractor to divide your circle into the number of sectors you chose.
Cut out the sectors.
Arrange the sectors to approximate a parallelogram.

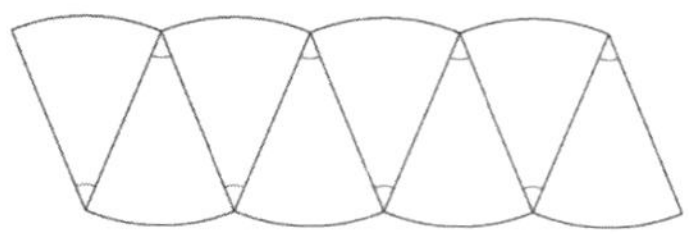

The area of a parallelogram is base × height.

Glue the sectors on paper.
Calculate the area of the parallelogram.
Estimate the area of the circle.

Reflect & Share

Compare your answer for the area of the circle with those of your group members.
Which area do you think is closest to the area of the circle? Explain.
How could you improve your estimate for the area?

6.3 Area of a Circle 247

Area of a Circle

LESSON ORGANIZER (80–100 min)

Curriculum Focus: Develop and use the formula for the area of a circle. (8m33, 8m35, 8m36, 8m62)

Teacher Materials
Optional
- blank overhead transparency
- overhead projector

Student Materials
- scissors
- glue
- protractors
- compasses
- 0.5-cm grid paper (PM 14)
- rulers
- calculators

Optional
- Step-by-Step 3 (Master 6.9)
- Extra Practice 3 (Master 6.18)

Vocabulary: congruent, sector, sector angle

Assessment: Master 6.2 Ongoing Observations: Circles

Key Math Learning

The ratio of the area A of a circle to the square of its radius r is π; that is $\frac{A}{r^2} = \pi$.

BEFORE Get Started

On the board or an overhead transparency, divide a circle into 6 congruent sectors. Ask:

- How many sectors does the circle have? (*Six*)
- Where are the sector angles?
(*The six angles are at the centre of the circle.*)
- The sectors are congruent. Without measuring, how could you determine the measure of each sector angle?
(*The angle at the centre of a circle is 360°. I could divide 360° by the number of sectors: 360 ÷ 6 = 60. So, each sector angle is 60°.*)

Present *Explore*. An alternative to having all groups work with the same size of circle is to assign each group a different size circle. Students could create a poster showing the results from their group and their prediction for the area of a circle.

Having students develop a formula by starting with a physical model supports long-term understanding rather than memorization.

DURING Explore

Ongoing Assessment: Observe and Listen

Students may need help to draw the congruent sectors. Show them how to align the centre of the protractor with the centre of the circle, so a radius of the circle aligns with the base line of the protractor. Students then mark a point for the sector angle along the circumference, join this point to the centre to make the first sector, move the protractor to align with the new radius, then repeat the process.

Once students have glued the sectors on paper, ask them to draw a parallelogram around this figure before they try to calculate the area of the parallelogram. Students may extend the two

REACHING ALL LEARNERS

Alternative Explore

Materials: paper, compasses, scissors, calculators

Students work in groups of 3. After students have drawn the circles, they cut them out and use folding, instead of protractors, to get these numbers of congruent sectors:
4, 8, 16. Students then proceed as described in *Explore*.

Early Finishers

Have students make a table of *Radius* and *Area* for each circle they calculated. Students graph *Area* against *Radius*, and make inferences from the graph.

Common Misconceptions

➤ Students think that squaring the radius is the same as multiplying the radius by 2.

How to Help: Have students square and multiply by 2, each number from 3 to 10, to see the difference. Students could explain in words that squaring a number is multiplying it by itself.

Number Strategies

Greatest number: 9 874 321
Least number: 1 234 789
Sum: 11 109 110
Difference: 8 639 532

Connect

A circle, with radius 10 cm, was cut into 24 congruent sectors.
The sectors were then arranged to form a parallelogram.

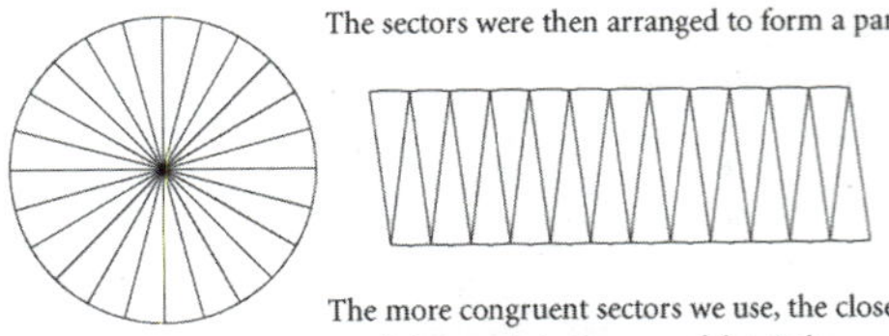

The more congruent sectors we use, the closer the area of the parallelogram is to the area of the circle.
If the number of sectors is large enough, the parallelogram is almost a rectangle.

The sum of the two longer sides of the rectangle is equal to the circumference, *C*.

$C = 2\pi r$
$= 2\pi \times 10$ cm
$= 20\pi$ cm

So, each longer side is: $\frac{20\pi \text{ cm}}{2} = 10\pi$ cm

Each of the two shorter sides is equal to the radius, 10 cm.

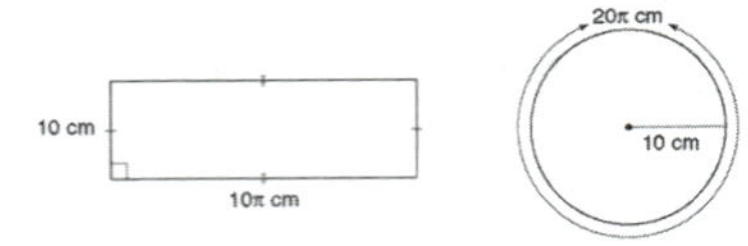

The area of the rectangle is: $10\pi \text{ cm} \times 10 \text{ cm} = 10^2\pi \text{ cm}^2$
$= 100\pi \text{ cm}^2$

So, the area of the circle with radius 10 cm is 100π cm^2.
We can apply this idea to a circle with radius *r*.

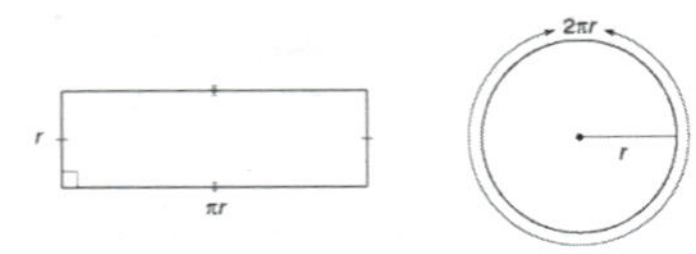

248 UNIT 6: Circles

radii that represent 2 sides of the parallelogram, so when the other 2 sides are drawn, they do not intersect the circles.

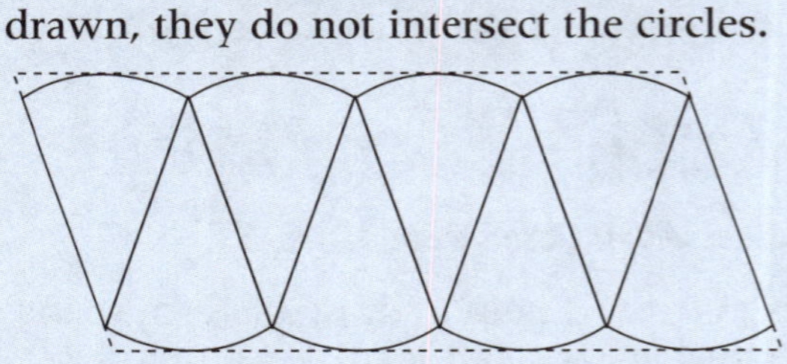

When students estimate the area of the circle after they calculate the area of the parallelogram, they may need prompting. Ask:

- Is the area of a parallelogram more or less than the area of a circle?
  (*If students draw the parallelogram shown above, its area will be greater than that of the circle. If students draw the parallelogram as shown above right, its area will be less than that of the circle.*)

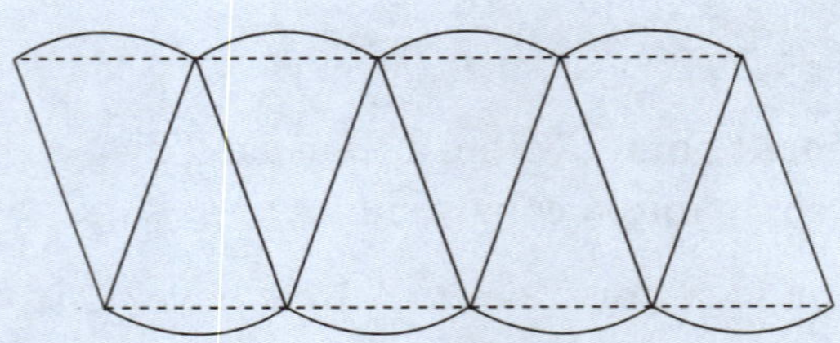

- How does the base of the parallelogram relate to the circle?
  (*The base of the parallelogram is approximately equal to one-half the circumference of the circle.*)
- How is the height of the parallelogram related to the radius of the circle?
  (*The answer will depend on the parallelogram students draw. For the first parallelogram above, the height is close to but greater than the radius. For the second parallelogram above, the height is close to but less than the radius.*)
- What happens to the height and radius when the number of congruent sectors increases?
  (*The height and radius get closer in value.*)

So, the area, A, of a circle with radius r is: $\pi r \times r = \pi r^2$
So, $A = \pi r^2$

We can use this formula to find the area of any circle when we know its radius.

Example

The face of a dime has diameter 1.8 cm.
a) Estimate the area of the face of the dime.
b) Calculate the area. Give the answer to 2 decimal places.

Solution

The diameter of the face of a dime is 1.8 cm.
So, its radius is:
$\frac{1.8 \text{ cm}}{2} = 0.9$ cm

a) The area of the face of the dime is about $3 \times r^2$.
$r \doteq 1$
So, $r^2 = 1$
and $3 \times r^2 = 3 \times 1$
$= 3$
The area of the face of the dime is approximately 3 cm^2.

b) Use the formula: $A = \pi r^2$
Substitute: $r = 0.9$
$A = \pi \times 0.9^2$
Use a calculator.
Key in: [π] [×] 0.9 [x^2] [ENTER] to display 2.544690049
$A \doteq 2.544\ 69$
The area of the face of the dime is 2.54 cm^2 to 2 decimal places.

If your calculator does not have an x^2 key, key in 0.9×0.9 instead of 0.9^2.

Since 1 mm = 0.1 cm
Then 1 mm^2 = 1 mm × 1 mm
= 0.1 cm × 0.1 cm
= 0.01 cm^2
This illustrates that when an area in square centimetres has 2 decimal places, the area is given to the nearest square millimetre. In the *Example*, the area 2.54 cm^2 is written to the nearest square millimetre.

Assignment Guidelines

If your students do not have time to complete all the *Practice* questions on pages 250 and 251, these questions provide minimum curriculum coverage: 1, 2, 3, 4, 7, 8, *Reflect*

To assess the 4 Achievement Chart categories listed in the curriculum document, have students complete these *Practice* questions:
Knowledge and Understanding: 2
Communication: 3
Application: 7
Thinking: 8

Sample Solutions

4. a) The area of the circle is between the areas of the two squares. So, I estimate that the area of my circle lies halfway between 49 cm^2 and 100 cm^2; that is, about 75 cm^2.

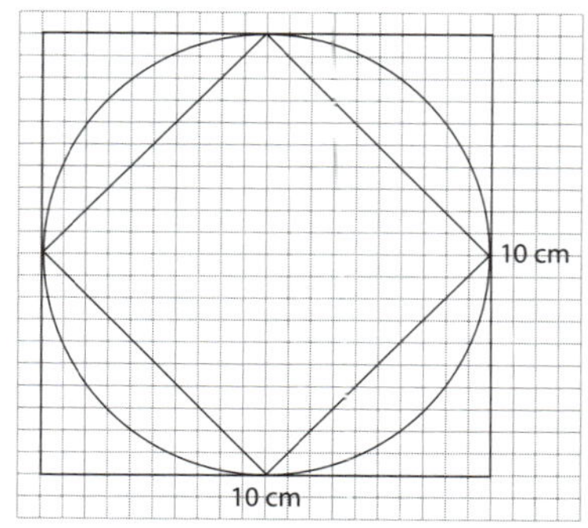

b) Use the formula:
$A = \pi r^2$
Substitute: $r = 5$
$A = \pi \times 5^2$
$\doteq 78.54$
The area of the circle is about 78.5 cm^2.

- In your group, whose parallelogram do you think best represents the area of the circle? (*The parallelogram with the most sectors, because it is closest in shape to a parallelogram; that is, there is less space in the parallelogram that is not part of the circle.*)
- What could you do to get a better estimate for the area? (*I could draw more congruent sectors. I could draw 36 sectors with each sector angle 10°, or even 72 sectors with each sector angle 5°. These figures would be very close to a parallelogram.*)

AFTER Connect

Use students' results and *Connect* to illustrate how the formula for the area of a circle is developed.

Review the *Example* that illustrates how to estimate and calculate the area of a circle. As with the circumference calculations, have students find the correct key sequence for their calculators. Ensure students understand the descriptions of area measurements that follow the *Example*. It may help students' understanding to sketch this diagram on the board.

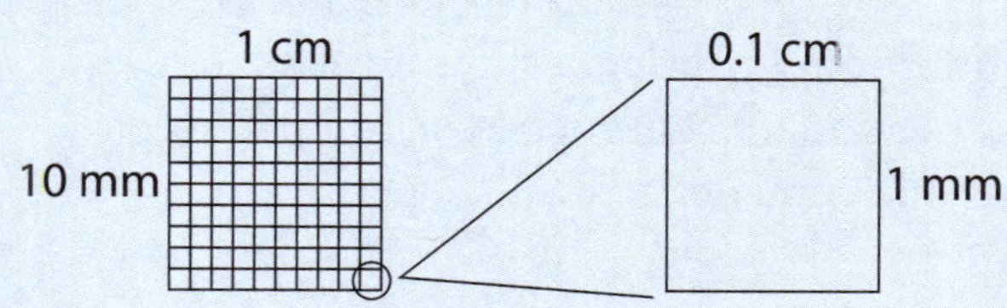

This illustrates 1 cm^2 and 1 mm^2.

Practice

Questions 2–9 require a calculator.

Question 4 requires 0.5-cm grid paper, a compass, and a ruler.

Question 8 requires students to first calculate the radius given the circumference, then to

c) Here are two circles I drew.

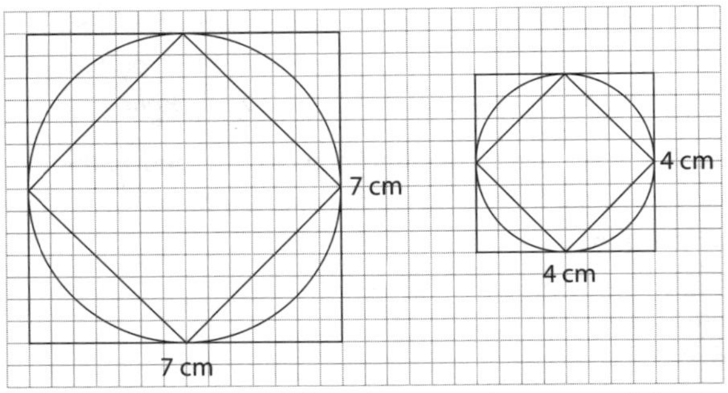

The area of the first circle is between the areas of the two squares. So, I estimate that the area of my circle lies halfway between 25 cm^2 and 49 cm^2; that is, about 37 cm^2.
Use the formula: $A = \pi r^2$
Substitute: $r = 3.5$
$A = \pi \times 3.5^2 \doteq 38.48$
The area of the first circle is about 38.5 cm^2.
The area of the second circle is between the areas of the two squares. So, I estimate that the area of my circle lies halfway between 8 cm^2 and 16 cm^2; that is, about 12 cm^2. Use the formula: $A = \pi r^2$
Substitute: $r = 2$
$A = \pi \times 2^2 \doteq 12.57$
The area of the second circle is about 12.6 cm^2.
It is possible to estimate the area of a circle by drawing a square that just encloses the circle and drawing another square inside the circle whose vertices are on the circle. The approximate area of the circle is the mean of the areas of the squares.

Practice

1. Estimate the area of each circle.

a) b) c)

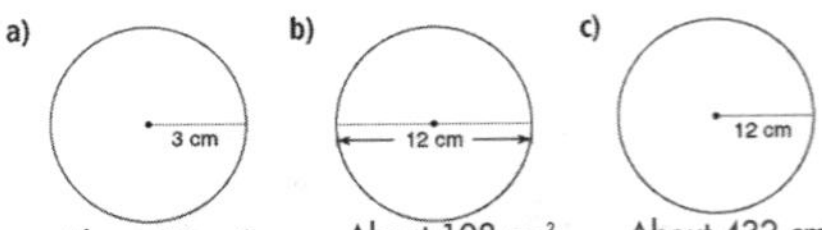

About 27 cm^2 About 108 cm^2 About 432 cm^2

2. Calculate the area of each circle in question 1.
Give the answers to the nearest square millimetre.
a) 28.27 cm^2 b) 113.10 cm^2 c) 452.39 cm^2

3. a) Use the results of questions 1 and 2.
What if you double the radius of a circle.
What happens to its area? The area quadruples.
b) What do you think happens to the area of a circle if you triple its radius? The area is 9 times as great.
Justify your answers.

Number Strategies

Arrange these digits to make the greatest number:
7, 1, 8, 2, 4, 3, 9
Arrange the same digits to make the least number.
Calculate the sum and the difference of the two numbers.

4. **Assessment Focus** Use 0.5-cm grid paper.
Draw a circle with radius 5 cm.
Draw a square outside the circle that just encloses the circle.
Draw a square inside the circle so that its vertices lie on the circle.
a) How can you use the areas of the two squares to estimate the area of the circle?
b) Check your estimate in part a by calculating the area of the circle.
c) Repeat the activity for circles with different radii.
Record your results.
Show your work.

5. In the biathlon, athletes shoot at targets.
Each target is 50 m from the athlete.
Find the area of each target.
a) The target for the athlete who is standing is a circle with diameter 11.5 cm. 104 cm^2
b) The target for the athlete who is prone is a circle with diameter 4.5 cm. 16 cm^2
Give the answers to the nearest square centimetre.

calculate the area using the calculated radius. Remind students to use the memory function of the calculator to store the radius, as rounding is not done until all calculations have been completed.

In question 9, students should calculate the cost per square centimetre for comparison to determine the better deal.

Assessment Focus: Question 4

Students can draw the diagonals for the first square and use the point where the diagonals intersect the circle as the vertices of the smaller square.

Students who need extra support to complete this Assessment Focus question may benefit from Step-by-Step 3 (Master 6.9).

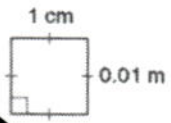

6. a) A square has side length 1 cm.
   i) What is the area of the square in square centimetres? 1 cm^2
   ii) What is the area of the square in square metres? 0.0001 m^2
   iii) Use the results of parts i and ii to write 1 cm^2 in square metres. 0.0001 m^2
   b) A calculator display shows the area of a circle as 7.068583471 m^2.
   What is this area rounded to the nearest square centimetre? 70 686 cm^2

7. In curling, the target area is a bull's eye series of 4 concentric circles.

Concentric circles have the same centre.

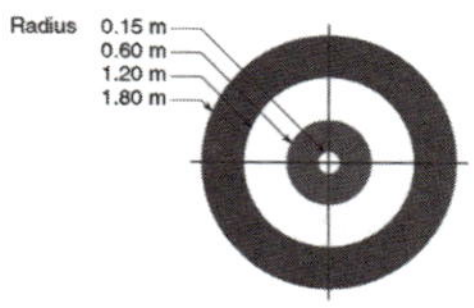

   a) Calculate the area of the smallest circle. 0.0707 m^2
   Write the area to the nearest square centimetre. 707 cm^2
   b) When a smaller circle overlaps a larger circle, a ring is formed. Calculate the area of each ring on the target area to the nearest square centimetre. Smallest ring: 10 603 cm^2; second smallest ring: 33 929 cm^2; largest ring: 56 549 cm^2

8. The bottom of a swimming pool is a circle with circumference 31.4 m. What is the area of the bottom of the pool? 78 m^2
   Give the answer to the nearest square metre.

Take It Further

9. A large pizza has diameter 35 cm.
   Two large pizzas cost $19.99.
   A medium pizza has diameter 30 cm.
   Three medium pizzas cost $24.99.
   Which is the better deal: 2 large pizzas or 3 medium pizzas?
   Justify your answer. 2 large pizzas

Reflect

When you know the radius of a circle, how can you calculate its area? Include an example in your explanation.

6.3 Area of a Circle 251

9. The diameter of a large pizza is 35 cm.
So, the radius is: $\frac{35 \text{ cm}}{2} = 17.5$ cm.
Use the formula: $A = \pi r^2$
Substitute: $r = 17.5$
$A = \pi \times 17.5^2$
$\doteq 962.113$
The area of a large pizza is about 962 cm^2.
The diameter of a medium pizza is 30 cm.
So, the radius is: $\frac{30 \text{ cm}}{2} = 15$ cm.
Use the formula: $A = \pi r^2$
Substitute: $r = 15$
$A = \pi \times 15^2$
$\doteq 706.858$
The area of a medium pizza is about 707 cm^2.
Two large pizzas have area about:
962 cm^2 + 962 cm^2 = 1924 cm^2
They cost $19.99.
So each $1 buys about 1924 cm^2 ÷ 20 = 96.2 cm^2 of pizza.
Three medium pizzas have area about:
707 cm^2 + 707 cm^2 + 707 cm^2 = 2121 cm^2
They cost $24.99.
So each $1 buys about 2121 cm^2 ÷ 25 = 84.84 cm^2 of pizza.
The better deal is the 2 large pizzas.

REFLECT: When I know the radius of a circle, I can calculate its area by squaring the radius, then multiplying by π.
For example, if the radius of a circle is 4 mm, then its area, in square millimetres, is $4^2 \times \pi \doteq 50.3$. The area of the circle is about 50 mm^2.

ASSESSMENT FOR LEARNING

What to Look For	What to Do
Thinking ✔ Students can solve multi-step problems including radius, diameter, area, and circumference of a circle.	***Extra Support:*** Students who have difficulty approximating a circle as a parallelogram could use plastic Fraction Circles instead of paper cutouts. Students can use Step-by-Step 3 (Master 6.9) to complete question 4.
Communication ✔ Students can explain how to calculate the area of a circle given its radius.	***Extra Practice:*** Have students find the areas of some of the circles in Lesson 6.2. Students can complete Extra Practice 3 (Master 6.18).
Application ✔ Students can use the formula $A = \pi r^2$ to calculate the area of a circle.	***Extension:*** Have students choose a radius and find the area of a circle with this radius. Students double the area and find the radius of the circle with this area. Students repeat for several pairs of circles related this way. For each pair, students divide the greater radius by the lesser radius, and describe what they find out. (The greater radius is about 1.4 times the lesser radius.)

Recording and Reporting
Master 6.2 Ongoing Observations: Circles

LESSON ORGANIZER

Student Materials

- calculators
- rulers
- compasses
- protractors

Assessment: Masters 6.1 Unit Rubric: Circles, 6.4 Unit Summary: Circles

Assignment Guidelines

To assess the 4 Achievement Chart categories listed in the curriculum document, have students complete these questions:
Knowledge and Understanding: 4
Application: 5
Communication: 6
Thinking: 11

Mid-Unit Review

LESSON

6.1 **1.** A circle has radius 3.6 cm. What is its diameter? 7.2 cm

2. A circle has diameter 3.6 cm. What is its radius? 1.8 cm

3. a) Draw a large circle. Label its centre C. Mark points P, Q, and R on the circle. Join P, Q, and R to form $\triangle PQR$. Join QC and RC. These line segments form 2 angles at C. Measure $\angle QPR$ and the smaller $\angle QCR$. How are these angles related?

b) Repeat part a for a different circle. Is the relationship in part a still true? Explain.

6.2 **4.** The face of a penny has radius 9.5 mm.

a) Estimate the circumference of the penny. About 60 mm

b) Calculate the circumference. Give the answer to the nearest tenth of a millimetre. About 59.7 mm

5. An auger is used to drill a hole in the ice, for ice fishing. The diameter of the hole is 25 cm. What is the circumference of the hole? About 78.5 cm

6. Explain how you could calculate the circumference of a paper plate.

7. There is a clock on the Peace T in Ottawa. The circumference of the clock face is approximately 15.02 m.

a) Estimate the diameter and radius of the clock face.

b) Calculate the diameter and radius of the clock face to the nearest centimetre. $d \doteq 4.78$ m, $r \doteq 2.39$ m

8. a) How is the circumference of a circle with radius 9 cm related to the circumference of a circle with diameter 9 cm?

b) Draw both circles in part a.

6.3 **9.** The radius of a circular tray is 14.4 cm. What is its area to the nearest square millimetre? 651.44 cm^2

10. The diameter of a circle is 58 m. What is its area to the nearest square centimetre? About 2642.0794 m^2

11. A circular table has radius 56 cm. A tablecloth covers the table. The edge of the cloth is 10 cm below the tabletop. What is the area of the tablecloth? About 13 685 cm^2

12. a) How is the area of a circle with radius 6 cm related to the area of a circle with diameter 6 cm?

b) Draw both circles in part a. Do the diagrams justify your answer in part a? Explain.

252 UNIT 6: Circles

Sample Solutions

3. a) The measure of $\angle QCR$ is twice the measure of $\angle QPR$.

b) Yes, the relationship is true for all circles.

4. a) The circumference is approximately 6 times the radius:

$6 \times 9.5 \text{ mm} \doteq 6 \times 10 \text{ mm}$
$= 60 \text{ mm}$

b) $C = 2\pi r$
$= 2 \times \pi \times 9.5$
$\doteq 59.690$
$\doteq 59.7$

6. Fold the plate in half to find the diameter. Measure the diameter. Multiply the diameter by π to get the circumference.

7. a) Since the circumference is approximately 3 times the diameter, then the diameter is about $\frac{1}{3}$ the circumference. One-third of 15.02 m is about 5 m. So, the diameter is about 5 m.
The radius is $\frac{1}{2}$ the diameter. One-half of 5 m is 2.5 m. So, the radius is about 2.5 m.

b) The diameter is: $d = \frac{C}{\pi}$
$= \frac{15.02}{\pi}$
$\doteq 4.781$

The radius is $\frac{1}{2}$ the diameter.
Divide the diameter by 2.
$r \doteq 2.391$
The diameter is 4.78 m to the nearest centimetre.
The radius is 2.39 m to the nearest centimetre.

8. a) A circle with radius 9 cm has double the circumference of a circle with diameter 9 cm.

b) The circles have diameters that measure 9 cm and 18 cm.

9. Use the formula: $A = \pi r^2$
Substitute: $r = 14.4$
$A = \pi \times 14.4^2$
$\doteq 651.441$

11. The radius of the tablecloth is 56 cm + 10 cm = 66 cm.
Use the formula: $A = \pi r^2$
Substitute: $r = 66$
$A = \pi \times 66^2$
$\doteq 13\,684.7776$

12. a) The area of a circle with radius 6 cm is 4 times the area of a circle with diameter 6 cm.

b) I drew the circles on grid paper, then counted squares and part squares. The diagrams did justify my answers in part a.

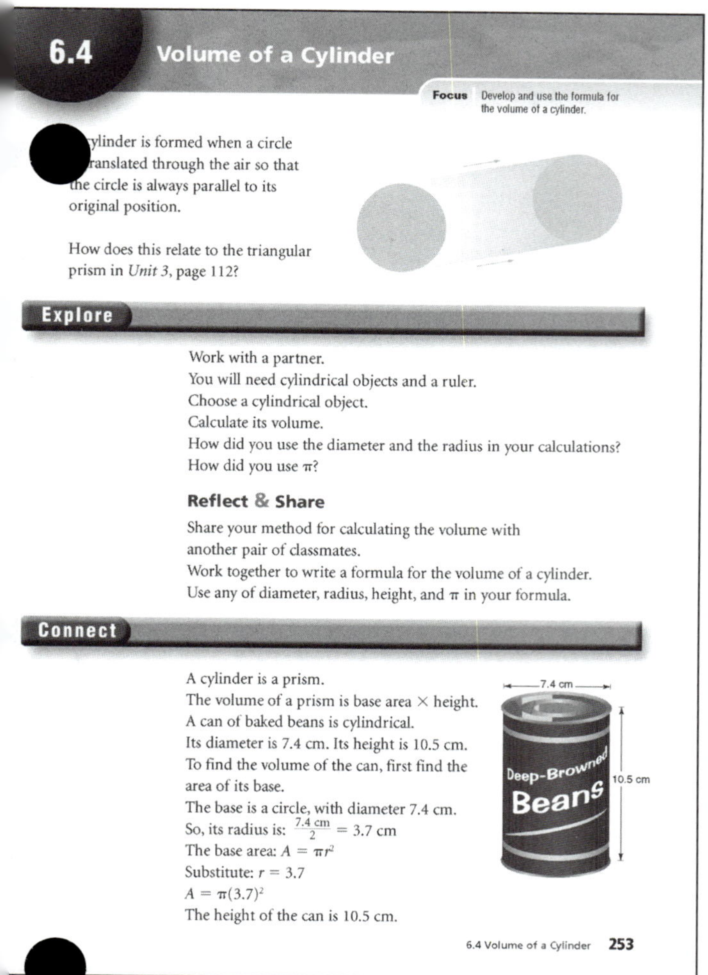

6.4 Volume of a Cylinder

Focus Develop and use the formula for the volume of a cylinder.

ylinder is formed when a circle ranslated through the air so that the circle is always parallel to its original position.

How does this relate to the triangular prism in *Unit 3*, page 112?

Explore

Work with a partner.
You will need cylindrical objects and a ruler.
Choose a cylindrical object.
Calculate its volume.
How did you use the diameter and the radius in your calculations?
How did you use π?

Reflect & Share

Share your method for calculating the volume with another pair of classmates.
Work together to write a formula for the volume of a cylinder.
Use any of diameter, radius, height, and π in your formula.

Connect

A cylinder is a prism.
The volume of a prism is base area × height.
A can of baked beans is cylindrical.
Its diameter is 7.4 cm. Its height is 10.5 cm.
To find the volume of the can, first find the area of its base.
The base is a circle, with diameter 7.4 cm.
So, its radius is: $\frac{7.4 \text{ cm}}{2} = 3.7$ cm
The base area: $A = \pi r^2$
Substitute: $r = 3.7$
$A = \pi(3.7)^2$
The height of the can is 10.5 cm.

6.4 Volume of a Cylinder 253

Volume of a Cylinder

LESSON ORGANIZER (80–100 min)

Curriculum Focus: Develop and use the formula for the volume of a cylinder. (8m33, 8m37, 8m39, 8m62)

Student Materials
- cylindrical objects
- dental floss
- rulers
- calculators

Optional
- Step-by-Step 4 (Master 6.10)
- Extra Practice 4 (Master 6.19)

Vocabulary: parallel, triangular prism, capacity, composite

Assessment: Master 6.2 Ongoing Observations: Circles

Key Math Learnings

1. A cylinder is a prism with circular bases.
2. The volume of a cylinder can be calculated using the same formula as that for a prism; that is, volume = base area × height.

Calculator Skills

A composite number has 2 or more factors, other than 1. Between 1 and 40, the composite numbers are: 4, 6, 8, 9, 10, 12, 14, 15, 16, 18, 20, 21, 22, 24, 25, 26, 27, 28, 30, 32, 33, 34, 35, 36, 38, and 39.

BEFORE Get Started

Have students review prisms from Unit 3. Ask questions, such as:

- How is a cylinder considered to be a prism? (*A prism has two congruent polygonal bases that are joined by rectangular faces. A cylinder has two congruent circular bases that are joined by a curved surface. Each has two bases and the distance between the bases is the height.*)
- How is the volume of a prism related to the volume of a cylinder? (*The volumes of a prism and cylinder are calculated by multiplying the base area by the height.*)

Present *Explore.*

DURING Explore

Ongoing Assessment: Observe and Listen

Instead of using a ruler to measure the radius of a base, students get a more accurate answer by using dental floss to first determine the circumference. They can then use the circumference to calculate the radius of the base, and then the area of the base.

As students work, ask questions, such as:

- How did you find the area of the base? (*I used a ruler to measure the diameter of the base. I divided the diameter by 2 to find the radius. I then used the area formula: $A = \pi r^2$.*)
- How did you determine the height? (*I measured the distance between the bases.*)

REACHING ALL LEARNERS

Alternative Explore

Materials: various prisms and cylinders

Show students examples of various prisms and cylinders. Ask students to examine the similarities and differences between cylinders and prisms. Have students adapt the formula they learned in Unit 3 for volume of a prism to the volume of a cylinder. Ask students if the formula would change if the cylinder were placed on its side.

Common Misconceptions

➤ Students have difficulty substituting numbers for variables in the formula, and evaluating the volume.

How to Help: Have students write the formula as $V = \pi \times r \times r \times h$. After they list the value of each variable, students substitute and multiply. Students may also say the formula in words: volume equals pi times radius times radius times height.

Assignment Guidelines

If your students do not have time to complete all the *Practice* questions on page 255, these questions provide minimum curriculum coverage: 1, 3, 5, *Reflect*

To assess the 4 Achievement Chart categories listed in the curriculum document, have students complete these *Practice* questions:

Knowledge and Understanding: 1
Application: 5
Thinking: 3
Communication: *Reflect*

So, its volume is: V = base area × height
$= \pi(3.7)^2 \times 10.5$

Use a calculator.

Key in: [π] [×] 3.7 [x^2] [×] 10.5 [ENTER] to display 451.588236

$V \doteq 451.6$

The volume of the can of baked beans is about 452 cm³.

We can apply this idea to write a formula for the volume of any cylinder.
Its radius is r.
So, its base area is πr^2.
Its height is h.
So, its volume is: V = base area × height
$= \pi r^2 \times h$
$= \pi r^2 h$

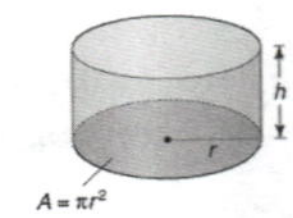

So, a formula for the volume of a cylinder is $V = \pi r^2 h$, where r is the radius of its base, and h its height.

Example

The base of a juice can is a circle with diameter 6.8 cm.
The height of the can is 12.2 cm.
What is the volume of the can?

Solution

The radius of the base is: $\frac{6.8 \text{ cm}}{2} = 3.4$ cm
Use the formula for the volume of a cylinder:
$V = \pi r^2 h$
Substitute: $r = 3.4$ and $h = 12.2$

Use a calculator.

$V = \pi(3.4)^2 \times 12.2$
Key in: [π] [×] 3.4 [x^2] [×] 12.2 [ENTER] to display 443.0650951
$V \doteq 443.07$
The volume of the can is about 443 cm³.

Capacity is measured in litres or millilitres.
Since 1 cm³ = 1 mL, the capacity of the can in the *Example* is about 443 mL.

254 UNIT 6: Circles

AFTER Connect

Ask each group to share its method for calculating the volume of a cylinder and how they developed a formula.

Use students' work or *Connect* to derive the formula for the volume of a cylinder. Review the *Example* to illustrate how to apply the volume formula.

Practice

All questions require a calculator.

Students need to be reminded that rounded answers are not to be used in further calculations. In cases where an answer must be used later, students should store the non-rounded number in the memory of the calculator, or copy it onto paper.

Assessment Focus: Question 5

Students find the radius of the column by dividing the diameter by 2. Students then use the formula for the volume of a cylinder to find the volume of one concrete column. The non-rounded answer to part a is multiplied by 127 to find the total volume of concrete. To find the dimensions of the cube, students find a number which, when multiplied by itself 3 times, gives the answer in part a.

Students who need extra support to complete this Assessment Focus question may benefit from the Step-by-Step 4 (Master 6.10).

Practice

Give each volume to the nearest cubic unit.

1. Calculate the volume of each cylinder.

a)

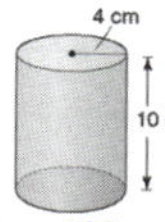

About 503 cm^3

b)

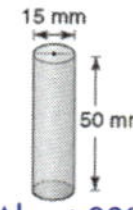

About 8836 mm^3

c)

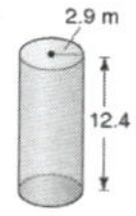

About 328 m^3

Calculator Skills

Find the sum of the composite numbers between 1 and 40.
582

2. A candle mould is cylindrical. Its radius is 5 cm and its height is 20 cm. What is the capacity of the mould? About 1571 cm^3

3. Frozen apple juice comes in cylindrical cans. A can is 12 cm high and has radius 3.5 cm.
   a) What is the capacity of the can? About 461.8 cm^3
   b) Apple juice expands when it freezes. The can is filled to 95% of its volume. What is the volume of apple juice in the can? About 438.7 cm^3

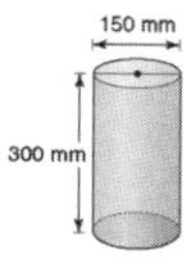

4. A core sample of earth is cylindrical. The length of the core is 300 mm. Its diameter is 150 mm. Calculate the volume of earth in cubic millimetres and cubic centimetres.
   About 5 301 438 mm^3; about 5301 cm^3

5. **Assessment Focus** A concrete column in a parkade is cylindrical. The column is 10 m high and has diameter 3.5 m.
   a) What is the volume of concrete in one column? About 96.2 m^3
   b) There are 127 columns in the parkade. What is the total volume of concrete? About 12 218 m^3
   c) What if the concrete in part a is made into a cube. What would the dimensions of the cube be? About 4.58 m by 4.58 m by 4.58 m

Reflect

How is the volume of a cylinder related to the volume of a triangular prism?
How are these volumes different?

6.4 Volume of a Cylinder 255

Sample Solutions

5. a) The radius of the base is: $\frac{3.5\text{ m}}{2} = 1.75$ m

$V = \pi r^2 h$

Substitute: $r = 1.75$ and $h = 10$

$V = \pi \times 1.75^2 \times 10$

$\doteq 96.2112$

The volume of concrete in one column is about 96.2 m^3.

b) The volume of 127 columns is about: 127×96.2112 m^3

$= 12\ 218.82$ m^3

$\doteq 12\ 218$ m^3

c) The volume of a cube is: $V = s^3$, where s is the edge length of the cube.

I used the calculator to find a number which, when multiplied by itself, was 96.2.

$4.58 \times 4.58 \times 4.58 \doteq 96.072$

The dimensions of the cube would be about:

4.58 m by 4.58 m by 4.58 m.

REFLECT: The volumes of a prism and cylinder are calculated by multiplying the base area by the height. A cylinder is a prism with circular bases. A triangular prism has triangular bases. To find the volume of a cylinder, use the formula $A=\pi r^2$ to find the area of a circular base, then multiply the area by the height. To find the volume of a triangular prism, use the formula $A = \frac{1}{2}bh$ to find the area of a triangular base, then multiply the area by the height.

ASSESSMENT FOR LEARNING

What to Look For

Thinking

✔ Students can use the formula for the volume of a cylinder to solve problems.

Communication

✔ Students can explain how the formulas for the volume of a prism and cylinder are related.

Application

✔ Students can use the formula $V = \pi r^2 h$ to calculate the volume of a cylinder.

What to Do

Extra Support: Students who have difficulty may benefit from using a model cylinder, with base area shaded on one base, radius drawn and labelled on another base, and the height drawn and labelled.
Students can use Step-by-Step 4 (Master 6.10) to complete question 5.

Extra Practice: Students can complete the Additional Activity *Cylinder Comparison* (Master 6.6).
Students can complete Extra Practice 4 (Master 6.19).

Extension: Suppose the number of columns in question 5 was doubled. How would that affect the length of the edges of the cube?

Recording and Reporting
Master 6.2 Ongoing Observations: Circles

Explaining Solutions

LESSON ORGANIZER

Student Materials

- calculators

This section addresses the mathematical processes of "Representing and Communicating." Students write the solution to each problem using words, numbers, pictures, or models. Review these ways of "Representing and Communicating" solutions to problems. Follow this by asking students to share the four steps of the problem-solving model with which they have worked.

Review the problem and its 2 solutions on page 256. You could have volunteer students read the material out loud. Ask students for other ways to solve the problem.

Explaining Solutions

To explain a solution using only words helps to communicate why you did what you did.
When you explain, show the numbers or models you used.

Reading/ Viewing

Here are two solutions to this problem:
Six students wrote a math test.
Their mean mark was 68%.
Another student wrote the test and scored 89%.
What is the mean mark for the 7 students?

Talking/ Listening

Jol explains:
I took the mean mark and multiplied it by 6, the number of students. This gave me the total marks for all of them. Next, I added the mark of the seventh student to get the total marks for everyone. I then divided the total marks by 7, the total number of students who took the test. This gave me the mean mark for the 7 students.

Writing/ Representing

Jol writes:

$$\frac{\text{(original mean)} \times \text{(number of students)} + \text{(7th mark)}}{\text{total number of students}} = \text{new mean}$$

$$\frac{68 \times 6 + 89}{7} = \frac{408 + 89}{7} = \frac{497}{7} = 71$$

The mean mark for the 7 students is 71%.

Talking/ Listening

Veronica explains:
I subtracted the mean from the mark of the 7th student. This told me how many marks above the mean the 7th student had. I shared these marks equally among the 7 students. Then I added the extra marks to the original mean to get the new mean.

Writing/ Representing

Veronica writes:

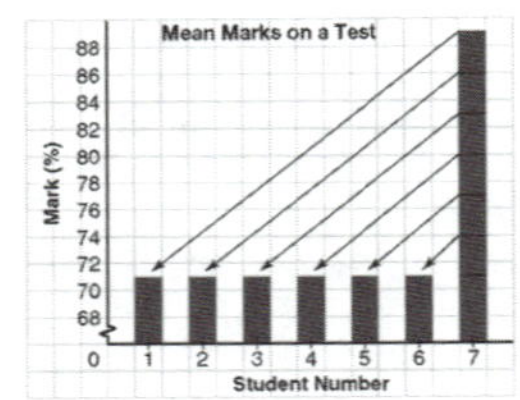

89 − 68 = 21
21 extra marks ÷ 7
= 3 extra marks each
68 + 3 = 71
The mean for 7 students is 71%.

Sample Solutions

1. I created a table of values where one row represents the cut number and the other the height of the pile.

Cut number	0	1	2	3	4	5
Height of pile (mm)	0.01	0.02	0.04	0.08	0.16	0.32

Cut number	6	7	8	9	10
Height of pile (mm)	0.64	1.28	2.56	5.12	10.24

The height of the pile doubles each time the pieces are cut in half and stacked. After the pieces have been cut and stacked 10 times, the height of the pile is 10.24 mm, or 1.024 cm.

2. I begin a table with the information I am given.

Day	1	2	3	4	5	6	7
Attendance	50	78	106	134	162	190	218

I can see that the show's attendance increases by 28 people each day. I continued the pattern until at least 200 people attend the show. This happens on Day 7.

3. There are 10 single triangles. There are 10 triangles made up of two other triangles. There are 5 triangles made up of three other triangles. There are 5 triangles that use a vertex and the side opposite the vertex. There are 5 triangles made up of two triangles and the centre pentagon. This is a total of 35 triangles.

4. I begin a table with the information I am given.

After bounce	Height (m)
0	2.3
1	0.92
2	0.368
3	0.1472
4	0.058 88
5	0.023 552
6	0.009 420 8

a) After each of the first 4 bounces, the heights are 0.92 m, 0.368 m, 0.1472 m, and 0.058 88 m.

b) After six bounces, the ball reaches a height of about 0.01 m, or 1 cm.

Check

Reading and Writing in Math

Write your solution to each problem using words, numbers, pictures, and/or models. Explain your solution using only words.

Strategies

- Make a table.
- Use a model.
- Draw a diagram.
- Solve a simpler problem.
- Work backward.
- Guess and check.
- Make an organized list.
- Use a pattern.
- Draw a graph.
- Use logical reasoning.

1. A large piece of construction paper is 0.01 mm thick. It is cut in half and one piece is placed on the other to make a pile. These two pieces are cut in half and all four pieces are placed in a pile. The process continues. After the pieces have been cut and piled 10 times, what is the height of the pile in centimetres? 10.24 mm, or 1.024 cm
2. A magician opened a show at the mall. On Day 1, 50 people attended the show. On Day 2, there were 78 people. On Day 3, there were 106 people. This pattern continues. When will there be at least 200 people in the audience? On Day 7
3. This pentagon has each vertex connected with every other. How many triangles are in the pentagon? 35

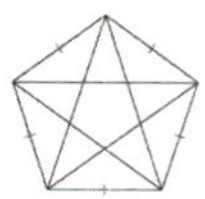

4. A ball is dropped from a height of 2.30 m. After each bounce, it reaches 40% of its height before the bounce.
   a) What height does it reach after each of the first four bounces?
   b) After how many bounces does the ball reach a height of about 1 cm? After 6 bounces

Lake	Area (km^2)
Superior	82 100
Michigan	57 800
Huron	59 600
Erie	25 700
Ontario	18 960

5. The Great Lakes are some of the largest freshwater lakes in the world. The areas are listed in the chart at the left. About what percent of the total area is each lake?
6. How many breaths have you taken in your lifetime?
7. A bag contains ten marbles. One marble is red, two are blue, three are white, and four are black. A marble is picked at random. What is the probability of picking:
   a) red? $\frac{1}{10}$, or 0.1
   b) not white? $\frac{7}{10}$, or 0.7
   c) neither black nor red? $\frac{1}{2}$, or 0.5
   d) either black or white? $\frac{7}{10}$, or 0.7

Reading and Writing in Math: Explaining Solutions 257

5. To calculate what percent of the total area each lake is, the total area must first be found. I do this by adding 82 100 km^2, 57 800 km^2, 59 600 km^2, 25 700 km^2, and 18 960 km^2. The total area of all of the lakes is 244 160 km^2. I divide the area of each lake by the total area, then write the decimal as a percent.

Lake Superior: $\frac{82\ 100}{244\ 160} \doteq 0.336 = 33.6\%$

Lake Michigan: $\frac{57\ 800}{244\ 160} \doteq 0.237 = 23.7\%$

Lake Huron: $\frac{59\ 600}{244\ 160} \doteq 0.244 = 24.4\%$

Lake Erie: $\frac{25\ 700}{244\ 160} \doteq 0.105 = 10.5\%$

Lake Ontario: $\frac{18\ 960}{244\ 160} \doteq 0.078 = 7.8\%$

6. I am 13 years old. I take 9 breaths in one minute.
There are 60 min in 1 h.
There are 24 h in one day.
There are about 365 days in one year.
$9 \times 60 \times 24 \times 365 \times 13 = 61\ 495\ 200$
I have taken about 60 million breaths in my lifetime.

7. There are 10 marbles.

a) The probability of picking a red marble is equal to the fraction of red marbles in the bag. Therefore, the probability is $\frac{1}{10}$, or 0.1.

b) The number of marbles that are not white is 7, so the probability of picking a marble that is not white is $\frac{7}{10}$, or 0.7.

c) The number of marbles that are neither black nor red is 5, so the probability of picking a marble that is neither black nor red is $\frac{5}{10} = \frac{1}{2}$, or 0.5.

d) The number of marbles that are either black or white is 7, so the probability of picking a marble that is either black or white is $\frac{7}{10}$, or 0.7.

Surface Area of a Cylinder

LESSON ORGANIZER 80–100 min

Curriculum Focus: Develop and use the formula for the surface area of a cylinder. (8m33, 8m38, 8m39, 8m62)

Student Materials
- cardboard tubes
- scissors
- sticky tape
- rulers
- calculators

Optional
- Nets for 6.5 *Practice* (Master 6.13)
- Step-by-Step 5 (Master 6.11)
- Extra Practice 5 (Master 6.20)

Assessment: Master 6.2 Ongoing Observations: Circles

Key Math Learnings

1. The surface area of a cylinder is the sum of the areas of its circular bases and its curved surface.
2. The formula for the surface area *SA* of a cylinder with base radius *r* and height *h* is $SA = 2\pi r^2 + 2\pi rh$.

6.5 Surface Area of a Cylinder

Focus Develop and use the formula for the surface area of a cylinder.

Explore

Work with a partner.
You will need a cardboard tube, scissors, and sticky tape.
Cut out two circles to fit the ends of the tube.
Tape a circle to each end of the tube.
You now have a cylinder.
Find a way to calculate the surface area of the cylinder.

Reflect & Share

Share your method for finding the surface area with that of another pair of classmates.
Work together to write a formula for the surface area of any cylinder.

Connect

A cylinder has height 10 cm and radius 4 cm.
To find the surface area of the cylinder, we think of its net.
The bases of the cylinder are 2 congruent circles.
The curved surface of the cylinder is a rectangle.

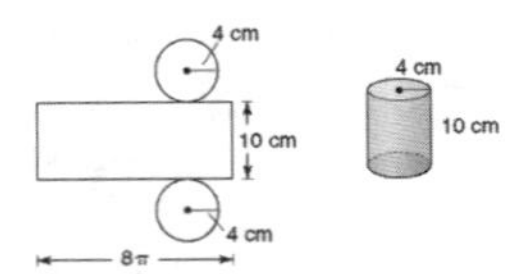

The height of the rectangle is equal to the height of the cylinder.
The base of the rectangle is equal to the circumference of the base of the cylinder, which is: $2\pi(4 \text{ cm}) = 8\pi$ cm
So, the surface area of the cylinder is:

$$\begin{aligned} SA &= \text{area of 2 congruent circles} + \text{area of rectangle} \\ &= 2(\pi(4)^2) + 10 \times 8\pi \\ &= 32\pi + 80\pi \end{aligned}$$

Use a calculator.

BEFORE Get Started

Have students share methods for finding surface area that they have used in the past. Students should understand that to find the surface area of an object, the area of each face should be calculated. The areas should then be added.

Present *Explore*.

DURING Explore

Ongoing Assessment: Observe and Listen

Ask questions, such as:

- What figures are involved in finding the surface area of the cylinder?
  (*A rectangle and two circles*)
- How can a net help to calculate the surface area? (*It helps me to see the dimensions better.*)
- How do the base and height of the rectangle relate to the dimensions of a cylinder?
  (*The base of the rectangle is the circumference of a base of the cylinder and the height of the rectangle is the height of the cylinder.*)

Some students may have difficulty understanding that the curved surface of the cylinder is a rectangle. Have these students make a net for the cylinder. Using a net is especially valuable for visual learners.

Key in: 32 [×] [π] [+] 80 [×] [π] [ENTER] to display 351.8583772
$SA \doteq 351.858$
The surface area of the cylinder is approximately 352 cm^2.

To find a formula for the surface area of any cylinder, we can apply this idea to a cylinder with height h and radius r.
Sketch the cylinder and its net.

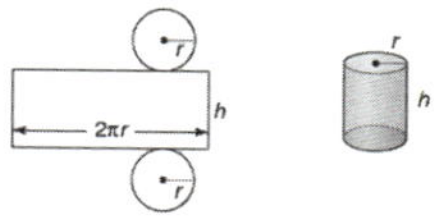

On the net:
The height of the rectangle is h.
The base of the rectangle is the circumference of the base of the cylinder: $2\pi r$
The surface area of the cylinder is:
$SA = 2(\pi r^2) + 2\pi r(h)$
$SA = 2\pi r^2 + 2\pi rh$

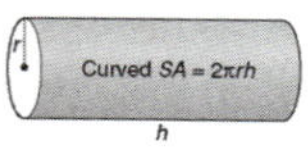

If a cylinder is like a cardboard tube, and has no circular bases, its surface area is the curved surface only: curved $SA = 2\pi rh$

Example

A manufacturer produces a can with height 7 cm and diameter 5 cm. What is the surface area of the can, to the nearest square millimetre?

Solution

The radius of the can:
$r = \frac{5\text{ cm}}{2} = 2.5$ cm
Use the formula for the surface area of a cylinder.
$SA = 2\pi r^2 + 2\pi rh$
Substitute: $r = 2.5$ and $h = 7$
$SA = 2\pi(2.5)^2 + 2\pi(2.5)(7)$

Use a calculator.

Key in: 2 [×] [π] [×] 2.5 [x^2] [+] 2 [×] [π] [×] 2.5 [×] 7 [ENTER]
to display 149.225651
$SA \doteq 149.2257$
The surface area of the can is 149.23 cm^2 to the nearest square millimetre.

6.5 Surface Area of a Cylinder 259

REACHING ALL LEARNERS

Alternative Explore

Materials: can with label, scissors
Students work in pairs to estimate the surface area of the can. (They cut the label and use the area of the resulting rectangle as an estimate of the curved surface area of the can. Students draw around the base of the can, then find the area of the resulting circle.)

Early Finishers

Have students find the radius r and height h of a cardboard tube that has surface area 215 cm^3. Students can find as many values of r and h as possible.

Common Misconceptions

➤ Students evaluate the surface area incorrectly after they substitute for the variables.

How to Help: Remind students of the order of operations: evaluate exponents first, then multiply, then add.

Number Strategies

$\frac{3}{2} + \frac{7}{12} = \frac{18}{12} + \frac{7}{12} = \frac{25}{12}$

$\frac{3}{2} - \frac{7}{12} = \frac{18}{12} - \frac{7}{12} = \frac{11}{12}$

$\frac{3}{2} \times \frac{7}{12} = \frac{21}{24} = \frac{7}{8}$

$\frac{3}{2} \div \frac{7}{12} = \frac{3}{2} \times \frac{12}{7} = \frac{36}{14} = \frac{18}{7}$

AFTER Connect

Have each group of students explain its formula for the surface area of any cylinder. Prompt those who need help.

Use *Connect* or the work of one group of students to derive the algebraic formula for the surface area of a cylinder.

Many cylinders are tubes, so show students how the surface area formula is different for a tube.

Review the *Example*, which illustrates an application of the surface area formula.

Practice

All questions require a calculator.

Assessment Focus: Question 6

To calculate the area of the label, the base and height of the rectangle, that is the label, must first be found. The base of the rectangle is 1 cm (overlap) plus the circumference of the can.

Students who need extra support to complete this Assessment Focus question may benefit from Step-by-Step 5 (Master 6.11).

Assignment Guidelines

If your students do not have time to complete all the *Practice* questions on page 260, these questions provide minimum curriculum coverage: 2, 3, 5, 6, *Reflect*

To assess the 4 Achievement Chart categories listed in the curriculum document, have students complete these *Practice* questions:

Knowledge and Understanding: 2 Application: 6
Thinking: 5 Communication: *Reflect*

Sample Solutions

6. The radius of the can is: $r = \frac{6.6 \text{ cm}}{2} = 3.3$ cm
   The circumference of the can in centimetres is:
   $C = 2\pi r = 2 \times \pi \times 3.3 \doteq 20.7345$
   There is a 1-cm overlap on the label, so add 1 cm to the circumference: 20.7345 cm + 1 cm = 21.7345 cm
   The label is a rectangle with base 21.7345 cm and height 8.8 cm.
   So, the area of label is base × height
   = 21.7345 cm × 8.8 cm
   $\doteq 191.264 \text{ cm}^2$
   The area of the label is about 191 cm^2.

REFLECT: The net of a cylinder is made up of two circles and a rectangle. Each circle represents a base of the cylinder. The area of each circle is πr^2. The rectangle represents the curved surface of the cylinder. The base of the rectangle is the circumference of the cylinder, $2\pi r$. The height of the rectangle is equal to the height of the cylinder, h. So the area of the rectangle is $2\pi r$. Therefore, the total surface area of the cylinder is: $2\pi r^2 + 2\pi rh$.

Practice

Give each area to the nearest square unit, unless stated otherwise.

1. Calculate the curved surface area of each tube.

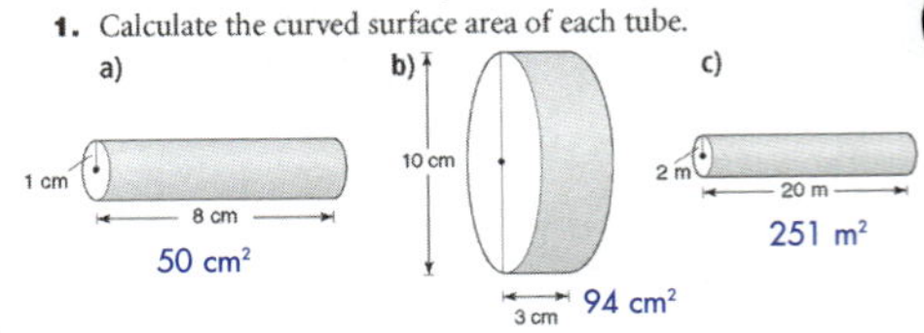

a) 50 cm^2 b) 94 cm^2 c) 251 m^2

Number Strategies

Evaluate.
- $\frac{3}{2} + \frac{7}{12} = \frac{25}{12}$
- $\frac{3}{2} - \frac{7}{12} = \frac{11}{12}$
- $\frac{3}{2} \times \frac{7}{12} = \frac{7}{8}$
- $\frac{3}{2} \div \frac{7}{12} = \frac{18}{7}$

2. Calculate the surface area of each cylinder.

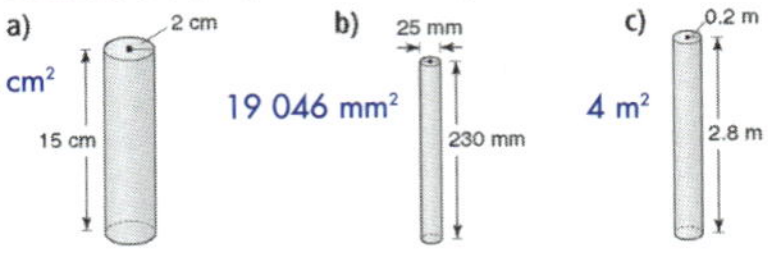

a) 214 cm^2 b) 19 046 mm^2 c) 4 m^2

3. A cylindrical tank has diameter 3.8 m and length 12.7 m. What is the surface area of the tank? 174 m^2

4. Cylindrical paper dryers are used in pulp and paper mills. One dryer has diameter 1.5 m and length 2.5 m. What is the area of the curved surface of this dryer? 12 m^2

5. A wooden toy kit has different painted solids. One solid is a cylinder with diameter 2 cm and height 14 cm.
   a) What is the surface area of the cylinder? 94 cm^2
   b) One can of paint covers 40 m^2. How many cylinders can be painted with one coat of paint? About 4244 cylinders

6. **Assessment Focus** A soup can has diameter 6.6 cm. The label on the can is 8.8 cm high. There is a 1-cm overlap on the label. What is the area of the label? About 191 cm^2

Reflect

How is the formula for the surface area of a cylinder related to the net of the cylinder? Include a diagram in your explanation.

260 UNIT 6: Circles

ASSESSMENT FOR LEARNING

What to Look For	What to Do
Knowledge and Understanding ✔ Students know the formulas for the surface area of a cylinder and a tube. ***Communication*** ✔ Students can explain how the formula for the surface area of a cylinder relates to a net of the cylinder. ***Application*** ✔ Students can use formulas to calculate the surface area of a cylinder and a tube.	***Extra Support:*** Students who have difficulty completing the *Practice* questions could use models of cylinders along with the nets on Master 6.13. Students label each net with its dimensions before they calculate the surface area. Students can use Step-by-Step 5 (Master 6.11) to complete question 6. ***Extra Practice:*** Have students find the surface areas of some of the cylinders in Lesson 6.4. Students can complete Extra Practice 5 (Master 6.20). ***Extension:*** For question 6, consider the tin used to make the can. Suppose there is 1 cm overlap for the curved surface, top, and bottom. How much tin is used to make the can?

Recording and Reporting
Master 6.2 Ongoing Observations: Circles

Unit Review

Review any lesson with etext online tutorial

What Do I Need to Know?

✓ **Measurements in a Circle**

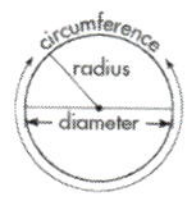

The distance from the centre to the circle is the *radius*.
The distance across the circle, through the centre, is the *diameter*.
The distance around the circle is the *circumference*.

✓ **Circle Formulas**

In a circle, let the radius be r, the diameter d, the circumference C, and the area A.

Then $d = 2r$

$r = \frac{1}{2}d$

$C = \pi d$, or $C = 2\pi r$

$d = \frac{C}{\pi}$

$A = \pi r^2$

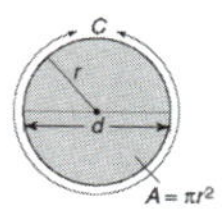

π is an irrational number that is approximately 3.14.

✓ **Cylinder Formulas**

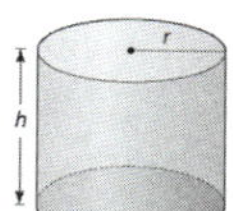

Let the height of a cylinder be h and its radius r.
The volume of a cylinder is: $V = \pi r^2 h$
The curved surface area of a cylinder is: Curved $SA = 2\pi rh$
The total surface area of a cylinder is: $SA = 2\pi r^2 + 2\pi rh$

Unit Review 261

LESSON ORGANIZER

Student Materials
- calculators
- rulers
- compasses
- large circular objects

Assessment: Masters 6.1 Unit Rubric: Circles; 6.4 Unit Summary: Circles

Correlation of Extra Practice questions on page 493:

Lesson	Questions
6.1	1, 2
6.2	1, 2, 3, 4
6.3	4, 5, 6
6.4	7, 8, 9
6.5	10

Remind students that they should not round their answers in intermediate steps. Students should round their *final* answers to the appropriate number of decimal places. Rounding at the *end* ensures that answers are more precise.

Sample Solutions

1. **a)** The diameter of the circle is twice the length of the line segment formed by joining the two points on the piece of paper.
   b) The radius is one-half the length of the line segment formed by joining the two points on the piece of paper.
2. Fold the circle in half twice. The radius is the distance from the intersection point (centre) of the folds to the circle. The diameter is double this length.
3. $C = \pi d$
   Substitute $d = 43$ mm
   $C = \pi \times 43$ mm
   $\doteq 135.0885$ mm
   The circumference to the nearest millimetre is 135 mm.
   To convert millimetres to centimetres, divide by 10.
   The circumference to the nearest centimetre is 14 cm.
4. $r = \frac{C}{2\pi}$
   Substitute $C = 219.91$.
   $r = \frac{219.91}{2\pi}$
   $\doteq 34.9998$
   The radius of the crater is about 35 m.
   To convert metres to centimetres, multiply by 100. The radius of the crater is about 35 × 100 cm = 3500 cm.
5. $A = \pi r^2$
   Substitute $r = 12$ m
   $A = \pi \times (12\text{ m})^2$
   $\doteq 452.3893\text{ m}^2$
   To convert square metres to square centimetres, multiply by $(100)^2$, or 10 000.
   The area is about 4 523 893 cm^2.
6. $r = \frac{d}{2}$
   Since $d = 28.5$ cm, $r = \frac{28.5\text{ cm}}{2}$, or 14.25 cm
   $A = \pi r^2$
   $A = \pi(14.25\text{ cm})^2$
   $\doteq 637.9396\text{ cm}^2$
   To convert square centimetres to square millimetres, multiply by $(10)^2$, or 100.
   The area of the mirror is about 63 794 mm^2.
7. **a)** Since $C = 2\pi r$, when the radius is halved, the circumference is also halved.
   b) To find the area, the radius is squared. If the radius is halved, the area is $(\frac{1}{2})^2$, or $\frac{1}{4}$ of what it was. So, the new area is $\frac{1}{4}$ of the original area.
8. **a)** The area is a circle; $A = \pi r^2$.
   The radius is equal to the length of the rope, 8 m.
   $A = \pi(8)^2$
   $\doteq 201.0619\text{ m}^2$

To the nearest square metre, the goat can graze on about 201 m^2 of the field.

b) $C = 2\pi r$; $r = 8$ m;
$C = 2\pi(8 \text{ m})$
$\doteq 50.2655$ m
To the nearest metre, the circumference is about 50 m.

9. a) To calculate the volume, find the area of the base and multiply it by the height.
$A = \pi r^2$; $r = \frac{d}{2}$; $d = 7.2$ cm; $r = \frac{7.2 \text{ cm}}{2}$, or 3.6 cm
$A = \pi r^2$
$= \pi(3.6)^2$
$\doteq 40.7150$
V = area of base × height
$= 40.7150 \times 10.5$
$= 427.5075 \text{ cm}^3$
Since 1 mL = 1 cm^3, the volume of the can is about 428 mL.

b) The can is likely not filled to the top.

10. Since the base of each column will not be painted, use the formula: $SA = \pi r^2 + 2\pi rh$
Shortest column: $SA = \pi \times 0.6^2 + 2 \times \pi \times 0.6 \times 3$
$\doteq 12.4407 \text{ m}^2$
Middle column: $SA = \pi \times 0.6^2 + 2 \times \pi \times 0.6 \times 4$
$\doteq 16.2106 \text{ m}^2$
Tallest column: $SA = \pi \times 0.6^2 + 2 \times \pi \times 0.6 \times 5$
$\doteq 19.9805 \text{ m}^2$
The total area is about: $12.4407 \text{ m}^2 + 16.2106 \text{ m}^2 + 19.9805 \text{ m}^2 = 48.6318 \text{ m}^2$
So, the total area to be painted is about 49 m^2.

What Should I Be Able to Do?

For extra practice, go to page 493.

LESSON

6.1 **1. a)** Mark two points on a piece of paper. Join the points. Use this line segment as the radius of a circle. Draw the circle. What is its diameter?
b) Mark two points. Join the points. Use this line segment as the diameter of a circle. Draw the circle. What is its radius?

2. Trace a large circular object. Explain how to find the radius and diameter of the circle you have drawn.

6.2 **3.** The diameter of a circle is 43 mm. What is its circumference? Give the answer to the nearest millimetre and to the nearest centimetre. 135 mm; 14 cm

4. The circumference of a large crater is 219.91 m. What is the radius of the crater to the nearest centimetre? About 3500 cm

6.3 **5.** The radius of a circle is 12 m. What is its area? Give the answer to the nearest square centimetre. About 4 523 893 cm^2

6. The diameter of a circular mirror is 28.5 cm. What is the area of the mirror? Give the answer to the nearest square millimetre. About 63 794 mm^2

6.2 6.3 **7.** Choose a radius. Draw a circle. What if you halve the radius.
a) What happens to the circumference?
b) What happens to the area? Explain.

8. A goat is tied to an 8-m rope in a field.
a) What area of the field can the goat graze? About 201 m^2
b) What is the circumference of the area in part a? About 50 m

6.4 **9.** A can of creamed corn has a label that indicates its capacity is 398 mL. The height of the can is 10.5 cm. The diameter of the can is 7.2 cm.
a) Calculate the capacity of the can in millilitres. About 428 mL
b) Give a reason why the answer in part a is different from the capacity on the label.

6.5 **10.** A piece of sculpture comprises 3 cylindrical columns. Each column has diameter 1.2 m. The heights of the columns are 3 m, 4 m, and 5 m. The surfaces of the cylinders are to be painted. Calculate the area to be painted. (The base each column sits on will *not* be painted.) About 49 m^2

262 UNIT 6: Circles

ASSESSMENT FOR LEARNING

What to Look For

Knowledge and Understanding

✔ **Question 1:** Student understands the relationship between the radius and diameter of a circle.

Thinking

✔ **Question 10:** Student can solve problems related to surface areas of cylinders.

Communication

✔ **Question 7:** Student can use mathematical language to describe the relationship between radius and circumference, and radius and area.

Application

✔ **Question 9:** Student can use the formula to find the volume of a can and relate volume to capacity and contents.

Recording and Reporting
Master 6.1 Unit Rubric: Circles
Master 6.4 Unit Summary: Circles

Practice Test

1. Draw a circle. Measure its radius.
Calculate its diameter, circumference, and area.

2. Calculate the circumference and area of each circle.
Give each answer to the nearest unit or square unit.

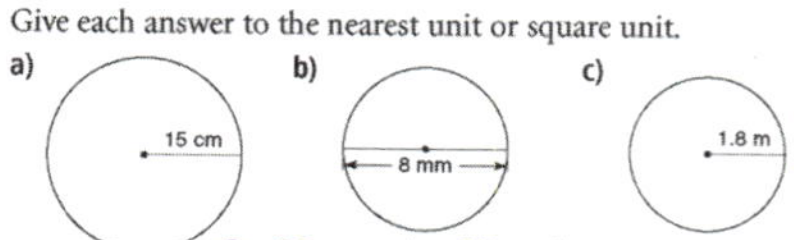

a) $C = 94$ cm, $A = 707$ cm^2
b) $C = 25$ mm; $A = 50$ mm^2
c) $C = 11$ m, $A = 10$ m^2

3. Arleen has 50 m of plastic edging.
She uses the edging to enclose a circular garden.
   a) What is the circumference of the garden? Explain. 50 m
   b) What is the radius of the garden? About 8 m
   c) What is the area of the garden? About 199 m^2
   d) Arleen fills the garden with topsoil to a depth of 15 cm.
   What is the volume of topsoil in the garden? About 30 m^3

4. What if you are asked to draw a circle with circumference 100 cm.
   a) You have a compass. Explain why it is not possible for you to draw a circle with this circumference.
   b) Draw a circle whose circumference is as close to 100 cm as possible.
      i) What is this circumference?
      ii) What is the radius of this circle?

5. Which has the greater volume? The paper rolled into a cylinder widthwise
   - a piece of paper rolled into a cylinder lengthwise, or
   - the same piece of paper rolled into a cylinder widthwise

   Justify your answer. Include diagrams in your answer.

Practice Test 263

LESSON ORGANIZER

Student Materials
- calculators
- rulers
- compasses

Assessment: Masters 6.1 Unit Rubric: Circles; 6.4 Unit Summary: Circles

To assess the 4 Achievement Chart categories listed in the curriculum document, use these test questions:
Knowledge and Understanding: 1
Application: 3
Communication: 4
Thinking: 5

Sample Solutions

1.

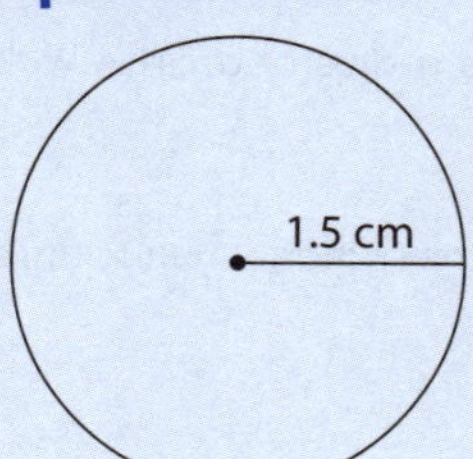

The radius of my circle is 1.5 cm.
The circumference is $C = \pi d$, or about 9 cm.
The area is: $A = \pi r^2$, or about 7cm^2.

4.a) The formula for circumference uses π — which is an irrational number. This irrational number is a decimal that never repeats and never terminates. So, when I multiply π by the diameter (which is a whole number), the circumference is also an irrational number, so it will never be exactly 100 cm.

b) i) ii) It is possible to get close to a circumference of 100. Begin by finding the radius of a circle with circumference 100 cm. This radius is about 15.915 494 cm. Since I would be using a ruler to draw the radius and the most exact value on my ruler is to the nearest 0.5 of a mm, the closest radius I could draw to the one calculated is 15.9 cm. With this radius, the circumference of the circle would be about 99.9 cm.

5. The greater volume occurs when the paper is rolled widthwise. I used a sheet of paper 21.6 cm by 28 cm. Rolling the paper lengthwise, the circumference of one circular base was 21.6 cm. Its radius was about 3.44 cm. The volume was about 1039.5746 cm^3. Rolling the paper widthwise, the circumference of one circular base was 28 cm. Its radius was about 4.46 cm. The volume was about 1347.5967 cm^3. I did not use the rounded values of the radii in my volume calculations.

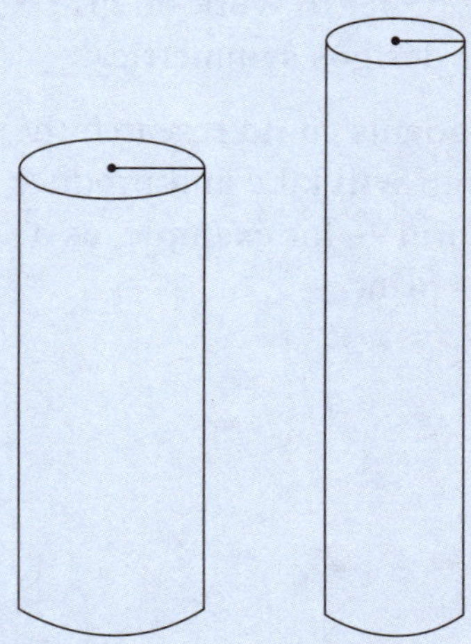

Lengthwise Widthwise

Circle Designs

LESSON ORGANIZER 80–100 min

Student Grouping: 2 or 3

Student Materials	*Optional*
■ rulers	■ 1-cm grid paper (PM 20)
■ compasses	■ 0.5-cm grid paper (PM 14)
■ coloured pencils	
■ calculators	

Assessment: Masters 6.3 Performance Assessment Rubric: Circle Designs; 6.4 Unit Summary: Circles

Sample Response

(Sample Response continues below, right.)

Unit Problem Circle Designs

Have you noticed how many designs use circles?

You will use circles to create a design.
Your design *must* include:

- a circle with area approximately 80 cm^2
- a circle with circumference approximately 50 cm

Your design may include:

- lines
- curves
- more than the two required circles

Here are some questions to consider:

- Will I use colour?
- What is the scale of my design?
- Which tools will I use?

Your design is to be in one of these forms:

- logo for a company
- wallpaper
- sign for a shop
- poster for an art show
- quilt sample
- sundial
- greetings card
- another idea (approved by your teacher)

Your finished project must include:

- the design
- any calculations you made
- a written description of the design and how you drew it

264 UNIT 6: Circles

Have one student read the *Check List* aloud. Remind students that they should use the *Check List* to assess their work before handing it in. You may also wish to provide students with copies of Master 6.3 Performance Assessment Rubric: Circle Designs so they will know how their work will be assessed.

Some students may prefer to work on grid paper to make their designs symmetrical.

As an extension, students could research the form that their design will take and produce the design in that form — for example, as a quilt sample or lino print.

(Sample Response continued)

I used guess and check to find the radius of a circle with area 80 cm^2.
I know that $A = \pi r^2$.
π is about 3, so I looked for a number that, when squared and multiplied by 3, equals 80.

I tried 3: $\pi \times 3^2 \doteq 27$
I tried 4: $\pi \times 4^2 \doteq 48$
I tried 5: $\pi \times 5^2 \doteq 75$
I tried 6: $\pi \times 6^2 \doteq 108$
The closest is $r = 5$.
I checked $A = \pi r^2 = \pi \times 25 \doteq 78.5$.
r is about 5 cm.
Calculations for a circle with circumference approximately 50 cm:
I used $d = \frac{C}{\pi}$.
$d = \frac{50}{\pi}$
$d \doteq 15.915\ 49$
$r = \frac{d}{2}$
So, $r = \frac{15.915\ 49}{2}$
$\doteq 7.96$
r is about 8 cm.

Check List

Your work should show:

- ✓ how you estimated and calculated area and circumference
- ✓ correct measurements and calculations
- ✓ a diagram of your design
- ✓ a clear explanation of your design, with correct use of mathematical language

Reflect on the Unit

How are circles and cylinders related?
Write a paragraph to explain what you learned about circles and cylinders.

Unit Problem: Circle Designs 265

I wanted to make a quilt square so I started with a square that would fit my largest circle, the one with an area of approximately 80 cm^2. I drew the circle. I then drew four circles, each with circumference approximately 50 cm. For balance, I put a circle at the centre, then drew the two diagonals of the square. I like the sun and the moon so I included these on my designs. I finished by choosing materials in a variety of colours and patterns to make my quilt square.

REFLECT ON THE UNIT: The parallel bases of a cylinder are circles. Therefore, the surface area and volume formulas for a cylinder include the area of a circle.

In this unit, I developed the formula for the circumference of a circle as $C = 2\pi r$ or $C = \pi d$. I also developed the formula for the area of a circle as $A = \pi r^2$. I found out that regardless of the dimension of a circle that I was given, the radius was always related to the circumference and area. I learned that a cylinder is made of two parallel circular bases and a rectangle. This understanding helped me to find the formula for the surface area of a cylinder to be $SA = 2\pi r^2 + 2\pi rh$. I also realized that a cylinder is a kind of prism, so using what I learned about the volumes of prisms, I developed a formula for the volume of a cylinder as $V = \pi r^2 h$.

ASSESSMENT FOR LEARNING

What to Look For	What to Do
Knowledge and Understanding ✔ Students' calculations show an understanding of the relationships among area, radius, and circumference. ***Communication*** ✔ Students write clear and complete descriptions of their design. ***Application*** ✔ Students are able to take their understanding of circumference and area, and create a design to certain specifications.	***Extra Support:*** Make the problem accessible by sharing a design that you have created. Encourage students to make a rough sketch of their design including the two required circles. The calculations should be done to find the radii of the two required circles. Students should draw the two required circles first, then finish the design around these circles.

Recording and Reporting

Master 6.3 Performance Assessment Rubric: Circle Designs
Master 6.4 Unit Summary: Circles

Evaluating Student Learning: Preparing to Report: Unit 6 Circles

This unit provides an opportunity to report on the **Measurement** and **Patterning and Algebra** strands.

Master 6.4: Unit Summary: Circles provides a comprehensive format for recording and summarizing evidence collected.

Here is an example of a completed summary chart for this Unit:

Strand: *Measurement/ Patterning and Algebra*	**Knowledge and Understanding**	**Thinking**	**Communication**	**Application**	***Overall***
Ongoing Observations	3	4	3	4	3/4
Work samples or portfolios; conferences	3	3	4	3	3
Unit Review	4	3	3	3	3
Unit Test	3	3	3	3	3
Unit Problem Circle Designs	3	3	4	4	3/4
Achievement Level for reporting					3

Recording	How to Report
Ongoing Observations	Use *Master 6.2 Ongoing Observations: Circles* to determine the most consistent level achieved in each category. Enter it in the chart. Choose to summarize by achievement category, or simply to enter an overall level. Observations from late in the unit should be most heavily weighted.
Portfolios or collections of work samples; conferences or interviews	Use *Master 6.1 Unit Rubric: Circles* to guide evaluation of collections of work and information gathered in conferences. Teachers may choose to focus particular attention on the Assessment Focus questions. Work from late in the unit should be most heavily weighted.
Unit Review	*Master 6.1 Unit Rubric: Circles* may be helpful in determining levels of achievement. #3, 4, 5, and 6 provide evidence of Knowledge and Understanding; #2, 8, and 9 provide evidence of Application; #7 and 10 provide evidence of Thinking; all questions provide evidence of Communication.
Unit Test	*Master 6.1 Unit Rubric: Circles* may be helpful in determining levels of achievement. #1 and 2 provide evidence of Knowledge and Understanding; #4 provides evidence of Application; #6 provides evidence of Thinking; all questions provide evidence of Communication.
Unit Problem	Use *Master 6.3 Performance Assessment Rubric: Circle Designs*. The *Unit Problem* offers a snapshot of students' achievement. In particular, it shows their ability to synthesize and apply what they have learned.
Student Self-Assessment	Note students' perceptions of their own progress. This may take the form of an oral or written comment, or a self-rating.
Comments	Analyse the pattern of achievement to identify strengths and needs. In some cases, specific actions may need to be planned to support the learner.

Learning Skills	**Ongoing Records**
PM 4: Learning Skills Check List Use to record and report throughout a reporting period, rather than for each unit and/or strand.	*PM 10: Summary Class Records: Strands* *PM 11: Summary Class Records: Achievement Categories* *PM 12: Summary Record: Individual* Use to record and report evaluations of student achievement over several clusters, a reporting period, or a school year. These can also be used in place of the Unit Summary.

Name ____________________ Date ____________________

Master 6.1

Unit Rubric: Circles

	Level 1	Level 2	Level 3	Level 4
Knowledge and Understanding • Shows understanding by explaining and demonstrating: – strategies for estimating, measuring, and calculating radius, circumference, and diameter (includes developing formulas) – relationships among radius, diameter, and circumference – development of formulas for surface area and volume of a cylinder	shows limited understanding in demonstrating and explaining: – strategies for estimating, measuring, and calculating radius, circumference, and diameter – relationships among radius, diameter, and circumference – development of formulas for surface area and volume of a cylinder	shows some understanding in demonstrating and explaining: – strategies for estimating, measuring, and calculating radius, circumference, and diameter – relationships among radius, diameter, and circumference – development of formulas for surface area and volume of a cylinder	shows considerable understanding in demonstrating and explaining: – strategies for estimating, measuring, and calculating radius, circumference, and diameter – relationships among radius, diameter, and circumference – development of formulas for surface area and volume of a cylinder	shows thorough understanding in demonstrating and explaining: – strategies for estimating, measuring, and calculating radius, circumference, and diameter – relationships among radius, diameter, and circumference – development of formulas for surface area and volume of a cylinder
Thinking • Plans and carries out appropriate strategies to solve problems that involve circumference and area of a circle; surface area and volume of a cylinder	uses appropriate strategies to solve problems that involve circumference and area of a circle, and surface area and volume of a cylinder with limited effectiveness	uses appropriate strategies to solve problems that involve circumference and area of a circle, and surface area and volume of a cylinder with some effectiveness	uses appropriate strategies to solve problems that involve circumference and area of a circle, and surface area and volume of a cylinder with considerable effectiveness	uses appropriate strategies to solve problems that involve circumference and area of a circle, and surface area and volume of a cylinder with a high degree of effectiveness
Communication • Explains concepts, procedures, and reasoning clearly, using appropriate terminology	limited effectiveness; unable to explain reasoning and procedures clearly; rarely uses appropriate terms	some effectiveness; explains reasoning and procedures with some clarity and some appropriate terms	considerable effectiveness; explains reasoning and procedures clearly, using appropriate terms	high degree of effectiveness; explains reasoning and procedures clearly and precisely, using the most appropriate terms
• Presents work, including diagrams, drawings, and calculations clearly, using appropriate conventions (for example, symbols and labels)	presents diagrams, drawings, and calculations with limited clarity and use of appropriate conventions	presents diagrams, drawings, and calculations with some clarity and use of conventions	presents diagrams, drawings, and calculations with considerable clarity and use of conventions	presents diagrams, drawings, and calculations with a high degree of clarity and use of appropriate conventions
Application • Applies measurement skills appropriately to: – draw a circle, given radius, area, or circumference – use formulas to calculate area and circumference of a circle; and volume and surface area of a cylinder	limited effectiveness; major errors or omissions in: – drawing a circle, given radius, area, or circumference – calculating area and circumference of a circle; and volume and surface area of a cylinder	some effectiveness; somewhat accurate with several minor errors or omissions in: – drawing a circle, given radius, area, or circumference – calculating area and circumference of a circle; and volume and surface area of a cylinder	considerable effectiveness; generally accurate with few minor errors or omissions in: – drawing a circle, given radius, area, or circumference – calculating area and circumference of a circle; and volume and surface area of a cylinder	high degree of effectiveness; accurate and precise with no errors in: – drawing a circle, given radius area, or circumference – calculating area and circumference of a circle; and volume and surface area of a cylinder

Name ____________________ Date ______________

Master 6.2

Ongoing Observations: Circles

The behaviours described under each heading are examples; they are not intended to be an exhaustive list of all that might be observed. More detailed descriptions are provided in each lesson under *Assessment for Learning*.

STUDENT ACHIEVEMENT: Circles				
Student	**Knowledge and Understanding** • Demonstrates and explains: – strategies for estimating, measuring, and calculating area and volume – relationships among radius, diameter, circumference, area, and volume	**Thinking** • Uses appropriate strategies to solve problems that involve estimating and calculating area and volume	**Communication** • Explains reasoning and procedures clearly, using appropriate terms • Presents diagrams, drawings, and calculations clearly, including symbols and labels	**Application** • Accurately: – measures radius and diameter of a circle – calculates area and circumference of a circle; volume and surface area of a cylinder

Level 1 – very limited; Level 2 – somewhat or limited; Level 3 – satisfactory; Level 4 – thorough

Name ____________________ Date ______________

Master 6.3

Performance Assessment Rubric: Circle Designs

	Level 1	Level 2	Level 3	Level 4
Knowledge and Understanding • Explanations show understanding of: – strategies for estimating and calculating area and circumference – relationships among area, radius, and circumference	explanations show limited understanding of: – strategies for estimating and calculating area and circumference – relationships among area, radius, and circumference	explanations show some understanding of: – strategies for estimating and calculating area and circumference – relationships among area, radius, and circumference	explanations show considerable understanding of: – strategies for estimating and calculating area and circumference – relationships among area, radius, and circumference	explanations show thorough understanding of: – strategies for estimating and calculating area and circumference – relationships among area, radius, and circumference
Thinking • Uses appropriate strategies (for example, estimating, calculating, sketching, measuring) to solve the problems	uses a few simple strategies with limited success	uses some appropriate strategies with partial success	uses appropriate strategies with considerable success	uses appropriate, often innovative, strategies with a high degree of success
Communication • Communicates procedures, solutions, and reasoning clearly, using appropriate measurement language and conventions	limited effectiveness; does not communicate clearly	some effectiveness; communicates with some clarity	considerable effectiveness; communicates clearly	a high degree of effectiveness; communicates clearly and precisely
Application • Accurately applies measurement skills to: – calculate area and circumference – draw circles, given area or circumference	limited effectiveness; major errors or omissions in: – calculating area and circumference – drawing circles with required area and circumference	some effectiveness; somewhat accurate in: – calculating area and circumference – drawing circles with required area and circumference	considerable effectiveness; generally accurate in: – calculating area and circumference – drawing circles with required area and circumference	high degree of effectiveness; accurate and precise in: – calculating area and circumference – drawing circles with required area and circumference

Name ____________________ Date ______________

Master 6.4

Unit Summary: Circles

Review assessment records to determine the most consistent achievement levels for the assessments conducted. Some cells may be blank. *Overall* achievement levels may be recorded in each row, rather than identifying levels for each achievement category.

	Most Consistent Level of Achievement*				
Strand: *Measurement/Patterning and Algebra*	**Knowledge and Understanding**	**Thinking**	**Communication**	**Application**	***Overall***
Ongoing Observations					
Work samples or portfolios; conferences					
Unit Review					
Unit Test					
Unit Problem Circle Designs					
Achievement Level for reporting					

*Use Ontario Achievement Levels 1, 2, 3, 4

Self-Assessment:

Comments: (Strengths, Needs, Next Steps)

Name ____________________ Date ______________

Master 6.5

Additional Activity 1: Circle Mania

Play with a partner.

Materials: rulers, compasses, calculators

How to Play:

1. Player A marks a point on a piece of paper.
   Player A says a radius; for example, 6 cm.
   Player B draws a circle with the marked point as the centre of the circle, and with radius 6 cm.
   One point is scored for a correct drawing.
   Players switch roles. Player B marks a point and says a radius.

2. In round 2, Player A marks 2 points on a piece of paper.
   He labels one point the centre and says that the other point is on the circle.
   Player B draws the circle.
   One point is scored for a correct drawing.
   Players switch roles.

3. Players repeat *Steps 1* and *2*, continuing to alternate between the two types of constructions.
   The player with more points after 5 rounds wins.

Take It Further: Play the game again. This time, calculate the circumference of each circle you draw. One point is awarded for a correct calculation.

Name ____________________ Date ________________

Master 6.6

Additional Activity 2: Cylinder Comparison

Work on your own.

Materials: a variety of cylindrical objects, ruler, calculator

Instructions:

1. Choose a cylindrical object.
Estimate which is greater: circumference or height
Measure the diameter of the object.
Use the diameter to calculate the circumference of the cylinder.
Measure the height of the cylinder.
Record your measures in the table below.

2. Repeat *Step 1* for at least 5 different cylindrical objects.
Each time, record your measures in the table.

3. Compare the circumference and height of each cylinder.
Which is the greater measure?
Write about your findings.

Cylindrical Object	Circumference	Height
1		
2		
3		
4		
5		
6		

Take It Further: Calculate the volume of each cylindrical object you used.

Name ____________________ Date ________________

Master 6.7

Step-by-Step 1

Lesson 6.1, Question 9

You will need a copy of Master 6.12, a ruler, and coloured pencils.

Step 1 Use a coloured pencil to outline one circle in the logo.

Step 2 Use the ruler to find the diameter of the circle you outlined.
To do this, hold the ruler across the circle and move it around until you find the greatest distance; this is the diameter.
Record the distance to the nearest millimetre in the table below.

Step 3 Divide the diameter you found in *Step 2* by 2 to find the radius.

Step 4 Record the radius to the nearest millimetre in the table.

Step 5 Repeat *Step 1* to *Step 4* for each different circle in the logo.

Pencil Colour	Diameter (cm)	Radius (cm)

Name ____________________ Date ________________

Master 6.8

Step-by-Step 2

Lesson 6.2, Question 7

Step 1 Look at this picture.

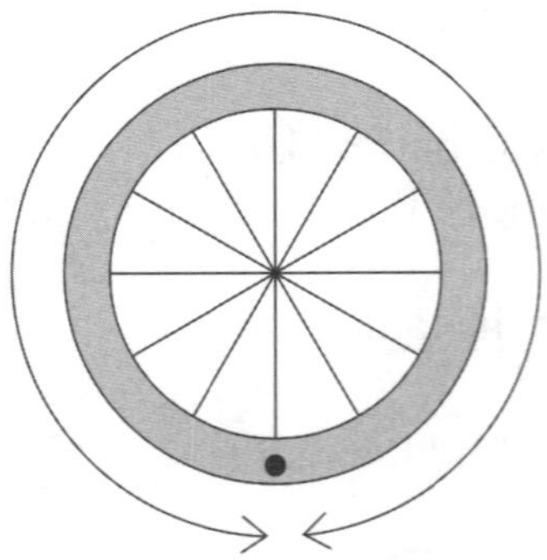

What do we call the distance the stone has to travel? ________________________

Step 2 What is the formula for calculating the distance around the circle? ____________

Step 3 The radius is 46 cm.
Use the formula in *Step 2* to calculate the distance around. ____________________

Step 4 Convert 1 km to centimetres. ____

Step 5 To find how many times the stone hits the ground when the bicycle travels 1 km, divide your answer in *Step 4* by your answer in *Step 3*. ______________________

Name ____________________ Date ______________

Master 6.9

Step-by-Step 3

Lesson 6.3, Question 4

Step 1 Assume the circle below has radius 5 cm.

What is its diameter? ______________________________

Step 2 What is the length of one side of the outside square? ______________

Calculate the area of the outside square. ______________________

Step 3 Measure the side length of the inside square. ______________________

Calculate the area of the inside square. ______________________

Step 4 Use the areas of the squares to estimate the area of the circle. ______________

Step 5 Use the formula $A = \pi r^2$ to calculate the area of the circle. ______________

Step 6 How does your estimate from *Step 4* compare with the area calculated in *Step 5*?

____

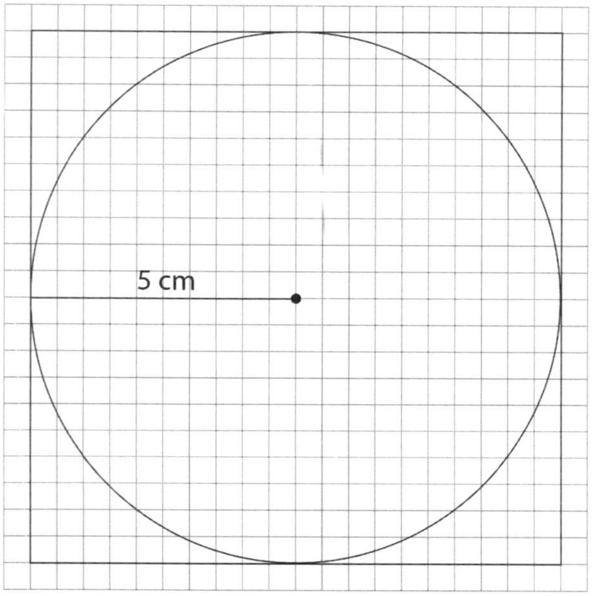

Name ______________________ Date ________________

Master 6.10

Step-by-Step 4

Lesson 6.4, Question 5

Step 1 The diameter of a cylinder is 3.5 m. What is its radius? ________________________

Step 2 Use $A = \pi r^2$ to find the area of the base of the cylinder. ________________________

Step 3 Multiply the area of the base by the height, 10 m, to calculate the volume of one column.

____

Step 4 Multiply your answer in *Step 3* by 127 to find the volume of 127 columns. __________

Step 5 The formula for the volume of a cube is $V = s^3$, where s represents the length of one edge of the cube.
Use your answer in *Step 4* as the total volume.
Use guess and check to find s.

Step 6 What are the dimensions of the cube? ______________________________________

Name ____________________ Date ______________

Master 6.11

Step-by-Step 5

Lesson 6.5, Question 6

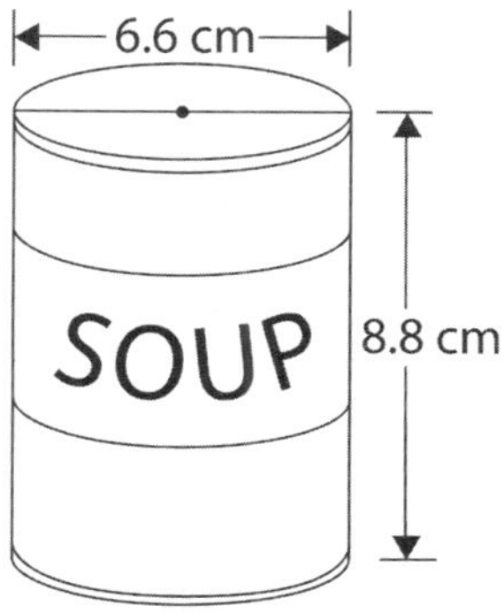

The label is a rectangle. The height of the label is 8.8 cm.
The length of the label is equal to the circumference of the can, plus 1 cm.

Step 1 Use $C = \pi d$ to calculate the circumference of the can. ______________________

Step 2 Add 1 cm to your answer in *Step 1*. ______________________

Step 3 Multiply your answer in *Step 2* by the height, 8.8 cm, to calculate the area of the label. ______________________

Step 4 What is the area of the label? ______________

Name ____________________ Date ________________

Master 6.12

Logo for 6.1 *Practice* Question 9

Name ______________________ Date ________________

Master 6.13

Nets for 6.5 *Practice*

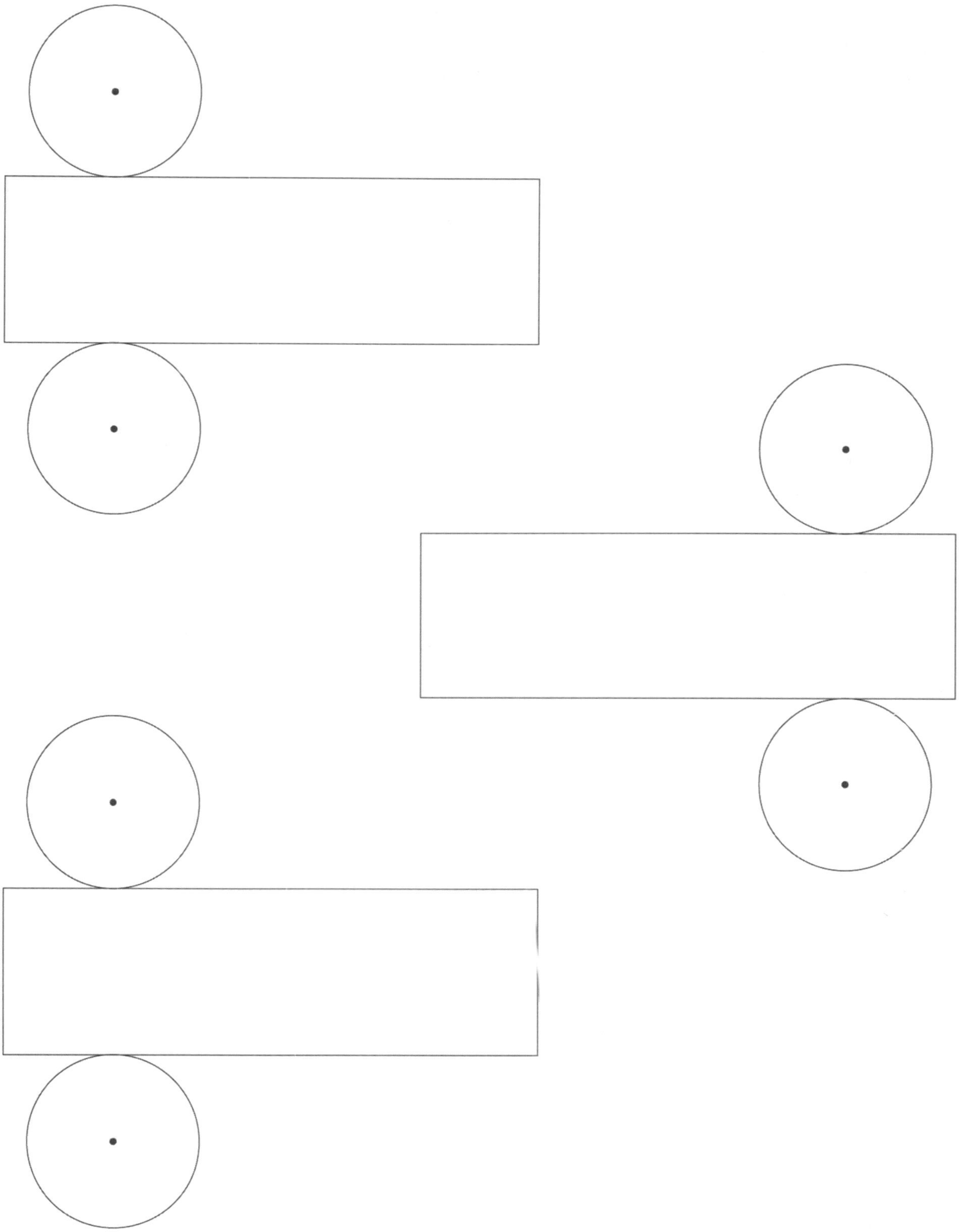

Name ____________________ Date ______________

Master 6.14a

Unit Test: Unit 6
Circles

1. For each circle, write the required measure.

a) Write the diameter.

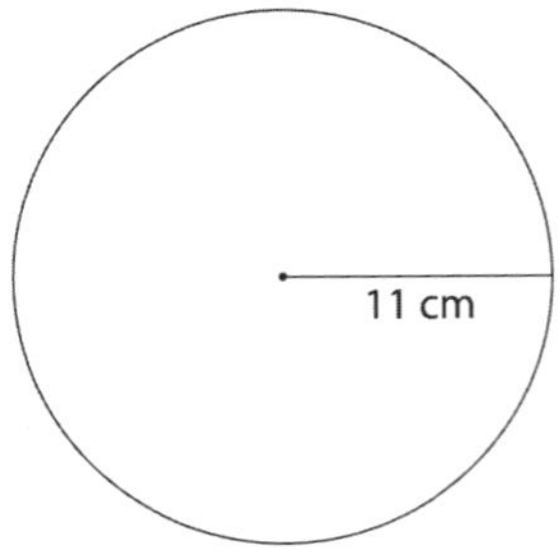

b) Write the radius.

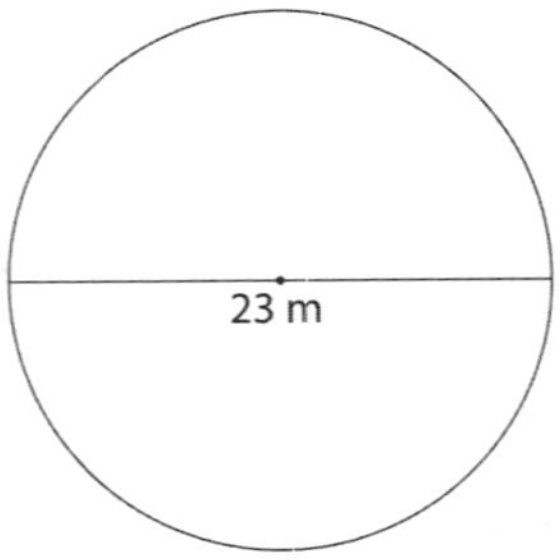

c) Write the radius.

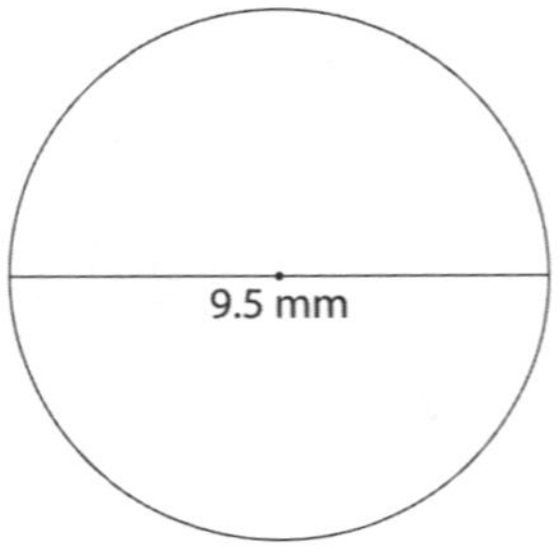

2. Find the circumference and area of each circle in question 1.

Name ________________ Date ______________

Master 6.14b **Unit Test continued**

3. Calculate the volume and surface area of each cylinder shown below.

a)

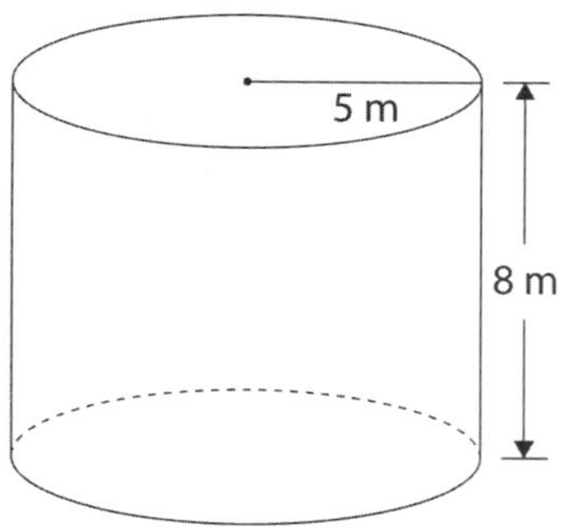

b)

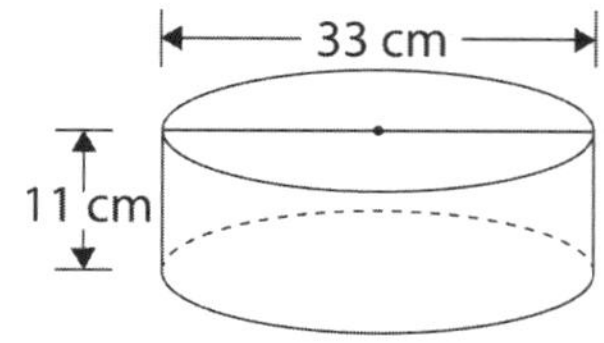

c)

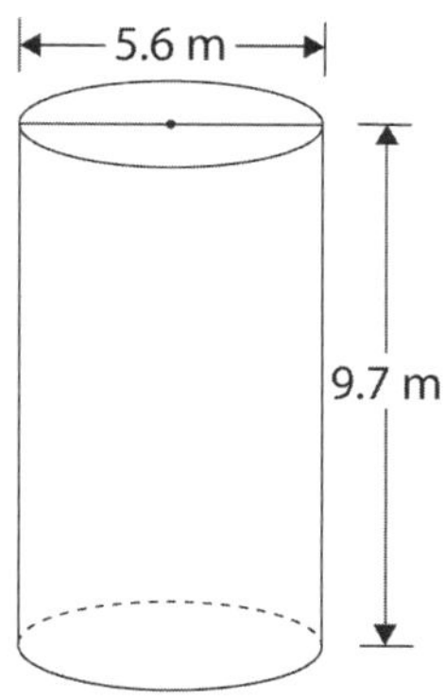

4. An electronic transmitter covers a circular area of 120 m^2.
What is the radius of the transmission area?

Name ____________________ Date ________________

Master 6.14c

Unit Test continued

5. A cardboard tube is used to mail a poster.
The diameter of the tube is 7 cm and its length is 1.2 m.
What is the surface area of the tube?

6. A cylinder has base radius less than 5 cm.
The surface area of the cylinder is greater than 400 cm^2.

a) Sketch a possible net for this cylinder.

b) Show how you found the height of the cylinder.

Name ______________________ Date ________________

Master 6.15

Sample Answers

Unit Test – Master 6.14

1. a) 22 cm **b)** 11.5 m **c)** 4.75 mm

2. a) $C \doteq 69.1$ cm; $A \doteq 380.1$ cm^2

b) $C \doteq 72.3$ m; $A \doteq 415.5$ m^2

c) $C \doteq 29.8$ mm; $A \doteq 70.9$ mm^2

3. a) $V \doteq 628.3$ m^3; $SA \doteq 408.4$ m^2

b) $V \doteq 9408.3$ cm^3; $SA \doteq 2851$ cm^2

c) $V \doteq 238.9$ m^3; $SA \doteq 219.9$ m^2

4. About 6 m

5. 2639 cm^2; I rounded up because if I rounded down, there would not be enough cardboard.

6. a)

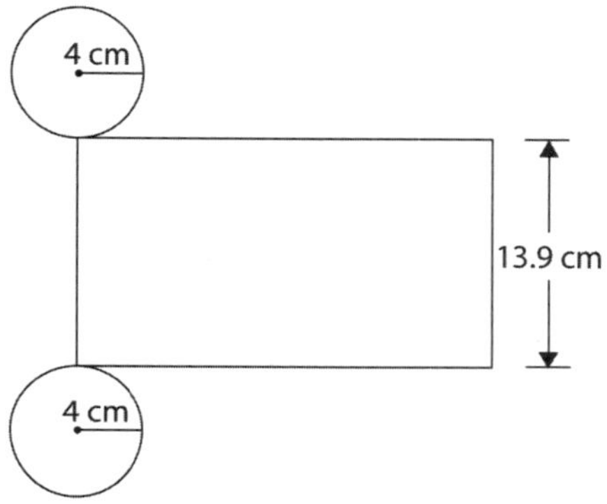

b) Since the radius must be less than 5 cm, suppose the radius is 4 cm.
Since the surface area must be greater than 400 cm^2, suppose the surface area is 450 cm^2.
SA = area of 2 circular bases + area of curved surface
Area of 2 circular bases $= 2 \times \pi(4)^2$
$\doteq 100.53$
So, area of curved surface $= 450 - 100.53$
$= 349.47$
Area of curved surface $= \pi dh$
$349.47 = \pi(8)h$
$h \doteq 13.9$
The height of the cylinder is about 13.9 cm.

Extra Practice Masters 6.16–6.21

Go to the CD-ROM to access editable versions of these Extra Practice Masters

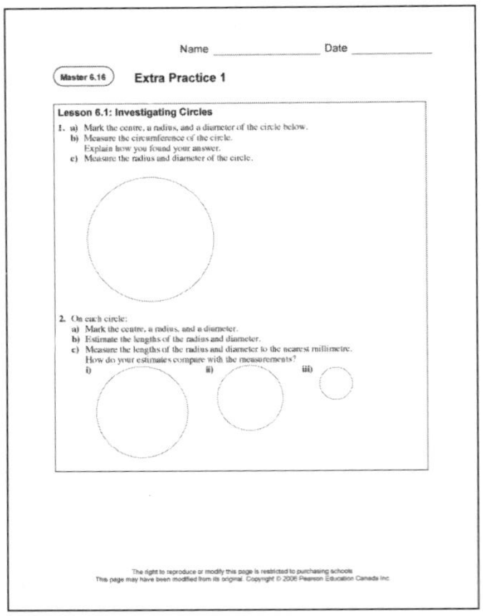
Name ______________ Date ______________

Master 6.16 **Extra Practice 1**

Lesson 6.1: Investigating Circles

1. a) Mark the centre, a radius, and a diameter of the circle below.
   b) Measure the circumference of the circle.
   Explain how you found your answer.
   c) Measure the radius and diameter of the circle.

2. On each circle:
   a) Mark the centre, a radius, and a diameter.
   b) Estimate the lengths of the radius and diameter.
   c) Measure the lengths of the radius and diameter to the nearest millimetre.
   How do your estimates compare with the measurements?
   i) ii) iii)

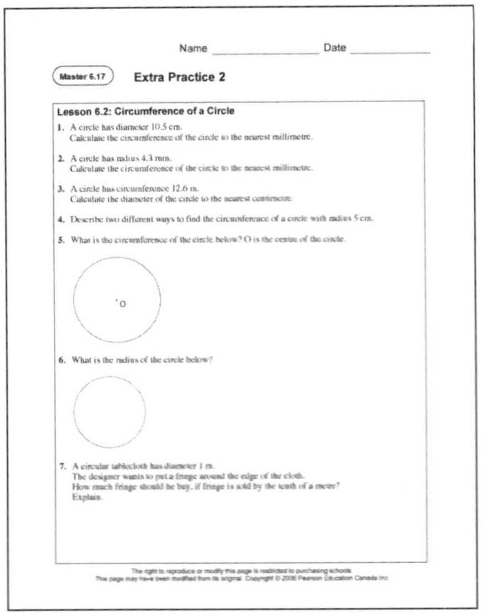
Name ______________ Date ______________

Master 6.17 **Extra Practice 2**

Lesson 6.2: Circumference of a Circle

1. A circle has diameter 10.5 cm.
   Calculate the circumference of the circle to the nearest millimetre.
2. A circle has radius 4.3 mm.
   Calculate the circumference of the circle to the nearest millimetre.
3. A circle has circumference 12.6 m.
   Calculate the diameter of the circle to the nearest centimetre.
4. Describe two different ways to find the circumference of a circle with radius 5 cm.
5. What is the circumference of the circle below? O is the centre of the circle.
6. What is the radius of the circle below?
7. A circular tablecloth has diameter 1 m.
   The designer wants to put a fringe around the edge of the cloth.
   How much fringe should he buy, if fringe is sold by the tenth of a metre?
   Explain.

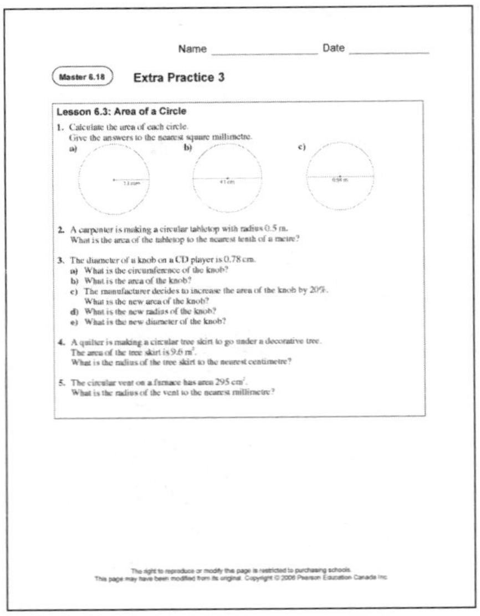
Name ______________ Date ______________

Master 6.18 **Extra Practice 3**

Lesson 6.3: Area of a Circle

1. Calculate the area of each circle.
   Give the answers to the nearest square millimetre.
   a) b) c)
2. A carpenter is making a circular tabletop with radius 0.5 m.
   What is the area of the tabletop to the nearest tenth of a metre?
3. The diameter of a knob on a CD player is 0.78 cm.
   a) What is the circumference of the knob?
   b) What is the area of the knob?
   c) The manufacturer decides to increase the area of the knob by 20%.
   What is the new area of the knob?
   d) What is the new radius of the knob?
   e) What is the new diameter of the knob?
4. A quilter is making a circular tree skirt to go under a decorative tree.
   The area of the tree skirt is 9.6 m².
   What is the radius of the tree skirt to the nearest centimetre?
5. The circular vent on a furnace has area 295 cm².
   What is the radius of the vent to the nearest millimetre?

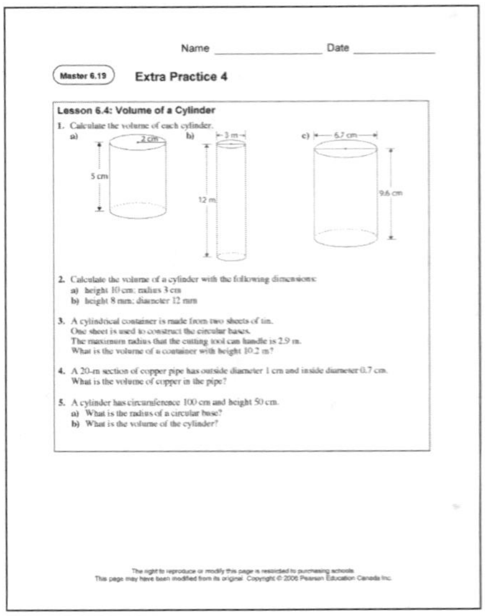
Name ______________ Date ______________

Master 6.19 **Extra Practice 4**

Lesson 6.4: Volume of a Cylinder

1. Calculate the volume of each cylinder.
   a) b) c)
2. Calculate the volume of a cylinder with the following dimensions:
   a) height 10 cm; radius 3 cm
   b) height 8 mm; diameter 12 mm
3. A cylindrical container is made from two sheets of tin.
   One sheet is used to construct the circular bases.
   The maximum radius that the cutting tool can handle is 2.9 m.
   What is the volume of a container with height 10.2 m?
4. A 20-m section of copper pipe has outside diameter 1 cm and inside diameter 0.7 cm.
   What is the volume of copper in the pipe?
5. A cylinder has circumference 100 cm and height 50 cm.
   a) What is the radius of a circular base?
   b) What is the volume of the cylinder?

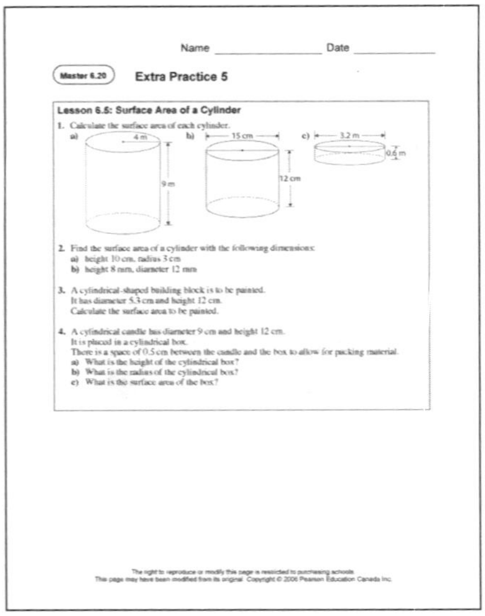
Name ______________ Date ______________

Master 6.20 **Extra Practice 5**

Lesson 6.5: Surface Area of a Cylinder

1. Calculate the surface area of each cylinder.
   a) b) c)
2. Find the surface area of a cylinder with the following dimensions:
   a) height 10 cm, radius 3 cm
   b) height 8 mm, diameter 12 mm
3. A cylindrical-shaped building block is to be painted.
   It has diameter 5.3 cm and height 12 cm.
   Calculate the surface area to be painted.
4. A cylindrical candle has diameter 9 cm and height 12 cm.
   It is placed in a cylindrical box.
   There is a space of 0.5 cm between the candle and the box to allow for packing material.
   a) What is the height of the cylindrical box?
   b) What is the radius of the cylindrical box?
   c) What is the surface area of the box?

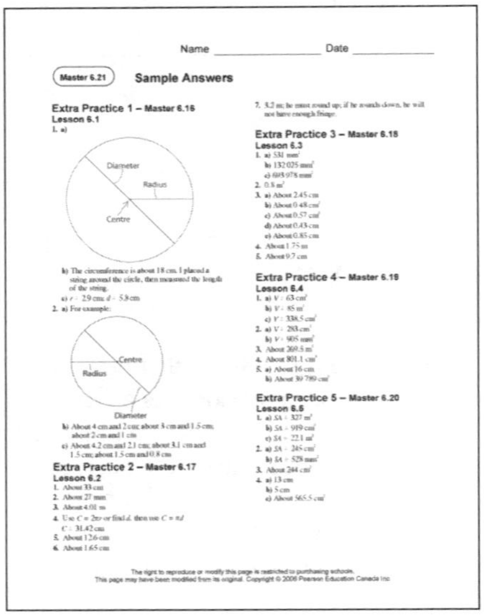
Name ______________ Date ______________

Master 6.21 **Sample Answers**

Extra Practice 1 – Master 6.16
Lesson 6.1

Extra Practice 2 – Master 6.17
Lesson 6.2

Extra Practice 3 – Master 6.18
Lesson 6.3

Extra Practice 4 – Master 6.19
Lesson 6.4

Extra Practice 5 – Master 6.20
Lesson 6.5

Addison Wesley
Mathematics
Makes Sense

Program Authors

Trevor Brown
Antonietta Lenjosek
Cathy Heideman
Jim Mennie
Georgia Konis-Chatzis
A.J. Keene
Margaret Sinclair
Craig Featherstone
Jason Johnston
Bryn Keyes
Elizabeth Wood
Elizabeth Milne
David Sufrin
Don Jones
Sharon Jeroski
Lynn Strangway

Printed and bound in Canada

2 3 4 5 – TC – 09 08 07 06

PEARSON
Education Canada

ADDISON WESLEY

Ontario

Math Makes Sense 8

Ontario

Teacher Guide

Unit 7: Geometry

PEARSON

Education Canada

UNIT 7

Geometry

"The student can, through construction and design, learn to perceive the world geometrically. Through construction of shapes and the use of these to build designs, the student can become aware of individual and group patterns in the natural and man-made environments."

Mary Laycock and Gene Watson, *The Fabric of Mathematics, A Resource Book for Teachers*, Revised Edition Activity Resources Co. Inc., 1975.

FOCUS STRAND
Geometry and Spatial Sense

SUPPORTING STRAND
Measurement

TIPS
Student centred investigations are learning contexts which require students to explore mathematics through inquiry, discovery, and research.

Mathematics Background

What Are the Big Ideas?

- Figures can be classified according to their geometric properties.
- Intersecting lines create equal, supplementary, and complementary angles.
- The sum of the angles in a triangle is 180°.
- The angles formed by two parallel lines and a transversal can be classified as alternate angles, corresponding angles, and interior angles.
- Angles, and bisectors of line segments and angles can be constructed using a ruler and compass.

How Will the Concepts Develop?

Students determine, through investigation, the angle relationships for intersecting lines, and the sum of the angles in a triangle.

Students use parallelograms and transformations to investigate the angles associated with parallel lines.

Students use a ruler and compass to construct bisectors of line segments and angles, and to construct an angle of a given measure.

Students use their knowledge of triangles, intersecting lines, and parallel lines and transversals to solve problems involving angle measurement.

Students investigate the geometric characteristics of quadrilaterals, and use these characteristics to sort and classify quadrilaterals.

Why Are These Concepts Important?

A knowledge of the geometric properties of lines, angles, and triangles is applied daily in many fields, such as carpentry, architecture, land surveying, interior design, manufacturing, and engineering. Geometric concepts occur in many aspects of the world in which we live. Understanding the properties of figures, lines, and angles will help students appreciate the use of geometry in artwork, and in the design and construction of buildings and monuments.

Geometry is connected to every strand in the math curriculum and to many real-life situations. Whether one is designing a circuit board, a house, a dress, a cabinet, or a poster, an understanding of geometric properties is required.

Curriculum Overview

The codes refer to the 2005 revised curriculum.

Overall Expectations

- Demonstrate an understanding of the geometric properties of quadrilaterals and circles and the applications of geometric properties in the real world. (8m40)
- Develop geometric relationships involving lines, triangles, and polyhedra, and solve problems involving lines and triangles. (8m41)

Specific Expectations

- Sort and classify quadrilaterals by geometric properties, including those based on diagonals, through investigation using a variety of tools. (8m43)
- Construct a circle, given its centre and radius, or its centre and a point on the circle, or three points on the circle. (8m44)
- Investigate and describe applications of geometric properties in the real world. (8m45)
- Determine through investigation using a variety of tools and strategies, the angle relationships for intersecting lines and for parallel lines and transversals, and the sum of the angles of a triangle. (8m47)
- Solve angle-relationship problems involving triangles, intersecting lines, and parallel lines and transversals. (8m48)

Launch

Lesson 7.1: Angle Properties of Intersecting Lines

Technology: Using *The Geometer's Sketchpad* to Investigate Intersecting Lines

Lesson 7.2: Angles in a Triangle

Technology: Using *The Geometer's Sketchpad* to Investigate Angles in a Triangle

Lesson 7.3: Angle Properties of Parallel Lines

Technology: Using *The Geometer's Sketchpad* to Investigate Parallel Lines and Transversals

Mid-Unit Review

Lesson 7.4: Constructing Bisectors

Lesson 7.5: Constructing Angles

Lesson 7.6: Creating and Solving Geometry Problems

Lesson 7.6A: Characteristics of Quadrilaterals

Unit Review
Practice Test

Unit Problem
Design a Banner

Curriculum across the Grades

Grade 7	Grade 8
Students construct related lines using angle properties. They sort and classify triangles and quadrilaterals by geometric properties related to symmetry, angles, and sides. Students construct angle bisectors and perpendicular bisectors, and represent equal angles and equal lengths using mathematical notation. Students identify the minimum side and angle information needed to describe a unique triangle.	Students sort and classify quadrilaterals by geometric properties, including those based on diagonals. They construct a circle, given its centre and radius, or its centre and a point on the circle, or three points on the circle. Students investigate and describe applications of geometric properties in the real world. Students determine the angle relationships for intersecting lines and for parallel lines and transversals, and the sum of the angles in a triangle. They solve angle-relationship problems.

Additional Activities

L-Game

For Extra Practice (Appropriate for use after Skills You'll Need)
Materials: *L-Game* (Master 7.6a), *L-Game Game Board* (Master 7.6b)
Playing this game provides practice in describing transformations.

The work students do: Students play with a partner. Students take turns to shade an L-shaped figure on the game board, then describe the transformation for which this figure is the image of Figure A. Students score one point for correctly describing the transformation. When no more Ls can be drawn, the round is over. The player with more points after 4 rounds wins.

Take It Further: Students create their own game boards, this time using a T-shaped figure. Students play the game again.

Mathematical/Social/Logical
Partner Activity

Can You Make It?

For Extra Practice (Appropriate for use after Lesson 7.2)
Materials: *Can You Make It?* (Master 7.7), 3 number cubes labelled 1 to 6
Playing this game reinforces the skills of recognizing and naming triangles.

The work students do: Students play with a partner. Students take turns rolling the 3 number cubes. The numbers rolled represent the possible side lengths of a triangle. Students decide whether a triangle can be formed. One point is scored for a correct answer. A second point is scored for stating the type of triangle that can be formed.
The student with more points after 6 rounds wins.

Take It Further: Students play the game again. This time, students must also draw any triangle that can be formed. Students get one point for a correct drawing.

Mathematical/Social/Logical
Partner Activity

Triangle Trial

For Extra Practice (Appropriate for use after lesson 7.4)
Materials: *Triangle Trial* (Master 7.8), rulers, protractors, compasses
This activity reinforces the skills of drawing line segments, angles, and triangles.

The work students do: Students work on their own. Students draw:

- an equilateral △ABC with side length 6 cm
- △ACD with ∠ACD = 120° and ∠CAD = 25°
- △ABE with ∠ABE = 120° and AE = 9 cm

Students measure ∠AED and ∠ADE, then record what they know about △AED.

Take It Further: Students draw quadrilateral PQRS, with PQ = 6 cm, QR = 5 cm, RS = 3 cm, PS = 7 cm, and ∠SPQ = 65°. Students measure ∠Q, ∠R, and ∠S, then find the sum of the angles in the quadrilateral.

Spatial/Kinesthetic/Mathematical
Individual Activity

Measuring Up

For Extra Practice (Appropriate for use after lesson 7.5)
Materials: *Measuring Up* (Master 7.9), rulers, protractors, and compasses
This activity reinforces the skills of using a ruler, protractor, and compass to construct figures.

The work students do: Students work on their own. Students follow instructions to construct a 5-pointed star. They use a protractor, a compass, and a ruler, and angles of 72° and 144°.

Take It Further: Students repeat the activity using angles of 60° and 120° to construct a 6-pointed star.

Spatial/Kinesthetic
Individual Activity

Planning for Unit 7

Planning for Instruction

Suggested Unit time: About 4 weeks

Lesson	Time	Materials	Program Support
Launch, page 2	15–20 min		
Skills You'll Need, page 4	65–80 min	protractors compasses	
7.1: Angle Properties of Intersecting Lines, page 7 Identify and calculate complementary, supplementary, and opposite angles.	80–100 min	protractors copies of Diagram in Lesson 7.1 *Explore*	Master 7.17: Diagram in Lesson 7.1 *Explore* Master 7.10: Step-by-Step 1 Master 7.23: Extra Practice 1
Technology: Using *The Geometer's Sketchpad* to Investigate Intersecting Lines, page 12 Use technology to investigate intersecting lines.	40–50 min	computers with *The Geometer's Sketchpad* software	
7.2: Angles in a Triangle, page 14 Explore the relationships of the angles in a triangle.	80–100 min	tracing paper scissors, protractors square dot paper calculators	PM 22: Square Dot Paper Master 7.11: Step-by-Step 2 Master 7.24: Extra Practice 2
Technology: Using *The Geometer's Sketchpad* to Investigate Angles in a Triangle, page 19 Use technology to investigate angles in a triangle.	40–50 min	computers with *The Geometer's Sketchpad* software	
7.3: Angle Properties of Parallel Lines, page 20 Investigate angles associated with parallel lines.	80–100 min	tracing paper isometric dot paper	PM 23: Isometric Dot Paper Master 7.12: Step-by-Step 3 Master 7.25: Extra Practice 3
Technology: Using *The Geometer's Sketchpad* to Investigate Parallel Lines and Transversals, page 26 Use technology to investigate parallel lines and transversals.	80–100 min	computers with *The Geometer's Sketchpad* software	
Mid-Unit Review, page 28			
7.4: Constructing Bisectors, page 29 Use a variety of methods to construct bisectors of line segments and angles.	optional but recommended	protractors, compasses tracing paper Miras, scissors	Master 7.13: Step-by-Step 4 Master 7.26: Extra Practice 4
7.5: Constructing Angles, page 35 Use a variety of methods to construct angles.	optional	compasses, tracing paper Miras, protractors	Master 7.14: Step-by-Step 5 Master 7.27: Extra Practice 5
7.6: Creating and Solving Geometry Problems, page 39 Create and solve problems involving angle measurement.	80–100 min	copies of Diagram for 7.6 *Explore* copies of Diagram for 7.6 *Practice* Question 5 (optional)	Master 7.18: Diagram for 7.6 *Explore* Master 7.19: Diagram for 7.6 *Practice* Question 5 Master 7.15: Step-by-Step 6 Master 7.28: Extra Practice 6
7.6A: Characteristics of Quadrilaterals, page 44 Investigate geometric properties of quadrilaterals.	80–100 min	copies of Quadrilaterals in *Explore* 7.6A Lesson 6A protractors isometric dot paper square dot paper Venn diagrams	Master 7.5: Lesson 6A Master 7.20: Quadrilaterals in *Explore* 7.6A PM 22: Square Dot Paper PM 23: Isometric Dot Paper PM 28: Venn Diagrams Master 7.16: Step-by-Step 6A Master 7.29: Extra Practice 6A
Reading and Writing in Math: Reasonable Solutions and Concluding Statements, page 48			

Lesson	Time	Materials	Program Support
Unit Review, page 51		tracing paper Miras, compasses	Extra Practice: Student Book page 494
Practice Test, page 55		tracing paper Miras, compasses	
Unit Problem: Design a Banner, page 56	80–100 min	tracing paper, Miras compasses, protractors chart paper scissors, tape coloured pencils or markers	

Planning for Assessment

Purpose	Tools and Process	Recording and Reporting
Diagnostic	*Unit Launch* Question; conference; scaffold problems throughout the unit	PM 8: Conference Prompts
Formative	*Explore* – Ongoing Assessment: Observe and Listen	Master 7.2: Ongoing Observations: Geometry PM 1: Inquiry Process Check List PM 6: Observation Record 1 PM 7: Observation Record 2 PM 8: Conference Prompts PM 2: Self-Assessment PM 3: Self-Assessment: Problem Solving PM 9: Work Sample Records
Summative	*Unit Review* *Unit Problem* – Performance Assessment Unit Test Review assessment records; add unit results to ongoing records	Master 7.1: Unit Rubric: Geometry Master 7.3: Performance Assessment Rubric: Design a Banner Master 7.4: Unit Summary: Geometry PM 10: Summary Class Records: Strands PM 11: Summary Class Records: Achievement Categories PM 12: Summary Record: Individual
Learning Skills/Mathematical Disposition	Observe and record throughout unit	PM 4: Learning Skills Check List PM 5: Mathematical Dispositions and Learning Skills

Program Masters (PM) are in the *Grade 8 Planning and Program Masters* module.
Extra Practice Masters are on the CD-ROM and printed in reduced format on pages 87 and 88 of this module

LESSON ORGANIZER

15–20 min

Curriculum Focus: Activate prior learning about geometry.

Teacher Materials

Optional

- examples of logos, badges, signs, and banners that use geometric concepts

ASSUMED PRIOR KNOWLEDGE

- ✓ Students can measure, construct, and classify angles.
- ✓ Students can use mathematical language to describe geometric concepts.

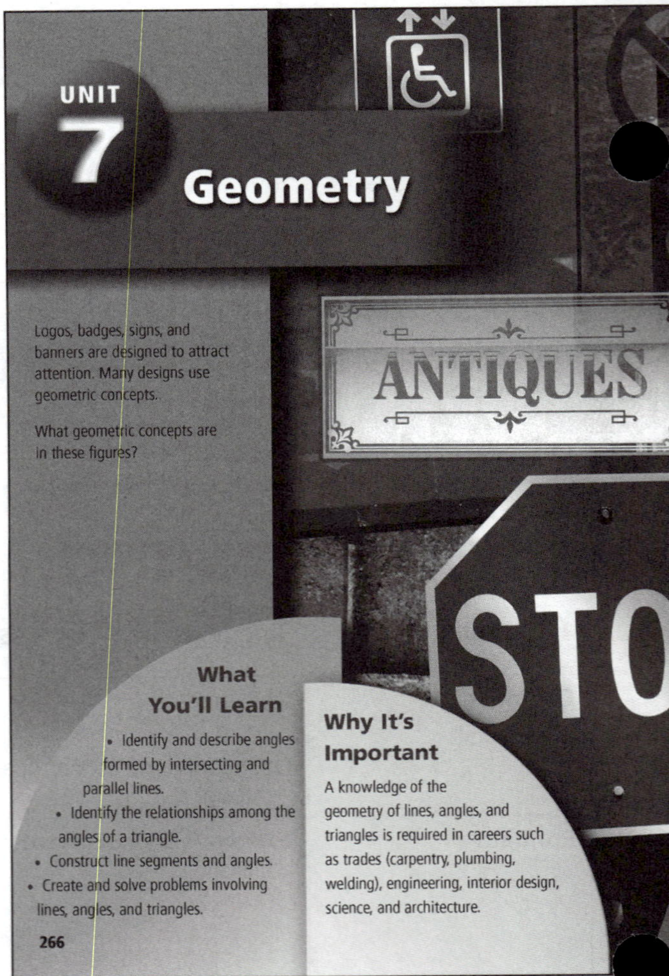

UNIT 7

Geometry

Logos, badges, signs, and banners are designed to attract attention. Many designs use geometric concepts.

What geometric concepts are in these figures?

What You'll Learn

- Identify and describe angles formed by intersecting and parallel lines.
- Identify the relationships among the angles of a triangle.
- Construct line segments and angles.
- Create and solve problems involving lines, angles, and triangles.

Why It's Important

A knowledge of the geometry of lines, angles, and triangles is required in careers such as trades (carpentry, plumbing, welding), engineering, interior design, science, and architecture.

266

ACTIVATE PRIOR LEARNING

Have students look at the pictures on pages 266 and 267 of the Student Book.

Ask questions, such as:

- What geometric concepts are in these figures? (*I see translations in the wheel chair sign and in the pedestrian crossing sign. I see reflections in the Antiques sign. I see rotations in the wheel rim. I see parallel lines and perpendicular lines in the frame of the house. I see a right angle in the No Right Turn sign. I see line symmetry in the Station Road sign. I see rotational symmetry in the Stop sign.*)
- Where have you seen designs that use geometric concepts? (*On banners hanging from lamp posts; in posters on bus shelters; and in logos used by sports teams and car manufacturers*)
- Why do you think the use of geometric concepts can make a design more appealing? (*The design may contain patterns, symmetry, transformations, or figures that make the design more interesting and attractive.*)

Have students work in groups to list as many examples of logos that contain geometric concepts as they can. Students then list the geometry used in each logo. For example, one group could list logos used by car manufacturers, while another group could list logos used by sports teams. Groups could make a collage of their logos for display in the classroom.

Tell students that, in this unit, they will work with geometric properties of straight lines and angles, triangles, intersecting lines, and parallel lines. They will also construct bisectors of line segments and angles, and construct angles of given measures. Students will expand on their knowledge of sorting and classifying quadrilaterals. At the end of the unit, students will demonstrate what they have learned about geometry by designing a banner.

Key Words

- complementary angles
- complement
- supplementary angles
- supplement
- opposite angles
- perpendicular
- transversal
- alternate angles
- corresponding angles
- interior angles
- bisect
- bisector
- perpendicular bisector
- angle bisector
- circumcentre
- circumcircle

267

FROM THE LIBRARY

Patty Paper Geometry by Michael Serra.
Key Curriculum Press, 1994.
ISBN: 1559530723
This book is designed to create interest in, and an understanding of, geometry. It uses a hands-on, cooperative approach to motivate students to read, write, and talk about geometry. *Patty Paper Geometry* contains dozens of activities covering such topics as intersecting lines, basic geometric constructions, angle properties of parallel lines, and transformations.

DIAGNOSTIC ASSESSMENT

What to Look For	What to Do
✔ Students can measure, construct, and classify angles.	***Extra Support:*** Students who have difficulty measuring, constructing, and classifying angles may benefit from working with a partner to write step-by-step instructions on how to use a ruler and a protractor to construct an angle with a given measure. *Work on this skill during Lessons 7.2 and 7.4.*
✔ Students can use mathematical language to describe geometric concepts.	Students who have difficulty using mathematical language to describe geometric properties may benefit from a review of terms such as, parallel lines, perpendicular, acute angle, right angle, obtuse angle, and straight angle. *Work on this skill during Lessons 7.2 and 7.3.*

LESSON ORGANIZER — 65–80 min

Skills in Review
- Using a protractor to measure angles
- Describing transformations
- Using a ruler and compass for constructions

Teacher Materials
Optional
- ruler and protractor for use on the overhead projector
- blank transparencies

Teacher Materials
- protractors
- compasses

Optional
- tracing paper
- Miras

Sample Solutions

4. i) a)

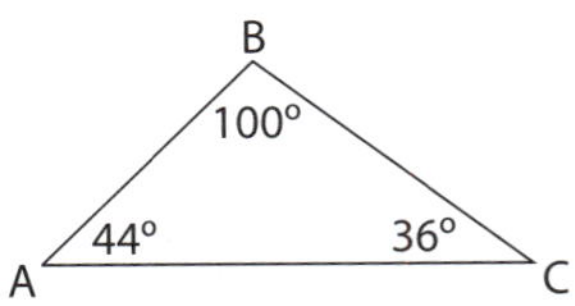

b) Scalene triangle
c) Scalene, obtuse, obtuse scalene

ii) a)

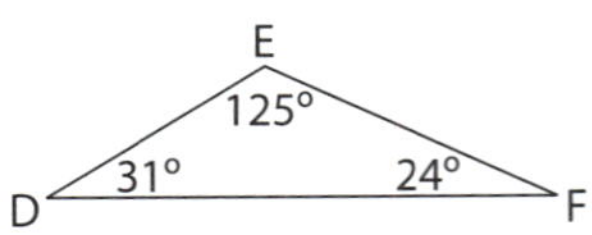

b) Scalene triangle
c) Scalene, obtuse, obtuse scalene

UNIT 7 **Skills You'll Need**

Using a Protractor to Measure Angles

To measure an angle:
Place the base line of a protractor along one arm of the angle, with the centre of the base line at the vertex of the angle.
Read the angle measure from the scale that has its 0 on the arm of the angle.

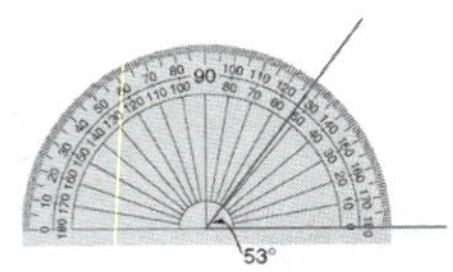

This acute angle measures 53°.

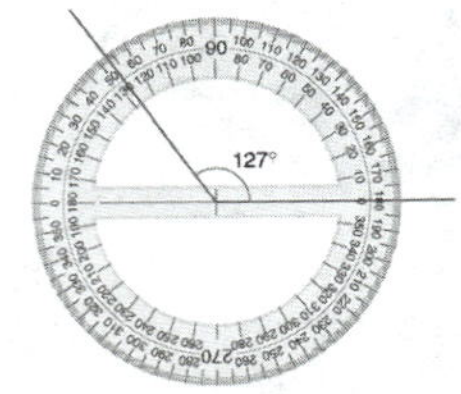

This obtuse angle measures 127°.

✓ Check

1. Draw a large irregular quadrilateral. Label it ABCD.
Measure each angle.
Label each angle with its measure.
Find the sum of the measures of the angles. 360°

Describing Transformations

Here is an example of 3 transformations of Figure A.

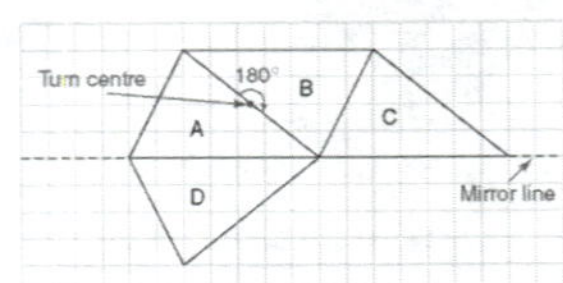

268 UNIT 7: Geometry

Using a Protractor to Measure Angles

Ensure students understand which is the base line on their protractor. On most semi-circular protractors, the baseline is about 0.5 cm from the bottom edge of the protractor. However, on some semi-circular protractors, the baseline is on the bottom edge of the protractor.

Ensure students understand how to correctly orient the protractor on the angle. Use an overhead projector, a blank transparency, and a clear protractor to demonstrate the steps for measuring an angle. Draw an angle on the transparency. Choose one arm of the angle to be the base. Align the baseline of the protractor with the base of the angle. The vertex of the angle must be at the centre of the protractor. Start at 0° on the arm along the base line. Count around the protractor until you reach the point where the other arm of the angle cuts the protractor. If the angle is acute, read the scale with the lesser numbers. If the angle is obtuse, read the scale with the greater numbers.

A circular protractor is used in the same way; its advantage is that it allows students to measure reflex angles (angles greater than 180°) more easily.

Review the meanings of acute angle, obtuse angle, right angle, and straight angle with students.

Common Misconceptions

➤ Students read from the wrong scale on the protractor.
How to Help: Encourage students to estimate the measure of an angle before measuring with a protractor. For example, if the angle is greater than a right angle (an obtuse angle), the measure must be greater than 90°. If the angle is less than a right angle (an acute angle) the measure must be less than 90°.

- Figure B is the image of Figure A after a 180° rotation about the midpoint of the side they share.
The midpoint is the turn centre.
- Figure C is the image of Figure A after a translation of 7 units right.
- Figure D is the image of Figure A after a reflection in a horizontal line through the side Figure A and Figure D share.
The reflection line is the mirror line.

✓ Check

2. In the drawing on page 268, which transformation relates Figure C to Figure B? A 180° rotation about the midpoint of the side Figure C and Figure B share

3. Look at this pattern.

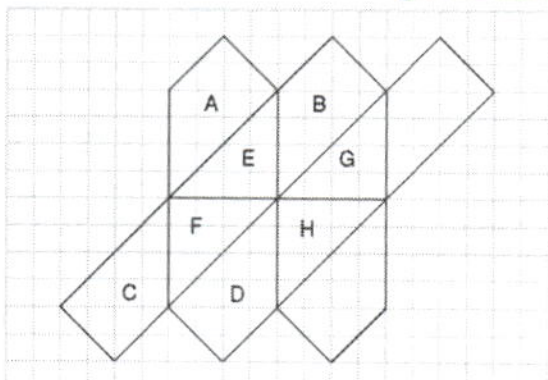

Describe the transformation for which:

a) Figure B is the image of Figure A. A translation of 4 units right

b) Figure C is the image of Figure A. A 180° rotation about the vertex they share

c) Figure E is the image of Figure G. A translation of 4 units left

d) Figure H is the image of Figure G. A 180° rotation about the midpoint of the side they share

e) Figure D is the image of Figure B. A 180° rotation about the vertex they share

Using a Ruler and Compass for Constructions

To construct △PQR with QR = 8 cm, PQ = 6 cm, and PR = 5 cm:
Sketch the triangle first.

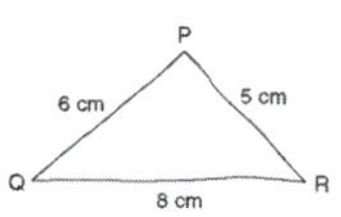

Skills You'll Need 269

Alternative Example 1

Describe the transformation for which:

a) Figure B is the image of Figure A

b) Figure C is the image of Figure A

c) Figure D is the image of Figure A

d) Figure E is the image of Figure A

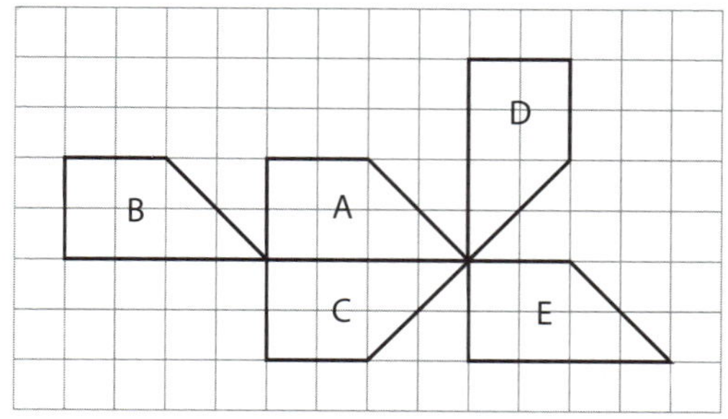

Solution

a) Figure B is the image of Figure A after a translation of 4 units left.

b) Figure C is the image of Figure A after a reflection in the horizontal line through the side Figure A and Figure C share.

c) Figure D is the image of Figure A after a 90° clockwise rotation about the point that Figure A and Figure D share.

d) Figure E is the image of Figure A after a translation of 4 units right and 2 units down.

Describing Transformations

Remind students that:

- A translation moves a figure along a straight line. The figure and its image face the same direction, and the slide can be described with a vertical and/or horizontal motion.
- A rotation is a clockwise or counterclockwise turn about a point. The point can be a vertex of the figure, a point on the side of the figure, or a point inside or outside the figure. The figure and its image may face different ways.
- A reflection is a flip in a mirror line. The mirror line can be a side of the figure, a line through the figure, or a line outside the figure. The figure and its image face opposite ways and are the same distance from the mirror line.

Tell students that transformations can be shown on plain paper, on a grid, or on a coordinate grid. The advantage of a grid is that it is often easier to draw and describe transformations.

Remind students they do not have to give a direction when a rotation is 180°. A figure rotated 180° clockwise, and the same figure rotated 180° counterclockwise result in the same image.

Students can complete the Additional Activity *L-Game* (Master 7.6).

Common Misconceptions

➤ Students have difficulty identifying a reflection and a rotation.

How to Help: Encourage students to use a Mira to help identify a reflection, and tracing paper to help identify a rotation. Remind students to try different mirror lines and turn centres. Show students that a rotation of 180° can also be described as a reflection.

(Sample Solutions continued)

4. iii) a)

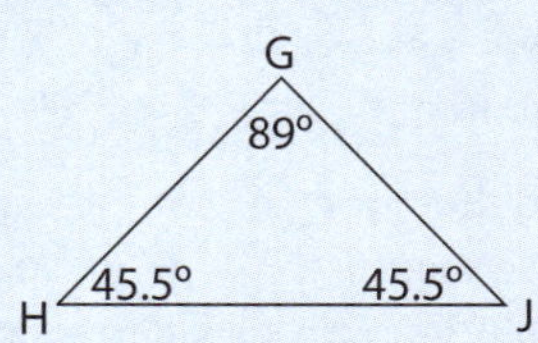

b) Acute triangle

c) Acute, isosceles, acute isosceles

iv) a)

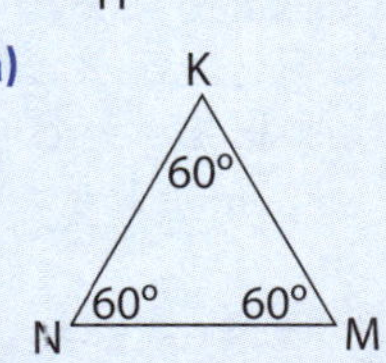

b) Equilateral triangle

c) Equilateral, acute

5. The sum of the lengths of two sides of the triangle must be greater than the length of the third side.

Alternative Example 2

Construct △ABC with BC = 10 cm, AB = 6 cm, and AC = 8 cm.
Sketch the triangle first.

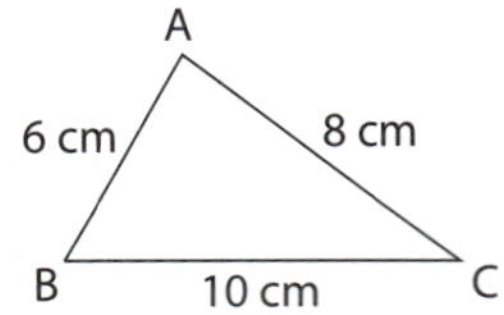

Solution

Use a ruler to draw BC = 10 cm.
With compass and pencil points 6 cm apart, place the compass point on B.
Draw an arc above BC.
With compass and pencil points 8 cm apart, place the compass point on C.
Draw an arc above BC.
Label the point of intersection A.
Join AB and AC.
Label each side with its length.
Use a protractor to measure the angles.
∠BAC = 90°, ∠ABC = 53°, ∠ACB = 37°

Label each angle with its measure.

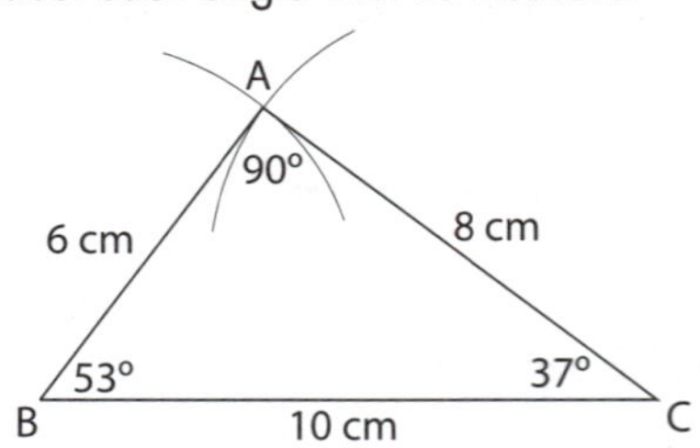

Use a ruler to draw QR = 8 cm.
With compass and pencil points 6 cm apart, place the compass point on Q.
Draw an arc above QR.
With compass and pencil points 5 cm apart, place the compass point on R.
Draw an arc above QR. Make sure the arcs intersect.
Label the point of intersection P.
Join PQ and PR. Label each side with its length.

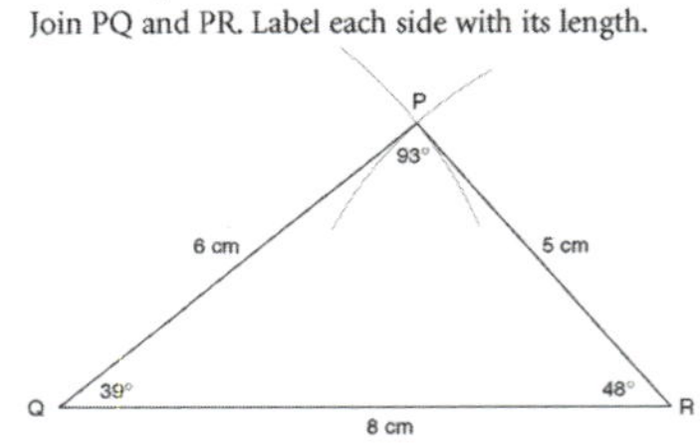

The arcs could have been drawn below QR.

The angles are measured with a protractor. They are accurate to the nearest degree.
Recall how to use 3 letters to label an angle:
∠PQR = 39°
∠PRQ = 48°
∠RPQ = 93°

✓ Check

4. For each triangle below:
   a) Draw the triangle, then measure all the angles.
   b) Name the triangle.
   c) How many different ways can you classify the triangle?
      i) △ABC with AB = 6 cm, BC = 7 cm, and AC = 10 cm
      ii) △DEF with DE = 4 cm, EF = 5 cm, and DF = 8 cm
      iii) △GHJ with GH = 5 cm, HJ = 7 cm, and GJ = 5 cm
      iv) △KMN with KM = 6 cm, MN = 6 cm, and KN = 6 cm

5. Suppose you are given the lengths of 3 line segments.
How can you tell if they can form a triangle?

6. A scalene triangle has side lengths 6, *x*, and 16.
The side lengths are listed from shortest to longest.
What are the possible whole-number values for *x*? *x* = 11, 12, 13, 14, 15

Using a Ruler and Compass for Constructions

Remind students that the minimum side and angle information needed to draw a unique triangle is the lengths of the three sides, the lengths of two sides and the measure of the angle between them, or the measures of two angles and the length of the side between them.
Ask:

- Suppose you were given the measures of the 3 angles. Could you construct a unique triangle? Explain. (*No, I could construct many triangles. All the triangles would have the same shape, but they would be of different sizes. The triangles would be similar.*)

Ensure students understand that triangles can be classified by side length and by angle measure.

By side length:	Equilateral triangle	all sides equal
	Isosceles triangle	2 sides equal
	Scalene triangle	all sides different
By angle measure:	Acute triangle	all angles less than 90°
	Right triangle	one 90° angle
	Obtuse triangle	one angle greater than 90°

Common Misconceptions

➤ Students do not understand how to tell if 3 line segments can form a triangle.

How to Help: Have students draw an acute triangle, ABC, an obtuse triangle, DEF, and a right triangle, PQR. Have students measure and label the lengths of the sides.
Have students copy and complete the following.
AB = __ cm, AC + CB = __ cm
AC = __ cm, AB + BC = __ cm
BC = __ cm, AB + AC = __ cm
DE = __ cm, DF + FE = __ cm
DF = __ cm, DE + EF = __ cm
EF = __ cm, DE + DF = __ cm
PR = __ cm, PQ + QR = __ cm
PQ = __ cm, PR + RQ = __ cm
QR = __ cm, QP + PR = __ cm

Students should discover that the sum of the lengths of any 2 sides of a triangle is always greater than the length of the third side.

7.1 Angle Properties of Intersecting Lines

Focus Identify and calculate complementary, supplementary, and opposite angles.

First Nations people use a drying rack to dry fish and animal hides.
The drying rack in this picture is used in a Grade 2 classroom to dry artwork.

Each end support of the drying rack forms 4 angles.
What do you notice about these angles?
What is the greatest possible value of each angle?
What is the least possible value of each angle?

Explore

Work on your own.
You will need a circular protractor and a large copy of this diagram.

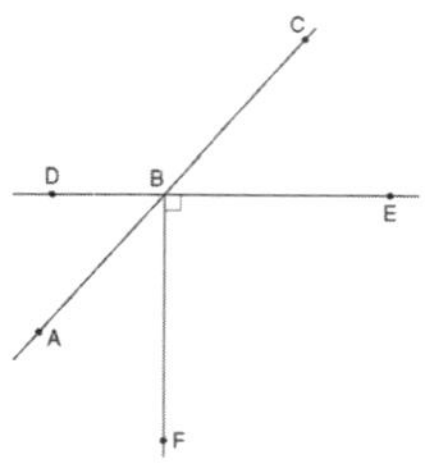

Measure all the angles.
Label each angle with its measure.

➢ Add these angles.
∠DBA + ∠DBC
∠DBC + ∠CBE
∠DBA + ∠ABF
What do you notice? Explain your results.

➢ What do you notice about ∠DBA and ∠CBE?
About ∠DBC and ∠ABE?

Reflect & Share

Compare your results with those of a classmate.
Suppose line AC were rotated about B.
How would the results change? Explain.
Suppose line FB were rotated about B.
How would the results change? Explain.

7.1 Angle Properties of Intersecting Lines 271

Angle Properties of Intersecting Lines

LESSON ORGANIZER (80–100 min)

Curriculum Focus: Identify and calculate complementary, supplementary, and opposite angles. (8m45, 8m48)

Teacher Materials
Optional
- transparencies of parts of Diagram in Lesson 7.1 *Explore* (Master 7.17)
- overhead protractor

Student Materials
- protractors
- copies of Diagram in Lesson 7.1 *Explore* (Master 7.17)

Optional
- Step-by-Step 1 (Master 7.10)
- Extra Practice 1 (Master 7.23)

Vocabulary: complement, complementary angles, supplement, supplementary angles, opposite angles

Assessment: Master 7.2 Ongoing Observations: Geometry

Key Math Learnings

1. Two angles whose sum is 90° are complementary.
2. Two angles whose sum is 180° are supplementary.
3. For any intersecting lines, the opposite angles are equal.

BEFORE Get Started

Have students look at the picture at the top of page 271 in the Student Book. Ask students if they remember using a drying rack in elementary school.

Ask:
- What other items have you seen with this type of support structure?
(*A clothes drying rack and a TV dinner tray*)
- What do you notice about the top and bottom angles in each end support?
(*The angles are equal.*)
- What do you notice about the other two angles in each end support?
(*The angles are equal.*)
- What happens to the angles if the frame is raised or lowered?
(*The angles that are opposite each other remain equal.*)
- What is the greatest possible value of each angle?
(*Since adjacent angles form a straight angle, the sum of adjacent angles is 180°. So, the greatest possible whole-number value of each angle is 179°, and the least possible whole-number value is 1°.*)

Present *Explore.* Distribute copies of Diagram in Lesson 7.1 *Explore* (Master 7.17). Ensure students remember how to use a circular or semi-circular protractor.

If you have not already done so, review *Skills You'll Need,* page 268, *Using a Protractor to Measure Angles.*

DURING Explore

As students work, ask questions, such as:
- Which angle is ∠DBA?
(*The angle formed by line segments DB and AB*)

REACHING ALL LEARNERS

Early Finishers

Have students write a problem, including a diagram, similar to *Practice* question 3. Students trade problems with a classmate and solve their classmate's problem.

Common Misconceptions

➤ Students have difficulty differentiating between complementary angles and supplementary angles.

How to Help: Point out that two angles whose sum is 180° are supplementary. An angle of 180° is described as a straight angle. The words supplementary and straight both begin with the letter s.

➤ Students think supplementary angles must share an arm.

How to Help: Draw this diagram on the board.

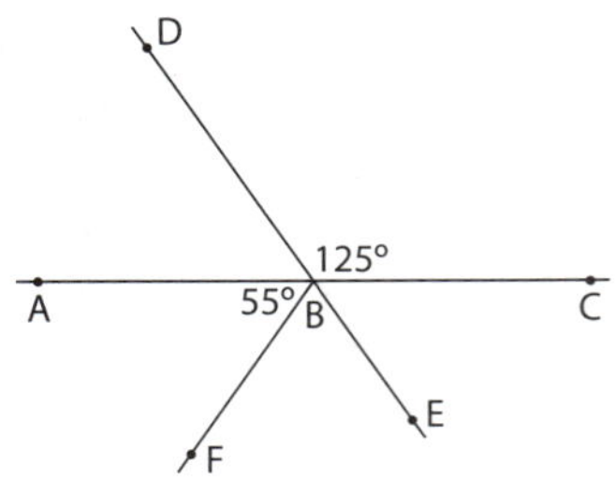

Point out that ∠DBC = 125° and ∠ABF = 55°. Since ∠DBC + ∠ABF = 125° + 55° = 180°, the angles are supplementary. The angles do not share an arm.

ESL Strategies

Have students for whom English is a second language draw diagrams to illustrate supplementary angles, complementary angles, and opposite angles. Students write a description below each diagram, both in English and in their native language.

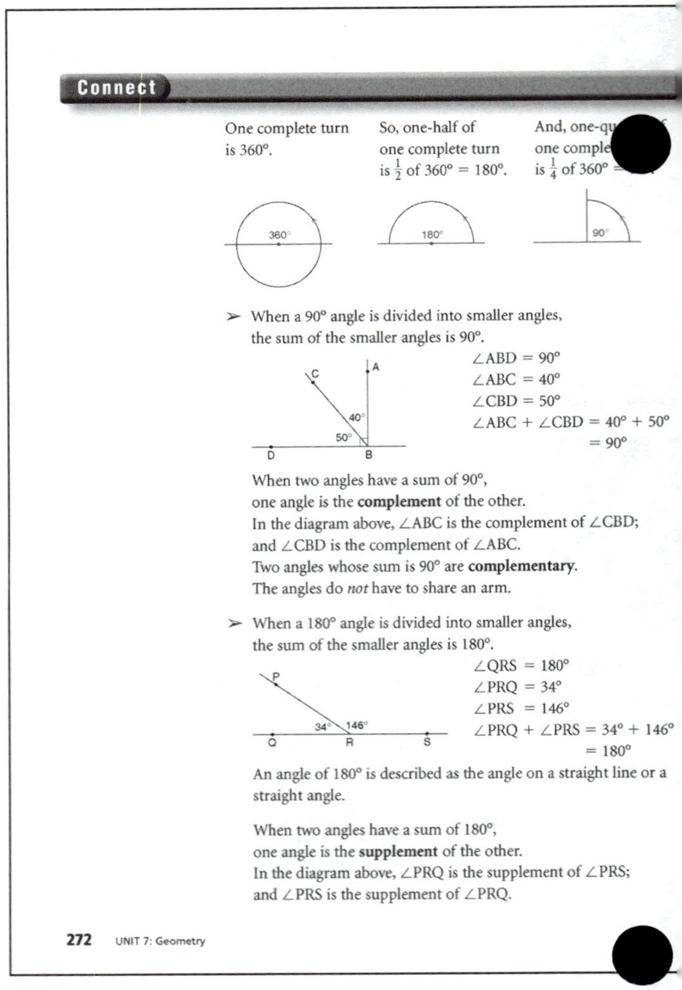

Connect

One complete turn is 360°.

So, one-half of one complete turn is $\frac{1}{2}$ of 360° = 180°.

And, one-qu… one comple… is $\frac{1}{4}$ of 360° = …

➤ When a 90° angle is divided into smaller angles, the sum of the smaller angles is 90°.

∠ABD = 90°
∠ABC = 40°
∠CBD = 50°
∠ABC + ∠CBD = 40° + 50°
= 90°

When two angles have a sum of 90°, one angle is the **complement** of the other.
In the diagram above, ∠ABC is the complement of ∠CBD; and ∠CBD is the complement of ∠ABC.
Two angles whose sum is 90° are **complementary**.
The angles do *not* have to share an arm.

➤ When a 180° angle is divided into smaller angles, the sum of the smaller angles is 180°.

∠QRS = 180°
∠PRQ = 34°
∠PRS = 146°
∠PRQ + ∠PRS = 34° + 146°
= 180°

An angle of 180° is described as the angle on a straight line or a straight angle.

When two angles have a sum of 180°, one angle is the **supplement** of the other.
In the diagram above, ∠PRQ is the supplement of ∠PRS; and ∠PRS is the supplement of ∠PRQ.

272 UNIT 7: Geometry

- How did you use your protractor to measure ∠DBA? (*I placed the base line of the protractor on BD, with the centre of the base line on point B. Since the angle is acute, I read the scale with the lesser numbers. BA meets the scale at 48°.*)
- How else could you have measured ∠DBA? (*I could have placed the base line of the protractor on BA, with the centre of the base line on point B, then found where BD meets the scale.*)
- What is the measure of ∠DBA? (*48°*) ∠DBC? (*132°*)
- What is the value of ∠DBA + ∠DBC? (*180°*)
- What is the value of ∠ABC? Explain. (*180°; it is a straight angle.*)
- Without measuring, what do you think the sum of ∠DBC and ∠CBE is? Explain. (*DBE is a straight line so I think the sum of ∠DBC and ∠CBE is 180°.*)
- What is the value of ∠CBE? (*48°*)
- What is the value of ∠DBC + ∠CBE? (*180°*)
- What is the measure of ∠ABF? (*42°*)
- What is the value of ∠DBA + ∠ABF? (*90°*)
- Does this answer seem reasonable? (*Yes, ∠FBE is 90°. Since DBE is a straight line, ∠DBF is also 90°. Since ∠DBF is made up of ∠DBA and ∠ABF, and ∠DBA = 48°, ∠ABF = 90° − 48° = 42°.*)
- What do you notice about ∠DBA and ∠CBE? (*They are equal.*)
- What do you notice about line segments AC and DE? (*They intersect.*)
- What is the measure of ∠ABE? (*∠ABE = ∠FBE + ∠ABF = 90° + 42° = 132°*)
- What do you notice about ∠DBC and ∠ABE? (*They are equal.*)

AFTER Connect

Invite students to share their results with the class.

Demonstrate the results on the overhead projector. Use Diagram in Lesson 7.1 *Explore* (Master 7.17).

Two angles whose sum is 180° are **supplementary**.
The angles do *not* have to share an arm.

➢ Extend PR to T.
Then ∠PRT = 180°
So, ∠SRT = ∠PRT − ∠PRS
∠SRT = 180° − 146°
= 34°
So, ∠PRQ = ∠SRT
These are **opposite angles**.

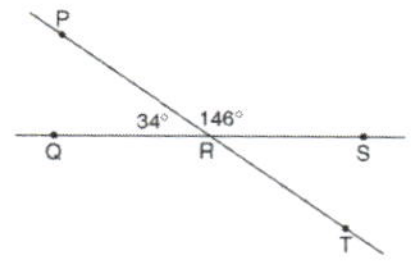

Similarly, ∠PRS = ∠QRT
These are opposite angles.

This property applies to any pair of intersecting lines.
So, for any intersecting lines, the opposite angles are equal.

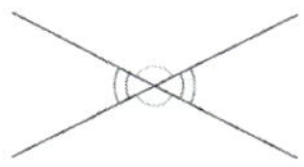

When two supplementary angles are equal, each angle is 90°.
∠MPN = 90° and ∠NPR = 90°
We say that NP is perpendicular to MR.

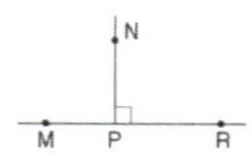

Example

Find the measure of each angle. Justify your answers.
a) ∠ACE b) ∠BCE c) ∠FCD

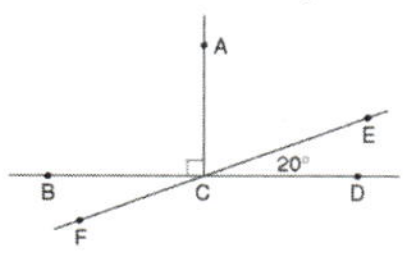

Solution

a) Since ∠BCD is a straight angle,
∠BCA and ∠DCA are supplementary.
∠BCA = 90°
So, ∠DCA = 180° − 90°
= 90°

7.1 Angle Properties of Intersecting Lines **273**

Assignment Guidelines

If your students do not have time to complete all the *Practice* questions on pages 274 and 275, these questions provide minimum curriculum coverage: 2, 3, 4, 6, 7, *Reflect*

To assess the 4 Achievement Chart categories listed in the curriculum document, have students complete these *Practice* questions:
Knowledge and Understanding: 2
Application: 4
Thinking: 6
Communication: 7

Mental Math

Remind students of the order of operations.

- Do the operations in brackets.
- Do the exponents.
- Multiply and divide, in order, from left to right.
- Add and subtract, in order, from left to right.

Sample Solutions

3. a) Since ∠PQR = 90°, ∠SQP and ∠RQS are complementary.
∠RQS = 56°
So, ∠SQP = 90° – 56° = 34°
Since ∠SQT is a straight angle, ∠PQT and ∠SQP are supplementary. ∠SQP = 34°
So, ∠PQT = 180° – 34° = 146°

b) Since ∠PQR = 90°, ∠SQP and ∠RQS are complementary.
∠RQS = 56°
So, ∠SQP = 90° – 56° = 34°

On an overhead transparency, trace line segments DE and BF. On another overhead transparency, trace line segment AC.

Rotate line segment AC around point B to different positions. Ask:

- What do you notice?
(The measures of ∠DBA and ∠DBC change, but their sum is always 180°. The measures of ∠DBC and ∠CBE change, but their sum is always 180°. The measures of ∠DBA and ∠ABF change, but their sum is always 90°. ∠DBA and ∠CBE are always equal. ∠DBC and ∠ABE are always equal.)

Use transparencies on the overhead projector to rotate line FB about B. Students should discover that the sum of each pair of angles does not change, and that opposite angles are always equal.

Use *Connect* to introduce the terms *supplement, supplementary angles, complement, complementary angles*, and *opposite angles*. Emphasize the spelling of complement – with an e.

Demonstrate that complementary angles do not have to share an arm.

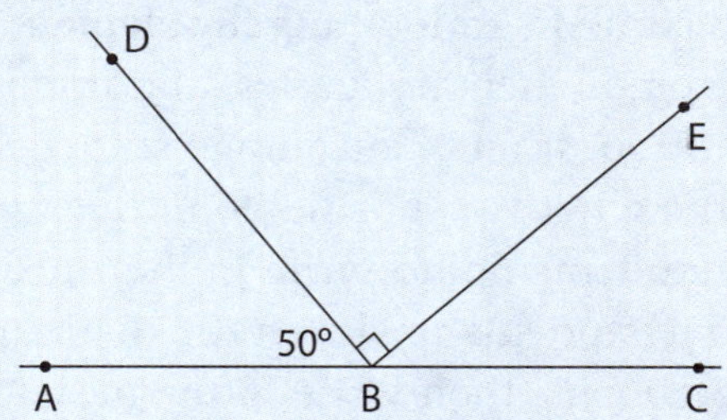

Since ∠ABC is a straight angle, and ∠DBE = 90°,
∠DBA + ∠EBC = 90°.
So, ∠DBA and ∠EBC are complementary.

Since ∠DBA = 50°, ∠EBC = 90° – 50° = 40°

Use the *Example* to show students how the angle measures can be determined without using a protractor to measure. In part c, show students another way to find the measure of ∠FCD. Since ∠FCE is a straight angle, ∠FCD and ∠ECD are supplementary. ∠ECD = 20°
So, ∠FCD = 180° – 20° = 160°

c) Since ∠SQT is a straight angle, ∠RQT and ∠SQR are supplementary. ∠SQR = 56°
So, ∠RQT = 180° – 56° = 124°

6. a) Opposite angles are equal. Supplementary angles have a sum of 180°.
Let the angle measure, in degrees, be a.

$a + a = 180$
$2a = 180$
$a = 90$

Each angle is 90°.
There is only one solution.

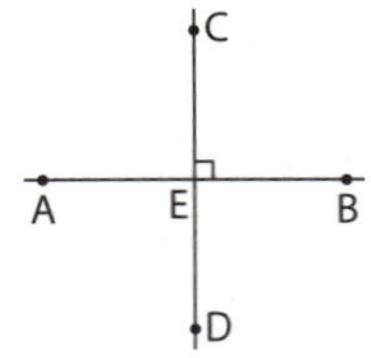

b) Opposite angles are equal. Complementary angles have a sum of 90°.
Let the angle measure, in degrees, be b.

$b + b = 90$
$2b = 90$
$b = 45$

Each angle is 45°.
There is only one solution.

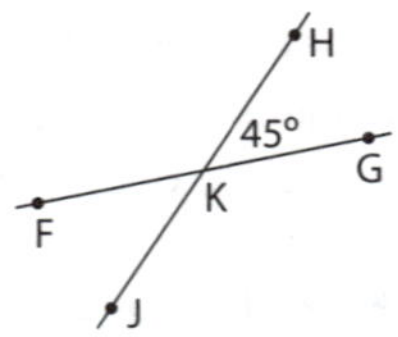

c) The two angles must have a sum of 180°, and the measures of the angles cannot be equal.
For example, 1° and 179°, 2° and 178°, ... 89° and 91°

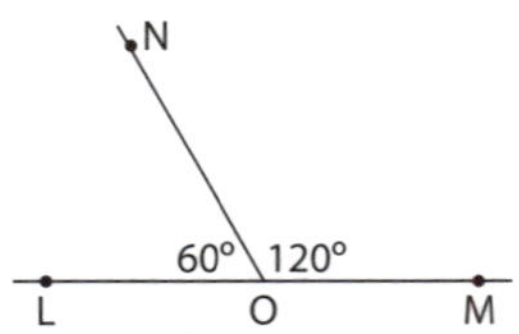

Since ∠DCA = 90°,
∠ACE and ∠DCE are complementary.
∠DCE = 20°
So, ∠ACE = 90° – 20°
= 70°

b) ∠BCE = ∠BCA + ∠ACE
We know that ∠BCA = 90° and ∠ACE = 70°.
So, ∠BCE = 90° + 70°
= 160°

Which other ways could you use to find these measures?

c) Since BD and FE intersect, then ∠FCD and ∠BCE are opposite angles.
So, ∠FCD = ∠BCE
= 160°

Practice

1. In the diagram, below left, what is the measure of each angle?
a) ∠AEC 34°
b) ∠DEB 34°
c) ∠CEB 146°
d) ∠CED 180°

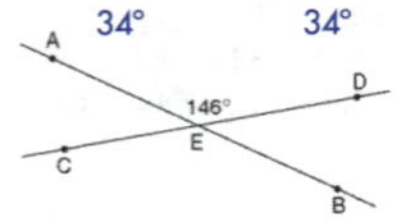

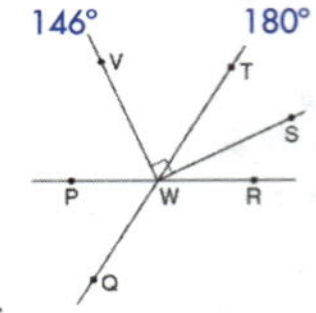

2. In the diagram, above right, name:
a) the angle opposite ∠PWQ ∠TWR
b) the complement of ∠VWT ∠TWS
c) two angles supplementary to ∠QWR ∠PWQ and ∠TWR
d) the supplement of ∠SWR ∠PWS

3. ∠RQS = 56° and ∠PQR is a right angle.
Find the measure of each angle.
Justify your answers.
a) ∠PQT 146°
b) ∠SQP 34°
c) ∠RQT 124°

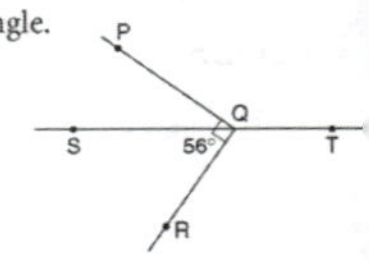

274 UNIT 7: Geometry

Practice

Remind students to look for supplementary angles, complementary angles, and opposite angles. In question 4, encourage students to sketch the other two positions. In question 5, remind students not to write in their textbooks. Encourage students to sketch the diagram in their notebooks, then write in the measures of the angles. In question 8, students could sketch the diagram in their notebooks, then extend DA, AB, BC, and CD to make it easier to see the angles Karen turns through at each point A, B, C, and D.

Assessment Focus: Question 6

In parts a and b, students should realize that opposite angles are equal. So, for two angles to be supplementary or complementary, and opposite, their measures must be equal, and have a sum of either 180° or 90°.

In parts c and d, students should realize that for two angles to be supplementary or complementary, but not opposite, their measures cannot be equal, and they must have a sum of either 180° or 90°.

Students who need extra support to complete the Assessment Focus questions may benefit from the Step-by-Step masters (Masters 7.10–7.16).

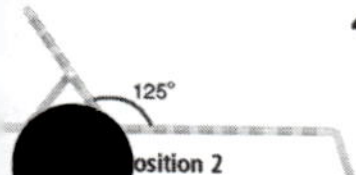

4. The back of a garden lounge chair has 3 possible positions.
a) In position 1, the obtuse angle is 100°. What is the acute angle? 80°
b) In position 2, the obtuse angle is 125°. What is the acute angle? 55°
c) In position 3, the acute angle is 28°. What is the obtuse angle? 152°

5. a) Name two 53° angles. ∠AFB and ∠EFD
b) Name two 127° angles. ∠DFB and ∠AFE
c) Name a 143° angle. ∠EFC

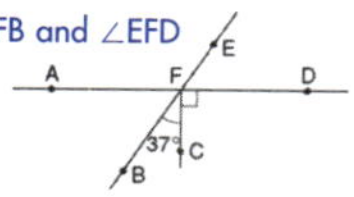

tal Math

ne pair of brackets
ke this statement
to 8.
15 ÷ (3 + 2) × 2 − 13 = 8

6. Assessment Focus
a) Sketch opposite angles that are supplementary. How many possible angles are there?
b) Sketch opposite angles that are complementary. How many possible angles are there?
c) Sketch two supplementary angles that could not be opposite angles. How many possible angles are there?
d) Sketch two complementary angles that could not be opposite angles. How many possible angles are there?

7. Find the measures of ∠EBD and ∠DBC. Explain your reasoning.

Remember that matching arcs in a diagram show equal angles.

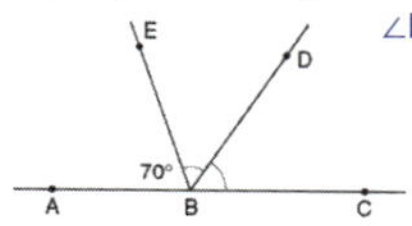

∠EBD = ∠DBC = 55°

Take It Further

8. On a cross-country trail, Karen runs round the course shown. Through which angle does she turn at each point A, B, C, and D? Explain. What is the total angle Karen turns through? Show how you know.
360°

At A: 120°
At B: 50°
At C: 90°
At D: 100°

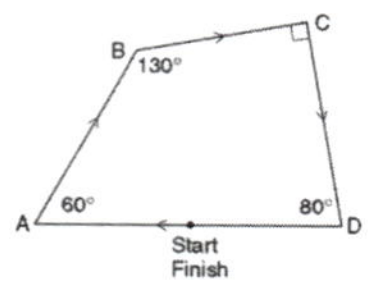

Reflect

Draw a diagram that contains at least one pair of complementary angles and one pair of supplementary angles. Explain how you know the angles are complementary or supplementary.

d) The two angles must have a sum of 90°, and the measures of the angles cannot be equal.
For example, 1° and 79°, 2° and 78°, ... 44° and 46°
In parts c and d, if you consider decimal angle measures, there are many more possible angles.

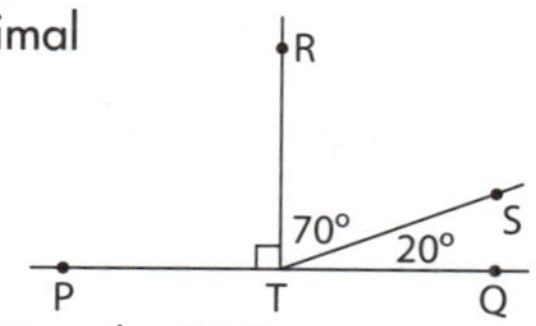

7. Since ∠ABC is a straight angle, ∠ABE and ∠EBC are supplementary. ∠ABE = 70°
So, ∠EBC = 180° − 70° = 110°
∠EBC = ∠EBD + ∠DBC
110° = ∠EBD + ∠DBC
Since ∠EBD = ∠DBC,
110° = 2 × ∠EBD
$\frac{110°}{2}$ = ∠EBD
∠EBD = 55°
So, ∠EBD = ∠DBC = 55°

8. At each vertex, Karen turns through an angle supplementary to the interior angle of the quadrilateral. The total angle Karen turns through is: 120° + 50° + 90° + 100° = 360°

REFLECT:

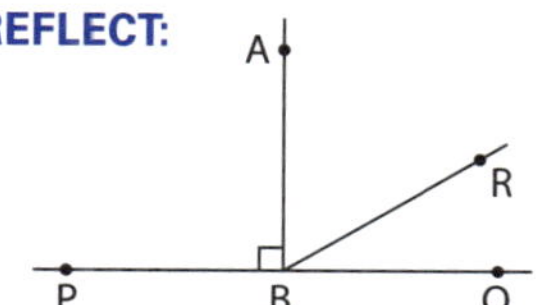

Since ∠PBQ is a straight angle, ∠PBA and ∠ABQ are supplementary. ∠PBA = 90°.
So, ∠ABQ = 180° − 90° = 90°
Since ∠ABQ = 90°,
∠ABR and ∠RBQ are complementary.
Since ∠PBQ is a straight angle, ∠RBQ and ∠RBP are supplementary.

ASSESSMENT FOR LEARNING

What to Look For	What to Do
Knowledge and Understanding ✔ Students understand the meaning of complementary, supplementary, and opposite angles. ***Communication*** ✔ Students can explain how they know angles are complementary, supplementary, or opposite. ***Application*** ✔ Students can identify and calculate complementary, supplementary, and opposite angles.	***Extra Support:*** Students who have difficulty with supplementary angles could first work with simpler diagrams. Students draw a straight line, then draw a line segment that makes an angle with the original line. Students use a protractor to find the measure of one of the angles formed, then predict the measure of the other angle. Students use a protractor to check their prediction. Students can use Step-by-Step 1 (Master 7.10) to complete question 6. ***Extra Practice:*** Have students repeat *Practice* question 2 with ∠SWR = ∠TWS = 25°. Students find the measures of all other angles in the diagram. Students can complete Extra Practice 1 (Master 7.23). ***Extension:*** Have students draw a diagram that contains at least 2 pairs of complementary angles, 2 pairs of supplementary angles, and 2 pairs of opposite angles. Students trade diagrams with a partner and identify the pairs of angles in their partner's diagram.

Recording and Reporting
Master 7.2 Ongoing Observations: Geometry

Using *The Geometer's Sketchpad* to Investigate Intersecting Lines

LESSON ORGANIZER 40–50 min

Curriculum Focus: Use technology to investigate intersecting lines. (8m47)

Student Materials

- computers with *The Geometer's Sketchpad* software

Assessment: Master 7.2 Ongoing Observations: Geometry

Key Math Learning

Computer software can be used to investigate the angle relationships for intersecting lines.

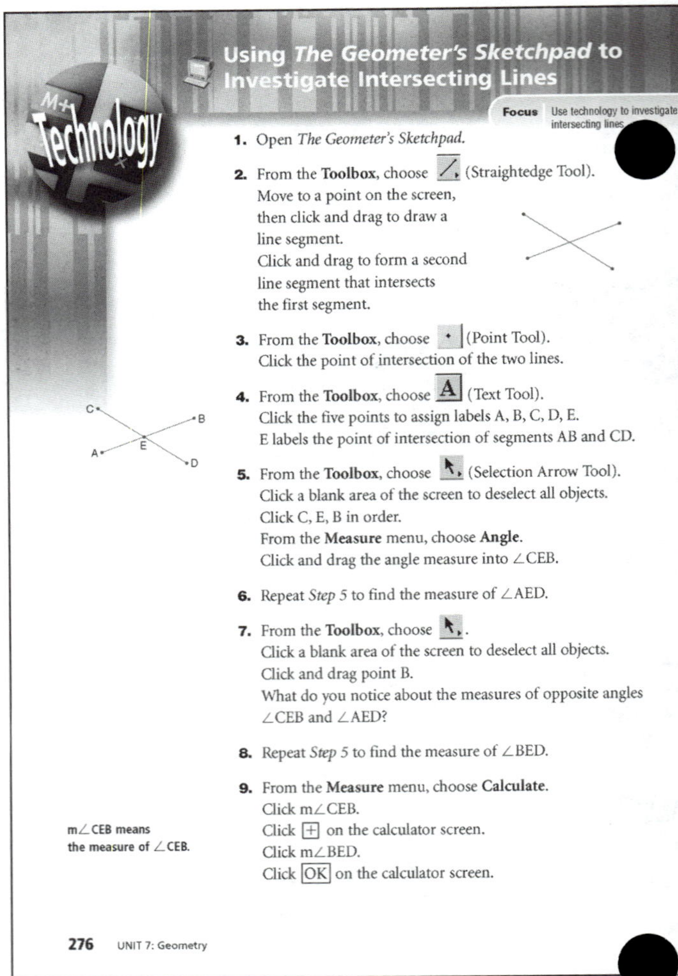

M+ Technology

Using *The Geometer's Sketchpad* to Investigate Intersecting Lines

Focus: Use technology to investigate intersecting lines.

1. Open *The Geometer's Sketchpad*.
2. From the **Toolbox**, choose (Straightedge Tool).
   Move to a point on the screen, then click and drag to draw a line segment.
   Click and drag to form a second line segment that intersects the first segment.
3. From the **Toolbox**, choose (Point Tool).
   Click the point of intersection of the two lines.
4. From the **Toolbox**, choose A (Text Tool).
   Click the five points to assign labels A, B, C, D, E.
   E labels the point of intersection of segments AB and CD.
5. From the **Toolbox**, choose (Selection Arrow Tool).
   Click a blank area of the screen to deselect all objects.
   Click C, E, B in order.
   From the **Measure** menu, choose **Angle**.
   Click and drag the angle measure into ∠CEB.
6. Repeat *Step 5* to find the measure of ∠AED.
7. From the **Toolbox**, choose .
   Click a blank area of the screen to deselect all objects.
   Click and drag point B.
   What do you notice about the measures of opposite angles ∠CEB and ∠AED?
8. Repeat *Step 5* to find the measure of ∠BED.
9. From the **Measure** menu, choose **Calculate**.
   Click m∠CEB.
   Click + on the calculator screen.
   Click m∠BED.
   Click OK on the calculator screen.

m∠CEB means the measure of ∠CEB.

276 UNIT 7: Geometry

Review the basic steps in using *The Geometer's Sketchpad.*

Have students work through *Steps 1* to *7*.

As they work, circulate to ensure all students are able to draw intersecting line segments and to find the measures of the angles.

When they have completed *Step 7*, ask:

- What do you notice about the measures of ∠CEB and ∠AED?
  (*The measures of the angles are equal.*)
- How does dragging point B affect the measures of ∠CEB and ∠AED?
  (*The measures of the angles change, but the angles are always equal.*)

Have students complete *Steps 8* to *11*.

Ask:

- What do you notice about m∠CEB + m∠BED?
  (*The sum is 180°.*)
- How does dragging point C affect the sum of the measures of ∠CEB and ∠BED?
  (*The sum of the angles is always 180°.*)

Have students complete *Steps 12* to *22*.

Ask:

- How does moving line segment ED affect the measures of ∠CDE and ∠EDB?
  (*As the size of one angle increases, the size of the other angle decreases. m∠CDE + m∠EDB is always 90°.*)

10. What do you notice about m∠CEB + m∠BED?

11. From the **Toolbox**, choose .
Click a blank area of the screen to deselect all objects.
Click and drag point C.
What do you notice about the sum of the measures of supplementary angles ∠CEB and ∠BED?

12. From the **File** menu, choose **New Sketch** to get a new screen.

13. From the **Toolbox**, choose .
Click and drag anywhere on the screen to draw a line segment.

14. From the **Toolbox**, choose .
Click the screen to create a point not on the line segment.

15. From the **Toolbox**, choose .
Click a blank area of the screen to deselect all objects.
Click the point and the line segment.

16. From the **Construct** menu, choose **Perpendicular Line**.

17. From the **Toolbox**, choose .
Draw a line segment with one endpoint at the intersection of the two segments.

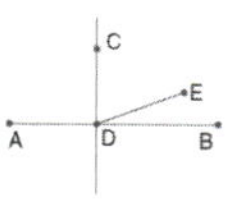

18. From the **Toolbox**, choose **A**.
Click the five points in order to assign labels A, B, C, D, E.

19. Repeat *Step 5* to find the measures of ∠CDE and ∠EDB.

20. Repeat *Steps 9* and *10* for ∠CDE and ∠EDB.

21. From the **Toolbox**, choose .
Click a blank area of the screen to deselect all objects.
Click and drag point E, ensuring that DE always lies between CD and DB.

22. What do you notice about the sum of the measures of complementary angles ∠CDE and ∠EDB?

REACHING ALL LEARNERS

Early Finishers

Have students use *The Geometer's Sketchpad* to draw a diagram that shows supplementary angles that do not share an arm, and to draw complementary angles that do not share an arm.

Common Misconceptions

➤ Students have difficulty getting the correct angle measure.
How to Help: Remind students they must click the points in order. For example, to find the measure of ∠AED, students should click A, then E, and then D. The vertex of the angle must be the second point clicked.

Sample Solutions

Step 11

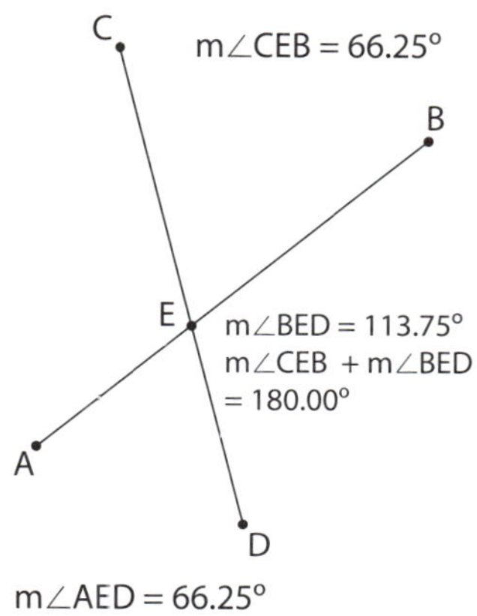

Step 22

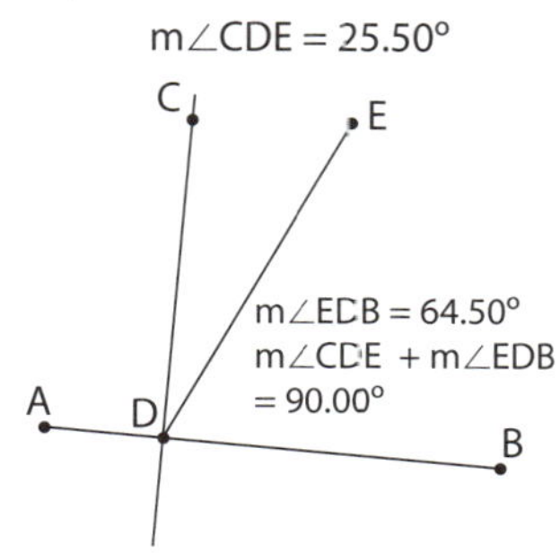

ASSESSMENT FOR LEARNING

What to Look For	What to Do
Knowledge and Understanding ✔ Students can connect the measures of the angles to their knowledge of the angle properties of intersecting lines. ***Application*** ✔ Students can use *The Geometer's Sketchpad* to verify the angle properties of intersecting lines.	***Extra Support:*** Pair students having difficulty with those who have good computer skills. ***Extra Practice:*** Have students find the measures of all angles in *Step 18*. Students find all supplementary angles, complementary angles, and opposite angles. ***Extension:*** Students use *The Geometer's Sketchpad* to construct a figure that has both complementary angles and supplementary angles; for example, a quadrilateral with angles 20°, 70°, 110°, 160°.

Recording and Reporting

Master 7.2 Ongoing Observations: Geometry

Angles in a Triangle

LESSON ORGANIZER 80–100 min

Curriculum Focus: Explore the relationships of the angles in a triangle. (8m45, 8m47, 8m48)

Teacher Materials
Optional
- cardboard triangle
- cardboard rectangle
- scissors

Student Materials
- tracing paper
- scissors
- protractors
- square dot paper (PM 22)
- calculators

Optional
- card or thin cardboard
- Step-by-Step 2 (Master 7.11)
- Extra Practice 2 (Master 7.24)

Assessment: Master 7.2 Ongoing Observations: Geometry

Key Math Learning

The sum of the angles in any triangle is 180°.

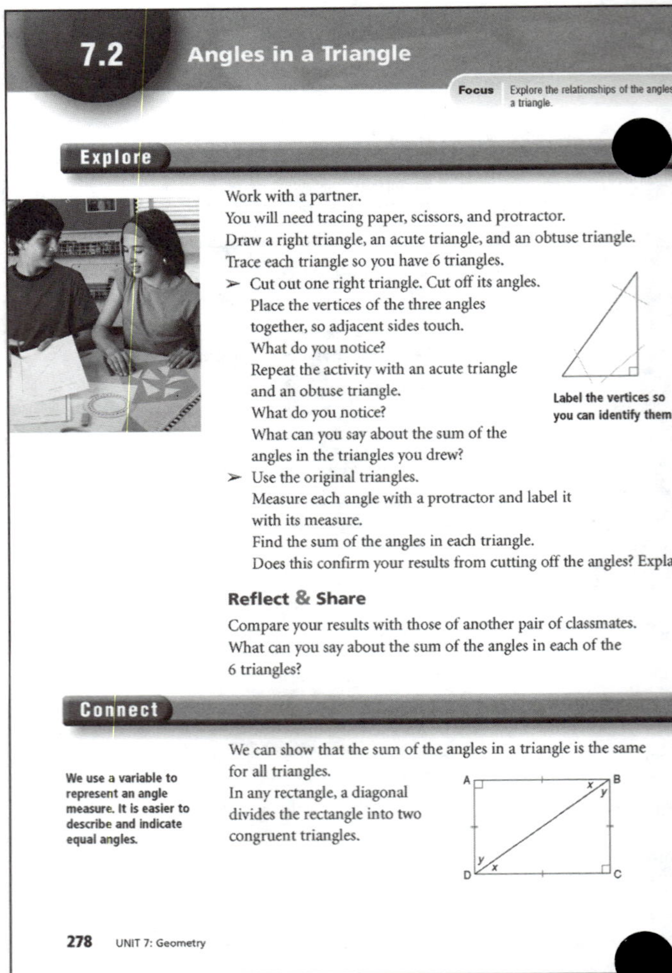

7.2 Angles in a Triangle

Focus Explore the relationships of the angles a triangle.

Explore

Work with a partner.
You will need tracing paper, scissors, and protractor.
Draw a right triangle, an acute triangle, and an obtuse triangle.
Trace each triangle so you have 6 triangles.

➢ Cut out one right triangle. Cut off its angles.
Place the vertices of the three angles together, so adjacent sides touch.
What do you notice?
Repeat the activity with an acute triangle and an obtuse triangle.
What do you notice?
What can you say about the sum of the angles in the triangles you drew?

➢ Use the original triangles.
Measure each angle with a protractor and label it with its measure.
Find the sum of the angles in each triangle.
Does this confirm your results from cutting off the angles? Explai

Label the vertices so you can identify them.

Reflect & Share

Compare your results with those of another pair of classmates.
What can you say about the sum of the angles in each of the 6 triangles?

Connect

We use a variable to represent an angle measure. It is easier to describe and indicate equal angles.

We can show that the sum of the angles in a triangle is the same for all triangles.
In any rectangle, a diagonal divides the rectangle into two congruent triangles.

278 UNIT 7: Geometry

BEFORE — Get Started

Review the different types of triangles with students. Ask:

- What is a right triangle? (*A triangle with one right angle*) An acute triangle? (*A triangle with all angles less than 90°*) An obtuse triangle? (*A triangle with one angle greater than 90°*)
- What other types of triangles can you name and describe?
(*A scalene triangle has all sides different. An equilateral triangle has all sides equal. An isosceles triangle has 2 sides equal.*)

Ensure students understand that combinations of these triangles are possible; such as a right isosceles triangle and a scalene obtuse triangle.

Present *Explore.* Encourage students to draw the triangles on cardboard (index cards or file folders) for better results. Students should make the triangles large enough to ensure that the angles can be measured accurately.

Students should cut out the tracing of each triangle. Suggest students colour the vertices of the triangles before cutting off the angles. This way, students will recognize the angles they are working with, and they will know which angles are to be combined.

DURING — Explore

Ongoing Assessment: Observe and Listen

As students work, ask questions, such as:

- Can you place 2 of the vertices of the right triangle together to form a right angle? Explain. (*Yes, if I use the two smaller angles*)
- What happens when you add the third angle? (*I get a straight line.*)
- What does this suggest about the sum of the angles in a right triangle?
(*The sum of the angles is 180°.*)

ere is only one a vertex, we can use a single letter to name the angle.

So, $\triangle ABD$ and $\triangle CDB$ are congruent because corresponding sides are equal.
Since the triangles are congruent, corresponding angles are equal.
That is, $\angle DAB = \angle BCD = 90°$
$\angle ABD = \angle CDB = x$
$\angle ADB = \angle CBD = y$

$\angle ABC = 90°$ because it is the angle in a rectangle.
So, $x + y = 90°$

Note that the sum of the acute angles in a right triangle is 90°.

In $\triangle ABD$, $\angle A + \angle ABD + \angle ADB = 90° + x + y$
$= 90° + 90°$
$= 180°$
Similarly, in $\triangle CDB$, the sum of the angles is 180°.

We can divide any triangle into 2 right triangles by drawing a perpendicular from the greatest angle to the base.
In $\triangle JKN$, draw the perpendicular from K to JN at M.

We use variables to label the acute angles.

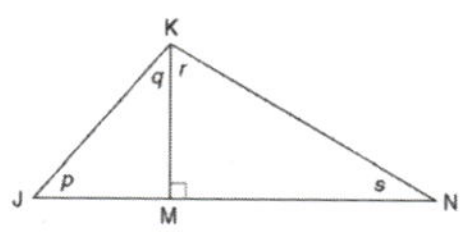

So, $\angle JMK = \angle NMK = 90°$
In $\triangle JKM$, $p + q = 90°$,
because the sum of the acute angles in a right triangle is 90°.
In $\triangle KMN$, $r + s = 90°$,
because the sum of the acute angles in a right triangle is 90°.
So, in $\triangle JKN$,
$\angle J + \angle JKN + \angle N = p + q + r + s$
$= (p + q) + (r + s)$
$= 90° + 90°$
$= 180°$
So, the sum of the angles in any triangle is 180°.
We can use this property to find angles in triangles and other figures.

REACHING ALL LEARNERS

Alternative Explore

Materials: protractors
Draw a large triangle. Use a protractor to measure the angles in the triangle. Label each angle with its measure, then calculate and record the sum of the angles. Repeat the activity for two different large triangles. Combine your answers with those of three classmates. What do you notice about the sum of the angles in a triangle?

Early Finishers

Have students use the sum of the angles in a triangle to find the measure of an angle in a regular hexagon, octagon, and decagon.

Common Misconceptions

➤ Students have difficulty finding the measures of angles in a triangle when only one interior angle and one exterior angle are given.

How to Help: Remind students to use their knowledge of supplementary angles. Use the diagram in *Practice* question 4. Since $\angle BCD$ is a straight angle, $\angle ACB$ and $\angle ACD$ are supplementary. So, $\angle ACB = 180° - 140° = 40°$
The measure of $\angle A$ can then be found using the sum of the angles in a triangle.

Calculator Skills

To calculate the amount received in US$, students could multiply by 0.82. To calculate the amount received in C$, students could divide by 0.82.

- Can you place the vertices of the three angles of the acute triangle together to form a straight line? Explain.
  (*Yes, if I place the three vertices so that adjacent sides touch, I get a straight line.*)
- What does this suggest about the sum of the angles in an acute triangle?
  (*The sum of the angles is 180°.*)
- Can you place the vertices of the three angles of the obtuse triangle together to form a straight line? (*Yes*) What does this suggest about the sum of the angles in an obtuse triangle? (*The sum of the angles is 180°.*)

In the second part of *Explore*, ensure students use the original, uncut triangles. Suggest students label each angle with its measure, then write the sum of the angles in the centre of each triangle.

Ask:

- What is the sum of the angles in each triangle? (*180°*)
- Does this confirm your results from cutting off the angles? Explain.
  (*Yes, I placed the vertices of the three angles in each triangle together to form a straight line. A straight line can be described as an angle of 180°. So, the sum of the angles in each triangle should be 180°.*)

AFTER Connect

Invite students to share their results with the class. Students who were unable to place the vertices of the three angles in each triangle together to form a straight line may not have labelled the vertices. They may have tried to combine the wrong angles.

Demonstrate the results of the first part of *Explore*. Use a cardboard triangle on the overhead projector. Cut off two of its angles. Rotate the angles to positions beside the third angle.

Assignment Guidelines

If your students do not have time to complete all the *Practice* questions on pages 281 and 282, these questions provide minimum curriculum coverage: 2, 3, 5, 6, 8, 10, 11, *Reflect*

To assess the 4 Achievement Chart categories listed in the curriculum document, have students complete these *Practice* questions:
Knowledge and Understanding: 4
Application: 7
Communication: 10
Thinking: 11

Sample Solutions

3. a) Since △ABC is an equilateral triangle, ∠A = ∠B = ∠C. So, each angle measures 180° ÷ 3 = 60°.

5. a) Since ∠QRS is a straight angle, ∠QRT and ∠TRS are supplementary.
So, ∠TRS = 180° − 70° = 110°

b) ∠PSQ = ∠TSR
Use the sum of the angles in △TRS.
∠PSQ = ∠TSR = 180° − 110° − 20° = 50°

c) Use the sum of the angles in △PQS.
∠PQS = 180° − 85° − 50° = 45°

6. a) Two angles whose sum is 180° are supplementary. The sum of the 3 angles in a triangle is 180°. So, it is not possible for 2 angles in a triangle to have a sum of 180°.

b) Two angles whose sum is 90° are complementary. So, if two angles in a triangle are complementary, the third angle

Example 1

Find the measure of ∠C in △ABC.

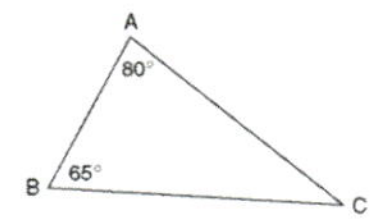

Solution

The sum of the angles is 180°.
∠A + ∠B + ∠C = 180°
Substitute for ∠A and ∠B.
80° + 65° + ∠C = 180° Add the angles.
145° + ∠C = 180°
To find the number to be added to 145 to make 180, subtract:
∠C = 180° − 145°
= 35°

We can also solve this equation by subtracting 145° from each side.

Example 2

Find the measures of ∠R and ∠P in △PQR.

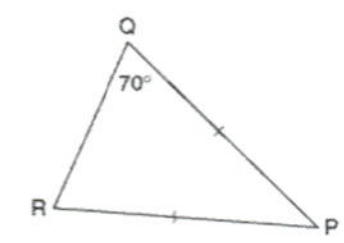

Solution

Since PQ = PR, the triangle is isosceles.
This means ∠R = ∠Q.
Since ∠Q = 70°, then ∠R = 70°
The sum of the angles is 180°.
∠P + ∠Q + ∠R = 180°
∠P + 70° + 70° = 180°
∠P + 140° = 180°
∠P = 180° − 140°
= 40°

280 UNIT 7: Geometry

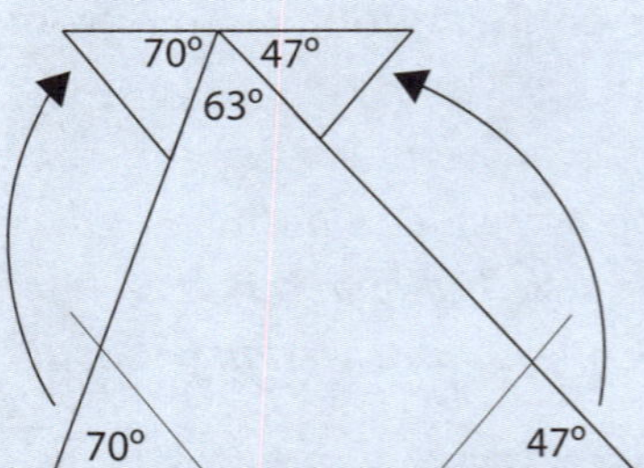

Discuss the convention for naming angles. An angle is usually described using three upper-case letters, with the middle letter representing the vertex of the angle. However, if there is only one angle at a vertex we can use a single upper-case letter to name the angle.

Have students look at the rectangle in *Connect*, at the bottom of page 278 of the Student Book. There is only one angle at vertex A. So, we can name the angle ∠A. At vertex D, there are two angles. To distinguish between the angles, we use 3 letters to name the angles: ∠ADB and ∠BDC.

We use lower-case variables, such as *w*, *x*, *y*, and *z*, to represent an angle measure. This way, we are able to distinguish between the angle and its measure. In higher levels of math, a lower-case letter is often used to represent the length of the side opposite an angle; for example, *b* represents the length of the side opposite ∠B.

Use a cardboard rectangle to demonstrate the sum of the angles in a right triangle. Cut the rectangle along a diagonal. Place one triangle on top of the other triangle to show they are congruent. Ask:

- How would you classify these triangles? (*They are both right triangles.*)
- What is the sum of the angles in a rectangle? (*360°*) How do you know? (*A rectangle has 4 right angles; 4 × 90° = 360°.*)
- What is the sum of the angles in each right triangle? (*180°*) How do you know? (*360° ÷ 2 = 180°*)

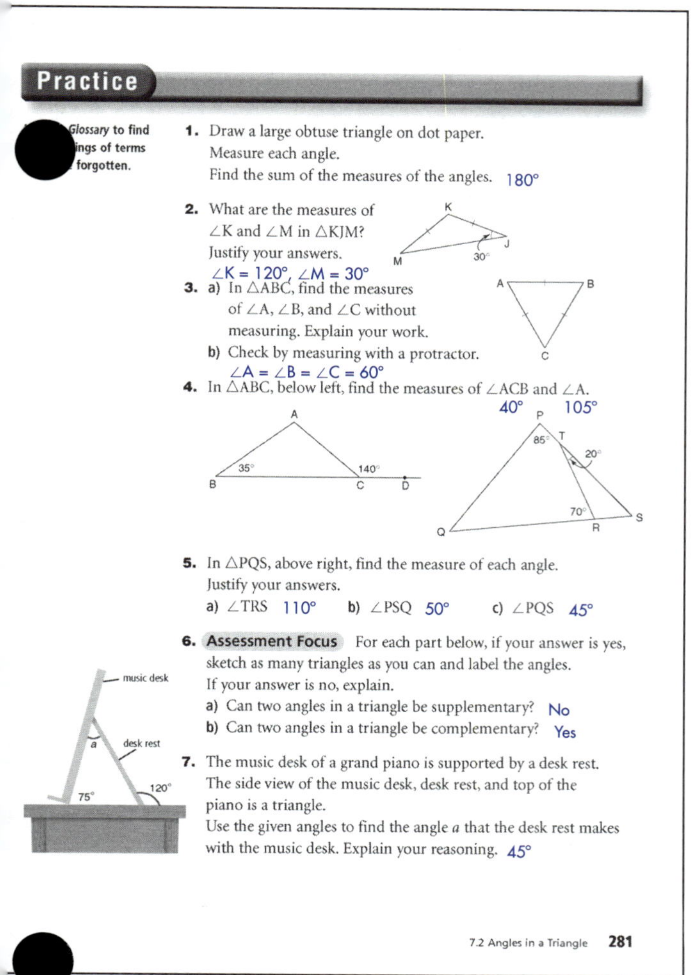

Practice

Check the *Glossary* to find meanings of terms forgotten.

1. Draw a large obtuse triangle on dot paper.
Measure each angle.
Find the sum of the measures of the angles. 180°

2. What are the measures of ∠K and ∠M in △KJM?
Justify your answers.
∠K = 120°, ∠M = 30°

3. a) In △ABC, find the measures of ∠A, ∠B, and ∠C without measuring. Explain your work.
b) Check by measuring with a protractor.
∠A = ∠B = ∠C = 60°

4. In △ABC, below left, find the measures of ∠ACB and ∠A. 40° 105°

5. In △PQS, above right, find the measure of each angle.
Justify your answers.
a) ∠TRS 110° b) ∠PSQ 50° c) ∠PQS 45°

6. **Assessment Focus** For each part below, if your answer is yes, sketch as many triangles as you can and label the angles.
If your answer is no, explain.
a) Can two angles in a triangle be supplementary? No
b) Can two angles in a triangle be complementary? Yes

7. The music desk of a grand piano is supported by a desk rest.
The side view of the music desk, desk rest, and top of the piano is a triangle.
Use the given angles to find the angle *a* that the desk rest makes with the music desk. Explain your reasoning. 45°

7.2 Angles in a Triangle 281

must be 180° – 90° = 90°. The triangle must be a right triangle. There are many different right triangles possible. Students' answers should include sketches of right triangles.

7. The angle supplementary to the 120° angle measures 180° – 120° = 60°.
Use the sum of the angles in a triangle.
a = 180° – 60° – 75° = 45°

8. ∠DEC = ∠AEB = 180° – 40° = 140° (supplementary angles)
The diagonals form 2 pairs of congruent isosceles triangles:
△AED and △BEC; △AEB and △DEC.

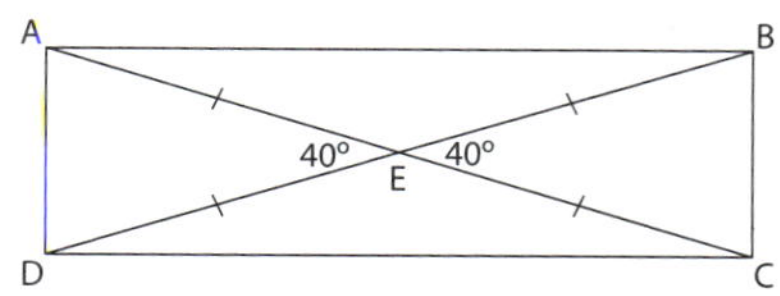

Using the sum of the angles in a triangle and the properties of an isosceles triangle, the measures of the angles in the first pair of triangles are 40°, 70°, and 70°, and the measures of the angles in the second pair of triangles are 140°, 20°, and 20°.

9. a)

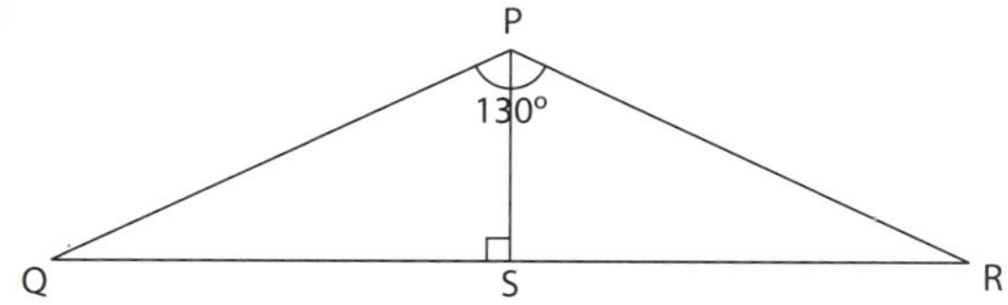

b) ∠PQR = ∠PRQ = 25°; ∠QPS = ∠RPS = 65°;
∠QSP = ∠RSP = 90°

10. a) An obtuse angle is greater than 90°. Since the sum of the angles in a triangle is 180°, a triangle can only have one obtuse angle.

Review the *Examples*. *Example 1* shows students how to determine one angle measure in a triangle, given the other two. *Example 2* shows students how to determine two angle measures in an isosceles triangle, given one.

Practice

Have protractors available for all questions. Question 1 requires square dot paper (PM 22). In questions 4 and 5, remind students not to write in their textbooks. Instead, encourage students to copy the diagrams in their notebooks, then mark any additional angle measures using a different colour. In question 11, suggest students divide the figure into triangles. In question 14, have students start by naming equal line segments.

Assessment Focus: Question 6

Students know two supplementary angles have a sum of 180°. Since the sum of the angles in a triangle is 180°, students should realize that two angles in a triangle cannot be supplementary.

The sum of the angles in a triangle is 180°. If two angles in a triangle are complementary (have a sum of 90°), the other angle must be a right angle. Students draw as many different right triangles as they can.

obtuse angle.

b) The sum of the 3 angles in a triangle is 180°. The sum of 3 right angles is 270° and the sum of two right angles is 180°. A right triangle can only have one right angle, and the sum of the other two angles must be 90°.

13. There are 12 different kinds of triangles: right; acute; obtuse; equilateral; isosceles; scalene; acute isosceles; obtuse isosceles; right isosceles; scalene obtuse; scalene acute; and scalene right. Students' answers should include a sketch of each triangle named.

14. OP = OQ = OR because they are radii of the circle
So, △OPQ and △ORQ are isosceles triangles.
So, ∠OPQ = ∠OQP = 40° (isosceles triangle)
∠QOR = 80° as it is supplementary to ∠QOP
∠OQR = ∠ORQ = 50° (isosceles triangle)
∠PQR = ∠PQO + ∠OQR = 40° + 50° = 90°

REFLECT: A diagonal can be drawn to divide a rectangle into 2 congruent right triangles. Since the sum of the angles in a rectangle is 360°, the sum of the angles in a right triangle is 360° ÷ 2 = 180°.
I can divide a scalene triangle into 2 right triangles by drawing a perpendicular from the greatest angle to the base. The sum of the angles in each right triangle is 180°, and each triangle has one right angle. So, the sum of the other two angles in each triangle must be 90°. These four acute angles combine to make the angles in the scalene triangle. So, the sum of the angles in the triangle is 90° + 90° = 180°.

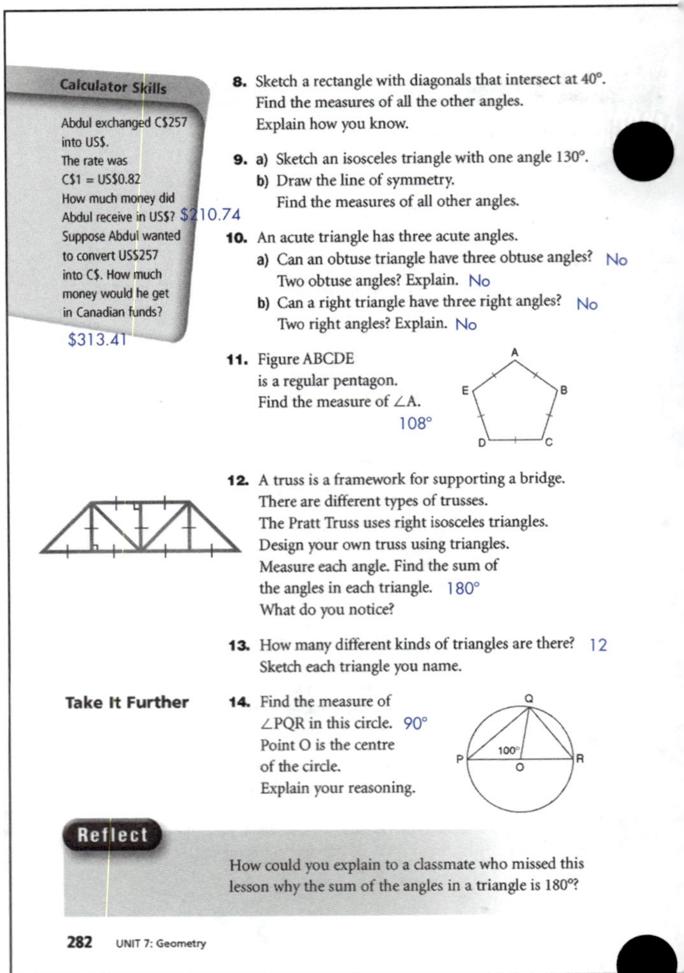

Calculator Skills

Abdul exchanged C$257 into US$.
The rate was C$1 = US$0.82
How much money did Abdul receive in US$? $210.74
Suppose Abdul wanted to convert US$257 into C$. How much money would he get in Canadian funds?
$313.41

8. Sketch a rectangle with diagonals that intersect at 40°. Find the measures of all the other angles. Explain how you know.

9. a) Sketch an isosceles triangle with one angle 130°.
b) Draw the line of symmetry. Find the measures of all other angles.

10. An acute triangle has three acute angles.
a) Can an obtuse triangle have three obtuse angles? No Two obtuse angles? Explain. No
b) Can a right triangle have three right angles? No Two right angles? Explain. No

11. Figure ABCDE is a regular pentagon. Find the measure of ∠A. 108°

12. A truss is a framework for supporting a bridge. There are different types of trusses. The Pratt Truss uses right isosceles triangles. Design your own truss using triangles. Measure each angle. Find the sum of the angles in each triangle. 180° What do you notice?

13. How many different kinds of triangles are there? 12 Sketch each triangle you name.

Take It Further

14. Find the measure of ∠PQR in this circle. 90° Point O is the centre of the circle. Explain your reasoning.

Reflect

How could you explain to a classmate who missed this lesson why the sum of the angles in a triangle is 180°?

282 UNIT 7: Geometry

ASSESSMENT FOR LEARNING

What to Look For

Knowledge and Understanding
✔ Students understand the sum of the angles in any triangle is 180°.

Thinking
✔ Students can solve problems that involve the sum of the angles in a triangle.

Application
✔ Students can use the sum of the angles in a triangle to find angles in triangles and other figures.

What to Do

Extra Support: Students who have difficulty finding the measures of angles may benefit from first identifying what information is missing and what is known. Students can use Step-by-Step 2 (Master 7.11) to complete question 6.

Extra Practice: Students can complete the Additional Activity *Can You Make It?* (Master 7.7). Students can complete Extra Practice 2 (Master 7.24).

Extension: Provide students with this diagram. Students find a relationship between w, x, and y.

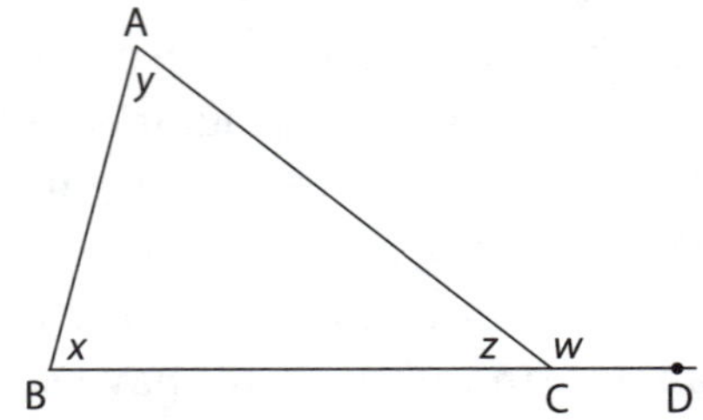

Recording and Reporting
Master 7.2 Ongoing Observations: Geometry

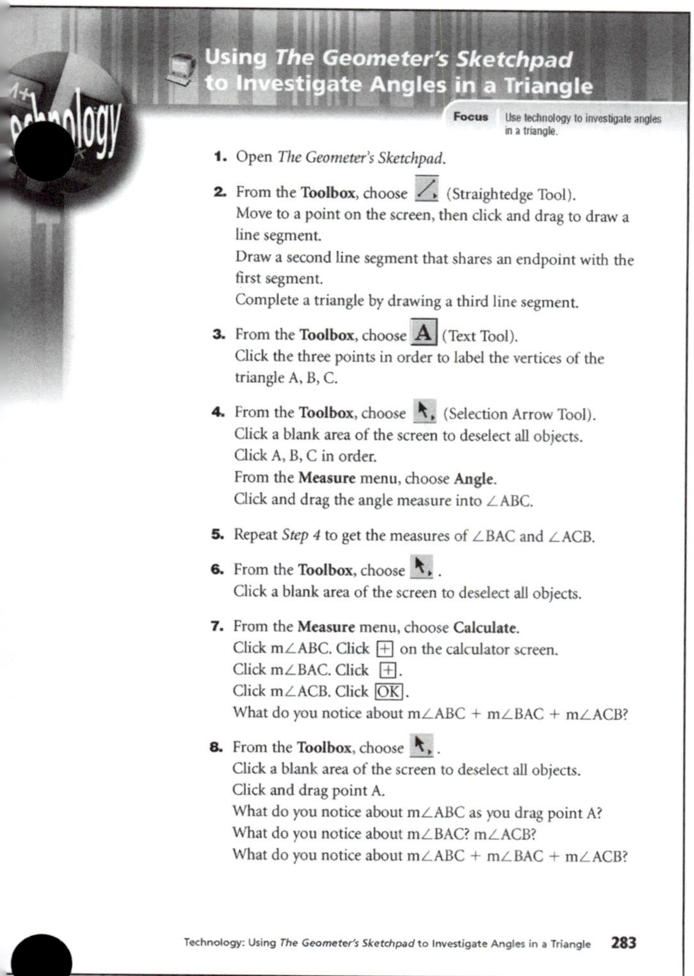

Using *The Geometer's Sketchpad* to Investigate Angles in a Triangle

Focus Use technology to investigate angles in a triangle.

1. Open *The Geometer's Sketchpad*.
2. From the **Toolbox**, choose [Straightedge Tool icon] (Straightedge Tool).
   Move to a point on the screen, then click and drag to draw a line segment.
   Draw a second line segment that shares an endpoint with the first segment.
   Complete a triangle by drawing a third line segment.
3. From the **Toolbox**, choose [A] (Text Tool).
   Click the three points in order to label the vertices of the triangle A, B, C.
4. From the **Toolbox**, choose [Selection Arrow Tool icon] (Selection Arrow Tool).
   Click a blank area of the screen to deselect all objects.
   Click A, B, C in order.
   From the **Measure** menu, choose **Angle**.
   Click and drag the angle measure into ∠ABC.
5. Repeat *Step 4* to get the measures of ∠BAC and ∠ACB.
6. From the **Toolbox**, choose [Selection Arrow Tool icon].
   Click a blank area of the screen to deselect all objects.
7. From the **Measure** menu, choose **Calculate**.
   Click m∠ABC. Click [+] on the calculator screen.
   Click m∠BAC. Click [+].
   Click m∠ACB. Click [OK].
   What do you notice about m∠ABC + m∠BAC + m∠ACB?
8. From the **Toolbox**, choose [Selection Arrow Tool icon].
   Click a blank area of the screen to deselect all objects.
   Click and drag point A.
   What do you notice about m∠ABC as you drag point A?
   What do you notice about m∠BAC? m∠ACB?
   What do you notice about m∠ABC + m∠BAC + m∠ACB?

Technology: Using *The Geometer's Sketchpad* to Investigate Angles in a Triangle 283

Using *The Geometer's Sketchpad* to Investigate Angles in a Triangle

LESSON ORGANIZER 40–50 min

Curriculum Focus: Use technology to investigate angles in a triangle. (8m47)

Student Materials

- computers with *The Geometer's Sketchpad* software

Assessment: Master 7.2 Ongoing Observations: Geometry

Key Math Learning

Computer software can be used to investigate the sum of the angles in a triangle.

Sample Solutions

What you might see:

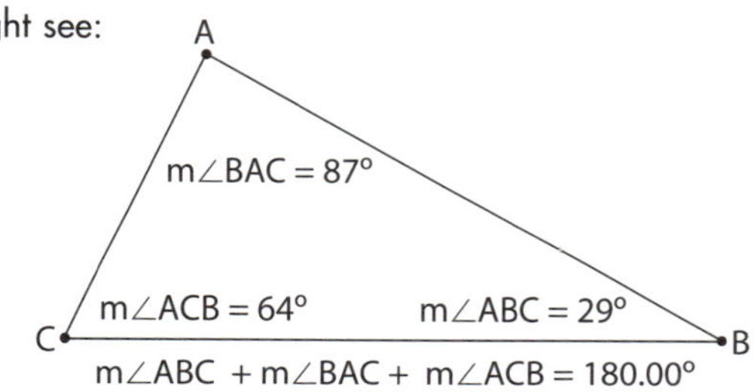

Have students work through *Steps 1* to *8*.

As they work, circulate to ensure all students are able to draw a triangle, and to find and label the measures of the angles.

When they have completed *Step 8*, ask:

- What do you notice about m∠ABC + m∠BAC + m∠ACB? (*The sum is 180°.*)
- What do you notice about the measures of the angles as you drag point B? (*The measures of the angles change.*)
- What do you notice about the sum of the angles as you drag point B? (*The sum of the angles is always 180°.*)

REACHING ALL LEARNERS

Early Finishers

Have students use *The Geometer's Sketchpad* to construct a quadrilateral with one diagonal drawn. Students use the sum of the angles in the triangles to find the sum of the angles in the quadrilateral. Students repeat the activity for different quadrilaterals. Students write about their findings.

Common Misconceptions

➤ Students are confused if the angle measures are not displayed as whole numbers.

How to Help: Show students how to change the display of the angle measures to whole numbers. From the **Edit** menu, choose **Preferences**. Select the **Units** tab. **Angle** should read **degrees**. Use the drop down menu to change **Precision** to **units**.

Angle Properties of Parallel Lines

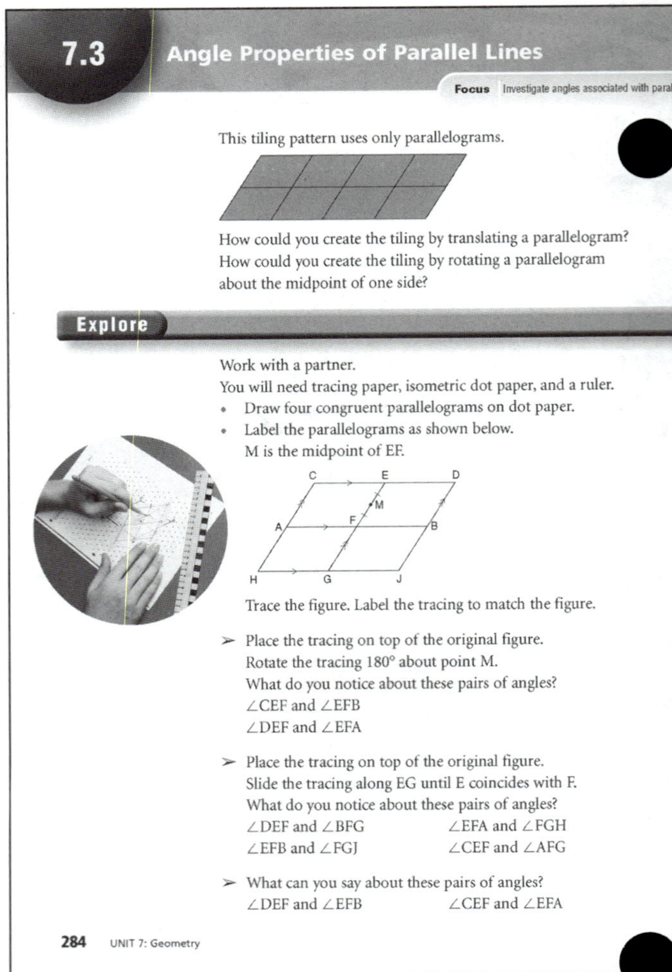

7.3 Angle Properties of Parallel Lines

Focus Investigate angles associated with parallel lines.

This tiling pattern uses only parallelograms.

How could you create the tiling by translating a parallelogram?
How could you create the tiling by rotating a parallelogram about the midpoint of one side?

Explore

Work with a partner.
You will need tracing paper, isometric dot paper, and a ruler.

- Draw four congruent parallelograms on dot paper.
- Label the parallelograms as shown below.
  M is the midpoint of EF.

C E D M A F B H G J

Trace the figure. Label the tracing to match the figure.

➢ Place the tracing on top of the original figure.
Rotate the tracing 180° about point M.
What do you notice about these pairs of angles?
∠CEF and ∠EFB
∠DEF and ∠EFA

➢ Place the tracing on top of the original figure.
Slide the tracing along EG until E coincides with F.
What do you notice about these pairs of angles?
∠DEF and ∠BFG ∠EFA and ∠FGH
∠EFB and ∠FGJ ∠CEF and ∠AFG

➢ What can you say about these pairs of angles?
∠DEF and ∠EFB ∠CEF and ∠EFA

284 UNIT 7: Geometry

LESSON ORGANIZER 80–100 min

Curriculum Focus: Investigate angles associated with parallel lines. (8m45, 8m47, 8m48)

Student Materials
- tracing paper
- isometric dot paper (PM 23)

Optional
- Step-by-Step 3 (Master 7.12)
- Extra Practice 3 (Master 7.25)

Vocabulary: transversal, alternate angles, corresponding angles, interior angles

Assessment: Master 7.2 Ongoing Observations: Geometry

Key Math Learning

When a transversal intersects parallel lines:
- alternate angles are equal
- corresponding angles are equal
- interior angles are supplementary

BEFORE Get Started

Have students look at the picture at the top of page 284 in the Student Book.

Ask:
- What is a tiling pattern? (*Congruent copies of a figure that cover a surface and leave no gaps*)
- What is a mathematical term for a tiling pattern? (*Tessellation*)
- How could you create the tiling by translating a parallelogram? (*I could slide the parallelogram to the right to form the first row, then slide the row down and to the left to form the second row.*)
- How would you create the tiling by rotating a parallelogram about the midpoint of one side? (*I would rotate the parallelogram 180° about the midpoint of the shorter side. I would continue to rotate in this way to complete the first row. To start the second row, I would rotate the original parallelogram 180° about the mid-point of the longer side. I would then complete the second row the same way as I completed the first row.*)

Remind students of the notations used to indicate parallel lines and equal line segments.

Small arrows (single, double, triple) are used to show lines that are parallel. Hatch marks (single, double, triple) are used to show equal sides.

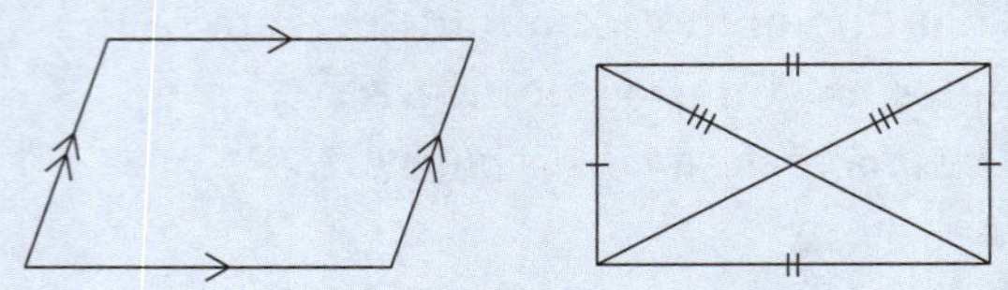

If you have not already done so, review *Skills You'll Need*, page 268, *Describing Transformations*.

Reflect & Share

Compare your results with those of another pair of classmates.
Work with your classmates. Write as many statements as you can about angle properties of parallel lines.

Connect

PQ and RS are parallel lines.
KN is a **transversal**.
F is the midpoint of JM.

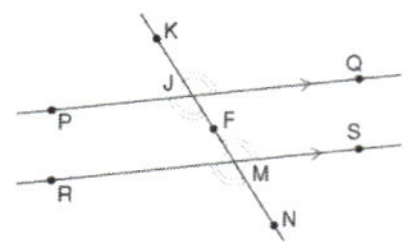

➢ After a rotation of 180° about point F,
∠PJM coincides with ∠JMS.
So, ∠PJM = ∠JMS
∠PJM and ∠JMS are between the parallel lines and are on opposite sides of the transversal.
They are called **alternate angles**.
Similarly, ∠QJM and ∠JMR are alternate angles.
So, ∠QJM = ∠JMR

➢ After a translation along line KN, ∠QJM coincides with ∠SMN.
So, ∠QJM = ∠SMN
Look at the parallel lines and the transversal.
∠QJM and ∠SMN are in the same relative position.
That is, each angle is below a parallel line and to the right of the transversal.
These angles are called **corresponding angles**.
Similarly, ∠KJQ and ∠JMS are corresponding angles.
Each angle is above a parallel line and to the right of the transversal.
∠KJQ = ∠JMS
And, ∠KJP and ∠JMR are corresponding angles.
Each angle is above a parallel line and to the left of the transversal.
∠KJP = ∠JMR

REACHING ALL LEARNERS

Alternative Explore

Materials: protractors

Draw a larger version of the diagram in *Connect*.

- Measure ∠PJM and ∠JMS.
  Measure ∠QJM and ∠JMR.
  What do you notice about these pairs of angles?
- Measure ∠KJP and ∠JMR.
  Repeat for ∠PJM and ∠RMN, ∠KJQ and ∠JMS, and ∠QJM and ∠SMN.
  What do you notice about these pairs of angles?
- Measure ∠PJM and ∠JMR. Find the sum of the measures.
  Repeat for ∠QJM and ∠JMS.
  What can you say about these pairs of angles?

Early Finishers

Have students draw and label 3 parallel lines crossed by a transversal. Students name sets of equal angles obtained by rotation, and sets of equal angles obtained by translation.

Common Misconceptions

➤ Students have difficulty identifying alternate, corresponding, and interior angles.

How to Help: Encourage students to look for patterns. Illustrate that alternate angles form a Z pattern, corresponding angles form an F pattern, and interior angles form a C pattern.

Mental Math

Students should use their knowledge of square numbers to see that 48 does not belong.
Forty eight should be replaced with 49, which is 7^2.

Present *Explore*. Encourage students to draw large parallelograms. Suggest students put a different coloured dot on ∠CEF, ∠EFA, ∠DEF, and ∠EFB. Students should use the same colour on the tracing of each figure. This makes it easier for students to see each angle in its original and final positions.

DURING Explore

Ongoing Assessment: Observe and Listen

As students work, ask questions, such as:

- What happens to the coloured dot on ∠CEF when the tracing is rotated 180° about point M? (*The dot moves to ∠EFB.*)
- What do you notice about ∠CEF and ∠EFB? (*The angles are equal.*)
- What happens to the coloured dot on ∠EFA when the tracing is rotated 180° about point M? (*The dot moves to ∠DEF.*)
- What do you notice about ∠EFA and ∠DEF? (*The angles are equal.*)
- How can you describe the positions of ∠CEF and ∠EFB in terms of EF and the parallel lines CD and AB? (*The angles are between the parallel lines and on opposite sides of EF.*)
- Is the same true for ∠DEF and ∠EFA? (*Yes, the angles are between the parallel lines and on opposite sides of EF.*)
- What happens to the coloured dot on ∠DEF when the tracing is slid along EG to the new position? (*The dot moves to ∠BFG.*)
- What do you notice about ∠DEF and ∠BFG? (*The angles are equal.*)
- What happens to the coloured dot on ∠EFB when the tracing is slid along EG to the new position? (*It moves to ∠FGJ.*)
- What do you notice about ∠EFB and ∠FGJ? (*The angles are equal.*)

Math Link

Students' lists might include: fences and gates, trellis work, bridge structures, hydro towers, metal shelving, road maps, buildings, transit maps, railroad tracks, and tiling patterns.

Assignment Guidelines

If your students do not have time to complete all the *Practice* questions on pages 287, 288, and 289, these questions provide minimum curriculum coverage: 2, 3, 5, 7, 8, 10, 12, *Reflect*

To assess the 4 Achievement Chart categories listed in the curriculum document, have students complete these *Practice* questions:
Knowledge and Understanding: 3
Communication: 6
Application: 8
Thinking: 10

Sample Solutions

4. a) ∠AGC and ∠AGD are supplementary angles.
So, ∠AGC = 180° – ∠AGD = 180° – 35° = 145°
∠CGB and ∠AGD are opposite angles.
So, ∠CGB = ∠AGD = 35°

b) ∠ABE and ∠AGC are corresponding angles.
So, ∠ABE = ∠AGC = 145°
∠ABF and ∠AGD are corresponding angles.
So, ∠ABF = ∠AGD = 35°
∠DGB and ∠AGD are supplementary angles.
So, ∠DGB = 180° – ∠AGD = 180° – 35° = 145°

The 4th pair of corresponding angles is ∠PJM and ∠RMN.
Each angle is below a parallel line and to the left of the transversal.
∠PJM = ∠RMN

➢ ∠QJM is the supplement of ∠KJQ because
∠QJM + ∠KJQ = 180°.
But, ∠KJQ = ∠JMS
So, ∠QJM is the supplement of ∠JMS.
That is, ∠QJM + ∠JMS = 180°
∠QJM and ∠JMS are between the parallel lines and are on the same side of the transversal. They are called **interior angles.**
Similarly, ∠PJM and ∠JMR are interior angles.
That is, ∠PJM + ∠JMR = 180°

Example

Two transversals intersect parallel lines.
Find the measure of each angle.
Justify each answer.

a) ∠HBC
b) ∠AFC
c) ∠AGB
d) ∠BGF

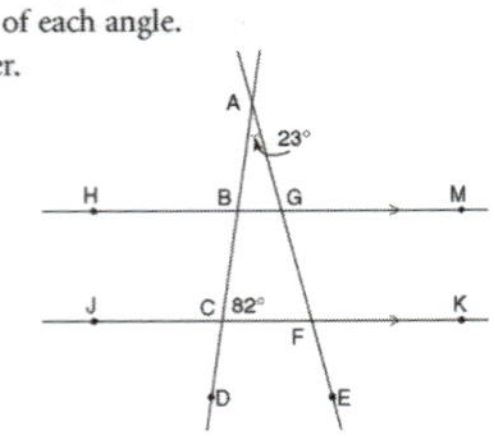

Solution

a) ∠HBC and ∠BCF are alternate angles.
So, ∠HBC = ∠BCF = 82°
∠HBC = 82°

b) In △AFC, the sum of the angles is 180°.
So, ∠A + ∠ACF + ∠AFC = 180°
23° + 82° + ∠AFC = 180°
105° + ∠AFC = 180°
∠AFC = 180° – 105°
= 75°

286 UNIT 7: Geometry

- What happens to the coloured dot on ∠EFA when the tracing is slid along EG to the new position? (*It moves to ∠FGH.*)
- What do you notice about ∠EFA and ∠FGH? (*The angles are equal.*)
- What happens to the coloured dot on ∠CEF when the tracing is slid along EG to the new position? (*It moves to ∠AFG.*)
- What do you notice about ∠CEF and ∠AFG? (*The angles are equal.*)
- How can you describe the positions of ∠DEF and ∠BFG in terms of EG and parallel lines CD and AB?
(*Each angle is below a parallel line and on the same side of EG. They form an F pattern.*)
- How can you describe the positions of ∠EFA and ∠FGH, ∠EFB and ∠FGJ, ∠CEF and ∠AFG in terms of EG and parallel lines CD and AB? (*In each pair, each angle is on the same side of a parallel line and on the same side of EG.*)
- How can you describe the positions of ∠DEF and ∠EFB in terms of EG and parallel lines CD and AB?
(*The angles are between the parallel lines and on the same side of EG.*)
- Can you name other pairs of angles in similar positions?
(*∠CEF and ∠EFA, ∠BFG and ∠FGJ, ∠AFG and ∠FGH*)
- What do you notice about the measures of ∠DEF and ∠EFB? Explain.
(*The sum of the angles is 180°. We showed that ∠DEF = ∠BFG. Since ∠EFB and ∠BFG are supplementary, ∠DEF and ∠EFB are also supplementary.*)
- What is the sum of pairs of angles that are between parallel lines and on the same side of the intersecting line? (*180°*)

c) ∠AGB and ∠AFC are corresponding angles.
So, ∠AGB = ∠AFC = 75°
∠AGB = 75°

∠BGC is the same angle as ∠AFC, which is 75°.

d) ∠BGF and ∠GFC are interior angles.
So, ∠BGF + ∠GFC = 180°
∠BGF + 75° = 180°
∠BGF = 180° − 75°
= 105°

Practice

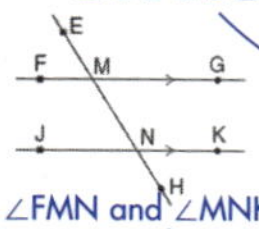

1. Use lined paper. Draw a larger copy of this diagram. Measure and mark all the angles.
   a) Name the corresponding angles. Are they equal? ∠HNJ and ∠NMF, ∠EMF and ∠MNJ, ∠NMG and ∠HNK, ∠EMG and ∠MNK; Yes
   b) Name the alternate angles. Are they equal? ∠FMN and ∠MNK, ∠GMN and ∠MNJ; Yes
   c) Name the interior angles. Are they supplementary? ∠GMN and ∠MNK, ∠FMN and ∠MNJ; Yes

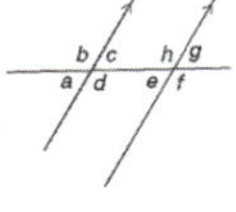

2. In this diagram, each angle is labelled with a variable. Use the variables to name:
   a) two pairs of corresponding angles b and h, c and g, a and e, d and f
   b) two pairs of alternate angles c and e, d and h
   c) two pairs of interior angles c and h, d and e

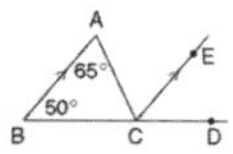

3. Look at this diagram.
   a) Name two parallel line segments. AB and EC
   b) Name two transversals. BD and AC
   c) Name two corresponding angles. ∠ABC and ∠ECD
   d) Name two alternate angles. ∠BAC and ∠ACE
   e) Find the measures of ∠ECD, ∠ACE, and ∠BCA. 50° 65° 65°

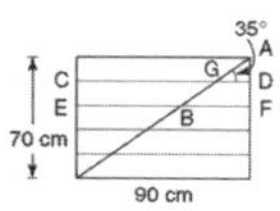

4. A gate is made of 5 parallel boards, with a cross piece for support. The plans for the gate are shown.
   a) What is the measure of ∠AGC? ∠CGB? 145°, 35°
   b) What is the measure of ∠ABE? ∠ABF? ∠DGB? 145° 35° 145°
   Justify each answer.

7.3 Angle Properties of Parallel Lines 287

5. ∠SPQ and ∠PQR are alternate angles.
So, ∠SPQ = ∠PQR = 55°
∠TPR and ∠PRQ are alternate angles.
So, ∠TPR = ∠PRQ = 25°
In ΔPQR, the sum of the angles is 180°.
So, 55° + 25° + ∠QPR = 180°
80° + ∠QPR = 180°
∠QPR = 180° − 80° = 100°

6. a) ∠SRY and ∠RTK are corresponding angles.
   b) ∠SQR and ∠SVT are corresponding angles.
   c) ∠RTK and ∠QRT are alternate angles.
   d) ∠YRT and ∠RTV are alternate angles.
   e) ∠QRT and ∠RTV are interior angles.
   f) ∠RTK and ∠VTW are opposite angles.
   g) ∠SQR = 90° and the sum of the angles in △SRQ is 180°.
   h) ∠SRY and ∠SRQ form a straight angle.

7. a) ∠GBD and ∠BDC are alternate angles.
So, ∠GBD = ∠BDC = 60°
∠BCD and ∠ABC are alternate angles.
So, ∠BCD = ∠ABC = 70°
In ΔBCD, the sum of the angles is 180°.
So, 60° + 70° + ∠DBC = 180°
130° + ∠DBC = 180°
∠DBC = 180° − 130° = 50°
∠BDC and ∠BDF are supplementary angles.
So, ∠BDF = 180° − ∠BDC = 180° − 60° = 120°
∠BCE and ∠ABC are interior angles.
So, ∠BCE = 180° − ∠ABC
= 180° − 70°
= 110°

AFTER Connect

Invite students to share their results with the class.

On the board, make a list of the different angle properties of parallel lines that students discover.

Draw the diagram in *Connect* on 2 different transparencies. Use different colours to mark ∠JMR and ∠QJM. Place the transparencies on top of each other so that the diagrams coincide. Rotate the upper transparency 180° about point F. Students can easily see the equal alternate angles.

Mark ∠KJQ and ∠JMS in different colours. Slide the upper transparency over the lower transparency until the angles coincide. Students can easily see the equal corresponding angles.

Use *Connect* to introduce the terms *transversal, alternate angles, corresponding angles,* and *interior angles.* Tell students that when two parallel lines are crossed by a transversal, two pairs of interior angles, two pairs of alternate angles, and four pairs of corresponding angles are formed.

Students may notice that alternate angles form a Z pattern and corresponding angles form an F pattern. Encourage students not to rely on these patterns too heavily, and to use the mathematical terms for these angles when justifying their answers.

Work through the *Example* together so students can see the type of justification expected in their solutions.

Ensure students understand that parallel lines should be named in the same direction.

b) Since ∠GBD, ∠DBC, and ∠ABC form a straight angle,
∠GBD + ∠DBC + ∠ABC = 180°.
By the properties of the angles between parallel lines,
∠BDC = ∠GBD and ∠BCD = ∠ABC (alternate angles).
So, ∠BDC + ∠DBC + ∠BCD = 180°
These are the angles of △BCD.
The sum of the angles in the triangle is 180°.

8. ∠KGH and ∠MFG are corresponding angles.
So, ∠KGH = ∠MFG = 125°
∠KGF and ∠MFG are interior angles.
So, ∠KGF = 180° – ∠MFG = 180° – 125° = 55°
∠HGJ and ∠KGF are opposite angles.
So, ∠HGJ = ∠KGF = 55°
In △GHJ, the sum of the angles is 180°.
So, 55° + 90° + ∠GHJ = 180°
145° + ∠GHJ = 180°
∠GHJ = 180° – 145° = 35°

9. ∠SRQ = ∠SRP + ∠PRQ = 50° + 85° = 135°
∠RQP and ∠SRQ are interior angles.
So, ∠RQP = 180° – ∠SRQ = 180° – 135° = 45°
△SPR is isosceles. So, ∠SRP = ∠SPR = 50°
In △SPR, the sum of the angles is 180°.
So, 50° + 50° + ∠PSR = 180°
100° + ∠PSR = 180°
∠PSR = 180° – 100° = 80°

10. a)

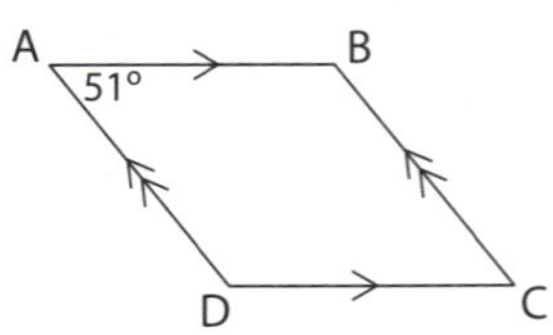

(Sample Solutions continue below, right.)

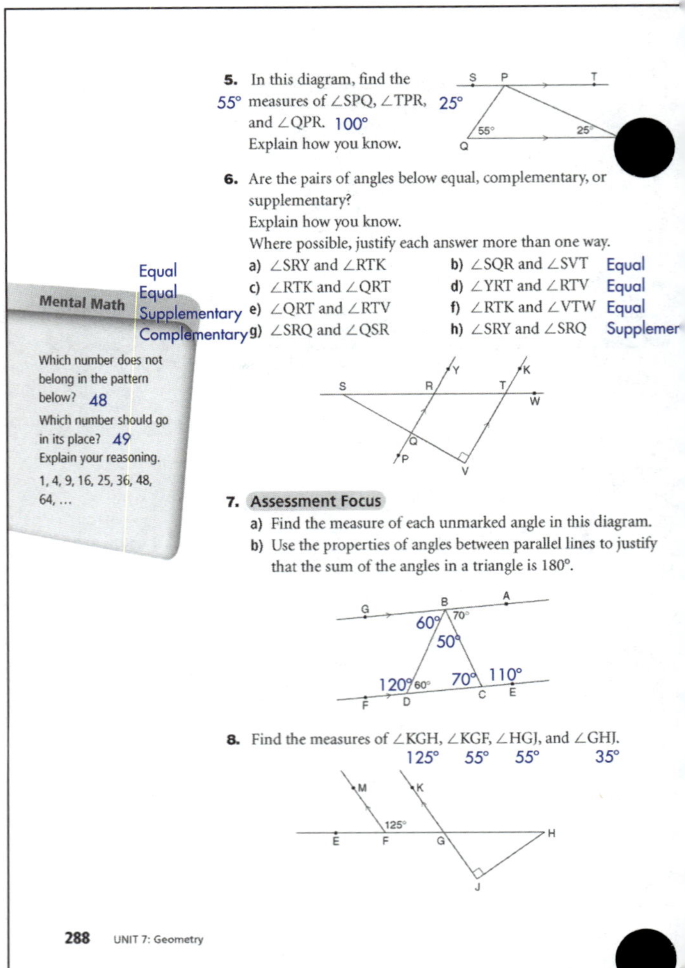

5. In this diagram, find the measures of ∠SPQ, ∠TPR, and ∠QPR. Explain how you know.
55° 25° 100°

6. Are the pairs of angles below equal, complementary, or supplementary?
Explain how you know.
Where possible, justify each answer more than one way.
a) ∠SRY and ∠RTK — Equal
b) ∠SQR and ∠SVT — Equal
c) ∠RTK and ∠QRT — Equal
d) ∠YRT and ∠RTV — Equal
e) ∠QRT and ∠RTV — Supplementary
f) ∠RTK and ∠VTW — Equal
g) ∠SRQ and ∠QSR — Complementary
h) ∠SRY and ∠SRQ — Supplemer

Mental Math

Which number does not belong in the pattern below? 48
Which number should go in its place? 49
Explain your reasoning.
1, 4, 9, 16, 25, 36, 48, 64, …

7. **Assessment Focus**
a) Find the measure of each unmarked angle in this diagram.
b) Use the properties of angles between parallel lines to justify that the sum of the angles in a triangle is 180°.

8. Find the measures of ∠KGH, ∠KGF, ∠HGJ, and ∠GHJ.
125° 55° 55° 35°

288 UNIT 7: Geometry

Practice

In question 2, students have to recognize corresponding, alternate, and interior angles with the parallel lines oriented differently. In question 4, students should realize that the dimensions of the gate are not relevant. In question 8, suggest students sketch the diagram in their notebooks, then write in the measures of the angles as they calculate them.

Assessment Focus: Question 7

Students could sketch the diagram in their notebooks and label the given angles in ink. Students could calculate the measure of each angle, then use pencil to label the angle with its measure. Remind students to justify each angle measure found, as well as the sum of the angles in a triangle.

(Sample Solutions, continued)

b) ∠A and ∠B are interior angles.
So, ∠B = 180° – ∠A = 180° – 51° = 129°
∠B and ∠C are interior angles.
So, ∠C = 180° – ∠B = 180° – 129° = 51°
∠C and ∠D are interior angles.
So, ∠D = 180° – ∠C = 180° – 51° = 129°

c) A quadrilateral is a parallelogram when opposite angles are equal. When opposite angles are equal, pairs of interior angles will add to 180°. This is one of the properties of angles between parallel lines.

11. I could draw a transversal, then measure the angles. If alternate angles and corresponding angles are equal, the lines are parallel.

12. The corresponding and alternate angles are not equal, and the interior angles are not supplementary.

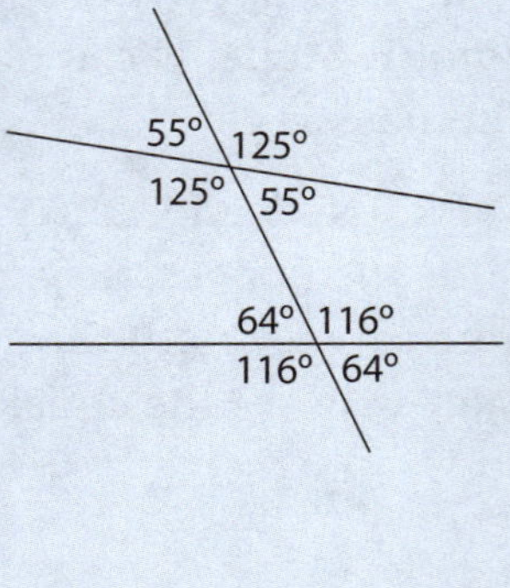

9. In trapezoid PQRS, PQ is parallel to SR, and diagonal PR is drawn. SP = SR, ∠SRP = 50°, and ∠PRQ = 85°
Find the measures of ∠RQP, ∠SPR, and ∠PSR.
Justify your answers. 45° 50° 80°

10. a) Sketch parallelogram ABCD with ∠A = 51°.
b) How can you use what you know about parallel line segments and a transversal to find the measures of the other 3 angles in the parallelogram? Explain your work.
c) When is a quadrilateral a parallelogram? Explain.

11. Suppose there are 2 line segments that look parallel. How could you tell if they are parallel?

12. Draw 2 line segments that are not parallel, and a transversal. Measure the alternate, corresponding, and interior angles. What do you notice?

Take It Further

13. Find the value of x, and the measures of ∠ADC and ∠CAD.
20° 60° 40°

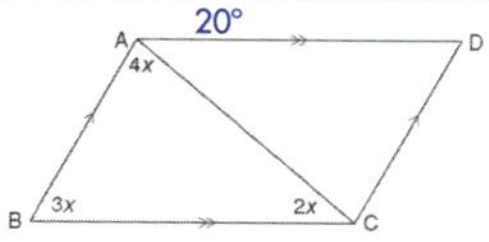

Math Link

Your World

Make a list of where you see parallel lines and transversals in your community, around the house, or on a construction site. Sketch diagrams to illustrate your list.

Reflect

Draw two parallel lines and a transversal. Label the angles. Explain how you remember which are corresponding angles, which are alternate angles, and which are interior angles.

13. In △ABC, the sum of the angles is 180°.
So, $4x + 3x + 2x = 180°$
$9x = 180°$
$x = 20°$
$\angle BAC = 4x = 4 \times 20° = 80°$
$\angle ACB = 2x = 2 \times 20° = 40°$
$\angle ABC = 3x = 3 \times 20° = 60°$
Since ABCD is a parallelogram, opposite angles are equal.
So, ∠ADC = ∠ABC = 60°
∠CAD and ∠ACB are alternate angles.
So, ∠CAD = ∠ACB = 40°

REFLECT:

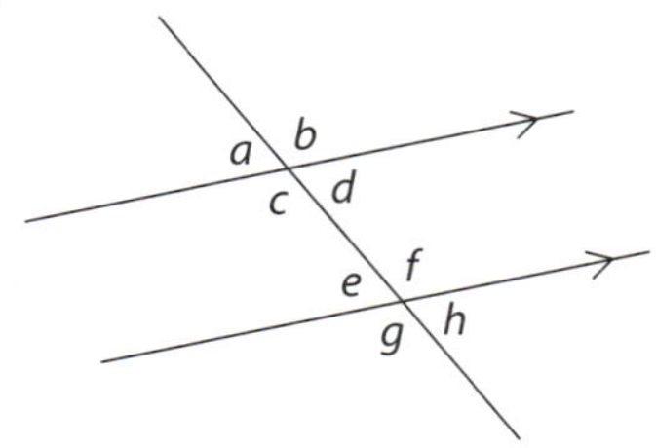

Corresponding angles are on the same side of the transversal and both are either above or below the parallel lines. They form an F pattern. Angles a and e, c and g, b and f, d and h are corresponding angles.
Alternate angles are between the parallel lines and on opposite sides of the transversal. They form a Z pattern. Angles c and f, and d and e are alternate angles.
Interior angles are between the parallel lines and on the same side of the transversal. They form a C pattern. Angles c and e, and d and f are interior angles.

ASSESSMENT FOR LEARNING

What to Look For	What to Do
Knowledge and Understanding ✔ Students understand the angle relationships for parallel lines and transversals.	***Extra Support:*** Students who have difficulty getting started may benefit from writing a checklist of angles to look for: alternate angles, corresponding angles, interior angles, opposite angles, supplementary angles, complementary angles, and angles in a triangle. Students can use Step-by-Step 3 (Master 7.12) to complete question 7.
Thinking ✔ Students can solve angle-relationship problems involving parallel lines and transversals.	***Extra Practice:*** Have students draw a diagram similar to the diagram in *Practice* question 1, and mark ∠GMN = 40°. Students find the measure of each unmarked angle, and justify their answers. Students can complete Extra Practice 3 (Master 7.25).
Communication ✔ Students can use appropriate mathematical terminology to justify the measures of angles found.	***Extension:*** Students consider the following: We know corresponding or alternate angles formed by 2 lines and a transversal are equal. Can we conclude that the lines are parallel? (Answer: Yes)

Recording and Reporting
Master 7.2 Ongoing Observations: Geometry

Using *The Geometer's Sketchpad* to Investigate Parallel Lines and Transversals

LESSON ORGANIZER 80–100 min

Curriculum Focus: Use technology to investigate parallel lines and transversals. (8m47)

Student Materials
- computers with *The Geometer's Sketchpad* software

Assessment: Master 7.2 Ongoing Observations: Geometry

Key Math Learning

Computer software can be used to investigate the angles formed by parallel lines.

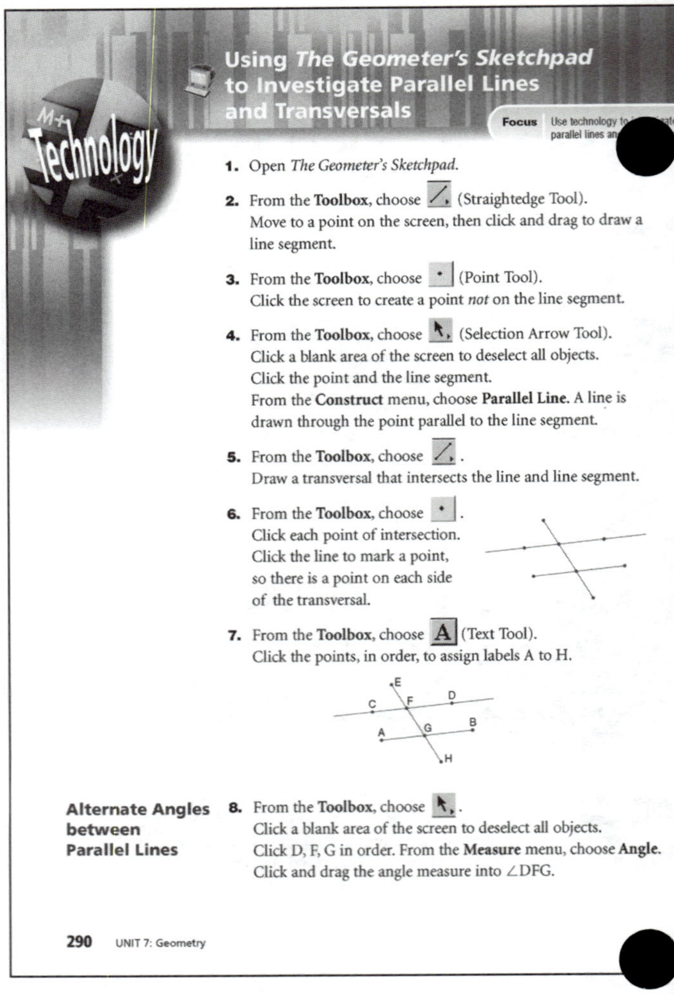

M+ Technology

Using *The Geometer's Sketchpad* to Investigate Parallel Lines and Transversals

Focus Use technology to [illegible] parallel lines an[illegible]

1. Open *The Geometer's Sketchpad*.
2. From the **Toolbox**, choose (Straightedge Tool). Move to a point on the screen, then click and drag to draw a line segment.
3. From the **Toolbox**, choose (Point Tool). Click the screen to create a point *not* on the line segment.
4. From the **Toolbox**, choose (Selection Arrow Tool). Click a blank area of the screen to deselect all objects. Click the point and the line segment. From the **Construct** menu, choose **Parallel Line.** A line is drawn through the point parallel to the line segment.
5. From the **Toolbox**, choose . Draw a transversal that intersects the line and line segment.
6. From the **Toolbox**, choose . Click each point of intersection. Click the line to mark a point, so there is a point on each side of the transversal.
7. From the **Toolbox**, choose (Text Tool). Click the points, in order, to assign labels A to H.

Alternate Angles between Parallel Lines

8. From the **Toolbox**, choose . Click a blank area of the screen to deselect all objects. Click D, F, G in order. From the **Measure** menu, choose **Angle.** Click and drag the angle measure into ∠DFG.

290 UNIT 7: Geometry

Tell students they will use *The Geometer's Sketchpad* to investigate alternate, corresponding, and interior angles formed by parallel lines and transversals.

Have students work through *Steps 1* to *11*. As they work, ensure students are able to produce the required diagram, with all points labelled correctly. When most students have completed *Step 11*, ask:

- What do you notice about the measures of alternate angles ∠DFG and ∠FGA as you drag point E?
  (*The alternate angles are always equal.*)
- What happens if you drag point D instead of point E?
  (*The alternate angles are always equal because line segments CD and AB are always parallel.*)

Have students complete *Steps 12* to *14*. Ask:

- What do you notice about the pairs of corresponding angles as you drag point E?
  (*The pairs of corresponding angles are always equal.*)
- What happens if you drag point B instead of point E? (*The pairs of corresponding angles are always equal because line segments CD and AB are always parallel.*)

Have students complete *Steps 15* to *19*. Ask:

- What do you notice about the sum of the measures of interior angles ∠DFG and ∠FGB as you drag point E?
  (*The sum of the measures is always 180°.*)
- What happens if you drag point C instead of point E?
  (*The sum of the measures is always 180° because line segments CD and AB are always parallel.*)

Have students repeat *Steps 1* to *19* for 2 non-parallel lines and a transversal. Ask:

- What do you notice?
  (*Alternate angles and corresponding angles are not equal. Interior angles are not supplementary.*)

9. Repeat *Step 8* for ∠FGA.

10. From the **Toolbox**, choose .
Click a blank area of the screen to deselect all objects.
Click and drag point E.
What do you notice about the measures of alternate angles ∠DFG and ∠FGA as you drag point E?

11. Repeat *Steps 8* to *10* for ∠CFG and ∠FGB.

Corresponding Angles between Parallel Lines

12. From the **File** menu, choose **New Sketch**.

13. Repeat *Steps 2* to *7* to create a new set of parallel lines cut by a transversal.

14. Repeat *Steps 8* to *10* for: ∠DFG and∠BGH; ∠CFG and ∠AGH; ∠EFD and ∠FGB; ∠EFC and ∠FGA
What do you notice about the pairs of corresponding angles?

Interior Angles between Parallel Lines

15. From the **File** menu, choose **New Sketch**. Repeat *Step 13*.

16. From the **Toolbox**, choose .
Use the **Measure** menu to measure ∠DFG and ∠FGB.

17. Use the **Measure** menu to calculate the sum of ∠DFG and ∠FGB.
What do you notice about ∠DFG + ∠FGB?

18. From the **Toolbox**, choose .
Click a blank area of the screen to deselect all objects.
Click and drag point E so that point F is always between point C and point D.
What do you notice about the sum of the measures of interior angles ∠DFG and ∠FGB?

19. Repeat *Steps 16* to *18* for ∠CFG and ∠FGA.

Angles between Non-Parallel Lines

20. Change *Steps 1* to *19*, as necessary, to find the angle measures between a transversal and 2 non-parallel lines.
What do you notice?

REACHING ALL LEARNERS

Early Finishers

Students draw △ABC with ∠A = 90°, then mark the midpoints P, Q, and R of AB, BC, and AC. Students join PQ, QR, and PR, then find pairs of parallel lines. They find a relationship between the measures of PR and BC, PQ and AC, and QR and AB.

Common Misconceptions

➤ In *Step 10*, students do not find that the measures of alternate angles are always equal.

How to Help: Ensure students understand that when they drag point E, point F must always be between point C and point D. This way, the angles are always on opposite sides of the transversal.

Sample Solutions

What you might see:

Step 11

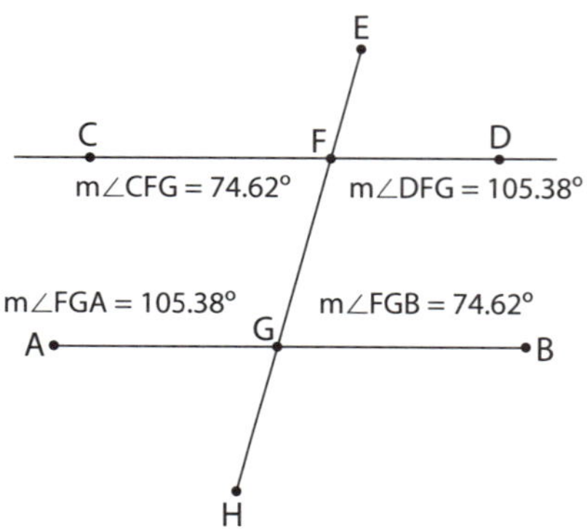

ASSESSMENT FOR LEARNING

What to Look For

Knowledge and Understanding

✔ Students can connect the measures of the angles to their knowledge of the angle properties of parallel lines and transversals.

Application

✔ Students can use *The Geometer's Sketchpad* to verify the angle properties of parallel lines and transversals.

What to Do

Extra Support: Pair students having difficulty with those who have good computer skills.

Extra Practice: Have students draw a trapezoid and one of its diagonals. Students use *The Geometer's Sketchpad* to investigate the relationships among all the angles.

Extension: Students use *The Geometer's Sketchpad* to draw 3 parallel lines and a transversal. Students identify all corresponding, alternate, and interior angles.

Recording and Reporting

Master 7.2 Ongoing Observations: Geometry

MID-UNIT REVIEW

LESSON ORGANIZER

Student Materials *Optional*
- calculators

Assessment: Masters 7.1 Unit Rubric: Geometry, 7.4 Unit Summary: Geometry

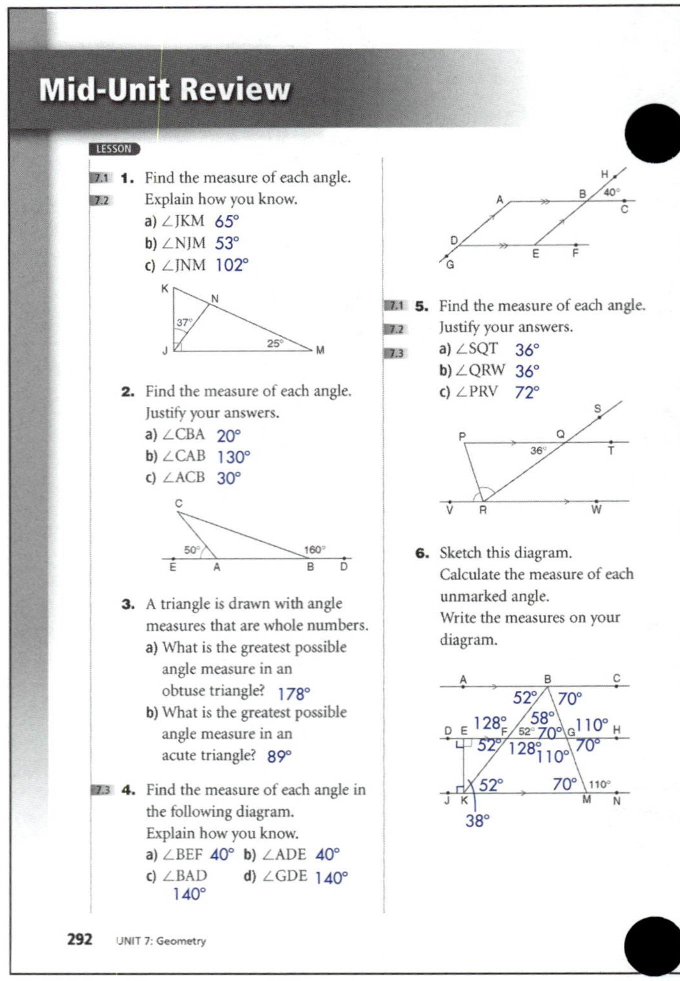

Mid-Unit Review

LESSON

7.1 7.2 **1.** Find the measure of each angle. Explain how you know.
a) ∠JKM 65°
b) ∠NJM 53°
c) ∠JNM 102°

2. Find the measure of each angle. Justify your answers.
a) ∠CBA 20°
b) ∠CAB 130°
c) ∠ACB 30°

3. A triangle is drawn with angle measures that are whole numbers.
a) What is the greatest possible angle measure in an obtuse triangle? 178°
b) What is the greatest possible angle measure in an acute triangle? 89°

7.3 **4.** Find the measure of each angle in the following diagram. Explain how you know.
a) ∠BEF 40° b) ∠ADE 40°
c) ∠BAD 140° d) ∠GDE 140°

7.1 7.2 7.3 **5.** Find the measure of each angle. Justify your answers.
a) ∠SQT 36°
b) ∠QRW 36°
c) ∠PRV 72°

6. Sketch this diagram. Calculate the measure of each unmarked angle. Write the measures on your diagram.

292 UNIT 7: Geometry

Assignment Guidelines

To assess the 4 Achievement Chart categories listed in the curriculum document, have students complete these questions:
Knowledge and Understanding: 1
Thinking: 3
Communication: 4
Application: 6

Sample Solutions

1. a) In ΔJKM, the sum of the angles is 180°.
So, 90° + 25° + ∠JKM = 180°
115° + ∠JKM = 180°
∠JKM = 180° – 115° = 65°

b) Since ∠KJM = 90°, ∠KJN and ∠NJM are complementary.
So, ∠NJM = 90° – 37° = 53°

c) In ΔJNM, the sum of the angles is 180°.
So, 53° + 25° + ∠JNM = 180°
78° + ∠JNM = 180°
∠JNM = 180° – 78° = 102°

2. a) Since ∠ABD is a straight angle, ∠CBD and ∠CBA are supplementary.
∠CBD = 160°
So, ∠CBA = 180° – 160° = 20°

b) Since ∠EAB is a straight angle, ∠CAE and ∠CAB are supplementary.
∠CAE = 50°
So, ∠CAB = 180° – 50° = 130°

c) In ΔABC, the sum of the angles is 180°.
So, 20° + 130° + ∠ACB = 180°
150° + ∠ACB = 180°
∠ACB = 180° – 150° = 30°

3. a) An obtuse triangle has one angle greater than 90°. The greatest possible angle measure in an obtuse triangle is 178°. This occurs when the other two angles each measure 1°.

b) An acute triangle has all angles less than 90°.
So, the greatest possible angle measure is 89°.

4. a) ∠BEF and ∠HBC are corresponding angles.
So, ∠BEF = ∠HBC = 40°

b) ∠ADE and ∠BEF are corresponding angles.
So, ∠ADE = ∠BEF = 40°

c) ∠BAD and ∠ADE are interior angles.
So, ∠BAD = 180° – ∠ADE
= 180° – 40°
= 140°

d) ∠GDE and ∠ADE are supplementary angles.
So, ∠GDE = 180° – 40° = 140°

5. a) ∠SQT and ∠PQR are opposite angles.
So, ∠SQT = ∠PQR = 36°

b) ∠QRW and ∠PQR are alternate angles.
So, ∠QRW = ∠PQR = 36°

c) Since ∠VRW is a straight angle,
∠PRV + ∠PRQ + ∠QRW = 180°.
∠QRW = 36°
So, ∠PRV + ∠PRQ + 36° = 180°
∠PRV + ∠PRQ = 144°
Since ∠PRV = ∠PRQ,
∠PRV = ∠PRQ = 144° ÷ 2 = 72°

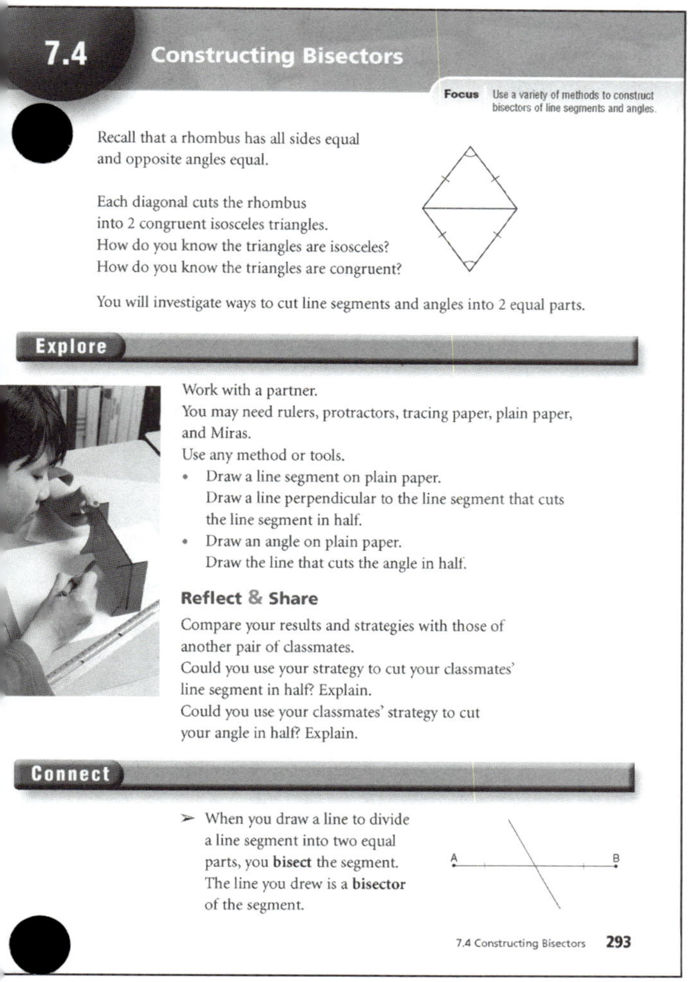
7.4 Constructing Bisectors

Focus Use a variety of methods to construct bisectors of line segments and angles.

Recall that a rhombus has all sides equal and opposite angles equal.

Each diagonal cuts the rhombus into 2 congruent isosceles triangles.
How do you know the triangles are isosceles?
How do you know the triangles are congruent?

You will investigate ways to cut line segments and angles into 2 equal parts.

Explore

Work with a partner.
You may need rulers, protractors, tracing paper, plain paper, and Miras.
Use any method or tools.

- Draw a line segment on plain paper.
  Draw a line perpendicular to the line segment that cuts the line segment in half.
- Draw an angle on plain paper.
  Draw the line that cuts the angle in half.

Reflect & Share

Compare your results and strategies with those of another pair of classmates.
Could you use your strategy to cut your classmates' line segment in half? Explain.
Could you use your classmates' strategy to cut your angle in half? Explain.

Connect

➢ When you draw a line to divide a line segment into two equal parts, you **bisect** the segment. The line you drew is a **bisector** of the segment.

7.4 Constructing Bisectors 293

LESSON 7.4

Constructing Bisectors

LESSON ORGANIZER (optional but recommended)

Curriculum Focus: Use a variety of methods to construct bisectors of line segments and angles. (8m44, 8m45)

Teacher Materials *Optional*
- ruler and overhead compass

Student Materials
- protractors
- tracing paper
- Miras
- compasses
- scissors

Optional
- Step-by-Step 4 (Master 7.13)
- Extra Practice 4 (Master 7.26)

Vocabulary: bisect, bisector, perpendicular bisector, angle bisector, circumcentre, circumcircle

Assessment: Master 7.2 Ongoing Observations: Geometry

Key Math Learning

The properties of a rhombus can be used to construct the perpendicular bisector of a line segment, and the bisector of an angle.

Curriculum Note

Although this lesson is no longer specifically required by the Grade 8 curriculum, it serves as a review of Grade 7 material. *Practice* questions 8 and 9 should be completed as they cover specific Grade 8 expectations.
This lesson should be taught in the first year of implementation.

BEFORE Get Started

Have students look at the picture at the top of page 293 in the Student Book.
Ask questions, such as:

- What is an isosceles triangle?
  (*A triangle with two equal sides*)
- How do you know the triangles are isosceles?
  (*By the definition of a rhombus, all sides are equal. So, in each triangle, the two sides that are sides of the rhombus are equal.*)

Remind students that congruent figures have the same size and shape. Review the conditions for congruence of triangles.Two triangles are congruent if:

- three pairs of corresponding sides are equal
- two pairs of corresponding sides are equal and the corresponding angles between these sides are equal
- two pairs of corresponding angles are equal and one pair of corresponding sides are equal

Ask:

- How do you know the triangles formed by the diagonal are congruent?
  (*Two pairs of corresponding sides and the angles between these sides are equal.*)
- How else can you describe the diagonal?
  (*It is a line of symmetry of the rhombus.*)
- How could you check that the diagonal is a line of symmetry?
  (*I could fold the rhombus along the line of symmetry to see one triangle coincides with the other*

REACHING ALL LEARNERS

Alternative Explore

Materials: ruler, protractor, Mira

Students draw line segment AB. They use a ruler and protractor to draw a line perpendicular to the line segment that goes through the midpoint of AB. Students check their results with a Mira. Students draw line segment CD. They use a Mira to draw a line perpendicular to the line segment that goes through the midpoint of CD. Students check their results with a ruler and protractor. Students repeat the activity for a line that cuts an angle in half.

Early Finishers

Students draw a large triangle. They use tracing paper and Miras to draw the bisector of each angle.

Common Misconceptions

➤ Students do not realize they are constructing the diagonal of a rhombus when they construct the bisector of a line segment or the bisector of an angle.

How to Help: Model the construction of the perpendicular bisector of a line segment. When you have completed the construction, use a coloured marker to highlight the rhombus, and a different coloured marker to highlight the bisector of the line segment. Students should see that the bisector of the line segment is also the diagonal of the rhombus. Repeat for the construction of the bisector of an angle if necessary.

When the bisector is drawn at right angles to the segment, the line is the **perpendicular bisector** of the segment.

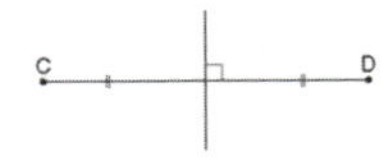

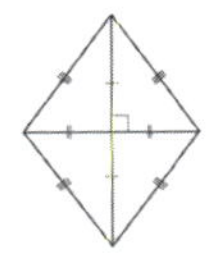

➤ Each diagonal of a rhombus is a line of symmetry.
The diagonals intersect at right angles.
The diagonals bisect each other.
So, each diagonal is the perpendicular bisector of the other diagonal.

We can use these properties of a rhombus to construct the perpendicular bisector of a line segment.
Think of the line segment as a diagonal of a rhombus.
As we construct the rhombus, we also construct the perpendicular bisector of the segment.

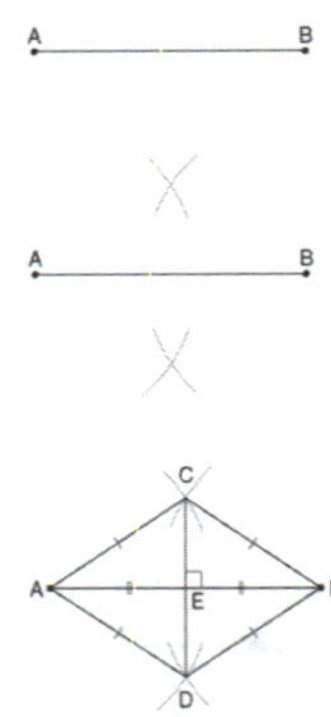

Use a ruler and compass.

- Draw any line segment AB.
- Set the compass so the distance between the compass and pencil points is greater than one-half the length of AB.
- Place the compass point on A.
  Draw an arc above and below the segment.
  Do not change the distance between the compass and pencil points. Place the compass point on B. Draw an arc above and below the segment to intersect the first 2 arcs you drew.
- Label the points C and D where the arcs intersect.
  Join the points to form rhombus ACBD. Draw the diagonal CD. The diagonals intersect at E. CD is the perpendicular bisector of AB. That is, AE = EB and ∠AEC = ∠CEB = 90°
  To check that the perpendicular bisector has been drawn correctly, measure the two parts of the segment to check they are equal, or measure the angles to check each is 90°.

Note that any point on the perpendicular bisector of a line segment is the same distance from the endpoints of the segment.
For example, AC = BC and AD = BD

294 UNIT 7: Geometry

triangle. I could also use a Mira. If I place the Mira along the diagonal, one triangle matches the other triangle.)

- What does this tell you about the triangles? (*Since the triangles coincide, they are congruent.*)

Present *Explore*. Suggest students label the line segment AB.

DURING Explore

Ongoing Assessment: Observe and Listen

As students work to construct a perpendicular bisector of a line segment, ask questions, such as:

- How could you use tracing paper to draw a line perpendicular to AB that cuts AB in half? (*Trace AB, then fold the tracing paper so that point A coincides with point B. Crease the fold line, then draw a line along the fold line. This line cuts AB in half and intersects AB at an angle of 90°.*)
- How could you use a Mira to draw a line perpendicular to AB that cuts AB in half? (*Place the Mira on AB so that the image of point A coincides with point B. Draw the mirror line. This line is perpendicular to AB and passes through the midpoint of AB.*)
- How could you use a ruler and protractor to draw a line perpendicular to AB that cuts AB in half? (*Measure the length of AB. Divide its length by 2 to get the midpoint of the line. Place the centre of the protractor on the midpoint, with the baseline of the protractor along AB. Mark an angle of 90°. Join this mark to the midpoint. This line is perpendicular to AB and passes through the midpoint of AB.*)

Introduce the second part of *Explore*. Have students label the angle ∠ABC. Have students brainstorm ideas for using tracing paper, Miras, or protractors to draw the line that cuts the angle in half.

As students work, ask questions, such as:

➢ When you divide an angle into two equal parts, you **bisect** the angle.
We can use the properties of a rhombus to construct the bisector of an angle.
Think of the angle as one angle of a rhombus.

BJ and BK are 2 sides of the rhombus; BJ = BK.

- Draw ∠B as one angle of a rhombus.
With compass point on B, draw an arc that intersects one arm at K and the other arm at J.

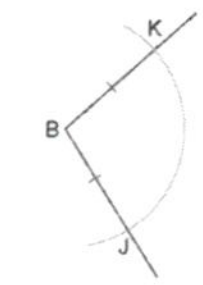

- Do not change the distance between the compass and pencil points.
Place the compass point on K.
Draw an arc between the arms of the angle.
Place the compass point on J.
Draw an arc to intersect the second arc you drew.
Label the point M where the arcs intersect.

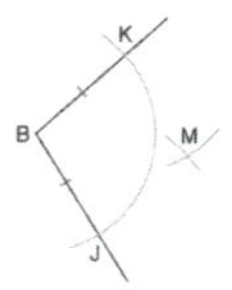

JM and MK are the other 2 sides of the rhombus.

BM is a diagonal of the rhombus.

- Join KM and MJ to form rhombus BKMJ.
Draw a line through BM.
This line is the **angle bisector** of ∠KBJ.
That is, ∠KBM = ∠MBJ

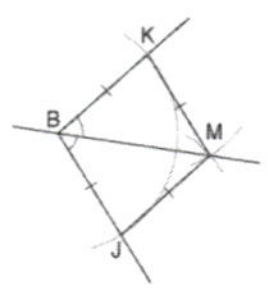

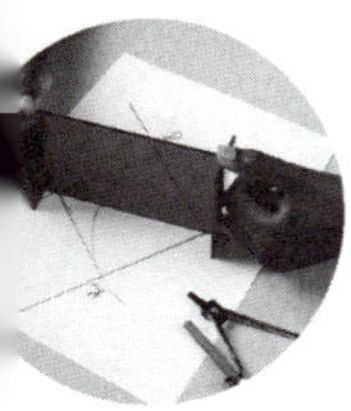

To check that the bisector of ∠B has been drawn correctly, we can:

- Measure the two angles formed by the bisector.
They should be equal.
- Fold the angle so the bisector is the fold line.
Arm JB should coincide with arm KB.
- Place a Mira along BM.
The reflection image of arm JB should coincide with arm KB, and vice versa.

Math Link

In an equilateral triangle, the angle bisectors, the perpendicular bisectors of the sides, and the lines joining the vertices of the triangle to the midpoint of their opposite sides are the same lines. In a scalene triangle, the angle bisectors, the perpendicular bisectors of the sides, and the lines drawn from the vertices to the midpoints of their opposite sides are different lines. To find the centre of gravity of a non-equilateral triangle, we find the midpoints of the sides of the triangle, then join these points to the opposite vertices. These lines are called *medians* and their point of intersection is the *centroid*, or centre of gravity of the triangle.

Assignment Guidelines

If your students do not have time to complete all the *Practice* questions on pages 296, 297, and 298, these questions provide minimum curriculum coverage: 1, 3, 4, 6, 8, 10, *Reflect*

To assess the 4 Achievement Chart categories listed in the curriculum document, have students complete these *Practice* questions:
Knowledge and Understanding: 1
Communication: 3
Application: 8
Thinking: 10

Number Strategies

Review the meanings of the terms mean, median, and mode.

- How could you use tracing paper to draw a line that cuts ∠ABC in half?
(*Trace ∠ABC. Fold the tracing paper so that arm AB coincides with arm BC. Crease the fold, then draw a line along the fold. This line cuts ∠ABC in half.*)
- How could you use a Mira to draw a line that cuts ∠ABC in half?
(*Place the Mira on point B, the vertex of the angle, so that the image of AB coincides with BC. Draw the mirror line. This line cuts ∠ABC in half.*)
- How could you use a ruler and protractor to draw a line that cuts ∠ABC in half?
(*Use a protractor to measure ∠ABC, then divide its measure by 2 to get the measure of one-half the angle. Place the centre of the protractor on point B, with the baseline of the protractor along BC. Mark an angle equal to one-half of ∠ABC. Join point B to this point, D. DB cuts ∠ABC in half.*)

AFTER Connect

Invite students to share their results and strategies with the class. Ensure students understand the different methods that can be used to find the bisectors of the line and of the angle.

Use *Connect* to introduce the terms *bisect, bisector,* and *perpendicular bisector*. Read through the steps for constructing the perpendicular bisector of a line segment together. Tell students that although all construction lines should be shown, students should make the construction lines faint. This will distinguish the construction lines from the required lines. Once students are comfortable with these steps, ask:

- How could you construct a line through a point C and perpendicular to AB?
(*Suppose point C is on AB. Place the compass point on C. Draw an arc on each side of C that intersects*

Sample Solutions

1. a)

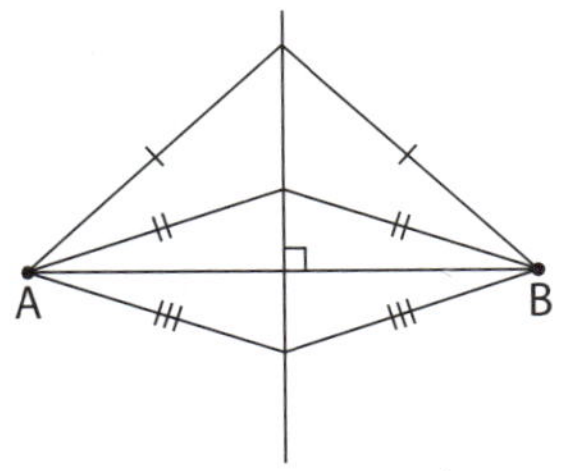

b) The distance to each point from A and from B is equal. The line segments joining each point on the bisector to A and to B form an isosceles triangle.

2. a) The arcs intersect at the midpoint of the line segment.
   b) The arcs do not intersect.
3. The ruler and compass method offers a greater degree of precision.
4. a)

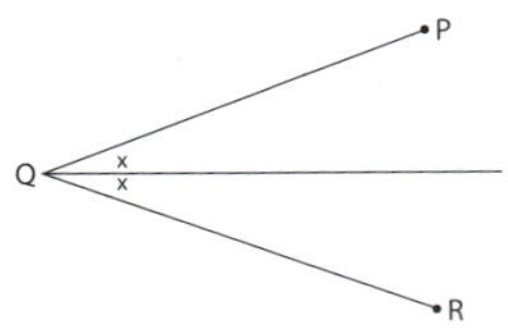

b)

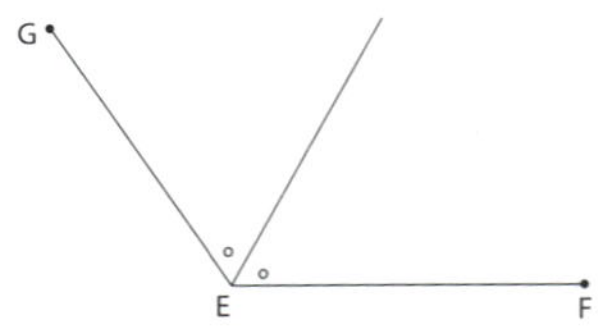

5. b) A reflex angle is an angle greater than 180°. The easiest way to bisect a reflex angle is to bisect the acute or obtuse angle formed by the arms of the angle, then extend the bisector through the reflex angle. For example, if the reflex angle measures 230°, I can bisect the obtuse angle that measures 360° – 230° = 130°. To do this, I can:
   - Trace the angle, then fold the tracing so that the arms of the angle coincide. The fold line is the bisector.
   - Place a Mira on the angle so that the image of one arm of the angle coincides with the other arm. The mirror line is the angle bisector.

Example

Draw any obtuse angle.
Use a ruler and compass to bisect the angle.
Measure the angles to check.

Solution

Draw obtuse ∠B.
With compass point on B, draw an arc to intersect the arms of the angle.
Label the points of intersection F and G.
Place the compass point on F. Draw an arc between the arms of the angle.
Do not adjust the compass. Place the compass point on G.
Draw an arc to intersect the second arc.
Label the point H where the arcs intersect.
Draw a line through BH.
This line is the bisector of ∠B.

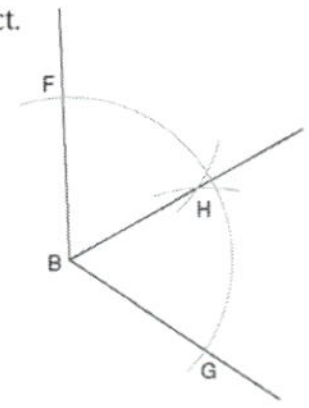

Use a protractor to check.
∠FBG = 126°
∠FBH = 63° and ∠GBH = 63°
∠FBH + ∠GBH = 63° + 63°
= 126°
= ∠FBG

Practice

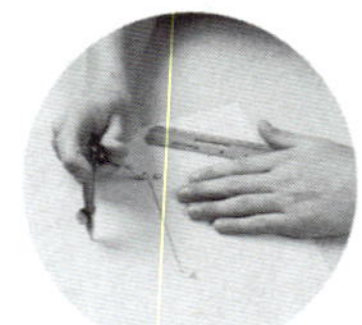

Show all construction lines.

1. a) Draw line segment AB.
   Use a ruler and compass to draw its perpendicular bisector.
   b) Choose three different points on the bisector.
   Measure the distance to each point from A and from B.
   What do you notice? Explain.
2. Find out what happens if you try to draw the perpendicular bisector of a segment when the distance between the compass and pencil points is:
   a) equal to one-half the length of the segment
   b) less than one-half the length of the segment

296 UNIT 7: Geometry

AB, keeping the distance between the compass and pencil points the same. Label the points of intersection D and E. Construct the perpendicular bisector of DE. This line passes through C and is perpendicular to AB.
Suppose point C is not on AB. Place the compass point on C. Draw an arc that intersects AB at 2 points. Label these points F and G. Construct the perpendicular bisector of FG. This line passes through C and is perpendicular to AB.)

Use a ruler and compass, and a transparency on the overhead projector to model these constructions.

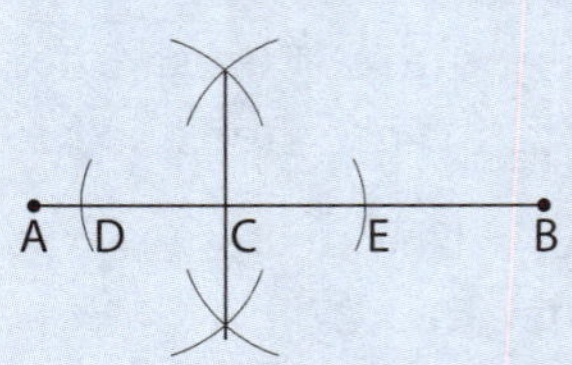

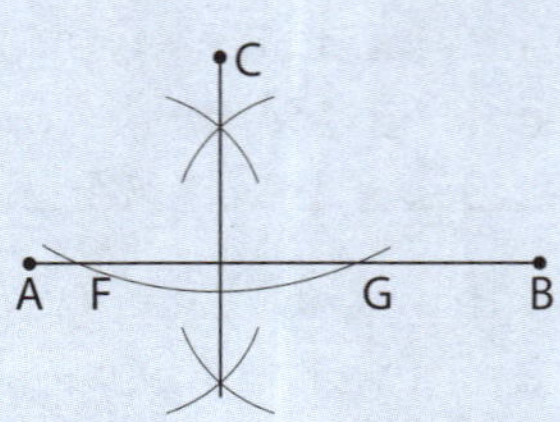

Introduce the term angle bisector. Work through the steps for constructing the bisector of an acute angle. Use the *Example* to show students how to construct the bisector of an obtuse angle. Students might benefit from writing step-by-step instructions for constructing the perpendicular bisector of a line and the bisector of an angle on index cards for reference purposes.

Practice

Remind students to use a sharp pencil and to draw all construction lines faintly.

In question 3, students may not see an advantage of using a ruler and compass. Students might think that Miras are the better tool as the required lines can be constructed quickly. Suggest students think about the accuracy of the construction rather than the speed at which it was made.

Use the *Glossary* if you have forgotten what a reflex angle is.

Number Strategies

...ean received these test ...marks in geography:
...2, 84, 88, 76, 64, 84
...ind the mean, median, ...and mode.
...78, 80, 84

"Circum" is Latin for "around." So, the circumcircle is the circle that goes around a triangle.

The point at which the perpendicular bisectors of the sides of a triangle intersect is called the circumcentre.

3. You have used Miras and paper folding to bisect an angle.
What is the advantage of using a ruler and compass?

4. Use a ruler and compass.
a) Draw acute ∠PQR. Bisect the angle.
b) Draw obtuse ∠GEF. Bisect the angle.

5. Draw a reflex angle.
a) How many different methods can you find to bisect this angle?
b) Describe each method.
Check that each bisector you draw is correct.

6. a) Draw line segment HJ.
Draw the perpendicular bisector of HJ.
b) Bisect each right angle in part a.
c) How many angle bisectors did you need to draw in part b? 2
Explain.

7. Draw a large △ABC. Cut it out.
Fold the triangle so B and C coincide. Open the triangle.
Fold it so A and B coincide. Open the triangle.
Fold it so A and C coincide. Open the triangle.
Use a ruler to draw a line along each crease.
a) Measure the angles each crease makes with one side.
What do you notice? Each angle measures 90°.
b) Label point K where the creases meet.
Measure KA, KB, and KC.
What do you notice? KA = KB = KC
c) What have you constructed by folding?
Perpendicular bisectors of the sides of the triangle

8. Draw a large △PQR.
Construct the perpendicular bisector of each side.
Label point C where the bisectors meet.
Draw the circle with centre C and radius CP.

9. a) How could you use the construction in question 8 to draw a circle through any 3 points that do not lie on a line?
b) Mark 3 points as far apart as possible.
Draw a circle through the points.
Describe your construction.

- Use a ruler and compass to bisect the angle, then extend the bisector through the reflex angle.

6. a), b)

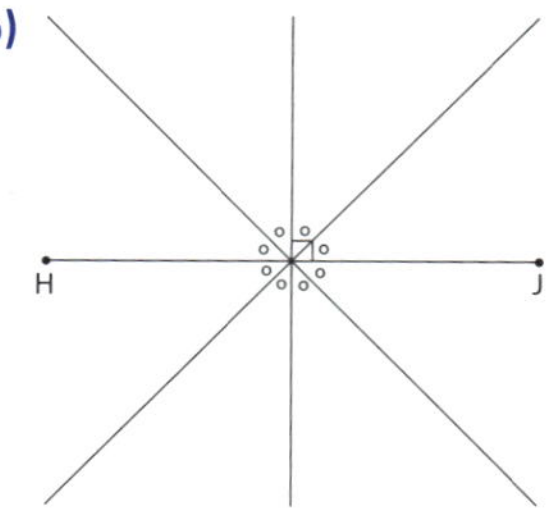

c) I needed to draw 2 angle bisectors because I was able to extend the bisectors into the opposite angles.

7. c) I have constructed the perpendicular bisectors of the sides of the triangle. I have also constructed a point that is equidistant from each vertex of the triangle.

8.

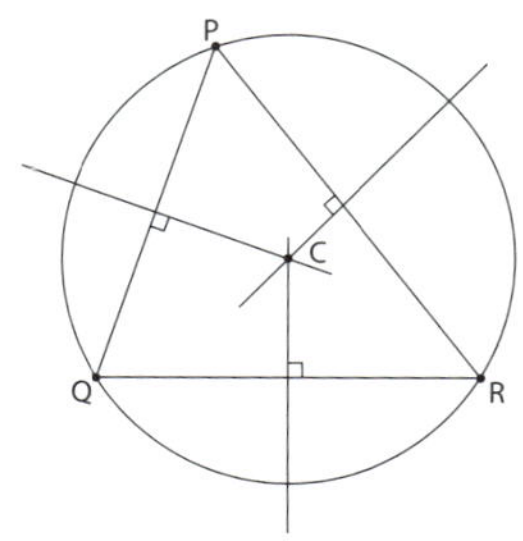

9. a) I could join the 3 points to form a triangle. I could construct the perpendicular bisector of each side, then label the point where the bisectors meet, C. I could draw a circle with centre C that passes through the vertices of the triangle.

(Sample Solutions continue below, right.)

In question 8, tell students they are constructing the circumcentre, or the centre of the circle that passes through the 3 vertices of the triangle. Encourage students to investigate acute, right, and obtuse triangles.

In question 11, encourage students to draw another quadrilateral PQRS, then draw the circumcircle of ∠PQR. It is unlikely the circle will pass through S. The only time the circle will pass through all 4 vertices of the quadrilateral is when opposite angles are supplementary.

Assessment Focus: Question 10

Remind students to construct, rather than draw, the isosceles triangle.

In part e, some students will have to repeat parts a to d for an equilateral triangle and a scalene triangle. Stronger math students may be able to draw conclusions from the results obtained from the isosceles triangle. Remind students to justify their answers in part e.

(Sample Solutions continued)

10. a), b), c),

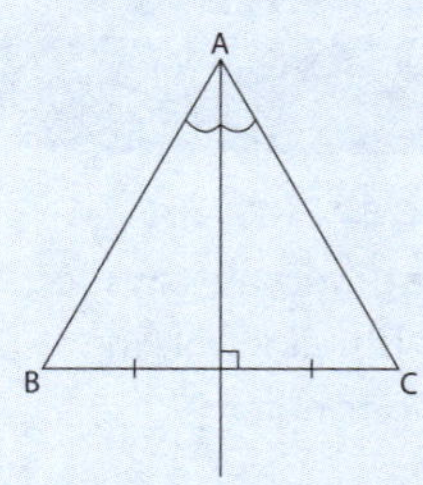

d) The bisector of ∠A is also the perpendicular bisector of BC.

e) i) The result will be true for all isosceles triangles because the angle bisector and the perpendicular bisector of the base are lines of symmetry.

ii) The result will be true for all equilateral triangles because each angle bisector and perpendicular bisector of a side is a line of symmetry.

iii) The result will not be true for all scalene triangles because they do not have lines of symmetry.

11.

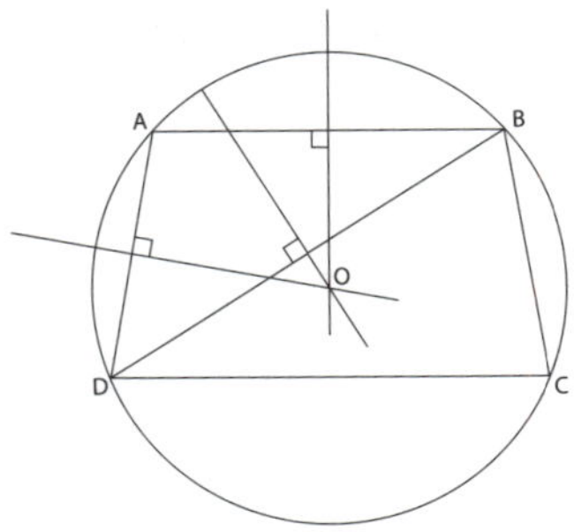

The circle passes through C. This result will only be true when the opposite angles of a quadrilateral are supplementary.

REFLECT: An angle can have only one bisector.

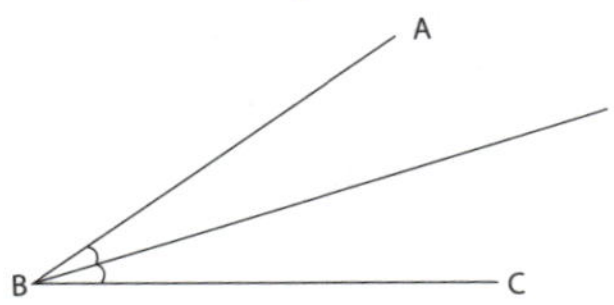

A line segment can have many bisectors. The angle at which the bisector intersects the line segment does not matter.

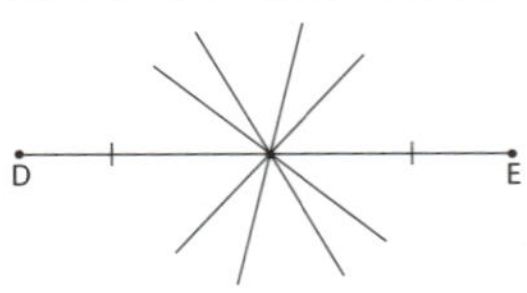

A line segment can have only one perpendicular bisector.

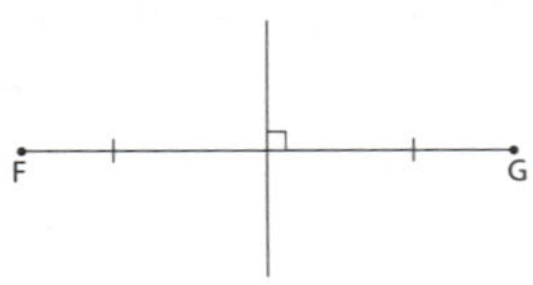

10. Assessment Focus

Use a ruler and compass.

a) Draw a large isosceles △ABC, with AB = AC.

b) Bisect ∠A.

c) Draw the perpendicular bisector of BC.

d) What do you notice about the bisectors?

e) Will the result in part d be true for:

i) all isosceles triangles? Yes

ii) all equilateral triangles? Yes

iii) all scalene triangles? No

Explain your answers. Show your work.

Take It Further

11. Use a ruler and protractor to draw quadrilateral ABCD.
AB = 7 cm, AD = 5 cm, ∠DAB = 105°, ∠ABC = 100°, and ∠ADC = 80°

Join BD. Construct the circumcircle of △ABD.

Does the circle pass through C? Yes

Do you think this would happen for all quadrilaterals? Investigate

Math Link

Science

The circumcentre of an equilateral triangle is also the balancing point of the triangle.
For example, you can balance the triangle on the tip of a pencil using the circumcentre.
Gravity acts on all parts of a structure. Gravity pulls a structure downward through a point called the **centre of gravity**. The centre of gravity of an equilateral triangle is its circumcentre.

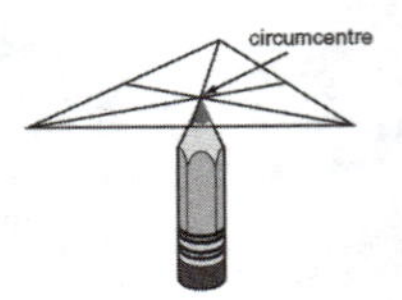

Reflect

How many bisectors can an angle have?
How many bisectors can a line segment have?
How many perpendicular bisectors can a line segment have?
Draw a diagram to illustrate each answer.

298 UNIT 7: Geometry

ASSESSMENT FOR LEARNING

What to Look For	What to Do
Knowledge and Understanding ✔ Students understand the different ways to construct perpendicular bisectors of line segments and bisectors of angles. ***Communication*** ✔ Students can describe and justify the methods used for constructing perpendicular bisectors of line segments and bisectors of angles. ***Application*** ✔ Students can use tracing paper, Miras, and rulers and compasses to construct perpendicular bisectors of line segments and bisectors of angles.	***Extra Support:*** Students who have difficulty with ruler and compass constructions should practise constructing perpendicular bisectors of line segments and bisectors of angles before they move on to constructions involving triangles and quadrilaterals. Students can use Step-by-Step 4 (Master 7.13) to complete question 10. ***Extra Practice:*** Students can complete the Additional Activity *Triangle Trial* (Master 7.8). Students can complete Extra Practice 4 (Master 7.26). ***Extension:*** Students draw a line segment AB at the bottom of a page. Students describe how to construct the perpendicular bisector of AB such that all construction lines are on the page.

Recording and Reporting

Master 7.2 Ongoing Observations: Geometry

7.5 Constructing Angles

Focus Use a variety of methods to construct angles.

You have used a protractor to construct an angle of a given measure.
What if you do not have a protractor.
How can you construct angles?

Explore

Work with a partner.
You will need a ruler, compass, Mira, and tracing paper.

- Use your knowledge of equilateral triangles and angle bisectors to construct a 30° angle.
- Use your knowledge of perpendicular bisectors and angle bisectors to construct a 45° angle.

Explain the steps you took to construct each angle.

Reflect & Share

Compare strategies with another pair of classmates.
How many different strategies can you use to construct a 30° angle?
A 45° angle?

Connect

You can construct a 60° angle by drawing two sides of an equilateral triangle.
You can construct a 90° angle by drawing the perpendicular bisector of a line segment.
You can use these constructions to draw other angles.

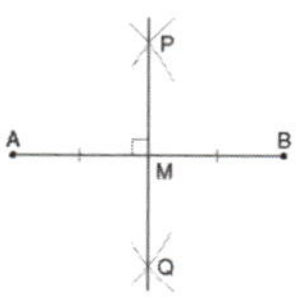

- Here is one method to draw a 135° angle.
  135° = 90° + 45°
  So, draw a 90° angle and a 45° angle at a common vertex.
  Draw line segment AB.
  Use a ruler and compass to draw the perpendicular bisector of AB.

Constructing Angles

LESSON ORGANIZER (optional)

Curriculum Focus: Use a variety of methods to construct angles.

Teacher Materials
Optional
- ruler and overhead compass

Student Materials
- tracing paper
- Miras
- compasses
- protractors

Optional
- Step-by-Step 5 (Master 7.14)
- Extra Practice 5 (Master 7.27)

Assessment: Master 7.2 Ongoing Observations: Geometry

Key Math Learning

The constructions of 60° and 90° angles can be used to draw other angles.

Assignment Guidelines

If your students do not have time to complete all the *Practice* questions on page 302, these questions provide minimum curriculum coverage: 1, 2, 3, 4, 5, 6, *Reflect*

To assess the 4 Achievement Chart categories listed in the curriculum document, have students complete these *Practice* questions:

Knowledge and Understanding: 3
Application: 5
Thinking: 4
Communication: 6

BEFORE Get Started

Remind students of the methods they used to construct bisectors of line segments and angles. Ask questions, such as:

- How can you construct a 90° angle?
  (I can use a ruler and compass to draw the perpendicular bisector of a line segment. The angle between the bisector and the line segment is 90°.)
- How can you construct a 45° angle?
  (I can construct a 90° angle, then use a Mira to draw the bisector of the angle. Each angle will be 45°.)

Tell students they will use their construction skills to construct specific angles. Remind students that protractors should only be used to check that angles have been drawn correctly. Present *Explore*.

DURING Explore

Ongoing Assessment: Observe and Listen

As students work, ask questions, such as:

- What is the measure of each angle in an equilateral triangle? *(60°)*
- How can you use an equilateral triangle to construct a 30° angle?
  (I can draw an equilateral triangle, then bisect one of the angles. Each angle will measure 60° ÷ 2 = 30°.)
- How can you construct an equilateral triangle?
  (Draw line segment AB. Place the compass point on A and the pencil point on B to fix the side length of the triangle. With the compass point on A, draw an arc above AB. Do not change the distance between the compass and pencil points. Place the compass point on B and draw an arc above AB that intersects the first arc. Label the point of intersection C. Join the points to form ∠ABC. Since AB = BC = AC, the triangle is equilateral, and each angle measures 60°.)

REACHING ALL LEARNERS

Alternative Explore

Materials: ruler, compass, protractor

➤ Draw line segment AB. Mark point C on AB. Draw ∠DCB = 60°. Construct EC, the bisector of ∠DCB. Construct FC, the bisector of ∠DCA. Measure ∠ECB and ∠ECD. Measure ∠DCF and ∠FCA. What do you notice about the pairs of angles?

➤ Draw line segment PQ. Construct TR, the perpendicular bisector of PQ. Construct KR, the bisector of ∠TRQ. Measure ∠TRK and ∠KRQ. What do you notice?

Early Finishers

Challenge students to construct an angle of 195° in two different ways.

Common Misconceptions

➤ Students always add combinations of angles to get the required angle.

How to Help: Remind students that subtraction is sometimes the easier choice. For example, to construct a 330° angle, students could combine angles of 180°, 90°, and 60°. Instead, students could draw a 30° angle and the resulting reflex angle would measure 360° – 30° = 330°.

Mental Math

Students could first subtract the hours: 2 h before 4:15 p.m. is 2:15 p.m.
23 min = 15 min + 8 min
Then subtract 15 min: 15 min before 2:15 p.m. is 2:00 p.m.
Then subtract 8 min: 8 min before 2:00 p.m. is 1:52 p.m.

∠AMP = ∠PMB = 90°
Use a ruler and compass to bisect ∠PMB.
Label point R on the angle bisector.

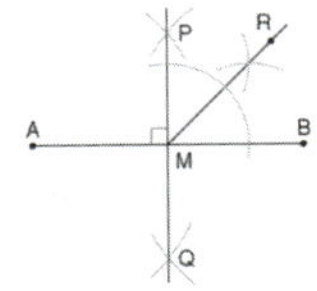

Then, ∠PMR = ∠RMB = $\frac{1}{2}$ of 90°
So, ∠PMR = 45°
And, ∠AMR = ∠AMP + ∠PMR
= 90° + 45°
= 135°

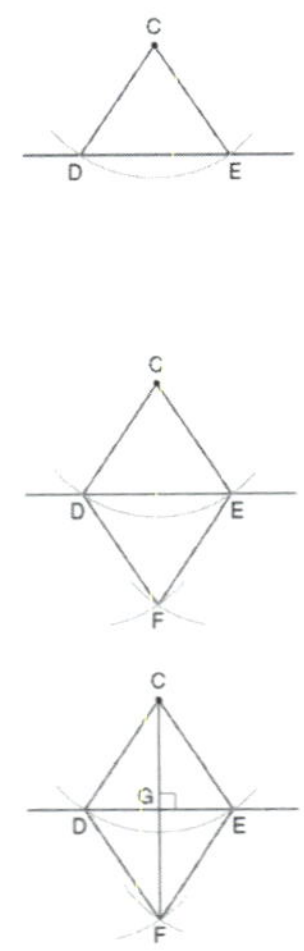

➢ We can use the properties of a rhombus to construct a 90° angle.
Use a ruler and compass.
Draw a line. Mark a point C away from the line.
C is on one arm of the 90° angle. The other arm is on the line.
Place the compass point on C.
Draw an arc that intersects the line at two points, D and E.
DE is one diagonal of the rhombus.
CD and CE are two sides of the rhombus.

Do not change the distance between the compass and pencil points.
Place the compass point on D. Draw an arc below DE.
Place the compass point on E.
Draw an arc below DE to intersect the previous arc.
Label point F where the arcs intersect.
Then, DF and EF are the other two sides of the rhombus.

Draw CF, the other diagonal of the rhombus.
Label point G where the diagonals intersect.
Since the diagonals of a rhombus intersect at right angles, ∠CGE = 90°.

- How could you use a Mira to bisect ∠BAC?
  (*Place a Mira so that the reflection image of AB coincides with AC. Draw the mirror line. The mirror line is the angle bisector. Each angle formed measures 60° ÷ 2 = 30°.*)
- How could you use tracing paper to bisect ∠BAC?
  (*I could trace ∠BAC, then fold the angle so that AB coincides with AC. The fold line is the angle bisector.*)
- How could you use a ruler and compass to bisect ∠BAC?
  (*Place the compass point on A and draw an arc that intersects AB at K and AC at L. Without changing the distance between the compass and pencil points, place the compass point on K and draw an arc between the arms of the angle. Place the compass point on L and draw an arc that intersects the second arc. Label the point of intersection D. Join AD. AD bisects ∠BAC, and ∠DAC = ∠DAB= 30°.*)
- How could you construct a 45° angle?
  (*I could bisect a 90° angle.*)
- How can you use a ruler and compass to construct a 90° angle?
  (*Draw line segment AB. Place the compass point on A and draw an arc above and below AB. Without changing the distance between the compass and pencil points, place the compass point on B and draw an arc above and below AB to intersect the first 2 arcs. Label the points C and D where the arcs intersect. Join CD. CD is perpendicular to AB.*)
- How could you use a ruler and compass to bisect the 90° angle?
  (*I could follow the same steps I used to bisect an angle in the equilateral triangle.*)

AFTER Connect

Invite students to share their strategies with the class. Ask:

- What other strategies can you use to create a 30° or 45° angle?
  (*I could construct a square, then draw a diagonal to*

The following *Example* explains how to draw a 120° angle.

Example

Use only a ruler and compass.

a) Construct △DBC, with ∠B = 120°.

b) Explain how you know ∠B = 120°.

Solution

a) Draw line segment AC. Mark point B on AC.
Make the distance between the compass and pencil points equal to AB.
Place the compass point on B. Draw an arc.
Do not change the distance between the compass and pencil points. Place the compass point on A.
Draw an arc to intersect the first arc.
Label point D where the arcs intersect. Join DB. Join DC.

Measure to check that the angle is correct.

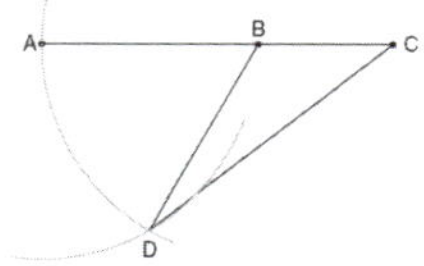

Then, ∠DBC = 120°

b) Sketch the construction.
Join AD.
Since the distance between the compass and pencil points is equal to AB,
then AB = BD = AD.
So, △ABD is equilateral.
And, ∠A = ∠ABD = ∠ADB = 60°
∠ABD and ∠DBC are supplementary angles.
So, ∠ABD + ∠DBC = 180°
60° + ∠DBC = 180°
∠DBC = 180° − 60°
= 120°

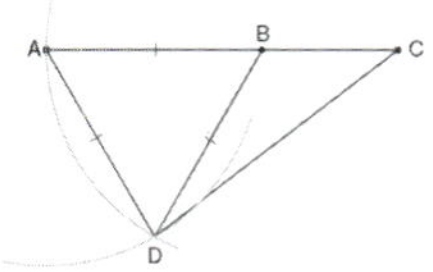

Sample Solutions

3. b) The method in the *Example* is easier. The method used in part a requires the construction of a 90° angle, then a 60° angle, which is then bisected to get an angle of 90° + 30° = 120°. The method in the *Example* only requires the construction of a 60° angle. The supplement of the 60° angle is a 120° angle.

4. There are many possible ways to construct each triangle. For example,

   a) Construct ∠ABC = 60°, then bisect the angle. With compass point on B, draw an arc that intersects BC and the bisector of ∠ABC. Label the points of intersection K and L. Join KL to form isosceles △KBL.

   b) Construct equilateral △ABC. Bisect ∠B and ∠C. Label the point D where the bisectors intersect. △DBC is an isosceles triangle with two 30° angles.

   Students' solutions should include a construction with each method.

get a 45° angle. I could construct an isosceles right triangle, then construct the perpendicular bisector of the hypotenuse. I could construct an equilateral triangle, then construct the perpendicular bisector of one side to get a 30° angle.)

Use a ruler and overhead compass to demonstrate the constructions of a 135° angle and a 120° angle.

Have the class brainstorm a list of other angles they might be able to construct, and how they could be constructed.

For example, some possible angles are: 15° (bisect a 30° angle); 75° (combine angles of 45° and 30°, or 60° and 15°); 105° (combine angles of 60° and 45°, or 90° and 15°); 120° (combine angles of 60° and 60°, or 90° and 30°); 150° (combine angles of 90° and 60°); 165° (combine angles of 120° and 45°, or 150° and 15°)

Practice

Remind students to draw large diagrams to ensure greater accuracy, and to draw all construction lines faintly.

In question 8, students should recall the sum of the angles in a triangle. Students can use algebra to write an equation, then solve the equation to find the measures of ∠C, ∠B, and ∠A.

Assessment Focus: Question 4

Students could use rulers, compasses, Miras, tracing paper, and protractors to construct the triangles. Students' answers should include a construction with each method they used.

5. I can construct a 60° angle. The reflex angle measures 360° – 60° = 300°.
I can also construct a 180° angle, a 90° angle, and a 30° angle at a common vertex.

6. I can construct a 120° angle. The reflex angle will measure 360° – 120° = 240°.
I can also construct a 180° angle and a 60° angle at a common vertex. This angle would measure 180° + 60° = 240°.

REFLECT: I can construct these angles using only a ruler and compass:
0°, 15°, 30°, 45°; 60°, 75°, 90°, 105°, 120°, 135°, 150°, 165°, 180°
To construct a 150° angle, draw a straight angle, then construct a 60° angle, with one arm of the angle on the straight angle.
Bisect the 60° angle to form two 30° angles.
The angle supplementary to the 30° angle is 180° – 30° = 150°.

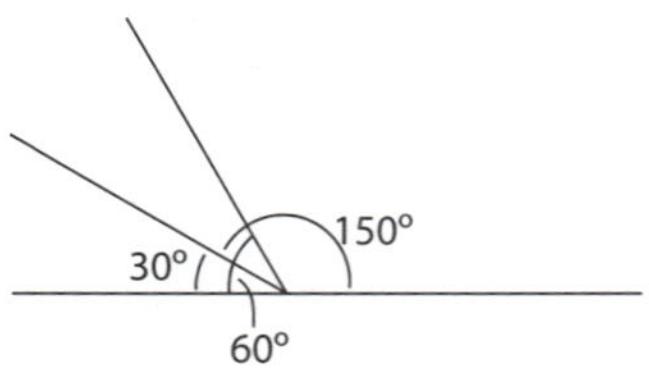

Practice

Use only a ruler and compass in questions 1 to 3.

1. Construct a large equilateral △PQR.
Bisect ∠P to construct a 30° angle.

2. Construct an isosceles right △DEF, with ∠D = 90°.
a) What is the measure of ∠E? ∠F? How do you know? 45°
b) How can you construct a 45° angle? Bisect angle of 90°.

3. a) Use your knowledge of constructing a 90° angle and a 30° angle to construct a 120° angle.
b) Compare your method with the method in the *Example.* Which is easier? Explain.

4. **Assessment Focus** Use any methods or tools.
a) Construct an isosceles triangle with one 30° angle.
b) Construct an isosceles triangle with two 30° angles.
How many different ways can you construct each triangle? Include a construction with each method.

5. Construct a 300° angle.
Can you do this in more than one way? Explain.

6. Describe one way to construct a 240° angle.

7. Construct parallelogram ABCD with:
∠A = ∠C = 150°, ∠B = ∠D = 30°, AD = BC = 3 cm, AB = CD = 5 cm

8. Triangle ABC has angle measures related this way:
∠A is 3 times ∠C, and ∠B is twice ∠C.
a) What is the measure of ∠A? ∠B? ∠C? 90°, 60°, 30°
b) Use only a ruler and compass. Construct △ABC.

Mental Math

Kenji completed a bicycle race in 2 h and 23 min.
He finished at 4:15 p.m.
At what time did the race start?
1:52 pm

Reflect

List all the angles between 0° and 180° you can construct using only a ruler and compass.
Choose one angle from the list. Construct the angle.
Describe how you did it.

ASSESSMENT FOR LEARNING

What to Look For	What to Do
Knowledge and Understanding ✔ Students understand angles can be combined to form other angles. ✔ Students understand how to construct angles of specified measures. ***Communication*** ✔ Students can describe the methods used to construct angles of different measures. ***Application*** ✔ Students can apply a variety of methods to construct angles.	***Extra Support:*** Students who have difficulty constructing a specified angle could make a list of all possible combinations of the angles they can draw which result in the given angle. For example, 120°: 90° + 30°, 180° – 60°, 60° + 60°, 45° + 45° + 30° Students choose the easiest possible construction. Students can use Step-by-Step 5 (Master 7.14) to complete question 4. ***Extra Practice:*** Students can complete the Additional Activity *Measuring Up* (Master 7.9). Students can complete Extra Practice 5 (Master 7.27). ***Extension:*** The measures of 4 angles in a pentagon are: 90°, 90°, 135°, and 135°. Have students construct the pentagon, then use a protractor to find the measure of the fifth angle. All construction lines should be shown.

Recording and Reporting
Master 7.2 Ongoing Observations: Geometry

7.6 Creating and Solving Geometry Problems

Focus Create and solve problems involving angle measurement.

Explore

Work with a partner.

➢ You will need a copy of this diagram.

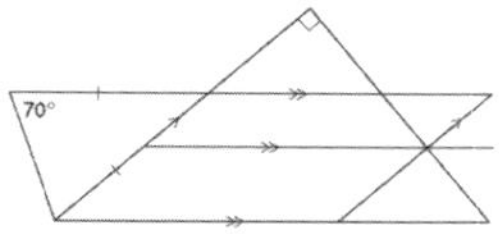

Find the measures of all the angles.

➢ Make up a geometry problem that involves a triangle and parallel lines.
Sketch your diagram.
Remember to mark equal side lengths, if appropriate.
Find the measures of all the angles.
On a copy of your diagram, write the fewest angle measures a person would need to find all the measures.
Trade diagrams with another pair of classmates.
Find the measures of the angles in your classmates' diagram.

Reflect & Share

Compare your answers with those of your classmates.
Were you able to find all the measures? Explain.
Were your classmates able to find all the measures on your diagram? If not, find out why.

Connect

Look back through the unit to review any concepts you are unsure about.

To solve problems that involve angle measures associated with triangles and parallel lines, you might need to use any or all of the geometry concepts you learned in this unit.
We often use variables to describe angle measures.
In each case, the variable represents one angle measure.

7.6 Creating and Solving Geometry Problems 303

LESSON 7.6

Creating and Solving Geometry Problems

LESSON ORGANIZER (80–100 min)

Curriculum Focus: Create and solve problems involving angle measurement. (8m43, 8m48)

Teacher Materials

Optional
- transparency of Diagram for 7.6 *Explore* (Master 7.18)

Student Materials
- Diagram for 7.6 *Explore* (Master 7.18)
- protractors

Optional
- Diagram for 7.6 *Practice* Question 5 (Master 7.19)
- Step-by-Step 6 (Master 7.15)
- Extra Practice 6 (Master 7.28)

Assessment: Master 7.2 Ongoing Observations: Geometry

Key Math Learning

Different strategies can be used to solve problems that involve angle measures associated with triangles and parallel lines.

BEFORE Get Started

Review the different geometry concepts students have studied in the unit.

Ask:

- What are the angle properties of intersecting lines?
  (*Opposite angles are equal, supplementary angles have a sum of 180°, and complementary angles have a sum of 90°.*)
- What have you learned about the angles in a triangle?
  (*The sum of the angles in a triangle is 180°.*)
- What are the angle properties of parallel lines and a transversal?
  (*Alternate angles are equal, corresponding angles are equal, and interior angles are supplementary.*)
- What have you learned about bisectors?
  (*The perpendicular bisector of a line segment divides the segment into two equal parts, and the bisector is perpendicular to the line segment. An angle bisector divides an angle into two equal angles.*)

Tell students they will use these concepts to solve problems that involve angle measurement.

Present *Explore*. Distribute copies of Diagram for 7.6 *Explore* (Master 7.18) to pairs of students. Remind students they should be able to justify the measures of all the angles they write in.

DURING Explore

Ongoing Assessment: Observe and Listen

As students work, ask questions, such as:

- How many sets of parallel line segments are there? Explain.
  (*There is one pair of parallel line segments that are on a slant, and a set of 3 parallel horizontal line segments.*)
- Show me an isosceles triangle. How do you know it is isosceles?
  (*The hatch marks indicate that the two sides are equal.*)

REACHING ALL LEARNERS

Early Finishers

Use a copy of the diagram from *Explore,* but remove the symbol indicating the right angle. Find the measures of as many angles as possible. Add one new condition that allows you to find the measures of all the angles.

Common Misconceptions

➤ Students think there is only one way to find the measure of an angle.

How to Help: Have students think of solving geometry questions as problem solving. There are often many different ways to find the solution to a problem. Remind students of the two different methods used to solve the problems in *Examples 1* and *2.*

Calculator Skills

Encourage students to use their knowledge of ratios.

Assignment Guidelines

If your students do not have time to complete all the *Practice* questions on pages 305, 306, and 307, these questions provide minimum curriculum coverage: 1, 3, 4, 5, 8, *Reflect*

To assess the 4 Achievement Chart categories listed in the curriculum document, have students complete these *Practice* questions:
Knowledge and Understanding: 1
Application: 4
Thinking: 5
Communication: 8

Example 1

Find the values of w, x, y, and z in this diagram.

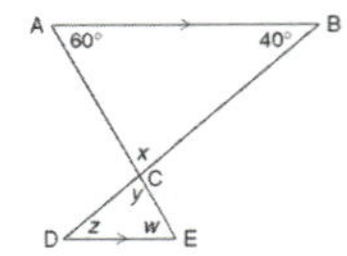

Solution

Each variable represents one angle measure.
In $\triangle ABC$, the sum of the angles is 180°.
So, $\angle A + \angle B + \angle ACB = 180°$
$60° + 40° + x = 180°$
$100° + x = 180°$
Solve this equation by inspection.

Think: What do we add to 100° to get 180°?

$x = 80°$

x and y are measures of opposite angles.
So, $y = x = 80°$
$y = 80°$

Transversal AE intersects parallel line segments AB and DE.
So, alternate angles are equal.
$\angle DEC = \angle BAC$
$w = 60°$

What other method could we use to find the value of z?

Transversal DB intersects parallel line segments AB and DE.
So, alternate angles are equal.
$\angle CDE = \angle ABC$
$z = 40°$

Example 2

Find the values of q, w, and y in this diagram.

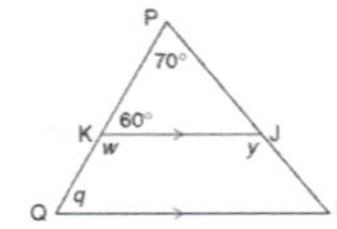

304 UNIT 7: Geometry

- What are the measures of the other angles in the triangle? How do you know? (*70°; the two sides are equal, so the corresponding angles are equal. 40°; the sum of the angles in a triangle is 180°: 180° – 70° – 70° = 40°.*)
- What are the measures of the other angles in the small right triangle at the top of the diagram? How do you know? (*40°, using opposite angles; and 50°, using the sum of the angles in a triangle: 180° – 90° – 40° = 50°*)
- What are the measures of the other angles in the large right triangle? How do you know? (*40° and 50°, using corresponding angles*)
- How many 40° angles did you find? (*Eight*) 50° angles? (*Five*)
- What are the measures of the other angles in the diagram? (*140° and 130°*)

Students who have difficulty making up a geometry problem could use this diagram.

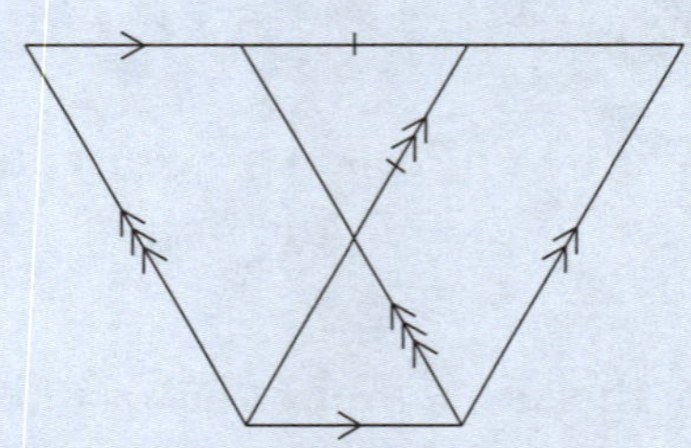

Students can mark in the measure of one angle, then try to find the measures of all other angles.

AFTER Connect

Invite students to share their answers and to describe the methods they used to justify their answers. Use a transparency of Diagram for 7.6 *Explore* (Master 7.18) on the overhead projector. Have volunteers give the measure of one angle at a time. Mark in the measure of each angle, and have students provide different justifications for the measure.

Solution

Transversal PQ intersects parallel line segments KJ and QR.
So, corresponding angles are equal.

$\angle KQR = \angle PKJ$

$q = 60°$

Angles that form a straight line are supplementary.

What other method could we use to find the value of *w*?

So, $\angle PKJ + \angle JKQ = 180°$

$60° + w = 180°$

$w = 120°$

Think: What do we add to 60° to get 180°?

We cannot find the value of *y* directly.
First, we need to find the measure of $\angle PJK$.
In $\triangle PKJ$, the sum of the angles is 180°.

So, $\angle P + \angle PKJ + \angle PJK = 180°$

$70° + 60° + \angle PJK = 180°$

$130° + \angle PJK = 180°$

$\angle PJK = 50°$

Angles that form a straight line are supplementary.

So, $\angle PJK + \angle KJR = 180°$

$50° + y = 180°$

$y = 130°$

Practice

1. Look at this diagram.
   a) Name a pair of parallel line segments. AB and EC
   b) Name two transversals. BD and AC
   c) Name two corresponding angles. $\angle ABC$ and $\angle ECD$
   d) Name two alternate angles. $\angle BAC$ and $\angle ACE$
   e) Name two complementary angles. $\angle ACE$ and $\angle ECD$
   f) Find the values of *x*, *y*, and *z*.
   $x = 35°$, $y = 35°$, $z = 55°$

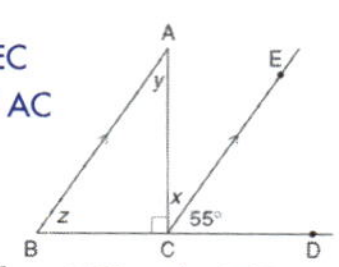

7.6 Creating and Solving Geometry Problems 305

Sample Solutions

4. $\angle KAB$ and $\angle JAB$ are supplementary angles.
   So, $\angle KAB = 180° - 125° = 55°$
   $\angle ABJ$ and $\angle BJM$ are alternate angles.
   So, $\angle ABJ = \angle BJM = 25°$
   The sum of the angles in $\triangle ABJ = 180°$.
   So, $\angle AJB = 180° - 125° - 25° = 30°$
   The sum of the angles in $\triangle BJM = 180°$.
   So, $\angle JMB = 180° - 90° - 25° = 65°$
   The sum of the angles in $\triangle KJM = 180°$. $\angle J = 30° + 25° = 55°$
   So, $\angle JKM = 180° - \angle J - \angle M$
   $= 180° - 55° - 65° = 60°$
   $\angle KBA$ and $\angle BMJ$ are corresponding angles.
   So, $\angle KBA = \angle BMJ = 65°$
5. Measure: $\angle CDA = 65°$
   Since $\triangle ADC$ is isosceles, $\angle ACD = \angle ADC = 65°$
   The sum of the angles in $\triangle ADC = 180°$.
   So, $\angle CAD = 180° - 65° - 65° = 50°$
   $\angle CAD$ and $\angle EAD$ are complementary angles.
   So, $\angle EAD = 90° - 50° = 40°$
   $\angle EDB$ and $\angle ACD$ are corresponding angles.
   So, $\angle EDB = \angle ACD = 65°$
   $\angle CAD$ and $\angle ADE$ are alternate angles.
   So, $\angle CAD = \angle ADE = 50°$
   $\angle A$ and $\angle BED$ are corresponding angles.
   So, $\angle BED = \angle A = 90°$
   The sum of the angles in $\triangle BED = 180°$.
   So, $\angle EBD = 180° - 90° - 65° = 25°$
   $\angle DEA$ and $\angle DEB$ are supplementary angles.
   So, $\angle DEA = 180° - 90° = 90°$

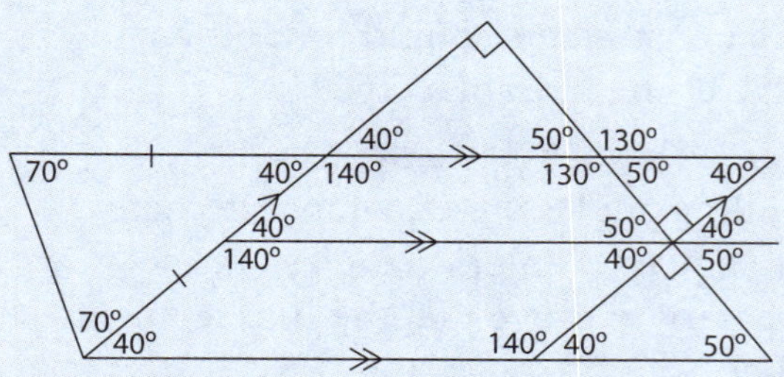

Discuss problems created by students, especially the more challenging ones.

It might be of interest to collect the student generated problems and make a worksheet of some, or all, of the questions.

Remind students that there may be more than one way to solve a problem involving angle measurement. Show students an alternative solution to *Example 1*.

Find the value of *w*: Transversal AE intersects parallel line segments AB and DE.

So, alternate angles are equal.

So, $\angle A = \angle E$

$w = 60°$

Find the value of *z*: Transversal BD intersects parallel line segments AB and DE.

So, alternate angles are equal.

So, $\angle D = \angle B$

$z = 40°$

Find the value of *y*: The sum of the angles of $\triangle CDE$ is 180°.

So, $y + z + w = 180°$

$y + 40° + 60° = 180°$

$y = 80°$

Find the value of *x*: $\angle ACB$ is opposite $\angle DCE$, so $\angle ACB = \angle DCE$.

$x = y = 80°$

Show students an alternative solution to *Example 2*.

Find the value of *w*: $\angle PKJ$ and $\angle QKJ$ are supplementary angles.

6. OE and OD are radii of the circle. So, OE = OD and △OED is isosceles, with ∠OED = ∠ODE, or $x = y$.
The sum of the angles in △OED = 180°.
So, ∠OED + ∠ODE + ∠EOD = 180°
$x + x + 100° = 180°$
$x = 40°$
So, $x = y = 40°$
∠OED and ∠EOB are alternate angles.
So, ∠EOB = ∠OED = 40°
The sum of the angles in △EOB = 180°.
So, ∠OEB = 180° − ∠EBO − ∠EOB
= 180° − 90° − 40°
= 50°

7. Sample diagram:

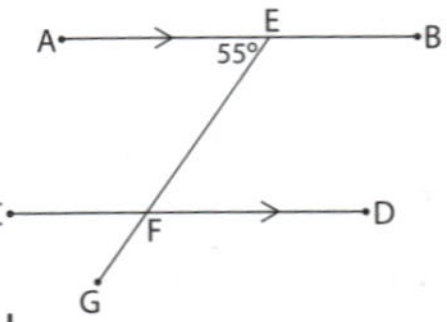

∠AEF = 55°
∠AEF and ∠EFD are alternate angles.
So, ∠AEF = ∠EFD = 55°
∠CFG and ∠AEF are corresponding angles.
So, ∠CFG = ∠AEF = 55°
∠BEF and ∠EFD are interior angles.
So, ∠BEF = 180° − 55° = 125°
∠DFG and ∠BEF are corresponding angles.
So, ∠DFG = ∠BEF = 125°
∠EFC and ∠BEF are alternate angles.
So, ∠EFC = ∠BEF = 125°

8. AB is parallel to CE.
So, ∠ABC and ∠BCE are alternate angles.
So, ∠ABC = ∠BCE = 90°
AD is a straight angle.

2. a) Write an equation for the sum of the angles in △ABC. $x + 60° + 80° = 180°$
b) Solve the equation to find the value of x. $x = 40°$

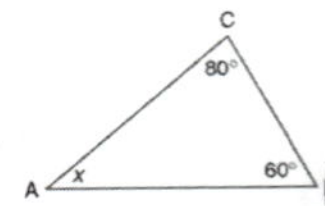

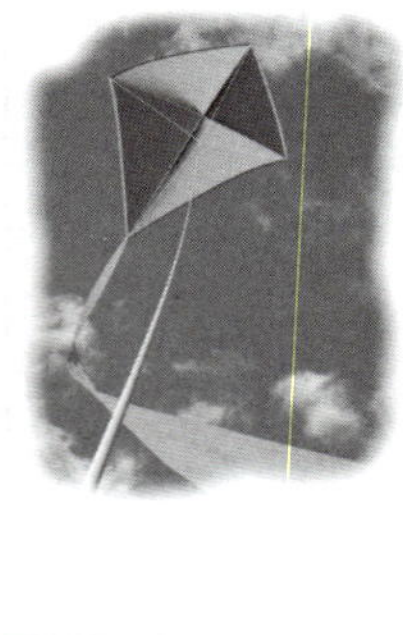

3. Look at the diagram below.
a) Name two isosceles triangles. △PQS and △RQS
b) Name two complementary angles. ∠PQS and ∠RQS
c) Find the values of x and y. ∠PSQ and ∠RSQ

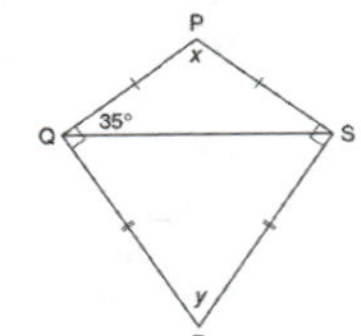

$x = 110°$
$y = 70°$

4. In the diagram below, find the values of x, y, z, w, t, and s. Show all your work. Justify your answers.

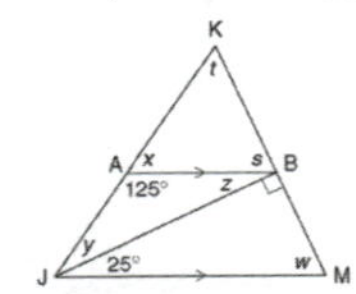

$x = 55°$, $z = 25°$
$y = 30°$, $w = 65°$
$t = 60°$, $s = 65°$

Calculator Skills

A map scale is 1 cm to 250 km.
Two cities are 4.8 cm apart on the map. What is the actual distance between the two cities? 1200 km
The actual distance between two different cities is 937 km. How far apart are the cities on the map?
3.748 cm

5. **Assessment Focus** Use a copy of this diagram, or draw your own diagram.
Measure and label one or more angles, the fewest you need to know to calculate the remaining measures.
Label each unmarked angle with a variable.
Find the value of each variable. Justify your answers.
Show your work.

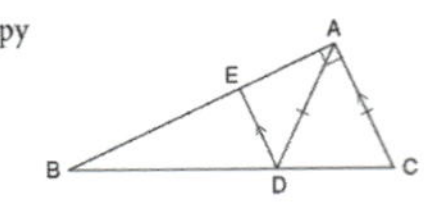

306 UNIT 7: Geometry

So, ∠QKJ = 180° − ∠PKJ
$w = 180° − 60°$
$= 120°$

Find the value of q: ∠QKJ and ∠KQR are interior angles formed by parallel line segments KJ and QR, and transversal KQ.

So ∠KQR = 180° − ∠QKJ
$q = 180° − w$
$= 180° − 120°$
$= 60°$

We can find the value of y in the same way as in *Example 2*.

Suggest students make a list of all geometric properties learned in this unit to which they can refer to when solving angle problems.

Practice

Questions 5 and 7 require protractors. In question 4, students can find the measures of the angles in the order listed. However, it might be easier to find the value of z before y.

In question 6, students should recall their knowledge of the radii of a circle.

In question 9, students use the fact that corresponding angles are equal, or alternate angles are equal, or interior angles are supplementary to prove that the line segments are parallel.

Assessment Focus: Question 5

It might save time to provide students with a copy of the Diagram for 7.6 *Practice* Question 5 (Master 7.19), rather than have them draw their own. If necessary, allow students to use a checklist of geometric properties as a way to find the measures of the angles.

Remind students to label only the fewest number of angles needed to calculate the remaining angles. Strong math students should only have to measure one non-right angle. Ensure students justify the value of each variable.

6. Point O is the centre of the circle.
Find the values of x, y, z, and w.
Explain how you know.

$x = 40°$, $y = 40°$
$z = 40°$, $w = 50°$

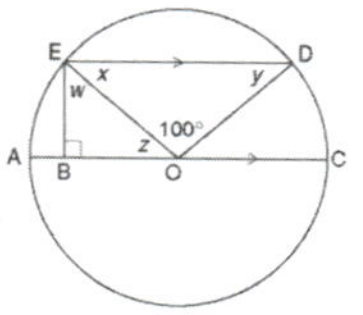

7. Use a ruler and lined paper.
Draw a diagram that has corresponding angles, alternate angles, and interior angles between parallel lines.
Use a protractor to measure and label one angle.
Calculate the measures of all the other angles.
Justify your answers.

8. Explain why ∠BCA and ∠ECD are complementary.

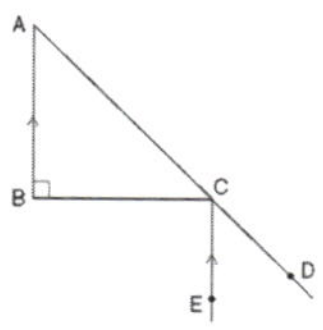

Take It Further

9. In this diagram, is AD parallel to BC? Explain. Yes

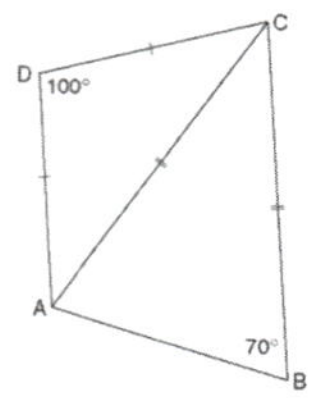

Reflect

How does the use of variables help solve some geometry problems?
Explain using examples.

7.6 Creating and Solving Geometry Problems **307**

So, ∠BCA + ∠BCE + ∠ECD = 180°
∠BCA + 90° + ∠ECD = 180°
∠BCA + ∠ECD = 180° − 90° = 90°
So, ∠BCA and ∠ECD are complementary angles.

9. △DAC is isosceles with ∠DAC = ∠DCA. ∠ADC = 100°
The sum of the angles in △DAC = 180°.
So, ∠DAC + ∠DCA + ∠ADC = 180°
∠DAC + ∠DCA + 100° = 180°
∠DAC + ∠DCA = 80°
Since ∠DAC = ∠DCA, ∠DAC = ∠DCA = 80° ÷ 2 = 40°
△CAB is isosceles. Since CA = CB, ∠CAB = ∠CBA = 70°
The sum of the angles in △CAB = 180°.
So, ∠ACB + ∠CAB + ∠CBA = 180°
∠ACB + 70° + 70° = 180°
∠ACB = 40°
So, ∠DAC = ∠ACB = 40°
Since these angles are equal alternate angles, AD is parallel to BC.

REFLECT: The use of variables allows us to set up algebraic equations that can be solved for unknown values. For example, in △ABC, it is easier to work with the equation x + 110° + 40° = 180° than it is to work with ∠ACB + ∠ABC + ∠BAC = 180°.
I can solve the algebraic equation easily.
x + 110° + 40° = 180°
x = 30°

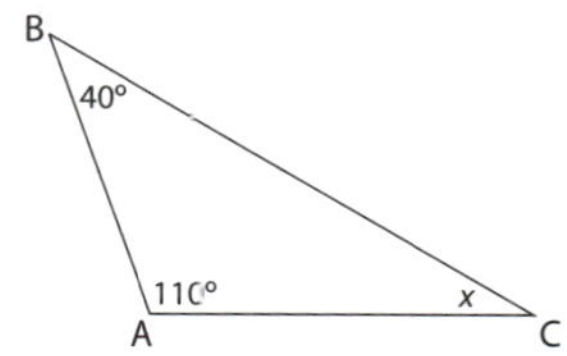

ASSESSMENT FOR LEARNING

What to Look For	What to Do
Knowledge and Understanding ✔ Students understand that the measures of angles can be calculated using properties of angles.	***Extra Support:*** Students who have difficulty solving problems involving angle measurement may benefit from repeating *Explore*, this time given the measure of a different angle. Students can use Step-by-Step 6 (Master 7.15) to complete question 5.
Communication ✔ Students can explain how they calculated the measures of unknown angles, using appropriate mathematical terminology.	***Extra Practice:*** Students draw a diagram that involves parallel lines, transversals, and triangles. Students mark the measure of one angle, then trade diagrams with a partner. Students find the measures of as many angles as they can in their partner's diagram. Students can complete Extra Practice 6 (Master 7.28).
Thinking ✔ Students can use the geometric properties of the unit to solve problems involving angle measurement.	***Extension:*** In △ABC, ∠A = 90°. P, Q, and R are the midpoints of AB, BC, and AC respectively. Prove that △APR, △PQB, △RQC, and △QRP are all right triangles.

Recording and Reporting
Master 7.2 Ongoing Observations: Geometry

Characteristics of Quadrilaterals

LESSON ORGANIZER

80–100 min

Curriculum Focus: Investigate the geometric properties of quadrilaterals. (8m43)

Teacher Materials

Optional
- large cut out of each of the special quadrilaterals

Student Materials
- Lesson 6A (Master 7.5)
- Quadrilaterals in *Explore* 7.6A (Master 7.20)
- protractors
- isometric dot paper (PM 23)
- square dot paper (PM 22)
- Venn diagrams (PM 28)

Optional
- computers with *The Geometer's Sketchpad* software
- Step-by-Step 6A (Master 7.16)
- Extra Practice 6A (Master 7.29)

Vocabulary: isosceles trapezoid

Assessment: Master 7.2 Ongoing Observations: Geometry

Assignment Guidelines

If your students do not have time to complete all the *Practice* questions, these questions provide minimum curriculum coverage: 1, 4, 5, 6, *Reflect*

To assess the 4 Achievement Chart categories listed in the curriculum document, have students complete these *Practice* questions:
Knowledge and Understanding: 4
Application: 5
Thinking: 6
Communication: *Reflect*

Key Math Learnings

1. Some quadrilaterals have special names that relate to the characteristics they possess.
2. A quadrilateral can be classified according to its side, angle, and diagonal characteristics.

BEFORE — Get Started

Have students find examples of different quadrilaterals in the classroom. Ask:

- What is a quadrilateral?
  (*A figure with 4 sides*)
- Which quadrilaterals do you see in the classroom?
  (*I see a square, a rectangle, a rhombus, and a parallelogram.*)
- Which other quadrilaterals do you know?
  (*I know a trapezoid and a kite.*)

Present *Explore*. Distribute copies of Lesson 6A (Master 7.5) and the Quadrilaterals in *Explore* 7.6A (Master 7.20) to pairs of students. Remind students that a diagonal joins two opposite vertices in a quadrilateral. Tell students that accurate measurements are necessary to ensure appropriate conclusions are made.

DURING — Explore

Ongoing Assessment: Observe and Listen

As students work, watch to see they are using the mathematical terms associated with parallel lines, bisectors, and angles. Ask:

- What is quadrilateral A? (*Parallelogram*) B? (*Rectangle*) C? (*Rhombus*) D? (*Square*) E? (*Trapezoid*) F? (*Kite*) G? (*Trapezoid*)
- How is Trapezoid G different from Trapezoid E?
  (*In Trapezoid G, the non-parallel sides are equal.*)
- Which quadrilaterals have opposite sides parallel?
  (*A parallelogram, rectangle, square, rhombus*)
- Which quadrilaterals have opposite angles equal?
  (*A parallelogram, rectangle, square, rhombus; a kite has one pair of opposite angles equal.*)

- Which characteristics did you find that relate to diagonals?
  (*The diagonals of a parallelogram, rectangle, square, rhombus, and kite all bisect each other. The rectangle, square, and Trapezoid G have diagonals equal.*)
- What are the characteristics of a trapezoid?
  (*One pair of parallel sides, and adjacent interior angles add to 180°.*)
- Do any of the quadrilaterals have more than one name? Explain.
  (*Yes, for example, a square is a rectangle, and a rhombus is a parallelogram.*)

AFTER — Connect

Invite students to share their results with the class. Have them compare their results to those in the Quadrilateral Characteristics chart in *Connect*.

The *isosceles trapezoid* might be new to some students. Ensure students understand that it is a special trapezoid, where the non-parallel sides are of equal lengths.

Tell students that each quadrilateral has a minimal list of characteristics that defines it. Any quadrilateral that has the characteristics in a particular list is that quadrilateral. If a characteristic is removed from the list, the quadrilateral is no longer uniquely defined. For example, a minimal list of characteristics that defines a square is: 4 equal sides
4 right angles

Any quadrilateral with these characteristics is a square. If one characteristic is removed from the list, for example, 4 equal sides, the quadrilateral is no longer uniquely defined as a square. The quadrilateral could now be a rectangle.

Have students suggest a possible minimal list of characteristics for different quadrilaterals.

Use the *Example* to show students how possible quadrilaterals are eliminated with each additional characteristic.

Practice

Have isometric dot paper (PM 23), square dot paper (PM 22), and protractors available. Question 4 requires Venn diagrams (PM 28). Some students may want to use *The Geometer's Sketchpad* to complete questions 1, 2, 6, and 7. Encourage students to present neat, accurate, well-labelled diagrams.

Assessment Focus: Question 6

Remind students that with each additional characteristic, possible quadrilaterals are eliminated. In each part, only one type of quadrilateral can be drawn. In parts b and c, there are many different possibilities for that particular quadrilateral. Students' answers should include a drawing of each possible quadrilateral.

REACHING ALL LEARNERS

Common Misconceptions

➤ Students have difficulty understanding that one type of quadrilateral is also another type of quadrilateral; for example, a square is also a rhombus.

How to Help: Tell students a square is a rhombus because it has the properties of a rhombus: all sides equal, opposite sides parallel, adjacent interior angles supplementary, opposite angles equal, diagonals bisect each other perpendicularly, diagonals bisect angles at vertices. A rhombus is not necessarily a square because it does not always have all right angles and diagonals equal.

Sample Solutions

1. a)

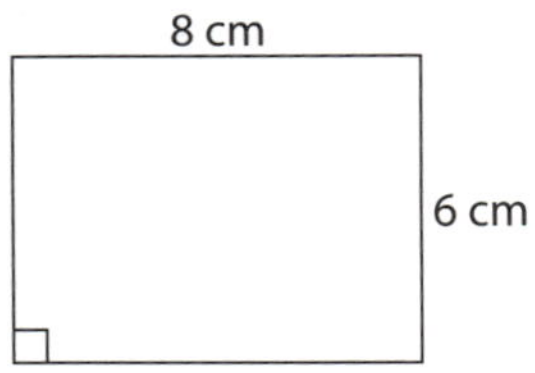

b)

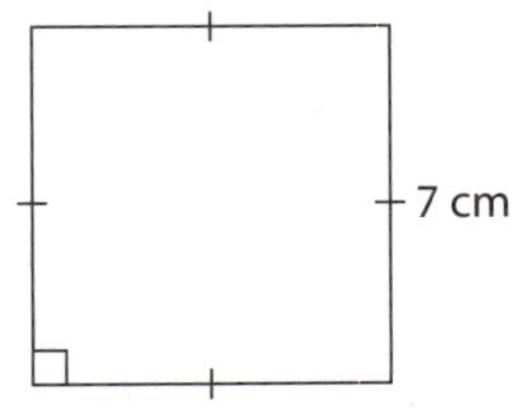

c)

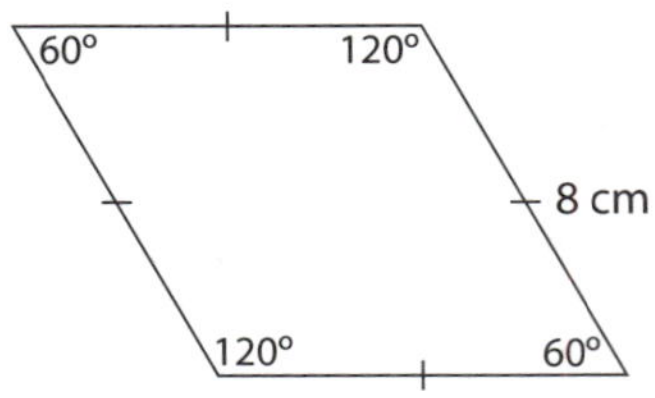

d)

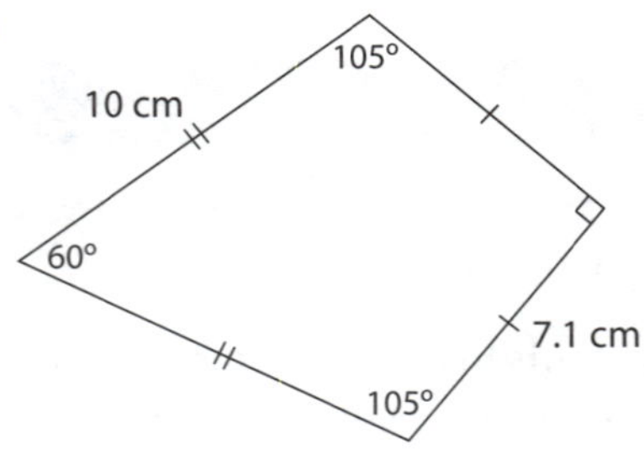

e)

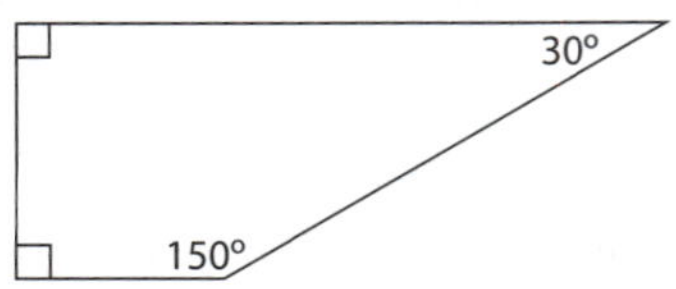

2. a) Diagonals are equal and bisect each other.

b) Diagonals are equal, bisect each other perpendicularly, and bisect angles at vertices.

c) Diagonals bisect each other perpendicularly and bisect angles at vertices.

d) Diagonals bisect each other. Only one diagonal bisects the other perpendicularly.

e) Diagonals are not equal, do not bisect each other, and do not bisect angles at vertices.

3. A square is a rectangle because it has the properties of a rectangle: opposite sides equal and parallel, all right angles, diagonals equal and bisect each other. A rectangle is not necessarily a square because it does not always have all sides equal and diagonals that bisect each other perpendicularly.

4. a)

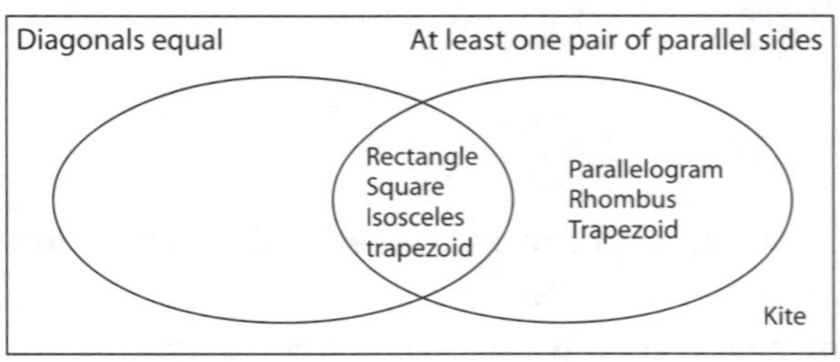

b) I chose: "Opposite sides equal," "Diagonals bisect each other," and "All right angles."

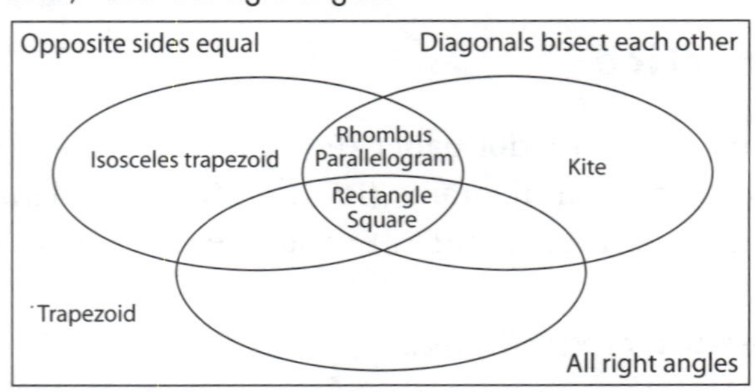

5. Place the same board diagonally between the supports. If the board fits each diagonal exactly, then the diagonals are equal. Since the diagonals are equal, the supports form rectangles, and the wall supports are at right angles.

6. a) A square and a rhombus have diagonals that bisect each other perpendicularly. Of these quadrilaterals, only a square has a right angle. So, the quadrilateral is a square with perimeter 24 cm, or side length 6 cm.

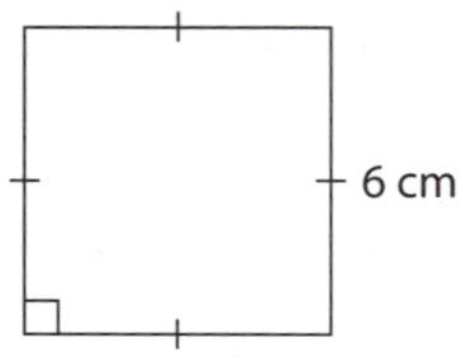

b) A parallelogram, rectangle, square, and rhombus have opposite sides parallel. Of these quadrilaterals, only the parallelogram and rectangle have diagonals that bisect each other, but not perpendicularly. Since a rectangle has all right angles, the quadrilateral is a parallelogram with one angle 60°. Many different parallelograms can be drawn because the lengths of the sides are not known.

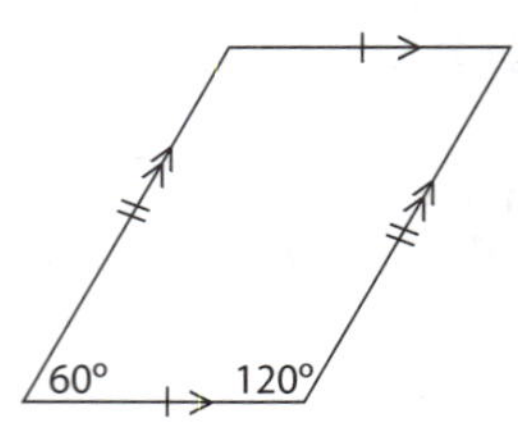

c) A trapezoid and isosceles trapezoid have one pair of parallel sides. Of these quadrilaterals, only the isosceles trapezoid has diagonals equal. So, the quadrilateral is an isosceles trapezoid with non-parallel sides of length 8.5 cm. Many different isosceles trapezoids can be drawn because the lengths of the parallel sides and the measures of angles are not known.

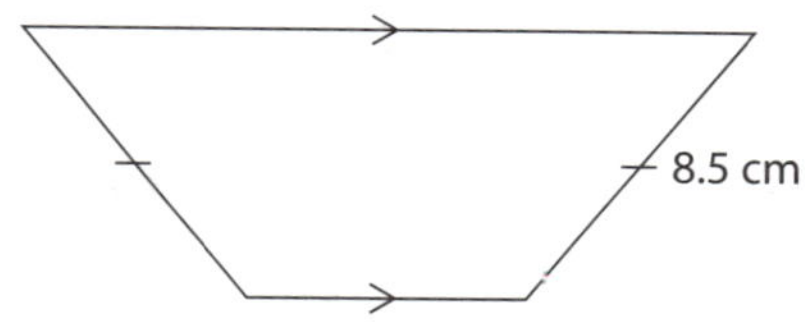

8. a) Square with side length 9 cm

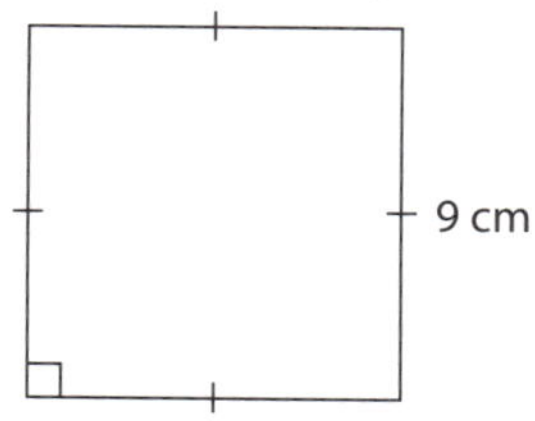

b) Any rectangle with perimeter 36 cm

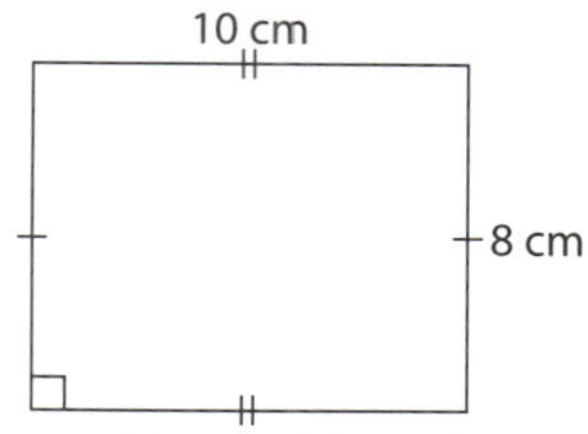

c) Rhombus with side length 9 cm

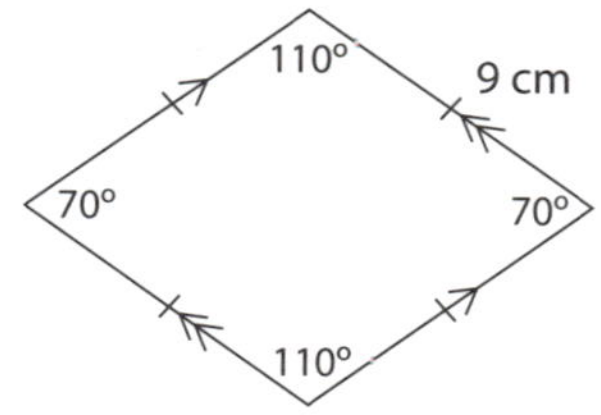

d) Any kite with perimeter 36 cm

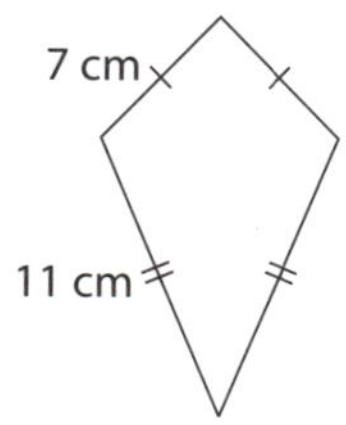

e) An irregular quadrilateral with perimeter 36 cm

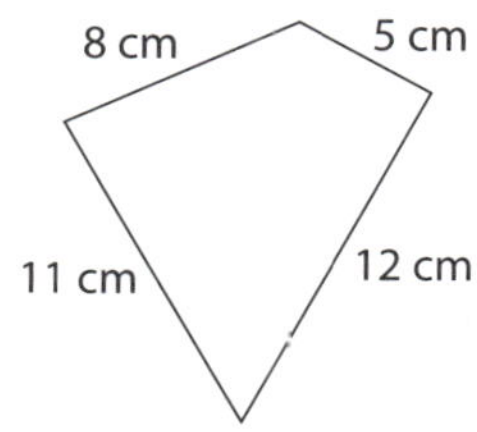

REFLECT: A quadrilateral indicates a figure with 4 sides.
The special name of a quadrilateral defines its characteristics.
For example, an isosceles trapezoid is a trapezoid with one pair of parallel sides, non-parallel sides equal, opposite angles supplementary, two pairs of adjacent interior angles supplementary, and diagonals equal. A parallelogram has opposite sides equal and parallel, adjacent interior angles supplementary, opposite angles equal, and diagonals that bisect each other. All figures that belong to the same type of quadrilateral share the same characteristics. Some figures have very specialized characteristics.

ASSESSMENT FOR LEARNING

What to Look For	What to Do
Knowledge and Understanding ✔ Students understand that quadrilaterals can be sorted according to side, angle, and diagonal characteristics.	***Extra Support:*** Students can cut out the quadrilaterals in *Explore*, then use paper folding to investigate the characteristics of diagonals. Students can use Step-by-Step 6A (Master 7.16) to complete question 6.
Communication ✔ Students can describe how the special name of a quadrilateral defines its characteristics.	***Extra Practice:*** Students use a Venn diagram to sort the quadrilaterals they drew in *Practice* question 1. Students can complete Extra Practice 6 (Master 7.29).
Application ✔ Students can sort quadrilaterals using given characteristics.	***Extension:*** Have students write problems similar to those in *Practice* question 6. Students trade problems with a classmate and solve their classmate's problem.

Recording and Reporting
Master 7.2 Ongoing Observations: Geometry

Reasonable Solutions and Concluding Statements

LESSON ORGANIZER

Student Materials	*Optional* ■ calculators

Reasonable Solutions and Concluding Statements

Katja invites 8 friends to her birthday party, which takes place in 4 days. Katja's age in years will be 2 less than twice the number of people she invites. How old will Katja be on her birthday? Which solution is reasonable?

a) 12 **b)** 14 **c)** 16 **d)** 18

Show why 14 is the reasonable solution.

To be sure you have a reasonable solution:

1. Identify the features of the problem (context, math information, problem statement) to help understand the problem. Think of what might be a reasonable answer.
2. Use words, numbers, pictures, models, graphic organizers, and/or symbols to solve the problem. Record how you solved it.
3. Think back on the problem:
   - Check if the solution makes sense with the *context*.
   - Check that the *math information* was used appropriately.
   - Check that the solution answers the *problem*.
4. Write a concluding statement to answer the problem.

308 UNIT 7: Geometry

Invite students to read the problem at the top of page 308 in the Student Book.

Ask:

- What is the context of the problem?
  (*Katja's birthday party*)
- What math information are we given?
  (*Katja has invited 8 friends; the party takes place in 4 days; Katja's age in years will be 2 less than twice the number of people she invites.*)
- What is the problem statement?
  (*How old will Katja be on her birthday?*)
- What information do we not need to solve the problem?
  (*We do not need to know the birthday party takes place in 4 days.*)

Solve the problem together as a class.

Solution

Katja invites 8 friends to her party.

Her age in years will be 2 less than twice the number of people she invites.

Twice the number of people she invites is:
$2 \times 8 = 16$

2 less than this number is: $16 - 2 = 14$

So, Katja will be 14 years old.

Encourage students to check the solution to be sure it makes sense, that it is accurate, and that the problem is answered.

Ensure students understand that a concluding statement can often be written by rearranging the words in the problem statement, then including the answer.

Reading and Writing in Math

It is common to use part of the problem statement in the concluding statement.

How old will Katja be on her birthday?

Katja will be 14 years old on her birthday.

Some Dos and Don'ts for Problem Solving

- Do keep asking yourself, "Does this make sense?"
- Don't work without writing anything down.
- Do look for patterns.
- Don't stay with a strategy when it is not working.

✓ Check

Show how you might use math information from the problem to find each answer. Which solutions are reasonable? Why? Write a concluding statement for each word problem.

1. You need enough cake to serve 18 people. A 20-cm square cake serves four people. How many 30-cm square cakes are needed to provide equal servings for 18 people?
a) 2 b) 4 c) 10 d) 12

2. Exactly five diagonals can be drawn from one vertex of a convex polygon. How many sides does the polygon have?
a) 4 b) 5 c) 6 d) 8

3. Mr. Davis wants to encourage his son Mike to save money. Every month, when Mike puts \$3 into a savings account, Mr. Davis doubles the amount of money in the account. Mike now has \$90 in the account. How many months ago did Mike start to save?
a) 2 b) 3 c) 4 d) 5

4. One hundred sixty-three students are going on a field trip. One bus holds 60 students. How many buses are needed?
a) 2 b) 2.72 c) 3 d) 4

Reading and Writing in Math: Reasonable Solutions and Concluding Statements 309

Sample Solutions

1. The area of a 20-cm square cake is:
20 cm × 20 cm = 400 cm^2
The cake serves 4 people.
So, each serving has an area of 400 cm^2 ÷ 4 = 100 cm^2.
The area of a 30-cm square cake is:
30 cm × 30 cm = 900 cm^2
The number of people this cake serves is:
900 cm^2 ÷ 100 cm^2 = 9
So, one 30-cm cake serves 9 people.
Two 30-cm cakes will serve 2 × 9 people = 18 people.
Two 30-cm square cakes are needed to provide equal servings for 18 people.

2. Look for a pattern.

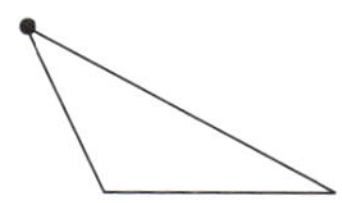

triangle

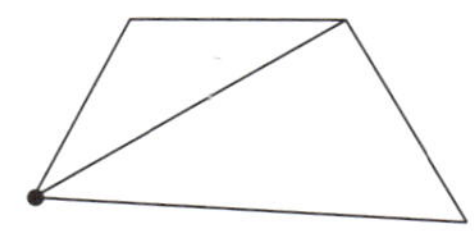

quadrilateral

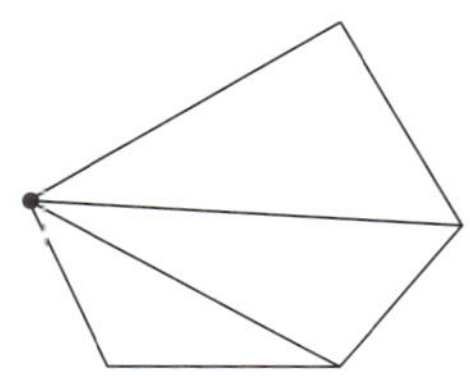

pentagon

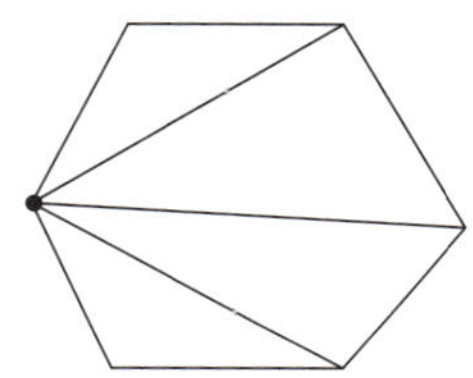

hexagon

In a 3-sided polygon, a triangle, I can draw 0 diagonals.
In a 4-sided polygon, a quadrilateral, I can draw 1 diagonal from each vertex.
In a 5-sided polygon, a pentagon, I can draw 2 diagonals from each vertex.
In a 6-sided polygon, a hexagon, I can draw 3 diagonals from each vertex.
In a polygon with n sides, I can draw $n - 3$ diagonals from each vertex.
So, when the number of diagonals is 5, $n - 3 = 5$.
$n = 8$
The polygon has 8 sides.

3. Make a table.

Month	Deposit	Balance	Balance doubled
1	\$3	\$3	\$3 × 2 = \$6
2	\$3	\$6 + \$3 = \$9	\$9 × 2 = \$18
3	\$3	\$18 + \$3 = \$21	\$21 × 2 = \$42
4	\$3	\$42 + \$3 = \$45	\$45 × 2 = \$90

From the table, the balance is \$90 after 4 months.
Mike started to save 4 months ago.

4. There are 163 students.
One bus holds 60 students.
So, the number of buses needed is: 163 ÷ 60 ≐ 2.72
We cannot have part of a bus.
So, round the number of buses up to 3.
Three buses are needed.

Robotics Engineer

Robotics Engineer

The robots from novels, movies, and television shows that lo act like humans exist only in science fiction. Scientists *are* de machines with certain human or animal capabilities, and lesse robots — such as automated arms like Canadarm — have been in use for years.

Imagine a human task: screwing a light bulb into a socket. Sounds simple, doesn't it? To design a robotic machine that can do this again and again without error is a major feat of engineering. The robot must have mobility: it has to grasp the bulb, pull it from a bin, line it up with the socket, turn the bulb into the socket, move up as the bulb goes in, and release it when done. It also needs agility: a light bulb is delicate — if the robot holds it too tightly or tries to force it into place when it isn't aligned, the bulb will break.

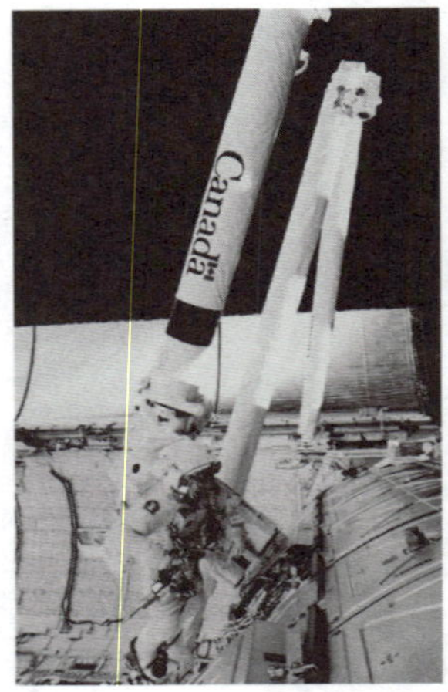

The mobility design of a robot is an exercise in geometry. How many joints should this robotic arm have? How long should each segment be? Through which angle must the arm bend and how much does it need to rotate? The robotics engineer calculates the best design for the robot's intended tasks. One advantage of robots over simple industrial machines is that a robot can be programmed to do different tasks. Today it might screw light bulbs into sockets; next week it might screw small bolts into pre-drilled holes. The tasks are similar, but the geometry has changed and the programming needs to change as well.

Providing robots with mobility and agility is one of the biggest challenges for today's robotics engineers.

310 UNIT 7: Geometry

A robot is a computer-controlled system that imitates the actions or appearance of a human being. It is able to get information from its surroundings and to perform physical tasks, such as move or manipulate objects.

The most common use of robotics is in the production of cars. In 2002, a leading automaker in Canada installed 'thinking' robots. These robots made history as the first robots of their kind to have 'eyes' and 'brains.' They are able to complete tasks faster and more accurately than any autoworker. With the advances in technology, new applications of robotics are occurring almost daily. There is even a robot that can be programmed to go to the fridge and bring you a can of pop! Other applications of robotics include building integrated circuits, arranging chocolates in boxes, managing air traffic, searching for and defusing bombs, and working in space. There is even an annual soccer competition for radio-controlled teams of robots.

Robotics has many applications in medicine and in the military, as well as in agriculture, mining, entertainment, and electronics.

Here are some jobs that involve robotics.

Engineer: An engineer might design and maintain robots, develop new applications, or research potential applications of robotics.

Technician: A technician might create blueprints for building robots, build robots, or test to ensure the robots perform properly.

Assembler: An assembler might put together hardware and electronic components for robots.

Systems analyst: A systems analyst might test for faults or troubleshoot to identify problem areas.

Unit Review

Review any lesson with etext online tutorial

What Do I Need to Know?

☑ **Intersecting Lines**
When two lines intersect,
opposite angles are equal.
∠MPN = ∠KPQ and ∠MPK = ∠NPQ

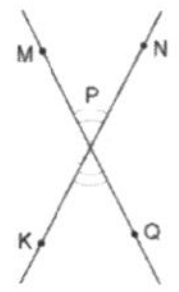

☑ **Supplementary Angles**
Angles that form a straight line are *supplementary*.
Supplementary angles have a sum of 180°.
∠KPM + ∠MPN = 180°

☑ **Complementary Angles**
Angles that form a right angle are *complementary*.
Complementary angles have a sum of 90°.
∠QRT + ∠TRS = 90°

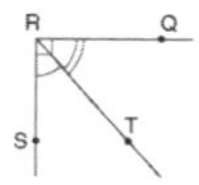

☑ **Angles in a Triangle**
The *sum of the angles* in a triangle is 180°.

- ∠A + ∠B + ∠C = 180°
- An *equilateral triangle* has all sides equal and all angles equal. Each angle in an equilateral triangle is 60°.
- An *isosceles triangle* has two sides equal and two angles equal.

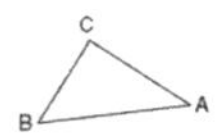

☑ **Perpendicular Bisector**
The *perpendicular bisector* of a line segment divides the segment into two equal parts.
Line CD is the perpendicular bisector of segment AB.
AE = EB
∠AEC = ∠CEB = 90°

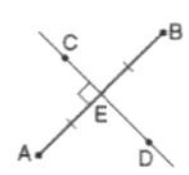

LESSON ORGANIZER

Student Materials

- tracing paper
- Miras
- compasses

Assessment: Masters 7.1 Unit Rubric: Geometry, 7.4 Unit Summary: Geometry

Correlation of Extra Practice questions on page 494:

Lesson	Questions
7.1	1, 5
7.2	2, 3, 4
7.3	6
7.4	7, 8
7.5	–
7.6	6

Sample Solutions

2. a) ∠AFE and ∠EFD are complementary angles.
∠EFD = 25°
So, ∠AFE = 90° – 25° = 65°

b) ∠AFE and ∠AFB are supplementary angles.
∠AFE = 65°
So, ∠AFB = 180° – 65° = 115°

c) ∠AFE and ∠BFC are opposite angles.
So, ∠BFC = ∠AFE = 65°

4. d) △ABE is isosceles. AE = BE
So, ∠ABE = ∠BAE = 70°
The sum of the angles in △ABE = 180°
So, 70° + 70° + ∠BEA = 180°
140° + ∠BEA = 180°
∠BEA = 40°
∠BEA and ∠CED are opposite angles.
So, ∠CED = ∠BEA = 40°
The sum of the angles in △CDE = 180°
90° + 40° + ∠ECD = 180°
130° + ∠ECD = 180°
∠ECD = 50°

5. Suppose you know the measure of ∠A.

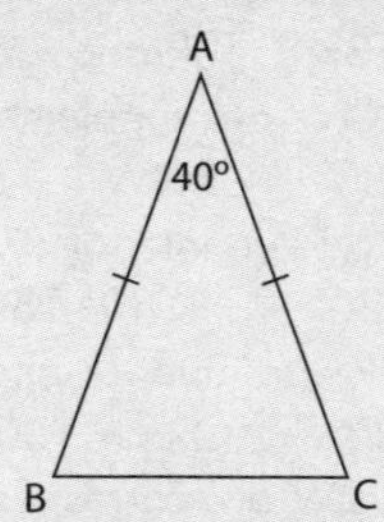

△ABC is isosceles, AB = AC, and ∠B = ∠C.
Use the sum of the angles in △ABC.
∠A + ∠B + ∠C = 180°
40° + ∠B + ∠C = 180°
∠B + ∠C = 140°
Since ∠B = ∠C, ∠B = ∠C = 140° ÷ 2 = 70°
Suppose you know the measure of one of the equal angles.

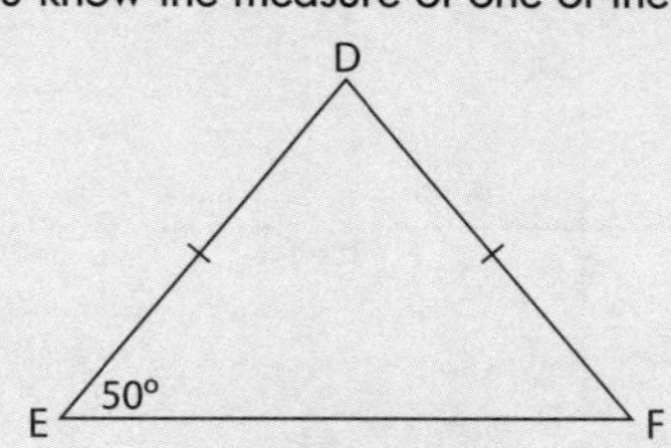

Since △DEF is isosceles and DE = DF, ∠E = ∠F = 50°.
Use the sum of the angles in △DEF.

$\angle D + \angle E + \angle F = 180°$
$\angle D + 50° + 50° = 180°$
$\angle D + 100° = 180°$
$\angle D = 80°$

6. a) The sum of the angles in $\triangle ABC$ is 180°.
$\angle A + \angle B + \angle C = 180°$
$75° + 62° + \angle C = 180°$
$137° + \angle C = 180°$
$\angle C = 43°$

b) $\angle A + \angle B + \angle C = 180°$

$75° + 79° + \angle C = 180°$
$154° + \angle C = 180°$
$\angle C = 26°$

7. a) The sum of the angles in a right triangle is 180°.
One angle is 90°.
So, the sum of the other two angles is
$180° - 90° = 90°$.
The greatest possible measure of an acute angle is 89°.

b) The greatest possible measure of an acute angle is 89°.
So, the least possible measure of an acute angle is
$90° - 89° = 1°$.

Bisector of an Angle
The *bisector of an angle* divides the angle into two equal angles.
Line QS is the bisector of $\angle PQR$.
$\angle PQS = \angle SQR$

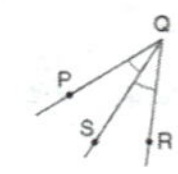

Parallel Lines and a Transversal
DE is a transversal that intersects parallel lines AC and FH.

- Alternate angles are equal.
  $\angle CBG = \angle BGF$ and $\angle ABG = \angle BGH$
- Corresponding angles are equal.
  $\angle DBC = \angle BGH$
  $\angle DBA = \angle BGF$
  $\angle CBG = \angle HGE$
  $\angle ABG = \angle FGE$
- Interior angles are supplementary.
  $\angle CBG + \angle BGH = 180°$
  $\angle ABG + \angle BGF = 180°$

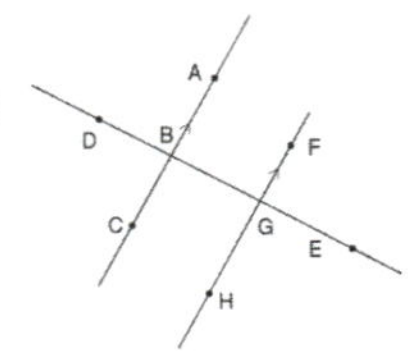

What Should I Be Able to Do?

For extra practice, go to page 494.

LESSON

7.1 **1.** Look at the diagram below. Name:
a) an angle supplementary to $\angle BFC$ $\angle BFA$ or $\angle EFC$
b) an angle complementary to $\angle EFD$ $\angle AFE$
c) an angle opposite $\angle AFB$ $\angle EFC$
d) an angle supplementary to $\angle EFC$ $\angle AFE$ or $\angle BFC$
e) an angle opposite $\angle BFC$ $\angle AFE$

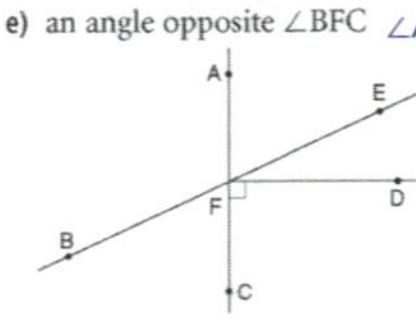

2. In the diagram in question 1, the measure of $\angle EFD$ is 25°. Find the measure of each other angle. Explain how you know.
a) $\angle AFE$ 65°
b) $\angle AFB$ 115°
c) $\angle BFC$ 65°

3. An angle measures 34°. What is the measure of:
a) its complementary angle? 56°
b) its supplementary angle? 146°
c) its opposite angle? 34°

312 UNIT 7: Geometry

8. b) $\angle RQT$ and $\angle QRS$; $\angle RQT$ and $\angle QTS$;
$\angle QTS$ and $\angle TSR$; $\angle TSR$ and $\angle SRQ$

c) $\angle RQT$ and $\angle RQW$ are supplementary angles.
So, $\angle RQT = 180° - \angle RQW = 180° - 130° = 50°$
$\angle QRS$ and $\angle RQT$ are interior angles.
So, $\angle QRS = 180° - \angle RQT = 180° - 50° = 130°$
$\angle RST$ and $\angle QRS$ are interior angles.
So, $\angle RST = 180° - \angle QRS = 180° - 130° = 50°$
$\angle STQ$ and $\angle RQW$ are corresponding angles.
So, $\angle STQ = \angle RQW = 130°$

d) Opposite angles in a parallelogram are equal.

9. a) Fold line segment AB so that A coincides with B.
The fold line is the perpendicular bisector.

b) Place the Mira so that C coincides with D.
The mirror line is the perpendicular bisector.

c)

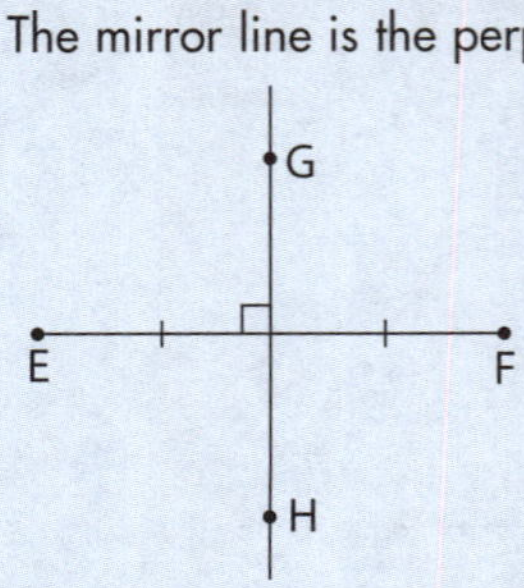

d) The ruler and compass method is most accurate because the fold line and the mirror line might not be exact.

10. a) Fold the paper so that arm AC coincides with arm BA.
The fold line is the angle bisector.

b) Place the Mira so that arm EF coincides with arm DE.
The mirror line is the angle bisector.

c)

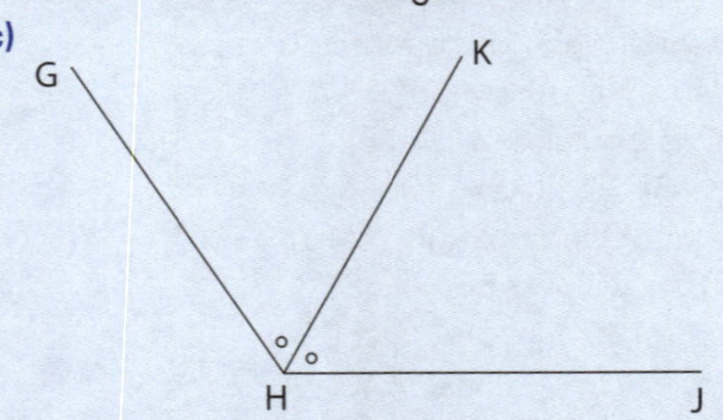

d) The ruler and compass method is most accurate because the fold line and the mirror line might not be exact.

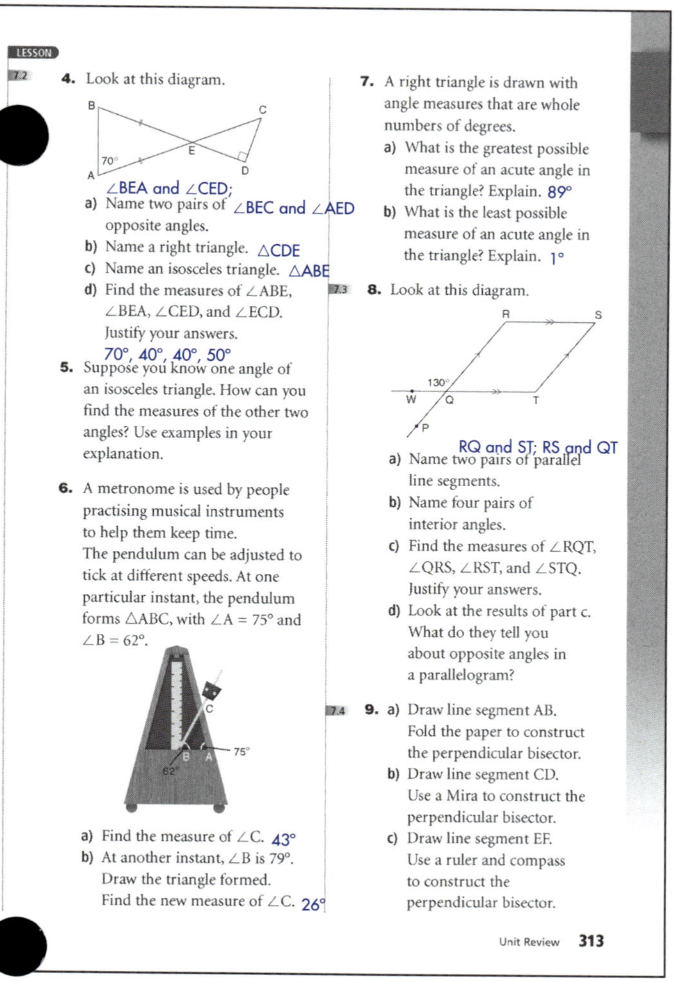

LESSON 7.2

4. Look at this diagram.

a) Name two pairs of opposite angles. ∠BEA and ∠CED; ∠BEC and ∠AED
b) Name a right triangle. △CDE
c) Name an isosceles triangle. △ABE
d) Find the measures of ∠ABE, ∠BEA, ∠CED, and ∠ECD. Justify your answers. 70°, 40°, 40°, 50°

5. Suppose you know one angle of an isosceles triangle. How can you find the measures of the other two angles? Use examples in your explanation.

6. A metronome is used by people practising musical instruments to help them keep time. The pendulum can be adjusted to tick at different speeds. At one particular instant, the pendulum forms △ABC, with ∠A = 75° and ∠B = 62°.

a) Find the measure of ∠C. 43°
b) At another instant, ∠B is 79°. Draw the triangle formed. Find the new measure of ∠C. 26°

7. A right triangle is drawn with angle measures that are whole numbers of degrees.
a) What is the greatest possible measure of an acute angle in the triangle? Explain. 89°
b) What is the least possible measure of an acute angle in the triangle? Explain. 1°

7.3 8. Look at this diagram.

a) Name two pairs of parallel line segments. RQ and ST; RS and QT
b) Name four pairs of interior angles.
c) Find the measures of ∠RQT, ∠QRS, ∠RST, and ∠STQ. Justify your answers.
d) Look at the results of part c. What do they tell you about opposite angles in a parallelogram?

7.4 9. a) Draw line segment AB. Fold the paper to construct the perpendicular bisector.
b) Draw line segment CD. Use a Mira to construct the perpendicular bisector.
c) Draw line segment EF. Use a ruler and compass to construct the perpendicular bisector.

Unit Review 313

11. a)

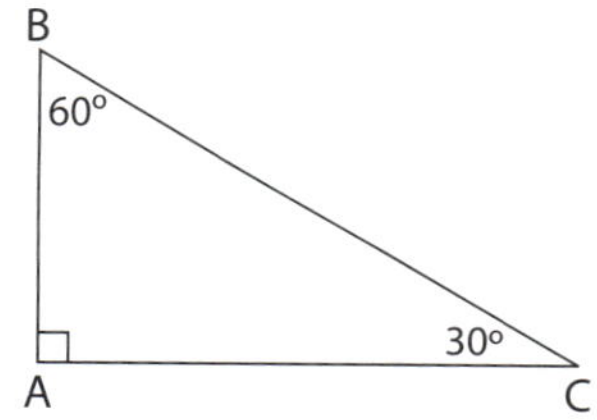

b)

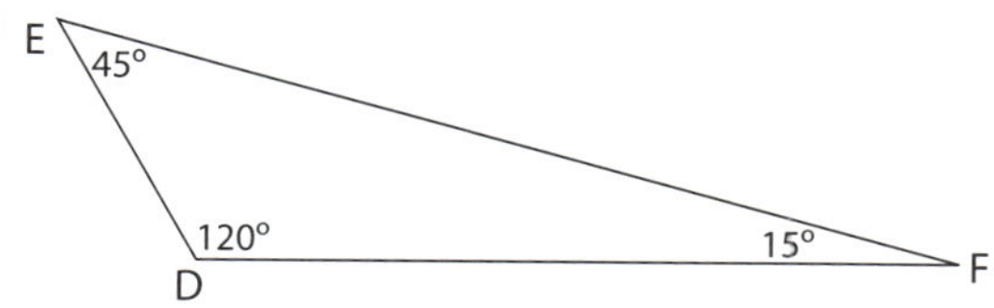

12. c), i) ∠EBC and ∠ABE are supplementary angles.
∠ABE = 156°
So, ∠EBC = 180° − 156° = 24°
△BEC is isosceles, with ∠EBC = ∠BCE
Since ∠EBC = 24°, ∠BCE = 24°

ii) ∠CEF and ∠BCE are alternate angles.
So, ∠CEF = ∠BCE = 24°

iii) ∠FEH and ∠CEF are complementary angles.
∠CEF = 24°
So, ∠FEH = 90° − 24° = 66°

iv) ∠EHG and ∠FEH are alternate angles.
So, ∠EHG = ∠FEH = 66°

v) ∠HED and ∠EHG are interior angles.
So, ∠HED = 180° − ∠EHG = 180° − 66° = 114°

vi) △BEC is isosceles and ∠BCE = ∠EBC = 24°.
∠BED and ∠EBC are alternate angles.
So, ∠BED = ∠EBC = 24°
∠HEB = ∠HED + ∠BED
= 114° + 24°
= 138°

13. a) The sum of the angles in △ABD is 180°.
So, $53° + 90° + x = 180°$
$143° + x = 180°$
$x = 37°$

b) The sum of the angles in △ACD is 180°.
So, $45° + 90° + y = 180°$
$135° + y = 180°$
$y = 45°$

c) ∠BAC = ∠BAD + ∠DAC
$= x + y$
$= 37° + 45°$
$= 82°$

d) The sum of the angles in
△ABC = ∠ABC + ∠BCA + ∠BAC
= 53° + 45° + 82°
= 180°

My answers are correct because the sum of the angles in a triangle is always 180°.

LESSON

d) Which of the three methods is most accurate? Justify your answer.

7.4 **10.** a) Draw acute ∠BAC. Fold the paper to construct the angle bisector.
b) Draw right ∠DEF. Use a Mira to construct the angle bisector.
c) Draw obtuse ∠GHJ. Use a ruler and compass to construct the angle bisector.
d) Which of the three methods is most accurate? Justify your answer.

7.5 **11.** Use only a ruler and compass. Construct each triangle.
a) △ABC with ∠A = 90°, ∠B = 60°, and ∠C = 30°
b) △DEF with ∠D = 120°, ∠E = 45°, and ∠F = 15°

7.6 **12.** Look at this diagram.

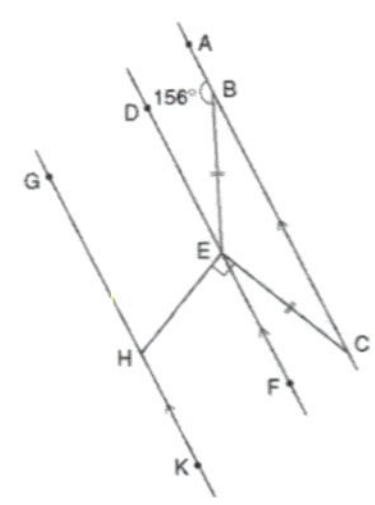

a) Name 3 parallel lines. GK, DF, and AC
b) Name an isosceles triangle. △BEC
c) Find the measure of each angle. Give reasons for your answers.

i) ∠BCE 24°		ii) ∠CEF 24°	
iii) ∠FEH 66°		iv) ∠EHG 66°	
v) ∠HED 114°		vi) ∠HEB 138°	

13. There are two buildings. A worker is standing on top of the shorter building. She looks up to the top of the taller building.

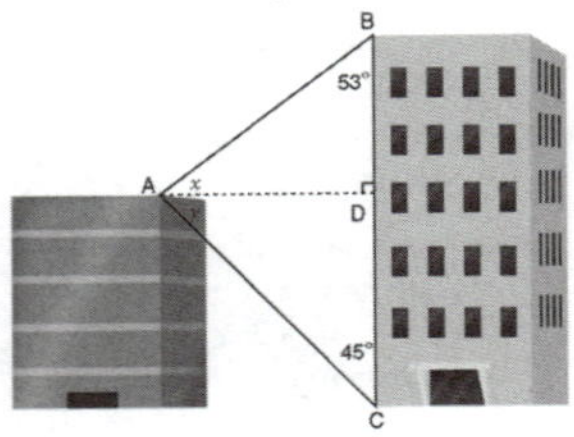

a) What is the angle of elevation, x? 37°
b) The worker then looks down to the base of the taller building. What is the angle of depression, y? 45°
c) What is the measure of ∠BAC? 82°
d) What is the sum of the angles in △ABC? Are your answers to parts a and b correct? 180° How do you know? Yes

314 UNIT 7: Geometry

ASSESSMENT FOR LEARNING

What to Look For

Knowledge and Understanding

✔ **Question 1:** Student understands the meaning of complementary, supplementary, and opposite angles.
✔ **Question 8:** Student understands the angle relationships for parallel lines and transversals.
✔ **Questions 9 and 10:** Student understands how to construct angle bisectors and perpendicular bisectors of lines.

Thinking

✔ **Question 6:** Student can solve problems that involve the sum of the angles in a triangle.
✔ **Questions 12 and 13:** Student can solve problems involving angle measurement.

Communication

✔ **Questions 5 and 7:** Student can explain how to find the measures of angles in a triangle.

Application

✔ **Questions 2 and 3:** Student can find the measures of angles formed by intersecting lines.
✔ **Question 4:** Student can find the measures of angles in a triangle.
✔ **Question 11:** Student can construct triangles given angle measures.

Recording and Reporting

Master 7.1 Unit Rubric: Geometry
Master 7.4 Unit Summary: Geometry

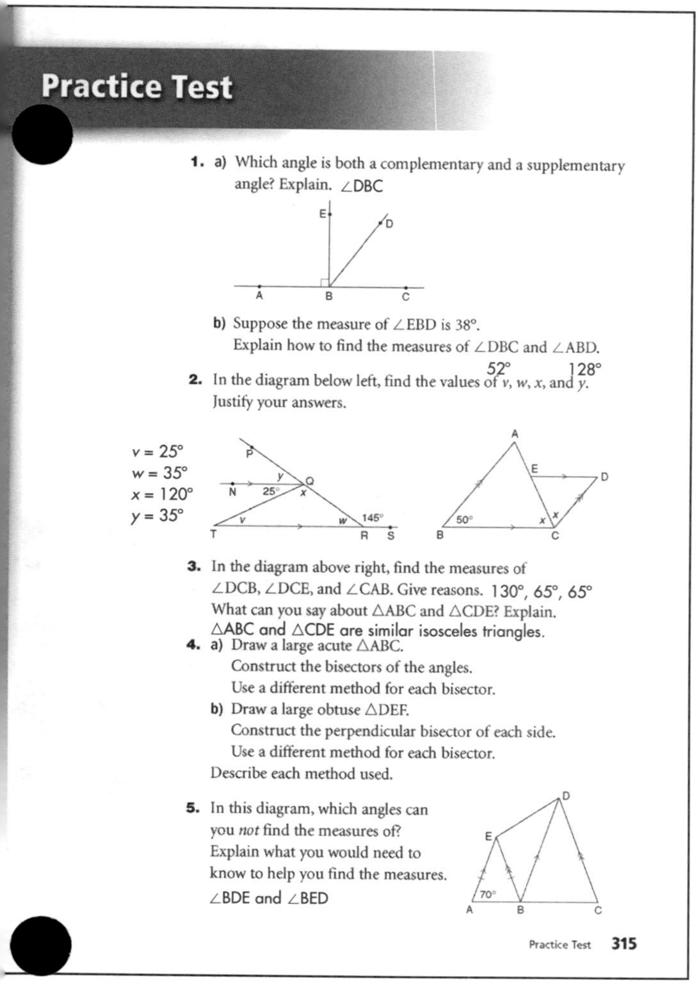

Practice Test

1. a) Which angle is both a complementary and a supplementary angle? Explain. ∠DBC
   b) Suppose the measure of ∠EBD is 38°. Explain how to find the measures of ∠DBC and ∠ABD. 52° 128°
2. In the diagram below left, find the values of *v*, *w*, *x*, and *y*. Justify your answers.
   $v = 25°$, $w = 35°$, $x = 120°$, $y = 35°$
3. In the diagram above right, find the measures of ∠DCB, ∠DCE, and ∠CAB. Give reasons. 130°, 65°, 65°
   What can you say about △ABC and △CDE? Explain.
   △ABC and △CDE are similar isosceles triangles.
4. a) Draw a large acute △ABC. Construct the bisectors of the angles. Use a different method for each bisector.
   b) Draw a large obtuse △DEF. Construct the perpendicular bisector of each side. Use a different method for each bisector.
   Describe each method used.
5. In this diagram, which angles can you *not* find the measures of? Explain what you would need to know to help you find the measures.
   ∠BDE and ∠BED

Practice Test 315

LESSON ORGANIZER

Student Materials
- tracing paper
- Miras
- compasses

Assessment: Master 7.1 Unit Rubric: Geometry; 7.4 Unit Summary: Geometry

To assess the 4 Achievement Chart categories listed in the curriculum document, use these test questions:
Communication: 1
Knowledge and Understanding: 2
Application: 4
Thinking: 5

Sample Solutions

1. a) ∠DBC and ∠EBD are complementary angles.
∠DBC and ∠ABD are supplementary angles.

b) ∠DBC and ∠EBD are complementary angles.
∠EBD = 38°
So, ∠DBC = 90° − 38° = 52°
∠DBC and ∠ABD are supplementary angles.
∠DBC = 52°
So, ∠ABD = 180° − 52° = 128°

2. ∠NQT and ∠QTR are alternate angles.
So, ∠QTR = ∠NQT = 25°
∠QRS and ∠QRT are supplementary angles.
So, ∠QRT = 180° − 145° = 35°
The sum of the angles in △QTR is 180°.
So, ∠RQT = 180° − ∠QTR − ∠QRT
= 180° − 25° − 35°
= 120°
∠PQN and ∠QRT are corresponding angles.
So, ∠PQN = ∠QRT = 35°

3. ∠DCB and ∠ABC are interior angles. ∠ABC = 50°
So, ∠DCB = 180° − 50° = 130°
∠DCB = ∠DCE + ∠ACB
$130° = x + x$
$= 2x$
$\frac{130°}{2} = \frac{2x}{2}$
$65° = x$
∠DCE = 65°
∠DCE and ∠CAB are alternate angles.
So, ∠CAB = ∠DCE = 65°
△ABC and △CDE are similar triangles because corresponding angles are equal.
In each triangle, 2 angles measure 65°. So, the triangles are isosceles.

4. a) I used paper folding, a Mira, and a ruler and compass to construct the bisectors of the angles. Students' answers should include a description of each method used, and a large acute △ABC, with each angle bisected.

b) I used paper folding, a Mira, and a ruler and compass to construct the perpendicular bisectors of each side. Students' answers should include a description of each method used, and a large obtuse △DEF with each side bisected perpendicularly.

5. ∠EBA = 70° because △EAB is isosceles.
∠AEB = 180° − 70° − 70° = 40°, using the sum of the angles in △AEB
∠EBD and ∠AEB are alternate angles.
So, ∠EBD = ∠AEB = 40°
∠EAB and ∠DBC are corresponding angles.
So, ∠DBC = ∠EAB = 70°
∠DCB and ∠EBA are corresponding angles.
So, ∠DCB = ∠EBA = 70°
∠CDB and ∠DBE are alternate angles.
So, ∠CDB = ∠DBE = 40°
I cannot find the measures of ∠BDE and ∠BED.
I would need to know the measure of ∠AED or ∠CDE.

Design a Banner

LESSON ORGANIZER — 80–100 min

Student Grouping: 4

Student Materials
- protractors
- Miras
- compasses
- tracing paper
- scissors
- chart paper
- tape
- coloured pencils or markers

Optional
- computers with *The Geometer's Sketchpad* software

Assessment: Master 7.3 Performance Assessment Rubric: Design a Banner, Master 7.4 Unit Summary: Geometry

Unit Problem — Design a Banner

You have to design one of a series of mathematical banners to be hung on posts outside the school.

Your design will be created on 4 large pieces of chart paper.
It has to include:
- geometric figures, including triangles
- parallel lines with transversals
- geometric constructions

Work in a group of 4.
Brainstorm a theme and design ideas for your banner.
Sketch your banner.
Each person is responsible for one piece of the banner.
Make sure the pattern or design continues across a seam.
Create your banner.

On a sketch of the banner, show all construction lines.

316 UNIT 7: Geometry

Have students turn to pages 316 and 317 of the Student Book.

Review *What You'll Learn,* the learning goals of the unit, and discuss the meanings of the Key Words. Tell students they will use the skills and concepts they learned in this unit to complete the *Unit Problem.*

Present the *Unit Problem*. Have one student read the *Check List* aloud. Remind students that they should use the *Check List* to assess their work before handing it in. You may also wish to provide students with copies of Master 7.3 Performance Assessment Rubric: Design a Banner so they will know how their work will be assessed.

Have students brainstorm ideas for a bright, colourful, and attractive banner. Banner designs can be abstract like a stained glass window; thematic such as the seasons, sports, music, travel, and advertising, and so on.

Ensure students understand they must also provide details of the figures, parallel and intersecting lines, constructions, and transformations used in their banner.

The banners could be displayed in the classroom for all to see.

Sample Response

My group chose sports as its theme. I chose swimming.
On my part of the banner, I constructed the angle bisectors of the two bottom corners of the chart paper to form an isosceles triangle.
I constructed the perpendicular bisector of the 2 equal sides of the triangle.
I joined the midpoints of the 2 sides of the triangle.
I joined the endpoints of the perpendicular bisectors to form an isosceles trapezoid.
I constructed the perpendicular bisector of each non-parallel side of the trapezoid.
I shaded the hexagon and the triangle on the right to represent the arm of a swimmer doing the front stroke.

My part of the banner has rectangles, 2 isosceles trapezoids, a hexagon, a concave heptagon, 2 right trapezoids, many right isosceles triangles, parallel lines and transversals, angle bisectors, perpendicular bisectors, opposite angles, alternate angles, corresponding angles, supplementary angles, complementary angles, and interior angles.
The other members of my group each chose a different sport. One member chose hockey and had a figure that resembled part of a hockey stick.

We continued the triangles on the right and left of my part of the banner across the seams, using reflections and rotations.

We used a ruler and compass to do all constructions because it is the most accurate method.

We taped the different parts of the banner together, then used markers and coloured pencils to colour the banner.

This is a sketch of my part.

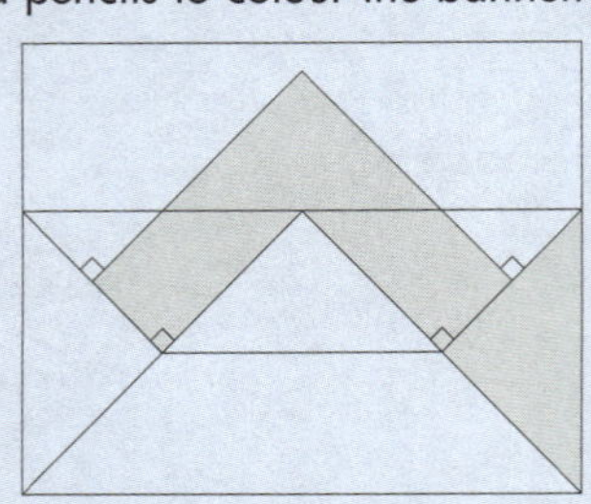

Alternatively, use *The Geometer's Sketchpad* to illustrate each construction on your banner.
Write about your banner.
Explain your choice of design or pattern, and how it relates to the geometric concepts in this unit.

Check List

Your work should show:

- ✓ a detailed sketch including construction lines
- ✓ a description of the figures and angles in your part of the banner
- ✓ your understanding of geometric language and ideas
- ✓ the construction methods you used

Reflect on the Unit

Summarize what you have learned about angles formed by intersecting and parallel lines, and angles of a triangle. Use words and diagrams in your summary.

REFLECT ON THE UNIT: When two lines intersect, opposite angles are equal.
Angles that form a straight line are supplementary.
Supplementary angles have a sum of 180°. Angles that form a right angle are complementary. Complementary angles have a sum of 90°.
The sum of the angles in a triangle is 180°.
When parallel lines are cut by a transversal:
Alternate angles are equal.
Corresponding angles are equal.
Interior angles are supplementary.

For example:

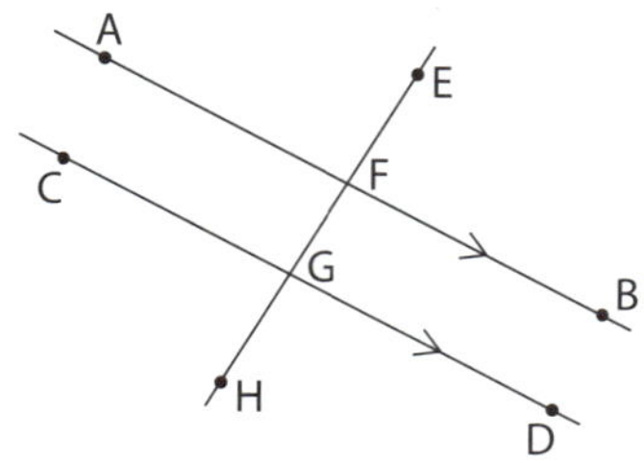

$\angle AFG = \angle FGD$ and $\angle BFG = \angle FGC$ (alternate angles)

$\angle EFA = \angle FGC$, $\angle EFB = \angle FGD$,
$\angle CGH = \angle AFG$, $\angle DGH = \angle BFG$ (corresponding angles)

$\angle AFG + \angle FGC = 180°$ and $\angle BFG + \angle FGD = 180°$ (interior angles)

Teaching notes for Cross Strand Investigation *Pack It Up!* are in the *Additional Assessment Support* module.

ASSESSMENT FOR LEARNING

What to Look For	What to Do
Knowledge and Understanding ✔ Students understand how to use geometric figures, parallel lines with transversals, and geometric constructions to create a banner. ***Communication*** ✔ Students can use correct mathematical terminology to explain how their banner relates to the geometric concepts in the unit. ***Application*** ✔ Students can apply geometric concepts to create a banner.	***Extra Support:*** Make the problem accessible. Groups of students who have difficulty coming up with a design could have each group member construct a different triangle, including angle bisectors, or perpendicular bisectors of sides, or medians. The figure could then be rotated about the midpoint of one side of the triangle. This would produce parallel lines cut by transversals. To produce a more attractive banner, and to make the task more enjoyable, suggest students make use of colour.

Recording and Reporting
Master 7.3 Performance Assessment Rubric: Design a Banner
Master 7.4 Unit Summary: Geometry

Evaluating Student Learning: Preparing to Report: Unit 7 Geometry

This unit provides an opportunity to report on the **Geometry and Spatial Sense** strand.

Master 7.4: Unit Summary: Geometry provides a comprehensive format for recording and summarizing evidence collected.

Here is an example of a completed summary chart for this Unit:

Strand: *Geometry and Spatial Sense*	**Knowledge and Understanding**	**Thinking**	**Communication**	**Application**	***Overall***
Ongoing Observations	2	2	3	3	2/3
Work samples or portfolios; conferences	3	3	3	2	3
Unit Review	2	3	2	3	2/3
Unit Test	3	3	3	3	3
Unit Problem Design a Banner	3	3	3	3	3
Achievement Level for reporting					3

Recording	How to Report
Ongoing Observations	Use *Master 7.2 Ongoing Observations: Geometry* to determine the most consistent level achieved in each category. Enter it in the chart. Choose to summarize by achievement category, or simply to enter an overall level. Observations from late in the unit should be most heavily weighted.
Portfolios or collections of work samples; conferences or interviews	Use *Master 7.1 Unit Rubric: Geometry* to guide evaluation of collections of work and information gathered in conferences. Teachers may choose to focus particular attention on the Assessment Focus questions. Work from late in the unit should be most heavily weighted.
Unit Review	*Master 7.1 Unit Rubric: Geometry* may be helpful in determining levels of achievement. #1, 8, 9, and 10 provide evidence of Knowledge and Understanding; #2, 3, 4, and 11 provide evidence of Application; #5, 6, 7, 12, and 13 provide evidence of Thinking; all questions provide evidence of Communication.
Unit Test	*Master 7.1 Unit Rubric: Geometry* may be helpful in determining levels of achievement. #1 and 2 provide evidence of Knowledge and Understanding; #3 provides evidence of Application; #5 provides evidence of Thinking; all questions provide evidence of Communication.
Unit Problem	Use *Master 7.3 Performance Assessment Rubric: Design a Banner*. The *Unit Problem* offers a snapshot of students' achievement. In particular, it shows their ability to synthesize and apply what they have learned.
Student Self-Assessment	Note students' perceptions of their own progress. This may take the form of an oral or written comment, or a self-rating.
Comments	Analyse the pattern of achievement to identify strengths and needs. In some cases, specific actions may need to be planned to support the learner.

Learning Skills	Ongoing Records
PM 4: Learning Skills Check List Use to record and report throughout a reporting period, rather than for each unit and/or strand.	*PM 10: Summary Class Records: Strands* *PM 11: Summary Class Records: Achievement Categories* *PM 12: Summary Record: Individual* Use to record and report evaluations of student achievement over several clusters, a reporting period, or a school year. These can also be used in place of the Unit Summary.

Name ____________________ Date ____________________

Master 7.1

Unit Rubric: Geometry

	Level 1	Level 2	Level 3	Level 4
Knowledge and Understanding • Shows understanding by describing and explaining: – angles formed by intersecting and parallel lines – the relationships among angles of a triangle – strategies for constructing bisectors – the geometric properties of different quadrilaterals	shows limited understanding in describing and explaining: – angles formed by intersecting and parallel lines – the relationships among angles of a triangle – strategies for constructing bisectors – the geometric properties of different quadrilaterals	shows some understanding in describing and explaining: – angles formed by intersecting and parallel lines – the relationships among angles of a triangle – strategies for constructing bisectors – the geometric properties of different quadrilaterals	shows considerable understanding in describing and explaining: – angles formed by intersecting and parallel lines – the relationships among angles of a triangle – strategies for constructing bisectors – the geometric properties of different quadrilaterals	shows thorough understanding in describing and explaining: – angles formed by intersecting and parallel lines – the relationships among angles of a triangle – strategies for constructing bisectors – the geometric properties of different quadrilaterals
Thinking • Plans and carries out appropriate strategies to create and solve problems that involve lines, angles, triangles, and quadrilaterals	uses appropriate strategies to create and solve problems that involve lines, angles, triangles, and quadrilaterals with limited effectiveness	uses appropriate strategies to create and solve problems that involve lines, angles, triangles, and quadrilaterals with some effectiveness	uses appropriate strategies to create and solve problems that involve lines, angles, triangles, and quadrilaterals with considerable effectiveness	uses appropriate strategies to create and solve problems that involve lines, angles, triangles, and quadrilaterals with a high degree of effectiveness
Communication • Explains concepts, procedures, and reasoning clearly, using appropriate terminology	limited effectiveness; unable to explain reasoning and procedures clearly; rarely uses appropriate terms	some effectiveness; explains reasoning and procedures with some clarity and some appropriate terms	considerable effectiveness; explains reasoning and procedures clearly, using appropriate terms	high degree of effectiveness; explains reasoning and procedures clearly and precisely, using the most appropriate terms
• Presents work, including diagrams, drawings, and calculations clearly, using appropriate conventions (for example, symbols and labels)	presents diagrams, drawings, and calculations with limited clarity and use of appropriate conventions	presents diagrams, drawings, and calculations with some clarity and use of conventions	presents diagrams, drawings, and calculations with considerable clarity and use of conventions	presents diagrams, drawings, and calculations with a high degree of clarity and use of appropriate conventions
Application • Applies geometry skills appropriately to: – identify angles and their properties – construct bisectors – sort and classify quadrilaterals	limited effectiveness; major errors or omissions in: – identifying angles and their properties – constructing bisectors – sorting and classifying quadrilaterals	some effectiveness; somewhat accurate with several minor errors or omissions in: – identifying angles and their properties – constructing bisectors – sorting and classifying quadrilaterals	considerable effectiveness; generally accurate with few minor errors or omissions in: – identifying angles and their properties – constructing bisectors – sorting and classifying quadrilaterals	high degree of effectiveness; accurate and precise with no errors in: – identifying angles and their properties – constructing bisectors – sorting and classifying quadrilaterals

Name ____________________ Date ______________

Master 7.2

Ongoing Observations: Geometry

The behaviours described under each heading are examples; they are not intended to be an exhaustive list of all that might be observed. More detailed descriptions are provided in each lesson under *Assessment for Learning*.

STUDENT ACHIEVEMENT: Geometry				
Student	**Knowledge and Understanding** • Demonstrates and explains: – angles formed by intersecting and parallel lines – relationships among angles of a triangle – strategies for constructing bisectors – the geometric properties of different quadrilaterals	**Thinking** • Uses appropriate strategies to create and solve problems that involve lines, angles, triangles, and quadrilaterals	**Communication** • Explains reasoning and procedures clearly using appropriate terms • Presents diagrams, drawings, and calculations clearly, including symbols and labels	**Application** • Accurately: – identifies angles and their properties – constructs bisectors – sorts and classifies quadrilaterals by geometric properties

Level 1 – very limited; Level 2 – somewhat or limited; Level 3 – satisfactory; Level 4 – thorough

Name ____________________ Date ________________

Master 7.3

Performance Assessment Rubric: Design a Banner

	Level 1	Level 2	Level 3	Level 4
Knowledge and Understanding • Explanations show understanding of angles, line segments, and triangles	explanations show limited understanding of angles, line segments, and triangles	explanations show some understanding of angles, line segments, and triangles	explanations show considerable understanding of angles, line segments, and triangles	explanations show thorough understanding of angles, line segments, and triangles
Thinking • Uses appropriate design strategies (for example, estimating, calculating, sketching, computer software) to create a design that meets the criteria given	uses a few simple design strategies with limited success in meeting criteria	uses some appropriate design strategies with partial success in meeting criteria	uses appropriate design strategies with considerable success in meeting criteria	uses appropriate, often innovative, design strategies with a high degree of success in meeting criteria
Communication • Communicates procedures, solutions, and reasoning clearly, using appropriate geometric language	limited effectiveness; does not communicate clearly	some effectiveness; communicates with some clarity	considerable effectiveness; communicates clearly	a high degree of effectiveness; communicates clearly and precisely
• Presents diagrams and drawings clearly, using appropriate geometric conventions (for example, symbols and labels)	presents diagrams and drawings with limited clarity and use of appropriate conventions	presents diagrams and drawings with some clarity and use of appropriate conventions	presents diagrams and drawings with considerable clarity and use of appropriate geometric conventions	presents diagrams and drawings with a high degree of clarity and use of appropriate geometric conventions
Application • Accurately applies measurement skills to construct appropriate geometric figures, angles, and line segments	limited effectiveness; major errors or omissions in constructions	some effectiveness; somewhat accurate constructions	considerable effectiveness; generally accurate constructions	high degree of effectiveness; accurate and precise constructions

Name ____________________ Date ______________

Master 7.4

Unit Summary: Geometry

Review assessment records to determine the most consistent achievement levels for the assessments conducted. Some cells may be blank. *Overall* achievement levels may be recorded in each row, rather than identifying levels for each achievement category.

	Most Consistent Level of Achievement*				
Strand: *Geometry and Spatial Sense*	**Knowledge and Understanding**	**Thinking**	**Communication**	**Application**	***Overall***
Ongoing Observations					
Work samples or portfolios; conferences					
Unit Review					
Unit Test					
Unit Problem Design a Banner					
Achievement Level for reporting					

*Use Ontario Achievement Levels 1, 2, 3, 4

Self-Assessment:

Comments: (Strengths, Needs, Next Steps)

Name ____________________ Date ______________

Master 7.5a

Lesson 7.6A: Characteristics of Quadrilaterals

Curriculum Focus: Investigate the geometric properties of quadrilaterals.

Look around the classroom.
Name the different quadrilaterals you see.

Explore

Work with a partner.
You will need a ruler and protractor.

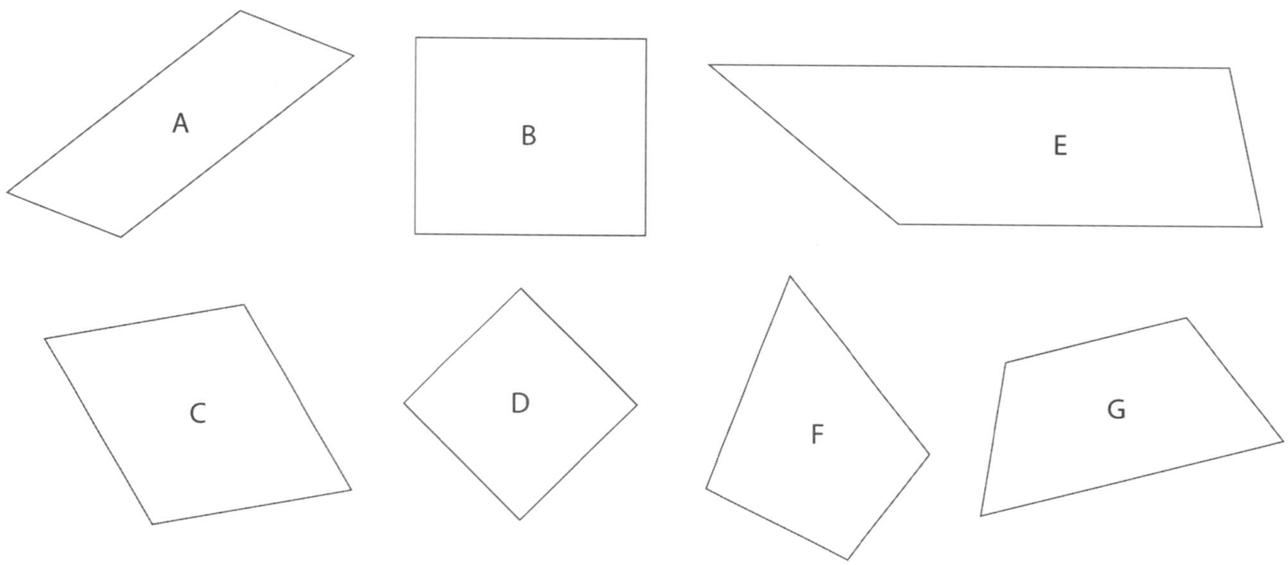

Your teacher will give you a large copy of the quadrilaterals above.

- Identify each figure.
- Measure and record the lengths of the sides of each quadrilateral.
  What do you notice?
- Measure and record the angles in each quadrilateral.
  What do you notice?
- Draw the diagonals in each quadrilateral.
  Measure and record the lengths of the diagonals and the angles formed.
  What do you notice?

Reflect & Share

Share your results with another pair of classmates.
Work together to make a list of the characteristics of each quadrilateral.

Name ____________________ Date ________________

Master 7.5b

Connect

All quadrilaterals have 4 sides and 2 diagonals.
Some quadrilaterals have special names that relate to the characteristics they possess: a parallelogram, rectangle, square, kite, rhombus, and trapezoid.

Quadrilateral Characteristics

Name	Side Characteristics	Angle Characteristics	Diagonal Characteristics
Parallelogram	opposite sides equal opposite sides parallel	adjacent interior angles supplementary opposite angles equal	diagonals bisect each other
Rectangle	opposite sides equal opposite sides parallel	all right angles	diagonals equal diagonals bisect each other
Square	all sides equal opposite sides parallel	all right angles	diagonals equal diagonals bisect each other perpendicularly diagonals bisect angles at vertices
Rhombus	all sides equal opposite sides parallel	adjacent interior angles supplementary opposite angles equal	diagonals bisect each other perpendicularly diagonals bisect angles at vertices
Kite	two pairs of equal adjacent sides	one pair of opposite angles equal	diagonals bisect each other only one diagonal bisects the other perpendicularly
Trapezoid	one pair of parallel sides	two pairs of adjacent interior angles supplementary	
Isosceles Trapezoid	one pair of parallel sides non-parallel sides equal	two pairs of adjacent interior angles supplementary opposite angles supplementary	diagonals equal

Many figures share the same characteristics. For example, a parallelogram, rectangle, square, and rhombus all have opposite sides equal.
Some figures have very specialized characteristics. For example, a kite has only one diagonal that bisects the other perpendicularly.

Name ______________________ Date ________________

Master 7.5c

Example

Draw a quadrilateral with these characteristics:
Diagonals bisect each other.
Side lengths are 7 cm and 9 cm.
One angle is 50°.

Solution

A parallelogram, rectangle, square, and rhombus have diagonals that bisect each other.
Of these quadrilaterals, only a parallelogram and a rectangle can have different side lengths.
Since all angles in a rectangle are right angles, this quadrilateral must be a parallelogram.
Since adjacent interior angles in a parallelogram are supplementary, the other adjacent interior angle measures: 180° – 50° = 130°

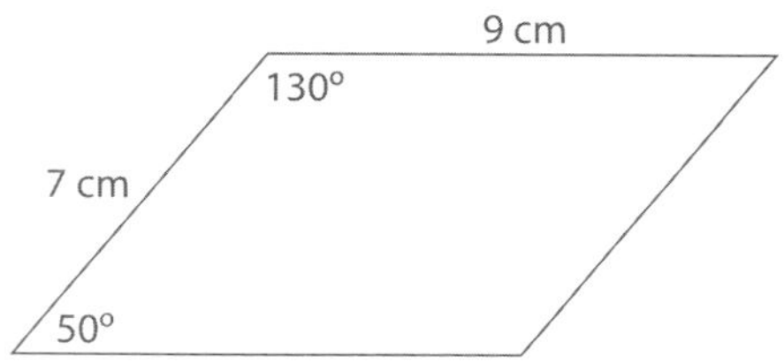

Practice

You might need isometric or square dot paper, plain paper, a ruler, and protractor.
Many of these questions can also be completed using *The Geometer's Sketchpad*.

1. Draw each quadrilateral.
a) a rectangle with side lengths 6 cm and 8 cm
b) a square with side length 7 cm
c) a rhombus with side length 8 cm, and angles of 60° and 120°
d) a kite with side lengths 7.1 cm and 10 cm, and angles of 105°, 90°, 105°, and 60°
e) a trapezoid with interior angles of 90°, 90°, 150°, and 30°

2. Draw the diagonals in each quadrilateral in question 1.
Measure and record the lengths of the diagonals and the angles formed.
Explain how these measures verify the characteristics of each quadrilateral.

3. A square is a rectangle, but a rectangle is not necessarily a square.
Is this statement correct?
Explain.

4. Use a Venn diagram to sort the quadrilaterals in *Explore*.
a) Use the characteristics: "Diagonals equal" and "At least one pair of parallel sides"
b) Choose three different characteristics.
Sort the quadrilaterals a different way.

Name ____________________ Date ______________

Master 7.5d

5. A builder wants wall supports to be perpendicular to both the bottom and top boards. How can a builder use the diagonal characteristics to check that the wall supports are at right angles?

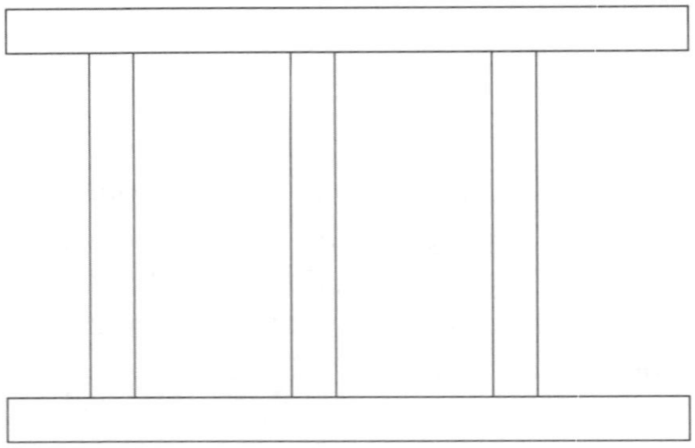

6. **Assessment Focus** Identify, then draw, a quadrilateral with the given characteristics. How many different quadrilaterals can you find each time? Explain.
   a) Diagonals bisect each other perpendicularly.
   One angle is 90°.
   Perimeter is 24 cm.
   b) Opposite sides are parallel.
   Diagonals bisect each other, but not perpendicularly.
   One angle is 60°.
   c) One pair of parallel sides
   Diagonals are equal.
   Non-parallel sides are 8.5 cm.

Take It Further

7. Use a ruler and protractor to construct a quadrilateral with a perimeter of 36 cm for each of these characteristics:
   a) diagonals equal and bisect each other perpendicularly
   b) diagonals equal and bisect each other, but not perpendicularly
   c) diagonals are not equal, but they bisect each other perpendicularly
   d) only one diagonal bisected perpendicularly
   e) all sides different lengths

Reflect

Describe how the special name of a quadrilateral defines its characteristics.

Name ____________________ Date ______________

Master 7.6a

Additional Activity 1: L-Game

Play with a partner.

Materials: You will need the *L-Game* game board.

How to Play:

1. Player A shades an image of the original L-shaped figure.
   He describes the transformation for which his figure is the image of the original figure.
   One point is scored for a correct description.
2. Player B shades an image of the original L-shaped figure.
   Squares on the game board can only be shaded once.
   She describes the transformation for which her figure is the image of the original figure.
   One point is scored for a correct description.
3. Players continue to take turns.
   The round is over when no more images can be drawn.
4. The player with more points after 4 rounds wins.

Take It Further: Students create their own game boards, this time using a T-shaped figure.
Students play the game again.

Name ______________________ Date ________________

Master 7.6b

L-Game Game Board

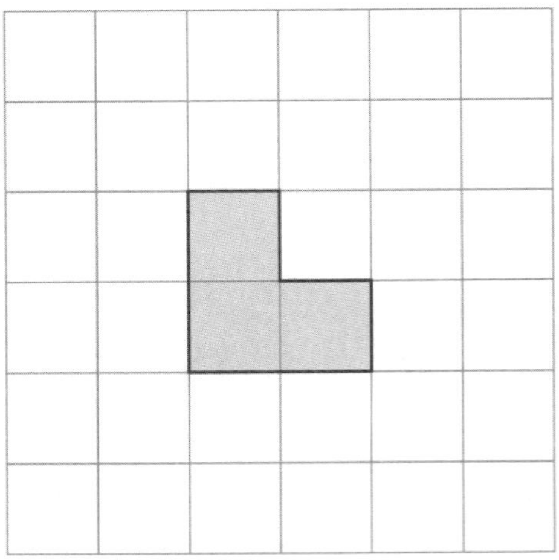

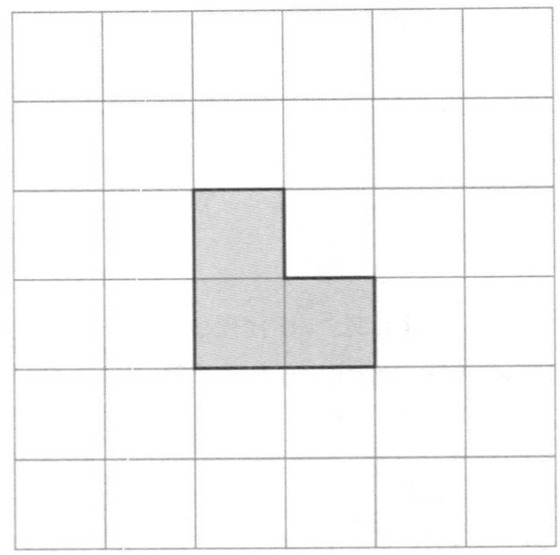

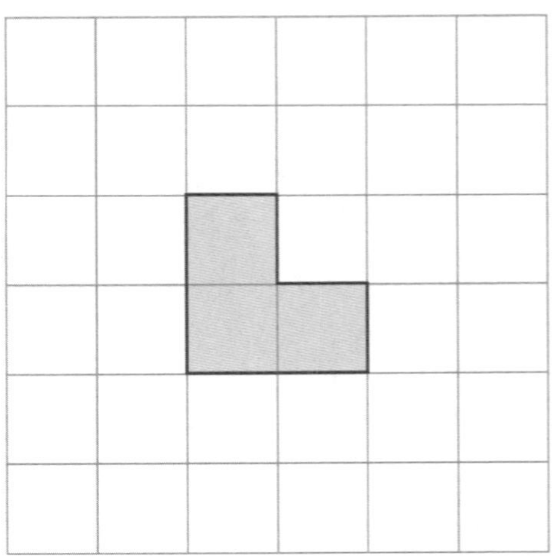

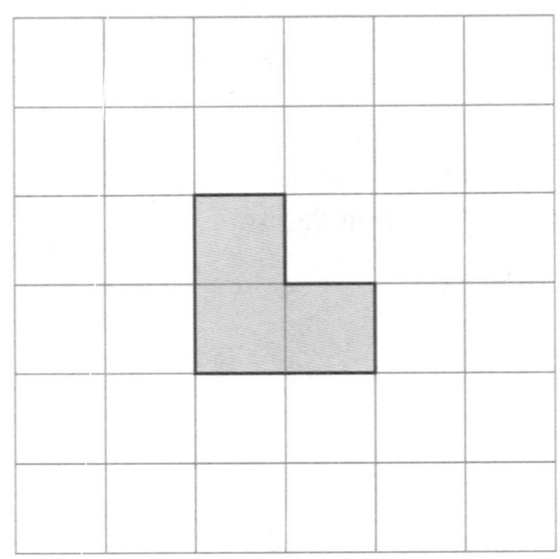

Name ______________ Date ______________

Master 7.7

Additional Activity 2: Can You Make It?

Play with a partner.

Materials: You will need three number cubes labelled 1 to 6.

How to Play:

1. Player A rolls the number cubes.
   The numbers rolled represent the possible side lengths of a triangle.
   Player A decides whether a triangle can be formed.
   One point is scored for a correct answer.
   A bonus point is scored for naming the type of triangle that can be formed.

2. Player B rolls the number cubes.
   Player B decides whether a triangle can be formed.
   One point is scored for a correct answer.
   A bonus point is scored for naming the type of triangle that can be formed.

3. Players continue to take turns.
   The player with more points after 6 rounds wins.

Take It Further: Students play the game again.
This time, students must also draw any triangle that can be formed.
Students get one point for a correct drawing.

Name ____________________ Date ________________

Master 7.8

Additional Activity 3: Triangle Trial

Work on your own.

Materials: You will need a ruler and compass, and a protractor.

Follow these instructions to construct several triangles with common sides.
Sketch the triangles before you draw them.

1. Construct an equilateral ΔABC with side length 6 cm.

2. Construct ΔACD with ∠ACD = 120°, and ∠CAD = 25°.

3. Construct ΔABE with ∠ABE = 120°, and AE = 9 cm.

4. Measure ∠AED and ∠ADE.

5. Describe ΔAED.

Take It Further: Students draw quadrilateral PQRS with PQ = 6 cm, QR = 5 cm, RS = 3 cm, PS = 7 cm, and ∠SPQ = 65°.
Students measure ∠Q, ∠R, and ∠S.
Students find the sum of the angles in a quadrilateral.

Name ____________________ Date ______________

Master 7.9

Additional Activity 4: Measuring Up

Work on your own.

Materials: You will need a ruler and compass, and a protractor.

Follow these instructions to draw a 5-pointed star.
Sketch the star before you draw it.

1. Draw a large circle. Label its centre O.
   Draw a radius. Label it OA.

2. Construct ∠BOA = 72°, with B on the circle.

3. Construct ∠COA = 144°, with C on the circle.

4. Construct ∠EOA = 72°, with E on the opposite side of OA from B and C.

5. Construct ∠DOA = 144°, with D on the circle.

6. Join AC, CE, EB, BD, and AD.

Take It Further: Repeat the activity using angles of 60° and 120° to construct a 6-pointed star.

Name ____________________ Date ______________

Master 7.10

Step-by-Step 1

Lesson 7.1, Question 6

Step 1 Opposite angles are equal.
Supplementary angles have a sum of ______°.
Name 2 equal angles whose sum is 180°. ______ + ______ = 180°
Sketch the angles.

How many possible opposite angles that are supplementary are there?

____

Step 2 Complementary angles have a sum of ______°.
Name 2 equal angles whose sum is 90°. ______ + ______ = 90°
Sketch the angles.

How many possible opposite angles that are complementary are there?

____

Step 3 Name 2 angles that are not equal whose sum is 180°. ______ + ______ = 180°
Could these angles be opposite angles? ______
Explain. ______________________________________
Sketch the angles.

How many possible supplementary angles that could not be opposite angles are there?

____

Step 4 Name 2 angles that are not equal whose sum is 90°. ______ + ______ = 90°
Could these angles be opposite angles? ______
Explain. ______________________________________
Sketch the angles.

How many possible complementary angles that could not be opposite angles are there?

____

Name ____________________ Date _______________

Master 7.11

Step-by-Step 2

Lesson 7.2, Question 6

Step 1 How many angles are in a triangle? _____
What is the sum of the angles in a triangle? _____°

Step 2 What is the sum of 2 supplementary angles? _____°

Step 3 Suppose 2 angles in a triangle are supplementary.
Find the measure of the third angle:
Subtract your answer in *Step 2* from the sum of the angles in a triangle from *Step 1*.

______ – ______ = ______
What is the measure of the third angle? ______°
Can two angles in a triangle be supplementary? Explain.

____

Step 4 What is the sum of 2 complementary angles? _____°

Step 5 Suppose 2 angles in a triangle are complementary.
Find the measure of the third angle:
Subtract your answer in *Step 4* from the sum of the angles in a triangle from *Step 1*.

______ – ______ = ______
What is the measure of the third angle? ______°
Can two angles in a triangle be complementary? Explain.

____

Step 6 Name two complementary angles. ______, _______
What is the measure of the third angle in the triangle? ______°
Sketch the triangle. Label the angles.

Step 7 Repeat *Step 6* for as many different complementary angles as you can.

Name ____________________ Date ______________

Master 7.12

Step-by-Step 3

Lesson 7.3, Question 7

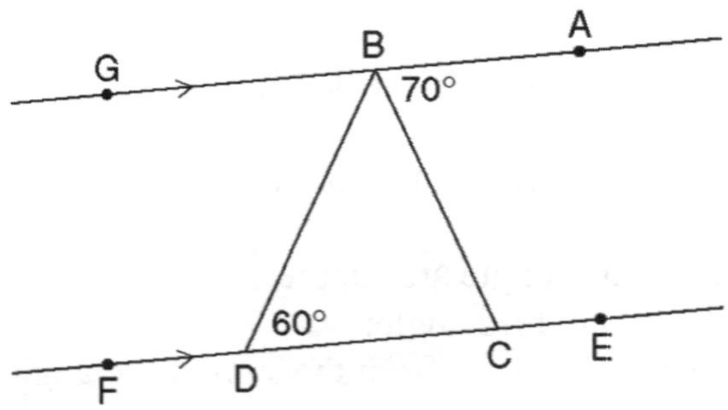

Step 1 Use alternate angles.
What is the measure of ∠BCD? ______°
Label the angle with its measure.

Step 2 Use supplementary angles.
What is the measure of ∠BCE? ______°
Label the angle with its measure.

Step 3 Use alternate angles.
What is the measure of ∠GBD? ______°
Label the angle with its measure.

Step 4 Use supplementary angles.
What is the measure of ∠BDF? ______°
Label the angle with its measure.

Step 5 Use supplementary angles.
What is the measure of ∠DBC? ______°
Label the angle with its measure.

Step 6 Name an angle equal to ∠GBD. _______
Name an angle equal to ∠ABC. _______

Step 7 ∠GBA is a straight angle.
So, ∠GBD + ∠DBC + ∠ABC = 180°.
Replace ∠GBD and ∠ABC with their equal angles form *Step 6*.
∠_____ + ∠DBC + ∠______ = 180°

Step 8 What is the sum of the angles in ΔBCD? _______°

Name ____________________ Date ______________

Master 7.13

Step-by-Step 4

Lesson 7.4, Question 10

You will need a ruler and compass, and plain paper.

Step 1 Draw a line segment. Label it AB.
Set the compass so the distance between the compass and pencil points is equal to AB.
Place the compass point on A.
Mark a point C. Join AC and CB to form isosceles ΔABC.

Step 2 Bisect $\angle$A.

Step 3 Draw the perpendicular bisector of BC.

Step 4 What do you notice about the bisectors? ______________________________
Will the result be true for all isosceles triangles? Explain.

____

____

Step 5 Draw a line segment. Label it AB.
Set the compass so the distance between the compass and pencil points is equal to AB.
Place the compass point on A. Draw an arc above AB.
Place the compass point on B. Draw an arc to intersect the first arc.
Label point C where the arcs intersect. Join AC and BC to form equilateral ΔABC.

Step 6 Repeat *Steps 2* and *3*.
What do you notice about the bisectors? ______________________________
Will the result be true for all equilateral triangles? Explain.

____

____

Step 7 Draw a large scalene ΔABC.
Repeat *Steps 2* and *3*.
What do you notice about the bisectors? ______________________________
Will the result be true for all scalene triangles? Explain.

____

____

Name ____________________ Date ______________

Master 7.14

Step-by-Step 5

Lesson 7.5, Question 4

You will need a ruler and compass, plain paper, and a protractor.

To construct an isosceles triangle with one 30° angle:

Step 1 Draw a line segment. Label it AB.
Set the compass so the distance between the compass and pencil points is equal to AB.
Place the compass point on A. Draw an arc above AB.
Place the compass point on B. Draw an arc to intersect the first arc.
Label point C where the arcs intersect. Join AC.
What is the measure of ∠A? _____°

Step 2 Bisect ∠A.

Step 3 Place the compass point on A.
Draw an arc that intersects AB and the angle bisector.
Label the points of intersection D and E.
Join DE.
What are the measures of the angles in ΔADE? _____°, _____°, _____°

Which type of triangle have you constructed? ______________________________

To construct an isosceles triangle with two 30° angles:

Step 4 Repeat *Step 1*. This time join AC and BC.
Which type of triangle have you constructed? ______________________________

Step 5 Bisect ∠A.
Bisect ∠B.
Label the point D where the angle bisectors intersect.

Step 6 What are the measures of the angles in ΔABD? _____°, _____°, _____°

Which type of triangle have you constructed? ______________________________

Step 7 How many different ways can you construct each triangle? ____________________
Include a construction with each method.

Name ____________________ Date ______________

Master 7.15

Step-by-Step 6

Lesson 7.6, Question 5

You will need a large copy of the diagram in *Practice* question 5, on page 306 of the Student Book.

Step 1 Choose an angle. ∠_____
Use a protractor.
Measure the angle. ∠_____ = _____°
Label the angle with its measure.

Step 2 Label the unmarked angles with the variables: p, q, r, s, t, u, v, w

Step 3 Use alternate angles, corresponding angles, supplementary angles, complementary angles, and the sum of the angles in a triangle.
Find the value of each variable.
Justify each answer.

p = _____°: ______________________________

q = _____°: ______________________________

r = _____°: ______________________________

s = _____°: ______________________________

t = _____°: ______________________________

u = _____°: ______________________________

v = _____°: ______________________________

w = _____°: ______________________________

Step 4 Were you able to find the value of each variable? _____
If not, repeat *Steps 1* to *3*. This time, measure a different angle.

Name ____________________ Date ______________

Master 7.16

Step-by-Step 6A

Lesson 7.6A, Question 6

Step 1 List all quadrilaterals with diagonals that bisect each other perpendicularly.

____

Step 2 Which quadrilateral in *Step 1* has a 90° angle? ____________________

What is true about the side lengths of this quadrilateral? ________________

____

Step 3 What is the side length of the quadrilateral in *Step 2* with perimeter 24 cm? ________
Draw this quadrilateral.

Step 4 List all quadrilaterals with opposite sides parallel.

____

Step 5 Which quadrilaterals in *Step 4* have diagonals that bisect each other, but not perpendicularly? ______________________________

Step 6 Which quadrilateral in *Step 5* can have a 60° angle? ____________________
Draw this quadrilateral.

Step 7 List all quadrilaterals with one pair of parallel sides.

____

Step 8 Which quadrilateral in *Step 7* has diagonals equal? ____________________
Draw this quadrilateral with non-parallel sides of length 8.5 cm.

Step 9 Can you change any of the quadrilaterals you have drawn and still satisfy the given characteristics? Explain.

____

Name ____________________ Date ______________

Master 7.17

Diagram in Lesson 7.1 *Explore*

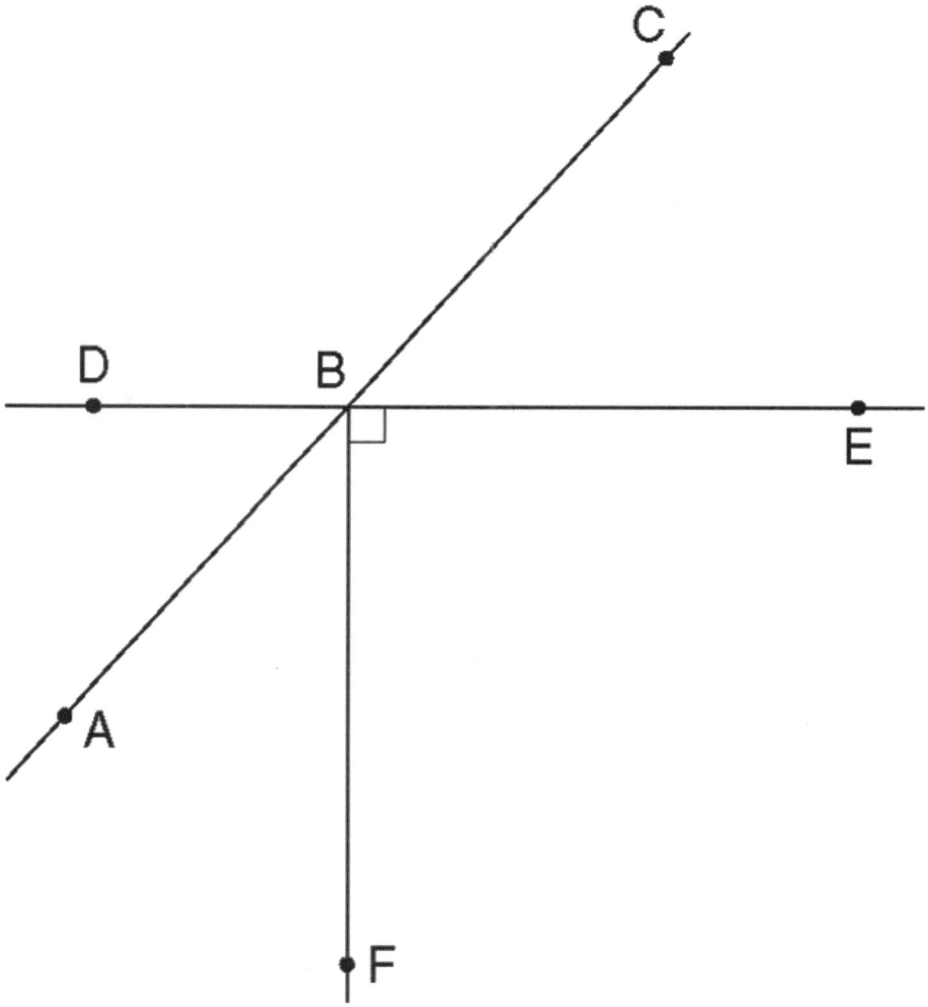

Name ____________________ Date ________________

Master 7.18

Diagram for 7.6 *Explore*

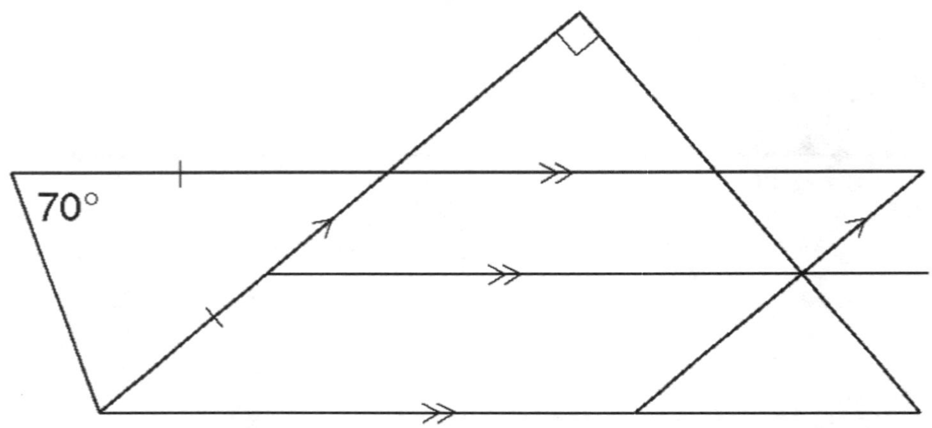

Name ______________________ Date ________________

Master 7.19

Diagram for 7.6 *Practice* Question 5

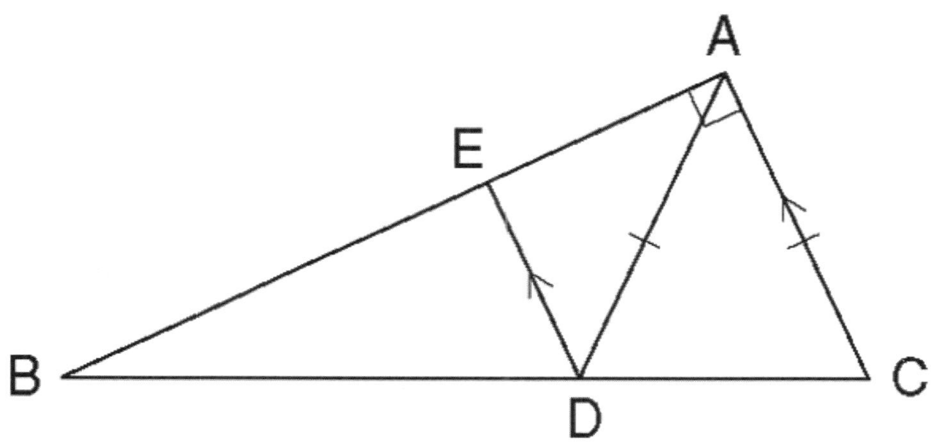

Name ____________________ Date ________________

Master 7.20

Quadrilaterals in *Explore* 7.6A

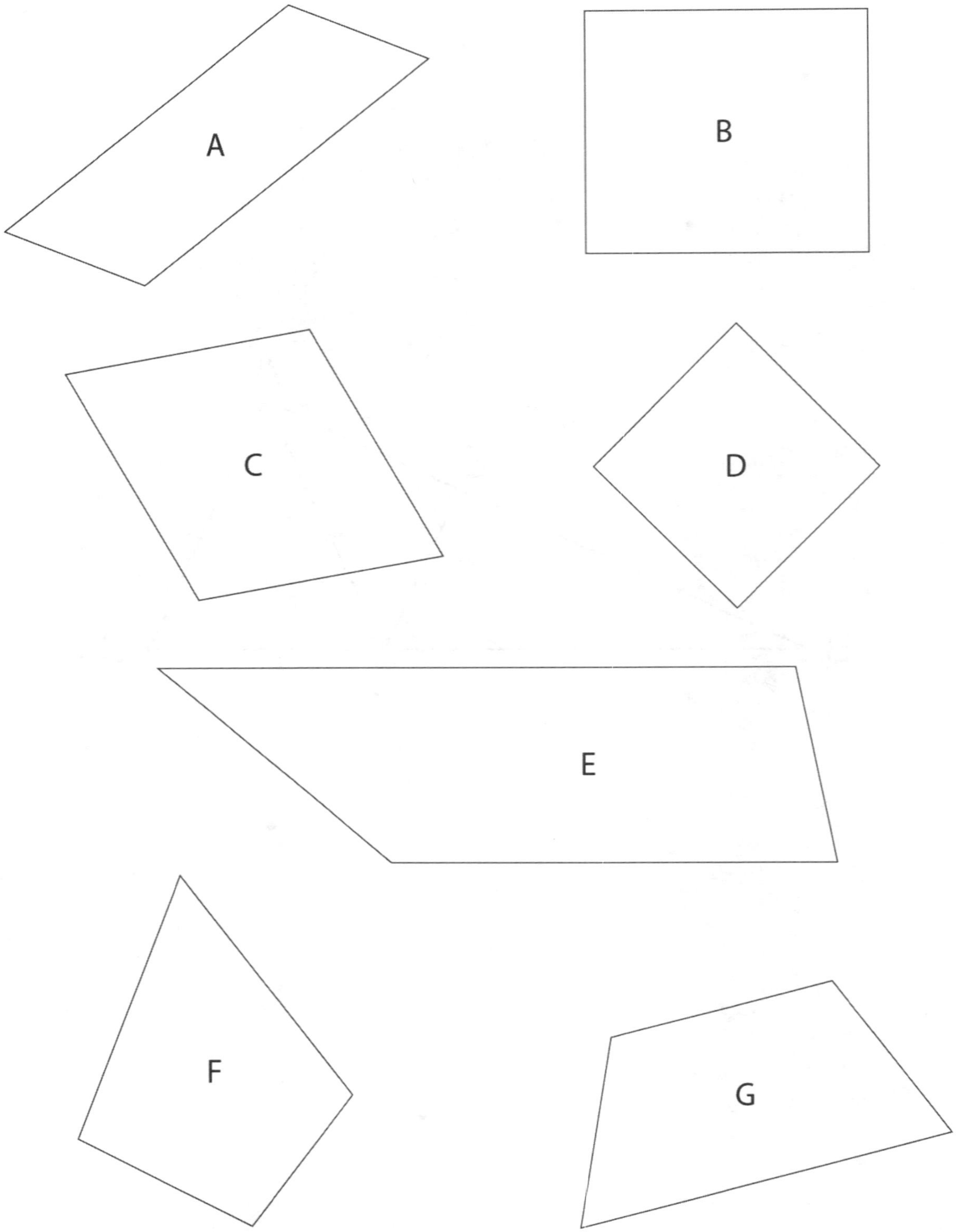

Name ____________________ Date ______________

Master 7.21a

Unit Test: Unit 7 Geometry

You will need a ruler, compass, and protractor.

1. Look at the diagram to the right. Name a pair of:

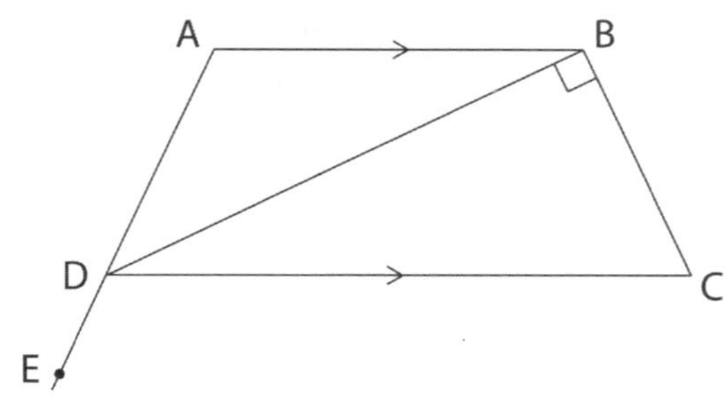

a) alternate angles ____________________

b) corresponding angles ________________

c) supplementary angles ________________

d) complementary angles ________________

e) interior angles ______________________

2. Look at the diagram.
Find the measure of each angle.
Justify your answers.

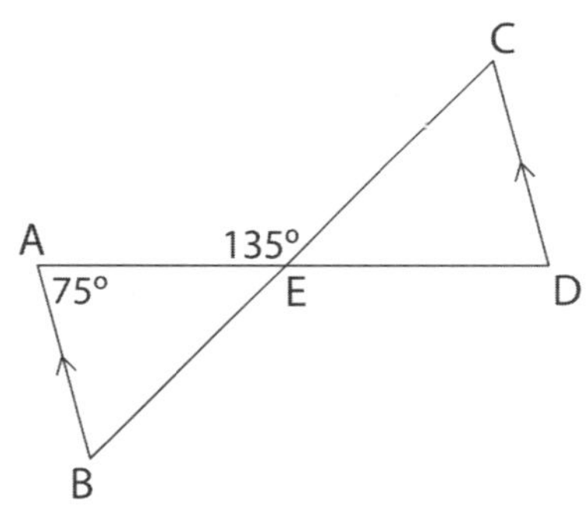

a) ∠AEB

b) ∠ABE

c) ∠EDC

3. Look at this diagram.
Find the values of *x*, *y*, *z*, *w*, and *t*. Justify your answers.

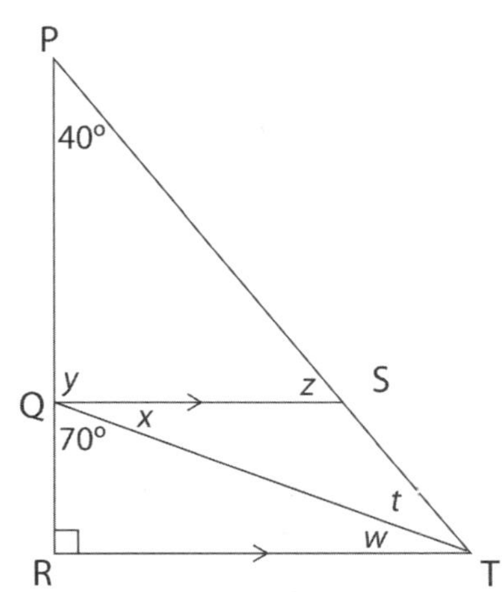

Name ____________________ Date ________________

Master 7.21b

Unit Test continued

4. Use ΔABC below. Show all construction lines.
Construct the bisector of ∠A. Label the point D where the bisector intersects BC.
Construct the bisector of ∠B. Label the point E where the bisector intersects AC.
Construct the bisector of ∠C. Label the point F where the bisector intersects AB.
Label point G where the bisectors meet.
Draw the circle with centre G and radius GD.
What do you notice?

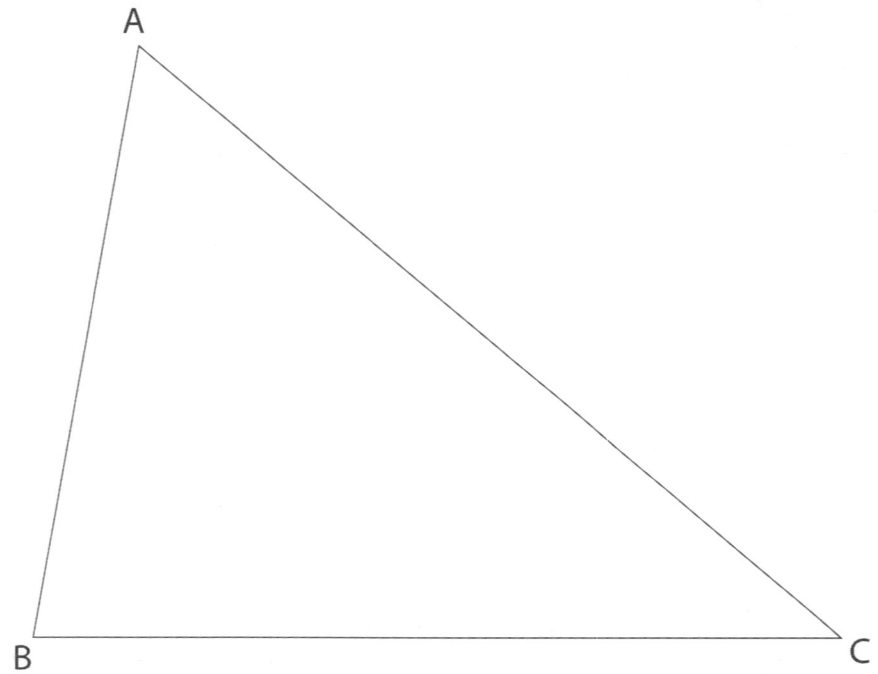

5. a) I have: opposite angles equal
diagonals that bisect angles at vertices
no right angles
What am I? Explain.

Name ______________________ Date __________________

Master 7.21c

Unit Test continued

b) Choose 3 characteristics.
Use the Venn diagram to sort these quadrilaterals:
Square, rectangle, kite, trapezoid, parallelogram, rhombus

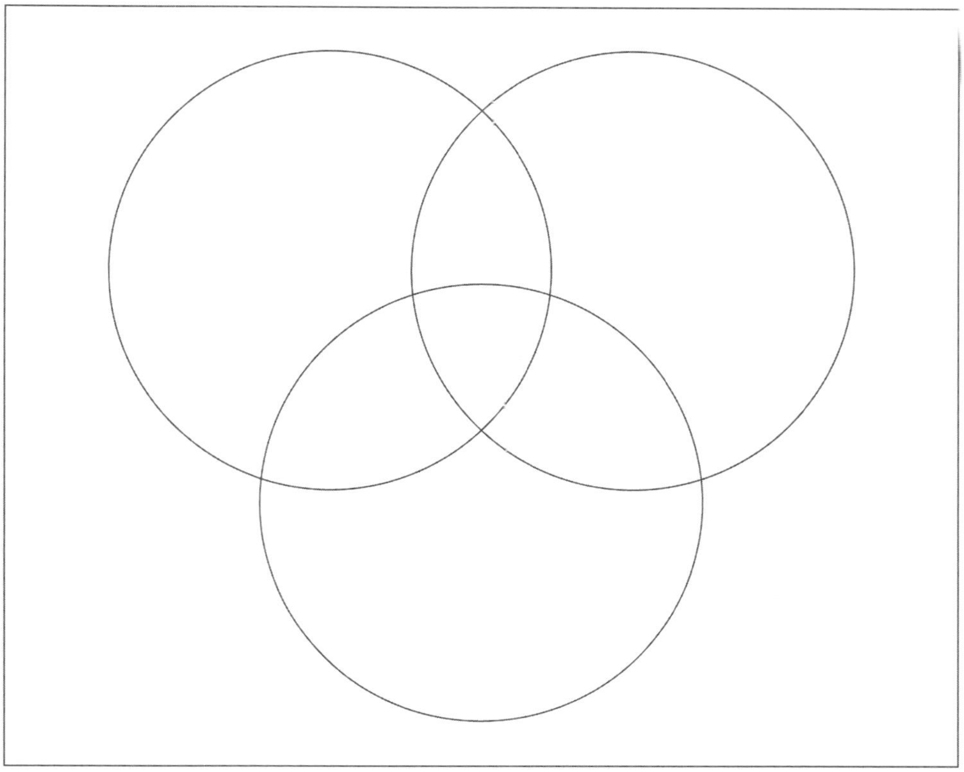

6. a) Calculate the measure of each unmarked angle. Mark the measures on the diagram.
b) Name all isosceles triangles.

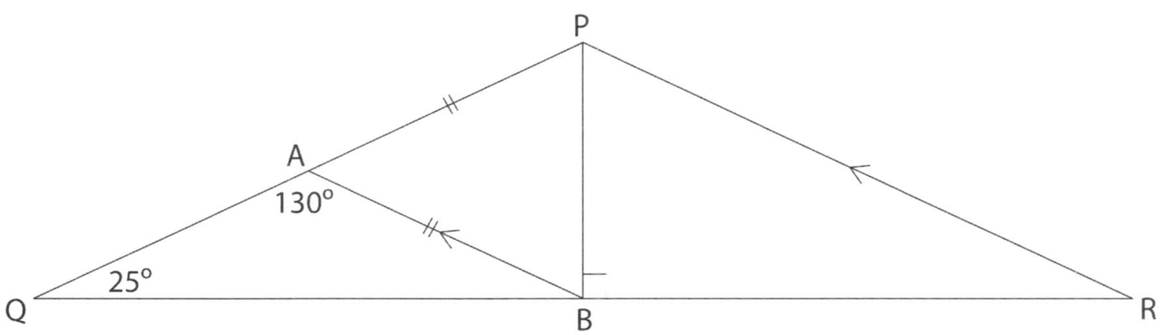

Name ____________________ Date ______________

Master 7.22

Sample Answers

Unit Test – Master 7.21

1. a) ∠ABD and ∠BDC
   b) ∠BAD and ∠CDE
   c) ∠BDA and ∠BDE, or ∠CDA and ∠CDE, or ∠BAD and ∠ADC, or ∠ABC and ∠BCD
   d) ∠BDC and ∠BCD, or ∠ABD and ∠BCD
   e) ∠BAD and ∠ADC, or ∠ABC and ∠BCD
2. a) ∠AEB and ∠AEC are supplementary angles. So, ∠AEB = 180° – ∠AEC
   = 180° – 135°
   = 45°
   b) The sum of the angles in ΔABE = 180°. So, ∠ABE = 180° – 75° – 45° = 60°
   c) ∠EDC and ∠BAE are alternate angles. So, ∠EDC = ∠BAE = 75°
3. w = 20°; the sum of the angles in ΔQRT = 180°.
   So, ∠QTR = 180° – 90° – 70° = 20°
   x = 20°; ∠QTR and ∠SQT are alternate angles. So, ∠SQT = ∠QTR = 20°
   y = 90°; ∠PQR is a straight angle.
   So, ∠PQS = 180° – 20° – 70° = 90°
   z = 50°; the sum of the angles in ΔPQS = 180°.
   So, ∠PSQ = 180° – 90° – 40° = 50°
   t = 30°; ∠PSQ and ∠PTR are corresponding angles. So, ∠PTR = ∠PSQ = 50°
   ∠PTR = t + w
   50° = t + 20°
   t = 30°
4. 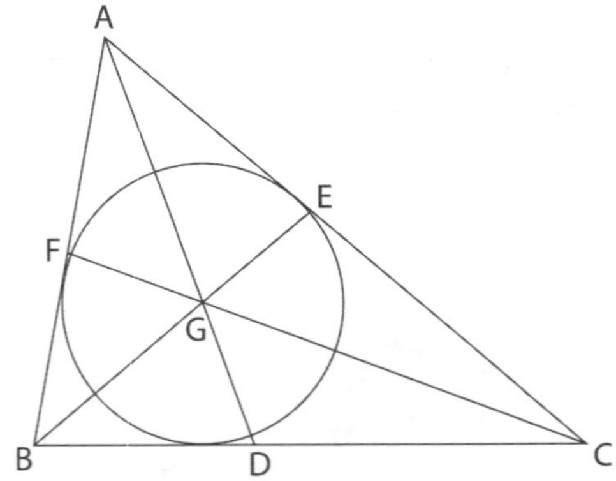

   The circle passes through the points D, E, and F. The circle is inscribed in the triangle.
5. a) A parallelogram, rectangle, square, rhombus, and kite have opposite angles equal. Of these quadrilaterals, only the square and rhombus have diagonals that bisect angles at vertices. Since a square has all right angles, the quadrilateral is a rhombus.
   b) 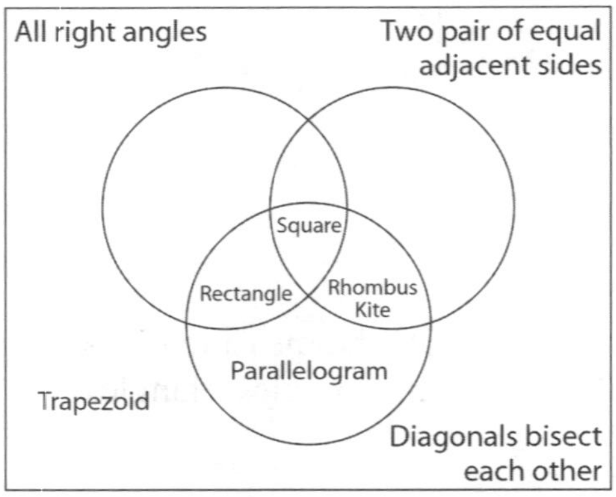

6. a) ∠ABQ = 25°, ∠BPA = 65°, ∠PBA = 65°, ∠PAB = 50°, ∠BPR = 65°, ∠PRB = 25°
   b) ΔPQR, ΔABP, ΔABQ

Extra Practice Masters 7.23–7.30

Go to the CD-ROM to access editable versions of these Extra Practice Masters

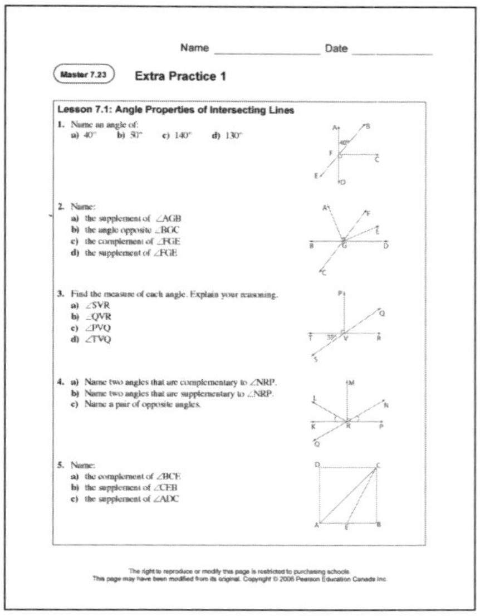

Name ______________ Date __________

Master 7.23 **Extra Practice 1**

Lesson 7.1: Angle Properties of Intersecting Lines

1. Name an angle of:
   a) 40° b) 50° c) 140° d) 130°
2. Name:
   a) the supplement of ∠AGB
   b) the angle opposite ∠BGC
   c) the complement of ∠FGE
   d) the supplement of ∠FGE
3. Find the measure of each angle. Explain your reasoning.
   a) ∠SVR
   b) ∠QVR
   c) ∠PVQ
   d) ∠TVQ
4. a) Name two angles that are complementary to ∠NRP.
   b) Name two angles that are supplementary to ∠NRP.
   c) Name a pair of opposite angles.
5. Name:
   a) the complement of ∠BCF
   b) the supplement of ∠CFB
   c) the supplement of ∠ADC

The right to reproduce or modify this page is restricted to purchasing schools. This page may have been modified from its original. Copyright © 2006 Pearson Education Canada Inc.

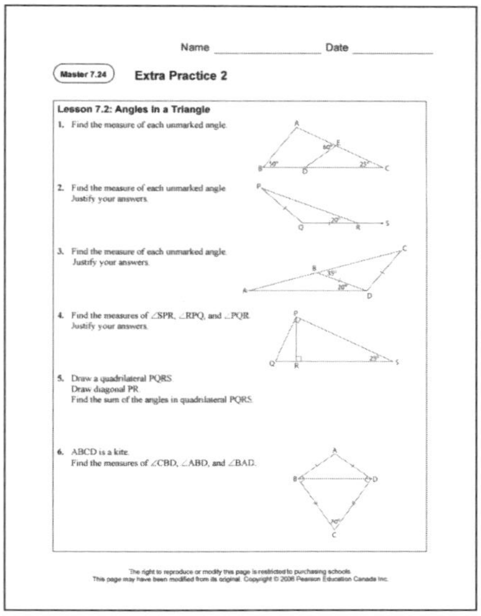

Name ______________ Date __________

Master 7.24 **Extra Practice 2**

Lesson 7.2: Angles in a Triangle

1. Find the measure of each unmarked angle.
2. Find the measure of each unmarked angle. Justify your answers.
3. Find the measure of each unmarked angle. Justify your answers.
4. Find the measures of ∠SPR, ∠RPQ, and ∠PQR. Justify your answers.
5. Draw a quadrilateral PQRS. Draw diagonal PR. Find the sum of the angles in quadrilateral PQRS.
6. ABCD is a kite. Find the measures of ∠CBD, ∠ABD, and ∠BAD.

The right to reproduce or modify this page is restricted to purchasing schools. This page may have been modified from its original. Copyright © 2006 Pearson Education Canada Inc.

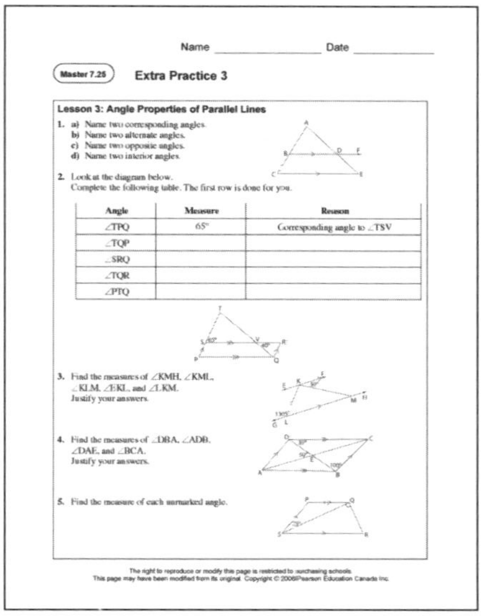

Name ______________ Date __________

Master 7.25 **Extra Practice 3**

Lesson 3: Angle Properties of Parallel Lines

1. a) Name two corresponding angles.
   b) Name two alternate angles.
   c) Name two opposite angles.
   d) Name two interior angles.
2. Look at the diagram below. Complete the following table. The first row is done for you.

Angle	Measure	Reason
∠TPQ	65°	Corresponding angle to ∠TSV
∠TQP		
∠SRQ		
∠TQR		
∠PTQ		

3. Find the measures of ∠KMH, ∠KML, ∠KLM, ∠EKL, and ∠LKM. Justify your answers.
4. Find the measures of ∠DBA, ∠ADB, ∠DAE, and ∠BCA. Justify your answers.
5. Find the measure of each unmarked angle.

The right to reproduce or modify this page is restricted to purchasing schools. This page may have been modified from its original. Copyright © 2006 Pearson Education Canada Inc.

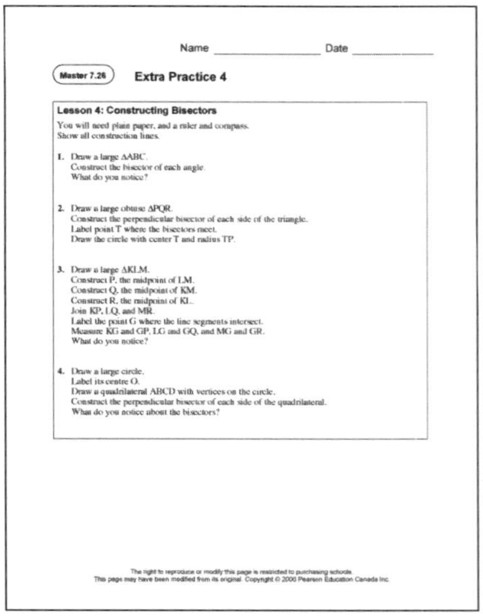

Name ______________ Date __________

Master 7.26 **Extra Practice 4**

Lesson 4: Constructing Bisectors

You will need plain paper, and a ruler and compass. Show all construction lines.

1. Draw a large ΔABC. Construct the bisector of each angle. What do you notice?
2. Draw a large obtuse ΔPQR. Construct the perpendicular bisector of each side of the triangle. Label point T where the bisectors meet. Draw the circle with center T and radius TP.
3. Draw a large ΔKLM. Construct P, the midpoint of LM. Construct Q, the midpoint of KM. Construct R, the midpoint of KL. Join KP, LQ, and MR. Label the point G where the line segments intersect. Measure KG and GP, LG and GQ, and MG and GR. What do you notice?
4. Draw a large circle. Label its centre O. Draw a quadrilateral ABCD with vertices on the circle. Construct the perpendicular bisector of each side of the quadrilateral. What do you notice about the bisectors?

The right to reproduce or modify this page is restricted to purchasing schools. This page may have been modified from its original. Copyright © 2006 Pearson Education Canada Inc.

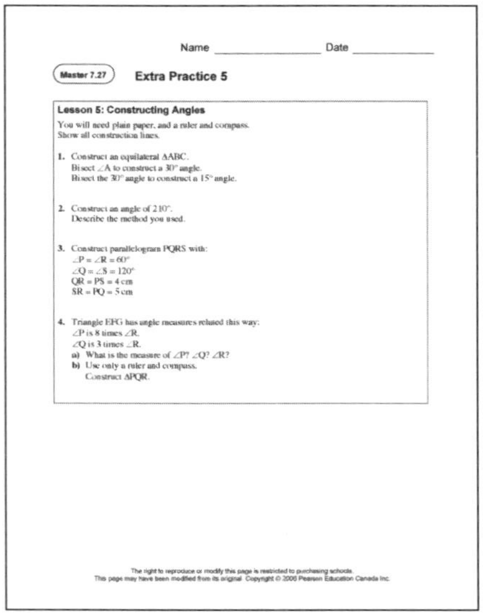

Name ______________ Date __________

Master 7.27 **Extra Practice 5**

Lesson 5: Constructing Angles

You will need plain paper, and a ruler and compass. Show all construction lines.

1. Construct an equilateral ΔABC. Bisect ∠A to construct a 30° angle. Bisect the 30° angle to construct a 15° angle.
2. Construct an angle of 210°. Describe the method you used.
3. Construct parallelogram PQRS with: ∠P = ∠R = 60°, ∠Q = ∠S = 120°, QR = PS = 4 cm, SR = PQ = 5 cm
4. Triangle EFG has angle measures related this way: ∠P is 8 times ∠R. ∠Q is 3 times ∠R.
   a) What is the measure of ∠P? ∠Q? ∠R?
   b) Use only a ruler and compass. Construct ΔPQR.

The right to reproduce or modify this page is restricted to purchasing schools. This page may have been modified from its original. Copyright © 2006 Pearson Education Canada Inc.

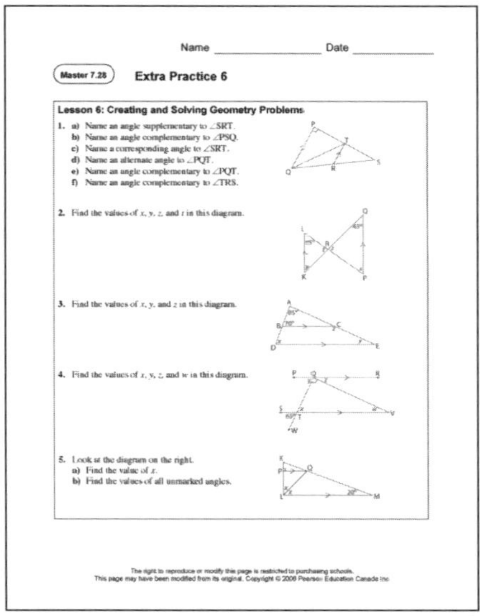

Name ______________ Date __________

Master 7.28 **Extra Practice 6**

Lesson 6: Creating and Solving Geometry Problems

1. a) Name an angle supplementary to ∠SRT.
   b) Name an angle complementary to ∠PSQ.
   c) Name a corresponding angle to ∠SRT.
   d) Name an alternate angle to ∠PQT.
   e) Name an angle complementary to ∠PQT.
   f) Name an angle complementary to ∠TRS.
2. Find the values of x, y, z, and t in this diagram.
3. Find the values of x, y, and z in this diagram.
4. Find the values of x, y, z, and w in this diagram.
5. Look at the diagram on the right.
   a) Find the value of x.
   b) Find the values of all unmarked angles.

The right to reproduce or modify this page is restricted to purchasing schools. This page may have been modified from its original. Copyright © 2006 Pearson Education Canada Inc.

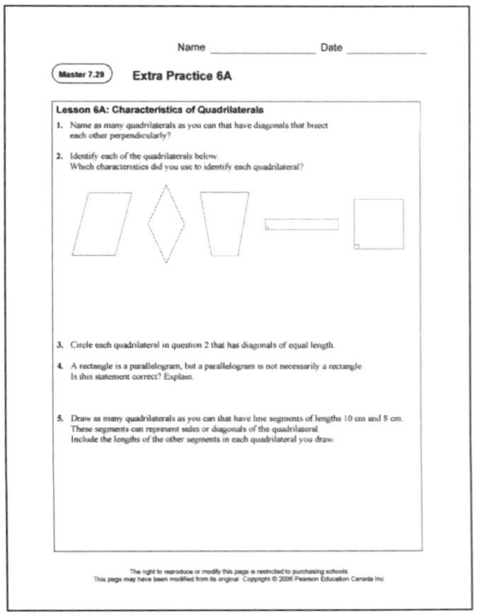

Name ______________ Date __________

Master 7.29 **Extra Practice 6A**

Lesson 6A: Characteristics of Quadrilaterals

1. Name as many quadrilaterals as you can that have diagonals that bisect each other perpendicularly?
2. Identify each of the quadrilaterals below. Which characteristics did you use to identify each quadrilateral?
3. Circle each quadrilateral in question 2 that has diagonals of equal length.
4. A rectangle is a parallelogram, but a parallelogram is not necessarily a rectangle. Is this statement correct? Explain.
5. Draw as many quadrilaterals as you can that have line segments of lengths 10 cm and 8 cm. These segments can represent sides or diagonals of the quadrilateral. Include the lengths of the other segments in each quadrilateral you draw.

The right to reproduce or modify this page is restricted to purchasing schools. This page may have been modified from its original. Copyright © 2006 Pearson Education Canada Inc.

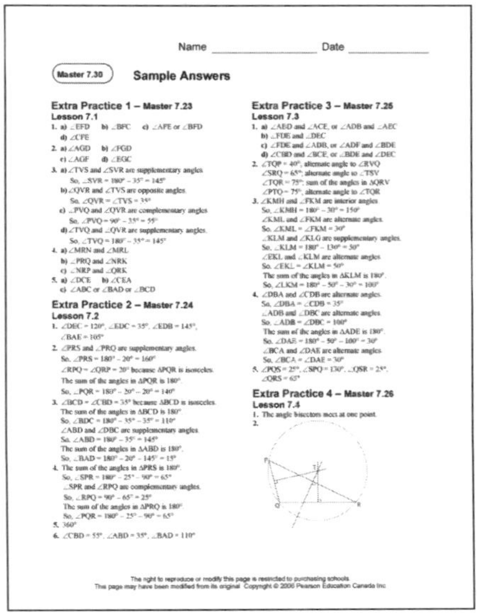

Name ______________ Date __________

Master 7.30 **Sample Answers**

Extra Practice 1 – Master 7.23
Lesson 7.1

Extra Practice 2 – Master 7.24
Lesson 7.2

Extra Practice 3 – Master 7.25
Lesson 7.3

Extra Practice 4 – Master 7.26
Lesson 7.4

The right to reproduce or modify this page is restricted to purchasing schools. This page may have been modified from its original. Copyright © 2006 Pearson Education Canada Inc.

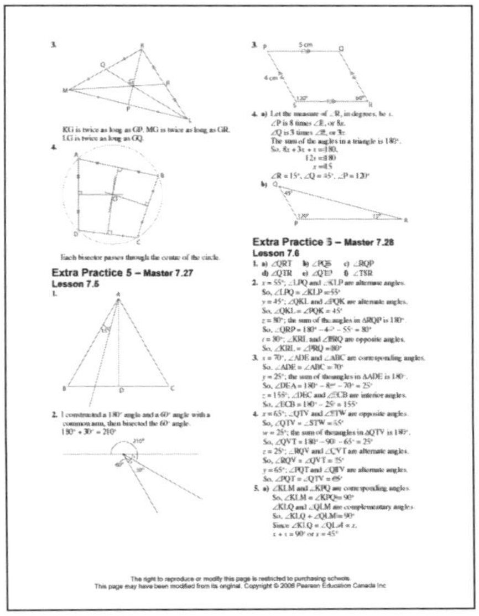

Extra Practice 5 – Master 7.27
Lesson 7.5

Extra Practice 3 – Master 7.28
Lesson 7.6

The right to reproduce or modify this page is restricted to purchasing schools. This page may have been modified from its original. Copyright © 2006 Pearson Education Canada Inc.

b) $\angle KLQ = \angle QLM = 45°$
$\angle PQL$ and $\angle QLM$ are alternate angles.
So, $\angle PQL = \angle QLM = 45°$
$\angle KQP$ and $\angle QML$ are corresponding angles.
So, $\angle KQP = \angle QML = 20°$
The sum of the angles in $\triangle KPQ$ is 180°.
So, $\angle PKQ = 180° - 90° - 20° = 70°$
$\angle LPQ$ and $\angle KPQ$ are supplementary angles.
So, $\angle LPQ = \angle KPQ = 90°$

Extra Practice 6A – Master 7.29

Lesson 7.6A

1. Square, rhombus
2. Parallelogram: opposite sides equal, opposite sides parallel, opposite angles equal
   Rhombus: all sides equal, opposite sides parallel, opposite angles equal
   Isosceles trapezoid: one pair of parallel sides, non-parallel sides equal
   Rectangle: opposite sides equal, opposite sides parallel, all right angles
   Square: all sides equal, opposite sides parallel, all right angles
3. Rectangle, isosceles trapezoid, square
4. A rectangle has opposite sides parallel, and opposite sides equal, so it is a parallelogram. However, a rectangle has all right angles and this characteristic is not true for all parallelograms.
5. For example:

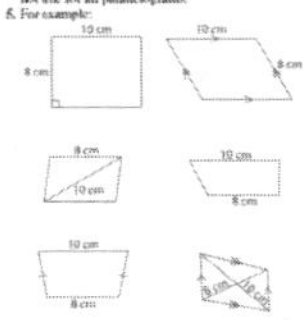

Addison Wesley Mathematics Makes Sense

Program Authors

Trevor Brown
Antonietta Lenjosek
Cathy Heideman
Jim Mennie
Georgia Konis-Chatzis
A.J. Keene
Margaret Sinclair
Craig Featherstone
Jason Johnston
Bryn Keyes
Elizabeth Wood
Elizabeth Milne
David Sufrin
Don Jones
Sharon Jeroski
Lynn Strangway

Printed and bound in Canada

2 3 4 5 – TC – 09 08 07 06

PEARSON Education Canada

ADDISON WESLEY

Ontario

Math Makes Sense 8

Ontario

Teacher Guide

Unit 8: Square Roots and Pythagoras

PEARSON
Education Canada

UNIT 8

Square Roots and Pythagoras

"He is unworthy of the name of man who is ignorant of the fact that the diagonal of a square is incommensurable with its side."

–Plato

FOCUS STRANDS
Number Sense and Numeration
Geometry and Spatial Sense

SUPPORTING STRAND
Measurement

TIPS
Providing regular formative and summative feedback to both students and parents is of importance to help students adjust to the demands of the mathematics program.

Mathematics Background

What Are the Big Ideas?

- An irrational number is a number that never repeats and never terminates. Square roots of non-perfect squares are irrational and can only be estimated with decimal numbers.
- The area of the square on the hypotenuse of a right triangle is equal to the sum of the areas of the squares on the legs. This relationship is called the Pythagorean Theorem.

How Will the Concepts Develop?

Students use the area of a square to find the length of a line segment. They develop strategies for estimating a square root: drawing squares, using a number line, and using a calculator.

Students use the properties of a right triangle to find the length of a line segment. They discover a relationship among the side lengths of a right triangle, the Pythagorean Theorem. Students use this relationship to find the length of any side of a right triangle, when the lengths of the other two sides are known.

Students use a computer to investigate the Pythagorean relationship. They use the Pythagorean Theorem to solve problems involving the estimation and calculation of side lengths of right triangles.

Why Are These Concepts Important?

The Pythagorean relationship is used extensively in construction, architecture, land surveying, and pure mathematics. Students will use this relationship in more advanced math; for example, to prove trigonometric identities and to calculate distances in a plane.

One of the most important applications of the Pythagorean Theorem is to calculate the distance between two points, especially when the distances are inaccessible, such as the distance across a lake. This relationship can be used to calculate distances in any situation that can be modelled using a right triangle, where the lengths of two sides are known.

Curriculum Overview

The codes refer to the 2005 revised curriculum.

Overall Expectations

- Solve problems involving whole numbers, decimal numbers … using a variety of computational strategies. (8m9)
- Demonstrate an understanding of the geometric properties … and the applications of geometric properties in the real world. (8m40)
- Develop geometric relationships involving lines, triangles, … and solve problems involving lines and triangles. (8m41)
- … solve and verify algebraic equations, using a variety of strategies, including inspection, guess and check, … (8m55)

Specific Expectations

- Solve multi-step problems arising from real-life contexts and involving whole numbers and decimals, using a variety of tools and strategies. (8m16)
- Estimate, and verify using a calculator, the positive square roots of whole numbers, and distinguish between whole numbers that have whole-number square roots and those that do not. (8m25)
- Investigate and describe applications of geometric properties in the real world. (8m45)
- Determine the Pythagorean relationship, through investigation using a variety of tools and strategies. (8m49)
- Solve problems involving right triangles geometrically, using the Pythagorean relationship. (8m50)
- Describe different ways in which algebra can be used in real-life situations. (8m59)
- Evaluate algebraic expressions, with up to three terms, by substituting … decimals … for the variables. (8m62)

Launch

Lesson 8.1: Constructing and Measuring Squares

Lesson 8.2: Estimating Square Roots

Technology: Investigating Square Roots with a Calculator

Mid-Unit Review

Lesson 8.3: The Pythagorean Relationship

Technology: Using *The Geometer's Sketchpad* to Verify the Pythagorean Theorem

Lesson 8.4: Applying the Pythagorean Theorem

Lesson 8.5: Special Triangles

Unit Review
Practice Test

Unit Problem
Pythagoras through the Ages

Curriculum across the Grades

Grade 7	Grade 8
Students represent perfect squares and square roots, using a variety of tools. Students sort and classify triangles by geometric properties related to symmetry, angles, and sides. Students solve multi-step problems involving whole numbers and decimals in real-life situations. They evaluate algebraic expressions by substituting natural numbers for the variables.	Students use a calculator to estimate and verify the positive square roots of whole numbers. They differentiate between whole numbers that are perfect squares and those that are not. Students determine the Pythagorean relationship through investigation. They use the Pythagorean relationship to solve problems involving right triangles. Students solve multi-step problems involving whole numbers and decimals in real-life situations. They evaluate algebraic expressions, with up to three terms, by substituting decimals for the variables.

Additional Activities

Area Challenge

For Extra Practice (Appropriate for use after Skills You'll Need)
Materials: *Area Challenge* (Master 8.5), 2 number cubes labelled 1 to 6, 1-cm grid paper (PM 20), rulers, calculators
Playing this game reinforces the skills of finding the areas of a square and a triangle.

The work students do: Students draw a square on grid paper with side length equal to the sum of the numbers rolled. They draw a triangle on grid paper using one of the numbers rolled as the base, and the other number as the height. Students find the area of each figure they drew.

Take It Further: Students use the numbers rolled to represent the dimensions of the base and height of a triangle. Students draw the triangle on grid paper, then draw a square that has the same area as the triangle.

Spatial/Social/Logical
Partner Activity

Inscribed Squares

For Extra Practice (Appropriate for use after Lesson 8.1)
Materials: *Inscribed Squares* (Master 8.6), 2 number cubes labelled 1 to 6, 1-cm grid paper (PM 20), rulers, calculators
Playing this game reinforces the skills of finding the area of a square by subtracting the areas of the enclosed triangles.

The work students do: Students play with a partner. Students draw a square on grid paper with side length equal to the sum of the numbers rolled. Students roll one number cube. They draw a point on each side of the square, moving clockwise, a number of grid squares from each vertex equal to the number rolled. Students join the points to form an inscribed square. Students find the area of the inscribed square.

Take It Further: Students find the side length of each inscribed square.

Mathematical/Social/Spatial
Partner Activity

From Here to There

For Extra Practice (Appropriate for use after Lesson 8.3)
Materials: *From Here to There* (Master 8.7), 2 number cubes labelled 1 to 6, 1-cm grid paper (PM 20), rulers, calculators
Playing this game reinforces the skills of finding the length of a line segment.

The work students do: Students work on their own. Students roll the number cubes to get the coordinates of a point. Students plot the point on a grid, then roll the number cubes again to get the coordinates of a second point. Students plot the second point, then join the points with a ruler. Students find the length of the line segment by drawing a right triangle with this line segment as the hypotenuse, then applying the Pythagorean relationship.

Take It Further: Students find the perimeter and area of each triangle formed.

Kinesthetic/Mathematical
Individual Activity

Planning for Unit 8

Planning for Instruction

Suggested Unit time: About 3 weeks

Lesson	Time	Materials	Program Support
Launch, page 2	15–20 min		
Skills You'll Need, page 4	40–50 min	calculators 0.5-cm grid paper	PM 14: 0.5-cm Grid Paper
8.1: Constructing and Measuring Squares, page 7 Use the area of a square to find the length of a line segment.	80–100 min	1-cm grid paper calculators square dot paper 3-column charts scissors glue or tape	PM 18: 3-Column Chart PM 20: 1-cm Grid Paper PM 22: Square Dot Paper Master 8.8: Step-by-Step 1 Master 8.18: Extra Practice 1
8.2: Estimating Square Roots, page 11 Develop strategies for estimating a square root.	80–100 min	number lines calculators 1-cm grid paper	Master 8.13: Number Lines for *Explore* PM 20: 1-cm Grid Paper Master 8.9: Step-by-Step 2 Master 8.19: Extra Practice 2
Game: Fitting In, page 15	20 min	scissors three sheets of game cards	Masters 8.14a, 8.14b, and 8.14c: *Fitting In* Game Cards
Technology: Investigating Square Roots with a Calculator, page 16 Use a calculator to investigate square roots.	40–50 min	scientific calculators 4-function calculators compasses	
Mid-Unit Review, page 18		1-cm grid paper calculators compasses	PM 20: 1-cm Grid Paper
8.3: The Pythagorean Relationship, page 19 Discover a relationship among the side lengths of a right triangle.	80–100 min	1-cm grid paper calculators	PM 20: 1-cm Grid Paper Master 8.10: Step-by-Step 3 Master 8.20: Extra Practice 3
Technology: Using *The Geometer's Sketchpad* to Verify the Pythagorean Theorem, page 24 Use a computer to investigate the Pythagorean relationship.	80–100 min	computers with *The Geometer's Sketchpad* software	
Reading and Writing in Math: Communicating Solutions, page 26		calculators	
8.4: Applying the Pythagorean Theorem, page 28 Solve problems using the Pythagorean Theorem.	80–100 min	1-cm grid paper calculators	PM 20: 1-cm Grid Paper Master 8.11: Step-by-Step 4 Master 8.21: Extra Practice 4
8.5: Special Triangles, page 33 Apply the Pythagorean Theorem to isosceles and equilateral triangles.	80–100 min	calculators protractors 1-cm grid paper	PM 20: 1-cm Grid Paper Master 8.12: Step-by-Step 5 Master 8.22: Extra Practice 5
Unit Review, page 37		calculators 1-cm grid paper	PM 20: 1-cm Grid Paper Extra Practice: Student Book page 495

Lesson	Time	Materials	Program Support
Practice Test, page 39		1-cm grid paper calculators	PM 20: 1-cm Grid Paper
Unit Problem: Pythagoras through the Ages, page 40	80–100 min	protractors 10-cm ruler	Master 8.15: The 10-cm Ruler

Planning for Assessment

Purpose	Tools and Process	Recording and Reporting
Diagnostic	*Unit Launch* Question; conference; scaffold problems throughout the unit	PM 8: Conference Prompts
Formative	*Explore* – Ongoing Assessment: Observe and Listen	Master 8.2 Ongoing Observations: Square Roots and Pythagoras PM 1: Inquiry Process Check List PM 6: Observation Record 1 PM 7: Observation Record 2 PM 8: Conference Prompts PM 2: Self-Assessment PM 3: Self-Assessment: Problem Solving PM 9: Work Sample Records
Summative	*Unit Review* *Unit Problem* – Performance Assessment Unit Test Review assessment records; add unit results to ongoing records	Master 8.1 Unit Rubric: Square Roots and Pythagoras Master 8.3 Performance Assessment Rubric: Pythagoras through the Ages Master 8.4 Unit Summary: Square Roots and Pythagoras PM 10: Summary Class Records: Strands PM 11: Summary Class Records: Achievement Categories PM 12: Summary Record: Individual
Learning Skills/ Mathematical Disposition	Observe and record throughout unit	PM 4: Learning Skills Check List PM 5: Mathematical Dispositions and Learning Skills

Program Masters (PM) are in the *Grade 8 Planning and Program Masters* module.
Extra Practice Masters are on the CD-ROM and are printed in reduced format on page 66 of this module.

LESSON ORGANIZER

15–20 min

Curriculum Focus: Activate prior learning about geometry.

ASSUMED PRIOR KNOWLEDGE

- ✓ Students can calculate the area of a square and a triangle.
- ✓ Students can represent perfect squares and square roots.

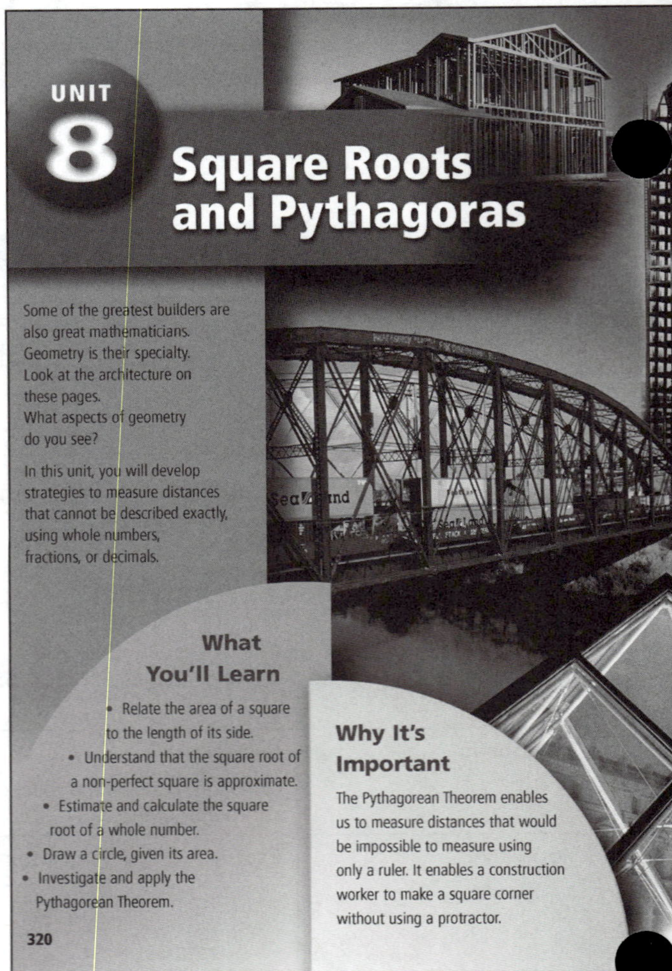

UNIT 8

Square Roots and Pythagoras

Some of the greatest builders are also great mathematicians. Geometry is their specialty. Look at the architecture on these pages. What aspects of geometry do you see?

In this unit, you will develop strategies to measure distances that cannot be described exactly, using whole numbers, fractions, or decimals.

What You'll Learn

- Relate the area of a square to the length of its side.
- Understand that the square root of a non-perfect square is approximate.
- Estimate and calculate the square root of a whole number.
- Draw a circle, given its area.
- Investigate and apply the Pythagorean Theorem.

Why It's Important

The Pythagorean Theorem enables us to measure distances that would be impossible to measure using only a ruler. It enables a construction worker to make a square corner without using a protractor.

320

ACTIVATE PRIOR LEARNING

Have students look at the pictures on pages 320 and 321 of the Student Book. Have students identify as many figures as they can.

Ask questions, such as:

- What figures do you see in the pictures?
  (I see triangles, kites, trapezoids, parallelograms, and hexagons in the frame of the dome. I see triangles, rectangles, and pentagons in the frame of the house. I see squares in the pyramid. I see rectangles and triangles in the tower and in the bridge.)
- Which types of triangles do you see?
  (I see an isosceles triangle in the tower, an equilateral triangle in the dome, and a right triangle in the bridge. I see acute and right triangles in the dome, right triangles in the bridge, and obtuse triangles in the frame of the house.)
- Which types of angles do you see?
  (I see right angles, acute angles, and obtuse angles.)
- What measurable attributes could you find?
  (I could find the side length, area, and perimeter of the figures. I could measure angles to classify triangles, and to verify parallel and perpendicular lines.)
- What other aspects of geometry do you see?
  (I see intersecting lines, perpendicular lines, parallel lines, and diagonal lines.)

Tell students that, in this unit, they will use the area of a square to find the length of a line segment, estimate the square roots of non-perfect squares, and discover a relationship among the side lengths of a right triangle. At the end of the unit, students will demonstrate what they have learned about right triangles by exploring some of the discoveries in the ancient world.

FROM THE LIBRARY

Pythagoras and the Pythagoreans: A Brief History by Charles H. Kahn.
Hackett Publishing Company, 2001.
ISBN: 0872205754
This book provides readers with a history of Pythagoras and his followers, the Pythagoreans. It is an ideal choice for students wanting to research Pythagoras.

Looking for Pythagoras: The Pythagorean Theorem (*Connected Mathematics Series*) by Glenda Lappan, James T. Fey (Editor), William M. Fitzgerald (Editor), Catherine Anderson (Editor).
Dale Seymour Publications, 1997.
ISBN: 1572321806
This book, designed for Grades 6 to 8 students, explores the Pythagorean Theorem. Students' knowledge and understanding of the Pythagorean Theorem is developed through connections between math, other school subjects, and the outside world.

DIAGNOSTIC ASSESSMENT

What to Look For	What to Do
✔ Students can calculate the area of a square and a triangle. ✔ Students can represent perfect squares and square roots.	***Extra Support:*** Students who have difficulty calculating the area of a square or a triangle should draw the figure on grid paper, count squares to estimate the area, then use the area formula to check. *Work on this skill during Skills You'll Need.* Students who have difficulty finding the square root of a perfect square should first write the perfect square as the product of two equal factors; for example, $25 = 5 \times 5$. *Work on this skill during Skills You'll Need and Lesson 8.1.*

LESSON ORGANIZER

40–50 min

Skills in Review
- Areas of a square and a triangle
- Square numbers
- Square roots

Student Materials
- calculators
- 0.5-cm grid paper (PM 14)

Vocabulary: square number, perfect square, square root

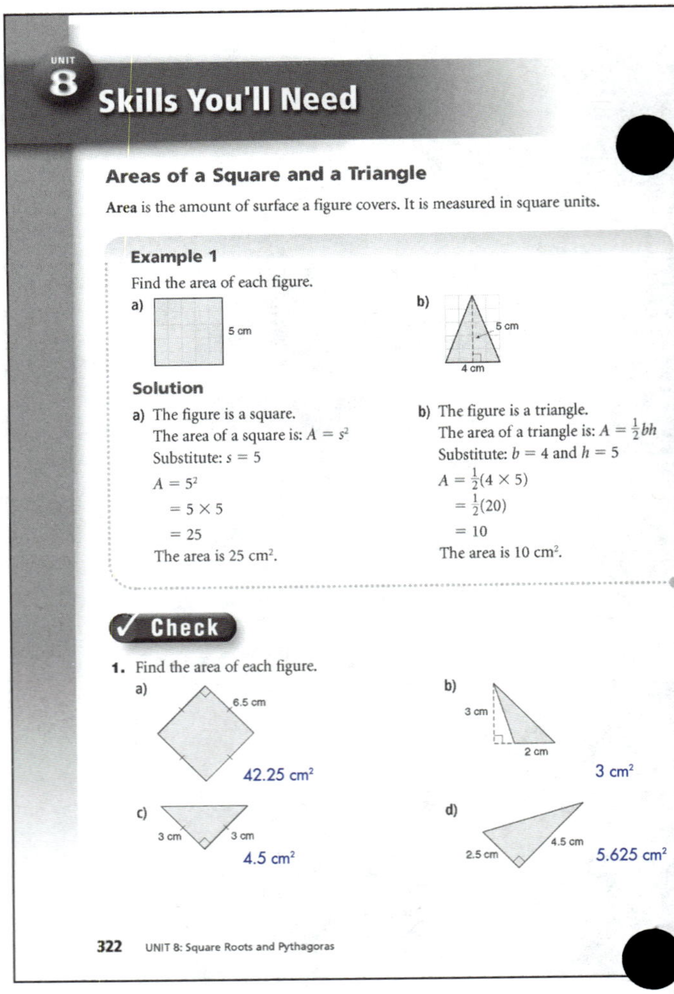

UNIT 8

Skills You'll Need

Areas of a Square and a Triangle

Area is the amount of surface a figure covers. It is measured in square units.

Example 1

Find the area of each figure.

a) [square, 5 cm]

b) [triangle, 5 cm, 4 cm]

Solution

a) The figure is a square.
The area of a square is: $A = s^2$
Substitute: $s = 5$
$A = 5^2$
$= 5 \times 5$
$= 25$
The area is 25 cm^2.

b) The figure is a triangle.
The area of a triangle is: $A = \frac{1}{2}bh$
Substitute: $b = 4$ and $h = 5$
$A = \frac{1}{2}(4 \times 5)$
$= \frac{1}{2}(20)$
$= 10$
The area is 10 cm^2.

✓ Check

1. Find the area of each figure.

a) 6.5 cm — 42.25 cm^2

b) 3 cm, 2 cm — 3 cm^2

c) 3 cm, 3 cm — 4.5 cm^2

d) 2.5 cm, 4.5 cm — 5.625 cm^2

322 UNIT 8: Square Roots and Pythagoras

Alternative Example 1

Find the area of each figure.

a)

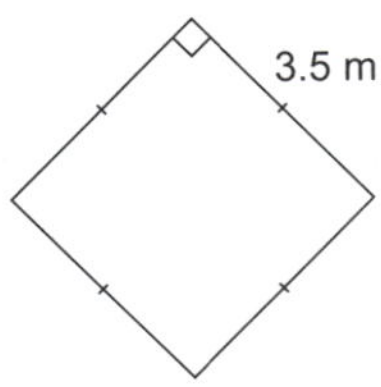

b)

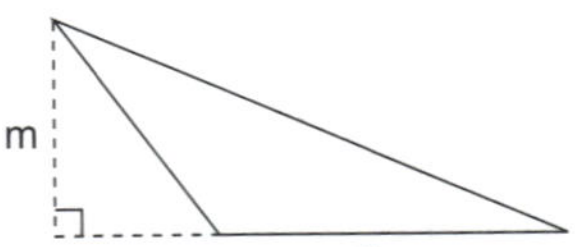

Solution

a) The figure is a square.
The area of a square is:
$A = s^2$
Substitute: $s = 3.5$
$A = 3.5^2$
$= 3.5 \times 3.5$
$= 12.25$
The area is 12.25 m^2.

b) The figure is a triangle.
The area of a triangle is:
$A = \frac{1}{2}bh$
Substitute: $b = 7$ and $h = 3$
$A = \frac{1}{2}(7 \times 3)$
$= \frac{1}{2}(21)$
$= 10.5$
The area is 10.5 m^2.

Areas of a Square and Triangle

Remind students that a square is a rectangle with all sides equal. The formula for the area of a square is:
A = side length $\times$ side length
Use s for the side length. Then $A = s \times s$, or s^2.
Students who have difficulty using this formula can draw the squares on 1-cm grid paper, then count grid squares to find the area.
Draw a parallelogram with base 6 cm and height 4 cm on the board. Draw a diagonal to make 2 congruent triangles. Remind students that the area of one triangle is $\frac{1}{2}$ the area of the parallelogram. The area of the parallelogram is 4 cm $\times$ 6 cm = 24 cm^2. So, the area of the triangle is $\frac{1}{2}$ of 24 cm^2, or 12 cm^2. Ensure students know the formula for the area of a triangle: $A = \frac{1}{2}bh$. Remind students that for an obtuse triangle, the height may be drawn outside the triangle, as in *Check* question 1b.
Students can complete the Additional Activity, *Area Challenge* (Master 8.5).

Common Misconceptions

➤ Students have difficulty identifying the base and height of a triangle.

How to Help: Ensure students understand that the base and height (or extension of the base) of a triangle meet at right angles. Encourage students to look for this "L" formation. Show students several triangles and have them identify the "L," then identify the dimensions of the base and height.

Square Numbers

When we multiply a number by itself, we square the number.
We can use exponents to write a **square number**.
4^2 means: $4 \times 4 = 16$
We say, "Four squared is sixteen."
16 is a square number, or a **perfect square**.
One way to model a square number is to draw a square whose area is equal to the square number.

Example 2

Show that 49 is a square number. Use symbols, words, and a diagram.

Solution

With symbols: $49 = 7 \times 7 = 7^2$
With words: "Seven squared is forty-nine."

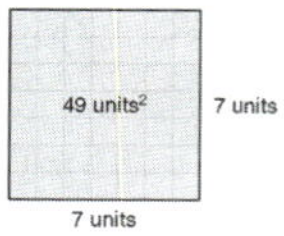

✓ Check

2. Show that 36 is a square number. Use a diagram, symbols, and words.

3. Write each number in exponent form.
a) 25 5^2 b) 81 9^2 c) 64 8^2 d) 169 13^2

4. List the first 15 square numbers. 1, 4, 9, 16, 25, 36, 49, 64, 81, 100, 121, 144, 169, 196, 225

5. Here are the first 3 triangular numbers.

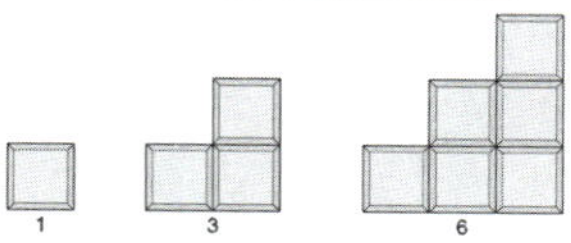

a) Write the next 3 triangular numbers. 10, 15, 21
b) Add consecutive triangular numbers. What do you notice? Explain.
4, 9, 16, 25, 36; the sums are all square numbers.

Alternative Example 2

Show that 121 is a square number. Use symbols, words, and a diagram.

Solution

With symbols: $121 = 11 \times 11 = 11^2$
With words: "Eleven squared is one hundred twenty-one."

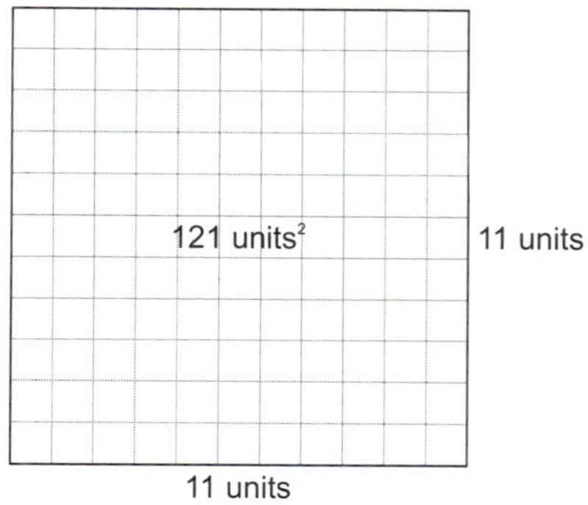

Sample Answers

2. With symbols: $36 = 6 \times 6 = 6^2$
With words: "Six squared is thirty-six."

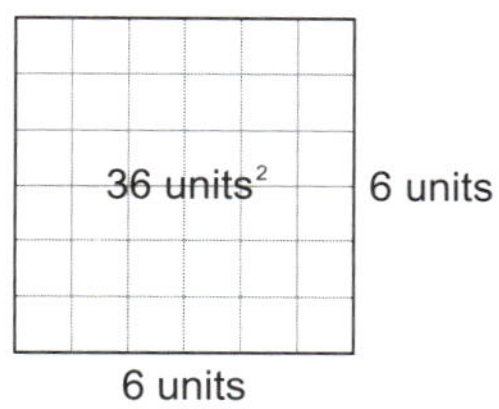

Square Numbers

Remind students that a square number, or perfect square, has an odd number of factors. For example, the factors of 100 are: 1, 2, 4, 5, 10, 20, 25, 50, and 100
100 has nine factors, and 9 is an odd number. So, 100 is a square number.
Ensure students understand that a square number can always be written as a power with exponent 2.
For example, $100 = 10^2$
Encourage students to model a square number with a diagram to enable students to make a visual connection.

Common Misconception

➤ Students misinterpret the exponent; for example, students think 5^2 means 5×2.

How to Help: Ensure students understand that the square of a number is the product of a number multiplied by itself; for example, $5^2 = 5 \times 5$. Remind students that a square has 4 equal sides, and the area of a square is: $A = s \times s$. Since a square number represents the area of a square, the two numbers multiplied to get the area must be equal.

Alternative Example 3

Find a square root of 144.

Solution

Method 1

Think of a number that, when multiplied by itself, produces 144.

$12 \times 12 = 144$

So, $\sqrt{144} = 12$

Method 2

Draw a square with area 144 units^2.

Find its side length.

$144 = 12 \times 12$

So, $\sqrt{144} = 12$

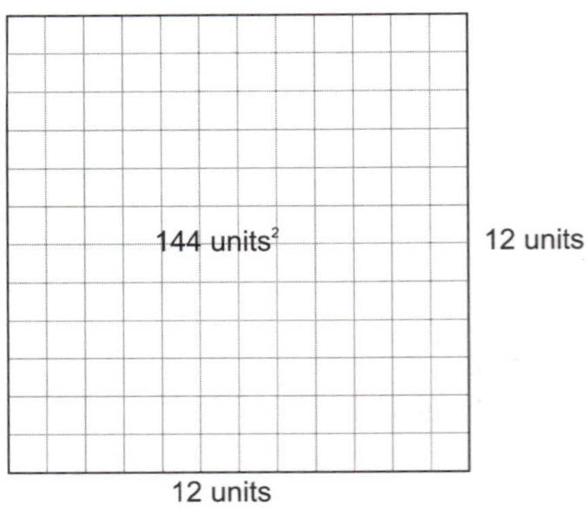

Square Roots

Squaring and finding a **square root** are inverse operations.
For example, $7^2 = 49$ and $\sqrt{49} = 7$
We can model a square root with a diagram.
The *area* of a square shows the *square number*.
The *side length* of the square shows a *square root* of the square number.
We say, "A square root of 36 is 6."
We write: $\sqrt{36} = 6$

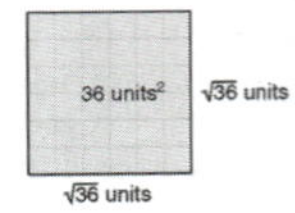

Example 3

Find a square root of 64.

Solution

Method 1

Think of a number that, when multiplied by itself, produces 64.

$8 \times 8 = 64$

So, $\sqrt{64} = 8$

Method 2

Visualize a square with an area of 64 units^2.
Find its side length.

$64 = 8 \times 8$

So, $\sqrt{64} = 8$

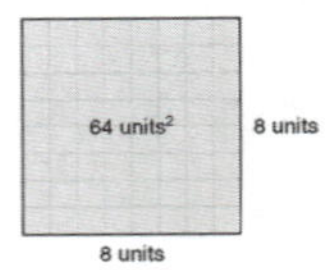

✓ Check

6. Find each square root.

a) $\sqrt{1}$ 1 b) $\sqrt{25}$ 5 c) $\sqrt{81}$ 9 d) $\sqrt{9}$ 3
e) $\sqrt{16}$ 4 f) $\sqrt{100}$ 10 g) $\sqrt{121}$ 11 h) $\sqrt{225}$ 15

324 UNIT 8: Square Roots and Pythagoras

Square Roots

Remind students that addition and subtraction, and multiplication and division are other inverse operations. That is, the operations undo each other. For example,
$5 + 6 = 11$ and $11 - 6 = 5$; $5 \times 3 = 15$ and $15 \div 3 = 5$
Similarly, $6 \times 6 = 36$ so, $6^2 = 36$ $\sqrt{36} = \sqrt{6^2} = 6$
In *Example 3*, students are asked to find *a* square root of 64. This is because 64 has two square roots, 8 and –8. Students will learn to multiply integers in Unit 9. They will learn that $(-8) \times (-8) = 64$. At that time, students could find a negative square root for each square number in *Check* question 6.

Common Misconceptions

➤ Students write the square root under a square root sign; for example, $\sqrt{36} = \sqrt{6^2} = \sqrt{6}$.

How to Help: Remind students that a square root represents the side length of a square.
A square with area 36 units^2 has side length 6 units because $6 \times 6 = 36$.
Have students estimate $\sqrt{6}$; 6 is close to 4 and $\sqrt{4} = 2$.
So, the area of a square with side length $\sqrt{6}$ is:
$\sqrt{6} \times \sqrt{6} \doteq \sqrt{4} \times \sqrt{4} = 2 \times 2 = 4$
This is much less than 36, the area of the given square.

8.1 Constructing and Measuring Squares

Focus Use the area of a square to find the length of a line segment.

All squares are *similar*.
They come in many sizes, but always have the same shape.
How many ways can you describe a square?

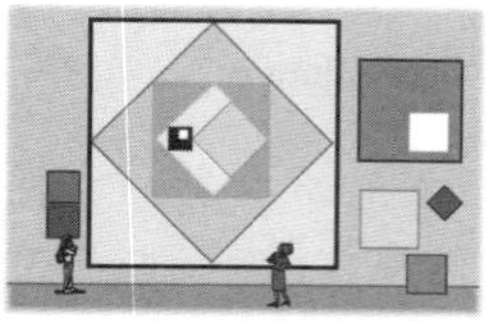

Explore

Work with a partner.
You will need 1-cm grid paper.
Copy the squares below.
Without using a ruler, find the area and side length of each square.

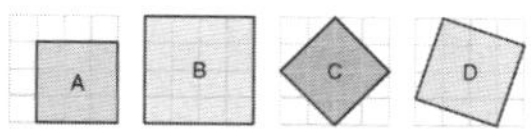

What other squares can you draw on a 4 by 4 grid?
Find the area and side length of each square.
Write all your measurements in a table.

Reflect & Share

How many squares did you draw?
Describe any patterns in your measurements.
How did you find the area and side length of each square?
How did you write the side lengths of squares C and D?

Connect

We can use the properties of a square to find its area or side length.

Area of a square = length × length
= $(\text{length})^2$
When the side length is l, the area is l^2.
When the area is A, the side length is $\sqrt{A}$.

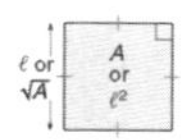

8.1 Constructing and Measuring Squares 325

Constructing and Measuring Squares

LESSON ORGANIZER 80–100 min

Curriculum Focus: Use the area of a square to find the length of a line segment. (8m25)

Teacher Materials
Optional
- enlarged 1-cm grid transparency (PM 20)
- scissors

Student Materials
- 1-cm grid paper (PM 20)
- square dot paper (PM 22)
- 3-column charts (PM 18)
- scissors
- glue or tape
- calculators

Optional
- Step-by-Step 1 (Master 8.8)
- Extra Practice 1 (Master 8.18)

Vocabulary: similar

Assessment: Master 8.2 Ongoing Observations: Square Roots and Pythagoras

Key Math Learnings

1. The properties of a square can be used to find its area or side length.
2. The length of any segment on a grid can be calculated by thinking of it as the side length of a square.

BEFORE Get Started

Have students look at the picture at the top of page 325 in the Student Book. Have students find as many squares as they can. Ask:

- What do we mean when we say two figures are similar? (*They have the same shape, but not necessarily the same size.*)
- How many ways can you describe a square? (*A square is a rectangle with all sides equal; a square has 4 sides, 4 right angles, and all sides have the same length; the diagonals of a square are equal; a square has 2 pairs of parallel sides; a square has 4 lines of symmetry and rotational symmetry of order 4.*)

If you have not already done so, review *Skills You'll Need*, pages 322, 323, and 324, *Areas of a Square and a Triangle*, *Square Numbers*, and *Square Roots*.

Present *Explore*. Distribute 1-cm grid paper (PM 20) and 3-column charts (PM 18) to pairs of students.

Remind students that they are only to use rulers to copy the squares on grid paper.

Some students may have difficulty finding "tilted" squares.

Remind students to check the area of each square to check that they are different.

DURING Explore

Ongoing Assessment: Observe and Listen

As students work, ask questions, such as:

- For which squares was it easier to find the area? Explain.
(*Squares A and B; I counted grid squares, and all the grid squares were whole squares.*)
- What is the area and side length of squares A and B?
(*Square A: Area = 9 cm^2, side length = 3 cm; Square B: Area = 16 cm^2, side length = 4 cm*)

REACHING ALL LEARNERS

Early Finishers

Have students draw a square for each area given in *Practice* question 3. Students explain how they know each square has the given area.

Common Misconceptions

➤ Students do not cut the square into smaller figures that result in only whole numbers of grid squares being covered.

How to Help: Remind students that the smaller triangles that are cut and rearranged should be congruent to the enclosed triangles. This will ensure that the pieces fit together, with side lengths along grid lines. The figure formed should only have vertical and horizontal sides. Students can then count whole squares to find the area.

Assignment Guidelines

If your students do not have time to complete all the *Practice* questions on pages 327 and 328, these questions provide minimum curriculum coverage: 2, 4, 5, 6, *Reflect*

To assess the 4 Achievement Chart categories listed in the curriculum document, have students complete these *Practice* questions:

Knowledge and Understanding: 2
Application: 4
Thinking: 6
Communication: *Reflect*

Example 1

A square has side length 10 cm.
What is the area of the square?

Solution

Area = (length)² or $A = l^2$
$A = 10^2$
$= 100$
The area is 100 cm².

Example 2

A square has area 81 cm².
What is the side length of the square?

Solution

Length = $\sqrt{\text{Area}}$ or $l = \sqrt{A}$
$l = \sqrt{81}$
$= 9$
The side length is 9 cm.

We can calculate the length of any segment on a grid by thinking of it as the side length of a square.

To find the length of the line segment AB:

Construct a square on the segment.
Find the area of the square.
Then, the length of the segment is the square root of the area.

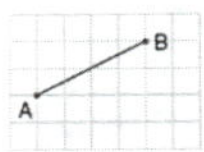

To construct a square on segment AB:
Rotate segment AB 90° counterclockwise about A, to get segment AC.
Rotate segment AC 90° counterclockwise about C, to get segment CD.
Rotate segment CD 90° counterclockwise about D, to get segment DB.

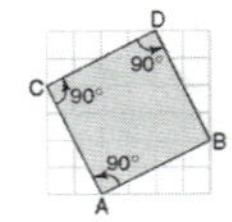

- How did you find the area of Square C?
  (I counted whole squares and half squares. There are 4 whole squares and 8 half squares. Eight half squares = 4 whole squares. 4 squares + 4 squares = 8 squares; the area is 8 cm².)
- How did you find the side length of Square C? *(I found a number that when multiplied by itself has the product 8. $\sqrt{8} \times \sqrt{8} = 8$, so the side length is $\sqrt{8}$ cm.)*
- How did you find the area of Square D?
  (I counted squares. There are 4 whole squares. There are 4 half squares; 4 half squares = 2 whole squares. There are 4 squares greater than $\frac{1}{2}$ a square, so I counted these squares as 4 whole squares. I ignored squares less than $\frac{1}{2}$ a square. The area is 4 + 2 + 4 = 10, or 10 cm².)
- Did anyone use a different method?
  (I found the area of the 4 triangles outside Square D, then subtracted their areas from the area of the grid. The area of each triangle is:
  $A = \frac{1}{2} \times 3$ cm $\times 1$ cm $= \frac{3}{2}$ cm². The area of the 4 triangles is: $4 \times \frac{3}{2}$ cm² = 6 cm²
  The area of Square D is: 16 cm² – 6 cm² = 10 cm²)
- What is the side length of Square D?
  ($\sqrt{10}$ cm)
- What patterns did you find in your measurements?
  (The area of each square is the square of its side length. The side length of each square is the square root of its area.)

AFTER Connect

Invite students to share the different squares they drew, the area and side length of each square, and any patterns they found.

What you might see:

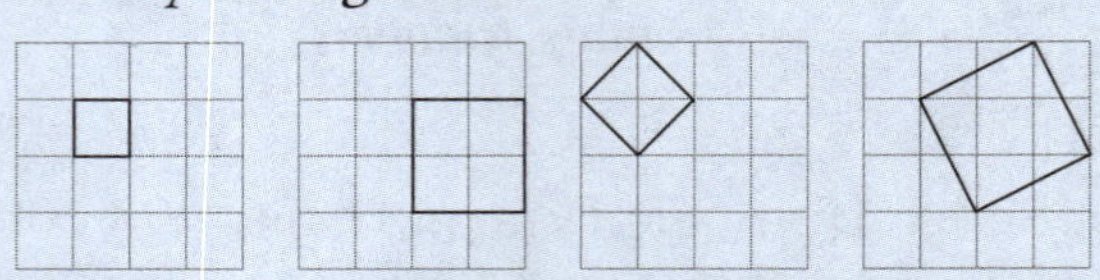

Square E　Square F　Square G　Square H

Here are two methods to find the area of the square.

Method 1

Draw an enclosing square and subtract areas.
Draw square EFGH along grid lines
so each vertex of ABDC lies on
one side of the enclosing square.
The area of EFGH = 6^2 units^2
= 36 units^2

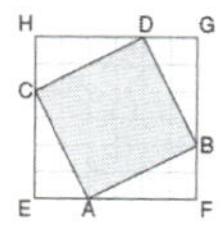

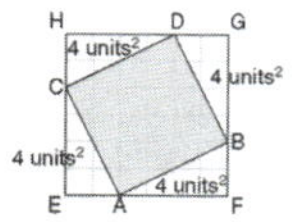

The triangles formed by the enclosing square are congruent.
Each triangle has area: $\frac{1}{2}(4)(2)$ units^2 = 4 units^2
So, the 4 triangles have area 4 × 4 units^2 = 16 units^2

The area of ABDC = Area of EFGH − Area of triangles
= 36 units^2 − 16 units^2
= 20 units^2

So, the side length of ABDC is: AB = $\sqrt{20}$ units

Method 2

Cut the square into smaller figures, then rearrange.
Cut and move two triangles to form a figure
with side lengths along grid lines.
Count squares to find the area.
The area of the new figure is 20 units^2.
So, the area of square ABDC = 20 units^2
And, the side length of the square, AB = $\sqrt{20}$ units

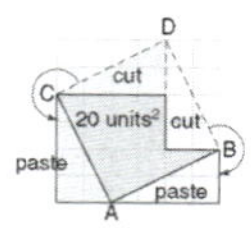

Since 20 is not a square number,
we cannot write $\sqrt{20}$ as a whole number.
Later in this unit, you will learn how to find an approximate value for $\sqrt{20}$ as a decimal.

Practice

1. Simplify.

a) 3^2 9	b) $\sqrt{1}$ 1	c) 4^2 16	d) $\sqrt{64}$ 8
e) 7^2 49	f) $\sqrt{144}$ 12	g) 10^2 100	h) $\sqrt{169}$ 13
i) 6^2 36	j) $\sqrt{121}$ 11	k) 12^2 144	l) $\sqrt{625}$ 25

8.1 Constructing and Measuring Squares 327

Number Strategies

Remind students of the formula for the surface area of a cube:
$SA = 6c^2$
Ensure students understand that the faces of a cube are congruent squares.

Sample Solutions

4. a)

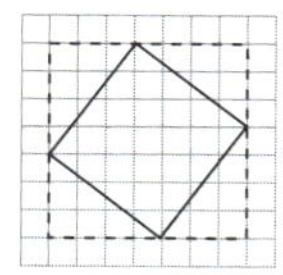

b)

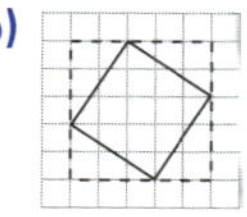

c)

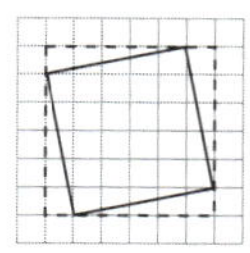

d)

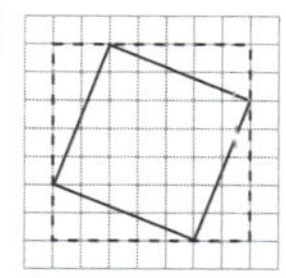

6. The area of the square is 2 units^2. I know that by drawing the diagonals of the square, I get 4 congruent triangles, each with an area of 2 units^2 ÷ 4 = $\frac{1}{2}$ unit^2. So, I drew a square with each triangle covering $\frac{1}{2}$ of a grid square.

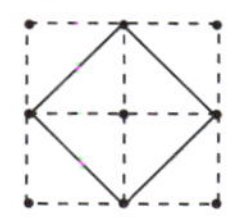

To check that the square has an area of 2 units^2, I drew an enclosing square.
The area of the enclosing square is:
2^2 units^2 = 4 units^2
The triangles formed by the enclosing squares are congruent.
Each triangle has area: $\frac{1}{2}(1)(1)$ unit^2 = $\frac{1}{2}$ unit^2
So, the 4 triangles have area: 4 × $\frac{1}{2}$ unit^2 = 2 units^2
The area of the given square
= Area of enclosing square − Area of triangles
= 4 units^2 − 2 units^2 = 2 units^2

Square	Area (cm²)	Side length (cm)
A	9	3
B	16	4
C	8	$\sqrt{8}$
D	10	$\sqrt{10}$
E	1	1
F	4	2
G	2	$\sqrt{2}$
H	5	$\sqrt{5}$

Use the *Examples* in *Connect* to show students how to use the formulas they developed to find the area of a square and the side length of a square.

Method 2 to find the area of a square may be challenging for students to follow. Work through this method as a class using an enlarged 1-cm grid transparency. Have volunteers cut out the two triangles and move them as shown. This will help students make the visual connection.

Practice

Students require 1-cm grid paper (PM 20) for questions 2 and 4. Students require square dot paper (PM 22) for question 6.

Assessment Focus: Question 6

Students understand that the area of 1 grid square is 1 unit^2. They draw a diagonal in a grid square to form 2 congruent triangles, each with area $\frac{1}{2}$ unit^2. Students use the diagonal to construct a square with area 2 units^2. They use one of the methods learned in the lesson to verify the area of the square they have drawn.

Students who need extra support to complete the Assessment Focus questions may benefit from the Step-by-Step masters (Masters 8.8-8.12).

7. Let the given diagonal be a diagonal for Square A.
Draw Square B with side length equal to the given diagonal.
Draw an enclosing square around Square B.
The area of Square A equals the sum of the areas of 2 of the enclosed triangles, or $\frac{1}{2}$ the area of Square B.
So, the side length of Square A is the square root of one-half the area of Square B.

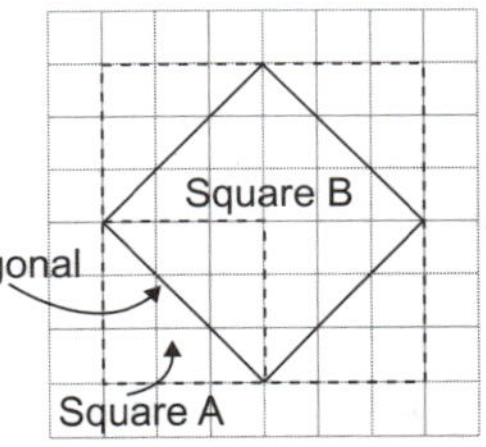

REFLECT: Finding a square root and squaring a number are inverse operations. When we square a number, we write it with the exponent 2. The area of a square is the square of its side length. To find the length of a line segment, we can construct a square on the segment, find the area of the square, then the length of the segment is the square root of the area.
For example, to find the length of this line segment:

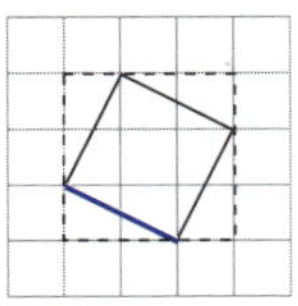

Construct a square on the segment.
Draw an enclosing square.
The area of the enclosing square is: 9 units^2
The triangles formed by the enclosing squares are congruent.
Each triangle has area: $\frac{1}{2}(2)(1)$ units^2 = 1 unit^2
So, the 4 triangles have area: 4 × 1 unit^2 = 4 units^2
The area of the given square
= Area of enclosing square − Area of triangles
= 9 units^2 − 4 units^2 = 5 units^2
So, the side length of the square is $\sqrt{5}$ units.

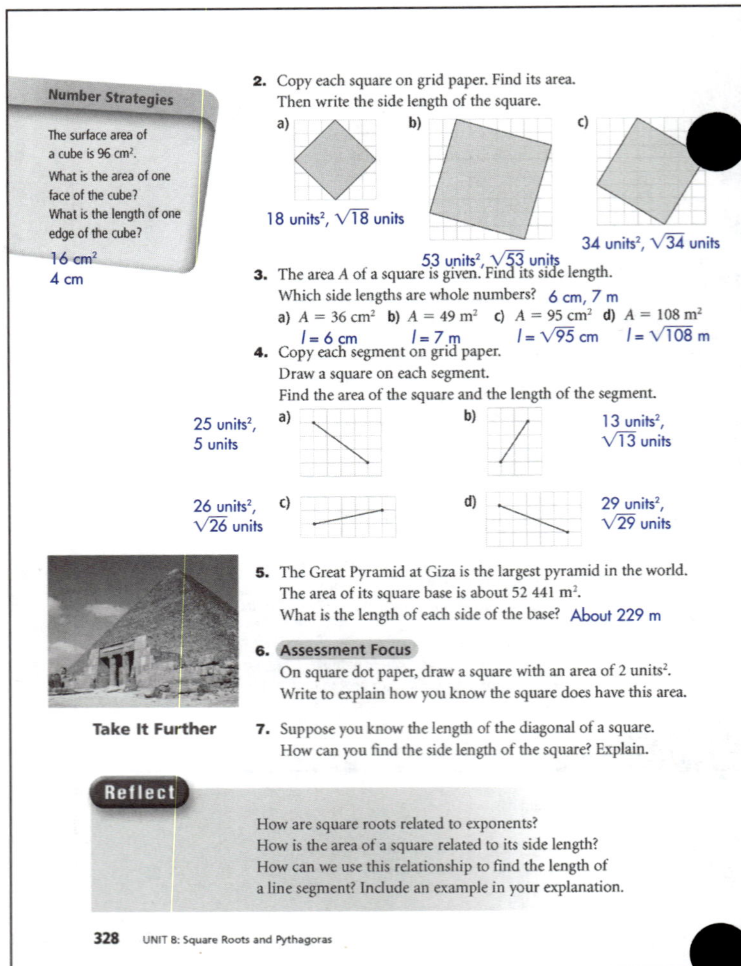

Number Strategies

The surface area of a cube is 96 cm^2.
What is the area of one face of the cube?
What is the length of one edge of the cube?
16 cm^2
4 cm

2. Copy each square on grid paper. Find its area. Then write the side length of the square.
a) 18 units^2, $\sqrt{18}$ units
b) 53 units^2, $\sqrt{53}$ units
c) 34 units^2, $\sqrt{34}$ units

3. The area A of a square is given. Find its side length. Which side lengths are whole numbers? 6 cm, 7 m
a) A = 36 cm^2 l = 6 cm
b) A = 49 m^2 l = 7 m
c) A = 95 cm^2 $l = \sqrt{95}$ cm
d) A = 108 m^2 $l = \sqrt{108}$ m

4. Copy each segment on grid paper. Draw a square on each segment. Find the area of the square and the length of the segment.
a) 25 units^2, 5 units
b) 13 units^2, $\sqrt{13}$ units
c) 26 units^2, $\sqrt{26}$ units
d) 29 units^2, $\sqrt{29}$ units

5. The Great Pyramid at Giza is the largest pyramid in the world. The area of its square base is about 52 441 m^2. What is the length of each side of the base? About 229 m

6. Assessment Focus
On square dot paper, draw a square with an area of 2 units^2. Write to explain how you know the square does have this area.

Take It Further

7. Suppose you know the length of the diagonal of a square. How can you find the side length of the square? Explain.

Reflect

How are square roots related to exponents? How is the area of a square related to its side length? How can we use this relationship to find the length of a line segment? Include an example in your explanation.

328 UNIT 8: Square Roots and Pythagoras

ASSESSMENT FOR LEARNING

What to Look For	What to Do
Knowledge and Understanding ✔ Students understand the relationship between the area of a square and its side length. ***Thinking*** ✔ Students can draw a square whose area is not a perfect square. ***Application*** ✔ Students can calculate the length of any segment on a grid.	***Extra Support:*** Students who have difficulty constructing a square on a line segment may benefit from tracing the line segment, then rotating it 90° each time. Students could use a protractor to check that the angles are right angles. Students can use Step-by-Step 1 (Master 8.8) to complete question 6. ***Extra Practice:*** Students can complete the Additional Activity, *Inscribed Squares* (Master 8.6). Students can complete Extra Practice 1 (Master 8.18). ***Extension:*** Students draw the diagonal of a square, with length $\sqrt{18}$ cm. Students find the side length of the square. (Answer: 3 cm)

Recording and Reporting
Master 8.2 Ongoing Observations: Square Roots and Pythagoras

8.2 **Estimating Square Roots**

Focus Develop strategies for estimating a square root.

You know that the square root of a given number is a number which, when multiplied by itself, results in the given number;
for example, $\sqrt{121} = \sqrt{11 \times 11}$
$= 11$

You also know that the square root of a number is the side length of a square with area that is equal to the number.
For example, $\sqrt{9} = 3$

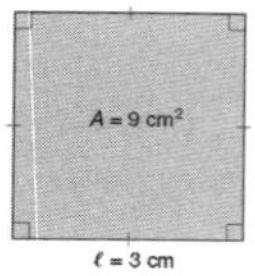

Explore

Work with a partner.
Use a copy of the number line below.
Place each square root on the number line to show its approximate value as a decimal: $\sqrt{2}$, $\sqrt{5}$, $\sqrt{9}$, $\sqrt{18}$, $\sqrt{24}$
Use grid paper if it helps.

Reflect & Share

Compare your answers with those of another pair of classmates.
What strategies did you use to estimate the square roots?
How could you use a calculator to check your square roots?

8.2 Estimating Square Roots 329

Estimating Square Roots

LESSON ORGANIZER 80–100 min

Curriculum Focus: Develop strategies for estimating a square root. (8m25)

Student Materials
- Number Lines for *Explore* (Master 8.13)
- 1-cm grid paper (PM 20)
- calculators

Optional
- Step-by-Step 2 (Master 8.9)
- Extra Practice 2 (Master 8.19)

Vocabulary: palindrome

Assessment: Master 8.2 Ongoing Observations: Square Roots and Pythagoras

Key Math Learning

The square root of a non-perfect square can be estimated by drawing squares, or by using a number line and a calculator.

Mental Math

Students could write a number that is close to the given number, and that is divisible by the denominator of the fraction. Students divide the number by the denominator of the fraction, then multiply the quotient by the numerator of the fraction.

BEFORE Get Started

Remind students that the perfect squares are the set of numbers 1, 4, 9, 16, 25, ...

They are formed by squaring the natural numbers: 1, 2, 3, 4, 5, ...

For example, $3^2 = 9$ and $5^2 = 25$

Numbers such as 2, 3, 5, and 6 are not perfect squares. They do not have whole-number square roots.

Present *Explore*. Distribute *Number Lines for Explore* (Master 8.13) and 1-cm grid paper (PM 20) to pairs of students. Tell students they will estimate the square roots of numbers that are not perfect squares. Ensure students understand they are to make a reasoned guess that is close to the actual value, without calculating it exactly.

Some students may need a quick review of decimals.

DURING Explore

Ongoing Assessment: Observe and Listen

As students work, ask questions, such as:

- Which square root was easiest to place? Explain.
  ($\sqrt{9}$; it has a whole-number square root, 3.)
- What strategy did you use to estimate the square roots?
  (I thought of the perfect squares closest to the number, then decided which perfect square the number was closer to, and how close it was to the perfect square.)
- How did you decide where to place $\sqrt{2}$?
  (I found whole numbers that $\sqrt{2}$ is between. Since $1 \times 1 = 1$ and $2 \times 2 = 4$, I know $\sqrt{2}$ is between 1 and 2, but a bit closer to 1. I estimated $\sqrt{2}$ to be about 1.4.)
- How did you decide where to place $\sqrt{5}$?
  (Since $2 \times 2 = 4$ and $3 \times 3 = 9$, I know $\sqrt{5}$ is between 2 and 3, but much closer to 2. I estimated $\sqrt{5}$ to be about 2.2.)

REACHING ALL LEARNERS

Alternative Explore

Materials: square tiles, scissors, 1-cm grid paper

Students work in pairs to estimate $\sqrt{42}$. Students use 42 tiles to make the largest square possible. Students note the dimensions of the square and any tiles left over. Students cut a square from grid paper to match the square made with tiles. They cut a strip of squares to match the leftover tiles. They cut the strip into 2 narrow strips, then place them against the square. Students use the results to estimate $\sqrt{42}$, then check their estimate with a calculator.

Early Finishers

Have students create a number line similar to the one in *Practice* question 2, where some placements are good estimates of the square roots and some are not. Students trade problems with a classmate, then explain which placements are good estimates, and estimate the value of each square root that is incorrectly placed.

Common Misconceptions

➤ Students think there is only one estimate of a square root.

How to Help: Remind students that we can often find a better estimate of a square root by writing the square root to more decimal places. For example, we can estimate $\sqrt{5}$ to be 2.2 to the nearest tenth, 2.24 to the nearest hundredth, 2.236 to the nearest thousandth, and so on. Generally, the more decimal places, the better the estimate. Often an estimate to one or two decimal places is adequate.

Connect

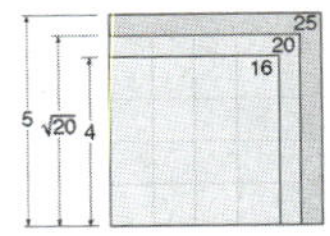

Here is one way to estimate the value of $\sqrt{20}$:
Find the square number closest to 20, but greater than 2
The number is 25.
On grid paper, draw a square with area 25.
Its side length is: $\sqrt{25} = 5$
Find the square number closest to 20, but less than 20.
The number is 16.
Draw a square with area 16.
Its side length is: $\sqrt{16} = 4$
Draw the squares so they overlap.

A square with area 20 lies between these two squares.
Its side length is $\sqrt{20}$.
20 is between 16 and 25, but closer to 16.
$\sqrt{20}$ is between $\sqrt{16}$ and $\sqrt{25}$, but closer to $\sqrt{16}$.
So, $\sqrt{20}$ is between 4 and 5, but closer to 4.
An estimate of $\sqrt{20}$ is 4.4.

The *Example* illustrates another method to estimate $\sqrt{20}$.

Example Use a number line and a calculator to estimate $\sqrt{20}$.

Solution Think of the perfect squares closest to $\sqrt{20}$.

$\sqrt{20}$ is between 4 and 5, but closer to 4.
With a calculator, use guess and check to refine the estimate.
Try 4.4: $4.4 \times 4.4 = 19.36$ (too small)
Try 4.5: $4.5 \times 4.5 = 20.25$ (too large)
Try 4.45: $4.45 \times 4.45 = 19.8025$ (too small)
Try 4.46: $4.46 \times 4.46 = 19.8916$ (too small)
Try 4.47: $4.47 \times 4.47 = 19.9809$ (very close)
A close estimate of $\sqrt{20}$ is 4.47.

330 UNIT 8: Square Roots and Pythagoras

- How did you decide where to place $\sqrt{18}$?
  (Since $4 \times 4 = 16$ and $5 \times 5 = 25$, I know $\sqrt{18}$ is between 4 and 5, but much closer to 4. I estimated $\sqrt{18}$ to be about 4.2.)
- How did you decide where to place $\sqrt{24}$?
  (Since $4 \times 4 = 16$ and $5 \times 5 = 25$, I know $\sqrt{24}$ is between 4 and 5, but very close to 5. I estimated $\sqrt{24}$ to be about 4.9.)

AFTER Connect

Invite students to share their answers and strategies with the class.

What you might see:

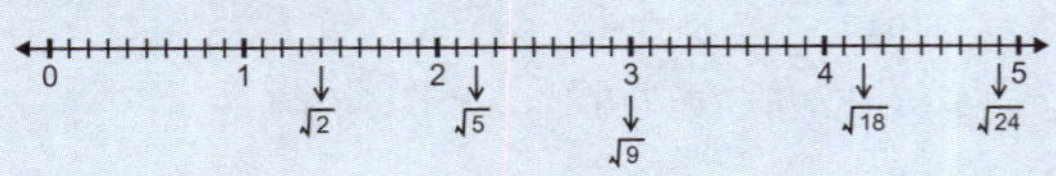

Ask:

- Did you get the same answers as those of another pair of classmates? Explain.
  (Three answers were the same and 2 answers were very close. We estimated $\sqrt{18}$ to be about 4.2 and $\sqrt{24}$ to be about 4.9. Our classmates estimated $\sqrt{18}$ to be about 4.3 and $\sqrt{24}$ to be about 4.8.)
- How could you use a calculator to check your square roots?
  (I could multiply the decimal number by itself, then check how close the product is to the given number.)

Have students use a calculator to check whether 4.8 or 4.9 is the better estimate of $\sqrt{24}$.

$4.8 \times 4.8 = 23.04$

$4.9 \times 4.9 = 24.01$

Ensure students understand that because 24.01 is closer to 24 than 23.04, 4.9 is the better estimate. Since students were not to use a calculator in *Explore*, both estimates should be considered good estimates.

Use the diagram in *Connect* to show students one way to estimate the square root of a non-perfect square.

Review the *Example*. Point out the 3 steps to estimating a square root with a calculator:

Practice

1. Copy this diagram on grid paper. Then estimate the value of $\sqrt{7}$.

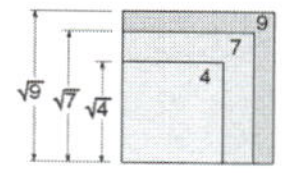

About 2.6

2. Use the number line below. $\sqrt{30}, \sqrt{64}, \sqrt{72}$
   a) Which placements are good estimates of the square roots? Explain your reasoning.
   b) Use the number line to estimate the value of each square root that is incorrectly placed.

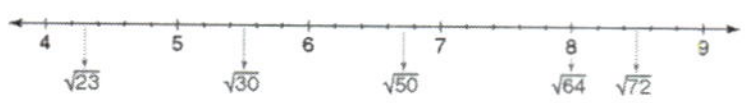

3. Which two consecutive whole numbers is each square root between? How do you know?

   a) $\sqrt{5}$ 2 and 3 b) $\sqrt{11}$ 3 and 4 c) $\sqrt{57}$ 7 and 8 d) $\sqrt{38}$ 6 and 7 e) $\sqrt{171}$ 13 and 14

4. Write five square roots whose values are between 9 and 10. Explain your strategy. $\sqrt{83}, \sqrt{87}, \sqrt{90}, \sqrt{95}, \sqrt{99}$

5. Is each statement true or false? Explain.
   a) $\sqrt{17}$ is between 16 and 18. False
   b) $\sqrt{5} + \sqrt{5}$ is greater than $\sqrt{10}$. True
   c) $\sqrt{131}$ is between 11 and 12. True

6. Use guess and check to estimate the value of each square root. Record each trial.

   a) $\sqrt{23}$ About 4.8 b) $\sqrt{13}$ About 3.61 c) $\sqrt{78}$ About 8.83 d) $\sqrt{135}$ About 11.62 e) $\sqrt{62}$ About 7.87

Mental Math

Estimate.
What strategies did you use?
- $\frac{3}{4}$ of 70 51 or 54
- $\frac{2}{3}$ of 55 36
- $\frac{5}{8}$ of 100 60 or 65
- $\frac{1}{5}$ of 299 60

To round a length in centimetres to the nearest millimetre, round to the nearest tenth.

7. Find the approximate side length of the square with each area. Give your answer to the nearest millimetre.

   a) 92 cm^2 About 9.6 cm b) 430 m^2 About 20.736 m c) 150 cm^2 About 12.2 cm d) 29 m^2 About 5.385 m

8. A square garden has an area of 138 m^2.
   a) What are the approximate dimensions of the garden? About 11.75 m by 11.75 m
   b) About how much fencing would be needed to go around the garden? About 47 m

Sample Solutions

2. a) $\sqrt{30}$; since $5 \times 5 = 25$ and $6 \times 6 = 36$, and 30 is about halfway between 25 and 36, I know that $\sqrt{30}$ is about 5.5.
   $\sqrt{64}$; $8 \times 8 = 64$
   $\sqrt{72}$; since $8 \times 8 = 64$ and $9 \times 9 = 81$, and 72 is about halfway between 64 and 81, I know that $\sqrt{72}$ is about 8.5.
   b) Since $4 \times 4 = 16$ and $5 \times 5 = 25$, I know that $\sqrt{23}$ is between 4 and 5, but much closer to 5. An estimate of $\sqrt{23}$ is 4.8.
   Since $7 \times 7 = 49$ and $8 \times 8 = 64$, I know that $\sqrt{50}$ is between 7 and 8, but much closer to 7. An estimate of $\sqrt{50}$ is 7.1.
3. a) $2 \times 2 = 4$ and $3 \times 3 = 9$, and 5 is between 4 and 9.
   b) $3 \times 3 = 9$ and $4 \times 4 = 16$, and 11 is between 9 and 16.
   c) $7 \times 7 = 49$ and $8 \times 8 = 64$, and 57 is between 49 and 64.
   d) $6 \times 6 = 36$ and $7 \times 7 = 49$, and 38 is between 36 and 49.
   e) $13 \times 13 = 169$ and $14 \times 14 = 196$, and 171 is between 169 and 196.
4. $9 \times 9 = 81$ and $10 \times 10 = 100$
   Any number between 81 and 100 will have a square root between 9 and 10.
5. a) $16 \times 16 = 256$ and $18 \times 18 = 324$, and 17 is not between 256 and 324.
   b) $\sqrt{5}$ is between 2 and 3, but much closer to 2.
   So, $\sqrt{5} + \sqrt{5}$ is a bit more than $2 + 2 = 4$.
   $\sqrt{10}$ is between 3 and 4, but much closer to 3.
   c) $11 \times 11 = 121$ and $12 \times 12 = 144$, and 131 is between 121 and 144.

- Find the whole numbers that the square root is between.
- Look at numbers with one decimal place.
- To get a better estimate, try numbers with two decimal places.

Encourage students not to use the $\sqrt{\ }$ key on their calculators. The calculator should only be used to check estimates by squaring. If it is difficult to limit the use of the calculator, have students work in pairs, with one student estimating square roots and the other student using the $\sqrt{\ }$ key to check.

Practice

Question 1 requires 1-cm grid paper (PM 20). Questions 6, 7, and 13 require a calculator. For question 7, ensure students understand that to round a length in metres to the nearest millimetre, they should round to the nearest thousandth. Question 10 requires a measuring tape or a metre stick.

Assessment Focus: Question 9

Students find the area of the canvas, multiply its area by 2 to get the area of the artwork, then estimate the square root of the area of the artwork to get the side length of the square frame. Students' work should include a diagram. Some students may find it easier to work in centimetres.

Assignment Guidelines

If your students do not have time to complete all the *Practice* questions on pages 331 and 332, these questions provide minimum curriculum coverage: 2, 3, 6, 8, 9, *Reflect*

To assess the 4 Achievement Chart categories listed in the curriculum document, have students complete these *Practice* questions:
Communication: 2
Knowledge and Understanding: 3
Application: 8
Thinking: 9

9. The area of the square canvas is: $A = l^2 = 1 \text{ m} \times 1 \text{ m} = 1 \text{ m}^2$
The area of the square artwork is:
$2 \times 1 \text{ m}^2 = 2 \text{ m}^2$
The side length of the square frame is:
Length = $\sqrt{\text{Area}}$ or $l = \sqrt{2}$
With a calculator, I used guess and check to estimate $\sqrt{2}$.
An estimate of $\sqrt{2}$ is 1.4.
The dimensions of the square frame are about 1.4 m by 1.4 m.

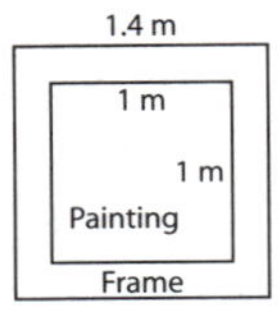

10. My classroom is a rectangle with length 10 m and width 9 m.
The area of the classroom is: $A = lw = 10 \text{ m} \times 9 \text{ m} = 90 \text{ m}^2$
Suppose the classroom was a square with area 90 m^2.
The side length of the classroom would be: $l = \sqrt{90}$
An estimate of $\sqrt{90}$ is 9.49.
The square classroom would be about 9.49 m by 9.49 m.

12. The product of two perfect squares is always a perfect square.
For example: $16 \times 25 = 4^2 \times 5^2$
$= 4 \times 4 \times 5 \times 5$ Order of multiplication does not matter.
$= (4 \times 5) \times (4 \times 5) = 20 \times 20 = 20^2 = 400$

REFLECT: The perimeter of a square is 4 times its side length. To find the side length of a square, I calculate the square root of its area.
My favourite method for estimating a square root of a number that is not a perfect square is to use guess and check with a calculator. I record each trial until I get an estimate that is very close. With a calculator, I can estimate to any number of decimal places. The other methods do not usually result in very close estimates.

9. **Assessment Focus** A student uses a 1-m square canvas for her painting. After framing, she wants her artwork to have an area twice the area of the canvas.
What are the dimensions of the square frame? About 1.4 m by 1.4 m
Show your work.

10. Most classrooms are rectangles.
Measure the dimensions of your classroom.
Calculate its area.
What if your classroom was a square.
What would its dimensions be?

Take It Further

11. A square carpet covers 75% of the area of a floor.
The floor is 8 m by 8 m.

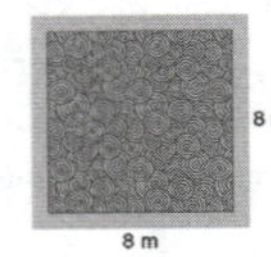

a) What are the dimensions of the carpet? About 6.93 m by 6.93 m
b) What area of the floor is not covered by carpet? 16 m^2

12. Is the product of two perfect squares sometimes a perfect square? Always a perfect square?
Investigate to find out. Write about your findings.

A palindrome is a number that reads the same forward and backward.

13. a) Find the square root of each palindrome.
i) $\sqrt{121}$ 11
ii) $\sqrt{12\,321}$ 111
iii) $\sqrt{1\,234\,321}$ 1111
iv) $\sqrt{123\,454\,321}$ 11 111
b) Continue the pattern.
Write the next 4 palindromes and their square roots.
$\sqrt{12\,345\,654\,321} = 111\,111$,
$\sqrt{1\,234\,567\,654\,321} = 1\,111\,111$,
$\sqrt{123\,456\,787\,654\,321} = 11\,111\,111$,
$\sqrt{12\,345\,678\,987\,654\,321} = 111\,111\,111$

Reflect

How can you find the perimeter of a square if you know its area?
What is your favourite method for estimating a square root of a number that is not a perfect square? Explain your choice.

332 UNIT 8: Square Roots and Pythagoras

ASSESSMENT FOR LEARNING

What to Look For	What to Do
Knowledge and Understanding ✔ Students understand that non-perfect squares do not have whole-number square roots. ***Thinking*** ✔ Students can solve problems that involve estimating square roots. ***Communication*** ✔ Students can explain whether placements of square roots on a number line are good estimates. ***Application*** ✔ Students can estimate the square root of a number using various strategies.	***Extra Support:*** Students who have difficulty using a number line to estimate square roots may benefit from writing each whole number on the number line as a square root. For example, students could write $\sqrt{9}$ below 3, and $\sqrt{16}$ below 4. Students can use Step-by-Step 2 (Master 8.9) to complete question 9. ***Extra Practice:*** Students use a calculator to estimate the side length of the squares in Lesson 8.1 *Practice* questions 2, 3c and d, and 4b, c, and d. Students can complete Extra Practice 2 (Master 8.19). ***Extension:*** Challenge students to find the width of the frame in *Practice* question 9. (Answer: About 20.71 cm or 0.21 m)

Recording and Reporting
Master 8.2 Ongoing Observations: Square Roots and Pythagoras

Fitting In

Fitting In

HOW TO PLAY THE GAME:

Your teacher will give you 3 sheets of game cards. Cut out the 54 cards.

1. Place the 1, 5, and 9 cards on the table.
   Spread them out so there is room for several cards between them.
   Shuffle the remaining cards.
   Give each player six cards.
2. All cards laid on the table must be arranged from least to greatest.
   Take turns to place a card so it touches another card on the table.
   - It can be placed to the right of the card if its value is greater.
   - It can be placed to the left of the card if its value is less.
   - It can be placed on top of the card if its value is equal.
   - However, it cannot be placed between two cards that are already touching.

In this example, the $\sqrt{16}$ card cannot be placed because the 3.5 and the 5 cards are touching.
The player cannot play that card in this round.

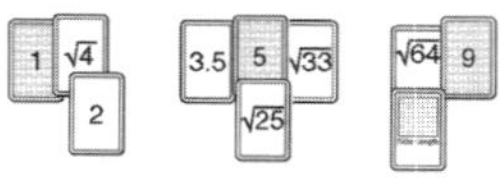

3. Place as many of your cards as you can. When no player can place any more cards, the round is over.
   Your score is the number of cards left in your hand.
   At the end of five rounds, the player with the lowest score wins.

OU WILL NEED
set of FITTING IN game rds; scissors

UMBER OF PLAYERS
to 4

OAL OF THE GAME
get the lowest score

hat other games could you lay with these cards? y out your ideas.

LESSON ORGANIZER — 20 min

Student Grouping: 2 to 4

Student Materials

- *Fitting In* Game Cards (Masters 8.14a, 8.14b, 8.14c)
- scissors

How to Play:

Students play in pairs.
Deal 27 cards to each player.
Place the cards face down in a pile.
The object of the game is to win all the cards.
Both players turn their top card face up and put them on the table.
The player whose card has the greater value takes both cards.
If both cards are of equal value, students shout "Challenge."

- In a challenge, both players turn up their next card.
- The player whose card has the greater value takes all 4 cards.

The game is over when one player has all the cards.
If time permits, allow students to try some of the suggested games.

BEFORE — Get Started

Invite a volunteer to read the game rules.

Ensure students understand that a card cannot be placed between two cards that are touching, and that a player can place only one card each turn.

DURING — Game

As students play, ask questions such as:

- How did you decide which card to play first?
  (*I played the card that was closest in value to a card on the table, to leave room for my next turn. For example, if I placed $\sqrt{36}$ to the left of 9, all the cards with values between 6 and 9 could not be played this round.*)
- Did anyone use a different strategy?
  (*Each turn, I placed the card that was furthest in value from a card on the table to try and block my opponents.*)

AFTER

After students have played the game a few times, have students suggest other games they could play with these cards.
Another possible game is *Challenge*.

Investigating Square Roots with a Calculator

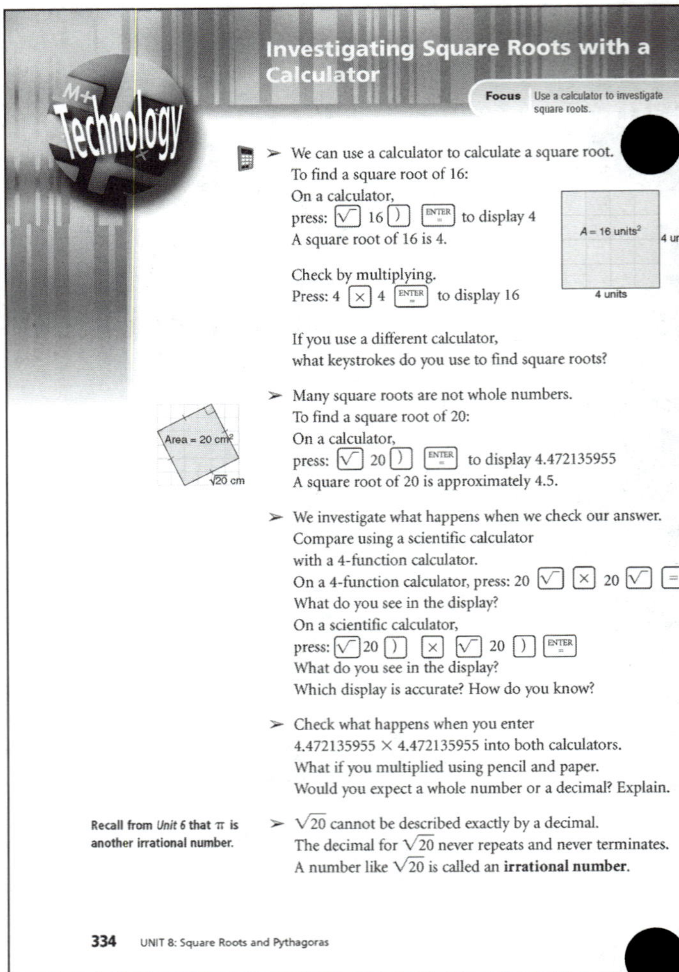

Investigating Square Roots with a Calculator

Technology

Focus Use a calculator to investigate square roots.

➢ We can use a calculator to calculate a square root.
To find a square root of 16:
On a calculator,
press: [√] 16 [)] [ENTER] to display 4
A square root of 16 is 4.

$A = 16$ units²
4 units
4 units

Check by multiplying.
Press: 4 [×] 4 [ENTER] to display 16

If you use a different calculator,
what keystrokes do you use to find square roots?

➢ Many square roots are not whole numbers.
To find a square root of 20:
On a calculator,
press: [√] 20 [)] [ENTER] to display 4.472135955
A square root of 20 is approximately 4.5.

Area = 20 cm²
$\sqrt{20}$ cm

➢ We investigate what happens when we check our answer.
Compare using a scientific calculator
with a 4-function calculator.
On a 4-function calculator, press: 20 [√] [×] 20 [√] [=]
What do you see in the display?
On a scientific calculator,
press: [√] 20 [)] [×] [√] 20 [)] [ENTER]
What do you see in the display?
Which display is accurate? How do you know?

➢ Check what happens when you enter
4.472135955 × 4.472135955 into both calculators.
What if you multiplied using pencil and paper.
Would you expect a whole number or a decimal? Explain.

Recall from *Unit 6* that π is another irrational number.

➢ $\sqrt{20}$ cannot be described exactly by a decimal.
The decimal for $\sqrt{20}$ never repeats and never terminates.
A number like $\sqrt{20}$ is called an **irrational number**.

334 UNIT 8: Square Roots and Pythagoras

LESSON ORGANIZER — 40–50 min

Curriculum Focus: Use a calculator to investigate square roots. (8m25)

Student Materials
- scientific calculators
- 4-function calculators
- compasses

Vocabulary: irrational number

Assessment: Master 8.2 Ongoing Observations: Square Roots and Pythagoras

Key Math Learnings

1. A calculator can be used to calculate a square root.
2. A number like $\sqrt{2}$ is an irrational number. It cannot be described exactly by a decimal.
3. Square roots can be used to calculate the radius of a circle, given its area.

Students may have different calculators. Have students write the keystrokes used to find square roots on the board if they are different from those in the Student Book. For example, the keystrokes for the TI-30XIIS are:

[2nd] [x^2] 16 [)] [ENTER =]

Ask questions, such as:

- What do you see in the display when we check our answer to $\sqrt{20}$ on a 4-function calculator? (*19.999999*)
- What do you see in the display when we check our answer to $\sqrt{20}$ on a scientific calculator? (*20*)
- Which display is accurate?
(*The scientific calculator*) How do you know?
(*I know that the square root of a number multiplied by itself gives the original number.*)
- What happened when you entered 4.472135955 × 4.472135955 into both calculators?
(*The 4-function calculator displayed 19.999999 and the scientific calculator displayed 20.*)
- Suppose you multiplied using pencil and paper. Would you expect a whole number or a decimal? Explain.
(*I would expect a decimal because the decimal 4.472 135 955 ends in 5, and 5 × 5 = 25. There is no decimal whose square is exactly 20.*)

Ensure students understand that the square root of 20 displayed on a calculator has been rounded to fit the screen. By the definition of an irrational number, $\sqrt{20}$ never repeats or terminates.

Tell students that although $\sqrt{20}$ never ends, there is a fixed length that we label $\sqrt{20}$; that is, a square of area 20 cm² has side length $\sqrt{20}$ cm.

Work through the example on using square roots to find the radius of a circle. Since π is an irrational number, the radius of a circle in this lesson will never be exact.

When we know the area of a circle, we can use square roots to calculate its radius.

The area of a circle, A, is about $3r^2$.
So, r^2 is about $\frac{1}{3}$ of A, or $\frac{A}{3}$.
Similarly, the area $A = \pi r^2$; so $r^2 = \frac{A}{\pi}$
To find r, we take the square root.
So, $r = \sqrt{\frac{A}{\pi}}$
We can use this formula to calculate the radius of a circle when we know its area.

A circular rug has area 11.6 m^2.
To calculate the radius of the rug, use: $r = \sqrt{\frac{A}{\pi}}$
Substitute: $A = 11.6$
$r = \sqrt{\frac{11.6}{\pi}}$
Use a calculator.
Key in: [√] 11.6 [÷] [π] [)] [ENTER]
to display 1.92156048
$r \doteq 1.92$
The radius of the rug is about 1.92 m, to the nearest centimetre.

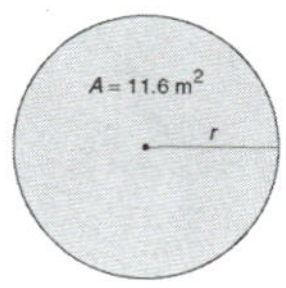

✓ Check

1. Calculate the radius and diameter of each circle.
Give the answers to 1 decimal place.

a)
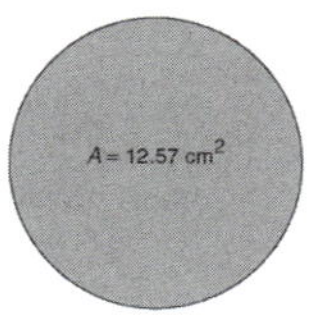

r = 2.0 cm
d = 4.0 cm

b)
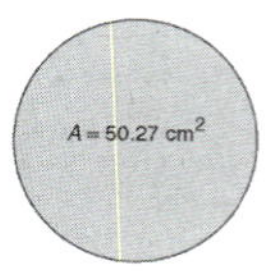

r = 4.0 cm
d = 8.0 cm

c)
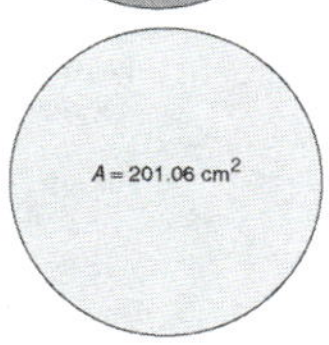

r = 8.0 cm
d = 16.0 cm

d)
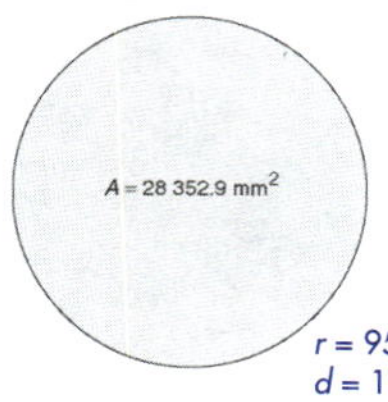

r = 95.0 mm
d = 190.0 mm

2. Draw each circle in question 1.

Technology: Investigating Square Roots with a Calculator 335

REACHING ALL LEARNERS

Early Finishers

Have students compare the calculator displays for the square roots of other non-perfect squares, such as 2, 5, and 41.

Common Misconceptions

➤ Students think that when they use the area of a circle to find its radius, the radius is exact.

How to Help: Remind students that the formula for the radius of a circle, given its area, is $r = \sqrt{\frac{A}{\pi}}$. Ensure students understand that π is an irrational number, and its value can never be known exactly. Since the formula contains π, the radius cannot be calculated exactly.

Sample Solutions

2. a)

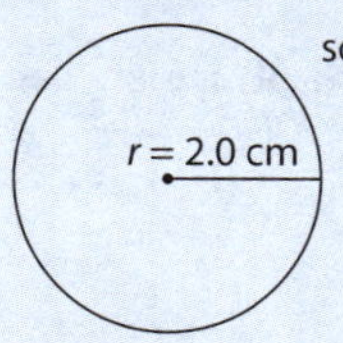

b)

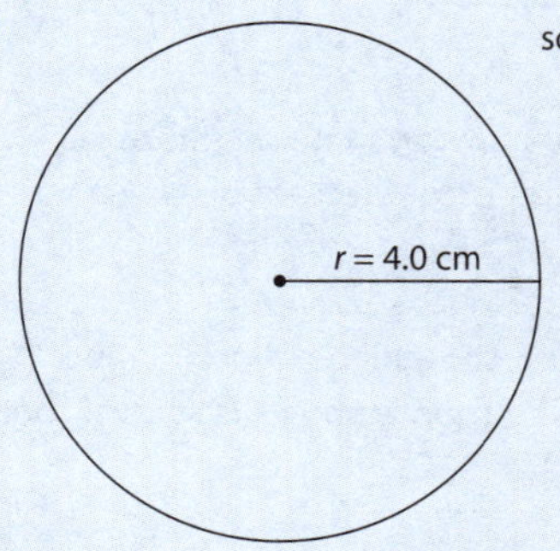

c)

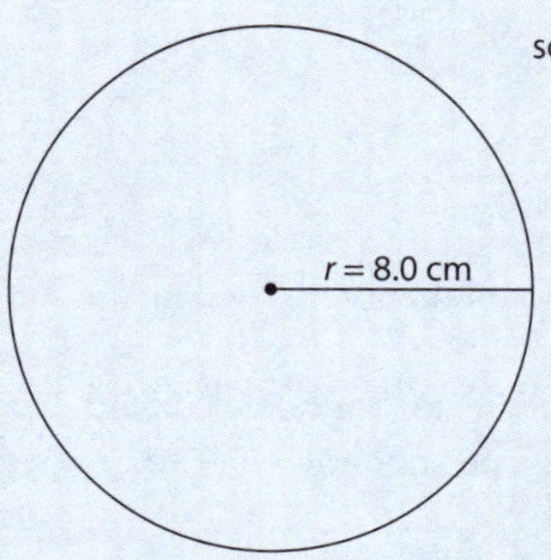

d)

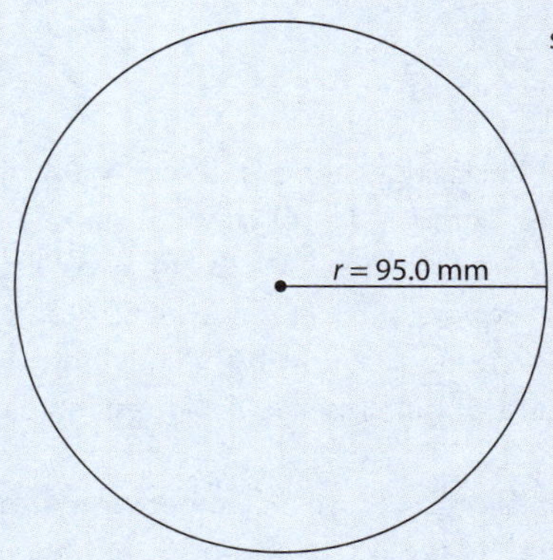

MID-UNIT REVIEW

LESSON ORGANIZER

Student Materials

- 1-cm grid paper (PM 20)
- calculators
- compasses

Assessment: Masters 8.1 Unit Rubric: Square Roots and Pythagoras, 8.4 Unit Summary: Square Roots and Pythagoras

Assignment Guidelines

To assess the 4 Achievement Chart categories listed in the curriculum document, have students complete these questions:
Knowledge and Understanding: 1
Communication: 2
Application: 5
Thinking: 7

Mid-Unit Review

LESSON

8.1 **1.** Copy each square onto 1-cm grid paper.
i) Find the area of each square.
ii) Write the side length of each square as a square root.
iii) Which areas can be written using exponents? Explain.

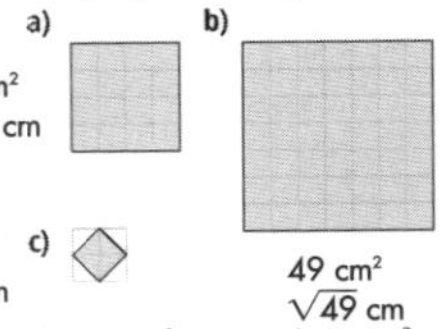

2. a) The area of a square is 24 cm². What is its side length? $\sqrt{24}$ cm
b) The side length of a square is 9 cm. What is its area? 81 cm²
c) Explain the relationship between square roots and square numbers. Use diagrams, symbols, and words.

8.1 8.2 **3.** Copy this square onto 1-cm grid paper.

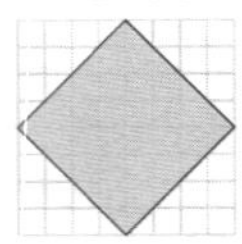

a) What is the area of the square? 32 cm²
b) Write the side length of the square as a square root. $\sqrt{32}$ cm
c) Estimate the side length to the nearest millimetre. About 5.7 cm

8.2 **4.** Between which two consecutive whole numbers does each square root lie? How do you know?
a) $\sqrt{3}$ 1 and 2 b) $\sqrt{65}$ 8 and 9
c) $\sqrt{57}$ 7 and 8 d) $\sqrt{30}$ 5 and 6

5. What is a square root of 100? Use this fact to predict the square root of each number. $\sqrt{100} = 10$ Use a calculator to check.
a) 900 30 b) 2500 50
c) 400 20 d) 8100 90
e) 10 000 100 f) 1 000 000 1000

6. a) Draw a circle with area 113 cm².
b) Does the circle in part a have an area of exactly 113 cm²? How do you know?

7. The opening of the fresh air intake pipe for a furnace is circular. Its area is 550 cm². What are the radius and diameter of the pipe? Give the answers to the nearest millimetre. $r \doteq 13.2$ cm $d \doteq 26.5$ cm

8. The top of a circular concrete footing has an area of 4050 cm². What is the radius of the circle? Give the answer to the nearest millimetre. About 35.9 cm

336 UNIT 8: Square Roots and Pythagoras

Sample Solutions

1. iii) Areas a and b: $4^2 = 16$ and $7^2 = 49$
$\sqrt{2}$ is not a whole number. I could write $2 = (\sqrt{2})^2$.

2. c) Squaring and finding a square root are inverse operations.
For example, $5^2 = 25$ and $\sqrt{25} = 5$
The area of a square shows the square number.
The side length of the square shows a square root of the square number.

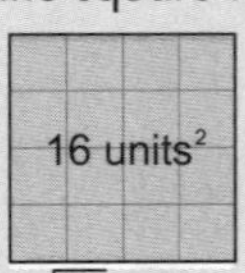

3. a) The area of the enclosing square is: 8^2 cm² = 64 cm²
Each triangle has area: $\frac{1}{2}(4)(4)$ cm² = 8 cm²
So, the 4 triangles have area 4×8 cm² = 32 cm².
The area of the square = 64 cm² − 32 cm² = 32 cm²

c) Since $5 \times 5 = 25$ and $6 \times 6 = 36$, I know that $\sqrt{32}$ is between 5 and 6, but closer to 6. An estimate of $\sqrt{32}$ is 5.7.

4. a) $1 \times 1 = 1$ and $2 \times 2 = 4$, and 3 is between 1 and 4.
b) $8 \times 8 = 64$ and $9 \times 9 = 81$, and 65 is between 64 and 81.
c) $7 \times 7 = 49$ and $8 \times 8 = 64$, and 57 is between 49 and 64.
d) $5 \times 5 = 25$ and $6 \times 6 = 36$, and 30 is between 25 and 36.

6. a)

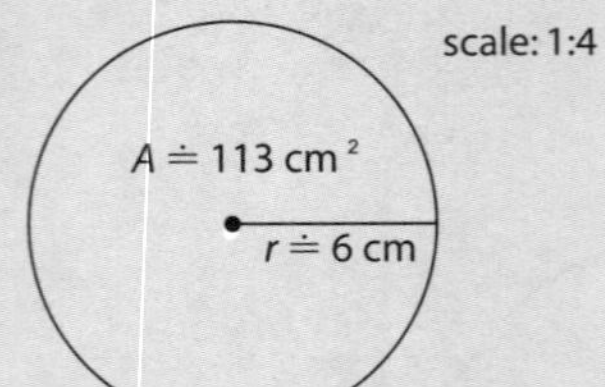

b) The formula for the area of a circle is: $A = \pi r^2$.
Since π is an irrational number, its value can never be known exactly.
So, the area of a circle cannot be calculated exactly.
The circle in part a does not have an area of exactly 113 cm².

7. $r = \sqrt{\frac{A}{\pi}}$
$= \sqrt{\frac{550}{\pi}} \doteq 13.2$
$d = 2r$
$= 2 \times \sqrt{\frac{550}{\pi}} \doteq 26.5$

8.3 The Pythagorean Relationship

Focus Discover a relationship among the side lengths of a right triangle.

In *Lesson 8.1*, you learned how to use the properties of a square to find the length of a line segment.

We will now use the properties of a right triangle to find the length of a line segment. A right triangle has two **legs** that form the right angle. The third side of the right triangle is called the **hypotenuse**.

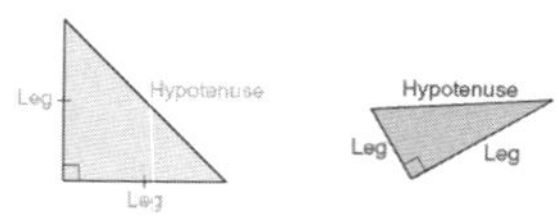

Isosceles right triangle   Scalene right triangle

Explore

Work on your own.
You will need grid paper.

- ➢ Copy segment AB.
  Find the length of the segment by drawing a square on it.
- ➢ Copy segment AB again.
  Draw a right triangle that has segment AB as its hypotenuse.
  Draw a square on each side.
  Find the area and side length of each square.
- ➢ Draw 3 different right triangles, with a square on each side.
  Find the area and side length of each square.
  Record your results in a table.

Use the corner of a sheet of paper or a protractor to check that the angles in the square are right angles.

	Area of Square on Leg 1	Length of Leg 1	Area of Square on Leg 2	Length of Leg 2	Area of Square on Hypotenuse	Length of Hypotenuse
Triangle 1						
Triangle 2						
Triangle 3						
Triangle 4						

Reflect & Share

Compare your results with those of another classmate.
What relationship do you see among the areas of the squares on the sides of a right triangle? How could this relationship help you find the length of a side of a right triangle?

8.3 The Pythagorean Relationship 337

LESSON 8.3

The Pythagorean Relationship

LESSON ORGANIZER (80–100 min)

Curriculum Focus: Discover a relationship among the side lengths of a right triangle. (8m49, 8m62)

Teacher Materials
Optional
- 1-cm grid transparency (PM 20)

Student Materials
- 1-cm grid paper (PM 20)
- calculators

Optional
- protractors
- Step-by-Step 3 (Master 8.10)
- Extra Practice 3 (Master 8.20)

Vocabulary: legs, hypotenuse, Pythagorean Theorem, Pythagorean triple

Assessment: Master 8.2 Ongoing Observations: Square Roots and Pythagoras

Key Math Learnings

1. In a right triangle, the area of the square on the hypotenuse is equal to the sum of the areas of the squares on the legs. This relationship is called the Pythagorean Theorem.
2. The Pythagorean relationship can be used to find the length of any side of a right triangle, given the lengths of the other two sides.

BEFORE Get Started

Have students look at the triangles at the top of page 337 in the Student Book. Remind students that a right triangle is a triangle with a right, or 90° angle. A right angle is often marked with a square.

Ask:

- How can you identify the hypotenuse of a right triangle?
  (It is the side opposite the right angle, and it is the longest side of a right triangle.)
- How can you identify the legs of a right triangle?
  (The legs meet to form the right angle. They form the letter "L.")

Present *Explore*. Tell students they will discover a relationship among the side lengths of a right triangle. Distribute 1-cm grid paper (PM 20) to students.

DURING Explore

Ongoing Assessment: Observe and Listen

Circulate to see that students are drawing the squares on the right triangles correctly.

As students work, ask questions, such as:

- How did you find the length of segment AB by drawing a square on it?
  (I drew a square on AB, then drew an enclosing square. I subtracted the areas of the 4 congruent triangles from the area of the enclosing square to find the area of the original square. Then, the length of AB was the square root of the area.)
- What is the length of AB?
  ($\sqrt{17}$ *cm*)
- How did you find the areas of the squares on the legs?
  (I counted grid squares. I could have squared the side length of each square.)

REACHING ALL LEARNERS

Early Finishers

Have students verify that the Pythagorean Theorem applies to right triangles whose side lengths are not whole numbers; for example, $\sqrt{7}$ units, $\sqrt{7}$ units, and $\sqrt{14}$ units.

Common Misconceptions

➤ When finding the length of a third side of a right triangle, students add the squares of the two known sides, regardless of whether the lengths are of two legs, or a leg and a hypotenuse.

How to Help: Remind students that the Pythagorean relationship states that the area of the square on the hypotenuse is equal to the sum of the areas of the squares on the legs. Have students copy the triangle on grid paper, then use a coloured pencil to circle the length of the hypotenuse. If its length is not known, students write h, then circle it. Remind students that the hypotenuse is the side opposite the right angle. Students are visually reminded that the sums of the squares on the other two sides should equal the square of the circled number, or the square of the value of the circled variable.

ESL Strategies

Students for whom English is a second language may benefit from drawing pictures on index cards to help them remember key words and concepts. Students could draw a diagram similar to the one at the top of page 338 in the Student Book. Instead of showing actual measures, students label Leg 1, Leg 2, Hypotenuse, Area of Square on Leg 1, Area of Square on Leg 2, and Area of Square on Hypotenuse. Students than write: Area of Square on Leg 1 + Area of Square on Leg 2 = Area of Square on Hypotenuse

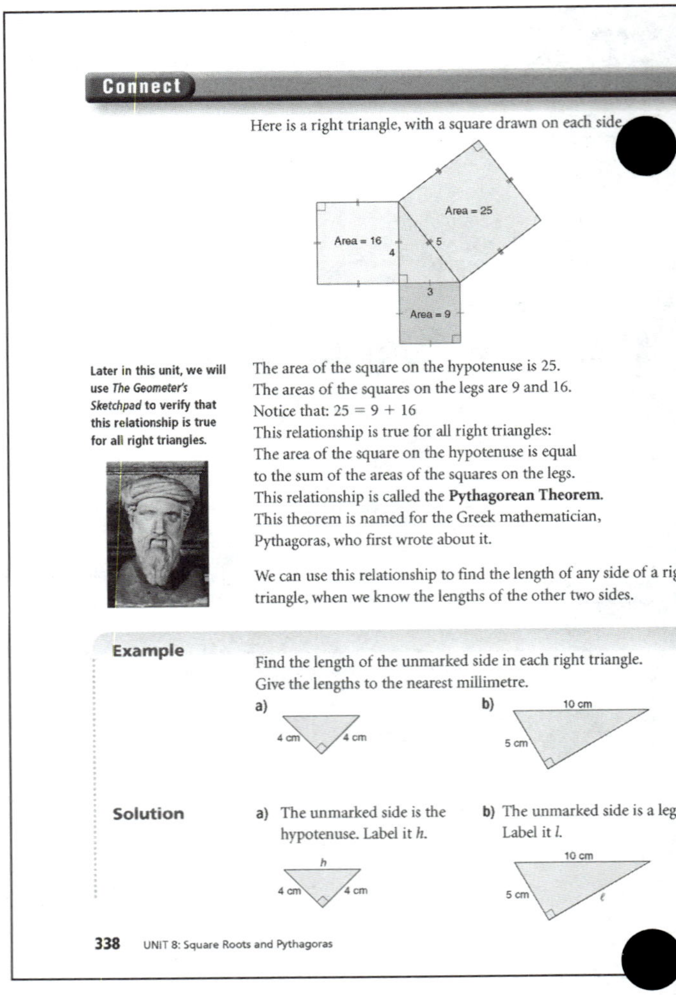

Connect

Here is a right triangle, with a square drawn on each side.

Later in this unit, we will use *The Geometer's Sketchpad* to verify that this relationship is true for all right triangles.

The area of the square on the hypotenuse is 25.
The areas of the squares on the legs are 9 and 16.
Notice that: 25 = 9 + 16
This relationship is true for all right triangles:
The area of the square on the hypotenuse is equal to the sum of the areas of the squares on the legs.
This relationship is called the **Pythagorean Theorem.**
This theorem is named for the Greek mathematician, Pythagoras, who first wrote about it.

We can use this relationship to find the length of any side of a right triangle, when we know the lengths of the other two sides.

Example

Find the length of the unmarked side in each right triangle.
Give the lengths to the nearest millimetre.

a) 4 cm, 4 cm b) 10 cm, 5 cm

Solution

a) The unmarked side is the hypotenuse. Label it h.

b) The unmarked side is a leg. Label it l.

- What were the areas of the squares on your right triangle?
  (1 cm², 16 cm², and 17 cm²)
- How did you find the side length of each square?
  (I took the square root of its area.)
- What were the side lengths of the squares on your right triangle?
  (1 cm, 4 cm, and $\sqrt{17}$ cm)

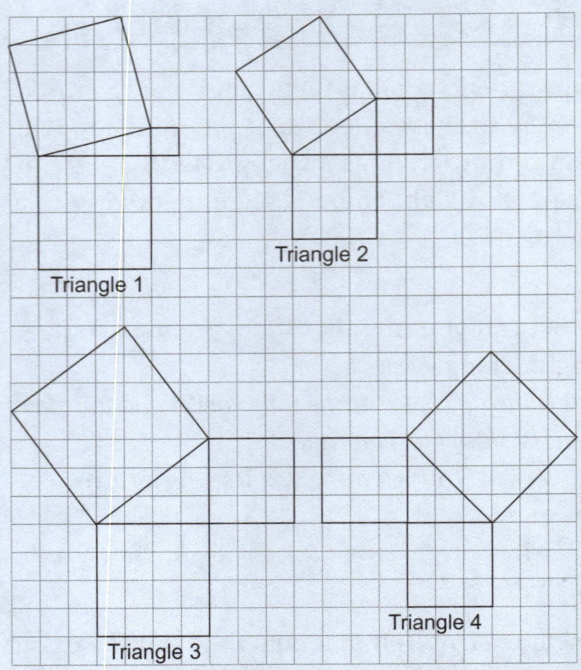

AFTER Connect

What you might see:

	Area of Square on Leg 1 (cm²)	Length of Leg 1 (cm)	Area of Square on Leg 2 (cm²)	Length of Leg 2 (cm)	Area of Square on Hypotenuse (cm²)	Length of Hypotenuse (cm)
Triangle 1	1	1	16	4	17	$\sqrt{17}$
Triangle 2	4	2	9	3	13	$\sqrt{13}$
Triangle 3	9	3	16	4	25	5
Triangle 4	9	3	9	3	18	$\sqrt{18}$

The area of the square on the hypotenuse is h^2.
The area of the squares on the legs are 4^2 and 4^2.
So, $h^2 = 4^2 + 4^2$
Use the order of operations.
Square, then add.
$h^2 = 16 + 16$
$h^2 = 32$
The area of the square on the hypotenuse is 32.
So, the side length of the square is: $h = \sqrt{32}$
Use a calculator.
$h \doteq 5.6569$
So, the hypotenuse is approximately 5.7 cm.

The area of the square on the hypotenuse is 10^2.
The areas of the squares on the legs are l^2 and 5^2.
So, $10^2 = l^2 + 5^2$
Square each number.
$100 = l^2 + 25$
To solve this equation, subtract 25 from each side.
$100 - 25 = l^2 + 25 - 25$
$75 = l^2$
The area of the square on the leg is 75.
So, the side length of the square is: $l = \sqrt{75}$
$l \doteq 8.66025$
So, the leg is approximately 8.7 cm.

Practice

1. The area of the square on each side of a triangle is given.
Is the triangle a right triangle? How do you know?

a)

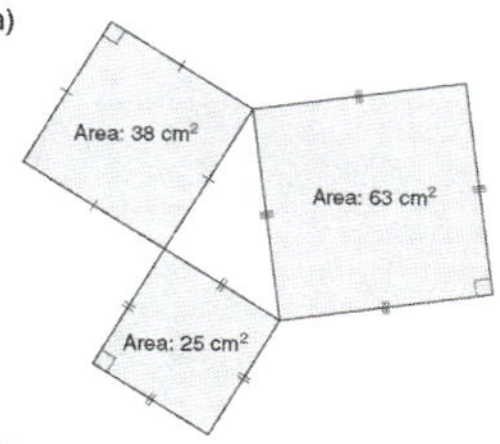

Yes
$38\text{ cm}^2 + 25\text{ cm}^2 = 63\text{ cm}^2$

b)

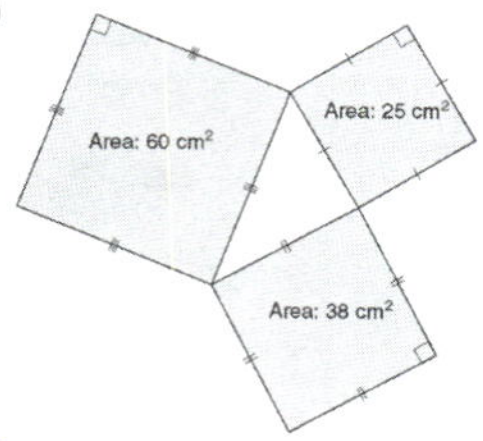

No
$25\text{ cm}^2 + 38\text{ cm}^2 \neq 60\text{ cm}^2$

Number Strategies

To find the lowest common multiple, students could work with 2 numbers at a time. Since 4 is a factor of 12, the lowest common multiple of 4 and 12 is 12. The lowest common multiple of 9 and 12 is 36. Since 11 and 36 have no common factors, the lowest common multiple of 11 and 36 is $11 \times 36 = 396$.

Sample Solutions

5. a)

Length of Leg 1 (cm)	Length of Leg 2 (cm)	Length of Hypotenuse (cm)
3	4	5
6	8	10
5	12	13
9	12	15
10	24	26
15	20	25
12	16	20

b) Each Pythagorean triple is a multiple of 3, 4, and 5, or 5, 12, and 13.

c) I can extend the pattern by multiplying the Pythagorean triples 3, 4, 5 and 5, 12, 13 by any whole number. For example, 12(3), 12(4), 12(5) = 36, 48, 60, and 25(5), 25(12), 25(13) = 125, 300, 325

6. If the triangle is a right triangle, the sum of the areas of the squares on the legs must equal the area of the square on the hypotenuse. I assume the hypotenuse has length 7 cm and the legs have lengths 3 cm and 5 cm.
The sum of the areas of the squares on the legs is:
$3^2 + 5^2 = 9 + 25 = 34$

Have students share their results with the class.
Ask:

- What patterns do you see in the table?
(*The sum of the areas of the squares on the legs is equal to the area of the square on the hypotenuse; for example, 1 cm² + 16 cm² = 17 cm²*)
- How could this relationship help you find the length of a side of a right triangle?
(*If the lengths of two sides are known, I could find the areas of the squares on these sides, then use the relationship to find the area of the square on the third side. I then take the square root of the area to find the length of the third side.*)

Review *Connect*. To help students understand that the Pythagorean Theorem is true for right triangles only, work through drawing squares on each side of a non-right triangle.

Use the overhead projector. Draw this triangle on a 1-cm grid transparency.

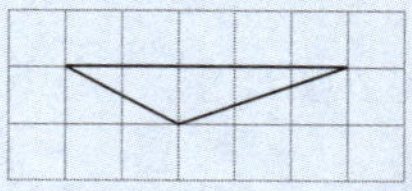

Show students that it is not a right triangle.
Draw squares on each side of the triangle, then find the areas of the squares.
The areas of the squares are: 5 units², 10 units², and 25 units².

Ask:

- Do you see a relationship among the areas of the squares on the non-right triangle? Explain.
(*No, the sum of the areas of the smaller squares does not equal the area of the larger square. $5 + 10 \neq 25$*)
- Do you think the Pythagorean Theorem is true for all triangles?
(*No, I think it is true for right triangles only.*)

The area of the square on the hypotenuse is: $7^2 = 49$
Since $34 \neq 49$, the triangle is not a right triangle.

7. The area of the square on the hypotenuse is: $(\sqrt{18})^2 = 18$
So, the sum of the areas of the squares on the legs must be 18. These numbers represent the areas of the squares on the legs. I took the square root of each number to find the lengths of the legs.

Area of Squares (units^2)	Lengths of Legs (units)
1, 17	1, $\sqrt{17}$
2, 16	$\sqrt{2}$, 4
3, 15	$\sqrt{3}$, $\sqrt{15}$
4, 14	2, $\sqrt{14}$
5, 13	$\sqrt{5}$, $\sqrt{13}$
6, 12	$\sqrt{6}$, $\sqrt{12}$
7, 11	$\sqrt{7}$, $\sqrt{11}$
8, 10	$\sqrt{8}$, $\sqrt{10}$
9, 9	3, 3

Students' answers should include a sketch of each triangle.

8. a) b) c) d)

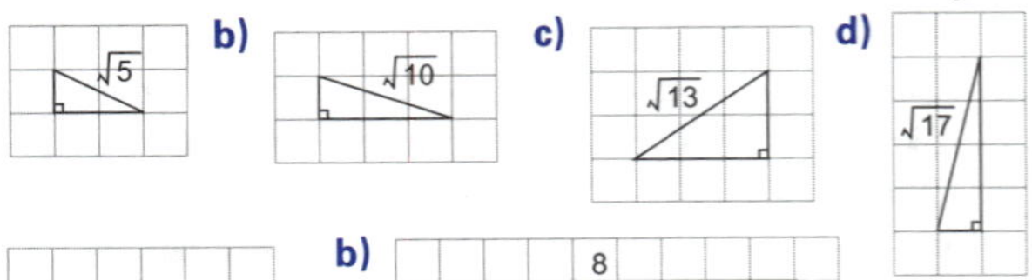

9. a) b)

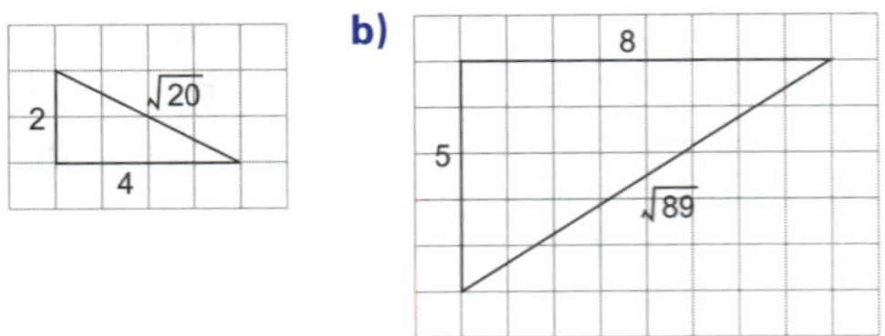

Number Strategies

Write the first 6 multiples of each number: 4, 9, 11, 12

Find the lowest common multiple of these numbers.

396

4: 4, 8, 12, 16, 20, 24
9: 9, 18, 27, 36, 45, 54
11: 11, 22, 33, 44, 55, 66
12: 12, 24, 36, 48, 60, 72

2. Find the length of the hypotenuse in each right triangle.

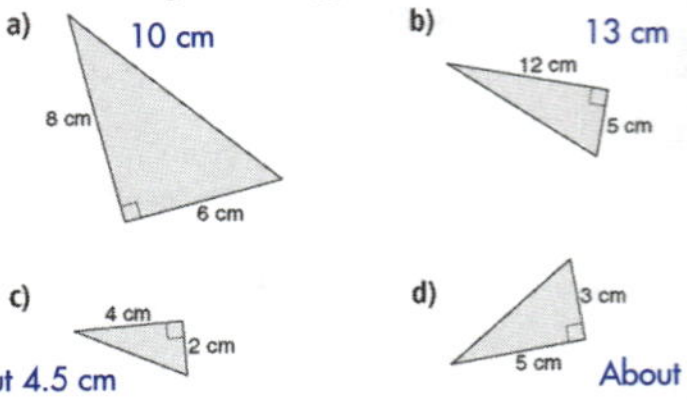

a) 10 cm b) 13 cm c) About 4.5 cm d) About 5.8 cm

3. Find the length of the unmarked leg in each right triangle.

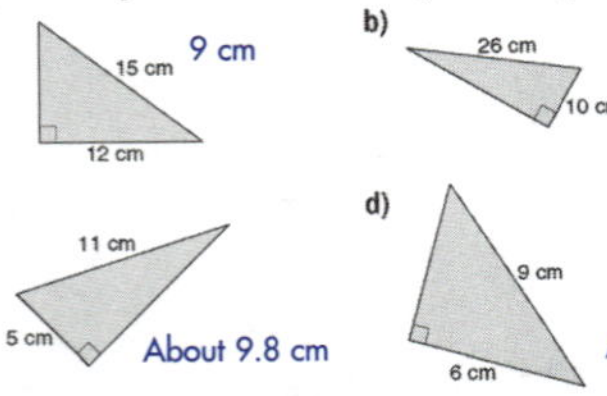

a) 9 cm b) 24 cm c) About 9.8 cm d) About 6.7 cm

4. Find the length of the unmarked side in each right triangle.

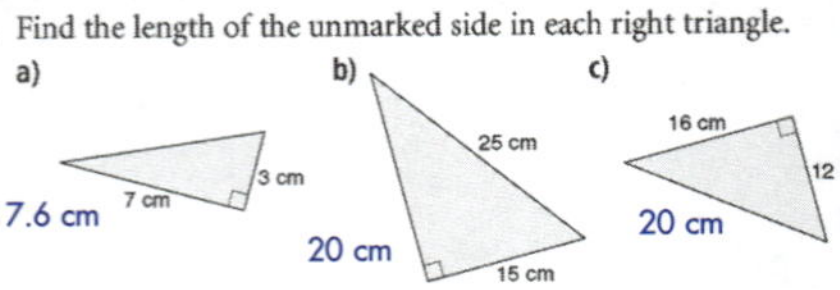

a) About 7.6 cm b) 20 cm c) 20 cm

Math Link

History

"Numbers Rule the Universe!" That was the belief held by a group of mathematicians called the Brotherhood of Pythagoreans. Their power and influence became so strong that fearful politicians forced them to disband. Nevertheless, they continued to meet in secret and teach Pythagoras' ideas.

340 UNIT 8: Square Roots and Pythagoras

Ensure students understand that the Pythagorean relationship applies to all right triangles.

Review the *Examples*. Some students may need to draw squares on the sides of the triangles. Encourage students to do this until they feel comfortable with the relationship and have made a strong visual connection. Remind students that to write a length given in centimetres to the nearest millimetre, round to the nearest tenth.

Practice

Have 1-cm grid paper (PM 20) and calculators available for all questions. In question 5, ensure students understand the meaning of *Pythagorean triple*.

Assessment Focus: Question 7

Students should realize that the square on the hypotenuse has area $(\sqrt{18})^2$, or 18 square units. Students use their knowledge of the Pythagorean relationship to find all possible whole-number areas for the other two squares that have a sum of 18. Students find the square roots of the areas to find the lengths of the legs of each triangle. There are 9 possible triangles. Students' work should include labelled sketches.

Assignment Guidelines

If your students do not have time to complete all the *Practice* questions on pages 339, 340, and 341, these questions provide minimum curriculum coverage:
1, 4, 6, 7, 8, *Reflect*

To assess the 4 Achievement Chart categories listed in the curriculum document, have students complete these *Practice* questions:
Knowledge and Understanding: 4
Application: 6
Communication: 7
Thinking: 8

The 3 whole-number side lengths of a right triangle are called a ...gorean triple.

5. Look at the answers to questions 1 to 4, and at the triangles in *Connect*. Identify the triangles that have all 3 side lengths that are whole numbers.
   a) List the lengths of the legs and the hypotenuse for each of these triangles. Try to arrange the measures to show patterns.
   b) What patterns do you see? Explain the patterns.
   c) Extend the patterns. Explain your strategy.

6. Mei Lin uses a ruler and compass to construct a triangle with side lengths 3 cm, 5 cm, and 7 cm. Before Mei Lin constructs the triangle, how can she tell if the triangle will be a right triangle? Explain.

7. **Assessment Focus**
   The hypotenuse of a right triangle is $\sqrt{18}$ units.
   What are the lengths of the legs of the triangle?
   How many different answers can you find?
   Sketch a triangle for each answer. Explain your strategies.

8. On grid paper, draw a line segment with each length.
   Explain how you did it.
   a) $\sqrt{5}$ b) $\sqrt{10}$ c) $\sqrt{13}$ d) $\sqrt{17}$

Take It Further

9. Use grid paper.
   Draw a right triangle with a hypotenuse with each length.
   a) $\sqrt{20}$ units b) $\sqrt{89}$ units c) $\sqrt{52}$ units

10. a) Sketch a right triangle with side lengths: 3 cm, 4 cm, 5 cm
    b) Imagine that each side is a diameter of a semicircle. Sketch a semicircle on each side.
    c) Calculate the area of each semicircle you drew. What do you notice? Explain.

Reflect

When you know the side lengths of a triangle, how can you tell if it is a right triangle?
Use examples in your explanation.

8.3 The Pythagorean Relationship 341

c)

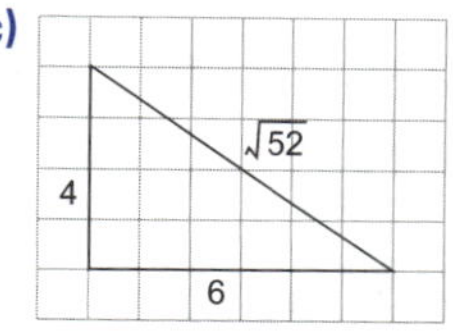

10. a) b)

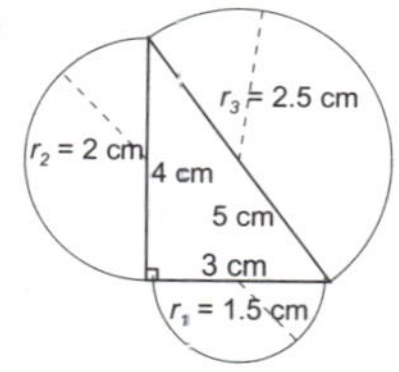

c) The area of a semicircle is: $A = \frac{1}{2}\pi r^2$
The radius of a circle is one-half the diameter.
The sum of the areas of the semicircles on the legs is:

$$A = \frac{1}{2}\pi r_1^2 + \frac{1}{2}\pi r_2^2$$
$$= \frac{1}{2}\pi(1.5)^2 + \frac{1}{2}\pi(2)^2$$
$$\doteq 3.534 + 6.283 = 9.817$$

The area of the semicircle on the hypotenuse is:
$A = \frac{1}{2}\pi r_3^2 = \frac{1}{2}\pi(2.5)^2 \doteq 9.817$
The sum of the areas of the semicircles on the legs of a right triangle is equal to the area of the semicircle on the hypotenuse.

REFLECT: If the triangle is a right triangle, the sum of the areas of the squares on the legs must equal the area of the square on the hypotenuse. Since the hypotenuse is the longest side of a right triangle, I let the greatest length be the hypotenuse.
For example, a triangle has side lengths 2 cm, 3 cm, 6 cm.
$2^2 + 3^2 = 4 + 9 = 13$
$6^2 = 36$
Since $13 \neq 36$, the triangle is not a right triangle.
A triangle has side lengths 5 cm, 12 cm, 13 cm.
$5^2 + 12^2 = 25 + 144 = 169$
$13^2 = 169$
Since 169 = 169, the triangle is a right triangle.

ASSESSMENT FOR LEARNING

What to Look For	What to Do
Knowledge and Understanding ✔ Students understand the relationship among the side lengths of a right triangle. ***Communication*** ✔ Students can explain how to tell if a triangle will be a right triangle, when all side lengths are known. ***Application*** ✔ Students can use the Pythagorean relationship to find the length of any side of a right triangle when the lengths of the other two sides are given.	***Extra Support:*** Students who have difficulty finding the length of a side of a right triangle should continue to draw squares on each side of the triangle. This may be time consuming, but it will allow students to develop a strong visual connection. Students can use Step-by-Step 3 (Master 8.10) to complete question 7. ***Extra Practice:*** Students can complete the Additional Activity, *From Here to There* (Master 8.7). Students can complete Extra Practice 3 (Master 8.20). ***Extension:*** Students can use the Internet to research some of the many proofs of the Pythagorean Theorem.

Recording and Reporting
Master 8.2 Ongoing Observations: Square Roots and Pythagoras

Using *The Geometer's Sketchpad* to Verify the Pythagorean Theorem

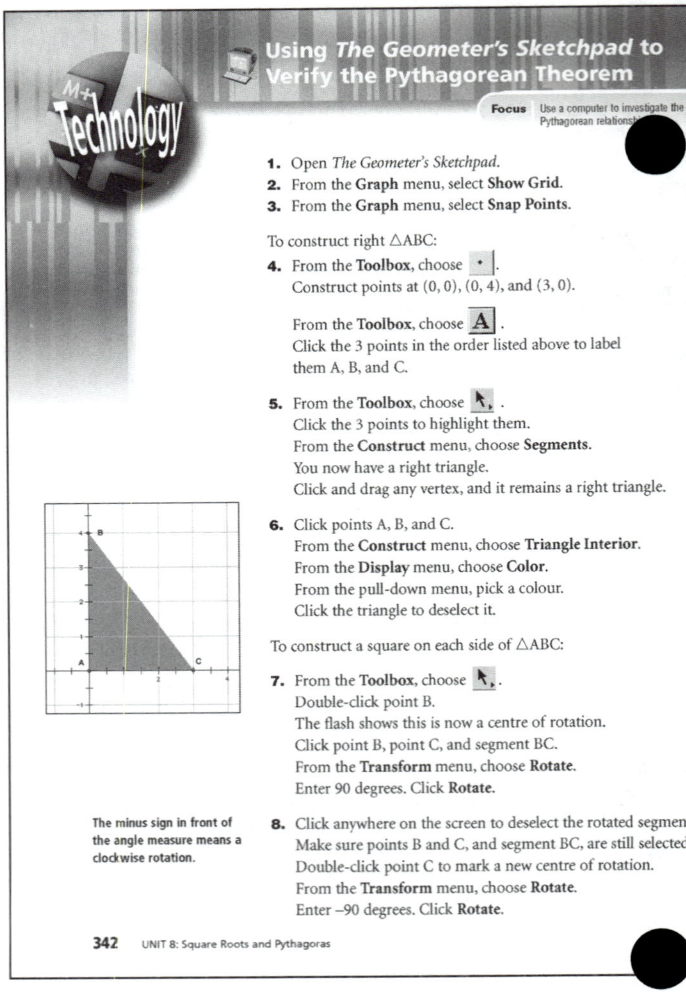

Using *The Geometer's Sketchpad* to Verify the Pythagorean Theorem

Focus Use a computer to investigate the Pythagorean relationship.

1. Open *The Geometer's Sketchpad.*
2. From the **Graph** menu, select **Show Grid.**
3. From the **Graph** menu, select **Snap Points.**

To construct right △ABC:

4. From the **Toolbox,** choose [point tool]. Construct points at (0, 0), (0, 4), and (3, 0).

   From the **Toolbox,** choose **A**. Click the 3 points in the order listed above to label them A, B, and C.

5. From the **Toolbox,** choose [arrow tool]. Click the 3 points to highlight them. From the **Construct** menu, choose **Segments.** You now have a right triangle. Click and drag any vertex, and it remains a right triangle.

6. Click points A, B, and C. From the **Construct** menu, choose **Triangle Interior.** From the **Display** menu, choose **Color.** From the pull-down menu, pick a colour. Click the triangle to deselect it.

To construct a square on each side of △ABC:

7. From the **Toolbox,** choose [arrow tool]. Double-click point B. The flash shows this is now a centre of rotation. Click point B, point C, and segment BC. From the **Transform** menu, choose **Rotate.** Enter 90 degrees. Click **Rotate.**

8. Click anywhere on the screen to deselect the rotated segment. Make sure points B and C, and segment BC, are still selected. Double-click point C to mark a new centre of rotation. From the **Transform** menu, choose **Rotate.** Enter –90 degrees. Click **Rotate.**

The minus sign in front of the angle measure means a clockwise rotation.

342 UNIT 8: Square Roots and Pythagoras

LESSON ORGANIZER 80–100 min

Curriculum Focus: Use a computer to investigate the Pythagorean relationship. (8m49)
- computers with *The Geometer's Sketchpad* software

Assessment: Master 8.2 Ongoing Observations: Square Roots and Pythagoras

Key Math Learning

Computer software can be used to verify the Pythagorean relationship.

Give students time to explore the features of *The Geometer's Sketchpad* before beginning the investigation. Remind students to read the instructions carefully. Ensure students understand the importance of following the steps in order, to ensure accurate results.

What you might see:

13.

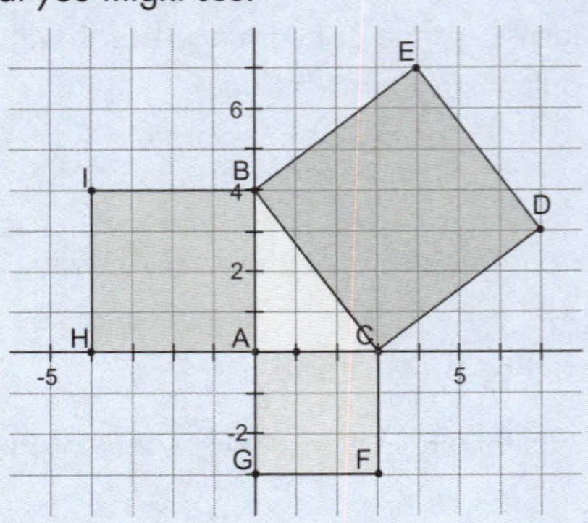

14. The sum of the areas of squares GACF and IBAH is equal to the area of Square BEDC.

Area BEDC = 24.90 cm²
Area GACF = 8.94 cm²
Area IBAH = 15.96 cm²
(Area GACF) + (Area IBAH) = 24.90 cm²

16. When I drag a vertex of the triangle, the measurements change, but the sum of the areas of squares GACF and IBAH always equals the area of Square BEDC.

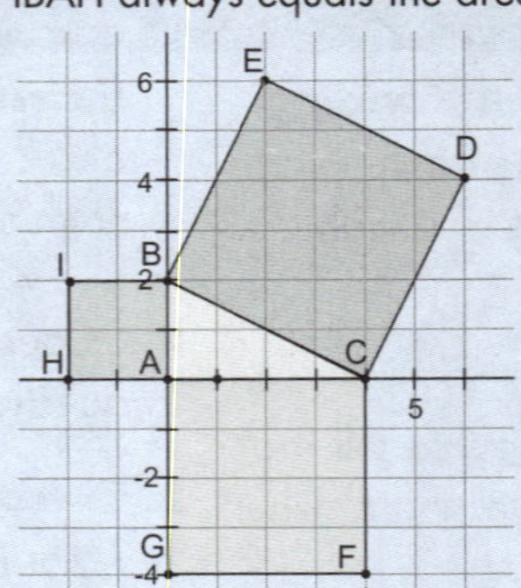

Area BEDC = 20.33 cm²
Area GACF = 16.39 cm²
Area IBAH = 3.94 cm²
(Area GACF) + (Area IBAH) = 20.33 cm²

The Geometer's Sketchpad shows that the sum of the areas of the squares on the legs of a right triangle is equal to the area of the square on the hypotenuse.

17. I repeated the investigation for a non-right triangle. The sum of the areas of squares AHJC and ABFG is not

9. From the **Toolbox**, choose .
Join the points at the ends of the rotated segments to form a square on side BC.

10. From the **Toolbox**, choose **A**.
Double-click one unlabelled vertex of the square. Type D. Click [OK].
Double-click the other unlabelled vertex. Type E. Click [OK].

11. From the **Toolbox**, choose .
Click the vertices of the square. If other points or segments are highlighted, deselect them by clicking them.
From the **Construct** menu, choose **Quadrilateral Interior**.
From the **Display** menu, choose **Color**.
From the pull-down menu, pick a colour.

12. From the **Measure** menu, choose **Area**.
The area of square BDEC appears.

13. Repeat *Steps 7* to *12* to construct and measure a square on each of the other two sides of the triangle.
Decide the direction of rotation for each line segment; it could be 90 degrees or –90 degrees.
Label the vertices F, G, and H, I.

14. Drag a vertex of the triangle and observe what happens to the area measurements.
What relationship is shown?

To use *The Geometer's Sketchpad* calculator:

15. From the **Measure** menu, choose **Calculate**.
Click the area equation for the smallest square.
Click [+].
Click the area equation for the next smallest square.
Click [OK].

16. Drag a vertex of the triangle. How do the measurements change?
How does *The Geometer's Sketchpad* verify the Pythagorean Theorem?

Use *The Geometer's Sketchpad* to investigate "what if" questions.

17. What if the triangle was not a right triangle.
Is the relationship still true?

REACHING ALL LEARNERS

Early Finishers

Have students circulate to help those who do not have strong computer skills.

Common Misconceptions

➤Students have difficulty rotating the segments.

How to Help: Remind students that the squares are to be constructed on the outside of the triangle. If a rotated line segment overlaps the triangle or another square, the rotation was in the wrong direction. Have students use the Edit menu to undo the rotation, then perform the rotation again, this time in the opposite direction (for example, change the sign in front of 90 degrees).

equal to the area of Square BCDE.
The Pythagorean relationship is not true for non-right triangles.

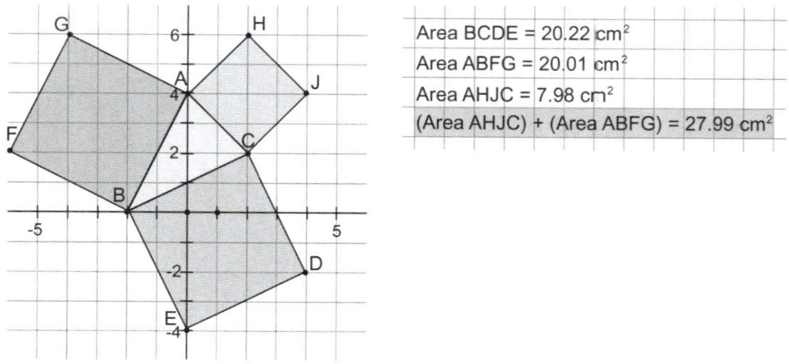

ASSESSMENT FOR LEARNING

What to Look For	What to Do
Knowledge and Understanding ✔ Students can connect the Pythagorean relationship to a pictorial representation.	***Extra Support:*** Pair a student who has good computer skills with a student who needs help.
Application ✔ Students can use the software to verify the Pythagorean Theorem.	***Extra Practice:*** Students repeat the investigation for a right triangle that does not have a vertex at the origin.
Communication ✔ Students can explain how *The Geometer's Sketchpad* verifies the Pythagorean relationship.	***Extension:*** Students use *The Geometer's Sketchpad* to construct an equilateral triangle or regular hexagon on each side of a right triangle. Students calculate the area of each figure they construct, then report on their findings.

Recording and Reporting
Master 8.2 Ongoing Observations: Square Roots and Pythagoras

Communicating Solutions

LESSON ORGANIZER

Student Materials
- calculators

Communicating Solutions

The draft solution to a problem is often messy. To commun solution clearly, the draft solution must be tidy. Communicating means talking, writing, drawing, or modelling to describe, explain, and justify your ideas to others. The draft solution is revised and edited for clear communication. The final solution presents only the steps needed to arrive at the answer. The steps are listed in the correct order.

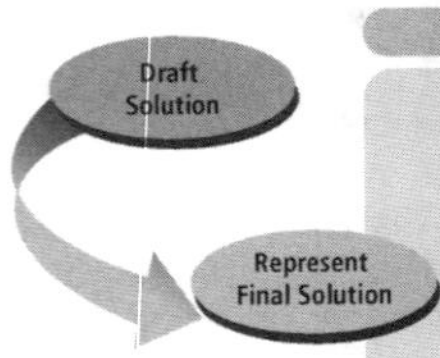

Communicate Solutions – Represent, justify, and prove to others

Revise and edit draft solutions:
1. Show all the math information you used; that is, words, numbers, drawings, tables, graphs, and/or models.
2. Remove any information that you did not use.
3. Arrange the steps in a logical order.
4. Create a concluding statement.
5. Check the criteria to assess your communication.

Here are some criteria for good communication of math solutions:
- The solution is complete. All steps are shown. Other students can follow the steps and come to the same conclusion.
- The steps are in a logical order.
- The calculations are accurate.
- The spelling and grammar are correct.
- The math conventions are correct; for example, units, position o equal sign, labels and scales on graphs/diagrams, symbols, brackets, and so on.
- Where appropriate, more than one possible solution is described
- The strategies are reasonable and are explained.
- Where appropriate, words, numbers, drawings, tables, graphs, and/or models are used to support the solution.
- The concluding statement fits the context and clearly answers the problem.

344 UNIT 8: Square Roots and Pythagoras

Sample Solutions

1. 23 + 25 + 27 occurs 5 times, so I found 5(23 + 25 + 27)
= 5(75) = 375
Each of the numbers 23, 25, and 27 occurs 5 times.
So, I found:
5(23) + 5(25) + 5(27) = 115 + 125 + 135
= 375
I used mental math. For each group of 23 + 25 + 27, I took 2 away from 27, then added 2 to 23 to get 25 + 25 + 25.
There are fifteen 25s.
(10 × 25) + (4 × 25) + 25 = 250 + 100 + 25 = 375

2. **a)** I used a table. I know that order does not count; for example, 1 shaking hands with 2 is the same as 2 shaking hands with 1.
Possible handshakes:

1 with 2	2 with 3	3 with 4	4 with 5	5 with 6
1 with 3	2 with 4	3 with 5	4 with 6	
1 with 4	2 with 5	3 with 6		
1 with 5	2 with 6			
1 with 6				

There are 15 handshakes.

b) I used a table. I know that order does not count; for example, line segment AB is the same as line segment BA.
Possible line segments:

AB	BC	CD	DE	EF
AC	BD	CE	DF	
AD	BE	CF		
AE	BF			
AF				

There are 15 different line segments.

c) I can model both problems in the same way, and both problems have the same number of different possibilities, 15.

3. The area of the large orange square is 20 cm × 20 cm = 400 cm².
The larger purple square is formed by joining the midpoints of the sides of the large orange square.
So, the length of each leg of a large orange triangle is 10 cm. The area of each large orange triangle, in square centimetres, is: $A = \frac{1}{2}bh = \frac{1}{2} \times 10 \times 10 = 50$
The area of the 4 large orange triangles is:
4 × 50 cm² = 200 cm²
So, the area of the largest purple square is:

Reading and Writing in Math

Check

Solve these problems. Share your work with a classmate for feedback and suggestions. Use the criteria as a guide.

1. Find this sum:
   23 + 25 + 27 + 23 + 25 + 27 + 23 +
   25 + 27 + 23 + 25 + 27 + 23 + 25 + 27 = 375
   Explain three different ways to solve this problem.
2. a) Six people met at a party. All of them exchanged handshakes. How many handshakes were there? 15
   b) How many different line segments can be named using the labelled points as end points? List them. 15

   A B C D E F

   c) How are these problems similar?

3. The side length of the largest square is 20 cm.
   a) What is the area of each purple section? 25 cm^2
   b) What is the area of each orange section? 12.5 cm^2
   Explain how you got your answers.
4. There are 400 students at a school. Is the following statement true? Yes
   There will always be at least two students in the school whose birthdays fall on the same day of the year.
   Explain.
5. Camden has a custard recipe that needs 6 eggs, 1 cup of sugar, 750 mL of milk, and 5 mL of vanilla. He has 4 eggs. He adjusts the recipe to use the 4 eggs. How much of each other ingredient will he need? $\frac{2}{3}$ cup sugar, 500 mL milk, and $3\frac{1}{3}$ mL vanilla

6. Lo Choi wants to buy a dozen doughnuts. She has a coupon. This week, the doughnuts are on sale for \$3.99 a dozen. If Lo Choi uses the coupon, each doughnut is \$0.35. Should Lo Choi use the coupon? Explain. No
7. How many times in a 12-h period does the sum of the digits on a digital clock equal 6? 36 times

Reading and Writing in Math: Communicating Solutions 345

$400\ cm^2 - 200\ cm^2 = 200\ cm^2$, or one-half the area of the large orange square
Similarly, the smaller orange square is formed by joining the midpoints of the sides of the larger purple square.
So, the area of the smaller orange square is:
$\frac{1}{2}$ the area of the large purple square,
or $\frac{1}{2} \times 200\ cm^2 = 100\ cm^2$
The area of the 4 purple triangles is:
$200\ cm^2 - 100\ cm^2 = 100\ cm^2$
So, the area of each purple triangle is:
$100\ cm^2 \div 4 = 25\ cm^2$
Similarly, the smaller purple square is formed by joining the midpoints of the sides of the smaller orange square.
So, the area of the smaller purple square is: $\frac{1}{2}$ the area of the smaller orange square,
or $\frac{1}{2} \times 100\ cm^2 = 50\ cm^2$
The area of the 4 small orange triangles is:
$100\ cm^2 - 50\ cm^2 = 50\ cm^2$
So, the area of each small orange triangle is:
$50\ cm^2 \div 4 = 12.5\ cm^2$

4. There are 365 days in one year.
   So, there are 365 possible birthdays.
   So, at least 400 – 365 = 35 students share a birthday with at least one other student in the school. The statement is true.
5. Camden uses $\frac{4}{6}$, or $\frac{2}{3}$ of the eggs needed in the recipe.
   So, Camden will need $\frac{2}{3}$ of each of the other ingredients.
   Sugar: $\frac{2}{3} \times 1$ cup $= \frac{2}{3}$ cup
   Milk: $\frac{2}{3} \times 750$ mL = 500 mL
   Vanilla: $\frac{2}{3} \times 5$ mL $= 3\frac{1}{3}$ mL
   Camden will need $\frac{2}{3}$ cup sugar, 500 mL milk, and $3\frac{1}{3}$ mL vanilla.
6. The cost of a dozen doughnuts with the coupon is:
   12 × \$0.35 = \$4.20
   The doughnuts are on sale for \$3.99 a dozen.
   The sale price is less than the price with a coupon.
   Lo Choi should not use the coupon.
7. The possible digits on a digital clock are 0, 1, 2, 3, 4, 5, 6, 7, 8, 9.
   I do not have to consider any time that has a digit greater than 6.
   When the first two digits are 01, I find all possible combinations for digits 3 and 4 that have a sum of 5.

First two digits	Sum of digits 3 and 4	Possible times
01	5	01:05, 01:14, 01:23, 01:32, 01:41, 01:50
02	4	02:04, 02:13, 02:22, 02:31, 02:40
03	3	03:03, 03:12, 03:21, 03:30
04	2	04:02, 04:11, 04:20
05	1	05:01, 05:10
06	0	06:00
10	5	10:05, 10:14, 10:23, 10:32, 10:41, 10:50
11	4	11:04, 11:13, 11:22, 11:31, 11:40
12	3	12:03, 12:12, 12:21, 12:30

The number of times in a 12-h period that the sum of the digits on a digital clock equals 6 is:
6 + 5 + 4 + 3 + 2 + 1 + 6 + 5 + 4 = 36

Applying the Pythagorean Theorem

LESSON ORGANIZER 80–100 min

Curriculum Focus: Solve problems using the Pythagorean Theorem. (8m16, 8m45, 8m50, 8m59, 8m62)

Student Materials
- calculators
- 1-cm grid paper (PM 20)

Optional
- Step-by-Step 4 (Master 8.11)
- Extra Practice 4 (Master 8.21)

Assessment: Master 8.2 Ongoing Observations: Square Roots and Pythagoras

Key Math Learnings

1. The Pythagorean Theorem can be described by the algebraic equation $c^2 = a^2 + b^2$, where c is the length of the hypotenuse, and a and b are the lengths of the legs.
2. The Pythagorean Theorem can be used to solve problems that involve right triangles.

Calculator Skills

Students should recall that $30^2 = 30 \times 30 = 900$. Students could use guess and check on a calculator, starting with 31. Students multiply each number by itself until they get the product 1089.

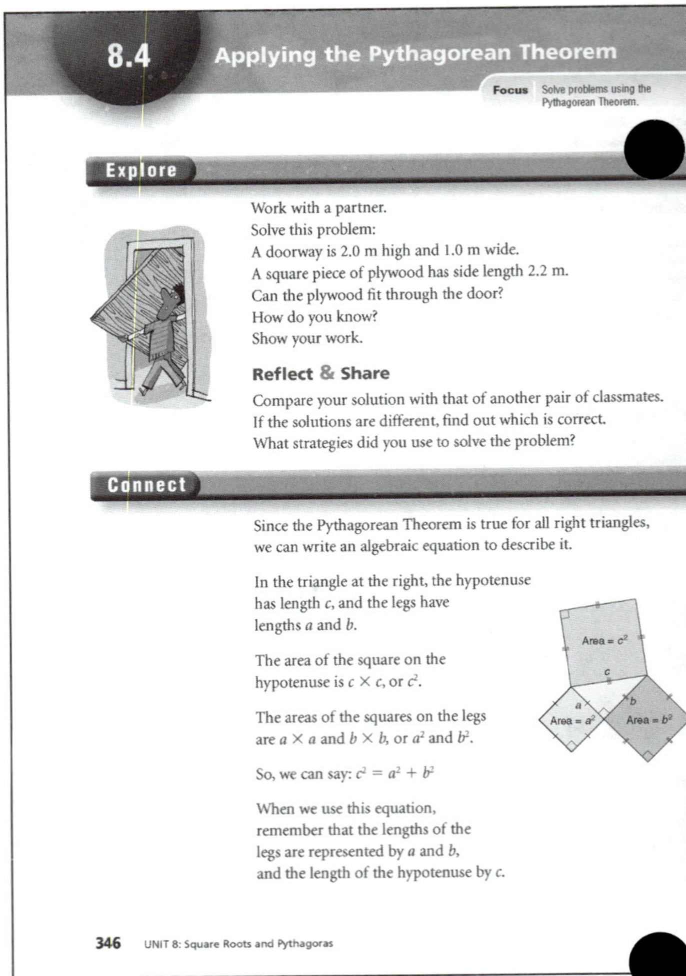
8.4 Applying the Pythagorean Theorem

Focus Solve problems using the Pythagorean Theorem.

Explore

Work with a partner.
Solve this problem:
A doorway is 2.0 m high and 1.0 m wide.
A square piece of plywood has side length 2.2 m.
Can the plywood fit through the door?
How do you know?
Show your work.

Reflect & Share

Compare your solution with that of another pair of classmates.
If the solutions are different, find out which is correct.
What strategies did you use to solve the problem?

Connect

Since the Pythagorean Theorem is true for all right triangles, we can write an algebraic equation to describe it.

In the triangle at the right, the hypotenuse has length c, and the legs have lengths a and b.

The area of the square on the hypotenuse is $c \times c$, or c^2.

The areas of the squares on the legs are $a \times a$ and $b \times b$, or a^2 and b^2.

So, we can say: $c^2 = a^2 + b^2$

When we use this equation, remember that the lengths of the legs are represented by a and b, and the length of the hypotenuse by c.

346 UNIT 8: Square Roots and Pythagoras

BEFORE Get Started

Invite students to recall the Pythagorean relationship. Draw a right triangle on the board with the legs and hypotenuse labelled. Remind students that the sum of the areas on the legs of a right triangle is equal to the area of the square on the hypotenuse.

Tell students that the Pythagorean Theorem is an important and useful mathematical tool. It can be used to solve many problems that involve right triangles.

Present *Explore*. Discuss with students how they might deal with the thickness of the plywood. Encourage students to represent the problem with a diagram.

DURING Explore

Ongoing Assessment: Observe and Listen

As students work, ask questions, such as:

- What assumptions did you make?
  (I assumed the doorframe had 4 right angles.)
- How did you begin to solve the problem?
  (I drew a rectangle to represent the doorway, then marked the right angles. I drew a diagonal of the rectangle to represent the plywood. I could see that I had constructed a right triangle.)
- What are the lengths of the legs of the right triangle?
  (2.0 m and 1.0 m)
- How can you find out if the plywood will fit through the door?
  (I can use the Pythagorean relationship to find the length of the hypotenuse of the triangle. If the length of the hypotenuse is greater than 2.2 m, the side length of the plywood, the plywood will fit through the door.)

Example 1

Find the length of each side labelled with a variable.
Give the lengths to the nearest millimetre.

a) 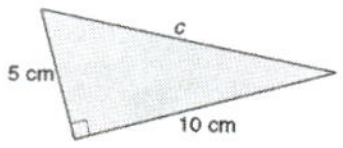

b) 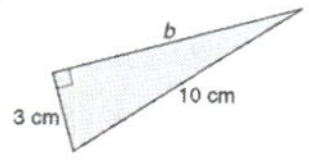

Solution

Use the Pythagorean Theorem: $c^2 = a^2 + b^2$

a) Substitute: $a = 5$ and $b = 10$
$c^2 = 5^2 + 10^2$
Square, then add.
$c^2 = 25 + 100$
$c^2 = 125$
The area of the square with side length c is 125.
So, $c = \sqrt{125}$
$c \doteq 11.180\ 34$
c is approximately 11.2 cm.

Use a calculator to calculate each square root.

b) Substitute: $a = 3$ and $c = 10$
$10^2 = 3^2 + b^2$
Square, then add.
$100 = 9 + b^2$
Subtract 9 from each side to isolate b^2.
$100 - 9 = 9 + b^2 - 9$
$91 = b^2$
The area of the square with side length b is 91.
So, $b = \sqrt{91}$
$b \doteq 9.539\ 39$
b is approximately 9.5 cm.

We can use the Pythagorean Theorem to solve problems that involve right triangles.

Example 2

A ramp has horizontal length 120 cm and sloping length 130 cm.
How high is the ramp?

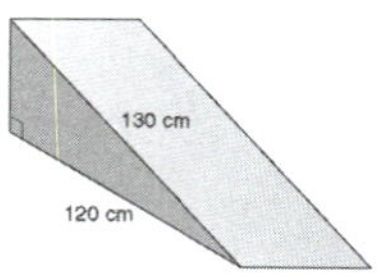

Solution

The height of the ramp is vertical, so the front face of the ramp is a right triangle.
The hypotenuse is 130 cm.

8.4 Applying the Pythagorean Theorem **347**

REACHING ALL LEARNERS

Early Finishers

In *Practice* question 9, have students find other pairs of points that are the same distance apart; for example, GF and CD, or GF and JB.

Common Misconceptions

➤Students add the lengths of the legs, then square the sum to find the square of the hypotenuse.

How to Help: Use numbers to show students that $a^2 + b^2 \neq (a + b)^2$.
For example, let $a = 3$ and $b = 4$.

$a^2 + b^2 = 3^2 + 4^2 = 9 + 16 = 25$

$(a + b)^2 = (3 + 4)^2 = 7^2 = 49$

Stress that students should square each number first, then add the squares.

Assignment Guidelines

If your students do not have time to complete all the *Practice* questions on pages 348, 349, and 350, these questions provide minimum curriculum coverage: 3, 4, 5, 8, 9, *Reflect*

To assess the 4 Achievement Chart categories listed in the curriculum document, have students complete these *Practice* questions:
Knowledge and Understanding: 3
Application: 8
Thinking: 9
Communication: *Reflect*

- How did you find the length of the hypotenuse?
  (*I drew the triangle on grid paper. I let 1 cm equal 1 m. I drew a square on each side of the triangle, then counted squares to find the areas of the squares on the legs: 1 m² and 4 m². I calculated the sum of these areas to find the area of the square on the hypotenuse: 1 m² + 4 m² = 5 m². To find the length of the hypotenuse, I used a calculator to find the square root of the area of the square on the hypotenuse: $\sqrt{5} \doteq 2.236$. The length of the hypotenuse is about 2.236 m. The plywood can fit through the door.*)
- How did you consider the thickness of the plywood?
  (*I wrote the lengths of the hypotenuse and the piece of plywood in centimetres: 200 cm and 223.6 cm. I subtracted to find how much leeway there was: 223.6 cm – 200 cm = 3.6 cm. I know that plywood is much less than 3.6 cm thick. So, the plywood can fit through the door.*)

AFTER — Connect

Have students share their solutions with the class. Look for specific references to the Pythagorean Theorem.

What you might see:

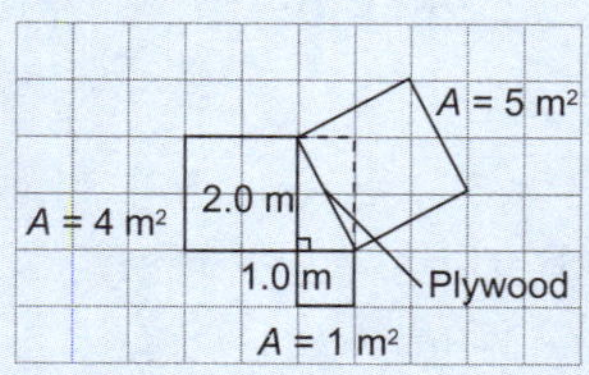

Review *Connect*.

Ensure students understand that the algebraic equation represents the same relationship discovered in Lesson 8.3. An equation is mathematical shorthand that shows the equal relationship between two expressions. This equation is a translation of the words previously used to describe the Pythagorean relationship.

Sample Solutions

5. b) There are two answers because we don't know whether the given side lengths are the lengths of the legs of the triangle, or the lengths of one leg and the hypotenuse.

6. a) The area of the square on the hypotenuse is 4.

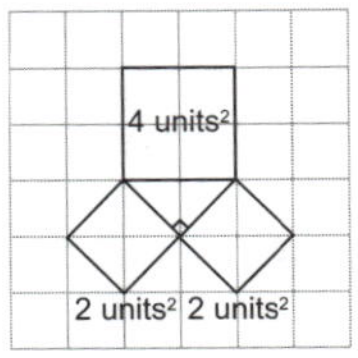

The areas of the squares on the legs are 2 and 2.

$4 = 2 + 2$

The area of the square on the hypotenuse is equal to the sum of the areas of the squares on the legs.

b) The length of the hypotenuse is:

$c^2 = 3^2 + 1^2$
$= 9 + 1$
$= 10$
$c = \sqrt{10}$

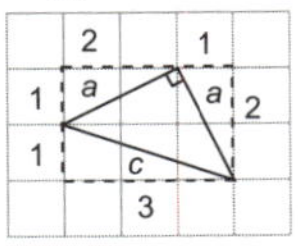

The length of each leg is: $a^2 = 2^2 + 1^2$
$= 5$
$a = \sqrt{5}$

$(\sqrt{10})^2 = (\sqrt{5})^2 + (\sqrt{5})^2$
$10 = 5 + 5$
$10 = 10$

The square of the length of the hypotenuse is equal to the sum of the squares of the lengths of the legs.

9. I copied the grid on 1-cm grid paper. I drew a right triangle with hypotenuse AB.

The length of AB is: $AB^2 = 4^2 + 3^2$

One leg is 120 cm.
The other leg is the height. Label it *a*.

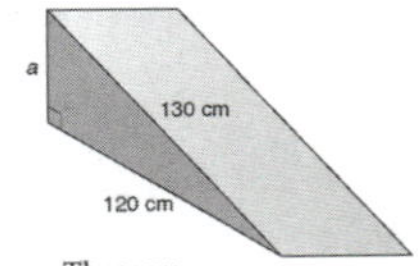

Use the Pythagorean Theorem.

$c^2 = a^2 + b^2$

Substitute: $c = 130$ and $b = 120$

$130^2 = a^2 + 120^2$ Use a calculator.

$16\,900 = a^2 + 14\,400$

Subtract 14 400 from each side to isolate a^2.

$16\,900 - 14\,400 = a^2 + 14\,400 - 14\,400$

$2500 = a^2$

The area of the square with side length *a* is 2500.

$a = \sqrt{2500}$
$= 50$

The ramp is 50 cm high.

Practice

Calculator Skills

Suppose your calculator does not have a $\sqrt{\ }$ key.
How can you find $\sqrt{1089}$?
33

1. Find the length of each hypotenuse labelled with a variable.

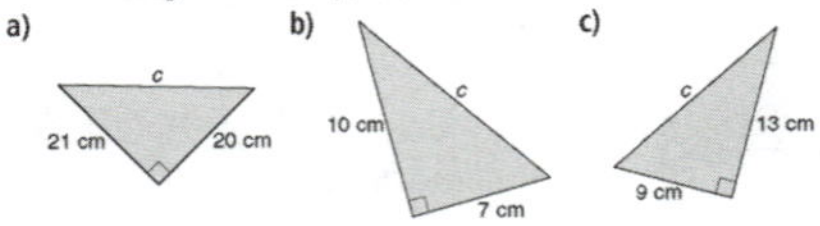

a) $c = 29$ cm b) $c \doteq 12.2$ cm c) $c \doteq 15.8$ cm

2. Find the length of each leg labelled with a variable.

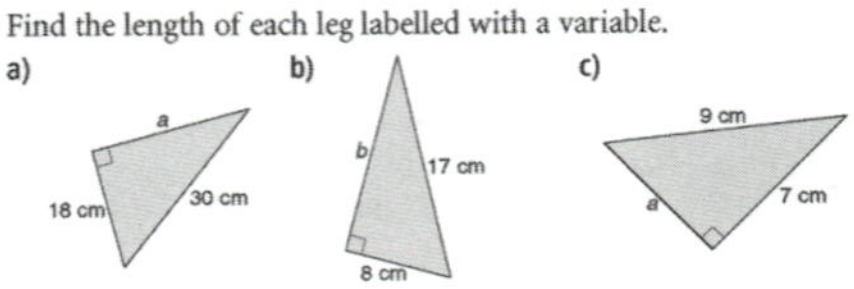

a) $a = 24$ cm b) $b = 15$ cm c) $a \doteq 5.7$ cm

Encourage students to use the variables *a, b,* and *c*. It is not wrong to use other variables, but students must remember to modify the equation accordingly. In Lesson 8.3, we labelled the length of the hypotenuse with the variable *h*. If students have grown accustomed to this, remind them that the equation then becomes $h^2 = a^2 + b^2$.

Example 1 covers the two possible scenarios that students will encounter when working with the Pythagorean Theorem:

- the length of the hypotenuse is unknown, and the lengths of the two legs are given
- the length of a leg is unknown, and the lengths of a leg and the hypotenuse are given

Remind students that to give a length in centimetres to the nearest millimetre, they round to the nearest tenth.

Review *Example 2*. Point out the small square that indicates a right angle. Have students use a protractor to measure this angle.

Ask:

- Does the angle marked as a right angle measure 90°? (*No*) What does it measure? (*120°*)
- Why is the angle marked as a right angle? (*The ramp is drawn in perspective, and because of the angle of view, the right angle looks larger than it actually is.*)

Tell students that the key to solving a problem using the Pythagorean relationship is recognizing the right triangle.

3. Find the length of each side labelled with a variable.

a) 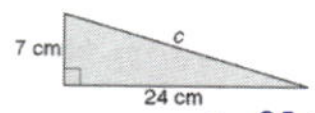

$c = 25$ cm

b) 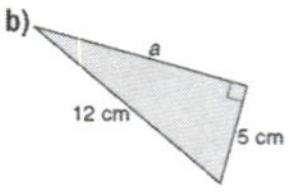

$a \doteq 10.9$ cm

c) 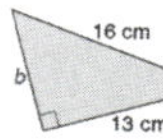

$b \doteq 9.3$ cm

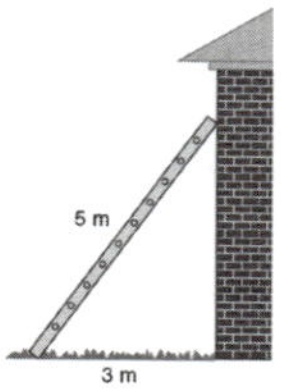

4. A 5-m ladder is leaning against a house. It is 3 m from the base of the wall. How high does the ladder reach? 4 m

5. Brandon constructed a right triangle with sides 10 cm and 24 cm.
a) How long is the third side? 26 cm or about 21.8 cm
b) Why are there two answers to part a?

6. Copy each diagram on grid paper. Explain how each diagram illustrates the Pythagorean Theorem.

a) 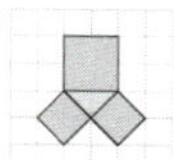

b) 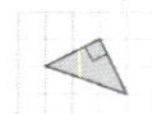

7. Alyssa has made a picture frame. The frame is 60 cm long and 25 cm wide. To check that the frame has square corners, Alyssa measures a diagonal. How long should the diagonal be? 65 cm Sketch a diagram to illustrate your answer.

8. The size of a TV set is described by the length of a diagonal of the screen. One TV is labelled as size 70 cm. The screen is 40 cm high. What is the width of the screen? Draw a diagram to illustrate your answer.

About 57.4 cm

$= 16 + 9$
$= 25$
$AB = \sqrt{25}$
$= 5$

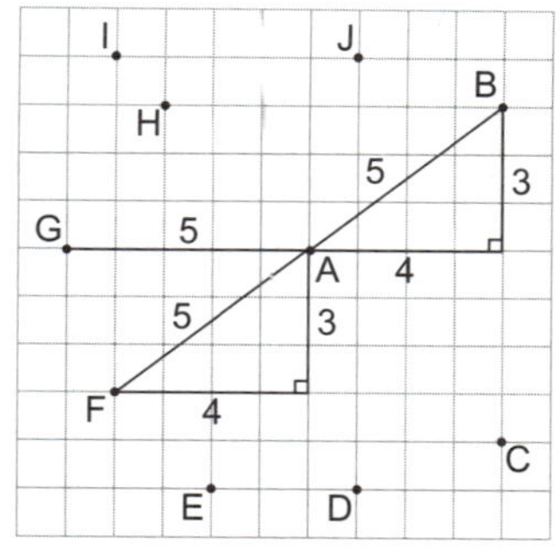

I drew a right triangle with hypotenuse AF. I notice that the legs of the triangle have lengths 4 and 3. So, the length of AF equals the length of AB, because the legs of the triangles have the same lengths. So, the distance from A to B is the same as the distance from A to F.

Point G is also 5 units from point A because it is 5 grid squares to the left of point A.

11. Use the Pythagorean Theorem to find h.

$45^2 = 27^2 + h^2$
$2025 = 729 + h^2$
$1296 = h^2$
$h = \sqrt{1296}$
$= 36$

The height of the kite above the ground is:
36 m + the height of the person flying it
= 36 m + 1.3 m
= 37.3 m

12. The base of the prism has sides of length 12 cm and 9 cm. The diagonal of the base, l, has length: $l^2 = 12^2 + 9^2 = 225$

$l = \sqrt{225} = 15$

Practice

Have calculators available for all questions. Encourage students to include diagrams to illustrate their answers whenever possible. In question 5, encourage students to use straws to construct the two possible triangles. This will help the kinesthetic learner. Students who choose to do this will need a ruler, straws, scissors, and a protractor. In question 9, students may benefit from copying the grid on 1-cm grid paper, then drawing right triangles to find the necessary distances. In question 13, remind students that distance = speed × time.

Assessment Focus: Question 9

Students may copy the grid on 1-cm grid paper. Students draw a right triangle with segment AB as its hypotenuse. Students use the Pythagorean relationship to find the length of AB. Students then join A to another point, and draw a right triangle with this segment as its hypotenuse. Students find the length of the hypotenuse. Students continue to do this until they find a hypotenuse equal to the length of AB. Some students may connect A to each of the other points, while stronger math students may look for right triangles with legs of lengths 3 units and 4 units. Some students may not see that G is 5 units from A because it does not involve the Pythagorean Theorem.

Use this as a leg of a right triangle with hypotenuse d.

$d^2 = 15^2 + 8^2 = 289$

$d = \sqrt{289} = 17$

The length of the diagonal of the rectangular prism is 17 cm.

13. After 3 h, the northbound car has travelled 240 km, and the eastbound car has travelled 165 km.
Use these distances as the legs of a right triangle.
Let the distance between the two cars be the hypotenuse, c.
Use the Pythagorean Theorem.

$c^2 = 240^2 + 165^2 = 84\ 825$

$c = \sqrt{84\ 825} \doteq 291.2$

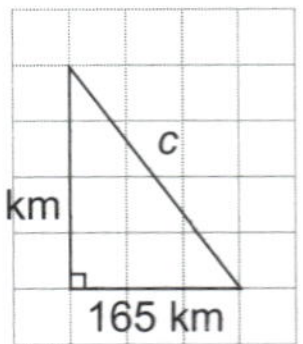

REFLECT: The Pythagorean Theorem can be used to solve problems that can be represented by a right triangle, when the lengths of two sides of the triangle are known.
For example:
A ladder reaches a distance of 10 m up a wall. The ladder is 11 m long. How far is the ladder from the base of the wall?
I draw a right triangle to model the problem.

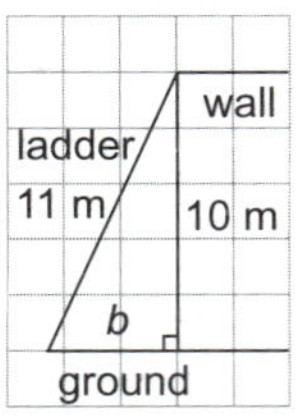

Use the Pythagorean Theorem.

$11^2 = 10^2 + b^2$

$121 = 100 + b^2$

$21 = b^2$

$b = \sqrt{21}$

$\doteq 4.6$

The ladder is about 4.6 m from the base of the wall.

---

9. Assessment Focus
Look at the grid.
Without measuring, find another point that is the same distance from A as B is.
Explain your strategy.
Show your work.
Point G and Point F

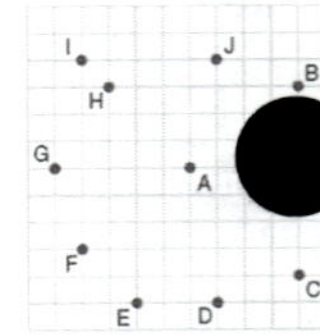

10. Joanna usually uses the sidewalk when she walks home from school. Today she is late, and so cuts through the field. How much shorter is Joanna's shortcut? About 216.9 m

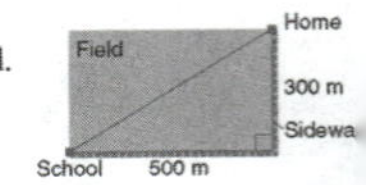

Take It Further

11. How high is the kite above the ground? 37.3 m

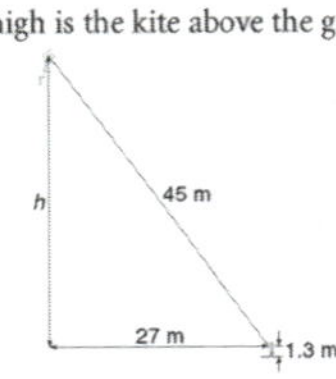

12. What is the length of the diagonal in this rectangular prism? 17 cm

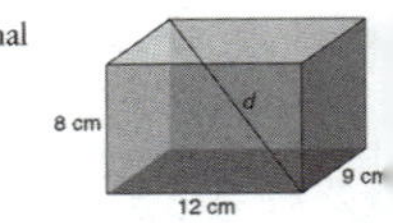

13. Two cars meet at an intersection.
One travels north at an average speed of 80 km/h.
The other travels east at an average speed of 55 km/h.
How far apart are the cars after 3 h? About 291.2 km

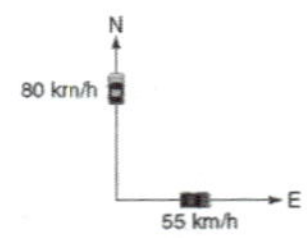

Reflect

When can you use the Pythagorean Theorem to solve a problem? Use examples in your explanation.

350 UNIT 8: Square Roots and Pythagoras

ASSESSMENT FOR LEARNING

What to Look For	What to Do
Knowledge and Understanding ✔ Students can interpret the algebraic equation that describes the Pythagorean relationship. ***Communication*** ✔ Students can present organized solutions, including well-labelled diagrams. ***Application*** ✔ Students can apply the equation to find the length of a side of a right triangle, given the lengths of the other two sides.	***Extra Support:*** Students who have difficulty using the algebraic equation should continue to draw a square on each side of the triangle, then find the area of each square. Students relate the steps in their solution to the algebraic equation, to develop a visual connection. Students can use Step-by-Step 4 (Master 8.11) to complete question 9. ***Extra Practice:*** Students can use the algebraic equation to check their answers to Lesson 8.3 *Practice* questions 2, 3, and 4. Students can complete Extra Practice 4 (Master 8.21). ***Extension:*** Have students measure the dimensions of any television screen at home, then check that the Pythagorean Theorem applies.

Recording and Reporting
Master 8.2 Ongoing Observations: Square Roots and Pythagoras

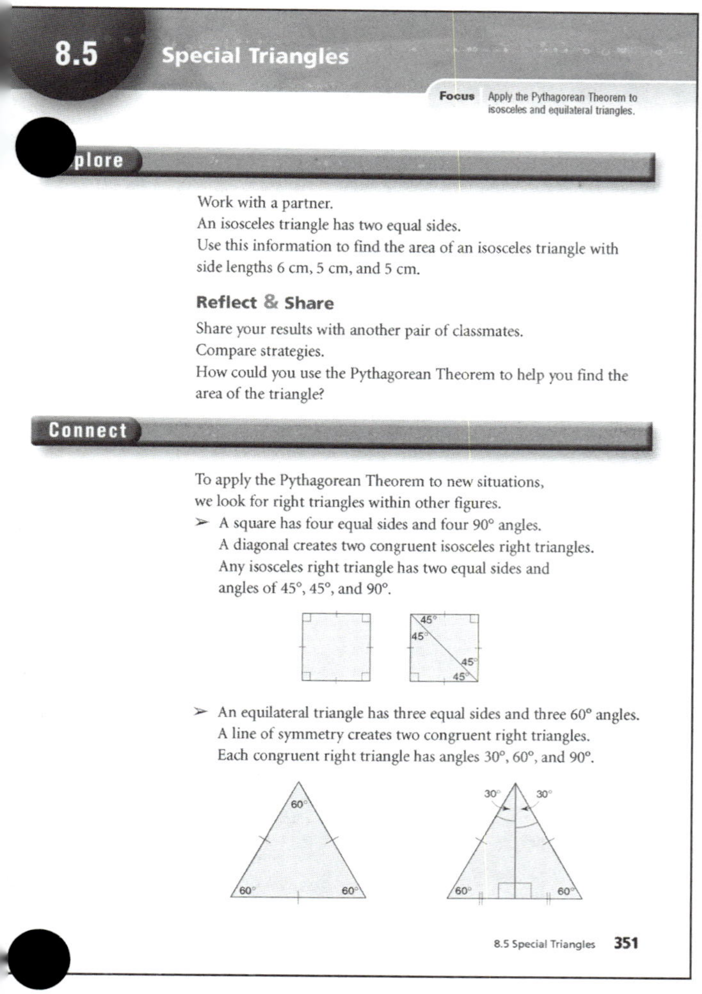

8.5 Special Triangles

Focus Apply the Pythagorean Theorem to isosceles and equilateral triangles.

Explore

Work with a partner.
An isosceles triangle has two equal sides.
Use this information to find the area of an isosceles triangle with side lengths 6 cm, 5 cm, and 5 cm.

Reflect & Share

Share your results with another pair of classmates.
Compare strategies.
How could you use the Pythagorean Theorem to help you find the area of the triangle?

Connect

To apply the Pythagorean Theorem to new situations, we look for right triangles within other figures.

➢ A square has four equal sides and four 90° angles.
A diagonal creates two congruent isosceles right triangles.
Any isosceles right triangle has two equal sides and angles of 45°, 45°, and 90°.

➢ An equilateral triangle has three equal sides and three 60° angles.
A line of symmetry creates two congruent right triangles.
Each congruent right triangle has angles 30°, 60°, and 90°.

8.5 Special Triangles 351

Special Triangles

LESSON ORGANIZER

80–100 min

Curriculum Focus: Apply the Pythagorean Theorem to isosceles and equilateral triangles. (8m16, 8m50, 8m62)

Student Materials
- calculators
- protractors
- 1-cm grid paper (PM 20)

Optional
- Step-by-Step 5 (Master 8.12)
- Extra Practice 5 (Master 8.22)

Assessment: Master 8.2 Ongoing Observations: Square Roots and Pythagoras

Key Math Learning

The Pythagorean Theorem can be used to solve problems that involve isosceles and equilateral triangles.

Assignment Guidelines

If your students do not have time to complete all the *Practice* questions on pages 353 and 354, these questions provide minimum curriculum coverage: 2, 3, 4, 5, *Reflect*

To assess the 4 Achievement Chart categories listed in the curriculum document, have students complete these *Practice* questions:
Knowledge and Understanding: 2
Application: 4
Thinking: 5
Communication: *Reflect*

BEFORE Get Started

Draw a right triangle and an isosceles triangle on the board. Ask:

- What is a right triangle? (*A right triangle has one right angle.*) What is an isosceles triangle? (*An isosceles triangle has two equal sides and two equal angles, and it is only in a special case that one of the angles is 90°.*)
- What is an isosceles acute triangle? (*A triangle with two equal sides and all angles less than 90°*)
- What is an isosceles obtuse triangle? (*A triangle with two equal sides and one angle greater than 90°*)
- What is an isosceles right triangle? (*A triangle with two equal sides and a 90° angle*)
- What else do all isosceles triangle have in common? (*They have one line of symmetry.*)

Have a volunteer draw an example of each type of isosceles triangle on the board.

Present *Explore*. Remind students of the formula for the area of a triangle: $A = \frac{1}{2}bh$

DURING Explore

Ongoing Assessment: Observe and Listen

As students work, ask questions, such as:

- What is the length of the base of the triangle? (*6 cm*)
- What is the angle between the base and height of a triangle? (*The base and height of a triangle intersect at an angle of 90°.*)
- How did you start to solve the problem? (*I drew the line of symmetry. I know that the line of symmetry is the height of the triangle, and the height and the base meet at right angles.*)
- What did you notice? (*I noticed that I made two congruent right triangles.*)
- How did you find the height of the triangle? (*I let the height of the right triangle be a centimetres. The length of the other leg of the*

REACHING ALL LEARNERS

Early Finishers

In *Practice* question 5, have students find the areas of Figures A, B, C, D, E, and G, and the perimeters of Figures A, C, F, and G.

Common Misconceptions

➤ Students use the dimensions of the base of the equilateral or isosceles triangle as the dimensions of the base of the right triangle.

How to Help: Draw an isosceles triangle on the board with side lengths 13 cm, 13 cm, and 10 cm.

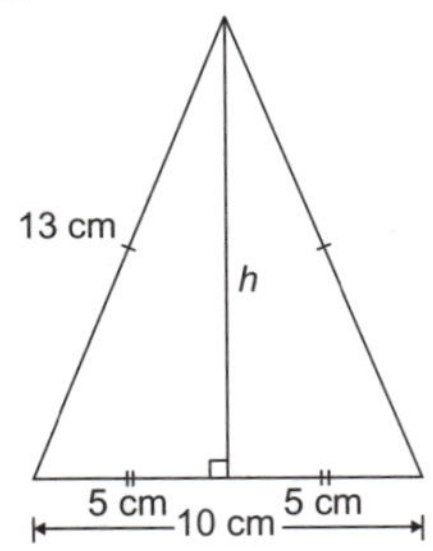

Draw the line of symmetry, or height, of the triangle. Show students that the line of symmetry bisects the base of the triangle and creates two congruent right triangles. Each right triangle has base 5 cm, because 10 cm ÷ 2 = 5 cm. When applying the Pythagorean Theorem to the right triangle to find the height, the base of the right triangle (5 cm) is used. Repeat using an equilateral triangle, if necessary.

Number Strategies

Students should recall the formula for the area of a rectangle ($A = lw$), the formula for the area of a circle ($A = \pi r^2$), and the formula for the circumference of a circle ($C = 2\pi r$).
Remind students that since π is involved in the calculations, the answer will not be exact.

We can use the area of an equilateral triangle to find the surface area and volume of a hexagonal prism when the base is a regular hexagon.

Example

The base of a prism is a regular hexagon with side length 8 cm.
The length of the prism is 12 cm.

a) Find the area of the hexagonal base.
b) Find the volume of the prism.
c) Find the surface area of the prism.

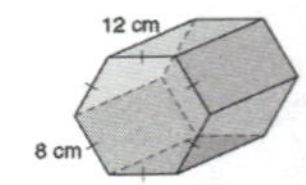

Solution

a) The diagonals through the centre of a regular hexagon divide it into 6 congruent equilateral triangles.
One of these triangles is $\triangle ABC$.
Draw the perpendicular from A to BC at D.
AD bisects BC, so: BD = DC = 4 cm
Label h, the height of $\triangle ABC$.

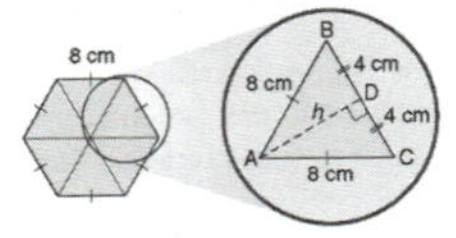

Use the Pythagorean Theorem in $\triangle ABD$.
$c^2 = a^2 + b^2$
Substitute: $c = 8$, $a = 4$, $b = h$
$8^2 = 4^2 + h^2$
$64 = 16 + h^2$
$64 - 16 = 16 + h^2 - 16$
$48 = h^2$
So, $h = \sqrt{48}$
The height of $\triangle ABD$ is $\sqrt{48}$ cm.
The base of the triangle is 8 cm.
So, the area of $\triangle ABC = \frac{1}{2} \times 8 \times \sqrt{48}$

There are 6 congruent triangles.

And, the area of the hexagon $= 6 \times \frac{1}{2} \times 8 \times \sqrt{48}$
$= 24 \times \sqrt{48}$ Use a calculator.
$\doteq 166.28$
The area of the hexagonal base is approximately 166 cm².

triangle is 6 cm ÷ 2 = 3 cm, and the length of the hypotenuse is 5 cm. I used the Pythagorean Theorem: $c^2 = a^2 + b^2$. So, $5^2 = 3^2 + a^2 \Rightarrow 25 = 9 + a^2 \Rightarrow 16 = a^2 \Rightarrow a = \sqrt{16} \Rightarrow a = 4$. The height of the right triangle is 4 cm.)

- How did you find the area of the isosceles triangle? (*I substituted b = 6 and h = 4 into the formula $A = \frac{1}{2}bh$: $A = \frac{1}{2} \times 6 \times 4 = 12$. The area of the triangle is 12 cm².*)

AFTER Connect

Have students share their results and strategies with the class. Look for specific references to the Pythagorean Theorem.

What you might see:

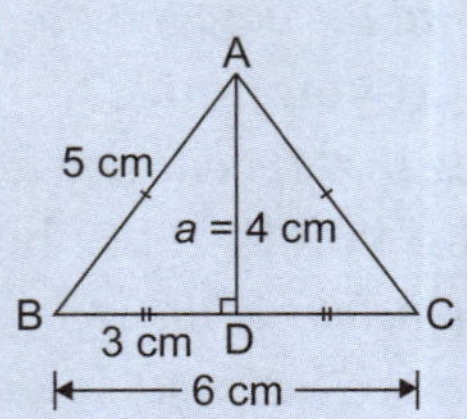

Review *Connect.*

In the *Example,* students may have difficulty understanding why the triangles are equilateral triangles. Explain that each diagonal shown is a line of symmetry of the hexagon. Each line of symmetry divides the hexagon into 2 equal parts. So, the 3 lines of symmetry shown produce 6 congruent triangles. Explain that the sum of the measures of the angles at the centre of the hexagon is 360°. Since there are 6 equal angles, each angle is 360° ÷ 6 = 60°. Since the two remaining angles in each triangle are equal, each angle must be 60°. So, the triangles are equilateral triangles with side length 8 cm.

Ensure students understand they should calculate an approximate square root only when an answer is required. When performing other calculations with the square root, students should use the exact value. For example, in *Example* part a, we calculate $\sqrt{48}$ to

b) The volume of the prism is: V = base area × length
Use the exact value of the base area: $24 \times \sqrt{48}$
The length of the prism is 12 cm.

So, $V = 24 \times \sqrt{48} \times 12$ Use a calculator.
$\doteq 1995.32$
The volume of the prism is approximately 1995 cm³.

c) The surface area A of the prism is the sum of the areas of the 6 rectangular faces and the two bases.
The rectangular faces are congruent.
So, $A = 6 \times (8 \times 12) + 2 \times (24 \times \sqrt{48})$
$\doteq 576 + 332.55$
$= 908.55$
The surface area of the prism is approximately 909 cm².

Practice

1. Find each length indicated.
Sketch and label the triangle first.

2. Find each length indicated.
Sketch and label the triangle first.

3. Find the area of each triangle.

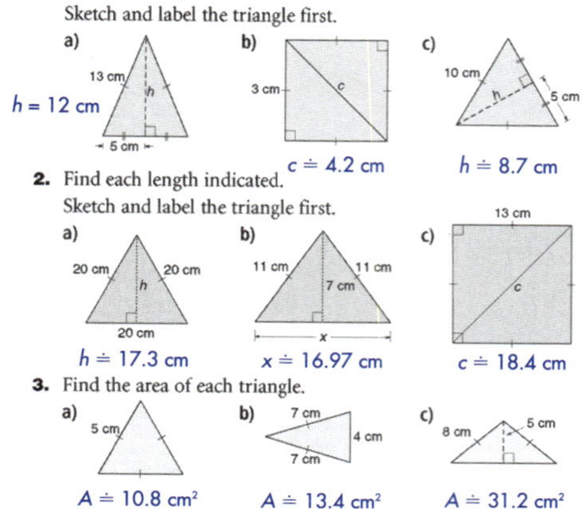

8.5 Special Triangles 353

Sample Solutions

5. a) I drew a horizontal diagonal through Figure F, creating two congruent right triangles.

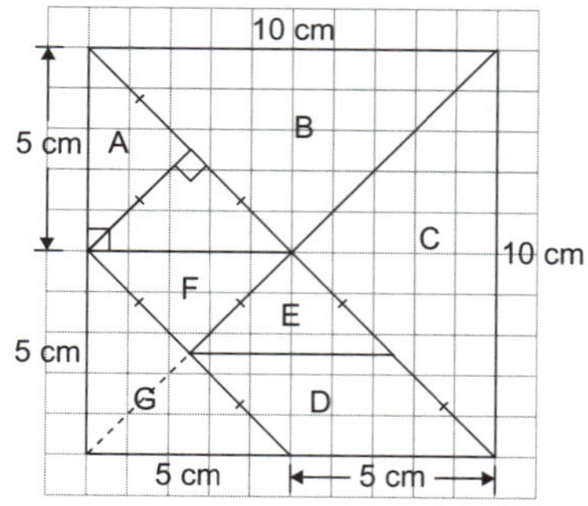

Figure A and one-half of Figure F form an isosceles right triangle. I found the area of this triangle:
$A = \frac{1}{2}bh$
$= \frac{1}{2} \times 5 \times 5 = 12.5$
I know the line of symmetry of this figure divides the triangle into two congruent, smaller right triangles.
So, the area of the right isosceles triangle I formed equals the area of Figure F.
The area of Figure F is 12.5 cm².
The side length of Figure F is the square root of its area, or $\sqrt{12.5}$ cm.

b) Figure B is an isosceles triangle. Its base is 10 cm. The length of each congruent side is 2 × side length of Figure F $= 2 \times \sqrt{12.5}$ cm.
So, the perimeter of Figure B
$= (2 \times \sqrt{12.5}\text{ cm}) + (2 \times \sqrt{12.5}\text{ cm}) + 10\text{ cm}$
$\doteq 24.14$ cm

c) The horizontal sides of Figure D have length 5 cm.
The diagonal of the tangram divides Figure G into 2 congruent triangles, each with a base equal to the side length of Figure F. So, the other pair of parallel sides in

find the area of the hexagonal base. In part b, we use the exact value of the base area in the formula for the volume of the prism. We calculate the square root at the end of the solution when an answer is required.
Show students how using the approximate base area affects the volume calculation.
V = base area × length
$\doteq 166 \times 12$
$= 1992$
The volume of the prism is approximately 1992 cm³.

By using the approximate base area, the volume is less accurate. It is 3 cm³ less than the volume obtained using the exact value of the base area.

Practice

Have calculators available for all questions. In questions 4 and 6, students need to know the formulas for the surface area and volume of a prism:
V = base area × height and
SA = the sum of the areas of the rectangular faces and the two bases.
In question 5, encourage students to copy the tangram on 1-cm grid paper (PM 20).

Assessment Focus: Question 5

Students should copy the tangram on 1-cm grid paper. Students could count squares or use the Pythagorean Theorem to find the area of Figure F. Students could then take the square root of the area of Figure F to find its side length. Students could then use the symmetry of the tangram, equal areas, parallel lines, and the relationships between the different figures to find the perimeters of Figures B, D, and E.

Figure D have length $\sqrt{12.5}$ cm.
The perimeter of Figure D
$= \sqrt{12.5}$ cm $+ \sqrt{12.5}$ cm + 5 cm + 5 cm
$\doteq$ 17.1 cm

d) Figure D and Figure E share a common side (5 cm).
Both Figure E (an isosceles triangle) and Figure D have two sides equal to the side length of Figure F.
So, the perimeter of Figure E = the perimeter of Figure D – 5 cm
$\doteq$ 17.1 cm – 5 cm
= 12.1 cm

7. Label each leg a.
Use the Pythagorean Theorem.
$12^2 = a^2 + a^2$
$144 = 2a^2$ Divide both sides by 2 to isolate a^2.
$72 = a^2$
$a = \sqrt{72}$
So, the base and height of the triangle have length $\sqrt{72}$ cm.
$A = \frac{1}{2} \times \sqrt{72} \times \sqrt{72} = 36$
The perimeter of the triangle $= \sqrt{72} + \sqrt{72} + 12$
$\doteq 28.97$

REFLECT: I can draw a line of symmetry in an isosceles or equilateral triangle to create two congruent right triangles. The base of each congruent right triangle is one-half the base of the original triangle. I can use the Pythagorean Theorem to find the height of the triangle, then use the height to find the area of the original triangle.
(Students' work should include an example.)

4. A prism has a base that is a regular hexagon with side length 6 cm. The prism is 14 cm long.
a) Find the area of the base of the prism.
b) Find the volume of the prism.
c) Find the surface area of the prism.

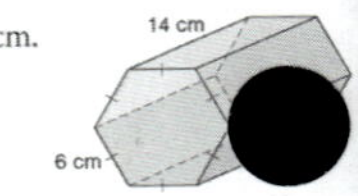

$A \doteq 94\ cm^2$
$V \doteq 1309\ cm^3$
$SA \doteq 691\ cm^2$

Number Strategies

A rectangular pool has length 12 m and width 7 m. A circular pool has the same area as the rectangular pool. What is the circumference of the circular pool?

About 32.5 m

5. Assessment Focus
Here is a tangram.
Its side length is 10 cm.
a) What is the area of Figure F? How long is each side of the square?
b) What is the perimeter of Figure B?
c) What is the perimeter of Figure D?
d) How can you use Figure D to find the perimeter of Figure E?
Show your work.

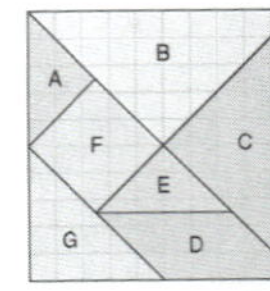

6. Here is one base of an octagonal prism. The prism is 30 cm long.

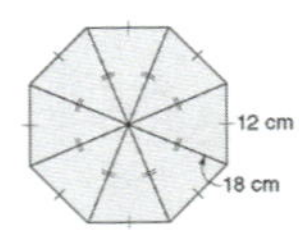

a) Find the volume of the prism. $V \doteq 24\ 438\ cm^3$
b) Find the surface area of the prism. $SA \doteq 4509\ cm^2$

Take It Further

7. Find the area and perimeter of this right isosceles triangle.

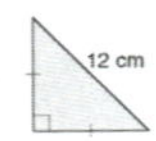

$A = 36\ cm^2$
$P \doteq 29$ cm

Reflect

How can the Pythagorean Theorem be used in isosceles and equilateral triangles?
Include examples in your explanation.

354 UNIT 8: Square Roots and Pythagoras

ASSESSMENT FOR LEARNING

What to Look For	What to Do
Knowledge and Understanding ✔ Students understand how the Pythagorean Theorem can be used in isosceles and equilateral triangles. ***Thinking*** ✔ Students can use the area of an equilateral triangle or an isosceles triangle to find the surface area and volume of regular prisms. ***Application*** ✔ Students can apply the Pythagorean Theorem to equilateral or isosceles triangles.	***Extra Support:*** Students who have difficulty focusing on the right triangle should draw the right triangle on its own to avoid any confusion with the other dimensions in the given diagram. Students can use Step-by-Step 5 (Master 8.12) to complete question 9. ***Extra Practice:*** Have students write a practical problem involving an isosceles or equilateral triangle, which would require the use of the Pythagorean Theorem in its solution. Students trade problems with a classmate and solve each other's problem. Students can complete Extra Practice 5 (Master 8.22). ***Extension:*** Have students use the Pythagorean Theorem to find the volume and surface area of other regular prisms.

Recording and Reporting
Master 8.2 Ongoing Observations: Square Roots and Pythagoras

Unit Review

Review any lesson with etext online tutorial

What Do I Need to Know?

✓ **Side Length and Area of a Square**
The side length of a square is equal to the square root of its area.
Length = $\sqrt{\text{Area}}$
Area = $(\text{Length})^2$

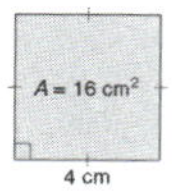

✓ **The Pythagorean Theorem**
In a right triangle, the area of the square on the hypotenuse is equal to the sum of the areas of the squares on the two legs.
$c^2 = a^2 + b^2$
Use the Pythagorean Theorem to find the length of a side in a right triangle, when two other sides are known.

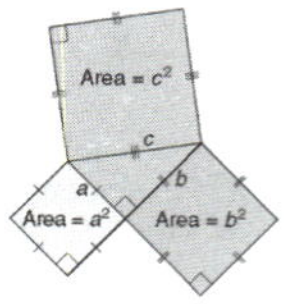

What Should I Be Able to Do?

For extra practice, go to page 495.

LESSON

8.1 8.2 **1.** Estimate each square root to the nearest whole number.
a) $\sqrt{6}$ 2 b) $\sqrt{11}$ 3
c) $\sqrt{26}$ 5 d) $\sqrt{35}$ 6
e) $\sqrt{66}$ 8 f) $\sqrt{86}$ 9

2. Estimate each square root to 1 decimal place.
Show your work.
a) $\sqrt{55}$ 7.4 b) $\sqrt{75}$ 8.7
c) $\sqrt{95}$ 9.7 d) $\sqrt{105}$ 10.2
e) $\sqrt{46}$ 6.8 f) $\sqrt{114}$ 10.7

3. Use a calculator to write each square root to 1 decimal place.
a) $\sqrt{46}$ 6.8 b) $\sqrt{84}$ 9.2
c) $\sqrt{120}$ 11.0 d) $\sqrt{1200}$ 34.6

4. A square blanket has an area of 16 900 cm². How long is each side of the blanket?
130 cm

Unit Review 355

LESSON ORGANIZER

Student Materials
- calculators
- 1-cm grid paper (PM 20)

Assessment: Masters 8.1 Unit Rubric: Square Roots and Pythagoras; 8.4 Unit Summary: Square Roots and Pythagoras

Correlation of extra practice questions on page 495:

Lesson	Questions
8.1	1, 2
8.2	3, 4
8.4	5, 7
8.5	6

Sample Solutions

6. a) The sum of the areas of the squares on the legs of a right triangle equals the area of the square on the hypotenuse.
If I draw a right triangle with hypotenuse $\sqrt{13}$, the area of the square on the hypotenuse is: $(\sqrt{13})^2 = 13$
So, the sum of the areas of the squares on the legs must be 13.
I found two whole numbers that have a sum of 13, and that are both perfect squares: 4 and 9
The areas of the squares on the legs are 4 cm² and 9 cm².
The lengths of the legs are the square roots of the areas: 2 cm and 3 cm
The treasure could be located 2 grid squares right and 3 grid squares up from X.

b) Yes, I can draw many different right triangles with legs of lengths 2 cm and 3 cm with a vertex at X.
For example:

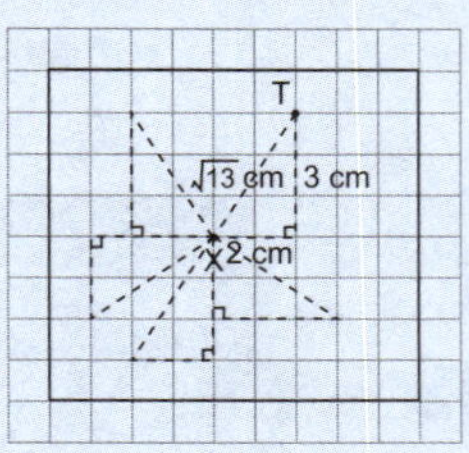

7. After 2 h, the eastbound boat has travelled 20 km, and the northbound boat has travelled 24 km.
Use these distances as the legs of a right triangle.
Let the distance between the two boats be the hypotenuse, c.
Use the Pythagorean Theorem.
$c^2 = 24^2 + 20^2 = 976$
$c = \sqrt{976} \doteq 31.2$
After 2 h, the boats are about 31.2 km apart.

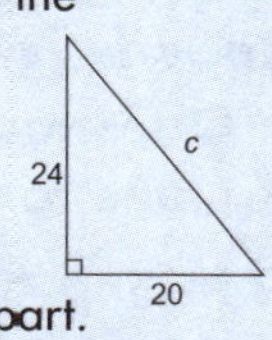

9. Draw an equilateral triangle with side length 15 cm.
Draw the line of symmetry, AD, to create two congruent right triangles with base 15 cm ÷ 2 = 7.5 cm.
Label h, the height of △ABC.
Use the Pythagorean Theorem in △ABD.

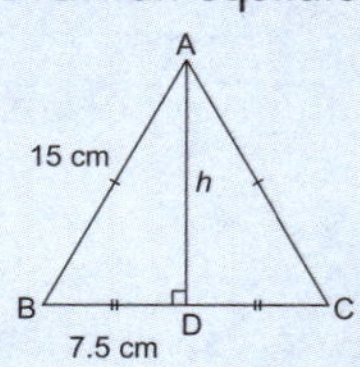

$15^2 = 7.5^2 + h^2$
$225 = 56.25 + h^2$
$168.75 = h^2$
$h = \sqrt{168.75}$
The area of $\triangle ABC = \frac{1}{2}bh$
$= \frac{1}{2} \times 15 \times \sqrt{168.75}$
$\doteq 97.43$
The area of the equilateral triangle is about 97.4 cm².

10. a)

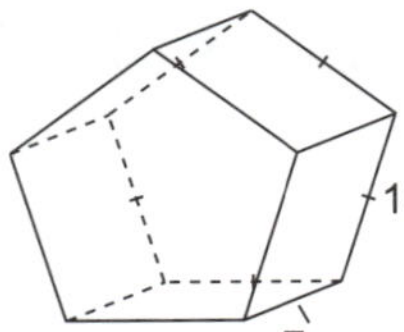

b) Find the area of one isosceles triangle.

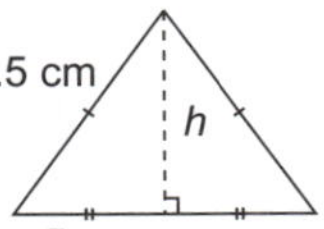

Use the Pythagorean Theorem.

$$8.5^2 = 5^2 + h^2$$
$$72.25 = 25 + h^2$$
$$47.25 = h^2$$
$$h = \sqrt{47.25}$$

Each isosceles triangle has height $\sqrt{47.25}$ cm and base 10 cm.

So, the area of each triangle is: $A = \frac{1}{2} \times 10 \times \sqrt{47.25}$

And the area of the pentagon $= 5 \times \frac{1}{2} \times 10 \times \sqrt{47.25}$
$= 25 \times \sqrt{47.25}$

SA = sum of the areas of the rectangular faces + sum of the areas of the two bases

$= 5 \times (10 \times 7) + 2 \times (25 \times \sqrt{47.25})$

$\doteq 693.7$

The surface area of the prism is approximately 694 cm^2.

c) V = base area × height

$= 25 \times \sqrt{47.25} \times 7$

$\doteq 1202.9$

The volume of the prism is approximately 1203 cm^3.

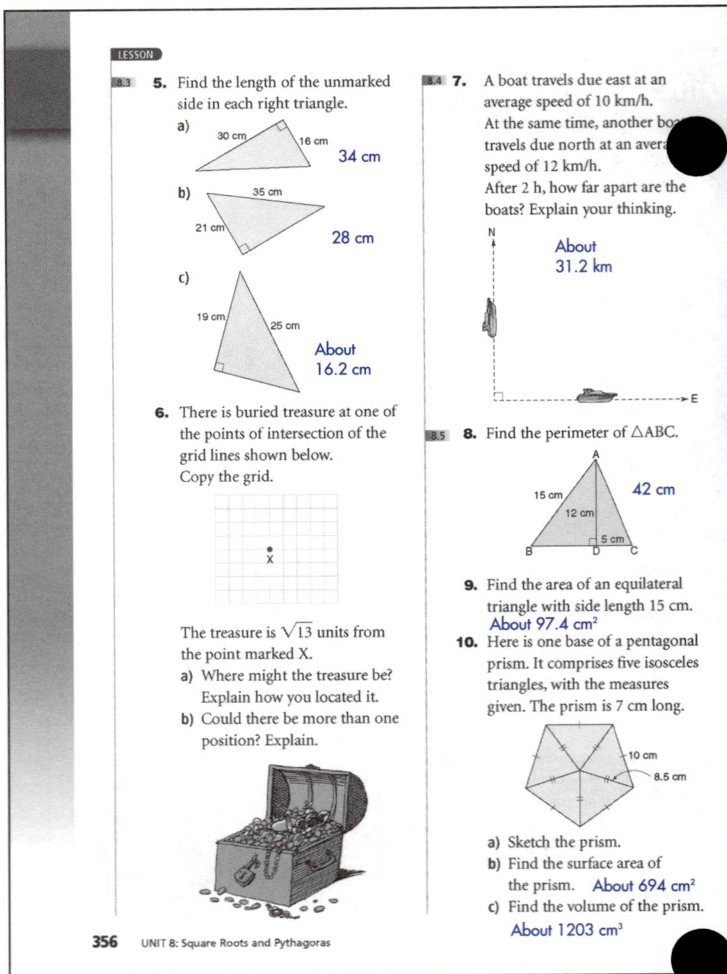

LESSON

8.3 **5.** Find the length of the unmarked side in each right triangle.

a) 30 cm, 16 cm — 34 cm

b) 35 cm, 21 cm — 28 cm

c) 19 cm, 25 cm — About 16.2 cm

6. There is buried treasure at one of the points of intersection of the grid lines shown below.
Copy the grid.

The treasure is $\sqrt{13}$ units from the point marked X.

a) Where might the treasure be? Explain how you located it.

b) Could there be more than one position? Explain.

8.4 **7.** A boat travels due east at an average speed of 10 km/h.
At the same time, another boat travels due north at an average speed of 12 km/h.
After 2 h, how far apart are the boats? Explain your thinking.
About 31.2 km

8.5 **8.** Find the perimeter of △ABC.
15 cm, 12 cm, 5 cm — 42 cm

9. Find the area of an equilateral triangle with side length 15 cm.
About 97.4 cm^2

10. Here is one base of a pentagonal prism. It comprises five isosceles triangles, with the measures given. The prism is 7 cm long.
10 cm, 8.5 cm

a) Sketch the prism.

b) Find the surface area of the prism. About 694 cm^2

c) Find the volume of the prism.
About 1203 cm^3

356 UNIT 8: Square Roots and Pythagoras

ASSESSMENT FOR LEARNING

What to Look For

Knowledge and Understanding

✔ **Question 4:** Student understands the relationship between the area of a square and its side length.

✔ **Question 5:** Student understands the relationship among the side lengths of a right triangle.

Thinking

✔ **Questions 8 and 9:** Student can use the Pythagorean Theorem to solve problems involving right triangles and equilateral triangles.

✔ **Question 10:** Student can use the area of an isosceles triangle to find the surface area and volume of a regular prism.

Communication

✔ **Questions 6 and 7:** Student can use mathematical language to describe how to locate points and find distances using the Pythagorean Theorem.

Application

✔ **Questions 1, 2, and 3:** Student can estimate the square root of a number using various strategies.

Recording and Reporting

Master 8.1 Unit Rubric: Square Roots and Pythagoras

Master 8.4 Unit Summary: Square Roots and Pythagoras

Practice Test

1. a) What is the area of square ABCD? 25 units^2
   b) What is the length of line segment AB? Explain your reasoning. 5 units

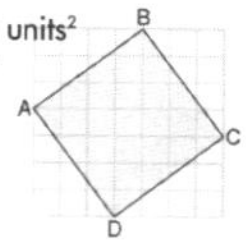

2. Find the side length of a square that has the same area as this rectangle.

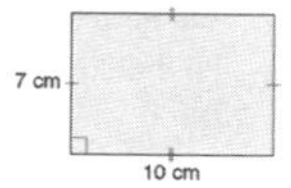

About 8.4 cm

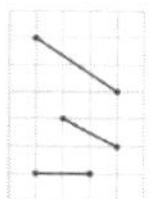

3. Draw these 3 line segments on 1-cm grid paper.
   a) Find the length of each line segment to the nearest millimetre.
   b) Could these segments be arranged to form a triangle? If your answer is no, explain why not. If your answer is yes, could they form a right triangle? Explain.

About 3.6 cm, about 2.2 cm, 2 cm

4. A parking garage has ramps from one level to the next.
   a) How long is each ramp? About 16.2 m
   b) What is the total length of the ramps?

About 80.8 m

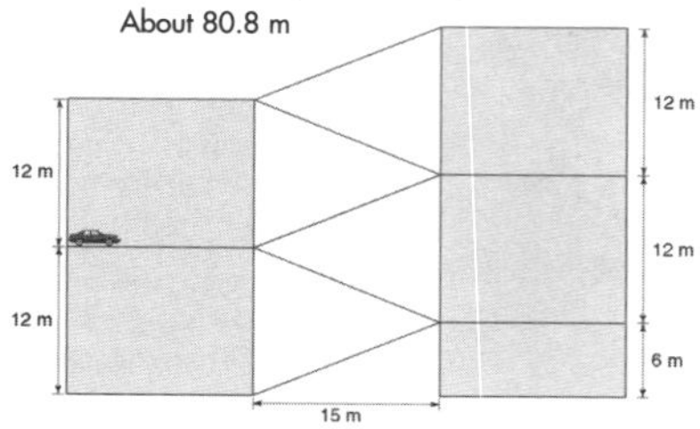

LESSON ORGANIZER

Student Materials
- calculators
- 1-cm grid paper (PM 20)

Assessment: Masters 8.1 Unit Rubric: Square Roots and Pythagoras; 8.4 Unit Summary: Square Roots and Pythagoras

Assignment Guidelines

To assess the 4 Achievement Chart categories listed in the curriculum document, use these test questions:
Knowledge and Understanding: 1
Application: 2
Communication: 3
Thinking: 4

Sample Solutions

1. a) The area of the enclosing square is: 7^2 units^2 = 49 units^2
The triangles formed by the enclosing squares are congruent.
Each triangle has area:
$\frac{1}{2} \times 4$ units $\times$ 3 units = 6 units^2
So, the 4 triangles have area: 4×6 units^2 = 24 units^2
The area of square ABCD = Area of enclosing square – Area of triangles
= 49 units^2 – 24 units^2
= 25 units^2

b) The length of line segment AB
$= \sqrt{\text{Area of square ABCD}}$
$= \sqrt{25 \text{ units}^2}$
= 5 units

2. Area of the rectangle: $A = lw$
= 7 cm $\times$ 10 cm
= 70 cm^2
Side length of square with area 70 cm^2: $l = \sqrt{A}$
$= \sqrt{70}$
$\doteq 8.37$
The side length of the square is about 8.4 cm.

3. a) The first line segment: Draw a right triangle with this segment as the hypotenuse. Use the Pythagorean Theorem to find its length.
$h^2 = 2^2 + 3^2$
$= 4 + 9$
$= 13$
$h = \sqrt{13}$

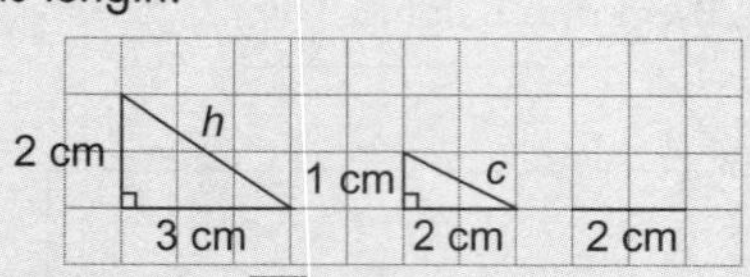

The line segment has length $\sqrt{13}$ cm, or about 3.6 cm.
The second line segment: Draw a right triangle with this segment as the hypotenuse. Use the Pythagorean Theorem to find its length.
$c^2 = 1^2 + 2^2$
$= 1 + 4$
$= 5$
$c = \sqrt{5}$
The line segment has length $\sqrt{5}$ cm, or about 2.2 cm.
The third line segment has length 2 cm.

b) The line segments could form a triangle because the sum of two side lengths is greater than the length of the third side: $2 + 2.2 > 3.6$. The line segments could not form a right triangle because $(3.6)^2 \neq (2.2)^2 + 2^2$.

4. a) Use the Pythagorean Theorem in the bottom right triangle.
Let the length of each ramp be c.
$c^2 = 15^2 + 6^2$
$= 225 + 36$
$= 261$
$c = \sqrt{261}$
$\doteq 16.16$
The length of each ramp is about 16.2 m.

b) Each ramp covers a horizontal distance of 15 m and a vertical distance of 6 m.
So, all the ramps are of equal length.
There are 5 ramps.
The total length of the ramps is: $5 \times \sqrt{261} \doteq 80.78$
The total length of the ramps is about 80.8 m.

Pythagoras through the Ages

LESSON ORGANIZER

80–100 min

Student Grouping: Individual
Student Materials
- protractors
- The 10-cm Ruler (Master 8.15)

Assessment: Masters 8.3 Performance Assessment Rubric: Pythagoras through the Ages; 8.4 Unit Summary: Square Roots and Pythagoras

Sample Response

Ancient Greece

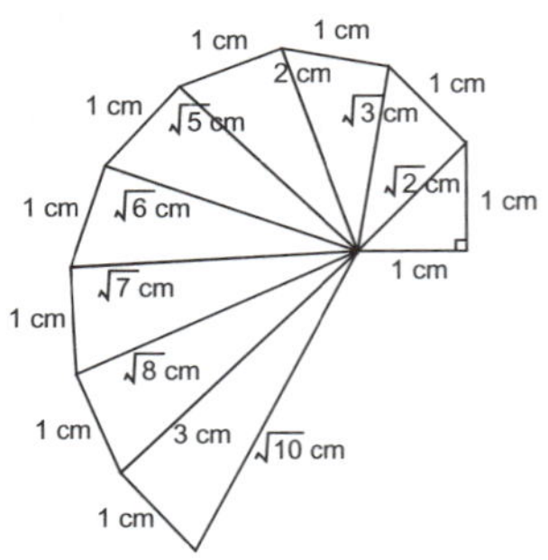

I see that the lengths of the hypotenuses are the square roots of consecutive whole numbers, starting at 1.

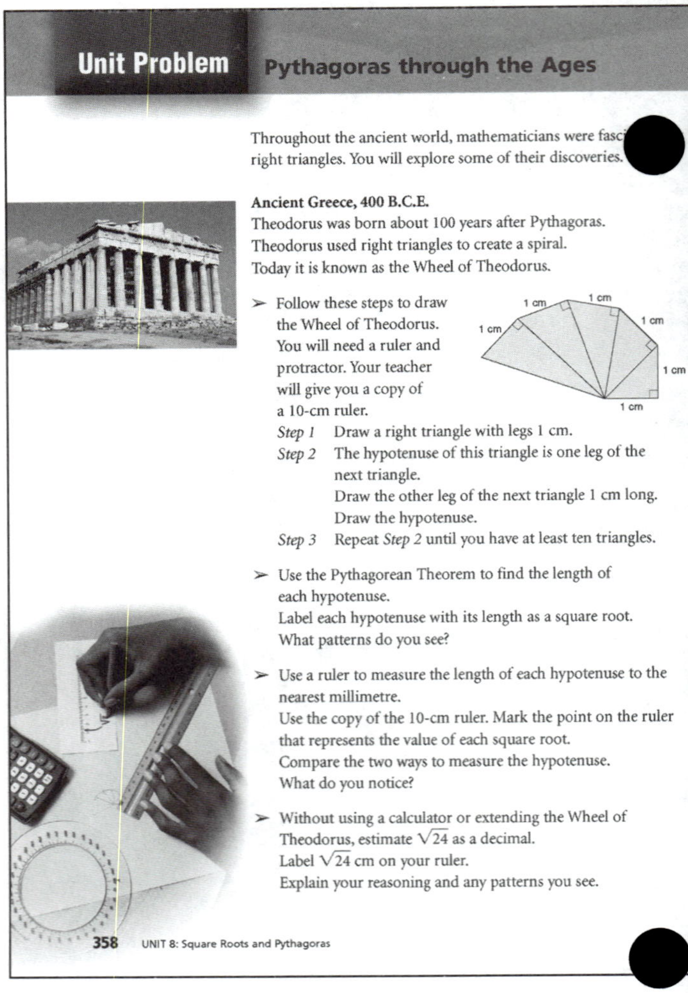

Unit Problem Pythagoras through the Ages

Throughout the ancient world, mathematicians were fasci[nated by] right triangles. You will explore some of their discoveries.

Ancient Greece, 400 B.C.E.
Theodorus was born about 100 years after Pythagoras.
Theodorus used right triangles to create a spiral.
Today it is known as the Wheel of Theodorus.

➢ Follow these steps to draw the Wheel of Theodorus. You will need a ruler and protractor. Your teacher will give you a copy of a 10-cm ruler.
Step 1 Draw a right triangle with legs 1 cm.
Step 2 The hypotenuse of this triangle is one leg of the next triangle.
Draw the other leg of the next triangle 1 cm long.
Draw the hypotenuse.
Step 3 Repeat *Step 2* until you have at least ten triangles.

➢ Use the Pythagorean Theorem to find the length of each hypotenuse.
Label each hypotenuse with its length as a square root.
What patterns do you see?

➢ Use a ruler to measure the length of each hypotenuse to the nearest millimetre.
Use the copy of the 10-cm ruler. Mark the point on the ruler that represents the value of each square root.
Compare the two ways to measure the hypotenuse.
What do you notice?

➢ Without using a calculator or extending the Wheel of Theodorus, estimate $\sqrt{24}$ as a decimal.
Label $\sqrt{24}$ cm on your ruler.
Explain your reasoning and any patterns you see.

358 UNIT 8: Square Roots and Pythagoras

Have students turn to pages 320 and 321 of the Student Book. Review *What You'll Learn,* the learning goals of the unit, and discuss the meanings of the Key Words. Tell students they will use the skills and concepts they learned in this unit to complete the *Unit Problem.*

Present the *Unit Problem.* Have one student read the *Check List* aloud. Remind students that they should use the *Check List* to assess their work before handing it in. You may also wish to provide students with copies of Master 8.3 Performance Assessment Rubric: Pythagoras through the Ages so they will know how their work will be assessed.

Tell students they will investigate how different ancient civilizations used the properties of right triangles. Distribute copies of *The 10-cm Ruler* (Master 8.15) to students. Remind students they should use calculators only to check their estimates of square roots.

REFLECT ON THE UNIT

The Pythagorean Theorem states that the area of the square on the hypotenuse of a right triangle is equal to the sum of the areas of the squares on the legs. We can use an algebraic equation to describe it: $c^2 = a^2 + b^2$, where the hypotenuse has length c, and the legs have lengths a and b. The Pythagorean Theorem can be used to find the distance between two points, to find the length of one side of a right triangle when the lengths of the two other sides are known, and to solve problems that involve isosceles and equilateral triangles.
For example, I can use the Pythagorean Theorem to find the length of the diagonal of a computer screen, with width 28 cm and height 21 cm.

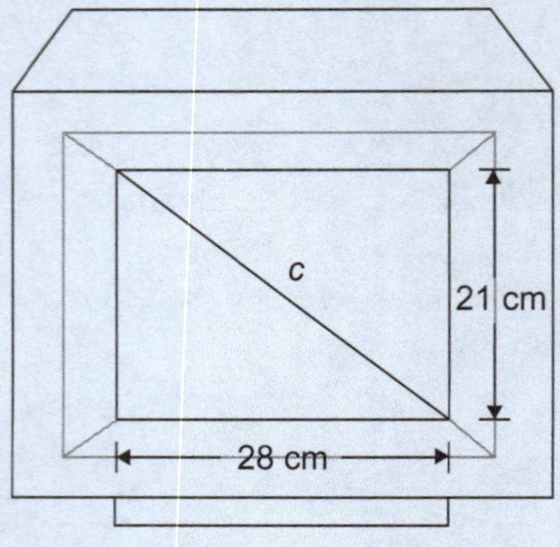

$$\begin{aligned} c^2 &= 28^2 + 21^2 \\ &= 784 + 441 \\ &= 1225 \\ c &= \sqrt{1225} \\ &= 35 \end{aligned}$$

The length of the diagonal is 35 cm.

Ancient Egypt, 2000 B.C.E.
In ancient Egypt, the Nile River overflowed every year and destroyed property boundaries.
Because the land plots were rectangular, the Egyptians needed a way to mark a right angle.

The Egyptians tied 12 evenly spaced knots along a piece of rope and made a triangle from it.
Explain how you think the Egyptians used the knotted rope to mark a right angle.

Check List

Your work should show:
- ✓ All constructions and diagrams correctly labelled
- ✓ Detailed and accurate calculations
- ✓ Clear descriptions of the patterns observed
- ✓ Reasonable explanations of your thinking and your conclusions about the Pythagorean Theorem

Ancient Babylon, 1700 B.C.E.
Archaeologists have discovered evidence that the ancient Babylonians knew about the Pythagorean Theorem over 1000 years before Pythagoras!

The archaeologists found this tablet.

When the tablet is translated, it looks like this.

What do you think the diagram on the tablet means? Explain your reasoning.

Reflect on the Unit

What is the Pythagorean Theorem? How is it used? Include examples in your explanation.

Unit Problem: Pythagoras through the Ages 359

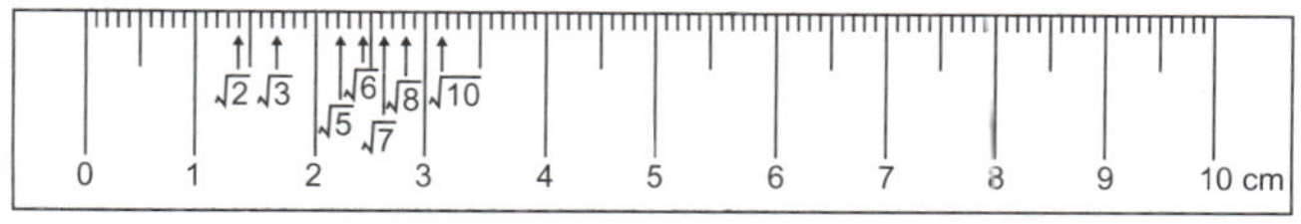

I notice that the decimal measures are the approximate square roots of the whole numbers from 1 to 10.
I estimate $\sqrt{24}$ to be about 4.9 because 24 is very close to 25, and $\sqrt{25} = 5$.

Ancient Egypt

By thinking of the knots as knots 1 through 12, I could hold knots 1, 4, and 8 to make a right triangle. The triangle has side lengths 3, 4, and 5. I can use the Pythagorean Theorem to check that the triangle is a right triangle.

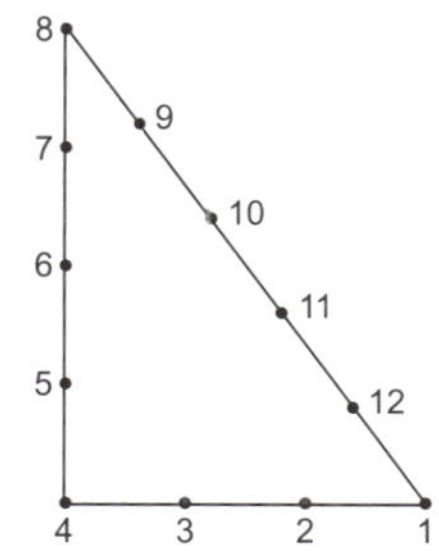

$3^2 + 4^2 = 5^2$
$9 + 16 = 25$
$25 = 25$
Since this statement is true, the triangle is a right triangle.

Ancient Babylon

The square has side length 30 units.
Use the Pythagorean Theorem on the right triangle to find the length of the diagonal.
$c^2 = 30^2 + 30^2 = 1800$
$c = \sqrt{1800} \doteq 42.4264$
The length of the diagonal of the square is about 42.4264 units.
This is equal to $30 \times \sqrt{2}$, or about $30 \times 1.414\ 21$.

ASSESSMENT FOR LEARNING

What to Look For	What to Do
Knowledge and Understanding ✔ Students show understanding by explaining how the Pythagorean Theorem was used in ancient Egypt. ***Communication*** ✔ Students present work clearly, including all constructions, diagrams, and calculations. ✔ Students give clear descriptions of the patterns they observed. ***Application*** ✔ Students can create an accurate drawing of the Wheel of Theodorus.	***Extra Support:*** Make the problem accessible. Encourage students to use a sharp pencil or fine tip pen when drawing the Wheel of Theodorus. It is important that the dimensions of the triangles are drawn accurately. Suggest students turn their paper after they have drawn each triangle so that the hypotenuse is parallel to the horizontal edge of the desk. It will be easier for students to see the hypotenuse as the leg of the next triangle. Encourage students to use a different coloured pen to draw each new leg and hypotenuse. Students use the matching coloured pen when calculating the length of each hypotenuse.

Recording and Reporting
Master 8.3 Performance Assessment Rubric: Pythagoras through the Ages
Master 8.4 Unit Summary: Square Roots and Pythagoras

Units 1–8

LESSON ORGANIZER

Student Materials
- calculators
- linking cubes
- isometric dot paper (PM 23)
- 0.5-cm grid paper (PM 14)
- compasses
- protractors

Assessment: PM 9 Work Sample Records

Sample Answers

3. b)

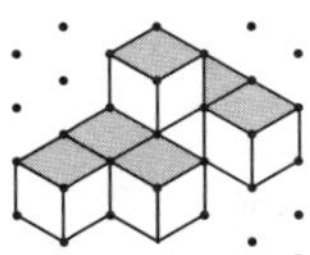

4. a) For example: $\frac{1}{4} \div \frac{1}{2}, \frac{2}{8} \div \frac{2}{4}, \frac{3}{12} \div \frac{3}{6}$
   b) For example: $\frac{1}{3} \div \frac{1}{2}, \frac{2}{6} \div \frac{2}{4}, \frac{3}{9} \div \frac{3}{6}$
   c) For example: $\frac{1}{5} \div \frac{1}{4}, \frac{2}{10} \div \frac{2}{8}, \frac{3}{15} \div \frac{3}{12}$
   d) For example: $\frac{1}{6} \div \frac{1}{5}, \frac{2}{12} \div \frac{2}{10}, \frac{3}{18} \div \frac{3}{15}$
   For each fraction, I wrote one division question, then used equivalent fractions to write other questions.
5. a) Only some cookies were tested.
   b) All family members were surveyed.

Units 1–8 Cumulative Review

UNIT

1 **1.** Evaluate.
a) 3.8 + 5.7 ÷ 1.9   6.8
b) $2.4^2 - (4.2 - 3.7)^2$ 5.51
c) (1.5 + 4.2) + 2.8 × 7.2   25.86
d) 1.5 + (4.2 + 2.8) × 7.2   51.9

2 **2.** Which is the better buy?
a) 8 cheese slices for $1.49 or 24 cheese slices for $3.29 (circled)
b) 1.89 L of cranberry-raspberry drink for $3.27 or 3.78 L for $5.98 (circled)
c) 100 g of iced tea mix for $0.29 (circled) or 500 g for $1.69
d) 1 can of chicken soup for $0.57 or a 12-pack for $5.99 (circled)

3 **3.** Use linking cubes.
a) Build the object for the set of views below.
b) Sketch the object on isometric dot paper.

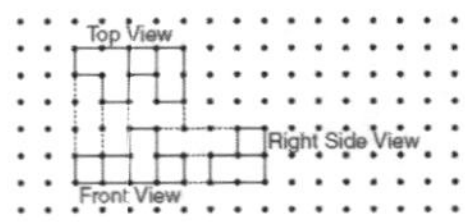

4 **4.** Write as many division questions as you can that have each fraction below as their quotient.
a) $\frac{1}{2}$ b) $\frac{2}{3}$ c) $\frac{4}{5}$ d) $\frac{5}{6}$
Write about the strategies you used to find the division questions.

5 **5.** In each case, identify the collected data as from a sample or a census. Justify your answer.
a) To find the mean number of chocolate chips in a cookie, every 100th cookie was tested. Sample
b) To find what type of movie the family wanted to rent, all 6 family members were asked. Census
c) To find the number of Ontario families that enjoy skiing, one in 10 households was surveyed by phone. Sample
d) To find out if the city should increase funding for snow removal, a questionnaire was enclosed in every tax bill. Sample

6. Adam recorded the heights of a bean plant and sunflower plant.

Time (days)	Height (cm)	
	Bean	Sunflower
0	2	6
3	6	8
6	9	11
9	13	14
12	20	17
15	28	21
18	35	26
21	41	33
24	47	38
27	56	42
30	63	48
33	68	53

360 Units 1–8

Students can use this review to evaluate their progress in the mathematical content of Units 1 through 8.

Remind students that the unit containing the content required to answer each question is listed in red beside the question.

Encourage students to refer to the *Connect* sections of the relevant units.

Encourage students to draw on each other's skills as they work through the review.

Students who have identified areas in which they are strong may wish to act as volunteer tutors for students who require assistance.

a) Display the data using the most suitable method. Justify your choice.
b) Describe any trends in the graph.
c) Predict the height of each plant after 39 days. Explain the method you used to make your prediction.

7. Draw a circle. Label its centre C. Choose two points G and H on the circle that are not the endpoints of a diameter. Join CG, GH, and CH. What type of triangle is △CGH? How do you know? Isosceles

8. Which has the greater area: a circle with circumference 1 m or a circle with radius 30 cm? Justify your answer.

9. A cardboard tube is used to send a poster by mail. The tube is 0.8 m long with diameter 7 cm. The ends of the tube are closed with tape. What is the area of cardboard in the tube? About 1759 cm²

10. a) Name the complement of ∠ABE. ∠CBD
b) Name the supplement of ∠ABE. ∠EBC

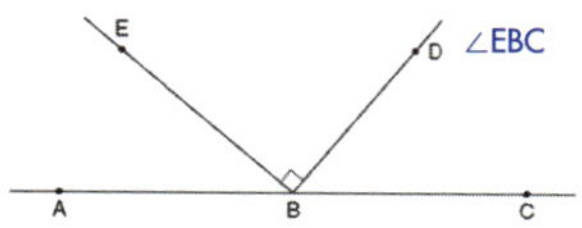

11. Look at this diagram.

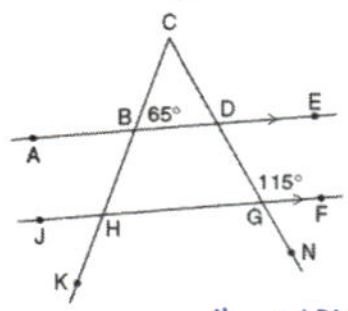

a) Name two pairs of:
i) interior angles — i) ∠ABH and ∠JHB; ∠EDG and ∠DGF
ii) alternate angles — ii) ∠ABH and ∠BHG; ∠BDG and ∠DGF
iii) corresponding angles — iii) ∠CDE and ∠DGF; ∠CBD and ∠BHG
b) Find the measures of ∠CHG, ∠JHK, ∠CGH, and ∠FGN. 65°, 65°, 65°, 65°
c) Find the measure of ∠BCD. 50°
What kind of triangle is △BCD? Isosceles

12. Estimate each square root to 1 decimal place. Show your work. Then check with a calculator.
a) $\sqrt{52}$ 7.2 b) $\sqrt{63}$ 7.9
c) $\sqrt{90}$ 9.5 d) $\sqrt{76}$ 8.7

13. The area of the square on each side of a triangle is given. Is the triangle a right triangle? How do you know?
a) 16 cm², 8 cm², 30 cm² No
b) 16 cm², 8 cm², 24 cm² Yes

14. The dimensions of a rectangle are 3 cm by 4 cm. What is the length of a diagonal? 5 cm
Explain your reasoning.

Cumulative Review 361

c) Not every household was surveyed.
d) Not every taxpayer would have returned the questionnaire.

6. a)

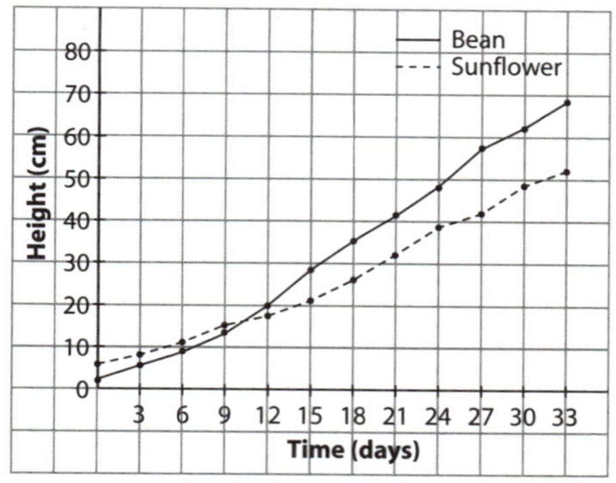

I used a double-line graph because there are two sets of data and the data are continuous.

b) The heights of the bean plant and sunflower plant increased over the 33 days.
After Day 9, the graph of the bean plant is steeper than that of the sunflower. So, after Day 9, the bean plant grew at a faster rate. The bean plant grew much taller than the sunflower plant.

c) For example: Bean plant: about 82 cm
Sunflower plant: about 65 cm
I assumed the plants would continue to grow at the same rates, so I extended the graphs to 39 days.

7.

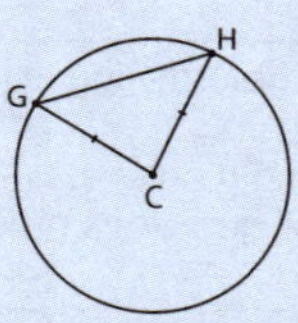

△CGH is an isosceles triangle. CG and CH are of equal length because they are both radii of the circle.

8. Use the formula for the circumference of a circle to find the radius of a circle with circumference 1 m.

$1\text{ m} = 100\text{ cm}$
$C = 2\pi r$
$100 = 2\pi r$ Divide both sides by 2π.
$\frac{100}{2\pi} = r$
$r \doteq 15.92$

The radius of the circle is about 16 cm.
Since the other circle has radius 30 cm and 30 > 16, the circle with radius 30 cm has the greater area.

9. The radius of the tube:
$r = \frac{d}{2} = \frac{7}{2} = 3.5$
The tube is 0.8 m or 0.8 × 100 = 80 cm long.
The tube does not have cardboard ends.
So, the formula for the surface area of the cylinder becomes:
$SA = 2\pi rh$
Substitute: $r = 3.5$ and $h = 80$
$SA = 2\pi(3.5)(80)$
$\doteq 1759.29$
The surface area of the tube is about 1759 cm².

11. c) ∠CGH = 65° from part b. ∠CDB = 65° because ∠CGH and ∠CDB are corresponding angles. The sum of the angles in a triangle is 180°.
So, ∠BCD = 180° − 65° − 65° = 50°.
△BCD is an isosceles triangle because there are two equal angles.

13. If a triangle is a right triangle, the sum of the areas of the squares on the legs is equal to the area of the square on the hypotenuse.
a) $8\text{ cm}^2 + 16\text{ cm}^2 \neq 30\text{ cm}^2$
b) $8\text{ cm}^2 + 16\text{ cm}^2 = 24\text{ cm}^2$

14.

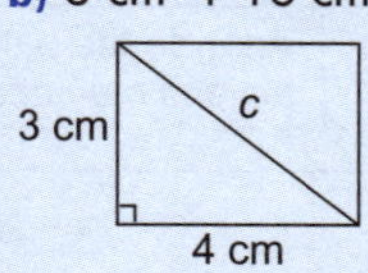

The two sides of a rectangle and its diagonal form a right triangle. Use the Pythagorean Theorem to find the length of the diagonal, c.

$c^2 = 3^2 + 4^2$
$= 9 + 16$
$= 25$
$c = \sqrt{25}$
$= 5$

The length of the diagonal is 5 cm.

Evaluating Student Learning: Preparing to Report: Unit 8 Square Roots and Pythagoras

This unit provides an opportunity to report on the **Number Sense and Numeration** and **Geometry and Spatial Sense** strands.

Master 8.4: Unit Summary: Square Roots and Pythagoras provides a comprehensive format for recording and summarizing evidence collected.

Here is an example of a completed summary chart for this Unit:

Strand: *Number Sense and Numeration/Geometry and Spatial Sense*	**Knowledge and Understanding**	**Thinking**	**Communication**	**Application**	***Overall***
Ongoing Observations	3	3	3	4	3
Work samples or portfolios; conferences	2	3	3	3	3
Unit Review	2	3	2	3	2/3
Unit Test	3	3	4	3	3
Unit Problem Pythagoras through the Ages	3	3	3	3	3
Achievement Level for reporting					3

Recording	**How to Report**
Ongoing Observations	Use *Master 8.2 Ongoing Observations: Square Roots and Pythagoras* to determine the most consistent level achieved in each category. Enter it in the chart. Choose to summarize by achievement category, or simply to enter an overall level. Observations from late in the unit should be most heavily weighted.
Portfolios or collections of work samples; conferences or interviews	Use *Master 8.1 Unit Rubric: Square Roots and Pythagoras* to guide evaluation of collections of work and information gathered in conferences. Teachers may choose to focus particular attention on the Assessment Focus questions. Work from late in the unit should be most heavily weighted.
Unit Review	*Master 8.1 Unit Rubric: Square Roots and Pythagoras* may be helpful in determining levels of achievement. #4 and 5 provide evidence of Knowledge and Understanding; #1, 2, 3, and 6 provide evidence of Application; #7, 8, 9, and 10 provide evidence of Thinking; all questions provide evidence of Communication.
Unit Test	*Master 8.1 Unit Rubric: Square Roots and Pythagoras* may be helpful in determining levels of achievement. #2 provides evidence of Knowledge and Understanding; #3 provides evidence of Application; #4 provides evidence of Thinking; all questions provide evidence of Communication.
Unit Problem	Use *Master 8.3 Performance Assessment Rubric: Pythagoras through the Ages*. The *Unit Problem* offers a snapshot of students' achievement. In particular, it shows their ability to synthesize and apply what they have learned.
Student Self-Assessment	Note students' perceptions of their own progress. This may take the form of an oral or written comment, or a self-rating.
Comments	Analyse the pattern of achievement to identify strengths and needs. In some cases, specific actions may need to be planned to support the learner.

Learning Skills	**Ongoing Records**
PM 4: Learning Skills Check List Use to record and report throughout a reporting period, rather than for each unit and/or strand.	*PM 10: Summary Class Records: Strands* *PM 11: Summary Class Records: Achievement Categories* *PM 12: Summary Record: Individual* Use to record and report evaluations of student achievement over several clusters, a reporting period, or a school year. These can also be used in place of the Unit Summary.

Name ____________________ Date ______________

Master 8.1

Unit Rubric: Square Roots and Pythagoras

	Level 1	Level 2	Level 3	Level 4
Knowledge and Understanding • Shows understanding by describing and explaining: – the relationship of the area of a square to the length of its side – that the square root of a non-perfect square is approximate – the Pythagorean relationship	shows limited understanding; may be unable to demonstrate or explain: – the relationship of the area of a square to the length of its side – that the square root of a non-perfect square is approximate – the Pythagorean relationship	shows some understanding; partially able to demonstrate or explain: – the relationship of the area of a square to the length of its side – that the square root of a non-perfect square is approximate – the Pythagorean relationship	shows considerable understanding; able to clearly and appropriately demonstrate or explain: – the relationship of the area of a square to the length of its side – that the square root of a non-perfect square is approximate – the Pythagorean relationship	shows a high degree of understanding; able to accurately and effectively demonstrate or explain: – the relationship of the area of a square to the length of its side – that the square root of a non-perfect square is approximate – the Pythagorean relationship
Thinking • Plans and carries out appropriate strategies to apply the Pythagorean Theorem to solve problems involving area and right triangles	uses appropriate strategies to solve problems using the Pythagorean Theorem with limited effectiveness	uses appropriate strategies to solve problems using the Pythagorean Theorem with some effectiveness	uses appropriate strategies to solve problems using the Pythagorean Theorem with considerable effectiveness	uses appropriate strategies to solve problems using the Pythagorean Theorem with a high degree of effectiveness
Communication • Explains concepts, procedures, and reasoning clearly, using appropriate terminology	limited effectiveness; unable to explain reasoning and procedures clearly; rarely uses appropriate terms	some effectiveness; explains reasoning and procedures with some clarity and some appropriate terms	considerable effectiveness; explains reasoning and procedures clearly, using appropriate terms	high degree of effectiveness; explains reasoning and procedures clearly and precisely, using the most appropriate terms
• Presents work, including diagrams, drawings, and calculations clearly, using appropriate conventions (for example, symbols and labels)	presents diagrams, drawings, and calculations with limited clarity and use of conventions	presents diagrams, drawings, and calculations with some clarity and use of conventions	presents diagrams, drawings, and calculations with considerable clarity and use of conventions	presents diagrams, drawings, and calculations with a high degree of clarity and use of appropriate conventions
Application • Applies geometric and number skills appropriately to: – estimate and calculate the square root of a whole number – draw a circle, given its area	limited effectiveness; major errors or omissions in: – estimating and calculating the square root of a whole number – drawing a circle, given its area	some effectiveness; somewhat accurate with several minor errors or omissions in: – estimating and calculating the square root of a whole number – drawing a circle, given its area	considerable effectiveness; generally accurate with few minor errors or omissions in: – estimating and calculating the square root of a whole number – drawing a circle, given its area	high degree of effectiveness; accurate and precise with no errors in: – estimating and calculating the square root of a whole number – drawing a circle, given its area

Name ____________________ Date ______________

Master 8.2

Ongoing Observations: Square Roots and Pythagoras

The behaviours described under each heading are examples; they are not intended to be an exhaustive list of all that might be observed. More detailed descriptions are provided in each lesson under *Assessment for Learning*.

STUDENT ACHIEVEMENT: Square Roots and Pythagoras

Student	Knowledge and Understanding	Thinking	Communication	Application
	• Demonstrates and explains: – the Pythagorean relationship – square roots	• Uses appropriate strategies to use the Phythagorean Theorem to solve problems	• Explains reasoning and procedures clearly, using appropriate terms • Presents diagrams, drawings, and calculations clearly, including symbols and labels	• Accurately: – estimates and calculates the square root of a whole number – draws a circle, given its area

Level 1 – very limited; Level 2 – somewhat or limited; Level 3 – satisfactory; Level 4 – thorough

Name ______________________ Date ________________

Master 8.3

Performance Assessment Rubric: Pythagoras through the Ages

	Level 1	Level 2	Level 3	Level 4
Knowledge and Understanding • Explanations show understanding of the Pythagorean relationship and square roots	explanations show limited understanding of the Pythagorean relationship and square roots	explanations show some understanding of the Pythagorean relationship and square roots	explanations show considerable understanding of the Pythagorean relationship and square roots	explanations show thorough understanding of the Pythagorean relationship and square roots
Thinking • Uses appropriate strategies (for example, drawing, estimating, calculating, logical reasoning) to solve the problems	uses a few simple strategies with limited success	uses some appropriate strategies with partial success	uses appropriate strategies with considerable success	uses appropriate, often innovative, strategies with a high degree of success
Communication • Communicates procedures, solutions, and reasoning clearly, using appropriate geometric language	limited effectiveness; does not communicate clearly	some effectiveness; communicates with some clarity	considerable effectiveness; communicates clearly	a high degree of effectiveness; communicates clearly and precisely
• Presents constructions and diagrams clearly, using appropriate geometric conventions (for example, symbols and labels)	presents constructions and diagrams with limited clarity and use of appropriate conventions	presents constructions and diagrams with some clarity and use of appropriate conventions	presents constructions and diagrams with considerable clarity and use of appropriate geometric conventions	presents constructions and diagrams with a high degree of clarity and use of appropriate geometric conventions
Application • Accurately applies geometric and number skills to: – draw required figures – estimate and measure – calculate length of each hypotenuse	limited effectiveness; major errors or omissions in: – drawing required figures – estimating and measuring – calculating length of each hypotenuse as a square root	some effectiveness; somewhat accurate in: – drawing required figures – estimating and measuring – calculating length of each hypotenuse as a square root	considerable effectiveness; generally accurate in: – drawing required figures – estimating and measuring – calculating length of each hypotenuse as a square root	high degree of effectiveness; accurate and precise in: – drawing required figures – estimating and measuring – calculating length of each hypotenuse as a square root

Name ____________________ Date ________________

Master 8.4

Unit Summary: Square Roots and Pythagoras

Review assessment records to determine the most consistent achievement levels for the assessments conducted. Some cells may be blank. *Overall* achievement levels may be recorded in each row, rather than identifying levels for each achievement category.

	Most Consistent Level of Achievement*				
Strand: *Number Sense and Numeration/Geometry and Spatial Sense*	**Knowledge and Understanding**	**Thinking**	**Communication**	**Application**	***Overall***
Ongoing Observations					
Work samples or portfolios; conferences					
Unit Review					
Unit Test					
Unit Problem Pythagoras through the Ages					
Achievement Level for reporting					

*Use Ontario Achievement Levels 1, 2, 3, 4

Self-Assessment:

Comments: (Strengths, Needs, Next Steps)

Name ____________________ Date ______________

Master 8.5

Additional Activity 1: Area Challenge

Play with a partner.

Materials: 2 number cubes labelled 1 to 6, 1-cm grid paper (PM 20), rulers, calculator

How to Play:

1. Player A rolls the two number cubes.
   The sum of the 2 numbers rolled represents the side length of a square, in centimetres.
   Draw the square on grid paper.
   Let the two numbers rolled represent the base and height of a triangle, in centimetres.
   Draw the triangle on grid paper.

2. Player A calculates the area of each figure he drew.
   Player B checks Player A's answers.
   One point is awarded for each correct area.

3. Players change roles. Repeat *Steps 1* and *2* to complete the round.

4. The player with the higher score after 4 rounds wins.

Take It Further: Play the game again. This time, use the numbers rolled to represent the dimensions of the base and height of a triangle. Draw the triangle on grid paper, then draw a square that has the same area as the triangle.

Name ____________________ Date ______________

Master 8.6

Additional Activity 2: Inscribed Squares

Play with a partner.

Materials: 2 number cubes labelled 1 to 6, 1-cm grid paper (PM 20), rulers, calculator

How to Play:

1. Player A rolls the two number cubes. Roll until you get a sum greater than 6.
   The sum of the 2 numbers rolled represents the side length of a square, in centimetres.
   Draw the square on grid paper.

2. Player A rolls one number cube.
   Draw a point on each side of the square a number of grid squares from each vertex equal to the number rolled. Always move in a clockwise direction.
   For example, suppose you rolled 2.

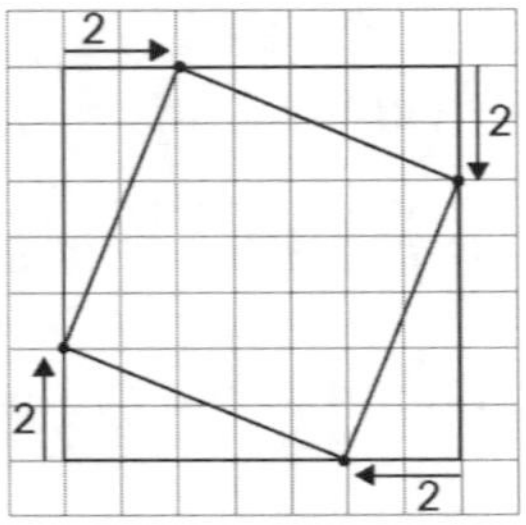

   Join the points to form an inscribed square.

3. Player A calculates the area of the inscribed square.
   Player B checks Player A's answer.
   Two points are awarded for a correct area.

4. Players change roles. Repeat *Steps 1* to *3* to complete the round.

5. The player with the higher score after 4 rounds wins.

Take It Further: Play the game again. This time, players must also find the side length of the inscribed square.

Name ______________________ Date ________________

Master 8.7

Additional Activity 3: From Here to There

Work on your own.

Materials: 2 number cubes labelled 1 to 6, 1-cm grid paper (PM 20), rulers, calculator

How to Play:

1. Draw a horizontal and vertical axis on grid paper.
   Label each axis from 0 to 6.

2. Roll the number cubes to get the coordinates of a point.
   For example, if you roll 3 and 5, the point could be (3, 5) or (5, 3).
   Plot the point on the grid.
   Roll the number cubes again to get the coordinates of a second point.
   Plot the point on the grid.
   Join the points with a ruler.
   If the line segment is horizontal or vertical, roll again to change the coordinates of the second point.
   The line segment should be slanted.

3. Draw a right triangle that has this line segment as its hypotenuse.
   Use the Pythagorean Theorem to find the length of the line segment.

4. Repeat the activity 3 times.

Take It Further: Repeat the activity again. This time, find the perimeter and area of each triangle formed.

Name ____________________ Date ________________

Master 8.8

Step-by-Step 1

Lesson 8.1, Question 6

You will need 1-cm grid paper.

Step 1 What is the area of 1 grid square? ______ cm^2

Draw a diagonal in one grid square.

What is the area of one-half of a grid square? ______ cm^2

Step 2 Construct a square on the diagonal in *Step 1*.

Label the square ABCD.

The area of ABCD is: 4 × ______ cm^2 = ______ cm^2

Step 3 Check to see that the area of ABCD is 2 cm^2.

Draw an enclosing square, EFGH.

What is the area of EFGH? ______ cm^2

What is the area of each triangle formed by the enclosing square?

_______ cm^2

The area of the 4 triangles is: 4 × ______ cm^2 = ______ cm^2

Step 4 The area of ABCD is: Area of EFGH – Area of triangles

= ______ cm^2 – _______ cm^2

= ______ cm^2

Step 5 Is the area of ABCD 2 cm^2? Explain.

____

____

Name ____________________ Date ________________

Master 8.9

Step-by-Step 2

Lesson 8.2, Question 9

Step 1 The canvas is square.

What is the side length of the canvas? ________ m

What is the area of the canvas? ______ m^2

Step 2 After framing, the area of the artwork is:

$2 \times$ Area of canvas $= 2 \times$ ______ m^2

$=$ _________ m^2

Step 3 The artwork is square.
Use your answer from *Step 2*.
The side length of the artwork is:

Side length $= \sqrt{\text{Area}}$

$= \sqrt{}$

Estimate the square root to one decimal place.
Show your work.

Step 4 What are the dimensions of the square frame? ___________________

Name ________________ Date ______________

Master 8.10

Step-by-Step 3

Lesson 8.3, Question 7

Step 1 The hypotenuse of a right triangle is $\sqrt{18}$ units.

What is the area of the square on the hypotenuse? ______ units^2

Step 2 What is the sum of the areas of the squares on the legs? ______ units^2

Step 3 Write two whole numbers with a sum equal to your answer in *Step 2*.

_______, _______

What are possible areas of the squares on the legs?

______ units^2 and ______ units^2

What are possible side lengths of the squares on the legs?

______ units and ______ units

Step 4 Sketch the triangle. Label the side lengths.

Step 5 Repeat *Steps 3* and *4* using two different whole numbers.

Step 6 How many different answers can you find?
Explain.

____

____

Name ____________________ Date ________________

Master 8.11

Step-by-Step 4

Lesson 8.4, Question 9

You will need 1-cm grid paper.

Step 1 Copy the grid onto grid paper.
Join points A and B.
Draw a right triangle that has segment AB as its hypotenuse.
What are the lengths of the legs? ______ cm and ______ cm

Step 2 Use the Pythagorean Theorem.
What is the length of AB? _______ cm

Step 3 Join points A and C.
Draw a right triangle that has segment AC as its hypotenuse.
What are the lengths of the legs? ______ cm and ______ cm
Use the Pythagorean Theorem.
What is the length of AC? _______ cm
Is C the same distance from A as B is? ________

Step 4 Repeat *Step 3* for points A and D, A and E, A and F, A and H, and A and I.

Step 5 Join points A and G.
What is the length of AG?
Is G the same distance from A as B is? ________

Step 6 Which points are the same distance from A as B is?

____

Name ____________________ Date ________________

Master 8.12

Step-by-Step 5

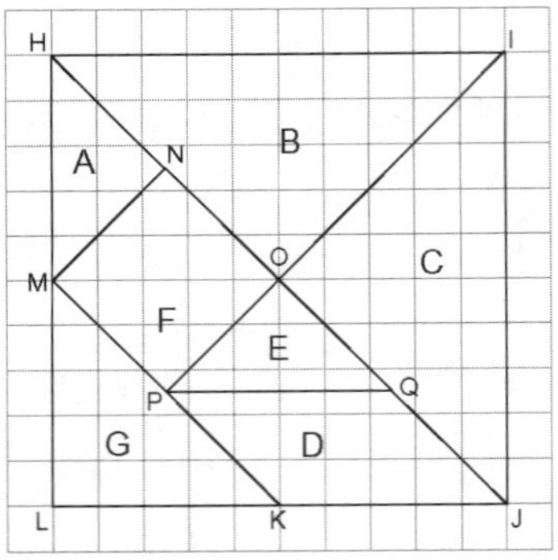

Lesson 8.5, Question 5

Step 1 Draw the diagonal MO of Figure F, to form 2 triangles.
What do you notice about these triangles?

____

Look at △HMO.
What do you notice about the 2 triangles formed by MN?

____

What can you say about Figure A and the two triangles in Figure F?

____

Step 2 Use the formula $A = \frac{1}{2}bh$.
What is the area of △HMO? __________ cm^2

Step 3 Use your answers in *Steps 1* and *2*.
What is the area of Figure F? __________ cm^2
What is the side length of Figure F? __________ cm

Step 4 Put a single hatch mark on each line segment whose length equals the side length of Figure F. You should find 8 line segments.

Step 5 Figure B is an isosceles triangle.
What are the lengths of HO and OI? ________ cm
What is the perimeter of Figure B?
________ cm + ________ cm + ________ cm = ________ cm

Step 6 Figure D is a parallelogram.
What is the length of PK? ________ cm
What is the length of PQ? ________ cm
What is the perimeter of Figure D?
_______ cm + _______ cm + _______ cm + _______ cm = _______ cm

Step 7 How can you use Figure D to find the perimeter of Figure E?

____

____

Step 8 What is the perimeter of Figure E? ________ cm

Name ________________ Date ______________

Master 8.13

Number Lines for *Explore*

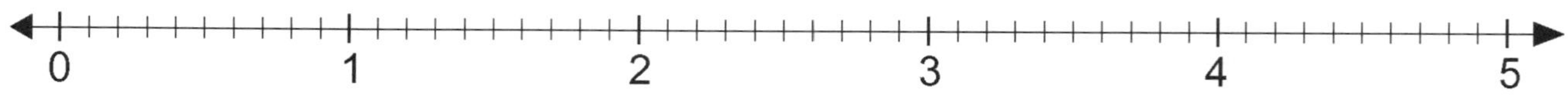

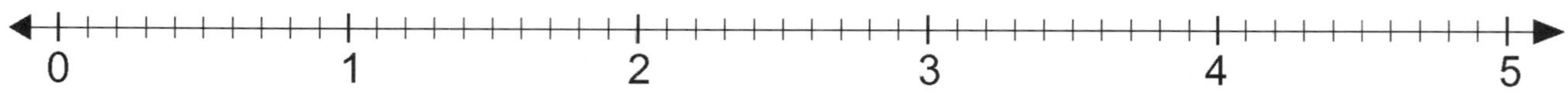

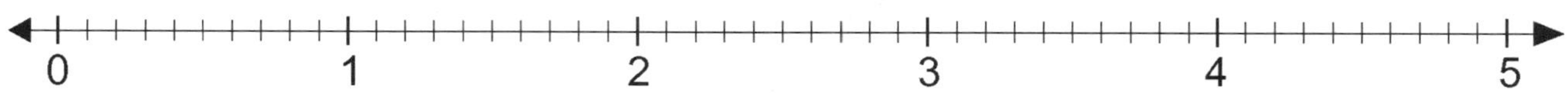

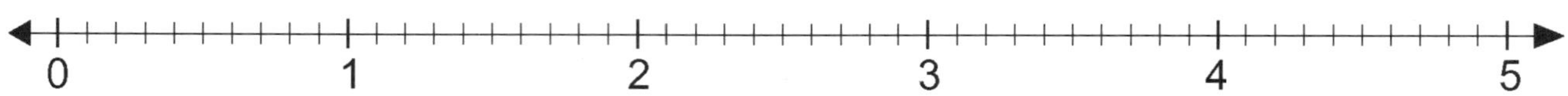

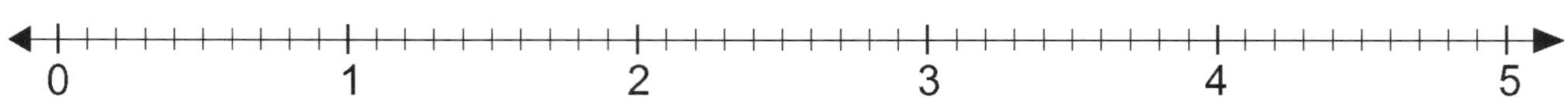

Name ____________________ Date ________________

Master 8.14a

Fitting In Game Cards

$\sqrt{50}$	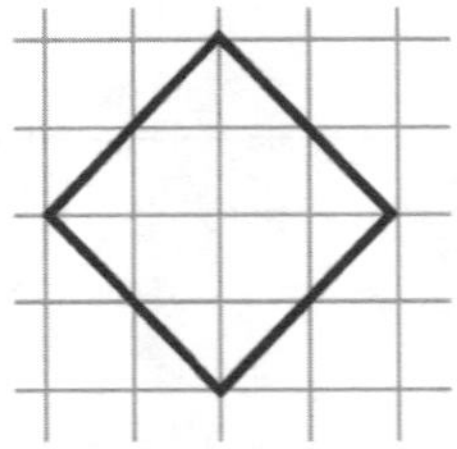 Area	3^2
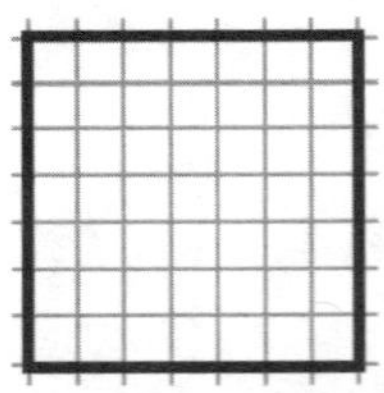 Side Length	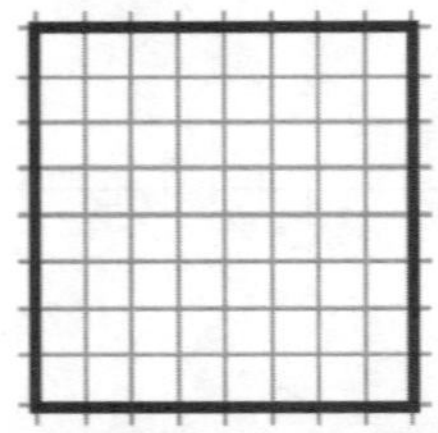 Side Length	 Side Length
$\sqrt{49}$	$\sqrt{64}$	$\sqrt{81}$
7	8	9
$\sqrt{45}$	$\sqrt{59}$	$\sqrt{74}$
6.5	7.5	8.5

Name ____________________ Date ______________

Master 8.14b

Fitting In Game Cards

2^2	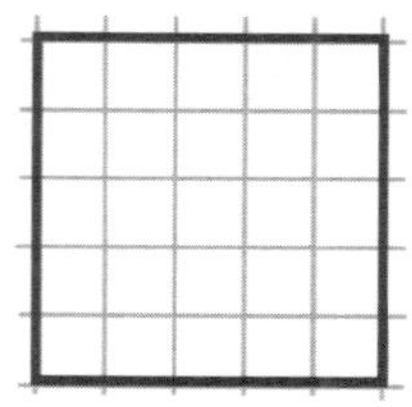 Side Length	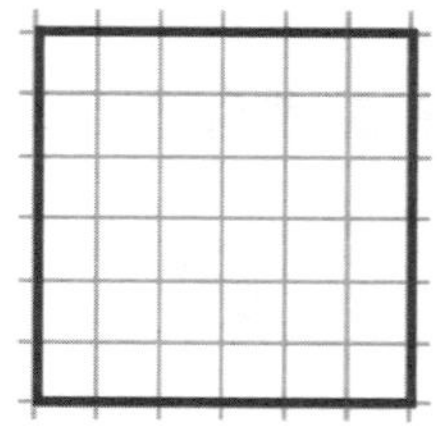 Side Length
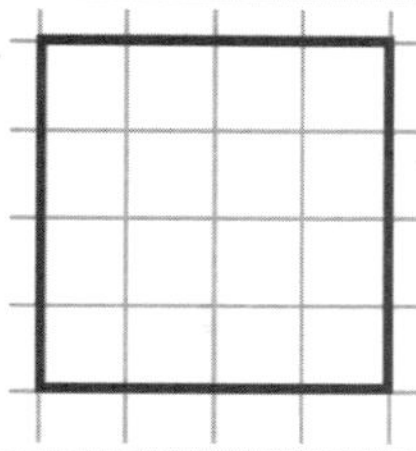 Side Length	$\sqrt{25}$	$\sqrt{36}$
$\sqrt{16}$	5	6
4	4.5	$\sqrt{33}$
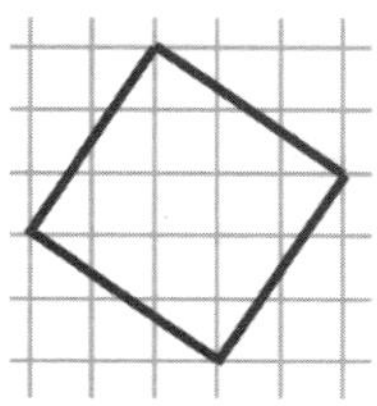 Side Length	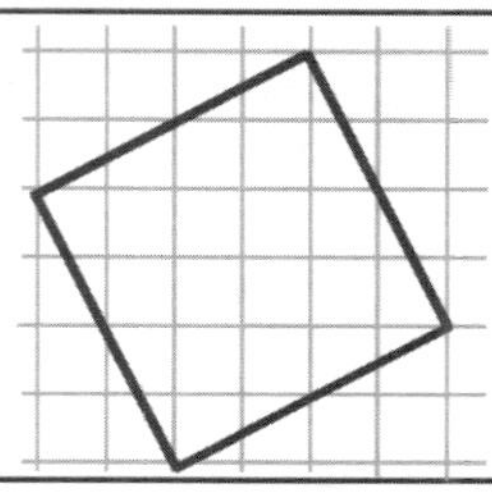 Side Length	5.5
$\sqrt{13}$	$\sqrt{20}$	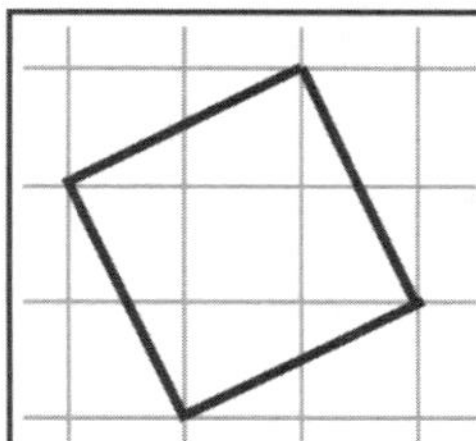 Area

Name ____________________ Date ________________

Master 8.14c

Fitting In Game Cards

$\sqrt{3}$	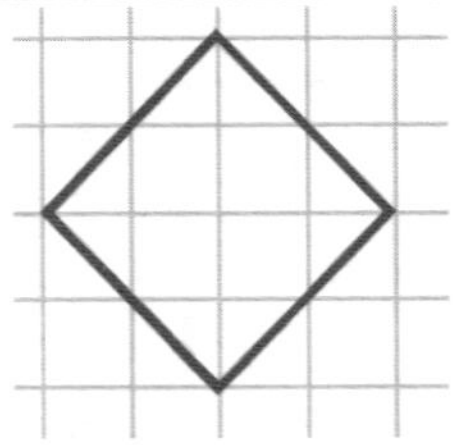 Side Length	3.5
1.5	2.5	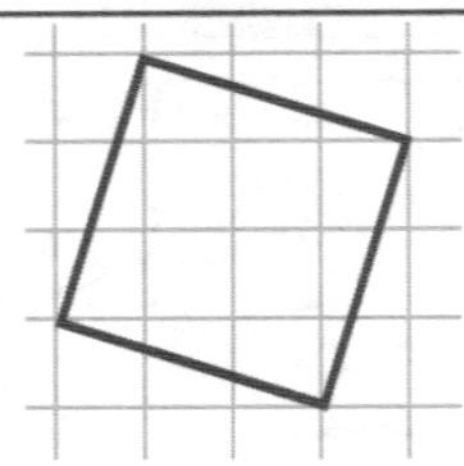 Side Length
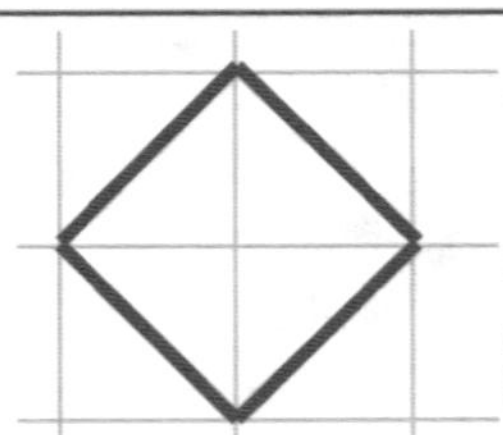 Side Length	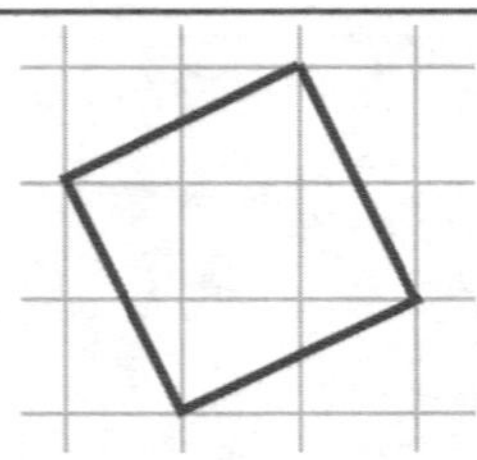 Side Length	$\sqrt{10}$
$\sqrt{2}$	$\sqrt{5}$	$\sqrt{9}$
$\sqrt{1}$	$\sqrt{4}$	3
1	2	$\sqrt{8}$

Name ______________________ Date ________________

Master 8.15

The 10-cm Ruler

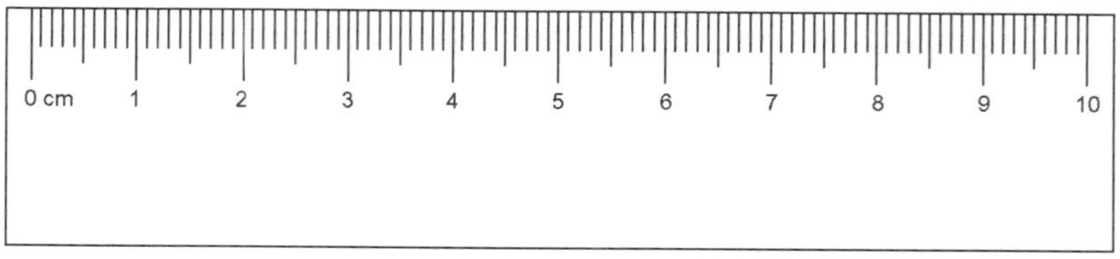

Name ____________________ Date ________________

Master 8.16a

Unit Test: Unit 8
Square Roots and Pythagoras

1. On the grid below, draw a line segment with a length of $\sqrt{41}$ cm.

Explain how you did it.

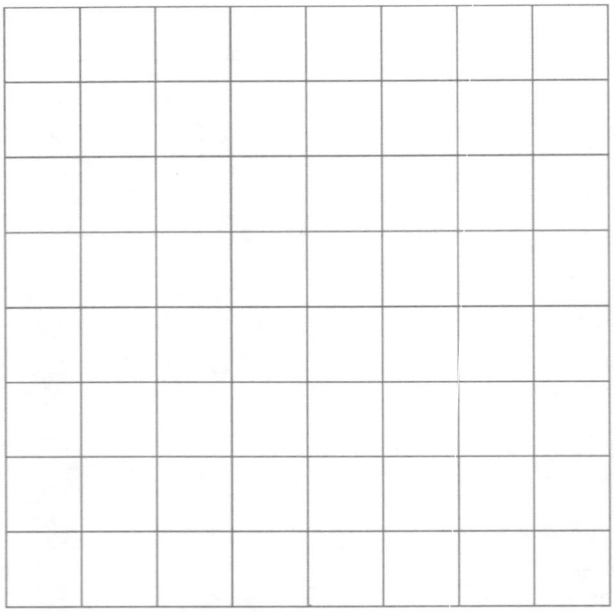

2. Find the length of the indicated side in each triangle.

a)

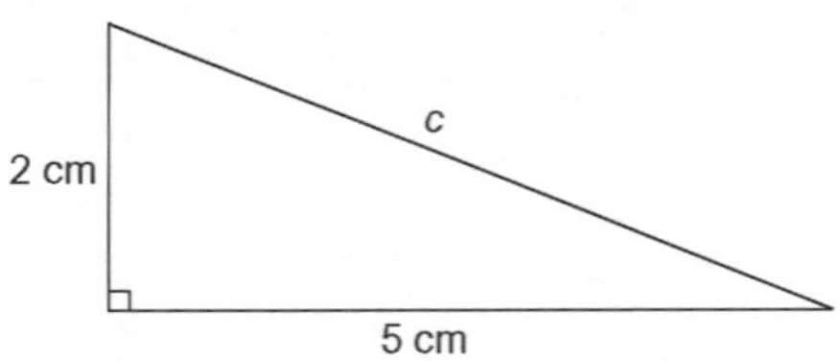

b)

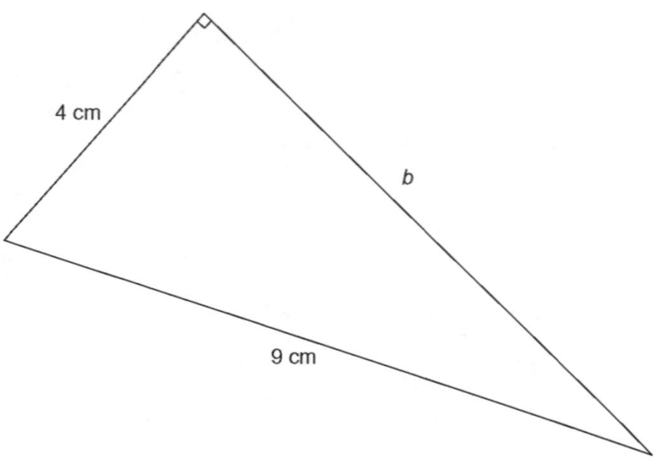

Name ______________________ Date ________________

Master 8.16b

Unit Test continued

c)

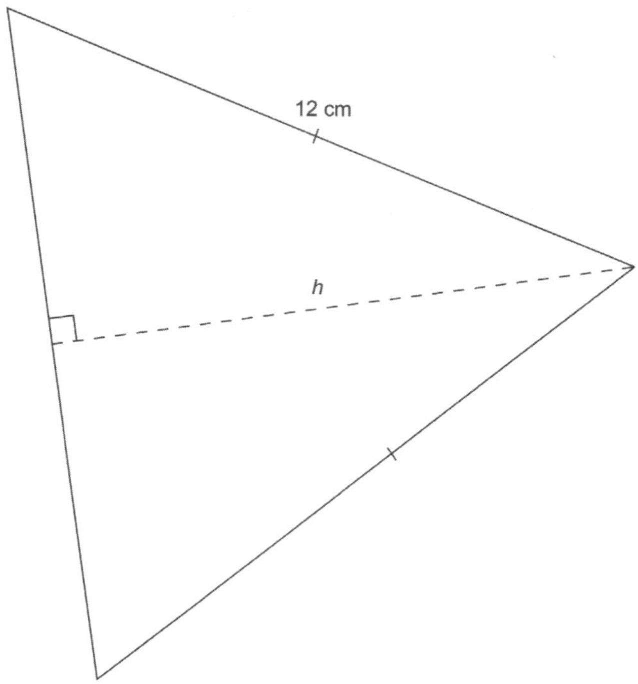

d)

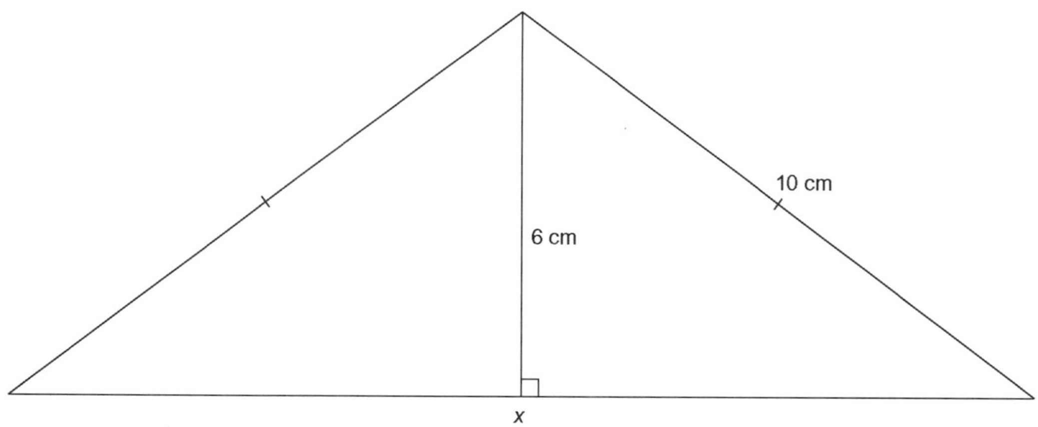

3. A bicycle travels due west at an average speed of 15 km/h.
At the same time, another bicycle travels due south at an average speed of 12 km/h.

a) After 90 min, how far has each bicycle travelled?

b) After 90 min, how far apart are the bicycles?

Name ____________________ Date ________________

Master 8.16c

Unit Test continued

4. A farmer wants to have a water pipe installed from the water source to his farmhouse.
He has two options.
He can have the water pipe follow the rural roads. This option costs $30/m.
He can have the water pipe go directly to the farmhouse, through his field.
This option costs $45/m.

a) What is the cost of running the water pipe directly from the water source to the farmhouse?

b) What is the cost of running the water pipe to the farmhouse along the rural roads?

c) Which is the better option? Explain.

Name ____________________ Date ______________

Master 8.17 **Sample Answers**

Unit Test – Master 8.16

1. I let the given length be the length of the hypotenuse of a right triangle.
The area of the square on the hypotenuse is:
$(\sqrt{41})^2 = 41$
The sum of the areas of the square on the legs must be 41.
So, I found two whole numbers that have a sum of 41, and that are both perfect squares: 16 and 25
The areas of the squares are 16 cm^2 and 25 cm^2.
The lengths of the legs are 4 cm and 5 cm.
I drew a right triangle with legs of lengths 4 cm and 5 cm. I knew the hypotenuse had length $\sqrt{41}$ cm.

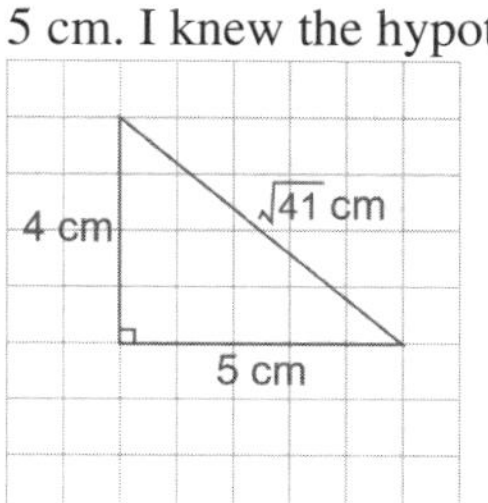

2. **a)** $\sqrt{29}$ cm, or about 5.4 cm

   b) $\sqrt{65}$ cm, or about 8.1 cm

   c) $\sqrt{108}$ cm, or about 10.4 cm

   d) 16 cm

3. **a)** The bicycle travelling due west has travelled 22.5 km. The bicycle travelling due south has travelled 18 km.

   b)

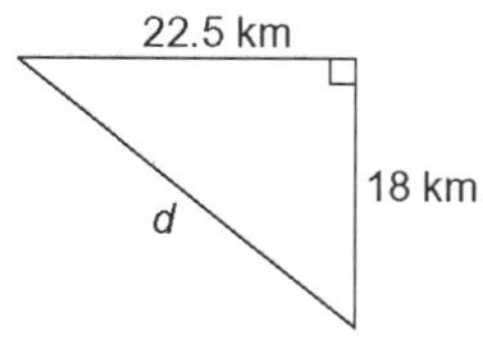

   The bicycles are about 28.8 km apart.

4. **a)** $\$45 \times 1100 = \$49\ 500$

   b) Use the Pythagorean Theorem to find the length of the longer rural road.
   $1100^2 = 200^2 + d^2$
   $1\ 210\ 000 = 40\ 000 + d^2$
   $d^2 = 1\ 170\ 000$
   $d = \sqrt{1\ 170\ 000}$

   The cost of running the water pipe along the rural roads is:
   $(200\text{ m} + \sqrt{1\ 170\ 000}\text{ m}) \times \$30 \doteq \$38\ 450$

   c) The better option is to run the water pipe through the farmer's field. It costs
   $\$49\ 500 - \$38\ 450 = \$11\ 050$ less.

Extra Practice Masters 8.18–8.23

Go to the CD-ROM to access editable versions of these Extra Practice Masters

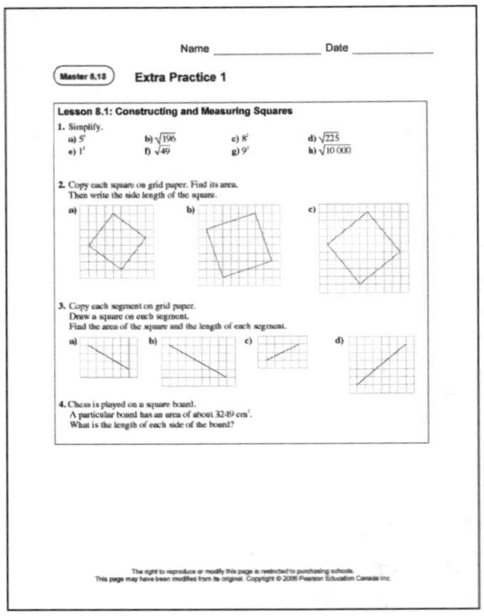

Name ______________ Date ______________

Master 8.18 Extra Practice 1

Lesson 8.1: Constructing and Measuring Squares

1. Simplify.

2. Copy each square on grid paper. Find its area. Then write the side length of the square.

3. Copy each segment on grid paper. Draw a square on each segment. Find the area of the square and the length of each segment.

4. Chess is played on a square board. A particular board has an area of about 32.49 cm². What is the length of each side of the board?

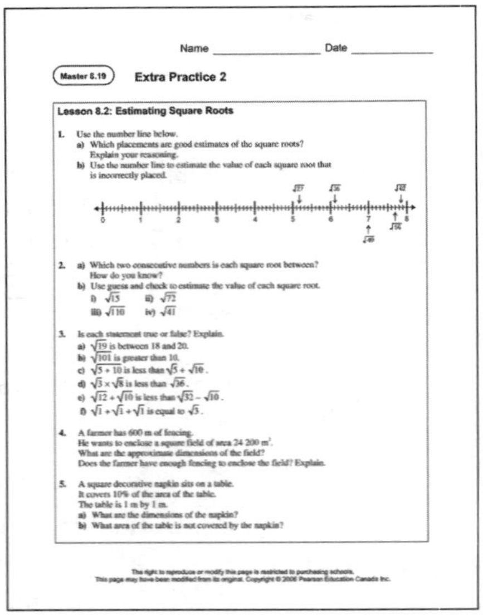

Name ______________ Date ______________

Master 8.19 Extra Practice 2

Lesson 8.2: Estimating Square Roots

1. Use the number line below.
a) Which placements are good estimates of the square roots? Explain your reasoning.
b) Use the number line to estimate the value of each square root that is incorrectly placed.

2. a) Which two consecutive numbers is each square root between? How do you know?
b) Use guess and check to estimate the value of each square root.

3. Is each statement true or false? Explain.

4. A farmer has 600 m of fencing. He wants to enclose a square field of area 24 200 m². What are the approximate dimensions of the field? Does the farmer have enough fencing to enclose the field? Explain.

5. A square decorative napkin sits on a table. It covers 10% of the area of the table. The table is 1 m by 1 m.
a) What are the dimensions of the napkin?
b) What area of the table is not covered by the napkin?

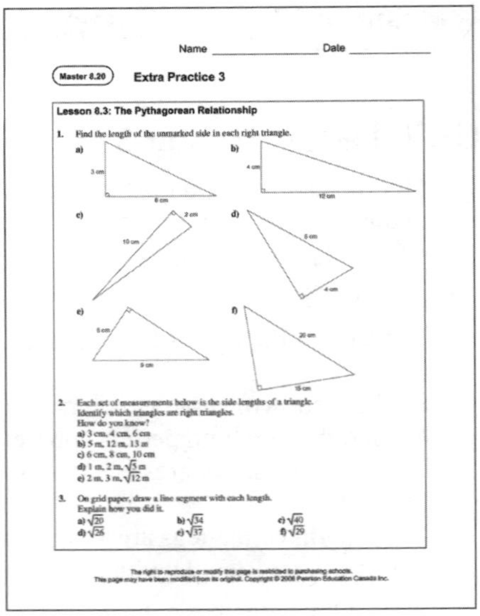

Name ______________ Date ______________

Master 8.20 Extra Practice 3

Lesson 8.3: The Pythagorean Relationship

1. Find the length of the unmarked side in each right triangle.

2. Each set of measurements below is the side lengths of a triangle. Identify which triangles are right triangles. How do you know?

3. On grid paper, draw a line segment with each length. Explain how you did it.

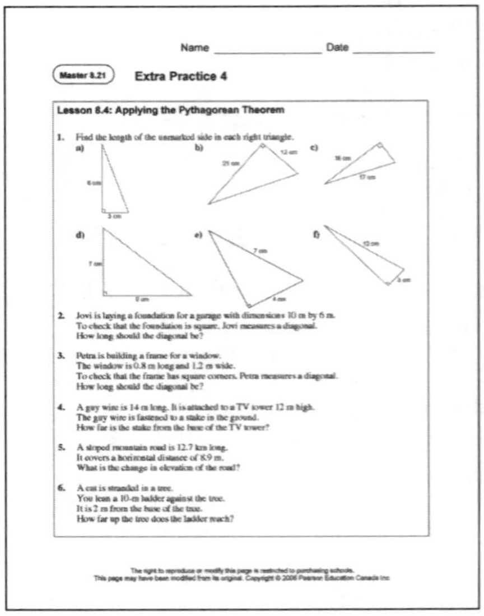

Name ______________ Date ______________

Master 8.21 Extra Practice 4

Lesson 8.4: Applying the Pythagorean Theorem

1. Find the length of the unmarked side in each right triangle.

2. Jovi is laying a foundation for a garage with dimensions 10 m by 6 m. To check that the foundation is square, Jovi measures a diagonal. How long should the diagonal be?

3. Petra is building a frame for a window. The window is 0.8 m long and 1.2 m wide. To check that the frame has square corners, Petra measures a diagonal. How long should the diagonal be?

4. A guy wire is 14 m long. It is attached to a TV tower 12 m high. The guy wire is fastened to a stake in the ground. How far is the stake from the base of the TV tower?

5. A sloped mountain road is 12.7 km long. It covers a horizontal distance of 8.9 m. What is the change in elevation of the road?

6. A cat is stranded in a tree. You lean a 10-m ladder against the tree. It is 2 m from the base of the tree. How far up the tree does the ladder reach?

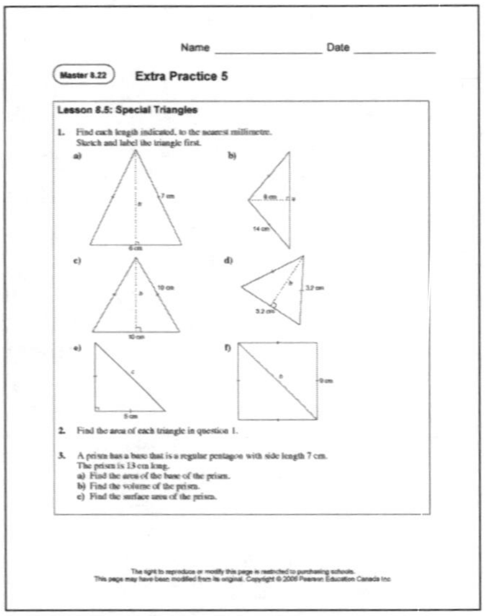

Name ______________ Date ______________

Master 8.22 Extra Practice 5

Lesson 8.5: Special Triangles

1. Find each length indicated, to the nearest millimetre. Sketch and label the triangle first.

2. Find the area of each triangle in question 1.

3. A prism has a base that is a regular pentagon with side length 7 cm. The prism is 13 cm long.
a) Find the area of the base of the prism.
b) Find the volume of the prism.
c) Find the surface area of the prism.

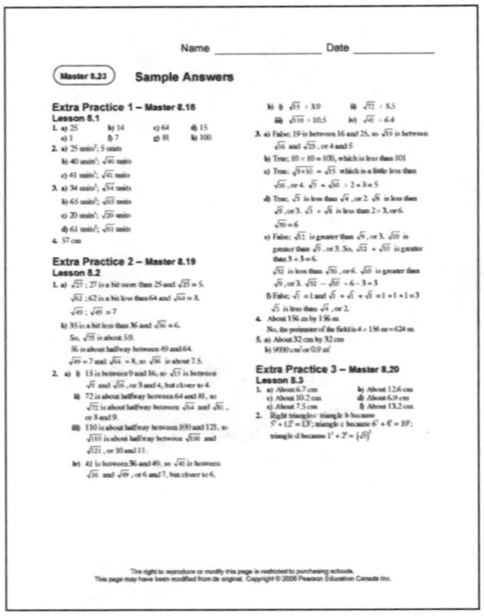

Name ______________ Date ______________

Master 8.23 Sample Answers

Extra Practice 1 – Master 8.18

Extra Practice 2 – Master 8.19

Extra Practice 3 – Master 8.20

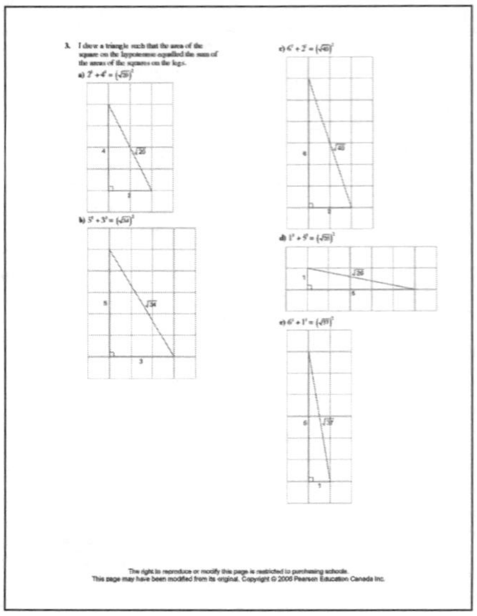

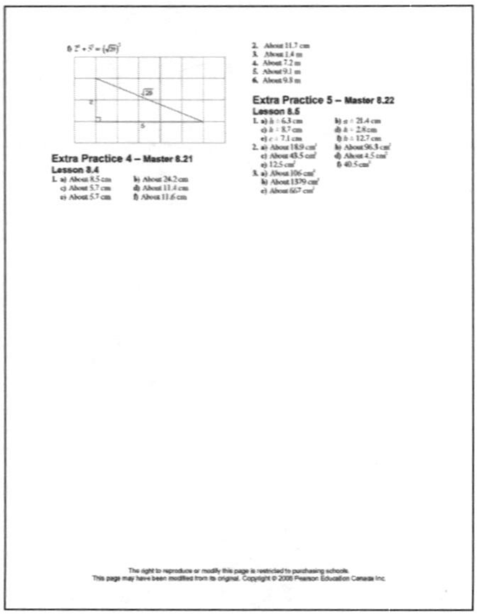

Extra Practice 4 – Master 8.21

Extra Practice 5 – Master 8.22

Addison Wesley Mathematics Makes Sense

Program Authors

Trevor Brown
Antonietta Lenjosek
Cathy Heideman
Jim Mennie
Georgia Konis-Chatzis
A.J. Keene
Margaret Sinclair
Craig Featherstone
Jason Johnston
Bryn Keyes
Elizabeth Wood
Elizabeth Milne
David Sufrin
Don Jones
Sharon Jeroski
Lynn Strangway

Printed and bound in Canada

2 3 4 5 – TC – 09 08 07 06

PEARSON Education Canada

ADDISON WESLEY

Ontario

Math Makes Sense 8

Ontario

Teacher Guide

Unit 9: Integers

PEARSON Education Canada

UNIT 9

Integers

"Students must understand numbers if they are to make sense of the ways numbers are used in their everyday world. They need to use numbers to quantify, to identify location, to identify a specific object in a collection, and to name and to measure."

— NCTM Standards, 1991

FOCUS STRANDS
Number Sense and Numeration
Geometry and Spatial Sense

SUPPORTING STRAND
Patterning and Algebra

TIPS
Students come to class with significant but varying prior knowledge. Such prior knowledge should be valued and used during instruction.

Mathematics Background

What Are the Big Ideas?

- The integers increase from left to right on a number line.
- The sum of an integer and its opposite is zero.
- Subtracting an integer is equivalent to adding the opposite integer.
- If two integers have the same sign, their product and quotient are positive. If two integers have different signs, their product and quotient are negative.
- Ordered pairs of integers can represent positions on a coordinate grid.

How Will the Concepts Develop?

Students review comparing and ordering integers. They continue to use coloured tiles and number lines to model integer addition and subtraction. As these models become internalized, students will be able to add and subtract integers without using manipulatives.

Students use patterns to discover the rules for multiplying and dividing integers.

Students apply the order of operations with integers.

Students pose problems involving integers and investigate solutions.

Students locate, graph, and transform points on a coordinate grid.

Why Are These Concepts Important?

Positive and negative integers are useful for representing real-life situations that involve relative changes or values. Proficiency with integers is necessary for future work in algebra such as evaluating expressions and solving equations. In this and later years, students will extend their concept of number beyond whole numbers and integers to rational, irrational, real, and complex numbers. With each extension, students will be able to solve a wider range of practical and theoretical problems.

Curriculum Overview

The codes refer to the 2005 revised curriculum.

Cluster 1: Integers

Overall Expectation
- Solve problems involving . . . integers, using a variety of computational strategies. (8m9)

Specific Expectations
- Represent, compare, and order rational numbers. (8m13)
- Represent the multiplication and division of integers, using a variety of tools. (8m21)
- Solve problems involving operations with integers, using a variety of tools. (8m22)
- Use estimation when solving problems involving operations with . . . integers . . . to help judge the reasonableness of a solution. (8m18)
- Evaluate expressions that involve integers, including expressions that contain brackets and exponents, using order of operations. (8m23)

Launch

Lesson 9.1: Adding Integers
Lesson 9.2: Subtracting Integers
Lesson 9.3: Adding and Subtracting Integers
Lesson 9.4: Multiplying Integers
Lesson 9.5: Dividing Integers
Lesson 9.5A: Rational Numbers
Mid-Unit Review
Lesson 9.6: Order of Operations with Integers

Cluster 2: Graphing on a Coordinate Grid

Overall Expectation
- Represent transformations using the Cartesian coordinate plane, and make connections between transformations and the real world. (8m42)

Specific Expectations
- Graph the image of a point, or set of points, on the Cartesian coordinate plane after applying a transformation to the original point(s). (8m52)
- Identify, through investigation, real-world movements that are translations, reflections, and rotations. (8m53)

Lesson 9.7: Graphing on a Coordinate Grid
Lesson 9.8: Graphing Translations and Reflections
Lesson 9.9: Graphing Rotations

Unit Review
Practice Test

Unit Problem
Charity Golf Tournament

Curriculum across the Grades

Grade 7	Grade 8
Students identify and compare integers found in real-life contexts. Students use a variety of tools to represent and order integers. Students use a variety of tools to add and subtract integers. Students plot points using all four quadrants of the Cartesian plane. Students identify, perform, and describe dilatations using a variety of tools. They create designs involving translations, reflections, dilatations, and/or simple rotations of two-dimensional figures. Students determine polygons or combinations of polygons that tile a plane, and describe the transformation(s) involved.	Students use a variety of tools to represent the multiplication and division of integers. Students use a variety of tools to solve problems involving operations with integers. They use estimation to help judge the reasonableness of a solution. Students use order of operations to evaluate expressions with integers, including expressions that contain brackets and exponents. Students graph the image of a point, or a set of points, on the Cartesian coordinate plane after applying a transformation to the original point(s). Students identify, through investigation, real-world movements that are translations, reflections, and rotations.

Additional Activities

Integer Alphabet

For Extra Support (Appropriate for use after Lesson 9.1)
Materials: *Integer Alphabet* (Master 9.6)

This game gives students practice in adding integers.

The work students do: Students work with a partner. Each letter of the alphabet is assigned an integer value. The "value" of a word is the sum of the values of its letters. Students find the values of words or make words whose values meet a specified condition.

Take It Further: Find a word whose value is 0.

Mathematical/Social
Partner Activity

What's the Temperature?

For Extension (Appropriate for use after Lesson 9.3)
Materials: *What's the Temperature?* (Master 9.7)

This game allows students to use their knowledge of integers to solve a problem.

The work students do: Students work with a partner to determine the daily low and daily high temperatures of the four cities based on the clues given. One student reads out the problem. The other sets up a chart similar to the one below.

	Daily Low	Daily High
Rome		
Oslo		
Orlando		
Toronto		

Students take turns reading out the clues and filling in the chart. The game ends when the chart is completely filled in.

Logical/Social
Partner Activity

What's My Product?

For Extra Practice (Appropriate for use after Lesson 9.4)
Materials: *What's My Product?* (Master 9.8), deck of cards with face cards removed

This game gives students practice in multiplying integers.

The work students do: Students play in pairs. Each player turns over two cards, and finds the product. Black cards are negative; red cards are positive. The player with the greater product wins all four cards. In the event of a tie, each player draws two more cards and finds the product. The player with the greater product wins all eight cards. Play continues until all the cards have gone. The player with more cards wins.

Take It Further: Students take 3 cards and find their sum.

Mathematical/Social
Partner Activity

Integer Bingo

For Extra Practice (Appropriate for use after Lesson 9.5)
Materials: *Integer Bingo* (Master 9.9a), *Expressions for Integer Bingo* (Master 9.9b), counters

This game gives students practice in solving problems involving operations with integers.

The work students do: Students randomly place an integer from −30 to +30 on each empty square of their Bingo cards. The caller calls out an integer expression. Students calculate the answer. If the answer is on their Bingo card, they cover it with a counter. Play continues. The winner is the first person with five counters in a row.

Mathematical/Social
Group Activity

Planning for Unit 9

Planning for Instruction

Suggested Unit time: About 3–4 weeks

Lesson	Time	Materials	Program Support
Launch, page 2	15–20 min		
Skills You'll Need, page 4	40–50 min	coloured tiles number lines	Master 9.20: Number Lines
9.1: Adding Integers, page 8 Use a number line and calculator to add integers.	40–50 min	number lines and transparency calculators deck of cards (optional)	Master 9.20: Number Lines Master 9.10: Step-by-Step 1 Master 9.24: Extra Practice 1
9.2: Subracting Integers, page 12 Use a calculator and number line to subtract integers.	40–50 min	number lines and transparency	Master 9.20: Number Lines Master 9.11: Step-by-Step 2 Master 9.25: Extra Practice 2
9.3: Adding and Subtracting Integers, page 17 Add and subtract integers.	40–50 min	number lines and transparency	Master 9.20: Number Lines Master 9.12: Step-by-Step 3 Master 9.26: Extra Practice 3
9.4: Multiplying Integers, page 20 Use patterns to develop the rules for multiplying integers.	40–50 min	multiplication charts (optional)	PM 15: 12 × 12 Multiplication Chart Master 9.13: Step-by-Step 4 Master 9.27: Extra Practice 4
9.5: Dividing Integers, page 25 Use patterns to develop the rules for dividing integers.	40–50 min	calculators	Master 9.14: Step-by-Step 5 Master 9.28: Extra Practice 5
9.5A: Rational Numbers, page 29 Represent, compare, and order rational numbers.	40–50 min	Lesson 5A number lines	Master 9.5: Lesson 5A Master 9.20: Number Lines Master 9.15: Step-by-Step 5A Master 9.29: Extra Practice 5A
Mid-Unit Review, page 33		number lines	Master 9.20: Number Lines
9.6: Order of Operations with Integers, page 34 Apply the order of operations with brackets and exponents.	40–50 min		Master 9.16: Step-by-Step 6 Master 9.30: Extra Practice 6
9.7: Graphing on a Coordinate Grid, page 37 Locate and graph points in four quadrants on a coordinate grid.	optional but recommended	overhead transparency of coordinate grid coordinate grids 0.5-cm grid paper	PM 14: 0.5-cm Grid Paper Master 9.21: Coordinate Grid Master 9.17: Step-by-Step 7 Master 9.31: Extra Practice 7
9.8: Graphing Translations and Reflections, page 42 Graph translation and reflection images on a coordinate grid.	80–100 min	overhead transparency of coordinate grid 0.5-cm grid paper coordinate grids	PM 14: 0.5-cm Grid Paper Master 9.21: Coordinate Grid Master 9.18: Step-by-Step 8 Master 9.32: Extra Practice 8
9.9: Graphing Rotations, page 47 Graph rotation images on a coordinate grid.	80–100 min	overhead transparency of coordinate grid 0.5-cm grid paper coordinate grids	PM 14: 0.5-cm Grid Paper Master 9.21: Coordinate Grid Master 9.19: Step-by-Step 9 Master 9.33: Extra Practice 9
Reading and Writing in Math: Creating a Study Sheet, page 52			
Unit Review, page 54		coloured tiles number lines coordinate grids 0.5-cm grid paper	Master 9.20: Number Lines Master 9.21: Coordinate Grid PM 14: 0.5-cm Grid Paper Extra Practice: Student Book page 496
Practice Test, page 57		coloured tiles number lines coordinate grids 0.5-cm grid paper	Master 9.20: Number Lines Master 9.21: Coordinate Grid PM 14: 0.5-cm Grid Paper
Unit Problem: Charity Golf Tournament, page 58	40–50 min	number lines (optional)	Master 9.20: Number Lines

Planning for Assessment

Purpose	Tools and Process	Recording and Reporting
Diagnostic	*Unit Launch* Question; conference; scaffold problems throughout the unit	PM 8: Conference Prompts
Formative	*Explore* – Ongoing Assessment: Observe and Listen	Master 9.2 Ongoing Observations: Integers PM 1: Inquiry Process Check List PM 6: Observation Record 1 PM 7: Observation Record 2 PM 8: Conference Prompts PM 2: Self-Assessment PM 3: Self-Assessment: Problem Solving PM 9: Work Sample Records
Summative	*Unit Review* *Unit Problem* — Performance Assessment Unit Test Review assessment records; add unit results to ongoing records	Master 9.1: Unit Rubric: Integers Master 9.3: Performance Assessment Rubric: Charity Golf Tournament Master 9.4: Unit Summary: Integers PM 10: Summary Class Records: Strands PM 11: Summary Class Records: Achievement Categories PM 12: Summary Record: Individual
Learning Skills/Mathematical Disposition	Observe and record throughout the unit	PM 4: Learning Skills Check List PM 5: Mathematical Dispositions and Learning Skills

Program Masters (PM) are in the *Grade 8 Planning and Program Masters* module.
Extra Practice Masters are on the CD-ROM and are printed in reduced format on page 89 of this module.

LESSON ORGANIZER 15–20 min

Curriculum Focus: Activate prior knowledge about integers.
Vocabulary: integer, par

ASSUMED PRIOR KNOWLEDGE

- ✓ Students can recognize positive and negative integers used in real-world situations.
- ✓ Students can place integers on a number line.
- ✓ Students can compare and order integers.

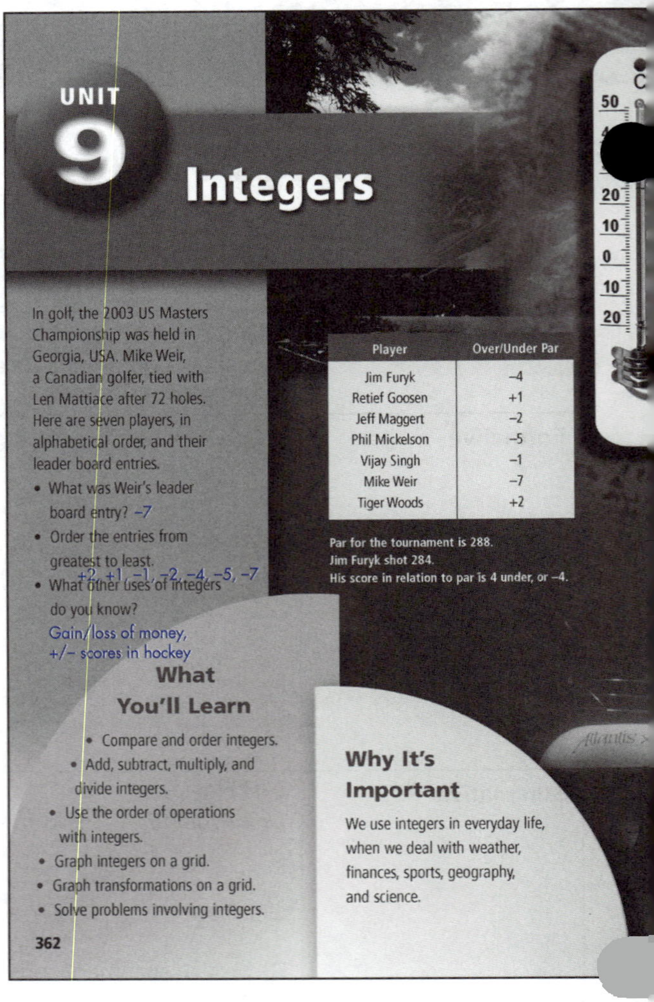

UNIT 9

Integers

In golf, the 2003 US Masters Championship was held in Georgia, USA. Mike Weir, a Canadian golfer, tied with Len Mattiace after 72 holes. Here are seven players, in alphabetical order, and their leader board entries.

- What was Weir's leader board entry? −7
- Order the entries from greatest to least. +2, +1, −1, −2, −4, −5, −7
- What other uses of integers do you know? Gain/loss of money, +/− scores in hockey

Player	Over/Under Par
Jim Furyk	−4
Retief Goosen	+1
Jeff Maggert	−2
Phil Mickelson	−5
Vijay Singh	−1
Mike Weir	−7
Tiger Woods	+2

Par for the tournament is 288.
Jim Furyk shot 284.
His score in relation to par is 4 under, or −4.

What You'll Learn

- Compare and order integers.
- Add, subtract, multiply, and divide integers.
- Use the order of operations with integers.
- Graph integers on a grid.
- Graph transformations on a grid.
- Solve problems involving integers.

Why It's Important

We use integers in everyday life, when we deal with weather, finances, sports, geography, and science.

362

ACTIVATE PRIOR LEARNING

Have students look at the chart on page 362 of the Student Book. Ask questions, such as:

- What does the statement "Par for the tournament is 288" mean?
  (*A player should take a total of 288 strokes to play the ball into all the given holes.*)
- Which number is assigned to par? (*0*)
- Jeff Maggert's score is −2 but Tiger Woods' score is +2. What do these numbers mean?
  (*−2 means two strokes less than par/zero; +2 means two strokes above par/zero.*)
- Of the players listed, who is doing the best? How do you know?
  (*Mike Weir; he has the lowest score, −7. He has taken the least number of strokes.*)
- Who is the next closest? How do you know?
  (*Phil Mickelson; his score is −5. After Mike Weir, he has taken the least number of strokes.*)

Have students look at the pictures on pages 362 and 363. Ask:

- Name two other real-life situations besides golf where positive and negative integers are used. (*Temperatures above/below 0°C, distances above/below sea level*)

Discuss the questions in the Student Book and record students' responses on the board.

Tell students that, in this unit, they will compare, order, add, subtract, multiply, and divide integers. They will extend their knowledge of order of operations to integers, and use integers to graph and transform points on a coordinate grid. At the end of this unit, they use integers to solve problems related to a charity golf tournament.

Key Words

- positive integer
- negative integer
- opposite integers
- zero pair
- rational number
- coordinate grid
- quadrants
- ordered pair
- x-axis
- y-axis
- origin

363

FROM THE LIBRARY

Algebra For Everyone: Videotape and Discussion Guide. NCTM (1992), third printing (2002)
ISBN: 087353350X
This videotape promotes the use of manipulatives in the classroom. Coloured tiles are used as a visual model for integers and to develop the meaning behind the algorithms for integer addition and subtraction.

REACHING ALL LEARNERS

Some students may benefit from using the virtual manipulatives on the e-Tools CD-ROM.
The e-Tools appropriate for this unit are *Counters*. If you do not have coloured tiles or counters, have students colour and cut out squares from 2-cm grid paper (PM 21).

DIAGNOSTIC ASSESSMENT

What to Look For	What to Do
✔ Students can recognize positive and negative integers used in real-world situations. ✔ Students can place integers on a number line. ✔ Students can compare and order integers.	***Extra Support:*** Have students continue to use integer tiles as needed. *Work on this skill during Skills You'll Need.* Have students check that they ordered the integers on page 362 correctly by having them place the integers on a number line. (*The integers decrease from right to left on a number line.*) *Work on this skill during Skills You'll Need.*

LESSON ORGANIZER (40–50 min)

Skills in Review
- Comparing and ordering integers
- Using models to add integers
- Using models to subtract integers

Teacher Materials
- coloured tiles for the overhead projector

Student Materials
- Number Lines (Master 9.20)
- coloured tiles

Vocabulary: positive integer, negative integer, opposite integer, zero pair

Alternative Example 1

Draw a vertical number line to represent the floors in a 12-storey office building, with 4 levels of underground parking.

a) Which floors are represented by the integers 0, +3, and −2?

b) Explain why −2 is greater than −4 by using the context of this office building.

Solution

a) Ground level; 3 floors above ground level; 2 floors below ground level

b) You are higher up when you are 2 floors below ground level than when you are 4 floors below ground level.

UNIT 9

Skills You'll Need

Comparing and Ordering Integers

Positive integers, such as +5, +9, +1, are greater than 0.
Negative integers, such as −5, −9, −1, are less than 0.
Positive and negative integers can be shown on a number line:

−4 −3 −2 −1 0 +1 +2 +3 +4

Any positive integer is greater than any negative integer.
For example, +1 is greater than −1000.

We use the symbols > and < to show order.

−3 is to the left of +1; so, −3 is less than +1, and we write: −3 < +1

+3 is to the right of −4; so, +3 is greater than −4, and we write: +3 > −4

Example 1

Order these integers from least to greatest: +5, −6, +3, −8, 0, −1, +8

Solution

+5, −6, +3, −8, 0, −1, +8
Sketch a number line from −8 to +8. Mark a point on the line for each integer.

−8 −7 −6 −5 −4 −3 −2 −1 0 +1 +2 +3 +4 +5 +6 +7 +8

For least to greatest, read the integers from left to right: −8, −6, −1, 0, +3, +5, +8

✓ Check

1. Sketch a number line. Use it to order these integers:
0, +2, −1, +4, −5, −7, +10 From least to greatest: −7, −5, −1, 0, +2, +4, +10

2. Copy each statement. Use < or > to show which number in each pair is greater. Use a number line if it helps.
a) +2 < +8 b) 0 > −5 c) −7 < 0
d) +250 > −251 e) −100 < −70 f) −361 < −360

364 UNIT 9: Integers

Comparing and Ordering Integers

Ask students to draw a horizontal number line from +5 to −5. Call out these pairs of integers.

+3 and 0	−4 and +4	−3 and +4
−2 and −1	+1 and −2	+5 and −5

Have students work with a partner to determine the greater integer in each pair.

As students work, ask questions, such as:
- How do you find out which integer is greater?
(*The integer farther to the right on a number line is greater.*)
- How do you know whether to use the > symbol or the < symbol?
(*> means greater than; < means less than.*)

Common Misconceptions

➤ Students confuse the symbols for *less than* and *greater than*.

How to Help: Remind students that the inequality symbol always points toward the lesser number.

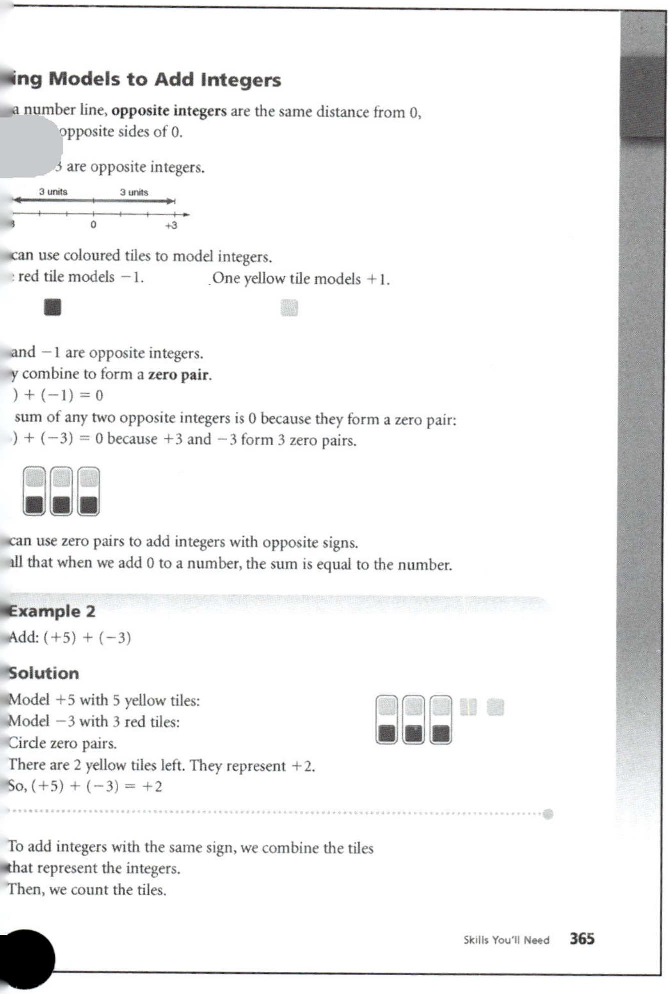

ing Models to Add Integers

a number line, **opposite integers** are the same distance from 0, opposite sides of 0.

3 are opposite integers.

can use coloured tiles to model integers.
red tile models −1. One yellow tile models +1.

and −1 are opposite integers.
y combine to form a **zero pair**.
) + (−1) = 0
sum of any two opposite integers is 0 because they form a zero pair:
) + (−3) = 0 because +3 and −3 form 3 zero pairs.

can use zero pairs to add integers with opposite signs.
ll that when we add 0 to a number, the sum is equal to the number.

Example 2

Add: (+5) + (−3)

Solution

Model +5 with 5 yellow tiles:
Model −3 with 3 red tiles:
Circle zero pairs.
There are 2 yellow tiles left. They represent +2.
So, (+5) + (−3) = +2

To add integers with the same sign, we combine the tiles that represent the integers.
Then, we count the tiles.

Skills You'll Need 365

Alternative Example 2

Add: (−2) + (+6)

Solution

Model −2 with 2 red tiles:
Model +6 with 6 yellow tiles:
Circle zero pairs.

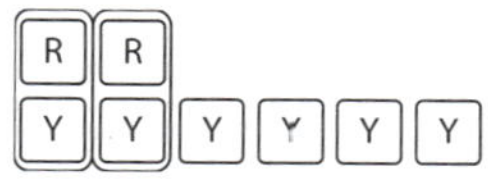

There are 4 yellow tiles left. They represent +4.
So, (−2) + (+6) = +4

Sample Solutions

1.

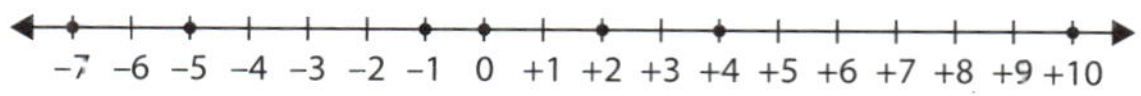

Using Models to Add Integers

Place a yellow tile and a red tile on the overhead projector.

- What is the value of each tile? (*Yellow tile: +1; Red tile: −1*)
- What is the result of combining a yellow tile with a red tile? (*They "cancel" each other out to form a zero pair.*)
- What is the value of a zero pair? (*0*)

Place two more yellow tiles and two more red tiles on the overhead projector.

- Which integer is represented by the yellow tiles? (*+3*)
- Which integer is represented by the red tiles? (*−3*)
- How do I use the tiles to find the sum of +3 and −3? (*Pair each red tile with a yellow tile to form a zero pair. No tiles are left, so (+3) + (−3) = 0.*)
- What are integers such as +3 and −3 called? (*Opposites*)
- Is the sum of any pair of opposites always 0? Explain. (*Yes, the number of red tiles equals the number of yellow tiles, so all the tiles can be paired. Since no tiles are left, the sum is 0.*)

Place four more yellow tiles on the overhead projector.

- What sum do the tiles now model? (*(+7) + (−3)*)
- How do I find the sum? (*3 yellow tiles and 3 red tiles form zero pairs. Four yellow tiles are left, so the sum is +4.*)

Common Misconceptions

➤ Students add integers incorrectly when coloured tiles are not used.

How to Help: Encourage students to continue using tiles. Alternatively, ask them to check that their answers make sense by relating them to real-life situations (for example, losing a $5 bill and then finding a toonie is a net loss of $3; this represents (−5) + (+2) = −3).

Alternative Example 3

Add: (+7) + (+4)

Solution

Model +7 with 7 yellow tiles: Y Y Y Y Y Y Y

Model +4 with 4 yellow tiles: Y Y Y Y

There are 11 yellow tiles altogether.

They represent +11.

So, (+7) + (+4) = +11

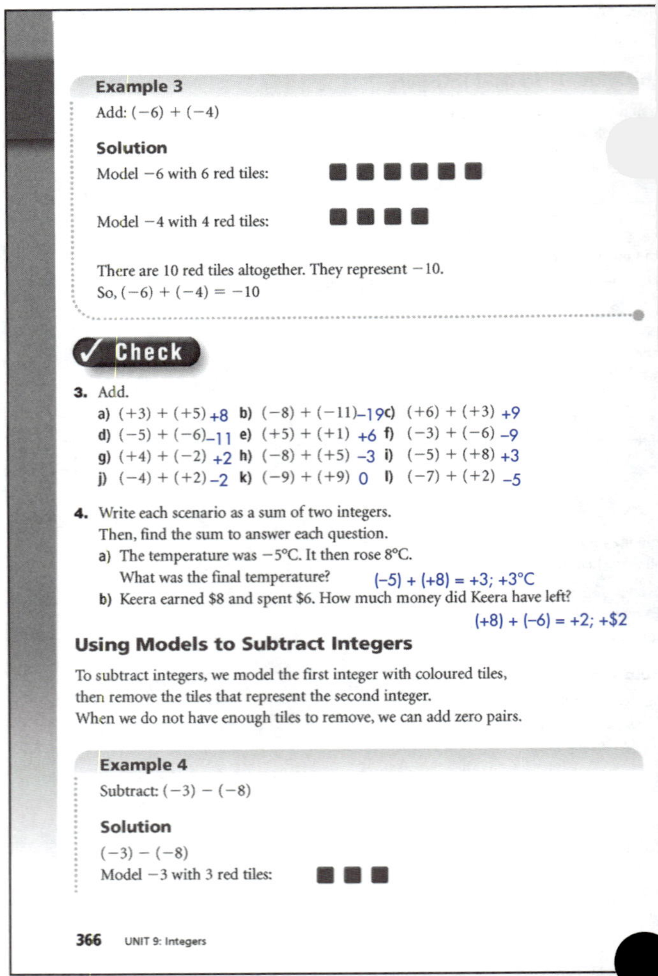

Example 3

Add: (−6) + (−4)

Solution

Model −6 with 6 red tiles:

Model −4 with 4 red tiles:

There are 10 red tiles altogether. They represent −10.

So, (−6) + (−4) = −10

✓ Check

3. Add.

a) (+3) + (+5) +8 b) (−8) + (−11) −19 c) (+6) + (+3) +9

d) (−5) + (−6) −11 e) (+5) + (+1) +6 f) (−3) + (−6) −9

g) (+4) + (−2) +2 h) (−8) + (+5) −3 i) (−5) + (+8) +3

j) (−4) + (+2) −2 k) (−9) + (+9) 0 l) (−7) + (+2) −5

4. Write each scenario as a sum of two integers. Then, find the sum to answer each question.

a) The temperature was −5°C. It then rose 8°C. What was the final temperature? (−5) + (+8) = +3; +3°C

b) Keera earned $8 and spent $6. How much money did Keera have left? (+8) + (−6) = +2; +$2

Using Models to Subtract Integers

To subtract integers, we model the first integer with coloured tiles, then remove the tiles that represent the second integer.
When we do not have enough tiles to remove, we can add zero pairs.

Example 4

Subtract: (−3) − (−8)

Solution

(−3) − (−8)

Model −3 with 3 red tiles:

366 UNIT 9: Integers

Using Models to Subtract Integers

Use an overhead projector to review how to subtract integers using tiles.

- How would you model (–5) – (–3)? (*Use 5 red tiles to represent –5. Remove 3 red tiles to represent subtracting –3. There are 2 red tiles left. This represents –2 so (–5) – (–3) = –2.*)
- How would you model (+4) – (–2)? (*Use 4 yellow tiles to represent +4. To subtract –2, you must remove 2 red tiles. Since there are no red tiles to remove, add 2 zero pairs. Now there are 6 yellow tiles and 2 red tiles. Remove the 2 red tiles. There are 6 yellow tiles left. This represents +6, so (+4) – (–2) = +6.*)

As you work through the examples, ask questions, such as:

- Why did we have to add zero pairs in the second example but not the first? (*In the first example, there were enough red tiles to take away the second integer. In the second example, there were not enough red tiles to take away the second integer.*)
- Why can we add zero pairs when we don't have enough tiles to take away the second integer? (*Adding zero pairs to the first integer does not change its numerical value because the sum of 0 and a number is equal to the number.*)

Common Misconceptions

➤ Students do not group all possible pairs of tiles that form zero pairs.

How to Help: Have students align the tiles in two rows, one below the other, so they can be paired easily. Students should see that after all zero pairs are formed, tiles of only one colour should remain. If both red and yellow tiles are left, more zero pairs can be made.

To take away −8, we need 5 more red tiles.
Add 5 zero pairs of tiles.
…is, add 5 red tiles and 5 yellow tiles. They represent 0.

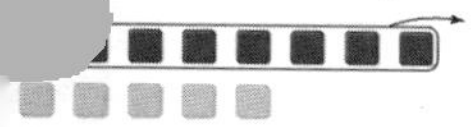

Take away 8 red tiles.
5 yellow tiles remain. They represent +5.
So, (−3) − (−8) = +5

Example 5

Subtract: (+2) − (−9)

Solution

(+2) − (−9)
Model +2 with 2 yellow tiles: 
To take away −9, we need 9 red tiles.
Add 9 zero pairs of tiles.
That is, add 9 red tiles and 9 yellow tiles. They represent 0.

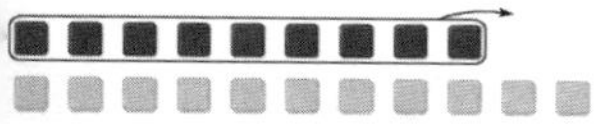

Take away 9 red tiles.
11 yellow tiles remain. They represent +11.
So, (+2) − (−9) = +11

Check

Subtract.

a) (+1) − (+5) −4 b) (+4) − (+1) +3 c) (−5) − (−9) +4
d) (−8) − (−1) −7 e) (+10) − (+5) +5 f) (−10) − (−3) −7

Subtract.

a) (+3) − (−8) +11 b) (+7) − (−2) +9 c) (−9) − (+3) −12
d) (−5) − (−11) +6 e) (+8) − (−8) +16 f) (−5) − (+5) −10

Alternative Example 4

Subtract: (−8) − (+5)

Solution

Model −8 with 8 red tiles:

R R R R R R R R

To take away +5, we need 5 yellow tiles.
Add 5 zero pairs of tiles.
That is, add 5 red tiles and 5 yellow tiles. They represent 0.

R R R R R R R R R R R R R
Y Y Y Y Y

Take away 5 yellow tiles.
13 red tiles remain. They represent −13.
So, (−8) − (+5) = −13

Adding Integers

LESSON ORGANIZER

40–50 min

Curriculum Focus: Use a number line and calculator to add integers. (8m18, 8m22)

Teacher Materials
- overhead transparency of a number line (Master 9.20)

Student Materials
- Number Lines (Master 9.20)
- calculators

Optional
- Step-by-Step 1 (Master 9.10)
- Extra Practice 1 (Master 9.24)
- deck of playing cards (face cards and jokers removed)

Assessment: Master 9.2 Ongoing Observations: Integers

Key Math Learnings

1. On a number line, positive integers are to the right of 0 and negative integers are to the left of 0.
2. On a number line, an arrow to the right represents a positive integer. An arrow to the left represents a negative integer. The length of the arrow is the numerical value of the integer.

9.1 Adding Integers

Focus Use a number line and calculator to add integers.

You have used coloured tiles to add integers.
We will now investigate other ways to add.

Explore

Work with a partner.
Use these integers: +5, −9, −16, +28, −34, +41
Choose two integers. Add them.
Choose two different integers. Add them.
Repeat this activity.
Add as many different pairs of integers as you can.
Sketch a number line to show each sum.
Write each addition equation.

Reflect & Share

Compare your addition equations with those of another pair of classmates.
How can you add two integers when their signs are the same?
When their signs are different?

Connect

Recall how to use a number line to add integers.
The integer +11 is represented by an arrow, 11 units long, pointing right.
The integer −5 is represented by an arrow, 5 units long, pointing left.

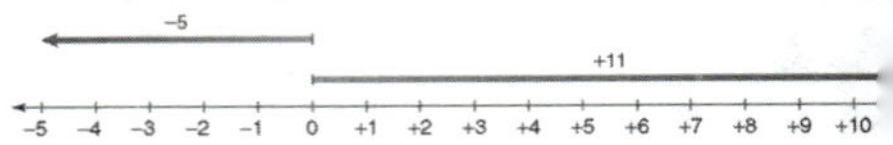

To add a positive integer, move right on a number line.

To add: (−5) + (+11)
Start at −5 on a number line. Move 11 units right.

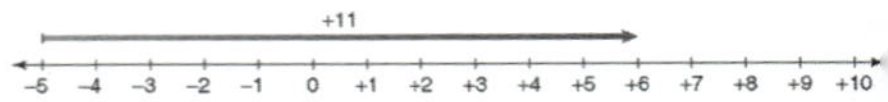

The arrow head is at +6.
So, (−5) + (+11) = +6

368 UNIT 9: Integers

BEFORE Get Started

Have students draw a number line from −7 to +7.

Ask:
- Where are the negative numbers located? (*To the left of zero*)
- Where are the positive numbers located? (*To the right of zero*)
- Why does a number line have arrows at the end? (*The line continues in both directions.*)
- Which integers are represented by arrows that point to the right? (*Positive integers*)
- Which integers are represented by arrows that point to the left? (*Negative integers*)

Present *Explore.* Distribute copies of *Number Lines* (Master 9.20) to pairs of students.

DURING Explore

Ongoing Assessment: Observe and Listen

As students work, ask questions, such as:
- Which integers are you adding? (*+5 and −9*)
- What is the addition statement? (*(+5) + (−9)*)
- Could you write this statement a different way? (*Yes, I could write (−9) + (+5).*)
- How did you add? (*I used a number line. I started at +5 and moved 9 units left. I ended up at −4.*)
- What is the addition equation? (*(+5) + (−9) = −4*)
- How would you add (−9) + (+5)? (*I would start at −9 and move 5 units right.*)
- How do you add two positive integers? (*I do not need a number line. I can add two positive integers the same way as I add two whole numbers. I added (+28) + (+41) as 28 + 41 = 69, so (+28) + (+41) = +69.*)

…l a negative
…e left on
…e.

And, to add: $(-12) + (-3)$
Start at -12 on a number line and move 3 units left.

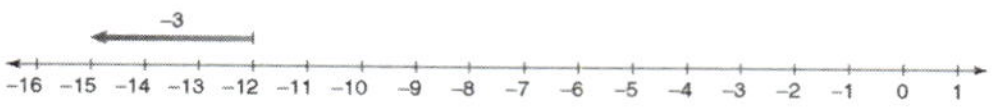

$(-12) + (-3) = -15$

…en you key in a
…sitive number, you
…not need to key in
positive sign.

When you use a calculator to add,
the keystrokes depend on the type of calculator.
When your calculator has this key [(−)],
you use it to input the negative sign.
When your calculator has this key [+/−],
you use it to change an input number to a negative number.

Example 1

Use a calculator to add. $(-325) + (-428)$

Solution

$(-325) + (-428)$

For a calculator with [(−)]:
Input:
[(−)] 325 [+] [(−)] 428 [=]
to display −753

For a calculator with [+/−]:
Input:
325 [+/−] [+] 428 [+/−] [=]
to display −753

So, $(-325) + (-428) = -753$

Example 2

The temperature in Calgary, Alberta, was −2°C. A chinook came through and the temperature rose 15°C. At nightfall, it fell 7°C.

a) Write an addition expression to show the temperature changes.
b) Use a number line to find the final temperature.

Solution

a) The addition expression is: $(-2) + (+15) + (-7)$
b) $(-2) + (+15) + (-7) = +6$

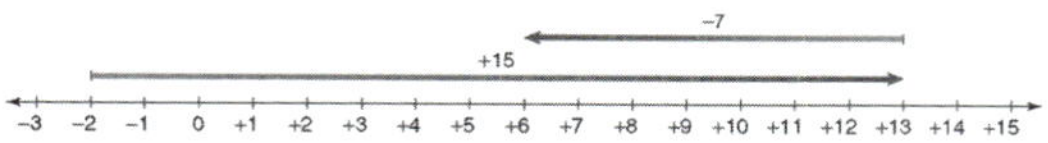

The final temperature is +6°C.

9.1 Adding Integers 369

REACHING ALL LEARNERS

Early Finishers

Have students create an application problem similar to question 9. Real-world scenarios that involve addition of integers are temperatures, bank statements, and wind chill factors. Have students share their problems and solutions.

Common Misconceptions

➤ Students think that (+3) + (−2) and (−2) + (+3) have different sums.

How to Help: Use coloured tiles to show that, when zero pairs have been made, only 1 yellow tile remains in each case. Students should see that the order of addition does not matter.

Sample Solutions

2. a) Start at −3. Move 4 units right, then 6 units left to end at −5.

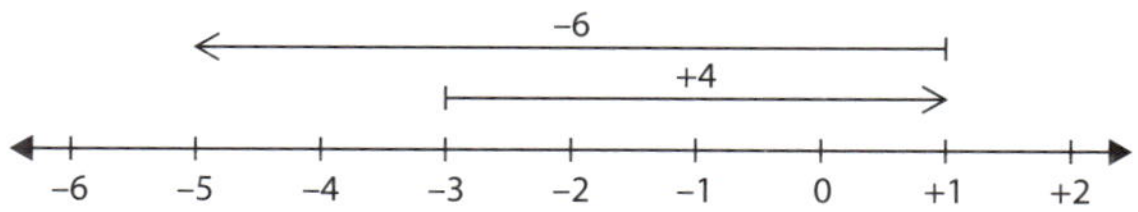

b) Start at +3. Move 5 units left, then 7 units right to end at +5.

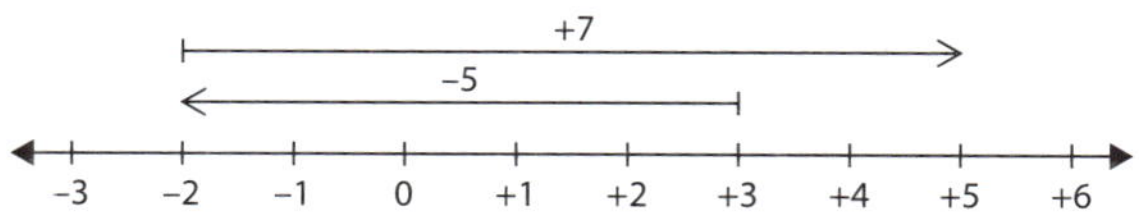

3. b) i) (+8) + (−8) = 0 **ii)** (−5) + (+5) = 0 **iii)** (+2) + (−2) = 0 **iv)** (−8) + (+8) =0

c) The sum of two opposite integers is 0.

- How do you add two negative integers? *(I do not need a number line. Because the signs are the same, I add the whole numbers, then make the sum negative. I added (−16) + (−34) as 16 + 34 = 50, so (−16) + (−34) = −50.)*
- Why does it work this way? *(If I used a number line, I could start at 0, move 16 units left, then 34 units left. This is the same as moving 50 units left, so I am finding the total number of units I move left by adding. Then I have to remember I moved left, so the sum is negative.)*

AFTER Connect

Have students write their addition equations and number lines on the board. What you should see:

(+5) + (−16) = −11	(−9) + (−16) = −25
(−16) + (+28) = +12	(+5) + (+28) = +33
(−9) + (+28) = +19	(−16) + (+41) = +25
(+5) + (−34) = −29	(−9) + (−34) = −43
(+28) + (−34) = −6	(+5) + (+41) = +46
(−9) + (+41) = +32	(−34) + (+41) = +7

Each equation should have a sketch of a number line.

For larger numbers, students may draw a number line to scale; for example, each hatch mark represents 2 units or 5 units.

Draw students' attention to the fact that drawing an arrow from 0 to the first integer always takes us to the location corresponding to that integer on the number line. Instead of drawing that arrow, we can start at the point that corresponds to the first integer.

Review *Connect* and the use of a number line to add: a negative integer and a positive integer; and two negative integers. If necessary, show another example that illustrates adding a positive integer and a negative integer.

4. b) The integers in all the expressions are positive.
Each sum is positive.
The sum of two positive integers is always a positive integer.
c) For example, (+13) + (+7) = +20

5. b) The integers in all the expressions are negative.
Each sum is negative.
The sum of two negative integers is always a negative integer.
c) For example, (−13) + (−7) = −20

7. The sum of two integers with opposite signs is:
- zero, when the integers are opposites; that is, they have the same numerical value; for example: (−5) + (+5) = 0
- a positive integer, when the numerically larger number is positive; for example, (−5) + (+8) is positive, because 8 > 5 and 8 is positive while 5 is negative.
- a negative integer, when the numerically larger number is negative; for example, (+5) + (−8) is negative, because 8 > 5 and 8 is negative while 5 is positive.

9. a) (+5) + (−6) + (−2) + (+4) + (+6) + (−2)

11. a) (−9) + (+7); (−8) + (+6); (−7) + (+5); (−6) + (+4); (−5) + (+3); (−4) + (+2); (−3) + (+1); (−2) + (0); (−1) + (−1)
I started with the greatest single-digit negative integer, then added +7 to get −2.
I then added +1 to the first integer, and −1 to the second integer to get a different way. I continued to do this with each new pair of integers to get all possible ways.
b) (−9) + (+5); (−8) + (+4); (−7) + (+3); (−6) + (+2); (−5) + (+1); (−4) + (+0); (−3) + (−1); (−2) + (−2)

Practice

1. Use a number line to add.
   a) (+5) + (−6) −1
   b) (−8) + (+6) −2
   c) (−2) + (−4) −6
   d) 0 + (−5) −5
   e) (−2) + (−4) −6
   f) (−5) + (+5) 0

2. Use a number line to add.
   a) (−3) + (+4) + (−6) −5
   b) (+3) + (−5) + (+7) +5
   c) (+6) + (−8) + (−1) −3
   d) (−10) + (+6) + (−2) −6

3. a) Write the opposite integer.
   i) +8 −8   ii) −5 +5   iii) +2 −2   iv) −8 +8
   b) Add each integer to its opposite in part a.
   c) What do you notice about the sum of two opposite integers?

4. a) Add.
   i) (+8) + (+6) +14   ii) (+3) + (+7) +10
   iii) (+5) + (+9) +14   iv) (+1) + (+12) +13
   b) Look at the integer expressions and sums in part a.
   How are they related?
   How can you use this relationship to add two positive integers without a number line or a calculator?
   c) Check the relationship in part b by adding two positive integers of your choice.

5. a) Add.
   i) (−8) + (−6) −14   ii) (−3) + (−7) −10
   iii) (−5) + (−9) −14   iv) (−1) + (−12) −13
   b) Look at the integer expressions and sums in part a.
   How are they related?
   How can you use this relationship to add two negative integers without a number line or a calculator?
   c) Check the relationship in part b by adding two negative integers of your choice.

6. a) Find 4 pairs of integers that have the sum −5.
   b) Find 4 pairs of integers that have the sum +4.

a) −2 and −3
−1 and −4
−10 and +5
+6 and −11

b) +3 and +1
+5 and −1
+6 and −2
+4 and 0

370 UNIT 9: Integers

Tell students that larger integers can be added on a calculator. Emphasize the difference between the negative key and the subtraction key. Students may have calculators that require keystrokes different from those illustrated.

Encourage students to estimate when using a calculator, so they can realize if an answer is incorrect because the wrong key was used.

For example, in *Example 1*, (−325) + (−428) is about (−300) + (−400) = −700. If students erroneously keyed in (−325) + (+428), their answer would be about +100, and they should realize that an error had been made.

Review *Example 2* that illustrates the sum of 3 integers.

Remind students that the addition of integers is commutative; that is, the order of the addition of integers does not matter.
For example: (−7) + (+3) = (+3) + (−7) = −4

Practice

Provide students with copies of *Number Lines* (Master 9.20).

Assessment Focus: Question 7

Students should look for and identify patterns in the relative sizes of the corresponding whole numbers, and the sign of the numerically greater number. Challenge students to give two explanations of when the sum of two integers is zero, positive, or negative. In one explanation, they should use counters; in the other explanation, they should use number lines.

Students who need extra support to complete the Assessment Focus questions may benefit from the Step-by-Step masters (Masters 9.10–9.19).

Number Strategies

... costs $125. ... is reduced ...%. Then, 15% sales tax is applied. Is the final price $125? Explain. No; $122.19

7. **Assessment Focus** When you add two integers with opposite signs, the sum may be 0, a positive integer, or a negative integer. When you look at an addition expression, how can you tell which of these sums it will be, without adding? Include examples in your explanation.

8. Add.

+331	a) $(+513) + (-182)$	b) $(+560) + (-266)$	+294
−296	c) $(+793) + (-1089)$	d) $(-563) + (+182) + (+363)$	−18
−109	e) $(-412) + (+382) + (-79)$	f) $(-114) + (+483) + (-293)$	+76

9. The value of a stock on the Toronto Stock Exchange has changed each week for six weeks as shown below:

Week 1	Week 2	Week 3	Week 4	Week 5	Week 6
Up $5	Down $6	Down $2	Up $4	Up $6	Down $2

a) Write an integer addition expression to represent the change in the value of the stock at the end of Week 6.

b) At the end of Week 6, how does the value of the stock compare with its value at the beginning of Week 1? $5 higher

c) At the beginning of Week 1, the stock was worth $40. How much was the stock worth at the end of Week 3? At the end of Week 6? $37, $45

Take It Further

10. Find each missing integer.

a) $-5 = (-2) + \square$ −3 b) $\square + (-8) = +2$ +10

11. Use only single-digit integers. How many ways can you complete each equation? How do you know you have found all possible ways?

a) $\square + \triangle = -2$ 9 ways b) $\square + \triangle = -4$ 8 ways

Reflect

Write an addition expression that has each sum: a positive sum, a negative sum, and a sum of 0. Show how to calculate each sum.

9.1 Adding Integers 371

REFLECT: For example:

Positive sum: (+3) + (+7) = +10

Negative sum: (+3) + (−7) = −4

Sum of zero: (+3) + (−3) = 0

Students' work should include a number line or illustration of coloured tiles for each addition equation.

Number Strategies

Students could multiply $125 by 0.85 to get the reduced price, then multiply the product by 1.15 to get the final price, including sales tax.

$125 × 0.85 = $106.25

$106.25 × 1.15 ≐ $122.19

Assignment Guidelines

If your students do not have time to complete all the *Practice* questions on pages 370 and 371, these questions provide minimum curriculum coverage: 2, 4, 5, 7, 8, 9

To assess the four Achievement Chart categories listed in the curriculum document, have students complete these *Practice* questions:

Knowledge and Understanding: 2 Thinking: 7

Communication: 5 Application: 9

ASSESSMENT FOR LEARNING

What to Look For

Knowledge and Understanding

✔ Students understand that to add a positive integer, move right on a number line. To add a negative integer, move left on a number line.

Communication

✔ Students can explain how they know the sign of a sum without doing the addition.

Application

✔ Students can use a number line and a calculator to add integers.

What to Do

Extra Support: Students can complete the Additional Activity *Integer Alphabet* (Master 9.6).
Students can use Step-by-Step 1 (Master 9.10) to complete question 7.

Extra Practice: Remove the face cards and jokers from a deck of playing cards. Red cards are negative, black cards are positive. Deal two cards. The first person who calls out their sum wins the cards. Continue play until all the cards have gone. The player with more cards wins.

Students can complete Extra Practice 1 (Master 9.24).

Extension: Have students find 3 or 4 different integers that have the sum +10 or −10. How many different addition equations can they write?

Recording and Reporting

Master 9.2: Ongoing Observations: Integers

LESSON 9.2

Subtracting Integers

LESSON ORGANIZER

40–50 min

Curriculum Focus: Use a calculator and number line to subtract integers. (8m22)

Teacher Materials

- transparency of Number Lines (Master 9.20)

Student Materials

- Number Lines (Master 9.20)

Optional

- coloured tiles
- Step-by-Step 2 (Master 9.11)
- Extra Practice 2 (Master 9.25)

Vocabulary: difference, adding the opposite

Assessment: Master 9.2 Ongoing Observations: Integers

Key Math Learnings

1. A number line can be used to subtract integers.
2. To subtract an integer, add its opposite.

Assignment Guidelines

If your students do not have time to complete all the *Practice* questions on pages 374, 375, and 376, these questions provide minimum curriculum coverage: 3, 4, 5, 7, 9, *Reflect*

To assess the 4 Achievement Chart categories listed in the curriculum document, have students complete these *Practice* questions:

Knowledge and Understanding: 3
Thinking: 7
Application: 5
Communication: *Reflect*

9.2 Subtracting Integers

Focus Use a calculator and number line to subtract integers.

Explore

Work with a partner.
You will need a calculator.

- Choose two positive integers between +150 and +300.
  Use a calculator to subtract them.
  Show the subtraction on a number line.
- Repeat the activity for a positive integer between +150 and +250, and a negative integer between −150 and −300.
- Repeat the activity for two negative integers between −150 and −300.

Reflect & Share

Compare expressions and number lines with those of another pair of classmates.
Suppose two integers are subtracted in reverse order.
What happens to their difference? Explain.
List the keystrokes to subtract two negative integers.

Connect

To subtract two integers, first think about how we subtract two whole numbers.
For example, to subtract: 13 − 6,
we think, "What do we add to 6 to get 13?"
The answer is 7, so: 13 − 6 = 7
To subtract two integers: (−6) − (+13),
we think, "What do we add to +13 to get −6?"

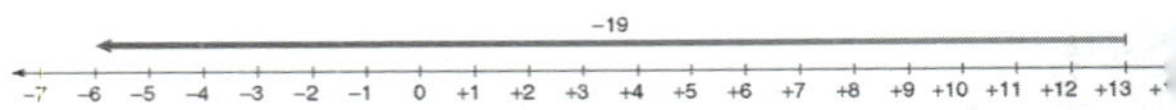

We add −19; that is, (+13) + (−19) = −6
So, (−6) − (+13) = −19
We also know that: (−6) + (−13) = −19

372 UNIT 9: Integers

BEFORE Get Started

Review subtracting integers by drawing a thermometer from –5°C to +20°C on the board. Present the following situation:

The temperature was +3°C this morning. Now it is –5°C.

Ask:

- By how much did the temperature drop?
  (–8°C)
- How do you know?
  (I started at +3°C on the thermometer and counted down 8°C. I reached –5°C.)

Present *Explore*. Distribute Number Lines (Master 9.20) to students.

DURING Explore

Ongoing Assessment: Observe and Listen

As students work, ask questions, such as:

- Which two positive integers did you choose?
  (+180 and +250)
- How did you use a calculator to subtract these integers? *(I entered 250, then –, then 180.)*
- What was the difference? *(70)*
- How did you show the subtraction on a number line?
  (I used a scale of 1 space for 10 units. I started at 250, then moved 180 units left. The arrowhead was at 70.)
- Which positive and negative integers did you subtract? *(+200 and –250)*
- Which expression did you write?
  ((+200) – (–250))
- How did you use a calculator to subtract these integers?
  (I entered 200, then –, then (–)250.)

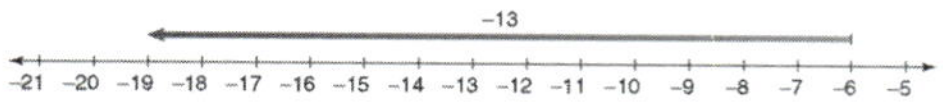

This example shows that subtracting an integer is the same as adding the opposite integer.

$(-6) - (+13) = -19$ — Subtract +13.

$(-6) + (-13) = -19$ — Add −13.

Example 1

Use a number line to subtract.

a) $(+14) - (+30)$ b) $(-18) - (-12)$

Solution

To subtract, add the opposite.

You can use coloured tiles to check.

a) Write $(+14) - (+30)$ as $(+14) + (-30)$.
Use a number line.
Start at +14. Move 30 units left.

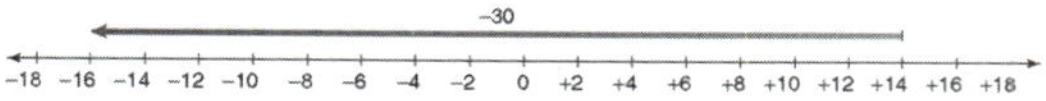

So, $(+14) - (+30) = -16$

b) Write $(-18) - (-12)$ as $(-18) + (+12)$.
Use a number line.
Start at −18. Move 12 units right.

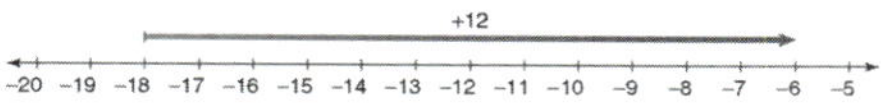

So, $(-18) - (-12) = -6$

Example 2

The mean temperature in January for Victoria, BC, is +4°C. In Thunder Bay, the mean January temperature is −11°C. Which temperature is lower and by how much?

Solution

Since $-11 < +4$, then −11°C is the lower temperature.
Subtract the temperatures to find their difference.

$(-11) - (+4) = (-11) + (-4)$
$= -15$

The temperature in Thunder Bay is 15°C lower than the temperature in Victoria.

9.2 Subtracting Integers **373**

REACHING ALL LEARNERS

Common Misconceptions

➤ Students think the order of subtraction does not matter.

How to Help: Have students use coloured tiles to subtract (+9) – (–2) and (–2) – (+9).
Students find that the first difference is +11 and the second difference is –11.

Early Finishers

Have students repeat Lesson 9.1, *Practice* questions 2 and 8, this time changing the addition signs to subtraction signs; for example, question 2a becomes (–3) – (+4) – (–6).

Number Strategies

- 1, 4, 9, 16, . . . can be rewritten as $1^2, 2^2, 3^2, 4^2$, . . .
  Therefore, the next three terms are: $5^2, 6^2, 7^2$, or 25, 36, 49
- In 1, 2, 4, 7, 11, . . ., the pattern is: Start at 1. Add +1, then +2, then +3, then +4, and so on. Therefore, the next three terms are: 11 + 5 = 16, 16 + 6 = 22, 22 + 7 = 29, or 16, 22, 29
- 1, 8, 27, 64, . . . can be rewritten as $1^3, 2^3, 3^3, 4^3$, . . .
  Therefore, the next three terms are: $5^3, 6^3, 7^3$, or 125, 216, 343

- What was the difference? *(450)*
- How did you show the subtraction on a number line? *(I used a scale of 1 space for 50 units. I started at 200, then moved 250 units right. The arrowhead was at 450.)*
- Why did you move 250 units right? *(I start at 200 and end at 450 so I have to move right. I remember that subtracting –250 is the same as adding +250.)*
- Which two negative integers did you choose? *(–200 and –250)*
- How did you use a calculator to subtract these integers? *(I entered (–)200, then –, then (–)250.)*
- What was the difference? *(50)*
- How did you show the subtraction on a number line? *(I used a scale of 1 space for 50 units. I started at –200, then moved 250 units right. The arrowhead was at 50.)*

AFTER **Connect**

Invite students to share their expressions and number lines with the class.
Ask questions, such as:

- What happens if you subtract +200 and –250 in the reverse order? Explain. *((–250) – (+200) = –450; the difference is numerically the same as it was with the integers subtracted the other way, but the difference changes from a positive integer to a negative integer.)*
- What are the keystrokes to subtract two negative integers on your calculator? *([(–)] [number] [–] [(–)] [number] [=])*

Ensure students understand that the subtraction of integers is *not* commutative; that is, the order of integers in a subtraction expression matters. For example,

$$(-7) - (+3) = -10$$
$$\text{and } (+3) - (-7) = +10$$
$$-10 \neq +10$$

Sample Solutions

1. a) (+8) + (–4) = +4 b) (–13) + (+8) = –5
   c) (–5) + (+5) = 0 d) (+20) + (+16) = +36
   e) (+30) + (+13) = +43 f) (+21) + (+18) = +39

2. a)

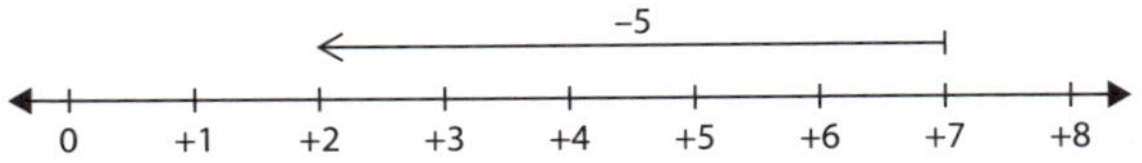

b)

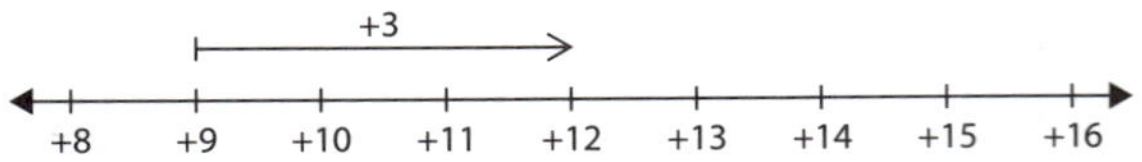

c)

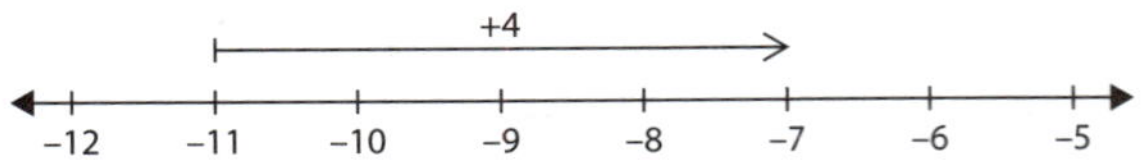

d)

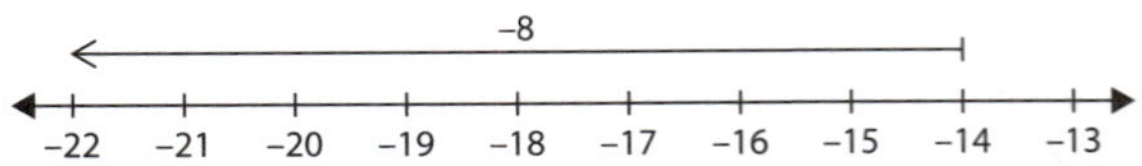

5. a) +7°C – (–5°C) = +7°C + (+5°C) = +12°C; 12°C above zero
   b) –15°C – (–8°C) = –15°C + (+8°C) = –7°C; 7°C below zero
   c) +51 m – (–17 m) = +51 m + (+17 m) = +68 m; 68 m above sea level
   d) +2 – (–6) = +2 + (+6) = +8; 8 over par
   e) +$21 – (–$14) = +$21 + (+$14) = +$35; a rise of $35

6. a) i) (+21) – (+6) = +15 ii) (+31) – (+22) = +9
   iii) (+20) – (–18) = (+20) + (+18) = +38
   iv) (+9) – (+25) = (+9) + (–25) = –16
   v) (+25) – (–4) = (+25) + (+4) = +29
   b) +38 is the greatest difference.
   c) Perth is in the southern hemisphere where it is winter, when in the northern hemisphere it is summer, and vice versa.

Some integer expressions require addition and subtraction.

Example 3

Evaluate. (+5) + (–3) – (+7)

Solution

(+5) + (–3) – (+7) Write the subtraction as an addition.

= (+5) + (–3) + (–7) Add the first two integers.

= (+2) + (–7) Then add.

= –5

So, (+5) + (–3) – (+7) = –5

We can use a calculator to subtract directly, without adding the opposite.

To use a calculator to subtract: (–137) – (+542)

For a calculator with [(–)]: Input: [(–)] 137 [–] 542 [=] to display –679

For a calculator with [+/–]: Input: 137 [+/–] [–] 542 [=] to display –679

Practice

1. Rewrite as an addition statement. Then evaluate.
   a) (+8) – (+4) +4 b) (–13) – (–8) –5 c) (–5) – (–5) 0
   d) (+20) – (–16) +36 e) (+30) – (–13) +43 f) (+21) – (–18) +39
2. Use a number line to subtract.
   a) (+7) – (+5) +2 b) (+9) – (–3) +12
   c) (–11) – (–4) –7 d) (–14) – (+8) –22
3. Subtract.
   a) (+4) – (+8) –4 b) (–9) – (–5) –4 c) (–7) – (+1) –8
   d) (+10) – (–3) +13 e) (+5) – (–5) +10 f) (–18) – (–3) –15
4. Subtract.
   a) (–256) – (+125) –381 b) (–103) – (–214) +111
   c) (+213) – (+133) +80 d) (+148) – (–222) +370

374 UNIT 9: Integers

Review *Connect*. Ask:

- When you subtract a positive integer, which way do you move on the number line? (*To the left*)
- When you subtract a negative integer, which way do you move on the number line? (*To the right*)

Introduce the concept of adding the opposite. For example: (–4) – (+9) = (–4) + (–9)

Review *Example 1*. Ask:

- How can you use coloured tiles to check (+14) – (+30)? (*I model +14 with 14 yellow tiles. To take away +30, I need 16 more yellow tiles. Add 16 zero pairs of tiles. I now have 30 yellow tiles and 16 red tiles. I take away 30 yellow tiles. 16 red tiles remain. So, (+14) – (+30) = –16*)
- How can you use coloured tiles to check (–18) – (–12)? (*I model –18 with 18 red tiles. To take away –12, I remove 12 red tiles. 6 red tiles remain. So, (–18) – (–12) = –6*)

Review *Example 2*. Extend the example by asking students which temperature is higher and by how much. Students may need to subtract the temperatures in reverse order ((+4) – (–11)) to get +15, or realize that the difference in temperatures is numerically the same as the previous difference, but with the opposite sign. This further reinforces that, when the order of subtracting integers is reversed, the difference changes sign.

Example 3 illustrates an expression involving addition and subtraction. As you review the solution, remind students of the order of operations: addition and subtraction are completed in the order they are presented.

Use a number line to show students how to subtract a negative integer from a positive integer; for example, (+18) – (–6):

5. For each scenario:
   i) Write each number as an integer.
   ii) Subtract the second integer from the first integer. Explain each answer.
   a) A temperature 7°C above zero and a temperature 5°C below zero +12°C
   b) A temperature 15°C below zero and a temperature 8°C below zero −7°C
   c) A height 51 m above sea level and a depth 17 m below sea level +68 m
   d) A golf score of 2 over par and a golf score of 6 under par +8
   e) A rise of $21 in the value of a stock, then a fall of $14 +$35

…trategies

…ext 3 terms …each pattern.
…ite each pattern rule.
1, 4, 9, 16, … 25, 36, 49
1, 2, 4, 7, 11, … 16, 22, 29
1, 8, 27, 64, … 125, 216, 343

6. The table shows the mean temperatures in January and July for several cities in a certain year.
   a) Find the difference between the temperatures in July and January for each city. Show your work.

	City	January Temperature (°C)	July Temperature (°C)	
i)	Victoria	+6	+21	+15°C
ii)	Miami, US	+22	+31	+9°C
iii)	Winnipeg	−18	+20	+38°C
iv)	Perth, Australia	+25	+9	−16°C
v)	Calgary	−4	+25	+29°C

   b) Which city has the greatest difference in temperatures? How do you know? Winnipeg
   c) In Perth, why is the July temperature less than the January temperature?

7. **Assessment Focus** For each integer below, write a subtraction expression that has this integer as its answer.
   a) −3 b) +2 c) 0
   Where possible, do this 4 different ways:
   - positive integer − positive integer
   - positive integer − negative integer
   - negative integer − positive integer
   - negative integer − negative integer

   Show your work.

9.2 Subtracting Integers 375

7. a) For example, (+6) − (+9) = −3
   (−1) − (+2) = −3
   (−9) − (−6) = (−9) + (+6) = −3
   I cannot subtract: positive integer − negative integer to get −3 because the difference is always positive.
   b) For example, (+5) − (+3) = +2
   (+1) − (−1) = (+1) + (+1) = +2
   (−2) − (−4) = (−2) + (+4) = +2
   I cannot subtract: negative integer − positive integer to get +2 because the difference is always negative.
   c) For example, (+6) − (+6) = 0
   (−8) − (−8) = (−8) + (+8) = 0
   The signs of the integers must be the same.
8. d) The median is the mean of the 2 middle temperatures: $\frac{+37 + (+40)}{2} = 38.5$
   e) The range is: (−50) − (−16) = (−50) + (+16) = −34
   f) What is the difference between the record high temperature for Thunder Bay and the record low temperature for Regina?
   Solution: +40 − (−50) = +40 + (+50) = +90; +90°C
10. a) Pattern rule: Start at +5. Add +7 each time.
   b) Pattern rule: Start at −4. Add +2 each time.
   c) Pattern rule: Start at −21. Add +4 each time.
   d) Pattern rule: Start at +1. Add −1 each time.
11. b) Find two integers with a sum of +10 and a difference of −4.
   I used trial and error.
   (+1) + (+9) = +10; (+1) − (+9) = −8; (+9) − (+1) = +8
   (+2) + (+8) = +10; (+2) − (+8) = −6; (+8) − (+2) = +6
   (+3) + (+7) = +10; (+3) − (+7) = −4
   The two integers are +3 and +7.

To subtract, add the opposite.
Write (+18) − (−6) as (+18) + (+6).
Use a number line.
Start at +18. Move 6 units right.

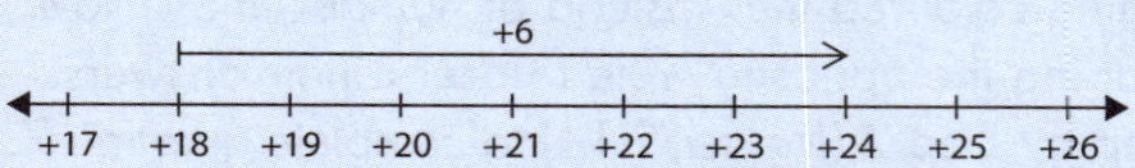

So, (+18) − (−6) = +24

If you did not remind students how to subtract integers with a calculator when you reviewed *Explore*, do so now before they begin *Practice*.

Review how to enter the subtraction sign as opposed to a negative number on a calculator. The keystrokes may vary depending on the calculator.

Have students try the following examples with their calculators before doing the *Practice* questions.

(+7) − (−5) (−9) − (+3)
(−15) − (+11) (−8) − (−4)

Practice

Provide students with copies of *Number Lines* (Master 9.20). In question 6, remind students that mean temperature is the sum of the daily temperatures divided by the number of days in the month.

Assessment Focus: Question 7

Students may use trial and error to solve this problem. Encourage students to use a number line or coloured tiles. They can work backward: for example, start with a positive integer and find what needs to be subtracted to get the given answer.

REFLECT: This is how I predict the sign of the answer when I subtract two integers:

(+10) – (+2) The answer will be positive because both integers are positive, and the first integer is greater than the second integer.

(–10) – (–2) The answer will be negative because both integers are negative, and the first integer is numerically larger than the second integer.

(+2) – (+10) The answer will be negative because both integers are positive, and the first integer is less than the second integer.

(–2) – (–10) The answer will be positive because both integers are negative, and the second integer is numerically larger than the first integer.

(+10) – (–2) The answer will be positive because the expression can be rewritten as (+10) + (+2) and both integers are positive.

(–2) – (+10) The answer will be negative because the expression can be rewritten as (–2) + (–10) and both integers are negative.

(–10) – (+2) The answer will always be negative because the expression can be rewritten as (–10) + (–2) and both integers are negative.

(–2) – (–2) The answer will be 0 because the two integers are equal.

(+2) – (+2) The answer will be 0 because the two integers are equal.

8. Use the table below.

City	Record High Temperature (°C)	Record Low Temperature (°C)
Halifax, NS	+37	–29
Regina, SK	+43	–50
Thunder Bay, ON	+40	–41
Victoria, BC	+36	–16

b) Halifax: 66°C, Regina: 93°C, Thunder Bay: 81°C, Victoria: 52°C

a) Which city has the greatest record high temperature? The least record low temperature? Regina; Victoria
b) Find the difference between the temperatures for each city.
c) Which city has the greatest difference in temperatures? Re
d) What is the median record high temperature? 38.5°C
e) What is the range of record low temperatures? –34°C
f) Make up your own problem about these temperatures. Solve your problem.

Use a calculator to check your answers.

9. Evaluate.

a) (−2) − (−8) − (+4) +2
b) (+5) − (−1) − (−3)
c) (+10) − (+3) − (−7) +14
d) (−5) − (+8) − (+6)
e) 0 + (−5) + (+8) + (–3) 0
f) (−42) + (−65) − (+2
g) (−1) − (+2) − (+3) − (+4) –10
h) (−241) − (+356) + (−

10. Write the next 3 terms in each pattern; then, write the pattern rule.

a) +5, +12, +19, … +26, +33, +40
b) −4, −2, 0, … +2, +4, +6
c) −21, −17, −13, … –9, –5, –1
d) +1, 0, −1, … –2, –3, –4

Take It Further

11. a) Find two integers with a sum of −12 and a difference of + –5
b) Create and solve a similar integer problem.

Reflect

When you subtract two integers, the answers can be positive, negative, or zero.
How can you predict the type of answer before you subtract?
Use examples in your explanation.

376 UNIT 9: Integers

ASSESSMENT FOR LEARNING

What to Look For	What to Do
Knowledge and Understanding ✔ Students understand that subtracting an integer is the same as adding its opposite.	***Extra Support:*** Students who have difficulty subtracting integers may benefit from using coloured tiles instead of number lines. Have students use the "adding the opposite" rule to check their answers. Students can use Step-by-Step 2 (Master 9.11) to complete question 7.
Thinking ✔ Students can create and solve their own subtraction problems. ✔ Students can solve multi-step problems involving integers.	***Extra Practice:*** Have students make up two more questions using the temperatures in question 6. Students trade questions with a classmate and solve each other's problems. Students can complete Extra Practice 2 (Master 9.25).
Application ✔ Students can use a calculator to subtract integers.	***Extension:*** Have students choose an integer between –40 and –50, and write as many addition and/or subtraction expressions as they can, involving 2 or more integers, for which the chosen integer is the answer.

Recording and Reporting
Master 9.2 Ongoing Observations: Integers

9.3 Adding and Subtracting Integers

Focus Add and subtract integers.

The whole numbers are 0, 1, 2, 3, 4, …, and so on.
The integers are …, −4, −3, −2, −1, 0, 1, 2, 3, 4, …, and so on.
We do not need to include the + sign to indicate a positive integer.
So, all whole numbers are integers.

Up until now, when we added and subtracted integers, the integers were written in brackets.
For example, (−3) + (+7) and (−5) − (+8)

We will now interpret sums and differences of numbers such as −3 + 7 and −5 − 8.

Explore

Work with a partner.
Use a number line to find each answer.

(+3) + (−7) and 3 − 7
(−3) + (−7) and −3 − 7
(+3) + (+7) and 3 + 7
(−3) + (+7) and −3 + 7

What patterns do you see?
Write your own two sets of expressions like these, then evaluate.

Reflect & Share

Compare solutions with those of another pair of classmates.
How could you find each answer without a number line?

Connect

➢ To add: −6 + 4, use a number line.

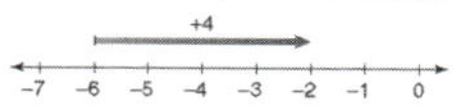

−6 + 4 = −2
We can also use mental math.
One number is negative: −6
One number is positive: +4

9.3 Adding and Subtracting Integers **377**

LESSON 9.3

Adding and Subtracting Integers

LESSON ORGANIZER (40–50 min)

Curriculum Focus: Add and subtract integers. (8m22)
Teacher Materials
- transparency of Number Lines (Master 9.20)

Student Materials
- Number Lines (Master 9.20)

Optional
- Step-by-Step 3 (Master 9.12)
- Extra Practice 3 (Master 9.26)

Assessment: Master 9.2 Ongoing Observations: Integers

Key Math Learning

Integers can be written without brackets and integer expressions can be evaluated using mental math.

Number Strategies

Change all the fractions to decimals. Order the decimals, then rewrite as fractions.

BEFORE Get Started

Students have modelled the addition and subtraction of integers with manipulatives such as coloured tiles and number lines. Most students have internalized these models, and are ready to add and subtract integers mentally.

Review the introduction. Point out that the positive sign (+) is not needed for a positive integer.

Present *Explore*. Provide each pair of students with a copy of *Number Lines* (Master 9.20).

DURING Explore

Ongoing Assessment: Observe and Listen

Ask questions, such as:

- How did you show (+3) + (−7) on a number line? (*Start at +3. Draw an arrow 7 units left. The arrowhead is at −4.*)
- How did you show 3 − 7 on the number line? (*Start at positive 3. Draw an arrow 7 units to the left to get to −4.*)
- What do you do to subtract a positive integer? (*Draw an arrow that many units to the left.*)
- What do you do to subtract a negative integer? (*Draw an arrow that many units to the right.*)
- What did you notice about each addition/subtraction pair? (*Their answers were equal.*)
- How can you explain what you observed? (*A positive integer, such as (+3), can be written without brackets and without the positive sign. A negative integer at the beginning of a statement can be written without brackets. A negative integer that is added, such as + (−7) can be written as −7; that is, the addition operation and negative sign combine to make a subtraction operation. Adding −7 is the same as subtracting +7, which is the same as subtracting 7.*)

REACHING ALL LEARNERS

Early Finishers

Have students draw a Tic-Tac-Toe board and place an integer addition or subtraction question in each square. As in regular Tic-Tac-Toe, players choose a square. If they answer the question in the square correctly, they place their initials in the square. The first person to correctly complete three questions in a row, column, or diagonal is the winner.

Common Misconceptions

➤ Students are confused by the two meanings of the – sign.

How to Help: Explain that when the – sign is between two numbers (5 – 7), it indicates subtraction. When the – sign is in front of a single number, it means negative. Reinforce this difference in meaning by having students say –5 – 7 as "negative 5 subtract 7."

Assignment Guidelines

If your students do not have time to complete all the *Practice* questions on page 379, these questions provide minimum curriculum coverage: 1, 4, 5, *Reflect*

To assess the 4 Achievement Chart categories listed in the curriculum document, have students complete these *Practice* questions:

Knowledge and Understanding: 1
Thinking: 4
Application: 5
Communication: *Reflect*

The answer to $-6 + 4$ is the difference of 6 and 4, and the sign of the difference matches the sign of -6, the numerically larger number:
$-6 + 4 = -2$

➤ To subtract: $4 - 10$, use a number line.

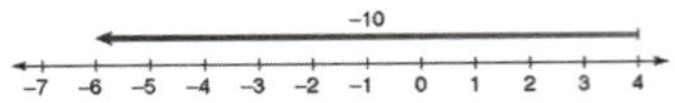

$4 - 10 = -6$

Use mental math.
One number is positive: 4
One number is negative: -10
The answer to $4 - 10$ is the difference of 10 and 4, and the sign of the difference matches the sign of -10, the numerically larger number:
$4 - 10 = -6$

➤ To evaluate: $-4 - 10$, use a number line.

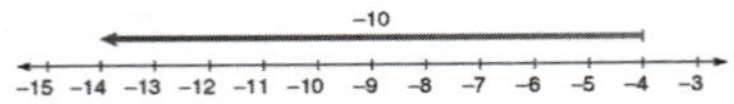

$-4 - 10 = -14$

Use mental math.
Both numbers are negative.
The answer is the sum of 4 and 10, and the sign of the answer matches the sign of both numbers.
So, $-4 - 10 = -14$

Example

Evaluate. $8 - 6 - 9$

Solution

$8 - 6 - 9$
$8 - 6 = 2$
So, $8 - 6 - 9 = 2 - 9$
$= -7$

378 UNIT 9: Integers

AFTER Connect

Invite students to share their results and the patterns they noticed with the rest of the class.

What you might see:

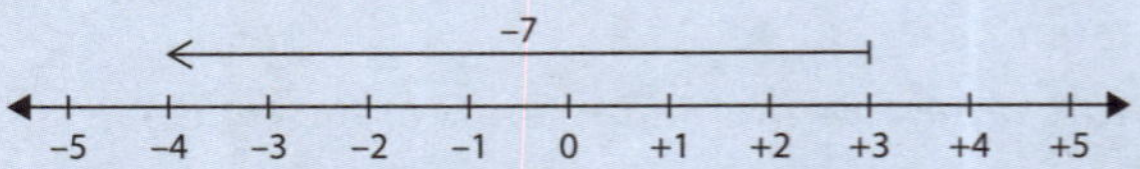

Addition: (+3) + (–7) = –4

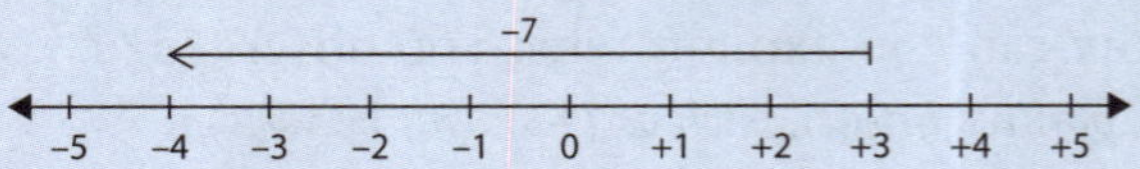

Subtraction: 3 – 7 = –4

In each pair, the first numbers are the same and the integer added is the opposite of the integer subtracted. Since subtraction is the same as adding the opposite, the answers are equal.

Some students are now ready to leave manipulatives behind and add and subtract integers mentally.

Review *Connect* and the *Example* for further illustrations of simplifying expressions with integers written without brackets.

Before students begin *Practice*, ask students to find 2 – 5 in four ways: using coloured tiles, drawing a number line, using a calculator, and by mental math.

Practice

Assessment Focus: Question 3

Students should understand that switching the order of the terms in a subtraction question changes the sign of the answer. For example: 6 – 4 = 2, while 4 – 6 = –2

Practice

1. Evaluate.
   a) $-5+7$ **+2** b) $3+4$ **+7** c) $-3+2$ **−1**
   d) $-6+8$ **+2** e) $-11+13$ **+2** f) $-21+36$ **+15**
   g) $5-12$ **−7** h) $-12-4$ **−16** i) $-6-9$ **−15**
   j) $11-13$ **−2** k) $-5-18$ **−23** l) $15-3$ **+12**

2. Evaluate.
   a) $6-1+3$ **+8** b) $-36+6-3$ **−33** c) $18-15-2$ **+1**

ber Strategies

from least to greatest.
, 3.6, $\frac{13}{4}$, 3.02
, 3.2, $\frac{13}{4}$, 3.6, $\frac{11}{3}$

3. **Assessment Focus**
   a) Evaluate each pair of expressions.
      i) $-6+4$; $4-6$ **−2, −2** ii) $-7+3$; $3-7$ **−4, −4**
      iii) $-8+2$; $2-8$ **−6, −6** iv) $-9+1$; $1-9$ **−8, −8**
   b) What patterns do you see in the expressions and the answers? Explain why these patterns occur.
   c) Write two more expressions that are related in the same way as those in part a.
   Show your work.

4. Evaluate each term. Each pattern continues. Write the next 3 terms in each pattern. Explain how you found each answer.
   a) $(-6+5), (-7+4), (-8+3), \ldots$ **(−9 + 2), (−10 + 1), (−11 + 0)**
   b) $(-3-1), (-4-2), (-5-3), \ldots$ **(−6 − 4), (−7 − 5), (−8 − 6)**

5. Last Monday, Suneel had \$283 in her bank account. On Tuesday, Suneel withdrew \$120 in cash, and wrote a cheque for \$200. On Thursday, Suneel deposited \$53. How much money did Suneel have in her account then? Show your work. **\$16**

Reflect

Do you prefer to use a number line or mental math to evaluate an expression involving integers? Use an example in your explanation.

9.3 Adding and Subtracting Integers 379

Sample Solutions

3. b) The answers in each pair are equal. In each pair, the numbers are interchanged and the negative integer is written as subtracting a positive integer. Each number decreases by 1 each time. The answer decreases by 2 each time.

c) For example, −10 + 8 and 8 − 10; −11 + 7 and 7 − 11
−10 + 8 = −2 and 8 − 10 = −2
−11 + 7 = −4 and 7 − 11 = −4

4. a) −1, −3, −5; (−9 + 2), (−10 + 1), (−11 + 0); in each term, each integer decreases by 1, so their sum decreases by 2.

b) −4, −6, −8; (−6 − 4), (−7 − 5), (−8 − 6); in each term, the first integer decreases by 1 and the second integer increases by 1, so their difference decreases by 2.

5. An expression to represent Suneel's bank account is:
\$283 − \$120 − \$200 + \$53
I evaluated the expression:
\$283 − \$120 − \$200 + \$53 = \$163 − \$200 + \$53
= −\$37 + \$53
= \$16
Suneel had \$16 in her account.

REFLECT: I prefer to use mental math when the integers are not written in brackets. For example, to find 8 − 11, I subtract 8 from 11 to get 3, and I know the answer is −3 because 11 is greater than 8, and 11 was subtracted from 8.

ASSESSMENT FOR LEARNING

What to Look For	What to Do
Knowledge and Understanding ✔ Students understand how integers can be written without brackets.	***Extra Support:*** Students who have difficulty could continue to use manipulatives to add and subtract integers. Students can use Step-by-Step 3 (Master 9.12) to complete question 3.
Thinking ✔ Students can identify and extend patterns involving integers.	***Extra Practice:*** Have students use a number cube labelled 11 to 16. Students roll the cube twice, then subtract the second number from the first number. Students can complete Extra Practice 3 (Master 9.26).
Application ✔ Students can add and subtract integers without brackets.	***Extension:*** Have students complete the Additional Activity *What's the Temperature?* (Master 9.7).

Recording and Reporting
Master 9.2 Ongoing Observations: Integers

Multiplying Integers

LESSON ORGANIZER

40–50 min

Curriculum Focus: Use patterns to develop the rules for multiplying integers. (8m21, 8m22)

Student Materials *Optional*
- 12 × 12 Multiplication Chart (PM 15)
- playing cards
- Step-by-Step 4 (Master 9.13)
- Extra Practice 4 (Master 9.27)

Vocabulary: properties of integers, order property, distributive property

Assessment: Master 9.2 Ongoing Observations: Integers

Key Math Learning

If two integers have the same sign, their product is positive.
If two integers have different signs, their product is negative.

Number Strategies

Students will probably identify the two perfect squares that each number under the square root sign lies between. Then, students use guess and check to approximate the square root to 1 decimal place.

9.4 Multiplying Integers

Focus Use patterns to develop the rules for multiplying integers.

We can write the number of tiles in this array in two ways.

As a sum:
$5 + 5 + 5 = 15$

As a product:
$(+3) \times (+5) = +15$

How can you use integers to write the number of tiles in this array in two ways?

In *Explore*, you will use patterns to find products such as $(-3) \times (+5)$ and $(-3) \times (-5)$, which cannot be represented as arrays.

Explore

Work on your own.
Your teacher will give you a large copy of this multiplication table.

Second Number

First Number

×	−5	−4	−3	−2	−1	0	+1	+2	+3	+4
−5										
−4										
−3										
−2										
−1										
0										
+1										
+2										
+3										
+4										
+5										

Start at the bottom right of the table.
Multiply the positive integers.
Then complete the bottom left of the table.
Multiply a positive integer by a negative integer.
Use patterns or any method you wish to complete the top right, then the top left of the table.

Reflect & Share

Compare your completed table with that of a classmate.
Use the patterns in your table.
How could you multiply any negative integer by a positive integer?
How could you multiply any two negative integers?

BEFORE Get Started

Review the introduction on page 380 of the Student Book. Ask:

- When a positive integer is multiplied by a positive integer, what is the sign of the product? (*Positive*)

Show students the 3-by-5 array of red tiles. Ask:

- What is the value of the array? (*–15*)
- Which addition equation models this array? (*(–5) + (–5) + (–5) = –15*)
- Which multiplication equation models this array? (*3 × (–5) = –15 or (+3) × (–5) = –15*)
- When a positive integer is multiplied by a negative integer, what is the sign of the product? (*Negative*)

Ask students why they cannot use tiles to model (–3) × (+5) and (–3) × (–5).

(*Because you cannot have negative 3 rows of 5 yellow tiles or negative 3 rows of 5 red tiles*).

Present *Explore*.

DURING Explore

Ongoing Assessment: Observe and Listen

As students work, ask questions, such as:

- Which part of the table involves multiplying two positive integers? (*Bottom right*)
- How do you multiply two positive integers? (*I think about an array of yellow tiles. The product of two positive integers is a positive integer.*)
- How do you fill in the bottom left? (*I think about arrays of red tiles. The positive integers in the left column are the numbers of rows. The negative integers in the heading of the table are the numbers of red tiles in each row.*)

Connect

These properties of whole numbers are also properties of integers.

Multiplying by 0

$3 \times 0 = 0$ and $0 \times 3 = 0$

So, $(-3) \times 0 = 0$ and $0 \times (-3) = 0$

Multiplying by 1

$3 \times 1 = 3$ and $1 \times 3 = 3$

So, $(-3) \times (+1) = -3$ and $(+1) \times (-3) = -3$

Order Property

$3 \times 4 = 12$ and $4 \times 3 = 12$

So, $(-3) \times (+4) = -12$ and $(+4) \times (-3) = -12$

Distributive Property

$$3 \times (4 + 5) = 3 \times 4 + 3 \times 5 \\ = 12 + 15 \\ = 27$$

$$\text{So, } (+3) \times [(-4) + (-5)] = [(+3) \times (-4)] + [(+3) \times (-5)] \\ = (-12) + (-15) \\ = -27$$

From the introduction on page 380, you know that

$(+3) \times (+5) = +15$

and $(+3) \times (-5) = -15$

We can use the order property to show that:

Since $(+3) \times (-5) = -15$, then $(-5) \times (+3) = -15$

We can use the distributive property to investigate the product of two negative integers.

Here are two ways to calculate: $(-5) \times [(+3) + (-3)]$

Method 1	Method 2
$(-5) \times [(+3) + (-3)]$	$(-5) \times [(+3) + (-3)]$
$= (-5) \times (+3) + (-5) \times (-3)$	
$= (-15) + (-5) \times (-3)$	$= (-5) \times (0)$
	$= 0$

These answers must be equal.

REACHING ALL LEARNERS

Early Finishers

Have students use question 5 as a model, to generate more number patterns using integers. Students write the first 4 terms of each pattern, then trade patterns with a classmate to continue the classmate's patterns.

Common Misconceptions

➤ Students do not understand why the product of two negative integers is a positive integer.

How to Help: Have students relate it to double negatives in language arts: "I did not do nothing" means "I did something;" that is, a double negative represents a positive statement.

ESL Strategies

Students for whom English is a second language should not have to learn the names of the properties on page 381; it is sufficient that they know when to apply them.

Sample Solutions

1. a), c) The product of two integers with opposite signs is negative.

b), d) The product of two integers with the same sign is positive.

5. a) Start at +1. Multiply by +2 each time.

b) Start at +1. Multiply by –6 each time.

c) Start at –1. Multiply by –3 each time.

d) Start at –4. Add –4 each time.

An alternative pattern is: Multiply each whole number by –4.

- What is the sign of each product in the bottom left? How do you know?
  (Negative; we found that a positive integer multiplied by a negative integer is negative when we worked with tiles earlier.)
- What patterns do you see in the products you know so far that will help you find the products that you do not know?
  (I start with the integers in the bottom left, and look at the integers in the first column. Start at the bottom; the integers are: –25, –20, –15, –10, –5. The pattern is add 5 each time. So, I continue the pattern upward to get (0) × (–5) = 0; (–1) × (–5) = +5; (–2) × (–5) = +10; (–3) × (–5) = +15; (–4) × (–5) = +20; (–5) × (–5) = +25. I do this for each column that extends from the bottom left to the top left.)
- How do you fill in the top right of the table?
  (I could do it two ways: extend the patterns in the rows in the top left or extend the patterns in the columns in the bottom right. I'll do it the second way. I start with the bottom of the column at the right. The integers are: +25, +20, +15, +10, +5. The pattern is subtract 5 each time. So, I continue the pattern upward to get (0) × (+5) = 0; (–1) × (+5) = –5; (–2) × (+5) = –10; (–3) × (+5) = –15; (–4) × (+5) = –20; (–5) × (+5) = –25. I do this for each column that extends from the bottom right to the top right.)
- How could you multiply a negative integer by a positive integer?
  (I look at the integers in the top right corner of the table. All of them are negative. So, to multiply a negative integer by a positive integer, I multiply the numbers and the product is negative.)
- How could you multiply two negative integers?
  (I look at the integers in the top left corner of the table. All of them are positive. So, to multiply two negative integers, I multiply the numbers and the product is positive.)

6. **b)** No, two integers can be multiplied in either order and their product is always the same.
7. **c)** There is not a greater product because I used the least negative numbers. There is not a lesser product because I used the greatest positive number and the least negative number.
8. **a)** (−2)(−3)(−4)(−5)(−6)(−7) = +5040
(−2)(−3)(−4)(−5)(−6)(−7)(−8) = −40 320
(−2)(−3)(−4)(−5)(−6)(−7)(−8)(−9) = +362 880
(−2)(−3)(−4)(−5)(−6)(−7)(−8)(−9)(−10) = −3 628 800
b) **i)** The product of an even number of negative factors is positive. Each pair of factors has a positive product. So, an even number of factors can be split into pairs of factors, with no factors left over. So, the final product is a product of positive integers.
ii) The product of an odd number of negative factors is negative. Each pair of factors has a positive product, and there is one factor left over that is negative. So, the final product is negative.
c) When the factors are positive and negative, we need only consider the negative factors. The same rules apply. When the number of negative factors is even, the product is positive. When the number of negative factors is odd, the product is negative.
9. When a number is multiplied by itself, the product is the product of two integers with the same sign, which is always positive. For example, (+6)(+6) = +36 and (−6)(−6) = +36

So, (−15) + (−5) × (−3) = 0
But: (−15) + (+15) = 0
So, (−5) × (−3) = +15
We could do this with any pair of opposite integers in the square brackets.
So, the product of two negative integers is positive.

The results above can be used to write these rules for multiplying integers:

- The product of two integers with the same sign is positive.
That is, (+7) × (+6) = +42 and (−7) × (−6) = +42
- The product of two integers with opposite signs is negative.
That is, (+8) × (−9) = −72 and (−8) × (+9) = −72

To multiply more than two integers, we use the order of operations.
That is, we multiply the integers in pairs, in the order they appear.

Example

Find each product.
a) (+3) × (−6) × (−2)
b) (−2) × (−4) × (−5)

Solution

a) (+3) × (−6) × (−2) — Multiply the first two integers.
= (−18) × (−2) — Then, multiply.
= +36

b) (−2) × (−4) × (−5) — Multiply the first two integers.
= (+8) × (−5) — Then, multiply.
= −40

When we write the product of integers, we do not need to write the multiplication sign.
That is, we may write (−8) × (−9) as (−8)(−9).
And, (+3) × (−6) × (−2) may be written as (+3)(−6)(−2).

382 UNIT 9: Integers

After students finish *Explore,* have students write the rules they discovered for multiplying integers.
Ask:

- When is the product of two integers positive? (*When the integers have the same sign*)
- When is the product of two integers negative? (*When the integers have opposite signs*)

AFTER **Connect**

What you should see:

×	−5	−4	−3	−2	−1	0	+1	+2	+3	+4	+5
−5	+25	+20	+15	+10	+5	0	−5	−10	−15	−20	−25
−4	+20	+16	+12	+8	+4	0	−4	−8	−12	−16	−20
−3	+15	+12	+9	+6	+3	0	−3	−6	−9	−12	−15
−2	+10	+8	+6	+4	+2	0	−2	−4	−6	−8	−10
−1	+5	+4	+3	+2	+1	0	−1	−2	−3	−4	−5
0	0	0	0	0	0	0	0	0	0	0	0
+1	−5	−4	−3	−2	−1	0	+1	+2	+3	+4	+5
+2	−10	−8	−6	−4	−2	0	+2	+4	+6	+8	+10
+3	−15	−12	−9	−6	−3	0	+3	+6	+9	+12	+15
+4	−20	−16	−12	−8	−4	0	+4	+8	+12	+16	+20
+5	−25	−20	−15	−10	−5	0	+5	+10	+15	+20	+25

Practice

1. Will each product be positive or negative? How do you know?
   a) $(-6) \times (+2)$ Negative b) $(+6) \times (+4)$ Positive
   c) $(+4) \times (-2)$ Negative d) $(-7) \times (-3)$ Positive

2. Find each product.
   a) $(+8)(-3)$ −24 b) $(-5)(-4)$ +20 c) $(-3)(+9)$ −27
   d) $(+7)(-6)$ −42 e) $(+10)(-3)$ −30 f) $(-7)(-6)$ +42
   g) $(0)(-8)$ 0 h) $(+10)(-20)$ −200 i) $(-14)(-30)$ +420

3. Find each product.
   a) $(-1)(-8)(-2)$ −16
   b) $(-11)(-12)(-1)$ −132
   c) $(-1)(-1)(-1)(-1)(-1)$ −1
   d) $(-2)(-3)(-4)(-5)$ +120

4. Copy each equation.
   Replace □ with an integer to make the equation true.
   a) $(+5) \times □ = +20$ +4 b) $□ \times (-9) = +27$ −3
   c) $(-9) \times □ = -54$ +6 d) $□ \times (-3) = +18$ −6
   e) $□ \times (+5) = -20$ −4 f) $□ \times (-12) = +144$ −12
   g) $□ \times (-6) = +180$ −30 h) $(+3) \times □ \times (-4) = +24$ −2

5. Write the next 3 terms in each pattern.
   Then write the pattern rule.
   a) +1, +2, +4, +8, … +16, +32, +64 b) +1, −6, +36, … −216, +1296, −7776
   c) −1, +3, −9, … +27, −81, +243 d) −4, −8, −12, … −16, −20, −24

6. a) Find the product of each pair of integers.
   i) $(+3)(-7)$ and $(-7)(+3)$ −21, −21 ii) $(+4)(+8)$ and $(+8)(+4)$ +32, +32
   iii) $(-5)(-9)$ and $(-9)(-5)$ +45, +45 iv) $(-6)(+10)$ and $(+10)(-6)$ −60, −60
   b) Use the results of part a. Does the order in which integers are multiplied affect the product? Explain. No

7. Use these integers: −5, +9, −8, +4, −2
   a) Which two integers have the greatest product? −5 and −8
   b) Which two integers have the least product? +9 and −8
   c) How do you know there is not a greater product or a lesser product?

9.4 Multiplying Integers 383

10. Write the factors of 36 as whole numbers, then include signs to make them integers.
    Two factors: +2, −18; −2, +18;
    +3, −9; −3, +9;
    +6, −6
    Three factors: −2, −2, −9; −2, +2, +9; −2, −3, −6;
    −2, +3, +6; +2, −3, +6; +2, +3, −6
    Four factors: −2, −2, −3, +3; −2, +2, −3, −3; −2, +2, +3, +3;
    +2, +2, −3, +3
    Exclude 1 as a factor because it is not possible to list all the possibilities if 1 is included. There are 15 ways if 1 is excluded.
11. I did not use +1, −1, or 0 as my integers. The product of two positive integers is always greater than either of the two integers, for example, $(+3) \times (+5) = +15$
    The product of two negative integers is always greater than either of the two integers, for example, $(-3) \times (-5) = +15$
    The product of a negative integer and a positive integer is less than both integers; for example, $(-3) \times (+5) = -15$
12. Use guess and check.
    Find two numbers with a product of −144 and add them:
    +1, −144; +2, −72; +3, −48; +4, −36; +6, −24;
    +8, −18; +9, −16
    +9 + (−16) = −7; so the integers are +9 and −16.

Review the multiplication properties of integers.
Students should find the rules for multiplying by 0 or 1 to be straightforward.
As you discuss the order property, ask:

- What is $(-5) \times (+3)$? *(−15)*
- What is $(+3) \times (-5)$? *(−15)*
- What do you notice? (*The products are equal.*)
- Describe the order property in words. (*You can change the order of two integers when you multiply them without affecting the answer.*)

Ask students to describe the distributive property in words (the product of an integer and the sum of two integers is equal to the sum of the products of the first integer with each of the other two integers.)

Review the *Example* that illustrates how to multiply more than two integers.
The Assessment Focus question has students investigate patterns in products of integers.

Practice

Assessment Focus: Question 8

Students use the products of consecutive integers to find rules for identifying the sign of the products of even and odd numbers of negative integers, and the products of positive and negative integers. Some students may need only a few examples to identify and describe the patterns.

Assignment Guidelines

If your students do not have time to complete all the *Practice* questions on pages 383 and 384, these questions provide minimum curriculum coverage:
1, 2, 3, 7, 8, 9, *Reflect*

To assess the 4 Achievement Categories listed in the curriculum document, have students complete these *Practice* questions:
Knowledge and Understanding: 3 Application: 9
Thinking: 7 Communication: *Reflect*

13. Find the factors of all numbers between 160 and 200 that have one factor between 20 and 40.
165 = 5 × 33; 170 = 5 × 34; 175 = 5 × 35;
180 = 5 × 36; 185 = 5 × 37; 190 = 5 × 38;
195 = 5 × 39
168 = 6 × 28; 174 = 6 × 29; 180 = 6 × 30;
186 = 6 × 31; 192 = 6 × 32; 198 = 6 × 33
168 = 7 × 24; 175 = 7 × 25; 182 = 7 × 26;
189 = 7 × 27; 196 = 7 × 28
168 = 8 × 21; 176 = 8 × 22; 184 = 8 × 23;
192 = 8 × 24
189 = 9 × 21; 198 = 9 × 22
Since the product is positive, and one integer is negative, the other integer must also be negative.

REFLECT: I would show my friend the completed multiplication chart from *Explore* and explain how the patterns are used to get the rules for multiplying integers. Then I would have my friend write the two rules:
The product of two integers with the same sign is positive.
The product of two integers with opposite signs is negative.
Then I would show my friend some examples:
Same sign: (−7) × (−8) = +56; (+10) × (+6) = +60
Opposite signs: (+3) × (−4) = −12; (−5) × (+2) = −10

Number Strategies

Estimate each square root to 1 decimal place.
$\sqrt{58}$, $\sqrt{47}$, $\sqrt{83}$, $\sqrt{31}$
Do not use the $\sqrt{\ }$ key on a calculator.
7.6, 6.9, 9.1, 5.6

8. Assessment Focus
a) Find each product. Then use a calculator to extend the pattern 4 more rows.
i) (−2)(−3) +6 ii) (−2)(−3)(−4) −24
iii) (−2)(−3)(−4)(−5) +120 iv) (−2)(−3)(−4)(−5)(−6) −720
b) Use the results of part a.
i) What is the sign of a product when it has an even number of negative factors? Explain. Positive
ii) What is the sign of a product when it has an odd number of negative factors? Explain. Negative
c) Investigate what happens when a product has positive and negative factors. Do the rules in part b still apply? Explain. Yes

9. Explain why the product of an integer multiplied by itself can never be negative.

Take It Further

10. How many different ways can you write −36 as the product of two or more integer factors?

The natural numbers are 1, 2, 3, 4, …, and so on.

11. When you multiply two natural numbers, the product is never less than either of the two numbers. Is the same statement true for the product of any two integers? No
Investigate, then write what you find out.

12. The product of two integers is −144. The sum of the integers is −7. What are the two integers?

13. The product of two integers is between +160 and +200. One integer is between −20 and −40.
a) What is the greatest possible value for the other integer? −5
b) What is the least possible value for the other integer? −9

Reflect

Suppose your friend missed this lesson. How would you explain to her how to multiply two integers? Use examples in your explanation.

384 UNIT 9: Integers

ASSESSMENT FOR LEARNING

What to Look For	What to Do
Knowledge and Understanding ✔ Students discover the rules for the multiplication of integers through patterning. ***Thinking*** ✔ Students can use patterns to explain the rules for multiplying integers. ***Application*** ✔ Students can multiply two or more integers.	***Extra Support:*** Students who have difficulty could use a completed multiplication chart for products of whole numbers up to 12 × 12 and refer to their completed table from *Explore* for the sign of the product of two integers. Students can use Step-by-Step 4 (Master 9.13) to complete question 8. ***Extra Practice:*** Students can complete the Additional Activity *What's My Product?* (Master 9.8). Students can complete Extra Practice 4 (Master 9.27). ***Extension:*** Have students make up problems similar to those in *Practice* questions 10, 12, and 13, then trade problems with a classmate, and solve the classmate's problems.

Recording and Reporting
Master 9.2 Ongoing Observations: Integers

9.5 Dividing Integers

Focus Use patterns to develop the rules for dividing integers.

Recall that, for any multiplication fact with two different factors, you can write two related division facts. For example:
$9 \times 7 = 63$
So, $63 \div 9 = 7$ and, $63 \div 7 = 9$
We can apply the same rules to the product of two integers.

Explore

Work with a partner.
Write each product below as many different ways as you can.
For each product, write two related division facts.

➢ Write 75 as the product of two positive integers.
➢ Write 126 as the product of two negative integers.
➢ Write −72 as the product of a negative integer and a positive integer.
➢ Write −80 as the product of a positive integer and a negative integer.

Reflect & Share

Compare your division facts with those of another pair of classmates. Work together to develop rules for:

- dividing two positive integers
- dividing two negative integers
- dividing a negative integer by a positive integer
- dividing a positive integer by a negative integer

Connect

To divide integers, we use the fact that division is the inverse of multiplication.

➢ We know that: $(+5) \times (+3) = +15$
So, $(+15) \div (+5) = +3$ and $(+15) \div (+3) = +5$
(arrows label: dividend, divisor, quotient)

When the dividend and divisor are positive, the quotient is positive.

9.5 Dividing Integers **385**

Dividing Integers

LESSON ORGANIZER — 40–50 min

Curriculum Focus: Use patterns to develop the rules for dividing integers. (8m21, 8m22)

Student Materials
- calculators

Optional
- Step-by-Step 5 (Master 9.14)
- Extra Practice 5 (Master 9.28)

Vocabulary: dividend, divisor, quotient, rational number

Assessment: Master 9.2 Ongoing Observations: Integers

Key Math Learning

If two integers have the same sign, their quotient is positive.
If two integers have different signs, their quotient is negative.

Assignment Guidelines

If your students do not have time to complete all the *Practice* questions on pages 387 and 388, these questions provide minimum curriculum coverage: 3, 4, 5, 6, 7, *Reflect*

To assess the 4 Achievement Chart categories listed in the curriculum document, have students complete these *Practice* questions:
Knowledge and Understanding: 3
Application: 5
Thinking: 6
Communication: *Reflect*

BEFORE — Get Started

Review the meanings of the words *dividend*, *divisor*, and *quotient*.

Use the division equation on page 385.

In $63 \div 9 = 7$, 63 is the dividend, 9 is the divisor, and 7 is the quotient.

On the board, draw an arrow from each word to the relevant number for students to refer to as they work through this lesson.

Present *Explore*.

DURING — Explore

Ongoing Assessment: Observe and Listen

Ask questions, such as:

- Which two factors that have 75 as a product did you choose?
  (I chose 5 and 15, so the product is $(+5) \times (+15) = +75$.)
- What are the two related division facts?
  ($(+75) \div (+5) = +15$ and $(+75) \div (+15) = +5$)
- Which two factors that have −80 as a product did you choose?
  (I chose −20 and +4, so the product is $(-20) \times (+4) = -80$. I also swapped the signs and wrote $(+20) \times (-4) = -80$.)
- What are the two related facts for each product? *($(-80) \div (+4) = -20$; $(-80) \div (-20) = +4$; $(-80) \div (+20) = -4$; and $(-80) \div (-4) = +20$)*

REACHING ALL LEARNERS

Early Finishers

Have students write problems involving division of integers. Each student trades problems with a classmate and solves the classmate's problems. Students then compare and discuss their solutions.

Common Misconceptions

➤ Students do not understand why there are two division facts for each multiplication fact.

How to Help: Have students use counters to review the two types of division; that is, equal groups with the size of the groups unknown and equal groups with the number of groups unknown. For example, have students divide 20 counters into 5 equal groups; there are 4 in each group and 20 ÷ 5 = 4. Then have students divide 20 counters into groups of 4; there are 5 groups; and 20 ÷ 4 = 5.

ESL Strategies

Have students create a poster to illustrate the rules for multiplying and dividing, with examples beside each rule.

Calculator Skills

Students should use the formulas $A = \pi r^2$, and $C = 2\pi r$ or $C = \pi d$, and substitute for r and/or d.

➢ We know that: $(-5) \times (+3) = -15$

So, $(-15) \div (+3) = -5$ and $(-15) \div (-5) = +3$

When the dividend is negative and the divisor is positive, the quotient is negative.

When both the d[...] divisor are negat[...] quotient is positive.

➢ We know that: $(-5) \times (-3) = +15$

So, $(+15) \div (-5) = -3$ and $(+15) \div (-3) = -5$

When the dividend is positive and the divisor is negative, the quotient is negative.

The results above are true for all integers related in the different ways illustrated.

We can use these results to write rules for dividing integers:

- The quotient of two integers with the same sign is positive. That is, $(+56) \div (+8) = +7$ and $(-56) \div (-8) = +7$
- The quotient of two integers with opposite signs is negative. That is, $(+63) \div (-9) = -7$ and $(-63) \div (+9) = -7$

A division expression can be written with a division sign: $(-48) \div (-6)$; or as a fraction: $\frac{-48}{-6}$

When the expression is written as a fraction, we do not need to use brackets.

Example

Divide.

a) $(-100) \div (-20)$

b) $\frac{-30}{+5}$

Solution

a) Since the signs are the same, the quotient is positive.
$(-100) \div (-20) = +5$

b) Since the signs are different, the quotient is negative.
$\frac{-30}{+5} = -6$

In *Example*, part b, the integer -6 can be written as $-\frac{6}{1}$. When the integer is written this way, it is written as a **rational number**.

386 UNIT 9: Integers

AFTER Connect

Have volunteers write their products and division facts on the board.

What you might see:

1 × 75 = 75; 75 ÷ 1 = 75; 75 ÷ 75 = 1
3 × 25 = 75; 75 ÷ 3 = 25; 75 ÷ 25 = 3
(–1) × (–126) = 126; (+126) ÷ (–1) = –126;
(+126) ÷ (–126) = –1
(–2) × (–63) = 126; (+126) ÷ (–2) = –63;
(+126) ÷ (–63) = –2
(–3) × (–42) = 126; (+126) ÷ (–3) = –42;
(+126) ÷ (–42) = –3
(–6) × (–21) = 126; (+126) ÷ (–6) = –21;
(+126) ÷ (–21) = –6
(–7) × (–18) = 126; (+126) ÷ (–7) = –18;
(+126) ÷ (–18) = –7
(–9) × (–14) = 126; (+126) ÷ (–9) = –14;
(+126) ÷ (–14) = –9
(–1) × (+72) = –72; (–72) ÷ (–1) = +72;
(–72) ÷ (+72) = –1
(+1) × (–72) = –72; (–72) ÷ (+1) = –72;
(–72) ÷ (–72) = +1
(–2) × (+36) = –72; (–72) ÷ (–2) = +36;
(–72) ÷ (+36) = –2
(+2) × (–36) = –72; (–72) ÷ (+2) = –36;
(–72) ÷ (–36) = +2
(–4) × (+18) = –72; (–72) ÷ (–4) = +18;
(–72) ÷ (+18) = –4
(+4) × (–18) = –72; (–72) ÷ (+4) = –18;
(–72) ÷ (–18) = +4
(–6) × (+12) = –72; (–72) ÷ (–6) = +12;
(–72) ÷ (+12) = –6
(+6) × (–12) = –72; (–72) ÷ (+6) = –12;
(–72) ÷ (–12) = +6
(–8) × (+9) = –72; (–72) ÷ (–8) = +9;
(–72) ÷ (+9) = –8
(+8) × (–9) = –72; (–72) ÷ (+8) = –9;
(–72) ÷ (–9) = +8

Practice

1. Copy and continue each pattern until you have 8 rows.
Which rules for division of integers does each pattern illustrate?

a) $(-12) \div (+3) = -4$	b) $(+25) \div (-5) = -5$
$(-9) \div (+3) = -3$	$(+15) \div (-3) = -5$
$(-6) \div (+3) = -2$	$(+5) \div (-1) = -5$
$(-3) \div (+3) = -1$	$(-5) \div (+1) = -5$
c) $(+8) \div (+2) = +4$	d) $(+14) \div (+7) = +2$
$(+6) \div (+2) = +3$	$(+10) \div (+5) = +2$
$(+4) \div (+2) = +2$	$(+6) \div (+3) = +2$
$(+2) \div (+2) = +1$	$(+2) \div (+1) = +2$
e) $(-14) \div (+7) = -2$	f) $(-10) \div (-5) = +2$
$(-10) \div (+5) = -2$	$(-5) \div (-5) = +1$
$(-6) \div (+3) = -2$	$(0) \div (-5) = 0$
$(-2) \div (+1) = -2$	$(+5) \div (-5) = -1$

2. a) Use each multiplication fact to find a related quotient.
   i) Given $(+8) \times (+3) = +24$, find $(+24) \div (+3) = \square$ +8
   ii) Given $(-5) \times (-9) = +45$, find $(+45) \div (-9) = \square$ −5
   iii) Given $(-7) \times (+4) = -28$, find $(-28) \div (+4) = \square$ −7
   iv) Given $(+11) \times (-6) = -66$, find $(-66) \div (+11) = \square$ −6
   b) For each division fact in part a, write a related division fact.

3. Divide.
   a) $(+12) \div (-6)$ −2 b) $(-9) \div (-3)$ +3 c) $\frac{-20}{-5}$ +4
   d) $\frac{+21}{-7}$ −3 e) $(-32) \div (-8)$ +4 f) $(-144) \div (+12)$ −12
   g) $(-250) \div (+10)$ −25 h) $0 \div (-8)$ 0 i) $(+125) \div (+5)$ +25

4. Nirmala borrowed \$7 every day.
She now owes \$56.
For how many days did Nirmala borrow money?
   a) Write this problem as a division expression using integers. (−56) ÷ (−7)
   b) Solve the problem. 8 days

9.5 Dividing Integers 387

Sample Solutions

1. a) (0) ÷ (+3) = 0 (+6) ÷ (+3) = +2
(+3) ÷ (+3) = +1 (+9) ÷ (+3) = +3
The quotient of two integers with opposite signs is negative.
The quotient of two integers with the same sign is positive.
   b) (−15) ÷ (+3) = −5 (−35) ÷ (+7) = −5
(−25) ÷ (+5) = −5 (−45) ÷ (+9) = −5
The quotient of two integers with opposite signs is negative.
   c) (0) ÷ (+2) = 0 (−4) ÷ (+2) = −2
(−2) ÷ (+2) = −1 (−6) ÷ (+2) = −3
The quotient of two integers with opposite signs is negative.
The quotient of two integers with the same sign is positive.
   d) (−2) ÷ (−1) = +2 (−10) ÷ (−5) = +2
(−6) ÷ (−3) = +2 (−14) ÷ (−7) = +2
The quotient of two integers with the same sign is positive.
   e) (+2) ÷ (−1) = −2 (+10) ÷ (−5) = −2
(+6) ÷ (−3) = −2 (+14) ÷ (−7) = −2
The quotient of two integers with opposite signs is negative.
   f) (+10) ÷ (−5) = −2
(+15) ÷ (−5) = −3
(+20) ÷ (−5) = −4
(+25) ÷ (−5) = −5
The quotient of two integers with opposite signs is negative.
The quotient of two integers with the same sign is positive.

(Sample Solutions continue below, right.)

Students will also write products and division facts for −80, which involve 1 and 80, 2 and 40, 4 and 20, 5 and 16, and 8 and 10.

Use students' responses to *Reflect and Share* to develop the rules for dividing integers.

Review *Connect*. Introduce the term *rational number* as the quotient of two integers.
In a later Teacher Guide lesson, students will compare and order rational numbers.

Practice

Assessment Focus: Question 6

Students need to consider the four ways to divide:
positive integer ÷ positive integer;
negative integer ÷ negative integer;
positive integer ÷ negative integer; and
negative integer ÷ positive integer.

(Sample Solutions continued)

2. b) i) (+24) ÷ (+8) = +3 ii) (+45) ÷ (−5) = −9
iii) (−28) ÷ (−7) = +4 iv) (−66) ÷ (−6) = +11

5. a) Start at −3. Multiply by −3 each time.
   b) Start at +6. Add 6 to the numerical value. Alternate the sign each time.
   c) Start at +5. Alternate between multiplying by +4 and dividing by −2.
   d) Start at −64. Divide by −2 each time.
   e) Start at +100 000. Divide by −10 each time.

6. a) The quotient is less than both integers when the divisor is greater than the quotient: for example,
(+6) ÷ (+3) = +2
(+6) ÷ (−2) = −3
   b) The quotient is greater than both integers when both the dividend and the divisor are negative: for example,
(−6) ÷ (−3) = +2
   c) The quotient is between the two integers when the divisor is less than the quotient: dividing two positive integers; for example: (+6) ÷ (+2) = +3, or dividing a positive integer by a negative integer: for example, (+6) ÷ (−3) = −2
Also, when a negative integer is divided by a positive integer: for example, (−6) ÷ (+2) = −3

d) The quotient is +1 when the dividend and divisor are equal: for example, (+6) ÷ (+6) = +1 and (–3) ÷ (–3) = +1

e) The quotient is –1 when the dividend and divisor are opposite integers: for example, (+6) ÷ (–6) = –1

f) The quotient is 0 when the dividend is 0: for example, 0 ÷ (+6) = 0

8. a) (–32) ÷ (+4) ÷ (–2) = (–8) ÷ (–2) = +4
   b) (–81) ÷ (–9) ÷ (–9) = (+9) ÷ (–9) = –1
   c) (+56) ÷ (–4) ÷ (–2) = (–14) ÷ (–2) = +7

9. All of the integers must be even numbers.
   For example:
   +2, –4, and +6; +2 – 4 + 6 = +4
   +2, +8, and –6; +2 + 8 – 6 = +4
   +4, –2, and +2; +4 – 2 + 2 = +4
   –6, +6, and +4; –6 + 6 + 4 = +4
   +4, –8, and +8; +4 – 8 + 8 = +4

REFLECT: To divide integers, I use these rules to find the sign of the quotient, then divide the whole numbers.
The quotient of two integers with the same sign is positive.
The quotient of two integers with opposite signs is negative.
For example, (+8) ÷ (+2): The integers have the same sign, so the quotient is positive, and 8 ÷ 2 = 4. So, (+8) ÷ (+2) = +4
(–14) ÷ (–7): The integers have the same sign, so the quotient is positive, and 14 ÷ 7 = 2. So, (–14) ÷ (–7) = +2
(+9) ÷ (–3): The integers have opposite signs, and 9 ÷ 3 = 3. So, (+9) ÷ (–3) = –3
(–12) ÷ (+4): The integers have opposite signs, and 12 ÷ 4 = 3. So, (–12) ÷ (+4) = –3

Calculator Skills

Calculate the area and circumference of a circle with diameter 9.8 cm.
Give the answers to 1 decimal place.
75.4 cm²
30.8 cm

5. Write the next three terms in each pattern.
What is each pattern rule?
a) −3, +9, −27, … +81, –243, +729
b) +6, −12, +18, −24, … +30, –36, +42
c) +5, +20, −10, −40, +20, +80, … –40, –160, +80
d) −64, +32, −16, … +8, –4, +2
e) +100 000, −10 000, +1000, … –100, +10, –1

6. **Assessment Focus** Suppose you divide two integers.
When is the quotient:
a) less than both integers?
b) greater than both integers?
c) between the two integers?
d) equal to +1?
e) equal to −1?
f) equal to 0?
Use examples to illustrate your answers.
Show your work.

7. Divide.
a) (+624) ÷ (−52) –12
b) (−2231) ÷ (−23) +97
c) (−1344) ÷ (+16) –84
d) (−2068) ÷ (−47) +44

Take It Further

8. Evaluate.
a) (−32) ÷ (+4) ÷ (−2) +4
b) (−81) ÷ (−9) ÷ (−9) –1
c) (+56) ÷ (−4) ÷ (−2) +7

9. Find as many examples as you can of three different 1-digit numbers that are all divisible by +2 and have a sum of +4.

Reflect

How do you divide two integers?
Include an example for each different possible division.

388 UNIT 9: Integers

ASSESSMENT FOR LEARNING

What to Look For	What to Do
Knowledge and Understanding ✔ Students understand the rules for division of integers. ✔ Students understand that division is the inverse operation for multiplication.	***Extra Support:*** Allow students to use calculators. Encourage them to determine the sign of the quotient before they divide, then they need only divide whole numbers. Students can use Step-by-Step 5 (Master 9.14) to complete question 6.
Communication ✔ Students can explain how multiplying and dividing integers are related.	***Extra Practice:*** Students can complete the Additional Activity *Integer Bingo* (Master 9.9a). Students can complete Extra Practice 5 (Master 9.28).
Application ✔ Students can use the rules of division of integers to solve problems.	***Extension:*** Have students use calculators and question 5 as a guide. They make up their own increasing and decreasing integer patterns. Students trade patterns with a classmate, identify the classmate's pattern rule, then write the next 3 terms of each pattern. If it is a decreasing pattern, students must ensure the next 3 terms are integers.

Recording and Reporting
Master 9.2 Ongoing Observations: Integers

Rational Numbers

Key Math Learnings

1. Rational numbers can be expressed as fractions or decimals.
2. Rational numbers can be ordered by using strategies similar to those used to order fractions, decimals, and integers.

LESSON ORGANIZER 40–50 min

Curriculum Focus: Represent, compare, and order rational numbers. (8m13)

Student Materials
- Lesson 5A (Master 9.5)
- Number Lines (Master 9.20)

Optional
- calculators
- Step-by-Step 5A (Master 9.15)
- Extra Practice 5A (Master 9.29)

Vocabulary: rational number
Assessment: Master 9.2 Ongoing Observations: Integers

BEFORE Get Started

On the board, write rational numbers in different forms, such as:

$\frac{3}{4}, -\frac{3}{4}, 0.75, -0.75, 5, \frac{5}{1}, -\frac{5}{1}$

Ensure students understand that a rational number is any number that can be written as a fraction, where the numerator and denominator are integers, but the denominator cannot be zero.

In Lesson 9.5, students learned that any integer can be written as a rational number, by writing the integer as a fraction with denominator 1; for example, $-4 = \frac{-4}{1}$. So, all integers are rational numbers.

Ensure students understand that the position of the negative sign may vary without affecting the value of the number. For example, $\frac{-2}{3}$, $\frac{2}{-3}$, and $-\frac{2}{3}$ are equivalent.

Review how to order fractions, decimals, and integers. Ask:

- How can you find which is greater: $\frac{3}{5}$ or $\frac{2}{3}$?
  (I could use fraction strips. I could write equivalent fractions ($\frac{9}{15}$ and $\frac{10}{15}$). I could use a calculator to write each fraction in decimal form (0.6 and $0.\overline{6}$).)
- How do you decide which decimal is greater: 0.6 or $0.\overline{6}$?
  (0.6 can be written as 0.600 and is $0.\overline{6}$ is 0.666 . . . I use place value. Both decimals have 6 tenths, so I look at the hundredths. 0.6 has zero hundredths and $0.\overline{6}$ has 6 hundredths. So, $0.\overline{6}$ is greater.)
- How do you know which is greater: –4 or –3?
  (I think about a number line. The greater number is to the right of the lesser number on the line, so –3 is greater than –4.)

Present *Explore.*

DURING Explore

Ongoing Assessment: Observe and Listen

As students work, ask questions, such as:

- How do you decide which number is least?
  (*All the numbers have 3 in the ones place, so I look for the least fraction or decimal part. One-quarter is 0.25,* $\frac{2}{3}$ *is* $0.\overline{6}$*, and* $\frac{2}{5}$ *is 0.4. So, the least number is* $3\frac{1}{4}$*.*)
- What is the order from least to greatest?
  (*When all the numbers are in decimal form, I sketch a number line and put each number on the line. Then I write them in order from left to right:* $3\frac{1}{4}$, *3.28,* $3\frac{2}{5}$, *3.5,* $3\frac{2}{3}$, *3.68*)
- How did you order the rational numbers?
  (*I looked at the negative numbers first because any negative number is less than a positive number. I used a number line. Both* $-2\frac{5}{8}$ *and –2.05 lie between –3 and –2, and* $-2\frac{5}{8}$ *is closer to –3, so* $-2\frac{5}{8}$ *is the least, with –2.05 the next number.* $-\frac{5}{4}$ *is* $-1\frac{1}{4}$*, so it comes next, followed by –0.45. Then I ordered the positive numbers.*)

AFTER Connect

What you might see:

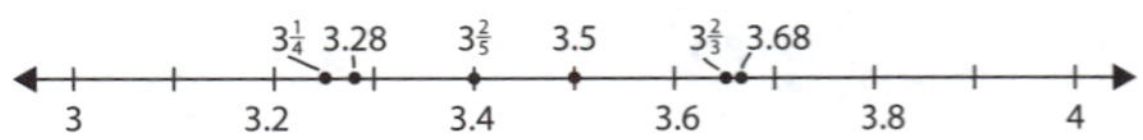

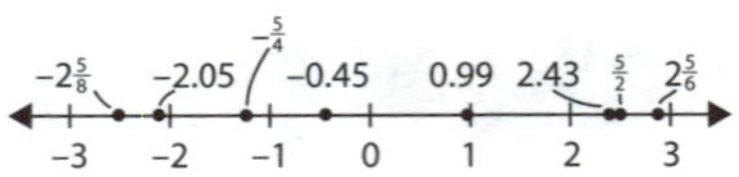

If necessary, review how to use a calculator to write a fraction in decimal form by dividing the numerator by the denominator; for example, $\frac{5}{6} = 0.8\overline{3}$.

Ensure students understand that to convert $-\frac{5}{6}$ to a decimal, they can ignore the negative sign when they divide but insert it in front of the decimal; that is, $-\frac{5}{6} = -0.8\overline{3}$.

Review the *Example*, reminding students that the lesser rational number is to the left of the greater rational number.

Practice

Students will need Number Lines (Master 9.20).

Assessment Focus: Question 8

Students order rational numbers and insert more rational numbers of their choice.

Sample Solutions

1.

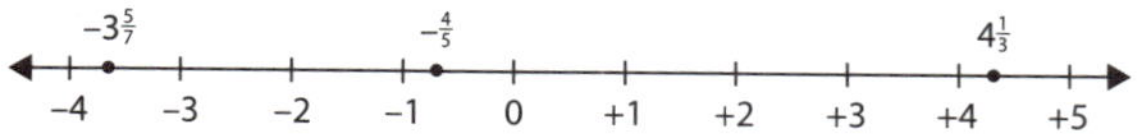

2. a) $1\frac{3}{4}$ is greater because it is positive.

b) $-1\frac{3}{4}$ is greater because it is to the right of $-2\frac{1}{2}$ on a number line.

c) $2\frac{1}{2}$ is greater because it is positive.

d) $2\frac{1}{2}$ is greater because it is to the right of $1\frac{3}{4}$ on a number line.

3.

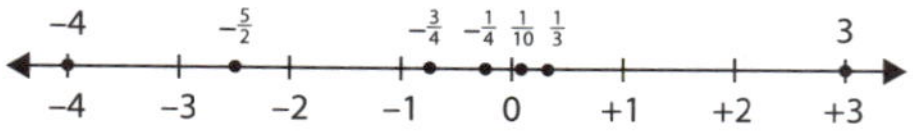

4. 1.80 m

5. −2.1, −1.8, −0.2, 0.1, 0.33, 2.4

Students' work should include a number line.

6. $-4.8, -2.2, -\frac{7}{10}, \frac{3}{2}, 2.5, \frac{8}{3}, 3.75$

Students' work should include a number line.

7. a) −10.6°C

b) −10.6, −6, −4.4, −0.8, 0.5, 3, 8.4

c) $\frac{-10.6 + 3 + 8.4 + (-4.4) + 0.5 + (-6) + (-0.8)}{7} \doteq -1.4$; about −1.4°C

8. a) $-4\frac{2}{3}, -3, -\frac{2}{5}, 7.38, 7\frac{5}{8}$

b)

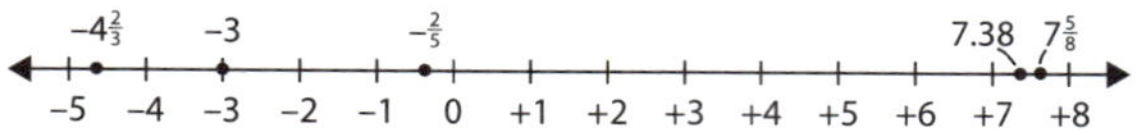

c) The new numbers are:

between $-4\frac{2}{3}$ and −3: −4

between −3 and $-\frac{2}{5}$: −2

between $-\frac{2}{5}$ and 7.38: 0

between 7.38 and $7\frac{5}{8}$: 7.4

I know the numbers are in the correct places because I used a number line to find them.

REFLECT: A rational number is a positive or negative fraction or a decimal or an integer. I chose $-4\frac{3}{5}$, $5\frac{1}{3}$, and $-3\frac{4}{9}$. First, I separate the negative numbers from the positive number. Then I look at the integer part of the numbers and order them from least to greatest. If two rational numbers have the same integer part, I would compare the fractional or decimal parts (by expressing both as decimals or as fractions with common denominators). With the numbers $-4\frac{3}{5}$, $5\frac{1}{3}$, and $-3\frac{4}{9}$, I would separate $-4\frac{3}{5}$ and $-3\frac{4}{9}$ from $5\frac{1}{3}$. Since $-4 < -3$, then $-4\frac{3}{5} < -3\frac{4}{9}$. Any positive number is greater than a negative number, so $5\frac{1}{3}$ is the greatest number. The numbers from least to greatest are: $-4\frac{3}{5}, -3\frac{4}{9}, 5\frac{1}{3}$

REACHING ALL LEARNERS

Early Finishers

Have students write their own rational numbers, then order them. Encourage students to use rational numbers expressed in a variety of forms: proper fractions, improper fractions, mixed numbers, integers, and decimals.

Common Misconceptions

➤ Students erroneously think that a negative mixed number, such as $-5\frac{1}{4}$, is greater than a negative mixed number such as $-4\frac{1}{3}$.

How to Help: Have students use number lines. $-5\frac{1}{4}$ is between −6 and −5. $-4\frac{1}{3}$ is between −5 and −4. Remind students that the order from least to greatest is always read from left to right. When students draw their own number lines, make sure they draw them correctly.

Assignment Guidelines

If students do not have time to complete all the *Practice* questions, these questions provide minimum curriculum coverage:
4, 5, 6, 7, *Reflect*

To assess the 4 Achievement Chart categories listed in the curriculum document, have students complete these *Practice* questions:
Knowledge and Understanding: 6
Application: 7
Thinking: 8
Communication: *Reflect*

ASSESSMENT FOR LEARNING

What to Look For	What to Do
Knowledge and Understanding ✔ Students understand what a rational number is.	***Extra Support:*** Students who have difficulty should use calculators and number lines. Students can use Step-by-Step 5A (Master 9.15) to complete question 8.
Communication ✔ Students can explain their strategies for ordering rational numbers.	***Extra Practice:*** Students can complete Extra Practice 5A (Master 9.29).
Application ✔ Students can order rational numbers.	***Extension:*** Have students add two rational numbers with different signs. They can use a calculator to check their work.

Recording and Reporting
Master 9.2 Ongoing Observations: Integers

LESSON ORGANIZER

Student Materials
- Number Lines (Master 9.20)

Assessment: Master 9.1 Unit Rubric: Integers, Master 9.4 Unit Summary: Integers

Mid-Unit Review

LESSON

9.1 **1.** a) Write these integers in order from least to greatest: +20, −4, −6, +13, 0, +2, −1
b) Show these integers on a number line.

2. Use a number line to add.
a) (−5) + (−7) −12
b) (−10) + (+7) −3
c) (−5) + (+12) +7
d) (−3) + (+5) + (−4) −2

3. a) Add: (−18) + (+5) −13
b) Find three other pairs of integers that have the same sum as part a.

9.2 **4.** Evaluate.
a) (−7) − (+2) −9
b) (−5) − (−2) −3
c) (+4) − (−3) +7
d) (−41) − (−17) −24
e) (−3) − (+4) + (−5) −12

5. Evaluate.
a) (−146) − (−571) +425
b) (−365) + (−198) − (+118) −681

6. The price of a new car is $27 599. The value of the car decreases by $2600 each year for five years. What will the value of the car be after five years?
a) Write an integer expression to represent this problem.
b) Solve the problem.

9.3 **7.** Evaluate.
a) 10 − 8 − 11 −9
b) −3 + 5 + 9 +11
c) −11 − 10 − 9 −30
d) 12 + 15 − 3 +24

9.4 **8.** Multiply.
a) (+8) × (−4) −32
b) (−120) × (−10) +1200
c) (−4) × (+7) −28
d) (+6)(−12) −72
e) (5)(0)(−1) 0
f) (−4)(−8)(−1) −32

9.3 9.4 **9.** Use integers to answer each question. Show your work.
a) The temperature drops 5°C, then drops another 3°C. What was the total drop in temperature? −8°C
b) A swimming pool drains at a rate of 35 L/min for 30 min. How much water drained out of the pool? +1050 L
c) The price of a house rose $25 000, dropped $28 999, then rose $14 500. What was the total change in the price of the house? +$10 501

9.5 **10.** Divide.
a) (−81) ÷ (+9) −9
b) (−12) ÷ (−6) +2
c) 0 ÷ (−9) 0
d) (+650) ÷ (−25) −26
e) (−1288) ÷ (−28) +46
f) (−100) ÷ (−100) +1

Mid-Unit Review 389

Sample Solutions

1. a) −6, −4, −1, 0, +2, +13, +20

b)

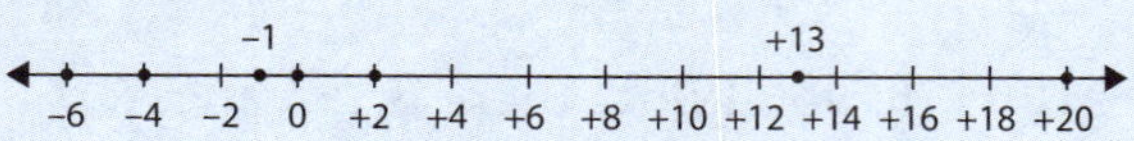

2. a)

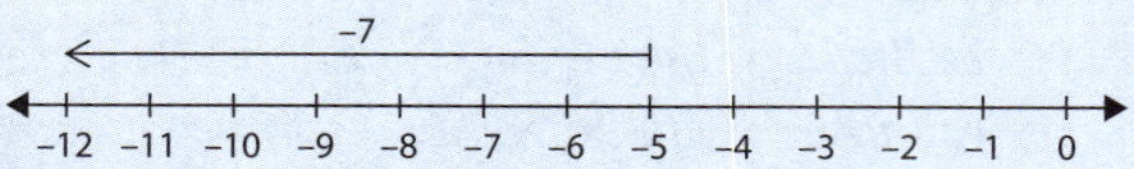

b)

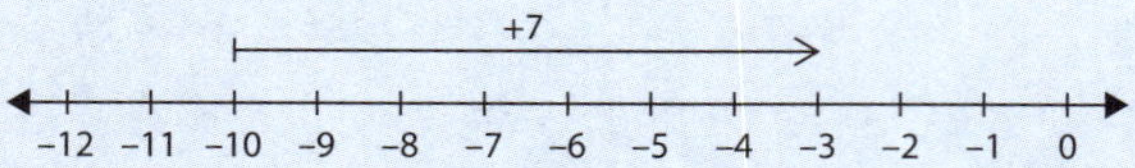

c)

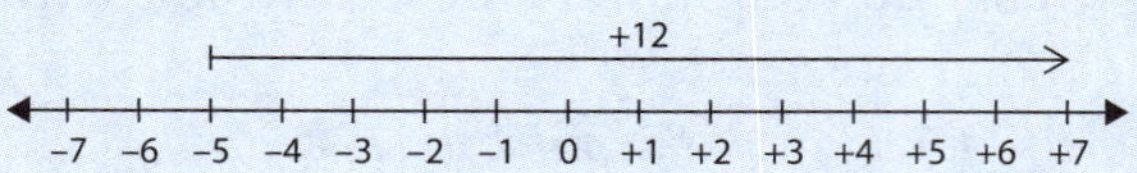

d)

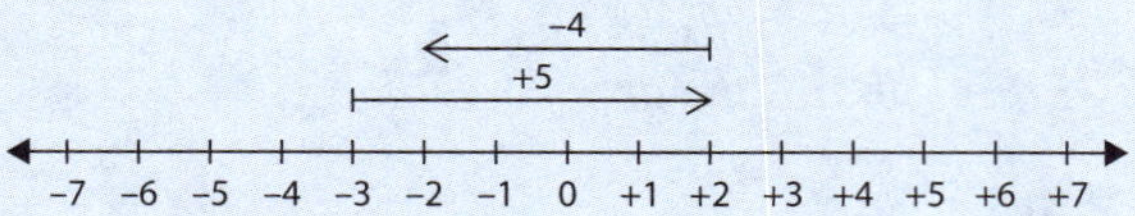

3. b) For example: −6 and −7; +1 and −14; +8 and −21

6. a) 27 599 − 2600 − 2600 − 2600 − 2600 − 2600, or 27 599 − (5 × 2600)

b) 27 599 − 13 000 = 14 599; the value of the car will be $14 599.

9. a) −5°C + (−3°C) = −8°C

b) 30 × 35 = +1050; 1050 L

c) $25 000 − $28 999 + $14 500 = +$10 501

LESSON 9.6

Order of Operations with Integers

LESSON ORGANIZER (40–50 min)

Curriculum Focus: Apply the order of operations with brackets and exponents. (8m23)

Student Materials

Optional
- calculators
- Step-by-Step 6 (Master 9.16)
- Extra Practice 6 (Master 9.30)

Vocabulary: order of operations, exponent

Assessment: Master 9.2 Ongoing Observations: Integers

Key Math Learning

The order of operations with whole numbers also applies to integers.

Assignment Guidelines

If your students do not have time to complete all the *Practice* questions on pages 391 and 392, these questions provide minimum curriculum coverage: 2, 3, 5, 7, 8

To assess the 4 Achievement Chart categories listed in the curriculum document, have students complete these *Practice* questions:

Knowledge and Understanding: 2	Communication: 6
Thinking: 5	Application: 8

9.6 Order of Operations with Integers

Focus Apply the order of operations with and exponents.

Recall the order of operations with whole numbers.
- Do the operations in brackets first.
- Do any work with exponents.
- Multiply and divide, in order, from left to right.
- Add and subtract, in order, from left to right.

It may help you to remember the order of operations when you think BEDMAS.

The same order of operations applies to all integers.

Explore

Work with a partner.
Use these integers: $-2, 4, -24, 7$
Use any operations or brackets.
Write the expression that has the greatest value.

Reflect & Share

Share your expression with that of another pair of classmates.
If the expressions are different, check that the expression with the greater answer is correct.
Work together to write an expression that has the least value.

Connect

Since we use curved brackets to show an integer; for example, (-2), we will use square brackets to group terms.

Example 1

Evaluate. $100 - 3[20 \div (-2)]$

Solution

$100 - 3[20 \div (-2)]$
$= 100 - 3 \times [20 \div (-2)]$ Do the operation in brackets first.
$= 100 - 3(-10)$
$= 100 + (-3)(-10)$ Multiply.
$= 100 + (+30)$ Add.
$= 130$

For clarity, we write positive integers as whole numbers.

390 UNIT 9: Integers

BEFORE — Get Started

Review the rules for the order of operations of whole numbers.

Present *Explore*.

DURING — Explore

Ongoing Assessment: Observe and Listen

As students work, ask questions, such as:

- Which two numbers multiplied together have the greatest product?
  ((–24) × (–2) = +48)
- How do you know there is no greater product?
  (To be the greatest, the product is positive. The product of two integers with the same sign is positive. The only other positive product is 4 × 7 = 28, which is less than 48.)
- Which two numbers multiplied together have the least product?
  ((–24) × (+7) = –168)
- How do you know there is not a lesser product?
  (To be the least, the product is negative. The product of two integers with different signs is negative. The other negative products are: (–2) × 4 = –8; (–2) × 7 = –14; 4 × (–24) = –96; none of these products is less than –168.)
- What do you think is the expression with the greatest value?
  (If I multiply all the numbers, I get (–2) × 4 × (–24) × 7 = 1344. I think that is the greatest value.)

Ask:

- How can you tell if a product will be positive or negative?
  (If there is an odd number of negative signs, the product will be negative. If there is an even number of negative signs, the product will be positive.)

When an expression is written as a fraction, the fraction bar has two meanings.

- The fraction bar indicates division.
- The fraction bar acts like brackets. That is, the operations in the numerator and denominator must be done before dividing the numerator by the denominator.

Example 2 Evaluate.

a) $\frac{4 \times (-8) + 2}{-6}$ b) $2 - (-3)^2$

Solution

a) $\frac{4 \times (-8) + 2}{-6}$ Multiply first.

$= \frac{(-32) + 2}{-6}$ Add the integers in the numerator.

$= \frac{-30}{-6}$ Divide.

$= 5$

b) $2 - (-3)^2$ Do the exponent first: $(-3)^2$ means $(-3)(-3)$

$= 2 - (-3)(-3)$ Multiply.

$= 2 - (+9)$ Subtract.

$= -7$

Practice

1. a) Evaluate.
   i) $12 \div (2 \times 3) - 2$ 0 ii) $12 \div 2 \times (3 - 2)$ 6
   b) Why are the answers different? Explain.

2. Evaluate. State which operation you do first.
   Multiply, +23 a) $(+7)(+4) - (+5)$ b) $(+6)[(+2) + (-5)]$ Add, −18
   Multiply, +25 c) $(-3) + (+4)(+7)$ d) $(-6) + (+4) \times (-2)$ Multiply, −14
   Division in brackets, −3 e) $(+15) \div [(+10) \div (-2)]$ f) $(+18) \div (-6) \times (+2)$ Divide, −6

3. Evaluate.
   a) $(-1)^3$ −1 b) $(-3)^2 + 9$ +18 c) $(5)^3 \times (-4)$ −500
   d) $\frac{(-2)^3}{-4}$ +2 e) $\frac{(-6)(-8)}{4}$ +12 f) $\frac{(-12)(-3)}{-6}$ −6

9.6 Order of Operations with Integers 391

REACHING ALL LEARNERS

Early Finishers

Have students make up their own order of operations questions with integers. If they include the division operation, they must ensure that the answer is an integer. Students could evaluate their own expression, then trade with a classmate.

Common Misconceptions

➤ Students do not understand the use of the different types of brackets or nested brackets.

How to Help: Remind students that they must evaluate the innermost brackets first, and then move outward. Some students may find it useful to highlight the first set of computations they need to do.

Number Strategies

654 = 600 + 50 + 4
7258 = 7000 + 200 + 50 + 8
83 507 = 80 000 + 3000 + 500 + 7
901 472 = 900 000 + 1000 + 400 + 70 + 2

Sample Solutions

1. b) Answers are different because you evaluate the expression in brackets first and there are different expressions in the brackets.

5. a) $-40 - 2[(-8) \div 2]$
$= -40 - 2[(-4)]$
$= -40 + 8$
$= -32$
Robert was correct.

- How did you find the expression with the least value?
(We knew the value had to be negative, so we thought the least number would be a product with the least negative integer as one factor, so we multiplied: 4 × (−24) × 7 = −672, then we added the remaining integer to get (−672) + (−2) = −674. Our expression is: 4 × (−24) × 7 + (−2) = −674)

AFTER Connect

Have students write their expressions on the board. Discuss what it is about the relevant expression that makes its value the greatest or the least.

Use *Example 1* to illustrate the need for different types of brackets to distinguish between those around a negative integer and those indicating a part of the expression that needs to be evaluated first.

In *Example 2*, review exponents. Have students investigate the difference between the answers for -3^2 and $(-3)^2$: $-3^2 = -9$, while $(-3)^2 = +9$. Point out how the locations of the negative signs produce the different answers.

Practice

In question 8, if students need to be reminded of the meaning of the word *mean*, direct them to the *Illustrated Glossary*. For question 4, remind students to show their work. Have students place each step of the solution directly under the calculation, as in *Example 1*.

Assessment Focus: Question 5

Students who are good at math might find it difficult to complete part b. They have to use the order of operations incorrectly to get the wrong answers.

b) Christian could have done this:

$-40 - 2[(-8) \div 2]$
$= -40 - 2[+4]$ He said $(-8) \div 2$ is +4 instead of −4.
$= -40 - 8$
$= -48$

c) Brenna did this:

$-40 - 2[(-8) \div 2]$
$= (-42)[(-8) \div 2]$ She subtracted before doing the operation in brackets.
$= (-42)(-4)$
$= 168$

6. $(-2)^2 \times (-100) \div 4 \times 5$
$= 4 \times (-25) \times 5$
$= -100 \times 5$
$= -500$ (closest to −500)

$376 \div 4 \times (-5)$
$= 94 \times (-5)$
$= -470$

$(-1360) \div 8 \times (-3)$
$= (-170)(-3)$
$= +510$

9. a) $\frac{(-24) + (+4)}{-5} = \frac{-20}{-5} = +4$

b) $(-4 + 10) \times -2 = 6(-2) = -12$

c) $\frac{(-10 - 4)}{-2} = \frac{-14}{-2} = +7$

REFLECT: I made up the expression: $\frac{3[(-12) + (-3)]}{5}$

I evaluated the expression:

$\frac{3[(-12) + (-3)]}{5} = \frac{3[-15]}{5}$ Do the operation in square brackets first.
$= \frac{-45}{5}$
$= -9$

Number Strategies

Write each number in expanded form.
- 654
- 7258
- 83 507
- 901 472

4. Evaluate. Show all the steps.
a) $(-3)(-2) + 4$ **+10** b) $(-8)(-2) + (-1)$ **+15**
c) $3(-4) - 2$ **−14** d) $-2(5 + 3)$ **−16**
e) $10 \div 2 + 4 \times (-3)$ **−7** f) $\frac{(-7)(4) + 8}{(-2)^2}$ **−5**

5. Assessment Focus Robert, Brenna, and Christian got different answers for this problem: $-40 - 2[(-8) \div 2]$
Robert's answer was −32, Christian's answer was −48, and Brenna's answer was 168.
a) Which student had the correct answer? **Robert**
b) Show and explain how the other two students got their answers. Where did they go wrong?

6. Which expression has a value that is closest to −500? Explain.
$(-2)^2 \times (-100) \div 4 \times 5$ (circled)
$376 \div 4 \times (-5)$
$(-1360) \div 8 \times (-3)$

7. Keisha had $405 in her bank account.
Over the summer, she made 4 withdrawals of $45 each.
What is the balance in Keisha's account?
Write an integer expression to represent this problem.
Solve the problem. **405 + 4(−45) = 225; $225**

8. The daily highest temperatures for one week in February were:
−2°C, +5°C, −8°C, −4°C, −11°C, −10°C, −5°C
Find the mean temperature. **−5°C**

Take It Further

9. Write an expression for each statement.
Evaluate each expression.
a) Divide the sum of −24 and 4 by −5. $\frac{(-24) + (+4)}{-5} = +4$
b) Multiply the sum of −4 and 10 by −2. $(-4 + 10) \times (-2) = -12$
c) Subtract 4 from −10, then divide by −2. $\frac{(-10 - 4)}{-2} = +7$

Reflect

Make up an integer expression that has three operations.
Evaluate the expression. Show your work.

392 UNIT 9: Integers

ASSESSMENT FOR LEARNING

What to Look For	What to Do
Knowledge and Understanding ✔ Students understand the rules for the order of operations involving integers and brackets. ***Thinking*** ✔ Students can solve multi-step problems using the order of operations with integers. ***Application*** ✔ Students evaluate exponents with an integer base.	***Extra Support:*** Students can use Step-by-Step 6 (Master 9.16) to complete question 5. ***Extra Practice:*** Have students complete question 2 after they have replaced each positive sign with a negative sign, and vice versa. Then they compare answers and explain why they are the opposites of the original answers. Have students investigate whether this always happens. Can they find an expression for which the answers are not opposites when all the signs are changed? Students can complete Extra Practice 6 (Master 9.30). ***Extension:*** Have students use question 5 as a guide. They write their own similar question, then trade with a classmate to identify the errors.

Recording and Reporting

Master 9.2 Ongoing Observations: Integers

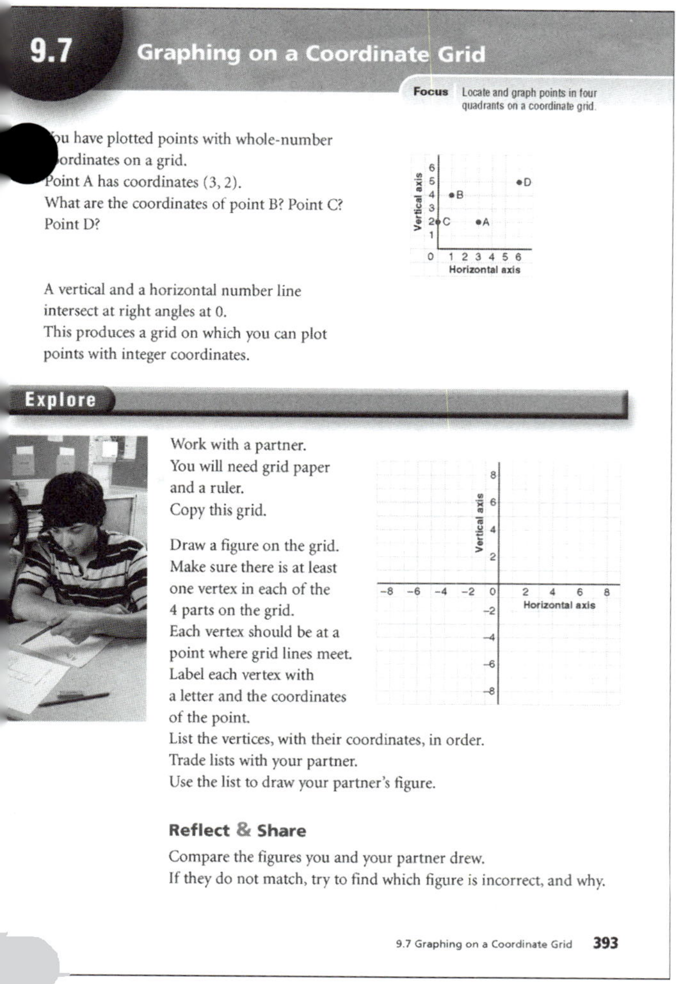
9.7 Graphing on a Coordinate Grid

Focus Locate and graph points in four quadrants on a coordinate grid.

You have plotted points with whole-number coordinates on a grid.
Point A has coordinates (3, 2).
What are the coordinates of point B? Point C?
Point D?

A vertical and a horizontal number line intersect at right angles at 0.
This produces a grid on which you can plot points with integer coordinates.

Explore

Work with a partner.
You will need grid paper and a ruler.
Copy this grid.

Draw a figure on the grid.
Make sure there is at least one vertex in each of the 4 parts on the grid.
Each vertex should be at a point where grid lines meet.
Label each vertex with a letter and the coordinates of the point.
List the vertices, with their coordinates, in order.
Trade lists with your partner.
Use the list to draw your partner's figure.

Reflect & Share

Compare the figures you and your partner drew.
If they do not match, try to find which figure is incorrect, and why.

9.7 Graphing on a Coordinate Grid 393

LESSON 9.7

Graphing on a Coordinate Grid

LESSON ORGANIZER (optional but recommended)

Curriculum Focus: Locate and graph points in four quadrants on a coordinate grid.

Teacher Materials

- overhead transparency of Coordinate Grid (Master 9.21)

Student Materials

- Coordinate Grid (Master 9.21)
- 0.5-cm grid paper (PM 14)

Optional

- Step-by-Step 7 (Master 9.17)
- Extra Practice 7 (Master 9.31)

Vocabulary: horizontal axis (x-axis), vertical axis (y-axis), coordinate grid, coordinate, ordered pair, origin, quadrant

Assessment: Master 9.2 Ongoing Observations: Integers

Key Math Learnings

1. An ordered pair of integers can be used to locate a point on a coordinate grid.
2. The x- and y-axes divide the coordinate grid into four quadrants.

Math Link

Have students research the life of René Descartes.
Read the story *The Fly on the Ceiling: A Math Reader* by Dr. Julie Glass to students.

Curriculum Note

This lesson is not directly required by the Grade 8 curriculum. However, it can be used to prepare students for Lessons 9.8 and 9.9, where students graph translations, reflections, and rotations on a coordinate grid.

BEFORE Get Started

Review graphing in the first quadrant. Ask:

- Point A is how many units to the right of the vertical axis? *(3)*
- Point A is how many units above the horizontal axis? *(2)*

Explain that the coordinates of A are written as the ordered pair (3, 2). Stress that the order of the numbers is important. Show that (2, 3) is not the same as (3, 2) by graphing both points. Have volunteers identify the coordinates of these points: B(1, 4), C(0, 2), D(6, 5).

Review how to identify and plot a point on the horizontal axis. Plot point E(2, 0) and have students identify the coordinates.

Present *Explore*.

DURING Explore

Ongoing Assessment: Observe and Listen

As students work, ask questions, such as:

- Now that there are four regions in your graph, what does the first coordinate of an ordered pair tell you?
(The distance right or left from the vertical axis)
- How could we distinguish between moving right and moving left?
(Use positive integers for moving right and negative integers for moving left.)
- What does the second coordinate of an ordered pair tell you?
(The distance up or down from the horizontal axis)

REACHING ALL LEARNERS

Alternative Explore

Materials: Coordinate Grid (Master 9.21)

Students work in pairs. They take turns to plot a point and have the partner write the coordinates. Then they take turns to say the coordinates and the partner plots the point.

Common Misconceptions

➤ Students write or say the numbers in an ordered pair in the incorrect order.

How to Help: Have students plot the points (3, –5) and (–5, 3) on a grid, then write the coordinates. Have them explain what happens if the coordinates are interchanged.

➤ Students forget to include the negative sign(s) in coordinate(s) when identifying the coordinates of points in Quadrants 2, 3, and 4.

How to Help: As before, on a separate grid, have students use the incorrect coordinates to plot a point, then compare the location of the points. Illustrating that the points are different should reinforce the importance of including negative signs when necessary.

➤ Students do not know the coordinates of points that lie on the x- or y-axis.

How to Help: Have students plot points on the x- and y-axes. Illustrate that when they plotted points on the x-axis, they did not move up or down, so the y-coordinates of the points are 0. Similarly when they plotted points on the y-axis, they did not move left or right, so the x-coordinates of the points are 0.

Connect

A vertical number line and a horizontal number line that intersect at right angles at 0 form a **coordinate grid**.
The horizontal axis is the ***x*-axis**.
The vertical axis is the ***y*-axis**.
The axes meet at the **origin**.
The axes divide the plane into four **quadrants**.
They are numbered counterclockwise.

We do not need arrows on the axes.

A pair of coordinates is called an ordered pair.

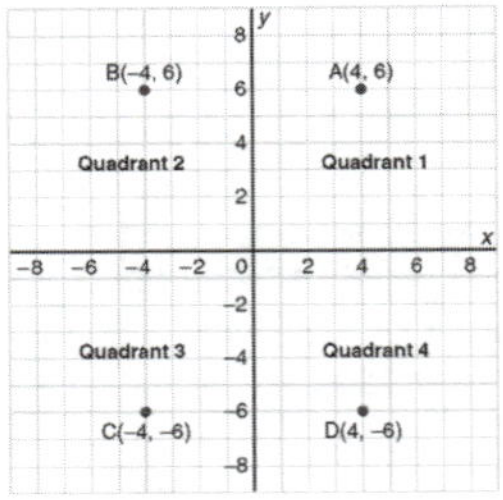

We do *not* include a + sign for a positive coordinate.

In Quadrant 1, point A has coordinates (4, 6).
In Quadrant 2, point B has coordinates (−4, 6).
In Quadrant 3, point C has coordinates (−4, −6).
In Quadrant 4, point D has coordinates (4, −6).

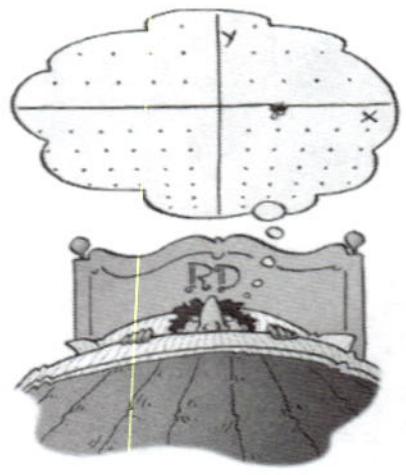

Math Link

History

René Descartes lived in the 17th century.
He developed the coordinate grid.
It is named the Cartesian grid in his honour.
There is a story that René was lying in bed and watching a fly on the ceiling.
He invented coordinates as a way to describe the fly's position.

394 UNIT 9: Integers

- How could we distinguish between moving up and moving down?
  (*Use positive integers for moving up and negative integers for moving down.*)

AFTER Connect

On an overhead transparency of a coordinate grid with 4 quadrants, have volunteers take turns to draw their figures and describe any problems their partners had.

Review *Connect* and introduce the terminology that labels the horizontal and vertical axes *x* and *y*, respectively.

On a grid, have volunteers plot several points in each quadrant and label them with their coordinates. Help students make these generalizations:

- If a point lies in Quadrant 1, both its coordinates are positive.
- If a point lies in Quadrant 2, its *x*-coordinate is negative and its *y*-coordinate is positive.
- If a point lies in Quadrant 3, both its coordinates are negative.
- If a point lies in Quadrant 4, its *x*-coordinate is positive and its *y*-coordinate is negative.

Have volunteers plot several points on each axis and label them with their coordinates.

Help students make these generalizations:

- If a point lies on the *x*-axis, its *y*-coordinate is 0.
- If a point lies on the *y*-axis, its *x*-coordinate is 0.

Review the *Example* and ensure students know how to plot points and identify their coordinates before they begin *Practice*.

Example

a) Write the coordinates of each point.
i) P ii) Q iii) R iv) S

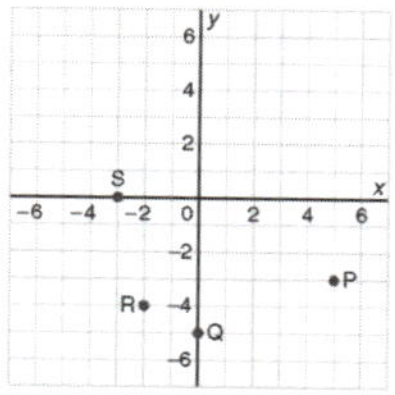

b) Plot each point on a grid.
i) D(−1, 3) ii) E(−3, −5) iii) F(0, −2) iv) G(−4, 0)

Solution

Remember, first move left or right, then up or down.

a) Start at the origin each time.
i) To get to P, move 5 units right and 3 units down. So, the coordinates of P are (5, −3).
ii) To get to Q, move 0 units right and 5 units down. So, the coordinates of Q are (0, −5)
iii) To get to R, move 2 units left and 4 units down. So, the coordinates of R are (−2, −4).
iv) To get to S, move 3 units left and 0 units down. So, the coordinates of S are (−3, 0).

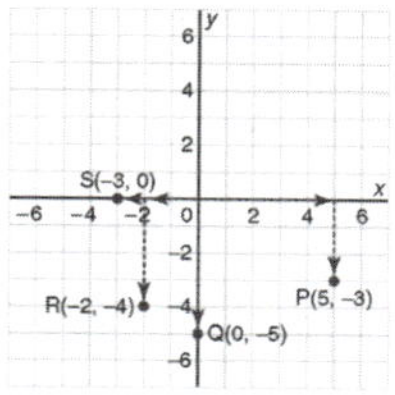

Calculator Skills

Students will use an algebraic or a word formula for the surface area of a rectangular prism.
$SA = 2((2.2)(4.4) + (2.2)(7.7) + (4.4)(7.7)) = 121$
The surface area is 121 cm^2.

Sample Solutions

2. a) B, E, F b) D, F, J
c) B, E, and F; H and K d) A and H; D, F, and J
e) F and G f) None

3.

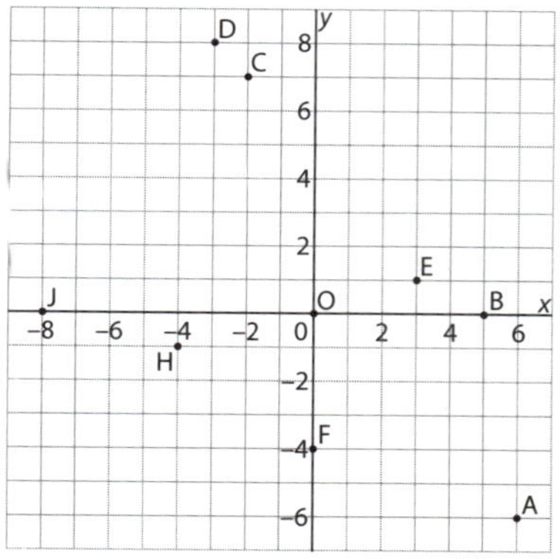

4. In Quadrant 1, both coordinates are positive. In Quadrant 2, the x-coordinate is negative and the y-coordinate is positive. In Quadrant 3, both coordinates are negative. In Quadrant 4, the x-coordinate is positive and the y-coordinate is negative.

(Sample Solutions continue below, left.)

Practice

Students require 0.5-cm grid paper (PM 14) or copies of *Coordinate Grid* (Master 9.21) for all questions.

Assessment Focus: Question 6

Students may begin by finding the factors of 12, and using each pair of factors as the base and height of a rectangle. A level 4 response could include bases and heights that are decimals.

(Sample Solutions continued)

5. Answers may vary. Here is a possible answer:

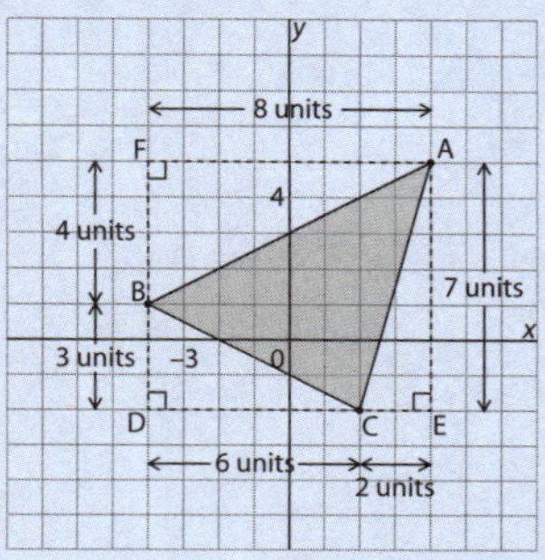

a) A (4, 5)
B (−4, 1)
C (2, −2)

b) Draw a rectangle around the triangle, so the sides of the rectangle are horizontal and vertical. To find the area of △ABC, find the area of rectangle AFDE, then subtract the areas of right triangles: △FBA, △AEC, and △BDC.
Area of AFDE = $8 \times 7 = 56$
Area of △FBA = $\frac{1}{2} \times 8 \times 4 = 16$
Area of △AEC = $\frac{1}{2} \times 7 \times 2 = 7$
Area of △BDC = $\frac{1}{2} \times 6 \times 3 = 9$
So, area of △ABC = $56 - 16 - 7 - 9 = 24$
The area of △ABC is 24 $units^2$.

6. For a rectangle to have area 12 $units^2$, the product of its base and height is 12. I found pairs of factors of 12: 1×12, 2×6, 3×4; then I thought about base and height that are decimals of a unit, such as 0.5×24; 1.5×8; 7.5×1.6.
I could plot a rectangle with base 0.5 units and height 24 units, and a 1.5-unit by 8-unit rectangle.

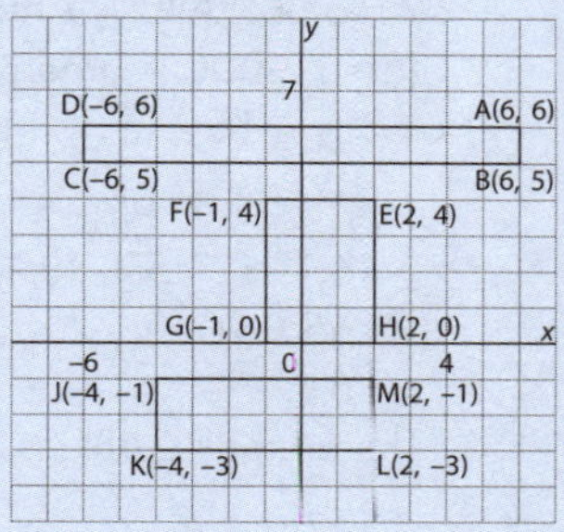

But a rectangle with base 7.5 units and height 1.6 units would be difficult to plot because I'd have to estimate a length of 1.6 units. To draw the rectangles, I counted squares, plotted points, then labelled them with their coordinates.

7. a)

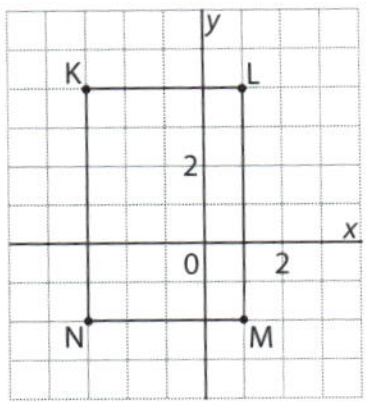

b) To find the coordinates of N, I drew a vertical line through K and a horizontal line through M. These lines meet at N. The coordinates of N are (–3, –2).

8. a)

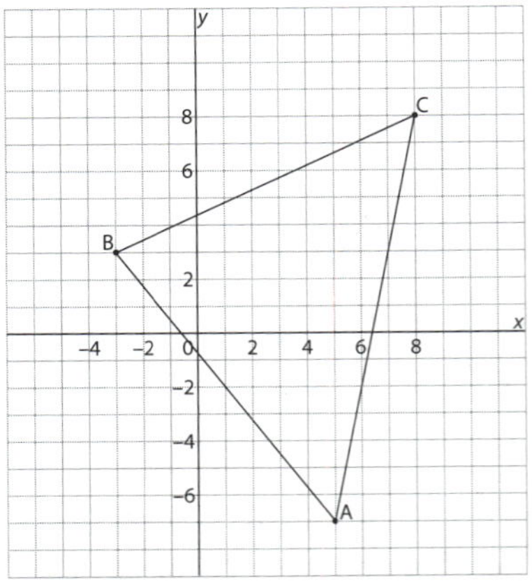

b) To find the area of △ABC, draw an enclosing rectangle, as in question 5.

b) **i)** D(–1, 3)
Start at –1 on the x-axis.
Move 3 units up. Mark point D.

ii) E(–3, –5)
Start at –3 on the x-axis.
Move 5 units down. Mark point E.

iii) F(0, –2)
Start at the origin.
Move 2 units down the y-axis. Mark point F.

iv) G(–4, 0)
Start at –4 on the x-axis.
Since there is no movement up or down, point G lies on the x-axis. Mark point G.

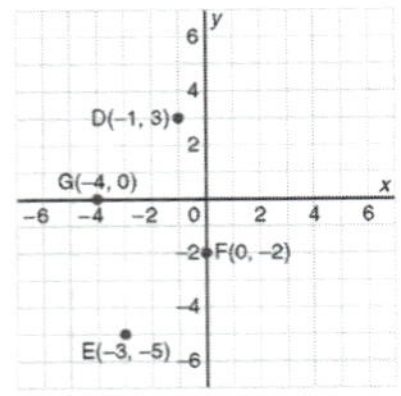

Practice

1. Write the coordinates of each point from A to K.

A(2, 3)	F(0, 0)
B(0, 5)	G(–1, –1)
C(1, –2)	H(–5, 3)
D(–6, 0)	J(4, 0)
E(0, –5)	K(–5, –6)

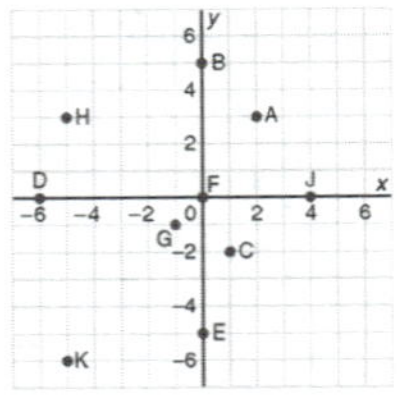

(Sample Solutions continue below.)

(Sample Solutions continued)

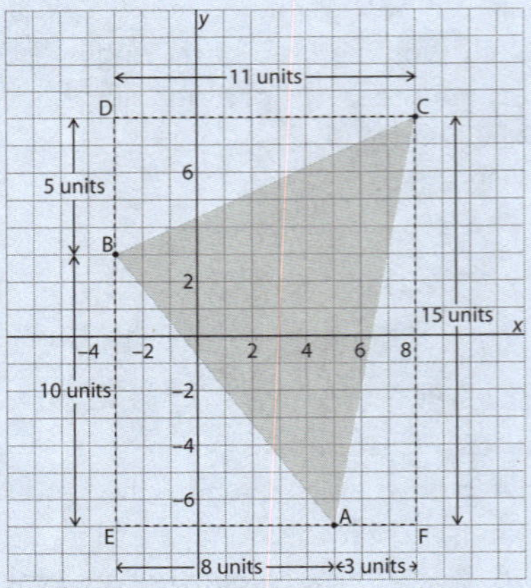

Draw rectangle DCFE.

Area of △ABC = Area rectangle DCFE – (area △BDC + area △BEA + area △CFA)

$= 11 \times 15 - (\frac{1}{2} \times 11 \times 5 + \frac{1}{2} \times 10 \times 8 + \frac{1}{2} \times 15 \times 3)$

$= 165 - (27.5 + 40 + 22.5)$

$= 165 - 90$

$= 75$

The area of △ABC is 75 units^2.

9.

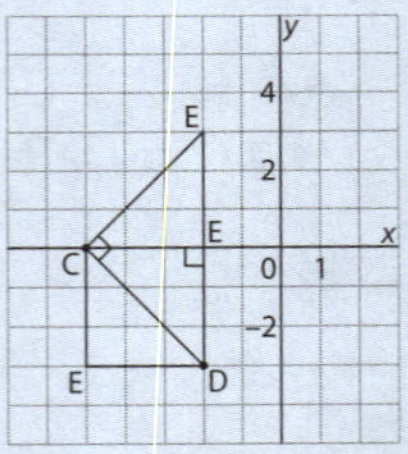

E can lie where the horizontal line through D meets the vertical line through C, at E(–5, –3).

E can lie where the vertical line through D meets the horizontal line through C (the x-axis) at E(–2, 0).

Use a protractor to draw a right angle at C.

Another point E lies anywhere on this line.

One point is at E(–2, 3).

lculator Skills

...e surface ...ctangular ...sm with dimensions ...cm by 4.4 cm ...7.7 cm.

...1 cm²

2. Use the coordinate grid in question 1. Which points have:
a) x-coordinate 0? b) y-coordinate 0?
c) the same x-coordinate? d) the same y-coordinate?
e) equal x- and y-coordinates? f) y-coordinate +2?

3. Draw a coordinate grid. Label the axes. Plot each point.
a) A(6, −6) b) B(5, 0) c) C(−2, 7)
d) D(−3, 8) e) E(3, 1) f) F(0, −4)
g) O(0, 0) h) H(−4, −1) i) J(−8, 0)

4. Suppose you are given the coordinates of a point.
You do not plot the point.
How can you tell which quadrant the point will be in?

5. Draw a scalene triangle on a coordinate grid.
Each vertex should be in a different quadrant.
a) Label each vertex with its coordinates.
b) What is the area of the triangle?

6. **Assessment Focus**
Use a coordinate grid.
How many different rectangles can you draw that have area 12 units²?
For each rectangle you draw, label its vertices.

...Remember that congruent rectangles are *not* different.

7. a) Plot these points: K(−3, 4), L(1, 4), M(1, −2)
b) Find the coordinates of point N that forms rectangle KLMN.
N(−3, −2)

Take It Further

8. a) Plot these points on a grid: A(5, −7), B(−3, 3), and C(8, 8).
Join the points.
b) Find the area of △ABC. 75 units²

9. Plot the points C(−5, 0) and D(−2, −3).
E is a point such that △CDE is a right triangle.
Find at least three possible positions for E.
Write the coordinates of each point.

Reflect

Choose four points, one in each quadrant. Write instructions to plot each point. Draw a grid to show your work.

9.7 Graphing on a Coordinate Grid **397**

REFLECT: I chose A(3, 2), B(−4, 6), C(−5, −1), and D(7, −2).

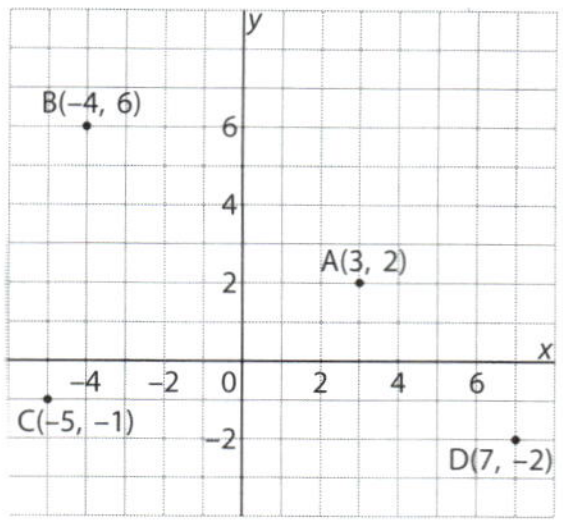

To plot point A, begin at 3 on the x-axis and move 2 units up.
To plot point B, begin at −4 on the x-axis and move 6 units up.
To plot point C, begin at −5 on the x-axis and move 1 unit down.
To plot point D, begin at 7 on the x-axis and move 2 units down.

Assignment Guidelines

If your students do not have time to complete all the *Practice* questions on pages 396 and 397, these questions provide minimum curriculum coverage: 1, 3, 4, 5, 6, *Reflect*

To assess the 4 Achievement Chart categories listed in the curriculum document, have students complete these *Practice* questions:
Knowledge and Understanding: 3
Communication: 4
Application: 5
Thinking: 6

ASSESSMENT FOR LEARNING

What to Look For

Knowledge and Understanding
✔ Students understand that the position of a point on a coordinate grid can be described by its coordinates.

Thinking
✔ Students can solve problems related to the areas of figures on a grid.

Communication
✔ Students can explain how to use coordinates to plot a point.

Application
✔ Students can plot ordered pairs on a coordinate grid.

What to Do

Extra Support: Students could use 12 square tiles to find the possible rectangles for question 6.
Students can use Step-by-Step 7 (Master 9.17) to complete question 6.

Extra Practice: Students could repeat question 6 for rectangles or other figures with different areas.
Students can complete Extra Practice 7 (Master 9.31).

Extension: Have students plot these points on a coordinate grid: (−1, 2), (2, −4). Ask them to graph and give the coordinates of ten other points that lie on the line through these points.

Recording and Reporting
Master 9.2 Ongoing Observations: Integers

LESSON 9.8

Graphing Translations and Reflections

LESSON ORGANIZER — 80–100 min

Curriculum Focus: Graph translation and reflection images on a coordinate grid. (8m52, 8m53)

Teacher Materials

- overhead transparency of Coordinate Grid (Master 9.21)

Student Materials

- 0.5-cm grid paper (PM 14)
- Coordinate Grid (Master 9.21)

Optional

- tracing paper
- Miras
- Step-by-Step 8 (Master 9.18)
- Extra Practice 8 (Master 9.32)

Vocabulary: transformation, translation, reflection, image

Assessment: Master 9.2 Ongoing Observations: Integers

Key Math Learning

When a figure is reflected in a mirror line, the reflection image is congruent to the figure, and its orientation is reversed.

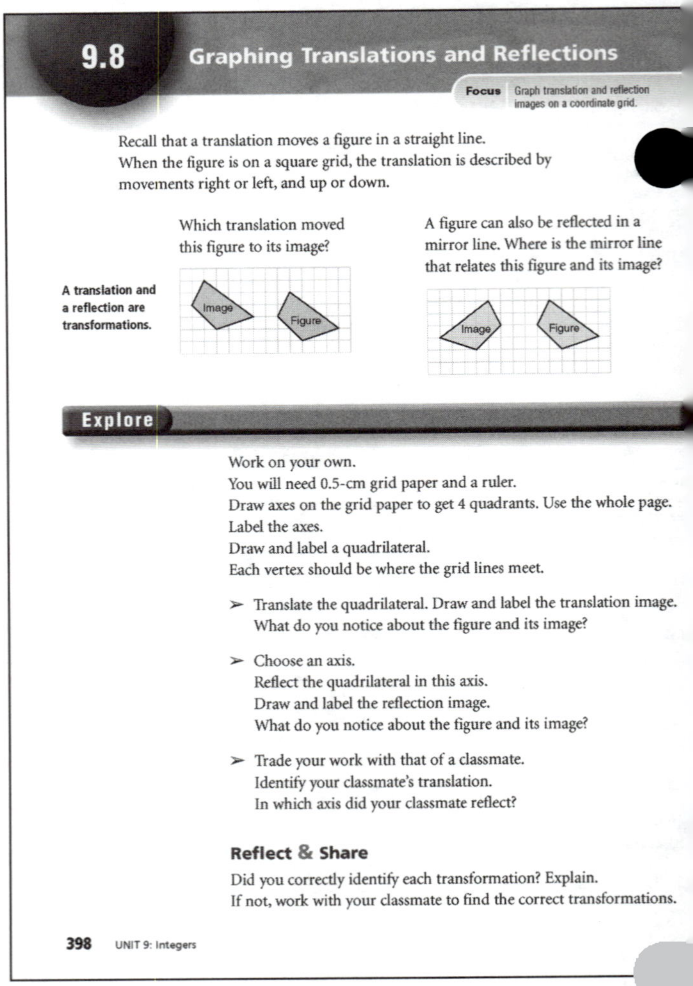

9.8 Graphing Translations and Reflections

Focus Graph translation and reflection images on a coordinate grid.

Recall that a translation moves a figure in a straight line.
When the figure is on a square grid, the translation is described by movements right or left, and up or down.

A translation and a reflection are transformations.

Which translation moved this figure to its image?

A figure can also be reflected in a mirror line. Where is the mirror line that relates this figure and its image?

Explore

Work on your own.
You will need 0.5-cm grid paper and a ruler.
Draw axes on the grid paper to get 4 quadrants. Use the whole page.
Label the axes.
Draw and label a quadrilateral.
Each vertex should be where the grid lines meet.

➢ Translate the quadrilateral. Draw and label the translation image.
What do you notice about the figure and its image?

➢ Choose an axis.
Reflect the quadrilateral in this axis.
Draw and label the reflection image.
What do you notice about the figure and its image?

➢ Trade your work with that of a classmate.
Identify your classmate's translation.
In which axis did your classmate reflect?

Reflect & Share

Did you correctly identify each transformation? Explain.
If not, work with your classmate to find the correct transformations.

398 UNIT 9: Integers

BEFORE — Get Started

Put a grid on the overhead projector. Draw △ABC on the grid. Write "translate 3 units left and 2 units up" beside the triangle.
Choose 3 volunteers. Have them come to the projector one at a time. Each student places an overhead pen at a vertex, moves it 3 units left and 2 units up, and plots the point.
When they have finished, draw the new triangle and label it △A′B′C′. Ask:

- Why are the image points labelled A′B′C′?
  (*So we do not confuse the original and image points*)

Redraw △ABC on a new overhead transparency. Draw a mirror line. Have a volunteer draw the reflection image of the triangle.

Present *Explore*. Instead of having students draw the coordinate grid, you could distribute copies of *Coordinate Grid* (Master 9.21).

DURING — Explore

Ongoing Assessment: Observe and Listen

As students work, ask:

- How are a figure and its translation image alike?
  (*The figure and its image are congruent and have the same orientation.*)
- How are a figure and its reflection image alike? (*The figure and its image are congruent.*) How are they different? (*The figure and its image have different orientations; that is, if I read Figure ABCD clockwise, then I read image A′B′C′D′ counterclockwise.*)
- How do you identify a translation?
  (*I check that each pair of corresponding points are related the same way. That is, to go from A to A′, B to B′, C to C′, and D to D′, I move the same distance horizontally and the same distance vertically each time.*)

Connect

ad A' as "A prime."

➢ To translate △ABC 5 units right and 6 units down:
Begin at vertex A(−2, 5).
Move 5 units right and 6 units down to point A′(3, −1).
From vertex B(2, 3), move 5 units right and 6 units down to point B′(7, −3).
From vertex C(−5, 1), move 5 units right and 6 units down to point C′(0, −5).

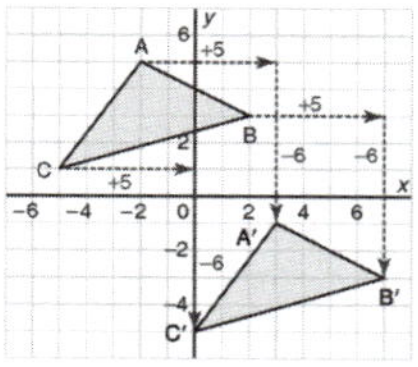

Then, △A′B′C′ is the image of △ABC after a translation 5 units right and 6 units down.
△ABC and △A′B′C′ are congruent.

➢ To reflect △ABC in the *y*-axis:
Reflect each vertex in turn.
The reflection image of A(−2, 5) is A′(2, 5).
The reflection image of B(2, 3) is B′(−2, 3).
The reflection image of C(−5, 1) is C′(5, 1).

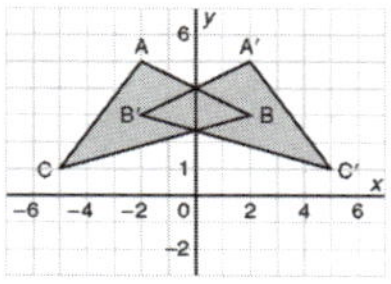

Then, △A′B′C′ is the image of △ABC after a reflection in the *y*-axis.
△ABC and △A′B′C′ are congruent.
The triangles have different orientations: we read △ABC clockwise; we read △A′B′C′ counterclockwise.

9.8 Graphing Translations and Reflections **399**

REACHING ALL LEARNERS

Alternative Explore

Materials: 11-pin by 11-pin geoboards, geobands, square dot paper (PM 22)
Have students use an erasable marker to draw coordinate axes to divide the board into 4 quadrants. Have students conduct *Explore* using geobands, and record their figures and images on dot paper.

Early Finishers

Have students choose a translation and reflection. Students draw a figure, translate it, then reflect the image. Then students draw the same figure, reflect it first, then translate the image. Before they begin, ask students if they think the final images will be the same in both cases. Have students explain any differences.

Common Misconceptions

➤ Students do not remember that the *x*-axis is horizontal and the *y*-axis is vertical.

How to Help: Have students think of a way to remember. Possibly, h in horizontal comes before v in vertical, and x comes before y, so h relates to x and v to y. Some students have difficulty differentiating between horizontal and vertical. Have them relate "horizontal" to "horizon."

- How do you identify a reflection?
(I check that the points in each pair of corresponding points are the same distance from the mirror line. Also, the figures are congruent but have opposite orientations.)

AFTER Connect

Review the translations and reflections in *Connect.*

The curriculum requires that students reflect in the line at 45° to the positive *x*-axis.

On the board or overhead projector, draw a line through the points (–10, –10), (0, 0), and (10, 10). This is the mirror line. Have students do the same on a copy of *Coordinate Grid* (Master 9.21). Then have students practise plotting a point on one side of the mirror line and its image point on the other side. It may help students to use tracing paper, and fold the paper along the mirror line, or use Miras to locate the image point.

If you feel your students might benefit from recognizing patterns in coordinates of corresponding points on the figure and its image, use the diagrams on page 399 to illustrate them.

Have students write the coordinates of △ABC and its image after the translation. Ask:

- What patterns do you see in the coordinates of the triangle and its image? Why does this pattern occur?
(The x-coordinates of △A′B′C′ are 5 more than the x-coordinates of △ABC. This is because △ABC was translated 5 units right. The y-coordinates of △A′B′C′ are 6 less than the y-coordinates of △ABC. This is because △ABC was also translated 6 units down.)

Number Strategies

Remind students of the formula for the volume of a cylinder:
$V = \pi r^2 h$.
Substitute: $h = 9$ and $r = \frac{7.5}{2} = 3.75$
$V = \pi \times 3.75^2 \times 9 \doteq 397.6$
The capacity of the mug is about 398 mL.

Assignment Guidelines

If your students do not have time to complete all the *Practice* questions on pages 400, 401, and 402, these questions provide minimum curriculum coverage: 1, 4, 5, 6, 9, 10, *Reflect*

To assess the 4 Achievement Chart categories listed in the curriculum document, have students complete these *Practice* questions:

Knowledge and Understanding: 1 | Application: 9
Thinking: 8 | Communication: 10

Sample Solutions

1. a) The line segment joining each point to its image is bisected by the y-axis and at right angles to the y-axis.
   b) Each image is 3 units right and 3 units down from the corresponding vertex.
2. a) A and C; the parallelograms are congruent and have the same orientations.
   b) A and B are related by a reflection in the y-axis. B and C are related by a reflection in the x-axis. In each case, the parallelograms are congruent but have different orientations.

Example

a) Plot these points: A(4, −4), B(6, 8), C(−3, 5), D(−6, −2)
Join the points to draw quadrilateral ABCD.
Reflect the quadrilateral in the x-axis.
Draw and label the reflection image A′B′C′D′.

b) What do you notice about the line segment joining each point to its reflection image?

Solution

a) After a reflection in the x-axis:
A(4, −4) → A′(4, 4)
B(6, 8) → B′(6, −8)
C(−3, 5) → C′(−3, −5)
D(−6, −2) → D′(−6, 2)

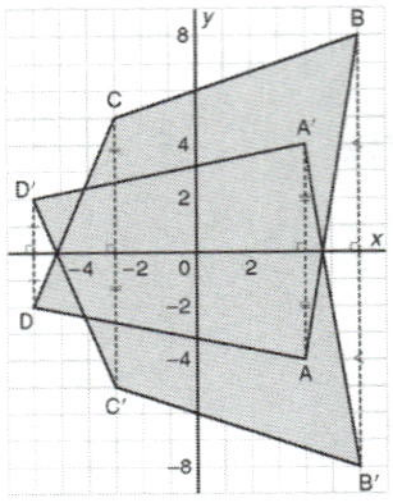

b) The line segments AA′, BB′, CC′, DD′ are vertical.
The x-axis is the perpendicular bisector of each line segment.
That is, the x-axis divides each line segment into 2 equal parts, and the x-axis intersects each line segment at right angles.

In *Practice* question 6, you will investigate a similar reflection in the y-axis.

Practice

1. Identify each transformation. Explain your reasoning.

a)

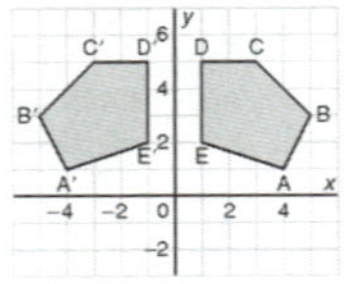

Reflection in the y-axis

b)

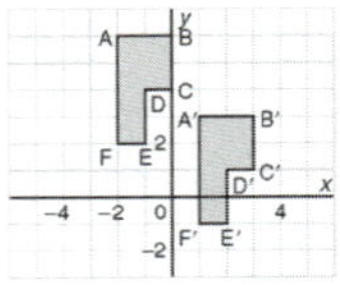

Translation 3 units right and 3 units down

- How do the coordinates of a point change if the point is translated up? (*The y-coordinates increase.*) Down? (*The y-coordinates decrease.*) Left? (*The x-coordinates decrease.*) Right? (*The x-coordinates increase.*)

Have students write the coordinates of △ABC and its image after the reflection in the y-axis. Ask:

- What patterns do you see in the coordinates of the triangle and its image? Why do these patterns occur?
(*The y-coordinates of △A′B′C′ are the same as those of △ABC. This is because a reflection in the y-axis does not move the triangle up or down. The x-coordinates of △A′B′C′ are the opposites of those in △ABC. This is because the triangle was reflected in the y-axis.*)

If time permits, have a student volunteer reflect △ABC in the x-axis, and label the image triangle with its coordinates.

- What patterns do you see in the coordinates now? (*The x-coordinates of △A′B′C′ are the same as those of △ABC. This is because a reflection in the x-axis does not move the triangle left or right. The y-coordinates of △A′B′C′ are the opposites of those in △ABC because the triangle is reflected in the x-axis.*)

Practice

Most questions require grid paper. Make sure students use a ruler to draw neat diagrams.

Assessment Focus: Question 9

Remind students that, for a figure to tessellate, it must completely fill the plane without overlapping or leaving any gaps. Remind them that, for a figure to tessellate, at any point where vertices meet the angles add up to 360°.

2. The diagram shows 4 parallelograms.

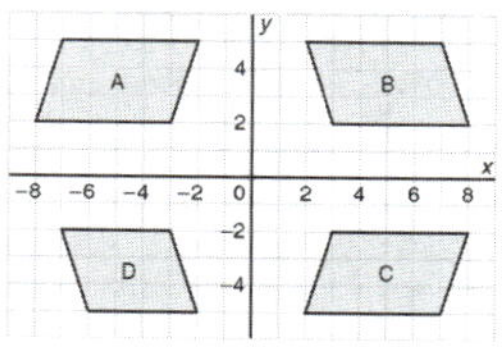

a) Are any 2 parallelograms related by a translation? Explain.
b) Are any 2 parallelograms related by a reflection? Explain.

3. Copy this pentagon on grid paper.
a) Draw the image after a translation 3 units left and 2 units up.
b) Draw the image after a reflection in the x-axis.
c) Draw the image after a reflection in the y-axis.

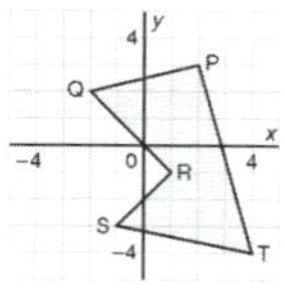

4. Plot these points on a coordinate grid:
A(1, 3), B(3, −2), C(−2, 5), D(−1, −4), E(0, −3), F(−2, 0)
a) Reflect each point in the x-axis.
Write the coordinates of each point and its reflection image.
What patterns do you see in the coordinates?
b) Reflect each point in the y-axis.
Write the coordinates of each point and its reflection image.
What patterns do you see in the coordinates?
c) How could you use the patterns in parts a and b to check that you have drawn the reflection image of a figure correctly?

5. a) Plot the points in question 4.
Translate each point 4 units left and 2 units down.
b) Write the coordinates of each point and its translation image.
What patterns do you see in the coordinates?
c) How could you use these patterns to write the coordinates of an image point after a translation, without plotting the points?

3. a)

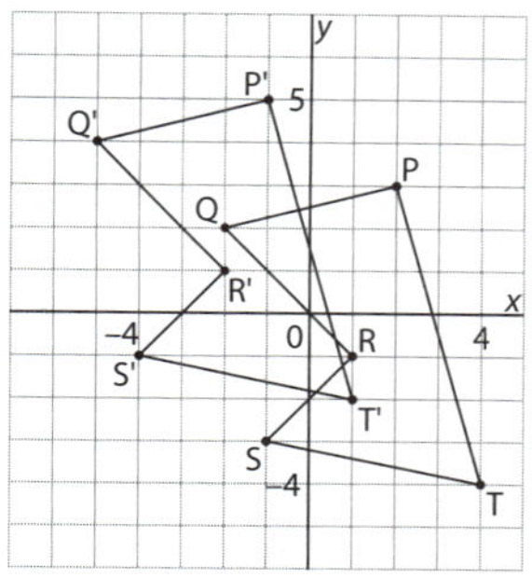

b)

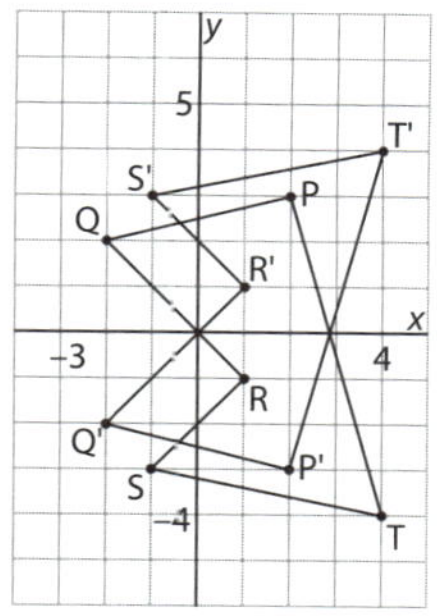

c)

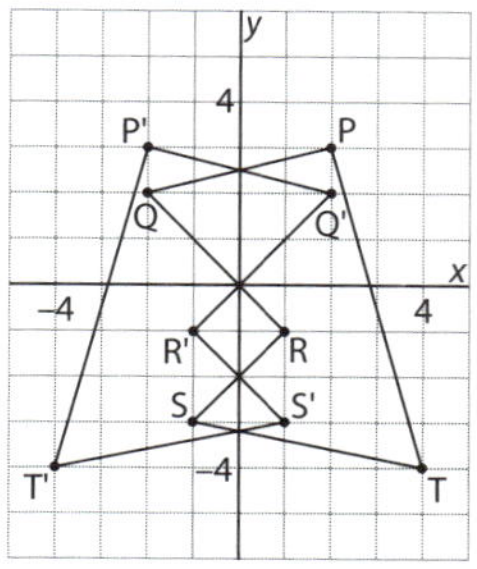

4. a) A(1, 3) → A′(1, −3); B(3, −2) → B′(3, 2);
C(−2, 5) → C′(−2, −5); D(−1, −4) → D′(−1, 4);
E(0, −3) → E′(0, 3); F(−2, 0) → F′(−2, 0);
the signs of the y-coordinates change.
b) A(1, 3) → A′(−1, 3); B(3, −2) → B′(−3, −2);
C(−2, 5) → C′(2, 5); D(−1, −4) → D′(1, −4);

(Sample Solutions continue below, left.)

(Sample Solutions continued)

E(0, −3) → E′(0, −3); F(−2, 0) → F′(2, 0);
the signs of the x-coordinates change.
c) I can check the coordinates of the reflection images. If they match the patterns, the images are drawn correctly.

5. a)

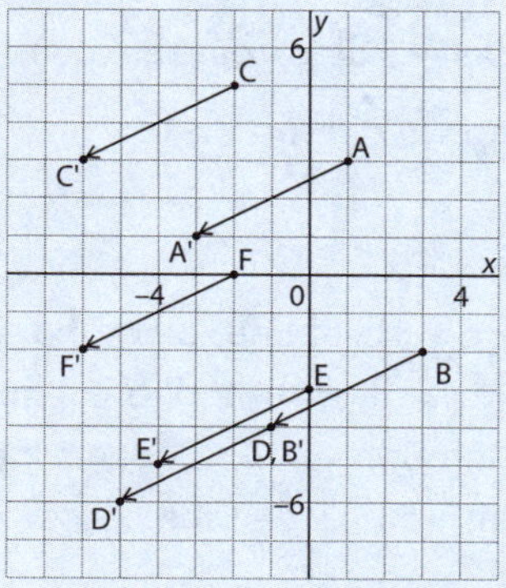

b) A(1, 3) → A′(−3, 1); B(3, −2) → B′(−1, −4);
C(−2, 5) → C′(−6, 3); D(−1, −4) → D′(−5, −6);
E(0, −3) → E′(−4, −5); F(−2, 0) → F′(−6, −2);
Each x-coordinate decreases by 4.
Each y-coordinate decreases by 2.

c) Add the number of units moved to the right, to the x-coordinate or, if the movement is to the left, subtract the number of units from the x-coordinate. Add the number of units moved up to the y-coordinate or, if the movement is down, subtract the number of units from the y-coordinate.

6. a)

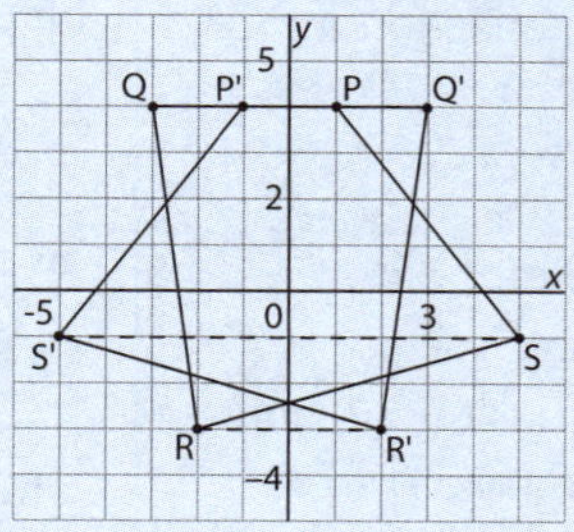

b) The line segments are horizontal. The y-axis is the perpendicular bisector of each line segment.

7. The coordinates of each point are interchanged to get the coordinates of its image.

8. a)

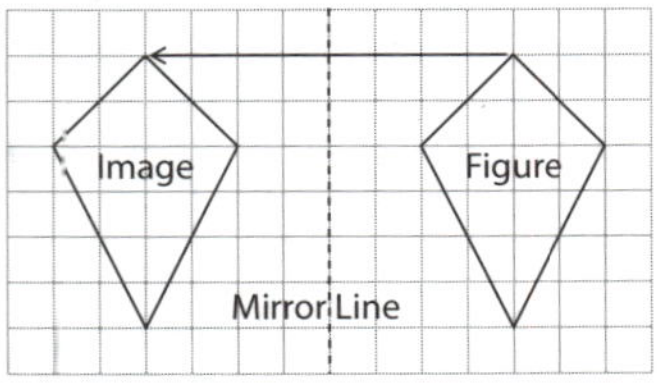

b) The figure has a line of symmetry parallel to the mirror line and perpendicular to the translation arrow.

9. a)

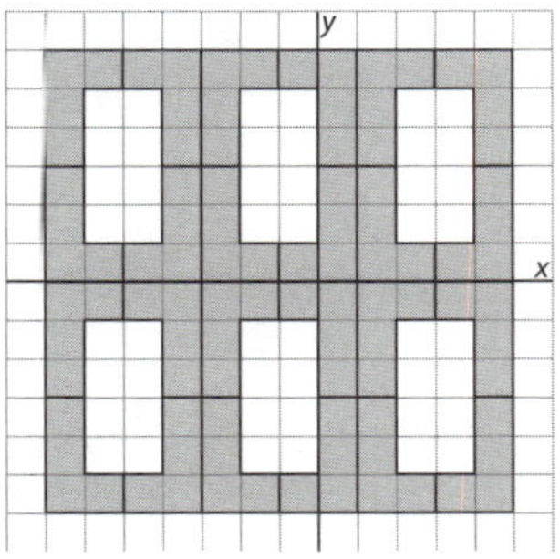

I chose an L-shaped hexagon that I only reflected in its horizontal and vertical sides to make a design. The figure did not tessellate but it covered the page with a rectangle inside 4 of the figures.

b) The L-shaped figure will tessellate if I also translate it.

REFLECT: Differences: All points move in a translation. In a reflection, points on the mirror line do not move. A reflection changes the orientation of a figure, but a translation does not. Similarities: Reflection and translation images are congruent to the figures. When I draw figures and their transformation images on a grid, I can easily see if a figure and its image have the same orientation for a translation. I can fold the grid so that a reflection image coincides with the figure, and the fold line is the mirror line.

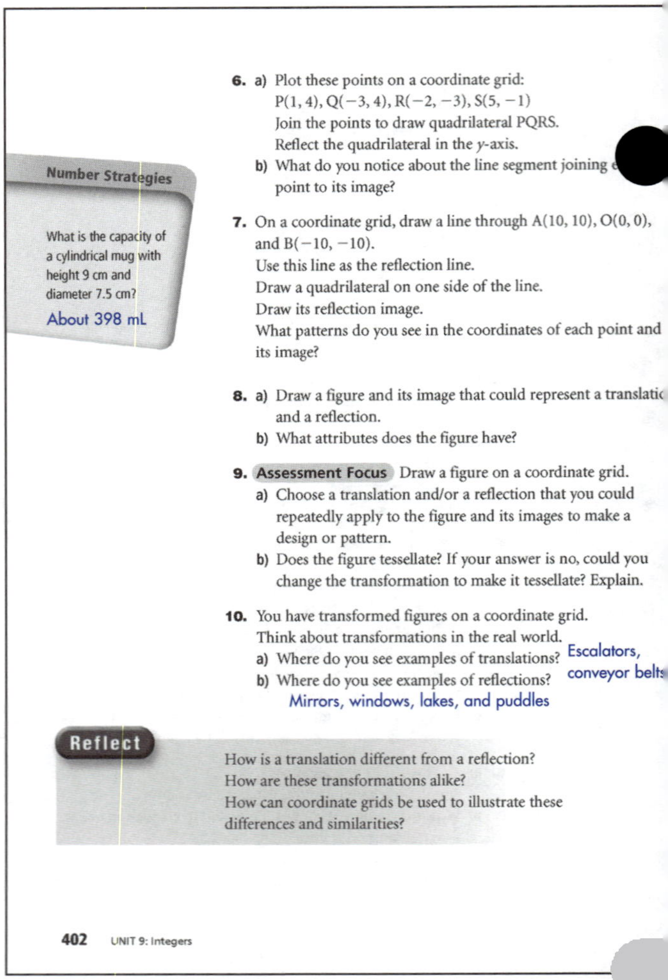

Number Strategies

What is the capacity of a cylindrical mug with height 9 cm and diameter 7.5 cm?

About 398 mL

6. a) Plot these points on a coordinate grid:
P(1, 4), Q(−3, 4), R(−2, −3), S(5, −1)
Join the points to draw quadrilateral PQRS.
Reflect the quadrilateral in the *y*-axis.
b) What do you notice about the line segment joining e
point to its image?

7. On a coordinate grid, draw a line through A(10, 10), O(0, 0), and B(−10, −10).
Use this line as the reflection line.
Draw a quadrilateral on one side of the line.
Draw its reflection image.
What patterns do you see in the coordinates of each point and its image?

8. a) Draw a figure and its image that could represent a translatio
and a reflection.
b) What attributes does the figure have?

9. **Assessment Focus** Draw a figure on a coordinate grid.
a) Choose a translation and/or a reflection that you could repeatedly apply to the figure and its images to make a design or pattern.
b) Does the figure tessellate? If your answer is no, could you change the transformation to make it tessellate? Explain.

10. You have transformed figures on a coordinate grid.
Think about transformations in the real world.
a) Where do you see examples of translations? Escalators, conveyor belts
b) Where do you see examples of reflections? Mirrors, windows, lakes, and puddles

Reflect

How is a translation different from a reflection?
How are these transformations alike?
How can coordinate grids be used to illustrate these differences and similarities?

402 UNIT 9: Integers

ASSESSMENT FOR LEARNING

What to Look For	What to Do
Knowledge and Understanding ✔ Students understand how a figure and its translation image are related and how a figure and its reflection image are related. ***Thinking*** ✔ Students use patterns and other strategies to create and solve problems involving translations and reflections on a coordinate grid. ***Application*** ✔ Students can graph translation and reflection images on a coordinate grid.	***Extra Support:*** Have students copy figures onto tracing paper so they can physically flip the paper to find the reflection image and slide the paper to find the translation image. Students can use Step-by-Step 8 (Master 9.18) to complete question 9. ***Extra Practice:*** Have students complete question 3 for different figures. Students can complete Extra Practice 8 (Master 9.32). ***Extension:*** Have students reflect in a vertical line, other than the y-axis, such as a vertical line through $x = 3$, or a horizontal line other than the x-axis, such as a line through $y = 4$. Students then investigate to see if there is a relationship between the coordinates of points and their images.

Recording and Reporting
Master 9.2 Ongoing Observations: Integers

9.9 Graphing Rotations

Focus Graph rotation images on a coordinate grid.

Recall that a rotation turns a figure about the turn centre.
The rotation may be clockwise or counterclockwise.
The turn centre may be:

On the figure

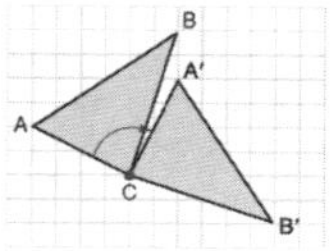

Off the figure

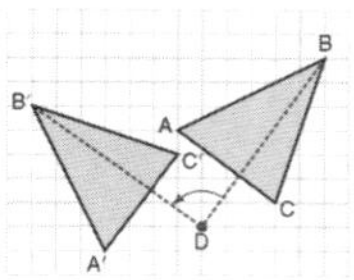

How would you describe each rotation?

Explore

Work with a partner.
You will need 0.5-cm grid paper, tracing paper, a protractor, and a ruler.
Draw axes on grid paper to get 4 quadrants.
Place the origin at the centre of the paper.
Label the axes.
Draw and label a figure in the 1st quadrant.
Use the origin as the turn centre.

➢ Rotate the figure 90° counterclockwise. Draw its image.
➢ Rotate the original figure 180° counterclockwise. Draw its image.
➢ Rotate the original figure 270° counterclockwise. Draw its image.

What do you notice about the figure and its 3 images?

Reflect & Share

Compare your work with that of another pair of classmates.
What strategies did you use to measure the rotation angle?
Would the images have been different if you had rotated clockwise instead of counterclockwise? Explain.

9.9 Graphing Rotations 403

Graphing Rotations

LESSON ORGANIZER	80–100 min

Curriculum Focus: Graph rotation images on a coordinate grid. (8m52, 8m53)

Teacher Materials
- overhead transparency of Coordinate Grid (Master 9.21)

Student Materials
- 0.5-cm grid paper (PM 14)
- Coordinate Grid (Master 9.21)
- tracing paper
- protractors
- rulers

Optional
- Step-by-Step 9 (Master 9.19)
- Extra Practice 9 (Master 9.33)

Vocabulary: rotation, clockwise, counterclockwise

Assessment: Master 9.2 Ongoing Observations: Integers

Key Math Learnings

1. A figure and its rotation image are congruent.
2. The rotation centre may be on or off the figure.

BEFORE Get Started

Review the concept of turns with students. Ask:

- How many degrees are there in a complete turn? *(360°)*
- Suppose you rotate the positive *x*-axis to coincide with the positive *y*-axis. The rotation centre is the origin. What is the angle of rotation? *(90° counterclockwise or 270° clockwise)*
- Why do we not use the terms *clockwise* and *counterclockwise* to describe a 180° rotation? *(A 180° clockwise turn moves a point to the same place as a 180° counterclockwise turn.)*

Show students how to use tracing paper to draw rotation images.

DURING Explore

Ongoing Assessment: Observe and Listen

As students work, for each rotation, have them write the coordinates of each point and its image.

Ask questions, such as:

- How did you rotate the figure 90° counterclockwise? *(I traced the figure on tracing paper and also traced the positive x-axis. When I rotated the figure about the origin, I knew I'd rotated 90° counterclockwise when the positive x-axis coincided with the positive y-axis.)*
- What do you notice about the images? *(The images are congruent. They have the same orientation.)*
- What if the figures had been rotated clockwise instead of counterclockwise. Would the images be different?

REACHING ALL LEARNERS

Alternative Explore

Materials: square dot paper (PM 22), tracing paper, protractor, ruler

Have students draw x- and y-axes on the dot paper, to form 4 quadrants. Students draw and label a figure in the 3rd quadrant, then rotate it 90°, 180°, and 270° clockwise. After each rotation, they draw and label the image. Students compare the images with the figure.

Early Finishers

Have students repeat the rotations in *Explore*, but draw the quadrilateral so one vertex is in each quadrant.

Common Misconceptions

➤ Students confuse clockwise and counterclockwise.

How to Help: Have students look at the classroom clock and identify the direction of rotation of the second hand or minute hand, to understand a clockwise rotation.

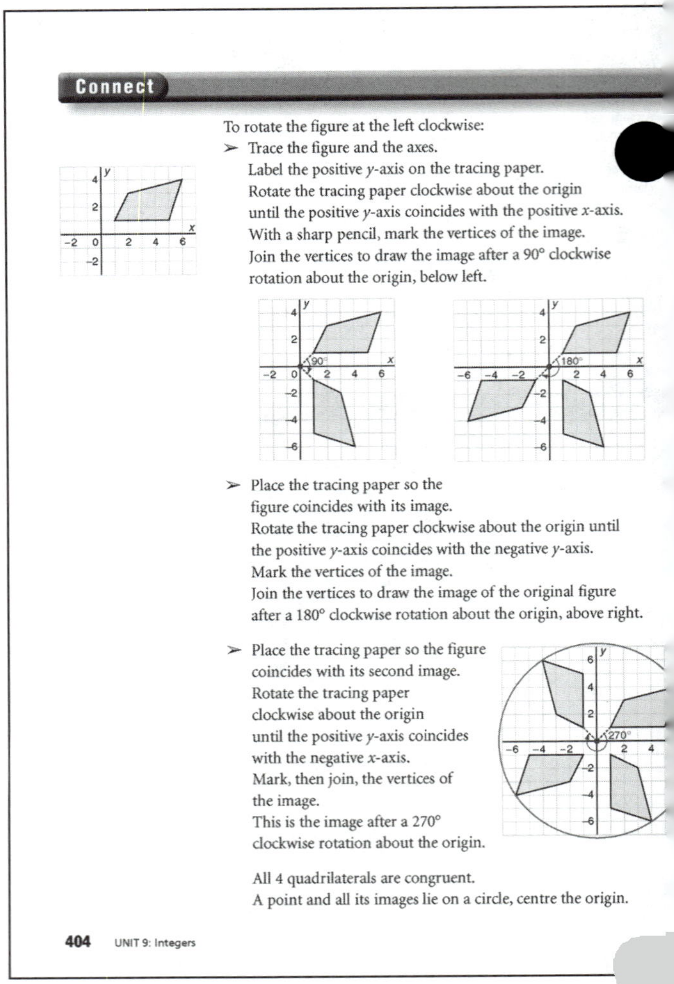

Connect

To rotate the figure at the left clockwise:

➢ Trace the figure and the axes.
Label the positive y-axis on the tracing paper.
Rotate the tracing paper clockwise about the origin until the positive y-axis coincides with the positive x-axis.
With a sharp pencil, mark the vertices of the image.
Join the vertices to draw the image after a 90° clockwise rotation about the origin, below left.

➢ Place the tracing paper so the figure coincides with its image.
Rotate the tracing paper clockwise about the origin until the positive y-axis coincides with the negative y-axis.
Mark the vertices of the image.
Join the vertices to draw the image of the original figure after a 180° clockwise rotation about the origin, above right.

➢ Place the tracing paper so the figure coincides with its second image.
Rotate the tracing paper clockwise about the origin until the positive y-axis coincides with the negative x-axis.
Mark, then join, the vertices of the image.
This is the image after a 270° clockwise rotation about the origin.

All 4 quadrilaterals are congruent.
A point and all its images lie on a circle, centre the origin.

404 UNIT 9: Integers

Assignment Guidelines

If your students do not have time to complete all the *Practice* questions on pages 405, 406, and 407, these questions provide minimum curriculum coverage: 2, 3, 4, 6, 8, *Reflect*

To assess the 4 Achievement Chart categories listed in the curriculum document, have students complete these *Practice* questions:
Knowledge and Understanding: 3
Thinking: 6
Application: 8
Communication: *Reflect*

(I did rotate clockwise and found that a 90° clockwise rotation produced the same image as a 270° counterclockwise rotation, and vice versa.)

AFTER Connect

Review *Connect* and the *Example* with its illustration of the properties of a rotation.

Practice

Most questions require grid paper and tracing paper. Have students use a ruler to draw neat diagrams.

Assessment Focus: Question 6

Encourage students to use a table to organize the coordinates of the figure and its images. It will also make it easier for them to find the patterns in the coordinates. Make sure students remember that a negative rotation angle is a clockwise rotation.

Example

A counterclockwise ...n is shown by a ...e angle such as ... or 90°. A clockwise rotation is shown by a negative angle such as −90°.

a) Plot these points: B(−5, 6), C(−3, 4), D(−8, 2)
Join the points to draw △BCD.
Rotate △BCD 90° about the origin, O.
Draw and label the rotation image △B′C′D′.

b) Join C, D, C′, D′ to O.
What do you notice about these line segments?

Solution

A rotation of 90° is a counterclockwise rotation.

a) Use tracing paper to draw the image △B′C′D′.
Rotate the paper counterclockwise until the positive *y*-axis coincides with the negative *x*-axis.

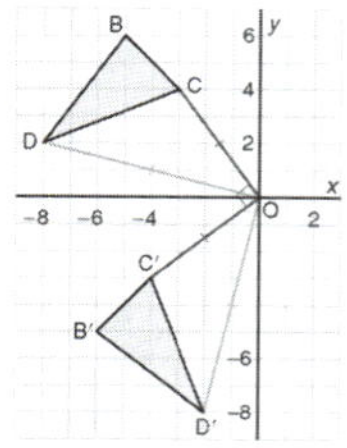

We could use the Pythagorean Theorem to verify that these line segments are equal.

b) From the diagram,
OC = OC′ and OD = OD′
∠COC′ = ∠DOD′ = 90°

The *Example* illustrates these properties of a rotation.

- A point and its image are the same distance from the rotation centre.
- The angle between the segments joining a point and its image to the rotation centre is equal to the rotation angle.

In the *Practice* questions, you will verify these properties for other angles of rotation.

Practice

1. Each grid shows a figure and its rotation image.
Identify the angle of rotation and the rotation centre.

a)

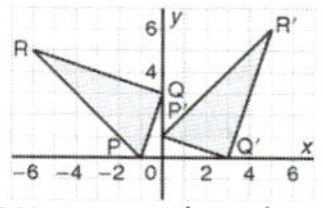

−90° rotation about the origin

b)

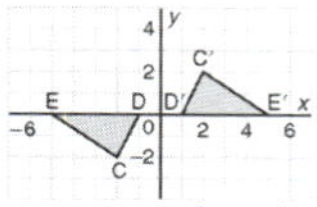

180° rotation about the origin

Sample Solutions

2. The figure was rotated 90° clockwise about the origin (Image 1), reflected in the *x*-axis (Image 2), and translated 5 units right and 5 units down (Image 3).

3. a), b), c)

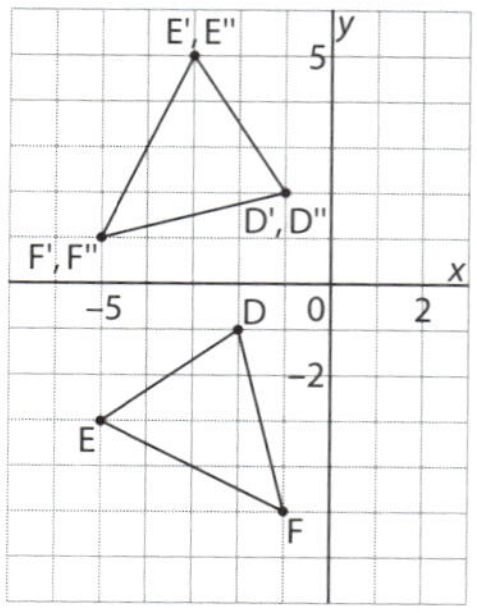

d) Both images have the same coordinates. Yes, a rotation of −90° is equivalent to a rotation of +270°.

4. a), b)

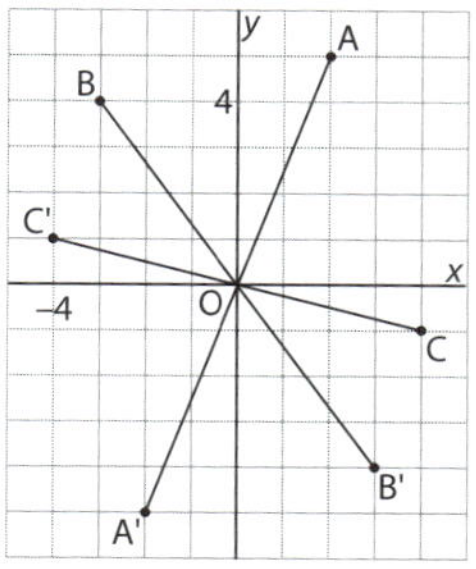

(Sample Solutions continue below, left.)

(Sample Solutions continued)

5. a)

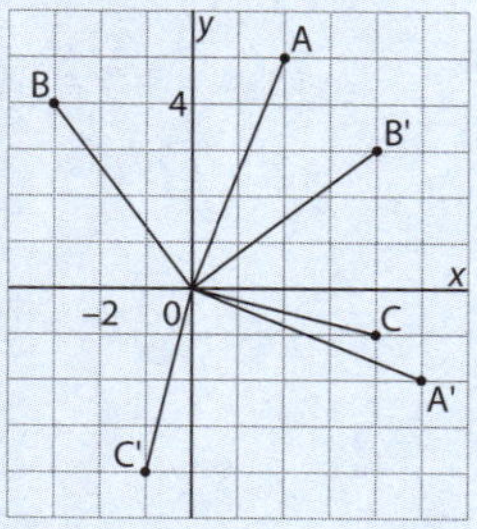

6.

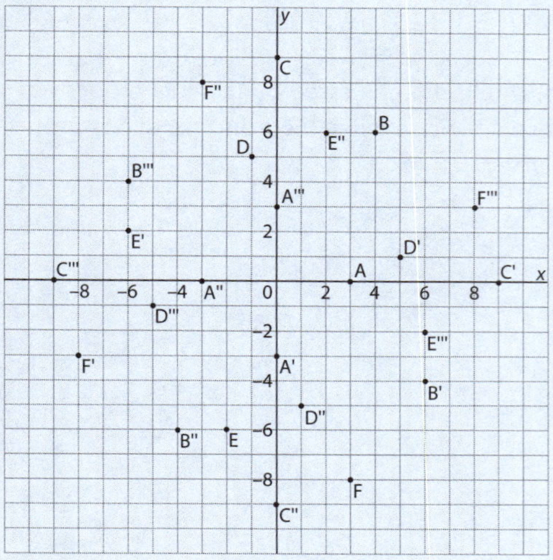

Point	−90° rotation	180° rotation	−270° rotation
A(3, 0)	A′(0, −3)	A′′(−3, 0)	A′′′(0, 3)
B(4, 6)	B′(6, −4)	B′′(−4, −6)	B′′′(−6, 4)
C(0, 9)	C′(9, 0)	C′′(0, −9)	C′′′(−9, 0)
D(−1, 5)	D′(5, 1)	D′′(1, −5)	D′′′(−5, −1)
E(−2, −6)	E′(−6, 2)	E′′(2, 6)	E′′′(6, −2)
F(3, −8)	F′(−8, −3)	F′′(−3, 8)	F′′′(8, 3)

a) To get the image coordinates from the original coordinates: change the sign of the *x*-coordinate, then interchange the coordinates. For example: Point (4, 6) rotates to (6, −4).

b) Change the sign of both the *x*-coordinate and the *y*-coordinate. For example: Point (−1, 5) rotates to point (1, −5).

c) Change the sign of the *y*-coordinate, then interchange the coordinates. For example: Point (3, −8) rotates to (8, 3).

d) To draw a rotation image of a point without tracing paper, I use whichever rule applies from parts a to c, then change the coordinates of the point according to the rule, and plot the image point.

8. a)

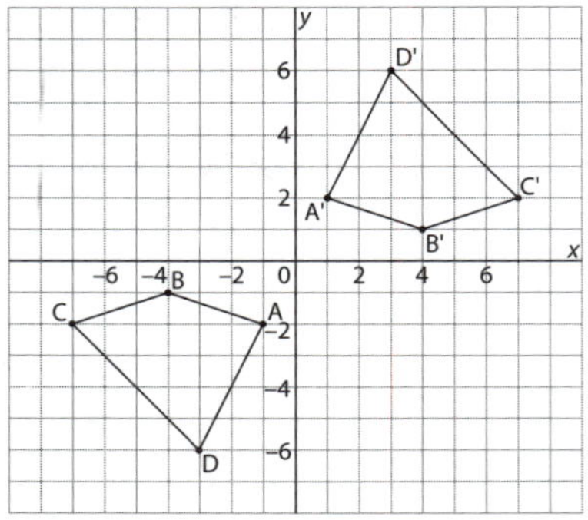

b)

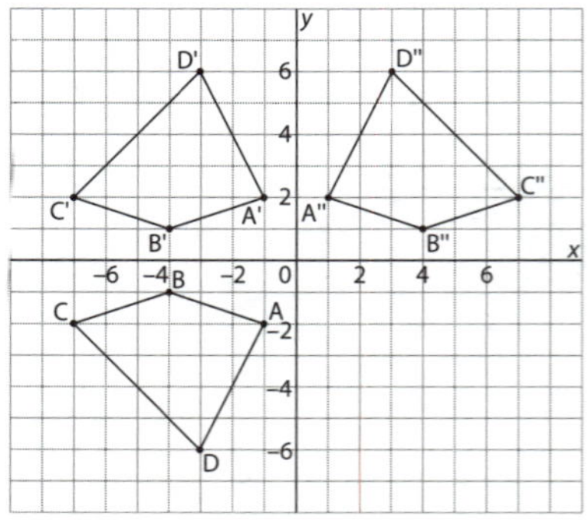

c) The images coincide.

(Sample Solutions continue below.)

2. Identify each transformation. Explain how you know.

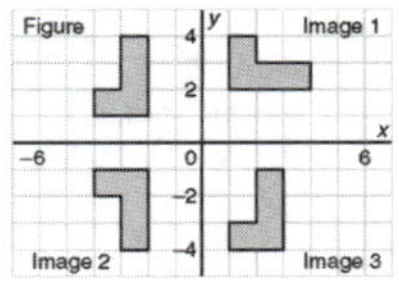

3. a) Copy △DEF on grid paper.

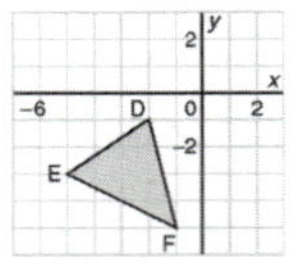

b) Rotate △DEF −90° about the origin to its image △D′E′F′.
c) Rotate △DEF +270° about the origin to its image △D″E″F″.
d) What do you notice about the images in parts b and c?
Do you think you would get a similar result with any figure that you rotate −90° and +270°? Explain.

When there are 2 rotation images, we use a "double" prime notation for the vertices of the second image.

4. Plot each point on a coordinate grid:
A(2, 5), B(−3, 4), C(4, −1)
a) Rotate each point 180° about the origin O to get image points A′, B′, C′.
b) Draw and measure:
i) OA and OA′ ii) OB and OB′ iii) OC and OC′
What do you notice? OA = OA′, OB = OB′, OC = OC′
c) Measure each angle.
i) ∠AOA′ ii) ∠BOB′ iii) ∠COC′
What do you notice? All the angles measure 180°.
d) What other rotation of A, B, and C would result in the image points A′, B′, C′? Explain. A rotation of −180° about the origin

5. Repeat question 4 for a rotation of −90° about the origin.

5. b) OA = OA′, OB = OB′, OC = OC′
c) All the angles measure 90°.
d) A rotation of +270° about the origin

406 UNIT 9: Integers

(Sample Solutions continued)

i) I would get a similar result with a different figure.
ii) I would get a similar result with a figure in a different quadrant.
Yes, a rotation of 180° is equivalent to a reflection in one axis, followed by a reflection in the other axis.

9. a)

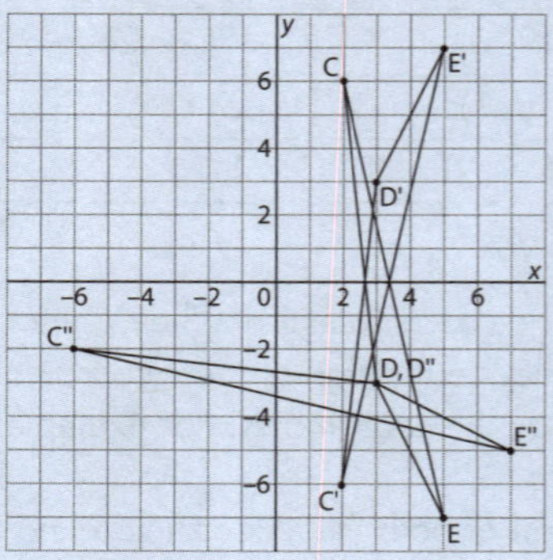

b)

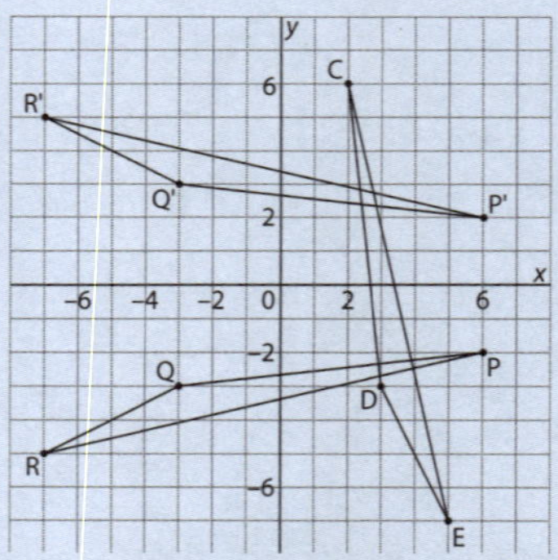

c) No, a reflection followed by a rotation does not give the same image when the transformations are reversed.

Number Strategies

...d each percent of ...75.00.

- 1% $3.75
- 10% $37.50
- 0.1% $0.38
- 15% $56.25
- 150% $562.50
- 1.5% $5.63

6. **Assessment Focus** Draw and label 6 points on a grid, one in each quadrant and one on each axis.
   a) Rotate each point −90° about the origin.
   Write the coordinates of each point and its image.
   What patterns do you see in the coordinates?
   b) Repeat part a for a rotation of 180° about the origin.
   c) Repeat part a for a rotation of −270° about the origin.
   d) How could you use the patterns in parts a, b, and c to draw a rotation image without using tracing paper?

7. You have rotated figures on a grid.
   Think about rotations in the real world.
   Where do you see examples of rotations outside of math class?
   Some examples of rotations are: merry-go-rounds, wheels on a bicycle, hands on a clock

8. Draw a quadrilateral in the 3rd quadrant.
   a) Rotate the quadrilateral 180° about the origin.
   b) Reflect the quadrilateral in the x-axis.
   Then reflect the image in the y-axis.
   c) What do you notice about the image in part a and the second image in part b?
   Do you think you would get a similar result if you started:
   i) with a different figure? ii) in a different quadrant?
   Investigate to find out.
   Write about what you discover.

Take It Further

9. Plot these points: C(2, 6), D(3, −3), E(5, −7)
   a) Reflect △CDE in the x-axis to its image △C′D′E′.
   Rotate △C′D′E′ −90° about the origin to its image △C″D″E″.
   b) Rotate △CDE −90° about the origin to its image △PQR.
   Reflect △PQR in the x-axis to its image △P′Q′R′.
   c) Do the final images in parts a and b coincide? Explain. No

Reflect

When you see a figure and its transformation image on a grid, how can you identify the transformation?
Include examples in your explanation.

REFLECT: If the figure and its image have corresponding sides parallel, the transformation is probably a translation. I count how many squares across and how many squares up or down to go from a point on the figure to a point on the image.
If the figure and its image have different orientations, the transformation is probably a reflection. I fold the paper so the figure and its image coincide. The fold line is the mirror line.
To identify a rotation, I join a point and its image to the rotation centre, the origin, and measure the angle between the line segments. This is the angle of rotation. I then decide if the line segment from the rotation centre to the point moves clockwise or counterclockwise to coincide with the line segment from the rotation centre to the image. This tells me the direction of the rotation.
Students' responses should include a diagram of each transformation.

Number Strategies

Students may use patterns to find certain percents. When 1% is known, multiply by 10 to get 10%, and divide by 10 to get 0.1%. When 15% is known, multiply by 10 to get 150%, and divide by 10 to get 1.5%.
Since we are considering money, each amount must be rounded to the nearest cent.

ASSESSMENT FOR LEARNING

What to Look For

Knowledge and Understanding

✔ Students understand that a rotation, with centre the origin, moves a figure to its rotation image on a coordinate grid.

Thinking

✔ Students use patterns and other strategies to create and solve problems involving rotations on a coordinate grid.

Application

✔ Students can graph rotation images on a coordinate grid.

What to Do

Extra Support: Students who have difficulty drawing rotation images should trace and label the axes as well as the figure. They can label the axes: $+x$, $+y$, $-x$, $-y$ to more easily see the angle the axes, and hence the figure, have turned through.
Students can use Step-by-Step 9 (Master 9.19) to complete question 6.

Extra Practice: Have students repeat question 3 for a triangle with each vertex in a different quadrant, then a quadrilateral, to verify that the results are true for all figures.
Students can complete Extra Practice 9 (Master 9.33).

Extension: Have students practise rotating figures about points on the coordinate grid, other than the origin. These rotation centres could be on the axes or off the axes.

Recording and Reporting

Master 9.2 Ongoing Observations: Integers

Creating a Study Sheet

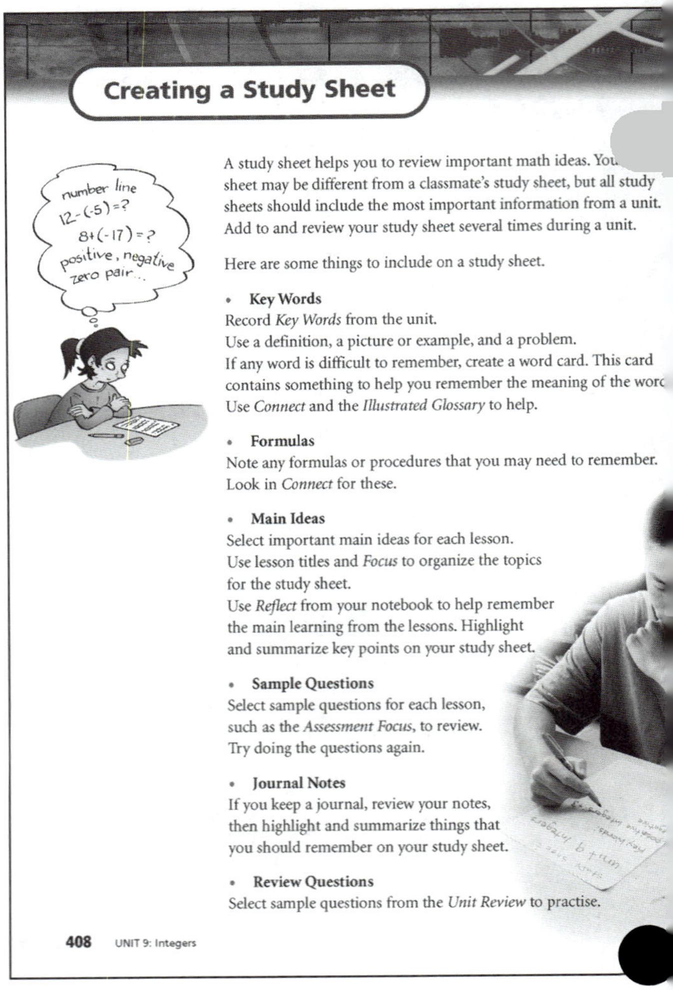

Creating a Study Sheet

A study sheet helps you to review important math ideas. You sheet may be different from a classmate's study sheet, but all study sheets should include the most important information from a unit. Add to and review your study sheet several times during a unit.

Here are some things to include on a study sheet.

- **Key Words**
  Record *Key Words* from the unit.
  Use a definition, a picture or example, and a problem.
  If any word is difficult to remember, create a word card. This card contains something to help you remember the meaning of the word. Use *Connect* and the *Illustrated Glossary* to help.
- **Formulas**
  Note any formulas or procedures that you may need to remember. Look in *Connect* for these.
- **Main Ideas**
  Select important main ideas for each lesson.
  Use lesson titles and *Focus* to organize the topics for the study sheet.
  Use *Reflect* from your notebook to help remember the main learning from the lessons. Highlight and summarize key points on your study sheet.
- **Sample Questions**
  Select sample questions for each lesson, such as the *Assessment Focus*, to review.
  Try doing the questions again.
- **Journal Notes**
  If you keep a journal, review your notes, then highlight and summarize things that you should remember on your study sheet.
- **Review Questions**
  Select sample questions from the *Unit Review* to practise.

408 UNIT 9: Integers

Engage students in a discussion of how to study for a math test.
Draw a web diagram on the board or overhead projector. Ask students to copy the web diagram in their notebooks.
Write "How to Study" at the centre of the web.
Write the various student responses on the web.
Brainstorm for five to ten minutes.
A possible web diagram is given.

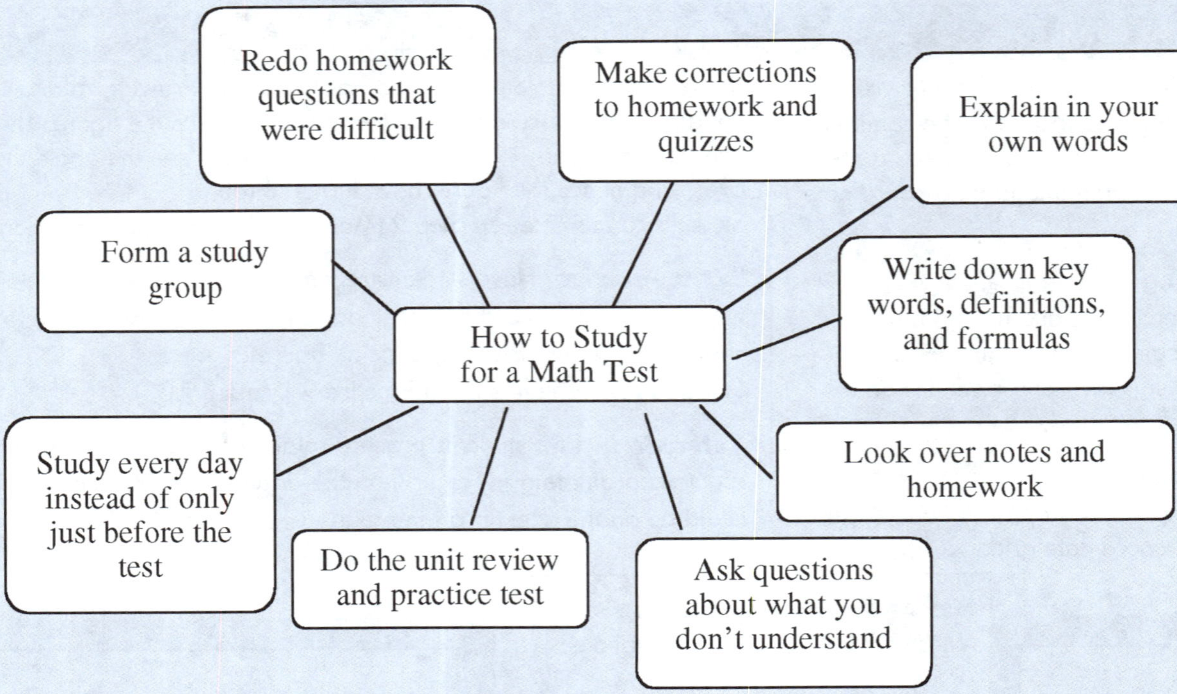

Reading and Writing in Math

Here is a study sheet for
Unit 8 Square Roots and Pythagoras.

Key Words

Square Numbers	Square Roots
1, 4, 9, 16, 25, 36, 49, 64, 81, 100	$\sqrt{1} = 1$ $\sqrt{16} = 4$ $\sqrt{36} = 6$ $\sqrt{81} = 9$

Formulas

$c^2 = a^2 + b^2$

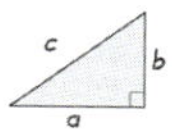

Pythagorean Theorem: In a right triangle, the area of the square on the hypotenuse is equal to the sum of the areas of the squares on the legs.

Main Idea

The Pythagorean Theorem can be used to find the length of one side in a right triangle when two other sides are known.

Sample Question

The size of a TV set is described by the length of a diagonal of the screen. One TV is labelled as size 70 cm.
The screen is 40 cm high.
What is the width of the screen?
Draw a diagram to illustrate your answer.

Journal Notes

To use the Pythagorean Theorem in an isosceles triangle, I draw a perpendicular from the vertex of the angle that is different from the equal angles, to the opposite side. Then I have two right triangles.

Review Questions

I need to review question 10, page 356, on finding the surface area of a pentagonal prism.

Reading and Writing in Math: Creating a Study Sheet 409

MATH TIPS

Preparing to Take a Test

Tests can be a major obstacle for students who suffer from math anxiety. It is important to help these students develop coping skills for test writing. These include:

1. Do a "mock" or practice test to simulate test-taking conditions.
2. Practise relaxation techniques such as deep breathing. Have students take a deep breath, hold their breath for a few seconds and slowly release the air. Do this three or four times before beginning the test.
3. Look over the test and start with problems the student feels sure about. This builds confidence and may lead to a better mark because the students will not loose "sure marks" if they run out of time. Then have students try the problems they think they can figure out, before finally trying the problems they are least sure about.
4. Pace themselves so that if they get stuck on a question, they move onto the next question. Come back to these questions at the end.
5. Read the questions carefully. Answer the question that was asked. Check answers. Do they make sense?
6. Show all work, so that partial credit can be given.

Tell students that a good way to review for a math test is to create a study sheet.
Point out that many of the suggestions on the web diagram can be included on the study sheet.
Invite volunteers to read each bulleted point on page 408 of the Student Book.

Review the study sheet for Unit 8 on page 409 of the Student Book.

Have students work with a partner and review the lessons in Unit 9. One partner explains the important relationships, concepts, and procedures in a lesson. The other partner takes notes and asks any questions he or she has. Partners trade roles for each lesson in the unit. When the unit has been reviewed, ask students to organize their notes into a study sheet.

Have students exchange study sheets with their classmates.

Ask students:

- How did writing things down in your own words help you understand concepts better?
- What did you think were the important concepts in Unit 9?
- Which concept(s) did you find most difficult? Why?
- How can you improve your understanding of these concepts before the test?

UNIT REVIEW

LESSON ORGANIZER

Student Materials
- coloured tiles
- Number Lines (Master 9.20)
- Coordinate Grid (Master 9.21)
- 0.5-cm grid paper (PM 14)

Assessment: Masters 9.1 Unit Rubric: Integers, 9.4 Unit Summary: Integers

Correlation of Extra Practice questions on page 496:

Lesson	Questions
9.1	1, 2, 3, 6
9.2	2, 3, 4, 5
9.3	3
9.4	7
9.5	7
9.6	8
9.7	9
9.8	9
9.9	9

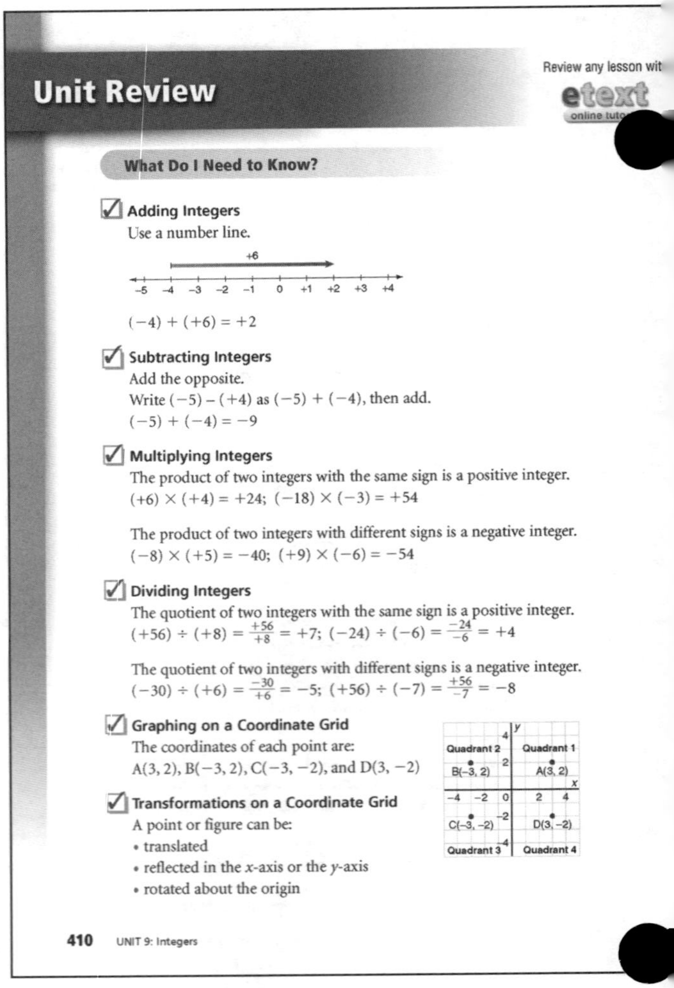
Unit Review

Review any lesson wit[h] etext online tuto[r]

What Do I Need to Know?

✓ **Adding Integers**
Use a number line.

$(-4) + (+6) = +2$

✓ **Subtracting Integers**
Add the opposite.
Write $(-5) - (+4)$ as $(-5) + (-4)$, then add.
$(-5) + (-4) = -9$

✓ **Multiplying Integers**
The product of two integers with the same sign is a positive integer.
$(+6) \times (+4) = +24$; $(-18) \times (-3) = +54$

The product of two integers with different signs is a negative integer.
$(-8) \times (+5) = -40$; $(+9) \times (-6) = -54$

✓ **Dividing Integers**
The quotient of two integers with the same sign is a positive integer.
$(+56) \div (+8) = \frac{+56}{+8} = +7$; $(-24) \div (-6) = \frac{-24}{-6} = +4$

The quotient of two integers with different signs is a negative integer.
$(-30) \div (+6) = \frac{-30}{+6} = -5$; $(+56) \div (-7) = \frac{+56}{-7} = -8$

✓ **Graphing on a Coordinate Grid**
The coordinates of each point are:
A(3, 2), B(−3, 2), C(−3, −2), and D(3, −2)

✓ **Transformations on a Coordinate Grid**
A point or figure can be:
- translated
- reflected in the x-axis or the y-axis
- rotated about the origin

410 UNIT 9: Integers

Sample Solutions

1. b)

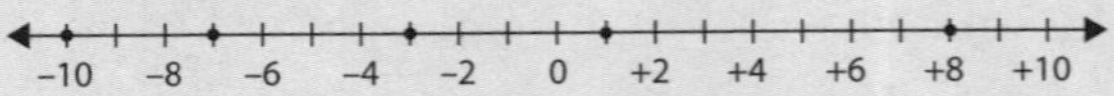

2. a)

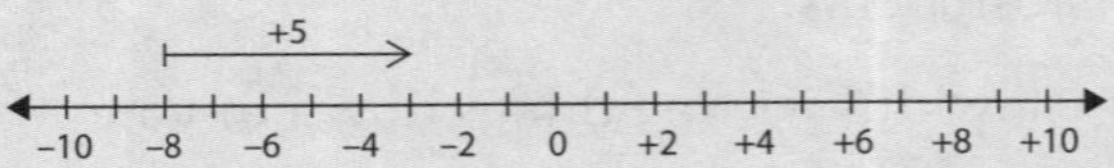

b)

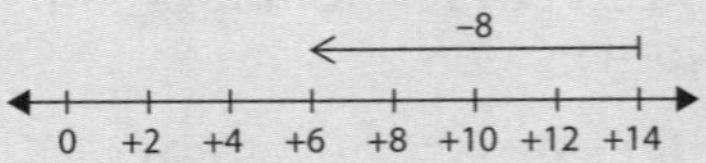

c)

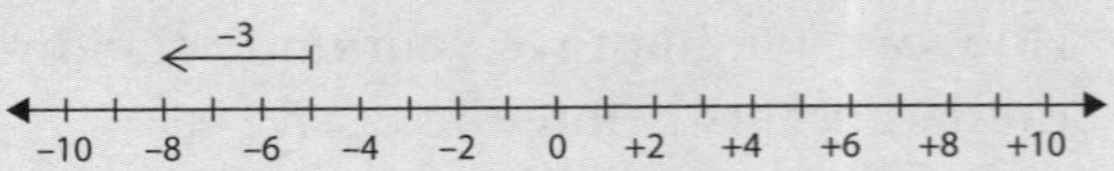

d)

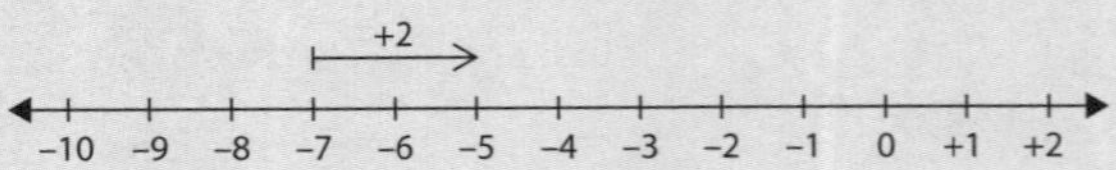

e)

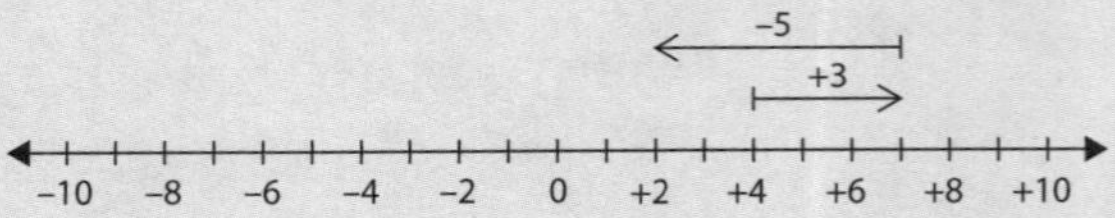

f)

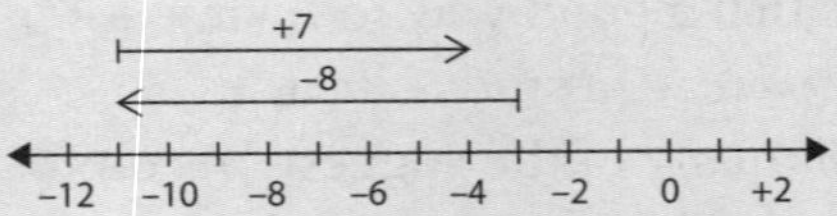

g)

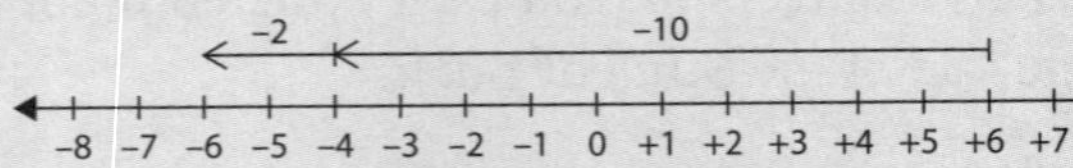

h)

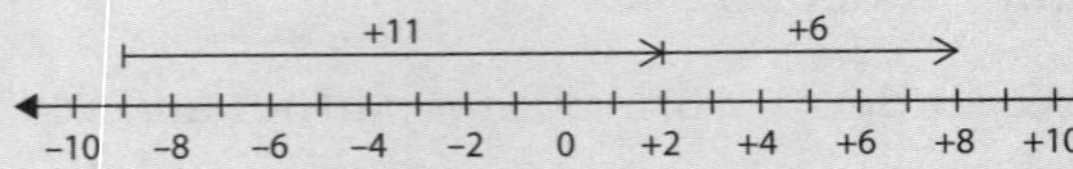

3. a) Reg is the winner. He had the lowest score.
b) 2 − (−5) = 7; 7 fewer strokes

4. −23 + 12 + (−8) = −19; the final temperature was −19°C.

7. 6 + 8(−2) = 6 + (−16) = −10; the final temperature was −10°C.

10. a) True; for example, +8 + (−8) = 0
b) False; for example, +4 − (+11) = −7
c) False; when two integers have different signs, their product is negative.
d) False; for example, (+4)(−4) = −16, not 0

What Should I Be Able to Do?

For extra practice, go to page 496.

1. a) List these integers from least to greatest: +8, −10, −3, +1, −7 −10, −7, −3, +1, +8
   b) Mark each integer in part a on a number line.

2. Use a number line to add or subtract.
   a) (−8) + (+5) −3
   b) (+14) + (−8) +6
   c) (−5) − (+3) −8
   d) (−7) − (−2) −5
   e) (+4) − (−3) + (−5) +2
   f) (−3) + (−8) − (−7) −4
   g) (+6) − (+10) + (−2) −6
   h) (−9) − (−11) − (−6) +8

3. Here are the results of a golf game.
   Al: −3; Lana: +2; Kirima: 0;
   Earl: +1; Reg: −5; Jody: −4
   a) Who won the game? Reg
   b) How many fewer strokes did the winner take than the person who came last? 7

4. At midnight in Winnipeg, the temperature was −23°C. During the next 24 h, the temperature rose 12°C, then dropped 8°C. What was the final temperature? Explain. −19°C

5. Evaluate.
   a) (+512) + (−173) +339
   b) (−879) − (−1092) +213
   c) (−243) + (+987) +744
   d) (+1591) − (−847) +2438

9.3 6. Evaluate.
   a) 3 − 5 −2 b) −1 + 10 +9
   c) −5 − 6 −11 d) 3 − 5 + 7 +5
   e) −4 + 3 −1 f) −3 + 5 − 7 −5

7. The temperature change in a chemistry experiment was −2°C every 30 min. The initial temperature was 6°C. What was the temperature after 4 h? −10°C

9.4 8. Multiply.
   a) (−7)(−5) +35
   b) (+10)(−6) −60
   c) (−3)(−9)(−1) −27
   d) (−2)(−2)(−2) −8
   e) (−7)(−8)(0) 0
   f) (−11)(+13)(−2) +286

9. Evaluate.
   a) 21 − 5 − 5 + 6 − 2 +15
   b) 0 − 6 + 4 + 8 − 1 + 2 + 7 +14

9.1 9.2 9.4 10. Answer true or false to each statement. Explain your answer.
   a) The sum of an integer and its opposite is always 0.
   b) When you subtract two positive integers, their difference is always a positive integer.
   c) The product of a positive integer and a negative integer is always positive.
   d) The product of an integer and its opposite is always 0.

Unit Review 411

12. a) $(-8) \div (-4) + 6 \times (-3)$
$= 2 + (-18)$
$= -16$

b) $(-5) + (-12) \div (-3)$
$= (-5) + 4$
$= -1$

c) $18 + 3[10 \div (-5)]$
$= 18 + 3[-2]$
$= 18 + (-6)$
$= +12$

d) $[(-16) \div 8]^2 - 12$
$= [-2]^2 - 12$
$= 4 - 12$
$= -8$

e) $\dfrac{4 \times (-5) - 4}{-6}$
$= \dfrac{-20 - 4}{-6}$
$= \dfrac{-24}{-6}$
$= +4$

f) $\dfrac{(-3)^2 + 5}{(-2)^2 - (-3)}$
$= \dfrac{9 + 5}{4 + 3}$
$= \dfrac{14}{7}$
$= +2$

13. a) $4[(-3) + 16]$
$= 4[+13]$
$= +52$

b) $3 - 2(10 \div 2)$
$= 3 - 2(5)$
$= 3 - 10$
$= -7$

c) $5 \times (-2) - 2[4 \div (-2)]$
$= -10 - 2(-2)$
$= -10 + 4$
$= -6$

d) $(-3)(-2)(4) + 3(-5)$
$= +24 + (-15)$
$= +9$

e) $\dfrac{3 \times (-6) - 3}{-7}$
$= \dfrac{-18 - 3}{-7}$
$= \dfrac{-21}{-7}$
$= +3$

f) $9 - 3[(-2)^3 + 4]$
$= 9 - 3[-8 + 4]$
$= 9 - 3[-4]$
$= 9 + 12$
$= +21$

15. a) i) −3 and −5 ii) −3 and +5
iii) −16 and +2 iv) +2 and −4
b) i) −3 and +1 ii) −3 and −1
iii) −2 and +1 iv) +1 and −2
c) i) −2 and −10 ii) −14 and −2
iii) −36 and +3 iv) +3 and −4
d) i) −1 and −2 ii) −7 and −4
iii) −21 and +7 iv) −3 and +1

16. a)

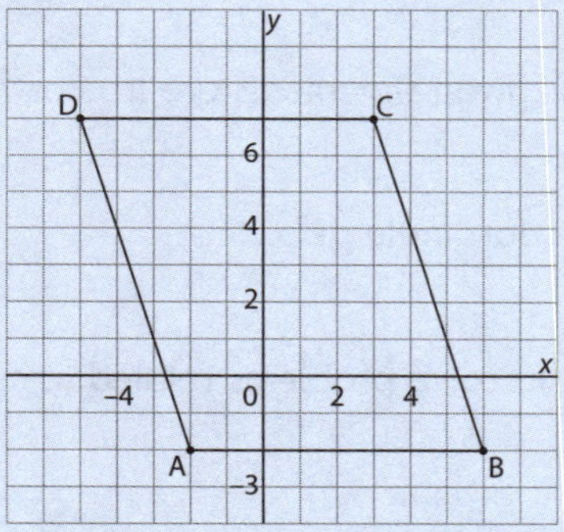

b) Point A : Quadrant 3
Point B : Quadrant 4
Point C : Quadrant 1
Point D : Quadrant 2

c) Parallelogram; 72 units^2

17. a)

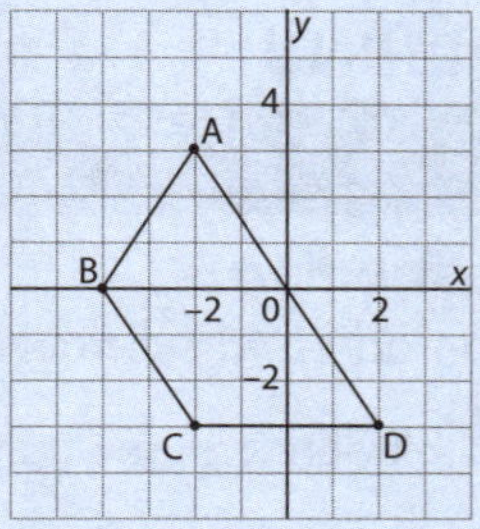

b) i)

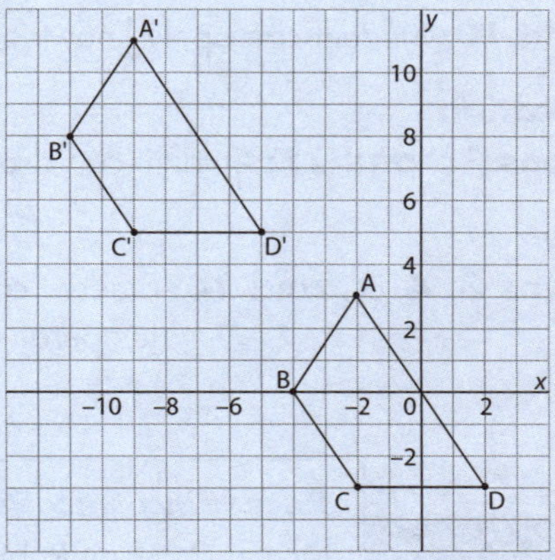

ii)

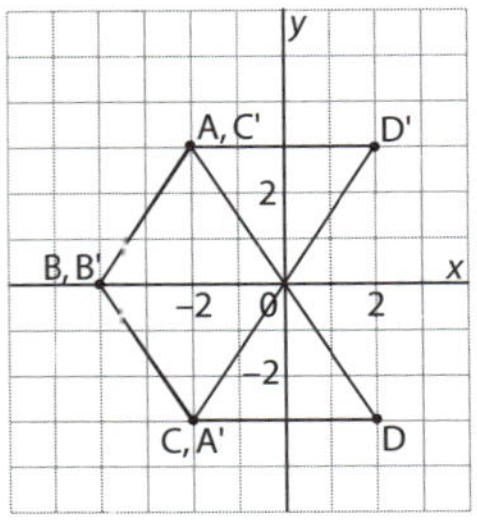

iii)

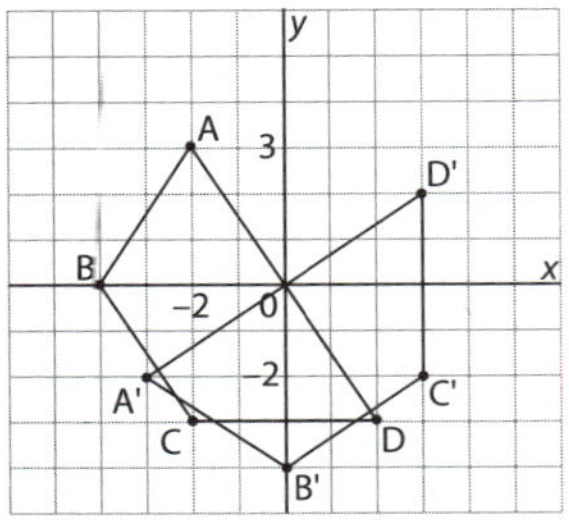

c) All images are congruent. Under the translation and rotation, the images have the same orientation as quadrilateral ABCD. Under the reflection, the orientation of the image is changed.

LESSON

9.5 **11.** Divide.

a) $(-56) \div (-7)$ +8

b) $(+40) \div (-5)$ –8

c) $(-121) \div (+11)$ –11

d) $\frac{-36}{-4}$ +9

e) $\frac{+72}{-4}$ –18

f) $\frac{-28}{+2}$ –14

9.6 **12.** Evaluate.

a) $(-8) \div (-4) + 6 \times (-3)$

b) $(-5) + (-12) \div (-3)$

c) $18 + 3[10 \div (-5)]$

d) $[(-16) \div 8]^2 - 12$

e) $\frac{4 \times (-5) - 4}{-6}$

f) $\frac{(-3)^2 + 5}{(-2)^2 - (-3)}$

13. Evaluate.

a) $4[(-3) + 16]$

b) $3 - 2(10 \div 2)$

c) $5 \times (-2) - 2[4 \div (-2)]$

d) $(-3)(-2)(4) + 3(-5)$

e) $\frac{3 \times (-6) - 3}{-7}$

f) $9 - 3[(-2)^3 + 4]$

14. In a darts game, Suzanne and Corey each threw the darts 10 times.
Corey had: three (+2) scores; three (–3) scores; and four (+1) scores.
Suzanne had four (+2) scores; four (–3) scores; and two (+1) scores.

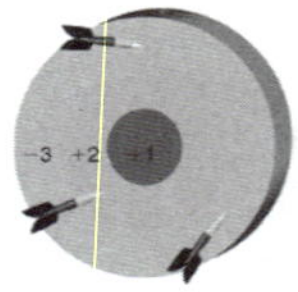

a) What was each person's final score? Corey: +1, Suzanne: –2

b) Who won the game? Explain. Corey; +1 > –2

9.1 9.2 9.4 9.5 **15.** For each number below, find two integers for which that number is:

i) the sum

ii) the difference

iii) the quotient

iv) the product

a) –8 b) –2

c) –12 d) –3

9.7 **16.** a) On a coordinate grid, plot each point. Join the points in order. Then join D to A.
A(–2, –2) B(6, –2)
C(3, 7) D(–5, 7)

b) Name the quadrant in which each point is located.

c) Identify the figure. Find its area.

9.8 9.9 **17.** a) Plot these points on a coordinate grid:
A(–2, 3), B(–4, 0), C(–2, –3), D(2, –3)
Join the points to draw quadrilateral ABCD.

b) Draw the image of quadrilateral ABCD after each transformation:

i) a translation 7 units left and 8 units up

ii) a reflection in the *x*-axis

iii) a rotation of 90° counterclockwise about the origin

c) How are the images alike? Different?

412 UNIT 9: Integers

ASSESSMENT FOR LEARNING

What to Look For

Knowledge and Understanding

✔ **Question 2:** Student can add and subtract integers.

✔ **Questions 8 and 11:** Student can multiply and divide integers.

Thinking

✔ **Question 10:** Student can apply knowledge of integers to decide whether given statements are true or false.

Communication

✔ **Questions 16 and 17:** Student can draw transformation images on a coordinate grid.

Application

✔ **Questions 3, 4, 7, and 14:** Student can apply knowledge of integers to solve problems related to temperatures and scores.

Recording and Reporting

Master 9.1 Unit Rubric: Integers
Master 9.4 Unit Summary: Integers

Practice Test

1. Use a number line to order these integers from least to greatest.
$+5, -3, 0, -11, -8, +7$
Least to greatest: $-11, -8, -3, 0, +5, +7$

2. Evaluate.
a) $(-4) + (-8)$ -12 b) $9 + (-17)$ -8
c) $(-8) \times 6$ -48 d) $(-56) + (-61)$ -117
e) $(-10) - (-3)$ -7 f) $(4)(-2)$ -8
g) $(-2)^4$ $+16$ h) $(-36) \div 9$ -4
i) $(-3) \times (-5) \times (-11)$ -165

3. Continue each pattern. Write the next 4 terms.
Write the pattern rule.
a) $-4, 8, -16, 32, \ldots$ $-64, +128, -256, +512$
b) $-9, -2, -5, 2, -1, 6, \ldots$ $+3, +10, +7, +14$

4. Evaluate.
a) $(-20) \times (-5) + 16 \div (-8)$ $+98$
b) $\frac{14 - 10 \div 2}{-3}$ -3
c) $(-3)^2 + 2 \times (-4)$ $+1$

5. A number is multiplied by -4.
Then 3 is subtracted from the product.
The answer is 13.
What is the number? -4

6. The temperature on Sunday was 4°C. The temperature dropped 8°C on Monday and dropped twice as much on Tuesday.
What was the temperature on Tuesday? -20°C

7. a) On a coordinate grid, draw a triangle with area 12 square units. Place each vertex in a different quadrant.
b) Write the coordinates of each vertex.
c) Explain how you know the area is 12 square units.
d) Translate the triangle 6 units right and 3 units down.
e) Reflect the triangle in the *y*-axis.
f) Rotate the triangle 90° clockwise about the origin.

Practice Test 413

LESSON ORGANIZER

Student Materials
- coloured tiles
- Number Lines (Master 9.20)
- Coordinate Grid (Master 9.21)
- 0.5-cm grid paper (PM 14)

Assessment: Masters 9.1 Unit Rubric: Integers, 9.4 Unit Summary: Integers

Assignment Guidelines

To assess the 4 Achievement Chart categories listed in the curriculum document, use these test questions:
Knowledge and Understanding: 1, 2, 4
Thinking: 3, 5
Application: 6
Communication: 7

Sample Solutions

1.
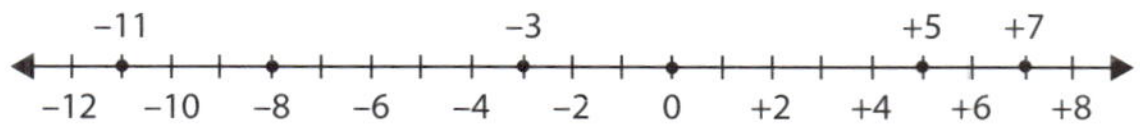

3. a) Start at −4. Multiply by −2 each time.
b) Start at −9. Alternate between adding +7 and −3.

6. $4 + (-8) + 2(-8)$
$= 4 - 8 - 16$
$= -20$
On Tuesday, the temperature was −20°C.

7. a), b) Answers can vary.
For example:
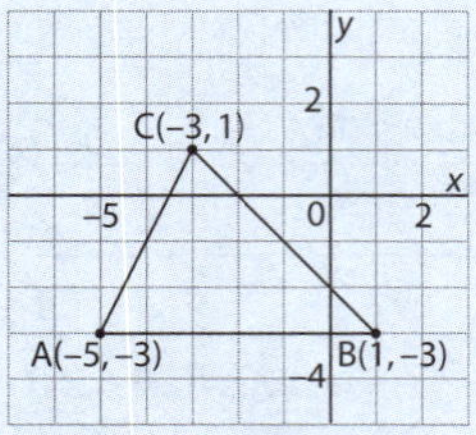

c) The base is 6 units and the height is 4 units.
Since $\frac{1}{2} \times 6 \times 4 = 12$, the triangle has an area of 12 units^2.

d)
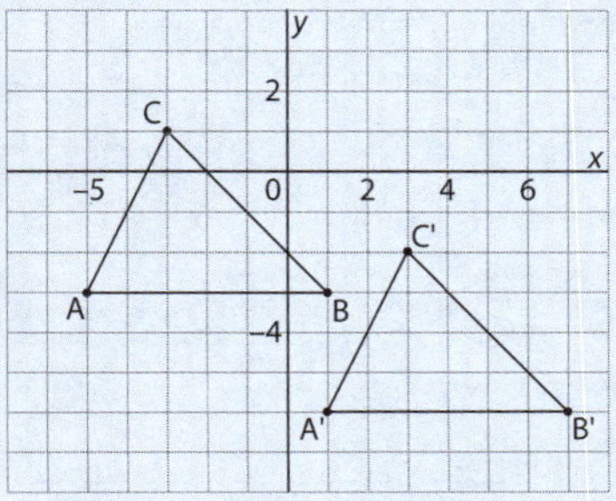

e)
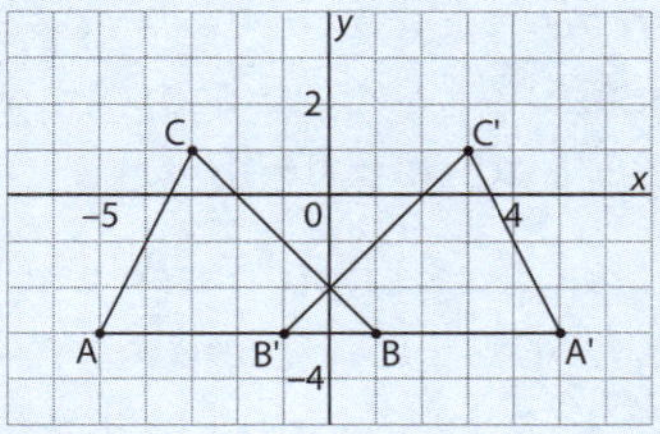

f)
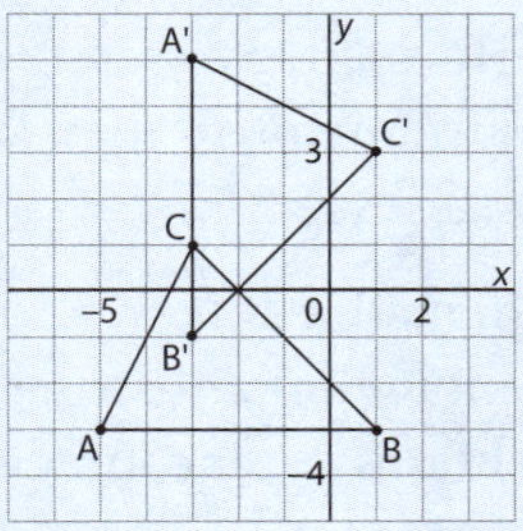

Charity Golf Tournament

LESSON ORGANIZER 40–50 min

Student Materials *Optional*
- Number Lines (Master 9.20)

Assessment: Masters 9.3 Performance Assessment Rubric: Charity Golf Tournament, 9.4 Unit Summary: Integers

Sample Response

1. a) 3(0) + 2(+1) + (−1) + (2)(−2) + (+2)
3. a) Kyle

Hole	1	2	3	4	5	6	7	8	9
Par	3	4	3	3	5	4	4	3	3
Under/Over Par	+1	0	+1	0	+1	−1	0	0	+1
Score	4	4	4	3	6	3	4	3	4

Kyle's total score was 35.

(Sample Response continues below, right.)

Unit Problem Charity Golf Tournament

A Grade 8 class and a local bank are partners to sponsor a golf tournament to raise money for local charities. The bank provides these prizes:

1st place—$5000 to a charity of the player's choice
2nd and 3rd places—$1000 to a charity of the player's choice

Golf Terms
Recall that "par" is the number of strokes it should take for a player to reach the hole.
If par is 3 and you take 5 strokes, then your score in relation to par is +2, or 2 over.
If par is 3 and you take 2 strokes, then your score in relation to par is −1, or 1 under.

A bogey is 1 stroke more than par, or 1 over par.
A double bogey is 2 strokes more than par, or 2 over par.
A birdie is 1 stroke less than par, or 1 under par.
An eagle is 2 strokes less than par, or 2 under par.

Here are the top 6 golfers:
Chai Kim, Delaney, Hamid, Hanna, Kyle, and Weng Kwong

1. The golf course has 9 holes. Here is one person's results: par on 3 holes, a bogey on 2 holes, a birdie on 1 hole, an eagle on 2 holes, and a double bogey on 1 hole
   a) Write an integer expression to represent these results.
   b) Evaluate the expression in part a to calculate the score in relation to par. −1, or 1 under par

2. Chai Kim wrote his results in a table like this.

Hole	1	2	3	4	5	6	7	8	9
Par	3	4	3	3	5	4	4	3	3
Under/Over Par	0	−1	+2	0	−1	0	0	−1	0
Score	3	3	5	3	4	4	4	2	3

414 UNIT 9: Integers

Present the *Unit Problem*. Ensure students understand the meaning of the words: par, birdie, bogey, eagle, and double bogey.

Remind students that they should use the *Check List* to assess their work before handing it in. You may also wish to provide students with copies of Master 9.3 Performance Assessment Rubric: Charity Golf Tournament so they know how their work will be assessed.

It is important that students be able to add and subtract integers. Students who still struggle with these operations should be encouraged to use coloured tiles or *Number Lines* (Master 9.20) as needed.

(Sample Response continued)

b) Delaney

Hole	1	2	3	4	5	6	7	8	9
Par	3	4	3	3	5	4	4	3	3
Under/Over Par	−1	−1	+1	+1	−2	+1	−1	−1	−1
Score	2	3	4	4	3	5	3	2	2

Delaney's total score was 28.

c) Hamid

Hole	1	2	3	4	5	6	7	8	9
Par	3	4	3	3	5	4	4	3	3
Under/Over Par	−1	−1	−1	−1	−1	−1	−1	+2	−1
Score	2	3	2	2	4	3	3	5	2

Hamid's total score was 26.

4. a)

Player	Chai Kim	Delaney	Hamid	Hannah	Kyle	Weng Kwong
Score	31	28	26	27	35	35

The players ranked from least to greatest score: Hamid, Hannah, Delaney, Chai Kim, Kyle, Weng Kwong.

a) Copy and complete the table. Use the following information:

Hole 1, 4, 6, 7, 9 Par

Hole 2, 5, 8 Birdie

Hole 3 Double bogey

b) What was Chai Kim's final score? +31

c) What was his final score in relation to par? 1 under par, or −1

3. For each person below, make a table similar to the table in question 2.

Use the information below. What is each golfer's final score?

a) Kyle: 35 — Bogey holes 1, 3, 5, 9; Birdie hole 6; Par holes 2, 4, 7, 8

b) Delaney: 28 — Bogey holes 3, 4, 6; Birdie holes 1, 2, 7, 8, 9; Eagle hole 5

c) Hamid: 26 — Birdie every hole except hole 8; Double bogey hole 8

Check List

Your work should show:

✓ how you used integers to solve the problems

✓ accurate calculations and ordering of integers

✓ tables you constructed to display the scores

✓ clear explanations, with correct use of mathematical language

4. a) Hannah had a score of −5 in relation to par.

Weng Kwong had a score of +3 in relation to par.

Use the information in questions 2 and 3.

Rank the players in order from least to greatest score.

b) Who won the tournament and the $5000 prize? Hamid

What was the score in relation to par? −6

c) Who won the $1000 prizes? Hannah; −5

What were the scores in relation to par? Delaney; −4

5. Use a table similar to that in question 2.

Complete the table with scores of your choice.

Calculate the final score, and the final score in relation to par.

Reflect on the Unit

What did you find easy about working with integers? What was difficult for you? Give examples to illustrate your answers.

Unit Problem: Charity Golf Tournament 415

b) Hamid won the tournament with a score of 6 under par.

c) Hannah was in second place with a score of 5 under par. Delaney was in third place with a score of 4 under par.

5.

Hole	1	2	3	4	5	6	7	8	9
Par	3	5	4	4	4	3	5	5	3
Under/Over Par	−1	0	+1	−1	+2	+1	−1	0	0
Score	2	5	5	3	6	4	4	5	3

Final score: 37, or +1

REFLECT ON THE UNIT: I found it easy to add integers that have the same sign, because I simply add the numbers and the sign of the answer is the sign of the integers; for example, (+5) + (+2) = +7, and (−3) + (−8) = −11.

It was also easy to multiply integers once I knew that if the signs are the same, the answer is positive and if the signs are different, the answer is negative; for example, (+5)(+2) = +10; (−7)(−1) = +7; (−3)(+8) = −24.

I did not find anything difficult about integers.

ASSESSMENT FOR LEARNING

What to Look For

Knowledge and Understanding

✔ Students understand that golf scores in relation to par are written as integers.

Communication

✔ Students can record their work with clear explanations and accurate answers.

Application

✔ Students can apply their knowledge of integers to solve problems related to golf.

What to Do

Extra Support: Make the problem accessible.

In question 1, have students add pairs of integers rather than attempt to add 9 integers at once.

Encourage students to use coloured tiles and number lines to add the integers and to order the integers.

Recording and Reporting

Master 9.3 Performance Assessment Rubric: Charity Golf Tournament

Master 9.4 Unit Summary: Integers

Evaluating Student Learning: Preparing to Report: Unit 9 Integers

This unit provides an opportunity to report on the **Number Sense and Numeration** and **Geometry and Spatial Sense** strands.

Master 9.4: Unit Summary: Integers provides a comprehensive format for recording and summarizing evidence collected.

Here is an example of a completed summary chart for this Unit:

Strands: *Number Sense and Numeration/ Geometry and Spatial Sense*	**Knowledge and Understanding**	**Thinking**	**Communication**	**Application**	***Overall***
Ongoing Observations	3	4	3	4	3/4
Work samples or portfolios; conferences	3	3	4	3	3
Unit Review	4	3	3	3	3
Unit Test	3	3	3	3	3
Unit Problem Charity Golf Tournament	3	3	4	4	3/4
Achievement Level for reporting					3

Recording	How to Report
Ongoing Observations	Use *Master 9.2 Ongoing Observations: Integers* to determine the most consistent level achieved in each category. Enter it in the chart. Choose to summarize by achievement category, or simply to enter an overall level. Observations from late in the unit should be most heavily weighted.
Portfolios or collections of work samples; conferences or interviews	Use *Master 9.1 Unit Rubric: Integers* to guide evaluation of collections of work and information gathered in conferences. Teachers may choose to focus particular attention on the Assessment Focus questions. Work from late in the unit should be most heavily weighted.
Unit Review	*Master 9.1 Unit Rubric: Integers* may be helpful in determining levels of achievement. #1, 2, 5, 6, 8, 9, 11, and 16 provide evidence of Knowledge and Understanding; #3, 4, 7, 12, 14, and 15 provide evidence of Application; #10 provides evidence of Thinking; all questions provide evidence of Communication.
Unit Test	*Master 9.1 Unit Rubric: Integers* may be helpful in determining levels of achievement. #1 and 5 provide evidence of Knowledge and Understanding; #8 provides evidence of Application; #7 and 9 provide evidence of Thinking; all questions provide evidence of Communication.
Unit Problem	Use *Master 9.3 Performance Assessment Rubric: Charity Golf Tournament*. The *Unit Problem* offers a snapshot of students' achievement. In particular, it shows their ability to synthesize and apply what they have learned.
Student Self-Assessment	Note students' perceptions of their own progress. This may take the form of an oral or written comment, or a self-rating.
Comments	Analyse the pattern of achievement to identify strengths and needs. In some cases, specific actions may need to be planned to support the learner.

Learning Skills	**Ongoing Records**
PM 4: Learning Skills Check List Use to record and report throughout a reporting period, rather than for each unit and/or strand.	*PM 10: Summary Class Records: Strands* *PM 11: Summary Class Records: Achievement Categories* *PM 12: Summary Record: Individual* Use to record and report evaluations of student achievement over several clusters, a reporting period, or a school year. These can also be used in place of the Unit Summary.

Name ______________________ Date ________________

Master 9.1

Unit Rubric: Integers

	Level 1	Level 2	Level 3	Level 4
Knowledge and Understanding • Shows understanding of integers by demonstrating and explaining: – comparisons and ordering – rules for multiplying and dividing – justifications for choice of methods and reasonableness of solutions	shows limited understanding in demonstrating and explaining: – comparing and ordering – rules for multiplying and dividing – justifications for methods and solutions	shows some understanding in demonstrating and explaining: – comparing and ordering – rules for multiplying and dividing – justifications for methods and solutions	shows considerable understanding in demonstrating and explaining: – comparing and ordering – rules for multiplying and dividing – justifications for methods and solutions	shows thorough understanding in demonstrating and explaining: – comparing and ordering – rules for multiplying and dividing – justifications for methods and solutions
Thinking • Plans and carries out appropriate strategies to pose and solve problems that involve integers	uses appropriate strategies to pose and solve problems that involve integers with limited effectiveness	uses appropriate strategies to pose and solve problems that involve integers with some effectiveness	uses appropriate strategies to pose and solve problems that involve integers with considerable effectiveness	uses appropriate strategies to pose and solve problems that involve integers with a high degree of effectiveness
Communication • Explains concepts, procedures, and reasoning clearly, using appropriate terminology	limited effectiveness; unable to explain reasoning and procedures clearly; rarely uses appropriate terms	some effectiveness; explains reasoning and procedures with some clarity and use of appropriate terms	considerable effectiveness; explains reasoning and procedures clearly, using appropriate terms	high degree of effectiveness; explains reasoning and procedures clearly and precisely, using the most appropriate terms
• Presents work, including diagrams, drawings, and calculations clearly, using appropriate conventions (e.g., symbols and labels)	presents diagrams, drawings, and calculations with limited clarity and use of appropriate conventions	presents diagrams, drawings, and calculations with some clarity and use of conventions	presents diagrams, drawings, and calculations with considerable clarity and use of conventions	presents diagrams, drawings, and calculations with a high degree of clarity and use of conventions
Application • Applies skills appropriately including: – adding, subtracting, multiplying, and dividing integers – order of operations – using integers to graph transformations on a grid	limited effectiveness; major errors or omissions in: – adding, subtracting, multiplying, and dividing integers – order of operations – using integers to graph transformations on a grid	some effectiveness; somewhat accurate with several minor errors or omissions in: – adding, subtracting, multiplying, and dividing integers – order of operations – using integers to graph transformations on a grid	considerable effectiveness; generally accurate with few minor errors or omissions in: – adding, subtracting, multiplying, and dividing integers – order of operations – using integers to graph transformations on a grid	high degree of effectiveness; accurate and precise with no errors in: – adding, subtracting, multiplying, and dividing integers – order of operations – using integers to graph transformations on a grid

Name ____________________ Date ________________

Master 9.2

Ongoing Observations: Integers

The behaviours described under each heading are examples; they are not intended to be an exhaustive list of all that might be observed. More detailed descriptions are provided in each lesson under *Assessment for Learning*.

STUDENT ACHIEVEMENT: Integers				
Student	**Knowledge and Understanding** • Demonstrates and explains: – comparing and ordering integers – rules for multiplying and dividing – justifications for choice of methods	**Thinking** • Uses appropriate strategies to pose and solve problems that involve integers	**Communication** • Explains reasoning and procedures clearly, using appropriate terms • Presents diagrams, drawings, and calculations clearly, including symbols and labels	**Application** • Accurately: – adds, subtracts, multiplies, and divides integers – applies order of operations – uses integers to graph transformations on a grid

Level 1 – very limited; Level 2 – somewhat or limited; Level 3 – satisfactory; Level 4 – thorough

Name ____________ Date ____________

Master 9.3

Performance Assessment Rubric: Charity Golf Tournament

	Level 1	Level 2	Level 3	Level 4
Knowledge and Understanding • Explanations show understanding of integers, including comparisons and ordering	explanations show limited understanding of integers, including comparisons and ordering	explanations show some understanding of integers, including comparisons and ordering	explanations show considerable understanding of integers, including comparisons and ordering	explanations show thorough understanding of integers, including comparisons and ordering
Thinking • Uses appropriate strategies to solve both single and multi-step problems involving integers	uses a few simple strategies with limited success	uses some appropriate strategies with partial success	uses appropriate strategies with considerable success	uses appropriate, often innovative, strategies with a high degree of success
Communication • Communicates procedures, solutions, and reasoning clearly, using appropriate language and conventions	limited effectiveness; does not communicate clearly	some effectiveness; communicates with some clarity	considerable effectiveness; communicates clearly	a high degree of effectiveness; communicates clearly and precisely
Application • Accurately: – writes and evaluates integer expressions – creates data from the information given – calculates total scores, and scores in relation to par – compares and orders integers to determine prize winners	limited effectiveness; major errors or omissions in: – writing and evaluating integer expressions – creating data from the information given – calculating total scores, and scores in relation to par – comparing and ordering integers to determine prize winners	some effectiveness; somewhat accurate in: – writing and evaluating integer expressions – creating data from the information given – calculating total scores, and scores in relation to par – comparing and ordering integers to determine prize winners	considerable effectiveness; generally accurate in: – writing and evaluating integer expressions – creating data from the information given – calculating total scores, and scores in relation to par – comparing and ordering integers to determine prize winners	high degree of effectiveness; accurate and precise in: – writing and evaluating integer expressions – creating data from the information given – calculating total scores, and scores in relation to par – comparing and ordering integers to determine prize winners

Name ____________________ Date ________________

Master 9.4

Unit Summary: Integers

Review assessment records to determine the most consistent achievement levels for the assessments conducted. Some cells may be blank. *Overall* achievement levels may be recorded in each row, rather than identifying levels for each achievement category.

	Most Consistent Level of Achievement*				
Strands: *Number Sense and Numeration/Geometry and Spatial Sense*	**Knowledge and Understanding**	**Thinking**	**Communication**	**Application**	***Overall***
Ongoing Observations					
Work samples or portfolios; conferences					
Unit Review					
Unit Test					
Unit Problem: Charity Golf Tournament					
Achievement Level for reporting					

*Use Ontario Achievement Levels 1, 2, 3, 4

Self-Assessment:

Comments: (Strengths, Needs, Next Steps)

Name ____________________ Date ______________

Master 9.5a

Lesson 9.5A: Rational Numbers

Curriculum Focus: Represent, compare, and order rational numbers.

In Lesson 9.5, you learned that a rational number is the quotient of two integers.
For example, $\frac{-6}{1}$, $\frac{-3}{4}$, and $\frac{1}{2}$ are rational numbers.

Since some decimals can be written as fractions, numbers such as –0.25, $3.\overline{6}$, and –1.8 are also rational numbers.

Explore

Work with a partner.
You will need a number line from –5 to +5.

- Order these numbers from least to greatest:
  $3.68, 3.5, 3\frac{1}{4}, 3\frac{2}{3}, 3.28, 3\frac{2}{5}$
  Use a calculator if it helps.

  How did you decide the correct order?
  Could you use a different strategy? If so, explain.
  Show each number on a number line.

- Order these numbers from least to greatest:
  $2.43, -2\frac{5}{8}, -2.05, \frac{5}{2}, -\frac{5}{4}, 2\frac{5}{6}, -0.45, 0.99$
  What strategies did you use for ordering these numbers?

Reflect & Share

Share your lists of numbers with another pair of students.
If the lists are different, which is correct? How do you know?
How is ordering rational numbers the same as ordering integers? How is it different?

Connect

Rational numbers can be ordered in a similar way to ordering integers.
On a number line, the negative numbers are to the left of zero and the positive numbers are to the right of zero.

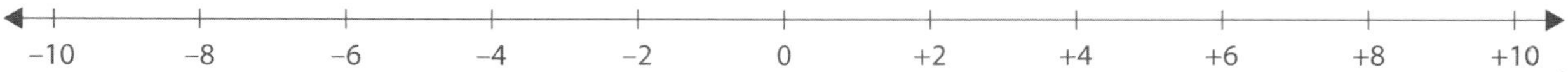

Name ____________________ Date ________________

Master 9.5b

Example

Place $-4\frac{3}{5}$ and –7.385 on a number line.

Which number is greater? How do you know?

Solution

$-4\frac{3}{5}$ is between –5 and –4.

Draw a number line from –5 to –4.
Divide the line in fifths.

Label the line. Mark a point at $-4\frac{3}{5}$.

–7.385 is between –8 and –7.
Draw a number line from –8 to –7.
Divide the line in tenths.
Label the line.
–7.385 is between –7.4 and –7.3, but closer to –7.4.

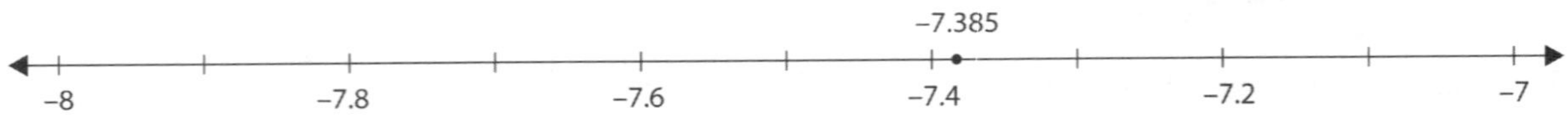

Draw one line to show both rational numbers.

Since $-4\frac{3}{5}$ is to the right of –7.385, then $-4\frac{3}{5} > -7.385$.

Practice

1. Place each rational number on a number line.

   a) $-\frac{4}{5}$ b) $4\frac{1}{3}$ c) $-3\frac{5}{7}$

2. Which rational number in each pair is greater? How do you know?

   a) $1\frac{3}{4}, -2\frac{1}{2}$ b) $-1\frac{3}{4}, -2\frac{1}{2}$ c) $-1\frac{3}{4}, 2\frac{1}{2}$ d) $1\frac{3}{4}, 2\frac{1}{2}$

Name ____________________ Date ______________

Master 9.5c

3. Order these rational numbers from least to greatest.
Show them on a number line.
$-\frac{3}{4}, \frac{1}{10}, -\frac{5}{2}, \frac{1}{3}, -\frac{1}{4}, 3, -4$

4. Jennifer wants to find the median height of her basketball team.
The team members' heights in metres are: 1.94, $1\frac{4}{5}$, 1.75, 1.88, $1\frac{3}{4}$, $1\frac{9}{10}$, $1\frac{7}{8}$, 1.80, 1.74
What is the median height?

5. Order these rational numbers from least to greatest.
Show them on a number line.
0.1, 0.33, –1.8, 2.4, –0.2, –2.1

6. Order these rational numbers from least to greatest.
Show them on a number line.
2.5, $\frac{3}{2}$, –2.2, 3.75, $-\frac{7}{10}$, $\frac{8}{3}$, –4.8

7. Karen recorded the temperature at noon everyday for one week in March.
The temperatures in degrees Celsius are: –10.6, 3, 8.4, –4.4, 0.5, –6, –0.8
a) Which is the lowest temperature?
b) Arrange the temperatures from least to greatest.
c) What is the mean temperature?

8. **Assessment Focus**

a) Arrange these numbers from least to greatest.
7.38, –3, $-\frac{2}{5}$, $7\frac{5}{8}$, $-4\frac{2}{3}$
b) Show the numbers in part a on a number line.
c) Between each two numbers in part a, mark and label another number.
Explain how you know the new numbers are in the correct places.

Reflect
What is a rational number?
Choose 3 rational numbers in fraction form.
Explain how to order the numbers from least to greatest.

Name ____________________ Date ________________

Master 9.6

Additional Activity 1: Integer Alphabet

Work with a partner.
The "value" of a word is the sum of the values of its individual letters.

Letter Values			
A	−1	N	+7
B	+1	O	−8
C	−2	P	+8
D	+2	Q	−9
E	−3	R	+9
F	+3	S	−10
G	−4	T	+10
H	+4	U	−11
I	−5	V	+11
J	+5	W	−12
K	−6	X	+12
L	+6	Y	−13
M	−7	Z	+13

1. Find the value of each phrase.

a) Maple Leaf ____________

b) Prince Edward Island ____________

c) Edmonton Eskimos ____________

2. Which partner's first name has the greater value? Show your work. ____________

3. Which partner's last name has the lesser value? Show your work. ____________

4. Write an 8-letter word whose value is greater than +15. ____________

5. Write a 6-letter word whose value is less than +5. ____________

6. Each partner writes a word from geometry.

a) Which word has the greater value? ____________

b) Which word has the lesser value? ____________

7. Each partner writes the name of a European country. Whoever writes the name with the lesser value wins. ____________

8. Each partner writes the name of a Canadian province. Whoever writes the name with the greater value wins. ____________

Take It Further: Find a word whose value is 0.

Name ____________________ Date ________________

Master 9.7

Additional Activity 2: What's the Temperature?

Work with a partner. Use the clues given below to solve the problem.

Problem

A newspaper listed the daily low and daily high temperatures of four cities: Rome, Orlando, Oslo, and Toronto. The low temperatures (in no particular order) were: –9°C, 16°C, –17°C, and 24°C. What were the low and high temperatures of each city?

Clue 1
Toronto's low temperature was less than 16°C.

Clue 2
Rome's high temperature was greater than 25°C.

Clue 3
Orlando's low temperature was greater than 14°C.

Clue 4
Toronto's high temperature was less than 16°C.

Clue 5
Rome's low temperature was not 24°C.

Clue 6
The difference between Toronto's high and low temperatures was 10°C.

Clue 7
Orlando's high temperature was 45°C greater than Oslo's low temperature.

Clue 8
Of the four cities, Oslo had the lowest temperature.

Clue 9
The difference between Rome's high temperature and Orlando's low temperature was 6° C.

Clue 10
Oslo's high temperature was 22°C less than Rome's low temperature.

Name ____________________ Date ________________

Master 9.8

Additional Activity 3: What's My Product?

Work with a partner.

You will need a deck of cards.

How to Play:

1. Remove the face cards (Jacks, Queens, Kings) from the deck.
   Use the remaining cards. An ace is 1.
   A red card represents a positive integer; for example, the 10 of diamonds is +10.
   A black card represents a negative integer; for example, the ace of spades is –1.

2. Place the cards face down in a pile.
   Players take turns to turn over the top 2 cards and find the product.
   The person with the greater product keeps all 4 cards.

3. If there is a tie, each player turns over 2 more cards and the person with the greater product keeps all 8 cards.

4. Play continues until all the cards have been used.
   The winner is the player with more cards.

Take It Further: Use the same cards. Take turns to turn over 3 cards and find their sum. The player with the lesser sum takes the cards. Play continues until 4 cards remain.

Name ____________________ Date ________________

Master 9.9a

Additional Activity 4: Integer Bingo

Play in groups of 4 or 5.
You will need *Expressions for Integer Bingo* (Master 9.9b) and counters.

Write an integer from –30 to +30 in each empty square below.
Each integer can only be used once.

Decide who will be the caller.
The caller calls out an integer expression (from Master 9.9b).
Players calculate the answer.
If the answer is on your Bingo card, cover the square with a counter.
Play continues.
The winner is the first person with 5 counters in a horizontal, vertical, or diagonal row.

B	I	N	G	O
		FREE		

Name ____________________ Date ________________

Master 9.9b

Expressions for Integer Bingo (For Caller Use Only)

Answers

1. Twice –4 .... (–8)
2. – 9 – 4 + 10 .... (–3)
3. Negative 8 minus negative 8 .... (0)
4. Which is greater: –18 or –36? .... (–18)
5. The opposite of –1 .... (1)
6. The sum of –7, –6, and –1 .... (–14)
7. 52 more than –30 .... (22)
8. The distance between –1 and 2 on a number line .... (3)
9. 10 subtracted from –6 .... (–16)
10. – 8 – (–14) .... (6)
11. – 8 × ☐ = – 88 .... (11)
12. – 6 × 5 .... (–30)
13. 19 multiplied by –1 .... (–19)
14. The quotient of – 22 ÷ (–11) .... (2)
15. 2 less than 0 .... (–2)
16. The product of –2 and –4 .... (8)
17. Which is greater: –19 or 17? .... (17)
18. – 7 – 10 .... (–17)
19. What is 4 – (–3) ? .... (7)
20. 15 minus 20 .... (–5)
21. –10 × (–3) .... (30)
22. 13 – 22 .... (–9)
23. 14 – (–1) .... (15)
24. –24 is twice what number? .... (–12)
25. – 6 + 4 + 12 .... (10)
26. What number multiplied by 3 equals –45? .... (–15)
27. –8 minus 3 .... (–11)
28. –3 times –6 .... (18)
29. Which is greater: –11 or –10? .... (–10)
30. –12 increased by 5 .... (–7)
31. –(–12) .... (12)
32. –4 minus –13 .... (9)
33. The opposite of 6 .... (–6)
34. The distance between –11 and –7 on a number line .... (4)
35. What number multiplied by 3 gives –3? .... (–1)
36. –1 plus what number gives –5? .... (–4)
37. What number times 5 gives 95? .... (19)
38. –18 + 5 .... (–13)
39. Twice what number is 32? .... (16)
40. 8 – (–5) .... (13)

Name ____________________ Date _______________

Master 9.10 **Step-by-Step 1**

Lesson 9.1, Question 7

You will need red and yellow coloured tiles and coloured pencils or markers.

Step 1 Pick some yellow tiles and an equal number of red tiles.
Which two integers are represented by these tiles? ______________
Add the integers. Sketch the tiles.
Write the addition equation. _______________________
Explain why the sum of opposite integers is zero.

____

Step 2 Pick tiles so you have more yellow than red.
Which two integers are represented by these tiles? ______________
Add the integers. Sketch the tiles.
Write the addition equation. _______________________
Explain why the sum has the sign it does.

____

Write two other addition expressions whose sum is positive. __________________

____

Step 3 Pick tiles so you have more red than yellow.
Which integers are represented by these tiles? ______________
Add the integers. Sketch the tiles.
Write the addition equation. _______________________
Explain why the sum has the sign it does.

____

Write two other addition expressions whose sum is negative. __________________

____

Step 4 When you look at an addition expression for two integers with opposite signs, how can you tell whether the sum will be zero, a positive integer, or a negative integer, without adding the integers?

____

____

____

____

Name ____________________ Date ________________

Master 9.11

Step-by-Step 2

Lesson 9.2, Question 7

In *Steps 1* to *3*, complete the pattern. Where possible, label each row of the pattern as:

- positive integer – positive integer
- positive integer – negative integer
- negative integer – positive integer
- negative integer – negative integer

Step 1

Pattern	Type of subtraction expression
(+4) – (+7) = _______	____________________
(+2) – (+5) = _______	____________________
(0) – (+3) = _______	____________________
(–2) – (+1) = _______	____________________
(–4) – (–1) = _______	____________________

Can you write a subtraction expression that equals –3 in the four ways listed above? Explain.

____

Step 2

Pattern	Type of subtraction expression
(+3) – (+1) = _______	____________________
(+2) – (0) = _______	____________________
(+1) – (–1) = _______	____________________
(0) – (–2) = _______	____________________
(–1) – (–3) = _______	____________________

Can you write a subtraction expression that equals +2 in the four ways listed above? Explain.

____

Step 3

Pattern	Type of subtraction expression
(+2) – (+2) = _______	____________________
(+1) – (+1) = _______	____________________
0 – 0 = _______	____________________
(–1) – (–1) = _______	____________________
(–2) – (–2) = _______	____________________

Can you write a subtraction expression that equals 0 in the four ways listed above? Explain.

____

Name ____________________ Date ______________

Master 9.12

Step-by-Step 3

Lesson 9.3, Question 3

Step 1 Evaluate each pair of expressions.

Addition Expression	Subtraction Expression
$-6 + 4 =$ _____	$4 - 6 =$ _____
$-7 + 3 =$ _____	$3 - 7 =$ _____
$-8 + 2 =$ _____	$2 - 8 =$ _____
$-9 + 1 =$ _____	$1 - 9 =$ _____

Step 2 Look across each row.

a) What patterns do you see in the expressions?

____

____

b) What patterns do you see in the answers?

____

____

Step 3 Write two more expressions that are related in the same way as those in *Step 1*.

____

____

Name ____________________ Date ________________

Master 9.13

Step-by-Step 4

Lesson 9.4, Question 8

Step 1 Complete the first four rows of the table.

Product	Answer	Number of negative factors in product	Sign of answer
(–2)(–3)			
(–2)(–3)(–4)			
(–2)(–3)(–4)(–5)			
(–2)(–3)(–4)(–5)(–6)			

Step 2 Extend the pattern 4 more rows. Use a calculator to complete the table.

Step 3 Use the results of *Steps 1* and *2*.

a) What is the sign of a product when it has an even number of negative factors? Explain.

____

b) What is the sign of a product when it has an odd number of negative factors? Explain.

____

Step 4 Complete this table. Use a calculator when necessary.

Product	Answer	Number of negative factors in product	Sign of answer
(–2)(+3)			
(–2)(+3)(–4)			
(–2)(+3)(–4)(+5)			
(–2)(+3)(–4)(+5)(–6)			
(–2)(+3)(–4)(+5)(–6)(+7)			
(–2)(+3)(–4)(+5)(–6)(+7)(–8)			

Do the rules from *Step 3* still apply when a product has positive and negative factors? Explain.

____

Name ____________________ Date ______________

Master 9.14

Step-by-Step 5

Lesson 9.5, Question 6

Step 1 Name the dividend, divisor, and quotient in the division statement $(+6) \div (-3) = -2$.

Dividend: _____ Divisor: _____ Quotient: _____

Step 2 Complete this table. The first row has been done for you.

Division Expression	Quotient	Quotient less than, more than, or between dividend and divisor?	Sign of dividend	Sign of divisor	Is divisor less than the quotient?
$(+10) \div (+2)$	+5	Between	+	+	Yes
$(+10) \div (+5)$					
$(+10) \div (-2)$					
$(+10) \div (-5)$					
$(-10) \div (+2)$					
$(-10) \div (+5)$					
$(-10) \div (-2)$					
$(-10) \div (-5)$					

When two integers are divided, the quotient is:

a) less than both integers when ______________________________

b) greater than both integers when ______________________________

c) between the two integers when ______________________________

Step 3 Evaluate.

$(+10) \div (+10) =$ ______ $(+10) \div (-10) =$ ______ $0 \div (+10) =$ ______

$(-10) \div (-10) =$ ______ $(-10) \div (+10) =$ ______ $0 \div (-10) =$ ______

When two integers are divided, the quotient is:

d) +1 when ______________________________

e) −1 when ______________________________

f) 0 when ______________________________

Name ____________________ Date ________________

Master 9.15

Step-by-Step 5A

Lesson 9.5A, Question 8

Use this number line.

Step 1 Between which two numbers on the line is:

7.38? ____________________

$-\frac{2}{5}$? ____________________

$7\frac{5}{8}$? ____________________

$-4\frac{2}{3}$? ____________________

Step 2 Use your answers in *Step 1* to place 7.38, –3, $-\frac{2}{5}$, $7\frac{5}{8}$, and $-4\frac{2}{3}$ on this line.

Step 3 Use the completed number line in *Step 2*.
Mark a point to represent a number between each pair of numbers in *Step 2*.
Write the new numbers.
Explain how you know the new numbers are in the correct places.

____

____

____

____

____

Name ______________________ Date __________________

Master 9.16

Step-by-Step 6

Lesson 9.6, Question 5

Look at the order of operations at the top of page 390 in the Student Book.

Step 1 Robert, Brenna, and Christian got different answers for this problem:

$-40 - 2[(-8) \div 2]$

Here is their work.

Robert	Brenna	Christian
$-40 - 2[\underbrace{(-8) \div 2}]$	$-40 - 2[\underbrace{(-8) \div 2}]$	$-40 - 2[\underbrace{(-8) \div 2}]$
$= -40 \underbrace{- 2[-4]}$	$= \underbrace{-40 - 2}[-4]$	$= -40 \underbrace{- 2[-4]}$
$= -40 + 8$	$= -42[-4]$	$= -40 - 8$
$= -32$	$= 168$	$= -48$

Step 2 Analyse the work in *Step 1*. Fill in the blanks.

______________________ has the correct answer.

________________ got the wrong answer because ______________________________

____

____

________________ got the wrong answer because ______________________________

____

____

Name ____________________ Date _______________

Master 9.17

Step-by-Step 7

Lesson 9.7, Question 6

You will need 12 congruent square tiles and two coordinate grids (Master 9.21).

Step 1 Make as many different rectangles as you can using all 12 tiles.
Draw the rectangles you make. Congruent rectangles are *not* different.

Step 2 **a)** How many different rectangles did you make? __________

b) How do you know that you made all the possible rectangles?

____

____

____

____

Step 3 Transfer the rectangles you made in *Step 1* onto a coordinate grid.
Label their vertices.

Step 4 How many different rectangles did you draw? __________________

Step 5 Suppose you did not use congruent square tiles to make the rectangles.
What other rectangles could you draw?
Show your work on a coordinate grid.

Name ____________________ Date ________________

Master 9.18

Step-by-Step 8

Lesson 9.8, Question 9

Step 1 Draw trapezoid A(–1, –1), B(1, –1), C(1, 3), D(–1, 1) on a coordinate grid.

Step 2 Translate and/or reflect the trapezoid and its images to make a design or pattern.

Step 3 Does the figure tessellate under these transformations? Explain.

____

____

Step 4 What could you do to the trapezoid so it does tessellate?
Try it to see if you are correct.
Explain what you did.

____

____

Name ____________________ Date ________________

Master 9.19

Step-by-Step 9

Lesson 9.9, Question 6

You will need a coordinate grid (Master 9.21) and tracing paper.

Step 1 Plot these points on a coordinate grid:
A(5, 0), B(2, 3), C(–4, 1), D(–2, –4), E(0, –2), F(4, –3).

Step 2 Rotate each point 90° clockwise about the origin.
Write the coordinates of the image points in the table below.
Complete the table.

Original	A(5, 0)	B(2, 3)	C(–4, 1)	D(–2, –4)	E(0, –2)	F(4, –3)
Image						

What patterns do you see in the coordinates of the points and their images?

____

Step 3 Rotate each point 180° about the origin.
Complete the table.

Original	A(5, 0)	B(2, 3)	C(–4, 1)	D(–2, –4)	E(0, –2)	F(4, –3)
Image						

What patterns do you see in the coordinates of the points and their images?

____

Step 4 Rotate each point 270° clockwise about the origin.
Complete the table.

Original	A(5, 0)	B(2, 3)	C(–4, 1)	D(–2, –4)	E(0, –2)	F(4, –3)
Image						

What patterns do you see in the coordinates of the points and their images?

____

Step 5 How could you use the patterns in *Steps 2* to *4* to draw rotation images without using tracing paper?

____

____

Name ____________________ Date ________________

Master 9.20

Number Lines

−10 −9 −8 −7 −6 −5 −4 −3 −2 −1 0 +1 +2 +3 +4 +5 +6 +7 +8 +9 +10

−10 −9 −8 −7 −6 −5 −4 −3 −2 −1 0 +1 +2 +3 +4 +5 +6 +7 +8 +9 +10

−10 −9 −8 −7 −6 −5 −4 −3 −2 −1 0 +1 +2 +3 +4 +5 +6 +7 +8 +9 +10

−10 −9 −8 −7 −6 −5 −4 −3 −2 −1 0 +1 +2 +3 +4 +5 +6 +7 +8 +9 +10

−10 −9 −8 −7 −6 −5 −4 −3 −2 −1 0 +1 +2 +3 +4 +5 +6 +7 +8 +9 +10

−10 −9 −8 −7 −6 −5 −4 −3 −2 −1 0 +1 +2 +3 +4 +5 +6 +7 +8 +9 +10

−10 −9 −8 −7 −6 −5 −4 −3 −2 −1 0 +1 +2 +3 +4 +5 +6 +7 +8 +9 +10

−100 −90 −80 −70 −60 −50 −40 −30 −20 −10 0 +10 +20 +30 +40 +50 +60 +70 +80 +90 +100

−100 −90 −80 −70 −60 −50 −40 −30 −20 −10 0 +10 +20 +30 +40 +50 +60 +70 +80 +90 +100

−50 −45 −40 −35 −30 −25 −20 −15 −10 −5 0 +5 +10 +15 +20 +25 +30 +35 +40 +45 +50

−20 −18 −16 −14 −12 −10 −8 −6 −4 −2 0 +2 +4 +6 +8 +10 +12 +14 +16 +18 +20

−200 −160 −120 −80 −40 0 +40 +80 +120 +160 +200

Name ____________________ Date ________________

Master 9.21

Coordinate Grid

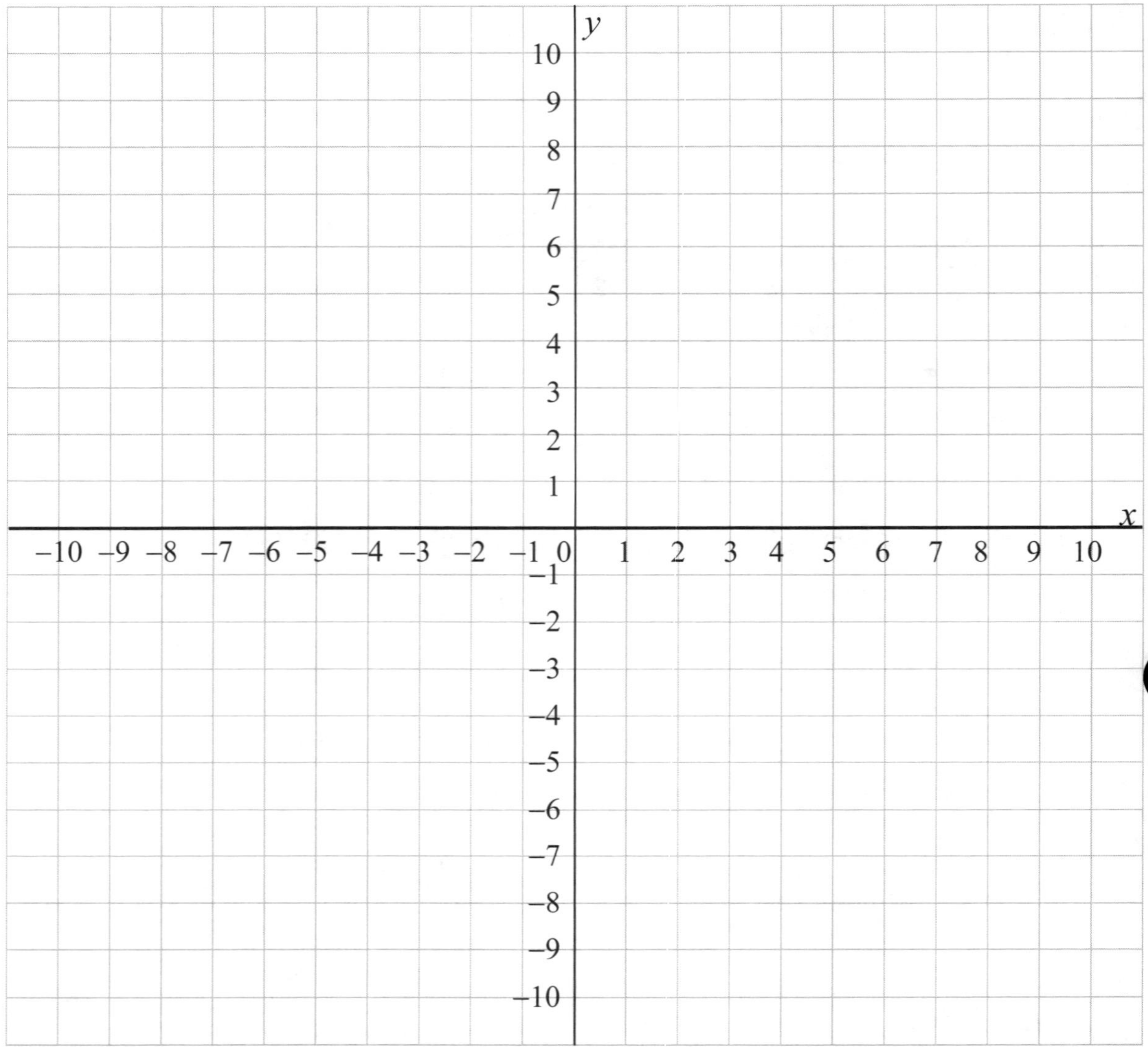

Name ______________________ Date ________________

Master 9.22a

Unit Test: Integers

1. Evaluate.

a) $(+2) + (-10)$ **b)** $(-3) + (-4) + (-6)$ **c)** $(+2) - (+4)$

d) $(-11) - (-5)$ **e)** $-7 + 11 - 10$ **f)** $(+6) \times (-5)$

g) $(-16) \times (-4)$ **h)** $(4)(-12)(-2)(-1)$ **i)** $(-15) \div (+3)$

j) $\frac{-30}{-30}$ **k)** $(-2)^3$ **l)** $\frac{(2)(-9)}{-3}$

2. Use any two of these integers: –12, –3, –7, and 10

a) What is the greatest product?

b) What is the greatest sum?

3. Write the next three terms in each pattern.
What is the pattern rule?

a) 4, –8, 16, –32, ___, ___, ___

b) 17, 12, 7, 2, ___, ___, ___

c) 5, –10, +15, –20, ___, ___, ___

Name ____________________ Date ______________

Master 9.22b

Unit Test continued

4. Draw a coordinate grid. Label the axes from –10 to +10. Copy △ABC. Draw the image of △ABC after each transformation.

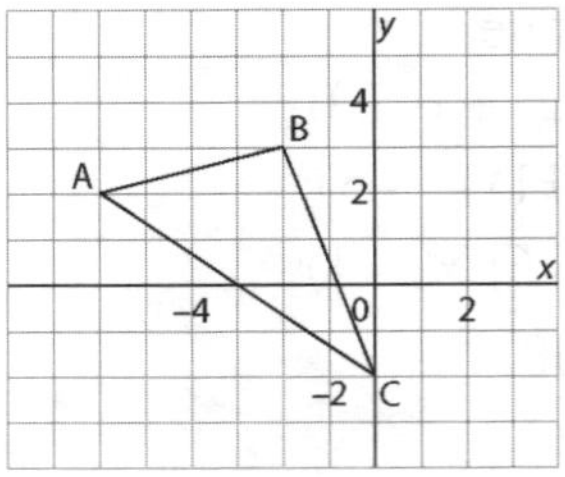

a) A translation 3 units left and 6 units up; label the image △ A′B′C′.

b) A reflection in the *x*-axis; label the image △ A″B″C″.

c) A rotation of –90° about the origin; label the image △ A‴B‴C‴.

d) A reflection in a line through (–10, –10) and (10, 10); label the image △ A⁗B⁗C⁗.

5. Evaluate each expression. Show all the steps.

a) $-20 \div (-5) - 2$

b) $3 - [(-15) \div (-5)]$

c) $-30 - (-5) \times (-10) \div 2$

d) $\dfrac{(-3)^2 + 1}{-2}$

6. One integer is 10 more than another. Their sum is 4. What are the two integers?

Name ______________________ Date ________________

Master 9.22c

Unit Test continued

7. When the sum of an integer and –4 is multiplied by 2, the answer is 4.

a) Write a number sentence to represent this situation.

b) Find the integer.

8. A golf tournament is five rounds. Pete shot –1 in two rounds, –2 on one round, and +1 on the other two rounds. The winning score was 5 under par.

a) What was Pete's final score?

b) Did Pete win the tournament? Explain.

9. Explain why the product of an integer multiplied by itself cannot be negative.

Name ______________________ Date ________________

Master 9.23

Sample Answers

Unit Test – Master 9.22

1. **a)** –8 **b)** –13 **c)** –2 **d)** –6 **e)** –6 **f)** –30
g) 64 **h)** –96 **i)** –5 **j)** 1 **k)** –8 **l)** 6

2. **a)** 84 **b)** 7

3. **a)** 64, –128, 256; Start at 4. Multiply by –2 each time.
b) –3, –8, –13; Start at 17. Subtract 5 each time.
c) +25, –30, +35; Start at 5. Skip count by 5s. Alternate the signs each time.

4. **a), b), c)**

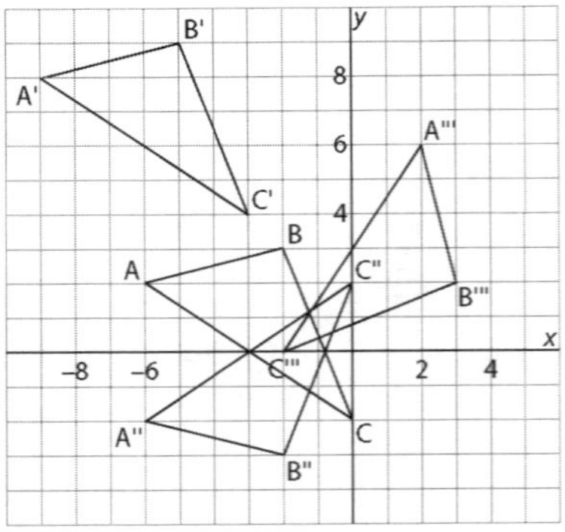

d)

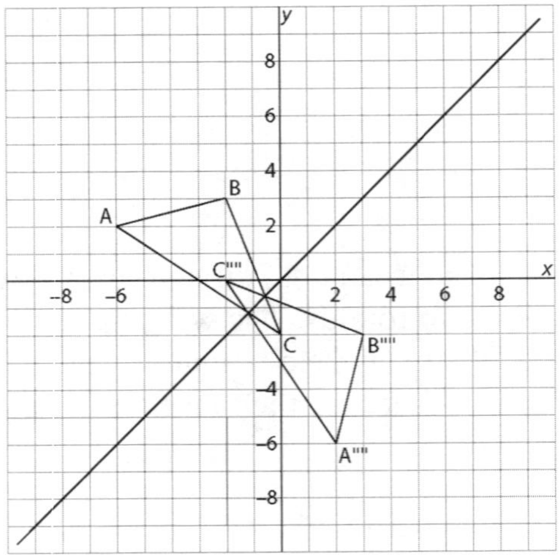

5. **a)** 2 **b)** 0
c) –55 **d)** –5

6. –3 and 7

7. **a)** 2[□ + (–4)] = 4 **b)** 6

8. **a)** –2
b) No. The winning score was –5. In golf, the lowest score wins.

9. An integer multiplied by itself cannot be negative because the product of any two integers with the same sign is positive.

Extra Practice Masters 9.24–9.34

Go to the CD-ROM to access editable versions of these Extra Practice Masters

Name ____________ Date ____________

Master 9.24 **Extra Practice 1**

Lesson 9.1: Adding Integers

1. Add. Sketch coloured tiles to show how you did it.
   a) $(+3)+(+5)$ b) $(+4)+(-4)$
   c) $(-5)+(+9)$ d) $(-5)+(-3)$
2. Add. Sketch number lines to show how you did it.
   a) $(+4)+(-6)$ b) $(-7)+(+10)$
   c) $(-3)+(+3)$ d) $(-3)+(-4)+(+5)$
3. a) Show three ways that -6 can be written as the sum of two integers.
   b) Show three ways that $+2$ can be written as the sum of a positive integer and a negative integer.
4. Which expressions have the same sum? What is this sum?
   a) $(+6)+(-2)$ b) $(+3)+(-6)$
   c) $(+8)+(-8)$ d) $(-8)+(+4)$
   e) $(+9)+(-4)$ f) $(-3)+(+7)$
   g) $(+12)+(-10)+(+2)$ h) $(-10)+(-2)+(+6)$
5. Add.
   a) $(-3)+(+15)$ b) $(-2)+(-3)+(-9)$
   c) $(-98)+(+48)$ d) $(+10)+(-9)+(-1)$
6. A submarine descends 42 m below the surface of the ocean. During the day, its changes in depth in metres are: $+5, -10, -16, +8, -12$. Write an integer that represents the submarine's depth at the end of the day.

Name ____________ Date ____________

Master 9.25 **Extra Practice 2**

Lesson 9.2: Subtracting Integers

1. Rewrite using addition, then evaluate.
   a) $(+5)-(+3)$ b) $(-8)-(+5)$
   c) $(-4)-(-4)$ d) $(+13)-(-6)$
   e) $(-35)-(-17)$ f) $(-71)-(+71)$
2. Complete each pattern. Extend the pattern for three more rows. Tell how you did it.
   a) $(+2)-(+3)=$ b) $(-2)-(+3)=$
   $(+2)-(+2)=$ $(-2)-(+2)=$
   $(+2)-(+1)=$ $(-2)-(+1)=$
   $(+2)-(0)=$ $(-2)-(0)=$
   $(+2)-(-1)=$ $(-2)-(-1)=$
3. Use a number line to subtract.
   a) $(+3)-(+2)$ b) $(-9)-(-2)$
   c) $(-6)-(+3)$ d) $(-4)-(-5)$
4. Evaluate.
   a) $(+4)-(+8)$ b) $(-5)-(-9)$
   c) $(-9)-(+4)$ d) $(-9)-(-10)$
   e) $(+5)-(-5)$ f) $(-9)-(-9)$
5. At 12:30, the temperature was -7°C. At 18:30, the temperature was -13°C. What was the change in temperature?

Name ____________ Date ____________

Master 9.26 **Extra Practice 3**

Lesson 9.3: Adding and Subtracting Integers

1. Evaluate.
   a) $(+25)-(+36)$ b) $25-36$
   c) $(+8)+(-9)$ d) $8-9$
2. Evaluate.
   a) $-25-4$ b) $16-(-8)$
   c) $18-22$ d) $-32-(-56)$
   e) $-16-(-24)$ f) $14-(-26)$
3. Evaluate.
   a) $12-4-8$ b) $-11-3-8$
   c) $-18-(-3)-5$ d) $-17-11-(-6)$
4. Darren and Jill are playing a game. Their total score is -8.
   a) Darren's score is 3. What is Jill's score?
   b) Show two other ways that Jill and Darren could have a total score of -8.

Name ____________ Date ____________

Master 9.27 **Extra Practice 4**

Lesson 9.4: Multiplying Integers

1. a) Evaluate.
   $(-3)+(-3)+(-3)+(-3)$
   b) Explain why $(+4)\times(-3)$ has the same answer as the expression in part a.
2. Complete each pattern. Extend the pattern for three more rows. Tell how you did it.
   a) $(+4)(+1)=$ b) $(+1)(+5)=$
   $(+4)(0)=$ $(0)(+5)=$
   $(+4)(-1)=$ $(-1)(+5)=$
   $(+4)(-2)=$ $(-2)(+5)=$
3. a) When is the product of two integers positive?
   b) When is the product of two integers negative?
4. Find each product.
   a) $(+2)(-9)$ b) $(-2)(-6)$
   c) $(+7)(-2)$ d) $(-3)(+4)$
   e) $(-1)(-1)(-1)$ f) $(-5)(+5)(-5)$
5. Find each product. Then order the answers from least to greatest.
   a) $(-3)(+6)$ b) $(-3)(+8)$
   c) $(+5)(-6)$ d) $(-4)(-5)$

Name ____________ Date ____________

Master 9.28 **Extra Practice 5**

Lesson 9.5: Dividing Integers

1. a) Evaluate each expression.

Multiplication	Division
$(+4)\times(-2)=$ ______	$(-8)\div(-2)=$ ______
$(-3)\times(+5)=$ ______	$(-15)\div(+5)=$ ______
$(-2)\times(-3)=$ ______	$(+6)\div(-3)=$ ______
$(+3)\times(+6)=$ ______	$(+18)\div(+6)=$ ______

   b) Look at the patterns in the signs in part a.
   How are the rules for the sign of a quotient of two integers related to the rules for the sign of a product of two integers?
2. a) When is the quotient of two integers positive?
   b) When is the quotient of two integers negative?
3. Divide.
   a) $(-100)\div(-10)$ b) $(-72)\div(+9)$
   c) $(+56)\div(-7)$ d) $(-42)\div(-6)$
   e) $(0)\div(-6)$ f) $(-9)\div(-9)$
4. Find each quotient. Then order the answers from least to greatest.
   a) $(+10)\div(-2)$ b) $(-15)\div(-5)$
   c) $(-36)\div(+12)$ d) $(0)\div(-10)$
   e) $(-8)\div(-8)$ f) $(-48)\div(+12)$
5. Maya recorded the noon temperature each day for a week.
   -12°C, -8°C, 3°C, 0°C, 1°C, -3°C, 5°C
   What was the mean temperature?

Name ____________ Date ____________

Master 9.29 **Extra Practice 5A**

Lesson 9.5A: Rational Numbers

1. Place each rational number on a number line.
   a) $-7\frac{2}{3}$ b) $-1\frac{3}{4}$ c) $6\frac{1}{4}$
2. Which rational number in each pair is greater? How do you know?
   a) $5\frac{3}{4}, 4\frac{7}{10}$ b) $-2\frac{4}{5}, -3\frac{1}{5}$ c) $-9\frac{2}{3}, 5\frac{1}{4}$
3. Arrange these rational numbers from least to greatest.
   $6\frac{5}{8}, -7\frac{3}{5}, -4\frac{1}{6}$
4. Arrange these rational numbers from least to greatest.
   $-1\frac{5}{6}, \frac{8}{9}, -3\frac{5}{12}$
5. Arrange each set of rational numbers from least to greatest.
   a) $2.3, -4\frac{2}{5}, 2\frac{1}{3}, -4\frac{4}{9}$
   b) $-0.524, \frac{3}{4}, -\frac{1}{3}, \frac{4}{9}, -\frac{1}{2}, 0.5$

Name ____________ Date ____________

Master 9.30 **Extra Practice 6**

Lesson 9.6: Order of Operations with Integers

1. Evaluate. State which operation you do first.
   a) $(+8)(+5)-(+4)$ b) $(-4)^2+9$
   c) $(+18)\div(-6)+2$ d) $(-3)+(-14)\div(-2)$
2. Evaluate.
   a) $(-2)^3$ b) $(-1)^2+5$
   c) $(2)^3\times(-2)$ d) $\frac{(-4)^3}{-4}$
   e) $\frac{(-5)(-4)}{2}$ f) $\frac{(-9)(-4)}{-3}$
3. Evaluate. Show all the steps.
   a) $(-4)(-2)+(-9)$ b) $(-7)(-2)-3$
   c) $4(-8)-9$ d) $-3(-8-11)$
   e) $-72\div9+4\times(-3)$ f) $\frac{-5(4)-4}{-6}$

Name ____________ Date ____________

Master 9.31 **Extra Practice 7**

Lesson 9.7: Graphing on a Coordinate Grid

1. Write the coordinates of each point from A to H.

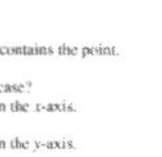

   A ______
   B ______
   C ______
   D ______
   E ______
   F ______
   G ______
   H ______
2. For each point in question 1, name the quadrant or axis that contains the point.
3. What can be said about the coordinates of a point P in each case?
   a) P is in Quadrant 2. b) P lies on the x-axis.
   c) P is in Quadrant 4. d) P lies on the y-axis.
   e) P is at the origin. f) P is in Quadrant 3.
4. a) Plot these points on a coordinate grid: K(−3, 4), A(4, 4), T(3, 2), E(−2, 2)
   b) Join the points. Which figure is formed?
5. a) Plot these points on a coordinate grid: A(3, 5), B(−4, 5), C(−4, 2)
   b) Find the coordinates of point D that forms rectangle ABCD.

Name ____________ Date ____________

Master 9.32 **Extra Practice 8**

Lesson 9.8: Graphing Translations and Reflections

1. Trapezoid ABCD has vertices A(−1, −1), B(1, −1), C(1, 3), and D(−1, 1).
   After a translation, the image of ABCD is A′(4, −3), B′(6, −3), C′(6, 1), D′(4, −1).
   a) Draw ABCD and A′B′C′D′ on a grid.
   b) Describe the translation.
2. Identify each reflection.
   a)

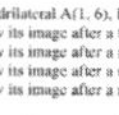

   b)

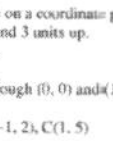

3. Plot quadrilateral A(1, 6), B(2, 4), C(4, 4), O(0, 0) on a coordinate grid.
   a) Draw its image after a translation 2 units left and 3 units up.
   b) Draw its image after a reflection in the x-axis.
   c) Draw its image after a reflection in the y-axis.
   d) Draw its image after a reflection in the line through (0, 0) and (10, 10).
4. Plot these points on a coordinate grid: A(2, 1), B(−1, 2), C(1, 5)
   a) Translate each point 3 units left and 4 units down to get image points A′, B′, C′.
   b) Write the coordinates of each point and its translation image.
   What patterns do you see in the coordinates?
5. Plot the points in question 4.
   a) Reflect each point in the x-axis to get image points A′, B′, C′.
   b) Write the coordinates of each point and its reflection image.
   What patterns do you see in the coordinates?
6. Plot the points in question 4.
   a) Reflect each point in the y-axis to get image points A′, B′, C′.
   b) Write the coordinates of each point and its reflection image.
   What patterns do you see in the coordinates?
7. Plot the points in question 4.
   a) Reflect each point in the line through (−10, −10) and (10, 10).
   b) Write the coordinates of each point and its reflection image.
   What patterns do you see in the coordinates?

Addison Wesley
Mathematics
Makes Sense

Program Authors

Trevor Brown

Antonietta Lenjosek

Cathy Heideman

Jim Mennie

Georgia Konis-Chatzis

A.J. Keene

Margaret Sinclair

Craig Featherstone

Jason Johnston

Bryn Keyes

Elizabeth Wood

Elizabeth Milne

David Sufrin

Don Jones

Sharon Jeroski

Lynn Strangway

Printed and bound in Canada

2 3 4 5 – TC – 09 08 07 06

PEARSON
Education
Canada

Addison Wesley

Ontario

Math Makes Sense 8

Ontario

Teacher Guide

Unit 10: Algebra

Pearson Education Canada

UNIT 10

Algebra

"Variables constitute an extremely powerful method of expressing the regularities found in mathematics. Variables enable us to use mathematical symbolism as a tool to think and help better understand mathematical ideas in the same way physical objects and drawings are used."

John A. Van de Walle

FOCUS STRAND
Patterning and Algebra

SUPPORTING STRAND
Number Sense and Numeration

TIPS
Adolescent students learn mathematics best in environments which allow for physical activity, social interaction, technological investigations, choice, variety, and meaningful input.

Mathematics Background

What Are the Big Ideas?

- An expression for the *n*th term of a pattern can be used to find the value of any term in the pattern.
- Algebra tiles can be used to solve equations where the coefficient of the variable is negative.
- An algebraic method can be used to solve an equation where the solution is a fraction or a decimal.

How Will the Concepts Develop?

Students investigate the distributive property of multiplication, and relate it and other properties to algebra.

Students use a table, a graph, and algebra to describe and extend a number pattern. They use a variable to write an expression for the *n*th term of a number pattern.

Students use algebra to describe and extend a geometric pattern, then write an algebraic expression for the *n*th term of a geometric pattern.

Students are introduced to the red variable tile, which represents $-x$. They use algebra tiles to solve linear equations with variables on both sides of the equal sign. Students use an algebraic method to solve equations where the solutions are fractions or decimals. They use equations to solve problems related to number patterns. They solve a word problem by solving a related equation.

Why Are These Concepts Important?

The ability to recognize patterns is key in many areas of mathematics, as well as in many other disciplines. For example, a lab technician may notice a pattern in data that leads to the discovery of a cure for a disease. Patterns are everywhere around us, and the ability to see these patterns and to make sense of them is essential.

Extending and generalizing patterns using variables helps students develop algebraic reasoning. Algebra is the language through which most of mathematics is communicated. The ability to analyse situations and to represent them algebraically are important skills.

Curriculum Overview

The codes refer to the 2005 revised curriculum.

Cluster 1: Patterns

Overall Expectations
- Represent linear growing patterns (where the terms are whole numbers) using graphs, algebraic expressions, and equations. (8m54)
- Model linear relationships graphically and algebraically . . . (8m55)

Specific Expectations
- Translate statements describing mathematical relationships into algebraic expressions and equations. (8m61)
- Evaluate algebraic expressions with up to three terms, by substituting fractions, decimals, and integers for the variables. (8m62)
- Represent, through investigation with concrete materials, the general term of a linear pattern, using one or more algebraic expressions. (8m56)
- Represent linear patterns graphically, using a variety of tools. (8m57)
- Determine a term, given its term number, in a linear pattern that is represented by a graph or an algebraic equation. (8m58)
- Model linear relationships using tables of values, graphs, and equations, through investigation using a variety of tools. (8m60)

Cluster 2: Algebraic Equations

Overall Expectations
- Model linear relationships . . . algebraically, and solve and verify algebraic equations, using a variety of strategies, including inspection, guess and check, . . . (8m55)

Specific Expectations
- Make connections between solving equations and determining the term number in a pattern, using the general term. (8m63)
- Translate statements describing mathematical relationships into algebraic . . . equations. (8m61)
- Solve and verify linear equations involving a one-variable term and having solutions that are integers, by using inspection, guess and check, . . . (8m64)

Launch

Lesson 10.1: Number Properties

Lesson 10.2: Describing Number Patterns

Lesson 10.3: Describing Geometric Patterns

Mid-Unit Review

Lesson 10.4: Solving Equations with Algebra Tiles

Lesson 10.5: Solving Equations Algebraically

Unit Review
Practice Test

Unit Problem
Choosing a Cell Phone Plan

Curriculum across the Grades

Grade 7	Grade 8
Students represent and make predictions about linear growing patterns. They develop and represent the general term of a linear growing pattern, using algebraic expressions involving one operation. Students compare pattern rules that generate a pattern by adding or subtracting a constant, or multiplying or dividing by a constant, to get the next term. Students translate phrases describing simple mathematical relationships into algebraic expressions, and evaluate algebraic expressions by substituting natural numbers for the variables. Students make connections between evaluating algebraic expressions and determining the term in a pattern using the general term. Students solve linear equations of the form $ax = c$, $c = ax$, and $ax + b = c$ by modelling with concrete materials, by inspection, or by guess and check.	Students represent the general term of a linear pattern, using one or more algebraic expressions. They represent linear patterns graphically. Students determine a term, given its term number, in a linear pattern that is represented by a graph or an algebraic equation. They model linear relationships using tables of values, graphs, and equations. Students translate statements describing mathematical relationships into algebraic expressions and equations, and evaluate expressions with up to three terms, by substituting fractions, decimals, and integers for the variables. Students make connections between solving equations and determining the term number in a pattern, using the general term. They solve and verify linear equations involving a one-variable term and having solutions that are integers.

Additional Activities

Number Pattern Search

For Extra Practice (*Appropriate for use after Lesson 10.2*)
Materials: *Number Pattern Search* (Master 10.5)
This activity provides practice in recognizing and describing number patterns.

The work students do: Students work alone. Students find as many number patterns as they can, and write a description of each pattern they find. The number patterns may appear horizontally, vertically, or diagonally. Students circle the number patterns as they find them. Each number pattern must contain at least 5 terms.

Take It Further: Students write an expression for the *n*th term of each number pattern.

Mathematical/Spatial/Logical
Individual Activity

Equation Concentration

For Extra Practice (*Appropriate for use after Lesson 10.4*)
Materials: *Equation Concentration* (Master 10.6a), *Concentration Cards* (Master 10.6b), scissors, algebra tiles (PM 27)
This activity reinforces the skills of solving equations.

The work students do: Students play with a partner. Students cut out the cards and lay them face down on the table. Player A turns over a card, then tries to find the matching card (a match consists of an equation and its solution). If Player A finds a matching card, she keeps the cards. If the cards do not match, Player A turns both cards over. Player B takes a turn. Play continues until all matches have been made.

Take It Further: Students make their own equation and solution cards, then add the cards to the game. Students play the game again.

Social/Kinesthetic/Mathematical
Partner Activity

Algebra Bingo

For Extra Practice (*Appropriate for use after Lesson 10.5*)
Materials: *Algebra Bingo* (Master 10.7a), *Algebra Bingo Problem Cards* (Master 10.7b), *Algebra Bingo Cards* (Master 10.7c), scissors, counters
Playing this game reinforces the skills of recognizing number patterns, evaluating expressions, writing equations, and solving equations.

The work students do: Students play in groups of 3. Each student plays with 2 bingo cards. Students place the problem cards face down in a pile. The cards are turned over one at a time. Students work on their own to solve the problem, then use counters to cover the solution wherever it appears on their cards. The first player to cover a row, column, or diagonal line wins.

Take It Further: Students play the game again. This time, students make their own bingo problem cards. Each problem must have a whole-number solution between 0 and 17. The first player to cover an entire card wins.

Mathematical/Social/Kinesthetic
Group Activity

Planning for Unit 10

Planning for Instruction

Suggested Unit time: About 2–3 weeks

Lesson	Time	Materials	Program Support
Launch, page 2	15–20 min		
Skills You'll Need, page 4	20–35 min		
10.1: Number Properties, page 6 Relate the distributive property and other properties to algebra.	optional but recommended	0.5-cm grid paper	PM 14: 0.5-cm Grid Paper Master 10.8: Step-by-Step 1 Master 10.15: Extra Practice 1
10.2: Describing Number Patterns, page 9 Write an expression for the *n*th term of a number pattern.	80–100 min	0.5-cm grid paper	PM 14: 0.5-cm Grid Paper Master 10.9: Step-by-Step 2 Master 10.16: Extra Practice 2
10.3: Describing Geometric Patterns, page 14 Write an expression for the *n*th term of a geometric pattern.	80–100 min	0.5-cm grid paper 1-cm grid paper	PM 14: 0.5-cm Grid Paper PM 20: 1-cm Grid Paper Master 10.10: Step-by-Step 3 Master 10.17: Extra Practice 3
Mid-Unit Review, page 20		0.5-cm grid paper calculators	PM 14: 0.5-cm Grid Paper
10.4: Solving Equations with Algebra Tiles, page 21 Use algebra tiles to solve equations involving whole numbers.	80–100 min	algebra tiles	PM 27: Algebra Tiles Master 10.11: Step-by-Step 4 Master 10.18: Extra Practice 4
10.5: Solving Equations Algebraically, page 26 Solve a problem by solving a related equation.	80–100 min		Master 10.12: Step-by-Step 5 Master 10.19: Extra Practice 5
Reading and Writing in Math: Writing a Journal, page 30			
Unit Review, page 33		0.5-cm grid paper isometric dot paper algebra tiles calculators	PM 14: 0.5-cm Grid Paper PM 23: Isometric Dot Paper PM 27: Algebra Tiles Extra Practice: Student Book page 497
Practice Test, page 35		calculators	
Unit Problem: Choosing a Cell Phone Plan, page 36	80–100 min	0.5-cm grid paper calculators coloured pencils or markers	PM 14: 0.5-cm Grid Paper

Planning for Assessment

Purpose	Tools and Process	Recording and Reporting
Diagnostic	*Unit Launch* Question; conference; scaffold problems throughout the unit	PM 8: Conference Prompts
Formative	*Explore* – Ongoing Assessment: Observe and Listen	Master 10.2 Ongoing Observations: Algebra PM 1: Inquiry Process Check List PM 6: Observation Record 1 PM 7: Observation Record 2 PM 8: Conference Prompts PM 2: Self-Assessment PM 3: Self-Assessment: Problem Solving PM 9: Work Sample Records
Summative	*Unit Review* *Unit Problem* – Performance Assessment Unit Test Review assessment records; add unit results to ongoing records	Master 10.1 Unit Rubric: Algebra Master 10.3 Performance Assessment Rubric: Choosing a Cell Phone Plan Master 10.4 Unit Summary: Algebra PM 10: Summary Class Records: Strands PM 11: Summary Class Records: Achievement Categories PM 12: Summary Record: Individual
Learning Skills/Mathematical Disposition	Observe and record throughout unit	PM 4: Learning Skills Check List PM 5: Mathematical Dispositions and Learning Skills

Program Masters (PM) are in the *Grade 8 Planning and Program Masters* module.
Extra Practice Masters are on the CD-ROM and printed in reduced format on page 58 of this module.

LESSON ORGANIZER (15–20 min)

Curriculum Focus: Activate prior learning about patterning.

ASSUMED PRIOR KNOWLEDGE

- ✓ Students can recognize patterns in a table of values.
- ✓ Students can write a pattern rule for a number pattern.
- ✓ Students can use a pattern rule to find the value of a given term.

UNIT 10

Algebra

Telecommunication companies offer telephone services.

These tables show the plans for cell phones for two companies. Each plan includes 200 free minutes.

What patterns do you see in the tables?

Write a pattern rule for each pattern. Describe each plan.

Assume the patterns continue. How could you find the total cost for 60 additional minutes for each plan?

Company A

Number of Additional Minutes	Total Cost ($)
0	35
4	36
8	37
12	38
16	39
20	40

Company B

Number of Additional Minutes
0
5
10
15
20
25

What You'll Learn

- Investigate number properties.
- Write an expression for the *n*th term of a pattern.
- Evaluate algebraic expressions by substituting fractions and integers.
- Read, write, and solve equations.
- Represent algebraic relationships using tables, graphs, and equations.

Why It's Important

- Algebra is used to communicate with symbols. It can be used to describe patterns.
- Patterns and equations are used to investigate changes in our world. For example, urban planners use equations to investigate population growth.

416

ACTIVATE PRIOR LEARNING

Have students look at the pictures and tables on pages 416 and 417 of the Student Book.

Ask questions, such as:

- What means of telecommunication do we have available today?
  (*Cell phones, the Internet, satellite dishes, pagers*)
- What patterns do you see in the table for Company A?
  (*The number of additional minutes increases by 4 each time. The total cost increases by $1 each time.*)
- What is a pattern rule for the number of additional minutes? (*Start at 0. Add 4 each time.*) For the total cost? (*Start at 35. Add 1 each time.*)
- What patterns do you see in the table for Company B?
  (*The number of additional minutes increases by 5 each time. The total cost increases by $1 each time.*)
- What is a pattern rule for the number of additional minutes? (*Start at 0. Add 5 each time.*) For the total cost? (*Start at 40. Add 1 each time.*)
- How could you find the total cost for 60 additional minutes for each plan?
  (*I could extend each table. I could graph each table of values, then extend the graph to 60 additional minutes. I could look for a relationship between the number of additional minutes and the total cost for each company.*)
- What is the cost for 60 additional minutes for Company A? (*$50*) Company B? (*$52*)

Tell students that, in this unit, they will evaluate expressions by substituting fractions and integers, investigate number properties, write an expression for the *n*th term of a pattern, use a table, a graph, and algebra to describe and extend a number pattern, and read, write, and solve equations. At the end of the unit, students will demonstrate what they have learned by choosing a cell phone plan.

FROM THE LIBRARY

Marvels of Math: Fascinating Reads and Awesome Activities by Kendall Haven.
Teacher Ideas Press, 1998.
ISBN: 1563085852
This book contains 16 stories of mathematical innovations. Each story is full of interesting facts, and includes a list of mathematical terms and definitions, discussion questions with answers, and activities and experiments related to the theme of the story. This book is sure to spark students' interest in math.

REACHING ALL LEARNERS

Some students may benefit from using the virtual manipulatives on the e-Tools CD-ROM.
The e-Tools appropriate for this unit are *Counters* and *Spreadsheet/Data/Grapher*.

DIAGNOSTIC ASSESSMENT

What to Look For	What to Do
✔ Students can recognize patterns in a table of values. ✔ Students can write a pattern rule for a number pattern. ✔ Students can use a pattern rule to find the value of a given term.	***Extra Support:*** Students who have difficulty recognizing the patterns in a table of values may benefit from subtracting or dividing consecutive terms to see if there is a constant number added or multiplied. *Work on this skill during Lessons 10.2 and 10.3.* Students who have difficulty writing a pattern rule may benefit from using these "starters" to help them find a pattern rule. Start at ___. Add ___ each time. Start at ___. Subtract ___ each time. Start at ___. Multiply by ___ each time. Start at ___. Divide by ___ each time. *Work on this skill during Lessons 10.2 and 10.3.* Students who have difficulty using a pattern rule to find the value of a given term may benefit from working with simple patterns, such as: Start at 3. Add 2 each time. What is the 5th term? *Work on this skill during Lessons 10.2 and 10.3.*

LESSON ORGANIZER 20–35 min

Skills in Review

- Writing expressions and equations (8m61)
- Evaluating expressions (8m62)

Alternative Example 1

a) Write an algebraic expression for this statement:
Five less than a number divided by three

b) Write an equation for this sentence:
Two more than six times a number is 20.

Solution

a) Five less than a number divided by three
Let x represent the number.
Then, a number divided by three is $\frac{x}{3}$.
Five less than $\frac{x}{3}$ is: $\frac{x}{3} - 5$

b) Two more than six times a number is 20.
Let n represent the number.
Six times a number is: $6n$
Two more than $6n$ is: $6n + 2$
The equation is: $6n + 2 = 20$

UNIT 10 **Skills You'll Need**

Writing Expressions and Equations

We use a letter, such as x or n, to represent a number.
We can write an algebraic expression to represent a word statement.
For example, "a number plus five," or "five more than a number" can be written as $n +$

When we write an algebraic expression as equal to a number or another expression, we have an equation.
For example, $n + 5 = 8$ is an equation.

Example 1

a) Write an algebraic expression for this statement:
Three more than four times a number

b) Write an equation for this sentence:
A number divided by four is 5.

Solution

a) Three more than four times a number
Let x represent the number.
Then, four times a number is $4x$.
Three more than $4x$ is:
$4x + 3$ or $3 + 4x$

b) A number divided by four is 5.
Let z represent the number.
z divided by four is: $\frac{z}{4}$
The equation is: $\frac{z}{4} = 5$

✓ **Check**

1. Write an algebraic expression for each statement.
   a) a number multiplied by seven $7x$
   b) six less than a number $n - 6$
   c) five more than three times a number $3x + 5$
   d) three less than five times a number $5n - 3$

2. Write an equation for each sentence.
   a) A number divided by seven is 6. $\frac{x}{7} = 6$
   b) The sum of eight and a number is 17. $8 + n = 17$
   c) Five more than two times a number is 11. $2x + 5 = 11$

418 UNIT 10: Algebra

Writing Expressions and Equations

Ensure students understand the difference between an expression and an equation. A sentence that contains the verb "is" or "equals" may be written as an equation. As soon as we equate an algebraic expression to a number, it becomes an equation. An equation must have an equal sign.

Review the words that can be used to suggest addition (more than, increased by, sum to), subtraction (less than, subtracted from, decreased by), multiplication (times, product, double, twice), and division (divided by). Ensure students understand that it makes no difference which letter they use as a variable; for example, $n + 5$ and $d + 5$ represent the same expression. Remind students that $3 \times n$ and $3n$ are equivalent.

Show students that an expression can often be put into words in several different ways. For example, these statements all represent $n + 9$: a number plus nine
9 more than a number
a number increased by 9
the sum of a number and 9

Common Misconceptions

➤ Students write the algebraic expression $3 - n$ for the statement 3 less than a number.

How to Help: Encourage students to check the expression using a specific example; for example, if the number is 10, "3 less than the number" is $10 - 3 = 7$. If we evaluate $3 - n$ for $n = 10$, we get $3 - 10 = -7$. Remind students that 3 less than a number is the same as a number decreased by 3. So, the expression must be $n - 3$.

aluating Expressions

aluate an algebraic expression for a particular value of the variable, the variable with a number. Then, find the value of the expression. mber we substitute can be a fraction or an integer.

Example 2

Evaluate the expression $2x + 3y + 4z$ for $x = -1$, $y = \frac{1}{3}$, and $z = \frac{1}{2}$.

Solution

$2x + 3y + 4z$

Substitute: $x = -1$, $y = \frac{1}{3}$, and $z = \frac{1}{2}$

$2x + 3y + 4z = 2(-1) + 3(\frac{1}{3}) + 4(\frac{1}{2})$

$= 2 \times (-1) + 3 \times \frac{1}{3} + 4 \times \frac{1}{2}$ Multiply first.

$= -2 + 1 + 2$ Then add.

$= -2 + 3$

$= 1$

Check

Evaluate each expression.

a) $3 + x$ for $x = \frac{1}{2}$ $\frac{7}{2}$ or $3\frac{1}{2}$ b) $3 - x$ for $x = -2$ 5 c) $3x$ for $x = \frac{1}{4}$ $\frac{3}{4}$

Evaluate each expression for $p = \frac{2}{3}$ and $q = \frac{1}{4}$.

a) $p + q$ $\frac{11}{12}$ b) $p - q$ $\frac{5}{12}$ c) pq $\frac{1}{6}$

Evaluate each expression for $m = \frac{2}{5}$ and $n = \frac{1}{2}$.

a) $2m + n$ $\frac{13}{10}$ b) $2n + m$ $\frac{7}{5}$ c) $2m + 2n$ $\frac{9}{5}$

d) $2m - n$ $\frac{3}{10}$ e) $2n - m$ $\frac{3}{5}$ f) $2n - 2m$ $\frac{1}{5}$

g) mn $\frac{1}{5}$ h) $2mn$ $\frac{2}{5}$ i) $\frac{1}{2}mn$ $\frac{1}{10}$

Evaluate each expression in question 5 for $m = -3$ and $n = -6$.

Evaluate each expression.

a) $3x - 2y + 4z$, when $x = \frac{3}{4}$, $y = \frac{1}{5}$, $z = \frac{5}{4}$ $\frac{137}{20}$ or $6\frac{17}{20}$

b) $3x + 5y - 3z$, when $x = \frac{5}{4}$, $y = \frac{1}{6}$, $z = \frac{2}{3}$ $\frac{31}{12}$ or $2\frac{7}{12}$

c) $3x + 3y - 2z$, when $x = \frac{1}{5}$, $y = \frac{4}{3}$, $z = \frac{1}{15}$ $\frac{67}{15}$ or $4\frac{7}{15}$

Evaluate each expression in question 7 for $x = 2$, $y = -4$, and $z = -1$.

Skills You'll Need 419

Alternative Example 2

Evaluate the expression $4x + 7y - 2z$ for $x = \frac{3}{4}$, $y = \frac{1}{5}$, and $z = \frac{1}{3}$.

Solution

$4x + 7y - 2z$

Substitute: $x = \frac{3}{4}$, $y = \frac{1}{5}$, and $z = \frac{1}{3}$

$4x + 7y - 2z = 4(\frac{3}{4}) + 7(\frac{1}{5}) - 2(\frac{1}{3})$

$= 4 \times \frac{3}{4} + 7 \times \frac{1}{5} - 2 \times \frac{1}{3}$ Multiply first.

$= 3 + \frac{7}{5} - \frac{2}{3}$ Write the fractions with a common denominator, 15.

$= \frac{45}{15} + \frac{21}{15} - \frac{10}{15}$ Add or subtract in order from left to right.

$= \frac{56}{15}$ or $3\frac{11}{15}$

Sample Answers

6. a) −12 **b)** −15 **c)** −18 **d)** 0

e) −9 **f)** −6 **g)** 18 **h)** 36

i) 9

8. a) 10 **b)** −11 **c)** −4

Evaluating Expressions

Ensure students understand that the order of operations must be followed when they evaluate an algebraic expression. Remind students of the order of operations:

- Do the operations in brackets first.
- Do any work with exponents.
- Multiply and divide, in order, from left to right.
- Add and subtract, in order, from left to right.

Use the *Alternative Example 2* to show students that when we substitute fractions for the variables, it is often necessary to find a common denominator before we can add or subtract.

Tell students that we often put negative integers in brackets to help us distinguish between the negative sign and the subtraction sign.

For example, evaluate $2x - 3y$ for $x = 5$ and $y = -2$.

$2x - 3y = 2(5) - 3(-2)$

$= 10 - (-6)$

$= 10 + 6$

$= 16$

Common Misconceptions

➤ Students have difficulty working with "unfriendly" fractions because they do not simplify before multiplying.

How to Help: Use this example to demonstrate the importance of simplifying:

Evaluate $4x + 5y$ for $x = \frac{1}{8}$ and $y = \frac{2}{15}$

$4x + 5y = 4(\frac{1}{8}) + 5(\frac{2}{15})$

$= \frac{4}{8} + \frac{10}{15}$ The lowest common denominator is $8 \times 15 = 120$.

This time, simplify first:

$4x + 5y = 4(\frac{1}{8}) + 5(\frac{2}{15})$ Notice that each numerator and denominator has common factors.

$= \not{4}^{1}(\frac{1}{\not{8}_{2}}) + \not{5}^{1}(\frac{2}{\not{15}_{3}})$ Simplify.

$= \frac{1}{2} + \frac{2}{3}$ These fractions are much easier to work with.

$= \frac{3}{6} + \frac{4}{6}$ Write each fraction with common denominator 6.

$= \frac{7}{6}$

Encourage students to simplify before multiplying to make "friendly" fractions.

Number Properties

LESSON ORGANIZER (optional but recommended)

Curriculum Focus: Relate the distributive property and other properties to algebra.

Student Materials
- 0.5-cm grid paper (PM 14)

Optional
- Step-by-Step 1 (Master 10.8)
- Extra Practice 1 (Master 10.15)

Vocabulary: distributive property, expand

Assessment: Master 10.2 Ongoing Observations: Algebra

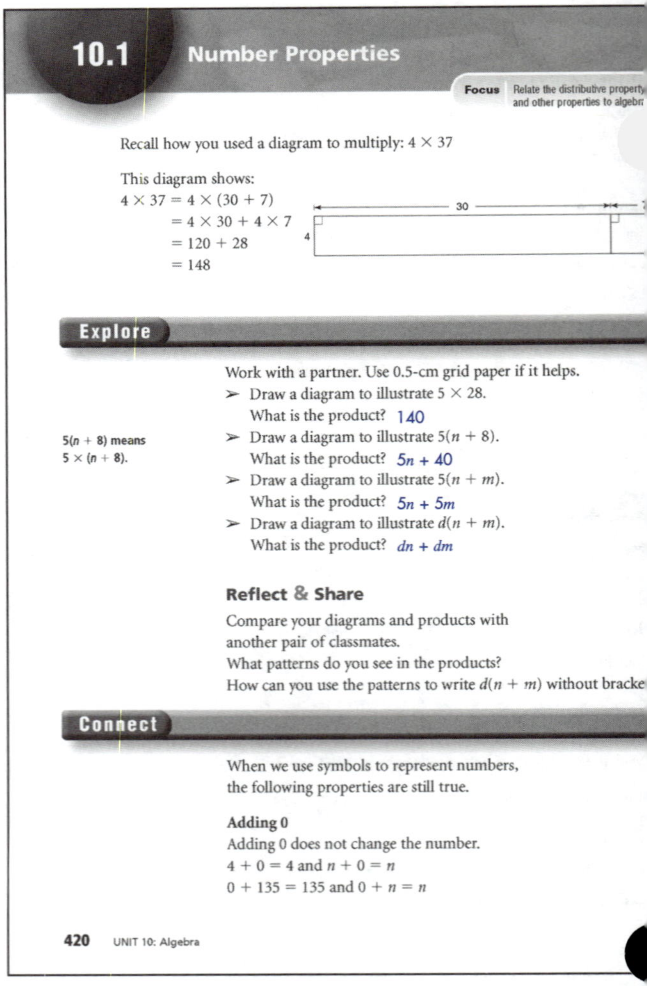

10.1 Number Properties

Focus Relate the distributive property and other properties to algebra

Recall how you used a diagram to multiply: 4×37

This diagram shows:

$$\begin{aligned} 4 \times 37 &= 4 \times (30 + 7) \\ &= 4 \times 30 + 4 \times 7 \\ &= 120 + 28 \\ &= 148 \end{aligned}$$

Explore

$5(n + 8)$ means $5 \times (n + 8)$.

Work with a partner. Use 0.5-cm grid paper if it helps.

➢ Draw a diagram to illustrate 5×28.
What is the product? 140

➢ Draw a diagram to illustrate $5(n + 8)$.
What is the product? $5n + 40$

➢ Draw a diagram to illustrate $5(n + m)$.
What is the product? $5n + 5m$

➢ Draw a diagram to illustrate $d(n + m)$.
What is the product? $dn + dm$

Reflect & Share

Compare your diagrams and products with another pair of classmates.
What patterns do you see in the products?
How can you use the patterns to write $d(n + m)$ without bracke

Connect

When we use symbols to represent numbers, the following properties are still true.

Adding 0

Adding 0 does not change the number.

$4 + 0 = 4$ and $n + 0 = n$

$0 + 135 = 135$ and $0 + n = n$

420 UNIT 10: Algebra

Key Math Learnings

1. The distributive property of multiplication states that the product of $a(b + c)$ is the same as the sum $ab + ac$.
2. The number properties adding 0, multiplying by 1, multiplying by 0, the order of addition and multiplication, and the distributive property are true for variables.

Curriculum Note

Although this material is not directly required by the Grade 8 curriculum, this lesson is recommended because the properties of number also apply to variables in algebraic expressions and equations.

BEFORE — Get Started

Have students think of an array for 13×3: 13 rows of 3 counters.

The product of 13×3 is equal to the sum of the products 10×3 and 3×3.

$$\begin{aligned} 13 \times 3 &= (10 \times 3) + (3 \times 3) \\ &= 30 + 9 \\ &= 39 \end{aligned}$$

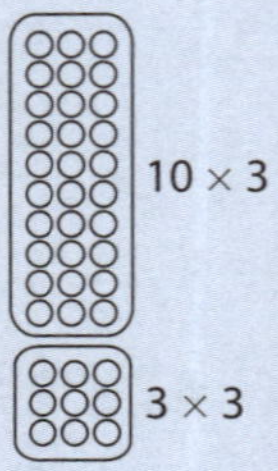

We can also use a diagram to illustrate multiplication, as shown at the top of page 420 of the Student Book. Ensure students understand that 37 is broken down into 2 lesser numbers, which make the multiplication easier.

Present *Explore*. Have 0.5-cm grid paper (PM 14) available.

DURING — Explore

As students work, ask questions, such as:

- What is the width of the diagram for 5×28? (5)
- How did you represent the length 28? (*As lengths of 20 and 8*)
- How did you illustrate 5×28? (*I drew a 5 by 28 rectangle, then divided the rectangle into 2 smaller rectangles, one of length 20 and the other of length 8.*)
- What is 5×28? ($5 \times 28 = (5 \times 20) + (5 \times 8) = 100 + 40 = 140$)
- How did you illustrate $5(n + 8)$? (*I used the illustration for 5×28 and replaced 20 with the variable n.*)
- What is the product of $5(n + 8)$? ($(5 \times n) + (5 \times 8) = 5n + 40$)
- What is the product of $5(n + m)$? ($(5 \times n) + (5 \times m) = 5n + 5m$)
- What is the product of $d(n + m)$? ($(d \times n) + (d \times m) = dn + dm$)

Multiplying by 1
When 1 is a factor, the product is always the other factor.
$1 \times 11 = 11$ and $1 \times n = n$
$256 \times 1 = 256$ and $n \times 1 = n$

Multiplying by 0
When 0 is a factor, the product is always 0.
$15 \times 0 = 0$ and $n \times 0 = 0$
$0 \times 137 = 0$ and $0 \times n = 0$

Order of addition and multiplication
When you add, the order does not matter.
$9 + 4 = 13$ and $4 + 9 = 13$ $\quad a + b = b + a$
When you multiply, the order does not matter.
$6 \times 8 = 48$ and $8 \times 6 = 48$ $\quad ab = ba$

Distributive Property
We will investigate $a(b + c)$ and $ab + ac$ for different values of a, b, and c.
Recall that $a(b + c)$ means $a \times (b + c)$, ab means $a \times b$, and ac means $a \times c$.

a	b	c	(b + c)	a(b + c)	ab	ac	ab + ac
2	4	7	11	22	8	14	22
3	6	2	8	24	18	6	24
7	1	1	2	14	7	7	14
12	8	3	11	132	96	36	132
0	7	5	12	0	0	0	0

can illustrate property with agram.

The numbers in these columns are the same.
This table illustrates the **distributive property** of multiplication:
$a(b + c) = ab + ac$
That is, the product of $a(b + c)$ is the same as the sum $ab + ac$.

Example

Use the distributive property to write each expression as a sum of terms.

a) $7(c + 2)$ **b)** $2(2a + 3b + 4)$

REACHING ALL LEARNERS

Early Finishers

Have students write two formulas for the surface area of a rectangular prism and two formulas for the surface area of a triangular prism. Students explain how both pairs of formulas illustrate the distributive property.

Common Misconceptions

➤ Students simplify expressions such as $6 + 5x$ to $11x$.
How to Help: Ensure students understand that only like terms can be added. $4x$ and $5x$ are like terms because they contain the same variable. 2 and 6 are like terms because they contain no variables. The terms 6 and $5x$ are not like terms and cannot be combined.

Calculator Skills

Students could work backward. A number divided by 43.2 is 35.
So, the number is $43.2 \times 35 = 1512$.
To find what the answer should have been, students then multiply:
$1512 \times 43.2 = 65\ 318.4$

Sample Solutions

1.

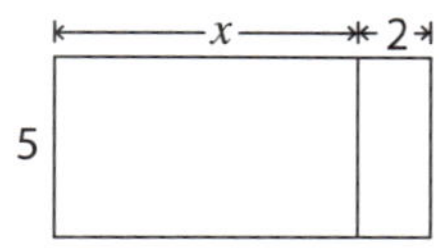

$5(x + 2) = (5 \times x) + (5 \times 2)$
$= 5x + 10$

3. $P = 2(b + h)$ and $P = 2b + 2h$
I used the distributive property to expand the first formula:
$P = 2(b + h) = 2b + 2h$. This is the second formula.

AFTER Connect

Invite students to share their diagrams and products with the class.

What you might see:

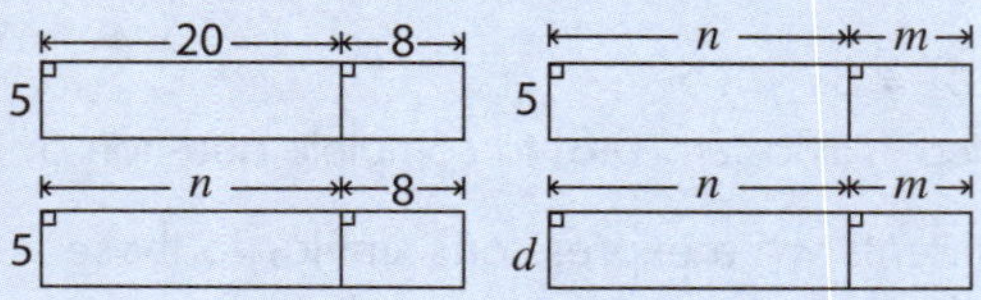

Ask:

- What patterns do you see in the products?
  (The first term is the product of the width and the first length. The second term is the product of the width and the second length. The product is the sum of these two terms.)
- How can you use the patterns to write $d(n + m)$ without brackets?
  (I multiply each variable in brackets by d, then write the sum of the products; dn + dm.)

Use *Connect* to review the number properties. Students should be familiar with these properties when they are applied to numbers. Ensure students understand that these properties are also true for variables. Use the *Example* to demonstrate how the distributive property can be applied to expressions that contain numbers and variables, and to expressions with more than 2 terms.

Practice

Have 0.5-cm grid paper (PM 14) available for question 1.

Assessment Focus: Question 6

In each of parts a and c, students could use the distributive property to expand the second expression, then compare their result to the first expression. In parts b and d, students should use their knowledge of the other properties of number.

4. When you multiply, the order does not matter.
For example, $3 \times 4 = 12$ and $4 \times 3 = 12$
So, $h \times b = b \times h$, or $hb = bh$

6. a) Using the distributive property, $2(x + 20) = (2 \times x) + (2 \times 20)$
$= 2x + 40$

$2x + 20 \neq 2x + 40$

b) Only like terms can be added. Since $3x$ and 7 are not like terms, $3x + 7 \neq 10x$

c) Using the distributive property, $2(t + 3) = (2 \times t) + (2 \times 3)$
$= 2t + 6$

Since the order of addition does not matter, $6 + 2t = 2t + 6$

d) Order of addition does not matter. So, $9 + x = x + 9$

REFLECT: The distributive property for multiplication states that the product of $a(b + c)$ is the same as the sum $ab + bc$.
For example, I can illustrate the distributive property with this diagram:

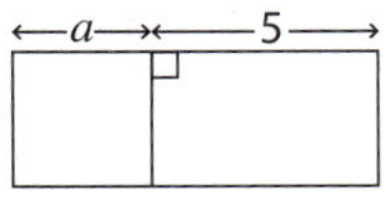

$3(a + 5) = (3 \times a) + (3 \times 5)$
$= 3a + 15$

Assignment Guidelines

If your students do not have time to complete all the *Practice* questions on page 422, these questions provide minimum curriculum coverage: 2, 4, 5, 6, *Reflect*

To assess the 4 Achievement Chart categories listed in the curriculum document, have students complete these *Practice* questions:

Knowledge and Understanding: 4
Thinking: 6
Application: 5
Communication: *Reflect*

Solution

a) $7(c + 2) = 7(c) + 7(2)$
$= 7c + 14$

b) $2(2a + 3b + 4) = 2(2a) + 2(3b) + 2(4)$
$= 4a + 6b + 8$

In the *Example*, when we use the distributive property, we expar

Practice

1. Draw a rectangle to show that $5(x + 2)$ and $5x + 10$ are equivalent.

2. Expand.
a) $2(x + 10)$ $2x + 20$
b) $5(x + 1)$ $5x + 5$
c) $10(x + 2)$ $10x + 20$
d) $6(12 + 6y)$ $72 + 36y$
e) $8(8 + 9y)$ $64 + 72y$
f) $5(7y + 6)$ $35y + 30$

3. Write two formulas for the perimeter, *P*, of a rectangle. Explain how the formulas illustrate the distributive property.

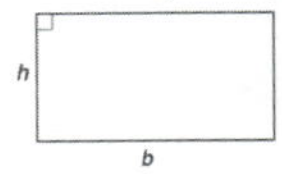

Calculator Skills

Instead of multiplying a number by 43.2, a student divided it by 43.2.
The student got the answer 35. What should the answer have been? 65 318.4

4. Explain how you know $hb = bh$.
Use an example to justify your answer.

5. Expand.
a) $5(2x + 2y + 2)$ $10x + 10y + 10$
b) $4(3x + 5y + 1)$ $12x + 20y + 4$
c) $8(7x + 3y +$ $56x + 24y +$

6. **Assessment Focus** Which expressions in each pair are equivalent? Explain your reasoning.
a) $2x + 20$ and $2(x + 20)$
b) $3x + 7$ and $10x$
c) $6 + 2t$ and $2(t + 3)$
d) $9 + x$ and $x + 9$

Reflect

What is the distributive property?
Include a diagram with your explanation.

422 UNIT 10: Algebra

ASSESSMENT FOR LEARNING

What to Look For	What to Do
Knowledge and Understanding ✔ Students understand the number properties and how they relate to algebra.	***Extra Support:*** Students who have difficulty expanding an expression may benefit from using arrows; for example, $3(x + 5) = (3 \times x) + (3 \times 5) = 3x + 15$ Students can use Step-by-Step 1 (Master 10.8) to complete question 6.
Communication ✔ Students can use a diagram to explain the distributive property.	***Extra Practice:*** Have students write expressions similar to those in *Practice* question 5. Students trade expressions with a classmate and expand their classmate's expression. Students can complete Extra Practice 1 (Master 10.15).
Application ✔ Students can use the distributive property to expand algebraic expressions.	***Extension:*** Have students use the distributive property to write $(3 + 2)(x + 3)$ as a sum of terms, without simplifying first. Students check their answer by using the distributive property to expand $5(x + 3)$.

Recording and Reporting
Master 10.2 Ongoing Observations: Algebra

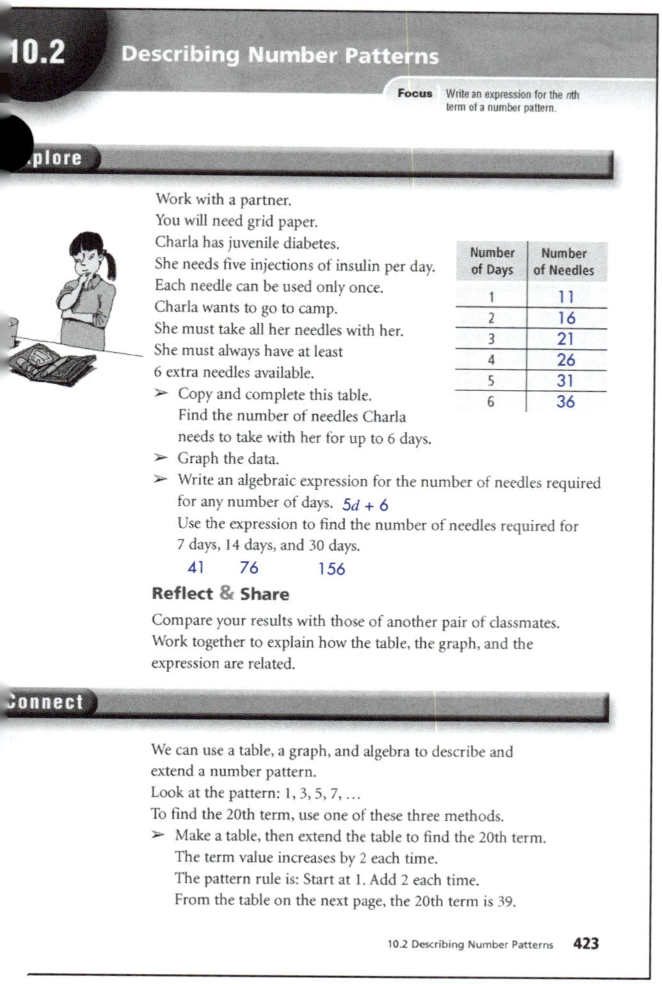
10.2 Describing Number Patterns

Focus Write an expression for the *n*th term of a number pattern.

Explore

Work with a partner.
You will need grid paper.
Charla has juvenile diabetes.
She needs five injections of insulin per day.
Each needle can be used only once.
Charla wants to go to camp.
She must take all her needles with her.
She must always have at least 6 extra needles available.

Number of Days	Number of Needles
1	11
2	16
3	21
4	26
5	31
6	36

➢ Copy and complete this table. Find the number of needles Charla needs to take with her for up to 6 days.
➢ Graph the data.
➢ Write an algebraic expression for the number of needles required for any number of days. $5d + 6$
Use the expression to find the number of needles required for 7 days, 14 days, and 30 days.
41 76 156

Reflect & Share

Compare your results with those of another pair of classmates. Work together to explain how the table, the graph, and the expression are related.

Connect

We can use a table, a graph, and algebra to describe and extend a number pattern.
Look at the pattern: 1, 3, 5, 7, …
To find the 20th term, use one of these three methods.
➢ Make a table, then extend the table to find the 20th term.
The term value increases by 2 each time.
The pattern rule is: Start at 1. Add 2 each time.
From the table on the next page, the 20th term is 39.

10.2 Describing Number Patterns 423

LESSON 10.2

Describing Number Patterns

LESSON ORGANIZER 80–100 min

Curriculum Focus: Write an expression for the *n*th term of a number pattern. (8m56, 8m57, 8m58, 8m60)

Student Materials
- 0.5-cm grid paper (PM 14)

Optional
- calculators
- Step-by-Step 2 (Master 10.9)
- Extra Practice 2 (Master 10.16)

Assessment: Master 10.2 Ongoing Observations: Algebra

Key Math Learnings

1. A table, a graph, and algebra can be used to describe and extend a number pattern.
2. An expression for the *n*th term of a number pattern can be used to find the value of any term in the pattern.

Number Strategies

Pairs of fractions must simplify to $\frac{1}{2}$ before multiplying. For example, the denominator of the first fraction could equal the numerator of the second fraction, and the denominator of the second fraction could be two times the numerator of the first fraction.

For example: $\frac{\not{3}^{1}}{\not{4}_{1}} \times \frac{\not{4}^{1}}{\not{6}_{2}} = \frac{1}{2}$

Math Note

The data in this lesson are discrete data; that is, the data are the counting numbers: 0, 1, 2, 3, 4, 5, . . . There are no values between these counting numbers. So, the graphs will consist of a series of points, rather than solid lines.

BEFORE Get Started

Initiate a discussion about juvenile diabetes. Tell students that diabetes is a disorder in which the body has trouble regulating its blood sugar levels. In juvenile diabetes, the body's immune system attacks the cells that produce insulin, a protein that absorbs sugar from the blood. Without insulin, your body cannot access the calories contained in the sugar. For this reason, people with juvenile diabetes must take insulin in order to stay alive. This means undergoing multiple injections daily and testing their blood sugar levels by pricking their fingers for blood six or more times a day.

Present *Explore*. Remind students that we can use a table, as well as a graph, to illustrate a number pattern. Distribute 0.5-cm grid paper (PM 14) to pairs of students. Students should find it easy to see a pattern in the table. Encourage students to also look for a relationship between the number of days and the number of needles. When writing an algebraic expression, suggest students use the variable *d* to represent the number of days. Remind students to label the axes and to give their graphs a title. Encourage students to use a scale on each axis that will allow them to extend the graph to find other terms.

REACHING ALL LEARNERS

Alternative Explore

Materials: 0.5-cm grid paper (PM 14)

A basic pizza costs \$7. Each additional topping costs \$2. Make a table for the cost of a pizza with 1, 2, 3, and 4 additional toppings. Graph the data. Write an algebraic expression for the cost of a pizza with any number of toppings. Use the expression to find the cost of a pizza with 5, 7, and 10 additional toppings.

Early Finishers

Have students graph the number patterns in *Practice* question 3. Students use the graph to verify each of their answers in part ii.

Common Misconceptions

➤ Students have difficulty writing an expression for the nth term of a number pattern.

How to Help: Encourage students to add a column to the table of values to help them see the relationship between the term value and the term number. Demonstrate with the pattern:
5, 11, 17, 23, 29, . . .
Each term is 6 more than the previous term.
Look for patterns that involve multiples of 6.

Term Number	Term Value	Pattern Rule for Term Value
1	5	5 = 6(1) – 1
2	11	11 = 6(2) – 1
3	17	17 = 6(3) – 1
4	23	23 = 6(4) – 1
5	29	29 = 6(5) – 1

Replace a term number with n. The nth term is: $6n - 1$

Term Number	Term Value
1	1
2	3
3	5
4	7
5	9
20	39

The 20th term is 39.

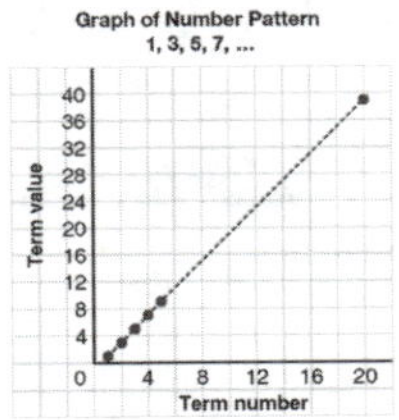

➤ Graph the pattern, then extend the graph to find the 20th term.
The points lie on a straight line.
To get from one point to another, move 1 unit right and 2 units up.

Use a ruler to draw a broken line through the points to show the trend.
Extend the broken line to the right to find that the 20th term

➤ The term values are consecutive odd numbers: 1, 3, 5, 7, 9, ..
The algebraic expression $2n$ produces even numbers, when we substitute $n = 1, 2, 3, 4, \ldots$
That is, $2(1) = 2$
$2(2) = 4$
$2(3) = 6$
$2(4) = 8$, and so on
Each odd number is 1 less than the following even number.
So, the expression $2n - 1$ produces odd numbers, when we substitute $n = 1, 2, 3, 4, \ldots$
That is, $2(1) - 1 = 2 - 1 = 1$
$2(2) - 1 = 4 - 1 = 3$
$2(3) - 1 = 6 - 1 = 5$
$2(4) - 1 = 8 - 1 = 7$
This table shows how the term value relates to the term num

Term Number	Term Value	Pattern Rule for Term Value
1	1	1 = 2(1) – 1
2	3	3 = 2(2) – 1
3	5	5 = 2(3) – 1
4	7	7 = 2(4) – 1
5	9	9 = 2(5) – 1

In each case, the term value is equal to: The term number multiplied by 2, then subtract 1

424 UNIT 10: Algebra

DURING Explore

Ongoing Assessment: Observe and Listen

As students work, ask questions, such as:

- How many needles does Charla need per day? (*5*)
- How many extra needles does Charla need to have available at all times? (*At least 6*)
- How many needles does Charla need to take with her for 1 day? (*11*) How do you know? (*5 × 1 = 5, and 5 + 6 = 11*)
- How many needles does Charla need to take with her for 2 days? (*16*) How do you know? (*5 × 2 = 10, and 10 + 6 = 16*)
- How many needles does Charla need to take with her for 3 days? (*21*) How do you know? (*5 × 3 = 15, and 15 + 6 = 21*) For 4 days? (*26*) For 5 days? (*31*) For 6 days? (*36*)
- What patterns do you see in the table? (*The number of days starts at 1 and increases by 1 each time. The number of needles starts at 11 and increases by 5 each time.*)
- What label did you put on the horizontal axis? (*Number of Days*) The vertical axis? (*Number of Needles*)
- What title did you give your graph? (*Charla's Needles for Camp*)
- What scale did you use on the horizontal axis? (*One grid square represents 1 day.*) On the vertical axis? (*One grid square represents 5 needles.*)
- Did you join the points with a solid line? Explain. (*No, the numbers of needles are whole numbers, and we cannot have part of a needle.*)

e natural numbers the counting s: 1, 2, 3, ...

Let t represent the term number.
Then an expression for the term value is $2t - 1$,
where t is any natural number.
To check that the expression for the term value is correct, substitute a number for t.
Substitute $t = 2$.

$$\begin{aligned} 2t - 1 &= 2 \times 2 - 1 \\ &= 4 - 1 \\ &= 3 \end{aligned}$$

So, the 2nd term is 3, which matches the 2nd term in the pattern given.

This method allows us to find the value of any term in the pattern.
For example, the 20th term has value: $2(20) - 1 = 39$

Example

Here is a number pattern.
8, 12, 16, 20, ...

a) Complete a table for the first 5 terms of this pattern. Extend the table to find the 10th term. Describe the pattern. Write a pattern rule.
b) Graph the pattern.
c) Write an expression for the nth term.
d) Use the expression in part c to verify the 10th term.

Solution

a) 8, 12, 16, 20, ...
The pattern begins with 8.
To get the next term, add 4 each time.
The pattern rule is: Start at 8. Add 4 each time.
Extend the table to find the 10th term is 44.

Term Number	1	2	3	4	5	6	7	8	9	10
Term Value	8	12	16	20	24	28	32	36	40	44

b) Graph the pattern.
The points lie on a straight line.
Use a ruler to draw a broken line through the points to show the trend.

10.2 Describing Number Patterns **425**

Sample Solutions

1. a) The pattern rule is: Start at 3. Add 2 each time.
   b) The pattern rule is: Start at 2. Add 3 each time.
   c) The pattern rule is: Start at 4. Add 2 each time.
   d) The pattern rule is: Start at 2. Add 4 each time.
3. a) i) Start at 1. Add 1 each time.
   b) i) Start at 2. Add 1 each time.
   c) i) Start at 3. Add 1 each time.
   d) i) Start at 4. Add 1 each time.
4. a) i) Start at 2. Add 2 each time.
   ii) Graph of Number Pattern 2, 4, 6, 8, 10, ...

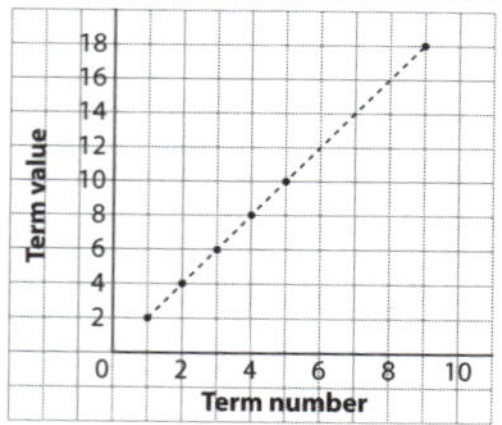

   b) i) Start at 6. Add 3 each time.
   ii) Graph of Number Pattern 6, 9, 12, 15, 18, ...

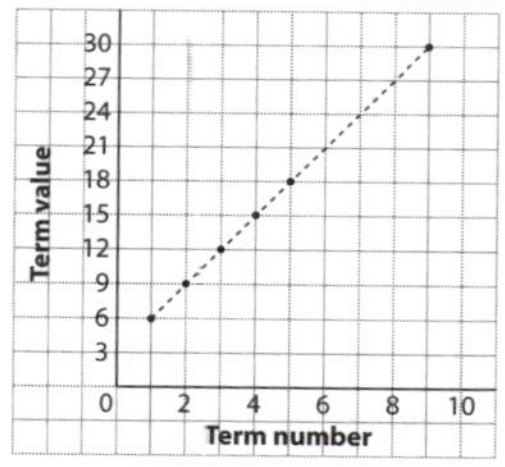

   c) i) Start at 3. Add 4 each time.
   ii) Graph of Number Pattern 3, 7, 11, 15, 19, ...

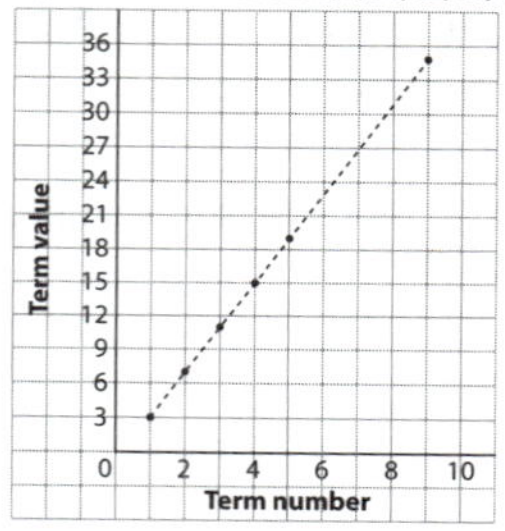

   d) i) Start at 10. Add 5 each time.
   ii) Graph of Number Pattern 10, 15, 20, 25, 30, ...

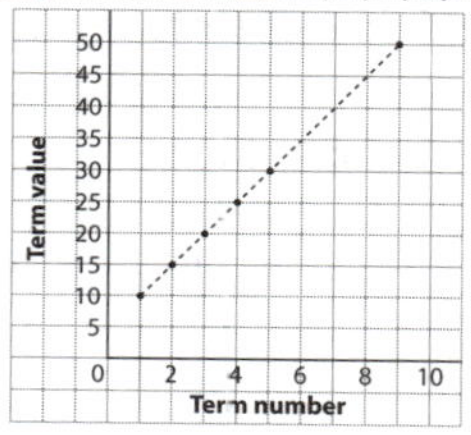

- **Do you see a relationship between the number of days and the number of needles? Explain.**
  (*Yes, if I multiply the number of days by 5, then add 6, I get the number of needles.*)
- **What is an algebraic expression for the number of needles required for any number of days?**
  (*I let the number of days be d. The algebraic expression is: 5d + 6*)
- **How did you use the expression to find the number of needles required for 7 days?**
  (*I substituted d = 7 into the algebraic expression to get 5 × 7 + 6 = 41.*)
- **How many needles are required for 14 days?** (*76*) **For 30 days?** (*156*)

AFTER Connect

Invite students to share their results with the class.

What you might see:

Charla's Needles for Camp

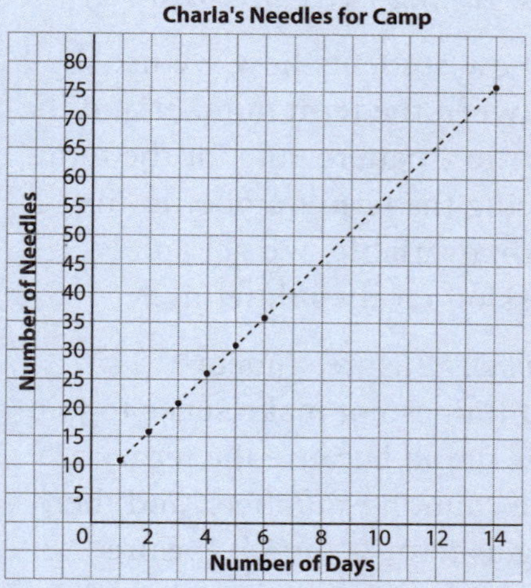

5. The nth term of the first pattern is: n^2
Since 512 is not a square number, 512 does not appear in the first pattern.
I could not find an expression for the nth term of the second pattern. So, I used a table to extend the pattern.

Term Number	Term Value
1	4
2	8
3	16
4	32
5	64
6	128
7	256
8	512

The 8th term in the second number pattern is 512.

6. a) For example: 10, 20, 30, 40, 50, 60, . . . and 10, 20, 40, 80, 160, 320, . . .

b) In the first pattern, each term is 10 more than the previous term. The pattern rule is: Start at 10. Add 10 each time.
In the second pattern, each term is twice the previous term. The pattern rule is: Start at 10. Multiply by 2 each time.

c) I can write an expression for the nth term of the first pattern: $10 = 10 \times 1$
$20 = 10 \times 2$
$30 = 10 \times 3$
So, the nth term is: $10n$

d) I cannot write an expression for the nth term of the second pattern because the difference between consecutive terms is not constant.

7. a) i) The pattern rule is: Start at $\frac{2}{2}$. Increase the numerator by 1 and the denominator by 3 each time.

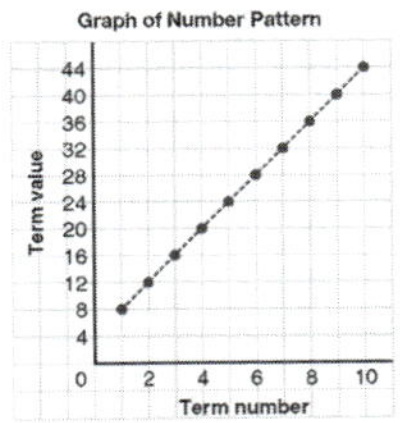

c) Find a pattern rule that relates the term value to the term number.
Each term is 4 more than the previous term.
Look for patterns that involve multiples of 4.

In each case, the term value is equal to: Four more than four times the term number

Term Number	Term Value	Pattern Rule for Term Value
1	$8 = 4 + 4$	$8 = 4(1) + 4$
2	$12 = (4 + 4) + 4$	$12 = 4(2) + 4$
3	$16 = (4 + 4 + 4) + 4$	$16 = 4(3) + 4$
4	$20 = (4 + 4 + 4 + 4) + 4$	$20 = 4(4) + 4$

To write an expression for the nth term, let n represent any te[rm] number. Then, the nth term is: $4n + 4$

d) To find the 10th term, substitute $n = 10$ into $4n + 4$.
$4n + 4 = 4(10) + 4$
$= 44$
The 10th term is 44. This verifies the value in the table in par[t]

Practice

1. Substitute $n = 1, 2, 3, 4, 5$, and 6 to generate a number patter[n]. Describe each pattern, then write a pattern rule. 2, 6, 10, 14
a) $2n + 1$ 3, 5, 7, 9, 11, 13 b) $3n - 1$ 2, 5, 8, 11, 14, 17 c) $2n + 2$ 4, 6, 8, 10, 12, 14 d) $4n - 2$

2. For each number pattern, write an expression for the nth ter[m].
a) $\frac{1}{1}, \frac{1}{2}, \frac{1}{3}, \frac{1}{4}, \frac{1}{5}, \frac{1}{6}, \ldots$ $\frac{1}{n}$ b) $\frac{1}{2}, \frac{2}{3}, \frac{3}{4}, \frac{4}{5}, \frac{5}{6}, \frac{6}{7}, \ldots$ $\frac{n}{n+1}$

426 UNIT 10: Algebra

Ask:

- How could you use the graph to find the number of needles required for 14 days? (*I could extend the graph to 14 on the horizontal axis. From the graph, I draw a horizontal line to the vertical axis. The line meets the axis at 76.*)

Use *Connect* to show students how we use the relationship between the term number and the term value to write a pattern rule for the term value. By replacing the term number in the pattern rule with a variable, we get an algebraic expression for the nth term.

Review the *Example*. Ensure students understand that it does not make sense to join the points in the graph because the term numbers are the counting numbers, and there is no such thing as term $1\frac{1}{2}$ or $3\frac{3}{4}$. Ensure students understand that they should not join the points for any graph they draw in this lesson.

Practice

Have 0.5-cm grid paper available for question 4.

Assessment Focus: Question 6

Students should be able to extend the pattern in at least two different ways. For example,

- Start at 10. Add 10 each time.
- Start at 10. Multiply by 2 each time.
- Start at 10. Add 10. Increase the number added by 1 each time.

Students are not expected to write an expression for the nth term of any pattern where the difference between consecutive terms is not constant. Stronger math students may be able to write algebraic expressions for these patterns.

Students who need extra support to complete Assessment Focus questions may benefit from the Step-by-Step masters (Masters 10.8–10.12).

3. For each number pattern below:
   i) Describe the pattern. Write the pattern rule.
   ii) Use a table to find the 12th term.
   iii) Write an expression for the nth term.
   iv) Use the expression to find the 100th term.

   a) 1, 2, 3, 4, 5, … n, 12, 100
   b) 2, 3, 4, 5, 6, … $n + 1$, 13, 101
   c) 3, 4, 5, 6, 7, … $n + 2$, 14, 102
   d) 4, 5, 6, 7, 8, … $n + 3$, 15, 103

4. For each number pattern below:
   i) Write a pattern rule. Justify your rule.
   ii) Graph the pattern. Use the graph to find the 9th term.
   iii) Write an expression for the nth term.
   iv) Use the expression to find the 60th term.

   a) 2, 4, 6, 8, 10, … $2n$, 18, 120
   b) 6, 9, 12, 15, 18, … $3n + 3$, 30, 183
   c) 3, 7, 11, 15, 19, … $4n - 1$, 35, 239
   d) 10, 15, 20, 25, 30, … $5n + 5$, 50, 305

5. Here are two number patterns.
   - 1, 4, 9, 16, 25, …
   - 4, 8, 16, 32, 64, …

   Does the number 512 appear in either pattern? Both patterns? Justify your answer.

Strategies

ct of two … $\frac{1}{2}$. … different pairs of … hat have a … $\frac{1}{2}$.

$\frac{5}{7} \times \frac{7}{10}$, $\frac{17}{15} \times \frac{15}{34}$

6. **Assessment Focus** Here is the beginning of a number pattern.
   10, 20, …
   a) Extend the pattern in two different ways.
   b) Describe each pattern. Write a pattern rule for each.
   c) Write an expression for the nth term for one pattern.
   d) Can you write an expression for the nth term of the other pattern? Explain.

ke It Further

7. For each number pattern below:
   i) Write a pattern rule. Justify your rule.
   ii) Find the 15th term.
   iii) Write an expression for the nth term.
   iv) Use the expression to find the 30th term.

   a) $\frac{2}{2}, \frac{3}{5}, \frac{4}{8}, \frac{5}{11}, \ldots$ $\frac{16}{44}$, $\frac{n+1}{3n-1}$, $\frac{31}{89}$
   b) 1, 3, 6, 10, 15, … 120, $\frac{n(n+1)}{2}$, 465

eflect

Name three ways to describe and extend a number pattern. Which way is the most efficient? Explain.

10.2 Describing Number Patterns **427**

b) i) The pattern rule is: Start at 1. Add 2. Increase the number added by 1 each time.

REFLECT: A number pattern can be described and extended using a table, a graph, and an expression for the nth term of the pattern.
The most efficient way to describe and extend a pattern is to use the algebraic expression for the nth term. This expression can be used to find the value of any term in the pattern by substituting the term number for the variable. It takes much more time to extend a table or graph to the required term number.

Assignment Guidelines

If your students do not have time to complete all the *Practice* questions on pages 426 and 427, these questions provide minimum curriculum coverage: 1, 3, 4, 6, *Reflect*

To assess the 4 Achievement Chart categories listed in the curriculum document, have students complete these *Practice* questions:
Knowledge and Understanding: 1
Application: 4
Thinking: 6
Communication: *Reflect*

ASSESSMENT FOR LEARNING

What to Look For

Knowledge and Understanding

✔ Students understand that a table, a graph, and algebra can be used to describe and extend a number pattern.

Communication

✔ Students can explain 3 ways to describe and extend a number pattern.

Application

✔ Students can write an expression for the nth term of a number pattern.
✔ Students can use an expression to find the value of a given term in a number pattern.

What to Do

Extra Support: Students who have difficulty finding the pattern rule for the term value should work with simple patterns first, such as 3, 5, 7, . . . Students find the difference between consecutive terms (2), multiply this number by the variable ($2n$), then find what must be added or subtracted each time to get each term value ($2n + 1$).
Students can use Step-by-Step 2 (Master 10.9) to complete question 6.

Extra Practice: Students can complete the Additional Activity *Number Pattern Search* (Master 10.5).
Students can complete Extra Practice 2 (Master 10.16).

Extension: Have students find an expression for the nth term of this number pattern: 2, 5, 10, 17, . . .
(Answer: $n^2 + 1$)

Recording and Reporting

Master 10.2 Ongoing Observations: Algebra

Describing Geometric Patterns

LESSON ORGANIZER — 80–100 min

Curriculum Focus: Write an expression for the *n*th term of a geometric pattern. (8m56, 8m57, 8m58, 8m60)

Student Materials
- 1-cm grid paper (PM 20)
- 0.5-cm grid paper (PM 14)

Optional
- isometric dot paper (PM 23)
- calculators
- toothpicks
- Step-by-Step 3 (Master 10.10)
- Extra Practice 3 (Master 10.17)

Assessment: Master 10.2 Ongoing Observations: Algebra

Key Math Learning

Algebra can be used to describe and extend a geometric pattern.

Number Strategies

Students should use their knowledge of the divisibility rule for 9: If the sum of the digits is divisible by 9, the number is also divisible by 9.

6 + 3 + 7 + 5 + 1 = 22

Students find all possible digits which, when added to 22, have a sum that is divisible by 9.

22 + 5 = 27, and 27 ÷ 9 = 3

10.3 Describing Geometric Patterns

Focus Write an expression for the *n*th term of a geometric pattern.

Explore

Work in a group.
Here is a pattern with squares.

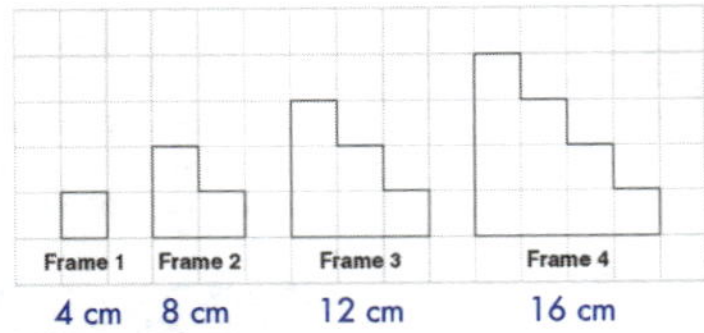

The pattern continues.
Find the perimeter of each frame.
What pattern do you see in the perimeters?
Use a table to show the pattern.
Graph the pattern.
Write a rule for the pattern.
Use a variable.
Write an algebraic expression you could use to find the perimeter of any frame. *4f*
Use the expression to find the perimeters of Frame 5, Frame 10, and Frame 100. *20 cm 40 cm 400 cm*

Reflect & Share

Share your algebraic expression with that of another group.
Are the expressions the same?
If not, how can you check if either expression is correct?
Could both expressions be correct? Explain.

Connect

We can use algebra to describe and extend a geometric pattern.
Here is a pattern of equilateral triangles drawn on isometric pap

428 UNIT 10: Algebra

BEFORE — Get Started

Remind students of some of the geometric patterns they studied in earlier grades. Draw these rectangles on a 1-cm grid transparency. Ask:

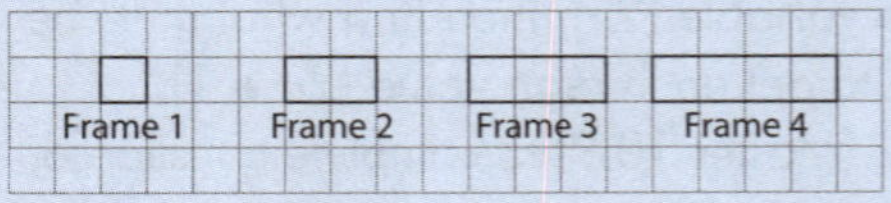

- What is the area of each rectangle?
  (1 cm², 2 cm², 3 cm², 4 cm²)
- What pattern do you see in the areas?
  (The area increases by 1 cm² each time.)
- What is the pattern rule for the areas?
  (Start at 1. Add 1 each time.)
- What is the area of the rectangle in Frame 15? How do you know?
  (15 cm²; the area of each rectangle, in square centimetres, equals the frame number.)

Present *Explore*. Remind students that we can use a table, as well as a graph, to illustrate a geometric pattern. Distribute 0.5-cm grid paper (PM 14) and 1-cm grid paper (PM 20) to groups of students. Encourage students to copy the pattern with squares onto 1-cm grid paper. Ensure students understand that perimeter is the distance around a closed figure. Suggest students use a coloured pencil to mark the sides as they count to find the perimeters. Encourage students to look for a relationship between the frame number and the perimeter of each frame. Remind students to label the axes and to give their graphs a title.

DURING — Explore

Ongoing Assessment: Observe and Listen

As students work, ask questions, such as:

- What are the perimeters of the first 4 frames?
  (4 cm, 8 cm, 12 cm, 16 cm)

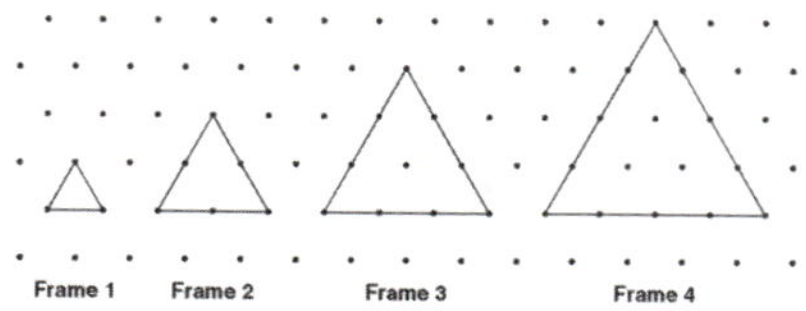

ame	Perimeter (units)
1	3
2	6
3	9
4	12

This table shows the perimeter of each frame.

The pattern rule for the perimeters is:
Start at 3. Add 3 each time.

If we use this pattern rule to find the perimeter of Frame 40, we would need to know the perimeter of all the frames from Frame 1 to Frame 39.
Instead, we look for a pattern rule for the perimeter in terms of the frame number.
The perimeters are multiples of 3, so write each perimeter as a product, with one factor of 3.

Frame	Perimeter (units)	Perimeter as a Product
1	3	$3 = 3 \times 1$
2	6	$6 = 3 \times 2$
3	9	$9 = 3 \times 3$
4	12	$12 = 3 \times 4$

In each case, the perimeter is equal to 3 times the frame number.
We can use this pattern to find the perimeter of Frame 40:
$3 \times 40 = 120$
The perimeter of Frame 40 is 120 units.
We write the pattern using algebra.
Let f represent the frame number.
Then, an algebraic expression for the perimeter of Frame f is: $3f$
f is any natural number.

10.3 Describing Geometric Patterns **429**

REACHING ALL LEARNERS

Early Finishers

Have students use an equation to find:

- Which frame in question 2 has 81 toothpicks? (*Frame 40*)
- Which frame in question 3 has perimeter 68 cm? (*Frame 32*)
- Which frame in question 5 has an arrangement of tables that can sit 146 people? (*Frame 36*)

Common Misconceptions

➤ Students think that every graph that represents a geometric pattern must be a set of points that lie on a straight line.

How to Help: Use the pattern for the areas of the equilateral triangles in *Connect*. Graph the data in the table of values:

Frame	Area (units^2)
1	1
2	4
3	9
4	16

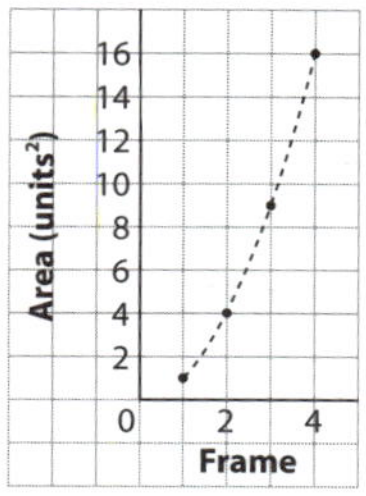

Students will see that the points lie on a curve. This is because the frame number is squared each time to get the area.

ESL Strategies

Have students for whom English is a second language write their own glossary for terms such as perimeter, area, variable, expression, equation, frame number, and so on. Students should illustrate their glossary with examples found in the Student Book.

- What patterns do you see in the perimeters? (*The perimeter of each frame is 4 cm greater than the perimeter of the previous frame.*)
- What is the pattern rule for the perimeter? (*Start at 4. Add 4 each time.*)
- How did you use a table to show the pattern? (*I completed a table with one column labelled "Frame" and the other column labelled "Perimeter (cm)."*)
- What label did you put on the horizontal axis of your graph? (*Frame*)
  The vertical axis? (*Perimeter (cm)*)
- What title did you give your graph? (*Perimeter of Frame against Frame Number*)
- What scale did you use on the horizontal axis? (*One grid square represents 1 frame number.*) On the vertical axis? (*One grid square represents 2 cm.*)
- Did you join the points with a solid line? Explain.
  (*No, the frame numbers are whole numbers, and there is no such thing as part of a frame.*)
- Do you see a relationship between the frame number and the perimeter? Explain.
  (*Yes, in each case, the perimeter is equal to 4 times the frame number.*)
- What is an algebraic expression for the perimeter?
  (*I let the frame number be f. The algebraic expression is: 4f*)
- How did you use the expression to find the perimeter of Frame 5?
  (*I substituted $f = 5$ into the algebraic expression to get $4 \times 5 = 20$; 20 cm.*)
- What is the perimeter of Frame 10?
  (*$4 \times 10 = 40$; 40 cm*) Frame 100?
  (*$4 \times 100 = 400$; 400 cm*)

AFTER **Connect**

Invite students to share their tables, graphs, and algebraic expressions with the class.

What you might see:

Sample Solutions

1. a)

Frame	Length (cm)
1	4
2	5
3	6
4	7

Each length is 1 cm more than the previous length.

b) **Length of Frame against Frame Number**

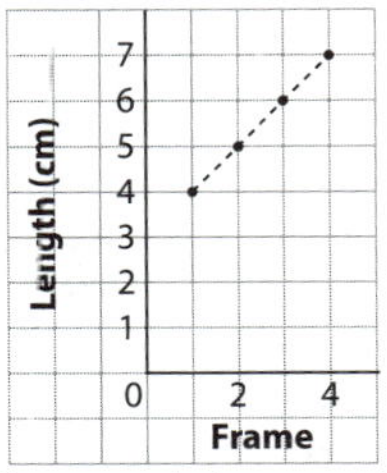

The graph is a straight line. The graph starts at (1, 4).
To get to the next point each time, move 1 right and 1 up.
Moving 1 right is the increase in the frame number.
Moving 1 up is the increase in the length.

2. a)

Frame	Number of Toothpicks
1	3
2	5
3	7
4	9

The number of toothpicks starts at 3 and increases by 2 each time.

To check that the expression is correct, substitute a number for f.
Substitute $f = 4$.
$3f = 3(4)$
$= 12$
So, Frame 4 has perimeter 12 units.
This is verified by the table on page 429.

Example

Picture frames are decorated with square tiles in the pattern show
Each tile has side length 1 cm.
The pattern continues.

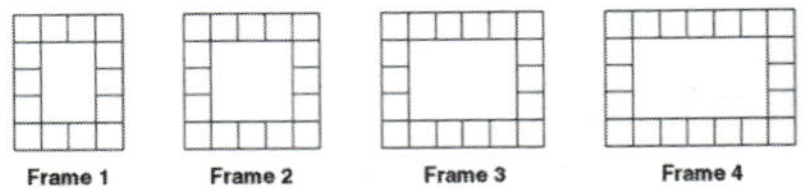

a) Find the area of the picture in each frame.
What pattern do you see in the areas?
b) Graph the pattern in part a.
How does the graph illustrate the pattern?
c) Use a variable.
Write an algebraic expression for the area of the picture in any frame.
d) Use the expression in part c.
Find the area of the picture in Frame 99.

Solution

a) Each picture is a rectangle.
Its area is length × width.
Write the areas in a table.

Frame	Area of Picture (
1	$3 \times 2 = 6$
2	$3 \times 3 = 9$
3	$3 \times 4 = 12$
4	$3 \times 5 = 15$

The areas are multiples of 3.
The pattern rule is:
Start at 6. Add 3 each time.

b) The graph starts at (1, 6).
To get the next point each time, move 1 right and 3 up.
Moving 1 right is the increase in the frame number.
Moving 3 up is the increase in the area.

Area of Picture agains Frame Number

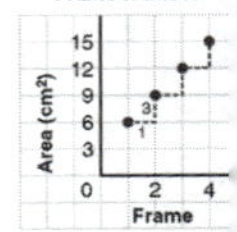

Frame	Perimeter (cm)
1	4
2	8
3	12
4	16

Perimeter of Frame against Frame Number

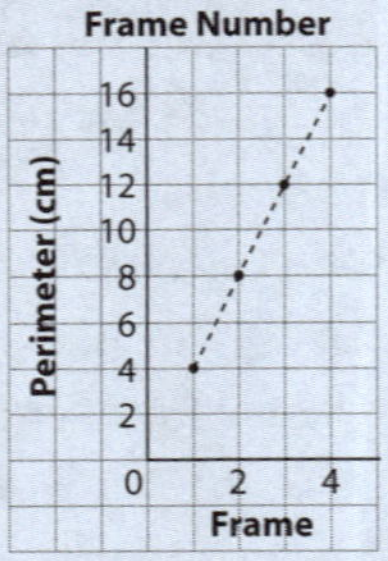

Ask:

- Did anybody get a different expression? Explain. (*I got the expression $f + 4$.*)
- How can we check if this expression is correct?
(*We can substitute a number for f. For example, substitute $f = 3$: $f + 4 = 3 + 4 = 7$. This does not agree with the table. The expression is not correct.*)

Ensure students understand that there is only one correct algebraic expression for this pattern.

Review *Connect*. Have students graph the pattern in the perimeter of the equilateral triangles. What you might see:

Perimeter of Frame against Frame Number

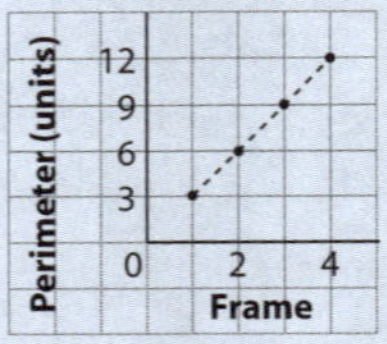

To cover the curriculum outcome "model linear relationships using . . . equations," show students an equation that represents the perimeter of the equilateral triangles: $P = 3f$, where P is the perimeter in units and f is the frame number. We can use this equation to see whether a frame has a given perimeter. For example, does a frame have perimeter 27 units? If so, which one?

Substitute $P = 27$ into the equation.

c) For an algebraic expression, look at each area in terms of the frame number.
Adding 3 each time indicates a pattern where the term number is multiplied by 3.
So, multiply each term number by 3 and find out what needs to be added each time to get the area.

Frame	Area of Picture (cm^2)	Area in Terms of Frame Number
1	6	$3 \times 1 + 3$
2	9	$3 \times 2 + 3$
3	12	$3 \times 3 + 3$
4	15	$3 \times 4 + 3$

Each area is: 3 times the frame number, then add 3
Use the variable n.
An algebraic expression for the area of the picture in Frame n is:
3 times n, then add 3
This is written: $3n + 3$

d) For the area of the picture in Frame 99, substitute $n = 99$ in $3n + 3$.

$$\begin{aligned} 3n + 3 &= 3(99) + 3 \\ &= 297 + 3 \\ &= 300 \end{aligned}$$

The picture in Frame 99 has area 300 cm^2.

Practice

1. Use the pattern of frames in the *Example*. Each frame has the same height of 5 cm.
   a) Find the length of each frame. Make a table. What patterns do you see in the lengths?
   b) Graph the pattern. How does the graph illustrate the pattern?
   c) Write an algebraic expression for the length of the nth frame. $n + 3$
   d) Use the expression in part c. Find the length of Frame 50. 53 cm

b) **Number of Toothpicks against Frame Number**

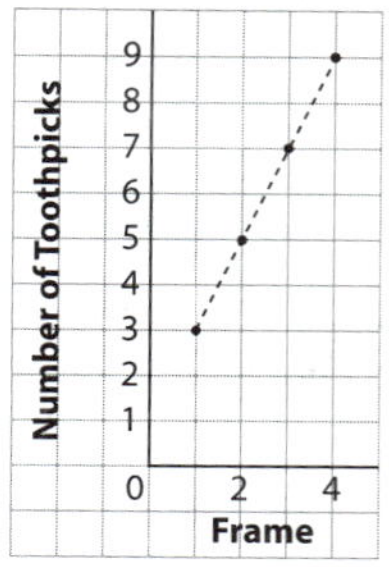

3. a) The perimeter starts at 6 cm and increases by 2 cm each time.

b) **Perimeter of Frame against Frame Number**

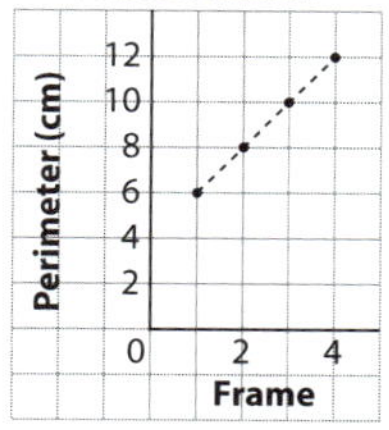

The graph is a straight line. The graph starts at (1, 6). To get to the next point each time, move 1 right and 2 up. Moving 1 right is the increase in the frame number. Moving 2 up is the increase in the perimeter.

4. a) The areas are square numbers.
The pattern rule is: Start at 1. Square the number. Increase the number squared by 1 each time.

d) An equation that represents the area is: $A = n^2$, where A is the area in square centimetres and n is the frame number.
Substitute $A = 625$ into the equation.

$625 = n^2$ Take the square root of each side to isolate n.

$\sqrt{625} = \sqrt{n^2}$

$25 = n$

$27 = 3f$ Divide both sides of the equation by 3 to isolate f.

$\frac{27}{3} = \frac{3f}{3}$

$9 = f$

Frame 9 has perimeter 27 units.

Show students how they can use the areas of the equilateral triangles to form a different pattern. Let the area of the equilateral triangle in Frame 1 be 1 $unit^2$. Make a table to show the area of each frame.

Frame	Area ($units^2$)
1	1
2	4
3	9
4	16

The pattern rule for the areas is: Start at 1. Square the number. Increase the number squared by 1 each time.

Look for a pattern rule for the area in terms of the frame number.

The areas are square numbers, so write each area with exponent 2.

Frame	Area ($units^2$)	Area as an Exponent
1	1	1^2
2	4	2^2
3	9	3^2
4	16	4^2

In each case, the area is the square of the frame number.
Let f represent the frame number.
Then, an algebraic expression for the area of Frame f is: f^2, where f is any natural number.

Work through the *Example* together. Show students an equation for the area of the picture: $A = 3n + 3$, where A is the area of the picture in square centimetres and n is the frame number. Use the equation to determine if a frame has a picture with area 50 cm^2.
Substitute $A = 50$.

5. a)

Frame	Number of People
1	6
2	10
3	14
4	18

The number of people starts at 6 and increases by 4 each time.

c) I could write an algebraic expression for the number of people who could be seated at the tables in the nth frame.
The expression is: $4n + 2$
I could substitute a frame number into the expression to find the number of people who could be seated at the table arrangement in that frame.

6. a)

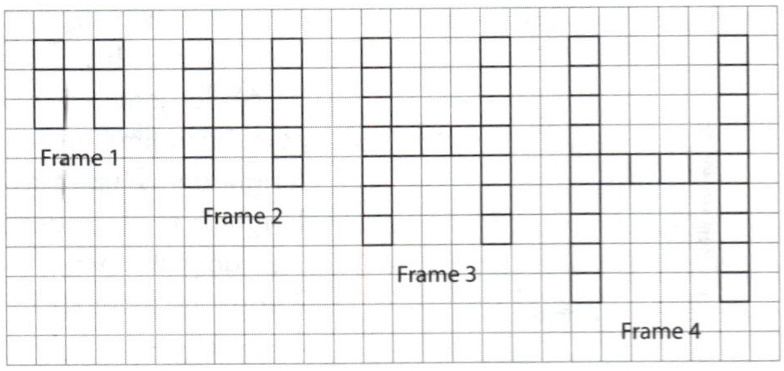

b) Each frame contains an H-shaped figure. The length of each horizontal section equals the frame number. The length of each vertical section starts at 3 units and increases by 2 units each time. The length of each vertical section is one more than twice the frame number.

c) Frame 5: The vertical sections are each of length 11 units and the horizontal section is of length 5 units.
Frame 10: The vertical sections are each of length 21 units and the horizontal section is of length 10 units.

2. Here is a pattern of triangles made with congruent toothpicks.

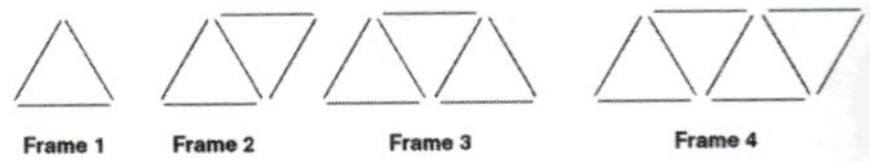

The pattern continues.

a) Find the number of toothpicks in each frame. What patterns do you see?
b) Graph the data in part a.
c) Write an algebraic expression for the number of toothpicks in the nth frame. $2n + 1$
d) Find the number of toothpicks in Frame 45. 91 toothpicks

3. Here is a pattern of squares.

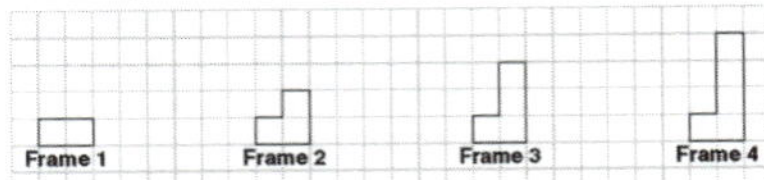

Each square has side length 1 cm.
The pattern continues.

Frame	Perimeter (cm)
1	6
2	8
3	10
4	12

a) Find the perimeter of each frame. Make a table. What pattern do you see in the perimeters?
b) Graph the pattern. Explain how the graph illustrates the pattern.
c) Write an algebraic expression for the perimeter of the nth frame. $2n + 4$
d) Find the perimeter of Frame 75. 154 cm

4. Here is a pattern made from congruent square tiles. Each tile has side length 1 cm. The pattern continues.

Frame	Area (cm^2)
1	1
2	4
3	9
4	16

a) Find the area of each frame. What patterns do you see in the areas?
b) Use a pattern to find the area of Frame 8. 64 cm^2
c) Write an algebraic expression for the area of the nth frame. n^2
d) Which frame has an area of 625 cm^2? Justify your answer. Frame 25

432 UNIT 10: Algebra

$50 = 3n + 3$ To isolate $3n$, subtract 3 from each side.

$50 - 3 = 3n + 3 - 3$

$47 = 3n$ Divide each side by 3.

$\frac{47}{3} = \frac{3n}{3}$

$15.\overline{6} = n$

Since n is not a natural number, no frame has a picture of area 50 cm^2.

Practice

Questions 1, 2, 3, and 6 require 0.5-cm grid paper. Have toothpicks available for question 2. Have isometric dot paper (PM 23) available for questions 5 and 6. Have sheets of newspaper available for question 7. Have students write equations to represent the frame length in question 1, the number of toothpicks in question 2, the perimeter in question 3, the area in question 4, the number of people in question 5, and the number of pieces in question 7.

Assessment Focus: Question 6

Students could use manipulatives such as Colour Tiles, toothpicks, or Pattern Blocks to create a growing pattern, then copy the pattern onto grid paper. Encourage students to be creative. Have students write an equation to represent the aspect they choose.

Assignment Guidelines

If your students do not have time to complete all the *Practice* questions on pages 431, 432, and 433, these questions provide minimum curriculum coverage: 2, 3, 5, 6, *Reflect*

To assess the 4 Achievement Chart categories listed in the curriculum document, have students complete these *Practice* questions:
Knowledge and Understanding: 2
Application: 5
Thinking: 6
Communication: *Reflect*

Strategies

...mber ...divisible by 9.
...t can go in the ...place? 5
...answers can ... One

5. Hexagonal tables are arranged as shown below.
One person sits at each side of a table.
The pattern continues.

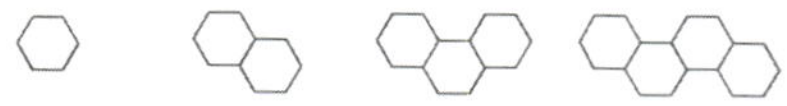

Frame 1 Frame 2 Frame 3 Frame 4

a) How many people can sit at the tables in each frame? What pattern do you see in the number of people?
b) How many people can sit at the tables in Frame 9? 38
c) Explain how you could find the number of people who could be seated at any table arrangement in this pattern.

...all that a growing ...tern is a pattern ...grows in a ...dictable way.

6. Assessment Focus Use grid paper.
a) Draw the first four frames of a growing pattern.
b) Describe the patterns in the frames.
c) Describe or draw Frame 5, Frame 10, and Frame 100.
d) Choose one aspect of your pattern; for example, area, perimeter, and so on. Write an algebraic expression for the nth frame of your pattern.

...ke It Further

7. Bryn has a sheet of paper. He cuts the paper in half to produce two pieces. Bryn places one piece on top of the other. He then cuts these pieces in half. The pattern continues. The table shows some of the results.

Number of Cuts	1	2	3	4	5	6	7	8	9	10
Number of Pieces	2	4	8	16	32	64	128	256	512	1024

a) Copy and complete this table.
b) What patterns do you see in the number of pieces?
c) Use a pattern to find the number of pieces after 15 cuts. 32 768
d) Write an algebraic expression for the number of pieces after n cuts. 2^n

...eflect

Explain the meaning of the term "nth frame."

Frame 100: The vertical sections are each of length 201 units and the horizontal section is of length 100 units.

d) I chose Area. Each grid square has area 1 unit^2.

Frame	Area (unit^2)	Area in Terms of Frame Number
1	7	$5 \times 1 + 2$
2	12	$5 \times 2 + 2$
3	17	$5 \times 3 + 2$
4	22	$5 \times 4 + 2$

Each area is: 5 times the frame number, then add 2
Use the variable n.
An algebraic expression for the area in Frame n is: $5n + 2$

7. b) The numbers of pieces are all powers of 2.
The pattern rule for the number of pieces is: Start at 2. Multiply by 2 each time.

c) I extended the pattern to 15 cuts: . . . 512, 1024, 2048, 4096, 8192, 16 384, 32 768
There are 32 768 pieces after 15 cuts.

REFLECT: The variable n is used to replace any frame number in an algebraic expression that represents a geometric pattern. n is a natural number. We can substitute a number for n to find the value of the aspect in that frame of the pattern. For example, we can substitute $n = 20$ into the expression for the area of the picture in the *Example* to get the area of Frame 20:

$3n + 3 = 3(20) + 3$
$= 63$

The area of the picture in Frame 20 is 63 cm^2.

ASSESSMENT FOR LEARNING

What to Look For

Knowledge and Understanding

✔ Students understand that a geometric pattern can be described and extended using a table, a graph, and algebra.

Communication

✔ Students can explain the meaning of the term "nth frame."

Application

✔ Students can write an expression for the nth frame and use the expression to make predictions.

✔ Students can write an equation to represent a linear pattern.

What to Do

Extra Support: Students who have difficulty recognizing patterns may benefit from using manipulatives. Students could use Colour Tiles to model the patterns in questions 1, 3, and 4, toothpicks to model the pattern in question 2, and yellow hexagonal Pattern Blocks to model the pattern in question 5. Students can use Step-by-Step 3 (Master 10.10) to complete question 6.

Extra Practice: Have students graph the patterns in *Practice* questions 4, 5, 6, and 7. Students describe each graph as linear or non-linear.
Students can complete Extra Practice 3 (Master 10.17).

Extension: Have students find an expression for the area of the nth frame in *Explore*. (Answer: $\frac{n(n + 1)}{2}$)

Recording and Reporting

Master 10.2 Ongoing Observations: Algebra

LESSON ORGANIZER

Student Materials
- 0.5-cm grid paper (PM 14)
- calculators

Optional
- Colour Tiles

Assessment: Masters 10.1 Unit Rubric: Algebra, 10.4 Unit Summary: Algebra

Assignment Guidelines

To assess the 4 Achievement Chart categories listed in the curriculum document, have students complete these questions:
Communication: 2
Knowledge and Understanding: 3
Application: 5
Thinking: 6

Mid-Unit Review

LESSON

10.1 **1.** Write two expressions for the area of the shaded rectangle.

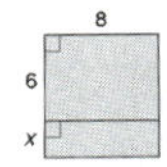

$8(6 + x)$; $48 + 8x$

2. Draw a rectangle to show that: $6(3 + a) = 18 + 6a$

3. Expand.
a) $3(x + 11)$ $3x + 33$
b) $5(12 + y)$ $60 + 5y$
c) $4(x + 5y + 9)$ $4x + 20y + 36$
d) $8(5x + 2y + 3)$ $40x + 16y + 24$

10.2 **4.** For each number pattern below:
a) Use a table to find the 8th term. Describe the pattern. Write a pattern rule.
b) Graph the pattern. Use the graph to find the 12th term.
c) Write an expression for the nth term.
d) Use the expression to find the 40th term.
i) 1, 7, 13, 19, 25, …
ii) 2, 7, 12, 17, 22, …
iii) 4, 7, 10, 13, 16, …

i) a) 43 b) 67 c) $6n - 5$ d) 235
ii) a) 37 b) 57 c) $5n - 3$ d) 197
iii) a) 25 b) 37 c) $3n + 1$ d) 121

5. Laurel buys a box of mechanical pencils, and a tube of 8 refill leads. Each pencil contains 3 leads. Laurel puts the tube of refill leads into her pencil case, then adds one pencil at a time.
a) Make a table to show the n[…] of leads in the pencil case for […] to 7 pencils. Describe the pattern. Write a pattern rule.
b) Graph the data in the table.
c) Write an algebraic expression […] the number of leads in the p[…] case for any number of penc[…]
d) Use the expression in part c t[…] find the number of leads in t[…] pencil case for 21 pencils. 7[…]

10.3 **6.** Here is a pattern made with congruent square tiles.

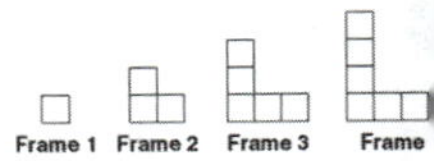

a) Count the number of tiles in each frame. What pattern do you see?
b) Make a table to show the pat[…]
c) Graph the pattern.
d) Write an algebraic expression for the number of tiles in the nth frame. $2n - 1$
e) Use the expression in part d to find the number of tiles in Frame 30. 59
f) Will any frame have each nu[…] of tiles?
i) 31 ii) 32 iii) 33
How do you know?
Yes No Yes

434 UNIT 10: Algebra

Sample Solutions

4. i) a) Each term is 6 more than the previous term. The pattern rule is: Start at 1. Add 6 each time.

b)

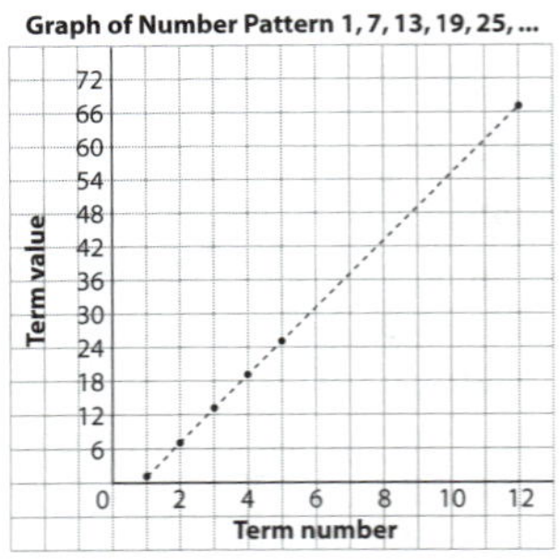

ii) a) Each term is 5 more than the previous term. The pattern rule is: Start at 2. Add 5 each time.

b)

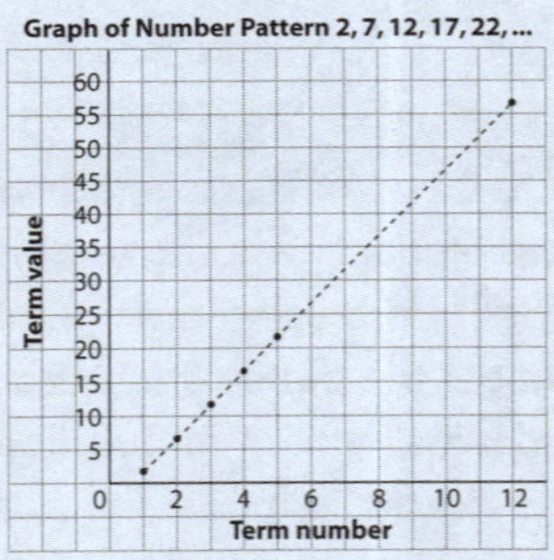

iii) a) Each term is 3 more than the previous term. The pattern rule is: Start at 4. Add 3 each time.

b)

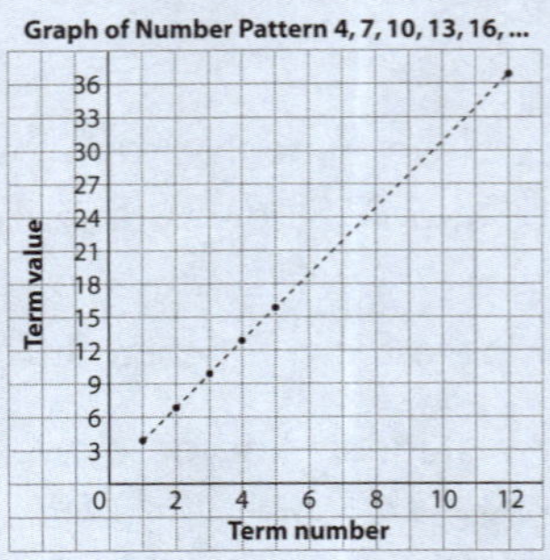

5. a)

Number of pencils	1	2	3	4	5	6	7
Number of leads	11	14	17	20	23	26	29

The number of leads increases by 3 each time.
The pattern rule is: Start at 11. Add 3 each time.

b)

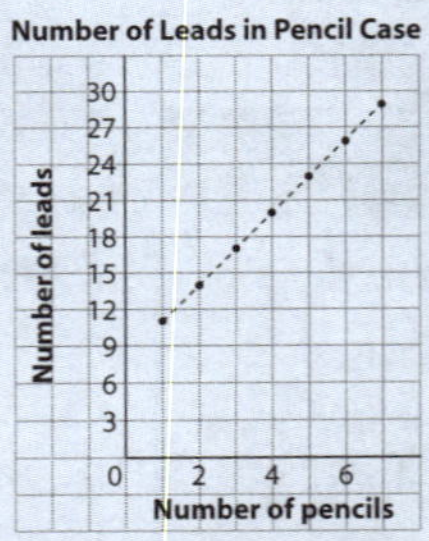

6. a) The number of tiles increases by 2 each time.

b)

Frame Number	Number of Tiles
1	1
2	3
3	5
4	7

c)

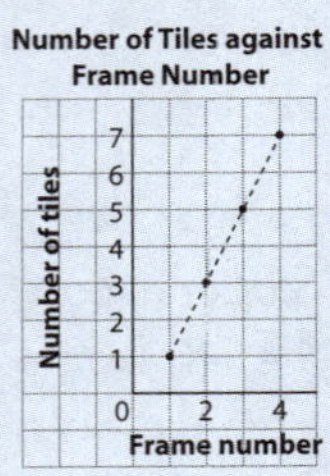

f) i) $31 = 2n - 1 \Rightarrow 16 = n$
ii) $32 = 2n - 1 \Rightarrow n = 16.5$
Since 16.5 is not a natural number, no frame will have 32 tiles.
iii) $33 = 2n - 1 \Rightarrow n = 17$

10.4 Solving Equations with Algebra Tiles

Focus Use algebra tiles to solve equations involving whole numbers.

'ecall that one red unit tile and one yellow unit tile ombine to model 0.
These two unit tiles form a zero pair.

−1 +1

The yellow variable tile represents x.
The opposite of x is $-x$.
So, the red variable tile represents $-x$.
One red variable tile and one yellow variable tile also combine to model 0.
These two variable tiles form a zero pair.

x
$-x$

Flip the yellow tile to get a red tile.

xplore

Work with a partner.
You will need algebra tiles.

➢ For the equation: $2x = 9 - x$
- Interpret the equation in words.
- Use algebra tiles to solve the equation. $x = 3$
- Sketch the tiles you used.

➢ Repeat the activity for this equation: $2 - 3x = 2x - 8$ $x = 2$

Reflect & Share

Compare the solutions for the equations with those of another pair of classmates.
What strategies did you use to solve the equations?
How did you use zero pairs?

onnect

Recall how we used algebra tiles to solve equations in *Unit 1*.
Remember that to keep the balance of an equation, what you do to one side you must also do to the other side.

To solve the equation $3x - 8 = -x$,
isolate the variable tiles on one side of the equation.

10.4 Solving Equations with Algebra Tiles 435

Solving Equations with Algebra Tiles

LESSON ORGANIZER (80–100 min)

Curriculum Focus: Use algebra tiles to solve equations involving whole numbers. (8m64)

Teacher Materials
Optional
- overhead algebra tiles

Student Materials
- algebra tiles (PM 27)

Optional
- Step-by-Step 4 (Master 10.11)
- Extra Practice 4 (Master 10.18)

Assessment: Master 10.2 Ongoing Observations: Algebra

Key Math Learning

Algebra tiles can be used to solve linear equations with variables on both sides of the equal sign.

Calculator Skills

Students could use a calculator to multiply 3 × \$45.00 and 327 × \$0.35, then find the sum of the products. Other students may use the calculator to find 3 × 45 + 327 × 0.35, knowing that the calculator follows the order of operations.

BEFORE Get Started

Review the algebra tiles used in Lesson 6 of Unit 1. Introduce the red x-tile or red variable tile. Ensure students understand this tile represents $-x$. Have students use algebra tiles to model $x + 1$, $1 - x$, $2x + 1$, $1 - 2x$, $3x + 2$, $2 - 3x$, and so on.

Have students use algebra tiles to create, then sketch, a "picture" worth zero.
Students should use both variable tiles and unit tiles.
For example:

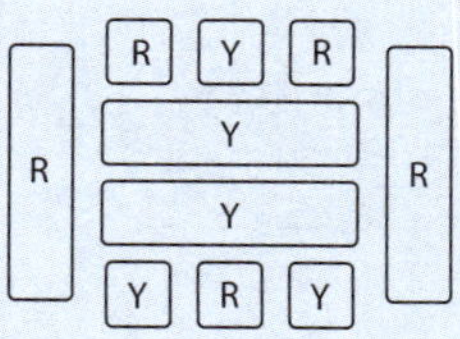

Present *Explore*.

DURING Explore

Ongoing Assessment: Observe and Listen

Ensure students know how to lay out tiles to represent $2x = 9 - x$.

As students work, ask questions, such as:

- How did you interpret the equation in words? (*Two times a number is equal to nine minus the number.*)
- Which algebra tiles did you use to represent the equation? (*I used 2 yellow x-tiles on the left side. I used 9 yellow unit tiles and 1 red x-tile on the right side.*)
- How did you solve the equation? (*I added 1 yellow x-tile to each side to isolate the unit tiles on the right side. I was left with 3 yellow x-tiles on one side and 9 yellow unit tiles on the other side. Since there are 3 yellow x-tiles, I arranged the yellow unit tiles into 3 groups. Each group had 3 yellow unit tiles. So, $x = 3$*)

REACHING ALL LEARNERS

Early Finishers

Have students write equations similar to those in *Practice* question 2. Equations must have an integer solution. Students trade equations with a classmate and solve their classmate's equation.

Common Misconceptions

➤ Students flip the tiles on one side of the equation only.

How to Help: Remind students that to keep the balance of an equation, what we do to one side of the equation we must also do to the other side. For example, solve the equation: $-4x = 8$
Use algebra tiles to model this equation.
There are 4 red x-tiles on the left side and 8 yellow unit tiles on the right side. So, arrange the unit tiles into 4 equal groups.
One red x-tile equals 2 yellow unit tiles.
To state the solution, x must be positive, or yellow.
So, flip the tiles on both sides of the equation to get $x = -2$.
Verify the solution:

Left side $= -4x$ $\quad$ Right side $= 8$
$= -4(-2)$
$= 8$

Since the left side equals the right side, $x = -2$ is correct.
If we only flip the red x-tiles on the left side of the equation, we get $x = 2$. Verify the solution:

Left side $= -4x$ $\quad$ Right side $= 8$
$= -4(2)$
$= -8$

Since the left side does not equal the right side, $x = -2$ is not correct. This illustrates the importance of doing the same to both sides of the equation.

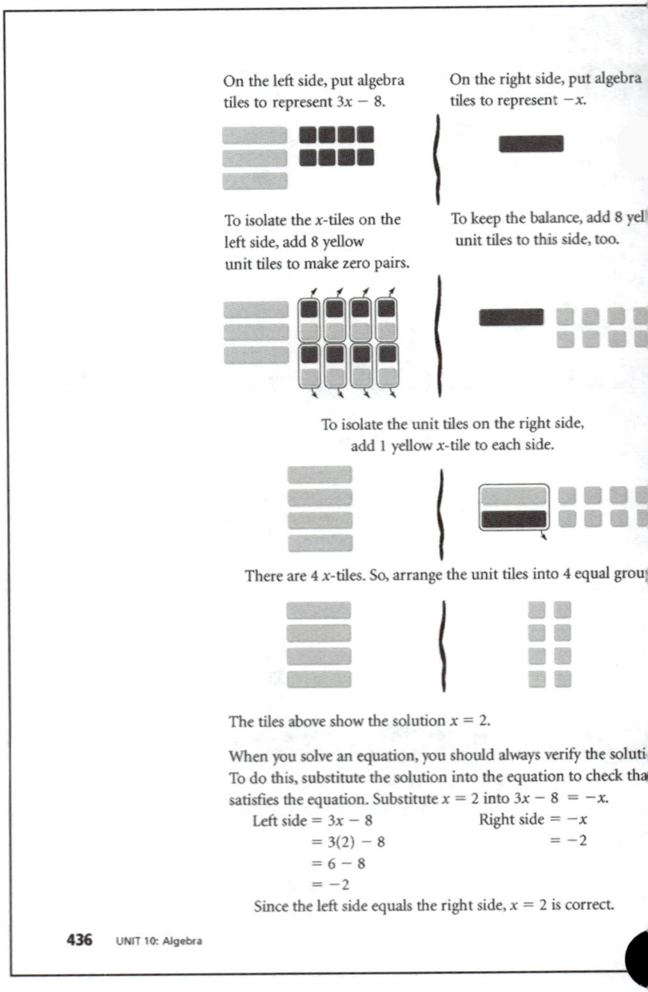

On the left side, put algebra tiles to represent $3x - 8$.

On the right side, put algebra tiles to represent $-x$.

To isolate the x-tiles on the left side, add 8 yellow unit tiles to make zero pairs.

To keep the balance, add 8 yel[low] unit tiles to this side, too.

To isolate the unit tiles on the right side, add 1 yellow x-tile to each side.

There are 4 x-tiles. So, arrange the unit tiles into 4 equal grou[ps].

The tiles above show the solution $x = 2$.

When you solve an equation, you should always verify the soluti[on]. To do this, substitute the solution into the equation to check tha[t it] satisfies the equation. Substitute $x = 2$ into $3x - 8 = -x$.

Left side $= 3x - 8$ $\quad$ Right side $= -x$
$= 3(2) - 8$ $\quad$ $= -2$
$= 6 - 8$
$= -2$

Since the left side equals the right side, $x = 2$ is correct.

436 UNIT 10: Algebra

- How did you interpret the equation $2 - 3x = 2x - 8$ in words?
  (Two minus three times a number is equal to two times the number minus eight.)
- Which algebra tiles did you use to represent the equation?
  (I used 2 yellow unit tiles and three red x-tiles on the left side. I used 2 yellow x-tiles and 8 red unit tiles on the right side.)
- What was the first step in solving this equation?
  (I added 2 red unit tiles to each side to isolate the x-tiles on the left side. I was left with 3 red x-tiles on the left side, and 2 yellow x-tiles and 10 red unit tiles on the right side.)
- What did you do next?
  (I added 2 red x-tiles to each side to isolate the unit tiles on the right side. I was left with 5 red x-tiles on the left side, and 10 red unit tiles on the right side.)
- What did you do next?
  (I flipped all the tiles because x must be positive to state the solution. There must not be a negative sign preceding x in the solution. All the tiles are now yellow.)
- What is the solution to the equation?
  (I arranged the unit tiles into 5 equal groups. There are 2 unit tiles in each group. So, x = 2)

AFTER Connect

Invite students to share their solutions with the class.

What you might see:

$2x = 9 - x$

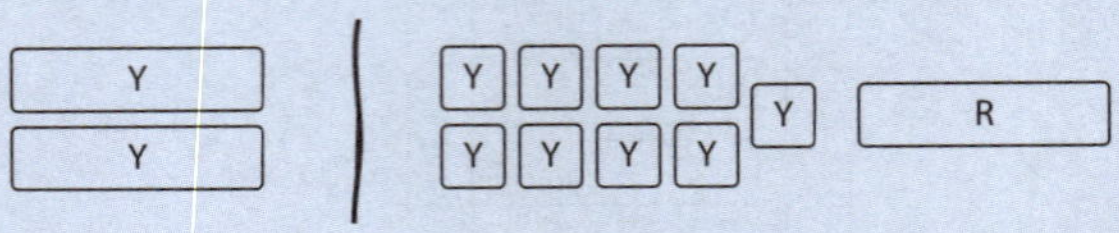

$2 - 3x = 2x - 8$

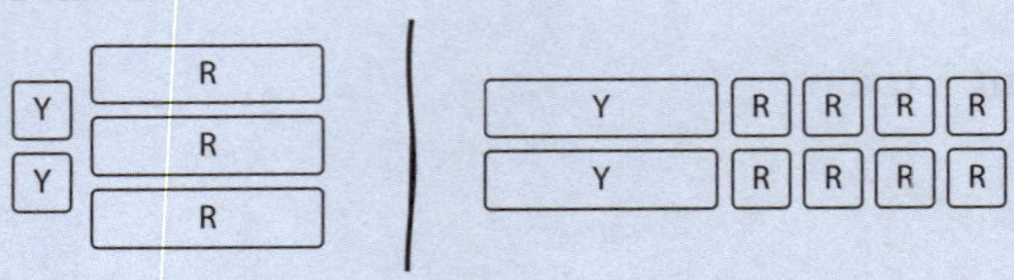

Example

a) Use algebra tiles to solve the equation $2x + 3 = 4x - 3$.
b) Verify the solution.
c) Interpret the equation in words.

Solution

a) $2x + 3 = 4x - 3$

Isolate the x-tiles on the left side.
Add 3 red unit tiles to each side.

Isolate the unit tiles on the right side.
Add 4 red x-tiles to each side.

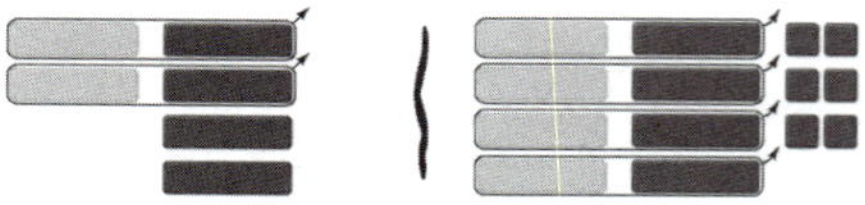

There are 2 x-tiles. So, arrange the unit tiles into 2 equal groups.

The tiles show that one red x-tile equals 3 red unit tiles.
Flip the tiles on each side.
One yellow x-tile equals 3 yellow unit tiles.
So, $x = 3$

b) To verify the solution, substitute $x = 3$ into $2x + 3 = 4x - 3$.

Left side $= 2x + 3$	Right side $= 4x - 3$
$= 2(3) + 3$	$= 4(3) - 3$
$= 6 + 3$	$= 12 - 3$
$= 9$	$= 9$

Since the left side equals the right side, $x = 3$ is correct.

10.4 Solving Equations with Algebra Tiles **437**

Sample Solutions

Students' answers should include a verification of each solution.

1. a) Two times a number is equal to the number plus five.
b) Three times a number minus two is equal to the number.
c) Seven times a number minus nine is equal to four times the number.
d) Six minus a number is equal to two times the number.

3. i) a) Two times a number plus two is equal to three times the number minus 5.
ii) a) Five times a number minus six is equal to eight minus two times the number.
iii) a) Three times a number minus thirteen is equal to the number minus seven.

7. b) Substitute $l = 6$ into $2l = 6 + l$.

Left side $= 2l$	Right side $= 6 + l$
$= 2(6)$	$= 6 + 6$
$= 12$	$= 12$

Since the left side equals the right side, $l = 6$ is correct.

c) The formula for the surface area of a cube is: $SA = 6l^2$, where l is the edge length of the cube.
Substitute $l = 6$ into $SA = 6l^2$.
$SA = 6(6)^2$
$= 6(36)$
$= 216$
The surface area of the cube is 216 cm^2.
The formula for the volume of a cube is: $V = l^3$, where l is the edge length of the cube.
Substitute $l = 6$ into $V = l^3$.
$SA = 6^3$
$= 216$
The volume of the cube is 216 cm^3.

Have students share the different ways they interpreted the equations in words. For example, for $2x = 9 - x$, some possible interpretations are:

- Double a number is equal to the number subtracted from nine.
- Two times a number is nine decreased by the number.
- Two times a number is equal to nine minus the number.

Ask:

- What strategies did you use to solve the equations?
  (I used zero pairs to help isolate tiles. For example, in the first equation, I added 1 yellow x-tile to each side. The yellow x-tile and the red x-tile on the right side of the equation formed a zero pair. So, the unit tiles were now isolated on the right side.) (When I had isolated the variable tiles on one side and the unit tiles on the other side, I arranged the tiles on each side into equal groups. When there were 5 x-tiles, I arranged the variable tiles into 5 equal groups.)

Introduce *Connect* and explain the process of solving equations using algebra tiles. Emphasize the use of zero pairs when using the tiles.

Remind students that an equation can be solved so that x is on the left side or the right side in the final line of the solution. Show students an alternative solution to the *Example*, a solution that does not involve flipping tiles.

Alternative Solution:

Isolate the x-tiles on the right side.
Add 3 yellow unit tiles to each side.
You are left with 6 yellow unit tiles and 2 yellow x-tiles on the left side, and 4 yellow x-tiles on the right side.

8. a) Let the first number be n.
Then, the next number is $n + 1$, and the next number is $n + 2$.
So, an equation you could use to solve the problem is:
$n + (n + 1) + (n + 2) = 63$, or $3n + 3 = 63$

REFLECT: To use algebra tiles to solve an equation with variables on both sides of the equal sign, I first model the equation.
I isolate the variable on one side of the equation. I must remember to do to one side of the equation what I do to the other side.
For example: Use algebra tiles to solve the equation
$5x + 5 = 3x + 13$

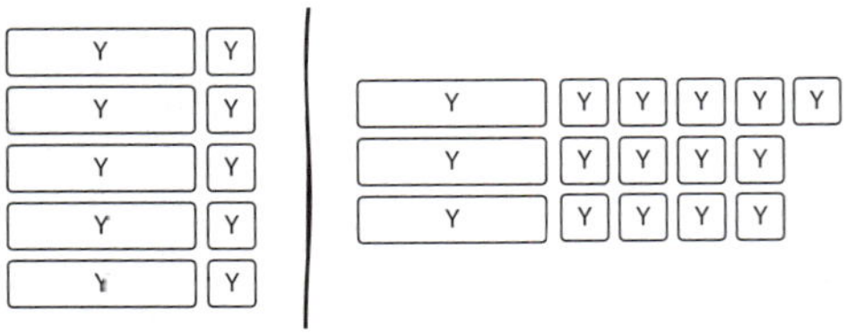

Isolate the x-tiles on the left side.
Add 5 red unit tiles to each side.

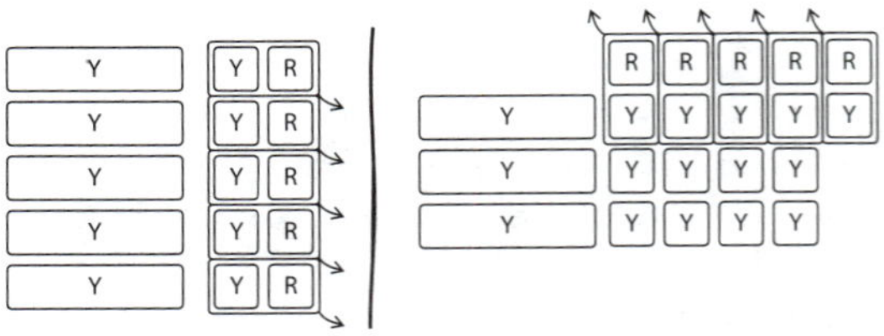

Isolate the unit tiles on the right side.
Add 3 red x-tiles to each side.

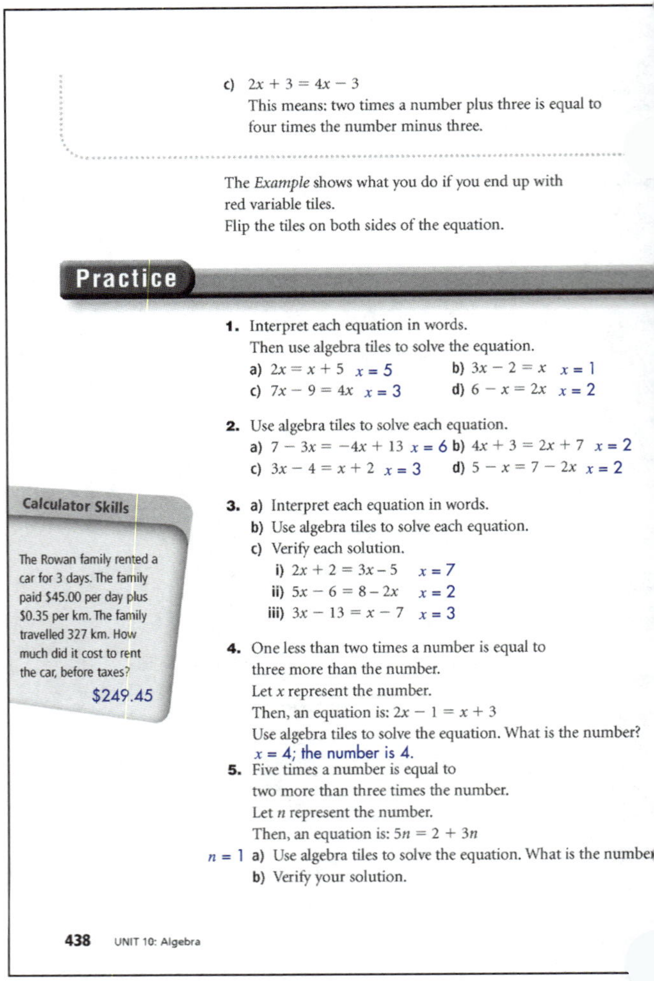

c) $2x + 3 = 4x - 3$
This means: two times a number plus three is equal to four times the number minus three.

The *Example* shows what you do if you end up with red variable tiles.
Flip the tiles on both sides of the equation.

Practice

1. Interpret each equation in words.
Then use algebra tiles to solve the equation.
a) $2x = x + 5$ $x = 5$ b) $3x - 2 = x$ $x = 1$
c) $7x - 9 = 4x$ $x = 3$ d) $6 - x = 2x$ $x = 2$

2. Use algebra tiles to solve each equation.
a) $7 - 3x = -4x + 13$ $x = 6$ b) $4x + 3 = 2x + 7$ $x = 2$
c) $3x - 4 = x + 2$ $x = 3$ d) $5 - x = 7 - 2x$ $x = 2$

3. a) Interpret each equation in words.
b) Use algebra tiles to solve each equation.
c) Verify each solution.
i) $2x + 2 = 3x - 5$ $x = 7$
ii) $5x - 6 = 8 - 2x$ $x = 2$
iii) $3x - 13 = x - 7$ $x = 3$

Calculator Skills
The Rowan family rented a car for 3 days. The family paid \$45.00 per day plus \$0.35 per km. The family travelled 327 km. How much did it cost to rent the car, before taxes?
\$249.45

4. One less than two times a number is equal to three more than the number.
Let x represent the number.
Then, an equation is: $2x - 1 = x + 3$
Use algebra tiles to solve the equation. What is the number?
$x = 4$; the number is 4.

5. Five times a number is equal to two more than three times the number.
Let n represent the number.
Then, an equation is: $5n = 2 + 3n$
$n = 1$ a) Use algebra tiles to solve the equation. What is the number?
b) Verify your solution.

438 UNIT 10: Algebra

Isolate the unit tiles on the left side.
Add 2 red x-tiles to each side.
You are left with 6 yellow unit tiles on the left side, and 2 yellow x-tiles on the right side.

There are 2 yellow x-tiles. So, arrange the unit tiles into 2 equal groups.

One yellow x-tile equals 3 yellow unit tiles.
So, $x = 3$

Ensure students understand the importance of verifying solutions.
Remind students that whatever is done to one side of the equation must also be done to the other side.

Practice

Have algebra tiles (PM 27) available for all questions.

Assessment Focus: Question 7

Remind students that the variable tile can represent other variables besides x. In this question, students should let the variable tile represent l. Remind students of the formulas for the surface area and volume of a cube ($SA = 6l^2$; $V = l^3$). Students substitute their solution to part a into the formulas for surface area and volume.

Assignment Guidelines

If your students do not have time to complete all the *Practice* questions on pages 438 and 439, these questions provide minimum curriculum coverage: 1, 3, 4, 7, *Reflect*

To assess the 4 Achievement Chart categories listed in the curriculum document, have students complete these *Practice* questions:
Knowledge and Understanding: 1 Application: 7
Thinking: 4 Communication: *Reflect*

6. The sum of a number and three more than the number is 23.
Let t represent the number.
Then, an equation is: $t + t + 3 = 23$

$t = 10$ a) Use algebra tiles to solve the equation. What is the number? 10
b) Verify your solution.

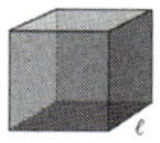

7. Assessment Focus Two times the edge length of a cube is 6 cm longer than the edge length.
Let l centimetres represent the edge length of the cube.
An equation for the edge length is: $2l = 6 + l$ $l = 6$
a) Use algebra tiles to solve the equation. What is the edge length of the cube? 6 cm
b) Verify the solution.
c) What are the surface area and the volume of the cube? 216 cm² 216 cm³

ke It Further

8. The sum of three consecutive numbers is 63.
a) Write an equation you could use to solve this problem.
$n = 20$ b) Solve the equation. What are the numbers? 20, 21, 22
c) Verify your solution.

9. Solve these equations. Verify your solutions.
a) $7x + 4 = 3x - 8$ $x = -3$
b) $3 - 2x = 13 + 3x$ $x = -2$

Math Link

Science
Pressure is force per unit area.
Pressure is measured in pascals (Pa).
A formula for pressure is:
$\text{Pressure} = \frac{\text{Force}}{\text{Area}}$
When we know the pressure in pascals and the area in square metres, we can solve this formula to find the force in newtons (N).

eflect

Explain how you can use algebra tiles to solve an equation with variables on both sides of the equal sign.
Include an example in your explanation.

10.4 Solving Equations with Algebra Tiles 439

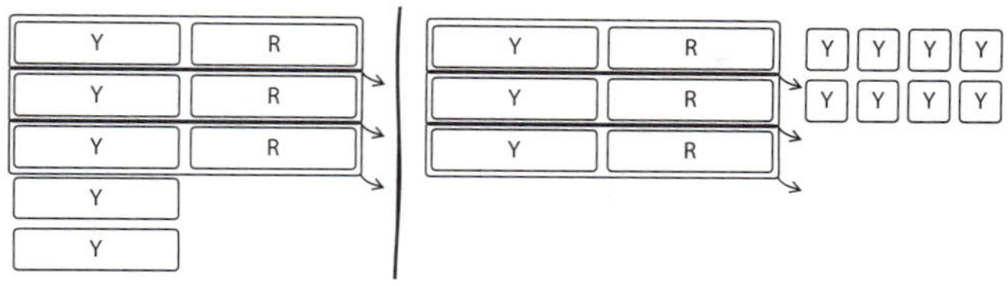

There are 2 yellow x-tiles. So, arrange the unit tiles into 2 equal groups.

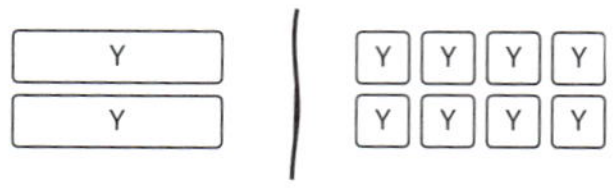

The tiles show that one yellow x-tile equals 4 yellow unit tiles. So, the solution is $x = 4$.

Math Link

The newton is named for Sir Isaac Newton (1642–1727), the British mathematician, physicist, and natural philosopher. He made three very important discoveries. He discovered the three universal laws of motion, the properties of light, and he invented the field of math known as calculus.

ASSESSMENT FOR LEARNING

What to Look For

Knowledge and Understanding

✔ Students understand that algebra tiles can be used to model and solve linear equations with variables on both sides of the equal sign.

Communication

✔ Students can explain how to use algebra tiles to solve an equation.

Application

✔ Students can interpret algebraic equations in words.

✔ Students can solve equations using algebra tiles, then verify the solutions.

What to Do

Extra Support: Students who have difficulty solving an equation with variables on both sides of the equal sign may benefit from first working with simpler equations such as $3x = 12$, $x + 3 = 12$, and $2x + 3 = 13$ to strengthen their skills and to build confidence. Students can use Step-by-Step 4 (Master 10.11) to complete question 7.

Extra Practice: Students can complete the Additional Activity *Equation Concentration* (Master 10.6).
Students can complete Extra Practice 4 (Master 10.18).

Extension: Have students use algebra tiles to solve the equations $6 + 2x = 6$ and $x + 4 = 4 + x$. Students report on their findings. (Solutions: *0; any integer*)

Recording and Reporting

Master 10.2 Ongoing Observations: Algebra

LESSON 10.5

Solving Equations Algebraically

LESSON ORGANIZER — 80–100 min

Curriculum Focus: Solve a problem by solving a related equation. (8m63, 8m64)

Student Materials *Optional*
- calculators
- Step-by-Step 5 (Master 10.12)
- Extra Practice 5 (Master 10.19)

Assessment: Master 10.2 Ongoing Observations: Algebra

Key Math Learnings

1. Equations, including those where the solution is a fraction or a decimal, can be solved using algebraic methods.
2. A word problem can be solved by solving a related equation.

Calculator Skills

Students could take the square root of the area to find the side length of the square: $\sqrt{225} = 15$.

Since the diagonal of a square creates two right triangles, students use the Pythagorean Theorem to find the length of the hypotenuse (the diagonal):

$$15^2 + 15^2 = c^2$$
$$225 + 225 = c^2$$
$$450 = c^2$$
$$c \doteq 21.21 \text{ m or } 2121 \text{ cm}$$

10.5 Solving Equations Algebraically

Focus Solve a problem by solving a related equation.

Explore

Work with a partner. Solve this problem.
My mother's age is 4 more than 2 times my brother's age.
My mother is 46 years old.
How old is my brother? 21 years old

Reflect & Share

Discuss the strategies you used for finding the brother's age with those of another pair of classmates.
Did you use an equation?
If not, how could you represent this problem with an equation?

Connect

In *Unit 1*, you learned how to solve equations algebraically.
All the equations in *Unit 1* had solutions that were whole numbe
We use the same method to solve an equation where the solution is a fraction or a decimal.

Example 1

Three more than two times a number is 4. What is the number?
a) Write an equation to represent this problem.
b) Solve the equation.
c) Verify the solution.

Solution

a) Let the number be n.
Then, two times the number is: $2n$
And, three more than two times the number is: $3 + 2n$
The equation is $3 + 2n = 4$

b) $3 + 2n = 4$
$3 + 2n - 3 = 4 - 3$ To isolate $2n$, subtract 3 from each
$2n = 1$
$\frac{2n}{2} = \frac{1}{2}$ Divide each side by 2.
$n = \frac{1}{2}$

Using the inverse operation here is the same as using zero pairs.

440 UNIT 10: Algebra

BEFORE — Get Started

Show students some simple word problems that can be solved mathematically.

Ask:
- Jeremy is 13 years old. The sum of his age and his sister's age is 23. How old is Jeremy's sister? How do you know?
(10 years old; 23 – 13 = 10)
- An ice cream cone costs $2. Josephine paid $12 for ice cream cones when she was shopping at the mall with her friends. How many ice cream cones did Josephine buy? How do you know?
(6 cones; $2 × 6 = $12)

Present *Explore*. Remind students that there are many different strategies that can be used to solve the problem.

DURING — Explore

Ongoing Assessment: Observe and Listen

As students work, ask questions, such as:
- Which strategies could you use to solve this problem?
(I could use guess and check. I could write an equation, then solve the equation by inspection, by systematic trial, or algebraically.)
- How did you use guess and check?
(I guessed a number for the brother's age, multiplied the number by 2, then added 4. I continued to do this until I got a solution of 46. The brother is 21 years old.)
- Which variable did you use in your equation?
(I let the brother's age in years be b.)
- How did you represent 4 more than 2 times the brother's age? *(2b + 4)*
- What equation did you write to represent this problem? *(2b + 4 = 46)*

c) To verify the solution, substitute $n = \frac{1}{2}$ into $3 + 2n = 4$.

Left side $= 3 + 2n$ $\quad$ Right side $= 4$

$= 3 + 2(\frac{1}{2})$

$= 3 + 1$

$= 4$

Since the left side equals the right side, $n = \frac{1}{2}$ is correct.

The number is $\frac{1}{2}$.

In *Example 1*, we could write the solution $n = \frac{1}{2}$ as a decimal, $n = 0.5$.

However, some fractions, such as $\frac{1}{3}$, are repeating decimals.

Do not convert a fraction of this type to a decimal.

We can use an equation to solve problems related to number patterns.

When we know the *n*th term and the term value, we can solve an equation to find the term number.

Example 2

The *n*th term of a number pattern is $5n - 2$.

What is the term number when the term value is 348?

Solution

The *n*th term is $5n - 2$.

The term value of an unknown term number is 348.

Write the equation: $5n - 2 = 348$

Solve this equation for *n*.

$5n - 2 = 348$

$5n - 2 + 2 = 348 + 2$ $\quad$ To isolate $5n$, add 2 to each side.

$5n = 350$

$\frac{5n}{5} = \frac{350}{5}$ $\quad$ Divide each side by 5.

$n = 70$

The 70th term has value 348.

In *Example 2*, the equation could have been solved by inspection:

$5n - 2 = 348$

Think: what do you subtract 2 from to get 348?

Answer: you subtract 2 from 350.

Think: what do you multiply 5 by to get 350?

Answer: you multiply 5 by 70.

So, $n = 70$

REACHING ALL LEARNERS

Alternative Explore

An indoor rock climbing facility charges an annual membership fee of $30, plus $8 per hour of climbing. Last year, Samantha paid $310. How many hours did Samantha climb?

Discuss the strategies you used to solve this problem.

How could you represent this problem with an equation?

Early Finishers

For each of *Practice* questions 8 and 9, have students use the information to write another problem that can be solved using an equation. Students write the equation, then solve the problem.

Common Misconceptions

➤ When students isolate the variable on the left side, they divide by the wrong number.

How to Help: Demonstrate using the equation $11 = 1 + 5x$.

Solve the equation: $11 = 1 + 5x$

$11 - 1 = 1 + 5x - 1$ $\quad$ To isolate $5x$, subtract 1 from each side.

$10 = 5x$

$\frac{10}{5} = \frac{5x}{5}$ $\quad$ To isolate x, divide each side by 5.

$2 = x$

Some students might divide each side of the equation by 10. Show students that this does not isolate the variable.

$\frac{10}{10} = \frac{5x}{10}$ $\quad$ Divide each side by 10.

$1 = \frac{x}{2}$

- How did you solve the equation? (*I solved the equation systematically. I chose a value for b. If the solution was too small, I chose a greater value for b. If the solution was too large, I chose a lesser value for b. I got the solution 46 when b = 21. The brother is 21 years old.*)
- How else could you solve the equation? (*I could solve the equation by inspection. I could find a number which, when multiplied by 2, has product 42, because 42 + 4 = 46. The number is 21.*)
- How else could you solve the equation? (*I could use algebra tiles.*)

AFTER Connect

Invite students to share their strategies with the class. Ask:

- How did you solve the equation algebraically? Explain. (*To isolate 2b, I subtracted 4 from each side:* $2b + 4 - 4 = 46 - 4$ ⇨ $2b = 42$. *I divided each side by 2 to isolate b:* $\frac{2b}{2} = \frac{42}{2}$ ⇨ $b = 21$. *The brother's age in years is 21.*)
- How do you know your solution is correct? (*I substituted the solution into the original equation: Left side = 2b + 4 = 2(21) + 4 = 46 = right side. Since the left side equals the right side, the solution is correct.*)

Introduce *Connect*. Ensure students understand that the first step to writing an equation is to write a statement that tells what the variable represents. In *Example 1*, students could not use algebra tiles to solve the equation because the solution is a fraction. Remind students that when solving an equation algebraically, the balance of the equation must always be retained. So, whatever you do to one side of the equation, you must also do to the other side. Remind students that an equation can be solved so that the variable is on the left side or the right side in the final line of the solution.

For example, show students an example where the variable is isolated on the right side.

Solve the equation: $8 = 4 + 3x$

Sample Solutions

3. In each case, let n represent the number.

a) $3n + 10 = 25 \Rightarrow 3n + 10 - 10 = 25 - 10 \Rightarrow 3n = 15 \Rightarrow$
$\frac{3n}{3} = \frac{15}{3} \Rightarrow n = 5$

b) $3n - 10 = 25 \Rightarrow 3n - 10 + 10 = 25 + 10 \Rightarrow 3n = 35 \Rightarrow$
$\frac{3n}{3} = \frac{35}{3} \Rightarrow n = \frac{35}{3}$

c) $\frac{n}{2} - 25 = 10 \Rightarrow \frac{n}{2} - 25 + 25 = 10 + 25 \Rightarrow \frac{n}{2} = 35 \Rightarrow$
$2(\frac{n}{2}) = 35 \times 2 \Rightarrow n = 70$

d) $25 - \frac{n}{2} = 10 \Rightarrow 25 - \frac{n}{2} - 25 = 10 - 25 \Rightarrow -\frac{n}{2} = -15 \Rightarrow$
$(-2)(-\frac{n}{2}) = (-2)(-15) \Rightarrow n = 30$

4. **c)** Substitute $w = 9$ into $72 + 24w = 288$; if the left side equals the right side, the solution is correct.

5. **a)** Let n represent the number of students who attended the dance. $85 + 2n = 197$

b) $85 + 2n = 197 \Rightarrow 85 + 2n - 85 = 197 - 85 \Rightarrow 2n = 112$
$\Rightarrow \frac{2n}{2} = \frac{112}{2} \Rightarrow n = 56$
Verify: Left side $= 85 + 2n = 85 + 2(56) = 197 =$ right side

8. **a)** Water flows into a bathtub at a rate of 15 L/min. There are 75 L of water in the bathtub. How long was the tap running?

b) Let the time in minutes be t.
$15t = 75 \Rightarrow \frac{15t}{15} = \frac{75}{15} \Rightarrow t = 5$
The tap was running for 5 min.

9. **a)** A family went on a fishing trip. They paid $300 to rent the boat. Each person rented a fishing rod at a cost of $20 per rod. The total cost of the trip was $380. How many people went on the fishing trip?

The equation could also have been solved by systematic trial:
$5n - 2 = 348$
Use a calculator to substitute different numbers for n until the left side of the equation equals 348.

In *Example 2*, there is only one value of n that makes the equatio[n] true. If $n = 69$, or if $n = 71$, or if n equals any number other than 70, the equation is not true.

Practice

Use algebra, systematic trial, or inspection to solve an equation.

1. Solve each equation.
   a) $2x = 3$ $x = \frac{3}{2}$ b) $3x = 2$ $x = \frac{2}{3}$ c) $4x = 6$ $x = \frac{3}{2}$ d) $5x = 12$ $x =$
2. Solve each equation. Verify the solution.
   a) $2x - 1 = 5$ $x = 3$ b) $7 = 1 + 3n$ $n = 2$
   c) $10 = 4a - 1$ $a = \frac{11}{4}$ d) $5 + 2m = 6$ $m = \frac{1}{2}$
3. Write, then solve, an equation to answer each question. Verify the solution.
   a) Ten more than three times a number is 25. What is the number? 5
   b) Ten less than three times a number is 25. What is the number? $\frac{35}{3}$
   c) Twenty-five subtracted from one-half a number is 10. What is the number? 70
   d) One-half of a number is subtracted from 25. The answer is 10. What is the number? 30
4. Navid has $72 in her savings account. Each week she saves $24. When will Navid have a total savings of $288?
   a) Write an equation you can use to solve the problem. $72 + 24w =$
   b) Solve the equation. When will Navid have $288 in her savings account? After 9 wee[ks]
   c) How can you check the answer?

442 UNIT 10: Algebra

$$8 = 4 + 3x$$
$$8 - 4 = 4 + 3x - 4$$ To isolate $3x$, subtract 4 from each side.
$$4 = 3x$$
$$\frac{4}{3} = \frac{3x}{3}$$ Divide each side by 3 to isolate x.
$$\frac{4}{3} = x$$
The solution is $x = \frac{4}{3}$.

Reinforce the importance of verifying solutions and checking the left side and the right side of an equation separately.

Students may solve some of the equations systematically or by inspection, but with practice, students should find the most efficient method is algebraically. This is especially true when the solution is a fraction or a decimal.

Practice

Encourage students to always verify their solutions. Questions 8 and 9 require students to write their own problems. Students will demonstrate the depth of their understanding by the problems they write.

Assessment Focus: Question 5

Ensure students understand that "flat rate" is the same as a one-time fee. Students could write one of the following equations: $85 + 2n = 197$, $2n + 85 = 197$, $197 = 85 + 2n$, $197 = 2n + 85$ (the variable used may differ). Students then solve the equation algebraically, by inspection, or systematically.

5. **Assessment Focus** The Grade 8 students had an end-of-the-year dance. The disc jockey they hired charged a flat rate of \$85, plus \$2 for each student who attended the dance. The disc jockey was paid \$197. How many students attended the dance?
   a) Write an equation you can use to solve the problem. $85 + 2n = 197$
   b) Solve your equation. Verify the solution. $n = 56$

6. The nth term of a number pattern is $4n - 3$.
   a) What is the term value for each term?
      i) the 10th term 37 ii) the 20th term 77
   b) What is the term number for each term value?
      i) 53 Term 14 ii) 97 Term 25

lator Skills

ea of a square m^2.
ate the length of onal of uare to the t centimetre.
or 2121 cm

7. The nth term of a number pattern is $9n + 1$. What is the term number for each term value?
   a) 154 $n = 17$ b) 118 $n = 13$ c) 244 $n = 27$

8. Use this information:
   Water flows into a bathtub at a rate of 15 L/min.
   a) Write a problem that can be solved using an equation.
   b) Write, then solve, the equation.

9. Use this information:
   Boat rental: \$300 Fishing rod rental: \$20
   a) Write a problem that can be solved using an equation.
   b) Write the equation, then solve the problem.
   c) How could you have solved the problem without writing an equation? Explain.

ke It Further

10. Two more than the square of a number is 123. What is the number?
    a) Write an equation you could use to find the number. $n^2 + 2 = 123$
    b) Solve the equation. What is the number? 11
    c) Verify the solution.

eflect

Choose one of the word problems in this section. Explain the steps you used to write the equation, then to solve the equation.

10.5 Solving Equations Algebraically 443

b) Let the number of people be n.
$300 + 20n = 380 \Rightarrow n = 4$
Four people went on the fishing trip.

c) I could have used guess and check. I could guess the number of people, multiply the number by 20, then add 300. When the solution is 380, the number is correct.

REFLECT: I chose question 3a. I let the number be n.
Three times a number is: $3n$
Ten more than three times a number is: $3n + 10$
The equation is: $3n + 10 = 25$
To solve the equation:

$$3n + 10 = 25$$

$$3n + 10 - 10 = 25 - 10$$

To isolate $3n$, I subtracted 10 from each side.

$$3n = 15$$

$$\frac{3n}{3} = \frac{15}{3}$$

To isolate n, divide each side by 3.

$$n = 5$$

The number is 5.

Assignment Guidelines

If your students do not have time to complete all the *Practice* questions on pages 442 and 443, these questions provide minimum curriculum coverage: 2, 3, 4, 5, 7, 9, *Reflect*

To assess the 4 Achievement Chart categories listed in the curriculum document, have students complete these *Practice* questions:

Knowledge and Understanding: 3
Thinking: 9
Application: 5
Communication: *Reflect*

ASSESSMENT FOR LEARNING

What to Look For

Knowledge and Understanding

✔ Students understand that a word problem can be represented by an equation.

Thinking

✔ Students can write a problem that can be solved using an equation, then use the equation to solve the problem.

Application

✔ Students can solve equations algebraically, by inspection, and systematically.

What to Do

Extra Support: Students who have difficulty writing an equation may benefit from breaking the problem down into parts. Students work to write an algebraic expression first, then use an equal sign to relate it to a number.
Students can use Step-by-Step 5 (Master 10.12) to complete question 5.

Extra Practice: Students can complete the Additional Activity *Algebra Bingo* (Master 10.7).
Students can complete Extra Practice 5 (Master 10.19).

Extension: Have students solve this equation algebraically, then verify the solution. $7x - 9 = 3x + 13$
(Solution: $x = \frac{11}{2}$, or $5\frac{1}{2}$)

Recording and Reporting

Master 10.2 Ongoing Observations: Algebra

Writing a Journal

Writing a Journal

A journal is a place to record ideas, observations, illustrations, and responses.
The responses to *Reflect* in each lesson are often recorded in a journal.
Here are some ideas for other items to include.

- ➢ Comment on thoughts and feelings, successes and challenges:
  - I worked well in the group today because…
  - I could improve my skills with integer operations by …
- ➢ Explain key math ideas, formulas, and words:
  - Write the word followed by a definition, picture, and example. Here is an example for *Unit 3*.

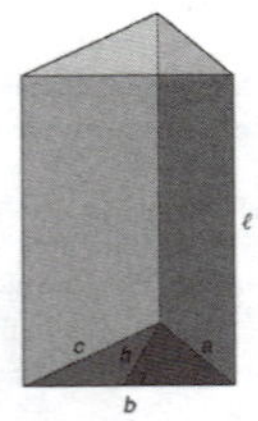

Triangular Prism

A triangular prism is a polyhedron with two congruent triangular bases, and its other faces are rectangles.

- *The volume is:*
  V = base area × height
  $V = \frac{1}{2}bh\ell$
- *The surface area is:*
  SA = sum of the areas of the faces
  $SA = a\ell + b\ell + c\ell + bh$

- ➢ Write the steps you would use to do a math task:
  - The steps I would follow to draw a circle graph…
- ➢ Create a math problem that uses the ideas from the lesson or unit:
  - Create a problem you could use an equation to solve.
- ➢ Make a list of examples of a math topic. Use headings to organize the list:
  - List the different types of problems that involve percents.
  - Draw different kinds of polygons with the same attributes.

444 UNIT 10: Algebra

Have students give examples from Unit 10 of what they might write in their journals for the given ideas. Students could share their examples with a partner.

Here are some sample responses for each idea:

➢ Comment on thoughts and feelings, successes, and challenges:
I worked well in the group today because *we cooperated and shared the work evenly.*
I could improve my skills with algebra by *getting more practice with algebra tiles.*

➢ Explain key math ideas, formulas, and words:
The Distributive Property
Definition: $a(b + c) = ab + ac$
Diagram:

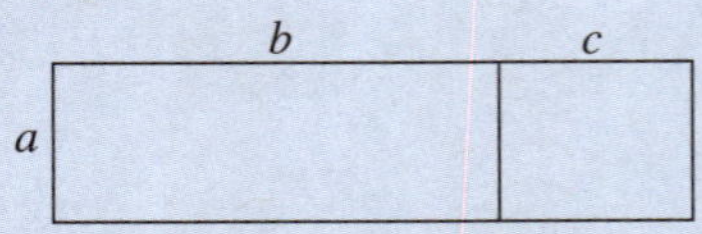

Example: $11(x + 4) = 11x + 44$

➢ Write the steps you would use to do a math task:
The steps I would follow to *solve an equation with algebra tiles are:*
Step 1: Represent the equation using algebra tiles.
Step 2: Isolate the variable tiles on one side.
Step 3: Isolate the unit tiles on the other side.
Step 4: Arrange the unit tiles into equal groups.

➢ Create a math problem that uses the lesson or unit:
Create a problem you could use an equation to solve.
Three less than seven times a number is 25.
What is the number?

➢ Make a list of examples of a math topic.
Use headings to organize the list:
List the different strategies that can be used to solve a word problem.
- *guess and check*
- *solve an equation systematically*
- *solve an equation by inspection*
- *solve an equation using algebra tiles*
- *solve an equation algebraically*

List different properties of number:
- *Adding 0:* $n + 0 = n$ *and* $0 + n = n$
- *Multiplying by 1:* $1 \times n = n$ *and* $n \times 1 = n$
- *Multiplying by 0:* $n \times 0 = 0$ *and* $0 \times n = 0$
- *Order of addition:* $n + m = m + n$
- *Order of multiplication:* $mn = nm$
- *Distributive property:* $a(b + c) = ab + ac$

Reading and Writing in Math

➢ Explain or justify a solution, pattern, or choice of strategy:
- This solution makes sense because…
- I chose to make a model because …

➢ Explain how you could apply the math:
- Who would need to calculate the area of a circle? Why?
- How does the media use charts and graphs when they want to persuade?
- Math was in the news today…

➢ Summarize what you learned:
- The main ideas I learned today (this week) are…
- Draw a concept map to show the key ideas today (this week). Here is a concept map for *Unit 10, Lesson 10.1.*

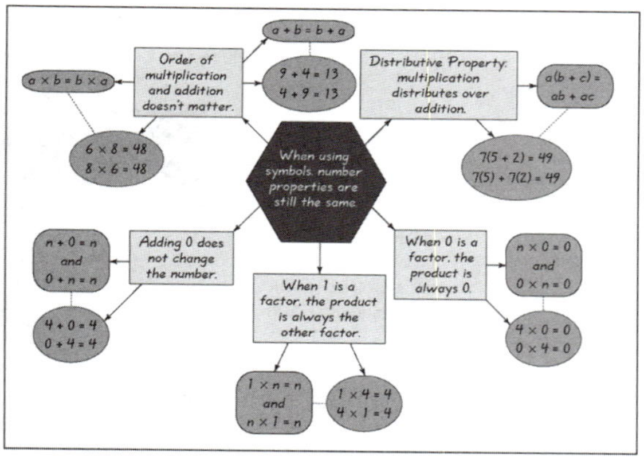

➢ Explain or justify a solution, pattern, or choice of strategy:
- This solution makes sense because *I substituted the solution into the original equation and the left side of the equation equals the right side.*
- In Lesson 3, I chose to *model the pattern of triangles in Practice question 2 with toothpicks because I was having difficulty recognizing the pattern.*

➢ Explain how you could apply the math:
- Who would need to solve an equation? Why?
A lab technician might use an equation to model the growth of a cell.
- Who would write an expression for the nth term of a number pattern?
Somebody who was studying population growth
- Algebra was in the news today when *the newspaper printed an equation that showed how to calculate interest paid on a deposit of $5000 at different financial institutions.*

➢ Summarize what you learned:
- The main ideas I learned this week are that *a number pattern or geometric pattern can be represented by a table, a graph, and an algebraic expression for the nth term, and that a word problem can be solved by solving a related equation.*
- Here is a concept map for Lessons 2 and 3 of Unit 10.

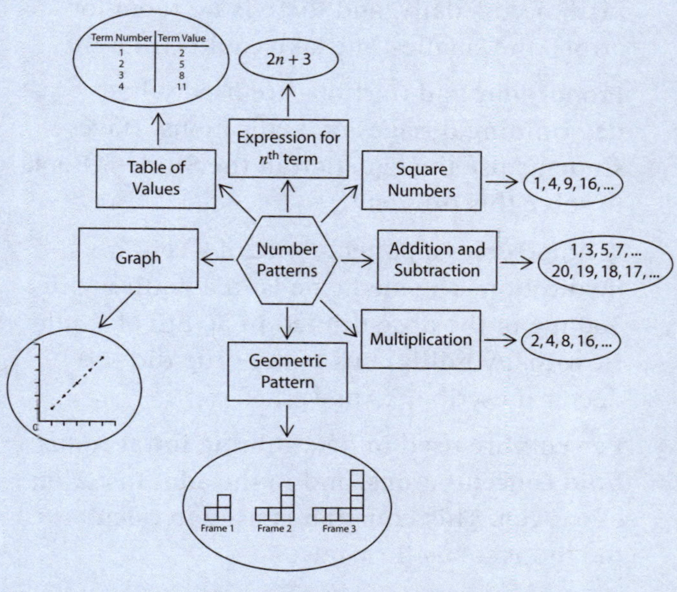

Health Care Professionals

Health Care Professionals

In the 16th century, a person who needed medical attention o went to the local hair-cutting shop for treatment. The patient be seen by a *barber-surgeon*, someone who was not only skilled a cutting hair, but also trained to cut into the human body. In fact, surgeon was often nicknamed "sawbones." The tool most often us by a barber-surgeon was a leech!

Today, hospitals and emergency rooms are staffed with medical e From the paramedic who may treat the patient on the way to the hospital, to the nurse in the recovery ward, everyone has extensiv training. Mathematics is an important part of this training.

Suppose a doctor prescribes a patient 30 mg of a certain drug. Th medicine is in a bottle, with 150 mg of the drug diluted in 20 mL liquid. How many millilitres of the medicine must the nurse give the patient? The nurse must be precise because too much or little of the drug could harm or even kill the patient. The nurse u this equation to determine the dosage, in millilitres:

$$\text{Dosage} = \frac{\text{amount of drug needed}}{\text{amount of drug diluted in bottle}} \times \text{the amount of liquid in}$$
$$= \frac{30}{150} \times 20$$
$$= \frac{1}{5} \times 20$$
$$= 4$$

The correct dose is 4 mL.

Calculating dosages for children is often based on their body mass, and the dosage will be a fraction of a typical adult dose.

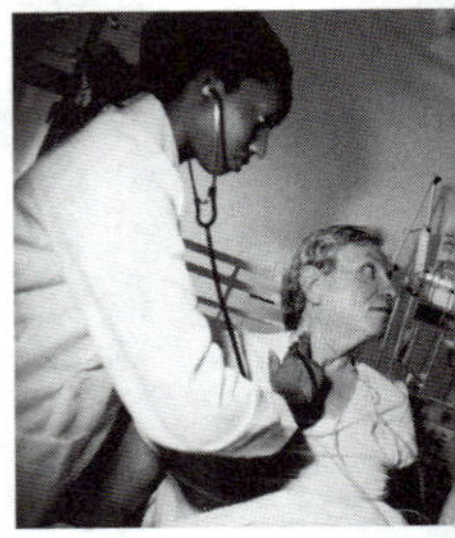

446 UNIT 10: Algebra

There are many different health care professionals working in a hospital. Whether they are anesthesiologists, dieticians, doctors, paramedics, medical technologists, nurses, radiologists, or respiratory technicians, a strong knowledge of math is essential. The use of math occurs daily, and there is no room for error—the smallest mistake could cost a life.

Proportions and fractions are used when determining dosages of medications. Have students use the equation in the Student Book to solve this problem.

A nurse gives a patient 5 mL of a certain medication. The medicine is in a bottle, with 360 mg of the drug diluted in 30 mL of liquid. How many milligrams of the drug did the doctor prescribe? (Answer: *60 mg*)

Percents are used in determining intravenous fluid concentrations, and in the administering of oxygen. This equation is used to calculate the intravenous flow rate:

$$\text{Flow rate} = \frac{\textit{Amount of fluid} \times \textit{number of drops per minute (IV setting)}}{\textit{Hours to administer} \times 60}$$

For example, 1000 mL of a certain medication is to be administered over an 8-h period. The IV is set to 15 drops/min. What should the flow rate be?

$$\text{Flow rate} = \frac{1000 \times 15}{8 \times 60}$$
$$= 31.25$$

The IV should flow at 31.25 mL/min.

Have students use the equation to find the flow rate when 500 mL of a medication is to be administered over a 4 h-period, and the IV is set at 10 drops/min. (Answer: *20.8$\overline{3}$ mL/min*)

A strong foundation in decimals is also important. Decimals are used in prescribing medications, and they also appear in the results of blood and urine tests.

Unit Review

Review any lesson with etext online tutorial

What Do I Need to Know?

Distributive Property

The product of a number and the sum of two numbers can be written as a sum of two products: $a(b + c) = ab + ac$

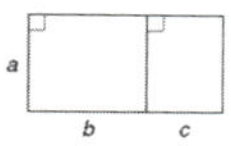

The *n*th Term of a Number Pattern

- The *n*th term can be used to find the term value of any term in a pattern.
  For example, for the pattern with *n*th term $3n + 2$, the 9th term is: $3(9) + 2 = 29$
- The *n*th term can also be used to find the term number when the term value is known.
  For example, for the pattern with *n*th term $3n + 2$, to find the term number with the term value 23, solve the equation $3n + 2 = 23$, to get $n = 7$.
  The 7th term has value 23.

What Should I Be Able to Do?

For extra practice, go to page 497.

LESSON

10.1 **1.** Expand.
a) $6(x + 9)$ $6x + 54$
b) $3(11 + 4x)$ $33 + 12x$
c) $5(7x + 6y + 5)$ $35x + 30y + 25$
d) $4(3a + 5b + 7c)$ $12a + 20b + 28c$

10.2 **2.** For each algebraic expression, substitute $n = 1, 2, 3, 4$, and 5 to generate a number pattern. Describe each pattern, then write a pattern rule.
a) $3n + 5$ 8, 11, 14, 17, 20
b) $5n + 15$ 20, 25, 30, 35, 40

3. For each number pattern below:
a) Write a pattern rule. Justify your rule.
b) Graph the pattern. Use the graph to find the 7th term.
c) Write an expression for the *n*th term.
d) Find the 70th term.

$4n + 4$ i) 8, 12, 16, 20, 24, … 32, 284
$2n + 3$ ii) 5, 7, 9, 11, 13, … 17, 143

LESSON ORGANIZER

Student Materials
- 0.5-cm grid paper (PM 14)
- isometric dot paper (PM 23)
- algebra tiles (PM 27)
- calculators

Assessment: Masters 10.1 Unit Rubric: Algebra, 10.4 Unit Summary: Algebra

Correlation of Extra Practice questions on page 497:

Lesson	Questions
10.1	1, 2
10.2	3, 4
10.3	
10.4	
10.5	5, 6, 7, 8, 9

Sample Solutions

2. a) Each term is 3 more than the previous term.
The pattern rule is: Start at 8. Add 3 each time.
b) Each term is 5 more than the previous term.
The pattern rule is: Start at 20. Add 5 each time.

3. i) a) The pattern rule is: Start at 8. Add 4 each time.
Each term is 4 more than the previous term.

b) Graph of Number Pattern 8, 12, 16, 20, 24, …

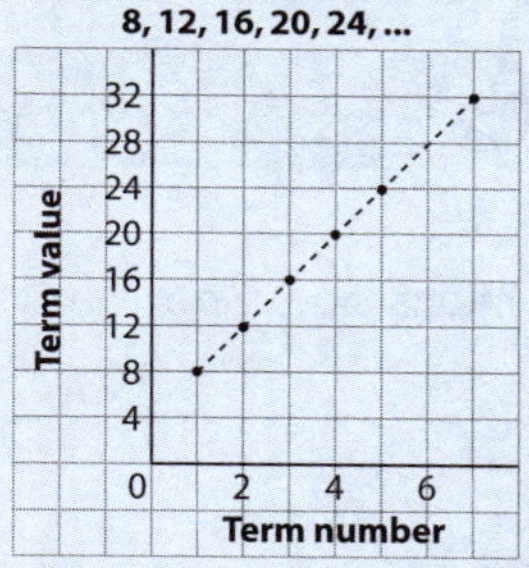

ii) a) The pattern rule is: Start at 5. Add 2 each time.
Each term is 2 more than the previous term.

b) Graph of Number Pattern 5, 7, 9, 11, 13, …

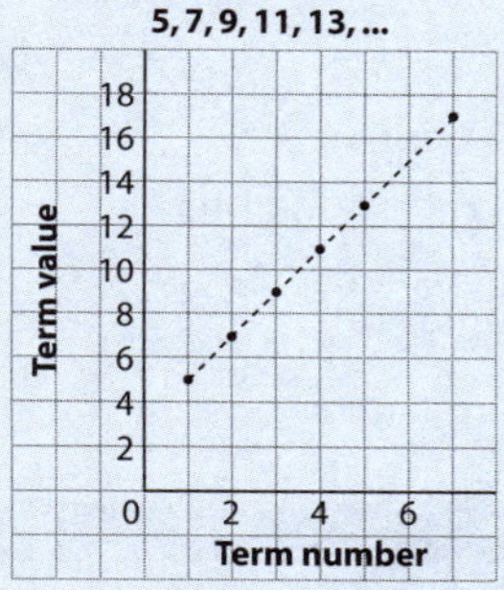

4. a) The perimeter starts at 6 units and increases by 2 units each time.

5. a) Twelve decreased by a number is equal to three times the number.
Verify: Left side $= 12 - x = 12 - 3 = 9$; Right side $= 3x = 3(3) = 9$
Since the left side equals the right side, $x = 3$ is correct.

b) Four times a number minus seven is equal to three more than two times the number.
Verify: Left side $= 4x - 7 = 4(5) - 7 = 13$; Right side $= 2x + 3 = 2(5) + 3 = 13$
Since the left side equals the right side, $x = 5$ is correct.

c) Three times a number minus eight is equal to the number.
Verify: Left side $= 3x - 8 = 3(4) - 8 = 4$; Right side $= x = 4$
Since the left side equals the right side, $x = 4$ is correct.

d) Three minus seven times a number is equal to seven minus nine times the number.
Verify: Left side $= 3 - 7x = 3 - 7(2) = -11$; Right side $= 7 - 9x = 7 - 9(2) = -11$
Since the left side equals the right side, $x = 2$ is correct.

6. b) Verify: Left side = $2n - 5$ Right side = $n - 1$

$= 2(4) - 5$ $= 4 - 1$

$= 3$ $= 3$

Since the left side equals the right side, $n = 4$ is correct.

7. a) $3x + 2 = 4 \Rightarrow 3x + 2 - 2 = 4 - 2 \Rightarrow 3x = 2 \Rightarrow \frac{3x}{3} = \frac{2}{3}$

$\Rightarrow x = \frac{2}{3}$

Verify: Left side = $3x + 2 = 3(\frac{2}{3}) + 2 = 2 + 2 = 4$ = right side

b) $4x = 10 \Rightarrow \frac{4x}{4} = \frac{10}{4} \Rightarrow x = \frac{10}{4} \Rightarrow x = \frac{5}{2}$

Verify: Left side = $4x = 4(\frac{5}{2}) = 2 \times 5 = 10$ = right side

c) $11 = 3x + 1 \Rightarrow 11 - 1 = 3x + 1 - 1 \Rightarrow 10 = 3x \Rightarrow$

$\frac{10}{3} = \frac{3x}{3} \Rightarrow \frac{10}{3} = x$

Verify: Right side = $3x + 1 = 3(\frac{10}{3}) + 1 = 11$ = left side

d) $4x - 7 = x + 1 \Rightarrow 4x - 7 - x = x + 1 - x \Rightarrow 3x - 7 = 1 \Rightarrow$

$3x - 7 + 7 = 1 + 7 \Rightarrow 3x = 8 \Rightarrow \frac{3x}{3} = \frac{8}{3} \Rightarrow x = \frac{8}{3}$

Verify: Left side = $4x - 7$ Right side = $x + 1$

$= 4(\frac{8}{3}) - 7$ $= \frac{8}{3} + 1$

$= \frac{32}{3} - \frac{21}{3}$ $= \frac{8}{3} + \frac{3}{3}$

$= \frac{11}{3}$ $= \frac{11}{3}$

Since the left side equals the right side, $x = \frac{8}{3}$ is correct.

8. b) $125 + 12n = 545 \Rightarrow 125 + 12n - 125 = 545 - 125 \Rightarrow$

$12n = 420 \Rightarrow \frac{12n}{12} = \frac{420}{12} \Rightarrow n = 35$

c) Verify: Left side = $125 + 12n = 125 + 12(35) = 545$ = right side

9. b) i) $4n - 1 = 79 \Rightarrow 4n - 1 + 1 = 79 + 1 \Rightarrow 4n = 80 \Rightarrow n = 20$

10. b) i) $6n + 1 = 151 \Rightarrow 6n + 1 - 1 = 151 - 1 \Rightarrow 6n = 150 \Rightarrow$

$n = 25$

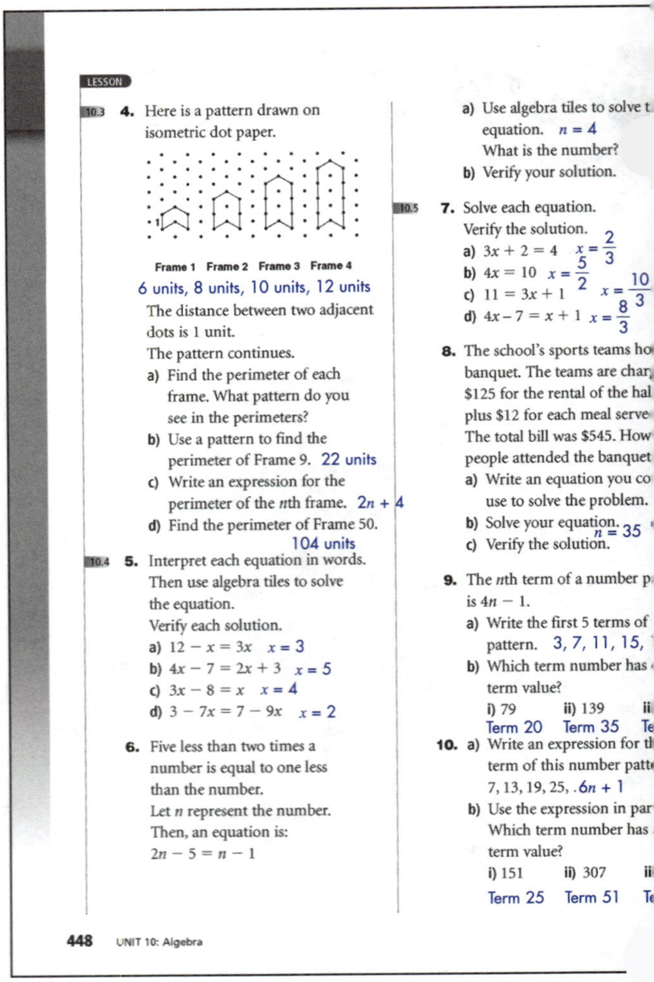

LESSON

10.3 4. Here is a pattern drawn on isometric dot paper.

Frame 1 Frame 2 Frame 3 Frame 4

6 units, 8 units, 10 units, 12 units

The distance between two adjacent dots is 1 unit.

The pattern continues.

a) Find the perimeter of each frame. What pattern do you see in the perimeters?

b) Use a pattern to find the perimeter of Frame 9. 22 units

c) Write an expression for the perimeter of the nth frame. $2n + 4$

d) Find the perimeter of Frame 50. 104 units

10.4 5. Interpret each equation in words. Then use algebra tiles to solve the equation. Verify each solution.

a) $12 - x = 3x$ $x = 3$

b) $4x - 7 = 2x + 3$ $x = 5$

c) $3x - 8 = x$ $x = 4$

d) $3 - 7x = 7 - 9x$ $x = 2$

6. Five less than two times a number is equal to one less than the number. Let n represent the number. Then, an equation is: $2n - 5 = n - 1$

a) Use algebra tiles to solve t equation. $n = 4$ What is the number?

b) Verify your solution.

10.5 7. Solve each equation. Verify the solution.

a) $3x + 2 = 4$ $x = \frac{2}{3}$

b) $4x = 10$ $x = \frac{5}{2}$

c) $11 = 3x + 1$ $x = \frac{10}{3}$

d) $4x - 7 = x + 1$ $x = \frac{8}{3}$

8. The school's sports teams ho banquet. The teams are char $125 for the rental of the hal plus $12 for each meal serve The total bill was $545. How people attended the banquet

a) Write an equation you co use to solve the problem.

b) Solve your equation. $n = 35$

c) Verify the solution.

9. The nth term of a number p is $4n - 1$.

a) Write the first 5 terms of pattern. 3, 7, 11, 15,

b) Which term number has term value?

i) 79 ii) 139 ii

Term 20 Term 35 Te

10. a) Write an expression for th term of this number patt 7, 13, 19, 25, . $6n + 1$

b) Use the expression in par Which term number has term value?

i) 151 ii) 307 ii

Term 25 Term 51 Te

448 UNIT 10: Algebra

ASSESSMENT FOR LEARNING

What to Look For

Knowledge and Understanding

✔ **Question 4:** Student understands that an expression can be used to make predictions about a given frame in a geometric pattern.

Thinking

✔ **Question 8:** Student can solve a problem by solving a related equation.

Communication

✔ **Question 5:** Student can interpret an algebraic equation in words.

Application

✔ **Question 1:** Student can use the distributive property to expand algebraic expressions.

✔ **Questions 5 and 6:** Student can solve equations using algebra tiles, then verify the solutions.

✔ **Question 7:** Student can solve equations algebraically.

✔ **Question 10:** Student can write an expression for the nth term of a number pattern.

Recording and Reporting

Master 10.1 Unit Rubric: Algebra

Master 10.4 Unit Summary: Algebra

Practice Test

1. Interpret each equation in words.
Solve the equation.
Verify the solution.
a) $x + 5 = 3x - 9$ $x = 7$
b) $2x - 5 = 10$ $x = \frac{15}{2}$

2. Whoopi saves pennies. She has 10¢ in her jar at the start.
Whoopi starts on January 1st. She saves 3¢ every day.
a) How many pennies does Whoopi have in the jar on each of January 1st, 2nd, 3rd, 4th, 5th, and 6th?
Record the results in a table.
What pattern do you see? Write a pattern rule.
b) Write an expression for the nth term. $3n + 10$
c) Use the expression to find the 25th term. 85
d) How could you find how much money Whoopi saved in January?

3. Anoki is holding a skating party.
The rental of the ice is \$75, plus \$3 per skater.
a) Write an expression for the cost in dollars for n skaters. $75 + 3n$
b) Use the expression in part a to find the total cost for 25 skaters. \$150
c) What if Anoki has a budget of \$204. Write an equation you can solve to find how many people can skate.
Solve the equation.

4. Two number patterns have these nth terms.
Pattern A: $6n + 4$
Pattern B: $5n - 3$
a) Find the 48th term of Pattern A. 292
b) Use the term value from part a.
Which term number in Pattern B has this term value? Term 59
How do you know?

LESSON ORGANIZER

Student Materials
- calculators

Assessment: Masters 10.1 Unit Rubric: Algebra, 10.4 Unit Summary: Algebra

To assess the 4 Achievement Chart categories listed in the curriculum document, use these test questions:
Knowledge and Understanding: 1
Application: 2
Thinking: 3
Communication: 4

Sample Solutions

1. a) Five more than a number is equal to three times the number minus nine.
$x + 5 = 3x - 9 \Rightarrow x + 5 - x = 3x - 9 - x \Rightarrow 5 = 2x - 9$
$\Rightarrow 5 + 9 = 2x - 9 + 9 \Rightarrow 14 = 2x \Rightarrow 7 = x$

Verify: Left side $= x + 5 = 7 + 5 = 12$ Right side $= 3x - 9 = 3(7) - 9 = 12$

Since the left side equals the right side, $x = 7$ is correct.

b) Two times a number minus five is equal to ten.
$2x - 5 = 10 \Rightarrow 2x - 5 + 5 = 10 + 5 \Rightarrow 2x = 15 \Rightarrow$
$\frac{2x}{2} = \frac{15}{2} \Rightarrow x = \frac{15}{2}$
Verify: Left side $= 2x - 5 = 2(\frac{15}{2}) - 5 = 15 - 5 = 10 =$ right side

2. a)

Day in January	Number of Pennies
1	13
2	16
3	19
4	22
5	25
6	28

The number of pennies starts at 13 and increases by 3 each time.
The pattern rule is: Start at 13. Add 3 each time.

d) Since January has 31 days, I could substitute $n = 31$ into the expression.

3. b) $75 + 3(25) = 150$; the total cost is \$150.

c) $75 + 3n = 204 \Rightarrow 75 + 3n - 75 = 204 - 75 \Rightarrow$
$3n = 129 \Rightarrow \frac{3n}{3} = \frac{129}{3} \Rightarrow n = 43$
43 people can skate on a budget of \$204.

4. b) Solve the equation $5n - 3 = 292$.
$5n - 3 = 292 \Rightarrow 5n - 3 + 3 = 292 + 3 \Rightarrow 5n = 295$
$\Rightarrow \frac{5n}{5} = \frac{295}{5} \Rightarrow n = 59$
In Pattern B, term 59 has value 292.

UNIT PROBLEM

Choosing a Cell Phone Plan

LESSON ORGANIZER (80–100 min)

Student Grouping: 2–4
Student Materials
- calculators
- 0.5-cm grid paper (PM 14)
- coloured pencils or markers

Assessment: Masters 10.3 Performance Assessment Rubric: Choosing a Cell Phone Plan, 10.4 Unit Summary: Algebra

Present the *Unit Problem*. Take a quick class survey to find how many students have their own cell phone, and approximately how many minutes they use each month.

Suggest students use the horizontal axis to represent the number of additional minutes, and the vertical axis to represent the total cost. Remind students to give the graph a title. Ensure students understand that to convert an amount in dollars to cents, we multiply by 100.

Unit Problem Choosing a Cell Phone Plan

Suppose your older sister has bought a cell phone.
She asks for your help to find the best cell phone plan.

Part 1

1. Here are three cell phone plans.
Each plan includes 200 free minutes.

CanTalk: $30.00 per month, plus $0.30 per additional minute
Connected: $35.00 per month, plus $0.25 per additional min
In-Touch: $40.00 per month, plus $0.20 per additional minut

Copy and complete this table.

Number of Additional Minutes	40	80	120	160	200
CanTalk	$42	$54	$66	$78	$90
Connected	$45	$55	$65	$75	$85
In-Touch	$48	$56	$64	$72	$80

2. Which plan would you choose if your sister uses 40 additional minutes per month? 120 additional minutes? 200 additional minutes? Explain.

3. Graph the data in the table.
Use a different colour for each plan.
Join each set of points with a broken line.
Label each line with the name of the plan.
What patterns do you see?
What happens to the lines when the number of additional minutes is 100?
What does this represent?
Which plan would you choose if your sister uses 100 additior minutes per month? Explain.

450 UNIT 10: Algebra

Sample Response

Part 1

2. I would choose CanTalk if my sister uses 40 additional minutes, and In-Touch if she uses 120 or 200 additional minutes. In each case, I chose the cheapest plan for that number of additional minutes.

3. **Comparison of 3 Cell Phone Plans**

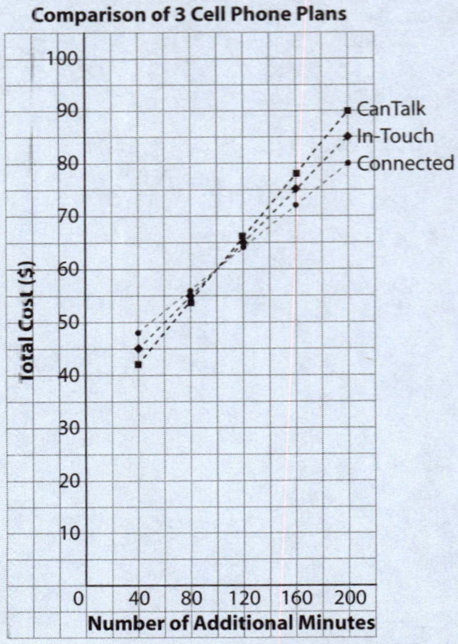

All lines are straight lines that go up to the right. The lines vary in steepness. The lines intersect at (100, 60).
Pattern rules: CanTalk: Start at 42. Add 12 each time.
Connected: Start at 45. Add 10 each time.
In-Touch: Start at 48. Add 8 each time.

At 100 additional minutes, the lines intersect at $60. This means that the cost for 100 additional minutes is the same for all 3 plans. If my sister uses 100 additional minutes per month, I would choose In-Touch so that if she uses more than her allowed minutes, she will pay the least amount possible.

Part 2

Expressions

CanTalk: $30 + 0.30n$ ⇨ $55.50
Connected: $35 + 0.25n$ ⇨ $56.25
In-Touch: $40 + 0.20n$ ⇨ $57.00

Equations

CanTalk: $3000 + 30n = 8000$ ⇨ $n \doteq 167$; 167 additional minutes
Connected: $3500 + 25n = 8000$ ⇨ $n = 180$; 180 additional minutes
In-Touch: $4000 + 20n = 8000$ ⇨ $n = 200$; 200 additional minutes

Part 2

For each plan, write an expression for the monthly cost of n additional minutes.

Use each expression to find the total monthly cost for 85 additional minutes for each plan.

Suppose your sister can spend $80 a month on her cell phone. Write an equation you can solve to find how many additional minutes she can afford with each plan.

Solve each equation. Explain what each solution means.

vert each money unt to cents before you e the equations.

Part 3

Write a paragraph to explain what decisions you have made about choosing the best cell phone plan.

heck List

Your work should show:

- all tables and graphs, clearly labelled
- he expressions and equations you wrote, and how you used hem to solve the problems
- detailed, accurate calculations
- clear explanations of your solutions and he patterns you observed

Reflect on the Unit

Explain how patterns, expressions, and equations are used to solve problems. Include an example in each case.

Each solution is the number of additional minutes my sister can use for a total cost of $80 per month.

Part 3

Choosing the best cell phone plan depends on how much my sister is going to use her phone. If my sister talks for less than 100 min per month, I would suggest she chooses CanTalk. If she talks for more than 100 min per month, I would suggest she chooses In-Touch. If she uses a wide range of additional minutes, I would suggest she chooses Connected as their costs are between the costs of the other 2 plans.

REFLECT ON THE UNIT

Patterns can be used to make predictions. For example, a pattern, which shows the number of needles needed by a child with juvenile diabetes over a 6-day period, can be extended to predict the number of needles needed for 10 days.

We can write an expression for the nth term of a pattern, then use the pattern to find the value of any term in the pattern. For example, we can write an expression for the number of needles required, then substitute into the expression to find the number of needles required for any number of days.

We can solve a word problem by solving a related equation. For example, if I know that four times a number plus five is 25, I can write the related equation, then solve the equation:

$4n + 5 = 25 \Rightarrow 4n + 5 - 5 = 25 - 5 \Rightarrow 4n = 20 \Rightarrow \frac{4n}{4} = \frac{20}{4}$

$\Rightarrow n = 5$

The number is 5.

ASSESSMENT FOR LEARNING

What to Look For	What to Do
Knowledge and Understanding ✔ Students understand that information can be presented as tables, graphs, algebraic expressions, and equations. ***Communication*** ✔ Students can justify decisions made about choosing the best cell phone plan. ***Application*** ✔ Students can identify number patterns, represent a pattern as a graph, write and evaluate algebraic expressions, and write and solve equations.	***Extra Support:*** Make the problem accessible. Students who have difficulty may benefit from being guided through the problem for the CanTalk plan, then completing the work for Connected and In-Touch on their own. Students who have difficulty interpreting the point of intersection of the graphs may benefit from using each expression in *Part 2* to find the total monthly cost for 100 additional minutes for each plan, then relating their findings to the graph.

Recording and Reporting

Master 10.3 Performance Assessment Rubric: Choosing a Cell Phone Plan

Master 10.4 Unit Summary: Algebra

Evaluating Student Learning: Preparing to Report: Unit 10 Algebra

This unit provides an opportunity to report on the **Patterning and Algebra** strand.
Master 10.4: Unit Summary: Algebra provides a comprehensive format for recording and summarizing evidence collected.

Here is an example of a completed summary chart for this Unit:

Strand: *Patterning and Algebra*	**Knowledge and Understanding**	**Thinking**	**Communication**	**Application**	***Overall***
Ongoing Observations	3	4	4	4	4
Work samples or portfolios; conferences	4	4	3	3	3/4
Unit Review	3	3	2	3	3
Unit Test	3	4	4	4	4
Unit Problem Choosing a Cell Phone Plan	4	3	3	3	3
Achievement Level for reporting					3/4

Recording	**How to Report**
Ongoing Observations	Use *Master 10.2 Ongoing Observations: Algebra* to determine the most consistent level achieved in each category. Enter it in the chart. Choose to summarize by achievement category, or simply to enter an overall level. Observations from late in the unit should be most heavily weighted.
Portfolios or collections of work samples; conferences or interviews	Use *Master 10.1 Unit Rubric: Algebra* to guide evaluation of collections of work and information gathered in conferences. Teachers may choose to focus particular attention on the Assessment Focus questions. Work from late in the unit should be most heavily weighted.
Unit Review	*Master 10.1 Unit Rubric: Algebra* may be helpful in determining levels of achievement. #2, 3, 4, and 9 provide evidence of Knowledge and Understanding; #1, 5, 6, 7, and 10 provide evidence of Application; #8 provides evidence of Thinking; all questions provide evidence of Communication.
Unit Test	*Master 10.1 Unit Rubric: Algebra* may be helpful in determining levels of achievement. #1 provides evidence of Knowledge and Understanding; #3 provides evidence of Application; #4 provides evidence of Thinking; all questions provide evidence of Communication.
Unit Problem	Use *Master 10.3 Performance Assessment Rubric: Choosing a Cell Phone Plan.* The *Unit Problem* offers a snapshot of students' achievement. In particular, it shows their ability to synthesize and apply what they have learned.
Student Self-Assessment	Note students' perceptions of their own progress. This may take the form of an oral or written comment, or a self-rating.
Comments	Analyse the pattern of achievement to identify strengths and needs. In some cases, specific actions may need to be planned to support the learner.

Learning Skills	**Ongoing Records**
PM 4: Learning Skills Check List Use to record and report throughout a reporting period, rather than for each unit and/or strand.	*PM 10: Summary Class Records: Strands* *PM 11: Summary Class Records: Achievement Categories* *PM 12: Summary Record: Individual* Use to record and report evaluations of student achievement over several clusters, a reporting period, or a school year. These can also be used in place of the Unit Summary.

Name ____________________ Date ______________

Master 10.1

Unit Rubric: Algebra

	Level 1	Level 2	Level 3	Level 4
Knowledge and Understanding • Shows understanding by demonstrating and explaining: – number properties – patterns – algebraic expressions and equations	shows limited understanding in demonstrating and explaining: – number properties – patterns – algebraic expressions and equations	shows some understanding in demonstrating and explaining: – number properties – patterns – algebraic expressions and equations	shows considerable understanding in demonstrating and explaining: – number properties – patterns – algebraic expressions and equations	shows thorough understanding in demonstrating and explaining: – number properties – patterns – algebraic expressions and equations
Thinking • Uses algebraic equations to create and solve problems	uses algebraic equations to create and solve problems with limited effectiveness	uses algebraic equations to create and solve problems with some effectiveness	uses algebraic equations to create and solve problems with considerable effectiveness	uses algebraic equations to create and solve problems with a high degree of effectiveness
Communication • Explains concepts, procedures, and reasoning clearly, using appropriate terminology	limited effectiveness; unable to explain reasoning and procedures clearly; rarely uses appropriate terminology	some effectiveness; explains reasoning and procedures with some clarity and use of appropriate terminology	considerable effectiveness; explains reasoning and procedures clearly, using appropriate terminology	high degree of effectiveness; explains reasoning and procedures clearly and precisely, using the most appropriate terminology
• Presents work, including tables, graphs, and equations clearly, using appropriate conventions (for example, variables and labels)	presents work, including tables, graphs, and equations, with limited clarity and use of appropriate conventions	presents work, including tables, graphs, and equations, with some clarity and use of conventions	presents work, including tables, graphs, and equations, with considerable clarity and use of conventions	presents work, including tables, graphs, and equations, with a high degree of clarity and use of conventions
Application • Accurately: – writes an expression for the *n*th term of a pattern – evaluates algebraic expressions – reads, writes, and solves equations – represents algebraic relationships in tables, graphs, and equations	limited effectiveness; major errors or omissions in: – writing an expression for the *n*th term of a pattern – evaluating algebraic expressions – reading, writing, and solving equations – representing algebraic relationships in tables, graphs, and equations	some effectiveness; somewhat accurate with several minor errors or omissions in: – writing an expression for the *n*th term of a pattern – evaluating algebraic expressions – reading, writing, and solving equations – representing algebraic relationships in tables, graphs, and equations	considerable effectiveness; generally accurate with few minor errors or omissions in: – writing an expression for the *n*th term of a pattern – evaluating algebraic expressions – reading, writing, and solving equations – representing algebraic relationships in tables, graphs, and equations	high degree of effectiveness; accurate and precise with no errors in: – writing an expression for the *n*th term of a pattern – evaluating algebraic expressions – reading, writing, and solving equations – representing algebraic relationships in tables, graphs, and equations

Name ____________________ Date ________________

Master 10.2

Ongoing Observations: Algebra

The behaviours described under each heading are examples; they are not intended to be an exhaustive list of all that might be observed. More detailed descriptions are provided in each lesson under *Assessment for Learning*.

STUDENT ACHIEVEMENT: Algebra				
Student	**Knowledge and Understanding** • Demonstrates and explains: – number properties – patterns – algebraic expressions and equations	**Thinking** • Uses algebraic equations to create and solve problems	**Communication** • Explains reasoning and procedures clearly, using appropriate terminology • Presents tables, graphs, and equations clearly	**Application** • Accurately: – writes and evaluates algebraic expressions – reads, writes, and solves equations – represents algebraic relationships

Level 1 – very limited; Level 2 – somewhat or limited; Level 3 – satisfactory; Level 4 – thorough

Name ______________________ Date ________________

Master 10.3

Performance Assessment Rubric: Choosing a Cell Phone Plan

	Level 1	Level 2	Level 3	Level 4
Knowledge and Understanding • Explanations show understanding of algebraic expressions and equations	explanations show limited understanding of algebraic expressions and equations	explanations show some understanding of algebraic expressions and equations	explanations show considerable understanding of algebraic expressions and equations	explanations show thorough understanding of algebraic expressions and equations
Thinking • Uses appropriate strategies to solve problems using algebra	uses a few simple strategies with limited success	uses some appropriate strategies with partial success	uses appropriate strategies with considerable success	uses appropriate, often innovative, strategies with a high degree of success
Communication • Communicates procedures, solutions, and reasoning clearly, using appropriate language	limited effectiveness; does not communicate clearly	some effectiveness; communicates with some clarity	considerable effectiveness; communicates clearly	a high degree of effectiveness; communicates clearly and precisely
• Presents tables and graphs clearly, using appropriate conventions (for example, variables and labels)	presents tables and graphs with limited clarity and use of appropriate conventions	presents tables and graphs with some clarity and use of appropriate conventions	presents tables and graphs with considerable clarity and use of appropriate conventions	presents tables and graphs with a high degree of clarity and use of appropriate conventions
Application • Accurately: – completes required tables and graphs – writes appropriate expressions and equations – evaluates expressions – solves equations	limited effectiveness; major errors or omissions in: – completing required tables and graphs – writing appropriate expressions and equations – evaluating expressions – solving equations	some effectiveness; somewhat accurate in: – completing required tables and graphs – writing appropriate expressions and equations – evaluating expressions – solving equations	considerable effectiveness; generally accurate in: – completing required tables and graphs – writing appropriate expressions and equations – evaluating expressions – solving equations	high degree of effectiveness; accurate and precise in: – completing required tables and graphs – writing appropriate expressions and equations – evaluating expressions – solving equations

Name ____________________ Date ______________

Master 10.4

Unit Summary: Algebra

Review assessment records to determine the most consistent achievement levels for the assessments conducted. Some cells may be blank. *Overall* achievement levels may be recorded in each row, rather than identifying levels for each achievement category.

	Most Consistent Level of Achievement*				
Strand: *Patterning and Algebra*	**Knowledge and Understanding**	**Thinking**	**Communication**	**Application**	***Overall***
Ongoing Observations					
Work samples or portfolios; conferences					
Unit Review					
Unit Test					
Unit Problem Choosing a Cell Phone Plan					
Achievement Level for reporting					

*Use Ontario Achievement Levels 1, 2, 3, 4

Self-Assessment:

Comments: (Strengths, Needs, Next Steps)

Name ____________________ Date ______________

Master 10.5

Additional Activity 1: Number Pattern Search

Work on your own.
Find as many number patterns as you can.
The patterns may appear horizontally, vertically, or diagonally.
Each pattern must contain at least 5 terms.
Circle the patterns as you find them.
Write a description of each pattern you find.

18	4	1	3	6	10	15	21
14	1	31	5	2	5	8	7
10	17	4	8	11	10	16	14
6	3	6	9	12	15	32	21
2	12	7	11	16	20	64	28
23	5	10	1	7	25	128	35
3	9	12	18	24	30	36	42
8	13	18	23	28	33	29	49

Take It Further: Write an expression for the *n*th term of each number pattern you find.

Name ____________________ Date ________________

Master 10.6a

Additional Activity 2: Equation Concentration

Play with a partner.
You will need *Concentration Cards* (Master 10.6b), algebra tiles, and a pair of scissors.

How to Play:

1. Cut out the Equation and Solution cards.
Shuffle the cards together.
Lay the cards in an array, face down on the table.

2. Player A turns over a card.
If the card contains an equation, she tries to find the matching solution.
If the card contains a solution, she tries to find the matching equation.
Player A turns over a second card.
Use algebra tiles to solve the equation, if necessary.

3. If Player A finds a matching pair, she keeps the cards.
If the two cards do not match, both cards are turned over.

4. Player B takes a turn.
Play continues until all matches have been made.
The player with the greater number of cards wins.

Take It Further: Students make their own equation cards and solution cards, then add the cards to the game. Students play the game again.

Name ______________________ Date ________________

Master 10.6b

Concentration Cards

Equation Cards

$2x + 3 = 5$	$5x - 7 = 3$	$4x - 7 = 5$
$x + 5 = 9$	$3x + 1 = 16$	$x - 4 = 2$
$6x - 12 = 30$	$6x = 48$	$3x - 3 = 24$
$2x + 3 = 23$	$2x - 6 = 16$	$3x = 36$

Solution Cards

1	2	3
4	5	6
7	8	9
10	11	12

Name ____________________ Date ________________

Master 10.7a

Additional Activity 3: Algebra Bingo

Play in groups of 3.
You will need *Algebra Bingo Problem Cards* (Master 10.7b), *Algebra Bingo Cards* (Master 10.7c), scissors, and counters.

How to Play:

1. Cut out the Bingo cards.
   Give 2 cards to each player.
   Cut out the Bingo Problem cards. Shuffle the cards.
   Place the cards face down in a pile.

2. Decide who will turn over the Problem cards.
   Turn over the top card.
   Each player works on his or her own to solve the problem.
   Use counters to cover the solution to the problem wherever it appears on your bingo cards.

3. Turn over another Problem card.
   Play continues until one player covers a horizontal, vertical, or diagonal line.
   He or she shouts "Bingo."

4. Players check to make sure all solutions covered are correct.

Take It Further: Students make their own bingo problem cards. Each problem must have a whole-number solution between 0 and 17. Students play the game again. The first player to cover an entire card wins.

Name ______________________ Date ________________

Master 10.7b

Algebra Bingo Problem Cards

Evaluate: $15n - 6m$ for $n = \frac{1}{5}$ and $m = \frac{1}{3}$	**Solve:** $6x = 30$	**Find the missing term:** 1, 4, __, 16, 25, …	**Solve:** $5x = 3x + 26$
Solve: $3x + 4 = x + 8$	**Evaluate:** $24x$ for $x = \frac{1}{4}$	**Solve:** $4x - 8 = 2x + 12$	**Find the next term:** 2, 5, 8, 11, …
Solve: $2x - 1 = 5$	**Solve:** $2x = x + 7$	**Two more than three times a number is 35. What is the number?**	**A number divided by three is 5. What is the number?**
One less than two times a number is 7. What is the number?	**Find the next term:** 2, 4, 6, …	**Evaluate:** $20x + 8y$ for $x = \frac{1}{2}$ and $y = \frac{1}{4}$	**Evaluate:** $a(b + c)$ for $a = 2, b = 3,$ and $c = 5$

Name ____________________ Date ________________

Master 10.7c

Algebra Bingo Cards

1	16	5
10	8	13
15	6	2

14	7	5
3	1	13
8	15	2

15	6	9
5	2	14
16	12	3

10	5	11
8	3	16
12	1	9

2	8	3
13	10	5
16	4	6

5	3	7
14	1	4
10	15	8

Name ____________________ Date ______________

Master 10.8

Step-by-Step 1

Lesson 10.1, Question 6

Step 1 Use the distributive property to expand $2(x + 20)$: ______________________

Is the product $2x + 20$? __________

Are $2x + 20$ and $2(x + 20)$ equivalent? __________

Step 2 Draw algebra tiles to represent $3x + 7$.

Draw algebra tiles to represent $10x$.

Are $3x + 7$ and $10x$ equivalent? __________

Step 3 Use the distributive property to expand $2(t + 3)$: ______________________

Is the product $6 + 2t$? __________

Use the order of addition. Write $6 + 2t$ in a different way. ________________

Are $2(t + 3)$ and $6 + 2t$ equivalent? __________

Step 4 Add: $3 + 4 =$ ____; $4 + 3 =$ ____

What number property does this represent? ______________________

Are $9 + x$ and $x + 9$ equivalent? Explain. ______________________

____

Name ____________________ Date ________________

Master 10.9

Step-by-Step 2

Lesson 10.2, Question 6

Step 1 Here is the beginning of a number pattern: 10, 20, …
Which number do you add to the first term to get the second term? ________

Add this number each time to extend the pattern to 5 terms:

____, ____, ____, ____, ____

Describe the pattern.

____

Write the pattern rule: Start at ____. Add ____ each time.

Step 2 Find a pattern rule that relates the term value to the term number.

Each term is ____ more than the previous term.

Look for patterns that involve this number.

Complete the table below.

Term Number	Term Value	Pattern Rule for Term Value
1	10	
2	20	
3		
4		
5		

Write an expression for the *n*th term, where *n* is any term number.

____

Step 3 Here is the beginning of a number pattern: 10, 20, …
Which number do you multiply the first term by to get the second term? __________
Multiply by this number each time to extend the pattern to 5 terms:

____, ____, ____, ____, ____

Describe the pattern. ____

Write the pattern rule: Start at ____. Multiply by ____ each time.

Step 4 Is the difference between consecutive terms the same? Explain. ____________

____

Can you write an expression for the *n*th term of this pattern? Explain.

____

Name ________________ Date ____________

Master 10.10

Step-by-Step 3

Lesson 10.3, Question 6

You will need 1-cm grid paper.

Step 1 Here are the first 2 frames of a growing pattern.
Copy this pattern onto 1-cm grid paper.

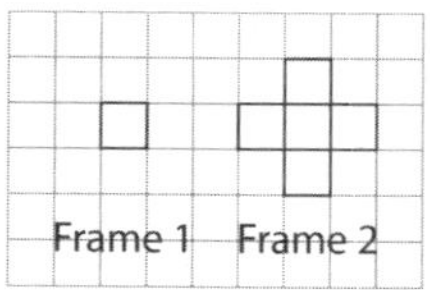

Step 2 How many squares are added to Frame 1 to get Frame 2? ____

Continue to add this number of squares. Draw Frame 3 and Frame 4.

Describe the patterns in the frames. ______________________________________

____

Describe or draw Frame 5, Frame 10, and Frame 100.

Step 3 Find the area of each of the first 4 frames.

____

Find a pattern rule that relates the area to the frame number.

The area increases by _____ each time.

Look for patterns that involve this number.

Complete the table below.

Frame	Area (cm^2)	Area in Terms of Frame Number
1	1	
2	5	
3		
4		

Write an expression for the *n*th frame, where *n* is any frame number.

____

Name ____________________ Date ______________

Master 10.11

Step-by-Step 4

Lesson 10.4, Question 7

You will need algebra tiles.

Step 1 Model the equation $2l = 6 + l$.
Put algebra tiles on the left side to represent $2l$.
Put algebra tiles on the right side to represent $6 + l$.
Add the same number of tiles to each side to isolate the unit tiles on the right side.
Remove zero pairs.
What solution do the tiles show? ______________

What is the edge length of the cube? ________ cm

Step 2 To verify the solution, substitute the solution from *Step 1* into $2l = 6 + l$.

Left side = $2l$ Right side = $6 + l$

= =

= =

Is your solution correct? Explain. ____

____

Step 3 What is the formula for the surface area of a cube? _______________
Use the formula to find the surface area of the cube.

$SA =$ ________ cm^2

Step 4 What is the formula for the volume of a cube? _______________
Use the formula to find the volume of the cube.

$V =$ ________ cm^3

Name ____________________ Date _______________

Master 10.12

Step-by-Step 5

Lesson 10.5, Question 5

Step 1 Let n represent the number of students who attended the dance.

The cost for each student is \$2.

The cost for n students is: ______

The disc jockey charged a flat rate of \$85.

An algebraic expression for the cost of the disc jockey for n students is: ____________

The disc jockey was paid \$197.

The equation is: _________________________

Step 2 Use algebra, systematic trial, or inspection to solve the equation.

How many students attended the dance? ________

Step 3 To verify the solution, substitute the solution from *Step 2* into the original equation.

Left side = Right side =

=

=

=

Is your solution correct? Explain. ____

____

Name ____________________ Date ______________

Master 10.13a

Unit Test: Unit 10 Algebra

1. A number pattern has this *n*th term: $6n - 3$

a) Write the first 5 terms of the pattern.

b) Describe the pattern, then write a pattern rule.

c) What is the value of the 35th term? The 52nd term?

d) Which term number has each term value?
i) 111 **ii)** 387 **iii)** 255

e) Will any term number have each value?
i) 123 **ii)** 198 **iii)** 430
How do you know?

Name ______________________ Date ________________

Master 10.13b

Unit Test continued

2. Interpret each equation in words.
Solve the equation.
Verify the solution.
a) $5x - 3 = 4$

b) $2x + 8 = 14 - x$

3. Alexi receives an allowance of \$7 per week. He has \$43 in his bank account.
He decides to deposit all of his allowance into the bank each week to save for a new bicycle.
Assume the bank pays no interest.
a) How much money does Alexi have in the bank after Week 1? Week 2? Week 3? Week 4? Week 5?
Record the results in a table.
What pattern do you see?
Write a pattern rule.

Name ____________________ Date ________________

Master 10.13c

Unit Test continued

b) Write an expression for the *n*th term.

c) Use the expression to find the 11th term.

d) The bicycle that Alexi wants to buy costs $253, including all taxes.
Write an equation you can solve to find when Alexi will be able to buy the bicycle.
Solve the equation.

4. Moira and Sammy were the only two people running for president of the Student Council. In the election, 536 students voted. The winner received 122 more votes than the other. How many votes were cast for each candidate?

a) Write an equation you could use to solve this problem.

b) Solve your equation.

c) Verify the solution.

Name ____________________ Date ________________

Master 10.14

Sample Answers

Unit Test – Master 10.13

1. a) 3, 9, 15, 21, 27

b) The pattern begins with 3. To get the next term, add 6 each time.
The pattern rule is:
Start at 3. Add 6 each time.

c) 207; 309

d) **i)** Term 19 **ii)** Term 65
iii) Term 43

e) **i)** Term 21 **ii)** No **iii)** No
In parts ii and iii, the value for n is not a counting number.

2. a) Three less than five times a number is 4.
$5x - 3 = 4 \Rightarrow 5x - 3 + 3 = 4 + 3 \Rightarrow$
$5x = 7 \Rightarrow \frac{5x}{5} = \frac{7}{5} \Rightarrow x = \frac{7}{5}$
Left side $= 5x - 3 = 5(\frac{7}{5}) - 3 = 7 - 3 = 4 =$ right side

b) Two times a number plus eight is equal to fourteen minus the number.
$2x + 8 = 14 - x \Rightarrow 2x + 8 + x = 14 - x + x \Rightarrow$
$3x + 8 = 14 \Rightarrow 3x + 8 - 8 = 14 - 8 \Rightarrow 3x = 6 \Rightarrow$
$x = 2$
Left side $= 2x + 8 = 2(2) + 8 = 4 + 8 = 12$
Right side $= 14 - x = 14 - 2 = 12$
Since the left side equals the right side, $x = 2$ is correct.

3. a)

Week Number	Money in Bank ($)
1	50
2	57
3	64
4	71
5	78

The amount of money starts at $50. It increases by $7 each week.
The pattern rule is: Start at 50. Add 7 each time.

b) $7n + 43$

c) $7(11) + 43 = 120$; $120

d) $7n + 43 = 253$
$7n + 43 = 253 \Rightarrow 7n + 43 - 43 = 253 - 43 \Rightarrow$
$7n = 210 \Rightarrow n = 30$
Alexi will be able to buy the bicycle after Week 30.

4. a) Let n be the number of votes the other candidate received. So, the winning candidate received $n + 122$ votes.
The equation is: $n + n + 122 = 536$ or
$2n + 122 = 536$

b) $2n + 122 = 536 \Rightarrow 2n + 122 - 122 = 536 - 122$
$\Rightarrow 2n = 414 \Rightarrow n = 207$
One candidate received 207 votes and the other candidate received $207 + 122 = 329$ votes.

c) Left side $= 2n + 122 = 2(207) + 122 =$
$414 + 122 = 536 =$ right side

Extra Practice Masters 10.15–10.20

Go to the CD-ROM to access editable versions of these Extra Practice Masters

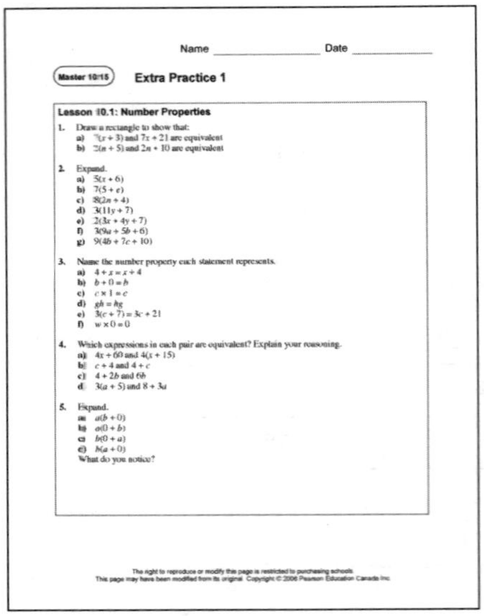

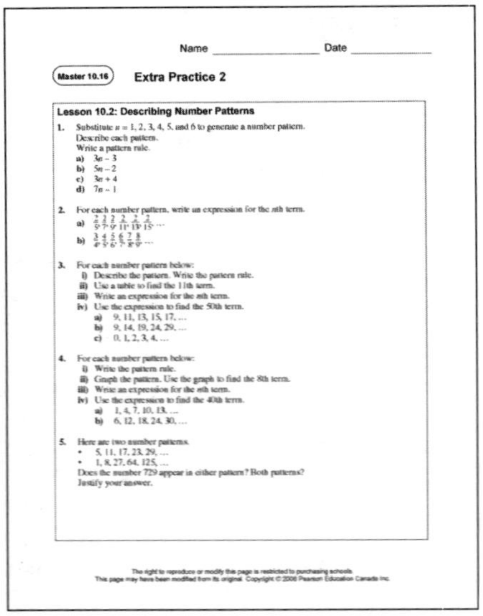

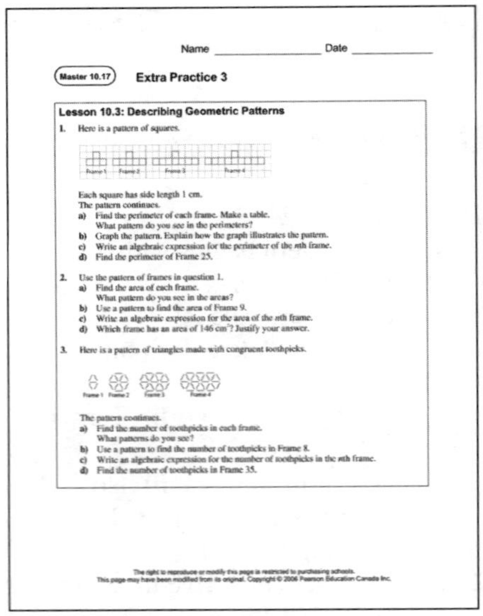

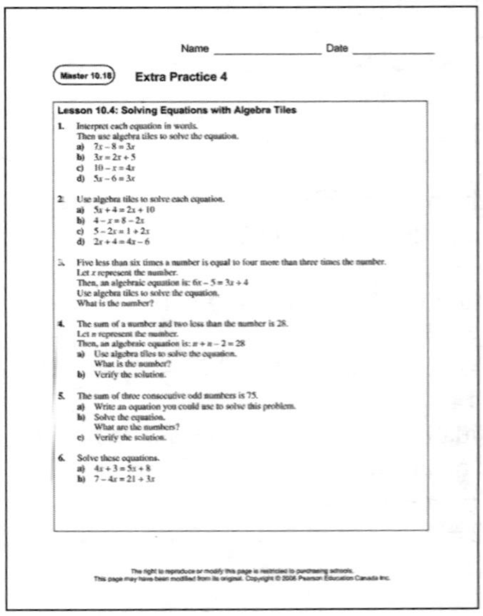

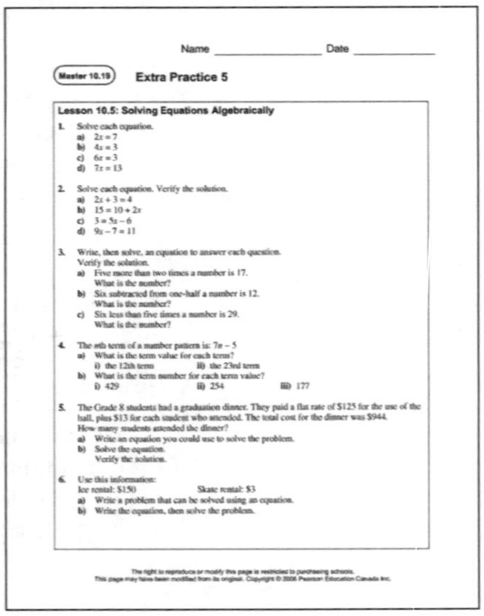

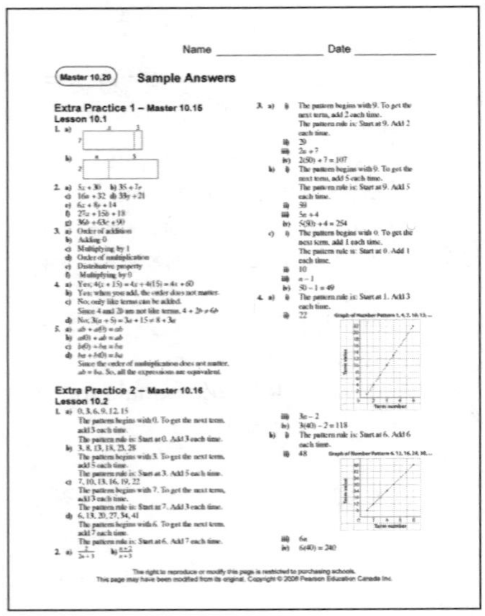

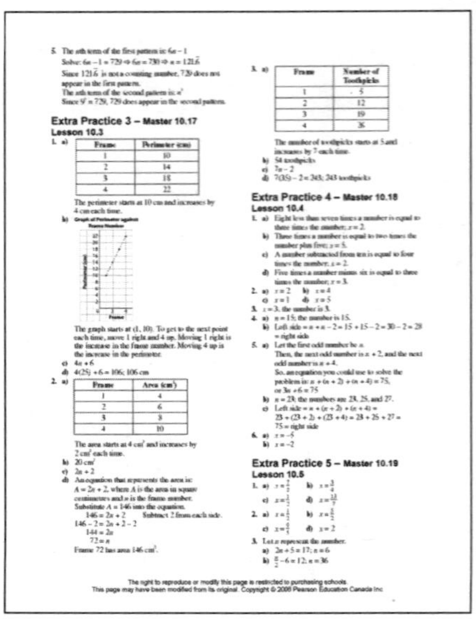

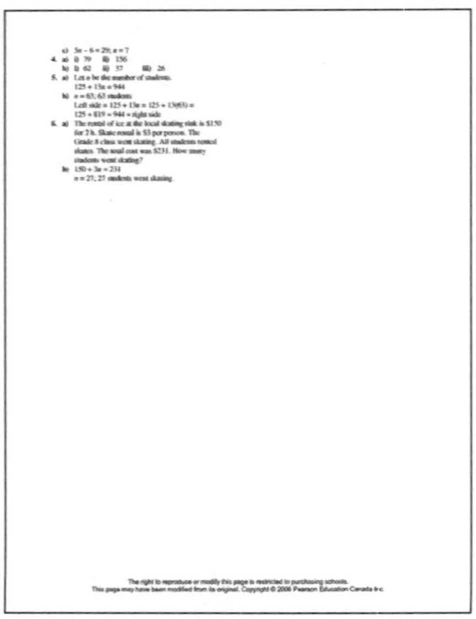

Addison Wesley

Mathematics Makes Sense

Program Authors

Trevor Brown

Antonietta Lenjosek

Cathy Heideman

Jim Mennie

Georgia Konis-Chatzis

A.J. Keene

Margaret Sinclair

Craig Featherstone

Jason Johnston

Bryn Keyes

Elizabeth Wood

Elizabeth Milne

David Sufrin

Don Jones

Sharon Jeroski

Lynn Strangway

Printed and bound in Canada

2 3 4 5 – TC – 09 08 07 06

PEARSON
Education Canada

ADDISON WESLEY

Ontario

Math Makes Sense 8

Ontario

Teacher Guide

Unit 11: Probability

PEARSON
Education Canada

UNIT 11

Probability

"Informal ideas about chance and probability, when developed early, provide necessary background for concepts to be constructed at the middle and secondary levels".

John A. Van de Walle

FOCUS STRAND
Data Management and Probability

SUPPORTING STRAND
Number Sense and Numeration

TIPS
In a balanced mathematics program, students become proficient with basic skills, develop conceptual understanding, and become adept at problem solving. All three areas are important and need to be included.

Mathematics Background

What Are the Big Ideas?

- In situations where outcomes are equally likely, tree diagrams may be used to determine the probability in experiments with one or more actions.
- Simulations are used to represent real-life situations for which gathering data and determining the corresponding probability may be complex. The model created to simulate the real-life situation must have the same number of outcomes as the real-life situation.
- Probability is applied in sports and games of chance to determine odds in favour and odds against.
- As the number of trials in an experiment increases, the experimental probability approaches the theoretical probability.

How Will the Concepts Develop?

Students use tree diagrams to determine theoretical probabilities and conduct simulations to estimate probabilities.

Students review that experimental probability is the number of times an event occurs divided by the total number of trials in an experiment. They also review that theoretical probability is the number of favourable outcomes divided by the number of possible outcomes. Students calculate theoretical probabilities by drawing tree diagrams and making lists. They review that a tree diagram can be used to find the outcomes of an experiment when the outcomes are equally likely.

Students learn that when an event is certain the probability is 1 and when an event is impossible the probability is 0. All other probabilities lie between 0 and 1.

Students conduct simulations to estimate probabilities with the understanding that the model must have the same number of outcomes as the real situation.

Students apply probability to determine odds in favour and odds against in sports and games of chance. They learn that odds in favour is the ratio of favourable outcomes to the number of unfavourable outcomes and that odds against is the ratio of unfavourable outcomes to the number of favourable outcomes.

Why Are These Concepts Important?

Probability concepts are used to make decisions in the areas of marketing, research, business, entertainment, and government policies. Understanding the language and concepts of probability will provide students with the basic knowledge to make informed observations about the likelihood of events, and to interpret and judge the validity of statistical claims encountered in everyday life.

Curriculum Overview

The codes refer to the 2005 revised curriculum.

Overall Expectations

- Use probability models to make predictions about real-life events. (8m67)

Specific Expectations

- Compare, through investigation, the theoretical probability of an event with experimental probability, and explain why they might differ. (8m80)
- Determine, through investigation, the tendency of experimental probability to approach theoretical probability as the number of trials in an experiment increases, using class-generated data and technology-based simulation models. (8m81)
- Identify the complementary event for a given event, and calculate the theoretical probability that a given event will not occur. (8m82)

Launch

Lesson 11.1:
Probability Range

Lesson 11.2:
Tree Diagrams

Mid-Unit Review

Lesson 11.3:
Simulations

Lesson 11.3A:
Probability Simulations Using a TI83-Plus

Lesson 11.4:
Odds For and Against

Unit Review
Practice Test

Unit Problem
What's Your Guess?

Curriculum across the Grades

Grade 7	Grade 8
Students compare experimental probabilities with the theoretical probability of an outcome involving two independent events. Students research and report on real-world applications of probabilities expressed in fraction, decimal, and percent form. Students make predictions about a population when given probability. Students represent all possible outcomes of a probability experiment involving two independent events in a variety of ways. Students determine the theoretical probability of a specific outcome involving two independent events. Students perform a simple probability experiment involving two independent events, and compare the experimental probability with the theoretical probability of a specific outcome.	Students compare, through investigation, the theoretical probability of an event with experimental probability, and explain why they might differ. Students determine, through investigation, the tendency of experimental probability to approach theoretical probability as the number of trials in an experiment increases. Students identify the complementary event for a given event, and calculate the theoretical probability that a given event will not occur.

Additional Activities

Growing Trees

For Extra Practice (Appropriate for use after Lesson 11.2)
Materials: *Growing Trees* (Master 11.5), *Spinners (Master 11.11), paper clip, coin, number cube, deck of cards, ruler, coloured pencils, calculator*
Completing this activity reinforces the relationship between experimental and theoretical probability.

The work students do: Students create an experiment using spinners, number cubes, or cards. They estimate the probability of a chosen event, and then carry out an experiment to determine the experimental probability. Students use tree diagrams to determine the theoretical probability of the event and compare it to their estimates and to the experimental probability.

Take It Further: Students create more complex events that require more complex tree diagrams. They estimate, then complete an experiment to calculate the experimental probability of an event. They draw a tree diagram to calculate the theoretical probability and compare their findings with their estimates and experimental findings.

When Is Your Birthday?

For Extra Practice (Appropriate for use after Lesson 11.3A)
Materials: *When Is Your Birthday?* (Master 11.6), *TI-83 Plus* calculators or simulation software, such as *Fathom*

Completing this activity reinforces the applicability of simulations and allows students to see the benefits in using technology to help with simulations.

The work students do: Students estimate the probability that 10 students in their class share the same birth month. They use a *TI-83 Plus* calculator or computer software to carry out a simulation to check their estimates.

Take It Further: Students estimate, then carry out a simulation to find the probability that 20 students in their class share the same birth month.

Planning for Unit 11

Planning for Instruction

Suggested Unit time: About 2 weeks

Lesson	Time	Materials	Program Support
Launch, page 2	15–20 min		
Skills You'll Need, page 4	20–30 min	calculators	
11.1: Probability Range, page 6 Investigate the range of 0 to 1 for probability.	80–100 min	calculators number lines (optional)	Master 11.12: Probability Number Lines Master 11.7: Step-by-Step 1 Master 11.16: Extra Practice 1
11.2: Tree Diagrams, page 11 Calculate probabilities from tree diagrams and lists.	80–100 min	spinners number cubes labelled 1 to 6 coins paper clips decks of cards rulers coloured pencils calculators	Master 11.11: Spinners Master 11.8: Step-by-Step 2 Master 11.17: Extra Practice 2
Mid-Unit Review, page 16		calculators spinners	Master 11.11: Spinners
11.3: Simulations, page 17 Use simulations to estimate probabilities.	80–100 min	coins, spinners (optional) number cubes labelled 1 to 6 paper clips decks of cards rulers coloured pencils calculators	Master 11.11: Spinners Master 11.9: Step-by-Step 3 Master 11.18: Extra Practice 3
11.3A: Probability Simulations Using a *TI-83 Plus*, page 21 Use technology-based simulation models.	80–100 min	*T1-83 Plus* calculators	Master 11.13: Alternative Explore for Technology-Based Simulations
11.4: Odds For and Against, page 23 Apply probability to sports and games.	Optional	number cubes decks of cards coins spinners	Master 11.11: Spinners Master 11.10: Step-by-Step 4 Master 11.19: Extra Practice 4
Reading and Writing in Math: Extending a Problem, page 26		calculators rulers	
Unit Review, page 28		spinners calculators	Master 11.11: Spinners Extra Practice: Student Book page 498
Practice Test, page 31		calculators	
Unit Problem: What's Your Guess?, page 32	40–50 min	calculators rulers coloured pencils spinners paper clips number cubes decks of cards, coins construction paper regular polyhedra with numbered faces	Master 11.11: Spinners

Planning for Assessment

Purpose	Tools and Process	Recording and Reporting
Diagnostic	*Unit Launch* Question; conference; scaffold problems throughout the unit	PM 8: Conference Prompts
Formative	*Explore* – Ongoing Assessment: Observe and Listen	Master 11.2 Ongoing Observations: Probability PM 1: Inquiry Process Check List PM 6: Observation Record 1 PM 7: Observation Record 2 PM 8: Conference Prompts PM 2: Self-Assessment PM 3: Self-Assessment: Problem Solving PM 9: Work Sample Records
Summative	*Unit Review* *Unit Problem* – Performance Assessment Unit Test Review assessment records; add unit results to ongoing records	Master 11.1 Unit Rubric: Probability Master 11.3 Performance Assessment Rubric: What's Your Guess? Master 11.4 Unit Summary: Probability PM 10: Summary Class Records: Strands PM 11: Summary Class Records: Achievement Categories PM 12: Summary Record: Individual
Learning Skills/Mathematical Disposition	Observe and record throughout unit	PM 4: Learning Skills Check List PM 5: Mathematical Dispositions and Learning Skills

Program Masters (PM) are in the *Grade 8 Planning and Program Masters* module.
Extra Practice Masters are on the CD-ROM and printed in reduced format on page 57 of this module.

LESSON ORGANIZER 15–20 min

Curriculum Focus: Activate prior learning about probability.

Student Materials *Optional*
- spinners with 5 sectors, 2 are one colour and 3 are another colour
- number cubes

Vocabulary: probability, equally likely, list, tree diagram

ASSUMED PRIOR KNOWLEDGE

✓ Students can relate favourable outcomes to total possible outcomes.

✓ Students recognize probabilities involving equally likely outcomes.

✓ Students can relate drawing a tree diagram to determining probability.

UNIT 11

Probability

- A quiz has two questions. Each question provides two answers. You guess each answer. What is the probability that you guess both answers correctly?
- Jason's golden retriever is about to have two puppies. Jason wants to sell the puppies. He gets more money for female puppies. What is the probability that both puppies are female?

How are these two problems alike?

What You'll Learn

- Identify 0 to 1 as a range of probabilities.
- List possible outcomes of experiments.
- Identify possible and favourable outcomes.
- Calculate probabilities from tree diagrams and lists.
- Compare theoretical and experimental probability.
- Apply probability to sports, weather predictions, and political polling.

Why It's Important

You need to be able to make sense of comments you read or hear in the media relating to odds, chance, and probability.

452

ACTIVATE PRIOR LEARNING

Invite students to answer the following questions:

- When a baby is born, what are the possible outcomes for gender?
  (When a baby is born there are two possible outcomes, it could be a girl or a boy.)
- How can these outcomes be described? Explain.
  (The outcomes are described as being equally likely because they each have the same chance of occurring.)
- When a baby is born, what is the probability that it will be male? Female?
  (The probability that a baby is a male is equal to the probability that it is a female: $\frac{1}{2}$ or 0.5, or 50%.)
- Suppose you are given a multiple choice question that has two possible choices and you guess the answer. What is the probability that you will guess the correct answer?
  (The probability of guessing the correct answer is $\frac{1}{2}$ because there are two choices and only one correct answer.)

Have students look at the problems on page 452.

Have them create tree diagrams to solve each problem.

First Question Response	Second Question Response	All Possible Responses
correct	correct	correct, correct
	incorrect	correct, incorrect
incorrect	correct	incorrect, correct
	incorrect	incorrect, incorrect

So, the probability of guessing both answers correctly is $\frac{1}{4}$.

First Puppy	Second Puppy	All Possibilities
female	female	female, female
	male	female, male
male	female	male, female
	male	male, male

So, the probability of both puppies being female is $\frac{1}{4}$.

FROM THE LIBRARY

Exploring Probability by Claire M. Newman, Thomas E. Obremski, and Richard L. Scheaffer. Dale Seymour Publications, 1987.
ISBN: 0866513337
This book serves as a good introduction to the study of probability. The activities are interesting and relate to a wide range of topics, including how to estimate probabilities from real data, and the relationship between estimated and theoretical probability.

Middle Grades Mathematics Project: Probability by Elizabeth Phillips, Glenda Lappan, Mary Jean Winter, and William Fitzgerald. Addison-Wesley Publishing Company, 1986.
ISBN: 0201214784
This book introduces the concepts of probability, including such topics as fair games, equally likely outcomes, expected value, and simulations.

REACHING ALL LEARNERS

Some students may benefit from using the virtual manipulatives on the e-Tools CD-ROM. The e-Tool appropriate for this unit is *Probability*.

DIAGNOSTIC ASSESSMENT

What to Look For	What to Do
✔ Students can relate favourable outcomes to total possible outcomes.	***Extra Support:*** Students who have difficulty identifying favourable outcomes might benefit from making a list of possible outcomes when a number cube is rolled (1, 2, 3, 4, 5, 6) and then identify a favourable outcome as rolling a number less than 4 (1, 2, 3). Work on this skill during *Lessons 11.1 and 11.4.*
✔ Students recognize probabilities involving equally likely outcomes.	Students who have difficulty recognizing probabilities involving equally likely outcomes may benefit from identifying equally likely actions such as tossing a coin or rolling a number cube, and comparing these to unequally likely actions such as spinning a spinner with 5 sections, 2 of which are one colour and 3 of which are another colour. Work on this skill during *Lesson 11.3.*
✔ Students can relate drawing a tree diagram to determining probability.	

LESSON ORGANIZER — 20–30 min

Skills in Review:
- Calculating experimental probability
- Calculating theoretical probability

Student Materials
- calculators

Vocabulary: experimental probability, relative frequency, theoretical probability

Alternative Example 1

Matt is practising basketball shots. He shoots the ball 55 times. The ball falls into the basket 34 times. What is the experimental probability for Matt making a basket?

Solution

Since Matt shoots the ball into the basket 34 out of 55 times, the experimental probability is: $\frac{34}{55} \doteq 0.62$

UNIT 11

Skills You'll Need

Experimental Probability

The **experimental probability** of an event occurring is:

$\frac{\text{Number of times the event occurs}}{\text{Total number of trials}}$

The experimental probability may be written as a fraction, decimal, or percent. Experimental probability is also called **relative frequency**.

Example 1

In baseball, a batting average is a relative frequency of the number of hits. The number of times a player goes to bat is the player's "at bats."

This table shows data for 3 girls from a baseball team.

Name	At Bats	Hits
Abba	29	11
Gina	35	17
Stacy	42	23

Calculate the batting average for each player.

Solution

To calculate each player's batting average, divide the number of hits by the number of at bats.

Abba $= \frac{11}{29} \doteq 0.379$ Gina $= \frac{17}{35} \doteq 0.486$ Stacy $= \frac{23}{42} \doteq 0.548$

A batting average is always written with 3 decimal places.

✓ **Check**

1. a) A quality control inspector tested 235 CDs and found 8 defective. What is the relative frequency of finding a defective CD?
   b) A rug cleaning service uses telemarketing to get business. For every 175 telephone calls made, on average, there will be about 28 new customers. What is the experimental probability of getting a new customer over the phone?

454 UNIT 11: Probability

Experimental Probability

Discuss the meaning of *experimental probability*, *event*, and *trial* in the context of a person tossing a ball into the air and catching it. The experiment is tossing the ball. The number of trials refers to the number of times the ball is tossed. The event refers to the number of times the person catches the ball. If the ball is tossed 40 times and the person catches it 32 times, then the experimental probability is: $\frac{32}{40} = \frac{4}{5}$ or 0.8. The *frequency* of catching the ball *relative* to tossing is 32 out of 40 times.

Ensure students know that experimental probability may differ when the same experiment is repeated.

Ask students to observe the numerator and denominator of each fraction in *Example 1*. The number of trials (the denominator) is always greater than (or equal to) the number of times the event occurs (the numerator).

Common Misconceptions

➤ Students do not understand the meaning of "equally likely."

How to Help: Write each of the numbers 1, 2, 3, 4, and 5 on five separate cards. Shuffle them and place them face down on the desk. Have students predict the chance of picking the number 3 and ask them to justify their reasoning. *($\frac{1}{5}$, because there are 5 different cards, and each has an equal chance of being picked.)*

Add a second card labelled 3 to the cards that are face down. Have students predict the chance of picking the number 3 and ask them to justify their reasoning. *($\frac{2}{6} = \frac{1}{3}$, because now there are six cards and two of them have the number 3. The outcomes are no longer equally likely.)*

Sample Solutions

1. a) Since 8 CDs out of 235 are defective, divide 8 by 235 to obtain the relative frequency: $\frac{8}{235} \doteq 0.03$.
   b) Since 28 new customers are obtained out of 175 telephone calls, divide 28 by 175 to obtain the experimental probability: $\frac{28}{175} = 0.16$.

eoretical Probability

he outcomes of an experiment are equally likely,
etical probability of an event is: $\frac{\text{Number of outcomes favourable to that event}}{\text{Number of possible outcomes}}$

ually we simply refer to the *probability*.
can use theoretical probability to predict how many times a particular
nt will occur when an experiment is repeated many times.

Example 2

A number cube is labelled from 1 to 6.

a) The number cube is rolled.
What is the probability of getting a number less than 4?
b) The cube is rolled 40 times.
Predict how many times a number less than 4 will show.

Solution

When a number cube is rolled, there are 6 possible outcomes: 1, 2, 3, 4, 5, 6
The outcomes are equally likely.
a) A number less than 4 is 1, 2, or 3.
So, 3 outcomes are favourable to the event
"a number less than 4."
The probability of rolling a 1 or 2 or 3 is: $\frac{3}{6} = \frac{1}{2}$
b) The predicted number of times a number less than 4 will show is:
$\frac{1}{2} \times 40 = 20$

Check

The pointer on this spinner is spun 80 times.
Is each statement true or false? Justify your answer.
The pointer will land:

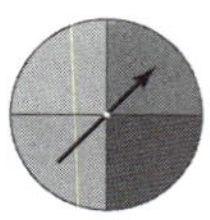

a) on blue exactly 20 times
b) on red or green about 40 times
c) on each colour an equal number of times
d) on each colour approximately 20 times

Skills You'll Need 455

Alternative Example 2

Ten cards, labelled from 1 to 10, are shuffled and placed face down in a pile. The top card is turned over.

a) What is the probability that the card has a number greater than 3?

b) The experiment is repeated 30 times. Predict how many times the top card will have a number greater than 3.

Solution

When the top card is turned over, there are 10 possible outcomes: 1, 2, 3, 4, 5, 6, 7, 8, 9, 10. The outcomes are equally likely.

a) A number greater than 3 is 4, 5, 6, 7, 8, 9, or 10. So, 7 outcomes are favourable to the event "a number greater than 3." The probability of rolling a 4, 5, 6, 7, 8, 9, or 10 is: $\frac{7}{10}$.

b) The predicted number of times a number greater than 3 will be turned over is: $\frac{7}{10} \times 30 = 21$.

Theoretical Probability

Discuss the meaning of *equally likely* outcomes in the context of tossing a coin. Students should understand that, when a coin is tossed, there are two possible outcomes when it lands: heads or tails. Each outcome has the same chance of happening and so is said to be equally likely.

Common Misconceptions

➤ Students do not understand the difference between experimental and theoretical probability.

How to Help: Have students predict the probability of a coin landing on heads when it is tossed. Students should predict that the probability of landing heads is $\frac{1}{2}$. Ask students to predict how many times it might land heads if the coin is tossed 10 times. They should predict that it might land on heads 5 times. Have students conduct the experiment of tossing a coin 10 times and then record the number of times the coin lands heads. They should observe that it may land heads more or less than 5 times. Have students repeat this experiment two or three times to see if they obtain the same result each time. They should observe (in most cases) that the results are not always the same. Then discuss that their predictions represent theoretical probability, while the results of tossing the coin represent experimental probability.

Sample Solutions

2. a) False. Since there are 4 colours, the theoretical probability of landing on blue is $\frac{1}{4}$. So, $\frac{1}{4} \times 80 = 20$ which means the spinner will land on blue *approximately* 20 times.

b) True. The theoretical probability of landing on red or green is $\frac{2}{4} = \frac{1}{2}$. The spinner will land on red or green approximately: $\frac{1}{2} \times 80$, or about 40 times.

c) False. The theoretical probability of landing on each colour is $\frac{1}{4}$, which means the pointer will land on each colour *approximately* an equal number of times.

d) True. The theoretical probability of landing on each colour is $\frac{1}{4}$. So, the pointer will land on each colour approximately: $\frac{1}{4} \times 80$, or about 20 times.

LESSON 11.1

Probability Range

LESSON ORGANIZER 80–100 min

Curriculum Focus: Investigate the range of 0 to 1 for probability. (8m82)

Student Materials
- calculators

Optional
- Probability Number Lines (Master 11.12)
- Step-by-Step 1 (Master 11.7)
- Extra Practice 1 (Master 11.16)

Vocabulary: impossible, unlikely, likely, certain, complementary events

Assessment: Master 11.2 Ongoing Observations: Probability

Key Math Learnings

1. The probability of an event that is certain is 1, and the probability of an event that is impossible is 0.
2. An event that is not impossible or not certain has a probability that is between 0 and 1.
3. Complementary events have probabilities whose sum is 1.

11.1 Probability Range

Focus Investigate the range of 0 to 1 for probability.

When your favourite hockey team is playing, you may ask: Will the team w
You may try to predict the outcome of the game.
By making a prediction, you are estimating the probability that the event will occ

Explore

Work on your own.
Use one of these words to describe the probability of each event below: impossible, unlikely, likely, certain

A Get a tail when a coin is tossed.
B Roll a 3 or 5 on a number cube labelled 1 to 6.
C Not roll a 3 or 5 on a number cube labelled 1 to 6.
D The same team will win the Grey Cup three years in a row.
E The sun will set tomorrow.
F A card drawn from a standard deck is a diamond.
G A card drawn from a standard deck is not a diamond.
H Roll a 4 on a number cube labelled 1 to 6.
I January immediately follows June.
J You will listen to a CD today.

Calculate the probability of each event where you can.
If you cannot calculate a probability, estimate it. Explain your est

Reflect & Share

Compare your results with those of a classmate.
Arrange the events in order from impossible to certain.
What is the probability of an impossible event?
What is the probability of a certain event?

Connect

On page 455, you reviewed the method to calculate the theoretic probability of an event. When *all* the outcomes are favourable to that event, then the fraction:

$$\frac{\text{Number of outcomes favourable to the event}}{\text{Number of possible outcomes}}$$

has numerator equal to denominator, and the probability is 1.

456 UNIT 11: Probability

BEFORE Get Started

Discuss with students the meaning of the words *impossible, unlikely, likely,* and *certain* in relation to probability and review how the probability of an event is determined. Ask:

- What does it mean when an event is impossible?
  (When an event is impossible, it means that the event will never happen; for example, the event that the sun is green is impossible.)
- What does it mean when an event is unlikely versus likely?
  (When an event is unlikely, it means that the event has a very small chance of happening. For example, suppose there are 15 cards in a bag; 14 are pink and 1 is blue. The probability of choosing the blue card is $\frac{1}{15}$. It is unlikely that choosing a card randomly will result in a blue card. The probability of choosing a pink card is $\frac{14}{15}$. It is likely that choosing a card randomly will result in a pink card.)

Present *Explore.*

DURING Explore

Ongoing Assessment: Observe and Listen

As students work, ask questions, such as:

- What are the possible outcomes when a coin is tossed?
  (The possible outcomes when a coin is tossed are heads or tails.)
- What is the probability of getting tails when a coin is tossed?
  (The probability of getting tails is $\frac{1}{2}$ or 0.5.)
- What are the possible outcomes when a number cube labelled 1 to 6 is rolled?
  (The possible outcomes are 1, 2, 3, 4, 5, and 6.)
- What is the probability of rolling a 3 or 5?
  (There are two favourable outcomes; so, the probability of rolling a 3 or 5 is $\frac{2}{6} = \frac{1}{3}$ or approximately 0.33. Since this is less than 0.5, it is unlikely that a 3 or 5 is rolled.)

When *no* outcomes are favourable to that event, then the fraction:

$$\frac{\text{Number of outcomes favourable to the event}}{\text{Number of possible outcomes}}$$

has numerator equal to 0, and the probability is 0.

So, the probability of an event occurring can be marked on a scale from 0 to 1.
When an event is impossible, the probability that it will occur is 0, or 0%.
When an event is certain, the probability that it will occur is 1, or 100%.
All other probabilities lie between 0 and 1.

Impossible — Certain

0.0 (0%) 0.1 0.2 0.3 0.4 0.5 0.6 0.7 0.8 0.9 1.0 (100%)

Example

Twenty cans of soup were immersed in water.
Their labels came off. The cans are identical.
There are: 2 cans of chicken soup; 3 cans of celery soup; 4 cans of vegetable soup; 5 cans of mushroom soup; and 6 cans of tomato soup
One can is opened.

a) What is the probability of each event?
- **i)** The can contains celery soup.
- **ii)** The can contains fish.
- **iii)** The can contains celery soup or chicken soup.
- **iv)** The can contains soup.

b) State which event in part a is:
- **i)** certain
- **ii)** impossible

Solution

a) There are 20 cans, so there are 20 possible outcomes.
- **i)** Three cans contain celery soup.
  The probability of opening a can of celery soup is:
  $\frac{3}{20} = \frac{15}{100} = 0.15$, or 15%
- **ii)** None of the cans contains fish.
  The probability of opening a can of fish is: 0, or 0%

11.1 Probability Range **457**

REACHING ALL LEARNERS

Early Finishers

For each event A to J in *Explore*, students write a similar event that would have the same probability.

Common Misconceptions

➤ Students have difficulty determining if an event is unlikely or likely.

How to Help: Ask students to write the probability of the event as a decimal. If the decimal is less than 0.5, the event is unlikely. In fact, the closer the probability of the event is to 0, the more unlikely that the event will happen. If the decimal is greater than 0.5, the event is likely. The closer the probability of the event is to 1, the more likely the event will happen.

ESL Strategies

Students for whom English is a second language may benefit from using a number line to associate probabilities with the numbers 0 to 1. Students label the number line. They write the word *impossible* for 0 probability, *unlikely* for probabilities between 0 and 0.5, *equally likely* for 0.5 probability, *likely* for values between 0.5 and 1, and *certain* for the probability value 1.

Students may also benefit from recording the expression "complementary events" in the vocabulary part of their notebook and then identifying on the number line a point A with probability, say, 0.3, and its complement point B, with probability $1 - 0.3 = 0.7$. They can write the equation $0.3 + 0.7 = 1$ for this situation.

- When a number cube is rolled and a 3 or 5 is not rolled, what are the possible numbers that might be rolled?
  (If a 3 or 5 is not rolled, the possible numbers that might be rolled are 1, 2, 4, and 6.)
- What is the probability of not rolling a 3 or 5?
  (The probability of not rolling a 3 or 5 is $\frac{4}{6} = \frac{2}{3}$ or approximately 0.66; so, it is likely that a 3 or 5 is not rolled, since the value is greater than 5.)
- What is the probability that the same team will win the Grey Cup three years in a row?
  (Answers may vary. I think there is very little chance, or it is unlikely, that the same team will win the Grey Cup three years in a row and I estimate the probability to be 0.1.)
- What is the probability of the sun setting tomorrow (or on any day)?
  (We know the sun sets each day; so, the probability is 1, because it is a certain event.)
- How many cards are in a standard deck?
  (There are 52 cards in a standard deck.)
- How many suits does the deck have?
  (The deck has 4 suits.)
- What are the suits?
  (Clubs, diamonds, hearts, and spades)
- How many cards have the same suit? How many cards are diamonds? What is the probability that the card is a diamond?
  (There are thirteen cards with the same suit. Thirteen cards are diamonds. The probability that the card is a diamond is $\frac{13}{52} = \frac{1}{4}$ or 0.25. Since this is less than 0.5, it is unlikely that the card will be a diamond.)
- How many cards are not diamonds? What is the probability the card is not a diamond? What is another way of calculating this probability?
  (Subtract 13 from 52: $52 - 13 = 39$. Therefore, 39 cards are not diamonds. The probability that the card is not a diamond is $\frac{39}{52} = \frac{3}{4}$ or 0.75. Since this number is greater than 0.5, it is likely that the card is not a diamond.)

Sample Solutions

5. Answers may vary.

a) Sunday immediately follows Saturday. An event with probability 1 is certain to happen.

b) Rolling 2 on a number cube has six possible outcomes and 1 favourable outcome.

c) Rolling an even number on a number cube has six possible outcomes and 3 favourable outcomes.

d) On a 4-sector spinner labelled A, B, C, D, the probability of spinning an A

e) Friday immediately follows Monday. An event that is impossible has probability 0.

8. c) There are 16 sums in total.

There is one 3; so, $\frac{1}{16}$ or 0.0625

There are two 4's; so, $\frac{2}{16} = \frac{1}{8}$ or 0.125

There are three 5's; so, $\frac{3}{16}$ or 0.1875

There are four 6's; so, $\frac{4}{16} = \frac{1}{4}$ or 0.25

There are three 7's; so, $\frac{3}{16}$ or 0.1875

There are two 8's; so, $\frac{2}{16} = \frac{1}{8}$ or 0.125

There is one 9; so, $\frac{1}{16}$ or 0.0625

d) $\frac{1}{16} + \frac{2}{16} + \frac{3}{16} + \frac{4}{16} + \frac{3}{16} + \frac{2}{16} + \frac{1}{16} = \frac{16}{16} = 1$

The sum 6 has the highest probability. Sums with the same probabilities are 3 and 9, 4 and 8, 5 and 7.

e) i) For example, getting the sum 6, or getting the sum 4 or 8, or getting the sum 3 or 5, or getting the sum 7 or 9

---

iii) Three cans contain celery soup and two contain chicken s
This is 5 cans in all.
The probability of opening a can of celery soup or ch
soup is:
$\frac{5}{20} = \frac{25}{100} = 0.25$, or 25%

iv) Since all the cans contain soup, the probability of opening
can of soup is:
$\frac{20}{20} = 1$, or 100%

b) i) The event that is certain to occur is opening a can that contains soup.
This event has the greatest probability, 1.

ii) The event that is impossible is opening a can that contains fish.
This event has zero probability, 0.

In the *Example*, there are 17 cans that do not contain celery soup
So, the probability of not opening a can of celery soup is $\frac{17}{20}$. The
the probability of opening a can of celery soup + the probability of not opening a can of celery soup $= \frac{3}{20} + \frac{17}{20} = 1$, or 10

The events "opening a can of celery soup" and "not opening a ca
soup" are complementary events. The sum of their probabilities

This is true in general:
the probability of an event occurring + the probability of that event not occurring = 1, or 100%

Practice

1. Copy this number line. Place the letter of each event on page
on the number line at the number that best matches the probability of the event.

Impossible — e 0.0 0%, d 0.1, 0.2, a 0.3, c, 0.4, 0.5, 0.6, 0.7, 0.8, 0.9

- What is the probability that January immediately follows June?
(January immediately follows December; so, this is an impossible event and the probability is 0.)
- How often do you listen to a CD each day? What is the probability that you will listen to a CD today?
(Answers will vary. I listen to a CD every day; so, the probability is 1. Another possible answer is: I never listen to a CD; so, the probability is 0.)

AFTER Connect

Invite students to share their results with a partner. Invite volunteers to write their results on the board and explain their reasoning to the class. What you might see:

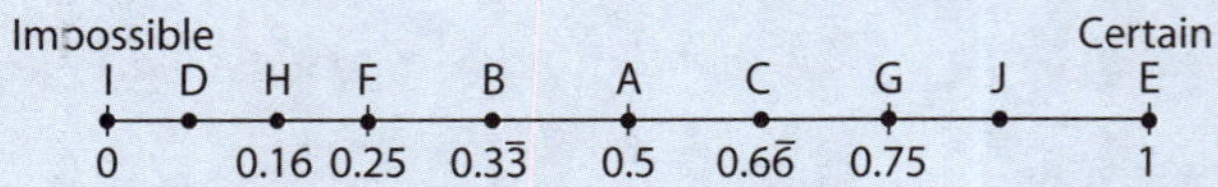

Invite students who have used different ways to display the arrangement of events to show their work on the board. Some students might arrange the letters horizontally without numbers or even vertically with numbers.

As a class, discuss if one method of display is more suitable than another. Point out that the horizontal arrangement from least to greatest corresponds to a number line and also takes up less space on paper.

Review *Connect*. Point out that events B and C in *Explore* are complementary events, as well as events F and G. Ensure students understand that a quick and efficient way to determine the probability of the complement of an event is to subtract the probability of that event occurring from 1. So:

1 – the probability of an event *not* occurring = the probability of an event occurring

a) Without looking, Jodi picks a pink block from a bucket with 5 pink blocks, 7 blue blocks, and 8 red blocks.
b) December immediately follows November.
c) Roll a 1 or 2 on a number cube labelled 1 to 6.
d) It will be warm in January in Ontario.
e) The colour of an apple is blue.

2. A TV weather channel reports a 35% chance of rain today. What is the probability that it will not rain today? 65%

3. An election poll predicts that, in one riding, 4 out of 7 voters will vote for a certain political party. There are 25 156 voters. If the prediction is true, how many voters will not vote for that political party? About 10 781 voters

4. A magazine subscription service uses telemarketing to get business. For every 400 telephone calls, on average, there will be 88 orders for which 80 are actually paid.
a) What is the probability that, on any given call, a telemarketer will receive an order? 0.22 or 22%
b) What is the probability that a telemarketer will receive an order that will be paid for? 0.2 or 20%

5. Give an example of an event with each probability. Explain your choice.
a) 1 b) $\frac{1}{6}$ c) $\frac{1}{2}$ d) $\frac{3}{4}$ e) 0

6. Light bulbs from a production line are tested. Of the 150 bulbs tested, 7 were defective.
a) What is the probability of a bulb not being defective? Describe two different ways to calculate this. $\frac{143}{150}$ or about 95%
b) What if 60 356 bulbs are produced in a week. How many may be defective? About 2817 bulbs

7. To play a board game, Marty and Shane roll a number cube labelled 1 to 6. The person with the greater number goes first. Marty rolls a 4.
a) What is the probability Marty will go first? $\frac{1}{2}$ or 0.5
b) What is the probability Marty will not go first? $\frac{1}{2}$ or 0.5
c) What is the probability that both Marty and Shane have to roll the number cube again? Explain. $\frac{1}{6}$ or $0.1\overline{6}$

11.1 Probability Range **459**

ii) For example, getting the sum 3 or 4 or 5 or 6 or 8, or getting the sum 5 or 6 or 7 or 8, or getting the sum 3 or 5 or 6 or 7 or 9

iii) The event of getting a sum of 3 or 4 or 5 or 6 or 7 or 8 or 9 has probability 1 since these are all the possible outcomes for this situation.

iv) The event of getting the sum 2 or 1 or 10 and higher is impossible and so has probability 0.

9. a) To win, the player needs any card that has 3, 4, 5, or 6. There are 4 suits, so there are 16 possible ways to win. So, the probability of winning is $\frac{16}{50}$, or $\frac{8}{25}$. The probability of not winning is $1 - \frac{8}{25} = \frac{17}{25}$

b) To win, the player needs any card that has 6, 7, 8, 9, 10, Jack, or Queen. The probability of winning is $\frac{28}{50}$, or $\frac{14}{25}$; so, the probability of not winning is $1 - \frac{14}{25} = \frac{11}{25}$.

c) To win, the player needs any card that has 2 or 3. The probability of winning is $\frac{8}{50}$, or $\frac{4}{25}$; so, the probability of not winning is $1 - \frac{4}{25} = \frac{21}{25}$.

d) There are no cards that can win. The probability of winning is 0; so, the probability of losing is 1.

REFLECT: Since the probability of an event lies between 0 and 1, the probability can be less than 1.
The probability of an event cannot be greater than 1 because probability is represented by the fraction:

$$\frac{\textit{number of favourable outcomes}}{\textit{number of possible outcomes}}$$

When all the outcomes are favourable to an event, the numerator is equal to the denominator and the fraction is equal to 1. The numerator can never be greater than the denominator.

1 – the probability of an event occurring = the probability of an event *not* occurring

Practice

Question 1. Students can use the Probability Number Line (Master 11.12). Encourage students to determine the probability of each event before placing the corresponding letter on the number line.

Question 2. To determine the probability of a complementary event, encourage students to subtract the probability of the event occurring from 1.

Questions 3 and 6. You may wish to ask students to solve this using two different methods and then explain which method they prefer and why. Using the probability of the complementary event is the most efficient way to solve the problem.

Question 9. Ensure students are aware that a standard deck of cards has 52 cards. There are 13 cards for each suit: ace, 2, 3, 4, 5, 6, 7, 8, 9, Jack, Queen, and King. Encourage students that are having difficulty to determine the cards that the player requires to win the game and find the probability of being dealt those cards. Then, students can determine the probability of the complementary event.

Assessment Focus: Question 8

Students who have difficulty with part e may benefit from knowing that they can combine two or more events for the sum of the faces of the tetrahedron.

Mental Math

5782.5, 57 825, 578 250
3.65, 36.5, 365
420.11, 4201.1, 42 011
14.32, 143.2, 1432
When each number is divided by 0.1, the decimal point moves one place to the right.
When each number is divided by 0.01, the decimal point moves two places to the right.
When each number is divided by 0.001, the decimal point moves three places to the right.
Dividing by 0.1 is the same as multiplying by 10.
Dividing by 0.01 is the same as multiplying by 100.
Dividing by 0.001 is the same as multiplying by 1000.

Assignment Guidelines

If your students do not have time to complete all the *Practice* questions on pages 458, 459, and 460, these questions provide minimum curriculum coverage: 1, 4, 7, 8, *Reflect*

To assess the 4 Achievement Chart categories listed in the curriculum document, have students complete these *Practice* questions:
Knowledge and Understanding: 1
Application: 7
Thinking: 8
Communication: *Reflect*

+	1	2	3	4
2	3	4	5	6
3	4	5	6	7
4	5	6	7	8
5	6	7	8	9

8. Assessment Focus A regular tetrahedron has 4 faces. The faces of one tetrahedron are labelled 1 to 4. The faces of the other tetrahedron are labelled 2 to 5. The two tetrahedrons are rolled. The numbers on the faces that land are added.

a) Copy and complete this table for the possible outcomes.
b) List the possible outcomes for the sum. 3, 4, 5, 6, 7, 8, 9
c) Calculate the probability of each outcome.
d) Add the probabilities in part c. What do you notice? Explain your result.
e) Which event has each probability?
i) 25% **ii)** 75% **iii)** 1 **iv)** 0

Take It Further

9. In the card game, *In Between*, a deck of cards is shuffled. Two cards are placed face up. A third card is dealt to the player. If the third card falls in between the two cards that are face up, the player wins. What is the probability that the player will not win for each pair of cards that are face up?

a) a 2 of hearts and a 7 of spades
b) a 5 of diamonds and a king of clubs

c) an ace of clubs and a 4 of spades
d) a 10 of diamonds and a jack of clubs

Mental Math

Divide each number by 0.1, 0.01, and 0.001:
- 578.25
- 0.365
- 42.011
- 1.432

What patterns do you see in your answers?

Reflect

Can the probability of an event be less than 1? Greater than 1? Explain.

460 UNIT 11: Probability

ASSESSMENT FOR LEARNING

What to Look For

Knowledge and Understanding
✔ Students understand that the probability of an event that is certain is 1 and the probability of an event that is impossible is 0.

Communication
✔ Students can describe what is meant by complementary events in terms of the sum of their probabilities.

Application
✔ Students can identify events that have probabilities that are between 0 and 1.

What to Do

Extra Support: Students who have difficulty arranging probabilities on a scale from 0 to 1 may benefit from converting all fractions to decimals and then placing them in order from least to greatest. Remind students that probabilities closer to 0 are unlikely while those closer to 1 are likely. Probabilities of 0.5 are equally likely.
Students can use Step-by-Step 1 (Master 11.7) to complete question 8.

Extra Practice: Students can complete Extra Practice 1 (Master 11.16).

Extension: Have students determine the probability of the complementary events for *Practice* question 5.

Recording and Reporting
Master 11.2 Ongoing Observations: Probability

11.2 Tree Diagrams

Focus Calculate probabilities from tree diagrams and lists.

Explore

Work with a partner.
You will need a number cube labelled 1 to 6 and a coin.

- One of you tosses the coin and one rolls the cube. Record the results.
- Calculate the experimental probability of the event "a head and a 2 show" after each number of trials.
  - 10 trials
  - 20 trials
  - 50 trials
  - 100 trials
- List the possible outcomes of this experiment.
- What is the theoretical probability of the event "a head and a 2 show"?
- How do the experimental and theoretical probabilities compare?

Reflect & Share

Compare your outcomes and probabilities with those of another pair of classmates.
Did you use a tree diagram to list the outcomes?
If not, work together to make a tree diagram.
Combine your results to get 200 trials.
What is the experimental probability of a head and a 2?
How do the experimental and theoretical probabilities compare?

Connect

Recall that a tree diagram can be used to find the outcomes of an experiment when the outcomes are equally likely.

11.2 Tree Diagrams 461

Tree Diagrams

LESSON ORGANIZER (80–100 min)

Curriculum Focus: Calculate probabilities from tree diagrams and lists. (8m80, 8m81)

Student Materials
- spinners (Master 11.11),
- number cubes labelled 1 to 6
- coins, paper clips, decks of cards, rulers, coloured pencils, calculators

Optional
- Step-by-Step 2 (Master 11.8)
- Extra Practice 2 (Master 11.17)

Vocabulary: tree diagram, experimental probability, theoretical probability

Assessment: Master 11.2 Ongoing Observations: Probability

Key Math Learnings

1. The greater the number of trials, the closer the experimental probability will be to the theoretical probability.
2. A tree diagram is useful to list the equally likely outcomes of an experiment and then determine the probability of related events.

BEFORE Get Started

Engage students in a discussion about experiments and how they can be used to determine the probability of an event. Ask:

- What are some different ways that the possible outcomes of an experiment can be recorded? *(The possible outcomes may be recorded using a list or a tree diagram.)*
- When determining the probability of an event, is it enough to conduct the experiment once, twice, five times? Explain. *(The more often the experiment is conducted, the better the estimate of the experimental probability. The number of trials also depends on the possible number of outcomes. The more outcomes possible, the larger the number of trials that should be repeated.)*

Present *Explore.* Distribute coins and number cubes to pairs of students. One student should toss the coin and the other should roll the number cube. Encourage students to draw a chart similar to the one below to record the results of each trial of their experiment. The chart will also allow students to keep track of the number of trials when determining the experimental probability after 10, 20, 50, and 100 trials.

Trial	Coin Toss	Number Cube Roll	Outcomes
1			
2			
3			
4			
5			

DURING Explore

Ongoing Assessment: Observe and Listen

As students work, ask questions, such as:

REACHING ALL LEARNERS

Alternative Explore

Have students work with a partner using a deck of cards and a coin. Students toss the coin and draw a card from the deck. They calculate the experimental probability of "tails and a king" after 10, 20, 50, and 100 trials. Students construct tree diagrams to determine the theoretical probability, then compare this with their findings.

Early Finishers

Have groups of four students combine their results from *Explore* with another group of four to get results for 400 trials. Have them complete *Reflect and Share* once more to confirm their findings. Have students look for a connection between the total number of possible outcomes (12) for the experiment, the number of possible first action outcomes (2), and the number of possible second action outcomes (6). Students should observe the relationship: $12 = 2 \times 6$.

Common Misconceptions

➤ Students think that each pair of students should obtain similar experimental results.

How to Help: Remind students that this is an experiment and it is possible for each pair of students to get different results.

➤ Students have difficulty drawing a tree diagram with two actions.

How to Help: Remind students that when drawing a tree diagram they are to begin with the word *Start*. The first column of the tree diagram should list all the possible results of the first action (for example, tossing a coin). For *each* possible outcome of the first action they are to list the possible outcomes of the second action (for example, rolling a number cube).

Example

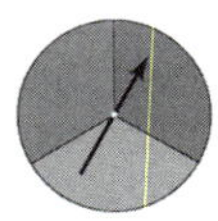

Carina and Paolo play the *Same/Different* game with the spinner at the left. A turn is two spins.
Player A scores 1 point if the colours are the same.
Player B scores 1 point if the colours are different.

a) Use a tree diagram to list the possible outcomes of this game.
b) Find the probability of getting the same colours.
c) Find the probability of getting different colours.
d) Is this a fair game? Explain.
e) If you think this game is fair, give your reasons. If the game is not fair, how could you change the rules to make it fair?

Solution

a) The first branch of the tree diagram lists the equally likely outcomes of the first spin: blue, green, pink
The second branch lists the equally likely outcomes of the second spin: blue, green, pink
For each outcome from the first spin, there are 3 possible outcomes for the second spin.
Follow the paths from left to right.
List all the possible outcomes.

	First Spin	Second Spin	Possible Outcomes
Start	blue	blue	blue/blue
		green	blue/green
		pink	blue/pink
	green	blue	green/blue
		green	green/green
		pink	green/pink
	pink	blue	pink/blue
		green	pink/green
		pink	pink/pink

b) From the tree diagram, there are 9 possible outcomes.
Three outcomes have: blue/blue, green/green, pink/pink
The probability of the same colour is:
$\frac{3}{9} = \frac{1}{3} \doteq 0.33$, or about 33%

- How many times did heads and a 2 appear after 10 trials? After 20 trials? After 50 trials? After 100 trials?
(Answers will vary. For example: After 10 trials, heads and a 2 appeared 1 time. After 20 trials, heads and a 2 appeared 2 times. After 50 trials, heads and a 2 appeared 4 times. After 100 trials, heads and a 2 appeared 8 times.)
- What is the experimental probability of getting heads and a 2 after 10 trials? After 20 trials? After 50 trials? After 100 trials?
(The experimental probability of getting heads and a 2 after 10 trials is $\frac{1}{10}$ or 0.1; after 20 trials is $\frac{2}{20} = \frac{1}{10}$ or 0.1; after 50 trials is $\frac{3}{50}$ or 0.06; after 100 trials is $\frac{8}{100} = \frac{2}{25}$ or 0.08.)
- What are the possible outcomes of the experiment?
(When a coin is tossed, the possible outcomes are heads or tails. These are equally likely outcomes. When a number cube labelled 1 to 6 is rolled, the possible outcomes are 1, 2, 3, 4, 5, or 6. These are also equally likely outcomes. The two actions together have 12 equally likely possible outcomes.)

	Coin Toss	Roll Number Cube	Possible Outcomes
Start	heads	1	(H, 1)
		2	(H, 2)
		3	(H, 3)
		4	(H, 4)
		5	(H, 5)
		6	(H, 6)
	tails	1	(T, 1)
		2	(T, 2)
		3	(T, 3)
		4	(T, 4)
		5	(T, 5)
		6	(T, 6)

- What is the theoretical probability of getting a head and a 2?
(There are 12 possible outcomes. Only 1 outcome (H, 2) has a head and a 2; so, the theoretical probability of this event is $\frac{1}{12} \doteq 0.083$.)
- What do you notice about the values of the experimental probability as more trials are performed compared to the theoretical probability?
(The theoretical probability is approximately 0.083. The experimental probabilities are 0.1, 0.1, 0.06,

c) Six outcomes have different colours: blue/green, blue/pink, green/blue, green/pink, pink/blue, pink/green
The probability of different colours is:
$\frac{6}{9} = \frac{2}{3} \doteq 0.67$, or about 67%

d) The game is not fair. The chances of scoring are not equal. Player A can score only 3 out of the possible 9 points, while Player B can score 6 out of the possible 9 points.

e) Here is one way to make the game fair: Player A should score 2 points when the colours are the same. When each player has 9 turns, the players have equal chances of winning.

Carina and Paolo played the *Same/Different* game 100 times.
There were 41 same colours and 59 different colours.
The experimental probability of the same colours is:
$\frac{41}{100} = 0.41$, or 41%
The experimental probability of different colours is:
$\frac{59}{100} = 0.59$, or 59%
These probabilities are different from the theoretical probabilities in the solution of the *Example*.
The greater the number of times the game is played, the closer the theoretical and experimental probabilities may be.

Practice

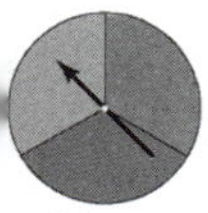
Spinner 1

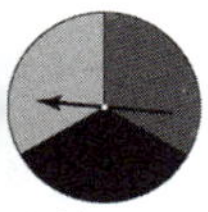
Spinner 2

1. Here is a spinner game called *Make Green*.
To play the game, a player spins the pointer on each spinner.
To win, a player must get blue on Spinner 1 and yellow on Spinner 2, because blue and yellow make green.
Your teacher will give you blank spinners.
Use an open paper clip as a pointer.
   a) Make these spinners. Play the game 10 times.
   Record your results.
   How many times did you make green?
   b) Combine your results with those of 9 classmates.
   How many times did make green occur in 100 tries?
   What is the experimental probability for make green?

Sample Solutions

1. a) Answers will vary.
   b) The experimental probability is found by counting the number of times all 10 students made green and dividing this number by 100.
   d) There are 9 possible outcomes and one favourable outcome (blue/yellow). The theoretical probability of making green is $\frac{1}{9}$, or about 0.11.
   e) Answers will vary depending on results in part b, but the probabilities should be close in value.
3. Students work should show tree diagrams.
Possible outcomes when rolling the tetrahedron and spinning the pointer: (blue, yellow), (blue, purple), (blue, blue), (blue, red), (blue, pink), (yellow, yellow), (yellow, purple), (yellow, red), (yellow, pink), (yellow, blue), (pink, yellow), (pink, purple), (pink, pink), (pink, red), (pink, blue), (red, yellow), (red, purple), (red, red), (red, pink), (red, blue)
The probability of making green with the tetrahedron and the spinner is $\frac{2}{20} = \frac{1}{10}$ or 0.1.
Possible outcomes when the tetrahedron is rolled twice: (b, y), (b, p), (b, r), (b, b), (y, y), (y, p), (y, r), (y, b), (p, y), (p, r), (p, b), (p, p), (r, y), (r, p), (r, r), (r, b)
The probability of making green when the tetrahedron is rolled twice is $\frac{2}{16} = \frac{1}{8}$ or 0.125.
Possible outcomes when spinning the pointer twice: (b, y), (b, pp), (b, r), (b, p), (b, b), (y, y), (y, p), (y, r), (y, pp), (y, b), (p, y), (p, pp), (p, r), (p, p), (p, b), (r, y), (r, pp), (r, r), (r, p), (r, b), (pp, y), (pp, pp), (pp, r), (pp, p), (pp, b)
The probability of making green when the pointer on the spinner is spun twice is $\frac{2}{25}$ or 0.08.

and 0.08. As more trials are performed, the values of the experimental probabilities are getting closer to the value of the theoretical probability.)

AFTER Connect

Invite students to share their findings. Ask questions, such as:

- What was the experimental probability of getting heads and a 2 after you combined your results with another pair or students for 200 trials?
(In 200 trials, the event occurred 17 times; so, the experimental probability is $\frac{17}{200} \doteq 0.085$.)
- How do the values of the experimental and theoretical probabilities compare after 200 trials?
(The experimental probability is approximately 0.085 and the theoretical probability is approximately 0.083; so, the two values are very close.)
- What conclusion can you make?
(The more often an experiment is repeated, the closer in value the experimental probability becomes to the theoretical probability.)
- What is an organized way of listing the possible outcomes of an experiment? Explain.
(A tree diagram is an organized way of listing the possible outcomes of an experiment. It can only be used when the outcomes are equally likely.)

Present *Connect*.

Ask:

- What is meant by a *fair* game?
(A game is fair when each person's chances of winning are equal.)

The greatest probability of making green is $\frac{1}{8}$ or 0.125, which occurs when the tetrahedron is rolled twice. Therefore, the player should choose to roll the tetrahedron twice to have the greatest chance of winning the game.

6. Possible outcomes: (h, h, h), (h, h, t), (h, t, h), (h, t, t), (t, h, h), (t, h, t), (t, t, h), (t, t, t)
Since David always picks tails, the outcome (t, t, t) represents the event of setting the table 3 days in a row. There are 8 possible outcomes and this event occurs only once; so, the probability that David sets the table 3 days in a row is $\frac{1}{8}$ or 0.125.

REFLECT: A tree diagram is useful to list all possible outcomes of an experiment in which the outcomes are equally likely.
For example, consider the experiment of tossing a coin three times and determining the probability of the coin landing on tails at least twice.

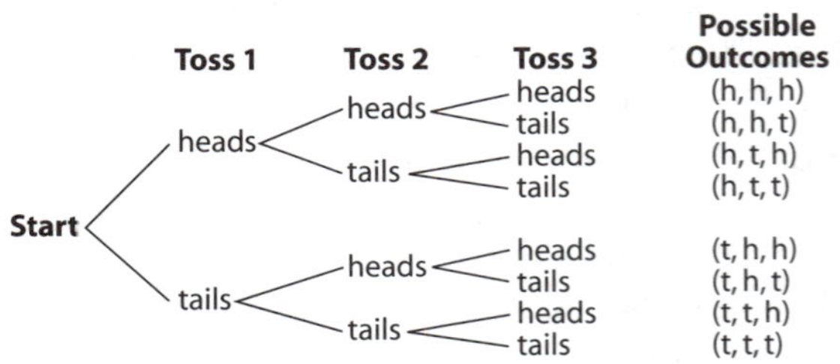

There are 8 possible outcomes. There are four favourable outcomes: (h, t, t), (t, h, t), (t, t, h) and (t, t, t). The probability of landing tails at least twice is $\frac{4}{8} = \frac{1}{2}$.

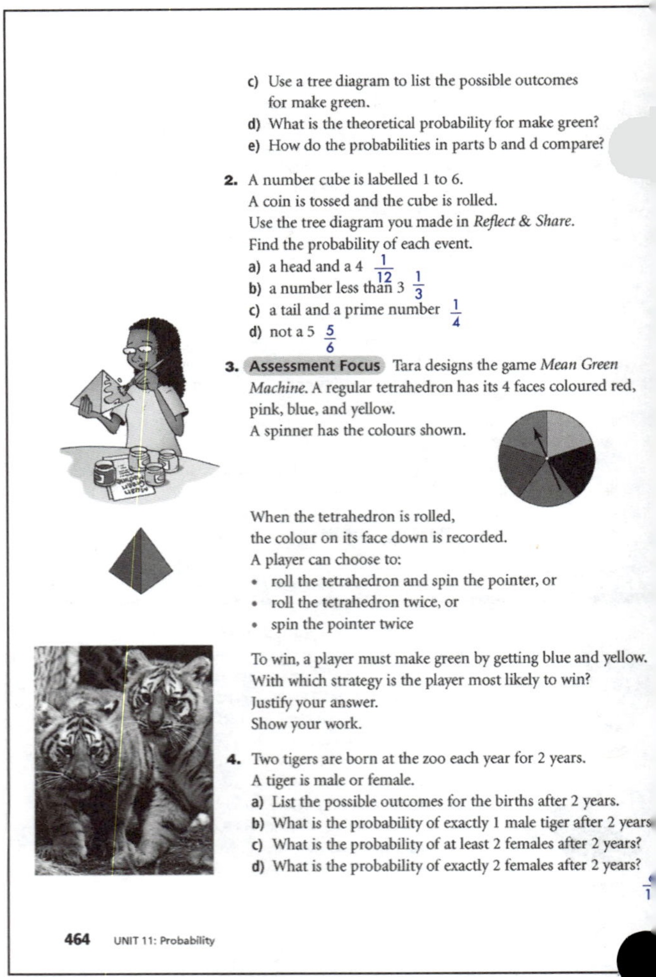

c) Use a tree diagram to list the possible outcomes for make green.
d) What is the theoretical probability for make green?
e) How do the probabilities in parts b and d compare?

2. A number cube is labelled 1 to 6.
A coin is tossed and the cube is rolled.
Use the tree diagram you made in *Reflect & Share.*
Find the probability of each event.
a) a head and a 4 $\frac{1}{12}$
b) a number less than 3 $\frac{1}{3}$
c) a tail and a prime number $\frac{1}{4}$
d) not a 5 $\frac{5}{6}$

3. **Assessment Focus** Tara designs the game *Mean Green Machine.* A regular tetrahedron has its 4 faces coloured red, pink, blue, and yellow.
A spinner has the colours shown.

When the tetrahedron is rolled,
the colour on its face down is recorded.
A player can choose to:
- roll the tetrahedron and spin the pointer, or
- roll the tetrahedron twice, or
- spin the pointer twice

To win, a player must make green by getting blue and yellow.
With which strategy is the player most likely to win?
Justify your answer.
Show your work.

4. Two tigers are born at the zoo each year for 2 years.
A tiger is male or female.
a) List the possible outcomes for the births after 2 years.
b) What is the probability of exactly 1 male tiger after 2 years?
c) What is the probability of at least 2 females after 2 years?
d) What is the probability of exactly 2 females after 2 years?

464 UNIT 11: Probability

Practice

Question 1: Students will require blank spinners and a paper clip.

Question 7: Encourage students to draw a tree diagram to list the outcomes and calculate the probability of each event. Remind students that for part a, the letters are not replaced and only used once; however, for part b the letters are replaced and can be used 3 times. For part c, students should know that they can use similar steps to the game described with the word WIN, but because the word CRUISE has 6 letters, the number of draws will be different. To determine the probabilities for the CRUISE game, encourage students to look for patterns in the WIN game and apply them.

Assessment Focus: Question 3

Encourage students to make a separate tree diagram to list the outcomes for each experiment:

i) roll the tetrahedron and spin the pointer
ii) roll the tetrahedron twice
iii) spin the pointer twice

From the tree diagram they can determine the required probabilities and then compare their values.

deck of playing cards
s 52 cards.
ere are 4 suits:
pades,
and clubs.
13 cards in
h suit.

r Strategies

h number in
form.
308.34
808 080.8

5. An experiment is: rolling a number cube labelled 1 to 6 and picking a card at random from a deck of cards.
The number on the cube and the suit of the card are recorded.
   a) Use a deck of cards and a number cube.
   Carry out this experiment 10 times. Record your results.
   b) Combine your results with those of 9 classmates.
   c) What is the experimental probability of each event?
      i) a heart and a 4 $\frac{1}{24}$
      ii) a heart or a diamond and a 2 $\frac{1}{12}$
      iii) a red card and an odd number $\frac{1}{4}$
   d) Draw a tree diagram to list the possible outcomes.
   e) What is the theoretical probability of each event in part c?
   f) Compare the theoretical and experimental probabilities of the events in part c.
   What do you think might happen if you carried out this experiment 1000 times?

6. Neither Andrew nor David likes to set the table for dinner. They toss a coin to decide who will set the table. David always picks tails. What is the probability David will set the table 3 days in a row? Justify your answer.

ke It Further

7. Each letter of the word WIN is written on a piece of paper.
The pieces of paper are placed in a can.
You make three draws.
You place the letters from left to right in the order drawn.
The pieces of paper are not replaced after each draw.
If you draw the letters that spell WIN, you win a prize.
   a) What is the probability of winning a prize? $\frac{1}{6}$ or $0.1\overline{6}$
   b) What if the pieces of paper are replaced after each draw.
   Is the probability of winning increased or decreased? Explain. Decreased
   c) Design a similar contest using the letters of CRUISE.
   Repeat parts a and b.

eflect

How is a tree diagram useful when calculating probabilities?
Use an example in your explanation.

11.2 Tree Diagrams 465

Number Strategies

- $12\ 006\ 308.34 = 1 \times 10\ 000\ 000 + 2 \times 1\ 000\ 000 + 6 \times 1000 + 3 \times 100 + 8 \times 1 + 3 \times \frac{1}{10} + 4 \times \frac{1}{100}$
- $8\ 080\ 808\ 080.8 = 8 \times 1\ 000\ 000\ 000 + 8 \times 10\ 000\ 000 + 8 \times 100\ 000 + 8 \times 1000 + 8 \times 10 + 8 \times \frac{1}{10}$
- $12.083 = 1 \times 10 + 2 \times 1 + 8 \times \frac{1}{100} + 3 \times \frac{1}{1000}$

Assignment Guidelines

If your students do not have time to complete all the *Practice* questions on pages 463, 464, and 465, these questions provide minimum curriculum coverage: 1, 3, 5, 6, *Reflect*

To assess the 4 Achievement Chart categories listed in the curriculum document, have students complete these *Practice* questions:
Knowledge and Understanding: 1
Thinking: 3
Application: 5
Communication: *Reflect*

ASSESSMENT FOR LEARNING

What to Look For

Knowledge and Understanding

✔ Students understand the difference between experimental probability and theoretical probability.

Communication

✔ Students can compare and explain how the values of experimental and theoretical probabilities are related as more trials are performed.

Application

✔ Students can perform experiments to determine experimental probabilities and use tree diagrams to find theoretical probabilities.

What to Do

Extra Support: Students can use Step-by-Step 2 (Master 11.8) to complete question 3.

Extra Practice: Students can complete the Additional Activity, *Growing Trees* (Master 11.5). Students can complete Extra Practice 2 (Master 11.17).

Extension: Have students use questions 4 and 6 as a guide. They make up their own questions, solve them, then trade with a classmate to solve their classmate's problem.

Recording and Reporting

Master 11.2 Ongoing Observations: Probability

MID-UNIT REVIEW

LESSON ORGANIZER

Student Materials
- calculators

Optional
- blank spinners (Master 11.11)

Assessment: Masters 11.1 Unit Rubric: Probability, 11.4 Unit Summary: Probability

Sample Solutions

3. a) Since 0.8 is closer to 1, the probability is best described by the word *likely*.
   b) An event with a probability of 0 is impossible.
   c) Since 0.2 is closer to 0, the probability is best described by the word *unlikely*.
   d) Since 0.4 is closer to 0 than it is to 1, the probability is best described by the word *unlikely*.

4. a) $\frac{1015}{1050}$, $\frac{35}{1050}$
   b) $\frac{1015}{1050} \times 8500 \doteq 8217$; about 8217 people

5. Fari's batting average is $\frac{97}{211}$ or approximately 0.460.
   Eric's batting average is $\frac{119}{234}$ or approximately 0.509.
   Eric's batting average is better than Fari's batting average.

Mid-Unit Review

LESSON

11.1 **1.** A TV news channel reports the results of a political poll. According to the poll, 53% of Canadians will reelect the current political party. What is the probability that the current political party will not be reelected? 0.47

2. Sal tossed a thumbtack 80 times. It landed point up 27 times. What is the experimental probability that the tack will land on its side? $\frac{53}{80}$

3. Each number below is the probability of an event. Which of these words best describe the probability?
certain, unlikely, likely, impossible
a) 0.8 likely b) 0 impossible c) 0.2 unlikely d) 0.4 unlikely

4. A dentist tested a new whitener for teeth. She found that, in 1050 tests, it worked 1015 times.
a) What is the experimental probability that the whitener works? That it does not work?
b) The whitener is used on 8500 people. About how many people can expect whiter teeth?

5. Fari was at bat 211 times and hit 97 times. Eric was at bat 234 times and hit 119 times. Which player has the better batting average? Explain.

11.2 **6.** Use a number cube labelled … Roll it twice. Record the results. Repeat this experiment until you have 10 results. Combine your results with those of 9 classmates. You now have 100 results.
a) Draw a tree diagram to list th… possible outcomes.
b) What is the theoretical probability of each event?
   i) rolling a 4 and a 5
   ii) rolling two even numbers
   iii) rolling the same number twice
   iv) rolling a 3
   v) not rolling a 1 or a 6
c) What is the experimental probability of each event in part b?
d) Compare the two probabilitie… for each event. What do you notice?

7. Red and black combine to make brown.
a) Sketch two different spinners with pointers that could be sp… to land on the two colours th… combine to make brown.
b) Draw a tree diagram to show possible outcomes of spinnin… the two pointers.
c) Calculate the probability of making brown.

466 UNIT 11: Probability

6. a)

First Roll	Second Roll	Possible Outcomes
1	1, 2, 3, 4, 5, 6	(1, 1) (1, 2) (1, 3) (1, 4) (1, 5) (1, 6)
2	1, 2, 3, 4, 5, 6	(2, 1) (2, 2) (2, 3) (2, 4) (2, 5) (2, 6)
3	1, 2, 3, 4, 5, 6	(3, 1) (3, 2) (3, 3) (3, 4) (3, 5) (3, 6)
4	1, 2, 3, 4, 5, 6	(4, 1) (4, 2) (4, 3) (4, 4) (4, 5) (4, 6)
5	1, 2, 3, 4, 5, 6	(5, 1) (5, 2) (5, 3) (5, 4) (5, 5) (5, 6)
6	1, 2, 3, 4, 5, 6	(6, 1) (6, 2) (6, 3) (6, 4) (6, 5) (6, 6)

b) i) $\frac{2}{36} = \frac{1}{18}$ ii) $\frac{9}{36} = \frac{1}{4}$ iii) $\frac{6}{36} = \frac{1}{6}$ iv) $\frac{11}{36}$ v) $\frac{16}{36} = \frac{4}{9}$
c) Answers may vary.
d) Answers may vary.

7. a) For example:

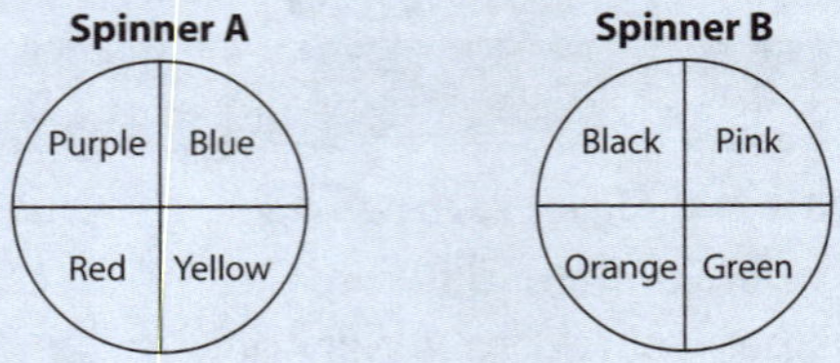

b)

Spinner A	Spinner B	Possible Outcomes
blue	black	not brown
	pink	not brown
	orange	not brown
	green	not brown
yellow	black	not brown
	pink	not brown
	orange	not brown
	green	not brown
red	black	brown
	pink	not brown
	orange	not brown
	green	not brown
purple	black	not brown
	pink	not brown
	orange	not brown
	green	not brown

c) There are 16 outcomes. One outcome makes brown; so, the probability of making brown is $\frac{1}{16}$ or approximately 0.063.

11.3 Simulations

Focus Use simulation to estimate probabilities.

A real-life situation can be simulated by a probability experiment.
For certain events, a **simulation** is more practical than gathering data.

Explore

Work with a partner.
You will need a number cube labelled 1 to 6.
A store has a "Scratch and Save" day.
The store gives each customer a card with 6 circles on it.
Under the circles there are two matching percents and four different percents.
You scratch two circles.

If you get the two matching percents, you have that discount on all items you buy in the store that day.
The percents are arranged randomly on the card.
What is the probability you will scratch two matching percents?

➢ How can you use the number cube to estimate the probability you will scratch two matching percents?
➢ Conduct the experiment as many times as you can. Record each result.
➢ What is the experimental probability you will scratch two matching percents?

Reflect & Share

Compare your results with those of another pair of classmates.
Are the probabilities equal? Explain.
Work together to sketch a spinner you could use, instead of a number cube, to carry out this experiment.

Simulations

LESSON ORGANIZER (80–100 min)

Curriculum Focus: Use simulations to estimate probabilities. (8m81)

Student Materials
- coins, number cubes labelled 1 to 6, paper clips, decks of cards, rulers, coloured pencils, calculators

Optional
- spinners (Master 11.11)
- Step-by-Step 3 (Master 11.9)
- Extra Practice 3 (Master 11.18)

Vocabulary: simulation, model, equally likely outcomes

Assessment: Master 11.2 Ongoing Observations: Probability

Key Math Learnings

1. A simulation models or imitates a real-life situation.
2. A simulation can be more practical than gathering data when determining the probability of an event.

Number Strategies

$72 = 2 \times 2 \times 2 \times 3 \times 3$
$73 = 1 \times 73$
$74 = 2 \times 37$
$75 = 3 \times 5 \times 5$
$76 = 2 \times 2 \times 19$

BEFORE Get Started

Prompt a short discussion about simulations. Have students share any information that they know about simulations.

Present *Explore.* Distribute the number cubes. Students may find it helpful to record the results of their experiment in a table with these headings.

Simulation	First Roll	Second Roll
1		
2		
3		
4		
5		
6		

DURING Explore

Ongoing Assessment: Observe and Listen

As students work, ask questions, such as:

- How can the situation of scratching circles on the Scratch and Save card be simulated with the number cubes?
  (Suppose the matching percents are in the 1st and 6th positions, as shown.

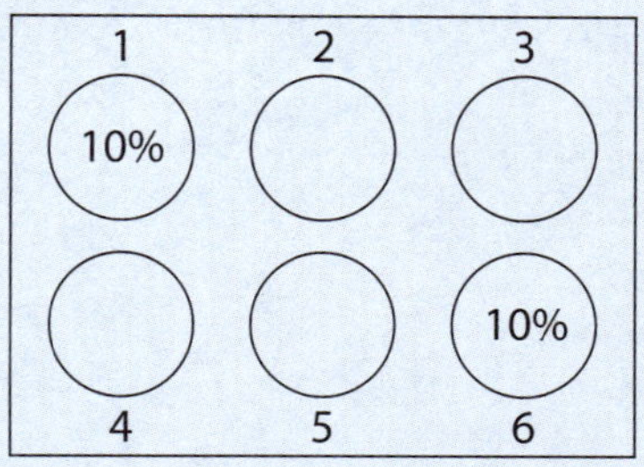

The possibilities for the first roll are: 1, 2, 3, 4, 5, or 6.
Rolling the second time also has six possibilities: 1, 2, 3, 4, 5, or 6.

REACHING ALL LEARNERS

Alternative Explore

Have students work with a partner. Students construct a spinner with four congruent sectors each having a different colour. Tell them that a Scratch and Win ticket has 4 circles on it. Under the circles there are three matching amounts and one different amount. Suppose they scratch 3 circles. If they get the three matching amounts, they win. The amounts are arranged randomly on the card.
Ask them to design a spinner to estimate the probability of scratching three matching amounts. Students conduct the experiment as many times as they can, and record their results.

Common Misconceptions

➤ Students may have difficulty understanding when and how an event can be simulated.

How to Help: Remind students that an event can only be simulated when the outcomes are equally likely. Encourage them to ask themselves the question: Are the outcomes equally likely? If the answer is yes, then the event can be simulated.
Remind students that once they know the event can be simulated, then the method of simulation depends on the number of equally likely outcomes. When there are two equally likely outcomes, a coin can be used to simulate the event. When there are 6 equally likely outcomes, a number cube can be used to simulate the event. For other numbers of outcomes, such as 3 or 4, use a spinner with the same number of congruent sections as the number of equally likely outcomes. For a large number of equally likely outcomes, combine a coin with a spinner or a coin with a cube or two cubes, as shown in the *Example*.

Connect

When we use a simulation to estimate probability, the mode must have the same number of outcomes as the real situati We use a coin when there are 2 equally likely outcomes.

We use a number cube, labelled 1 to 6, when there are 6 equally likely outcomes.

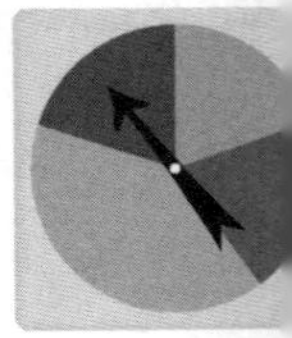

We use a spinner divided into congruent sectors, where the number of sectors matches the number of equally likely outcomes.

Example In a Grade 8 class, for a group of 4 students, what is the probability that 2 or more students will have birthdays the same month? Design a simulation to find out.

Solution There are 12 months in a year.
So, the probability of being born in a particular month is $\frac{1}{12}$.
We need a simulation that has 12 equally likely outcomes.
Use a number cube labelled 1 to 6, and a coin.
For each number on the cube, assign a head or a tail.
Then, let each month be represented by one of these pairs:
January H1, February T1,
March H2, April T2,
May H3, June T3,
July H4, August T4,
September H5, October T5,
November H6, December T6
Toss a coin and roll a number cube 4 times;
one for each student in the group.
Record if any month occurred two or more times.
Conduct the experiment 100 times.
An estimate of the probability is:
$\frac{\text{The number of times a month occurred two or more times}}{100}$

468 UNIT 11: Probability

Let a roll of 1 and 6 represent the favourable event of scratching two matching percents. This is represented by (1, 6) or (6, 1).

I can draw a tree diagram to show the possible outcomes, but I need to consider something else.

Suppose the first circle is scratched on the card. On the next scratch, it is not possible to scratch the first circle again. The same is true if I scratch the second circle on my first scratch. That is, it is not possible to scratch the second circle on the second scratch, and so on. So, cross out (1, 1), (2, 2), (3, 3), (4, 4), (5, 5), and (6, 6) from the possible outcomes.

So, here is my tree diagram:

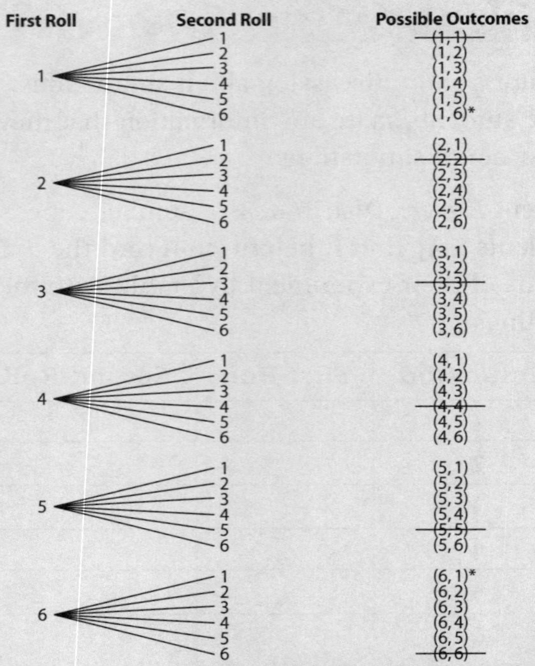

* represents a favourable outcome

In my experiment, I will record all the results of 2 rolls. If (1, 1), (2, 2), (3, 3), (4, 4), (5, 5), or (6, 6) is the

Practice

1. Work with a partner.
You will need a coin and a number cube labelled 1 to 6.
Conduct the experiment in the *Example* 25 times.
Combine your results with those of 3 other pairs of students.
Estimate the probability that, in a group of 4 people,
2 or more people have birthdays in the same month.

2. What if you want to estimate the probability that, in a group of 6 students, at least 3 students have birthdays in the same month.
How could you change the experiment in the *Example* to do this?

3. a) When a child is born, the child is either female or male.
What could you use to simulate this?
b) You want to estimate the probability there are exactly 3 girls in a family of 4 children.
Describe a simulation you could use.
c) Conduct the simulation in part b.
What is the estimated probability?
d) Use a tree diagram to calculate the probability of exactly 3 girls.
e) How do your answers to parts c and d compare? Explain.

4. What if you wanted to estimate or calculate the probability of exactly 1 boy in a family of 4 children.
How could you use the results in question 3 to do this?

5. **Assessment Focus** A multiple-choice test has 5 questions.
Each question has 4 answers.
For each question, a student randomly chooses an answer.
a) Design a spinner you could use to estimate the probability of getting 1 question correct.
b) Make this spinner. Conduct a simulation to estimate the probability of getting 3 correct answers out of the 5 questions.
c) How many times did you conduct the simulation?
What is your estimate for the probability?
Show your work.

Sample Solutions

1. For example: We combined our results with those of three other pairs of students for 100 simulations. There were 21 times where a month occurred 2 or more times. Therefore, the estimated probability that in a group of 4 people, 2 or more people have their birthdays in the same month is about 0.21.
4. These events have the same probability, 0.25.
5. a) Each question has 4 answers that are equally likely. Design a spinner that has 4 congruent sectors, each a different colour. Choose a colour to represent the correct answer, say red. Spin the pointer on the spinner. If it lands on red, the correct answer has been selected, if not, the answer is incorrect.
b) Spin the pointer 5 times and record the colour the pointer lands on each time. Getting three correct answers is represented by landing on the colour red three times in 5 spins.
c) Results may vary. In 100 simulations, the event "the pointer landed on red 3 times" occurred 13 times. The estimated probability of getting 3 correct answers out of five is $\frac{13}{100} = 0.13$.
8. a) Use 10 cards from a standard deck. Seven cards should be red and 3 cards should be black. A red card indicates a successful foul shot. A black card indicates a missed shot. Shuffle the cards. Choose a card randomly. Record the colour of the card, then replace it. Shuffle the cards again, choose one card, record its colour, and replace the card. Repeat the simulation of choosing a card, replacing it, shuffling the pile, then choosing a card again, many times.

outcome, I will repeat the trial.
The favourable outcomes are (1, 6) and (6, 1).
There are 2 favourable outcomes.
So, the probability of scratching 2 matching percents is: $\frac{2}{30} = \frac{1}{15}$*)*

AFTER Connect

Ask:

- What criteria did you use to design a spinner for this experiment?
(The spinner had to have six equally likely outcomes; so, we divided the spinner into six equal sectors and each sector is labelled with a percent.)

Present *Connect.*

Practice

Question 1: Students will need coins, number cubes, spinners, paper clips, and cards. Students are required to combine results with 3 other pairs of students.

Assessment Focus: Question 5

Encourage students to conduct the simulation many times for a better probability estimate.

b) Results may vary.

Successful shots	0	1	2
Frequency	2	3	15

c) Results may vary. According to my results, the probability of the team winning the game is $\frac{15}{20} = \frac{3}{4}$.

REFLECT: A simulation is used to estimate a probability for an event where it is not practical to gather data. For example, to estimate the probability that a bitch will have exactly 2 females in a litter of 5 pups, you can use a simulation. Toss a coin 5 times. Complete the simulation many times. Let heads represent females. Record the number of times that you get exactly 2 heads.

Assignment Guidelines

If your students do not have time to complete all the *Practice* questions on pages 469 and 470, these questions provide minimum curriculum coverage: 1, 3, 5, 7, *Reflect*

To assess the 4 Achievement Chart categories listed in the curriculum document, have students complete these *Practice* questions:

Knowledge and Understanding: 3
Thinking: 5
Application: 7
Communication: *Reflect*

Number Strategies

Write each number as a product of its prime factors.

72, 73, 74, 75, 76

6. Moira is on the school baseball team.
On average, Moira gets 1 hit every 3 times at bat.
Moira goes up to bat 4 times during a game.

a) How can this spinner be used to simulate Moira's batting average? Justify your answer.

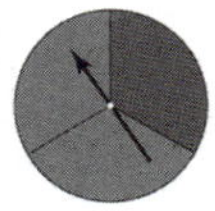

b) Conduct the simulation 30 times. Copy and complete this table. Record the frequency of each number of hits per gar

Hits per Game	0	1	2	3	4
Frequency					

c) Estimate the probability that, in a game, Moira will get each number of hits.
i) 0 hits ii) 1 hit iii) 2 hits iv) 3 hits v) 4 hits

7. The weather forecast for each of the next 6 days is a 50% chance of rain.
Describe a simulation to estimate the probability that it will rain on 3 of those 6 days.
Conduct the simulation. Explain the result.

Take It Further

8. A basketball player has a 70% shooting average.
He is about to take 2 foul shots.
There is very little time remaining in the game, and his team is behind by 1 point.

a) Describe a simulation to represent the player's shooting ability.

b) Conduct 20 simulations of the player's 2 foul shots.

c) What is the experimental probability that the player's team will win the game?

Reflect

When would you use a simulation to estimate a probability? Include an example in your explanation.

470 UNIT 11: Probability

ASSESSMENT FOR LEARNING

What to Look For	What to Do
Knowledge and Understanding ✔ Students understand what model to use to conduct a simulation for an event. ***Communication*** ✔ Students can describe when a simulation can be used to estimate the probability of an event. ***Application*** ✔ Students can design and apply a simulation to estimate the probability of an event.	***Extra Support:*** Students who are having difficulty understanding what model to use to conduct a simulation may benefit from counting the number of equally likely outcomes of the event and then identifying if it is appropriate to use a coin, number cube, spinner or a combination of these to model that event. Students can use Step-by-Step 3 (Master 11.9) to complete question 5. ***Extra Practice:*** Have students design a simulation for *Practice* question 4 on page 464 of the Student Book. Have students conduct the simulation in *Practice* question 2 on page 469 of the Student Book to estimate the required probability. Students can complete Extra Practice 3 (Master 11.18). ***Extension:*** Have students write a problem that can be modelled using a simulation, then design and conduct a simulation to solve the problem.

Recording and Reporting

Master 11.2 Ongoing Observations: Probability

LESSON 11.3A

Probability Simulations Using a *TI-83 Plus*

When estimating the probability of an event using a simulation, the more simulations that are conducted, the better the estimate. Repeated simulations can be very time consuming. At times it may be more efficient to conduct the simulation using technology.

LESSON ORGANIZER (80–100 min)

Curriculum Focus: Use technology-based simulation models (8m81)

Student Materials

- *TI-83 Plus* calculators

Key Math Learning

Technology-based models can be used to simulate events so that experimental probability may be determined.

Alternative Explore

Students who do not have access to *TI-83 Plus* calculators may use *Fathom* software to complete technology-based simulations. Have these students complete *Alternative Explore for Technology-Based Simulations* (Master 11.13).

BEFORE

Ask:

- Suppose you are going to write a multiple-choice test made up of 20 questions. Each question has 4 possible answers. Describe a simulation that may be used to estimate the probability that you will pass the test by guessing the answers.
  (I could create a spinner with four sectors. I could spin the pointer 20 times to see how often the spinner would land on one particular colour – representing the correct answer – in 20 spins.)

DURING

The following experiment will simulate this situation using the *TI-83 Plus* graphing calculator.

Generate random numbers from 1 to 4 to correspond to the four possible answers on the multiple-choice test. Any one of the four numbers can be chosen to correspond to the correct answer. Suppose we choose 3 to correspond with the correct answer. Then, 1, 2, and 4 will correspond to the incorrect answers. Since there are 20 questions on the test, use 20 for the number of trials.

Follow the steps below to perform this simulation.

1. Clear All Lists

   To view lists L1 and L2, press [STAT].

   To clear L1 use ▲ to select L1, then press [CLEAR] [ENTER].

   Repeat to clear L2 or other lists that may be present.

2. Generate Random Numbers

   Press ▲ to select **L1**.

   Press [MATH] ▶▶▶ [5]

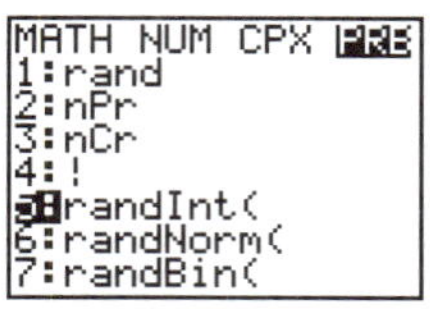

   You will see **L1(1)=randInt(**.

   Press [1] (for lower limit). Press [,] (comma).

   Press [4] (for upper limit). Press [,] (comma).

   Press [20] (for number of trials). Press [)] (close brackets).

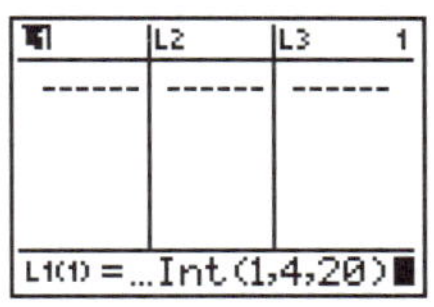

Press ENTER .

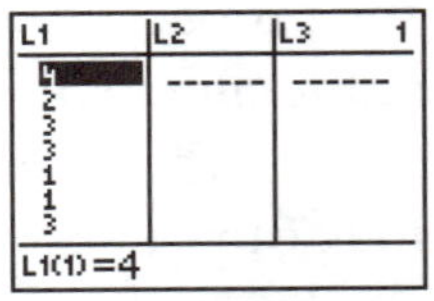

You will see L1 filled with 20 random integers between 1 and 4.

3. Sort the List of Random Numbers

Press 2nd STAT for *LIST*. Press ▶ to get *OPS*. Press 1 to get *SortA(*.

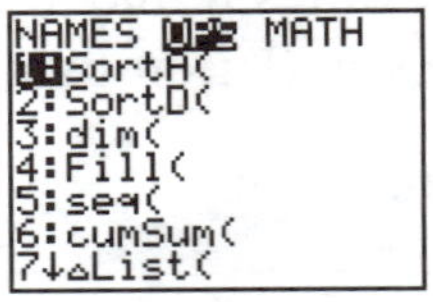

Press 2nd 1) ENTER and this will sort L1.

4. Return to L1.

Press STAT ENTER to find the random numbers in ascending order.

5. Favourable Outcomes

Scroll down the list to count the number of favourable outcomes, in this case the number 3. Enter the number of correct answers in L2.

6. Repeat the Experiment

The above steps represent one simulation. To simulate 25 tests, repeat steps 1 to 5 twenty-five times — but do *not* clear L2 in Step 1.

Record the number of correct answers for each simulation in L2.

7. Estimated Probability

a) Use the values you recorded for each simulation to find the experimental probability of passing the multiple choice test by guessing.

b) Compare your results with a partner. Explain any similarities or differences.

8. More simulations

a) For 100 simulations, combine your results with three other classmates. Repeat Step 7a.

b) Compare your estimate in part a with the estimate you found in part 7a.

Explain similarities or differences.

AFTER

Invite students to share their opinions on technology-based simulations.

Ask:

- How do technology-based simulations compare with simulations using coins, dice, or spinners? *(The technology-based simulations were much easier and quicker to complete. The calculator can complete 100 simulations in seconds.)*

Have students design a simple experiment. Then, have students determine the theoretical probability of one outcome. Have students complete a technology-based simulation to find the experimental probability of the experiment. Have them complete more simulations and compare the experimental probabilities with the theoretical probability.

Have students complete the Additional Activity, *When Is Your Birthday?* (Master 11.6).

11.4 Odds For and Against

Focus Apply probability to sports and games.

Explore

Work with a partner.
You will need a number cube labelled 1 to 6, and a deck of cards.

➢ Suppose you roll the number cube.
What is the probability of getting a number greater than 2?
What is the probability of getting a number less than 2?
Which event is more likely?
How many times as likely is it?

➢ Suppose you remove a card, at random, from the deck.
What is the probability it is a heart?
What is the probability it is not a heart?
Which event is more likely?
How many times as likely is it?

Reflect & Share

How are the two events in each experiment alike?
How are they different?
Think of another experiment you could conduct that would have two events related the same way as those in *Explore.*

Connect

In the media, you may hear or read about the likelihood of the Toronto Maple Leafs winning the Stanley Cup.
This likelihood may be referred to in terms of **odds**.
For example, if the Maple Leafs are likely to win, then the **odds in favour** of their winning could be 5 to 1.
If the Maple Leafs are likely to lose, then the **odds against** their winning could be 3 to 1.

11.4 Odds For and Against 471

Odds For and Against

LESSON ORGANIZER — optional

Curriculum Focus: Apply probability to sports and games.

Student Materials
- number cubes
- decks of cards
- spinners (Master 11.11)
- coins

Optional
- coloured pencils
- Step-by-Step 4 (Master 11.10)
- Extra Practice 4 (Master 11.19)

Vocabulary: odds in favour, odds against, favourable outcomes

Assessment: Master 11.2 Ongoing Observations: Probability

Key Math Learnings

1. The likelihood of an event occurring or an event not occurring may be referred to in terms of *odds in favour* or *odds against*.
2. When probability is expressed as a percent, the word *chance* is used.

Number Strategies

This situation is similar to rolling a number cube twice. When a number cube is rolled twice, there are 36 outcomes. Subtract 6 outcomes that represent a team playing against itself:
36 – 6 = 30. Therefore 30 games will be played.

BEFORE — Get Started

Review the meaning of *more likely* and *less likely* with students in regards to probabilities.

Present *Explore*. Remind students that they are to work in pairs. Distribute number cubes and decks of cards to pairs of students.

DURING — Explore

Ongoing Assessment: Observe and Listen

Ask:
- What are the possible outcomes when a number cube labelled 1 to 6 is rolled? *(There are 6 possible outcomes: 1, 2, 3, 4, 5, and 6.)*
- How many numbers are greater than 2? What is the probability of rolling one of these numbers? *(There are 4 numbers greater than 2: 3, 4, 5, and 6. The probability of rolling one of these numbers is $\frac{4}{6} \doteq 0.67$)*
- What is the probability of rolling a number less than 2? *(Only the number 1 is less than 2 so the probability of rolling a number less than 2 is $\frac{1}{6}$.)*
- Compare the two probabilities. Which is greater? How many times greater is it? *($\frac{4}{6}$ is greater than $\frac{1}{6}$; it is 4 times greater.)*
- How many cards in a deck are hearts? What is the probability of picking a heart? *(13 out of 52 cards are hearts, so the probability of picking a heart is $\frac{13}{52} = \frac{1}{4}$.)*
- How many cards in a deck are not hearts? What is the probability of not picking a heart? *(52 – 13 = 39 cards are not hearts, so the probability of not picking a heart is $\frac{39}{52} = \frac{3}{4}$.)*
- Compare the two probabilities. Which is greater? How many times greater is it? *($\frac{3}{4}$ is greater than $\frac{1}{4}$; it is 3 times greater.)*

REACHING ALL LEARNERS

Alternative Explore

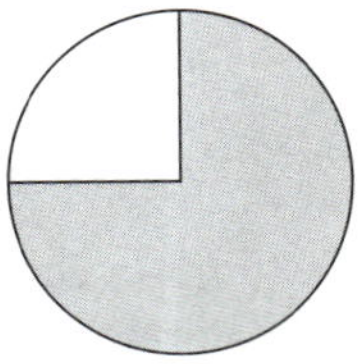

Have students examine this spinner. Ask them to determine the probability of landing on black and landing on white. Then, ask them to determine the probability of not landing or black and not landing on white. Have students compare the two situations and comment on the similarities and differences.

Early Finishers

Have students consider each experiment in *Explore*. Ask them to list the favourable outcomes and the unfavourable outcomes for each experiment. Have them describe how these outcomes are related to the probabilities and the likelihood of each event. Have students answer questions similar to *Explore* in regards to the experiment they described in *Reflect & Share.*

Common Misconceptions

➤ Students may accidentally use the total number of outcomes when determining odds in favour or odds against.

How to Help: Remind students that when finding odds in favour, the ratio represents the number of favourable outcomes to the number of unfavourable outcomes.

Similarly, for odds against, students may use the odds in favour of the event, as long as they transpose the terms of the odds-in-favour ratio.

In a bag, there are 12 counters.
A counter is picked at random.
The number of outcomes favourable to the counter being yell…
The number of outcomes not favourable to the counter bei…
is 8.
So, the odds in favour of the counter being yellow are 4 to 8.
This is a ratio, so it can be written in simplest form.
Divide each term by 4.
The odds in favour of the counter being yellow are 1 to 2.
The odds against the counter being yellow are 2 to 1.

In general,
odds in favour = number of favourable outcomes to number of unfavourable outcomes
odds against = number of unfavourable outcomes to number of favourable outcomes

Example

A card is drawn at random from a deck of cards.
a) What are the odds in favour of drawing a face card?
b) What are the odds against drawing a face card?

Solution

There are 3 face cards in each suit: Jack, Queen, King
There are 4 suits.
So, there are 3 × 4, or 12 favourable outcomes.
There are 52 cards in the deck.
So, there are 52 − 12, or 40 unfavourable outcomes.
a) The odds in favour of drawing a face card are 12 to 40.
Divide the terms by their common factor 4.
The odds in favour of drawing a face card are 3 to 10.
b) The odds against drawing a face card are 10 to 3.

Practice

1. What are the odds in favour of each event?
a) Getting a number greater than 1 when a number cube labelled 1 to 6 is rolled 5:1

472 UNIT 11: Probability

AFTER Connect

Have volunteers share their results with the class.

Ask:

- What similarities did you notice in the second experiment?
(The events were complementary.)
- How do you know?
(The probabilities add to 1.)
- Describe a different experiment that you designed similar to this experiment.
(Spin the pointer on a spinner that has 4 congruent sectors coloured yellow, orange, green, and blue. What is the probability of landing on green? What is the probability of not landing on green? Which event is more likely? How many times more likely?)

Work through the example in *Connect.* Have volunteers provide real-life examples of odds in favour and odds against. (For example, from sports statistics, or from weather predictions, or election predictions)

Practice

Question 6: Students who have difficulty with this question should use the fact that 25% represents favourable outcomes. From this, they can then determine what percent represents unfavourable outcomes.

Assessment Focus: Question 8

Students should consider how the two numbers are related. Students having difficulty with designing an experiment may benefit from using coins, spinners, cards, and other objects to determine combinations of actions that would help them visualize and design the experiment. Drawing tree diagrams is also useful to count possible outcomes.

b) Getting a 2 when a card is randomly picked from a deck of playing cards 4:48 or 1:12

c) Getting the sum 7 when two number cubes labelled 1 to 6 are rolled and the numbers are added 6:30 or 1:5

2. What are the odds against each event in question 1? a) 1:5 b) 12:1 c) 5:1

3. What are the odds against each event?

a) Getting a number less than 3 when a number cube labelled 1 to 6 is rolled 4:2 or 2:1

b) Getting a black card when a card is randomly picked from a deck of playing cards 26:26 or 1:1

c) Getting the sum 5 when two number cubes labelled 1 to 6 are rolled and the numbers are added 32:4 or 8:1

4. What are the odds in favour of each event in question 3? a) 1:2 b) 1:1 c) 1:8

5. Sera has 5 toonies, 8 loonies, 7 dimes, and 3 quarters in her piggy bank. One coin falls out at random.

a) What are the odds in favour of the coin being a dime? 7:16

b) What are the odds against the coin being a quarter? 20:3

6. The probability that David will be first in the 50-m backstroke is 25%. What are the odds in favour of his being first? 25:75 or 1:3

7. A weather report for Eastern Ontario was for a 40% probability of snow the next day. What are the odds against it snowing the next day? 60:40 or 3:2

8. **Assessment Focus** Use any materials or items you wish.

a) Design an experiment where the odds in favour of one event are 3 to 7.

b) Describe the experiment. List all possible outcomes and the odds in favour of each one.

Show your work.

Reflect

Explain how odds in favour and odds against are related. Include an example in your explanation.

Sample Solutions

8. For example: Construct a spinner with 10 equal sectors labelled with the numbers 1 to 10. Spin the pointer on the spinner. The odds in favour of spinning the numbers 2, 4, or 6 are 3 to 7. The odds in favour of spinning the numbers 1, 2, or 3 are 3 to 7.

REFLECT: Odds in favour are the number of favourable outcomes to the number of unfavourable outcomes, while odds against are the reverse of this. When added together the two parts give the total number of outcomes. For example, when a number cube is rolled there are 6 possible outcomes. The odds in favour of rolling a number that is a perfect square is 1 to 5 because there is only 1 perfect square number and 5 that are not. The odds against rolling a perfect square number are 5 to 1. Notice that the sum 5 + 1 = 6 gives the total number of possible outcomes. (Note that the ratio might be in simplest form, in which case, the sum may be less than the total number of possible outcomes.)

Assignment Guidelines

If your students do not have time to complete all the *Practice* questions on pages 472 and 473, these questions provide minimum curriculum coverage: 1, 5, 6, 8, *Reflect*

To assess the 4 Achievement Chart categories listed in the curriculum document, have students complete these *Practice* questions: Knowledge and Understanding: 5; Application: 6; Thinking: 8; Communication: *Reflect*

ASSESSMENT FOR LEARNING

What to Look For	What to Do
Knowledge and Understanding ✔ Students understand how to determine odds in favour and odds against from experiments. ***Communication*** ✔ Students can explain the relationship between odds and probability. ***Application*** ✔ Students can use odds in favour to find odds against and vice versa.	***Extra Support:*** Students can use Step-by-Step 4 (Master 11.4) to complete question 8. ***Extra Practice:*** Have students complete Extra Practice 4 (Master 11.19). ***Extension:*** Have students create and answer their own odds in favour and odds against problems based on questions 2, 3, 4, 6, and 7 from Lesson 11.1.

Recording and Reporting

Master 11.2 Ongoing Observations: Probability

Extending a Problem

LESSON ORGANIZER

Student Materials
- calculators
- rulers

Extending a Problem

- Read each question 1 to 7 carefully.
- Solve the problem using numbers, materials, pictures, graph tables, equations, and/or words.
  Try to find a solution in two different ways.
- Communicate your different solutions.
- Explain the solutions to someone else.
  Try to use only words in your explanation.
  Point to the numbers and other math information you used while you explain.
- Make up a similar problem by changing something (context, math information, problem statement). Solve the new problem.

✓ Check

1. You earn $20 a week doing yard work for a neighbour. You can either be paid the $20, or you can pull two bills from a brown paper bag containing:
   - two $5 bills
   - two $10 bills
   - one $20 bill

   For example, you might pull out a $5 bill followed by a $10 bill, and earn only $15. Or you might pull out the $20 bill followed by a $10 bill, and earn $30.
   Which is the better way for you to be paid?
   Justify your answer.

2. Use squares to make the next similar figure in this pattern.

   a) How many squares would be needed to make the 10th figure? The 20th figure?
   b) Suppose the pattern had been made with congruent equilateral triangles or congruent parallelograms. Would the numbers of figures needed to make the pattern change? Explain.

3. Suppose you have an unlimited supply of three masses: 3 kg, 11 kg, and 17 kg
   How many different ways can you combine at least one of each mass to make a total mass of exactly 100 kg?

474 UNIT 11: Probability

Sample Solutions

1. Here are the possibilities, should I pull bills from a bag:

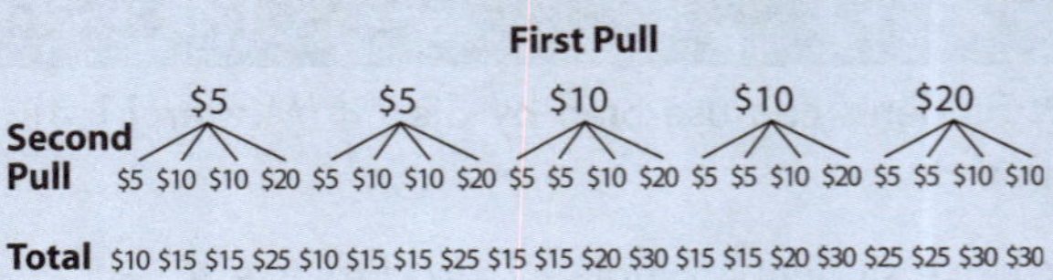

So, on $\frac{8}{20}$, or $\frac{2}{5}$ (40%) of the time I'll pull more than $20. I'd not be willing to take this chance.

2. a)

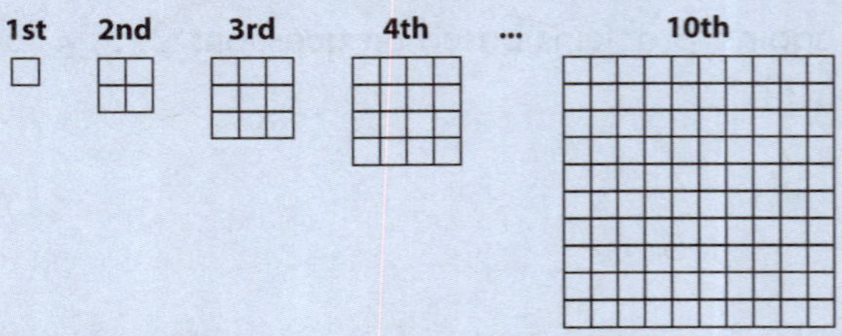

The 1st figure has side length 1, the 2nd has side length 2, the 3rd has side length 3, and so on. The 10th figure has side length 10, so it is a 10 × 10 figure. It has 100 squares. The 20th figure has side length 20, and therefore has 20 × 20, or 400 squares.

b) The number of figures needed to make the pattern remains the same.

3. Here are the ways I can combine the given masses to make 100 kg:

	Number of Masses					
3 kg	24	13	2	11	9	7
11 kg	1	4	7	3	2	1
17 kg	1	1	1	2	3	4

4. Myles' fuel consumption:
1 L/22 km means that his car uses $0.0\overline{45}$ L per kilometre.
So, for 8 km, his car used $0.0\overline{45}$ L × 8 ≐ 0.37 L
His 2 min at a stop used 0.16 L × 2 = 0.32 L
So, Myles used 0.37 L + 0.32 L = 0.69 L

Marlee's fuel consumption:
1 L/20 km means that her car uses about 0.05 L per kilometre.
So, for 9 km, her car used 0.05 × 9 = 0.45 L.
Myles used more gas.

5. I made a table to find the steps needed for a 20-step staircase.
The first row shows the number of steps.
The second row shows the number of blocks.
To find the number of blocks, I added the number of stairs to the number of blocks in the previous column.

Reading and Writing in Math

4. Myles' car has an automatic transmission.
He drove 8 km. He spent 2 min at a stoplight.
Marlee's car has a manual shift.
She drove 9 km with no stops.
Use the table below. Who used more gas?

Action	Automatic	Manual
Idling	0.16 L/min	0.16 L/min
Starting	0.05 L	0.05 L
Driving	1 L/22 km	1 L/20 km

5. This staircase has 3 steps.
How many blocks would you need for a 20-step staircase?

6. The cost of renting a truck for a day is \$45.
There is an additional charge of \$0.20/km.
The cost, *C* dollars, for renting the truck and driving it *k* kilometres is $C = 45 + 0.2k$.

a) The truck is driven 70 km. What was the rental cost?

b) Armand rented the truck. He paid a total of \$65. How far was the truck driven?

c) Jasmine rented the truck. She paid a total of \$58.20. How far did she drive the truck?

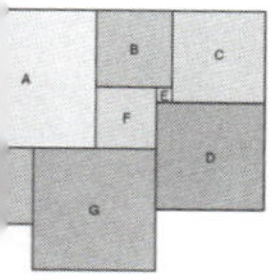

7. The area of Square F is 16 square units.
The area of Square B and of Square H is 25 square units.
The measure of each side is a whole number of units.
What is the area of each square?

a) A b) C c) D d) E e) G

8. This table shows the temperatures on 5 consecutive days in four Canadian cities during February. Create a math problem from these data. Solve the problem.

City	Monday	Tuesday	Wednesday	Thursday	Friday
Kamloops, BC	4°C	6°C	8°C	9°C	5°C
Fredericton, NB	−10°C	−6°C	−3°C	−5°C	−6°C
Windsor, ON	3°C	2°C	−1°C	−4°C	0°C
Swift Current, SK	−5°C	4°C	6°C	8°C	6°C

Reading and Writing in Math: Extending a Problem 475

1	2	3	4	5	6	7	8	9	10	11	12	13	14	15	16	17	18	19	20
1	3	6	10	15	21	28	36	45	55	66	78	91	105	120	136	153	171	190	210

For a 20-step staircase, I would need 210 blocks.

6. a) $C = 45 + 0.2k$
So, $C = 45 + 0.2(70)$
$= 59$
The rental cost is \$59.

b) $C = 45 + 0.2k$
$65 = 45 + 0.2k$
$20 = 0.2k$
$k = 100$
The truck was driven 100 km.

c) $C = 45 + 0.2k$
$58.20 = 45 + 0.2k$
$k = 66$
The truck was driven 66 km.

7. One way to solve the problem would be to draw the squares on 1-cm grid paper, beginning with the squares whose areas are given.
Here is a solution that uses logical reasoning.
As each side length is identified, label it on the copy of the figure.
Square F has area 16 square units, so its side length is 4 units.
Square B has area 25 square units, so its side length is 5 units.
Since the side lengths of squares B and F (5 + 4 = 9) equal the side length of Square A, then Square A has side length 9 units and area 81 square units.
Since the side lengths of squares E and F equal the side length of Square B, then Square E has side length 1 unit and area 1 square unit.
Since the side lengths of squares B and E (5 + 1 = 6) equal the side length of Square C, then Square C has side length 6 units and area 36 square units.
Since the side lengths of squares E and C (1 + 6 = 7) equal the side length of square D, then Square D has side length 7 units and area 49 square units.
Since the side lengths of squares A and F equal the side lengths of squares H and G (5 + side length of G), then the side length of Square G is (13 − 5) units = 8 units, and area of Square G is 64 square units.

8. What is the mean temperature for each city over these 5 days?
(Kamloops: 6.4°C, Fredericton: −6°C, Windsor 0°C, Swift Current: 3.8°C)

LESSON ORGANIZER

Student Materials
- spinners (Master 11.11)
- calculators

Assessment: Masters 11.1 Unit Rubric: Probability, 11.4 Unit Summary: Probability

Correlation of Extra Practice questions on page 498:

Lesson	Questions
11.1	1, 2
11.2	3, 6
11.3	4
11.4	7

Unit Review

Review any lesson with etext online tutorial

What Do I Need to Know?

Experimental Probability
The experimental probability of an event is:
$\frac{\text{The number of times the event occurred}}{\text{The number of times the experiment is conducted}}$
Experimental probability is also called relative frequency.

Theoretical Probability
The theoretical probability of an event is:
$\frac{\text{The number of outcomes favourable to that event}}{\text{Total number of outcomes}}$

Probability Range
All probabilities are greater than or equal to 0, and less than or equal to 1.
The probability of an event that is impossible is 0, or 0%.
The probability of an event that is certain is 1, or 100%.

(The probability that an event occurs) = 1 − (The probability that the event does not occur) These events are complementary events.

The sum of the probabilities of all possible outcomes is 1.

Odds
Odds in favour = number of favourable outcomes to number of unfavourable outcomes
Odds against = number of unfavourable outcomes to number of favourable outcomes

Math Link

Your World
The Princess Margaret Hospital Foundation runs a lottery every year to raise money for the hospital. One year, the chances of winning were given as 1 in 15. So, the odds in favour of winning were 1 to 14.

476 UNIT 11: Probability

Sample Solutions

1. c) iv) Answers may vary. Since the Arctic is usually cold in the winter, I estimate 0.99.

v) Answers may vary. Since I usually have homework on school nights, I estimate 0.9.

4. a)

×	1	2	3	4	5	6
1	**1**	2	**3**	4	**5**	6
2	2	4	6	8	10	12
3	**3**	6	9	12	15	18
4	4	8	12	16	20	24
5	**5**	10	15	20	25	30
6	6	12	18	24	30	36

b) There are 36 possible outcomes. There are 5 products that result in prime numbers. The probability that the product is a prime number is $\frac{5}{36}$. The probability of getting a composite number is $1 - \frac{5}{36} = \frac{31}{36}$. If the number cubes are rolled 60 times, the product is likely to be a prime number: $\frac{5}{36} \times 60 \doteq 8$ times; so, Player A would get $8 \times 10 = 80$ points. In 60 rolls, the product is likely to be a composite number: $\frac{31}{36} \times 60 \doteq 52$ times; Player B would get $52 \times 1 = 52$ points.

c) No, this is not a fair game because the chances of winning are not equal. Player A has a greater chance of getting more points than Player B.

d) Students work should show tree diagrams.
For each number 1 to 6 on one number cube, there would be 6 outcomes on the second number cube. The tree diagram would have 36 outcomes which would be the products of the numbers rolled on the the number cubes.
For example, the roll (1, 1) represents the product 1. The roll (3, 4) represents the product 12.

5. a)

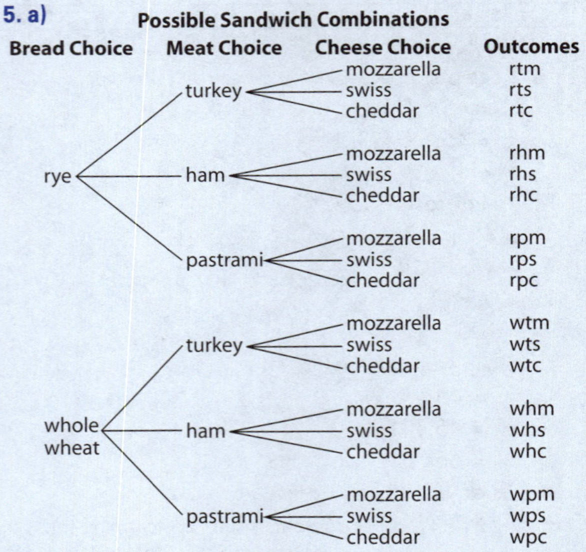

b) There are 18 possible outcomes.

i) There are 3 outcomes that have Swiss cheese on rye bread: rts, rhs, and rps, so the probability is $\frac{3}{18} = \frac{1}{6}$ or about 0.167.

ii) There are 4 outcomes with cheddar and no turkey: rhc, rpc, whc, and wpc, so the probability is $\frac{4}{18} = \frac{2}{9}$ or about 0.222.

What Should I Be Able to Do?

For extra practice, go to page 498.

LESSON

1. a) What is the probability of a certain event? 1
   b) What is the probability of an impossible event? 0
   c) Estimate or calculate the probability of each event.
      i) Chris randomly picks an orange out of a basket that contains 2 oranges, 6 apples, and 8 peaches. $\frac{1}{8}$ or 0.125
      ii) March immediately follows April. 0
      iii) Roll a 1, 2, 3, or 4 on a number cube labelled 1 to 6. $\frac{2}{3}$ or $0.\overline{6}$
      iv) It will be cold in January in the Arctic.
      v) You will have homework tonight.

2. A TV weather channel reports there is a 60% chance of snow tomorrow.
   What is the probability that it will not snow tomorrow? 0.4 or 40%

3. An election poll predicts that, in a certain riding, 5 out of 8 voters will vote for the Liberal Party in the next provincial election.
   According to this prediction, how many voters out of 180 000 voters would not vote Liberal?
   67 500

11.2 4. For the *Prime Numbers* game, roll two number cubes labelled 1 to 6. Then multiply the two numbers. When the product is a prime number, Player A gets 10 points. When the product is a composite number, Player B gets 1 point.
   a) Draw a multiplication table to list the outcomes.
   b) What if the number cubes are rolled 60 times. Estimate the number of points each player might get.
   c) Is this a fair game? Explain.
   d) Could you draw a tree diagram to list the outcomes? Explain.

5. Merio's Deli offers sandwiches on rye or whole wheat bread with one choice of meat: turkey, ham, or pastrami; and one choice of cheese: mozzarella, Swiss, or cheddar.
   Mya could not make up her mind. She requested a sandwich that would surprise her.
   a) Draw a tree diagram to list the possible sandwiches.
   b) What is the probability Mya will get each sandwich?
      i) Swiss cheese on rye bread
      ii) cheddar cheese but no turkey
   Justify your answers.

Unit Review 477

6. a) The possible pairs of numbers and their product are:
$1 \times 2 = 2$, $1 \times 3 = 3$, $1 \times 4 = 4$
$2 \times 2 = 4$, $2 \times 3 = 6$, $2 \times 4 = 8$
$3 \times 2 = 6$, $3 \times 3 = 9$, $3 \times 4 = 12$
So, the possible products are: 2, 3, 4, 6, 8, 9, 12

b) There is one of each of these products: 2, 3, 8, 9, and 12.
The probability of each of these is: $\frac{1}{9}$.
There are two of each of these products: 4 and 6.
The probability of each of these is: $\frac{2}{9}$.

c) The products 2, 3, 8, 9, and 12 have the same probability, so they are equally likely.
The products 4 and 6 have the same probability so they are equally likely.

d) There are two products that are perfect squares: 4 and 9; so, the probability of getting one of them is $\frac{2}{9}$.

e) There are 8 products less than 10, or only 1 greater than 10. So the probability of a product less than 10 is $\frac{8}{9}$.

7. a)

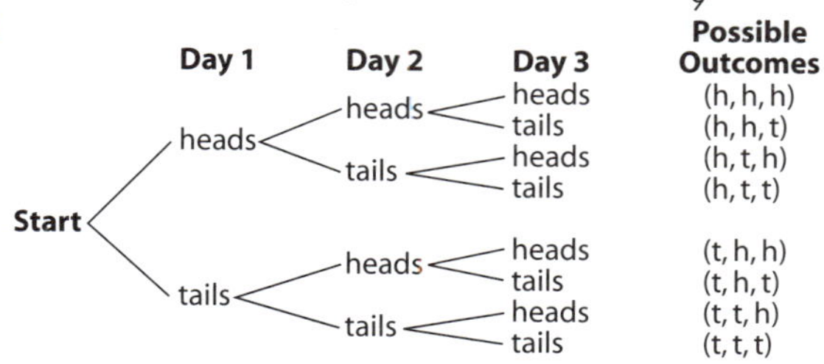

b) There are 8 possible outcomes. The outcome htt represents Irina's choices. This outcome occurs once so, the probability that Irina will be the first to ride the dirt bike 3 days in a row is $\frac{1}{8}$.

8. The birth of a male or female puppy represents 2 equally likely outcomes.

a) When a coin is tossed, the two equally likely outcomes are heads or tails. Let tails represent the birth of a female puppy and let heads represent the birth of a male puppy. Toss the coin once. If heads shows, the puppy is male; if tails shows, the puppy is female.

b) A number cube has 6 equally likely outcomes. Let the even numbers represent the birth of a female puppy and the odd numbers represent the birth of a male puppy. This simulates 2 equally likely outcomes.
Roll the number cube to see if an even or odd number occurs. (Another possibility is to let the numbers 1, 2, 3 represent the birth of a female puppy and the numbers 4, 5, and 6 represent the birth of a male puppy.)

c) Let the spinner have 2 congruent sectors such that one sector is yellow and the other is blue. Let yellow represent the birth of a female puppy and let blue represent the birth of a a male puppy. Spin the spinner once.

9. a) If 1 out of 4 computers is defective, design a spinner with 4 congruent sectors, each of a different colour. Let one colour — for example orange — represent a defective computer. Since 6 computers are delivered, spin the pointer on the spinner 6 times. Complete the simulation 50 times. In how many simulations did the spinner land on orange 3 out of 6 spins? This represents 3 out of 6 computers being defective.

b) Results will vary. For example: In 50 simulations, there were 9 where the pointer landed on orange 3 out of 6 spins. The estimated probability that 3 out of 6 computers are defective is $\frac{9}{50}$.

10.

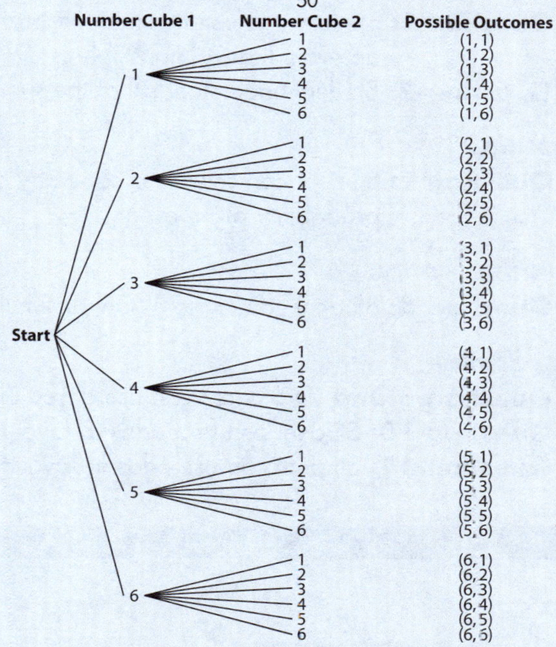

a) There are 36 possible outcomes.

i) There are 10 outcomes with numbers whose difference is 1: (1, 2), (2, 1), (2, 3), (3, 2), (3, 4), (4, 3), (4, 5), (5, 4), (5, 6), and (6, 5).
There are 36 − 10 = 26 outcomes whose difference is not 1.

ii) There are 6 outcomes with numbers whose difference is greater than 3:
(1, 5), (1, 6), (2, 6), (5, 1), (6, 1), and (6, 2).
There are 36 − 6 = 30 outcomes whose difference is not greater than 3.

b) i) There are 18 outcomes with numbers whose difference is an odd number:
(1, 2), (1, 4), (1, 6), (2, 1), (2, 3), (2, 5), (3, 2), (3, 4), (3, 6), (4, 1), (4, 3), (4, 5), (5, 2), (5, 4), (5, 6), (6, 1), (6, 3), and (6, 5). Therefore, there are 36 − 18 = 18 outcomes with numbers whose difference is an even number.

ii) There are 2 outcomes with numbers whose difference is 5: (1, 6) and (6, 1). Therefore, there are 36 − 2 = 34 outcomes with numbers whose difference is not 5.

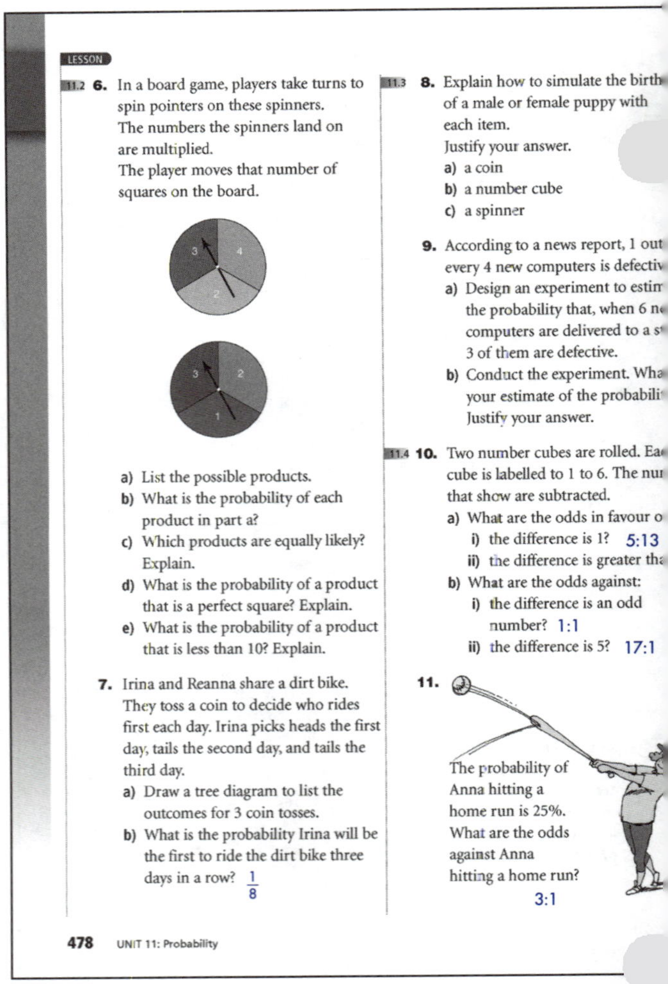

LESSON

11.2 **6.** In a board game, players take turns to spin pointers on these spinners.
The numbers the spinners land on are multiplied.
The player moves that number of squares on the board.

a) List the possible products.
b) What is the probability of each product in part a?
c) Which products are equally likely? Explain.
d) What is the probability of a product that is a perfect square? Explain.
e) What is the probability of a product that is less than 10? Explain.

7. Irina and Reanna share a dirt bike. They toss a coin to decide who rides first each day. Irina picks heads the first day, tails the second day, and tails the third day.
a) Draw a tree diagram to list the outcomes for 3 coin tosses.
b) What is the probability Irina will be the first to ride the dirt bike three days in a row? $\frac{1}{8}$

11.3 **8.** Explain how to simulate the birth of a male or female puppy with each item.
Justify your answer.
a) a coin
b) a number cube
c) a spinner

9. According to a news report, 1 out every 4 new computers is defectiv
a) Design an experiment to estir the probability that, when 6 n computers are delivered to a s 3 of them are defective.
b) Conduct the experiment. Wha your estimate of the probabili Justify your answer.

11.4 **10.** Two number cubes are rolled. Ea cube is labelled 1 to 6. The nu that show are subtracted.
a) What are the odds in favour o
i) the difference is 1? 5:13
ii) the difference is greater th
b) What are the odds against:
i) the difference is an odd number? 1:1
ii) the difference is 5? 17:1

11. The probability of Anna hitting a home run is 25%. What are the odds against Anna hitting a home run?
3:1

478 UNIT 11: Probability

ASSESSMENT FOR LEARNING

What to Look For

Knowledge and Understanding

✔ **Question 1:** Student understands that the probability of an event that is certain is 1 and the probability of an event that is impossible is 0.
✔ **Question 2:** Student understands that the sum of the probabilities of complementary events is 1.

Thinking

✔ **Question 9:** Student can solve a problem by designing and applying a simulation to estimate the probability of an event.

Communication

✔ **Question 8:** Student can explain how to simulate a situation using different items.

Application

✔ **Question 5 and 7:** Student can use a tree diagram to find theoretical probabilities.
✔ **Question 10:** Student can find odds in favour and odds against.
✔ **Question 11:** Student can use odds in favour to find odds against.

Practice Test

1. A coffee shop states that if you buy an extra large coffee, you have a 15% chance of getting a free bagel. Out of 45 550 extra large coffee cups, 7280 cups have the word FREE BAGEL written under the rim.
   a) What is the probability of getting a free bagel if you buy an extra large coffee? 0.16 or 16%
   b) Is the coffee shop's statement correct? Explain. No

2. Weng-Wai and Sarojinee make up games that can be played with two tetrahedrons labelled 2 to 5.
   In Weng-Wai's game, players add the numbers rolled.
   If the sum is even, Player A gets 1 point.
   If the sum is odd, Player B gets 1 point.
   In Sarojinee's game, players multiply the numbers rolled.
   If the product is even, Player A gets 1 point.
   If the product is odd, Player B gets 1 point.
   a) What is the probability that Player A will win in Weng-Wai's game? Sarojinee's game?
   b) Is each game fair? Justify your answer.
   c) How could you use tree diagrams to solve this problem?

3. Keyna used this tangram as a dart board. Calculate the probability that a randomly thrown dart will land in each area. Justify your answers.
   a) orange $\frac{2}{16}$ or $\frac{1}{8}$
   b) purple $\frac{1}{4}$
   c) blue or yellow $\frac{3}{16}$
   d) green or orange $\frac{1}{4}$

4. Describe a simulation you could conduct to estimate the probability that 3 people with birthdays in September were all born on an odd-numbered day.

Practice Test **479**

LESSON ORGANIZER

Student Materials
- calculators

Assignment Guidelines

To assess the 4 Achievement Chart categories listed in the curriculum document, use these test questions:
Knowledge and Understanding: 1
Application: 2
Thinking: 3
Communication: 4

Sample Solutions

2. a) In Weng-Wai's game there are 16 possible outcomes. There are 8 outcomes with even sums, so the probability of getting an even sum is $\frac{1}{2} = 0.5$. There are 8 outcomes with odd sums, so the probability of getting an odd sum is $\frac{1}{2} = 0.5$. The outcomes are equally likely; since each receives 1 point, the probability that Player A will win in this game is 0.5.
In Sarojinee's game there are 16 possible outcomes. There are 4 outcomes with odd products, so the probability of getting an odd product is $\frac{4}{16} = \frac{1}{4}$ or 0.25. The complementary event, getting an even product, has probability $1 - \frac{1}{4} = \frac{3}{4}$ or 0.75. Since 1 point is given for each type of product, the probability that Player A wins is 0.75.
   b) Weng-Wai's game is fair because each player has an equal chance of winning.
Sarojinee's game is not fair because Player A has a much greater chance of winning than Player B.
   c) A tree diagram may be drawn for each of the games.

Tetrahedron 1	Tetrahedron 2	Sum	Product
2	2	4	4
	3	5	6
	4	6	8
	5	7	10
3	2	5	6
	3	6	9
	4	7	12
	5	8	15
4	2	6	8
	3	7	12
	4	8	16
	5	9	20
5	2	7	10
	3	8	15
	4	9	20
	5	10	25

(Start)

3. The dartboard area can be divided into 16 pieces that are of the size of the blue or red triangle. Use these to determine the fraction of area represented by each colour of the total area: each of purple and pink is $\frac{1}{4}$; each of orange, yellow, and green is $\frac{1}{8}$; each of red and blue is $\frac{1}{16}$. Use the areas to determine the probability that a dart will land in each area.

What's Your Guess?

LESSON ORGANIZER 40–50 min

Student Grouping: 2
Student Materials
calculator, ruler, coloured pencils, spinners (Master 11.11), paper clips, number cubes labelled 1 to 6, coin, cards, construction paper, regular polyhedra with numbered faces
Assessment: Masters 11.3 Performance Assessment Rubric: What's Your Guess?, Master 11.4 Unit Summary: Probability

Teaching notes for Cross Strand Investigation *Integer Probabilty* are in the *Additional Assessment Support* module.

Unit Problem What's Your Guess?

A company that makes fortune cookies has 4 different mes[sages] in the cookies.
There are equal numbers of each message in a batch of cookies.
Design a simulation you could use to solve these problems.

- What if you have 2 fortune cookies.
  What is the probability you will get 2 different messages?
- What if you have 3 fortune cookies.
  What is the probability you will get 3 different messages?
- What if you have 4 fortune cookies.
  What is the probability you will get 4 different messages?
- Estimate how many cookies you will need to get 4 different messages.

480 UNIT 11: Probability

Sample Solution

Since there are four different messages and an equal number of messages in each batch of cookies, design a simulation with 4 equally likely outcomes. For example, construct a spinner with 4 congruent sectors — each of a different colour: red, yellow, blue, and green.

Problem with 2 fortune cookies: Use the pointer on the spinner. Spin it twice to represent the 2 fortune cookies. Record the number of times the pointer lands on two different colours. This is one simulation. Repeat the simulation 100 times to estimate the probability.
Sample Answer: We repeated the simulation 100 times and the pointer landed on two different colours 73 times. Therefore, we estimate the probability of getting 2 different messages to be 0.73 if we have 2 fortune cookies.

Problem with 3 fortune cookies: Use the pointer on the spinner. Spin it three times to represent the 3 fortune cookies. Record the number of times the pointer lands on three different colours. This is one simulation. Repeat the simulation 100 times to estimate the probability.
Sample Answer: We repeated the simulation 100 times and the pointer landed on three different colours 55 times. Therefore, we estimate the probability of getting 3 different messages to be 0.55 if we have 3 fortune cookies.

Problem with 4 fortune cookies: Use the pointer on the spinner. Spin it four times, to represent the 4 fortune cookies. Record the number of times the pointer lands on four different colours. This is one simulation. Repeat the simulation 100 times to estimate the probability.
Sample Answer: We repeated the simulation 100 times and the pointer landed on four different colours 22 times. Therefore, we estimate the probability of getting 4 different messages to be 0.22 if we have 4 fortune cookies.

REFLECT ON THE UNIT: I learned to estimate probability by conducting a simulation. For example, to estimate the probability that 3 or more students in a group of 5 students will have birthdays in the same month, I need to simulate 12 equally likely outcomes because there are 12 months in a year. I can use a number cube and a coin and label each month as January T1, February T2, . . ., June T6, July H1,. . ., December H6. For the simulation I roll the number cube and toss the coin 5 times (since there are 5 students in a group), and I record the number of simulations in which the same month occurs 3 or more times. I repeat as many simulations as possible. To estimate the required probability, I divide the number of simulations in which the same month appears 3 or more times, by the total

Conduct each simulation. Use any materials you think will help. Explain your choice of materials.
Answer each problem.
Show your work.

Check List

Your work should show:

- the steps and procedures you used in your simulations
- an explanation of why you chose each simulation
- all records and calculations, in detail
- clear explanations of your results, with correct use of the language of probability

Reflect on the Unit

List the different methods you have learned to estimate and calculate probability. Include an example of how each method is used.

Unit Problem: What's Your Guess? **481**

number of simulations. I learned that I can also make a prediction to estimate a probability. For example, the probability that the sun will set is 1, and the probability that it will snow in Ontario in July is 0.01. I learned to calculate probability by making lists and drawing a tree diagram. To find the probability of getting 3 tails when a coin is tossed 3 times, I can use the following tree diagram.

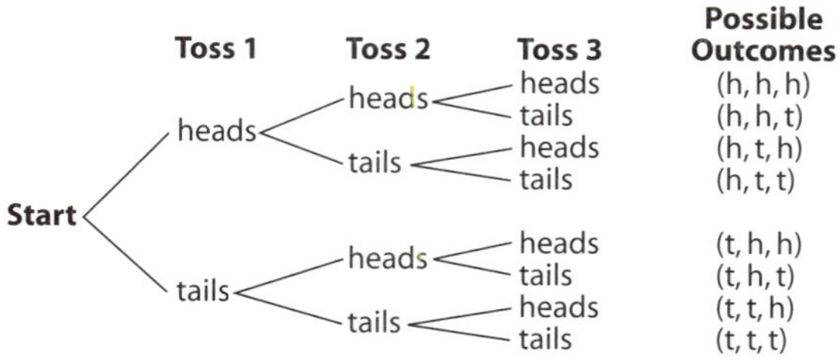

From the diagram, there are 8 possible outcomes. Only 1 outcome has 3 tails so, the probability of getting 3 tails when a coin is tossed 3 times is: $\frac{1}{8}$.

ASSESSMENT FOR LEARNING

What to Look For

Knowledge and Understanding

✔ Students understand the relationship between the number of equally likely outcomes and the simulation.

Communication

✔ Students can describe how the simulation they designed represents the situation in the problem.

Application

✔ Students conduct their simulations and estimate the experimental probability for each situation.

What to Do

Extra Support: Make the problem accessible.
Remind students to consider the number of equally likely outcomes in their simulation.

Encourage students to use ideas from Lesson 11.3 *Simulations* to design their simulations.

Encourage students to look at different objects, such as spinners, coins, and number cubes to help them design their simulation.

Recording and Reporting

Master 11.3 Performance Assessment Rubric: What's Your Guess?
Master 11.4 Unit Summary: Probability

Units 1–11

LESSON ORGANIZER

Student Materials
- grid paper (PM 20)
- calculators
- compasses
- rulers
- protractors
- spinners (Master 11.11)

Optional
- linking cubes

Units 1–11 Cumulative Review

UNIT

1 **1.** Write each number in expanded form and in scientific notation.
a) 335
b) 6272
c) 24 242

2. Solve each equation.
a) $x + 4 = 11$ $x = 7$
b) $x - 4 = 9$ $x = 13$
c) $4 + x = 7 + 9$ $x = 12$
d) $23 - 7 = x + 6$ $x = 10$

2 **3.** a) The longest snake is the reticulated python. The record length for this python is 985 cm. Which scale would you use to draw this snake in your notebook? Justify your choice.
i) 1:2 ii) 1:50
iii) 1:100 iv) 1:1000
b) Use the scale you chose in part a. Draw a line segment to represent a scale drawing of the snake. Is the scale you chose reasonable? Explain.

4. About 96% of the students at Westlake Middle School take at least one course from drama, music, or art. One thousand one hundred fifty-two students take at least one of these courses. How many students attend the school?

3 **5.** A rectangular sheet of card used to make a box. The cardboard is cut to make an open box with a base that measu 5 cm by 4 cm. The volume of the box is 60 cm³. Find the original a of the cardboard.

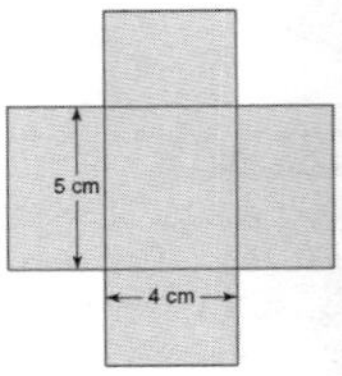

4 **6.** Use the fact that $\frac{1}{4} = 0.25$ to writ each number as a decimal.
a) $\frac{1}{2}$ b) $\frac{3}{4}$ c) $1\frac{1}{2}$ d) $1\frac{3}{4}$

7. a) Find the number of hours in fraction of a day.
i) $\frac{2}{3}$ ii) $\frac{5}{6}$
iii) $\frac{3}{4}$ iv) $\frac{3}{8}$
b) Write each time in minutes as fraction of an hour.
i) 12 min ii) 20 min
iii) 6 min iv) 136 min

5 **8.** The times, in minutes, that 14 students spent doing math homework over the weekend are 27, 36, 48, 35, 8, 40, 41, 39, 74, 47, 44, 125, 37, 47

484 Units 1–11

Students can use this review to evaluate their progress with the mathematical content of Units 1 through 11.

Remind students that the unit containing the content required to answer each question is listed in red beside or above the question.

Encourage students to refer to the *Connect* sections of the relevant units.

Encourage students to draw on each other's skills as they work through the review.

Students who have identified areas in which they are strong may wish to act as volunteer tutors for students who require assistance.

Sample Solutions

1. a) $335 = 300 + 30 + 5$; $335 = 3.35 \times 10^2$
b) $6272 = 6000 + 200 + 70 + 2$; $6272 = 6.272 \times 10^3$
c) $24\,242 = 20\,000 + 4000 + 200 + 40 + 2$;
$24\,242 = 2.4242 \times 10^4$

3. a) iii) 1:100; The drawing will be 9.85 cm long.
b) This is reasonable.

4. Let x represent the number of students at the school.
Then the number of students at the school multiplied by the percent that take one of the three courses should equal 1152.
$0.96x = 1152$
$x = 1200$
So, 1200 students attend the school.

a) Organize the data in a stem-and-leaf plot.
b) Calculate the mean, median, and mode for the data.
c) What are the outliers? Calculate the mean without the outliers. What do you notice? Explain.
d) Which measure of central tendency best describes the data? Explain.

9. *Census at School*, Canada, surveyed elementary students in 2003 to find how much time they spent travelling to school. The results are shown in the table.

Number of Minutes	Number of Students
0–10	3531
11–20	2129
21–30	994
31–40	292
41–50	433
51–60	193
More than 60	111

a) Use a circle graph to display these data.
b) You will go to high school next year. Suppose the high school has an enrolment of 1200 students. How many students would you expect to take more than 30 min to get to school? What assumptions did you make?

6 **10.** a) Draw a circle with radius 12 cm. Calculate its circumference and area.
b) Draw a circle with diameter 6 cm. Calculate its circumference and area.
c) How are the circumferences in parts a and b related? Explain.
d) How are the areas in parts a and b related? Explain.

11. A can of tuna has height 3.5 cm and diameter 8.5 cm.
a) Calculate the volume of the can.
b) The label covers the curved surface of the can. Calculate the area of the label.

7 **12.** Find the measure of each angle labelled *a*, *b*, *c*. Explain your reasoning.

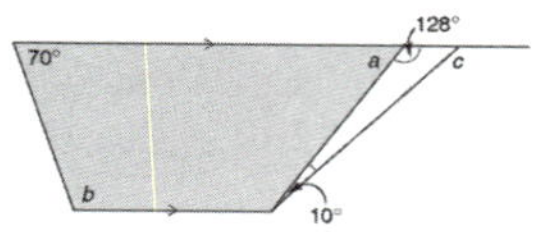

13. a) Draw a large triangle. Construct the perpendicular bisector of each side. Use this construction to draw a circle through the vertices of the triangle.
b) Explain why you can use this method to draw a circle through 3 points that are not on a line.

5. Let x represent the height of the box.
The volume of box is 60 cm³.
$V = lwh$
So, $60 = (4)(5)(x)$
$60 = 20x$
$x = 3$
Length of the cardboard: 3 + 4 + 3 = 10; 10 cm
Width: 5 + 3 + 3 = 11; 11 cm
The cardboard measures 10 cm by 11 cm.
So, the area of the cardboard is: 10 cm × 11 cm = 110 cm²

6. a) $\frac{1}{2} = \frac{1}{4} \times 2 = 0.25 \times 2 = 0.5$
b) $\frac{3}{4} = \frac{1}{4} \times 3 = 0.25 \times 3 = 0.75$
c) $1\frac{1}{2} = \frac{1}{4} \times 6 = 0.25 \times 6 = 1.5$
d) $1\frac{3}{4} = \frac{1}{4} \times 7 = 0.25 \times 7 = 1.75$

7. a) There are 24 h in a day.
i) $24 \times \frac{2}{3} = 16$ **ii)** $24 \times \frac{5}{6} = 20$
iii) $24 \times \frac{3}{4} = 18$ **iv)** $24 \times \frac{3}{8} = 9$
b) There are 60 min in one hour.
i) $\frac{12}{60} = \frac{1}{5}$ **ii)** $\frac{20}{60} = \frac{1}{3}$ **iii)** $\frac{6}{60} = \frac{1}{10}$ **iv)** $\frac{136}{60} = 2\frac{4}{15}$

8. a)

Time Spent Doing Homework

Stem	Leaf
0	8
1	
2	7
3	5, 6, 7, 9
4	0, 1, 4, 7, 7, 8
5	
6	
7	4
8	
9	
10	
11	
12	5
13	

b) Mean ≐ 46.3; Median = 40.5; Mode = 47
c) The outliers are 8, 74, and 125.
The mean without the outliers is about 40.1.
d) The median is less affected by the outliers; it is the best measure of central tendency.

9. a)

Time Travelling to School

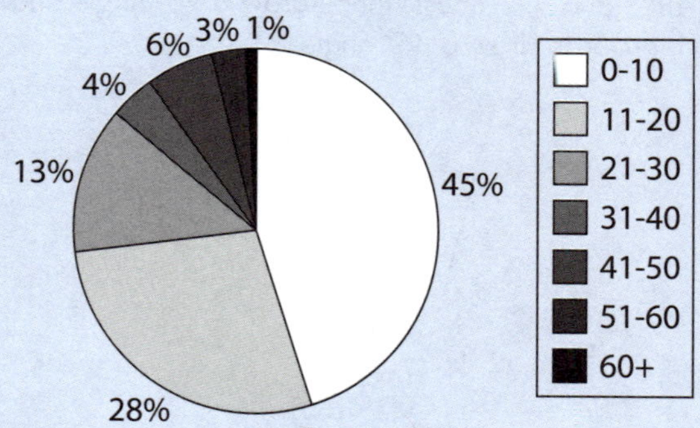

b) $\frac{1029}{7683}$ take 30 min or more to travel to school.
$\frac{1029}{7683} \times 1200 \doteq 161$
About 161 students take 30 min or more to travel to school.

10. a) $C = 2\pi r = 2\pi(12) \doteq 75.40$ $A = \pi r^2 = \pi(12)^2 \doteq 452.39$
b) $C = \pi d = \pi(6) \doteq 18.85$ $A = \pi r^2 = \pi(3)^2 \doteq 28.27$

c) The circumference in part a is about 4 times as great as the circumference in part b.

d) The area in part a is about 16 times as great as the area in part b.

11. a) $V = \pi r^2 h$
$= \pi(4.25)^2(3.5)$
$\doteq 198.61 \text{ cm}^3$

b) $A = \pi dh$
$= \pi(8.5)(3.5)$
$\doteq 93.46 \text{ cm}^2$

12. $a = 180° - 128° = 52°$
$b = 110°$ because interior angles add to 180°
$c = 128° + 10° = 138°$

13. a)

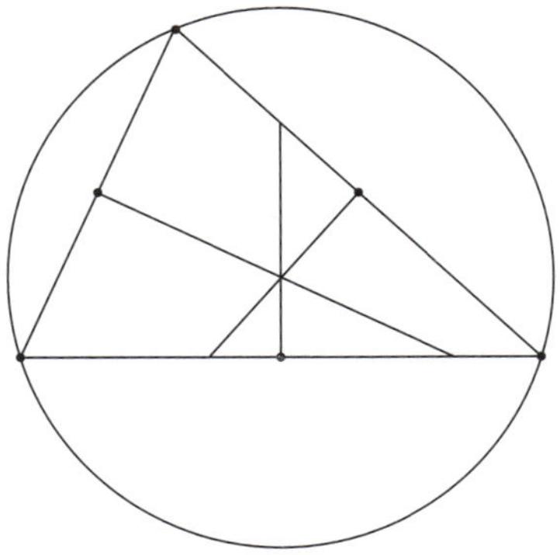

b) 3 points that are not on a line make a triangle. The intersection of the perpendicular bisectors of the sides is the circumcentre of the triangle.

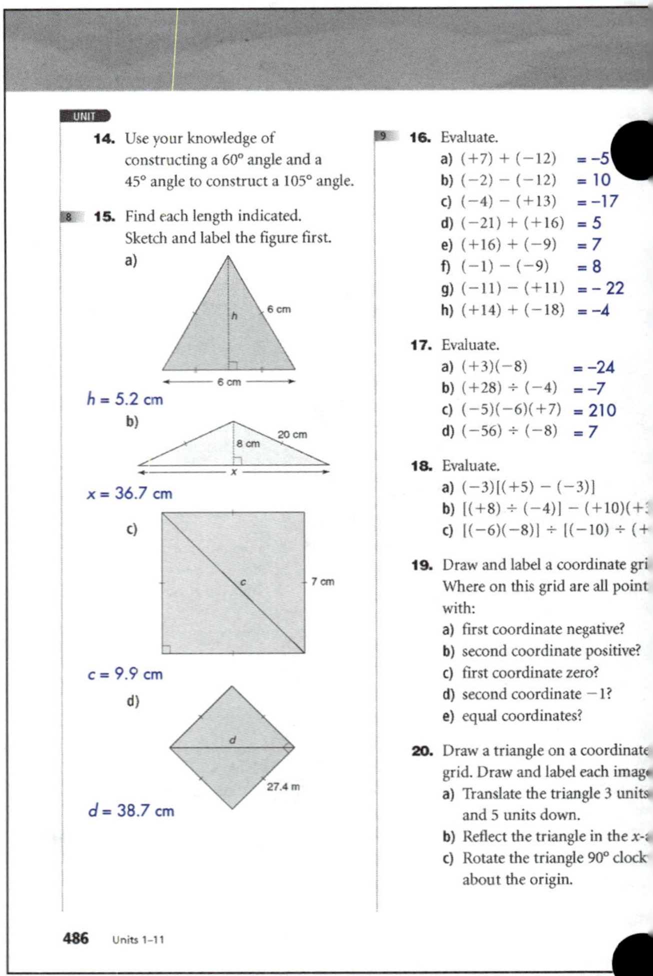

UNIT

14. Use your knowledge of constructing a 60° angle and a 45° angle to construct a 105° angle.

8 **15.** Find each length indicated. Sketch and label the figure first.

a) 6 cm, h, 6 cm
$h = 5.2$ cm

b) 20 cm, 8 cm, x
$x = 36.7$ cm

c) 7 cm, c
$c = 9.9$ cm

d) d, 27.4 m
$d = 38.7$ cm

9 **16.** Evaluate.
a) (+7) + (−12) = −5
b) (−2) − (−12) = 10
c) (−4) − (+13) = −17
d) (−21) + (+16) = 5
e) (+16) + (−9) = 7
f) (−1) − (−9) = 8
g) (−11) − (+11) = − 22
h) (+14) + (−18) = −4

17. Evaluate.
a) (+3)(−8) = −24
b) (+28) ÷ (−4) = −7
c) (−5)(−6)(+7) = 210
d) (−56) ÷ (−8) = 7

18. Evaluate.
a) (−3)[(+5) − (−3)]
b) [(+8) ÷ (−4)] − (+10)(+
c) [(−6)(−8)] ÷ [(−10) ÷ (+

19. Draw and label a coordinate gri
Where on this grid are all point
with:
a) first coordinate negative?
b) second coordinate positive?
c) first coordinate zero?
d) second coordinate −1?
e) equal coordinates?

20. Draw a triangle on a coordinate
grid. Draw and label each image
a) Translate the triangle 3 units
and 5 units down.
b) Reflect the triangle in the x-
c) Rotate the triangle 90° clock
about the origin.

486 Units 1–11

14. 60° + 45° = 105°. So, I draw first a 60° angle using a ruler and a compass; then I draw a 90° angle and its bisector to draw a 45° angle.

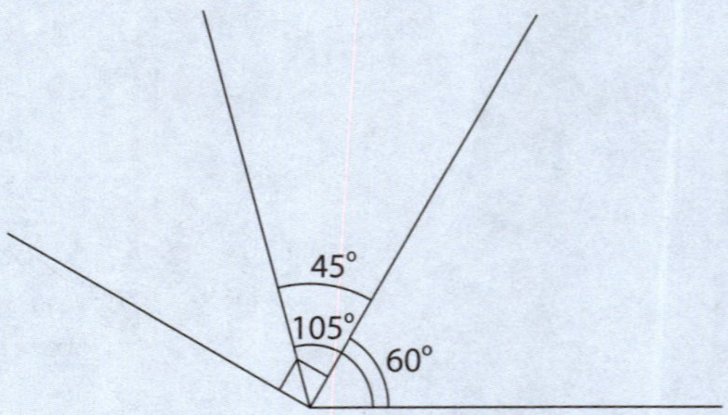

15. a) $h = 5.2$ cm **b)** $x = 36.7$ cm
c) $c = 9.9$ cm **d)** $d = 38.7$ cm

19. a) Quadrants 2 and 3
b) Quadrants 1 and 2
c) y-axis
d) On the line $y = -1$

e) Along the line $y = x$, as shown below:

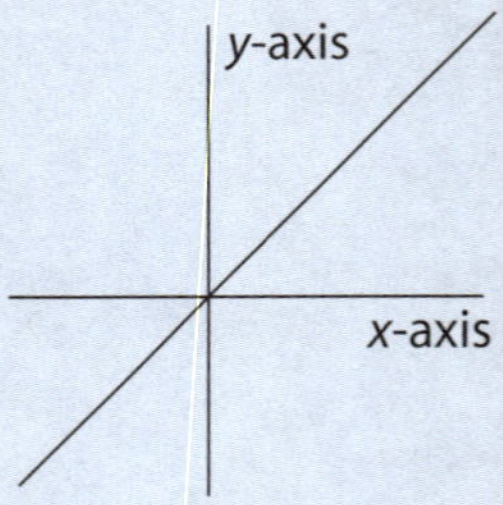

20.

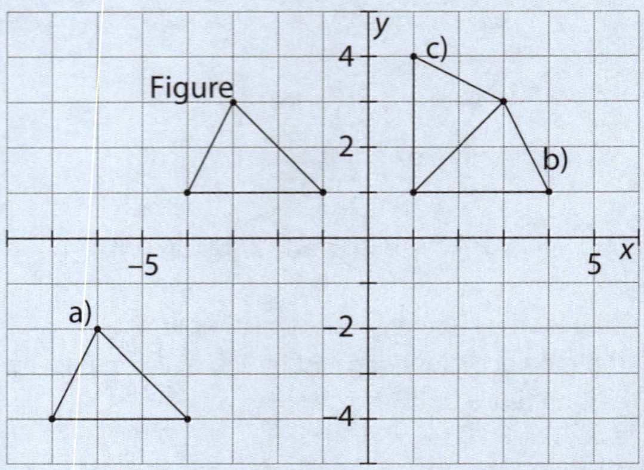

21. For each number pattern below:
   i) Describe the pattern. Write the pattern rule.
   ii) Use a table to find the 11th term.
   iii) Write an expression for the nth term.
   iv) Use the expression to find the 70th term.

a) 3, 5, 7, 9, 11, …
b) 5, 8, 11, 14, 17, …
c) 7, 11, 15, 19, 23, …
d) 9, 14, 19, 24, 29, …

22. Four times the side length of an equilateral triangle is 9 cm longer than the side length.

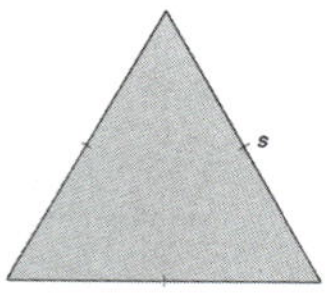

Let s centimetres represent the side length of the triangle.
An equation for the side length is:
$4s = s + 9$

a) Use algebra tiles to solve the equation. What is the side length of the equilateral triangle?
b) Verify the solution.
c) What is the perimeter of the triangle?

11 **23.** A spinner has 3 congruent sectors labelled D, E, and F.
A bag contains 3 linking cubes: 2 green and 1 red
The pointer is spun and a cube is picked at random.

a) Use a tree diagram to list the possible outcomes.
b) What is the probability of:
   i) spinning E?
   ii) picking a green cube?
   iii) spinning E and picking a green cube?
   iv) spinning D and picking a red cube?

24. Conduct the experiment in question 23.

a) Record the results for 10 trials.
   i) State the experimental probability for each event in question 23, part b.
   ii) How do the experimental and theoretical probabilities compare?
b) Combine your results with those of 9 other students. You now have the results of 100 trials. Repeat part a, parts i and ii.
c) What happens to the experimental and theoretical probabilities of an event when the experiment is repeated hundreds of times?

21. a) i) Start at 3 and add 2 each time.
ii) 23
iii) $2n + 1$
iv) 141

b) i) Start at 5 and add 3 each time.
ii) 35
iii) $3n + 2$
iv) 212

c) i) Start at 7 and add 4 each time.
ii) 47
iii) $4n + 3$
iv) 283

d) i) Start at 9 and add 5 each time.
ii) 59
iii) $5n + 4$
iv) 354

22. a) $3s = 9$; $s = 3$ cm
b) $4 \times 3 = 4(3) = 3 + 9$
$12 = 12$
So, the solution is true.
c) The side length, s, is 3 cm.
So, the perimeter is 9 cm.

23. a)

Spinner	Cube	Possible Outcomes
D	Green	DG
	Green	DG
	Red	DR
E	Green	EG
	Green	EG
	Red	ER
F	Green	FG
	Green	FG
	Red	FR

b) i) $\frac{1}{3}$
ii) $\frac{6}{9} = \frac{2}{3}$
iii) $\frac{2}{9}$
iv) $\frac{1}{9}$

24. Answers may vary. For example:
a) i) $\frac{4}{10}$ **ii)** $\frac{4}{10}$ **iii)** $\frac{2}{10}$ **iv)** 0
ii) The experimental and theoretical probabilities are close.
b) i) $\frac{31}{100}$ **ii)** $\frac{54}{100}$ **iii)** $\frac{19}{100}$ **iv)** $\frac{7}{100}$
c) The experimental probabilities get closer to the theoretical probabilities as the number of trials increases.

Evaluating Student Learning: Preparing to Report: Unit 11 Probability

This unit provides an opportunity to report on the **Data Management and Probability** strand.

Master 11.4: Unit Summary: Probability provides a comprehensive format for recording and summarizing evidence collected.

Here is an example of a completed summary chart for this Unit:

Strand: *Data Management and Probability*	**Knowledge and Understanding**	**Thinking**	**Communication**	**Application**	***Overall***
Ongoing Observations	3	4	3	4	3/4
Work samples or portfolios; conferences	3	3	4	3	3
Unit Review	4	3	3	3	3
Unit Test	3	3	3	3	3
Unit Problem What's Your Guess?	3	3	4	4	3/4
Achievement Level for reporting					3

Recording	How to Report
Ongoing Observations	Use *Master 11.2 Ongoing Observations: Probability* to determine the most consistent level achieved in each category. Enter it in the chart. Choose to summarize by achievement category, or simply to enter an overall level. Observations from late in the unit should be most heavily weighted.
Portfolios or collections of work samples; conferences or interviews	Use *Master 11.1 Unit Rubric: Probability* to guide evaluation of collections of work and information gathered in conferences. Teachers may choose to focus particular attention on the Assessment Focus questions. Work from late in the unit should be most heavily weighted.
Unit Review	*Master 11.1 Unit Rubric: Probability* may be helpful in determining levels of achievement. #1, 2, and 5 provide evidence of Knowledge and Understanding; #3, 4, 7, and 10 provide evidence of Application; #8 and 9 provide evidence of Thinking; all questions provide evidence of Communication.
Unit Test	*Master 11.1 Unit Rubric: Probability* may be helpful in determining levels of achievement. #1 provides evidence of Knowledge and Understanding; #2 provides evidence of Application; #4 provides evidence of Thinking; #3 provides evidence of Communication.
Unit Problem	Use *Master 11.3 Performance Assessment Rubric: What's Your Guess?* The *Unit Problem* offers a snapshot of students' achievement. In particular, it shows their ability to synthesize and apply what they have learned.
Student Self-Assessment	Note students' perceptions of their own progress. This may take the form of an oral or written comment, or a self-rating.
Comments	Analyse the pattern of achievement to identify strengths and needs. In some cases, specific actions may need to be planned to support the learner.

Learning Skills

PM 4: Learning Skills Check List

Use to record and report throughout a reporting period, rather than for each unit and/or strand.

Ongoing Records

PM 10: Summary Class Records: Strands
PM 11: Summary Class Records: Achievement Categories
PM 12: Summary Record: Individual

Use to record and report evaluations of student achievement over several clusters, a reporting period, or a school year.
These can also be used in place of the Unit Summary.

Name ________________ Date ________________

Master 11.1

Unit Rubric: Probability

	Level 1	Level 2	Level 3	Level 4
Knowledge and Understanding • Shows understanding by describing and explaining: – 0 to 1 as a range of probabilities – how probability relates to sports, weather predictions, and political polling – comparisons between theoretical and experimental probability – justifications for the methods	shows limited understanding in demonstrating and explaining: – how probability relates to sports, weather predictions, and political polling – comparisons between theoretical and experimental probebility – justifications for the methods	shows some understanding in demonstrating and explaining: – how probability relates to sports, weather predictions, and political polling – comparisons between theoretical and experimental probebility – justifications for the methods	shows considerable understanding in demonstrating and explaining: – how probability relates to sports, weather predictions, and political polling – comparisons between theoretical and experimental probebility – justifications for the methods	shows thorough understanding in demonstrating and explaining: – how probability relates to sports, weather predictions, and political polling – comparisons between theoretical and experimental probebility – justifications for the methods
Thinking • Uses a range of strategies (e.g., tree diagrams, lists, modelling, tables, logical reasoning) to design investigations and solve problems involving probability	uses appropriate strategies to solve problems that involve probability with limited effectiveness	uses appropriate strategies to solve problems that involve probability with some effectiveness	uses appropriate strategies to solve problems that involve probability with considerable effectiveness	uses appropriate strategies to solve problems that involve probability with a high degree of effectiveness
Communication • Explains concepts, procedures, and reasoning clearly using appropriate terminology	limited effectiveness; unable to explain reasoning and procedures clearly; rarely uses appropriate terms	some effectiveness; explains reasoning and procedures with some clarity and use of appropriate terms	considerable effectiveness; explains reasoning and procedures clearly, using appropriate terms	high degree of effectiveness; explains reasoning and procedures clearly and precisely, using the most appropriate terms
• Presents work, including diagrams, lists and tables, clearly, using appropriate conventions (e.g., symbols and labels)	presents work with limited clarity and use of appropriate conventions	presents work with some clarity and use of conventions	presents work with considerable clarity and use of conventions	presents work with a high degree of clarity and use of conventions
Application • Applies skills appropriately to: – list possible outcomes – identify favourable outcomes and state associated probability – calculate probabilities from tree diagrams and lists	limited effectiveness; makes major errors or omissions in: – listing possible outcomes – identifying favourable outcomes and stating associated probability – calculating probabilities from tree diagrams and lists	some effectiveness; somewhat accurate with several minor errors or omissions in: – listing possible outcomes – identifying favourable outcomes and stating associated probability – calculating probabilities from tree diagrams and lists	considerable effectiveness; generally accurate with few minor errors or omissions in: – listing possible outcomes – identifying favourable outcomes and stating associated probability – calculating probabilities from tree diagrams and lists	high degree of effectiveness; accurate and precise with very few or no errors in: – listing possible outcomes – identifying favourable outcomes and stating associated probability – calculating probabilities from tree diagrams and lists

Name ____________________ Date ______________

Master 11.2

Ongoing Observations: Probability

The behaviours described under each heading are examples; they are not intended to be an exhaustive list of all that might be observed. More detailed descriptions are provided in each lesson under *Assessment for Learning*.

STUDENT ACHIEVEMENT: Probability				
Student	**Knowledge and Understanding** • Demonstrates and explains: – how probability relates to sports, weather predictions, and political polling – comparisons between theoretical and experimental probability	**Thinking** • Uses appropriate strategies to design investigations and solve problems that involve probability	**Communication** • Explains reasoning and procedures clearly using appropriate terms • Presents diagrams, list, tables and calculations clearly, including symbols and labels	**Application** • Accurately: – lists possible outcomes – identifies favourable outcomes and associated probability – calculates probabilities from tree diagrams and lists

Level 1 – very limited; Level 2 – somewhat or limited; Level 3 – satisfactory; Level 4 – thorough

Name ____________________

Master 11.3

Performance Assessment Rubric: What's Your Guess?

	Level 1	Level 2	Level 3	Level 4
Knowledge and Understanding • Explanations show understanding of: – 0 to 1 as a range of probabilities – the difference between theoretical and experimental probability	explanations show limited understanding of: – 0 to 1 as a range of probabilities – the difference between theoretical and experimental probability	explanations show some understanding of: – 0 to 1 as a range of probabilities – the difference between theoretical and experimental probability	explanations show considerable understanding of: – 0 to 1 as a range of probabilities – the difference between theoretical and experimental probability	explanations show thorough understanding of: – 0 to 1 as a range of probabilities – the difference between theoretical and experimental probability
Thinking • Uses appropriate strategies to design appropriate simulations and solve the problems	uses a few simple strategies to design simulations and solve the problems with limited success	uses few appropriate strategies to design simulations and solve the problems with partial success	uses appropriate strategies to design simulations and solve the problems with considerable success	uses appropriate, often innovative, strategies to design simulations and solve the problems with a high degree of success
Communication • Communicates procedures, solutions, and reasoning clearly, using appropriate language	limited effectiveness; does not communicate clearly	some effectiveness; communicates with some clarity	considerable effectiveness; communicates clearly	a high degree of effectiveness; communicates clearly and precisely
• Presents work clearly, including diagrams, lists and tables, using appropriate conventions (e.g., symbols and labels)	presents calculations and any diagrams, lists, or tables with limited clarity and use of appropriate conventions	presents calculations and any diagrams, lists, or tables with some clarity and use of conventions	presents calculations and any diagrams, lists, or tables with considerable clarity and use of conventions	presents calculations and any diagrams, lists, or tables with a high degree of clarity and use of conventions
Application • Accurately: – determines probabilities based on 2, 3, and 4 fortune cookies – estimates number of cookies needed to get 4 different messages	limited effectiveness; makes major errors or omissions in: – determining probabilities based on 2, 3, and 4 fortune cookies – estimating number of cookies needed to get 4 different messages	some effectiveness; somewhat accurate in: – determining probabilities based on 2, 3, and 4 fortune cookies – estimating number of cookies needed to get 4 different messages	considerable effectiveness; generally accurate in: – determining probabilities based on 2, 3, and 4 fortune cookies – estimating number of cookies needed to get 4 different messages	high degree of effectiveness; accurate and precise in: – determining probabilities based on 2, 3, and 4 fortune cookies – estimating number of cookies needed to get 4 different messages

Name ______________ Date ______________

Master 11.3

Performance Assessment Rubric: What's Your Guess?

	Level 1	Level 2	Level 3	Level 4
Knowledge and Understanding • Explanations show understanding of: – 0 to 1 as a range of probabilities – the difference between theoretical and experimental probability	explanations show limited understanding of: – 0 to 1 as a range of probabilities – the difference between theoretical and experimental probability	explanations show some understanding of: – 0 to 1 as a range of probabilities – the difference between theoretical and experimental probability	explanations show considerable understanding of: – 0 to 1 as a range of probabilities – the difference between theoretical and experimental probability	explanations show thorough understanding of: – 0 to 1 as a range of probabilities – the difference between theoretical and experimental probability
Thinking • Uses appropriate strategies to design appropriate simulations and solve the problems	uses a few simple strategies to design simulations and solve the problems with limited success	uses few appropriate strategies to design simulations and solve the problems with partial success	uses appropriate strategies to design simulations and solve the problems with considerable success	uses appropriate, often innovative, strategies to design simulations and solve the problems with a high degree of success
Communication • Communicates procedures, solutions, and reasoning clearly, using appropriate language	limited effectiveness; does not communicate clearly	some effectiveness; communicates with some clarity	considerable effectiveness; communicates clearly	a high degree of effectiveness; communicates clearly and precisely
• Presents work clearly, including diagrams, lists and tables, using appropriate conventions (e.g., symbols and labels)	presents calculations and any diagrams, lists, or tables with limited clarity and use of appropriate conventions	presents calculations and any diagrams, lists, or tables with some clarity and use of conventions	presents calculations and any diagrams, lists, or tables with considerable clarity and use of conventions	presents calculations and any diagrams, lists, or tables with a high degree of clarity and use of conventions
Application • Accurately: – determines probabilities based on 2, 3, and 4 fortune cookies – estimates number of cookies needed to get 4 different messages	limited effectiveness; makes major errors or omissions in: – determining probabilities based on 2, 3, and 4 fortune cookies – estimating number of cookies needed to get 4 different messages	some effectiveness; somewhat accurate in: – determining probabilities based on 2, 3, and 4 fortune cookies – estimating number of cookies needed to get 4 different messages	considerable effectiveness; generally accurate in: – determining probabilities based on 2, 3, and 4 fortune cookies – estimating number of cookies needed to get 4 different messages	high degree of effectiveness; accurate and precise in: – determining probabilities based on 2, 3, and 4 fortune cookies – estimating number of cookies needed to get 4 different messages

Name ____________________ Date ________________

Master 11.4

Unit Summary: Probability

Review assessment records to determine the most consistent achievement levels for the assessments conducted. Some cells may be blank. *Overall* achievement levels may be recorded in each row, rather than identifying levels for each achievement category.

	Most Consistent Level of Achievement*				
Strand: *Data Management and Probability*	**Knowledge and Understanding**	**Thinking**	**Communication**	**Application**	***Overall***
Ongoing Observations					
Work samples or portfolios; conferences					
Unit Review					
Unit Test					
Unit Problem What's Your Guess					
Achievement Level for reporting					

*Use Ontario Achievement Levels 1, 2, 3, 4

Self-Assessment:

Comments: (Strengths, Needs, Next Steps)

Name ____________________ Date ____________________

Master 11.5

Additional Activity 1: Growing Trees

Students can complete this activity individually or in pairs.

Materials: spinners (Master 11.11), paper clip, coin, number cube, deck of cards, ruler, coloured pencils, calculator

1. Select two items (for example, a spinner and a coin).
Design an experiment that uses both of these items.

____

____

2. Choose and describe an event.

____

____

3. a) Conduct the experiment 50 times.
Record the number of times the event occurred in 50 trials. ____________
b) Use your results to estimate the theoretical probability of the event. ____________

4. a) On a separate sheet of paper, draw a tree diagram to represent the possible outcomes of the experiment.
b) Use the tree diagram to determine the theoretical probability of the event. ____________

5. Compare the experimental probability for the event and the theoretical probability.
Explain any similarities and differences.

____

____

____

6. Repeat *Steps 1* to *5* choosing two different items for the experiment.

Take It Further:
Repeat *Steps 1* to *5* using either more than 2 items (such as a coin, spinner, and number cube) or using items more than once (such as toss the coin twice and then roll a number cube).

Name ____________________ Date ______________

Master 11.6

Additional Activity 2: When Is Your Birthday?

In *Lesson 11.3* you carried out simulations to determine the probability of sharing a birth month.

Work with a partner.

Materials: a *TI-83 Plus* calculator or a computer with simulation software, such as *Fathom*.

1. Estimate the following:
What is the probability that 10 students in your class share the same birth month?

2. Use a *TI-83 Plus* calculator or simulation software to carry out the simulation.
Refer to *Lesson 11.3A* to review the steps to use to carry out the simulation.

3. Complete 100 simulations.
Review your results.

4. Combine your results with 10 other pairs of classmates.
What is the probability that 10 students in your class share the same birth month?
How close was your estimate?

5. Survey the class to determine birth months of your classmates.
How close were the results from the simulation?

Take It Further:
Estimate, then carry out the simulation to find the probability that 20 students in your class are born in the same month. Combine your results with 10 other pairs of classmates.
Use your previous survey results of actual birth months of your classmates.
Compare your estimate to the simulation and actual results.

Name ____________________ Date ______________

Master 11.7

Step-by-Step 1

Lesson 11.1, Question 8

Step 1 Complete the table.

+	1	2	3	4
2	3			
3				
4				
5				

Step 2 To list the possible outcomes of the sum, list all the *different* sums in the table.

Step 3 Use your answers in *Steps 1* and *2*.
Complete the table to determine the probability for each outcome.
The first one has been done for you.

Sum	Number of Times Sum Occurs	Probability = $\frac{\textit{number of times sum occurs}}{\textit{total number of sums}}$
3	1	$\frac{1}{16}$

Step 4 Add the probabilities that you found in *Step 3*. What do you notice?

Step 5
i) Express 25% as a fraction.
Which event has a probability equal to this fraction?
Which events have probabilities that add to equal this fraction?
ii) Express 75% as a fraction.
Which events have probabilites that add to equal this fraction?
iii) Which events have probabilities that add to 1?
iv) Which events are impossible? What is the probability of these events?

Name ____________________ Date ________________

Master 11.8

Step-by-Step 2

Lesson 11.2, Question 3

Step 1 Draw a tree diagram to represent the possible outcomes of rolling the tetrahedron and then spinning the pointer on a spinner.

i) State the number of possible outcomes. ________
ii) State the number of favourable outcomes (yellow/blue or blue/yellow). ________
iii) Write a fraction to represent the probability of making green when the tetrahedron is rolled and the pointer on the spinner is spun. _______

Step 2 Draw a tree diagram to represent the possible outcomes of rolling the tetrahedron twice.

i) State the number of possible outcomes. ________
ii) State the number of favourable outcomes (yellow/blue or blue/yellow). ________
iii) Write a fraction to represent the probability of making green when the tetrahedron is rolled twice. _______

Step 3 Draw a tree diagram to represent the possible outcomes of spinning the pointer on the spinner twice.

i) State the number of possible outcomes. ________
ii) State the number of favourable outcomes (yellow/blue or blue/yellow). ________
iii) Write a fraction to represent the probability of making green when the pointer on the spinner is spun twice. _______

Step 4 a) Write the probabilities you found in part iii) of *Steps 1*, *2*, and *3*.

____________, ____________, ____________

b) Which of the three probabilities is the greatest? _________
c) Which strategy should the player choose to have the greatest chance of winning the game?

____

____

Name ____________________ Date ________________

Master 11.9

Step-by-Step 3

Lesson 11.3, Question 5

Materials: markers or pencil crayons, spinners (Master 11.11), paper clip

Step 1 How many answers does each question have? ______
How many equally likely outcomes are there for each question? ______
How many equal sectors will your spinner have? _______

Step 2 Draw the spinner you described in *Step 1.*
Choose a sector to represent the favourable outcome (getting the correct answer).

Step 3 How many questions are on the test? ______
How many times should you spin the pointer on the spinner for one simulation?_______

Step 4 Describe an event on the spinner that will simulate getting 3 correct answers out of the 5 questions.

____

____

____

Step 5 Conduct the simulation as often as possible.
Record your results in a table similar to the one below.

Number of Simulations	Number of Simulations with Desired Event

Step 6 How many times did you conduct the simulation? _____
How many times did you achieve the desired result?______
What is your estimate for the probability of getting 3 correct answers out of the 5 questions?______

Name ____________________ Date ________________

Master 11.10

Step-by-Step 4

Lesson 11.4, Question 8

Materials: spinners (Master 11.11), cards, coloured pencils, ruler, coins

Step 1 For an event that has odds in favour 3 to 7, what is the number of:

a) favourable outcomes? ____________

b) unfavourable outcomes? ____________

c) total outcomes? ____________

Step 2 Design an experiment that has the same number (or multiple of this number) of total outcomes as your answer in *Step 1* part c.
(*Hint:* You may use a spinner or cards or any other items.)

____

____

____

Step 3 For the experiment you designed in *Step 2*, describe an event that has the same number of favourable outcomes as your answer in *Step 1* part a and the same number of unfavourable outcomes as your answer in *Step 1* part b.

____

____

____

Step 4 List other possible outcomes for your experiment.
State the odds in favour of each one.

____

____

____

____

____

____

____

____

____

Name ______________________ Date ________________

Master 11.11

Spinners

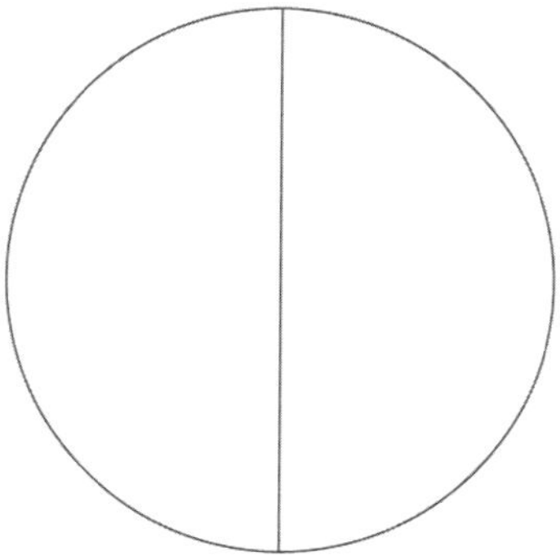
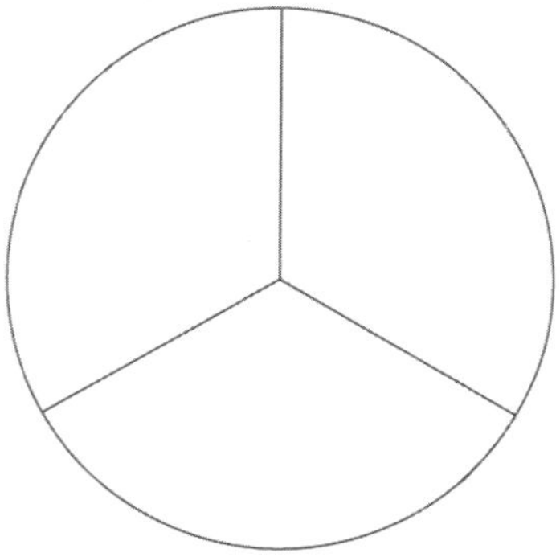
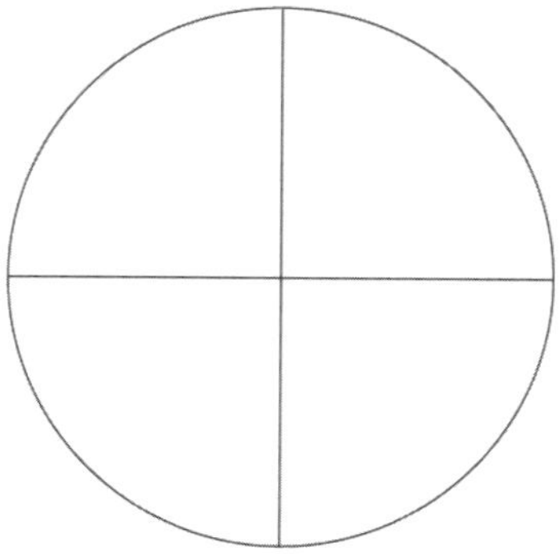

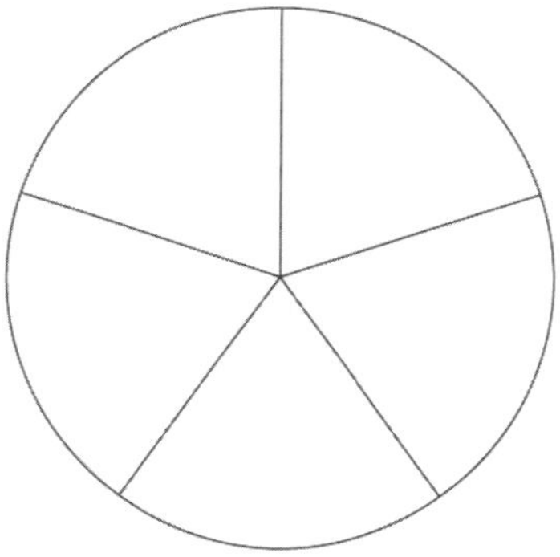
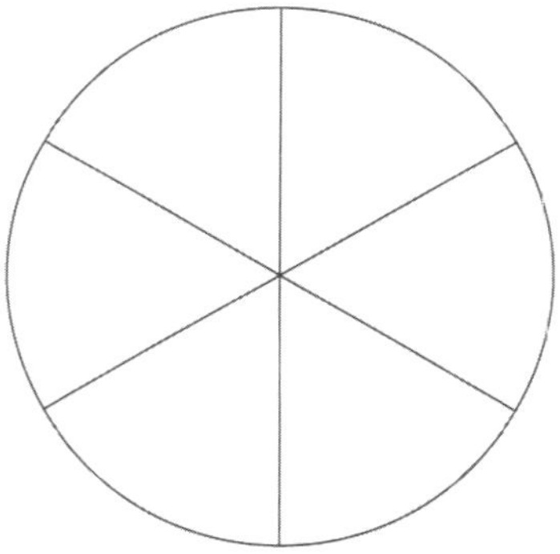
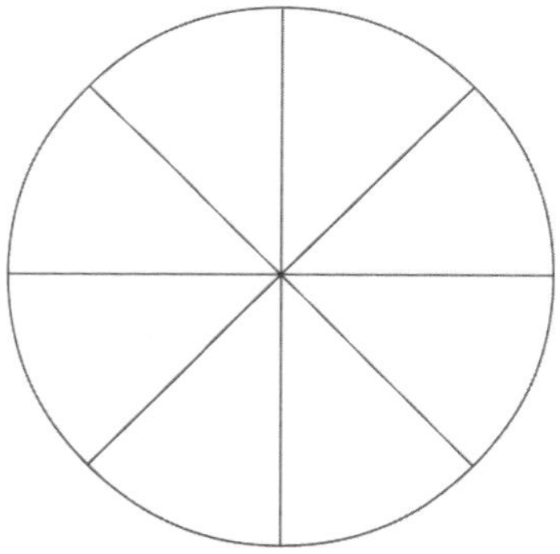

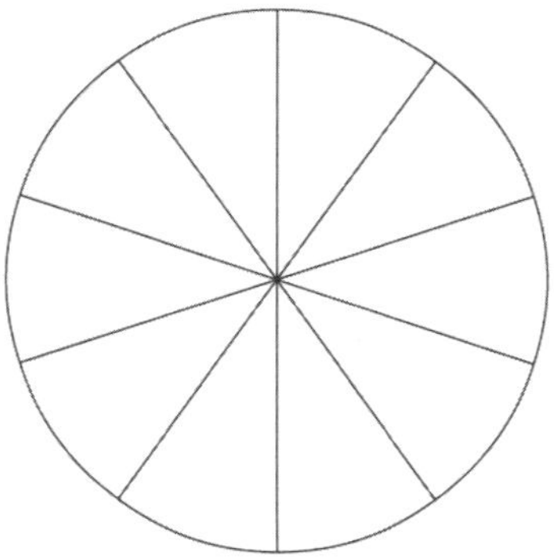
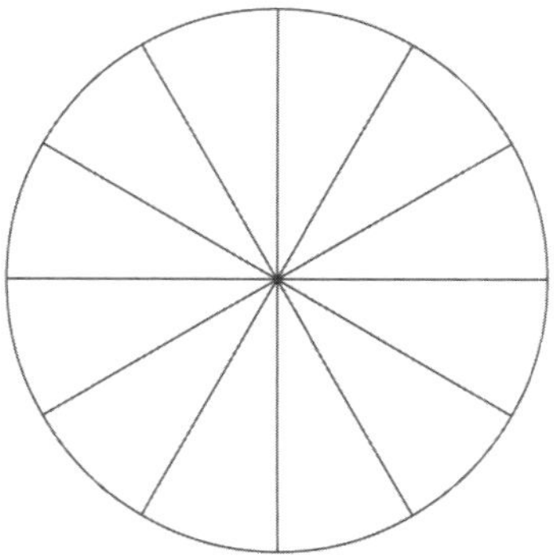
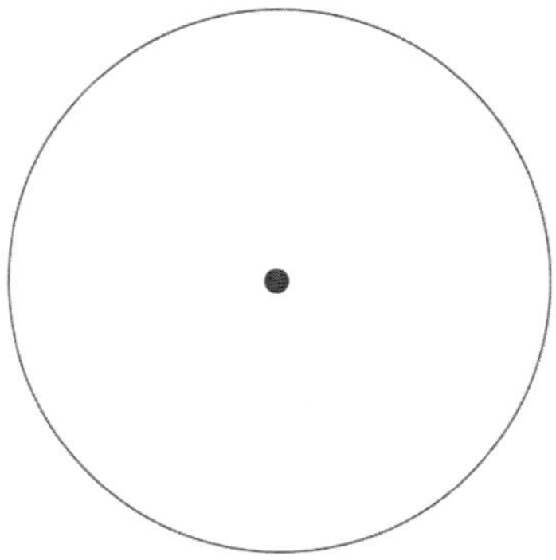

Name ____________________ Date ________________

Master 11.12

Probability Number Lines

Impossible Certain

0.0 0.1 0.2 0.3 0.4 0.5 0.6 0.7 0.8 0.9 1

0% 100%

Impossible Certain

0.0 0.1 0.2 0.3 0.4 0.5 0.6 0.7 0.8 0.9 1

0% 100%

Impossible Certain

0.0 0.1 0.2 0.3 0.4 0.5 0.6 0.7 0.8 0.9 1

0% 100%

Impossible Certain

0.0 0.1 0.2 0.3 0.4 0.5 0.6 0.7 0.8 0.9 1

0% 100%

Impossible Certain

0.0 0.1 0.2 0.3 0.4 0.5 0.6 0.7 0.8 0.9 1

0% 100%

Name ____________________ Date ________________

Master 11.13

Alternative Explore for Technology-Based Simulations

Probability Simulations Using *Fathom*

When estimating the probability of an event using a simulation, the more simulations that are conducted, the better the estimate. Repeated simulations can be very time consuming. At times it may be more efficient to conduct the simulation using technology.

Suppose you are going to write a multiple-choice test made up of 20 questions. Each question has 4 possible answers. Describe a simulation that may be used to estimate the probability that you will pass the test by guessing the answers.

The following experiment will simulate this situation using *Fathom.*

Generate random numbers from 1 to 4 to correspond to the four possible answers on the multiple choice test. Any one of the four numbers can be chosen to correspond with the correct answer. Suppose we choose 3 to correspond to the correct answer; then 1, 2, and 4 will correspond to the incorrect answers. Since there are 20 questions on the test, use 20 for the number of trials.

Follow the steps below to perform this simulation.

1. Open *Fathom.*

2. Click on a new collection box in the toolbox and drag it to the document.

3. Double click on "Collection 1."
Type: "Multiple Choice Test."

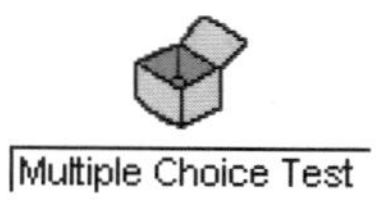

4. Right click on the collection box and select "New Cases.".
Enter 20 for the number of new cases. Click "OK."
If you expand the box, you will see 20 cases in it (represented by the gold balls).

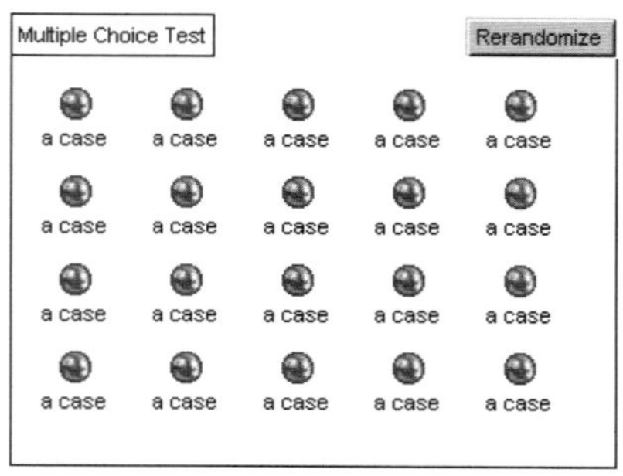

5. Click on a case table in the toolbar and drag it to the document. You will see the numbers 1 to 20 in the first column. These represent your 20 cases. To see all the numbers, you can expand the table by left-clicking on the bottom right corner and dragging it to open up the table.

Multiple Choice Test

	<new>
1	
2	
3	
4	

6. In the second column that says <**new**>, type the word **Guess** as shown at the right.

Multiple Choice Test

	Guess
1	
2	
3	
4	
5	
6	
7	
8	
9	
10	
11	
12	
13	
14	
15	
16	
17	
18	
19	
20	

7. Right-click the word **Guess** to open a menu.
Left-click **Edit Formula.** This opens the calculator.
Select **+ Functions** by left-clicking on **+.**
Scroll down to **+ Random numbers** and left-click +.
Scroll down to **randomInteger**. Double-click on it and it will automatically appear as **randomInteger( )**, in a different colour, in the top screen of the calculator. The cursor will be flashing inside the bracket. Inside the bracket type in **1, 4.**
Click **OK** in the bottom right corner of the calculator.

8. In the **Guess** column of the chart, you will now see the random numbers 1 to 4, as shown at the right.

Multiple Choice Test	
	Guess
1	1
2	4
3	2
4	4
5	2
6	2
7	1
8	4
9	3
10	2
11	4
12	3
13	3
14	2
15	1
16	3
17	2
18	1
19	4
20	1

9. Scroll down the column to count the number of favourable outcomes; in this case, the number 3 represents a correct answer. Record this number for simulation 1.

10. To run another simulation, press Ctrl and Y on your keyboard as often as you wish. Remember to record the number of 3s each time.

11. **a)** Use the numbers you recorded for each simulation to find the experimental probability of passing the multiple choice test by guessing.

b) Compare your results with a partner. Explain similarities or differences.

12. **a)** For 100 simulations, combine your results with three other classmates. Repeat *Step 11a.*

b) Compare your estimate in part a with the estimate you found in *Step 11a.* Explain similarities or differences.

Name ____________________ Date ______________

Master 11.14a

Unit Test: Unit 11 Probability

1. i) Place the letter of each event below on the number line at the number that best matches the probability of the event.

ii) Describe each event as impossible, unlikely, likely, or certain. Justify your answer.

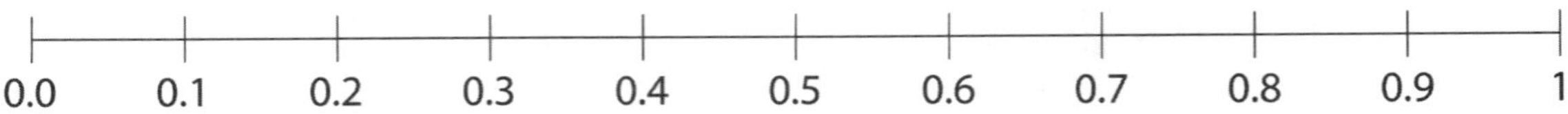

a) Julia randomly picks a peach or a plum from a bag that has 9 plums, 7 nectarines, 6 apples, and 8 peaches.

b) Saturday immediately follows Sunday.

c) Select a spade from a standard set of cards.

d) Roll a 1, 2, 3, 4, 5, or 6 on a number cube labelled 1 to 6.

2. The student council predicts that the odds in favour of a student choosing to ski on winter carnival day are 4 to 5. If the prediction is true, determine the following:

a) What are the odds against a student choosing to ski on winter carnival day?

b) What is the probability that a student will choose to ski on winter carnival day?

c) If there are 1782 students in the school, approximately how many students will not choose to ski on winter carnival day?

Name ______________________ Date ________________

Master 11.14b

Unit Test continued

3. Describe a simulation that you could use to estimate the probability of guessing answers and scoring 70% on a multiple choice test that has 10 questions, each of which has 5 answers.

4. In a game, the pointer on the following spinner is spun and a number cube labelled 1 to 6 is rolled.

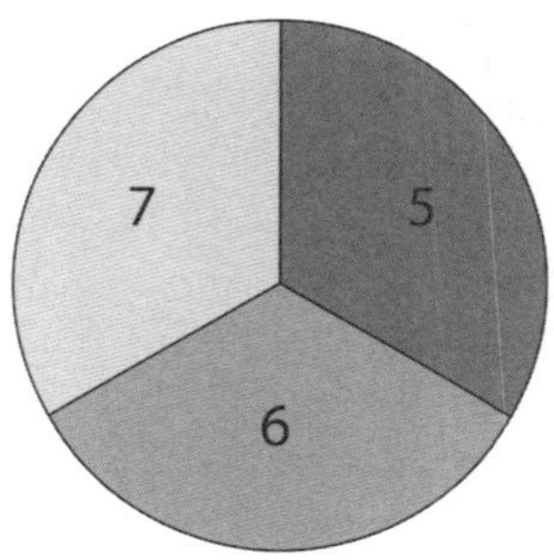

The two numbers are recorded. If the difference of the two numbers is 1, 2, or 3, Player A gets 1 point. If the difference of the two numbers is 0, 4, 5, or 6, Player B gets 1 point.

a) Is this a fair game? Include a tree diagram to justify your answer.

b) If it is not a fair game, how could you make it fair? Explain.

Name ____________________ Date ______________

Master 11.15

Sample Answers

Unit Test – Master 11.14

1.

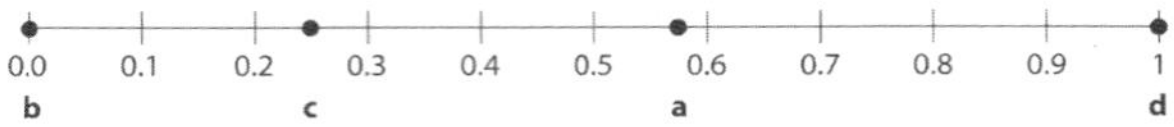

a) $\frac{17}{30}$ or about 0.57; this event is likely because the probability is between 0.5 and 1.

b) 0; this event is impossible, so the probability is 0.

c) $\frac{13}{52} = 0.25$; this event is unlikely because the probability is between 0 and 0.5.

d) 1; this event is certain because the probability is 1.

2. a) 5 to 4

b) $\frac{4}{9}$

c) $\frac{5}{9} \times 1782$ students = 990 students

3. Answers may vary.
A score of 70% is equivalent to getting 7 out of 10 answers correct on the test. Since each question has 5 answers, use a spinner with 5 congruent sectors, each of a different colour. If the colours are yellow, red, orange, blue, and green, choose one colour to represent the correct answer. Pick orange. This means that every time the pointer lands on orange, the answer is correct. Since there are 10 questions, one simulation requires that the pointer on the spinner is spun 10 times. To estimate the probability of scoring 70% or getting 7 correct answers, record the number of simulations in which the pointer lands on orange 7 times.

4.

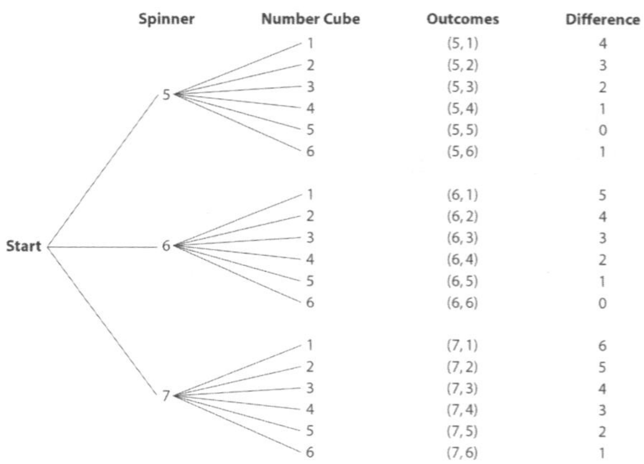

There are 18 possible outcomes.
The following table shows the differences of the numbers and their frequencies.

Difference	0	1	2	3	4	5	6
Frequency	2	4	3	3	3	2	1

Player A gets one point when the difference is 1, 2, or 3.
The frequency of these differences is $4 + 3 + 3 = 10$.
So, the probability that Player A will win the game is $\frac{10}{18}$ or approximately 0.556.

Player B gets one point when the difference is 0, 4, 5 or 6. The frequency of these numbers is $2 + 3 + 2 + 1 = 8$ so the probability that Player B will win the game is $\frac{8}{18}$ or approximately 0.444. Since the probabilities of winning are not equal, this is not a fair game.

b) Answers may vary. Sample answer: One way to make the game fair is to let Player A get one point when the difference is 0, 1, or 2 and let Player B get one point when the difference is 3, 4, 5, or 6. Each of these has a total frequency of 9 and so the probability of winning for each player will then be $\frac{9}{18}$ or 0.5.

Extra Practice Masters 11.16–11.20

Go to the CD-ROM to access editable versions of these Extra Practice Masters

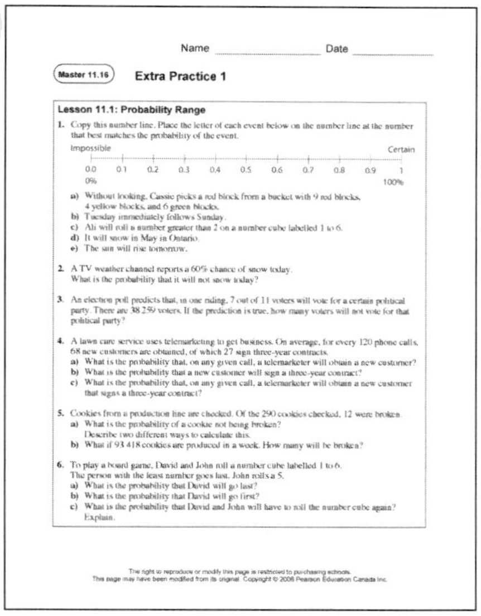

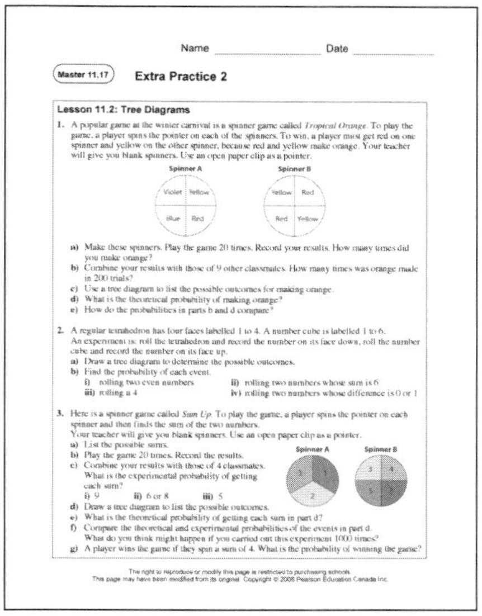

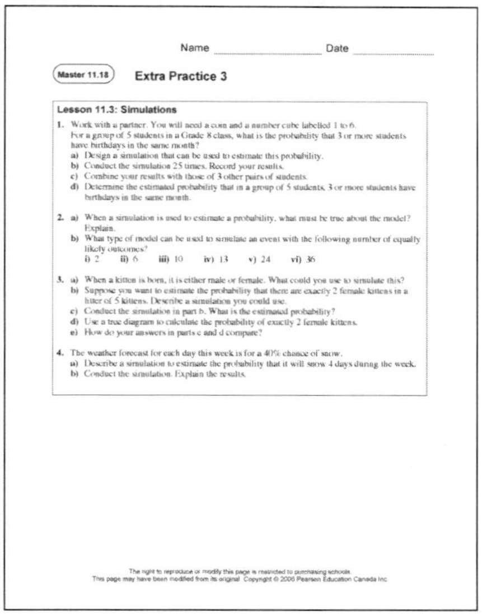

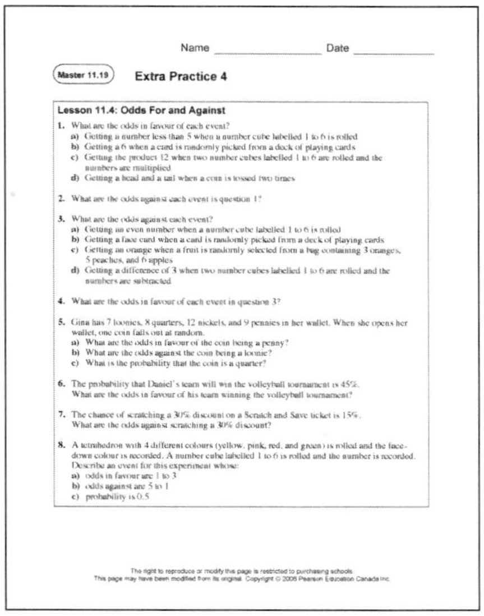

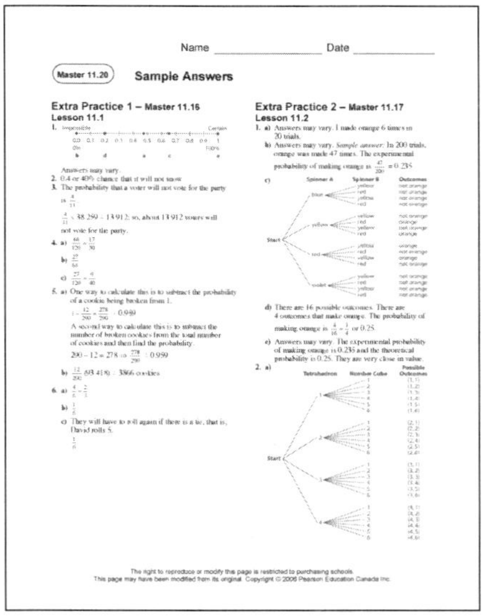

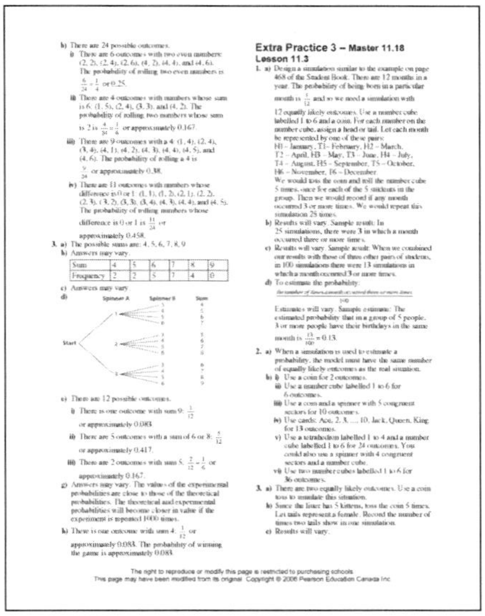

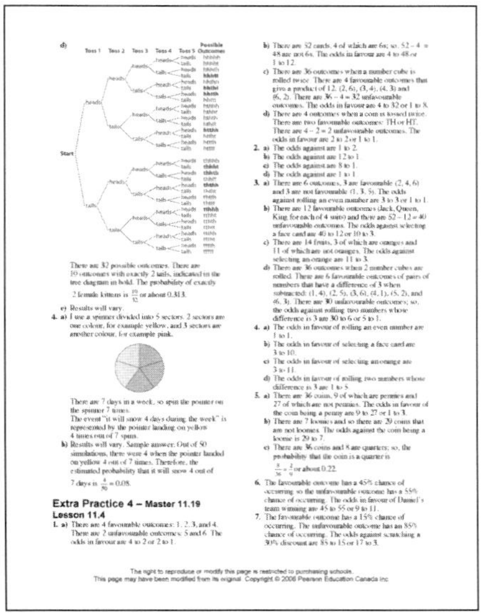

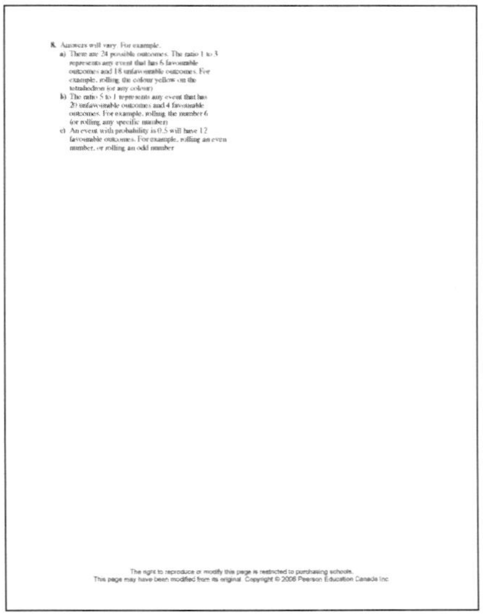

Addison Wesley

Mathematics
Makes Sense

Program Authors

Trevor Brown

Antonietta Lenjosek

Cathy Heideman

Jim Mennie

Georgia Konis-Chatzis

A.J. Keene

Margaret Sinclair

Craig Featherstone

Jason Johnston

Bryn Keyes

Elizabeth Wood

Elizabeth Milne

David Sufrin

Don Jones

Sharon Jeroski

Lynn Strangway

Printed and bound in Canada

2 3 4 5 – TC – 09 08 07 06

PEARSON

Education Canada